THE HISTORY OF PSYC

Fundamental Questions

THE HISTORY OF PSYCHOLOGY

Fundamental Questions

Edited by

Margaret P. Munger
Davidson College

New York   Oxford
OXFORD UNIVERSITY PRESS
2003

Oxford University Press

Oxford   New York
Auckland   Bangkok   Buenos Aires   Cape Town   Chennai
Dar es Salaam   Delhi   Hong Kong   Istanbul   Karachi   Kolkata
Kuala Lumpur   Madrid   Melbourne   Mexico City   Mumbai
Nairobi   São Paulo   Shanghai   Taipei   Tokyo   Toronto

Copyright © 2003 by Oxford University Press, Inc.

Published by Oxford University Press, Inc.,
198 Madison Avenue, New York, New York 10016
http://www.oup-usa.org

Oxford is a registered trademark of Oxford University Press

Library of Congress Cataloging-in-Publication Data
The history of psychology : fundamental questions / edited by Margaret P. Munger.
    p. cm.
  Includes bibliographical references.
  ISBN 0-19-515154-2 (alk. paper)
   1. Psychology–History. I. Munger, Margaret P., 1967–

BF81 .F86 2002
150′.9–dc21   2002025023

9   8   7   6   5   4   3   2   1

Printed in the United States of America
on acid-free paper

CONTENTS

PREFACE

It has been my pleasure to teach the history of psychology course at Davidson College for the past nine years. When confronted with the challenge of teaching history, my initial thought was that I needed to visit the library and start reading. I had enjoyed a history of western science course as an undergraduate at the University of Chicago and brought from that experience an expectation that I should read from primary sources. So I started my crash course, reading Helmholtz and James alongside a variety of history textbooks. As I started working on my syllabus, I realized that I had enjoyed reading Wilhelm Wundt and Charles Darwin more than any of the texts—the historical writings got to the core of what I wanted my students to think about more directly than did the textbooks. And so while I did choose a textbook, I also put a weighty list of readings on reserve at the library. It would be fair to say that my students were initially startled by the opening readings—Aristotle was not what they had in mind when they thought about the history of psychology. Happily, as I talked to them about listening to the questions the early philosophers were asking, along with examining the methods they were using, my students began to understand that these various ancient scholars were also looking at behavior and trying to understand what it means. By the end of the semester, when the students were reading more recent works, the connections abounded, and the point of starting with the ancients was underscored as the same issues, now sparked by more modern commentary, were discussed in class.

One approach to the history of psychology is to chronicle the fascinating stories and interconnections among various key players, watching for spheres of influence and overlap. Another approach is to highlight the critical observations and resulting theories and systems of psychological thought. A third approach is to examine what questions were being asked—questions that could not be answered by existing fields of study—starting with philosophy, but later including biology: What made it necessary for psychology to become a separate discipline? Readers and textbooks exist for the first two approaches, but not for the third. This book adopts just such an approach.

The History of Psychology: Fundamental Questions provides the words of the philosophers, theologians, and early scientists that contributed to the development of psychology. It also includes some more recent works, covering issues and ideas from cognitive psychology and neuroscience. My hope is that it is comprehensive in the range of ideas and issues covered, but limited enough to be manageable in a single-semester undergraduate course. The purpose of this book is to allow the reader the opportunity to consider the fundamental questions, not present and defend a particular point of view. This collection of readings developed as part of a senior capstone seminar experience at Davidson College. The goal of the capstone is to allow the seniors time to think through the foundations of psychology, inspired by the deeply rooted issues that make it necessary. This process is, by nature, contemplative, requiring careful study of these great works alongside careful study of developing opinions and intuitions.

When students find themselves interested in psychology, it's important for them to think about the field's underlying goals and their own intellectual focus and goals. To start this process, they need a selection of readings that covers a healthy range of what psychologists have thought and written. The selections in my book are important works from intellectual leaders as they developed and reflected on the discipline. In fact, many of the readings are transcripts of lectures or introductory or concluding chapters—moments in which the individual is seeking to summarize and expand on observed points. The readings are organized in a roughly chronological order, but also grouped by shared topic. The sequence leads to interesting comparisons and useful juxtapositions as it traces the roots of various issues in psychology.

Almost all the readings included in *The History of Psychology: Fundamental Questions* come from my senior seminar on the history of psychology. These readings have been "road tested" by a number of different classes, and each year students are thrilled to discover that they do, indeed, have something in common with these past scholars. As you may expect, not all the readings from my first syllabus were successful, and I am still actively thinking about what my students should read. For example, the theological work of Augustine and Aquinas and the writings of Margaret Floy Washburn and Milicent W. Shinn are new additions to my list. The added discussions of mind contributed by Saint Augustine and Saint Thomas Aquinas complement Plato and Aristotle. Washburn's writings on the animal mind and appropriate methods for studying comparative psychology provide a wonderful foil for both Darwin and William James. Shinn's careful observations of babies from 1900 complement issues raised by Sigmund Freud and Alfred Binet around the same time.

The sequencing of the readings is roughly chronological, but I have found it helpful and intriguing to arrange the works to highlight similar topics and debates. Some pairings are obvious, like reading John Locke and the next day reading Gottfried Wilhelm Leibniz's response to Locke, or assigning selections from B. F. Skinner's book *Verbal Behavior* to be followed by Noam Chomsky's critical review. But I have also gone a bit out of sequence in order to highlight key issues. For example, I think John B. Watson's "Behaviorist Manifesto" makes much more sense to the students if they have just read examples of Wundt's psychophysics, Max Wertheimer's Gestalt theory, and particularly E. B. Titchener's lab-manual exercise about introspection and imagery, even though some of these works were published after Watson's 1913 paper.

The book is arranged into nine sections. Each section includes readings that cohere thematically and encourage discussion and comparison, but often readings across section boundaries also invite comparison and discussion (e.g., Aquinas and René Descartes, Titchener and Watson). Each reading is preceded by a paragraph-length biography of the author, with some note about his or her range of interests and influence. The book does not have discussion questions or offer explicit links to other readings—the point of this book is to allow readers to find their own connections. There are 37 readings included in *The History of Psychology: Fundamental Questions*—each one chosen to accommodate a range of instructor and student interests. Over the course of a semester, I typically assign 32 readings, shifting the particular set a bit from year to year.

These works endure. Sharing this journey with students is a wonderful opportunity to watch opinions shift and alter and intuitions reverse and return throughout the semester, highlighting the fascinating questions that make psychology exciting. I hope the readers of this book find this course as fresh and as interesting as I do, every time.

Any project of this magnitude involves an enormous number of people, and so it is only appropriate that I try to thank the folks who made this possible: to the faculty of the University of Chicago, for teaching me how to read anything; to the department of psychology at Davidson College, for letting me teach this wonderful course; to the students of my history of psychology class, for sharing their exploration of the questions; to the amazing editorial and production staff at Oxford University Press, for helping me see this through, with particular thanks to Karita dos Santos, Sean Mahoney, Karen Shapiro, Terry Michelet, Wendy Almeleh, and Sheridan Books who all made this book so beautiful; to the authors from antiquity to today, for writing such interesting things to read and think about; and, finally, I'd like to thank my family—Jimmy and Nora for being kids, my dad for reading all those biographies, and my husband Dave, who not only convinced me that there was a book to put together, but who helped me see the entire project through to the end.

M. P. M.
Davidson College

THE HISTORY OF PSYCHOLOGY

Fundamental Questions

WHAT IS THE MIND?

1

PLATO

Plato (428–347 B.C.) wrote poetry as a young man, before turning to philosophy and the question of virtue. His given name was Aristocles, but he was called Platon at school because of his broad shoulders. Plato grew up during the Peloponnesian War, unfortunately on the losing Athenian side. The resulting conservative religious movement in Athens led to the execution of Socrates, Plato's teacher, who was convicted of corrupting the youths and introducing new gods. This background may explain Plato's interest in moral and political questions, rooted in the question of virtue. After leaving Athens to study and travel for several years, Plato returned to found the Academy at age 40. The Academy was not simply a classroom for discussing philosophy, but included gardens; shrines to various gods and goddesses; and, naturally, a gymnasium. Plato was a prolific writer; his dialogues included discussions not only of philosophy, but of geometry, religion, and geography, to name but a few topics. He also invented a completely fictional land, Atlantis, that sinks into the sea for lack of virtue. Around 367 B.C., Plato went to Syracuse to tutor its young ruler, Dionysus II. He returned after several years complicated by war just as his most famous student, Aristotle (p. 20), entered the Academy. His final years were peaceful, and he apparently died in his sleep following a student's wedding feast. Plato's Academy remained open for almost a thousand years, until it was finally closed by Emperor Justinian in A.D. 529.

THE REPUBLIC

THE CAVE

SOCRATES, GLAUCON. AND now, I said, let me show in a figure how far our nature is enlightened or unenlightened: Behold! human beings living in an underground den, which has a mouth open toward the light and reaching all along the den; here they have been from their childhood, and have their legs and necks chained so that they cannot move, and can only see before them, being prevented by the chains from turning round their heads. Above and behind them a fire is blazing at a distance, and between the fire and the prisoners there is a raised way; and you will see, if you look, a low wall built along the way, like the screen which marionette-players have in front of them, over which they show the puppets.

I see.

And do you see, I said, men passing along the wall carrying all sorts of vessels, and statues and figures of animals made of wood and stone and various materials, which appear over the wall? Some of them are talking, others silent.

You have shown me a strange image, and they are strange prisoners.

Like ourselves, I replied: and they see only their own shadows, or the shadows of one another, which the fire throws on the opposite wall of the cave?

True, he said; how could they see anything but the shadows if they were never allowed to move their heads?

And of the objects which are being carried in like manner they would only see the shadows?

From Plato, "Book VII, Story of the Cave." In B. Jowett (Trans.), *The Republic of Plato* (pp. 209–212). New York: Colonial Press, 1901. (Original work written 380 B.C.)

Yes, he said.

And if they were able to converse with one another, would they not suppose that they were naming what was actually before them?[1]

Very true.

And suppose further that the prison had an echo which came from the other side, would they not be sure to fancy when one of the passers-by spoke that the voice which they heard came from the passing shadow?

No question, he replied.

To them, I said, the truth would be literally nothing but the shadows of the images.

That is certain.

And now look again, and see what will naturally follow if the prisoners are released and disabused of their error. At first, when any of them is liberated and compelled suddenly to stand up and turn his neck round and walk and look toward the light, he will suffer sharp pains; the glare will distress him, and he will be unable to see the realities of which in his former state he had seen the shadows; and then conceive someone saying to him, that what he saw before was an illusion, but that now, when he is approaching nearer to being and his eye is turned toward more real existence, he has a clearer vision—what will be his reply? And you may further imagine that his instructor is pointing to the objects as they pass and requiring him to name them—will he not be perplexed? Will he not fancy that the shadows which he formerly saw are truer than the objects which are now shown to him?

Far truer.

And if he is compelled to look straight at the light, will he not have a pain in his eyes which will make him turn away to take refuge in the objects of vision which he can see, and which he will conceive to be in reality clearer than the things which are now being shown to him?

True, he said.

And suppose once more, that he is reluctantly dragged up a steep and rugged ascent, and held fast until he is forced into the presence of the sun himself, is he not likely to be pained and irritated? When he approaches the light his eyes will be dazzled, and he will not be able to see anything at all of what are now called realities.

Not all in a moment, he said.

He will require to grow accustomed to the sight of the upper world. And first he will see the shadows best, next the reflections of men and other objects in the water, and then the objects themselves; then he will gaze upon the light of the moon and the stars and the spangled heaven; and he will see the sky and the stars by night better than the sun or the light of the sun by day?

Certainly.

Last of all he will be able to see the sun, and not mere reflections of him in the water, but he will see him in his own proper place, and not in another; and he will contemplate him as he is.

Certainly.

He will then proceed to argue that this is he who gives the season and the years, and is the guardian of all that is in the visible world, and in a certain way the cause of all things which he and his fellows have been accustomed to behold?

Clearly, he said, he would first see the sun and then reason about him.

And when he remembered his old habitation, and the wisdom of the den and his fellow-prisoners, do you not suppose that he would felicitate himself on the change, and pity him?

Certainly, he would.

And if they were in the habit of conferring honors among themselves on those who were quickest to observe the passing shadows and to remark which of them went before, and which followed after, and which were together; and who were therefore best able to draw conclusions as to the future, do you think that he would care for such honors and glories, or envy the possessors of them? Would he not say with Homer,

"Better to be the poor servant of a poor master,"

and to endure anything, rather than think as they do and live after their manner?

Yes, he said, I think that he would rather suffer anything than entertain these false notions and live in this miserable manner.

Imagine once more, I said, such a one coming suddenly out of the sun to be replaced in his old situation; would he not be certain to have his eyes full of darkness?

To be sure, he said.

And if there were a contest, and he had to compete in measuring the shadows with the prisoners who had never moved out of the den, while his sight was still weak, and before his eyes had become steady (and the time which would be needed to acquire this new habit of sight might be very considerable), would he not be ridiculous? Men would say of him that up he went and down he came without his eyes; and that it was better not even to think of ascending; and if anyone tried to loose another and lead him up to the light, let them only catch the offender, and they would put him to death.

No question, he said.

1. Reading παρόντα

2

HIPPOCRATES

Hippocrates (460–377 B.C.) may have been a single individual, a fine physician, and a teacher, but little record of his life exists. In fact, the "Hippocratic Collection" does not appear to have been written by a single hand: its style, addressed audience, and even opinions shift through the 60–70 items. For example, around A.D. 100, both Seribonius Largus, a physician traveling in Britain with Emperor Claudius, and the Greek Soranus, working in Rome, followed the principles in the "Hippocratic Collection." Yet Scribonius Largus's refusal to perform any abortion and Soranus's choice to perform safe, alternative procedures are both supported by the collection. It is likely that the collection formed the heart of a medical library at Cos and was transferred to the library at Alexandria around 300–200 B.C.

THE HIPPOCRATIC COLLECTION

TRADITION IN MEDICINE

An explanation of the empirical basis of medicine as practised about the end of the fifth century B.C. This treatise is sometimes referred to as On Ancient Medicine.

1. In all previous attempts to speak or to write about medicine, the authors have introduced certain arbitrary postulates[1] into their arguments, and have reduced the causes of death and the maladies that affect mankind to a narrow compass. They have supposed that there are but one or two causes: heat or cold, moisture, dryness or anything else they may fancy. From many considerations their mistake is obvious; indeed, this is proved from their own words. They are specially to be censured since they are concerned with no bogus science, but one which all employ in a matter of the greatest importance, and one of which the good professors and practitioners are held in high repute. But besides such there are both sorry practitioners and those who hold widely divergent opinions. This could not happen were medicine a bogus science to which no consideration had ever been given and in which no discoveries had been made. For if it were so, all would be equally inexperienced and ignorant, and the condition of their patients due to nothing but the law of chance. But this is not so, and the practitioners of medicine differ greatly among themselves both in theory and practice just as happens in every other science. For this reason I do not think that medicine is in need of some new postulate, dealing, for instance, with invisible or problematic substances, and about which one must have some postulate or another in order to discuss them seriously. In such matters, medicine differs from subjects like astronomy and geology, of which a man might know the truth and lecture on it without either he or his audience being able to judge whether it were the truth or not, because there is no sure criterion.

2. Medicine has for long possessed the qualities necessary to make a science. These are a starting point

From Hippocrates "Tradition in Medicine," "Dreams," and "Nature of Man." In G. E. R. Lloyd (Ed.), J. Chadwick and W. N. Mann (Trans.), *Hippocratic Writings* (pp. 70–86, 252–271). New York: Penguin, 1986.

and a known method according to which many valuable discoveries have been made over a long period of time. By such a method, too, the rest of the science will be discovered if anyone who is clever enough is versed in the observations of the past and makes these the starting point of his researches. If anyone should reject these and, casting them aside, endeavour to proceed by a new method and then assert that he has made a discovery, he has been and is being deceived. A discovery cannot be made thus, and the reason why such a thing is impossible I shall endeavour to show by expounding the true nature of the science. My exposition will demonstrate clearly the impossibility of making discoveries by any other method but the orthodox one.

It seems to me to be of the greatest importance that anyone speaking of the science should confine himself to matters known to the general public, since the subject of inquiry and discourse is none other than the maladies of which they themselves fall sick. Although it were no easy matter for common people to discover for themselves the nature of their own diseases and the causes why they get worse or get better, yet it is easy for them to follow when another makes the discoveries and explains the events to them. Then when a man hears about a disease he will only have to remember his own experience of it. But if anyone departs from what is popular knowledge and does not make himself intelligible to his audience, he is not being practical. For such reasons we have no need of a postulate.

3. In the first place, the science of medicine would never have been discovered nor, indeed, sought for, were there no need for it. If sick men fared just as well eating and drinking and living exactly as healthy men do, and no better on some different regimen, there would be little need for the science. But the reason why the art of medicine became necessary was because sick men did not get well on the same regimen as the healthy, any more than they do now. What is more, I am of the opinion that our present way of living and our present diet would not have come about if it had proved adequate for a man to eat and drink the same things as an ox or a horse and all the other animals. The produce of the earth, fruits, vegetables and grass, is the food of animals on which they grow and flourish without needing other articles of diet. In the beginning I believe that man lived on such food and the modern diet is the result of many years' discovery. Such devising was necessary because, in primitive times, men often suffered terribly from their indigestible and animal-like diet, eating raw and uncooked food, difficult to digest. They suffered as men would suffer now from such a diet, being liable to violent pain and sickness and a speedy death. Certainly such ills would probably prove less serious then than now because they were accustomed to this kind of food, but even then, such illnesses would have been serious and would have carried off the majority of a weak constitution although the stronger would survive longer, just as now some people easily digest strong meats while others suffer much pain and illness from them. For this reason I believe these primitive men sought food suitable to their constitutions and discovered that which we now use. Thus, they took wheat and wetted it, winnowed it, ground it, sifted it, and then mixed it and baked it into bread, and likewise made cakes from barley. They boiled and baked and mixed and diluted the strong raw foods with the weaker ones and subjected them to many other processes, always with a view to man's nature and his capabilities. They knew that if strong food was eaten the body could not digest it and thus it would bring about pain, sickness and death, whereas the body draws nourishment and thus grows and is healthy from food it is able to digest. What fairer or more fitting name can be given to such research and discovery than that of medicine, which was founded for the health, preservation and nourishment of man and to rid him of that diet which caused pain, sickness and death?

4. It is perhaps not unreasonable to assert that this is no science, for no one can properly be called the practitioner of a science of which the facts are unknown to none and with which all are acquainted by necessity and experience. The discoveries of medicine are of great importance and are the result of thought and skill on the part of many people. For instance, even now trainers in athletics continue to make discoveries according to the same method; they determine what men must eat and drink to gain the greatest mastery over their bodies and to achieve the maximum strength.

5. Turning now to what is generally admitted to be the science of medicine, namely, discoveries concerning the sick, which is a science in name and boasts practitioners, let us consider whether it has the same purposes and from what origins it arose. As I have already said, I do not believe anyone would ever have looked for such a science if the same regimen were equally good for the sick and the healthy. Even now some people, the barbarians and some Greeks, who have no knowledge of medicine, go on behaving when they are ill just as they do in health. They neither abstain from nor moderate the use of the things they like. Those who sought for and found the science of medicine held the same opinion as those whom I mentioned before. First of all, I imagine, they

cut down the quantity without changing the quality of the food, making the sick eat very little. But when it became clear to them that such a regimen suited and helped some of the sick but not all, and that there were some even who were in such a condition that they could not digest even a very little food, then they concluded that in some cases a more easily digested food was necessary. Thus they invented gruel by mixing a little strong food with much water, so taking away its strength by dilution and cooking. For those that could not digest even gruel, they substituted liquid nourishment, taking care that this should be of moderate dilution and quantity, neither too weak nor too strong.

6. It must be clearly understood, however, that gruel is not necessarily of assistance to everyone who is sick. In some diseases it is evident that on such a diet, the fever and pains increase, the gruel serving as nourishment to the disease, but as a source of decline and sickness to the body. In such cases were dry food to be taken, barley-cakes or bread for example, even in very small quantities, the patients would become ten times worse than they would be on a diet of gruel, simply because of the strength of the food. Again, a man who was helped by gruel but not by dry food would be worse if he ate more of the latter than if he took only a little, and even a small quantity would give him pain. In fact, it is obvious that all the causes of such pains come to the same thing; the stronger foods are the most harmful to man whether he be in health or sickness.

7. What then is the difference in intention between the man who discovered the mode of life suitable for the sick, who is called a physician and admitted to be a scientist, and him who, from the beginning, discovered the way to prepare the food we eat now instead of the former wild and animal-like diet? I can see no difference; the discovery is one and the same thing. The one sought to do away with those articles of diet which, on account of their savage and undiluted nature, the human frame could not digest, and on which it could not remain healthy; the other discovered what a sick man could not digest in view of his particular malady. What difference is there save in the appearance, and that the one is more complicated and needs more study? Indeed, one is the fore-runner of the other.

8. A comparison between the diets of a sick man and a healthy one shows that the diet of a healthy man is no more harmful to a sick man than that of a wild beast to a healthy man. Suppose a man be suffering from a disease, neither something malignant nor incurable, nor yet some trifling ailment, but nevertheless of which he is well aware. If he were to eat bread or meat or anything else which is nourishing to a healthy man, but in smaller quantities than if he were well, he would suffer pain and run some risk. Now suppose a healthy man with neither an utterly weak nor a strong constitution were to take small quantities of a diet which would give strength and nourishment to an ox or a horse, such as vetch or barley-corn, he would suffer no less pain and run no less risk than the sick man who inopportunely ate bread or barley-cake. This proves that the whole science of medicine might be discovered by research according to these principles.

9. If it were all as simple as this, that the stronger foods are harmful and the weaker good and nourishing for men both in health and sickness, the matter were an easy one. The safest course would be to keep to the weaker food. But if a man were to eat less than enough he would make as big a mistake as if he were to eat too much. Hunger is a powerful agent in the human body; it can maim, weaken and kill. Undernourishment gives rise to many troubles and, though they are different from those produced by over-eating, they are none the less severe because they are more diverse and more specific. One aims at some criterion as to what constitutes a correct diet, but you will find neither number nor weight to determine what this is exactly, and no other criterion than bodily feeling. Thus exactness is difficult to achieve and small errors are bound to occur. I warmly commend the physician who makes small mistakes; infallibility is rarely to be seen. Most doctors seem to me to be in the position of poor navigators. In calm weather they can conceal their mistakes, but when overtaken by a mighty storm or a violent gale, it is evident to all that it is their ignorance and error which is the ruin of the ship. So it is with the sorry doctors who are the great majority. They cure men but slightly ill, in whose treatment even the biggest mistakes would have no serious consequences. Such diseases are many and much more common than the more serious ones. When doctors make mistakes over such cases, their errors are unperceived by the layman, but when they have to treat a serious and dangerous case, a mistake or lack of skill is obvious to all, and vengeance for either error is not long delayed.

10. That over-eating should cause no less sickness than excessive fasting is easily understood by reference to the healthy. Some find it better to dine but once a day and consequently make this their custom. Others, likewise, find it is better for them to have a meal both at noon and in the evening. Then there are some who adopt one or other of these habits merely because it pleases them or because of chance circumstances. On the

grounds of health it matters little to most people whether they take but one meal a day or two. But there are some who, if they do not follow their usual custom, do not escape the result and they may be stricken with a serious illness within a day. Some there are who, if they take luncheon when this practice does not agree with them, at once become both mentally and physically dull; they yawn and become drowsy and thirsty. If subsequently they should dine as well, they suffer from wind, colic and diarrhoea and, not infrequently, this has been the start of a serious illness even though they have taken no more than twice the amount of food they have been accustomed to. Similarly, a man who is accustomed to taking luncheon because he finds that this agrees with him, cannot omit the meal without suffering great weakness, fear and faintness. In addition, his eyes become sunken, the urine more yellow and warmer, the mouth bitter, and he has a sinking feeling in his stomach. He feels dizzy, despondent and incapable of exertion. Then later when he sits down to dine, food is distasteful to him and he cannot eat his customary dinner. Instead, the food causes colic and rumblings and burns the stomach; he sleeps poorly and is disturbed by violent nightmares. With such people this too has often been the start of some illness.

11. Let us consider the reason for these things. The man who is accustomed to dine only once a day suffers, in my opinion, when he takes an extra meal because he has not waited long enough since the last. His stomach has not fully benefited from the food taken on the previous day and has neither digested nor discarded it, nor calmed down again. This new food is introduced into the stomach while it is still digesting and fermenting the previous meal. Such stomachs are slow in digestion and need rest and relaxation. The man who is accustomed to a meal at midday suffers when he has to go without, because his body needs nourishment and the food taken at the previous meal has already been used up. If no fresh food be taken his body wastes through starvation, and I attribute to this the symptoms from which I described such a man to suffer. I maintain that other healthy people will suffer from these same troubles if they fast for two or three days.

12. Those constitutions which react rapidly and severely to changes in habit are, in my opinion, the weak ones. A weak man is next to a sick man, while a sick man is made still weaker by indiscretions in his diet. In matters requiring such nicety, it is impossible for science to be infallible. There are many things in medicine which require just as careful judgement as this matter of diet, and of these I will speak later. I contend that the

science of medicine must not be rejected as non-existent or ill-investigated because it may sometimes fail in exactness. Even if it is not always accurate in every respect, the fact that it is able to approach close to a standard of infallibility as a result of reasoning, where before there was great ignorance, should command respect for the discoveries of medical science. Such discoveries are the product of good and true investigation, not chance happenings.

13. I wish now to return to those whose idea of research in the science is based upon the new method: the supposition of certain postulates. They would suppose that there is some principle harmful to man: heat or cold, wetness or dryness, and that the right way to bring about cures is to correct cold with warmth, or dryness with moisture and so on. On such an assumption let us consider the case of a man of weak constitution. Suppose he eats grains of wheat as they come straight from the threshing-floor and raw meat, and suppose he drinks water. If he continues with such a diet I am well aware that he will suffer terribly. He will suffer pain and his body will become enfeebled; his stomach will be disordered and he will not be able to live long. What remedy, then, should be employed for someone in this condition? Heat or cold or dryness or wetness? It must obviously be one of them because these are the causes of disease, and the remedy lies in the application of the opposite principle according to their theory. Really, of course, the surest remedy is to stop such a diet and to give him bread instead of grains of wheat, cooked instead of raw meat and wine to drink with it. Such a change is bound to bring back health so long as this has not been completely wrecked by the prolonged consumption of his former diet. What conclusion shall we draw? That he was suffering from cold and the remedy cured him because it was hot, or the reverse of this? I think this is a question which would greatly puzzle anyone who was asked it. What was taken away in preparing bread from wheat; heat, cold, moisture or dryness? Bread is subjected to fire and water and many other things in the course of its preparation, each of which has its own effect. Some of the original qualities of wheat are lost, some are mixed and compounded with others.

14. I know too that the body is affected differently by bread according to the manner in which it is prepared. It differs according as it is made from pure flour or meal with bran, whether it is prepared from winnowed or unwinnowed wheat, whether it is mixed with much water or little, whether well mixed or poorly mixed, over-baked or under-baked, and countless other points besides. The same is true of the preparation of

barley-meal. The influence of each process is considerable and each has a totally different effect from another. How can anyone who has not considered such matters and come to understand them, possibly know anything of the diseases that afflict mankind? Each one of the substances of a man's diet acts upon his body and changes it in some way and upon these changes his whole life depends, whether he be in health, in sickness, or convalescent. To be sure, there can be little knowledge more necessary. The early investigators in this subject carried out their researches well and along the right lines. They referred everything to the nature of the human body, and they thought such a science worthy of being ascribed to a god, as is now believed. They never imagined that it was heat or cold, or wetness or dryness, which either harmed a man or was necessary to his health. They attributed disease to some factor stronger and more powerful than the human body which the body could not master. It was such factors they sought to remove. Every quality is at its most powerful when it is most concentrated; sweetness at its sweetest, bitterness at its bitterest, sharpness at its sharpest and so forth. The existence of such qualities in the body of man was perceived together with their harmful effects. There exists in man saltness, bitterness, sweetness, sharpness, astringency, flabbiness and countless other qualities having every kind of influence, number and strength. When these are properly mixed and compounded with one another, they can neither be observed nor are they harmful. But when one is separated out and stands alone it becomes both apparent and harmful. Similarly, the foods which are unsuitable for us and harm us if eaten, all have some such characteristic; either they are bitter or salt or sharp or have some other strong and undiluted quality. For that reason we are disturbed by them, just as similar qualities when retained in the body harm us. Those things which form the ordinary and usual food of man, bread and barley-cakes and the like, are clearly farthest removed from those things which have a strong or strange taste. In this way they differ from those that are prepared and designed for pleasure and luxury. The simple foods least often give rise to bodily disturbance and a separation of the forces located there. In fact, strength, growth and nourishment come from nothing but what is well mixed and contains no strong nor undiluted element.

15. I am utterly at a loss to know how those who prefer these hypothetical arguments and reduce the science to a simple matter of "postulates" ever cure anyone on the basis of their assumptions. I do not think that they have ever discovered anything that is purely "hot" or

"cold," "dry" or "wet," without it sharing some other qualities. Rather, I fancy, the diets they prescribe are exactly the same as those we all employ, but they impute heat to one substance, cold to another, dryness to a third and wetness to a fourth. It would be useless to bid a sick man to "take something hot." He would immediately ask "What?" Whereupon the doctor must either talk some technical gibberish or take refuge in some known solid substance. But suppose "something hot" is also astringent, another is hot and soothing as well, while a third produces rumbling in the belly. There are many varied hot substances with many and varied effects which may be contrary one to another. Will it make any difference to take that which is hot and astringent rather than that which is hot and soothing, or even that which is cold and astringent or cold and soothing? To the best of my knowledge the opposite is the case; everything has its own specific effect. This is not only true of the human body but is seen in the various substances used for working hides and wood and other things less sensitive than flesh and blood. It is not the heating effect of the application which is so important as its astringent or soothing qualities and so on, and this is true whether the substance be taken internally or applied as an ointment or plaster.

16. I think cold and heat are the weakest of the forces which operate in the body, and for these reasons. So long as cold and heat are present together they are harmless, for heat is tempered by cold and cold by heat. But when the two principles are separated from each other then they become harmful. However, when the body is chilled, warmth is spontaneously generated by the body itself so there is no need to take special measures, and this is true both in health and in disease. For instance, if a healthy man cools his body by taking a cold bath or by any other means, the more he cools himself the warmer he feels when he resumes his garments and comes into shelter again. This is only true, of course, so long as he does not wholly freeze. Again if he should warm himself thoroughly with a hot bath or at a fire, and then go into a cool place, it will seem to be much colder than formerly and he will shiver more. Should anyone cool himself with a fan on a very hot day, the heat seems ten times more suffocating when the fan is stopped than if its cooling properties had not been used at all. Let us consider now a more extreme example. If people get their feet, hands or head frozen by walking through snow or from exposure to cold, think of what they suffer from burning and irritation at night when they are wrapped up and come into a warm place; in some cases blisters come up like those formed by a

burn. But these things do not happen before they get warm. This shows how readily each of this pair replaces the other. There are countless other examples I might give to illustrate this subject. Is it not true of sick men that those who have the severest chill develop the highest fever? And even when the fever abates its fury a little, the patient remains very hot. Then subsequently as it passes through the body, it finishes in the feet, that is the first part of the body to be attacked by the chill and the part which remained cold the longest. Again when the patient sweats as the fever falls, he feels much colder than if he had not had the fever at all. What great or fearful effect, then, can a thing have when its opposite appears of itself with such speed and removes any effect that the former may have had? What need is there, also, for further assistance when nature neutralizes the effect of such an agent spontaneously?

17. Some may raise the objection that the fever of patients suffering from *causus,* pneumonia or other serious diseases does not rapidly decline. Neither in such cases is the fever intermittent. I think that such observations constitute a good proof of my own view that a high temperature is not the only element of a fever nor the only cause of the weak constitution of a febrile patient. May it not be said of a thing that it is both bitter and hot, sharp and hot, salt and hot, and countless other combinations both with heat and cold? In each combination, the effect of any two qualities acting together will be different. Such qualities may be harmful but there is as well the heat of physical exertion which increases as the strength increases and has no ill effects.

18. The truth of this may be demonstrated by the following consideration of certain signs. An obvious one, and one we have all experienced and shall continue to do so, is that of the common cold. When we have a running at the nose and there is a discharge from the nostrils, the mucus is more acrid than that which is present when we are well. It makes the nose swell and renders it hot and extremely inflamed, if you apply your hand to it. And if it lasts a long time, the part, being fleshless and hard, becomes ulcerated. The fever does not fall when the nose is running, but when the discharge becomes thicker, less acrid, milder and more of its ordinary consistency. Similar changes may be seen as the result of cold alone, but the same observations can be made. There is the same change from cold to hot and hot to cold and the changes take place readily and do not require any process of "digestion." I assert too that all other illnesses that are caused by acrid or undiluted humours within the body follow a similar course; they subside as these humours become less potent and are diluted.

19. Those humours which affect the eyes are very acrid and cause sores upon the eyelids; sometimes they cause destruction of the cheeks and the parts beneath the eyes. The discharge destroys anything it may touch, even eating away the membrane which surrounds the eye. Pain, heat and swelling obtain until such time as the discharges are "digested" and become thicker and give rise to a serum. The process of "digestion" is due to their being mixed and diluted with one another and warmed together. Again, the humours of the throat which cause hoarseness and sore throats, those of erysipelas or pneumonia are at first salt, moist and acrid and during this phase the maladies flourish. But when the discharges become thicker and milder and lose their acridity, the fevers cease as well as the other effects of the disease which are harmful to the body. The cause of these maladies is found in the presence of certain substances, which, when present, invariably produce such results. But when the nature of these substances becomes changed, the illness is at an end. Any abnormal condition which arose purely as a result of heat or cold and into which no other factor entered at all would be resolved when a change occurred from hot to cold or vice versa. However, the changes which take place really occur in the manner I described above. All the ills from which man suffers are due to the operation of "forces." For instance, if a sufferer from biliousness, complaining of nausea, fever and weakness, gets rid of a certain bitter material which we call yellow bile either by himself or with the assistance of purging, it is evident how he gets rid of both the fever and the pain at the same time. As long as this material is unabsorbed and undiluted, no device will terminate either the pain or the fever. When there are pungent rust-coloured acids present in the body, there is frenzy and severe pain in the bowels and in the chest and distress which cannot be cured until they have been purged of the acrid humours responsible and their poisonous effects neutralized by being mixed with other fluids. It is in the processes of digestion, change, dilution or thickening by which the nature of a humour is altered that the causes of disease lie. It is for this reason that the occurrence of crises and the periodicity of certain diseases are so important. It is most improper that all these changes should be attributed to the effects of heat and cold, for such principles are not subject to degeneration or thickening. The changes of disease cannot be due to the effect of varying mixtures of such principles, for the only thing that will mix with heat and reduce its warmth is coldness and vice versa. The various forces in the body become milder and more health-giving when they are adjusted

to one another. A man is healthiest when these factors are co-ordinated and no particular force predominates.

20. I think I have discussed this subject sufficiently, but there are some doctors and sophists who maintain that no one can understand the science of medicine unless he knows what man is; that anyone who proposes to treat men for their illnesses must first learn of such things. Their discourse then tends to philosophy, as may be seen in the writings of Empedocles and all the others who have ever written about Nature; they discuss the origins of man and of what he was created. It is my opinion that all which has been written by doctors or sophists on nature has more to do with painting than medicine. I do not believe that any clear knowledge of Nature can be obtained from any source other than a study of medicine and then only through a thorough mastery of this science. It is my intention to discuss what man is and how he exists because it seems to me indispensable for a doctor to have made such studies and to be fully acquainted with Nature. He will then understand how the body functions with regard to what is eaten and drunk and what will be the effect of any given measure on any particular organ. It is not enough to say "cheese is harmful because it produces pain if much of it is eaten." One should know what sort of pain, why it is produced and which organ of the body is upset. There are many other harmful items of food and drink which affect the body in different ways. For example, the taking of large quantities of undiluted wine has a certain effect upon the body and it is recognized, by those who understand, that the wine is the cause and we know which organs are particularly affected. I want to show that the same sort of thing is true of other cases. Cheese, since that is the example I used, is not equally harmful to all. Some can eat their fill of it without any unpleasant consequences and those whom it suits are wonderfully strengthened by it. On the other hand, there are some who have difficulty in digesting it. There must, then, be a difference in their constitutions and the difference lies in the fact that, in the latter case, they have something in the body which is inimical to cheese and this is aroused and disturbed by it. Those who have most of this humour and in whom it is at its strongest, naturally suffer most. If cheese were bad for the human constitution in general, it would affect everyone. Knowledge of this would avoid harm.

21. Both during convalescence as well as in the course of prolonged illnesses, complications are often seen. Some of them occur naturally in the course of the disease, others are occasioned by some chance happening. Most doctors, like laymen, tend to ascribe some such event to some particular activity that has been indulged in. In the same way they may ascribe something as being due to an alteration in their habits of bathing or walking or a change of diet, whether this is the actual case or not. As a result of jumping to conclusions, the truth may escape them. One must know with exactitude what is the effect of a bath or of fatigue indulged in at the wrong time. Neither such actions, nor eating too much, nor eating the wrong food will always produce the same effects; it depends upon other factors as well. No one who is unacquainted with the specific effects of such action on the body in different circumstances can know the results which follow and consequently he cannot make proper use of them as therapeutic measures.

22. I think it should also be known what illnesses are due to "forces" and what to "forms." By "forces" I mean those changes in the constitution of the humours which affect the working of the body; by "forms" I mean the organs of the body. Some of the latter are hollow and show variations in diameter, being narrow at one end and wide at the other, some are elongated, some solid and round, some flat and suspended, some are stretched out, some large, some thick, some are porous and sponge-like. For instance, which type of hollow organ should be the better able to attract and absorb moisture from the rest of the body: those which are all broad or those which are wide in part and narrow down? The latter kind. Such things have to be deduced from a consideration of what clearly happens outside the body. For instance, if you gape with your mouth wide open you cannot suck up any fluid, but if you pout and compress the lips and then insert a tube you can easily suck up as much as you like. Again, cupping glasses are made concave for the purpose of drawing and pulling the flesh up within them, and there are other examples of this kind of thing. Among the inner organs of the body, the bladder, the skull and the womb have such a shape and it is well known that these organs specially attract moisture from other parts of the body and are always filled with fluid. On the other hand organs which are more spread out, although they hold fluid which flows into them well, do not attract it to the same extent. Further, the solid and round organs neither attract it nor hold it because there is nowhere for the fluid to lodge. Those which are spongy and of loose texture such as the spleen, the lungs and the female breasts easily absorb fluid from the nearby parts of the body and when they do so become hard and swollen. Such organs do not absorb fluid and then discharge it day after day as would a hollow organ containing fluid, but when they have absorbed fluid and all the spaces and interstices are filled up, they become

hard and tense instead of soft and pliant. They neither digest the fluid nor discharge it, and this is the natural result of their anatomical construction. The organs of the body that cause flatulence and colic, such as the stomach and chest, produce noise and rumbling. For any hollow organ that does not become full of fluid and remain so but instead undergoes changes and movement, must necessarily produce noises and the signs of movement. The organs which are soft and fleshy tend to become obstructed and then they are liable to sluggishness and fullness. Sometimes an organ which is diseased comes up against some flat tissue which is neither strong enough to resist the force of the swollen organ nor sufficiently mobile to accommodate the diseased organ by yielding. For instance, the liver is tender, full-blooded and solid and on account of these qualities is resistant to the movement of other organs. Thus wind, being obstructed by it, becomes more forceful and attacks the thing which obstructs it with greater power. In the case of an organ such as the liver, which is both full-blooded and tender, it cannot but experience pain. For this reason, pain in the hepatic area is both exceedingly severe and frequently encountered. Abscesses and tumours also occur very commonly here, as well as beneath the diaphragm. This latter condition, although less common, is more serious. The extent of the diaphragm is considerable and is opposed to other organs; nevertheless, its more sinewy and stronger nature makes it less liable to pain although both pains and tumours may occur in this region.

23. There are many individual variations in the shape of the different organs of the body from one person to another and they react differently both in health and in disease. There are large and small heads; thin and thick, long and short necks. The belly may be large and round; the chest narrow and flat. There are countless other differences and the effects of such variation must be known so that one can understand the exact cause when they become diseased. Only thus can proper care be given.

24. Again, the effect of each type of humour on the body must be learnt and, as I said before, their relationships with one another must be understood. I mean this sort of thing: if a sweet humour should change its nature, not by admixture with something else but spontaneously, what characteristic would it show? Bitter, salt, astringent or sharp? Sharp, I fancy. A sharp humour, compared with the others, would be specially inimical to the digestion of food. At least it would be so if, as we believe, a sweet humour is the most suited.

Thus, if anyone were able to light upon the truth by experiment outside the body, he would always be able to make the best pronouncements of all. The best advice is that which is least unsuitable.

NOTE

1. The term translated "postulate" is *hypothesis*.

DREAMS

(REGIMEN IV)

This short treatise on the medical significance of dreams forms the conclusion to a long work on Regimen; this explains the numbering of the paragraphs, and the last sentence must be understood to refer to the whole work.

86. Accurate knowledge about the signs which occur in dreams will be found very valuable for all purposes. While the body is awake, the soul is not under its own control, but is split into various portions each being devoted to some special bodily function such as hearing, vision, touch, locomotion and all the various actions of the body. But when the body is at rest, the soul is stirred and roused and becomes its own master, and itself performs all the functions of the body. When the body is sleeping it receives no sensations, but the soul being awake at that time perceives everything; it sees what is visible, it hears what is audible, it walks, it touches, it feels pain and thinks. In short, during sleep the soul performs all the functions of both body and soul. A correct appreciation of these things implies considerable wisdom.

87. There are special interpreters, with their own science of these matters, for the god-given dreams which give to cities or to individuals foreknowledge of the future. Such people also interpret the signs derived from the soul which indicate bodily states; excess or lack of what is natural, or of some unusual change. In such matters they are sometimes right and sometimes wrong, but in neither case do they know why it happens, whether they are right or wrong, but nevertheless they give advice so you shall "beware of taking harm." Yet they never show you how you ought to beware, but merely tell you to pray to the gods. Prayer is a good thing, but one should take on part of the burden oneself and call on the gods only to help.

88. The facts about dreams are as follows: those that merely consist of a transference to the night of a person's daytime actions and thoughts, which continue to happen in normal fashion just as they were done and thought during the day, are good for they indicate a healthy state. This is because the soul remains true to its daytime cogitations, and is overcome neither by excess nor by emptiness, nor by any other extraneous circumstance. But when dreams take on a character contrary to daytime activities and involve conflict or victory over them, then they constitute a sign of bodily disturbance. The seriousness of the conflict is an indication of the seriousness of the mischief. Now concerning this, I make no judgement whether or not you ought to avert the consequence by appropriate rites or not. But I do advise treatment of the body, for an excretion resulting from some bodily superfluity has disturbed the soul. If the opposing force be strong, it is a good thing to give an emetic and to administer a gradually increasing light diet for five days, to order frequent early-morning walks gradually becoming more brisk, and gymnastics for those accustomed to this form of exercise, proportionate in severity to the increase of diet. If the opposing force be weaker, dispense with the emetic, reduce the diet by a third and restore the cut by a gradual measure over five days. Strenuous walks and the use of vocal exercises will put an end to the disturbance.

89. It is a good sign to see the sun, moon, sky and stars clear and undimmed, each being placed normally in its right place, since it shows that the body is well and free from disturbing influences. But it is necessary to follow a régime which will ensure that such a condition is maintained. On the contrary, if any of these celestial bodies appear displaced or changed then such a sign indicates bodily disease, the severity of which depends upon the seriousness of the interference.

Now the orbit of the stars is the outermost, that of the sun is intermediate, while that of the moon is nearest to the hollow vault of the sky. Should one of the stars seem to be injured, or should it disappear or stop in its revolution as a result of mist or cloud, this is a weak sign. If such a change be produced by rain or hail, it is stronger and signifies that an excretion of moisture and phlegm has occurred into the corresponding outermost parts. In such cases, prescribe long runs well wrapped up, increasing the exercise so as to cause as much sweating as possible. The exercise should be followed by long walks and the patient should go without breakfast. Food should be cut by a third and the normal diet restored gradually over five days. If the disorder appears more severe, prescribe vapour baths in addition. It is advisable to cleanse through the skin because the harm is in the outermost parts. Therefore prescribe dry, pungent, bitter, undiluted foods and the most dehydrating exercises.

If the moon is involved, it is advisable to draw off the harmful matter internally; therefore to use an emetic following the administration of pungent, salty and soft foods. Also, prescribe brisk runs on a circular track, walks and vocal exercises. Forbid breakfast and reduce the food intake, restoring it as before. The cleansing should be done internally because the harm appeared in the hollows of the body.

If the sun encounters any of these changes, the trouble is more violent and less easy to expel. The drawing-off should be produced both ways; prescribe runs on the stadium track and on the circular track, walks and all other forms of exercise. Give an emetic, cut the food and restore the diet gradually over five days as before.

If the heavenly bodies are seen dimly in a clear sky, and shine weakly and seem to be stopped from revolving by dryness, then it is a sign that there is a danger of incurring sickness. Exercise should be stopped while a fluid diet, frequent baths and plenty of rest and sleep should be prescribed until there is a return to normal.

If the heavenly bodies are opposed by a fiery atmosphere, the excretion of bile is indicated. If the opposing powers get the upper hand, sickness is portended; but if they completely overcome the stars and these vanish, then there is danger that the sickness may terminate fatally. If the opposing influences, however, are put to flight and it seems as if they are pursued by the heavenly bodies, then there is danger of the patient going mad unless he be treated. In all these cases, it is best to start treatment by purging with hellebore. If this is not done, the diet should be fluid and no wine should be taken unless it be white, thin, soft and watery. Warm, pungent, dehydrating and salt things should be avoided. Prescribe as much natural exercise as possible and plenty of runs with the patients well wrapped-up. Avoid massage, wrestling and wrestling in dust. Soften them with plenty of sleep and, apart from natural exercise, let them rest. Let them take a walk after dinner. It is also good to take a vapour bath followed by an emetic. For thirty days the patient should not eat his fill, but when he is restored to a full diet he should take an emetic thrice monthly after partaking of a sweet, fluid and light meal.

When the heavenly bodies wander in different directions, some mental disturbance as a result of anxiety is indicated. In this case, ease is beneficial. The soul should be turned to entertainments, especially amusing ones, or failing these, any that may give special pleasure, for two or three days. This may effect a cure; if not, the mental anxiety may engender disease.

It is a sign of health if a star, which is clear and bright, appears to fall out of its orbit and to move eastwards. The separation of any clear substance and its natural excretion from the body is good. Thus excretion of substances into the bowels and the formation of abscessions in the skin are examples of things falling out of their orbit.

It is a sign of sickness if the star appears dark and dim and moves either westward, or down into the earth or sea, or upwards. Upward movement indicates fluxes in the head; movement into the sea, disease of the bowels; earthward movement, the growing of tumours in the flesh. In these cases it is wise to reduce the food intake by a third and, after an emetic, to increase it over five days. Then a normal diet should be taken for a further five days, after which another emetic should be taken followed by an increase in the same way.

It is a healthy sign if any of the heavenly bodies appears clear and moist, because the influx from the ether acting on the person is clear and the soul perceives this as it enters. If it be dark, and not clean and transparent, then sickness is indicated, not due to some internal excess or lack of something, but coming from the external environment. In this case it is advisable to take brisk runs on a circular track so as to restrict the wasting of the body. Also, the quickened respiration causes excretion of the intruding influence, and brisk walks should follow the runs. The diet should be soft and light, being increased to reach the normal in four days.

When a person appears to receive something pure from a pure deity, it is good for health because it means that the things entering his body are pure. If he seems to see the opposite of this, it is not good because it indicates that some element of disease has entered his body. Such a case should be treated as the one described above.

If it seems to rain with gentle rain from clear skies, and without any violent downpour or heavy storm, it is good. Such indicates that the breath drawn from the air is proportionate and pure. If the reverse happens, violent rain, storm and tempest, and the rain is not clear, it indicates the onset of disease from the respired air. A similar régime should be prescribed for this sort of case and very little food should be taken.

From the information which comes from this knowledge of the heavenly bodies, one must take precautions and follow the prescribed regimens. Pray to the gods: when the signs are good to the Sun, to Zeus of the sky, Zeus of the home, Athena of the home, to Hermes and Apollo. When the signs are the opposite, pray to the gods who avert evil, to Earth and to the Heroes, that all ills may be turned aside.

90. The following are some of the signs that foretell health: to see clearly and to hear distinctly things on the earth, to walk safely and to run safely and swiftly without fear, to see the earth smooth and well tilled and trees flourishing, laden with fruit and well-kept; to see rivers flowing normally with water clear and neither in flood nor with their flow lessened, and springs and wells similarly. All these things indicate the subject's health, and that the body, its flows, the food ingested and the excreta, are normal.

Anything seen which is the contrary, however, indicates something wrong in the body. Interference with sight or hearing indicates some malady of the head and longer early morning and after dinner walks than in the previous regimen should be ordered. If the legs are harmed, a contrary pull should be exerted by emetics and a greater indulgence in wrestling. Rough land indicates impurity in the flesh; longer walks after exercise should be ordered.

Trees that do not bear fruit indicate destruction of the human semen; if the trees are losing their leaves the cause of the trouble is wet and cold; if they are flourishing but barren, heat and dryness. In the one case, the regimen should aim at warming and drying; in the other, at cooling and moistening.

Abnormality in rivers relates to the flow of the blood. If the flow of a river be greater than usual, a superfluity of blood; if it be less, a deficiency. The regimen should aim at a decrease or an increase respectively. If the water is cloudy, some disturbance is indicated. This can be remedied by runs on a track or by walking; increased breathing disperses it.

Springs and wells relate to the bladder and in these cases diuretics should be employed.

A rough sea indicates disease of the bowels. Light

and gentle laxatives should be used to effect a thorough purgation.

An earth-tremor or the shaking of a house predicts the onset of sickness when it is observed by a healthy man; a change and the restoration of health for a sick one. In the healthy, it is wise to change the regimen because it is the existing régime which is disturbing the whole body; therefore first give an emetic so that, after this, he may be fed up again gradually. But in the case of a sick man, because the body itself is undergoing a change, the same regimen should be continued.

To see land flooded with water or by the sea is a sign of illness, indicating excess fluid in the body. Prescribe emetics, fasting, exercise and a dry diet increasing little by little. Nor is it good to see the earth looking black or scorched; this shows excessive dehydration of the body and there is the risk of severe or fatal illness. Stop exercise and forbid all dry, pungent and diuretic food. Prescribe boiled barley-water and a small quantity of light food together with plenty of watery white wine to drink and lots of baths. The patient should not bath till he has eaten; then let him lie soft and relax, avoiding cold and sun. Pray to Earth, Hermes and the Heroes. To dream of diving into a lake, the sea or rivers is not a good sign as it too indicates an excess of moisture. It is advisable to use a dehydrating regimen and more exercise. In those suffering from fever, however, it is a good sign, indicating that the heat is being quenched by moisture.

91. It is a good sign for health to see anything normal about one's clothing, the size being neither too large nor too small but in accordance with one's own size. It is good to have white garments of one's own and the finest footwear. Anything too large or too small for one's limbs is not good; in the one case the regimen should aim at a decrease, and in the other, an increase. Black things indicate a more sickly or dangerous condition. Softening and moistening measures should be applied. New things denote a change.

92. To see the dead, clean, in white clothes, is good; while to receive something clean from them denotes health both of the body and the things which enter it. This is because the dead are a source of nourishment, increase and propagation, and it is a sign of health that what enters the body should be clean. On the contrary, if the dead appear naked, or in dark garments, or unclean, or taking or carrying anything out of the house, this is an inexpedient sign indicating disease because the things entering the body are harmful. These should be purged away by circular runs and walks and, after an emetic, a soft and light diet should be given which is gradually increased.

93. The appearance of monstrous creatures which appear during sleep and frighten the dreamer indicate a surfeit or unaccustomed food, a secretion, cholera and a dangerous illness. An emetic should be followed by an increasing diet of the lightest foods for five days; the food should neither be excessive nor pungent, nor dry nor warm. Prescribe also exercise, especially natural exercise, but not walks after dinner. Warm baths and relaxation are also advisable, and both the sun and the cold should be avoided.

To seem, while sleeping, to eat or to drink one's normal diet indicates undernourishment and a mental hunger. The stronger the meats seem, the greater the degree of inadequacy of the diet; weaker meats indicate a smaller deficiency, as if it were good to partake of whatever were seen in the dream. . . .[1] The diet should therefore be reduced, as it indicates a surfeit of nourishment. To dream of loaves made with cheese and honey has a similar significance.

Drinking clear water is not harmful; all other sorts of water are. Any normal things seen in a dream indicate a similar appetite of the soul.

If the dreamer flies in fright from anything, this means an obstruction to the blood as a result of dehydration. It is then wise to cool and moisten the body.

Fighting, being stabbed or bound by another indicates that some secretion, inimical to the flows, has taken place into the body. It is then advisable to take an emetic, to go on a reducing diet and to go for walks. A light diet, increasing over four days, should be taken after the emetic. Wandering and difficult climbs have the same meaning.

Fording rivers, enemy soldiers and monstrous apparitions denote illness or madness. After an emetic give a small diet of light soft food, increasing gently for five days, together with plenty of natural exercise—except walks after dinner—warm baths and relaxation. Avoid cold and sun.

By following the instructions I have given, one may live a healthy life; and I have discovered the best regimen that can be devised by a mere mortal with the help of the gods.

NOTE

1. A sentence is probably lost here.

THE NATURE OF MAN

A POPULAR LECTURE ON PHYSIOLOGY

1. This lecture is not intended for those who are accustomed to hear discourses which inquire more deeply into the human constitution than is profitable for medical study. I am not going to assert that man is all air, or fire, or water, or earth, or in fact anything but what manifestly composes his body; let those who like discuss such matters. Nevertheless, when these things are discussed I perceive a certain discrepancy in the analyses for, although the same theory is employed, the conclusions do not agree. They all, theorizing, draw the same deduction, asserting that there is one basic substance which is unique and the basis of everything; but they call it by different names, one insisting that it is air, another that it is fire, another water, another earth. Each adds arguments and proofs to support his contention, all of which mean nothing. Now, whenever people arguing on the same theory do not reach the same conclusion, you may be sure that they do not know what they are talking about. A good illustration of this is provided by attending their disputations when the same disputants are present and the same audience; the same man never wins the argument three times running, it is first one and then the other and sometimes the one who happens to have the glibbest tongue. Yet it would be expected that the man who asserts that he can provide the correct explanation of the subject, if, that is, he really knows what he is talking about and demonstrates it correctly, should always win the argument. I am of the opinion that these people wreck their own theories on the problem of the terms they use for the One because they fail to understand the issue. Thus they serve, rather, to establish the theory of Melissus.[1]

2. I need say no more about these theorists. But when we come to physicians, we find that some assert that man is composed of blood, others of bile and some of phlegm. But these, too, all make the same point, asserting that there is a basic unity of substance, although they each give it a different name and so change its appearance and properties under stress of heat and cold, becoming sweet or bitter, white or black, and so forth. Now I do not agree with these people either, although the majority will declare that this, or something very similar, is the case. I hold that if man were basically of one substance, he would never feel pain, since, being one, there would be nothing to hurt. Moreover, if he should feel pain, the remedy likewise would have to be single. But in fact there are many remedies because there are many things in the body which when abnormally heated, cooled, dried or moistened by interaction, engender disease. As a result, disease has a plurality of forms and a plurality of cures.

I challenge the man who asserts that blood is the sole constituent of the human body, to show, not that it undergoes changes into all sorts of forms, but that there is a time of year or of human life when blood is obviously the sole constituent of the body. It is reasonable to suppose, were this theory true, that there is one period at which it appears in its proper form. The same applies to those who make the body of phlegm or bile.

I propose to show that the substances I believe compose the body are, both nominally and essentially, always the same and unchanging; in youth as well as in age, in cold weather as well as in warm. I shall produce proofs and demonstrate the causes both of the growth and decline of each of the constituents of the body.

3. In the first place, generation cannot arise from a single substance. For how could one thing generate another unless it copulated with some other? Secondly, unless the things which copulated were of the same species and had the same generative capabilities, we should not get these results. Again, generation would be impossible unless the hot stood in a fair and reasonable proportion to the cold, and likewise the dry to the wet; if, for instance, one preponderated over the other, one being much stronger and the other much weaker. Is it likely, then, that anything should be generated from one thing, seeing that not even a number of things suffice unless they are combined in the right proportions? It follows, then, such being the nature of the human body and of everything else, that man is not a unity but each of the elements contributing to his formation preserves in the body the power which it contributed. It also follows that each of the elements must return to its original nature when the body dies; the wet to the wet, the dry to the dry, the hot to the hot and the cold to the cold. The constitution of animals is similar and of everything else too. All things have a similar generation and a similar dissolution, for all are formed of the substances mentioned

and are finally resolved in the same constituents as produced them; that too is how they disappear.

4. The human body contains blood, phlegm, yellow bile and black bile. These are the things that make up its constitution and cause its pains and health. Health is primarily that state in which these constituent substances are in the correct proportion to each other, both in strength and quantity, and are well mixed. Pain occurs when one of the substances presents either a deficiency or an excess, or is separated in the body and not mixed with the others. It is inevitable that when one of these is separated from the rest and stands by itself, not only the part from which it has come, but also that where it collects and is present in excess, should become diseased, and because it contains too much of the particular substance, cause pain and distress. Whenever there is more than slight discharge of one of these humours outside the body, then its loss is accompanied by pain. If, however, the loss, change or separation from the other humours is internal, then it inevitably causes twice as much pain, as I have said, for pain is produced both in the part whence it is derived and in the part where it accumulates.

5. Now I said that I would demonstrate that my proposed constituents of the human body were always constant, both nominally and essentially. I hold that these constituents are blood, phlegm and yellow and black bile. Common usage has assigned to them specific and different names because there are essential differences in their appearance. Phlegm is not like blood, nor is blood like bile, nor bile like phlegm. Indeed, how could they be alike when there is no similarity in appearance and when they are different to the sense of touch? They are dissimilar in their qualities of heat, cold, dryness and moisture. It follows then that substances so unlike in appearance and characteristics cannot basically be identical, at least if fire and water are not identical. As evidence of the fact that they are dissimilar, each possessing its own qualities and nature, consider the following case. If you give a man medicine which brings up phlegm, you will find his vomit is phlegm; if you give him one which brings up bile, he will vomit bile. Similarly, black bile can be eliminated by administering a medicine which brings it up, or, if you cut the body so as to form an open wound, it bleeds. These things will take place just the same every day and every night, winter and summer, so long as the subject can draw breath and expel it again, or until he is deprived of any of these congenital elements. For they must be congenital, firstly because it is obvious that they are present at every age so long as life is present and, secondly, because they

were procreated by a human being who had them all and mothered in a human being similarly endowed with all the elements which I have indicated and demonstrated.

6. Those who assert that the human body is a single substance seem to have reasoned along the following lines. Having observed that when men died from excessive purgation following the administration of drugs, some vomited bile and some phlegm, they concluded from this that whatever was the nature of the material voided at death, this was indeed the fundamental constituent of man. Those who insist that blood is the basic substance use a similar argument; because they see blood flowing from the body in the fatally wounded, they conclude that blood constitutes the soul. They all use similar arguments to support their theories. But, to begin with, no one ever yet died from excessive purgation and brought up only bile; taking medicine which causes the bringing up of bile, produces first the vomiting of bile, but subsequently, the vomiting of phlegm as well. This is followed by the vomiting of black bile in spite of themselves and they end up by vomiting pure blood and that is how they die. The same effects result from taking a drug which brings up phlegm; the vomiting of phlegm is followed by yellow bile, then black bile, then pure blood, and so death ensues. When a drug is ingested, it first causes the evacuation of whatever in the body is naturally suited to it, but afterwards, it causes the voiding of other substances too. It is similar in the case of plants and seeds; when these are put into the ground, they first absorb the things which naturally suit them; they may be acid, bitter, sweet, salty and so forth. But although at first the plant takes what is naturally suited to it, afterwards it absorbs other things as well. The action of drugs in the body is similar; those which cause the bringing up of bile at first bring it up undiluted, but later on it is voided mixed with other substances; the same is true of drugs which bring up phlegm. In the case of men who have been fatally wounded the blood at first runs very warm and red, but subsequently it becomes more like phlegm and bile.

7. Now the quantity of phlegm in the body increases in winter because it is that bodily substance most in keeping with the winter, seeing that it is the coldest. You can verify its coldness by touching phlegm, bile and blood; you will find that the phlegm is the coldest. It is however the most viscous and is brought up with greater force than any other substance with the exception of black bile. Although those things which are forcibly expelled become warmer owing to the force to which they are subjected, nevertheless phlegm remains the coldest substance, and obviously so, owing to its natural charac-

teristics. The following signs show that winter fills the body with phlegm: people spit and blow from their noses the most phlegmatic mucus in winter; swellings become white especially at that season and other diseases show phlegmatic signs.

During the spring, although the phlegm remains strong in the body, the quantity of blood increases. Then, as the cold becomes less intense and the rainy season comes on, the wet and warm days increase further the quantity of blood. This part of the year is most in keeping with blood because it is wet and hot. That this is so, you can judge by these signs: it is in spring and summer that people are particularly liable to dysentery and to epistaxis, and these are the seasons too at which people are warmest and their complexions are ruddiest.

During the summer, the blood is still strong but the bile gradually increases, and this change continues into the autumn when the blood decreases since the autumn is contrary to it. The bile rules the body during the summer and the autumn. As proof of this, it is during this season that people vomit bile spontaneously, or, if they take drugs, they void the most bilious sort of matter. It is plain too from the nature of fevers and from people's complexions in that season. During the summer, the phlegm is at its weakest since this season, on account of its dryness and heat, is most contrary to that substance.

The blood in the body reaches its lowest level in autumn, because this is a dry season and the body is already beginning to cool. Black bile is strongest and preponderates in the autumn. When winter sets in the bile is cooled and decreases while the phlegm increases again owing to the amount of rain and the length of the nights.

All these substances, then, are all always present in the body but vary in their relative quantities, each preponderating in turn according to its natural characteristics. The year has its share of all the elements: heat, cold, dryness and wetness. None of these could exist alone for a moment, while, on the other hand, were they missing, all would disappear, for they are all mutually interdependent. In the same way, if any of these primary bodily substances were absent from man, life would cease. And just as the year is governed at one time by winter, then by spring, then by summer and then by autumn; so at one time in the body phlegm preponderates, at another time blood, at another time yellow bile and this is followed by the preponderance of black bile. A very clear proof of this can be obtained by giving the same man the same emetic at four different times in the year; his vomit will be most phlegmatic in winter, most wet in spring, most bilious in summer and darkest in autumn.

8. In these circumstances it follows that the diseases which increase in winter should decrease in summer and vice versa. Those which come to an end in a given number of days are exceptions and I will discuss periodicity later on. You may expect diseases which begin in spring to end in the autumn; likewise autumnal diseases will disappear in the spring. Any disease which exceeds these limits must be put down as belonging to a whole year. In applying his remedies, the physician must bear in mind that each disease is most prominent during the season most in keeping with its nature.

9. In addition to these considerations, certain further points should be known. Diseases caused by over-eating are cured by fasting; those caused by starvation are cured by feeding up. Diseases caused by exertion are cured by rest; those caused by indolence are cured by exertion. To put it briefly: the physician should treat disease by the principle of opposition to the cause of the disease according to its form, its seasonal and age incidence, countering tenseness by relaxation and vice versa. This will bring the patient most relief and seems to me to be the principle of healing.

Some diseases are produced by the manner of life that is followed; others by the life-giving air we breathe. That there are these two types may be demonstrated in the following way. When a large number of people all catch the same disease at the same time, the cause must be ascribed to something common to all and which they all use; in other words to what they all breathe. In such a disease, it is obvious that individual bodily habits cannot be responsible because the malady attacks one after another, young and old, men and women alike, those who drink their wine neat and those who drink only water; those who eat barley-cake as well as those who live on bread, those who take a lot of exercise and those who take but little. The régime cannot therefore be responsible where people who live very different lives catch the same disease.

However, when many different diseases appear at the same time, it is plain that the regimen is responsible in individual cases. Treatment then should aim at opposing the cause of the disease as I have said elsewhere; that is, treatment should involve a change in regimen. For, in such a case, it is obvious that all, most, or at least one of the factors in the regimen does not agree with the patient; such must be sought out and changed having regard to the constitution of the patient, his age and appearance, the season of the year and the nature of the disease. The treatment prescribed should vary accordingly by lessening this or increasing that, and the regimen and drugs should be appropriately adapted to the various factors already mentioned.

When an epidemic of one particular disease is established, it is evident that it is not the regimen but the air breathed which is responsible. Plainly, the air must be harmful because of some morbid secretion which it contains. Your advice to patients at such a time should be not to alter the regimen since this is not to blame, but they should gradually reduce the quantity of food and drink taken so that the body is as little loaded and as weak as possible. A sudden change of regimen involves the risk of starting a fresh complaint, so you should deal with the regimen in this way when it is clearly not the cause of the patient's illness. Care should be taken that the amount of air breathed should be as small as possible and as unfamiliar as possible. These points may be dealt with by making the body thin so that the patient will avoid large and frequent breaths, and, wherever practicable, by a change of station from the infected area.

10. The most serious diseases are those which arise from the strongest part of the body, since if a disease remains in the place where it begins, it is inevitable that the whole body should sicken if its strongest part does. Alternatively, if the disease passes from the stronger part to a weaker part, it proves difficult to dispel. Those which pass from a weak part to a stronger are more easily cured because the in-flowing humours are easily spent by the strength of the part.

11. The blood-vessels of largest calibre, of which there are four pairs in the body, are arranged in the following way: one pair runs from the back of the head, through the neck, and, weaving its way externally along the spine, passes into the legs, traverses the calves and the outer aspect of the ankle, and reaches the feet. Venesection for pains in the back and loins should therefore be practised in the hollow of the knee or externally at the ankle.

The second pair of blood-vessels runs from the head near the ears through the neck, where they are known as the jugular veins. Thence they continue deeply close to the spine on either side. They pass close to the muscles of the loins, entering the testicles and the thighs. Thence they traverse the popliteal fossa on the medial side and passing through the calves lie on the inner aspect of the ankles and the feet. Venesection for pain in the loin and in the testicles should therefore be done in the popliteal area or at the inner side of the ankle.

The third pair of blood-vessels runs from the temples, through the neck and under the shoulder-blades. They then come together in the lungs; the right-hand one crossing to the left, the left-hand one crossing to the right. The right-hand one proceeds from the lungs, passes under the breast and enters the spleen and the kid-

neys. The left-hand one proceeds to the right on leaving the lungs, passes under the breast and enters the liver and the kidneys. Both vessels terminate in the anus.

The fourth pair runs from the front of the head and the eyes, down the neck and under the clavicles. They then course on the upper surface of the arms as far as the elbows, through the forearms into the wrists and so into the fingers. They then return from the fingers running through the ball of the thumb and the forearms to the elbows where they course along the inferior surface of the arms to the axillae. Thence they pass superficially down the sides, one reaching the spleen and its fellow the liver. Thence they course over the belly and terminate in the pudendal area.

Apart from the larger vessels which are thus accounted for, there are a large number of vessels of all sizes running from the belly to all parts of the body; these carry foodstuffs to the body. They also form connections between the large main vessels which run to the belly and the rest of the body. In addition they join up with each other and form connections between the deep and superficial vessels.

The following are therefore rules for venesection. Care should be taken that the cuts are as close as possible to the determined source of the pain and the place where the blood collects. By doing this a sudden, violent change is avoided but at the same time the customary site of collection of blood will be changed.

12. If a patient over the age of thirty-five expectorates much without showing fever, passes urine exhibiting a large quantity of sediment painlessly, or suffers continuously from bloody stools as in cases of dysentery, his complaint will arise from the following single cause. He must, when a young man, have been hardworking, fond of physical exertion and work and then, on dropping the exercises, have run to soft flesh very different from that which he had before. There must be a sharp distinction between his previous and his present bodily physique so that the two do not agree. If a person so constituted contracts some disease, he escapes for the time being but, after the illness, the body wastes. Fluid matter then flows through the blood-vessels wherever the widest way offers. If it makes its way to the lower bowel it is passed in the stools in much the same form as it was in the body; as its course is downwards it does not stay long in the intestines. If it flows into the chest, suppuration results because, owing to the upward tread of its path, it spends a long time in the chest and there rots and forms pus. Should the fluid matter, however, be expelled into the bladder, it becomes warm and white owing to the warmth of that region. It becomes separated in

the urine; the lighter elements float and form a scum on the surface while the heavier constituents fall to the bottom forming pus.

Children suffer from stones owing to the warmth of the whole body and of the region about the bladder in particular. Adult men do not suffer from stone because the body is cool; it should be thoroughly appreciated that a person is warmest the day he is born and coldest the day he dies. So long as the body is growing and advancing towards strength it is necessarily warm; but when it begins to wither and to fade away to feebleness, it cools down. From this principle it follows that a person is warmest the day he is born because he grows most on that day; he is coldest the day he dies because on that day he withers most.

People of the constitution mentioned above, that is athletic people who have got soft, generally recover of their own accord within forty-five days of the wasting beginning. If such a period be exceeded, natural recovery takes a year so long as no other malady intervenes.

13. Prognosis is safest to foretell in those diseases which develop quickly and those whose causes are apparent. They should be cured by opposing whatever is the cause of the disease, of which the body will thus be rid.

14. The presence of a sandy sediment or of stones in the urine means that originally tumours grew in relation to the aorta and suppurated. Then, because the tumour did not burst rapidly, stones were formed from the pus and these were squeezed out through the blood-vessels together with urine into the bladder. When the urine is only blood-stained, the blood-vessels have been attacked. Sometimes the urine is thick and small hair-like pieces of flesh are voided with it which, it must be realized, come from the kidneys and the joints. When in an otherwise clear urine, a substance like bran is present in it, the bladder is inflamed.

15. Most fevers are caused by bile. Apart from those arising from local injury, they are of four types. These are called continued, quotidian, tertian and quartan.

Continued fever is produced by large quantities of the most concentrated bile and the crisis is reached in the shortest time; as the body enjoys no periods of coolness, the great heat it endures results in rapid wasting.

Quotidian fever is caused by a large quantity of bile, but less than that which causes continued fever. This is quicker than the others to depart although it lasts longer than a continued fever by as much as there is less bile causing it, and because the body has some respite from the fever whereas continued fever allows none.

Tertian fever lasts longer than quotidian fever and is caused by less bile. A tertian fever is longer in proportion to the longer respites from fever allowed to the body compared with quotidian fevers.

Quartans behave similarly to the tertians but last longer, as they arise from still less of the heat-producing bile and because they give the body longer respites in which to cool down. A secondary reason for their chronic character and difficult resolution is that they are caused by black bile; this is the most viscous of the humours in the body and remains the longest. As evidence of this note the association of quartan fevers with melancholy. Quartan fever has its highest incidence in the autumn and in those between the ages of twenty-five and forty-five. This is the time of life when the body is most subject to black bile, and the autumn is the corresponding season of the year. If a quartan fever occurs at any other time of the year, or at any other age, you may be sure that it will not be chronic unless some other malady be present.

NOTE

1. Flourished about 440 B.C.; like Parmenides, he denied plurality and change and held that what is is one and unchanging.

3

~

ARISTOTLE

Aristotle (384–322 B.C.) was raised in the court of Amyntas III, king of Macedonia and grandfather of Alexander the Great, which may account for his distaste of court intrigue. Aristotle's father was the court physician Nicomachus, who may have instructed his son in the rudiments of medicine and thus be the ultimate source of Aristotle's love of biology and zoology. Aristotle joined Plato's (p. 2) Academy in 367 B.C., and gained considerable fame as a rhetorician during his 20 years there. Following Plato's death, Aristotle traveled with some fellow students to Assos and established a new school in the Platonic tradition at the invitation of a Hermeias of Atraneus. There Aristotle married his first wife Pythias, the daughter of Hermeais. Soon after her death, Aristotle established a new philosophical circle on the island of Lesbos with fellow traveler Theophrastus. It was on Lesbos that Aristotle began his extensive study of biology, spending hours investigating the lagoon of Pyrrha. Aristotle's perspective on the soul is clearly influenced by his biological observations, particularly of plants and mollusks. In 343 or 342 B.C., Philip II of Macedon invited Aristotle to tutor his son, Alexander, who would later earn the title "Great" by conquering most of the known world. However, it is clear that the later conqueror did not pay particular attention to his tutor's lectures on politics: he used both interracial marriage and imperial power to achieve his goals. Aristotle returned to Athens to found the Lyceum, a rival to Plato's Academy, around 335 B.C. One of the interesting differences between the schools was that Platonic science focused on mathematics, while science at the Lyceum was founded on biology. With Alexander the Great's death in 323 B.C., an understandable wave of anti-Macedonian aggression led Aristotle to retreat to his mother's estates on the island of Euboea, where he remained until his death. In his will, he left kind words and generous settlements for his survivors, who included his companion Herpyllis and their son Nicomachus, and even arranged for the bones of his first wife to be buried next to him.

DE ANIMA

ON THE SOUL

Book I

402ᵃ 1. Holding as we do that, while knowledge of any kind is a thing to be honoured and prized, one kind of it may, either by reason of its greater exactness or of a higher dignity and greater wonderfulness in its objects, be more honourable and precious than another, on both accounts we should naturally be led to place in the front rank the study of the soul.

The knowledge of the soul admittedly contributes greatly to the advance of truth in general, and, above all, to our understanding of Nature, for the soul is in some sense the principle of animal life. Our aim is to grasp and understand, first its essential nature, and secondly its properties; of these some are thought to be affections proper to the soul itself, while others are considered to attach to the animal[1] owing to the presence within it of soul.

To attain any assured knowledge about the

From Aristotle *De Anima*, Books 1 and 3. In J. S. Smith (Trans.), *Introduction to Aristotle*, (pp. 155–159, 216–245). Chicago: University of Chicago Press, 1973.

soul is one of the most difficult things in the world. As the form of question which here presents itself, viz. the question "What is it?," recurs in other fields, it might be supposed that there was some single method of inquiry applicable to all objects whose essential nature we are endeavouring to ascertain (as there *is* for derived properties the single method of demonstration); in that case what we should have to seek for would be this unique method. But if there is no such single and general method for solving the question of essence, our task becomes still more difficult; in the case of each different subject we shall have to determine the appropriate process of investigation. If to this there be a clear answer, e. g. that the process is demonstration or division, or some other known method, difficulties and hesitations still beset us—with what facts shall we begin the inquiry? For the facts which form the starting-points in different subjects must be different, as e. g. in the case of numbers and surfaces.

First, no doubt, it is necessary to determine in which of the *summa genera* soul lies, what it *is;* is it "a this-somewhat," a substance, or is it a quale or a quantum, or some other of the remaining kinds of predicates which we have distinguished? Further, does soul belong to the class of potential existents, or is it not rather an actuality? Our answer to this question is of the greatest importance.

402ᵇ We must consider also whether soul is divisible or is without parts, and whether it is everywhere homogeneous or not; and if not homogeneous, whether its various forms are different specifically or generically: up to the present time those who have discussed and investigated soul seem to have confined themselves to the human soul. We must be careful not to ignore the question whether soul can be defined in a single unambiguous formula, as is the case with animal, or whether we must not give a separate formula for each sort of it, as we do for horse, dog, man, god (in the latter case the "universal" animal—and so too every other "common predicate"—being treated either as nothing at all or as a later product²). Further, if what exists is not a plurality of souls, but a plurality of parts of one soul, which ought we to investigate first, the whole soul or its parts? (It is also a difficult problem to decide which of these parts are in nature distinct from one another.) Again, which ought we to investigate first, these parts or their functions, mind or thinking, the faculty or the act of sensa-

tion, and so on? If the investigation of the functions precedes that of the parts, the further question suggests itself: ought we not before either to consider the correlative objects, e. g. of sense or thought? It seems not only useful for the discovery of the causes of the derived properties of substances to be acquainted with the essential nature of those substances (as in mathematics it is useful for the understanding of the property of the equality of the interior angles of a triangle to two right angles to know the essential nature of the straight and the curved or of the line and the plane) but also conversely, for the knowledge of the essential nature of a substance is largely promoted by an acquaintance with its properties: for, when we are able to give an account conformable to experience of all or most of the properties of a substance, we shall be in the most favourable position to say something worth saying about the essential nature of that subject; in all demonstration a definition of the essence is required as a starting-point, so that 403ᵃ definitions which do not enable us to discover the derived properties, or which fail to facilitate even a conjecture about them, must obviously, one and all, be dialectical and futile.

A further problem presented by the affections of soul is this: are they all affections of the complex of body and soul, or is there any one among them peculiar to the soul by itself? To determine this is indispensable but difficult. If we consider the majority of them, there seems to be no case in which the soul can act or be acted upon without involving the body; e. g. anger, courage, appetite, and sensation generally. Thinking seems the most probable exception; but if this too proves to be a form of imagination or to be impossible without imagination, it too requires a body as a condition of its existence. If there is any way of acting or being acted upon proper to soul, soul will be capable of separate existence; if there is none, its separate existence is impossible. In the latter case, it will be like what is straight, which has many properties arising from the straightness in it, e. g. that of touching a bronze sphere at a point, though straightness divorced from the other constituents of the straight thing cannot touch it in this way; it cannot be so divorced at all, since it is always found in a body. It therefore seems that all the affections of soul involve a body—passion, gentleness, fear, pity, courage, joy, loving, and hating; in all these there is a concurrent affection of the body. In support of this we may point to the fact that, while sometimes on the occasion of violent and striking occurrences there is no excitement or fear felt, on others faint and feeble stimulations produce these emotions, viz. when the body is already in a state of tension resembling its condition when we are angry. Here is a still clearer case: in the absence of any external cause of terror we find ourselves experiencing the feelings of a man in terror. From all this it is obvious that the affections of soul are enmattered formulable essences.

Consequently their definitions ought to correspond, e. g. anger should be defined as a certain mode of movement of such and such a body (or part or faculty of a body) by this or that cause and for this or that end. That is precisely why the study of the soul must fall within the science of Nature, at least so far as in its affections it manifests this double character. Hence a physicist would define an affection of soul differently from a dialectician; the latter would define e. g. anger as the appetite for returning pain for pain, or something like that, while the former would define it as a boiling of the blood or warm substance surrounding the heart. The latter assigns the material conditions, the former the form or formulable essence; for what he states is the formulable essence of the fact, though for its actual existence there must be embodiment of it in a material such as is described by the other. Thus the essence of a house is assigned in such a formula as "a shelter against destruction by wind, rain, and heat"; the physicist would describe it as "stones, bricks, and timbers"; but there is a third possible description which would say that it was that form in that material with that purpose or end. Which, then, among these is entitled to be regarded as the genuine physicist? The one who confines himself to the material, or the one who restricts himself to the formulable essence alone? Is it not rather the one who combines both in a single formula? If this is so, how are we to characterize the other two? Must we not say that there is no type of thinker who concerns himself with those qualities or attributes of the material which are in fact inseparable from the material, and without attempting even in thought to separate them? The physicist is he who concerns himself with all the properties active and passive of bodies or materials thus or thus defined; attributes not considered as being of this character he leaves to others, in

certain cases it may be to a specialist, e. g. a carpenter or a physician, in others (a) where they are inseparable in fact, but are separable from any particular kind of body by an effort of abstraction, to the mathematician, (b) where they are separate both in fact and in thought from body altogether, to the First Philosopher or metaphysician. But we must return from this digression, and repeat that the affections of soul are inseparable from the material substratum of animal life, to which we have seen that such affections, e.g. passion and fear, attach, and have not the same mode of being as a line or a plane.

Book III

1. That there is no sixth sense in addition to the five enumerated—sight, hearing, smell, taste, touch—may be established by the following considerations:

If we have actually sensation of everything of which touch can give us sensation (for all the qualities of the tangible *qua* tangible are perceived by us through touch); and if absence of a sense necessarily involves absence of a sense-organ; and if (1) all objects that we perceive by immediate contact with them are perceptible by touch, which sense we actually possess, and (2) all objects that we perceive through media, i. e. without immediate contact, are perceptible by or through the simple elements, e. g. air and water (and this is so arranged that (a) if more than one kind of sensible object is perceivable through a single medium, the possessor of a sense-organ homogeneous with that medium has the power of perceiving both kinds of objects; for example, if the sense-organ is made of air, and air is a medium both for sound and for colour; and that (b) if more than one medium can transmit the same kind of sensible objects, as e. g. water as well as air can transmit colour, both being transparent, then the possessor of either alone will be able to perceive the kind of objects transmissible through both); and if of the simple elements two only, air and water, go to form sense-organs (for the pupil is made of water, the organ of hearing is made of air, and the organ of smell of one or other of these two, while fire is found either in none or in all—warmth being an essential condition of all sensibility—and earth either in none or, if anywhere, specially mingled with the components of the organ of touch; wherefore it would remain that there can be no sense-organ formed of anything except water and air); and if these sense-organs are actually found in certain animals;—then all the possible senses are possessed by those animals that are not imperfect or mutilated (for even the mole is observed to have eyes beneath its skin); so that, if there is no fifth element and no property other than those which belong to the four elements of our world, no sense can be wanting to such animals.

Further, there cannot be a special sense-organ for the common sensibles either, i. e. the objects which we perceive incidentally through this or that special sense, e. g. movement, rest, figure, magnitude, number, unity; for all these we perceive by movement, e. g. magnitude by movement, and therefore also figure (for figure is a species of magnitude), what is at rest by the absence of movement: number is perceived by the negation of continuity, and by the special sensibles; for each sense perceives one class of sensible objects. So that it is clearly impossible that there should be a special sense for any one of the common sensibles, e. g. movement; for, if that were so, our perception of it would be exactly parallel to our present perception of what is sweet by vision. *That* is so because we have a sense for each of the two qualities, in virtue of which when they happen to meet in one sensible object we are aware of both contemporaneously. If it were not like this our perception of the common qualities would always be incidental, i. e. as is the perception of Cleon's son, where we perceive him not as Cleon's son but as white, and the white thing which we really perceive happens to be Cleon's son.

But in the case of the common sensibles there is already in us a general sensibility which enables us to perceive them directly; there is therefore no special sense required for their perception: if there were, our perception of them would have been exactly like what has been above described.

The senses perceive each other's special objects incidentally; not because the percipient sense is this or that special sense, but because all form a unity: this incidental perception takes place whenever sense is directed at one and the same moment to two disparate qualities in one and the same object, e. g. to the bitterness and the yellowness of bile; the assertion of the identity of both cannot be the act of either of the senses; hence the illusion of sense, e. g. the belief that if a thing is yellow it is bile.

It might be asked why we have more senses than one. Is it to prevent a failure to apprehend the common sensibles, e. g. movement, magnitude, and number, which go along with the special sensibles? Had we no sense but sight, and that sense no object but white, they would have tended to escape our notice and everything would have merged for us into an indistinguishable identity because of the concomitance of colour and magnitude. As it is, the fact that the common sensibles are given in the objects of more than one sense reveals their distinction from each and all of the special sensibles.

2. Since it is through sense that we are aware that we are seeing or hearing, it must be either by sight that we are aware of seeing, or by some sense other than sight. But the sense that gives us this new sensation must perceive both sight and its object, viz. colour: so that either (1) there will be two senses both percipient of the same sensible object, or (2) the sense must be percipient of itself. Further, even if the sense which perceives sight were different from sight, we must either fall into an infinite regress, or we must somewhere assume a sense which is aware of itself. If so, we ought to do this in the first case.

This presents a difficulty: if to perceive by sight is just to see, and what is seen is colour (or the coloured), then if we are to see that which sees, that which sees originally must be coloured. It is clear therefore that "to perceive by sight" has more than one meaning; for even when we are not *seeing*, it is by sight that we discriminate darkness from light, though not in the same way as we distinguish one colour from another. Further, in a sense even that which sees *is* coloured; for in each case the sense-organ is capable of receiving the sensible object without its matter. That is why even when the sensible objects are gone the sensings and imaginings continue to exist in the sense-organs.

The activity of the sensible object and that of the percipient sense is one and the same activity, and yet the distinction between their being remains. Take as illustration actual sound and actual hearing: a man may have hearing and yet not be hearing, and that which has a sound is not always sounding. But when that which can hear is active-

30   ly hearing and that which can sound is sounding,
      then the actual hearing and the actual sound are
426ᵃ merged in one (these one might call respectively
      hearkening and sounding).

         If it is true that the movement, both the acting
      and the being acted upon, is to be found in that
      which is acted upon,³ both the sound and the hear-
      ing so far as it is actual must be found in that
      which has the faculty of hearing; for it is in the
5   passive factor that the actuality of the active or
      motive factor is realized; that is why that which
      causes movement may be at rest. Now the actuali-
      ty of that which can sound is just sound or sound-
      ing, and the actuality of that which can hear is
      hearing or hearkening; "sound" and "hearing" are
10   both ambiguous. The same account applies to the
      other senses and their objects. For as the-acting-
      and-being-acted-upon is to be found in the pas-
      sive, not in the active factor, so also the actuality
      of the sensible object and that of the sensitive sub-
      ject are both realized in the latter. But while in
      some cases each aspect of the total actuality has a
      distinct name, e. g. sounding and hearkening, in
      some one or other is nameless, e. g. the actuality
      of sight is called seeing, but the actuality of colour
15   has no name: the actuality of the faculty of taste is
      called tasting, but the actuality of flavour has no
      name. Since the actualities of the sensible object
      and of the sensitive faculty are *one* actuality in
      spite of the difference between their modes of be-
      ing, actual hearing and actual sounding appear
      and disappear from existence at one and the same
20   moment, and so actual savour and actual tasting,
      &c., while as potentialities one of them may exist
      without the other. The earlier students of nature
      were mistaken in their view that without sight
      there was no white or black, without taste no
      savour. This statement of theirs is partly true, part-
      ly false: "sense" and "the sensible object" are am-
25   biguous terms, i. e. may denote either potentiali-
      ties or actualities: the statement is true of the
      latter, false of the former. This ambiguity they
      wholly failed to notice.

         If voice always implies a concord, and if the
      voice and the hearing of it are in one sense one
      and the same, and if concord always implies a ra-
30   tio, hearing as well as what is heard must be a ra-
      tio. That is why the excess of either the sharp or
      the flat destroys the hearing. (So also in the case
426ᵇ of savours excess destroys the sense of taste, and
      in the case of colours excessive brightness or

darkness destroys the sight, and in the case of
smell excess of strength whether in the direction
of sweetness or bitterness is destructive.) This
shows that the sense is a ratio.

   That is also why the objects of sense are (1)
pleasant when the sensible extremes such as acid
or sweet or salt being pure and unmixed are
brought into the proper ratio;⁴ then they are pleas-   5
ant: and in general what is blended is more pleasant than the sharp or the flat alone; or, to touch,
that which is capable of being either warmed or
chilled: the sense and the ratio are identical: while
(2) in excess the sensible extremes are painful or
destructive.

   Each sense then is relative to its particular
group of sensible qualities: it is found in a sense-
organ as such⁵ and discriminates the differences
which exist within that group; e. g. sight discriminates white and black, taste sweet and bitter, and   10
so in all cases. Since we also discriminate white
from sweet, and indeed each sensible quality from
every other, with what do we perceive that they are
different? It must be by sense; for what is before us
is sensible objects. (Hence it is also obvious that
the flesh cannot be the ultimate sense-organ: if it   15
were, the discriminating power could not do its
work without immediate contact with the object.)

   Therefore (1) discrimination between white
and sweet cannot be effected by two agencies
which remain separate; both the qualities discriminated must be present to something that is one
and single. On any other supposition even if I perceived sweet and you perceived white, the difference between them would be apparent. What says   20
that two things are different must be one; for
sweet is different from white. Therefore what asserts this difference must be self-identical, and as
what asserts, so also what thinks or perceives.
That it is not possible by means of two agencies
which remain separate to discriminate two objects
which are separate is therefore obvious; and that
(2) it is not possible to do this in separate moments of time may be seen if we look at it as follows. For as what asserts the difference between
the good and the bad is one and the same, so also   25
the time at which it asserts the one to be different
and the other to be different is not accidental to
the assertion (as it is for instance when I now assert a difference but do not assert that there is now
a difference); it asserts thus—both now and that
the objects are different now; the objects therefore

must be present at one and the same moment. Both the discriminating power and the time of its exercise must be one and undivided.

But, it may be objected, it is impossible that what is self-identical should be moved at one and
30 the same time with contrary movements in so far as it is undivided, and in an undivided moment of time. For if what is sweet be the quality perceived,
427ª it moves the sense or thought in this determinate way, while what is bitter moves it in a contrary way, and what is white in a different way. Is it the case then that what discriminates, though both numerically one and indivisible, is at the same time divided in its being? In one sense, it is what is divided that perceives two separate objects at once, but in another sense it does so *qua* undivided; for it is divisible in its being, but spatially and numerically undivided.

5 But is not this impossible? For while it is true that what is self-identical and undivided may be both contraries at once *potentially,* it cannot be self-identical in its being—it must lose its unity by being put into activity. It is not possible to be at once white and black, and therefore it must also be impossible for a thing to be affected at one and the same moment by the forms of both, assuming it to be the case that sensation and thinking are properly so described.[6]

10 The answer is that just as what is called a "point" is, as being at once one and two, properly said to be divisible, so here, that which discriminates is *qua* undivided one, and active in a single moment of time, while so far forth as it is divisible it twice over uses the same dot at one and the same time. So far forth then as it takes the limit as two, it discriminates two separate objects with what in a sense is divided: while so far as it takes it as one, it does so with what is one and occupies in its activity a single moment of time.

15 About the principle in virtue of which we say that animals are percipient, let this discussion suffice.

3. There are two distinctive peculiarities by reference to which we characterize the soul—(1) local movement and (2) thinking, discriminating, and perceiving. Thinking, both speculative and
20 practical, is regarded as akin to a form of perceiving; for in the one as well as the other the soul discriminates and is cognizant of something which *is.* Indeed the ancients go so far as to identify thinking and perceiving; e. g. Empedocles says

"For 'tis in respect of what is present that man's wit is increased," and again "whence it befalls them from time to time to think diverse thoughts," 25 and Homer's phrase[7] "For suchlike is man's mind" means the same. They all look upon thinking as a bodily process like perceiving, and hold that like is *known* as well as *perceived* by like, as I explained at the beginning of our discussion.[8] Yet they ought at the same time to have accounted for 427ᵇ error also; for it is more intimately connected with animal existence and the soul continues longer in the state of error than in that of truth. They cannot escape the dilemma: either (1) whatever seems is true (and there are some who accept this) or (2) error is contact with the unlike; for that is the opposite of the knowing of like by like.

But it is a received principle that error as well as knowledge in respect to contraries is one and 5 the same.

That perceiving and practical thinking are not identical is therefore obvious; for the former is universal in the animal world, the latter is found in only a small division of it. Further, speculative thinking is also distinct from perceiving—I mean that in which we find rightness and wrongness— 10 rightness in prudence, knowledge, true opinion, wrongness in their opposites; for perception of the special objects of sense is always free from error, and is found in all animals, while it is possible to think falsely as well as truly, and thought is found only where there is discourse of reason as well as sensibility. For imagination is different from ei- 15 ther perceiving or discursive thinking, though it is not found without sensation, or judgement without it. That this activity is not the same kind of thinking as judgement is obvious. For imagining lies within our own power whenever we wish (e. g. we can call up a picture, as in the practice of mnemonics by the use of mental images), but in 20 forming opinions we are not free: we cannot escape the alternative of falsehood or truth. Further, when we think something to be fearful or threatening, emotion is immediately produced, and so too with what is encouraging; but when we merely imagine we remain as unaffected as persons who are looking at a painting of some dreadful or encouraging scene. Again within the field of judgement itself we find varieties—knowledge, opinion, prudence, and their opposites; of the differences between these I must speak elsewhere.[9]

Thinking is different from perceiving and is

held to be in part imagination, in part judgement: we must therefore first mark off the sphere of imagination and then speak of judgment. If then imagination is that in virtue of which an image arises for us, excluding metaphorical uses of the term, is it a single faculty or disposition relative to images, in virtue of which we discriminate and are either in error or not? The faculties in virtue of which we do this are sense, opinion, science, intelligence.

428ᵃ

That imagination is not sense is clear from the following considerations: (1) Sense is either a faculty or an activity, e. g. sight or seeing: imagination takes place in the absence of both, as e. g. in dreams. (2) Again, sense is always present, imagination not. If actual imagination and actual sensation were the same, imagination would be found in all the brutes: this is held not to be the case; e. g. it is not found in ants or bees or grubs. (3) Again, sensations are always true, imaginations are for the most part false. (4) Once more, even in ordinary speech, we do not, when sense functions precisely with regard to its object, say that we imagine it to be a man, but rather when there is some failure of accuracy in its exercise. And (5), as we were saying before, visions appear to us even when our eyes are shut. Neither is imagination any of the things that are never in error: e. g. knowledge or intelligence; for imagination may be false.

5

10

15

It remains therefore to see if it is opinion, for opinion may be either true or false.

But opinion involves belief (for without belief in what we opine we cannot have an opinion), and in the brutes though we often find imagination we never find belief. Further, every opinion is accompanied by belief, belief by conviction, and conviction by discourse of reason: while there are some of the brutes in which we find imagination, without discourse of reason. It is clear then that imagination cannot, again, be (1) opinion *plus* sensation, or (2) opinion mediated by sensation, or (3) a blend of opinion and sensation;¹⁰ this is impossible both for these reasons and because the content of the supposed opinion cannot be different from that of the sensation (I mean that imagination must be the blending of the perception of white with the opinion that it is white: it could scarcely be a blend of the opinion that it is good with the perception that it is white): to imagine is therefore (on this view) identical with the thinking of exactly the same as what one in the strictest sense perceives.

20

25

30

428ᵇ

ceives. But what we imagine is sometimes false though our contemporaneous judgement about it is true; e. g. we imagine the sun to be a foot in diameter though we are convinced that it is larger than the inhabited part of the earth, and the following dilemma presents itself. Either (*a*) while the fact has not changed and the observer has neither forgotten nor lost belief in the true opinion which he had, that opinion has disappeared, or (*b*) if he retains it then his opinion is at once true and false. A true opinion, however, becomes false only when the fact alters without being noticed.

5

Imagination is therefore neither any one of the states enumerated, nor compounded out of them.

But since when one thing has been set in motion another thing may be moved by it, and imagination is held to be a movement and to be impossible without sensation, i. e. to occur in beings that are percipient and to have for its content what can be perceived, and since movement may be produced by actual sensation and that movement is necessarily similar in character to the sensation itself, this movement must be (1) necessarily (*a*) incapable of existing apart from sensation, (*b*) incapable of existing except when we perceive, (2) such that in virtue of its possession that in which it is found may present various phenomena both active and passive, and (3) such that it may be either true or false.

10

15

The reason of the last characteristic is as follows. Perception (1) of the special objects of sense is never in error or admits the least possible amount of falsehood. (2) That of the concomitance of the objects concomitant with the sensible qualities comes next: in this case certainly we may be deceived; for while the perception that there is white before us cannot be false, the perception that what is white is this or that may be false. (3) Third comes the perception of the universal attributes which accompany the concomitant objects to which the special sensibles attach (I mean e. g. of movement and magnitude); it is in respect of these that the greatest amount of sense-illusion is possible.

20

The motion which is due to the activity of sense in these three modes of its exercise will differ from the activity of sense; (1) the first kind of derived motion is free from error while the sensation is present; (2) and (3) the others may be erroneous whether it is present or absent, especially when the object of perception is far off. If then

25

30

imagination presents no other features than those enumerated and is what we have described, then 429ª imagination must be a movement resulting from an actual exercise of a power of sense.

As sight is the most highly developed sense, the name *phantasia* (imagination) has been formed from *phaos* (light) because it is not possible to see without light.

And because imaginations remain in the organs of sense and resemble sensations, animals in 5 their actions are largely guided by them, some (i. e. the brutes) because of the non-existence in them of mind, others (i. e. men) because of the temporary eclipse in them of mind by feeling or disease or sleep.

About imagination, what it is and why it exists, let so much suffice.

4. Turning now to the part of the soul with 10 which the soul knows and thinks (whether this is separable from the others in definition only, or spatially as well) we have to inquire (1) what differentiates this part, and (2) how thinking can take place.

If thinking is like perceiving, it must be either a process in which the soul is acted upon by what is capable of being thought, or a process different from but analogous to that. The thinking part of the soul must therefore be, while impassible, ca-15 pable of receiving the form of an object; that is, must be potentially identical in character with its object without being the object. Mind must be related to what is thinkable, as sense is to what is sensible.

Therefore, since everything is a possible object of thought, mind in order, as Anaxagoras says, to 20 dominate, that is, to know, must be pure from all admixture; for the co-presence of what is alien to its nature is a hindrance and a block: it follows that it too, like the sensitive part, can have no nature of its own, other than that of having a certain capacity. Thus that in the soul which is called mind (by mind I mean that whereby the soul thinks and judges) is, before it thinks, not actually 25 any real thing. For this reason it cannot reasonably be regarded as blended with the body: if so, it would acquire some quality, e. g. warmth or cold, or even have an organ like the sensitive faculty: as it is, it has none. It was a good idea to call the soul "the place of forms," though (1) this description holds only of the intellective soul, and (2) even this is the forms only potentially, not actually.

Observation of the sense-organs and their employment reveals a distinction between the impas-30 sibility of the sensitive and that of the intellective faculty. After strong stimulation of a sense we are 429ᵇ less able to exercise it than before, as e. g. in the case of a loud sound we cannot hear easily immediately after, or in the case of a bright colour or a powerful odour we cannot see or smell, but in the case of mind, thought about an object that is highly intelligible renders it more and not less able afterwards to think objects that are less intelligible: the reason is that while the faculty of sensation is dependent upon the body, mind is separable from it.

Once the mind has become each set of its pos-5 sible objects, as a man of science has, when this phrase is used of one who is actually a man of science (this happens when he is now able to exercise the power on his own initiative), its condition is still one of potentiality, but in a different sense from the potentiality which preceded the acquisition of knowledge by learning or discovery: the mind too is then able to think *itself.*

Since we can distinguish between a spatial 10 magnitude and what it is to be such, and between water and what it is to be water, and so in many other cases (though not in all; for in certain cases the thing and its form are identical), flesh and what it is to be flesh are discriminated either by different faculties, or by the same faculty in two different states: for flesh necessarily involves matter and is like what is snub-nosed, a *this* in a *this.*¹¹ Now it is by means of the sensitive faculty that we discriminate the hot and the cold, i. e. the factors 15 which combined in a certain ratio constitute flesh: the essential character of flesh is apprehended by something different either wholly separate from the sensitive faculty or related to it as a bent line to the same line when it has been straightened out.

Again in the case of abstract objects what is straight is analogous to what is snub-nosed; for it necessarily implies a continuum as its matter: its constitutive essence is different, if we may distinguish between straightness and what is straight: 20 let us take it to be two-ness. It must be apprehended, therefore, by a different power or by the same power in a different state. To sum up, in so far as the realities it knows are capable of being separated from their matter, so it is also with the powers of mind.

The problem might be suggested: if thinking is

a passive affection, then if mind is simple and impassible and has nothing in common with anything else, as Anaxagoras says, how can it come to think at all? For interaction between two factors is held to require a precedent community of nature between the factors. Again it might be asked, is mind a possible object of thought to itself? For if mind is thinkable *per se* and what is thinkable is in kind one and the same, then either (*a*) mind will belong to everything, or (*b*) mind will contain some element common to it with all other realities which makes them all thinkable.

(1) Have not we already disposed of the difficulty about interaction involving a common element, when we said[12] that mind is in a sense potentially whatever is thinkable, though actually it is nothing until it has thought? What it thinks must be in it just as characters may be said to be on a writing-tablet on which as yet nothing actually stands written: this is exactly what happens with mind.

(2) Mind is itself thinkable in exactly the same way as its objects are. For (*a*) in the case of objects which involve no matter, what thinks and what is thought are identical; for speculative knowledge and its object are identical. (Why mind is not always thinking we must consider later.)[13] (*b*) In the case of those which contain matter each of the objects of thought is only potentially present. It follows that while *they* will not have mind in them (for mind is a potentiality of them only in so far as they are capable of being disengaged from matter) mind may yet be thinkable.

5. Since in every class of things, as in nature as a whole, we find two factors involved, (1) a matter which is potentially all the particulars included in the class, (2) a cause which is productive in the sense that it makes them all (the latter standing to the former, as e. g. an art to its material), these distinct elements must likewise be found within the soul.

And in fact mind as we have described it[14] is what it is by virtue of becoming all things, while there is another which is what it is by virtue of making all things: this is a sort of positive state like light; for in a sense light makes potential colours into actual colours.

Mind in this sense of it is separable, impassible, unmixed, since it is in its essential nature activity (for always the active is superior to the passive factor, the originating force to the matter which it forms).

Actual knowledge is identical with its object: in the individual, potential knowledge is in time prior to actual knowledge, but in the universe as a whole it is not prior even in time. Mind is not at one time knowing and at another not. When mind is set free from its present conditions it appears as just what it is and nothing more: this alone is immortal and eternal (we do not, however, remember its former activity because, while mind in this sense is impassible, mind as passive is destructible), and without it nothing thinks.

6. The thinking then of the simple objects of thought is found in those cases where falsehood is impossible: where the alternative of true or false applies, there we always find a putting together of objects of thought in a quasi-unity. As Empedocles said that "where heads of many a creature sprouted without necks" they afterwards by Love's power were combined, so here too objects of thought which were given separate are combined, e. g. "incommensurate" and "diagonal": if the combination be of objects past or future the combination of thought includes in its content the date. For falsehood always involves a synthesis; for even if you assert that what is white is not white you have included not-white in a synthesis. It is possible also to call all these cases division as well as combination. However that may be, there is not only the true or false assertion that Cleon is white but also the true or false assertion that he *was* or *will be* white. In each and every case that which unifies is mind.

Since the word "simple" has two senses, i. e. may mean either (*a*) "not capable of being divided" or (*b*) "not actually divided," there is nothing to prevent mind from knowing what is undivided, e. g. when it apprehends a length (which is actually undivided) and that in an undivided time; for the time is divided or undivided in the same manner as the line. It is not possible, then, to tell what part of the line it was apprehending in each half of the time: the object has no actual parts until it has been divided: if in thought you think each half separately, then by the same act you divide the time also, the half-lines becoming as it were new wholes of length. But if you think it as a whole consisting of these two possible parts, then also you think it in a time which corresponds to both parts together. (But what is not quantitatively but qualitatively simple is thought in a simple time and by a simple act of the soul.)

But that which mind thinks and the time in which it thinks are in this case divisible only incidentally and not as such. For in them too there is something indivisible (though, it may be, not isolable) which gives unity to the time and the whole of length; and this is found equally in every continuum whether temporal or spatial.

Points and similar instances of things that divide, themselves being indivisible, are realized in consciousness in the same manner as privations.

A similar account may be given of all other cases, e. g. how evil or black is cognized; they are cognized, in a sense, by means of their contraries. That which cognizes must have an element of potentiality in its being, and one of the contraries must be in it.[15] But if there is anything that has no contrary, then it knows itself and is actually and possesses independent existence.

Assertion is the saying of something concerning something, e. g. affirmation, and is in every case either true or false: this is not always the case with mind: the thinking of the definition in the sense of the constitutive essence is never in error nor is it the assertion of something concerning something, but, just as while the seeing of the special object of sight can never be in error, the belief that the white object seen is a man may be mistaken, so too in the case of objects which are without matter.

7. Actual knowledge is identical with its object: potential knowledge in the individual is in time prior to actual knowledge but in the universe it has no priority even in time; for all things that come into being arise from what actually is. In the case of sense clearly the sensitive faculty already was potentially what the object makes it to be actually; the faculty is not affected or altered. This must therefore be a different kind from movement; for movement is, as we saw,[16] an activity of what is imperfect, activity in the unqualified sense, i. e. that of what has been perfected, is different from movement.

To perceive then is like bare asserting or knowing; but when the object is pleasant or painful, the soul makes a quasi-affirmation or negation, and pursues or avoids the object. To feel pleasure or pain is to act with the sensitive mean towards what is good or bad as such. Both avoidance and appetite when actual are identical with this: the faculty of appetite and avoidance are not different,

either from one another or from the faculty of sense-perception; but their being *is* different.

To the thinking soul images serve as if they were contents of perception (and when it asserts or denies them to be good or bad it avoids or pursues them). That is why the soul never thinks without an image. The process is like that in which the air modifies the pupil in this or that way and the pupil transmits the modification to some third thing (and similarly in hearing), while the ultimate point of arrival is one, a single mean, with different manners of being.

With what part of itself the soul discriminates sweet from hot[17] I have explained before[18] and must now describe again as follows: That with which it does so is a sort of unity, but in the way just mentioned,[19] i. e. as a connecting term. And the two faculties it connects,[20] being one by analogy and numerically, are each to each as the qualities discerned are to one another (for what difference does it make whether we raise the problem of discrimination between disparates or between contraries, e. g. white and black?). Let then C be to D as A is to B:[21] it follows *alternando* that $C:A::D:B$. If then C and D belong to one subject, the case will be the same with them as with A and B; A and B form a single identity with different modes of being; so too will the former pair. The same reasoning holds if A be sweet and B white.

The faculty of thinking then thinks the forms in the images, and as in the former case[22] what is to be pursued or avoided is marked out for it, so where there is no sensation and it is engaged upon the images it is moved to pursuit or avoidance. E. g. perceiving by sense that the beacon is fire, it recognizes in virtue of the general faculty of sense that it signifies an enemy, because it sees it moving; but sometimes by means of the images or thoughts which are within the soul, just as if it were seeing, it calculates and deliberates what is to come by reference to what is present; and when it makes a pronouncement, as in the case of sensation it pronounces the object to be pleasant or painful, in this case it avoids or pursues; and so generally in cases of action.

That too which involves no action, i. e. that which is true or false, is in the same province with what is good or bad: yet they differ in this, that the one set imply and the other do not a reference to a particular person.

The so-called abstract objects the mind thinks just as, if one had thought of the snub-nosed not as snub-nosed but as hollow, one would have thought of an actuality without the flesh in which it is embodied: it is thus that the mind when it is thinking the objects of Mathematics thinks as separate, elements which do not exist separate. In every case the mind which is actively thinking is the objects which it thinks. Whether it is possible for it while not existing separate from spatial conditions to think anything that is separate, or not, we must consider later.[23]

8. Let us now summarize our results about soul, and repeat that the soul is in a way all existing things; for existing things are either sensible or thinkable, and knowledge is in a way what is knowable, and sensation is in a way what is sensible: in *what* way we must inquire.

Knowledge and sensation are divided to correspond with the realities, potential knowledge and sensation answering to potentialities, actual knowledge and sensation to actualities. Within the soul the faculties of knowledge and sensation are *potentially* these objects, the one what is knowable, the other what is sensible. They must be either the things themselves or their forms. The former alternative is of course impossible: it is not the stone which is present in the soul but its form.

It follows that the soul is analogous to the hand; for as the hand is a tool of tools,[24] so the mind is the form of forms and sense the form of sensible things.

Since according to common agreement there is nothing outside and separate in existence from sensible spatial magnitudes, the objects of thought are in the sensible forms, viz. both the abstract objects and all the states and affections of sensible things. Hence (1) no one can learn or understand anything in the absence of sense, and (2) when the mind is actively aware of anything it is necessarily aware of it along with an image; for images are like sensuous contents except in that they contain no matter.

Imagination is different from assertion and denial; for what is true or false involves a synthesis of concepts. In what will the primary concepts differ from images? Must we not say that neither these nor even our other concepts are images, though they necessarily involve them?

9. The soul of animals is characterized by two faculties, (*a*) the faculty of discrimination which is the work of thought and sense, and (*b*) the faculty of originating local movement. Sense and mind we have now sufficiently examined. Let us next consider what it is in the soul which originates movement. Is it a single part of the soul separate either spatially or in definition? Or is it the soul as a whole? If it is a part, is that part different from those usually distinguished or already mentioned by us, or is it one of them? The problem at once presents itself, in what sense we are to speak of parts of the soul, or how many we should distinguish. For in a sense there is an infinity of parts: it is not enough to distinguish, with some thinkers,[25] the calculative, the passionate, and the desiderative, or with others[26] the rational and the irrational; for if we take the dividing lines followed by these thinkers we shall find parts far more distinctly separated from one another than these, namely those we have just mentioned: (1) the nutritive, which belongs both to plants and to all animals, and (2) the sensitive, which cannot easily be classed as either irrational or rational; further (3) the imaginative, which is, in its being, different from all, while it is very hard to say with which of the others it is the same or not the same, supposing we determine to posit *separate* parts in the soul; and lastly (4) the appetitive, which would seem to be distinct both in definition and in power from all hitherto enumerated.

It is absurd to break up the last-mentioned faculty: as these thinkers do, for wish is found in the calculative part and desire and passion in the irrational;[27] and if the soul is tripartite appetite will be found in all three parts. Turning our attention to the present object of discussion, let us ask what that is which originates local movement of the animal.

The movement of growth and decay, being found in all living things, must be attributed to the faculty of reproduction and nutrition, which is common to all: inspiration and expiration, sleep and waking, we must consider later:[28] these too present much difficulty: at present we must consider local movement, asking what it is that originates forward movement in the animal.

That it is not the nutritive faculty is obvious; for this kind of movement is always for an end and is accompanied either by imagination or by appetite; for no animal moves except by compulsion unless it has an impulse towards or away from an object. Further, if it were the nutritive fac-

ulty, even plants would have been capable of originating such movement and would have possessed
the organs necessary to carry it out. Similarly it
cannot be the sensitive faculty either; for there are
many animals which have sensibility but remain
20   fast and immovable throughout their lives.

If then Nature never makes anything without a
purpose and never leaves out what is necessary
(except in the case of mutilated or imperfect
growths; and that here we have neither mutilation
nor imperfection may be argued from the facts
that such animals (a) can reproduce their species
and (b) rise to completeness of nature and decay
25   to an end), it follows that, had they been capable
of originating forward movement, they would
have possessed the organs necessary for that purpose. Further, neither can the calculative faculty
or what is called "mind" be the cause of such
movement; for mind as speculative never thinks
what is practicable, it never says anything about
an object to be avoided or pursued, while this
movement is always in something which is avoiding or pursuing an object. No, not even when it is
aware of such an object does it at once enjoin pur-
30   suit or avoidance of it; e. g. the mind often thinks
of something terrifying or pleasant without enjoying the emotion of fear. It is the heart that is
433ᵃ moved (or in the case of a pleasant object some
other part). Further, even when the mind does
command and thought bids us pursue or avoid
something, sometimes no movement is produced;
we act in accordance with desire, as in the case of
moral weakness. And, generally, we observe that
the possessor of medical knowledge is not necessarily healing, which shows that something else is
5   required to produce action in accordance with
knowledge; the knowledge alone is not the cause.
Lastly, appetite too is incompetent to account fully for movement; for those who successfully resist temptation have appetite and desire and yet
follow mind and refuse to enact that for which
they have appetite.

10. These two at all events appear to be
sources of movement: appetite and mind (if one
10   may venture to regard imagination as a kind of
thinking; for many men follow their imaginations
contrary to knowledge, and in all animals other
than man there is no thinking or calculation but
only imagination).

Both of these then are capable of originating
local movement, mind and appetite: (1) mind, that

is, which calculates means to an end, i. e. mind
practical (it differs from mind speculative in the
character of its end); while (2) appetite is in every
form of it relative to an end: for that which is the
object of appetite is the stimulant of mind practical; and that which is last in the process of thinking is the beginning of the action. It follows that
there is a justification for regarding these two as
the sources of movement, i. e. appetite and practical thought; for the object of appetite starts a
movement and as a result of that thought gives
rise to movement, the object of appetite being to
it a source of stimulation. So too when imagination originates movement, it necessarily involves
appetite.

That which moves therefore is a single faculty
and the faculty of appetite; for if there had been
two sources of movement—mind and appetite—
they would have produced movement in virtue of
some common character. As it is, mind is never
found producing movement without appetite (for
wish is a form of appetite; and when movement is
produced according to calculation it is also according to wish), but appetite can originate movement contrary to calculation, for desire is a form
of appetite. Now mind is always right, but appetite and imagination may be either right or
wrong. That is why, though in any case it is the
object of appetite which originates movement,
this object may be either the real or the apparent
good. To produce movement the object must be
more than this: it must be good that can be
brought into being by action; and only what can
be otherwise than as it is can thus be brought into
being. That then such a power in the soul as has
been described, i. e. that called appetite, originates movement is clear. Those who distinguish
parts in the soul, if they distinguish and divide in
accordance with differences of power, find themselves with a very large number of parts, a nutritive, a sensitive, an intellective, a deliberative, and
now an appetitive part; for these are more different from one another than the faculties of desire
and passion.

Since appetites run counter to one another,
which happens when a principle of reason and a
desire are contrary and is possible only in beings
with a sense of time (for while mind bids us hold
back because of what is future, desire is influenced by what is just at hand: a pleasant object
which is just at hand presents itself as both pleas-

15

20

25

30

433ᵇ

ant and good, without condition in either case, because of want of foresight into what is farther
away in time), it follows that while that which
originates movement must be specifically one,
viz. the faculty of appetite as such (or rather farthest back of all the object of that faculty; for it is
it that itself remaining unmoved originates the
movement by being apprehended in thought or
imagination), the things that originate movement
are numerically many.

All movement involves three factors, (1) that
which originates the movement, (2) that by means
of which it originates it, and (3) that which is
moved. The expression "that which originates the
movement" is ambiguous: it may mean either (*a*)
something which itself is unmoved or (*b*) that
which at once moves and is moved. Here that
which moves without itself being moved is the realizable good, that which at once moves and is
moved is the faculty of appetite (for that which is
influenced by appetite so far as it is actually so influenced is set in movement, and appetite in the
sense of actual appetite *is* a kind of movement),
while that which is in motion is the animal. The
instrument which appetite employs to produce
movement is no longer psychical but bodily:
hence the examination of it falls within the
province of the functions common to body and
soul.[29] To state the matter summarily at present,
that which is the instrument in the production of
movement is to be found where a beginning and
an end coincide as e. g. in a ball and socket joint;
for there the convex and the concave sides are respectively an end and a beginning (that is why
while the one remains at rest, the other is moved):
they are separate in definition but not separable
spatially. For everything is moved by pushing and
pulling. Hence just as in the case of a wheel, so
here there must be a point which remains at rest,
and from that point the movement must originate.

To sum up, then, and repeat what I have said,
inasmuch as an animal is capable of appetite it is
capable of self-movement; it is not capable of appetite without possessing imagination; and all
imagination is either (1) calculative or (2) sensitive. In the latter all animals, and not only man,
partake.

11. We must consider also in the case of imperfect animals, sc. those which have no sense but
touch, what it is that in them originates movement. Can they have imagination or not? or de-

sire? Clearly they have feelings of pleasure and
pain, and if they have these they must have desire.
But how can they have imagination? Must not we
say that, as their movements are indefinite, they
have imagination and desire, but indefinitely?

Sensitive imagination, as we have said,[30] is
found in all animals, deliberative imagination
only in those that are calculative: for whether this
or that shall be enacted is already a task requiring
calculation; and there must be a single standard to
measure by, for that is pursued which is *greater*. It
follows that what acts in this way must be able to
make a unity out of several images.

This is the reason why imagination is held not
to involve opinion, in that it does not involve
opinion based on inference, though opinion involves imagination. Hence appetite contains no
deliberative element. Sometimes it overpowers
wish and sets it in movement: at times wish acts
thus upon appetite, like one sphere imparting its
movement to another, or appetite acts thus upon
appetite, i. e. in the condition of moral weakness
(though by *nature* the higher faculty is *always*
more authoritative and gives rise to movement).
Thus *three* modes of movement are possible.

The faculty of knowing is never moved but remains at rest. Since the one premiss or judgment
is universal and the other deals with the particular
(for the first tells us that such and such a kind of
man should do such and such a kind of act, and
the second that *this* is an act of the kind meant,
and I a person of the type intended), it is the latter
opinion that really originates movement, not the
universal; or rather it is both, but the one does so
while it remains in a state more like rest, while the
other partakes in movement.

12. The nutritive soul then must be possessed
by everything that is alive, and every such thing is
endowed with soul from its birth to its death. For
what has been born must grow, reach maturity,
and decay—all of which are impossible without
nutrition. Therefore the nutritive faculty must be
found in everything that grows and decays.

But sensation need not be found in all things
that live. For it is impossible for touch to belong
either (1) to those whose body is uncompounded
or (2) to those which are incapable of taking in the
forms without their matter.

But animals must be endowed with sensation,
since Nature does nothing in vain. For all things
that exist by Nature are means to an end, or will

434^b be concomitants of means to an end. Every body capable of forward movement would, if unendowed with sensation, perish and fail to reach its end, which is the aim of Nature; for how could it obtain nutriment? Stationary living things, it is true, have as their nutriment that from which they have arisen; but it is not possible that a body which is not stationary but produced by generation should have a soul and a discerning mind without also having sensation. (Nor yet even if it were not produced by generation. Why should it not have sensation? Because it were better so either for the body or for the soul? But clearly it would not be better for either: the absence of sensation will not enable the one to think better or the other to exist better.) Therefore no body which is not stationary has soul without sensation.

But if a body *has* sensation, it must be either simple or compound. And simple it cannot be; for then it could not have touch, which is indispensable. This is clear from what follows. An animal is a body with soul in it: every body is tangible, i.e. perceptible by touch; hence necessarily, if an animal is to survive, its body must have tactual sensation. All the other senses, e. g. smell, sight, hearing, apprehend through media; but where there is immediate contact the animal, if it has no sensation, will be unable to avoid some things and take others, and so will find it impossible to survive. That is why taste also is a sort of touch; it is relative to nutriment, which is just tangible body; whereas sound, colour, and odour are innutritious, and further neither grow nor decay. Hence it is that taste also must be a sort of touch, because it is the sense for what is tangible and nutritious.

Both these senses, then, are indispensable to the animal, and it is clear that without touch it is impossible for an animal to be. All the other senses subserve well-being and for that very reason belong not to any and every kind of animal, but only to some, e. g. those capable of forward movement must have them; for, if they are to survive, they must perceive not only by immediate contact but also at a distance from the object. This will be possible if they can perceive through a medium, the medium being affected and moved by the perceptible object, and the animal by the medium. Just as that which produces local movement causes a change extending to a certain point, and that which gave an impulse causes another to produce a new impulse so that the movement traverses a medium—the first mover impelling without being impelled, the last moved being impelled without impelling, while the medium (or media, for there are many) is both—so is it also in the case of alteration, except that the agent produces it without the patient's changing its place. Thus if an object is dipped into wax, the movement goes on until submersion has taken place, and in stone it goes no distance at all, while in water the disturbance goes far beyond the object dipped: in air the disturbance is propagated farthest of all, the air acting and being acted upon, so long as it maintains an unbroken unity. That is why in the case of reflection it is better, instead of saying that the sight issues from the eye and is reflected, to say that the air, so long as it remains one, is affected by the shape and colour. On a smooth surface the air possesses unity; hence it is that it in turn sets the sight in motion, just as if the impression on the wax were transmitted as far as the wax extends.

13. It is clear that the body of an animal cannot be simple, i.e. consist of one element such as fire or air. For without touch it is impossible to have any other sense; for every body that has soul in it must, as we have said,[31] be capable of touch. All the other elements with the exception of earth can constitute organs of sense, but all of them bring about perception only through something else, viz. through the media. Touch takes place by direct contact with its objects, whence also its name. All the other organs of sense, no doubt, perceive by contact, only the contact is mediate: touch alone perceives by immediate contact. Consequently no animal body can consist of these other elements.

Nor can it consist solely of earth. For touch is as it were a mean between all tangible qualities, and its organ is capable of receiving not only all the specific qualities which characterize earth, but also the hot and the cold and all other tangible qualities whatsoever. That is why we have no sensation by means of bones, hair, &c., because they consist of earth. So too plants, because they consist of earth, have no sensation. Without touch there can be no other sense, and the organ of touch cannot consist of earth or of any other single element.

It is evident, therefore, that the loss of this one sense alone must bring about the death of an animal. For as on the one hand nothing which is not an animal can have this sense, so on the other it is

435^a

435^b

the only one which is indispensably necessary to what is an animal. This explains, further, the following difference between the other senses and touch. In the case of all the others excess of intensity in the qualities which they apprehend, i. e. excess of intensity in colour, sound, and smell, destroys not the animal but only the organs of the sense (except incidentally, as when the sound is accompanied by an impact or shock, or where through the objects of sight or of smell certain other things are set in motion, which destroy by contact); flavour also destroys only in so far as it is at the same time tangible. But excess of intensity in tangible qualities, e. g. heat, cold, or hardness, destroys the animal itself. As in the case of every sensible quality excess destroys the organ, so here what is tangible destroys touch, which is the essential mark of life; for it has been shown that without touch it is impossible for an animal to be. That is why excess in intensity of tangible qualities destroys not merely the organ, but the animal itself, because this is the only sense which it must have.

All the other senses are necessary to animals, as we have said,[32] not for their being, but for their well-being. Such, e. g., is sight, which, since it lives in air or water, or generally in what is pellucid, it must have in order to see, and taste because of what is pleasant or painful to it, in order that it may perceive these qualities in its nutriment and so may desire to be set in motion, and hearing that it may have communication made to it, and a tongue that it may communicate with its fellows.

NOTES

1. i.e. the complex of soul and body.
2. i.e. as presupposing the various sorts instead of being presupposed by them.
3. Cf. *Phys.* iii. 3.
4. i. e. that which is involved in the structure of the sense-organ.
5. The qualification appears to mean that the sense-organ may in other respects have other qualities. Thus the tongue can touch as well as taste.
6. i. e. as the being affected by the forms of sensible qualities.
7. *Od.* xviii. 136.
8. 404ᵇ 8–18.
9. The reference is perhaps to *E. N.* 1139ᵇ 15 ff.
10. For these three views Cf. Pl. *Tim.* 52 A, *Soph.* A, B, *Phil.* 39 B.
11. i. e. a particular form in a particular matter.
12. 15–24.
13. Ch. 5.
14. In ch. 4.
15. i. e. it must be characterized actually by one and potentially by the other of the contraries.
16. Cf. 417ᵇ 2–16.
17. i. e. the sweetness and the heat in a sweet-hot object.
18. 426ᵇ 12–427ᵃ 14.
19. i. e. as one thing with two aspects; cf. 1. 19.
20. i. e. the faculty by which we discern sweet and that by which we discern hot.
21. i. e. let the faculty that discerns sweet be to that which discerns hot as sweet is to hot.
22. i. e. that of sense-data.
23. This promise does not seem to have been fulfilled.
24. i. e. a tool for using tools.
25. Pl. *Rep.* 435–41.
26. A popular view, Cf. *E. N.* 1102ᵃ 26–8.
27. All three being forms of appetite.
28. Cf. *De Respiratione, De Somno.*
29. Cf. *De Motu An.* 702ᵃ 21–703ᵃ 22.
30. 433ᵇ 29.
31. 434ᵇ 10–24.
32. 434ᵇ 24.

4

SAINT AUGUSTINE OF HIPPO

Saint Augustine (354–430) was not initially attracted to Christianity, but instead joined an alternative group, the Manichees, who were generally disgusted by the physical nature of humans, particularly reproduction. Educated in rhetoric at Carthage, on the northern tip of Tunisia, Augustine rose from humble beginnings to an appointment as the imperial professor of rhetoric in Milan, Italy. However, advancement in his chosen career was stymied, not so much by his mistress of many years and their son, but by his failure to secure a rich wife. After being baptized into the Christian faith by St. Ambrose, a champion of orthodox Christianity preaching in Milan, he returned home to Tagaste in northern Africa to raise his son and tend to the family property. With the early death of his son, Augustine was pressed into the clergy at Hippo, in northeastern Algeria. His exquisite writing in the highest Latin and stunning oratory in a fiery style that worked well from the pulpit attracted controversy as he attacked various sects he considered a threat to Roman Christianity, including the Manicheism of his youth. In 430, the city of Hippo lay under siege by the Vandals, and shortly after Augustine's death, the walls fell.

CONFESSIONS

BOOK X

Memory

i (1). May I know you, who know me. May I "know as I also am known" (1 Cor. 13: 12). Power of my soul, enter into it and fit it for yourself, so that you may have and hold it "without spot or blemish" (Eph. 5: 27). This is my hope, and that is why I speak. In this hope I am placing my delight when my delight is in what it ought to be. As to the other pleasures of life, regret at their loss should be in inverse proportion to the extent to which one weeps for losing them. The less we weep for them, the more we ought to be weeping. "Behold, you have loved the truth" (Ps. 51: 8), for he who "does the truth comes to the light" (John 3: 21). This I desire to do, in my heart before you in confession, but before many witnesses with my pen.

ii (2). Indeed, Lord, to your eyes, the abyss of human consciousness is naked (Heb. 4: 13). What could be

hidden within me, even if I were unwilling to confess it to you? I would be hiding you from myself, not myself from you. Now, however, my groaning is witness that I am displeased with myself. You are radiant and give delight and are so an object of love and longing that I am ashamed of myself and reject myself. You are my choice, and only by your gift can I please either you or myself. Before you, then, Lord, whatever I am is manifest, and I have already spoken of the benefit I derive from making confession to you. I am not doing this merely by physical words and sounds, but by words from my soul and a cry from my mind, which is known to your ear. When I am evil, making confession to you is simply to be displeased with myself. When I am good, making confession to you is simply to make no claim on my own behalf, for you, Lord, "confer blessing on the righteous" (Ps. 5: 13) but only after you have first "justified the ungodly" (Rom. 4: 5). Therefore, my God, my confession before you is made both in silence and not in silence. It is silent in that it is no audible sound; but in

From Saint Augustine, "Book X, Memory." In H. Chadwick (Trans.), *Saint Augustine Confessions* (pp. 179–201). New York: Oxford University Press, 1998. (Original work written 397)

love it cries aloud. If anything I say to men is right, that is what you have first heard from me. Moreover, you hear nothing true from my lips which you have not first told me.

iii (3). Why then should I be concerned for human readers to hear my confessions? It is not they who are going to "heal my sicknesses" (Ps. 102: 3). The human race is inquisitive about other people's lives, but negligent to correct their own. Why do they demand to hear from me what I am when they refuse to hear from you what they are? And when they hear me talking about myself, how can they know if I am telling the truth, when no one "knows what is going on in a person except the human spirit which is within" (1 Cor. 2: 11)? But if they were to hear about themselves from you, they could not say "The Lord is lying." To hear you speaking about oneself is to know oneself.[1] Moreover, anyone who knows himself and says "That is false" must be a liar. But "love believes all things" (1 Cor. 13: 7), at least among those love has bonded to itself and made one. I also, Lord, so make my confession to you that I may be heard by people to whom I cannot prove that my confession is true. But those whose ears are opened by love believe me.

(4). Nevertheless, make it clear to me, physician of my most intimate self, that good results from my present undertaking. Stir up the heart when people read and hear the confessions of my past wickednesses, which you have forgiven and covered up to grant me happiness in yourself, transforming my soul by faith and your sacrament. Prevent their heart from sinking into the sleep of despair and saying "It is beyond my power." On the contrary, the heart is aroused in the love of your mercy and the sweetness of your grace, by which every weak person is given power, while dependence on grace produces awareness of one's own weakness. Good people are delighted to hear about the past sins of those who have now shed them. The pleasure is not in the evils as such, but that though they were so once, they are not like that now.[2]

My Lord, every day my conscience makes confession, relying on the hope of your mercy as more to be trusted than its own innocence. So what profit is there, I ask, when, to human readers, by this book I confess to you who I now am, not what I once was? The profit derived from confessing my past I have seen and spoken about. But what I now am at this time when I am writing my confessions many wish to know, both those who know me and those who do not but have heard something from me or about me; their ear is not attuned to my heart at the point where I am whatever I am. So as I

make my confession, they wish to learn about my inner self, where they cannot penetrate with eye or ear or mind. Yet although they wish to do that and are ready to believe me, they cannot really have certain knowledge. The love which makes them good people tells them that I am not lying in confessing about myself, and the love in them believes me.

iv (5). But what edification do they hope to gain by this? Do they desire to join me in thanksgiving when they hear how, by your gift, I have come close to you, and do they pray for me when they hear how I am held back by my own weight? To such sympathetic readers I will indeed reveal myself. For it is no small gift, my Lord God, if "many give you thanks on our account" (2 Cor. 1: 11), and if many petition you on our behalf. A brotherly mind will love in me what you teach to be lovable, and will regret in me what you teach to be regrettable. This is a mark of a Christian brother's mind, not an outsider's—not that of "the sons of aliens whose mouth speaks vanity, and their right hand is a right hand of iniquity" (Ps. 143: 7 f.). A brotherly person rejoices on my account when he approves me, but when he disapproves, he grieves on my behalf. Whether he approves or disapproves, he is loving me. To such people I will reveal myself. They will take heart from my good traits, and sigh with sadness at my bad ones. My good points are instilled by you and are your gifts. My bad points are my faults and your judgements on them. Let them take heart from the one and regret the other. Let both praise and tears ascend in your sight from brotherly hearts, your censers. But you Lord, who take delight in the odour of your holy temple, "have pity on me according to your mercy for your name's sake" (Ps. 50: 3). You never abandon what you have begun. Make perfect my imperfections.

(6). When I am confessing not what I was but what I am now, the benefit lies in this: I am making this confession not only before you with a secret exaltation and fear and with a secret grief touched by hope, but also in the ears of believing sons of men, shares in my joy, conjoined with me in mortality, my fellow citizens and pilgrims, some who have gone before, some who follow after, and some who are my companions in this life. They are your servants, my brothers, who by your will are your sons and my masters. You have commanded me to serve them if I wish to live with you and in dependence on you. This your word would have meant little to me if it had been only a spoken precept and had not first been acted out.[3] For my part, I carry out your command by actions and words; but I discharge it under the protection of your wings (Ps. 16:8; 35: 8). It would be a far too perilous responsibility unless under your wings my soul were submissive to you. My weakness is known to you. I am a child. But my Father ever lives and my protector is sufficient to guard me. He is one and the same who begat me and watches over me. You yourself are all my good qualities. You are the omnipotent one, who are with me even before I am with you. So, to those whom you command me to serve, I will reveal not who I was, but what I have now come to be and what I continue to be. "But I do not sit in judgement on myself" (1 Cor. 4: 3). It is, therefore, in this spirit that I ask to be listened to.

v (7). You, Lord, are my judge. For even if "no man knows the being of man except the spirit of man which is in him" (1 Cor. 2: 11), yet there is something of the human person which is unknown even to the "spirit of man which is in him." But you, Lord, know everything about the human person; for you made humanity. Although in your sight I despise myself and estimate myself to be dust and ashes (Gen. 18: 27), I nevertheless know something of you which I do not know about myself. Without question "we see now through a mirror in an enigma," not yet "face to face" (1 Cor. 13: 12). For this cause, as long as I am a traveller absent from you (2 Cor. 5: 6), I am more present to myself than to you. Yet I know that you cannot be in any way subjected to violence,[4] whereas I do not know which temptations I can resist and which I cannot. There is hope because "you are faithful and do not allow us to be tempted beyond what we can bear, but with the temptation make also a way of escape so that we can bear it" (1 Cor. 10: 13). Accordingly, let me confess what I know of myself. Let me confess too what I do not know of myself. For what I know of myself I know because you grant me light, and what I do not know of myself, I do not know until such time as my darkness becomes "like noonday" before your face (Isa. 58: 10).

vi (8). My love for you, Lord, is not an uncertain feeling but a matter of conscious certainty. With your word you pierced my heart, and I loved you. But heaven and earth and everything in them on all sides tell me to love you. Nor do they cease to tell everyone that "they are without excuse" (Rom. 1: 20). But at a profounder level you will have mercy on whom you will have mercy and will show pity on whom you will have pity (Rom. 9: 15). Otherwise heaven and earth would be uttering your praises to the deaf. But when I love you, what do I love? It is not physical beauty nor temporal glory nor the brightness of light dear to earthly eyes, nor the sweet melodies of all kinds of songs, nor the gentle odour of flowers and ointments and perfumes, nor man-

na or honey, nor limbs welcoming the embraces of the flesh; it is not these I love when I love my God. Yet there is a light I love, and a food, and a kind of embrace when I love my God—a light, voice, odour, food, embrace of my inner man, where my soul is floodlit by light which space cannot contain, where there is sound that time cannot seize, where there is a perfume which no breeze disperses, where there is a taste for food no amount of eating can lessen, and where there is a bond of union that no satiety can part. That is what I love when I love my God.[5]

(9). And what is the object of my love? I asked the earth and it said: "It is not I." I asked all that is in it; they made the same confession (Job 28: 12 f.). I asked the sea, the deeps, the living creatures that creep, and they responded: "We are not your God, look beyond us." I asked the breezes which blow and the entire air with its inhabitants said: "Anaximenes was mistaken; I am not God."[6] I asked heaven, sun, moon and stars; they said: "Nor are we the God whom you seek." And I said to all these things in my external environment: "Tell me of my God who you are not, tell me something about him." And with a great voice they cried out: "He made us" (Ps. 99: 3). My question was the attention I gave to them, and their response was their beauty.

Then I turned towards myself, and said to myself: "Who are you?" I replied: "A man." I see in myself a body and a soul, one external, the other internal. Which of these should I have questioned about my God, for whom I had already searched through the physical order of things from earth to heaven, as far as I could send the rays of my eyes[7] as messengers? What is inward is superior. All physical evidence is reported to the mind which presides and judges of the responses of heaven and earth and all things in them, as they say "We are not God" and "He made us." The inner man knows this—I, I the mind through the sense-perception of my body. I asked the mass of the sun about my God, and it replied to me: "It is not I, but he made me."

(10). Surely this beauty should be self-evident to all who are of sound mind. Then why does it not speak to everyone in the same way? Animals both small and large see it, but they cannot put a question about it. In them reason does not sit in judgement upon the deliverances of the senses. But human beings can put a question so that "the invisible things of God are understood and seen through the things which are made" (Rom. 1: 20). Yet by love of created things they are subdued by them,[8] and being thus made subject become incapable of exercising judgement. Moreover, created things do not answer those who question them if power to judge is lost. There is no alteration in the voice which is their beauty. If one person sees while another sees and questions, it is not that they appear one way to the first and another way to the second. It is rather that the created order speaks to all, but is understood by those who hear its outward voice and compare it with the truth within themselves. Truth says to me: "Your God is not earth or heaven or any physical body." The nature of that kind of being says this. They see it: nature is a physical mass, less in the part than in the whole.[9] In that respect, my soul, I tell you that you are already superior. For you animate the mass of your body and provide it with life, since no body is capable of doing that for another body.[10] But your God is for you the life of your life.

vii (11). What then do I love when I love my God? Who is he who is higher than the highest element in my soul? Through my soul I will ascend to him. I will rise above the force by which I am bonded to the body and fill its frame with vitality. It is not by that force that I find my God. For then he would be found by "the horse and mule which have no understanding" (Ps. 31: 9), since it is the same force by which their bodies also have life. There exists another power, not only that by which I give life to my body but also that by which I enable its senses to perceive. The Lord made this for me, commanding the eye not to hear, the ear not to see, but providing the eye to see and the ear to hear, and each of the other senses in turn to be in its proper place and carry out its proper function.[11] I who act through these diverse functions am one mind. I will also rise above this power. For this also is possessed by the horse and the mule. They also perceive through the body.

viii (12). I will therefore rise above that natural capacity in a step by step ascent to him who made me. I come to the fields and vast palaces of memory,[12] where are the treasuries of innumerable images of all kinds of objects brought in by sense-perception. Hidden there is whatever we think about, a process which may increase or diminish or in some way alter the deliverance of the senses and whatever else has been deposited and placed on reserve and has not been swallowed up and buried in oblivion. When I am in this storehouse, I ask that it produce what I want to recall, and immediately certain things come out; some things require a longer search, and have to be drawn out as it were from more recondite receptacles. Some memories pour out to crowd the mind and, when one is searching and asking for something quite different, leap forward into the centre as if saying "Surely we are what you want?" With the hand of my heart I chase them away from the face of my memory until what I want is freed of mist and emerges from its hiding places. Other memories come before me on demand with ease and without any confusion in their order. Memories of earlier events give way to those which followed, and as they pass are stored away available for retrieval when I want them. All that is what happens when I recount a narrative from memory.

(13). Memory preserves in distinct particulars and general categories all the perceptions which have penetrated, each by its own route of entry. Thus light and all colours and bodily shapes enter by the eyes; by the ears all kinds of sounds; all odours by the entrance of the nostrils; all tastes by the door of the mouth. The power of sensation in the entire body distinguishes what is hard or soft, hot or cold, smooth or rough, heavy or light, whether external or internal to the body. Memory's huge cavern, with its mysterious, secret, and indescribable nooks and crannies, receives all these perceptions, to be recalled when needed and reconsidered. Every one of them enters into memory, each by its own gate, and is put on deposit there. The objects themselves do not enter, but the images of the perceived objects are available to the thought recalling them. But who can say how images are created, even though it may be clear by which senses they are grasped and stored within. For even when I am in darkness and silence, in my memory I can produce colours at will, and distinguish between white and black and between whatever other colours I wish. Sounds do not invade and disturb my consideration of what my eyes absorb, even though they are present and as it were hide in an independent storehouse. On demand, if I wish, they can be immediately present. With my tongue silent and my throat making no sound, I can sing what I wish. The images of colours, which are no less present, do not intrude themselves or interrupt, when I draw upon another treasury containing sounds which flowed in through the ears. So I recall at pleasure other memories which have been taken in and collected together by other senses. I distinguish the odour of lilies from that of violets without smelling anything at all. I prefer honey to a sweet wine, a smooth taste to a rough one, not actually tasting or touching at the moment, but by recollection.

(14). These actions are inward, in the vast hall of my memory. There sky, land, and sea are available to me together with all the sensations I have been able to experience in them, except for those which I have forgotten. There also I meet myself and recall what I am, what I have done, and when and where and how I was affected when I did it. There is everything that I remember, whether I experienced it directly or believed the word of others. Out of the same abundance in store, I combine with past events images of various things, whether experienced directly or believed on the basis of what I have experienced; and on this basis I reason about future actions and events and hopes, and again think of all these things in the present. "I shall do this and that," I say to myself within that vast recess of my mind which is full of many, rich images, and this act or that follows. "O that this or that were so," "May God avert this or that." I say these words to myself and, as I speak, there are present images of everything I am speaking of, drawn out of the same treasure-house of memory. I would never say anything like that if these images were not present.

(15). This power of memory is great, very great, my God. It is a vast and infinite profundity. Who has plumbed its bottom? This power is that of my mind and is a natural endowment, but I myself cannot grasp the totality of what I am. Is the mind, then, too restricted to compass itself, so that we have to ask what is that element of itself which it fails to grasp? Surely that cannot be external to itself; it must be within the mind. How then can it fail to grasp it? This question moves me to great astonishment. Amazement grips me. People are moved to wonder by mountain peaks,[13] by vast waves of the sea, by broad waterfalls on rivers, by the all-embracing extent of the ocean, by the revolutions of the stars. But in themselves they are uninterested. They experience no surprise that when I was speaking of all these things, I was not seeing them with my eyes. On the other hand, I would not have spoken of them unless the mountains and waves and rivers and stars (which I have seen) and the ocean (which I believe on the reports of others) I could see inwardly with dimensions just as great as if I were actually looking at them outside my mind. Yet when I was seeing them, I was not absorbing them in the act of seeing with my eyes. Nor are the actual objects present to me, but only their images. And I know by which bodily sense a thing became imprinted on my mind.

ix (16). But these are not the only things carried by the vast capacity of my memory. Here also are all the skills acquired through the liberal arts which have not been forgotten. They are pushed into the background in some interior place—which is not a place. In their case I carry not the images but the very skills themselves. For what literature is, what the art of dialectical debate is, how many kinds of question there are—all that I know about these matters lies in my memory in this distinctive way. It is not that I retain the images and leave the object outside me. It is not a sound which has passed away, like a voice which makes its impression through the ears and leaves behind a trace allowing it to be recalled, as if it

were sounding though in fact it is no longer sounding. Nor does it resemble an odour which, as it passes and evaporates in the winds, affects the sense of smell and so puts into the memory an image of itself, which we recover through an act of recollection. Nor is it like food which cannot actually be tasted once it is in the stomach, and yet leaves the memory of its taste. Nor is it analogous to something which the body touches and feels, which even after contact with us has ceased, can be imagined by the memory. These objects have no entry to the memory: only their images are grasped with astonishing rapidity, and then replaced as if in wonderful storerooms, so that in an amazing way the memory produces them.

x (17). When I hear that there are three kinds of question, viz. "Does P exist? What is P? What kind of a thing is P?"[14] I retain images of the sounds which constitute these words. I know that they have passed through the air as a noise, and that they no longer exist. Moreover, the ideas signified by those sounds I have not touched by sense-perception, nor have I seen them independently of my mind. I hid in my memory not their images but the realities. How they came to me let them explain if they can. I run through all the entrance doors of my body but do not find one by which they have entered in. My eyes say: "If they are coloured, we have informed you about them." My ears say: "If they made any sound, we were responsible for telling you." My nostrils say: "If they gave off any odour, they passed our way." The sense of taste also says: "If they are tasteless, do not ask me." Touch says: "If the object is not physical, I have no contact with it, and if I have no contact, I have no information to give on the subject." Then how did these matters enter my memory? I do not know how. For when I learnt them, I did not believe what someone else was telling me, but within myself I recognized them and assented to their truth. I entrusted them to my mind as if storing them up to be produced when required. So they were there even before I had learnt them, but were not in my memory. Accordingly, when they were formulated, how and why did I recognize them and say, "Yes, that is true"? The answer must be that they were already in the memory, but so remote and pushed into the background, as if in most secret caverns, that unless they were dug out by someone drawing attention to them, perhaps I could not have thought of them.[15]

xi (18). On this theme of notions where we do not draw images through our senses, but discern them inwardly not through images but as they really are and through the concepts themselves, we find that the process of learning is simply this: by thinking we, as it were, gather together ideas which the memory contains in a dispersed and disordered way, and by concentrating our attention we arrange them in order as if ready to hand, stored in the very memory where previously they lay hidden, scattered, and neglected. Now they easily come forward under the direction of the mind familiar with them. How many things in this category my memory carries which were once discovered and, as I have said, were ordered ready to hand—things we are said to have learnt and to know! Yet if for quite short periods of time I cease to recollect them, then again they sink below the surface and slip away into remote recesses, so that they have to be thought out as if they were quite new, drawn again from the same store (for there is nowhere else for them to go). Once again they have to be brought together (*cogenda*) so as to be capable of being known; that means they have to be gathered (*colligenda*) from their dispersed state. Hence is derived the word cogitate. To bring together (*cogo*) and to cogitate (*cogito*) are words related as *ago* (I do) to *agito* (agitate) or *facio* (I make) to *factito* (I make frequently).[16] Nevertheless the mind claims the verb cogitate for its own province. It is what is collected (that is, by force) in the mind, not elsewhere, which is strictly speaking the object of recollection.

xii (19). Moreover, the memory contains the innumerable principles and laws of numbers and dimensions. None of them has been impressed on memory through any bodily sense-perception. They are not coloured. They give out no sound or odour. They cannot be tasted or touched. I have heard the sounds of the words which signify these things when they are the subject of discussion. But the sounds are one thing, the principles another. The sounds vary according to whether the terms are Latin or Greek. But numerical principles are neither Greek nor Latin nor any other kind of language. I have seen the lines drawn by architects. They are extremely thin, like a spider's web. But in pure mathematics lines are quite different. They are not images of the lines about which my bodily eye informs me. A person knows them without any thought of a physical line of some kind; he knows them within himself. I am also made aware of numbers which we use for counting on the basis of all the senses of the body. But they are different from the numbers by which we are able to think mathematically.[17] Nor are they the images of numbers as mental concepts, which truly belong to the realm of being. A person who does not see that mental numbers exist may laugh at me for saying this, but I am sorry for the person who mocks me.

xiii (20). All these ideas I hold in my memory, and the way I hold them in the memory is the way that I learnt them. Many quite mistaken objections to these ideas I have heard and hold in my memory. Although they are false, yet it is not false that I remember them. I have seen the difference between the ideas which are true and the objections which are false, and this too I remember. Moreover, in one way in the present I see that I make this distinction, and in another way I remember how I often made this distinction whenever I used to give the matter thought. So I both remember that I often thought about these questions and also store up in the memory what in the present I discern and understand, so that afterwards I remember that at this time I understood them. Accordingly, I also remember that I remember, just as, in the future, if I recall the fact that at this present time I could remember these things, I shall certainly be recalling this by the power of memory.

xiv (21). The affections of my mind are also contained in the same memory. They are not there in the same way in which the mind itself holds them when it experiences them, but in another very different way such as that in which the memory's power holds memory itself. So I can be far from glad in remembering myself to have been glad, and far from sad when I recall my past sadness. Without fear I remember how at a particular time I was afraid, and without any cupidity now I am mindful of cupidity long ago. Sometimes also, on the contrary, I remember with joy a sadness that has passed and with sadness a lost joy. So far as the body is concerned, that is no cause for surprise. The mind is one thing, the body another. Therefore it is not surprising if I happily remember a physical pain that has passed away. But in the present case, the mind is the very memory itself. For when we give an order which has to be memorized, we say "See that you hold that in your mind," and when we forget we say "It was not in my mind" and "It slipped my mind." We call memory itself the mind. Since that is the case, what is going on when, in gladly remembering past sadness, my mind is glad and my memory sad? My mind is glad for the fact that gladness is in it, but memory is not saddened by the fact that regret is in it. Surely this does not mean that memory is independent of the mind? Who could say that? No doubt, then, memory is, as it were, the stomach of the mind, whereas gladness and sadness are like sweet and bitter food. When they are entrusted to the memory, they are as if transferred to the stomach and can there be stored; but they cannot be tasted. It is ridiculous to think this illustration offers a real parallel; nevertheless, it is not wholly inapposite.

(22). Note also that I am drawing on my memory

when I say there are four perturbations of the mind—cupidity, gladness, fear, sadness[18] and from memory I produce whatever I say in discussing them, when I am dividing particular cases according to their species and genus, and when I am offering a definition. I find in memory what I have to say and produce it from that source. Yet none of these perturbations disturbs me when by act of recollection I remember them. And even before I recalled and reconsidered them, they were there. That is why by reminding myself I was able to bring them out from memory's store. Perhaps then, just as food is brought from the stomach in the process of rumination, so also by recollection these things are brought up from the memory. But then why in the mind or "mouth" of the person speaking, that is to say reminiscing, about past gladness or sadness is there no taste of sweetness or bitterness? Or is this a point where the incomplete resemblance between thought and rumination makes the analogy misleading? Who would willingly speak of such matters if, every time we mentioned sadness or fear, we were compelled to experience grief or terror? Yet we would not speak about them at all unless in our memory we could find not only the sounds of the names attaching to the images imprinted by the physical senses, but also the notions of the things themselves. These notions we do not receive through any bodily entrance. The mind itself perceives them through the experience of its passions and entrusts them to memory; or the memory itself retains them without any conscious act of commitment.

xv (23). Whether this happens through the medium of images or otherwise, who could easily tell? For example, I mention a stone, or I mention the sun, when the objects themselves are not present to my senses. Of course images of them are available to me in memory. I may mention physical pain when it is not present to me and I feel no discomfort. Yet if its image were not present in my memory, I would not know what I was talking about, and in discussing it I could not distinguish it from pleasure. I mention physical health. When I am in good health, the thing itself is present to me. But unless the image of it were also present in my memory, I would in no way remember what the sound of this word signified, nor would sick people know what was meant when health was mentioned, unless by the power of memory they held the same image, even though the thing itself was absent from their body. I mention the numbers by which we count things. It is remarkable that in my memory are present not their images but the numbers themselves. I mention the image of the sun, and this is present in my memory. I recall not the image of its image,

but the image itself. In my act of remembering this image is available to me. I mention memory and I recognize what I am speaking about. Where is my recognition located but in memory itself? Surely memory is present to itself through itself, and not through its own image.

xvi (24). What then? When I mention forgetfulness, I similarly recognize what I am speaking of. How could I recognize it except through memory? I refer not to the sound of the word but to the thing which it signifies. If I had forgotten what the force of the sound was, I would be incapable of recognizing it. So when I remember memory, memory is available to itself through itself. But when I remember forgetfulness, both memory and forgetfulness are present—memory by means of which I could remember, forgetfulness which I did remember. But what is forgetfulness except loss of memory? How then is it present for me to remember when, if it is present, I have no power of remembering? What we remember, we retain by memory. But unless we could recall forgetfulness, we could never hear the word and recognize the thing which the word signifies. Therefore memory retains forgetfulness. So it is there lest we forget what, when present, makes us forget. Should the deduction from this be that, when we are remembering forgetfulness, it is not through its actual presence in the memory but through its image? If forgetfulness were present through itself, it would cause us not to remember but to forget. Who can find a solution to this problem? Who can grasp what is going on?

(25). I at least, Lord, have difficulty at this point, and I find my own self hard to grasp. I have become for myself a soil which is a cause of difficulty and much sweat (Gen. 3: 17 f.). For our present inquiry is not to "examine the zones of heaven,"[19] nor are we measuring the distances between stars or the balancing of the earth. It is I who remember, I who am mind. It is hardly surprising if what I am not is distant from me. But what is nearer to me than myself? Indeed the power of my memory is something I do not understand when without it I cannot speak about myself. What shall I say when it is certain to me that I remember forgetfulness? Shall I say that what I recall is not in my memory? Or shall I say that forgetfulness is in my memory for this very purpose that I should not be forgetful? Both propositions are quite absurd. What of a third solution? Can I say that my memory holds the image of forgetfulness, not forgetfulness itself, when I am remembering it? How can I say this when, for the image of an object to be impressed upon the memory, it is first necessary for the object itself to be present, so that an impression of the image becomes possible? That is how I remember

Carthage, and all places where I have been, the faces of people I have seen, and information derived from the other senses. That is also how I know of the healthy or painful condition of my body. When these things were present, memory took images of them, images which I could contemplate when they were present and reconsider in mind when I recollected them even though absent from me. If, then, memory holds forgetfulness not through itself but through its image, forgetfulness must itself have been present for its image to be registered. But when it was present, how did it inscribe its image upon the memory, when, by its very presence, forgetfulness deletes whatever it finds already there? Yet in some way, though incomprehensible and inexplicable, I am certain that I remember forgetfulness itself, and yet forgetfulness destroys what we remember.

xvii (26). Great is the power of memory, an awe-inspiring mystery, my God, a power of profound and infinite multiplicity. And this is mind, this is I myself. What then am I, my God? What is my nature? It is characterized by diversity, by life of many forms, utterly immeasurable. See the broad plains and caves and caverns of my memory. The varieties there cannot be counted, and are, beyond any reckoning, full of innumerable things. Some are there through images, as in the case of all physical objects, some by immediate presence like intellectual skills, some by indefinable notions or recorded impressions, as in the case of the mind's emotions, which the memory retains even when the mind is not experiencing them, although whatever is in the memory is in the mind. I run through all these things, I fly here and there, and penetrate their working as far as I can. But I never reach the end. So great is the power of memory, so great is the force of life in a human being whose life is mortal. What then ought I to do, my God? You are my true life. I will transcend even this my power which is called memory. I will rise beyond it to move towards you, sweet light. What are you saying to me? Here I am climbing up through my mind towards you who are constant above me. I will pass beyond even that power of mind which is called memory, desiring to reach you by the way through which you can be reached, and to be bonded to you by the way in which it is possible to be bonded.

Beasts and birds also have a memory. Otherwise they could not rediscover their dens and nests, and much else that they are habitually accustomed to. Habit could have no influence on them in any respect except by memory. So I will also ascend beyond memory to touch him who "set me apart from quadrupeds and made me wiser than the birds of heaven" (Job 35: 11). As I rise above memory, where am I to find you? My true good and gentle source of reassurance, where shall I find you? If I find you outside my memory, I am not mindful of you. And how shall I find you if I am not mindful of you?

xviii (27). The woman who lost her drachma searched for it with a lamp (Luke 15: 8). She would not have found it unless she had remembered it. When she found it, how could she know that it was the one she lost, if she had failed to remember it? I recall myself to have searched for and found many lost items. From this experience I know that, when I was searching for one of them and someone said to me "Perhaps this is it, perhaps that is," I would always say "No" until I was offered the object which I sought. Unless I had it in my memory, whatever it was, even if an offer was being made to me, I would not have found it because I would not have recognized it. That is also what happens when we seek and find something lost. If anything such as a visible body disappears from sight but not from memory, its image is retained within, and the search continues until it is once more seen. When it is found, it is recognized from the image which is within. We do not say we have found the thing which was lost unless we recognize it, and we cannot recognize it if we do not remember it. The object was lost to the eyes, but held in the memory.

xix (28). What when the memory itself loses something? This happens when we forget and attempt to recall. The only place to search is in the memory itself. If something other than what we want is offered us, we reject it until the thing we are looking for turns up. And when it comes, we say "That is it." We would not say this unless we recognized it, and we would not recognize it unless we remembered. It seems certain, then, that we had forgotten.

Or perhaps it had not totally gone: part was retained, and was used to help in the search for another part. That would presuppose that memory felt itself to be working with a whole to which it was accustomed; as if limping from being deprived of support to which it was accustomed, it would demand the return of the missing element. For instance, our eyes may happen on a person known to us or we may think of him, and we try to recall his name. Other names that occur will not fit the case, because we are not in the habit of associating them with him, and so we reject them until that one comes up which at once corresponds to the familiarly known and is accepted as correct. Where does the right name come from if not from memory itself? Even when we recognize it after being prompted by someone else, memory is its source. We do not believe it as something we are hearing for the first time but, because we remember it, agree that the name mentioned is correct. If, however, it were wholly effaced from the mind, we would not remember even when prompted. When at least we remember ourselves to have forgotten, we have not totally forgotten. But if we have completely forgotten, we cannot even search for what has been lost.

xx (29). How then am I to seek for you, Lord? When I seek for you, my God, my quest is for the happy life. I will seek you that "my soul may live" (Isa. 55: 3), for my body derives life from my soul, and my soul derives life from you. How then shall I seek for the happy life? It is not mine until I say: "It is enough, it is there." But then I ought to say how my quest proceeds; is it by remembering, as if I had forgotten it and still recall that I had forgotten? Or is it through an urge to learn something quite unknown, whether I never had known it or had so forgotten it that I do not even remember having forgotten it? Is not the happy life that which all desire, which indeed no one fails to desire? But how have they known about it so as to want it? Where did they see it to love it? Certainly we have the desire for it, but how I do not know. There is also another sense in which a person who has it is happy at a particular time, and there are some who are happy in hope of becoming so. The kind of happiness they have is inferior to that of those who have the real thing. But they are better than those who are happy neither in actuality nor in hope. Even they would not wish to be happy unless they had some idea of happiness. That this is what they want is quite certain, but how they came to know it I do not know. So also I do not know what kind of knowledge is theirs when they have it. My inquiry is whether this knowing is in the memory because, if it is there, we had happiness once. I do not now ask whether we were all happy individually or only corporately in that man who first sinned, in whom we all died [Adam, 1 Cor. 15: 22] and from whom we were all born into a condition of misery.[20] My question is whether the happy life is in the memory. For we would not love it if we did not know what it is. We have heard the term, and all of us acknowledge that we are looking for the thing. The sound is not the cause of our pleasure. When a Greek hears the Latin term, it gives him no pleasure when he does not understand what has been said. But we are given pleasure, as he would be too if he heard this expressed in Greek. The thing itself is neither Greek nor Latin. Greeks and Latins and people of other languages yearn to acquire it. Therefore it is known to everyone. If they could be asked if they want to be happy, without hesitation they would answer with one voice that they so wish. That would not be the case unless the thing itself, to which this term refers, was being held in the memory.

xxi (30). That is surely not the way in which a person who has seen Carthage remembers it. For the happy life is not seen by the eyes, because it is no physical entity. It is surely not the way in which we remember numbers. A person who has a grasp of numbers does not still seek to acquire this knowledge. But the happy life we already have in our knowledge, and so we love it; and yet we still wish to acquire it so that we may be happy. Surely it is not the way in which we remember eloquence? No. When this word is heard, the thing itself is recalled by those who, though not yet eloquent, in many cases desire to be so. That shows that they already have a knowledge of it. It is through the bodily senses that they have seen other people who were eloquent, were given pleasure, and desired to possess it too. Yet without the basis of inward knowledge, they would not have been pleased nor wished to be eloquent unless they were given pleasure. But it is not by any bodily sense that we discern the happy life in others.

Surely this is not the way in which we recall joy? Well, perhaps it is. For even when sad, I remember my times of joy, like a wretched person thinking of the happy life. It is never by bodily sense that I have seen my joy or heard or smelt or tasted or touched it. I experienced it in my mind when I was glad, and the knowledge of it stuck in my memory, so that I could remind myself of it, sometimes with scorn, sometimes with desire, according to the varied character of the things which I remember myself delighting in. For I derived a sprinkling of pleasure even from discreditable acts which I now recall with hatred and execration. But sometimes my delight was in good and honourable things, which I recall with longing even though they are no longer part of my life. In this sense I am sad as I remember joy of long ago.

(31). Where and when, then, have I experienced the happy life for myself, so that I can remember and love and long for it? The desire for happiness is not in myself alone or in a few friends, but is found in everybody.[21] If we did not know this with certain knowledge, we would not want it with determination in our will. But what does this mean? If two people are asked if they want to serve in the army, it may turn out that one of them replies that he would like to do so, while the other would not. But if they are asked whether they would like to be happy, each would at once say without the least hesitation that he would choose to be so. And the reason why one would wish to be a soldier and the other would not is only that they want to be happy. Is it then the case that one person finds joy in one way, another in a different way? What all agree upon is that they want to be happy, just as they would concur, if asked, that they want to experience joy and would call that joy the happy life. Even if one person pursues it in one way, and another in a different way, yet there is one goal which all are striving to attain, namely to experience joy. Since no one can say that this is a matter outside experience, the happy life is found in the memory and is recognized when the words are uttered.

xxii (32). Far be it from me, Lord, far from the heart of your servant who is making confession to you, far be it from me to think myself happy, whatever be the joy in which I take my delight. There is a delight which is given not to the wicked (Isa. 48: 22), but to those who worship you for no reward save the joy that you yourself are to them. That is the authentic happy life, to set one's joy on you, grounded in you and caused by you. That is the real thing, and there is no other. Those who think that the happy life is found elsewhere, pursue another joy and not the true one. Nevertheless their will remains drawn towards some image of the true joy.[22]

xxiii (33). It is uncertain, then, that all want to be happy since there are those who do not want to find in you their source of joy. That is the sole happy life, but they do not really want it. But perhaps everyone does have a desire for it and yet, because "the flesh lusts against the spirit and the spirit against the flesh so that they do not do what they wish" (Gal. 5: 17), they relapse into whatever they have the strength to do, and acquiesce in that, because in that for which they lack the strength their will is insufficient to give them the strength. For if I put the question to anyone whether he prefers to find joy in the truth or in falsehood, he does not hesitate to say that he prefers the truth, just as he does not hesitate to say he wants to be happy. The happy life is joy based on the truth. This is joy grounded in you, O God, who are the truth, "my illumination, the salvation of my face, my God" (Ps. 26: 1;41: 12). This happy life everyone desires; joy in the truth everyone wants. I have met with many people who wished to deceive, none who wished to be deceived. How then did they know about this happy life unless in the same way that they knew about the truth? They love the truth because they have no wish to be deceived, and when they love the happy life (which is none other than joy grounded in truth) they are unquestionably loving the truth. And they would have no love for it unless there were some knowledge of it in their memory. Why then do they not find their joy in this? Why are they not happy? It is because they are more occupied in other things which make them more wretched than their tenuous consciousness of the truth makes them happy. For among humanity there is "still a little light." May they

walk, may they indeed walk, "so that the darkness does not capture them" (John 12: 35).

(34). But why is it that "truth engenders hatred?"[23] Why does your man who preaches what is true become to them an enemy (Gal. 4: 16) when they love the happy life which is simply joy grounded on truth? The answer must be this: their love for truth takes the form that they love something else and want this object of their love to be the truth; and because they do not wish to be deceived, they do not wish to be persuaded that they are mistaken. And so they hate the truth for the sake of the object which they love instead of the truth. They love truth for the light it sheds, but hate it when it shows them up as being wrong (John 3: 20; 5: 35). Because they do not wish to be deceived but wish to deceive, they love truth when it shows itself to them but hate it when its evidence goes against them. Retribution will come to them on this principle: those who resist being refuted the truth will make manifest against their will, and yet to them it will not be manifest. Yes indeed: the human mind, so blind and languid, shamefully and dishonourably wishes to hide, and yet does not wish anything to be concealed from itself. But it is repaid on the principle that while the human mind lies open to the truth, truth remains hidden from it. Yet even thus, in its miserable condition, it prefers to find joy in true rather than in false things. It will be happy if it comes to find joy only in that truth by which all things are true—without any distraction interfering.

xxiv (35). See how widely I have ranged, Lord, searching for you in my memory. I have not found you outside it. For I have found nothing coming from you which I have not stored in my memory since the time I first learnt of you. Since the day I learnt of you, I have never forgotten you. Where I discovered the truth there I found my God, truth itself, which from the time I learnt it, I have not forgotten. And so, since the time I learnt of you, you remain in my consciousness, and there I find you when I recall you and delight in you. These my holy delights you have given me, in your mercy looking upon my poverty.

xxv (36). But where in my consciousness, Lord, do you dwell? Where in it do you make your home? What resting-place have you made for yourself? What kind of sanctuary have you built for yourself? You conferred this honour on my memory that you should dwell in it. But the question I have to consider is, In what part of it do you dwell? In recalling you I rose above those parts of the memory which animals also share, because I did not find you among the images of physical objects. I came to the parts of my memory where I stored the emotions of my mind, and I did not find you there. I entered into the very seat of my mind, which is located in my memory, since the mind also remembers itself. But you were not there because, just as you are not a bodily image nor the emotional feeling of a living person such as we experience when glad or sad, or when we desire, fear, remember, forget, and anything of that kind, so also you are not the mind itself. For you are the Lord God of the mind. All these things are liable to change. But you remain immutable above all things, and yet have deigned to dwell in my memory since the time I learnt about you.

Why do I ask in which area of my memory you dwell, as if there really are places there? Surely my memory is where you dwell, because I remember you since first I learnt of you, and I find you there when I think about you.

xxvi (37). Where then did I find you to be able to learn of you? You were not already in my memory before I learnt of you. Where then did I find you so that I could learn of you if not in the fact that you transcend me? There is no place, whether we go backwards or forwards;[24] there can be no question of place. O truth, everywhere you preside over all who ask counsel of you. You respond at one and the same time to all, even though they are consulting you on different subjects. You reply clearly, but not all hear you clearly. All ask your counsel on what they desire, but do not always hear what they would wish. Your best servant is the person who does not attend so much to hearing what he himself wants as to willing what he has heard from you.

xxvii (38). Late have I loved you, beauty so old and so new: late have I loved you. And see, you were within and I was in the external world and sought you there, and in my unlovely state I plunged into those lovely created things which you made. You were with me, and I was not with you. The lovely things kept me far from you, though if they did not have their existence in you, they had no existence at all. You called and cried out loud and shattered my deafness. You were radiant and resplendent, you put to flight my blindness. You were fragrant, and I drew in my breath and now pant after you. I tasted you, and I feel but hunger and thirst for you. You touched me, and I am set on fire to attain the peace which is yours.[25]

NOTES

1. Like Plotinus and Porphyry, Augustine understood the Delphic maxim "Know yourself" as the path to know-

ing God; conversely, knowing God is the way to self-knowledge. Plotinus 5. 3. 7. 2 f.

2. The paragraph shows Augustine sensitive to the possibility that some among his readers may have a prurient interest in the record of his sexual excesses in youth.

3. By Jesus Christ.

4. Manichees held the opposite opinion.

5. Cf. above VIII. iv (9). The mystical idea of five spiritual senses (repeated in x. xxvii (38)) was developed already by Origen in the third century. For the ecstasy of Christ's arrow, like Cupid, see above IX. ii (3).

6. Anaximenes of Miletus, in the sixth century B.C., held air to be the origin of all else, and to be divine (cf. *City of God* 8. 5). The argument of Augustine here is strikingly like Plotinus 3. 2. 3. 20 ff.

7. In ancient optics the eyes are not merely passive recipients of images transmitted from the objects seen. A ray comes from the eyes: cf. Plotinus 4. 5. 7. 24; 5. 5. 7. 24 ff.

8. Plotinus 5. 1. 1. 18: "To be in admiring pursuit is to admit inferiority." Plotinus goes on (5. 1. 2) to argue the soul's superiority to all matter in earth or sky.

9. Plotinus 5. 1. 2. 30 ff. has this argument.

10. Plotinus 4. 3. 7. 14 f.; 4. 3. 10. 38.

11. Echo of Plotinus 5. 5. 12. 1–6.

12. *Memoria* for Augustine is a deeper and wider term than our "memory." In the background lies the Platonic doctrine of *anamnesis,* explaining the experience of learning as bringing to consciousness what, from an earlier existence, the soul already knows. But Augustine develops the notion of memory by associating it with the unconscious ("the mind knows things it does not know it knows"), with self-awareness, and so with the human yearning for true happiness found only in knowing God.

13. This passage was found intensely moving by Petrarch.

14. School questions (Cicero, *De partitione oratoria* 62), interestingly different from those of Aristotle's *Posterior Analytics* 2. 1. (Is it the case that P? Why it is the case that P; if X is; what X is. Aristotle does not ask if P exists, or what P is.) The Neoplatonic schools started from Plato (?), *Ep.* 7, 343b 8, as in Plotinus 5. 5. 2. 7.

15. Augustine echoes Plato (*Meno*) that learning is remembering, bringing to the conscious mind something already present.

16. Augustine follows Varro, "On the Latin language" 6. 43. *Cogo,* derived from con + ago, means both "collect" and "compel." *Cogito* is derived from con + agito.

17. Aristotle, *Physics* 4. 11, observed "Number has two senses: what is counted or countable, and that by which we count." Ancient Pythagoreans and Platonists were fascinated by the problem of numbers, especially outside the world

of the senses in the realm of mind. The impact of these debates on Aristotle is evident in the last two books of his *Metaphysics.* A wholly independent discussion of the nature of number (without influence on Augustine) is in Plotinus 6. 6.

18. Cicero, *De finibus* 3. 10. 35; *Tusculan Disputations* 4. 6. 11.

19. Ennius, *Iphigeneia,* quoted by Cicero, *On Divination* 2. 30; *Republic* 1. 30.

20. For Augustine Adam was not merely the start of the human race, but the representative of humanity, so that "we are all Adam."

21. From Cicero's *Hortensius;* cf. *Tusculan Disputations* 5. 28.

22. Plotinus 3. 5. 9. 47 writes of the sense of need, aspiration, and the memory of rational principles coming together in the soul to direct it towards the good.

23. Terence, *Andria* 68.

24. Echo of Plotinus 4. 4. 10. 5 (of time).

25. Augustine's Latin in this chapter is a work of high art, with rhymes and poetic rhythms not reproducible in translation. He is fusing imagery from the Song of Solomon with Neoplatonic reflection on Plato's *Phaedrus* and *Symposium,* and simultaneously summarizing the central themes of the *Confessions.* For the five spiritual senses see above x. vi (8).

5

SAINT THOMAS AQUINAS

Saint Thomas Aquinas (ca. 1224–1274) was traveling to his first assignment as a Dominican monk when he was kidnapped by order of his parents. It was not that the family objected to a religious career; in fact, they had enrolled Aquinas as a child in a Benedictine abbey at Montes Cassino with hopes that he would become a monk, and eventually a powerful abbot. The Dominicans, however, were a relatively new order with an emphasis on preaching Christian doctrine and teaching, rejecting the temporal wealth associated with some of the other orders. In 1245, after a year's captivity, Aquinas was finally allowed to continue his journey to Paris, where he began to study with Albertus Magnus, the magnificent scholar who five centuries later was declared the patron saint of those who study the natural sciences. The writings of Aristotle (p. 20) were just becoming known in Europe, preserved through the previous centuries by Muslim scholars; and it was in Paris, with Albertus Magnus, that Aquinas began his study of "the Philosopher." Aquinas traveled throughout his career, teaching and working at various Dominican houses and universities. He earned his master of theology from the University of Paris in 1256 and returned to Paris in 1268 as debate was escalating regarding whether the faithful Christian should integrate or reject Aristotelian philosophy. In 1274, Aquinas was summoned to the second Council of Lyons, an attempt to reunite the Roman Catholic and Greek Orthodox churches, but fell ill on the journey and died at the Cistercian abbey of Fossanova, near present-day Terracina, Papal States.

Excerpts from St. Thomas Aquinas, "Book 5, Human Nature—Embodied Spirit. Human Abilities—Bodily and Spiritual. How Man Knows." In T. McDermott (Ed.), *St. Thomas Aquinas Summa theologiae* (pp. 108–142). Allen, TX: Christian Classics, 1989. (Original work published 1265)

SUMMA THEOLOGIAE

HUMAN NATURE—
EMBODIED SPIRIT

[vol 11]

What is man? We turn now to man, a creature who is neither pure spirit nor pure body, but has a nature compounded of both. The theologian considers man's nature primarily from the point

75 1 of view of his soul. And if we want to know what sort of thing soul is we must start from how we use the word *anima* [which *soul* translates]. *Animate* means living and *inanimate* non-living, so *soul* means that which first *animates* or makes alive the living things with which we are familiar. Life mostly shows itself in the two activities of awareness and movement; and though these activities have particular sources (the eye for sight, for instance), those sources are organs or instruments of a first source of life. That first source cannot itself be a part of the body: bodily parts are not alive, or sources of life like the heart, simply by being bodily, but by being bodies of such-and-such a sort (otherwise all bodies would be alive and sources of life). Now what *makes* the body actually of such-and-such a sort we call its soul, its first source of life: not itself body but an actuation of body (just as the heat of hot bodies is not itself body, but an energy of bodies).

2 The human soul, however, because it is a source of mental activity, must itself subsist, even though it is not a body. For the mind understands all physical things. But if what knows has the nature of some particular thing it knows, that nature hinders it from knowing anything else (everything tastes sour to a soured tongue); mind, then, cannot have any determinate physical nature. And for the same reason it can't use a bodily organ with a determinate physical nature: for coloured glass colours what is seen through it just as much as colour in the eye itself. Mind then has an activity of its own in which the body has no part. Now to act on its own, it must exist on its own; since the way a thing acts depends on the way in which it exists. So the human soul or mind though non-bodily must be self-subsistent. Sometimes anything that subsists is called an individual thing, at other times only what is whole according to the nature of some species. The first use of individual

excludes things that exist only as properties and forms of something subsistent; the second use excludes component parts as well. A hand is individual in the first sense, not the second; and the human soul too, though subsistent, because it is only part of man, is individual only in the first sense. Only the whole composed of body and soul is an individual in the second sense. If a thing is properly to subsist on its own it must neither exist in nor be a component part of something else: we don't talk of eyes and hands subsisting or acting on their own. What we talk loosely of parts doing, is really done by the whole acting through the parts. Thus, men see with their eyes and feel with their hands (in a stronger sense though than hot things heat with their heat, for properly speaking heat does not *do* any heating). Saying souls understand is like saying eyes see, and what we mean is that men understand with their souls.

Mind needs body not as an organ or instrument of its activity but to present it with objects, for images are to mind as colour to eyes. Needing body in this way doesn't make minds non-subsistent, any more than sensation's need of external sense-objects makes animals non-subsistent. Animal 3 souls however, because they do not act on their own—sensation being an activity of body and soul—do not exist on their own. Physical changes accompany the action of sense-objects on the senses, and too intense an object can injure the sense. But this doesn't happen to the mind; rather understanding what is most intelligible helps with understanding what is less. What tires our bodies is not understanding as such, but the use of our 4 senses to supply the mind with images. Man then is not soul alone. Sensing is one of man's activities, though not peculiar to him, and this shows that individual men are not simply souls, but composed of body and soul. This particular man comprises this soul in this flesh and these bones, and man as such comprises soul and flesh and bones, for whatever is essential to every member of a species is essential to the species. Not everything individual is an individual substance or person: for that its nature must be complete; my soul is only a part of my nature, and no more a person than my hands or my feet are.

5   **Man's soul is immortal.**   To know things is to take in their form; and since our minds know things precisely as instantiations of natures—stones *qua* stones—they must take in the form of stone as such, as form. Now the way a thing is taken in depends on what takes it in; so the receptive mind itself must be form as such, not matter under some form. If minds were matter under some form, then the forms they take in would be individualized; and minds would know only particular things, as the senses do which receive forms into material organs. For matter individualizes form. Minds then, because they know forms as such, are not themselves composed of matter and form. The way mind takes in forms is quite different from the way matter takes them on, and this shows in the forms received; for matter individualizes any form it takes on, but the mind takes in the pure form as such.

6   The human soul, then, as source of our intelligence, cannot decompose. Because it is self-subsistent, it doesn't perish with the body as the souls of other animals do; but neither can it decompose itself. For forms are precisely what make things actual and give them existence. Material things come to be precisely by being formed, and perish when they lose their form. But subsistent forms cannot lose themselves. Even if souls *were* composed of matter and form, as some people think, they still couldn't decompose. For things decompose only when their forms are displaced by incompatible forms; the stars of heaven whose matter is not subject to such forms never decompose. Minds too do not take on forms; they take them in by knowing them. But *knowing* a form is compatible with knowing the forms that are incompatible with it; indeed knowing a thing entails knowing its contrary. So there is no way in which minds can decompose. An indication of this is the special way in which we manifest the general natural desire for survival. In things which possess awareness this desire reflects that awareness: now, whereas the senses are aware only of here-and-now existence, minds grasp existence as such, whenever and wherever, and as a result things with minds naturally desire to live for ever. But a drive of nature can't be pointless, so no substance with mind can decompose. The soul can cease to exist, but that means only that the creator can stop holding it in being; it doesn't

7   imply a tendency in the created soul itself to de-compose. Soul's substance doesn't contain body, but must of its nature be joined to body; for properly speaking, it is not soul that has a specific nature, but the thing body and soul compose. The soul needs a body even to exercise its own activity, and this very fact shows that souls are lesser minds than angels, who exist without bodies.

Embodied mind.   Mind is the form of man's   76 1 body. Active things must have forms by which they act; only healthy bodies heal themselves, and only instructed minds know. Activity depends on actuality, and what makes things actual makes them active. Now the soul is what makes our body live; so the soul is the primary source of all those activities that differentiate levels of life: growth, sensation, movement, understanding. So, whether we call our primary source of understanding mind or soul, it is the form of our body. This is Aristotle's proof in his book *On the Soul;* and to deny it one would have to find some other way in which each man's activity of understanding is his own (as we experience it to be). Aristotle says actions can be ascribed to things in three ways: *with intrinsic appropriateness to them as a whole (as healing to doctors), or to a part of them (as seeing to men because they have eyes), or entirely coincidentally (as building to white men, since their whiteness is irrelevant to their building).* Clearly I don't understand coincidentally: I understand as a man and I am a man by nature. So either I understand as a whole (which is Plato's position identifying man with his mind) or I understand with a part of myself. Now Plato's position is untenable, because I experience myself both understanding and sensing, and, since I cannot sense without a body, my body must be part of me. So the mind with which I understand, must also be part of me, united in some way to my body.

Ibn Roschd, in his commentary on Aristotle's *On the Soul,* maintained that mind and body were united through the forms of mind's objects. These he said had two subjects: the receptive mind and the images present in our bodily senses; so that they served to link the receptive mind to the body of this or that man. But such linking would not be enough to make the mind's activity my activity. The analogy with the senses that Aristotle uses to explain mind shows us why. Mind, he says, is related to images as sight is to colours; as sight conforms to colours, so the receptive mind conforms itself to our images. But clearly the fact that the colours to which our sight conforms are in a wall doesn't mean that the wall sees, but only that it is seen. So the fact that the receptive mind conforms to my images doesn't mean that I understand, but only that I and my images are understood.

So other thinkers have argued that mind is united to body by acting on it, and that this unites mind and body enough for understanding to be ascribable to the composite whole. But this fails on many counts. First, the only way my mind acts on my body is by arousing its desire, and that presupposes understanding. So I don't understand because I am acted on by mind, but on the contrary I am acted on by mind because I understand. Secondly, I am an individual with a single nature composed of matter and form, and if the mind is not that form then it must act from outside my nature, on the whole of me. But understanding is an activity that remains interior to its agent, not crossing over into other things in the way that, say, heating does. So I can't be said to understand because I am acted on by mind. Thirdly, the only sort of thing to which you can ascribe an action acting on it is a tool, like the carpenter's saw. So understanding ascribed to me because I am acted on by mind must belong to me as a tool; and that contradicts Aristotle's statement that understanding uses no bodily organ. Fourthly, though the action of a part can be ascribed to the whole, it can't be ascribed to another part, except coincidentally: men see with their eyes but their hands don't. So if I and some mind together made up some whole, the actions of the mind couldn't be ascribed to me. And if I were the whole, composed of mind and the rest of me, with the mind united to my other parts only by acting on them, then I would have no unity strictly speaking and therefore no existence simply speaking, since things exist in the way they are one. So we are left with only one way in which we can ascribe understanding to a man: Aristotle's way, in which the mind is man's form.

The same conclusion emerges if we ask what constitutes humankind a species. The natures of things are known from their activities, and the activity marking human animals out from all other animals is understanding (which is why Aristotle locates man's final happiness in this activity). So what decides man's species must be what makes him understand; and since what decides a thing's

species is the form that makes the thing what it is, this in man must be mind. Note then that successive levels of form master physical matter more and more, displaying behaviour and abilities less and less confined by matter. Chemical compounds behave in ways irreducible to the behaviour of their elements; and the abilities of higher forms transcend those of elemental matter even further: plant forms more than metal forms and animal forms more than plant forms. Of all these the human form is the highest, with abilities so transcending physical matter that it possesses an activity and ability which physical matter in no way shares: the power of mind.

Aristotle calls the human soul the highest form in nature, and thinks natural philosophy should culminate in its study. He says it is *separate, yet in matter, since men and the sun generate men from matter:* separate, because mind is not the power of a bodily organ in the way sight is the power of our eyes; in matter, because it is the form of our body and the term of human reproduction. The existence the soul itself has it shares with the physical matter it forms, so that the existence of the composite whole is the existence of the soul itself. This does not happen with other forms because they are not self-subsistent. And this is why when the body decays the human soul continues to exist of itself whereas other forms don't. But to be united with a body is as natural to the soul as floating upward is to lightweight things. Held down, light things remain light, with an affinity and inclination to float upward. So too the human soul, existing away from its body, has a natural affinity and inclination to be one with it again.

Each man has his own individual mind.   It 2
is quite impossible for all men to share one mind. If Plato is right and a man is his mind, then, if we shared one mind, you and I would be one man with different accessories, like a man now in a shirt and now in a coat; which is quite ridiculous. And if Aristotle is right and the mind is an ability of soul and soul is man's form: then a number of individuals could no more share a single form than they can share a single existence, since it is form that gives existence. And so also with every other model of a single mind united with one man here and another man there. For however mind is united to this or that man, the rest of him will obviously be mind's tool, since his animal powers

all obey mind and minister to it. Now clearly one agent using two tools does two actions while remaining one agent: a man using both hands is a single toucher even if he touches twice. And many agents using one tool do one action, while remaining many: many people pulling on one rope are many pullers giving a single pull. A single agent using a single tool does a single action: a workman using a hammer is one hammerer doing one hammering. So if you and I had two minds but shared one eye we would be two seers with but a single seeing; but if we shared one mind, then whatever number of other things we had as tools of mind, you and I would never be anything but one knower. Add the fact that mind in knowing uses no other tool than the mind itself, and it will follow that a shared mind would do only one action: that is, that all men would be one knower engaged in one act of knowing per known object. Some have thought they could differentiate my knowing from yours by the different images in our heads, for my image of a stone is not yours, and these different images received into the one receptive mind could produce different actions, just as different images of things in one eye produce different acts of seeing. But what the mind receives into itself are not images themselves, but forms abstracted from the images to make them ready for understanding. From different images of one sort of thing, a single mind would abstract a single understandable form, just as a man abstracts from his many images of stones one understandable definition of a stone through which his mind can know the nature of all stones in one act, despite the diversity of his images. So if all men had one mind, the different images in you and me could not, as Ibn Roschd imagined, differentiate my knowing from yours. It goes against all reason, then, to maintain that all men share one mind.

That minds and ideas exist individually does not prevent them knowing generalities, as existing materially would. The multitude of things that share one nature are distinguished by material features peculiar to them as individuals; and if the likenesses by which these things were known were also material, embedded in matter, then they would reflect the general nature under these many distinguishing features, and fail to yield knowledge of the nature in its generality. But a likeness that has been abstracted from its embodiments in particular matter will reflect the nature without

these many distinguishing features, and give general knowledge. So generality of knowledge says nothing about whether minds are one or many: even if we all shared one mind it would still be an individual one, and the likenesses by which it knew things in general would be individuals. Multiplying minds doesn't multiply what mind knows, for as Aristotle says it is not the stone that is in our mind but its likeness. Yet it is the stone that we know, not its likeness (unless we are reflecting on our own knowing), for otherwise we would know not things but ideas. So just as many eyes with many images see the same colour, so many minds know the same known thing. The only difference, in Aristotle's opinion, is that whereas we sense things in their particularity just as they exist outside, we know the natures of extra-mental things not in their extra-mental mode of existing, but in general, abstracted from any particularizing features.

Each man has a single soul.   If Plato is right and souls are not the forms bodies have but agents acting on them, one and the same body could well be acted on by several souls, especially if they acted on different parts of it. But if souls are forms of bodies then it doesn't seem possible for several essentially different souls to unite with one body. Firstly, an animal with more than one soul wouldn't be one animal in any straightforward sense of the word *one.* For oneness is an accompaniment of existence; and what makes a thing one strictly speaking is the single form making it what it is. Whatever is designated by two or more forms—a *white man,* for example—is not one thing, simply speaking. Secondly, predicates arising from different forms connect coincidentally (*per accidens*) if independent of one another (*what's white is sweet*), or with that type of intrinsic appropriateness (*per se type 2*) in which the subject helps define the predicate (*surfaces are coloured,* since colour presupposes surface). So, if we were animals by one form and men by another, *what's man is animal* would be coincidentally true if the two forms were independent, else intrinsically appropriate *type 2* if animality presupposed humanity. Now clearly neither alternative is true: men are animals *per se,* not coincidentally, but humanity presupposes animality and not vice versa. Now animal can be predicated *per se* of man in this way (*per se type I*) only if the same

3

form makes us both men and animals. Thirdly, the fact that the soul's activities when intense interfere with one another shows they must have the same source: one and the same soul in man is the source of his sense life and mental life and vegetative life. Aristotle compares the sequence of grades of life with that of geometrical shapes, each shape overlaying and extending the one before. Just as the area of a pentagon hasn't two shapes—pentagon and quadrilateral—but the quadrilateral area is included in the pentagonal, so one and the same soul is the basis of our mental activity and includes in its potential the sense-potential and metabolic potential of animal and plant souls. To begin with, the embryo has only animal soul, but this is later displaced by a more perfect soul with both mind and senses. [When we distinguish what is generically common from what differentiates a species of that genus] we are abstracting in thought things that are in reality one. The potential of the human soul includes and extends that of the animal soul, so we abstractly conceive the potential of sense-activity separately as something incomplete and material and generically common to men and animals, and the potential of mind as something added in man to complete and differentiate and give specific form to him.

4   If the human soul or form supervened on a body already existing as a substance under some other form, then the human form wouldn't give man his existence as a substance: indeed, man wouldn't exist strictly speaking but merely be one of the ways something else existed. The mind then is the only form in man under which he exists as a substance; including in its potential the potentials of the animal soul, the vegetative soul and all the more elementary forms. The human soul in man, the animal soul in animals, the vegetative soul in plants—in general the higher forms of higher substances—all effect what elementary forms effect in lower things. Aristotle defined soul as *that which actuates an organized physical body with the potential of life, a potential not existing apart from the soul.* Clearly he is including soul in what it actuates, as one might say heat actuates hot bodies and light actuates things that shine, not meaning things that are already shining without the light but the things light makes shine. When Aristotle says soul actuates the body he describes, he means that it is soul which makes it a physical body and organizes it

and gives it the potential of life. This first actuation he calls potential in relation to a second possible actuation, namely activity; and *apart from the soul* no such potential would exist. Once the soul is united to the body as form by its very existence, it goes on to move the body to activity. Through this power of movement the soul is the activating part of man, and the already animated body the activated part. Ibn Sina thought elements maintained their own substantial forms intact in compounds, the compound merely averaging out their conflicting properties. But this is impossible, for the different forms would have to exist in different parts of the matter, and so there would be no true fusion of elements, but only juxtaposition of minute particles that the senses could not discriminate. Ibn Roschd thought elements had forms halfway between accidental and substantial forms, and that they varied in intensity, becoming less intense in compounds and striking a sort of equilibrium from which a single form emerged. But this is even more inconceivable: a thing either is substantial or it isn't, substantial forms can't vary in intensity, and there is no halfway house between substances and concomitant accidents. So we prefer Aristotle's position: the forms of elements don't actually exist in compounds but only virtually, by way of their peculiar behavioural properties, which persist less intensely in the compound; and these properties dispose the matter to become the new compound substance, be it animal or mineral.

The human body.   Matter exists for the sake   5
of its forms, not the forms for the sake of their matter, so we explain the sort of body a man has by looking at what his soul needs. Now the human soul is the lowest grade of mind in nature's hierarchy, since its knowledge of truth is not inborn (like angels) but gathered from sense-experience of things spatially outside it. As such, it needs a body suited to sensing. Now the basis of all sensation is touch and an organ of touch must balance the opposing qualities of hot and cold and moist and dry in order to sense them all acutely. So men's bodies are made more sensitive to touch than animals' in this way, and intelligent men's even more then others: *tender flesh goes with a quick mind,* says Aristotle. But why not join an imperishable soul to an imperishable body? It is no use answering that originally Adam's body was imperishable, because that was not by nature

but by a grace of God; otherwise Adam's sin would have left him immortal. Rather we must admit that, whereas some characteristics of its matter suit a form, others are just unavoidable consequences. Carpenters make saws of iron for cutting hard things, but as a result the teeth will blunt and rust in time. In the same way the mind needs a body of balanced composition, but that means it will one day die. If you say God could have avoided this remember what Augustine says: the way things are in nature depends more on what nature needs than on what God can do. Anyway God does provide grace to heal death; and mind's grasp of generalities sets no limit to what man himself can do; so although nature can't endow him with the fixed instinctive responses, defence mechanisms and protective covering which it gives to other animals of limited awareness and powers, still it gives him reason and hands—those tools of tools—with which to make his own tools to suit every sort of purpose.

6   Since bodily matter is dimensioned, the mind can think of it first as dimensioned, then as divided, then as diversified according to its grade of form. But really one form gives matter all these
8   attributes, even if the mind distinguishes them. You can divide a whole into quantitative parts, or into the parts of its definition, or into various things it has the ability to do. When a homogeneous whole is divided quantitatively, its form is also coincidentally divided (whiteness with the white surface); but the same is not true of heterogeneous wholes. So to the question whether whiteness exists whole in every part of a white surface or only in the whole, we would have to make a distinction: the quantitative wholeness (which whiteness possesses only coincidentally) is not whole in every part, and no part of the white surface is as able to affect our sight as the whole; but the definition of whiteness is realized in every part. To a similar question about the soul, however, we can dismiss quantitative division, and say simply that whereas the whole essence of the soul is realized in every part of the body, not the whole of what it can do: for only the eye sees and only the ear hears. Note too that, since the soul requires a heterogeneous body, it relates principally and immediately to the whole body as to its appropriate matter, and only secondarily to parts of the body according to their place in the whole. Some powers of the soul, like intellect and will, belong

to its transcendence of the capacity of the whole body, and are not located in any part of it, but other powers are shared with the body and are located, not everywhere the soul is, but in the parts of the body appropriate to their activity.

HUMAN ABILITIES—BODILY AND SPIRITUAL

Abilities belong to the same category of being as   77 1
do the ways of actually existing they make possible; our abilities to act can no more constitute our substance than can the activities themselves. Only God is his own activity, and so only God is his own ability to act. To have soul is to be alive (the actualization achieved in us by being born); but if it were also to be engaged in activity then we would be in non-stop activity all our life long. Our first actualization, life, is capable of further actualization, activity, but this belongs not to soul's substance but to its potential, not to what it is but to what it can do. So we distinguish a soul's powers and abilities from its substance; for no actuality precisely as such is potential. If *accident* or *concomitant* means what can exist only in a preexistent subject then the soul's abilities, not being its substance, must be its concomitants: there is no halfway house between needing or not needing a subject. But if *concomitant* means a property not necessitated by the nature of a thing, then there is a halfway house between substance and concomitants: namely those properties which derive necessarily from a thing's nature. In this sense the soul's abilities are neither its substance nor its concomitants but its natural properties.

Abilities are potentials for activity, and we dif-   3
ferentiate them as we do activities according to different ways in which things can be objects of activity. The object of a receptive power's activity is whatever initially stimulates it (colour in the case of sight); the object of an agent power's activity is its final goal (adult size in the case of our power of growth). So what begins and what ends an activity can decide its type. Not that every difference in object defines a new type of ability, but only differences relevant to the object as object. Thus, the objects of sense are qualities that affect us, and any relevant differences in such qualities (colour, sound, etc) differentiate types of sense (sight, hearing, etc); but differences in objects ir-

relevant to their colour (musician, grammarian, big, small, man, stone) don't differentiate types of sight. Abilities, though they pre-exist their activities, are defined in terms of them, just as agencies are defined by their goals. Though the objects of an activity are external to it, the activity begins

4 and ends with them and is internally adapted to them. Our soul's many abilities derive from it in an order. Certain abilities are of their nature subordinate to others: vegetative powers to sense-powers, and sense-powers to the mind which controls and directs them; though we develop such powers in the reverse order.

5 Abilities like mind and will, which exercise no bodily organ, are properties of soul; but sense-powers and vegetative powers do exercise bodily organs and are properties of the composite of body and soul, but are called powers of soul because

6 it is through soul that the composite possesses them. A subject which previously existed only potentially acquires actual existence when it acquires its substantial form; a supervening concomitant or accidental form, on the other hand, acquires actual existence from its subject, which already existed actually even if it only potentially possessed this supervening form. Subjects as potential take on such supervening forms, but as actual they themselves produce them. I am thinking of supervening forms characteristic of their subjects: non-characteristic forms are produced in their subjects by external agents, but characteristic forms or properties derive from the subject's own actuality, not by a subject acting to modify itself in some way, but by its actuality overflowing naturally into that property, as light naturally overflows into colour. So the soul's abilities, whether they be properties of the soul itself or the body-soul composite, derive from their subject's actuality and thus from the soul, the source of that actuality.

78 1 **Bodily life.** We distinguish three sorts of soul, four levels of life, and five types of ability in souls: vegetative, sense, appetitive, locomotive and mental. Sorts of soul we distinguish by the degree to which their activity transcends that of physical nature. The rational soul's activity so far transcends the physical that it is not the activity of any bodily organ; the sense-soul's activities are activities of bodily organs consequent on physical changes of the organs, but are not themselves physical changes; whereas vegetative activities

such as digestion proceed in bodily organs by the instrumentality of physical changes, and transcend physical action only by being internally, not externally, caused (a characteristic of all living activities). Types of ability we distinguish by their objects. The only object of the vegetative powers is the body in which they reside, so they differ in type from abilities which relate to any object that can be sensed (sense abilities) or that can exist (mental abilities). Relating us to such external objects we have abilities that unite objects to us by taking in their forms (the senses less generally, the mind for all objects whatever), and abilities that incline and draw us towards objects (appetites, the objects of which are initial goals to be aimed at, and locomotive abilities, the objects of which are terms of the movements which achieve our aims). The levels of life are plants (with only vegetative abilities), immobile animals such as shellfish (adding sense), the higher animals (adding locomotion), and men (adding mind). Appetitive abilities add no new level to life, since *anything with sense-power has appetite.* Anything at all has its natural tendency (its *natural desire*); and any ability tends naturally towards its object in this way. But there is a special tendency consequent on awareness, called *animal desire,* which requires a special ability over and above awareness's natural tendencies. For desire seeks the thing itself, not just that likeness of things in us that makes us aware of them. An animal's sight will tend naturally towards what is visible to fulfil its function of seeing; but the animal itself seeks the actual thing it sees, with an animal desire, not just for seeing but for other purposes. If all we needed things for was perception, we wouldn't need this 2 special ability called appetite. By vegetative powers we mean the abilities to reproduce and bring living bodies into existence, to grow to a proper size, and to digest food so as to maintain that existence and size. The last two abilities affect the actual body they reside in, but the reproductive ability acts to produce other bodies, and so approaches the dignity of sense-powers. Digesting food serves growth; both serve reproduction. Such powers are often called natural powers, because their effects—existence, size and self-preservation—are similar to effects in [inanimate] nature, though more perfectly achieved; and because they act by means of natural [physico-chemical] forces.

3 **Our senses.**   Nature doesn't give us sense-powers to fit our sense-organs, but organs to fit our powers. Every sense-power is an ability to receive a particular stimulus from external objects, and what differentiates our sense-powers are different types of stimuli. But being physically affected by this stimulus [e.g. heated by heat] is not enough for the sensing of it [otherwise everything heated would feel heat]; the stimulus must be received intentionally, in the way eyes receive colour without becoming coloured. Sight—the least physical of the senses—is the only entirely intentional sense; in hearing and smell the objects sensed undergo physical change (for sounds are movements of the air, and smells arise when things are heated), and in taste and touch the sensing organs undergo change as well. Size and shape haven't got a particular sense to themselves: they are objects common to the senses (all attributes of extension) affecting a sense not immediately but by way of the quality that stimulates that particular sense (extension being the immediate subject of such qualities: surface, for example, of colour). Size and shape are however genuinely sensed, not merely known because of what is sensed [as the meanings of spoken words

4 are]; for size and shape modify the sense-stimulus itself. Higher animals must be aware of something not only when it is present to their senses but also in its absence, so that they can be prompted to seek it. So they not only need to receive, but also to retain, impressions of sense-objects presently affecting them. The senses reside in material organs, and since matter must be moist to receive impressions but dry to retain them, the ability to receive sense impressions differs from the ability to retain them. In addition, animals need to be attracted and repelled not only by what pleases or displeases their senses but by what is useful or harmful in other ways: the straws birds collect must look good for nest-building. So animals must be able to perceive a significance in things that is not merely an externally perceptible quality. In addition to their particular senses (and the common root of those senses) for receiving sense impressions and their imagination for storing them, animals must therefore have an instinctive judgment for certain further significances of things, and a memory for storing those (for what is memorable to animals is what is harmful or agreeable, and pastness itself is important to them

in this way). Judgment of this sort in men includes an element of calculation, working out particular significances as reason does general ones; and memory in man doesn't just have immediate recall of things past, but by a quasi-logical process of recollection searches out past memories guided by their particular significances. Particular senses discern the particular sense-stimuli proper to them, but to distinguish white from sweet we need some common root sensitivity in which all sense-perceptions meet, and where we can perceive perception itself and become aware that we see. When a particular sense is aware of the quality that is affecting it we see, but when affections of sense affect some common root sensitivity we see that we see.

Mental ability.   Aristotle says *mind is a sort* 79 2 *of susceptibility.* In the strict sense of the word, we are susceptible to unnatural and uncongenial things like sickness or sadness; less strictly, to any alteration in which something is lost, be it congenial or not; and most broadly of all, to any sort of fulfilling alteration, even if nothing is lost. It is in this last sense that man's mind is a susceptibility to being in general. God's mind is his very substance in which all being pre-exists originally and virtually as in its first cause. So God's mind is not potential or receptive of being in general but its active creator. Created minds, on the other hand, because their being is not infinite, are only potential of being in general, and actualized by the things they understand. Angels' minds are so actualized from the first moment of their creation, but the human mind, being the lowest and furthest away from God's perfect mind, starts as a sheer potential of understanding—*a blank page on which nothing is written*—and only later acquires actual understanding. This is why human understanding is a susceptibility in the third sense above, and why we call it a *receptive mind.*

But Aristotle also says that *in the mind, just as* 3 *in the rest of nature, besides what is receptive of existence there is what makes things exist.* According to Plato the forms physical matter takes on exist on their own account outside matter as actual objects of understanding called *Ideas.* Physical matter and mind are both *formed* by *participating* these Ideas: matter into particular things with their own specific and generic natures, and mind into knowledge of such species and genera. But according to Aristotle the forms of physical things exist only in matter and not as actually understandable. Since we can only understand what is actually understandable (just as we can only sense what is actually there to be sensed), our minds need to make things actually understandable by abstracting their forms from their material conditions. Our ability to do this we call our *agent mind.* Things outside us are already actually able to be sensed, so our senses need only to be receptive; but the mind must be part active, part receptive, for nothing material is actually understandable, and an immaterial receptive mind would be no use to us without an agent mind to make material things actually understandable by abstraction. Each of us has such an agent mind, for we are aware of ourselves abstracting. It doesn't activate our receptive mind as if it were itself an object of knowledge (if it did, its universality would give us all knowledge at a stroke). Rather it produces the objects that do activate our mind, given the help of imagination and the senses and practice in understanding (for understanding one thing leads to understanding others: we pass from terms to propositions, and from premises to conclusions).

If memory means only our ability to retain knowledge then mind is itself memory; but if we define it as knowing the pastness of what is past then it must be a sense-power able to grasp the particular: for the past as past is some particular then. Pastness can qualify both what we know and our act of knowing it. The two go together in sensation, where we sense what is presently affecting our senses; so that animals simultaneously remember past sensing and the sensed past. But to the mind the pastness of what we understand is irrelevant; we understand human nature as such, common to past, present and future men. Yet our acts of understanding are particulars occurring now, tomorrow or yesterday, just like acts of sensing. They, like the mind itself, are immaterial particulars, so the mind knows them in the same way it knows itself. In a sense then the mind too remembers the past by knowing its own past acts, though it cannot understand the material particular there-then-ness of the past. Sometimes the mind is merely capable of knowing something, sometimes it is actually attending to something it knows, and sometimes it is in a knowledgeable state or disposition halfway between potentiality and act, in which it possesses knowledge but is not actually attending to it.

Reasoning relates to understanding as journeying to rest. Journeys start and end in states of rest, and human reasoning journeys from what it immediately understands (its first premises) along the road of investigation and discovery, later returning along the road of judgment to analyse its findings and test them against those first premises. Even in nature one and the same tendency moves things to places and then keeps them at rest there. All the more then is it one and the same ability that we exercise when reasoning and understanding. Some philosophers make a fourfold division of mind: as agent, as receptive, as disposed and as fulfilled. Of these the agent mind and the receptive mind are distinct abilities (an ability to do always differs from an ability to be). But the other two are states of the receptive mind, which is sometimes only capable of knowing (receptive), sometimes actually knowledgeable (disposed to know), and sometimes actually attending to what it knows (fulfilled). We don't have one mind for planning action and one for pursuing truth. It is irrelevant to understanding as such whether we make practical use of what we understand or merely attend to its truth. *Practical understanding differs from theorizing only in intention.* The practical mind only plans what we do, it doesn't actually do it; and planning is a kind of understanding. Being good and being true imply one another: we value truth as a good, we perceive goodness as a truth about things. We can desire to know what is true, and know how to do what is good. In pursuit of truth we reason to what is true from theoretical premises, in planning action we reason to what to do from practical premises. Understanding these premises needs no other ability than mind; but it is a special competence or disposition of that ability. In the case of practical principles we call it *synteresis* [or moral sense], and talk of it as *prompting to good and crying out against evil,* since first principles initiate all our investigations and judge all our findings. Conscience on the other hand is neither ability nor disposition, strictly speaking, but the activity of consciously applying our knowledge to what we do: witnessing to what we do and don't do, legislating about what we should and shouldn't do, and defending or accusing us when we have or haven't done well. We are not always engaged in such activities, but our disposition to engage in them, and especially our competence of first principles called *synteresis,* is always there, so sometimes this moral sense itself gets called our conscience.

80 1   **Urges, inclinations and desires.**   Forms are accompanied by tendencies: matter under the form of fire, for example, tends to rise skyward and to propagate itself. Things lacking awareness have just the natural form that constitutes them the unique things they are and the natural tendencies accompanying such a form are called natural inclinations or desires. But things with awareness are so constituted by their natural forms that they can take in the forms of other things: the senses taking in all forms perceptible to sense and the mind all forms that can be understood, so that through mind and the senses the human soul is in a fashion everything, and bears a resemblance to God *in whom everything pre-exists.* Because they possess forms in this more perfect way, creatures with awareness possess a more perfect sort of inclination or tendency directed to things they are aware of, and not merely to things they incline to naturally. This more perfect inclination is the soul's ability to desire. We are aware of things as perceptible or understandable, but we desire them as congenial or good. Since there are different ways in which things can be objects of our activities, they require different abilities in the soul. Each ability is a sort of form or nature with a natural tendency towards its own natural object. But over and above all this is the animal desire that follows on awareness, tending not to what suits

2   this or that ability (to sights or sounds), but to what suits the whole animal. Our abilities to desire are abilities to respond to perceived stimuli. To respond to sense-perceptible stimuli we need sense-appetite, and to respond to stimuli which we mentally perceive we need a mental appetite. It is precisely because things stimulate our desires through our perceptions of them that different types of perception differentiate desirability as such. Mental appetite can be stimulated by individual things existing outside the mind, but this happens by way of some general stimulus they instantiate, such as being good. As Aristotle remarks, *we can hate the whole genus of robbers.* Moreover, with our mental appetite we can desire immaterial things like knowledge and virtue, which the senses cannot perceive. Both mind and

sense, however, command the same motor abilities: the higher appetite by way of the lower, in the way general principles affect us by way of their particular applications.

Sense-appetite.   Sense-appetite takes two dif- 81 2 ferent forms: one pleasure-seeking or *affective* and the other *aggressive.* The former drives animals to pursue what pleases their senses and avoid what hurts them, the latter drives them to resist whatever threatens pleasure or introduces danger, to confront difficulties and to overcome obstacles. These two drives cannot be reduced to one; for sometimes animals put up with pain (against their pleasure-seeking instincts) in order to fight obstacles (in accordance with their aggressive instincts). Nevertheless all aggressive emotions begin and end in pleasure-seeking: discomfort breeds anger and this, if it cures the situation, restores contentment. What animals fight about is their pleasures: food and sex. Reason can control   3 such emotion. In other animals emotions follow *instinctive judgment* (sheep fear wolves because they instinctively judge them to be hostile); but in man, a sort of *calculation* replaces instinctive judgment, making particular associations and connections. These particular connections are subject to the influence and control of general connections; we argue to particular conclusions from general premises. So reason can command the appetites of sense, both affective and aggressive, and control feeling. Arguing from general premises to particular conclusions is the work of reason rather than of simple understanding, so it is better to talk of us controlling our affections and our aggression by reasoning than by understanding. And we experience this in ourselves: we appeal to general considerations in order to calm or to incite our anger and our fears. The motor activities consequent on feeling are also under the control of our wills. Other animals react straightaway to feelings of pleasure or aggression (when sheep are afraid of wolves they run away immediately) for no higher appetite opposes them; but human beings do not react immediately but wait for will's command, since our lower appetites need our higher appetite's consent. Aristotle says *our soul rules our physical body like a tyrant ruling slaves:* its commands are irresistible, and every member of the body subject to will reacts immediately in the way the soul desires it to. But *our mind rules* *our appetites like a president ruling free men:* our sense-appetites have a domain of their own in which they can oppose reason's decisions. Appetite responds not only to instinctive judgment (in other animals) and calculation guided by general reasoning (in man), but also to sensation and imagination. We experience conflict between our feelings of pleasure or aggression and our reason when we sense or imagine pleasurable things that reason forbids or painful things it commands. Such conflict is still compatible with obedience. Our external senses require stimulus from external objects the presence of which reason cannot totally control. But our interior powers of knowledge and desire don't need external objects, and are subject to reason, which can excite or temper feeling and conjure up images.

82 1 **Will.** What can't be otherwise is necessary. The necessity may be absolute, a necessity of intrinsic nature: either of matter (things composed of opposing elements must decompose) or of form (the three angles of a triangle must equal two right angles). Or the necessity may be need, imposed extrinsically by goals which can't otherwise be achieved or achieved properly (food is needed for survival, a horse for a journey). Or the necessity may be coercion, imposed extrinsically by an agent which won't allow one to act otherwise. Coercion is altogether incompatible with will: our will inclines us to things, and movement in accord with such inclinations is called voluntary, just as movement in accord with natural inclination is called natural; but movement that goes against inclination is called forced or coerced. So movements can no more be both coerced and voluntary than they can be both forced and natural. Need, however, is compatible with will, when there is only one way of achieving a goal: if we will a voyage we must needs will a ship. And necessity of nature is also compatible with will: indeed just as mind must by nature assent to the first principles of thought, so will must by nature consent to our ultimate goal of happiness (goals playing the same role in activity as premises do in thought). For everything must have a basic invariant nature underlying and presupposed to everything else. We can control our behaviour by choosing this or that means to our ends, but our desire for our ultimate end is not something in our control.

However not everything we will has to be 2 willed [, just as not everything we think has to be thought]. The mind doesn't have to think thoughts that have no necessary connection with first principles (merely factual propositions, for instance, that can be denied without falsifying such principles); but it has to give assent to necessary propositions (demonstrable conclusions, for example, that cannot be denied without falsifying first principles), once their necessary connection with first principles has been demonstrated. And so it is with the will. The will doesn't have to want limited goods that have no necessary connection with happiness and that a person can be happy without; but other things do have a necessary connection with happiness, joining men to God, in whom alone true happiness is to be found. Before we see God and are sure of this necessary connection, our will doesn't have to want either God or the things of God; but when we see him as he is, our wills won't be able to help wanting him, just as now we can't help wanting to be happy.

Mind and will. To will a desirable good we 3 must know the way in which it is good and desirable, something more abstractly simple and more excellent than the actual object willed. [So in the abstract the mind is the more excellent faculty.] Understanding, however, takes things in and is concerned with their truth in the mind, whereas willing tends towards the goodness of things in themselves; so when things exist more excellently in themselves than in the mind, willing them is preferable to knowing them (loving God to knowing him); but when they exist more excellently in the mind, knowing them is preferable to loving 4 them. Our mind sees the good in things and this motivates our will (as goals motivate agents); but it is our will, as agent of our overall goal, which impels our mind and all our other powers to pursue their own particular goals. For what motivates a power is a particular goal suited to it: colour attracts sight and truth attracts the mind; but what attracts will is every good and goal as such. So the will is the overall motive power behind all human activity, save only those vegetative activities that are involuntary and natural. Mind and will can be regarded either as particular abilities with their own distinct activities, or as concerned with all-embracing objects: the mind as an awareness open to all that exists and is true, and the will as attracted towards everything good. If we consider the mind as all-embracing and the will as a special ability, then the mind includes the will and the act and object of willing as special instances of mind's object: existent true things. But if we consider the will as all-embracing and the mind as something special, then the will includes the mind and its act of understanding and its object (truth) as special goods. The actions and objects of mind and will mutually include each other: the mind understands the will's willing, the will wills the mind's understanding, good is something true and understandable, truth is something good and desirable. The mutual inclusion is not circular, but is grounded in mind to begin with. For every movement of will presupposes an act of knowledge, but not every act of knowledge presupposes our will: ultimately our planning and understanding issue from the mind of God, as even Aristotle says in his Eudemian Ethics.

5   **Emotion and will.**   Sense-appetite is not concerned with all good in general because sensation cannot perceive generalities, and that is why the sense-appetite has two parts concerned with particular kinds of good: the affective part concerned with what pleases the senses and is naturally congenial, and the aggressive concerned with repelling and attacking dangers. Will, however, is concerned with good in general, whatever its form, and does not divide into these two parts. Ordinarily by *love* and *desire* we mean the emotions and excited feelings that characterize sense-appetite; but we can also mean simple attraction without emotion or excitement, and then we can use the words of acts of will, such as characterize even angels and God.

83 1   **Free will.**   *God made man in the beginning, and left him free to make his own decisions.* Men make free decisions; otherwise advice and encouragement, directives and prohibitions, rewards and penalties would all be pointless. Things without awareness—stones and suchlike—act without judging; dumb animals judge instinctively, but not freely: sheep decide by nature, not by argument, to run away from the wolf; but men make up their own minds: in place of a natural repertoire of particular instincts they have a general capacity to reason, and since particular matters like what to do in this or that situation are not subject to con-

clusive argument men are not determined to any one course. Because they reason they are free to make their own decisions. Freedom is self-determination, but being a cause of action doesn't imply being its ultimate cause, even when the action is our own. God is the ultimate cause of all causes, natural and voluntary, working in each in a way appropriate to it. That God is at work in them doesn't prevent natural causes acting naturally or voluntary causes acting voluntarily; rather it enables them so to act. Jeremiah says *man's course is not in his control,* but he means that man can't always put his choices into effect, that he can be obstructed, like it or not. But the choices themselves are ours, given God's help. [Aristotle says *the goals we pursue are determined by the sort of persons we are.*] If he means the sort of persons we are by nature, then we all by nature have minds which desire happiness naturally and not freely, and our own natural bodily constitutions and temperaments which, unlike our non-bodily minds, are determined by physical causes and dispose us to choose this goal rather than that (though since our lower appetites are subject to reason this leaves our freedom intact). If however Aristotle means the sort of person we develop into, then all of us have dispositions and emotions which dispose us one way rather than another, though these again are subject to reason, and in any case we chose to acquire them. Freedom is a   2
fundamental capability of the soul, not just a disposition. A disposition to freedom couldn't be natural like our disposition to know the first premises of all reasoning, for what we are disposed to naturally we can't control, so that our freedom itself would be unfree. But neither could freedom be an acquired disposition, since we are free by nature. Moreover, dispositions incline us to do things well or badly whereas what we do freely can be done either way. So freedom is an ability, not a disposition. Man *lost by sin* not this natural   3
freedom from compulsion, but his freedom from guilt and unhappiness. Freedom is properly an ability to choose, and involves both the mind deciding what is preferable, and the will accepting this decision. But what we choose is what best serves our goal, what is *usefully* good, and since goods and goals are objects of desire, choice must fundamentally be a sort of desire and freedom an   4
ability to desire. Indeed freedom is nothing other than the will itself. Just as we distinguish under-

standing (assenting to something in itself) from reasoning (deriving one thing from another), so we distinguish willing (consenting to something for its own sake) from choice (desiring something for the sake of something else). For means are to goals as conclusions are to premises. Now we have already pointed out that understanding and reasoning are two actions of one power, related as resting in a place and moving from one place to another. In the same way, willing and choosing are actions of the same power: the ability to will and the ability to choose are one and the same ability.

HOW MAN KNOWS

[vol 12] 84 **Knowing material things.** The earliest philosophers thought the world contained only material things, continually changing, about which nothing could be known with certainty: as Heraclitus put it, *you can't step in the same river twice.* So Plato, to account for what we do know with certainty, said that each particular thing we sense we classify as a man or a horse or whatever because of a share it has in some Form or Idea that exists independently of matter and change. Scientific definitions and proofs and other products of intellectual activity relate to these Forms and not to the material things we sense. But this is a mistake: firstly, it rules out natural science, which deduces truths about matter and change by appealing to material causes of change; and secondly, it seems ludicrous to interpose between ourselves and the obvious objects of our enquiries other objects so essentially different that knowing them can't help us judge the objects we sense. Plato was apparently misled by the opinion that *like knows like* into thinking that since knowing is characterized by generality, necessity and invariance, what is known must exist in immaterial and unchanging ways outside the mind. But this is unnecessary. Even the qualities we sense exist in different ways in different objects (more or less intensely or with different associated qualities), and exist differently again in the senses themselves (where the colour of the gold exists without the gold itself). In the mind too then forms of bodies that are material and changeable can be received in a way appropriate to the recipient: immaterially and unchangeably. Changes presuppose some-

thing that doesn't change: qualitative change presupposes a persistent substance, and change of substance some identity of the underlying matter. Moreover, changing things are subject to invariant relations: though Socrates is not always seated, still it is invariably true that when seated he isn't walking about. So an unchanging science of changing things is quite possible.

Philosophers before Plato all held that *like knows like;* and recognizing that what we know is material they thought what knows must share the nature of some material element, like fire. But how would it be enough to have the nature of an element? We would have to share the nature of every compound too, bones and flesh and every sort of thing. Moreover if we understand fire by being like fire, why doesn't fire outside the mind understand itself? The truth is that material things are present in the mind not materially but immaterially: when we know a thing it remains other than us, [we don't become it,] whereas when matter takes on some form a new individual results. Clearly then, being aware is exactly the opposite of being material. Things that take on forms only through their matter, like plants, are not aware at all; whereas minds which take in likenesses of things' forms abstracted from matter and from all the particularities that go with it, know things better than the senses which take in forms without matter but particularized by it. The only person who knows everything by his own nature is God, who contains everything immaterially by nature (since his effects pre-exist in his power). [Men do not know things by nature.] They come to know things that previously they were only able to know: in the case of sensation the change is brought about by objects acting on the senses, in the case of mind by study or research. For the mind is not born possessed of the likenesses by which we sense and understand, but must acquire them [:as Aristotle says, it starts life *as a clean slate*]. Plato had believed the mind was filled with such likenesses by nature and that union with the body prevented it considering them. But it is surely impossible for minds so to forget what they possess by nature as not to know they know; and especially if what is supposed to obstruct this natural activity is an equally natural union with the body. In any case, men born blind know nothing of colour, so they aren't born with the likenesses of all things in their mind.

2

3

6   **Our dependence on our senses.**   Democritus
and other early philosophers confused mind with
the senses, and thought we know by means of images that sensed objects transmit and impress on
our senses. Plato on the other hand thought mind
was an immaterial power using no bodily organ
but knowing by participating Forms that exist abstractly; and he also thought (and Augustine
echoes this opinion) that external objects don't act
on our senses as such, but that the soul forms our
sense-images when objects act on our sense-
organs. Aristotle trod a middle path: he agreed
with Plato that mind differs from the senses, but
maintained that sensation is an activity in our
body caused by external bodies impressing themselves on our senses (acting on them rather than
transmitting something to them, as Democritus
had said). Body however has no share in the
mind's activity, which must be caused by something higher than impressions made on us by bodies: not impressions from higher things such as
Plato posited, but a higher agency in the mind itself (our *agent mind*) making sense-images actually understandable by abstracting ideas from
them. Sense provides the images, but they are not
enough to affect the receptive mind; they provide
only the material for knowledge which must be
7   made actually understandable by the agent mind.
The mind itself then makes no use of a bodily organ, but in this life it exists in a body acted on by
things, and actually to understand those things it
must have recourse to our sense-images of them:
not only to learn about the things in the first place
but also to make use of what it learns. Organic
disorders that affect imagination (as in delirium)
or memory (as in paralysis) prevent us actually
understanding things we have already learnt.
Moreover, we know by experience that when we
try to understand something we imagine examples
in which we can inspect, so to speak, what we
want to understand; and when helping others we
proffer examples to stimulate their imaginations
and thus their understanding. Now why is this?
Because every ability to know has an object that
specially suits it. The minds of angels, being quite
separate from bodies, know firstly other such separate substances and through them material substances. But human minds, existing in bodies,
know first the natures of material things, and by
knowing the natures of what they see derive some
knowledge of what they cannot see. Now by defi-

nition such natures belong in individual bodies: a
stone must be a *this stone* and a horse must be a
this horse. We haven't full and true knowledge of
what it is to be a stone (or any other material
thing) unless we know it in particular stones, in
stones we sense and imagine. So in order actually
to understand the things we are suited to understand we must have recourse to how we imagine
them, to see how general natures exist in particular instances. A knowledgeable man has a likeness
of what he knows stored in his receptive mind
even when not actually attending to it. But when
he actually attends he applies this stored knowledge to the thing of which it is a likeness, namely
the nature as it exists in particulars. Even immaterial things which can't be imagined are known by
way of analogies with material things which can;
so to know them we must have recourse to images   8
of material things. Aristotle says that just as practical knowledge aims at doing things, natural science aims at understanding what we sense. A
smith can't make proper judgments about knives
unless he knows what they are supposed to do,
and a natural scientist can't make proper judgments about natural objects unless he can sense
them. We know nothing in this life except by way
of the natural things we sense, so, if our senses are
out of commission, we can't judge anything properly. In sleep we are more or less gassed. When
we eat and drink well a lot of gas is formed, and
both senses and imagination cease to function. In
fever there is less gas but we have disordered and
distorted dream-images. As sleep wears off, especially in sober and strongly imaginative men,
these dreams are better ordered; and sometimes
even the inner root of our senses starts to operate
and while still asleep we perceive that we dream.
The more the senses and imagination are released
the more the mind's judgment is freed, but never
altogether. When we awake we always find flaws
in reasoning done while asleep.

Abstraction of ideas.   What we know de-   85 1
pends on the level at which we know. Sense-powers are functions animating bodily organs and
know forms as they exist in bodily matter, instantiated and particularized. Angels' minds exist
without bodies and know forms existing out of
matter, and material things as reflected in such
forms (in God or the angels themselves). In between, the human mind, which though not a func-

tion animating a bodily organ is nevertheless an ability of a soul animating a body, knows forms which exist only instantiated in bodily matter, but knows them in abstraction from any particular instance sensed or imagined. Our minds understand material things by abstracting ideas of them from their images, and then use such knowledge to acquire knowledge of immaterial things. Plato overlooked the way mind is joined to body in man and thought its immateriality enabled it to know not by abstracting ideas, but by participating in Ideas already existing abstractly and apart. Abstracting *A* from *B* can mean denying *A*'s connection with *B,* or simply thinking *A* without thinking *B*. Abstracting what in reality is connected generates falsehood if done the first way, but not if done the second. To say, for example, that an apple's colour exists somewhere else than in the apple would be a lie, but to think the colour without thinking the apple, and to express it in words, involves no lie; for apples don't enter our definition of colour and colour can be understood without understanding anything about apples. In the same way we can think what defines a material thing, stone, man or horse, without thinking of any additional individual peculiarities it may have; and this is precisely what we do when we abstract the general nature of what we understand from any particular way in which we imagine it. Understanding things otherwise than the way they exist is false understanding if *otherwise* describes the way we understand them to exist in themselves, but not if it describes the way they exist in our understanding. A man would falsely abstract the form of stone from matter if he denied its connection with matter, as Plato did; but there is nothing false about what a man understands existing immaterially in his mind, though materially in the thing understood. To understand natural things is not, as some have thought, to abstract their forms wholly from matter; for matter is part of the definition of natural things. We must rather distinguish matter in general (flesh and bones, say) from particular designated matter (this flesh and these bones), allowing that mind abstracts the species of natural things from any particular matter we perceive but not from perceptible matter in general. The nature of man, for example, cannot be mentally abstracted from flesh and bones in general, though it can be abstracted from this flesh and these bones, which belong only to this individual and not to the defi-

nition of his species. Objects of mathematics, however, abstract from perceived matter both in particular and in general; though from thought matter only in particular and not in general. By perceived matter I mean matter as underlying perceptible qualities (hot, cold, hard, soft, etc), and by thought matter I mean substance as underlying quantity. Clearly a substance must have quantity before it can have perceptible qualities. So numeric and dimensive quantity and boundary shape can be thought without thinking perceptible qualities, and thus be abstracted from all perceived matter. But they cannot be thought without thinking underlying substance, and so cannot be abstracted from thought matter in general. Nevertheless, because they can be thought apart from this or that substance they can be abstracted from particular thought matter. There are even things we can abstract from thought matter in general: things like being and oneness and potentiality and realization; for these can exist without any matter at all as immaterial substances prove. Plato overlooked these two ways of abstracting, and thought that everything mind abstracts really has an abstract existence. [Aristotle said that images are to mind as colours to sight.] However, colours exist in particular bodily matter in the same way as eyesight exists and can therefore affect our sight. But sense images represent particulars and exist in bodily organs, and since that is not the way our receptive mind exists, they can't of themselves affect our mind. The agent mind must itself turn to those images, and produce by its own power in the receptive mind a representation as to species of whatever the images represent as individual. This we call abstracting the species from the sense-images. What we don't mean is that numerically one and the same form moves from image to receptive mind, in the way a body moves from place to place. The agent mind by its very union with the body's senses lights up the imagination and prepares it for abstraction; and then it goes on to do the abstracting, producing from representations of particular instances of things in the imagination a representation of the species of the things in the receptive mind. Our mind both abstracts the species *from* images when it attends to the general natures of things, and understands the species *in* the images when it has recourse to the images in order to understand the things whose species it has abstracted.

2   **The general and the particular.**   [What we see is not the images in our eyes, but the things they image.] In the same way, what we know is not the abstracted species in our mind. If we did, all science would be about ideas, not about real things outside the mind; and (as some ancient philosophers wrongly thought) all appearances would be true. Rather the abstracted species is the means by which we know what we know. Just as the form that makes a natural thing externally active reproduces itself in an effect (heat producing heat), so the form that makes a thing interiorly active represents its object. By the image in the eye we see the thing it represents; and by the abstracted species imaging things in the mind we understand the things it images. Though, because our minds are self-reflective, we can also reflect on our own understanding and understand, in a secondary sense, the abstract species by which we understand. [If we ask *But where is what we actually understand, since, as actually understood, it must be immaterial and so cannot exist outside the mind?,*] we will have to distinguish what is understood from our actual understanding of it, just as we must distinguish what is conceived in an abstract general concept from the abstract generality of the conception. The nature that is being understood or abstracted or thought with generality exists only in particular things; but the understanding or abstracting or generality of it exists in the mind. We see the same thing in sense-perception. Sight perceives the colour of an apple but not its scent. Where then is the colour that is seen without the scent? In the apple, clearly. Though that it is seen without the scent belongs to it only in relation to sight, where colour can be imaged without scent. In the same way, the human nature we understand exists only in this or that man, but that this nature is perceived apart from its particular instantiations, that it is abstracted and clothed in generality, belongs to it only as perceived by mind, where the species of man is represented without any particularities of instantiation. [But, since Aristotle said, *words express mental concepts,* are abstract ideas what we talk and think about?] Mental activity combines two activities which in the senses are distinct: external perception in which we are simply affected by what we sense, and interior imagination in which we create images of things that are not and perhaps never have been present. The receptive mind is affected by an abstracted species, but when so affected it formulates definitions and propositional connections, which we express in words. Words express not the abstracted species themselves but judgments formulated by the mind about external things.

What do we know first, the particular or the general? Well, our mind's knowledge arises out of sense-perception, and so, in this sense, knowledge of the particular (sense-knowledge) precedes knowledge of the general (mental knowledge). But since our mind is not born with actual knowledge but acquires it, to arrive at complete, distinct, determinate knowledge it must go through a stage in which its knowledge is incomplete, indistinct and confused, knowing wholes without properly and precisely knowing their parts. We know animals, for example, indistinctly when we know them in general simply as animals; but we know them distinctly when we know rational and non-rational animals, men and lions. So our minds know animal first and man later, and similarly with whatever is more and less general. Sense-knowledge is ordered in the same way for the same reason: something approaching is first seen as a body, then as an animal, then as a man, and finally as Plato or Socrates; and *children begin by calling all men Daddy,* distinguishing men from non-men before they distinguish this man from that. The generality attaching to a nature—its relatedness to many particular instances—results from abstraction, so in this sense a generalized nature presupposes its instances, and does not, as Plato thought, precede them. But the nature existing in the instances can be thought of in two ways. In the genetic process the more general precedes the less (foetuses are animal before they are human), but in nature's purposes the perfectly actual precedes the imperfect and potential (nature, in producing the animal foetus, is aiming at producing a man). So our minds know animals in general before distinguishing men and horses; yet know man in general before distinguishing in him animality and rationality. Thus when defining *A* in terms of *B* we presuppose knowledge of *B* as such (otherwise the definition would give no information); but we know *A* before we know that *B* contributes to defining it: we know men in a confused sort of way before we know how to define them.

In what sense has the general a causative role? The generalized nature which results from ab-

3

straction does in a sense cause knowledge; but—*pace* Plato—not every cause of knowledge is a cause of existence (for causes can be known by effects and substances by their properties); and in any case, as Aristotle said, generalized natures in this sense are neither causes nor substances. Instances, however, of generic or specific natures existing in particular things are in a sense formal causes of those particulars: matter makes the particulars particular and form determines their species. However, the generic nature of something is material to its specific nature, being based on what is more material in the thing: we are animals because we have senses, men because we have minds. So neither the particular nor the genus, but the species, is the final cause ultimately aimed at by nature; the goal of reproduction is the form, and matter serves that goal. None of these ways of seeing the general nature as causative, however, implies that it is less known to us: sometimes effects reveal causes but sometimes causes reveal effects.

5   **The simple and the composite.**   In order to understand, human minds make and unmake connections. They acquire knowledge, and so bear a certain resemblance to things which get born and grow to completion by stages. For we don't grasp a thing completely from the start, but our first grasp of what it is opens it to understanding, and from that we come to understand the properties and relationships that are peculiar (or maybe coincidental) to what it is. To do this we make and unmake connections between what we grasp, and reason from one connection to another. The minds, of God and angels, however, resemble things perfect from the outset, and in their first grasp of what a thing is they know everything that we find out by making connections and reasoning. Though the mind abstracts from sense-images, it cannot actually understand what it abstracts without turning again to sense-images; and this introduces tense into the connections mind makes or unmakes. Two sorts of combination in material things correspond (with differences) to our mental making and unmaking of connections. To matter combining with form correspond all mental connections attributing a general nature to some instance of it (for generic natures are based on what is general but material, differentiated into species by what is formal; whilst particulars derive from

this or that particular matter). And to the combination of something's substance with its supervening properties correspond mental connections attributing properties to subjects. But there are differences between mental connections and combinations in things. The elements that combine in a thing differ from each other, but mental connections express the identity of what they connect. Thus we do not say *Man is whiteness,* but *Man is white,* for it is the same subject that is both man and white. Similarly with form and matter: one and the same thing is animal (possessing a sense nature), rational (possessing a mental nature), man (possessing both), and Socrates (combining all this with some particular matter); and we make mental connections attributing one to the other based on this identity. A sense can make a mistake 6 about its own particular stimulus (sight about colour, for instance) only indirectly, because of some deficiency in its organ. But it can err about stimuli not peculiar to that sense—misjudging shape and size—and especially about what it senses only indirectly—as when it mistakes gall for honey because it is the same colour. The reason is obvious: the object peculiar to an ability defines it; it cannot err about that and still be the same ability. Now understanding is defined as understanding what a thing is, so it cannot as such err about that. But it can make mistakes when connecting up and reasoning about anything else relating to that thing. It will not err about those propositions which we understand immediately we know what they are about (the first premises of science), or about conclusions derived with certainty from such premises. However, the mind can, indirectly, err about what a composite thing is: not because of some deficiency in an organ (since mind is not a function of an organ), but because defining such a thing presupposes making connections, and a definition can either get applied to the wrong thing (circle to triangle) or itself include impossible combinations (*winged rational animal*). Noncomposite things cannot be defined erroneously, though we can fail altogether to understand them.

   In our present life what we first understand are 8 the natures of material things as we abstract them from sense-images. Thinking about this will tell us whether we understand the simple before the composite or vice versa. In one sense, extended wholes are non-composite, actually undivided though divisible, and are understood as such before we have any understanding of their parts; we know things indistinctly before we know them distinctly. In another sense, every specific nature (humanity, for example) is understood as an indivisible whole before we analyse it into its defining elements, and begin to make and unmake connections with affirmations and denials; for specific natures are the very first things we understand. Finally, there are altogether simple elements, like points in a line or the units of counting, which we only know after divisibility, as lacking it: thus we define a point as that which has no parts, and unity, as indivisibility. To be indivisible in this way is opposed to being bodily, and bodies are what we primarily understand. It would be Platonist to think that what we primarily understand are separately existing simples. In the process of acquiring scientific knowledge, we don't always argue from principles and elements, since our knowledge of such intelligible principles sometimes comes through their sensible effects. But when a science is complete all such effects are explained in terms of their causes.

86 1 **What don't we know?**   This or that matter gives material things their particularity; but since we understand such things by abstracting their general nature from such matter, our mind has no direct knowledge of material objects in their particularity. Indirectly by a sort of reflection it does know particulars, for we can actually understand by way of abstracted species only by turning back to view them in sense-images. This is how our minds formulate propositions such as *Socrates is a man,* and choose particular actions as conclusions of a reasoning process premised by general practical principles but mediated by particular
2 sense-perceptions. Our mind is proportioned to knowing material things, so infinity applies to it in the way it applies to material things, not actually but potentially: our mind can understand one thing after another without ever exhausting its capacity to understand more. We cannot however actually consider an infinite number of things: for what we consider together must have a single form, which infinity can't have, since it is never whole (however much you take of infinity, as Aristotle said, there is always something over). Nor could we be potentially knowledgeable about an infinite number of things without previously

having actually considered them. Infinity in material things is matter undetermined by form, and unformed infinity is as such unknowable; but God's infinity is form unlimited by matter, and as such knowable, though not by us in the present life where we are naturally adapted to know material things and God only in his effects. There may be infinite species of numbers and geometrical figures, but our mind naturally knows them by abstraction from sense-images; so someone who has not imagined them cannot know them except generically, as implicit in some general rule, in-
3 distinctly and potentially. Nothing is so unnecessary that no necessity at all attaches to it: even if it is not necessary for Socrates to be running, it is nevertheless necessary that when he runs he moves. Non-necessity in things is due to their matter; necessity is a consequence of form. Now matter particularizes, whereas generality follows on the mind's abstraction of form from particularizing matter: the mind as such knows the general directly, whereas the senses (and the mind indirectly) know particulars. So what may or may not be so is known directly by the senses and indirectly by the mind; whilst any general necessity attaching to it is known by mind. All science then is concerned with what can be known generally and necessarily, either about things that must exist (in some sciences) or about things that need not exist
4 (in others). Future things are in time and particular, so mind can know them only by a sort of reflection on sense; though they may instantiate general notions that mind can itself grasp and prove scientifically. Only God knows the future as it will be in itself, for it presents itself to his eternal gaze together with the whole course of time. We know the future only as foreshadowed in present causes: with scientific certainty if these causes totally determine it (as when we predict eclipses), but otherwise with varying degrees of probability depending on how inclined the causes are to those effects.

Knowing ourselves.   The human mind is 87 1 only potentially a mind, holding the same place in the world of understanding as matter holds in the world of sense (which is why we call mind receptive). Of itself then it is able to understand, but not able to be understood until actualized. In our present life our mind turns naturally to the material things we sense, and only understands itself when brought to act by species abstracted from things sensed. This abstraction is caused by the light of the agent mind, the source of the actual intelligibility of everything we understand and hence of the receptive mind itself. So our mind knows itself not by its own substance but by its activity: each man through his experience of his own acts of understanding perceives himself to possess a mind (for that there is required only the mind's presence to itself), and through consideration of those acts he can come to a general understanding of the

3   mind's nature (but that requires diligent and subtle investigation). For God understanding himself and understanding his act of understanding is the same thing. For angels they differ but happen together; for in understanding itself an angel realizes itself, and any act of understanding a thing must understand what realizes it. But the human mind primarily understands not itself but external material things; secondarily its own act of understanding such things; and finally itself, the power of understanding realized in that act. The act of human understanding does not perfect and realize the material thing it understands: so the act by which we understand a stone is not the same act as that which understands us understanding the stone, and so on. But there is nothing awkward about the mind being potentially subject to an infinite regress. What activates the external senses is an external object operating on a material organ. Since nothing material can operate on itself, external sense activity is not perceptible to the external sense itself, but only to a central common sensitivity. Our minds however are not activated by

4   material operation on an organ, and can perceive their own activity. A thing's tendencies are of the sort the thing itself is: natural tendencies exist in natural things by nature, the desires sensation arouses are themselves sensibly perceptible to the desirer, and a person's acts of will (tendencies consequent on his understanding) exist understandably *in his mind* as in their origin and subject. But that means they can be understood by his mind: he can both perceive that he wills, and understand what willing is. Mind and will are different powers, but they are powers of one subject, the soul, deriving one from the other in a certain

88 2   sense, so that whatever is in will is also in mind. Created immaterial things have quite a different nature from material things (the potentiality they have is not a material potentiality [to decom-

pose]); they are nevertheless logically categorizable as substances, since they are something other than their own existence. God however is neither naturally nor logically similar to material things; so that images drawn from material things, though they give us positive but non-specific knowledge of angels, give us no such knowledge of God.

The soul after death.   It is hard to see how,   89 1 out of its body, the soul could know anything. In the body, experience shows that we understand only by turning to sense-images. Now if that was unnatural for the soul, resulting only from being tied to a body (as Platonists think), then obviously, once the hindrance of body went, the soul would act naturally again and understand things in a simple angelic way without recourse to sense-images. But that would mean the union of soul and body had served the body but not the soul, and form serving matter rather than vice versa is nonsensical. However, if it is natural to the soul to understand by turning to sense-images, then death won't change the soul's nature, and after death, when the soul has no sense-images to turn to, it presumably won't understand anything naturally. This difficulty disappears if we remember that activity realizes a thing's being, so that the way something exists determines the way it acts. The soul doesn't change its nature but it exists in two ways, one natural (united to a body) and one unnatural (separated from its body); just as heavy bodies, without changing their nature, can exist grounded (their natural place) or suspended. When naturally united to its body the soul understands in a natural way through recourse to sense-images, but when unnaturally separated from its body it understands without sense-images, in a way unnatural to it though natural to angels. The soul is united to a body in order that it can exist and operate naturally, understanding with the help of sense-images; but it can exist separately and understand in a different way. In this separate state the soul doesn't understand by way of innate ideas (for at birth the mind is a clean slate), nor by way of ideas it abstracts at that time (for it no longer possesses the senses and imagination by means of which it can make such abstractions), nor by ideas previously abstracted and stored (for then infants could understand nothing after death); but by ideas deriving from God's mind, in the way angels understand. As soon as it stops

2 turning to the body, the soul turns to this higher source. Such knowledge is not for that reason graced, but still natural, God being the author of both nature and grace. In its separate state the soul is immediately intelligible to itself, not merely re-flectively known as that which is understanding

4 the ideas it is abstracting from sense-images. God, as we saw, knows all things in general and in par-ticular, since he knows himself as causing every-thing in general and in particular; and immaterial things share this knowledge through ideas which are likenesses of God. But separated souls know in this way only the particular things to which they are already bound by some previous knowl-edge or affection or natural relationship or divine ordering: for what we receive we receive in ways

5 appropriate to what we already are. We acquire knowledge in this life through acts of understand-ing in which our minds are turned towards sense-images; our minds acquire the facility to attend to abstracted ideas, and our imaginations and memo-ries the aptitude to provide abstractable images. So the knowledge we acquire, like the acts which acquire it, resides primarily and formally in the mind, but materially and dispositively in our sen-sitive powers. These dispositions to knowledge disappear when the body dies, but the knowledge

8 in the mind remains. The souls of the dead are barred from converse with the living, and Gregory the Great and Augustine agree that they know nothing of what goes on among us. As to the souls in heaven, Augustine thinks it unlikely they know about us, since after his mother died she no longer visited and consoled him as she had before, and her happier state of life would surely not have made her less kind. But Gregory's opinion that those who see God know all that passes here be-low seems more probable. But because they are perfectly attuned to God's just will they remain content and do not intervene in our lives unless God plans it so.

PART 2

MECHANISMS OF MIND

6

RENÉ DESCARTES

René Descartes (1596–1650) tried to keep the details of his private life secret, including concealing his birth date so as to avoid embarrassing speculation from contemporary astrologers. The son of a wealthy magistrate, he was born near La Haye, France, and raised on his grandmother's estate. He attended college at La Fleche, a prestigious school in Anjou run by Jesuits, where he studied mathematics, physics, and philosophy. He was a stellar student and thinker, able to convince his teachers that he was most productive while lying in bed in the morning, when other students went about doing their chores. Following college, he spent some apparently wild years in Paris before joining William of Orange's army. It was during his army stint that a crisis of skepticism overtook him, leading to a new approach to philosophy, indeed developed as he lay in bed. Descartes took great care to ensure that his writings were acceptable to the Catholic Church, only to find his works temporarily banned from Dutch universities by the Protestant clergy of Holland. He died of pneumonia, contracted as he discussed his new philosophy with Queen Cristina of Sweden, who insisted that these conversations with her philosopher-in-residence occur at 5 o'clock in the morning.

TREATISE OF MAN

These men will be composed, as we are, of a soul and a body; and I must first separately describe for you the body; then, also separately, the soul; and finally I must show you how these two natures would have to be joined and united to constitute men resembling us.

I assume their body to be but a statue, an earthen machine formed intentionally by God to be as much as possible like us. Thus not only does He give it externally the shapes and colors of all the parts of our bodies; He also places inside it all the pieces required to make it walk, eat, breathe, and imitate whichever of our own functions can be imagined to proceed from mere matter and to depend entirely on the arrangement of our organs.

We see clocks, artificial fountains, mills, and similar machines which, though made entirely by man, lack not the power to move, of themselves, in various ways. And I think you will agree that the present machine could have even more sorts of movements than I have imagined and more ingenuity than I have assigned, for our supposition is that it was created by God.

Now I shall not pause to describe to you the bones, nerves, muscles, veins, arteries, stomach, liver, spleen, heart, brain, nor all the other different pieces of which the machine must be composed; for I suppose them all to be quite like the parts of our own body that have the same names. If you do not already know them sufficiently, you can have them shown to you by some learned anatomist, those at least that are large enough to be seen. As for those which because of their smallness are invisible, I shall be able to make them known to you most simply and clearly by speaking of the movements which depend upon them; so that it remains only for me to explain these movements to you here in proper order and by that means to tell you which of the machine's [latent] functions these [patent] movements represent. . . .

As for those parts of the blood that penetrate as far as the brain, they serve not only to nourish and sustain its

From René Descartes, "Selections." In T. S. Hall (translator), *Treatise of Man* (pp. 1–5, 19–23, 33–40, 59–90). Cambridge, MA: Harvard University Press, 1972. (Original work published 1650)

substance, but also and principally to produce there a certain very subtle wind, or rather a very lively and very pure flame, which is called the "animal spirits." For one must know that the arteries that bring blood from the heart, having divided into an infinity of little branches and having composed the little tissues that are stretched like tapestries at the bottom of the concavities of the brain [the choroid plexus], reassemble around a certain little gland [the pineal] situated near the middle of the brain's substance just at the entrance to its cavities. [And one must know also] that the arteries in this region have many little holes through which the subtlest parts of the blood can flow into this gland, but which are so narrow that they refuse passage to larger particles.

It is also necessary to know that the arteries do not stop there but, being gathered several into one [the great vein of Galen], they rise straight up [through the straight sinus] and enter into that great vessel [the sagittal sinus and connections] by which like a Euripos the whole external surface of the brain is bathed. It is further necessary to note that the coarsest parts of the blood can lose much of their agitation in the turnings of these little tissues through which they pass, inasmuch as they have the power to push the smaller ones that are among them and so to transfer to them some of their movement. The smaller ones, however, cannot lose their movement in this way, since [a] their agitation is augmented by that which the coarser ones transfer to them, and [b] there are no other bodies around them to which they themselves can as easily transfer theirs.

Whence it is easy to conceive that when the coarsest [particles in the blood] mount directly toward the external surface of the brain, where they serve to nourish its substance, they cause the smallest and most agitated [particles] to turn aside, and all of them to enter this gland, which must be imagined as a very full-flowing spring, whence they flow simultaneously in every direction into the cavities of the brain. And thus, without any preparation or alteration except that they are separated from the coarser ones and still retain the extreme rapidity that the heat of the heart has given them, they cease to have the form of blood and are designated animal spirits.

Now in the same measure that spirits enter the cavities of the brain they also leave them and enter the pores [or conduits] in its substance, and from these conduits they proceed to the nerves. And depending on their entering (or their mere tendency to enter) some nerves rather than others, they are able to change the shapes of the muscles into which these nerves are inserted and in this way to move all the members. Similarly you may

have observed in the grottoes and fountains in the gardens of our kings that the force that makes the water leap from its source is able of itself to move divers machines and even to make them play certain instruments or pronounce certain words according to the various arrangements of the tubes through which the water is conducted.

And truly one can well compare the nerves of the machine that I am describing to the tubes of the mechanisms of these fountains, its muscles and tendons to divers other engines and springs which serve to move these mechanisms, its animal spirits to the water which drives them, of which the heart is the source and the brain's cavities the water main. Moreover, breathing and other such actions which are ordinary and natural to it, and which depend on the flow of the spirits, are like the movements of a clock or mill which the ordinary flow of water can render continuous. External objects which merely by their presence act on the organs of sense and by this means force them to move in several different ways, depending on how the parts of the brain are arranged, are like strangers who, entering some of the grottoes of these fountains, unwittingly cause the movements that then occur, since they cannot enter without stepping on certain tiles so arranged that, for example, if they approach a Diana bathing they will cause her to hide in the reeds; and if they pass farther to pursue her they will cause a Neptune to advance and menace them with his trident; or if they go in another direction they will make a marine monster come out and spew water into their faces, or other such things according to the whims of the engineers who made them. And finally when there shall be a rational soul in this machine, it will have its chief seat in the brain and will there reside like the turncock who must be in the main to which all the tubes of these machines repair when he wishes to excite, prevent, or in some manner alter their movements.

But to make you understand all this distinctly, I wish to speak to you first of the fabric of the nerves and the muscles, and to show you how from the sole fact that the spirits in the brain are ready to enter into certain of the nerves they have the ability to move certain members at that instant. Then, having touched briefly on breathing and other such simple and ordinary movements, I shall tell how external objects act upon the sense organs. After that I shall explain in detail all that happens in the cavities and pores of the brain, what pathway the animal spirits follow there, and which of our functions this machine can imitate by means of them. For, were I to begin with the brain and merely follow in order the course of the spirits, as I did for the blood, I believe my discourse would be much less clear. . . .

To understand, next, how external objects that strike the sense organs can incite [the machine] to move its members in a thousand different ways: think that

[*a*] the filaments (I have already often told you that these come from the innermost part of the brain and compose the marrow of the nerves) are so arranged in every organ of sense that they can very easily be moved by the objects of that sense and that

[*b*] when they are moved, with however little force, they simultaneously pull the parts of the brain from which they come, and by this means open the entrances to certain pores in the internal surface of this brain; [and that]

[*c*] the animal spirits in its cavities begin immediately to make their way through these pores into the nerves, and so into muscles that give rise to movements in this machine quite similar to [the movements] to which we [men] are naturally incited when our senses are similarly impinged upon.

Thus [in Fig. 6.1], if fire *A* is near foot *B,* the particles of this fire (which move very quickly, as you know) have force enough to displace the area of skin that they touch; and thus pulling the little thread *cc,* which you

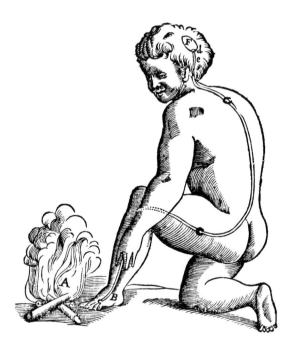

FIGURE 6.1

see to be attached there, they simultaneously open the entrance to the pore [or conduit] *de* where this thread terminates [in the brain]: just as, pulling on one end of a cord one simultaneously rings a bell which hangs at the opposite end.

Now the entrance of the pore or small conduit *de,* being thus opened, the animal spirits from cavity *F* enter and are carried through it—part into the muscles that serve to withdraw this foot from the fire, part into those that serve to turn the eyes and head to look at it, and part into those that serve to advance the hands and bend the whole body to protect it.

But they can also be carried through the same conduit *de* into many other muscles. And before stopping to explain more precisely in what way the animal spirits follow their course through the pores of the brain and how these pores are arranged, I wish to speak to you now in particular of all the senses that exist in this machine and to tell you how they are related to our own.

Know first, then, that a great many filaments like *cc* begin to separate one from another as soon as they arise at the internal surface of the brain [of the machine] and that proceeding to spread thence through the rest of its body they serve there as an organ of touch. For although external objects do not ordinarily touch these filaments, but touch the skin that surrounds them, there is no more reason to think of the skin as the sense organ than to think of gloves as sense organs when we feel something while wearing gloves.

And note that although the threads I speak of are very thin, yet they extend safely all the way from the brain to parts that are farthest therefrom, nor is there anything in between that breaks them or that prevents their activity through pressure, even though the parts are bent in myriad ways: because [*a*] the threads are enclosed in the same tubules that carry the animal spirits to the muscles, and [*b*] these spirits, always somewhat inflating the tubes, protect the fibers against crowding and keep them always maximally taut all the way from the brain whence they arise to the places where they terminate.

And now I assert that when God will later join a rational soul to this machine, as I intend to explain further on, He will place its chief seat in the brain and will make its nature such that, according to the different ways in which the entrances of the pores in the internal surface of this brain are opened through the intervention of the nerves, the soul will have different feelings.

Thus, firstly, if the filaments that compose the marrow of these nerves are pulled with force enough to be broken and thus are separated from the part to which they were joined, so that the structure of the whole machine is somehow less intact, the movement they then cause in the brain will cause the soul (to which it is essential that its place of residence be preserved) to experience a feeling of *pain.*

And if they are pulled by a force almost as great as the preceding without, however, being broken or separated from the parts to which they are attached, they will cause a movement in the brain which, testifying to the good constitution of the other parts, will cause the soul to feel a certain corporeal sensual pleasure referred to as tingling, which as you see, being very close to pain in its cause, is quite the opposite in effect.

If many of these filaments are pulled equally and all together, they will make the soul sense that the surface of the object touching the member where they terminate is smooth; and if they are pulled unequally, they will cause the soul to feel that it is uneven and rough.

If they [the nerve filaments] are set in motion only slightly, and separately from one another, as they continually are by the heat that the heart communicates to other members, the soul will have no more sensation of this than of all other ordinary actions; but if this movement is augmented or diminished by some unusual cause, its augmentation will make the soul have a feeling of heat; its diminution, a feeling of cold. And finally, according to the divers other ways in which they are moved, they will cause [the soul] to sense all the other qualities which belong to touch in general, such as humidity, dryness, weight, and the like. . . .

I shall not add here in detail what will make it possible for this soul to conceive all differences in color, since I have already spoken of that heretofore. Nor shall I say what objects of vision must be agreeable or disagreeable. For, from what I have explained about the other senses, it is easy for you to understand that light that is too strong must injure the eyes and that moderate light must refresh them. Also that among the colors, green, which consists in the most moderate action (which, by analogy, one can speak of as a ratio of 1 to 2), is like the octave among musical consonances or like bread among the foods that one eats. That is to say, green is the most universally agreeable [color]. Nor finally [will I add here] that all those different fashionable colors which often refresh much more than green are like the chords and passages of a new tune struck up by some excellent lutanist, or like the ragouts of a good cook, which titillate the sense and make it feel more pleasure at first, but which become tedious sooner than do simple and ordinary objects.

It only remains for me to tell you what it is that will give the soul a way of sensing [*a*] position, [*b*] shape, [*c*] distance, [*d*] size, and [*e*] other similar qualities, not qualities related to one particular sense (as are those of which I have spoken hitherto), but ones that are common to touch and vision and even in some way to the other senses.

Notice first [Fig. 6.2a], that if hand *A* touches body *C,* for example, the parts of brain *B* from which its nerve filaments come will be otherwise arranged than if it [the hand] touches a body of different shape or size or situated in a different place. It is by this means, then, that the soul will be able to know the situation of the body, and its shape and size and all other like qualities. Similarly, if eye *D* is turned toward object *E* [Fig. 6.2b], the soul will be able to know the *position* of this object, inasmuch as [in the brain] the nerves from this eye are differently arranged than if it were turned toward some other object. And [the soul] will be able to know the *shape* [of *E*], inasmuch as rays from point *1* assembling on the nerve termed optic [the retina] at point *2*—and those from point *3* at point *4,* and so forth—will trace there a shape corresponding exactly to the shape of *E.* Note also that the soul will be able to know the *distance* of point *1,* for, as has just been mentioned, in order to

FIGURE 6.2a

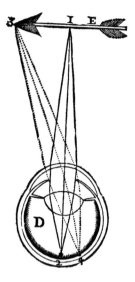

FIGURE 6.2b

FIGURE 6.3

make all the rays coming from point *1* assemble precisely at point *2* at the center of the back of the eye, the crystalline humor will be of a different shape than if the object were nearer or farther away. And [note] in addition that the soul will know the distance of point *3,* and of all others whose rays enter at the same time because, the crystalline humor being properly arranged, the rays from point *3* will not assemble as precisely at point *4* as will those from point *1* at point *2,* and so with the others; and their action will be proportionately less strong, as has also been said earlier. And [realize] finally that the soul will be able to know the *size* and all similar qualities of visible objects simply through its knowledge of the *distance* and *position* of all points thereof; just as, vice versa, it will sometimes judge their *distance* from the opinion it holds concerning their *size.*

Notice also [in Fig. 6.3] that if the two hands *f* and *g* each hold a stick, *i* and *h,* with which they touch object *K,* although the soul is otherwise ignorant of the length of these sticks, nevertheless because it knows the distance between the two points *f* and *g* and the size of angles *fgh* and *gfi,* it will be able to know, as if through a natural geometry, where object *K* is. And quite in the same way [Fig. 6.4], if the two eyes *L* and *M* are turned toward the object *N,* the magnitude of line *LM* and of the two angles *LMN* and *MLN* will cause it [the soul] to know where point *N* is.

But it will often enough be possible for the soul to be deceived in all this. For first of all, suppose that the po-

sition of hand or eye or brain is forced upon the organ by some external [that is, some other than muscular] cause. [In such a case] the position [of the part] will correspond less exactly to the position of the particles of the brain where the nerves arise than if it depended on muscles alone. Thus the soul, which will only sense [the position or orientation of the part] through the mediation of the parts of the brain, cannot fail to be deceived at such times.

Suppose for example [Fig. 6.5] that hand *f,* being dis-

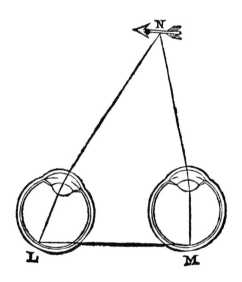

FIGURE 6.4

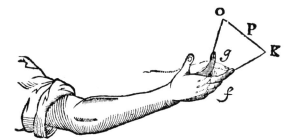

FIGURE 6.5

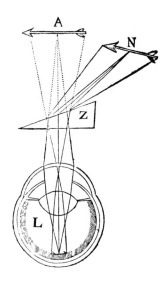

FIGURE 6.7

posed in itself to be turned toward *o,* finds itself constrained by some external force to remain turned toward
K. In that case, the parts of the brain whence the nerves
come will not be arranged in quite the same way as they
would be if it were by muscular force alone that the
hand was thus turned toward *K.* Nor will they be
arranged as they would be if the hand were in fact
turned toward *o.* They are rather arranged in a manner
intermediate between the two, that is, as if turned toward *P.* And thus the arrangement that this constraint
will give to the particles of the brain will cause the soul
to judge that the object *K* is at point *P* and that it is a different object from that which is touched by hand *g.*

Similarly [in Fig. 6.6], the two fingers *t* and *v,* touching the little ball *X,* will make the soul judge that they
are touching two different things because they are
crossed and kept forcibly in an unnatural position.

Moreover, if the rays (or other lines through whose
mediation the actions of distant objects pass toward the
senses) are curved, the soul, which would ordinarily
suppose them to be straight, will have occasion to be deceived. And if eye *L* [Fig. 6.7] receives rays from object
N through a glass *Z* [a prism] that curves them, it will
seem to the soul that this object is in the direction of *A.*
Again, suppose [in Fig. 6.8] that eye *B* receives rays
from point *D* through glass *C* [a magnifying glass],

which I assume bends them as though they were coming
from point *E* and bends those from point *F* as though
they were coming from point *G,* and so with other rays.
[In such a case] it would seem to the soul that the object
DFH is as far away and as large as *EGI* would seem to
be.

To conclude, it must be noted that none of the soul's

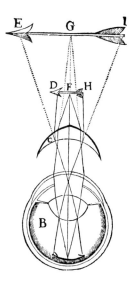

FIGURE 6.8

FIGURE 6.6

means of knowing the distance of objects will be quite sure, for the following [three] reasons. [First,] as for angles like *LMN* and *MLN* and so forth [see Fig. 6.4], these no longer change appreciably with distance for objects fifteen or twenty feet away or more. [Second,] as for the shape of the crystalline humor, it changes even less appreciably than the foregoing for objects more than two or three feet from the eye. And [third and] finally, what about judging the distances of objects from one's opinion of their size, or from the fact that rays from different points of the object differ in the precision with which they assemble at the back of the eye? The example of *tableaux de perspective* shows us amply how easy it is to be deceived. For if [peculiarities of] shape make us overestimate the size of visual objects, or if their colors are somewhat obscure, or their outlines somewhat indefinite, these things make them appear to be more distant, and larger, than they actually are.

Now having explained to you the five external senses as represented in this machine, I must tell you something of certain internal senses it contains.

When the liquids which serve, as mentioned earlier, as a sort of aqua fortis in the stomach, and which enter ceaselessly from the whole mass of the blood through the extremities of the arteries, do not find there enough food to dissolve so as to employ their whole force, they turn against the stomach itself and, agitating the filaments of its nerves more strongly than is usual, they cause motion in the parts of the brain from which the filaments come. This will cause the soul, when united to this machine, to conceive the general idea of *hunger.* And if these liquids are so disposed as to employ their action against certain particular foods rather than others, much as ordinary aqua fortis dissolves metals more easily than wax, they will act in a particular fashion also against the nerves of the stomach. This will cause the soul at such times to conceive an appetite to eat certain foods rather than others. (*Hic notari potest mira huius machinae conformatio, quod fames oriatur ex jejunio: sanguis enim circulatione acrior sit, & ita liquor ex eo in stomachum veniens nervos magis vellicat, idque modo peculiari, si peculiaris sit constitutio sanguinis: unde pica mulierum.*) Now these liquids are assembled chiefly at the bottom of the stomach, and it is there that they cause the feeling of hunger.

But many part[icle]s [of the gastric fluid] rise continuously toward the gullet, and when they do not come there in sufficient numbers to moisten it and fill its pores in the form of water, they rise instead in the form of air or smoke. At such times, acting against its nerves in an unusual fashion, they cause a movement in the brain that will make the soul conceive the idea of *thirst.*

Similarly, when the blood that goes into the heart is more pure and subtle and is kindled more easily than usual, this arranges the little nerve that is there in the manner required to cause the sensation of *joy.* And when this blood has quite contrary qualities, [it arranges the nerve] in the manner required to cause the sensation of *sadness.*

From this you can well enough understand what there is in this machine that corresponds to all the other internal sensations in us; whence it is time that I commence to explain to you [a] how the animal spirits pursue their course in the cavities and pores of its brain, and [b] what funtions depend upon them.

If you have ever had the curiosity to look closely at the organs in our churches, you know how their bellows push air into certain receptacles called—for this reason, presumably—wind trunks. [You know] also how from there the air enters the pipes, now one, now another, as the organist moves his fingers on the keyboard. And you can think of the heart and arteries of our machine (which push animal spirits into the cavities of its brain) as similar to the bellows (which push air into the wind trunks of organs); and of external objects (which, by displacing certain nerves, make spirits from the brain cavities enter certain pores) as similar to the organist's fingers (which, by pressing certain keys, make air from the wind trunks enter certain pipes).

Now the harmony of the organ depends not at all on the externally visible arrangement of the pipes nor on the shape of the wind trunks or other parts, but only on three things, namely, [a] the air that comes from the bellows, [b] the pipes that sound, and [c] the distribution of this air to those pipes. And let me call to your attention that, here too, the functions under consideration in no wise depend on the external shape of the visible parts which the anatomists distinguish in the substance of the brain nor on the shape of its cavities, but only [a] on the spirits that come from the heart, [b] on the pores of the brain through which they pass, and [c] on the way in which these spirits are distributed to these pores. Whence it is only necessary that I explain to you in proper order what is of most importance in connection with these three things.

Firstly, as to animal spirits, they can be more or less *abundant,* and their part[icle]s can at different times be more or less *coarse,* more or less *agitated,* and more or less *uniform* [in size, shape, and force—see below]; and it is by means of these four differences that all of the various humors or natural inclinations present in us are also represented in this machine (at least insofar as these do not depend on the constitution of the brain or on particular affections of the soul). For if these spirits are unusually abundant, they are appropriate for exciting movements in this machine like movements that give evidence in us of *generosity, liberality,* and *love.* And [they excite movements that give evidence] of *confidence* or *courage* if their part[icle]s are unusually strong and coarse; and of *constancy* if, in addition, they are unusually uniform in shape, force, and size; and of *promptness, diligence,* and *desire* if unusually agitated; and of *tranquility of spirit* if unusually uniform in their agitation. Whereas, on the contrary, if the same qualities are lacking, these same spirits are appropriate for exciting movements in [the machine] entirely like movements in us that bear witness to *malice, timidity, inconstancy, tardiness,* and *ruthlessness.*

And know that all the other humors or natural inclinations are dependent on those mentioned above. Thus the *joyous humor* is composed of promptitude and tranquility of spirit; and generosity and confidence serve to make the joyous humor more perfect. The *sad humor* is composed of tardiness and restlessness and can be augmented by malice and timidity. The *choleric humor* is composed of promptitude and restlessness, and malice and confidence fortify it. Finally, as I have just said, liberality, generosity, and love depend upon an abundance of spirits, and form in us that humor which renders us complaisant and benevolent to everyone. Curiosity and the other impulses depend upon the agitation of the part[icle]s of [the animal spirits]; and so with the other inclinations.

But because these same humors or at least the passions to which they predispose us are also very dependent on the impressions that are made in the substance of the brain, you will be able to understand them better hereafter; and I shall content myself here with telling you the causes whence differences in spirits arise.

The juice of the food that passes from the stomach into the veins on being mixed with the blood always communicates some of its own qualities thereto and, among other things, usually makes it more coarse when it first mixes freshly therewith. Whence, at this time, the particles of blood that the heart sends to the brain to constitute the animal spirits are generally not so agitated, strong, or abundant [as they are at other times]. Consequently they do not usually make this machine so nimble or quick as it becomes a while after digestion is finished and after the same blood, having passed and

repassed through the heart several times, has become more subtle.

The air of respiration, likewise, being mixed in some way with the blood before it enters the left cavity of the heart, makes the blood kindle more strongly, and produces more lively and agitated spirits [in the heart] in dry weather than in humid weather: just as flames of every sort are found at such times to be more ardent.

When the liver is well disposed and elaborates perfectly the blood that goes to the heart, the spirits that leave this blood are correspondingly *more abundant* and *more uniformly agitated.* And should the liver happen to be incited by its nerves, the subtlest part of the blood it contains, rising directly to the heart, will produce spirits correspondingly *more abundant* and lively than is usual—though *not so uniformly agitated.*

If the gall [bladder], which is intended to purge the blood of those of its parts that are *most suited* to be enkindled in the heart, fails in its task, or if being contracted through [the action of] its nerve it regorges into the veins the matter it contains, then the spirits will be, to that extent, *more lively* and *more unevenly agitated* withal.

Per contra, if the spleen, which is intended to purge the blood of parts *least suited* to be enkindled in the heart, is ill disposed, or if, under pressure from its nerves or from any other body whatever, it regorges into the veins the matter that it contains, then the spirits will be to that extent *less abundant,* and *less agitated,* and *less uniformly agitated withal.*

In sum, whatever can cause any change in the blood can also cause change in the spirits. But above all, the little nerve that ends in the heart is able to dilate and contract both [*a*] the two entrances through which the blood of the veins and air of the lung descend, and [*b*] the two exits through which blood is exhaled and driven into the arteries. [Hence this nerve] can cause a thousand differences in the nature of the spirits: just as the heat of certain enclosed lamps which the alchemists use can be moderated in several ways according as one opens, to a greater or less degree, now the conduit through which the oil or other aliment of the flame comes in and now that by which the smoke goes out.

Secondly, concerning the pores of the brain, they must be imagined as no different from the spaces that occur between the threads of some tissue [for example, a woven or felted fabric]; because, in effect, the whole brain is nothing but a tissue constituted in a particular way, as I shall try to explain to you here.

[In Figs. 6.9 and 6.10] conceive surface *AA* facing

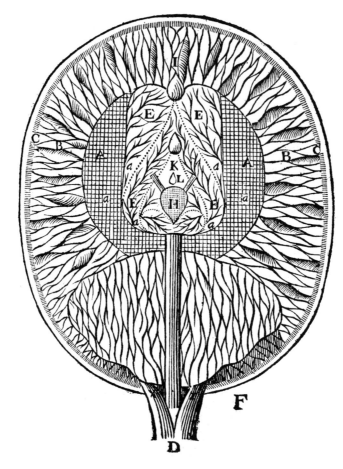

FIGURE 6.9

cavities *EE* to be a rather dense and compact net or mesh, all of whose links are so many little conduits which the spirits can enter and which, always facing toward gland *H* [the pineal] whence these spirits emanate, can easily turn hither and thither toward different points on this gland—as you see that they are turned differently in the 48th than in the 49th diagram [right and left sides of Fig. 6.11]. And assume that from each part of this net arise several very thin threads of which some as a rule are longer than others; and that after these threads have been differently interlaced through the space marked *B,* the longer of them descend toward *D,* and from there, comprising the marrow of the nerves, proceed to spread through all the members [see Fig. 6.10].

Assume also that the chief characteristics of these filaments are [*a*] that they can be flexed rather easily in all sorts of ways merely by the force of the spirits that

strike them, and [*b*] that they can retain, as if made of lead or wax, the flexure last received until something exerts a contrary pressure upon them.

Finally, assume that the pores we are considering are nothing but the intervals between these threads and [that they] can be diversely enlarged and constricted by the force of the spirits that enter them according as that force is more or less strong and [according as the spirits] are more or less abundant; and that the shortest of these threads betake themselves to the space *cc* [Fig. 6.9], where each terminates against the extremity of one of the little vessels that are there and receives nourishment from it.

Thirdly—in order to explain all the particularities of this tissue more conveniently, I must begin to speak to you now about the distribution of these spirits.

The spirits never stop for a single moment in any one

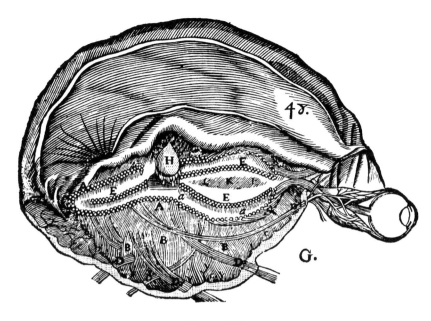

FIGURE 6.10

place, but as fast as they enter the brain cavities *EE* [Figs. 6.10 and 6.11], through apertures in the little gland marked *H,* they tend first toward those tub[ule]s, *a* and *a,* which are most directly opposite them; and if those tubules are not sufficiently open to receive them all, they receive at least the strongest and liveliest of the particles thereof, while the feeblest and most superflu-

ent particles are pushed aside toward the conduits *I, K, L* which face the nostrils and the palate. Specifically, the most agitated [are pushed] toward *I,* through which—if they still have much force and do not find the passage free enough—they sometimes pass out with so much violence that they tickle the internal parts of the nose which causes *sneezing.* Then other [particles are pushed] toward *K* and *L,* through which they can leave quite easily because the passages there are very large; or if they fail to do so, being forced to turn back toward tubules *a* and *a* in the internal surface of the brain, they promptly cause a *dizziness* or *vertigo* which disturbs the functioning of the *imagination.*

And note in passing that the weaker part[icle]s of the spirits come less from the arteries inserted in gland *H* [the pineal] than from those which divide into a myriad of very small branches and thus carpet the cavities of the brain. Note also that these particles can easily thicken into phlegm. Only in grave illness, however, do they do this in the brain itself; ordinarily it occurs in those large spaces beneath the base of the brain between the nostrils and the gullet, just as smoke converts easily into soot in the flues of the chimney but never in the hearth where the fire burns.

Note also that when I say that spirits leaving the gland tend toward the most directly "opposite" regions of the internal surface of the brain, I mean merely that

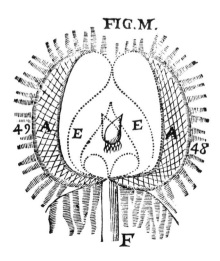

FIGURE 6.11

they tend where the arrangement of the brain at the time impels them, not necessarily to regions that face them rectilineally.

Now the substance of the brain being soft and pliant, if no spirits entered its cavities these cavities would be very narrow and almost entirely closed, as they appear in the brain of a dead man. But the source that produces these spirits is ordinarily so copious that they have a capability, corresponding to the amount of them entering the cavities, to push outward in all directions the matter that surrounds them, thus causing this matter to expand and tighten all nerve filaments that arise there [Fig. 6.12]: just as the wind when somewhat strong can inflate the sails of a ship and tighten all the ropes to which the sails are attached. Whence it follows that at such times this machine, being so arranged as to obey all the actions of the spirits, represents the body of a man who is *awake.* Or at the least the spirits have strength enough to push some [of the nervous filaments] in the way indicated and [thus] to stretch certain parts of the brain while others remain free and lax: as do different parts of a sail when the wind is a little too weak to fill it. And at

such times this machine represents the body of a man who sleeps and who has various dreams while sleeping. Imagine, for example, that the difference between the two diagrams *M* and *N* [Figs. 6.13 and 6.14] is the same as that between the brains [*a*] of a man who is awake and [*b*] of a man who is sleeping and dreaming.

But before I speak to you in greater detail concerning *sleep* and *dreams,* I would have you first consider whatever is most noticeable about the brain during the time of waking: namely, how ideas of objects are formed in the place destined for *imagination* and for *common sense,* how these ideas are preserved by *memory,* and how they cause the *movement of all the members.*

You can see in the diagram marked *M* [Fig. 6.13], that the spirits that leave gland *H,* having dilated the part of the brain marked *A* [the ventricle] and having partly opened all its pores, flow thence to *B* [the fibrous mesh of the brain substance], then to *C* [the membrane en-

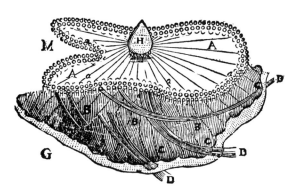

FIGURE 6.13

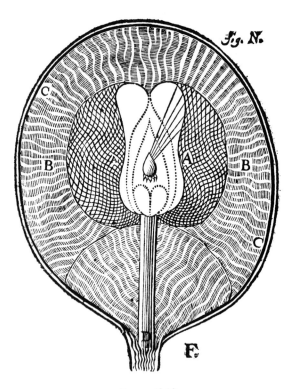

FIGURE 6.12

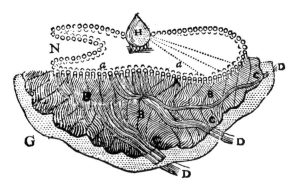

FIGURE 6.14

veloping this mesh], and finally into *D* [the origins of the cranial nerves], whence they spill out into all the nerves. And by this means they keep all the filaments that compose the nerves and the brain so tense that even those actions that have barely force enough to move them are easily communicated from one of their extremities to the other, nor do the roundabout routes they follow prevent this.

But lest this circuitousness keep you from seeing clearly how this [mechanism] is used to form ideas of objects that impinge on the senses, notice in the adjacent drawing [Fig. 6.15] the filaments 1–2, 3–4, 5–6, and the like that compose the optic nerve and extend from the back of the eye (1, 3, 5) to the internal surface of the brain (2, 4, 6). Now assume that these threads are so arranged that if the rays that come, for example, from point *A* of the object happen to exert pressure on the back of the eye at point 1, they in this way pull the whole of thread 1–2 and enlarge the opening of the tubule marked 2. And similarly, the rays that come from point *B* enlarge the opening of tubule 4, and so with the others. Whence, just as the different ways in which these rays exert pressure on points 1, 3, and 5 trace a figure at the back of the eye corresponding to that of object *ABC* (as has already been said), so, evidently, the different ways in which tubules 2, 4, 6, and the like are opened by filaments 1–2, 3–4, and 5–6 must trace [a corresponding figure] on the internal surface of the brain.

Suppose next that the spirits that tend to enter each of the tubules 2, 4, 6, and the like do not come indifferently from all points on the surface of gland *H* but each from one particular point; those that come from point *a*

of this surface, for example, tend to enter tube 2, those from points *b* and *c* tend to enter tubes 4 and 6, and so on. As a result, at the same instant that the orifices of these tubes enlarge, the spirits begin to leave the facing surfaces of the gland more freely and rapidly than they otherwise would. And [suppose] that just as [*a*] the different ways in which tubes 2, 4, and 6 are opened trace on the internal surface of the brain a figure corresponding to that of object *ABC*, so [*b*] [the different ways] in which the spirits leave the points *a, b,* and *c* trace that figure on the surface of this gland.

And note that by "figures" I mean not only things that somehow represent the position of the edges and surfaces of objects [that is, their shape], but also everything which, as indicated above, can cause the soul to sense movement, size, distance, colors, sounds, odors, and other such qualities; and even things that can make it sense titillation, pain, hunger, thirst, joy, sadness, and other such passions. For it is easy to understand that tube 2, for example, will be differently opened by the action that I said causes a red, or titillating, sensation than by the [action] that I said causes a white, or painful, sensation; and the spirits that leave from point *a* will tend differently toward this tube according as it is differently open, and so with other differences as well.

Now among these figures, it is not those imprinted on the organs of external sense, or on the internal surface of the brain, but only those traced in spirits on the surface of gland *H, where the seat of imagination and common sense is,* that should be taken to be ideas, that is to say, to be the forms or images that the rational soul will consider directly when, being united to this machine, it will imagine or will sense any object.

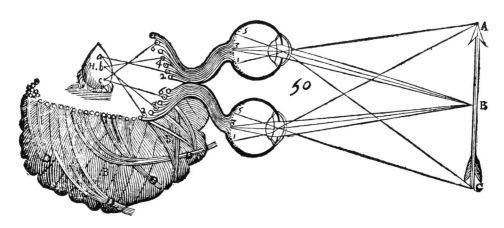

FIGURE 6.15

And note that I say "will imagine or will sense" inasmuch as I wish to include under the designation *Idea* all impressions that spirits receive in leaving gland *H;* and these [*a*] are all to be attributed to the common sense when they depend on the presence of objects, but [*b*] can also proceed from several other causes, as I shall later explain, and should then be attributed to imagination.

And I could add something here about how the traces of these ideas pass through the arteries toward the heart and thus radiate through all the blood; and about how they can sometimes even be caused, by certain actions of the mother, to be imprinted on the limbs of the child being formed in her entrails. But I shall content myself with telling you more about how they are imprinted in the internal part of the brain, marked *B,* which is the seat of *Memory.*

With this end in view, imagine that after leaving gland *H* [see Fig. 6.15] spirits pass through tubes 2, 4, 6, and the like, and into the pores or intervals that occur between the filaments composing part *B* [the solid part] of the brain. And [assume] that they are forceful enough to enlarge these intervals somewhat and to bend and rearrange any filaments they encounter, according to the differing modes of movement of the spirits themselves and the differing degrees of openness of the tubes into which they pass. [Assume also] that the first time they accomplish this they do so less easily and effectively here than on gland *H,* but that they accomplish it increasingly effectively in the measure that their action is stronger, or lasts longer, or is more often repeated. Which is why in such cases these patterns are no longer so easily erased, but are retained there in such a way that by means of them the ideas that existed previously on this gland can be formed again long afterward, without requiring the presence of the objects to which they correspond. And it is in this that *Memory* consists.

For example, when the action of the object *ABC,* by enlarging the degree of openness of the tubes 2, 4, and 6, causes the spirits to enter therein in greater quantity than they otherwise would, it gives these spirits force enough, as they pass on farther toward *N,* to form certain passageways there [no letter *N* used to represent indicated part of brain substance]. These passageways remain open even after the action of object *ABC* has ceased; or at least, if they close again, they leave a cer-

tain arrangement of the filaments composing this part of brain *N* by means of which they can be opened more easily later than if they had not been opened before. Similarly, if one were to pass several needles or engravers' points through a linen cloth as you see in the cloth marked *A* [see Fig. 6.16], the little holes that one would make would stay open as at *a* and at *b* after the needles had been withdrawn; or if they closed again, they would leave traces in this cloth, as at *c* and at *d,* which would enable them to open quite easily again.

And it is similarly necessary to remark that if one were merely to reopen some, like *a* and *b,* that fact alone could cause others like *c* and *d* to reopen at the very same time, especially if they all had been opened several times together and had not customarily been opened separately. Which shows how the recollection of one thing can be excited by that of another which was imprinted in the memory at the same time. For example, if I see two eyes with a nose, I at once imagine a forehead and a mouth and all the other parts of a face, because I am unaccustomed to seeing the former without the latter; and seeing fire, I am reminded of heat, because I have felt the latter in the past when seeing the former.

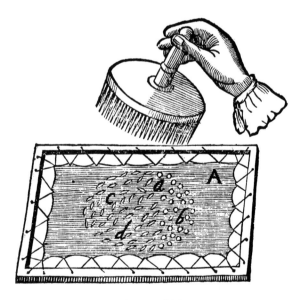

FIGURE 6.16

7

JOHN LOCKE

John Locke (1632–1704) enjoyed maintaining an air of mystery about his life, at one point spending five years in Holland under the assumed name Dr. van der Linden because of political turmoil in England (though he claimed his sudden preference for Dutch living was the beer). Locke's father was a minor attorney, with an influential client who was able to sponsor the boy's admission to the Westminster School in London. A scholarship allowed Locke to further his education at Christ's Church College at Oxford University, where he received not only a classical education, but also extracurricular instruction from anti-authoritarian scientists who were practicing the new methods of concrete observation and experiment. Robert Boyle, famous for the eponymous law relating pressure and volume in gases, became one of Locke's lifelong friends and advisers. In later years, the two helped found the Royal Society, Britain's most important scientific organization. Locke's career included work as the personal physician to Lord Shaftesbury, a diplomat, and a commissioner on the Board of Trade. He wrote several important treatises on government and spent 19 years developing and polishing his *Essay*. For his epitaph he wrote, "A scholar by training, he devoted his studies wholly to the pursuit of truth. Such you may learn from his writings, which will also tell you whatever else there is to be said about him more faithfully than the dubious eulogies of an epitaph."

AN ESSAY CONCERNING HUMAN UNDERSTANDING

BOOK II

Chapter 1

Of Ideas in General, and their Original

1. *Idea is the object of thinking.*—Every man being conscious to himself, that he thinks, and that which his mind is applied about, whilst thinking, being the ideas that are there, it is past doubt that men have in their mind several ideas, such as are those expressed by the words, "whiteness, hardness, sweetness, thinking, motion, man, elephant, army, drunkenness," and others. It is in the first place then to be inquired, How he comes by them? I know it is a received doctrine, that men have native ideas and original characters stamped upon their minds in their very first being. This opinion I have at large examined already; and, I suppose, what I have said

in the foregoing book will be much more easily admitted, when I have shown whence the understanding may get all the ideas it has, and by what ways and degrees they may come into the mind; for which I shall appeal to every one's own observation and experience.

2. *All ideas come from sensation or reflection.*—Let us then suppose the mind to be, as we say, white paper, void of all characters, without any ideas; how comes it to be furnished? Whence comes it by that vast store, which the busy and boundless fancy of man has painted on it with an almost endless variety? Whence has it all the materials of reason and knowledge? To this I answer, in one word, From experience: in that all our knowledge is founded, and from that it ultimately derives itself. Our observation, employed either about external sensible objects, or about the internal operations of our minds, perceived and reflected on by ourselves, is

From John Locke "Of Ideas in General, and their Original." In *An Essay Concerning Human Understanding* (pp. 59–70, 92–107). Amherst, NY: Prometheus Books, 1995. (Original work published 1689)

that which supplies our understandings with all the materials of thinking. These two are the fountains of
knowledge, from whence all the ideas we have, or can
naturally have, do spring.

3. *The object of sensation one source of ideas.*—
First. Our senses, conversant about particular sensible
objects, do convey into the mind several distinct perceptions of things, according to those various ways wherein
those objects do affect them; and thus we come by those
ideas we have of yellow, white, heat, cold, soft, hard,
bitter, sweet, and all those which we call sensible qualities; which when I say the senses convey into the mind,
I mean, they from external objects convey into the mind
what produces there those perceptions. This great
source of most of the ideas we have, depending wholly
upon our senses, and derived by them to the understanding, I call "sensation."

4. *The operations of our minds the other source of
them.*—Secondly. The other fountain, from which experience furnisheth the understanding with ideas, is the
perception of the operations of our own minds within
us, as it is employed about the ideas it has got; which
operations, when the soul comes to reflect on and consider, do furnish the understanding with another set of
ideas which could not be had from things without; and
such are perception, thinking, doubting, believing, reasoning, knowing, willing, and all the different actings of
our own minds; which we, being conscious of, and observing in ourselves, do from these receive into our understanding as distinct ideas, as we do from bodies affecting our senses. This source of ideas every man has
wholly in himself; and though it be not sense as having
nothing to do with external objects, yet it is very like it,
and might properly enough be called "internal sense."
But as I call the other "sensation," so I call this "reflection," the ideas it affords being such only as the mind
gets by reflecting on its own operations within itself. By
reflection, then, in the following part of this discourse, I
would be understood to mean that notice which the
mind takes of its own operations, and the manner of
them, by reason whereof there come to be ideas of these
operations in the understanding. These two, I say, viz.,
external material things as the objects of sensation, and
the operations of our own minds within as the objects of
reflection, are, to me, the only originals from whence all
our ideas take their beginnings. The term "operations"
here, I use in a large sense, as comprehending not barely the actions of the mind about its ideas, but some sort
of passions arising sometimes from them, such as is the
satisfaction or uneasiness arising from any thought.

5. *All our ideas are of the one or the other of*
these.—The understanding seems to me not to have the
least glimmering of any ideas which it doth not receive
from one of these two. External objects furnish the mind
with the ideas of sensible qualities, which are all those
different perceptions they produce in us; and the mind
furnishes the understanding with ideas of its own operations.

These, when we have taken a full survey of them,
and their several modes, combinations, and relations,
we shall find to contain all our whole stock of ideas; and
that we have nothing in our minds which did not come
in one of these two ways. Let any one examine his own
thoughts, and thoroughly search into his understanding,
and then let him tell me, whether all the original ideas
he has there, are any other than of the objects of his
senses, or of the operations of his mind considered as
objects of his reflection; and how great a mass of knowledge soever he imagines to be lodged there, he will,
upon taking a strict view, see that he has not any idea in
his mind but what one of these two hath imprinted,
though perhaps with infinite variety compounded and
enlarged by the understanding, as we shall see hereafter.

6. *Observable in children.*—He that attentively considers the state of a child at his first coming into the
world, will have little reason to think him stored with
plenty of ideas that are to be the matter of his future
knowledge. It is by degrees he comes to be furnished
with them; and though the ideas of obvious and familiar
qualities imprint themselves before the memory begins
to keep a register of time and order, yet it is often so late
before some unusual qualities come in the way, that
there are few men that cannot recollect the beginning of
their acquaintance with them; and, if it were worth
while, no doubt a child might be so ordered as to have
but a very few even of the ordinary ideas till he were
grown up to a man. But all that are born into the world
being surrounded with bodies that perpetually and diversely affect them, variety of ideas whether care be tak-
en about it, or no, are imprinted on the minds of children. Light and colours are busy at hand everywhere
when the eye is but open; sounds and some tangible
qualities fail not to solicit their proper senses, and force
an entrance to the mind; but yet I think it will be granted
easily, that if a child were kept in a place where he never saw any other but black and white till he were a man,
he would have no more ideas of scarlet or green, than he
that from his childhood never tasted an oyster or a pine-
apple has of those particular relishes.

7. *Men are differently furnished with these accord-*
ing to the different objects they converse with.—Men
then come to be furnished with fewer or more simple

ideas from without, according as the objects they converse with afford greater or less variety; and from the operations of their minds within, according as they more or less reflect on them. For, though he that contemplates the operations of his mind cannot but have plain and clear ideas of them; yet, unless he turn his thoughts that way, and considers them attentively, he will no more have clear and distinct ideas of all the operations of his mind, and all that may be observed therein, than he will have all the particular ideas of any landscape, or of the parts and motions of a clock, who will not turn his eyes to it, and with attention heed all the parts of it. The picture or clock may be so placed that they may come in his way every day; but yet he will have but a confused idea of all the parts they are made of, till he applies himself with attention to consider them each in particular.

8. *Ideas of reflection later, because they need attention.*—And hence we see the reason why it is pretty late before most children get ideas of the operations of their own minds; and some have not any very clear or perfect ideas of the greatest part of them all their lives:—because, though they pass there continually, yet like floating visions, they make not deep impressions enough to leave in the mind clear, distinct, lasting ideas, till the understanding turns inwards upon itself, reflects on its own operations, and makes them the object of its own contemplation. Children, when they come first into it, are surrounded with a world of new things, which, by a constant solicitation of their senses, draw the mind constantly to them, forward to take notice of new, and apt to be delighted with the variety of changing objects. Thus the first years are usually employed and diverted in looking abroad. Men's business in them is to acquaint themselves with what is to be found without; and so, growing up in a constant attention to outward sensations, seldom make any considerable reflection on what passes within them till they come to be of riper years; and some scarce ever at all.

9. *The soul begins to have ideas when it begins to perceive.*—To ask, at what time a man has first any ideas, is to ask when he begins to perceive; having ideas, and perception, being the same thing. I know it is an opinion, that the soul always thinks; and that it has the actual perception of ideas within itself constantly, as long as it exists; and that actual thinking is as inseparable from the soul, as actual extension is from the body: which, if true, to inquire after the beginning of a man's ideas is the same as to inquire after the beginning of his soul. For, by this account, soul and its ideas, as body and its extension, will begin to exist both at the same time.

10. *The soul thinks not always; for this wants proofs.*—But whether the soul be supposed to exist antecedent to, or coeval with, or some time after, the first rudiments or organization, or the beginnings of life in the body, I leave to be disputed by those who have better thought of that matter. I confess myself to have one of those dull souls that doth not perceive itself always to contemplate ideas; nor can conceive it any more necessary for the soul always to think, than for the body always to move; the perception of ideas being, as I conceive, to the soul, what motion is to the body; not its essence, but one of its operations; and, therefore, though thinking be supposed never so much the proper action of the soul, yet it is not necessary to suppose that it should be always thinking, always in action: that, perhaps, is the privilege of the infinite Author and Preserver of things, "who never slumbers nor sleeps;" but it is not competent to any finite being, at least not to the soul of man. We know certainly, by experience, that we sometimes think; and thence draw this infallible consequence,—that there is something in us that has a power to think; but whether that substance perpetually thinks, or no, we can be no farther assured than experience informs us. For to say that actual thinking is essential to the soul and inseparable from it, is to beg what is in question, and not to prove it by reason; which is necessary to be done, if it be not a self-evident proposition. But whether this—that "the soul always thinks," be a self-evident proposition, that everybody assents to on first hearing, I appeal to mankind. It is doubted whether I thought all last night, or no; the question being about a matter of fact, it is begging it to bring as a proof for it an hypothesis which is the very thing in dispute; by which way one may prove anything; and it is but supposing that all watches, whilst the balance beats, think, and it is sufficiently proved, and past doubt, that my watch thought all last night. But he that would not deceive himself ought to build his hypothesis on matter of fact, and make it out by sensible experience, and not presume on matter of fact because of his hypothesis; that is, because he supposes it to be so; which way of proving amounts to this,—that I must necessarily think all last night because another supposes I always think, though I myself cannot perceive that I always do so.

But men in love with their opinions may not only suppose what is in question, but allege wrong matter of fact. How else could anyone make it an inference of mine, that a thing is not, because we are not sensible of it in our sleep? I do not say there is no soul in a man because he is not sensible of it in his sleep; but I do say, he cannot think at any time, waking or sleeping, without being sensible of it. Our being sensible of it is not necessary to anything but to our thoughts; and to them it is, and to them it will always be, necessary, till we can think without being conscious of it.

11. *It is not always conscious of it.*—I grant that the soul in a waking man is never without thought, because it is the condition of being awake; but whether sleeping without dreaming be not an affection of the whole man, mind as well as body, may be worth a waking man's consideration; it being hard to conceive that any thing should think and not be conscious of it. If the soul doth think in a sleeping man without being conscious of it, I ask, whether, during such thinking, it has any pleasure or pain, or be capable of happiness or misery? I am sure the man is not, no more than the bed or earth he lies on. For to be happy or miserable without being conscious of it, seems to me utterly inconsistent and impossible. Or if it be possible that the soul can, whilst the body is sleeping, have its thinking, enjoyments, and concerns, its pleasure or pain, apart, which the man is not conscious of, nor partakes in, it is certain that Socrates asleep, and Socrates awake, is not the same person; but his soul when he sleeps, and Socrates the man, consisting of body and soul, when he is waking, are two persons; since waking Socrates has no knowledge of, or concernment for that happiness or misery of his soul which it enjoys alone by itself whilst he sleeps, without perceiving anything of it, no more than he has for the happiness or misery of a man in the Indies, whom he knows not. For if we take wholly away all consciousness of our actions and sensations, especially of pleasure and pain, and the concernment that accompanies it, it will be hard to know wherein to place personal identity.

12. *If a sleeping man thinks without knowing it, the sleeping and waking man are two persons.*—"The soul, during sound sleep, thinks," say these men. Whilst it thinks and perceives, it is capable, certainly, of those of delight or trouble, as well as any other perceptions; and it must necessarily be conscious of its own perceptions. But it has all this apart. The sleeping man, it is plain, is conscious of nothing of all this. Let us suppose, then, the soul of Castor, whilst he is sleeping, retired from his body; which is no impossible supposition for the men I have here to do with, who so liberally allow life without a thinking soul to all other animals. These men cannot, then, judge it impossible, or a contradiction, that the body should live without the soul; nor that the soul should subsist and think, or have perception, even perception of happiness or misery, without the body. Let us, then, as I say, suppose the soul of Castor separated, during his sleep, from his body, to think apart. Let us sup-

pose, too, that it chooses for its scene of thinking the body of another man, v.g. Pollux, who is sleeping without a soul: for if Castor's soul can think whilst Castor is asleep, what Castor is never conscious of, it is no matter what place it chooses to think in. We have here, then, the bodies of two men with only one soul between them, which we will suppose to sleep and wake by turns; and the soul still thinking in the waking man, whereof the sleeping man is never conscious, has never the least perception. I ask, then, whether Castor and Pollux, thus, with only one soul between them, which thinks and perceives in one what the other is never conscious of, nor is concerned for, are not two as distinct persons as Castor and Hercules, or as Socrates and Plato, were? and whether one of them might not be very happy and the other very miserable? Just by the same reason they make the soul and the man two persons, who make the soul think apart what the man is not conscious of. For, I suppose, nobody will make identity of persons to consist in the soul's being united to the very same numerical particles of matter; for if that be necessary to identity, it will be impossible, in that constant flux of the particles of our bodies, that any man should be the same person two days or two moments together.

13. *Impossible to convince those that sleep without dreaming that they think.*—Thus, methinks, every drowsy nod shakes their doctrine who teach that their soul is always thinking. Those, at least, who do at any time sleep without dreaming can never be convinced that their thoughts are sometimes for hours busy without their knowing of it; and if they are taken in the very act, waked in the middle of that sleeping contemplation, can give no manner of account of it.

14. *That men dream without remembering it, in vain urged.*—It will perhaps be said, that the soul thinks even in the soundest sleep, but the memory retains it not. That the soul in a sleeping man should be this moment busy a-thinking, and the next moment in a waking man not remember, nor be able to recollect one jot of all those thoughts, is very hard to be conceived, and would need some better proof than bare assertion to make it be believed. For who can without any more ado but being barely told so, imagine that the greatest part of men do, during all their lives, for several hours every day think of something which, if they were asked even in the middle of these thoughts, they could remember nothing at all of? Most men, I think, pass a great part of their sleep without dreaming. I once knew a man that was bred a scholar, and had no bad memory, who told me, he had never dreamed in his life till he had that fever he was then newly recovered of, which was about the five-or-

six-and-twentieth year of his age. I suppose the world affords more such instances; at least, every one's acquaintance will furnish him with examples enough of such as pass most of their nights without dreaming.

15. *Upon this hypothesis, the thoughts of a sleeping man ought to be most rational.*—To think often and never to retain it so much as one moment, is a very useless sort of thinking; and the soul, in such a state of thinking, does very little if at all excel that of a looking-glass, which constantly receives a variety of images, or ideas, but retains none; they disappear and vanish, and there remain no footsteps of them; the looking-glass is never the better for such ideas, nor the soul for such thoughts. Perhaps it will be said, "that in a waking man the materials of the body are employed and made use of in thinking; and that the memory of thoughts is retained by the impressions that are made on the brain, and the traces there left after such thinking; but that in the thinking of the soul which is not perceived in a sleeping man, there the soul thinks apart, and, making no use of the organs of the body, leaves no impressions on it and consequently no memory of such thoughts." Not to mention again the absurdity of two distinct persons, which follows from this supposition, I answer farther, that whatever ideas the mind can receive and contemplate without the help of the body, it is reasonable to conclude it can retain without the help of the body too; or else the soul, or any separate spirit, will have but little advantage by thinking. If it has no memory of its own thoughts; if it cannot lay them up for its use, and be able to recall them upon occasion; if it cannot reflect upon what is past, and make use of its former experiences, reasonings, and contemplations; to what purpose does it think? They who make the soul a thinking thing, at this rate will not make it a much more noble being than those do whom they condemn for allowing it to be nothing but the subtilest parts of matter. Characters drawn on dust that the first breath of wind effaces, or impressions made on a heap of atoms or animal spirits, are altogether as useful, and render the subject as noble, as the thoughts of a soul that perish in thinking; that, once out of sight, are gone for ever, and leave no memory of themselves behind them. Nature never makes excellent things for mean or no uses; and it is hardly to be conceived that our infinitely wise Creator should make so admirable a faculty as the power of thinking, that faculty which comes nearest the excellency of his own incomprehensible being, to be so idly and uselessly employed, at least a fourth part of its time here, as to think constantly without remembering any of those thoughts, without doing any good to itself or others, or being any

way useful to any other part of the creation. If we will examine it, we shall not find, I suppose, the motion of dull and senseless matter anywhere in the universe made so little use of, and so wholly thrown away.

16. *On this hypothesis, the soul must have ideas not derived from sensation or reflection, of which there is no appearance.*—It is true, we have sometimes instances of perception whilst we are asleep, and retain the memory of those thoughts: but how extravagant and incoherent for the most part they are, how little conformable to the perfection and order of a rational being, those who are acquainted with dreams need not be told. This I would willingly be satisfied in: Whether the soul, when it thinks thus apart, and as it were separate from the body, acts less rationally than when conjointly with it, or no? If its separate thoughts be less rational, then these men must say that the soul owes the perfection of rational thinking to the body; if it does not, it is a wonder that our dreams should be for the most part so frivolous and irrational, and that the soul should retain none of its more rational soliloquies and meditations.

17. *If I think when I know it not, nobody else can know it.*—Those who so confidently tell us, that the soul always actually thinks, I would they would also tell us what those ideas are that are in the soul of a child before or just at the union with the body, before it hath received any by sensation. The dreams of sleeping men are, as I take it, all made up of the waking man's ideas, though for the most part oddly put together. It is strange, if the soul has ideas of its own that it derived not from sensation or reflection (as it must have, if it thought before it received any impression from the body), that it should never in its private thinking (so private, that the man himself perceives it not), retain any of them the very moment it wakes out of them, and then make the man glad with new discoveries. Who can find it reasonable that the soul should in its retirement, during sleep, have so many hours' thought, and yet never light on any of those ideas it borrowed not from sensation or reflection, or at least preserve the memory of none but such which, being occasioned from the body, must needs be less natural to a spirit? It is strange the soul should never once in a man's whole life recall over any of its pure, native thoughts, and those ideas it had before it borrowed anything from the body; never bring into the waking man's view any other ideas but what have a tang of the cask, and manifestly derive their original from that union. If it always thinks, and so had ideas before it was united, or before it received any from the body, it is not to be supposed but that during sleep it recollects its native ideas and during that retirement from communicating with the

body, whilst it thinks by itself, the ideas it is busied about should be, sometimes at least, those more natural and congenial ones which it had in itself, underived from the body, or its own operations about them; which since the waking man never remembers, we must from this hypothesis conclude, either that the soul remembers something that the man does not, or else that memory belongs only to such ideas as are derived from the body, or the mind's operations about them.

18. *How knows anyone that the soul always thinks! For if it be not a self-evident proposition, it needs proof.*—I would be glad also to learn from these men, who so confidently pronounce that the human soul, or, which is all one, that a man, always thinks, how they come to know it; nay, how they come to know that they themselves think, when they themselves do not perceive it? This, I am afraid, is to be sure without proofs, and to know without perceiving. It is, I suspect, a confused notion taken up to serve an hypothesis; and none of those clear truths that either their own evidence forces us to admit, or common experience makes it impudence to deny. For the most that can be said of it is, that it is possible the soul may always think, but not always retain it in memory; and I say, it is as possible that the soul may not always think, and much more probable that it should sometimes not think, than that it should often think, and that a long while together, and not be conscious to itself, the next moment after, that it had thought.

19. *That a man should be busy in thinking, and yet not retain it the next moment, very improbable.*—To suppose the soul to think, and the man not to perceive it, is, as has been said, to make two persons in one man; and if one considers well these men's way of speaking, one should be led into a suspicion that they do so. For they who tell us that the soul always thinks, do never, that I remember, say, that a man always thinks. Can the soul think, and not the man? or a man think, and not be conscious of it? This perhaps would be suspected of jargon in others. If they say, "The man thinks always, but is not always conscious of it," they may as well say, his body is extended without having parts. For it is altogether as intelligible to say, that a body is extended without parts, as that anything thinks without being conscious of it, or perceiving that it does so. They who talk thus may, with as much reason, if it be necessary to their hypothesis, say, that a man is always hungry, but that he does not always feel it: whereas hunger consists in that very sensation, as thinking consists in being conscious that one thinks. If they say, that a man is always conscious to himself of thinking, I ask how they know it? Consciousness is the perception of what passes in a man's own

mind. Can another man perceive that I am conscious of any thing, when I perceive it not myself? No man's knowledge here can go beyond his experience. Wake a man out of a sound sleep, and ask him what he was that moment thinking on. If he himself be conscious of nothing he then thought on, he must be a notable diviner of thoughts that can assure him that he was thinking: may he not with more reason assure him he was not asleep? This is something beyond philosophy; and it cannot be less than revelation that discovers to another thoughts in my mind when I can find none there myself: and they must needs have a penetrating sight who can certainly see that I think, when I cannot perceive it myself, and when I declare that I do not; and yet can see that dogs or elephants do not think, when they give all the demonstration of it imaginable, except only telling us that they do so. This some may suspect to be a step beyond the Rosicrucians; it seeming easier to make one's self invisible to others than to make another's thoughts visible to me, which are not visible to himself. But it is but defining the soul to be a substance that always thinks, and the business is done. If such definition be of any authority, I know not what it can serve for, but to make many men suspect that they have no souls at all, since they find a good part of their lives pass away without thinking. For no definitions that I know, no suppositions of any sect, are of force enough to destroy constant experience; and perhaps it is the affectation of knowing beyond what we perceive that makes so much useless dispute and noise in the world.

20. *No ideas but from sensation or reflection evident, if we observe children.*—I see no reason therefore to believe that the soul thinks before the senses have furnished it with ideas to think on; and as those are increased and retained, so it comes by exercise to improve its faculty of thinking in the several parts of it; as well as afterwards, by compounding those ideas and reflecting on its own operations, it increases its stock, as well as facility in remembering, imagining, reasoning, and other modes of thinking.

21. He that will suffer himself to be informed by observation and experience, and not make his own hypothesis the rule of nature, will find few signs of a soul accustomed to much thinking in a new-born child, and much fewer of any reasoning at all. And yet it is hard to imagine, that the rational soul should think so much and not reason at all. And he that will consider that infants newly come into the world, spend the greatest part of their time in sleep, and are seldom awake, but when either hunger calls for the teat, or some pain (the most importunate of all sensations), or some other violent im-

pression on the body, forces the mind to perceive and attend to it:—he, I say, who considers this will, perhaps, find reason to imagine, that a fœtus in the mother's womb differs not much from the state of a vegetable; but passes the greatest part of its time without perception or thought, doing very little but sleep in a place where it needs not seek for food, and is surrounded with liquor always equally soft, and near of the same temper; where the eyes have no light, and the ears so shut up are not very susceptible of sounds; and where there is little or no variety or change of objects to move the senses.

22. Follow a child from its birth, and observe the alterations that time makes, and you shall find, as the mind by the senses comes more and more to be furnished with ideas, it comes to be more and more awake, thinks more the more it has matter to think on. After some time it begins to know the objects which, being most familiar with it, have made lasting impressions. Thus it comes by degrees to know the persons it daily converses with, and distinguish them from strangers; which are instances and effects of its coming to retain and distinguish the ideas the senses convey to it: and so we may observe how the mind, by degrees, improves in these, and advances to the exercise of those other faculties of enlarging, compounding, and abstracting its ideas, and of reasoning about them, and reflecting upon all these; of which I shall have occasion to speak more hereafter.

23. If it shall be demanded, then, when a man begins to have any ideas? I think, the true answer is, When he first has any sensation. For since there appear not to be any ideas in the mind before the senses have conveyed any in, I conceive that ideas in the understanding are coeval with sensation; which is such an impression or motion made in some part of the body as produces some perception in the understanding. It is about these impressions made on our senses by outward objects, that the mind seems first to employ itself in such operations as we call "perception, remembering, consideration, reasoning," &c.

24. *The original of all our knowledge.*—In time the mind comes to reflect on its own operations about the ideas got by sensation, and thereby stores itself with a new set of ideas, which I call "ideas of reflection." These are the impressions that are made on our senses by outward objects, that are extrinsical to the mind; and its own operations, proceeding from powers intrinsical and proper to itself, which, when reflected on by itself, become also objects of its contemplation, are, as I have said, the original of all knowledge. Thus the first capacity of human intellect is, that the mind is fitted to receive the impressions made on it, either through the senses by outward objects, or by its own operations when it reflects on them. This is the first step a man makes towards the discovery of anything, and the ground-work whereon to build all those notions which ever he shall have naturally in this world. All those sublime thoughts which tower above the clouds, and reach as high as heaven itself, take their rise and footing here: in all that great extent wherein the mind wanders in those remote speculations it may seem to be elevated with, it stirs not one jot beyond those ideas which sense or reflection have offered for its contemplation.

25. *In the reception of simple ideas, the understanding is for the most part passive.*—In this part the understanding is merely passive; and whether or no it will have these beginnings and, as it were, materials of knowledge, is not in its own power. For the objects of our senses do many of them obtrude their particular ideas upon our minds, whether we will or no; and the operations of our minds will not let us be without at least some obscure notions of them. No man can be wholly ignorant of what he does when he thinks. These simple ideas, when offered to the mind, the understanding can no more refuse to have, nor alter when they are imprinted, nor blot them out and make new ones itself, than a mirror can refuse, alter or obliterate the images or ideas, which the objects set before it do therein produce. As the bodies that surround us do diversely affect our organs, the mind is forced to receive the impressions, and cannot avoid the perception of those ideas that are annexed to them.

Chapter IX

Of Perception

1. *Perception the first simple idea of reflection.*—Perception, it is the first faculty of the mind exercised about our ideas, so it is the first and simplest idea we have from reflection, and is by some called "thinking" in general. Though thinking, in the propriety of the English tongue, signifies that sort of operation of the mind about its ideas wherein the mind is active; where it, with some degree of voluntary attention, considers anything: for in bare, naked perception, the mind is, for the most part, only passive, and what it perceives it cannot avoid perceiving.

2. *Is only when the mind receives the impression.*—What perception is, everyone will know better by reflecting on what he does himself, when he sees, hears, feels, &c., or thinks, than by any discourse of mine.

Whoever reflects on what passes in his own mind, cannot miss it; and if he does not reflect, all the words in the world cannot make him have any notion of it.

3. This is certain, that whatever alterations are made in the body, if they reach not the mind; whatever impressions are made on the outward parts, if they are not taken notice of within; there is no perception. Fire may burn our bodies with no other effect than it does a billet, unless the motion be continued to the brain, and there the sense of heat or idea of pain be produced in the mind, wherein consists actual perception.

4. How often may a man observe in himself, that whilst his mind is intently employed in the contemplation of some objects, and curiously surveying some ideas that are there, it takes no notice of impressions of sounding bodies made upon the organ of hearing with the same alteration that uses to be for the producing the idea of sound! A sufficient impulse there may be on the organ; but it not reaching the observation of the mind, there follows no perception: and though the motion that uses to produce the idea of sound be made in the ear, yet no sound is heard. Want of sensation in this case is not through any defect in the organ, or that the man's ears are less affected than at other times when he does hear: but that which uses to produce the idea, though conveyed in by the usual organ, not being taken notice of in the understanding, and so imprinting no idea on the mind, there follows no sensation. So that wherever there is sense or perception, there some idea is actually produced, and present in the understanding.

5. *Children, though they have ideas in the womb, have none innate.*—Therefore, I doubt not but children, by the exercise of their senses about objects that affect them in the womb, receive some few ideas before they are born, as the unavoidable effects either of the bodies that environ them, or else of those wants or diseases they suffer; amongst which (if one may conjecture concerning things not very capable of examination) I think the ideas of hunger and warmth are two, which probably are some of the first that children have, and which they scarce ever part with again.

6. But though it be reasonable to imagine that children receive some ideas before they come into the world, yet these simple ideas are far from those innate principles which some contend for, and we above have rejected. These here mentioned, being the effects of sensation, are only from some affections of the body which happen to them there, and so depend on something exterior to the mind; no otherwise differing in their manner of production from other ideas derived from sense, but only in the precedency of time; whereas those innate principles are supposed to be quite of another nature, not coming into the mind by any accidental alterations in or operations on the body; but, as it were, original characters impressed upon it in the very first moment of its being and constitution.

7. *Which ideas first, is not evident.*—As there are some ideas which we may reasonably suppose may be introduced into the minds of children in the womb, subservient to the necessities of their life and being there; so after they are born those ideas are the earliest imprinted which happen to be the sensible qualities which first occur to them: amongst which, light is not the least considerable, nor of the weakest efficacy. And how covetous the mind is to be furnished with all such ideas as have no pain accompanying them, may be a little guessed by what is observable in children new born, who always turn their eyes to that part from whence the light comes, lay them how you please. But the ideas that are most familiar at first being various, according to the divers circumstances of children's first entertainment in the world, the order wherein the several ideas come at first into the mind is very various and uncertain also, neither is it much material to know it.

8. *Ideas of sensation often changed by the judgment.*—We are farther to consider concerning perception, that the ideas we receive by sensation are often in grown people altered by the judgment without our taking notice of it. When we set before our eyes a round globe of any uniform colour, *v.g.,* gold, alabaster, or jet, it is certain that the idea thereby imprinted in our mind is of a flat circle variously shadowed, with several degrees of light and brightness coming to our eyes. But we having by use been accustomed to perceive what kind of appearance convex bodies are wont to make in us, what alterations are made in the reflections of light by the difference of the sensible figures of bodies, the judgment presently, by an habitual custom, alters the appearances into their causes: so that, from that which truly is variety of shadow or colour collecting the figure, it makes it pass for a mark of figure, and frames to itself the perception of a convex figure and an uniform colour; when the idea we receive from thence is only a plane variously coloured, as is evident in painting. To which purpose I shall here insert a problem of that very ingenious and studious promoter of real knowledge, the learned and worthy Mr. Molineux, which he was pleased to send me in a letter some months since: and it is this: "Suppose a man born blind, and now adult, and taught by his touch to distinguish between a cube and a sphere of the same metal, and nighly of the same bigness, so as to tell, when he felt one and the other, which is the cube, which

the sphere. Suppose then the cube and sphere placed on a table, and the blind man to be made to see; query, Whether by his sight, before he touched them, he could now distinguish and tell which is the globe, which the cube?" To which the acute and judicious proposer answers: "Not. For though he has obtained the experience of how a globe, how a cube, affects his touch; yet he has not yet attained the experience, that what affects his touch so or so, must affect his sight so or so; or that a protuberant angle in the cube, that pressed his hand unequally, shall appear to his eye as it does in the cube." I agree with this thinking gentleman, whom I am proud to call my friend, in his answer to this his problem; and am of opinion, that the blind man, at first sight, would not be able with certainty to say which was the globe, which the cube, whilst he only saw them; though he could unerringly name them by his touch, and certainly distinguish them by the difference of their figures felt. This I have set down, and leave with my reader, as an occasion for him to consider how much he may be beholden to experience, improvement, and acquired notions, where he thinks he has not the least use or help from them; and the rather, because this observing gentleman farther adds, that having upon the occasion of my book proposed this to divers very ingenious men, he hardly ever met with one that at first gave the answer to it which he thinks true, till by hearing his reasons they were convinced.

9. But this is not, I think, usual in any of our ideas but those received by sight; because sight, the most comprehensive of all our senses, conveying to our minds the ideas of light and colours, which are peculiar only to that sense; and also the far different ideas of space, figure and motion, the several varieties whereof change the appearances of its proper objects, viz., light and colours; we bring ourselves by use to judge of the one by the other. This, in many cases, by a settled habit in things whereof we have frequent experience, is performed so constantly and so quick, that we take that for the perception of our sensation which is an idea formed by our judgment; so that one, viz., that of sensation, serves only to excite the other, and is scarce taken notice of itself; as a man who reads or hears with attention and understanding, takes little notice of the characters or sounds, but of the ideas that are excited in him by them.

10. Nor need we wonder that this is done with so little notice, if we consider how very quick the actions of the mind are performed: for as itself is thought to take up no space, to have no extension, so its actions seem to require no time, but many of them seem to be crowded into an instant. I speak this in comparison to the actions of the body. Anyone may easily observe this in his own thoughts who will take the pains to reflect on them. How, as it were in an instant, do our minds with one glance see all the parts of a demonstration, which may very well be called a long one, if we consider the time it will require to put it into words, and step by step show it another! Secondly. We shall not be so much surprised that this is done in us with so little notice, if we consider how the facility which we get of doing things, by a custom of doing, makes them often pass in us without our notice. Habits, especially such as are begun very early, come at last to produce actions in us which often escape our observation. How frequently do we in a day cover our eyes with our eye-lids, without perceiving that we are at all in the dark! Men, that by custom have got the use of a by-word, do almost in every sentence pronounce sounds which, though taken notice of by others, they themselves neither hear nor observe. And therefore it is not so strange that our mind should often change the idea of its sensation into that of its judgment, and make one serve only to excite the other, without our taking notice of it.

11. *Perception puts the difference between animals and inferior beings.*—This faculty of perception seems to me to be that which puts the distinction betwixt the animal kingdom and the inferior parts of nature. For however vegetables have, many of them, some degrees of motion, and, upon the different application of other bodies to them, do very briskly alter their figures and motions, and so have obtained the name of "sensitive plants" from a motion which has some resemblance to that which in animals follows upon sensation; yet I suppose it is all bare mechanism, and no otherwise produced than the turning of a wild oat-beard by the insinuation of the particles of moisture, or the shortening of a rope by the affusion of water. All which is done without any sensation in the subject, or the having or receiving any ideas.

12. Perception, I believe, is in some degree in all sorts of animals; though in some possibly the avenues provided by nature for the reception of sensations are so few, and the perception they are received with so obscure and dull, that it comes extremely short of the quickness and variety of sensations which is in other animals: but yet it is sufficient for and wisely adapted to the state and condition of that sort of animals who are thus made; so that the wisdom and goodness of the Maker plainly appears in all the parts of this stupendous fabric, and all the several degrees and ranks of creatures in it.

13. We may, I think, from the make of an oyster or

cockle, reasonably conclude that it has not so many nor so quick senses as a man, or several other animals; nor, if it had, would it, in that state and incapacity of transferring itself from one place to another, be bettered by them. What good would sight and hearing do to a creature that cannot move itself to or from the objects wherein at a distance it perceives good or evil? And would not quickness of sensation be an inconvenience to an animal that must lie still where chance has once placed it, and there receive the afflux of colder or warmer, clean or foul, water, as it happens to come to it?

14. But yet I cannot but think there is some small dull perception whereby they are distinguished from perfect insensibility. And that this may be so, we have plain instances even in mankind itself. Take one in whom decrepit old age has blotted out the memory of his past knowledge, and clearly wiped out the ideas his mind was formerly stored with; and has, by destroying his sight, hearing, and smell quite, and his taste to a great degree, stopped up almost all the passages for new ones to enter; or if there be some of the inlets yet half open, the impressions made are scarce perceived, or not at all retained. How far such an one (notwithstanding all that is boasted of innate principles) is in his knowledge and intellectual faculties above the condition of a cockle or an oyster, I leave to be considered. And if a man had passed sixty years in such a state, as it is possible he might as well as three days, I wonder what difference there would have been, in any intellectual perfections, between him and the lowest degree of animals.

15. *Perception the inlet of knowledge.*—Perception, then, being the first step and degree towards knowledge, and the inlet of all the materials of it, the fewer senses any man as well as any other creature hath, and the fewer and duller the impressions are that are made by them, and the duller the faculties are that are employed about them, the more remote are they from that knowledge which is to be found in some men. But this, being in great variety of degrees (as may be perceived amongst men), cannot certainly be discovered in the several species of animals, much less in their particular individuals. It suffices me only to have remarked here, that perception is the first operation of all our intellectual faculties, and the inlet of all knowledge into our minds. And I am apt, too, to imagine that it is perception in the lowest degree of it which puts the boundaries between animals and the inferior ranks of creatures. But this I mention only as my conjecture by the by, it being indifferent to the matter in hand which way the learned shall determine of it.

Chapter X

Of Retention

1. *Contemplation.*—The next faculty of the mind, whereby it makes a farther progress towards knowledge, is that which I call retention or the keeping of those simple ideas which from sensation or reflection it hath received. This is done two ways. First, by keeping the idea which is brought into it for some time actually in view, which is called contemplation.

2. *Memory.*—The other way of retention is the power to revive again in our minds those ideas which after imprinting have disappeared, or have been as it were laid aside out of sight; and thus we do, when we conceive heat or light, yellow or sweet, the object being removed. This is memory, which is, as it were, the storehouse of our ideas. For the narrow mind of man, not being capable of having many ideas under view and consideration at once, it was necessary to have a repository to lay up those ideas, which at another time it might have use of. But our ideas being nothing but actual perceptions in the mind, which cease to be anything when there is no perception of them, this laying up of our ideas in the repository of the memory signifies no more but this,—that the mind has a power, in many cases, to revive perceptions which it has once had, with this additional perception annexed to them,—that it has had them before. And in this sense it is that our ideas are said to be in our memories, when indeed they are actually nowhere, but only there is an ability in the mind when it will to revive them again, and, as it were, paint them anew on itself, though some with more, some with less, difficulty; some more lively, and others more obscurely. And thus it is by the assistance of this faculty that we are said to have all those ideas in our understandings, which though we do not actually contemplate, yet we can bring in sight, and make appear again and be the objects of our thoughts, without the help of those sensible qualities which first imprinted them there.

3. *Attention, repetition, pleasure, and pain fix ideas.*—Attention and repetition help much to the fixing any ideas in the memory; but those which naturally at first make the deepest and most lasting impression, are those which are accompanied with pleasure or pain. The great business of the senses being to make us take notice of what hurts or advantages the body, it is wisely ordered by nature (as has been shown) that pain should accompany the reception of several ideas; which, supplying the place of consideration and reasoning in children, and acting quicker than consideration in grown men,

makes both the young and old avoid painful objects with that haste which is necessary for their preservation, and in both settles in the memory a caution for the future.

4. *Ideas fade in the memory.*—Concerning the several degrees of lasting wherewith ideas are imprinted on the memory, we may observe, that some of them have been produced in the understanding by an object affecting the senses once only, and no more than once: others, that have more than once offered themselves to the senses, have yet been little taken notice of: the mind, either heedless as in children, or otherwise employed as in men, intent only on one thing, not setting the stamp deep into itself; and in some, where they are set on with care and repeated impressions, either through the temper of the body or some other default, the memory is very weak. In all these cases, ideas in the mind quickly fade, and often vanish quite out of the understanding, leaving no more footsteps or remaining characters of themselves, than shadows do flying over fields of corn: and the mind is as void of them as if they never had been there.

5. Thus many of those ideas which were produced in the minds of children in the beginning of their sensation (some of which perhaps, as of some pleasures and pains, were before they were born, and others in their infancy), if in the future course of their lives they are not repeated again, are quite lost, without the least glimpse remaining of them. This may be observed in those who by some mischance have lost their sight when they were very young, in whom the ideas of colours, having been but slightly taken notice of, and ceasing to be repeated, do quite wear out; so that some years after there is no more notion nor memory of colours left in their minds, than in those of people born blind. The memory in some men, it is true, is very tenacious, even to a miracle; but yet there seems to be a constant decay of all our ideas, even of those which are struck deepest, and in minds the most retentive; so that if they be not sometimes renewed by repeated exercise of the senses, or reflection on those kinds of objects which at first occasioned them, the print wears out, and at last there remains nothing to be seen. Thus the ideas, as well as children, of our youth often die before us; and our minds represent to us those tombs to which we are approaching; where though the brass and marble remain, yet the inscriptions are effaced by time, and the imagery moulders away. The pictures drawn in our minds are laid in fading colours; and if not sometimes refreshed, vanish and disappear. How much the constitution of our bodies, and the make of our animal spirits, are concerned in this; and whether the temper of the brain makes this difference, that in some it retains the charac-

ters drawn on it like marble, in others like free-stone, and in others little better than sand, I shall not here inquire: though it may seem probable that the constitution of the body does sometimes influence the memory; since we oftentimes find a disease quite strip the mind of all its ideas, and the flames of a fever in a few days calcine all those images to dust and confusion, which seemed to be as lasting as if graved in marble.

6. *Constantly repeated ideas can scarce be lost.*—But concerning the ideas themselves it is easy to remark, that those that are oftenest refreshed (amongst which are those that are conveyed into the mind by more ways than one) by a frequent return of the objects or actions that produce them, fix themselves best in the memory, and remain clearest and longest there: and therefore those which are of the original qualities of bodies, viz., solidity, extension, figure, motion, and rest; and those that almost constantly affect our bodies, as heat and cold; and those which are the affections of all kinds of beings, as existence, duration, and number, which almost every object that affects our senses, every thought which employs our minds, bring along with them: these, I say, and the like ideas, are seldom quite lost whilst the mind retains any ideas at all.

7. *In remembering, the mind is often active.*—In this secondary perception, as I may so call it, or viewing again the ideas that are lodged in the memory, the mind is oftentimes more than barely passive; the appearances of those dormant pictures depending sometimes on the will. The mind very often sets itself on work in search of some hidden idea, and turns, as it were, the eye of the soul upon it; though sometimes too they start up in our minds of their own accord, and offer themselves to the understanding, and very often are roused and tumbled out of their dark cells into open daylight by some turbulent and tempestuous passion; our affections bringing ideas to our memory which had otherwise lain quiet and unregarded. This farther is to be observed concerning ideas lodged in the memory, and upon occasion revived by the mind,—that they are not only (as the word "revive" imports) none of them new ones, but also that the mind takes notice of them as of a former impression, and renews its acquaintance with them as with ideas it had known before. So that though ideas formerly imprinted are not all constantly in view, yet in remembrance they are constantly known to be such as have been formerly imprinted, *i.e.,* in view, and taken notice of before by the understanding.

8. *Two defects in the memory, oblivion and slowness.*—Memory, in an intellectual creature, is necessary in the next degree to perception. It is of so great mo-

ment, that where it is wanting all the rest of our faculties are in a great measure useless; and we in our thoughts, reasonings, and knowledge, could not proceed beyond present objects, were it not for the assistance of our memories, wherein there may be two defects.

First, That it loses the idea quite; and so far it produces perfect ignorance. For since we can know nothing further than we have the idea of it, when that is gone we are in perfect ignorance.

Secondly, That it moves slowly, and retrieves not the ideas that it has, and are laid up in store, quick enough to serve the mind upon occasions. This, if it be to a great degree, is stupidity; and he who through this default in his memory has not the ideas that are really preserved there ready at hand when need and occasion calls for them, were almost as good be without them quite, since they serve him to little purpose. The dull man who loses the opportunity whilst he is seeking in his mind for those ideas that should serve his turn, is not much more happy in his knowledge than one that is perfectly ignorant. It is the business therefore of the memory to furnish to the mind those dormant ideas which it has present occasion for; in the having them ready at hand on all occasions, consists that which we call invention, fancy, and quickness of parts.

9. These are defects we may observe in the memory of one man compared with another. There is another defect which we may conceive to be in the memory of man in general, compared with some superior created intellectual beings, which in this faculty may so far excel man, that they may have constantly in view the whole sense of all their former actions, wherein no one of the thoughts they have ever had may slip out of their sight. The omniscience of God, who knows all things, past, present, and to come, and to whom the thoughts of men's hearts always lie open, may satisfy us of the possibility of this. For who can doubt but God may communicate to those glorious spirits, his immediate attendants, any of his perfections in what proportion he pleases, as far as created finite beings can be capable? It is reported of that prodigy of parts, Monsieur Pascal, that, till the decay of his health had impaired his memory, he forgot nothing of what he had done, read, or thought in any part of his rational age. This is a privilege so little known to most men, that it seems almost incredible to those who, after the ordinary way, measure all others by themselves; but yet, when considered, may help us to enlarge our thoughts towards greater perfections of it in superior ranks of spirits. For this of Mr. Pascal was still with the narrowness that human minds are confined to here—of having great variety of ideas

only by succession, not all at once: whereas the several degrees of angels may probably have larger views, and some of them be endowed with capacities able to retain together and constantly set before them, as in one picture, all their past knowledge at once. This, we may conceive, would be no small advantage to the knowledge of a thinking man, if all his past thoughts and reasonings could be always present to him; and therefore we may suppose it one of those ways wherein the knowledge of separate spirits may exceedingly surpass ours.

10. *Brutes have memory.*—This faculty of laying up and retaining the ideas that are brought into the mind, several other animals seem to have to a great degree, as well as man. For to pass by other instances, birds' learning of tunes, and the endeavours one may observe in them to hit the notes right, put it past doubt with me that they have perception, and retain ideas in their memories, and use them for patterns. For it seems to me impossible that they should endeavour to conform their voices to notes (as it is plain they do) of which they had no ideas. For though I should grant sound may mechanically cause a certain motion of the animal spirits in the brains of those birds whilst the tune is actually playing, and that motion may be continued on to the muscles of the wings, and so the bird mechanically be driven away by certain noises, because this may tend to the bird's preservation; yet that can never be supposed a reason why it should cause mechanically either whilst the tune was playing, much less after it has ceased, such a motion in the organs of the bird's voice as should conform it to the notes of a foreign sound, which imitation can be of no use to the bird's preservation. But, which is more, it cannot with any appearance of reason be supposed (much less proved) that birds without sense and memory can approach their notes, nearer and nearer by degrees, to a tune played yesterday; which if they have no idea of it in their memory is now nowhere, nor can be a pattern for them to imitate, or which any repeated essays can bring them nearer to; since there is no reason why the sound of a pipe should leave traces in their brains, which not at first, but by their after endeavours, should produce the like sounds; and why the sounds they make themselves should not make traces which they should follow, as well as those of the pipe, is impossible to conceive.

Chapter XI

Of Discerning, and Other Operations of the Mind

1. *No knowledge without discerning.*—Another faculty we may take notice of in our minds, is that of discerning

and distinguishing between the several ideas it has. It is not enough to have a confused perception of something in general: unless the mind had a distinct perception of different objects and their qualities, it would be capable of very little knowledge; though the bodies that affect us were as busy about us as they are now, and the mind were continually employed in thinking. On this faculty of distinguishing one thing from another, depends the evidence and certainty of several even very general propositions, which have passed for innate truths; because men, overlooking the true cause why those propositions find universal assent, impute it wholly to native uniform impressions: whereas it in truth depends upon this clear discerning faculty of the mind, whereby it perceives two ideas to be the same or different. But of this more hereafter.

2. *The difference of wit and judgment.*—How much the imperfection of accurately discriminating ideas one from another lies either in the dulness or faults of the organs of sense, or want of acuteness, exercise, or attention in the understanding, or hastiness and precipitancy natural to some tempers, I will not here examine; it suffices to take notice, that this is one of the operations that the mind may reflect on and observe in itself. It is of that consequence to its other knowledge, that so far as this faculty is in itself dull, or not rightly made use of for the distinguishing one thing from another, so far our notions are confused, and our reason, and judgment disturbed or misled. If in having our ideas in the memory ready at hand consists quickness of parts; in this of having them unconfused, and being able nicely to distinguish one thing from another where there is but the least difference, consists in a great measure the exactness of judgment and clearness of reason which is to be observed in one man above another. And hence, perhaps, may be given some reason of that common observation—that men who have a great deal of wit and prompt memories, have not always the clearest judgment or deepest reason. For, wit lying most in the assemblage of ideas, and putting those together with quickness and variety wherein can be found any resemblance or congruity, thereby to make up pleasant pictures and agreeable visions in the fancy; judgment, on the contrary, lies quite on the other side, in separating carefully one from another ideas wherein can be found the least difference, thereby to avoid being misled by similitude and by affinity to take one thing for another. This is a way of proceeding quite contrary to metaphor and illusion, wherein for the most part lies that entertainment and pleasantry of wit which strikes so lively on the fancy, and therefore so acceptable to all people; because its

beauty appears at first sight, and there is required no labour of thought to examine what truth or reason there is in it. The mind, without looking any farther, rests satisfied with the agreeableness of the picture and the gaiety of the fancy: and it is a kind of an affront to go about to examine it by the severe rules of truth and good reason; whereby it appears that it consists in something that is not perfectly conformable to them.

3. *Clearness alone hinders confusion.*—To the well distinguishing our ideas, it chiefly contributes that they be clear and determinate; and when they are so, it will not breed any confusion or mistake about them, though the senses should (as sometimes they do) convey them from the same object differently on different occasions, and so seem to err. For though a man in a fever should from sugar have a bitter taste, which at another time would produce a sweet one, yet the idea of bitter in that man's mind would be as clear and distinct from the idea of sweet, as if he had tasted only gall. Nor does it make any more confusion between the two ideas of sweet and bitter, that the same sort of body produces at one time one and at another time another idea by the taste, than it makes a confusion in two ideas of white and sweet, or white and round, that the same piece of sugar produces them both in the mind at the same time. And the ideas of orange-colour and azure that are produced in the mind by the same parcel of the infusion of *lignum nephriticum,* are no less distinct ideas than those of the same colours taken from two very different bodies.

4. *Comparing.*—The comparing them one with another, in respect of extent, degrees, time, place, or any other circumstances, is another operation of the mind about its ideas, and is that upon which depends all that large tribe of ideas, comprehended under relation; which of how vast an extent it is, I shall have occasion to consider hereafter.

5. *Brutes compare, but imperfectly.*—How far brutes partake in this faculty is not easy to determine; I imagine they have it not in any great degree: for though they probably have several ideas distinct enough, yet it seems to me to be the prerogative of human understanding, when it has sufficiently distinguished any ideas so as to perceive them to be perfectly different, and so consequently two, to cast about and consider in what circumstances they are capable to be compared. And therefore, I think, beasts compare not their ideas farther than some sensible circumstances annexed to the objects themselves. The other power of comparing which may be observed in men, belonging to general ideas, and useful only to abstract reasonings, we may probably conjecture beasts have not.

6. *Compounding.*—The next operation we may observe in the mind about its ideas is composition; whereby it puts together several of those simple ones it has received from sensation and reflection, and combines them into complex ones. Under this of composition may be reckoned also that of enlarging; wherein though the composition does not so much appear as in more complex ones, yet it is nevertheless a putting several ideas together, though of the same kind. Thus, by adding several units together we make the idea of a dozen, and putting together the repeated ideas of several perches we frame that of a furlong.

7. *Brutes compound but little.*—In this also I suppose brutes come far short of men. For though they take in and retain together several combinations or simple ideas (as possibly the shape, smell, and voice of his master, make up the complex idea a dog has of him, or rather, are so many distinct marks whereby he knows him); yet I do not think they do of themselves ever compound them and make complex ideas. And perhaps even where we think they have complex ideas, it is only one simple one that directs them in the knowledge of several things, which possibly they distinguish less by their sight than we imagine. For I have been credibly informed that a bitch will nurse, play with, and be fond of young foxes, as much as and in place of her puppies, if you can but get them once to suck her so long that her milk may go through them. And those animals which have a numerous brood of young ones at once, appear not to have any knowledge of their number; for though they are mightily concerned for any of their young that are taken from them whilst they are in sight or hearing, yet if one or two of them be stolen from them in their absence or without noise, they appear not to miss them, or to have any sense that their number is lessened.

8. *Naming.*—When children have by repeated sensations got ideas fixed in their memories, they begin by degrees to learn the use of signs. And when they have got the skill to apply the organs of speech to the framing of articulate sounds, they begin to make use of words to signify their ideas to others. These verbal signs they sometimes borrow from others, and sometimes make themselves, as one may observe among the new and unusual names children often give to things in their first use of language.

9. *Abstracting.*—The use of words then being to stand as outward marks of our internal ideas, and those ideas being taken from particular things, if every particular idea that we take in should have a distinct name, names must be endless. To prevent this, the mind makes the particular ideas, received from particular objects, to become general; which is done by considering them as they are in the mind such appearances separate from all other existences, and the circumstances of real existence, as time, place, or any other concomitant ideas. This is called "abstraction," whereby ideas taken from particular beings become general representatives of all of the same kind; and their names, general names, applicable to whatever exists conformable to such abstract ideas. Such precise, naked appearances in the mind, without considering how, whence, or with what others they came there, the understanding lays up (with names commonly annexed to them) as the standards to rank real existences into sorts, as they agree with these patterns, and to denominate them accordingly. Thus, the same colour being observed to-day in chalk or snow, which the mind yesterday received from milk, it considers that appearance alone, makes it a representative of all of that kind, and, having given it the name "whiteness," it by that sound signifies the same quality wheresoever to be imagined or met with; and thus universals, whether ideas or terms, are made.

10. *Brutes abstract not.*—If it may be doubted whether beasts compound and enlarge their ideas that way to any degree, this, I think, I may be positive in, that the power of abstracting is not at all in them, and that the having of general ideas is that which puts a perfect distinction between man and brutes, and is an excellency which the faculties of brutes do by no means attain to. For it is evident we observe no footsteps in them of making use of general signs for universal ideas; from which we have reason to imagine, that they have not the faculty of abstracting or making general ideas, since they have no use of words or any other general signs.

11. Nor can it be imputed to their want of fit organs to frame articulate sounds, that they have no use or knowledge of general words: since many of them, we find, can fashion such sounds and pronounce words distinctly enough, but never with any such application. And, on the other side, men who, through some defect in the organs, want words, yet fail not to express their universal ideas by signs, which serve them instead of general words; a faculty which we see beasts come short in. And therefore, I think, we may suppose that it is in this that the species of brutes are discriminated from man; and it is that proper difference wherein they are wholly separated, and which at last widens to so vast a distance. For if they have any ideas at all, and are not bare machines (as some would have them), we cannot deny them to have some reason. It seems as evident to me that they do, some of them, in certain instances, reason, as that they have sense; but it is only in particular

ideas, just as they received them from their senses. They are, the best of them, tied up within those narrow bounds, and have not (as I think) the faculty to enlarge them by any kind of abstraction.

12. *Idiots and madmen.*—How far idiots are concerned in the want of weakness of any or all of the foregoing faculties, an exact observation of their several ways of faltering would no doubt discover. For those who either perceive but dully, or retain the ideas that come into their minds but ill, who cannot readily excite or compound them, will have little matter to think on. Those who cannot distinguish, compare, and abstract, would hardly be able to understand and make use of language, or judge, or reason, to any tolerable degree; but only a little and imperfectly about things present and very familiar to their senses. And indeed any of the forementioned faculties, if wanting or out of order, produce suitable defects in men's understandings and knowledge.

13. In fine, the defect in naturals seems to proceed from want of quickness, activity, and motion in the intellectual faculties, whereby they are deprived of reason; whereas madmen, on the other side, seem to suffer by the other extreme. For they do not appear to me to have lost the faculty of reasoning; but, having joined together some ideas very wrongly, they mistake them for truths, and they err as men do that argue right from wrong principles. For by the violence of their imaginations having taken their fancies for realities, they make right deductions from them. Thus you shall find a distracted man, fancying himself a king, with a right inference, require suitable attendance, respect, and obedience; others, who have thought themselves made of glass, have used the caution necessary to preserve such brittle bodies. Hence it comes to pass, that a man who is very sober and of a right understanding in all other things, may in one particular be as frantic as any in Bedlam; if either by any sudden very strong impression, or long fixing his fancy upon one sort of thoughts, incoherent ideas have been cemented together so powerfully as to remain united. But there are degrees of madness, as of folly; the disorderly jumbling ideas together is in some more and some less. In short, herein seems to lie the difference between idiots and madmen, that madmen put wrong ideas together, and so make wrong propositions, but argue and reason right from them; but idiots make very few or no propositions, and reason scarce at all.

14. *Method.*—These, I think, are the first faculties and operations of the mind which it makes use of in understanding; and though they are exercised about all its ideas in general, yet the instances I have hitherto given have been chiefly in simple ideas; and I have subjoined

the explication of these faculties of the mind to that of simple ideas, before I come to what I have to say concerning complex ones, for these following reasons:—

First, Because, several of these faculties being exercised at first principally about simple ideas, we might, by following nature in its ordinary method, trace and discover them in their rise, progress, and gradual improvements.

Secondly, Because, observing the faculties of the mind, how they operate about simple ideas, which are usually in most men's minds much more clear, precise, and distinct than complex ones, we may the better examine and learn how the mind abstracts, denominates, compares, and exercises its other operations about those which are complex, wherein we are much more liable to mistake.

Thirdly, Because these very operations of the mind about ideas received from sensation are themselves, when reflected on, another set of ideas, derived from that other source of our knowledge which I call "reflection;" and therefore fit to be considered in this place after the simple ideas of sensation. Of compounding, comparing, abstracting, &c., I have but just spoken, having occasion to treat of them more at large in other places.

15. *These are the beginnings of human knowledge.*—And thus I have given a short and, I think, true history of the first beginnings of human knowledge, whence the mind has its first objects, and by what steps it makes its progress to the laying in and storing up those ideas out of which is to be framed all the knowledge it is capable of; wherein I must appeal to experience and observation whether I am in the right: the best way to come to truths being to examine things as really they are, and not to conclude they are as we fancy of ourselves, or have been taught by others to imagine.

16. *Appeal to experience.*—To deal truly, this is the only way that I can discover whereby the ideas of things are brought into the understanding: if other men have either innate ideas or infused principles, they have reason to enjoy them; and if they are sure of it, it is impossible for others to deny them the privilege that they have above their neighbours. I can speak but of what I find in myself, and is agreeable to those notions which, if we will examine the whole course of men in their several ages, countries, and educations, seem to depend on those foundations which I have laid, and to correspond with this method in all the parts and degrees thereof.

17. *Dark room.*—I pretend not to teach, but to inquire; and therefore cannot but confess here again, that external and internal sensation are the only passages that I can find of knowledge to the understanding. These

alone, as far as I can discover, are the windows by which light is let into this dark room. For methinks the understanding is not much unlike a closet wholly shut from light, with only some little opening left to let in external visible resemblances or ideas of things without: would the pictures coming into such a dark room but stay there, and lie so orderly as to be found upon occasion, it would very much resemble the understanding of a man in reference to all objects of sight, and the ideas of them.

These are my guesses concerning the means whereby the understanding comes to have and retain simple ideas and the modes of them, with some other operations about them. I proceed now to examine some of these simple ideas and their modes a little more particularly.

8

GOTTFRIED WILHELM LEIBNIZ

Gottfried Wilhelm Leibniz (1646–1716) was insatiably curious about everything. Educated at home by his professor father, he was able to read Latin texts at the university level at the age of 6, prompting some debate about just what a 6 year old should be reading. He received his doctorate in law from the University of Altdorf when the University of Leipzig was unable to grant the degree because of annual quotas. Leibniz attached himself to wealthy patrons, working on a variety of projects encompassing history, public health, theology, engineering, teaching, and diplomacy. While in Paris on a failed diplomatic mission, Leibniz became interested in mathematics and developed binary arithmetic and calculus. The latter had been independently discovered, but not yet published, by Sir Issac Newton. The volume of Leibniz's work, including some 15,000 letters, simultaneously reveals a refreshing openness to new ideas and the exchange of information and a failure to focus and truly complete any of his work. Wearing a huge black wig and declaring a variety of catastrophes as the best of all possible worlds, Voltaire's character Pangloss, from the satire *Candide,* was modeled after Leibniz.

NEW ESSAYS ON HUMAN UNDERSTANDING

BOOK II

"Of Ideas"

Chapter i

IN WHICH WE DISCUSS "IDEAS IN GENERAL," AND INCIDENTALLY CONSIDER WHETHER THE SOUL OF MAN ALWAYS THINKS

Philalethes. **§1.** Having examined whether ideas are innate, let us consider what they are like and what varieties of them there are. Is it not true that an "idea is the object of thinking?"

Theophilus. I agree about that, provided that you add that an idea is an immediate inner object, and that this object expresses the nature or qualities of things. If the idea were the *form* of the thought, it would come into and go out of existence with the actual thoughts which correspond to it, but since it is the *object* of thought it can exist before and after the thoughts. Sensible outer objects are only *mediate,* because they cannot act

From Gottfried Wilhelm Leibniz, "Book 2, Of Ideas." In P. Remnant and J. Bennett (Trans. and Eds.) *New Essays on Human Understanding* (Section 109–145). Cambridge: Cambridge University Press, 1996. (Original work published 1765)

immediately on the soul. God is the only *immediate outer* object. One might say that the soul itself is its own immediate inner object; but that is only to the extent that it contains ideas, i.e. something corresponding to things. For the soul is a little world where distinct ideas represent God and confused ones represent the universe.

Phil. §2. Our gentlemen who take the soul to be initially a blank page, "void of all characters, without any ideas; [ask] How comes it to be furnished? Whence comes it by that vast store . . .? To this [they] answer, in one word, from experience."

Theo. This *tabula rasa* of which one hears so much is a fiction, in my view, which nature does not allow and which arises solely from the incomplete notions of philosophers—such as vacuum, atoms, the state of rest (whether absolute, or of two parts of a whole relative to one another), or such as that prime matter which is conceived without any form. Things which are uniform, containing no variety, are always mere abstractions: for instance, time, space, and the other entities of pure mathematics. There is no body whose parts are at rest, and no substance which does not have something which distinguishes it from every other. Human souls differ not only from other souls but also from one another, though the latter differences are not of the sort that we call specific. And I think I can demonstrate that every substantial thing, be it soul or body, has a unique relationship to each other thing; and that each must always differ from every other in respect of *intrinsic denominations*. Not to mention the fact that those who hold forth about the "blank page" cannot say what is left of it once the ideas have been taken away—like the Scholastics who leave nothing in their prime matter. It may be said that this "blank page" of the philosophers means that all the soul possesses, naturally and inherently, are bare faculties. But inactive faculties—in short, the pure powers of the Schoolmen—are also mere fictions, unknown to nature and obtainable only by abstraction. For where will one ever find in the world a faculty consisting in sheer power without performing any act? There is always a particular disposition to action, and towards one action rather than another. And as well as the disposition there is an endeavour towards action—indeed there is an infinity of them in any subject at any given time, and these endeavours are never without

some effect. Experience is necessary, I admit, if the soul is to be made to have such and such thoughts, and if it is to take heed of the ideas that are in us. But how could experience and the senses provide the ideas? Does the soul have windows? Is it similar to writing-tablets, or like wax? Clearly, those who take this view of the soul are treating it as fundamentally corporeal. Someone will confront me with this accepted philosophical axiom, that there is nothing in the soul which does not come from the senses. But an exception must be made of the soul itself and its states. *Nihil est in intellectu quod non fuerit in sensu, excipe: nisi ipse intellectus.* Now the soul includes being, substance, one, same, cause, perception, reasoning, and many other notions which the senses cannot provide. That agrees pretty well with your author of the *Essay,* for he looks for a good proportion of ideas in the mind's reflection on its own nature.

Phil. I hope then that you will concede to this able author that all ideas come through sensation or through reflection; that is, through "our observation employed either about external, sensible objects; or about the internal operations of our" soul.

Theo. In order to keep away from an argument upon which we have already spent too long, let me say in advance, sir, that when you say that ideas come from one or other of those causes, I shall take that to mean the actual perception of the ideas; for I believe I have shown that in so far as they contain something distinct they are in us before we are aware of them.

Phil. With that in mind, let us see when the soul should be said to start perceiving and actually thinking of ideas. §9. "I know it is an opinion, that the soul always thinks, . . . and that actual thinking is as inseparable from the soul, as actual extension is from the body." §10. But I cannot "conceive it any more necessary for the soul always to think, than for the body always to move; the perception of ideas being . . . to the soul, what motion is to the body." That appears to me quite reasonable, at least; and I would be very pleased, sir, to have your opinion on it.

Theo. You have said it, sir: action is no more inseparable from the soul than from the body. For it appears to me that a thoughtless state of the soul and absolute rest in a body are equally contrary to nature, and never occur in the world. A substance which is in action at some time will be so forever after, for all the impressions linger on, merely being mixed with new ones. When one strikes a body one causes or rather induces[1] an infinity of swirls, as in a liquid—for fundamentally every solid is in some degree liquid, every liquid in some degree solid—and there is no way of ever entirely stopping this internal turbulence. Now you may believe that since the body is never without movement, the soul which corresponds to it will never be without perception either.

Phil. But "that, perhaps, is the privilege of the . . . Author and Preserver" of all things, that being infinite in his perfection he "never[2] slumbers nor sleeps; but is not competent to any finite being, at least not to [a being such as] the soul of man."

Theo. Certainly, we slumber and sleep, and God has no need to. But it does not follow that when asleep we have no perceptions; rather, if the evidence is considered carefully it points the other way.

Phil. "There is something in us, that has a power to think." But that does not imply that thinking is always occurring in us.

Theo. True powers are never simple possibilities; there is always endeavour, and action.

Phil. But "that the soul always thinks [is not] a self-evident proposition."

Theo. I do not say that it is either. It cannot be found without a little attention and reasoning: the common man is no more aware of it than of the pressure of the air or the roundness of the earth.

Phil. "'Tis doubted whether I thought all last night"; this is a question "about a matter of fact," and it must be settled "by sensible experience."

Theo. One settles it in the same way that one proves that there are imperceptible bodies and invisible movements, though some people make fun of them. In the same way there are countless inconspicuous perceptions, which do not stand out enough for one to be aware of or to remember them but which manifest themselves through their inevitable consequences.

Phil. A certain author has objected that we maintain that the soul goes out of existence because we are not sensible of its existence during sleep. But that objection can only arise from a strange prejudice. For we "do not say there is no soul in a man, because he is not sensible of it in his sleep; but [we] do say, he cannot think . . . without being" aware of it.[3]

Theo. I have not read the book where that objection occurs. But there would have been nothing wrong with objecting against you simply that thought need not stop just because one is not aware of it; for if it did, then by parity of argument we could say that there is no soul while one is not aware of it. To meet that objection, you must show that it is of the essence of thought in particular that one be aware of it.

Phil. **§11.** It is "hard to conceive, that any thing should think, and not be conscious of it."

Theo. That is undoubtedly the crux of the matter—the difficulty by which able people have been perplexed. But here is the way to escape from it. Bear in mind that we do think of many things all at once, but pay heed only to the thoughts that stand out most distinctly. That is inevitable; for if we were to take note of everything, we should have to direct our attention on an infinity of things at the same time—things which impress themselves on our senses and which are all sensed by us. And I would go further: something remains of all our past thoughts, none of which can ever be entirely wiped out. When we are in dreamless sleep, or when we are dazed by some blow or a fall or a symptom of an illness or other mishap, an infinity of small, confused sensations occur in us. Death itself cannot affect the souls of animals in any way but that; they must certainly regain their distinct perceptions sooner or later, for in nature everything is orderly. I admit, though, that in that confused state the soul would be without pleasure and pain, for they are noticeable perceptions.

Phil. **§12.** Is it not true that "the men [we] have here to do with," namely the Cartesians who believe that the soul always thinks,[4] "allow life, without a thinking [and knowing] soul to all other animals"? And that they see no difficulty about saying that the soul can think without being joined to a body?

Theo. Speaking for myself, my view is different; for although I share the Cartesians' view that the soul always thinks, I part company with them on the other two points. I believe that beasts have imperishable souls, and that no soul—human or otherwise—is ever without some body. I hold that God alone is entirely exempt from this because he is pure act.

Phil. If you had accepted the Cartesian view, I would have drawn the following conclusion from it. Since the bodies of Castor and of Pollux can stay alive while sometimes having a soul and sometimes not; and since a soul can stay in existence while sometimes being in a given body and sometimes out of it; it could be supposed that Castor and Pollux shared a single soul which acted in their bodies by turn, with each being asleep while the other was awake. In that case, it would make two persons as distinct as Castor and Hercules could be.

Theo. I in turn shall offer you a different supposition which appears to be more real. Must it not be agreed that after some passage of time or some great change one may suffer a total failure of memory? They say that Sleidan before his death forgot everything he knew, and there are plenty of other examples of this sad phenomenon. Now, suppose that such a man were made young again, and learned everything anew—would that make him a different man? So it is not memory that makes the very same man. But as for the fiction about a soul which animates different bodies, turn about, with the things that happen to it in one body being of no concern to it in the other: that is one of those fictions which go against the nature of things—like space without body, and body without motion—which arise from the incomplete notions of philosophers, and which vanish when one goes a little deeper. For it must be borne in mind that each soul retains all its previous impressions, and could not be separated into two halves in the manner you have described: within each substance there is a perfect bond between the future and the past, which is what creates the identity of the individual. Memory is not necessary for this, however, and is sometimes not even possible, because of the multitude of past and present impressions which jointly contribute to our present thoughts; for I believe that each of a man's thoughts has some effect, if only a confused one, or leaves some trace which mingles with the thoughts which follow it. One may forget many 115 things, but one could also retrieve them, much later, if one were brought back to them in the right way.

Phil. **§13.** Those "who do at any time sleep without dreaming, can never be convinced, that their thoughts are . . . busy."

Theo. While sleeping, even without dreams, one always has some faint sensing going on. Waking up is itself a sign of this: the easier someone is to awaken, the more sense he has of what is going on around him, though often this sense is not strong enough to cause him to wake.

Phil. **§14.** "That the soul in a sleeping man should be this moment busy a thinking, and the next moment in a waking man, not remember, [appears][5] very hard to be conceived."

Theo. Not only is it easy to conceive, but something like it can be observed during every day of our waking lives. For there are always objects which strike our eyes and ears, and therefore touch our souls as well, without our paying heed to them. For our attention is held by other objects, until a given object becomes powerful enough to attract it, either by acting more strongly upon us or in some other way. It is as though we had been selectively asleep with regard to that object; and when we withdraw our attention from everything all together, the sleep becomes general. It is also a way of getting to sleep—dividing one's attention so as to weaken it.

Phil. "I once knew a man, that was bred a scholar, and had no bad memory, who told me, he had never dreamed in his life, till he had that fever, he was then newly recovered of, which was about the five or six and twentieth year of his age."

Theo. I have also been told of a scholar, much older than that, who had never dreamed. But the case for saying that the soul perceives continually does not rest entirely on dreams, since I have shown how even when asleep it has some perception of what is happening around it.

Phil. **§15.** "To think often, and never to retain [the memory of what one thinks] so much as one moment, is a . . . useless sort of thinking."

Theo. Every impression has an effect, but the effects are not always noticeable. When I turn one way rather than another, it is often because of a series of tiny impressions of which I am not aware but which make one movement slightly harder than the other. All our undeliberated actions result from a conjunction of minute perceptions; and even our customs and passions, which have so 116 much influence when we do deliberate, come from the same source; for these tendencies come into being gradually, and so without the minute perceptions we would not have acquired these noticeable dispositions. I have already remarked that anyone who excluded these effects from moral philosophy would be copying the ill-informed people who exclude insensible corpuscles from natural science; and yet I notice that among those who speak of liberty there are some who, ignoring these insensible impressions which can suffice to tilt the balance, fancy that moral actions can be subject to sheer indifference like that of Buridan's ass half-way between two pastures. We shall discuss that more fully later on. I admit, though, that these impressions tilt the balance without necessitating.

Phil. Perhaps it will be said that in a man who is awake, his body plays a part in his thinking, and that the memory is preserved by traces in the brain; whereas when he sleeps the soul has its thoughts separately, in itself.

Theo. I would say nothing of the sort, since I think that there is always a perfect correspondence between the body and the soul, and since I use bodily impressions of which one is not aware, whether in sleep or waking states, to prove that there are similar impressions in the soul. I even maintain that something happens in the soul corresponding to the circulation of the blood and to every internal movement of the viscera, although one is unaware of such happenings, just as those who live near a water-mill are unaware of the noise it makes. The fact is that if during sleep or waking there were impressions in the body which did not touch or affect the soul in any way at all, there would have to be limits to the union of body and soul, as though bodily impressions needed a certain shape or size if the soul was to be able to feel them. And that is indefensible if the soul is incorporeal, for there is no relation of proportion between an incorporeal substance and this or that modification of matter. In short, many errors can flow from the belief that the only perceptions in the soul are the ones of which it is aware.

Phil. **§16.** Most of the dreams which we remember are extravagant and incoherent . . . So we should have to say either that the soul owes its capacity for rational thinking to the body or else that it retains none of its "rational soliloquies."

Theo. The body has counterparts of all the thoughts of the soul, rational or otherwise, and dreams have traces in the brain just as much as do the thoughts of those who are awake.

117 *Phil.* **§17.** Since you are so confident "that the soul always actually thinks, I [wish that you could tell me] what those ideas are, that are in the soul of a child, before, or just at the union with

the body, before it hath received any by sensation."

Theo. It is easy to satisfy you on my principles. The perceptions of the soul always correspond naturally to the state of the body; and when there are many confused and indistinct motions in the brain, as happens with those who have had little experience, it naturally follows that the thoughts of the soul cannot be distinct either. But the soul is never deprived of the aid of "sensation"; for it always expresses its body, and this body is always affected in infinitely many ways by surrounding things, though often they provide only a confused impression.

Phil. **§18.** But here is yet another question posed by the author of the *Essay.* "I would be glad [he says] to learn from these men, who so confidently pronounce, that the human soul, or which is all one, that a man always thinks, how they . . . know it."

Theo. I suggest that it needs even more "confidence" to deny that anything happens in the soul of which we are not aware. For anything which is noticeable must be made up of parts which are not: nothing, whether thought or motion, can come into existence suddenly. In short, it is as though someone were to ask, these days, how we know about insensible particles.

Phil. **§19.** "They who tell us, that the soul always thinks, do never, that I remember, [tell us] that a man always thinks."

Theo. I suppose that that is because they are talking about the separated soul too, and that they would readily admit that the man always thinks while his soul and body are united. As for my own views: since I have reason to hold that the soul is never completely separated from all body, I think it can be said without qualification that the man does and will always think.

Phil. To say that a body is extended without having parts, and that anything thinks without being aware that it does so, are two assertions which seem equally unintelligible.

Theo. Forgive me, sir, but I must point out that when you contend that there is nothing in the soul of which it is not aware, you are begging the question. That contention has already held sway all through our first meeting, when you tried to use it to tear down innate ideas and truths. If I conceded it, I would not only be flying in the face of experience and of reason, but would also be gratuitously relinquishing my own view, for which I think I have made a good enough case. My opponents, accomplished as they are, have adduced no proof of their own firmly and frequently repeated contention on this matter; and what is more, there is an easy way of showing them that they are wrong, i.e. that it is impossible that we should always reflect explicitly on all our thoughts; for if we did, the mind would reflect on each reflection, *ad infinitum,* without ever being able to move on to a new thought. For example, in being aware of some present feeling, I should have always to think that I think about that feeling, and further to think that I think of thinking about it, and so on *ad infinitum.* It must be that I stop reflecting on all these reflections, and that eventually some thought is allowed to occur without being thought about; otherwise I would dwell for ever on the same thing.

Phil. But could one not "with as much reason . . . say, that a man is always hungry," adding that he can be hungry without being aware of it?

Theo. There is a great deal of difference: hunger arises from special conditions which do not always obtain. Still, it is true that even when one is hungry one does not think about the hunger all the time; but when one thinks about it, one is aware of it, for it is a very noticeable disposition: there are always disturbances in the stomach, but they do not cause hunger unless they become strong enough. One should always observe this distinction between thoughts in general and noticeable thoughts. Thus, a point which was offered in mockery of my view really serves to confirm it.

119 *Phil.* **§23.** It may be asked now "when a man begins to have any ideas" in his thought.[6] And it seems to me that one ought to reply that it is "when he first has any sensation."

Theo. That is my view too, though only for a somewhat special reason. For I believe that we are never without ideas, never without thoughts, and never without sensations either. But I distinguish ideas from thoughts. For we always have all our pure or distinct ideas independently of the senses, but thoughts always correspond to some sensation.

Phil. **§25.** But the mind is "merely passive" in the perception of simple ideas, which are the 'be-

ginnings [or] materials of knowledge'; whereas in the forming of composite ideas it is active.[7]

Theo. How can it be wholly passive with respect to the perception of all simple ideas, when by your own admission some simple ideas are perceived through reflection? The mind must at least give itself its thoughts of reflection, since it is the mind which reflects. Whether it can shut them out is another matter; no doubt it cannot do so unless some circumstance prompts it to turn aside.

Phil. So far we seem to have been in open disagreement. Now that we are moving on to consider ideas in detail, I hope that we shall find more to agree on and that our disagreements will be restricted to minor matters.

Theo. I shall be delighted to see able people accepting views which I hold to be true, for they can cause the views to be appreciated and can show them in a good light.

Chapter ii 120

"OF SIMPLE IDEAS"

Philalethes. **§1.** I hope then that you will still agree, sir, that some ideas are simple and some composite.[8] Thus, the warmth and softness of wax, the hardness and coldness of ice, provide simple ideas; for of these the soul has a uniform conception which is not distinguishable into different ideas.

Theophilus. It can be maintained, I believe, that these sensible ideas appear simple because they are confused and thus do not provide the mind with any way of making discriminations within what they contain; just like distant things which appear rounded because one cannot discern their angles, even though one is receiving some confused impression from them. It is obvious that green, for instance, comes from a mixture of blue and yellow; which makes it credible that the idea of green is composed of the ideas of those two colours, although the idea of green appears to us as simple as that of blue, or as that of warmth. So these ideas of blue and of warmth should also be regarded as simple only in appearance. I freely admit that we treat them as simple ideas, because we are at any rate not aware of any divisions within them; but we should undertake the analysis of them by means of further experiments, and by means of reason in so far they can be made more capable of being treated by the intellect.

121   *Chapter iii*

"OF IDEAS OF ONE SENSE"

Philalethes. **§1.** Now we can classify simple ideas according to how we come to perceive them, namely (1) by one sense only, (2) by more senses than one, (3) by reflection, or (4) by all the ways of sensation and reflection. As for those "which have admittance only through one sense, which is peculiarly adapted to receive them[,] light and colours . . . come in only by the eyes: all kinds of noises, sounds, and tones only by the ears": the several tastes by the palate, and smells by the nose. The organs or nerves convey them to the brain, and if some of the organs become disordered, those sensations have no side-entrance to be admitted by. "The most considerable of those, belonging to the touch, are heat and cold, and solidity." The rest consist either in the arrangement of sensible parts, "as smooth and rough; or else [in the] adhesion of the parts, as hard and soft, tough and brittle."

Theophilus. I am pretty much in agreement with what you say, sir. But I might remark that, judging by the late Monsieur Mariotte's experiment on the blind spot in the region of the optic nerve, it seems that membranes receive the sensation more than nerves do; and that there is a side-entrance for hearing and for taste, since the teeth and the cranium contribute to the hearing of sounds, and tastes can be experienced in a fashion through the nose because the organs are connected. But none of that makes any fundamental difference as regards the elucidation of ideas. As for tactile qualities: smooth and rough, like hard and soft, can be described as mere modifications of resistance or solidity.

122   *Chapter iv*

"OF SOLIDITY"

Philalethes. **§1.** No doubt you will also agree that the sensation[9] of solidity "arises from the resistance which we find in body, to the entrance of any other body into the place it possesses, till it

has left it. [Accordingly, that which] hinders the approach of two bodies, when they are moving one towards another, I call solidity. . . . If any one think it better to call it impenetrability, he has my consent. [But I think that] *solidity* . . . carries something more of positive in it[. This idea appears the] most intimately connected with, and essential to body," and one can find it only in matter.

Theophilus. It is true that we find resistance in the sense of touch, when there is difficulty in getting another body to give way to our own. It is true also that bodies are reluctant[10] jointly to occupy a single place. Yet some people are not convinced that this reluctance is unconquerable; and it is worth bearing in mind that the resistance which occurs in matter arises from it in more than one way, and for rather different reasons. One body resists another when it either has to leave the place it is already in or fails to enter the place it was about to enter, because the other body exerts itself to enter there too; and in that case it can happen, if neither yields, that each brings the other to a halt or pushes it back. The resistance is manifested in the change in the body which is resisted—whether a loss of force or a change of direction or both at once. Now, it can be said in a general way that this resistance comes from the reluctance of two bodies to share the same place, which can be called impenetrability; for when one exerts itself to enter the place, it also exerts itself to drive the other out or prevent it from entering. But having granted that there is this kind of incompatibility which makes one or both of them yield, there are in addition several other sources for a body's resistance to another body which tries to make it give way. Some lie in the body itself, the others in neighbouring bodies. Within the body itself there are two—one passive and constant, and the other active and changing. The former is what I follow Kepler and Descartes in calling *inertia*. This renders matter resistant to motion, so that force must be expended to move a body, independently of its having weight or being bonded to other things. Thus a body which seeks to drive another along must encounter such resistance as a result. The other cause—the active and changing one—consists in the body's own impetus: the body will not yield without resistance at a time when its own impetus is carrying it to a given place. These sources of resistance recur in the neighbouring bodies when the resisting body can-

123

not yield without making others yield in their turn. But now a new element enters the picture, namely *firmness* or the bonding of one body to another. This bonding often results in one's being unable to push one body without at the same time pushing another which is bonded to it, so that there is a kind of *traction* of the second body. Because of this bonding, there would be resistance even if there were no inertia or manifest impetus. For if space is conceived as full of perfectly fluid matter which has neither inertia nor impetus, and a single hard body is placed in it, there will be no resistance to the body's being moved; but if space were full of small cubes, a hard body would encounter resistance to its being moved among them. This is because the little cubes—just because they were hard, i.e. because their parts were 124 bonded together—would be difficult to split up finely enough to permit circular movement in which the position being evacuated by the moving body would at once be refilled by something else. But if two bodies were simultaneously inserted into the two open ends of a tube into which each of them fitted tightly, the matter which was already in the tube, however fluid it might be, would resist just because of its sheer impenetrability. So the phenomenon of resistance which we are considering involves the impenetrability of bodies, inertia, impetus, and bonding. It is true that in my opinion this bonding of bodies results from more attenuated movements of bodies towards one another; but since the point is disputable, it ought not to be assumed from the start. Nor, for the same reason, should it be initially assumed that there is an inherent, essential solidity which makes the place occupied always equal to the thing which occupies it, i.e. that the incompatibility (or, to put it more accurately, the *disagreement*) of two bodies in one place is a matter of perfect impenetrability, not admitting of degrees; since some people say that perceptible solidity may be due to a body's having a certain reluctance—but not an unconquerable one—to share a place with another body. For all the ordinary Peripatetics and some others believe that what they call rarefaction and condensation can occur, i.e. that the very same matter could occupy more or less space: not merely in appearance (as when water is squeezed out of a sponge), but really, as the Schoolmen think is the case with air. I do not hold this view, but I do not think that one ought to as-

sume its contradictory from the start; for the senses unaided by reasoning do not suffice to establish that perfect impenetrability which I hold obtains in the natural realm but which is not apprehended by mere sensation. And someone could claim that bodies' resistance to compression is due to an effort by their parts to spread out when they are subject to confinement. Two final points. In detecting these qualities, the eyes can very usefully come to the aid of the sense of touch. And solidity, in so far as there is a distinct notion of it, is fundamentally conceived through pure reason, though the senses provide a basis for reasoning to prove that solidity occurs in nature.

Phil. §4. We are in agreement, at least, that a body's "solidity consists in repletion, and so an utter exclusion of other bodies out of the space it possesses" unless it can find some new space for itself;[11] but hardness (or rather stability, which some call firmness) is "a firm cohesion of the parts of matter, making up masses of a sensible 125 bulk, so that the whole does not easily change its figure."

Theo. As I have already remarked, the special function of rigidity is to make it difficult to move one part of a body without also moving the remainder, so that when one part is pushed the other is also taken in the same direction by a kind of *traction,* although it is not itself pushed and does not lie on the line along which the endeavour is exercised; and, furthermore, if the latter part meets an obstacle which holds it still or forces it back, it in turn will pull back or hold still the former part—this is always reciprocal. The same thing happens sometimes with two bodies which are not in contact and are not contiguous parts of a single continuous body; for even then it can happen that the one, on being pushed, makes the other move without pushing it, so far as our senses can tell. Examples of this are provided by the magnet, electrical attraction, and the attraction which used to be attributed to nature's fear of a vacuum.

Phil. It seems that in general "hard and soft are names that we give to things, only in relation to the constitutions of our own bodies."

Theo. But then there would not be many philosophers attributing hardness to their "atoms." The notion of hardness does not depend on the senses: the possibility of it can be conceived through reason, although it is the senses which convince us that it also actually occurs in nature. However, rather than the word "hardness" I would prefer "firmness," if I may be allowed to use it in this sense, for there is always some firmness even in soft bodies. I would even look for a broader and more general word such as "stability" or "cohesion." Thus, I would contrast hard with soft, and firm with fluid; for wax is soft, but unless melted by heat it is not fluid and retains its boundaries; and even in fluids there is usually some cohesion, as can be seen in drops of water and of mercury. My opinion is that all bodies have a degree of cohesion; just as I think that there are none which are entirely without fluidity or possessed of a cohesion which cannot be overcome; so that in my view the atoms of Epicurus, which are supposed to be unconquerably hard, cannot exist, any more

126 than can the rarefied and perfectly fluid matter of the Cartesians. But this is not the place to defend this view or to explain what gives rise to cohesion.

Phil. There seems to be experimental proof that bodies are perfectly solid. For example, in Florence a golden globe filled with water was put into a press; the water could not give way, and so it passed out through the pores of the globe.

Theo. There is something to be said about the conclusion you draw from what happened to the water in that experiment. Air is a body just as much as water is, and yet the same thing would not happen to air, since it is—at least so far as the senses can tell—compressible. And those who hold with genuine rarefaction and condensation will say that water is already too compressed to yield to our machines, just as very compressed air resists further compression. But I admit on the other hand that if some tiny change were noticed in the volume of the water, that could be ascribed to the air which it contains; but I shall not now discuss the question of whether pure water is itself compressible, as it is found to be expansible when it evaporates. Still, fundamentally I share the view of those who think that bodies are perfectly impenetrable, and that there is only apparent rarefaction and condensation. But this cannot be proved by the sort of experiment you have described, any more than the Torricellian tube or Guericke's machine suffices to prove a perfect vacuum.

Phil. If body could be strictly rarefied or compressed, it could change its volume or its extension; but since that cannot happen, a body will al-

ways be equal to the same space.[12] §5. Yet its extension will always be distinct from the extension of the space.

Theo. Body could have its own extension 127 without that implying that the extension was always determinate or equal to the same space. Still, although it is true that in conceiving body one conceives something in addition to space, it does not follow that there are two extensions, that of space and that of body. Similarly, in conceiving several things at once one conceives something in addition to the number, namely the things numbered; and yet there are not two pluralities, one of them abstract (for the number) and the other concrete (for the things numbered). In the same way, there is no need to postulate two extensions, one abstract (for space) and the other concrete (for body). For the concrete one is as it is only by virtue of the abstract one: just as bodies pass from one position in space to another, i.e. change how they are ordered in relation to one another, so things pass also from one position to another within an ordering or enumeration—as when the first becomes the second, the second becomes the third, etc. In fact, time and place are only kinds of order; and an empty place within one of these orders (called 'vacuum' in the case of space), if it occurred, would indicate the mere possibility of the missing item and how it relates to the actual.

Phil. I am still very pleased that you are fundamentally in agreement with me that matter does not alter its volume. But when you refuse to allow that there are two extensions, sir, you seem to go too far, and to come close to the Cartesians, who do not distinguish space from matter. Now, it seems to me that if there are people who do not have these distinct ideas of space and of the solidity which fills it, but rather confound them and turn the two ideas into one, it is impossible to see how such people can communicate with anyone else. They are as a blind man would be, in relation to someone who was telling him about the colour scarlet, if the blind man believed that it is like the sound of a trumpet.

Theo. But I also hold that the ideas of extension and solidity do not consist in a *je ne sais quoi*, like the idea of the colour scarlet. I distinguish extension from matter, opposing the Cartesians' 128 view, but I do not believe that there are two extensions. Also, since those who dispute about the difference between extension and solidity do agree on some truths in this area, and have some distinct notions, they should be able to find a way of resolving their conflict, and so the alleged differences in their ideas ought not to serve as an excuse for letting the debate go on for ever; though I know that certain Cartesians—very able ones too—are given to sheltering behind ideas which they claim to have. But if they would avail themselves of means which I formerly presented ["Meditations on knowledge, truth and ideas"] for telling true ideas from false—means which we shall also say something about later on—they would withdraw from their untenable position.

Chapter v

"Of Simple Ideas of Divers Senses"

Philalethes. The ideas the perception of which comes to us "by more than one sense, are of space, or extension, figure, rest, and motion."

Theophilus. These ideas which are said to come from more than one sense—such as those of space, figure, motion, rest—come rather from the common sense, that is, from the mind itself; for they are ideas of the pure understanding (though ones which relate to the external world and which the senses make us perceive), and so they admit of definitions and of demonstrations.

Chapter vi

"Of Simple Ideas of Reflection"

Philalethes. §§1–2. The simple ideas which come through reflection are the ideas of the understanding and of the will; for we are aware of these when we reflect upon ourselves.

129 *Theophilus.* It is doubtful whether these are all simple ideas; for it is evident for instance that the idea of the will includes that of the understanding, and that the idea of movement contains the idea of figure.

Chapter vii

"Of . . . Ideas of Both Sensation and Reflection"

Philalethes. §1. There are simple ideas which come to be perceived in[13] "the mind, by all the

ways of sensation and reflection, viz. Pleasure . . . Pain . . . Power . . . Existence . . . Unity."

Theophilus. It seems that the senses could not convince us of the existence of sensible things without help from reason. So I would say that the thought of existence comes from reflection, that those of power and unity come from the same source, and that these are of a quite different nature from the perceptions of pleasure and pain.

Chapter viii

"Some Farther Considerations Concerning . . . Simple Ideas"

Philalethes. §2. What shall we say about privative qualities? It seems to me that the ideas of rest, darkness and cold are just as positive as those of motion, light and heat. §6. However, "the privative causes I have here assigned of positive ideas, are according to the common opinion; but in truth 130 it will be hard to determine, whether there be really any ideas from a privative cause, till it be determined, whether rest be any more a privation than motion."

Theophilus. I had never thought there could be any reason to doubt the privative nature of rest. All it involves is a denial of motion in the body. For motion, on the other hand, it is not enough to deny rest; something else must be added to determine the degree of motion, for it is essentially a matter of more and less, whereas all states of rest are equal. It is different when the cause of rest is in question, for that must be positive in secondary matter, i.e. mass. But I should still think that the *idea* of rest is privative, that is, that it consists only in negation. It is true that the act of denial is something positive.

Phil. §8. The *qualities* of things are their faculties for producing the perception of ideas in us. §9. We should make a distinction within them. There are primary and secondary qualities. Extension, solidity, figure, number, and mobility are what I call "primary" qualities: they are the original qualities of body and are inseparable from it. §10. And I designate as "secondary qualities" the faculties or powers which bodies have to produce certain sensations in us, or certain effects in other bodies, as for example the effect of the fire on the wax which it melts.

Theo. I think it could be said that when a pow-

er is intelligible and admits of being distinctly explained, it should be included among the primary
qualities, but when it is merely sensible and yields
only a confused idea it should be put among the
secondary qualities.

Phil. **§11.** These primary qualities show "how
bodies operate one upon another." Bodies act only
by impulse, at least so far as we can conceive, "it
being impossible to [understand], that body
should operate on what it does not touch, (which
is all one as to imagine it can operate where it is
not)."[14]

Theo. I am also of the opinion that bodies act
only by impulse, but there is a problem for the argument you have just given. For attraction sometimes involves touching: one can touch something
and draw it along apparently without impulse, as I
showed earlier in discussing hardness. If one part
of an Epicurean atom (supposing there were such
things) were pushed, it would draw the rest along
131   with it, being in contact with it while setting
it into motion without impulse; and when there is
an attraction between two contiguous things, the
one which draws the other along with it cannot be
said to "operate where it is not." This argument
would be valid only against attraction at a distance, such as would be involved in the so-called
centripetal force which some worthy people have
advanced.

Phil. **§13.** Now, when certain particles strike
our organs in various ways, they cause in us certain sensations of colours or of tastes, or of other
secondary qualities which have the power to produce those sensations. "It being no more impossible, to conceive, that God should annex such ideas
[as that of heat] to such motions, with which they
have no similitude; than that he should annex the
idea of pain to the motion of a piece of steel dividing our flesh, with which that idea hath no resemblance."

Theo. It must not be thought that ideas such as
those of colour and pain are arbitrary and that between them and their causes there is no relation or
natural connection: it is not God's way to act in
such an unruly and unreasoned fashion. I would
say, rather, that there is a resemblance of a kind—
not a perfect one which holds all the way through,
but a resemblance in which one thing expresses
another through some orderly relationship between them. Thus an ellipse, and even a parabola
or hyperbola, has some resemblance to the circle

of which it is a projection on a plane, since there
is a certain precise and natural relationship between what is projected and the projection which
is made from it, with each point on the one corresponding through a certain relation with a point
on the other. This is something which the Cartesians have overlooked; and on this occasion, sir,
you have deferred to them more than is your wont
and more than you had grounds for doing.

Phil. I tell you what appears to me true; and it
appears to be the case that **§15.** "the ideas of primary qualities of bodies, are resemblances of
[those qualities]; but the ideas, produced in us by
[the] secondary qualities, have no resemblance of
them at all."

Theo. I have just pointed out how there is a resemblance, i.e. a precise relationship, in the case
of secondary qualities as well as of primary. It is
thoroughly reasonable that the effect should correspond to the cause; and how could one ever be
sure that it does not, since we have no distinct
knowledge either of the sensation of blue (for instance) or of the motions which produce it? It is   132
true that pain does not resemble the movement of
a pin; but it might thoroughly resemble the motions which the pin causes in our body, and might
represent them in the soul; and I have not the least
doubt that it does. That is why we say that the pain
is in our body and not in the pin, although we say
that the light is in the fire;[15] because there are motions in the fire which the senses cannot clearly
detect individually, but which form a confusion—
a running together—which is brought within
reach of the senses and is represented to us by the
idea of light.

Phil. **§21.** But if the relation between the object and the sensation were a natural one, how
could it happen, as we observe it to do, that the
same water can appear cold to one hand and warm
to the other? That phenomenon shows that the
warmth is no more in the water than pain is in the
pin.

Theo. The most that it shows is that warmth is
not a sensible quality (i.e. a power of being senso-
rily detected) of an entirely absolute kind, but
rather depends upon the associated organs; for a
movement in the hand itself can combine with
that of warmth, altering its appearance. Again,
light does not appear to malformed eyes, and
when eyes are full of bright light they cannot see a
dimmer one. Even the primary qualities (as you

call them), such as unity and number, can fail to appear as they should; for, as M. Descartes has already reported [*Optics* VI], a globe appears double when it is touched with the fingers in a certain way, and an object is multiplied when seen in a mirror or through a glass into which facets have been cut. So, from the fact that something does not always appear the same, it does not follow that it is not a quality of the object, or that its image does not resemble it. As for warmth: when our hand is very warm, the lesser warmth of the water does not make itself felt, and serves rather to moderate the warmth of the hand, so that the water appears to us to be cold; just as salt water from the Baltic, when mixed with water from the Sea of Portugal, lessens its degree of salinity even though it is itself saline. So there is a sense in which the warmth can be said to inhere in the water in a bath, even if the water appears cold to someone; just as we describe honey in absolute terms as sweet, and silver as white, even though to certain invalids one appears sour and the other yellow; for things are named according to what is most usual. None of this alters the fact that when the organ and the intervening medium are properly constituted, the internal bodily motions and the ideas which represent them to the soul resemble 133 the motions of the object which cause the colour, the warmth, the pain etc.; or—what is here the same thing—they express the object through some rather precise relationship; though this relation does not appear distinctly to us, because we cannot disentangle this multitude of minute impressions, whether in our soul or in our body or in what lies outside us.

Phil. §24. The qualities which the sun has of blanching and softening wax, or hardening mud, we consider only as simple powers, without conceiving anything in the sun which resembles this whiteness and this softness, or this hardness. Yet warmth and light "are commonly thought real qualities [of] the sun. . . . Whereas, if rightly considered, these qualities of light and warmth, which are perceptions in me . . . , are no otherwise in the sun, than the changes made in the wax, when it is blanched or melted, are in the sun."

Theo. Some have pushed this doctrine so far that they have tried to persuade us that if someone could touch the sun he would find no heat in it. The counterfeit sun which can be felt at the focus of a mirror or a burning glass should disabuse

them of that. But as for the comparison between the warming faculty and the melting one: I would venture to say that if the melted or blanched wax were sentient, it too would feel something like what we feel when the sun warms us, and it would say if it could that the sun is hot. This is not because the wax's whiteness resembles the sun, for in that case the brown of a face tanned by the sun would also resemble it; but because at that time there are motions in the wax which have a relationship with the motions in the sun which cause them. There could be some other cause for the wax's whiteness, but not for the motions which it has undergone in receiving whiteness from the sun.

Chapter ix

"Of Perception"

Philalethes. §1. This brings us specifically to ideas of reflection. "Perception, as it is the first faculty of the [soul], exercised about our ideas; so it is the first and simplest idea we have from reflection [. *Thinking* often] signifies that sort of operation of the mind about its ideas, wherein the mind is active; where it with some degree of voluntary attention, considers any thing. [But in what is called] *perception,* the mind is, for the most part, only passive; and what it perceives, it cannot avoid perceiving." 134

Theophilus. It might perhaps be added that beasts have perception, and that they don't necessarily have thought, that is, have reflection or anything which could be the object of it. We too have minute perceptions of which we are not aware in our present state. We could in fact become thoroughly aware of them and reflect on them, if we were not distracted by their multiplicity, which scatters the mind, and if bigger ones did not obliterate them or rather put them in the shade.

Phil. §4. I admit that while the "mind is intently employed in the contemplation of some objects; [it is no way aware][16] of impressions of [certain] bodies, made upon the organ of hearing. . . . A sufficient impulse there may be . . . ; but it not reaching the observation of the [soul], there follows no perception."

Theo. I would prefer to distinguish between *perception* and *being aware.* For instance, a perception of light or colour of which we are aware is made up of many minute perceptions of which we are unaware; and a noise which we perceive but do not attend to is brought within reach of our awareness by a tiny increase or addition. If the previous noise had no effect on the soul, this minute addition would have none either, nor would the total. (I have already touched on this point at 11.i.11, 12, 15 etc.)

Phil. **§8.** This is a good time to remark that the ideas which are received by sensation are often altered by the judgment of the mind in grown people, without their being aware of it. The idea of a "globe, of any uniform colour, . . . is of a flat circle variously shadowed" and lighted. But as we are accustomed to distinguish the appearances of bodies, and the alterations in the reflections of light according to the shapes of their surfaces, we substitute the cause of the image for what actually appears to us, and confound judging with seeing.[17]

135   *Theo.* That is perfectly true: this is how a painting can deceive us, by means of an artful use of perspective. When bodies have flat surfaces they can be depicted merely by means of their outlines, without use of shading, painting them simply in the Chinese manner but with better proportions. This is how drawings of medallions are usually done, so that the draftsman can stay closer to the precise lineaments of the ancient originals. But such a drawing, unaided by shading, cannot distinguish definitely between a flat circular surface and a spherical surface—since neither contains any distinct points or distinguishing features—and yet there is a great difference between them which ought to be marked. That is why M. Desargues has offered rules about the effects of hue and shading.

So when we are deceived by a painting our judgments are doubly in error. First, we substitute the cause for the effect, and believe that we immediately see the thing that causes the image, rather like a dog barking at a mirror. For strictly we see only the image, and are affected only by rays of light. Since rays of light need time—however little—to reach us, it is possible that the object should be destroyed during the interval and no longer exist when the light reaches the eye; and something which no longer exists cannot be the present object of our sight. Secondly, we are further deceived when we substitute one cause for another and believe that what comes merely from

a flat painting actually comes from a body. In such cases our judgments involve both metonymy and metaphor (for even figures of rhetoric turn into sophisms when they mislead us). This confusion of the effect with the real or the putative cause frequently occurs in other sorts of judgments too. This is how we come to believe that it is by an immediate real influence that we sense our bodies and the things which touch them, and move our arms, taking this influence to constitute the interaction between the soul and the body; whereas really all that we sense or alter in that way is what is within us.

Phil. Here is a problem for you, which "that very ingenious and studious promoter of real knowledge, the learned and worthy Mr Molyneux," sent to the distinguished Mr Locke. This is   136 more or less how he worded it: "Suppose a man born blind, and now adult, and taught by his touch to distinguish between a cube, and a sphere of the same metal, and nighly of the same bigness, so as to tell, when he felt one and t'other, which is the cube, which the sphere. Suppose then the cube and sphere placed on a table, and the blind man to be made to see. *Quaere,* whether by his sight, before he touched them, he could now distinguish, and tell, which is the globe, which the cube." Now, sir, please tell me what your view is about this.

Theo. The question strikes me as a rather interesting one. I would need to spend time thinking about it; but since you urge me to reply at once I will risk saying, just between the two of us, that I believe that if the blind man knows that the two shapes which he sees are those of a cube and a sphere, he will be able to identify them and to say without touching them that this one is the sphere and this the cube.

Phil. I am afraid I have to include you among the many who have given Mr Molyneux the wrong answer. In the letter containing this question he recounts that having, on the occasion of Mr Locke's *Essay,* "proposed this to divers very ingenious men, he hardly ever met with one, that at first gave the answer to it, which he thinks true, [although after] hearing his reasons they were convinced" of their mistake. The answer which this "acute and judicious proposer" gives is negative. For, he says, though this blind man "has obtained the experience of, how a globe, how a cube affects his touch; yet he [does not yet know] that what affects his touch so or so, must affect his sight so or so; or that a protuberant angle in the cube, that pressed his hand unequally, shall appear to his eye, as it does in the cube." The author of the *Essay* declares that he entirely agrees.

Theo. It may be that Mr Molyneux and the author of the *Essay* are not as far from my opinion as at first appears, and that the reasons for their view—contained in Mr Molyneux's letter, it appears, and successfully used by him to convince people of their mistake—have been deliberately suppressed by our author in order to make his readers exercise their minds the harder. If you will just consider my reply, sir, you will see that I have included in it a condition which can be taken to be implicit in the question: namely that it is merely a problem of telling which is which, and that the blind man knows that the two shaped bodies which he has to discern are before him and thus that each of the appearances which he sees is either that of a cube or that of a sphere. Given this condition, it seems to me past question that the blind man whose sight is restored could discern them by applying rational principles to the senso-

137 ry knowledge which he has already acquired by touch. I am not talking about what he might actually do on the spot, when he is dazzled and confused by the strangeness—or, one should add, unaccustomed to making inferences. My view rests on the fact that in the case of the sphere there are no distinguished points on the surface of the sphere taken in itself, since everything there is uniform and without angles, whereas in the case of the cube there are eight points which are distinguished from all the others. If there were not that way of discerning shapes, a blind man could not learn the rudiments of geometry by touch, nor could someone else learn them by sight without touch. However, we find that men born blind are capable of learning geometry, and indeed always have some rudiments of a natural geometry; and we find that geometry is mostly learned by sight alone without employing touch, as could and indeed must be done by a paralytic or by anyone else to whom touch is virtually denied. These two geometries, the blind man's and the paralytic's, must come together, and agree, and indeed ultimately rest on the same ideas, even though they have no images in common. Which shows yet again how essential it is to distinguish *images* from *exact ideas* which are composed of defini-

tions. It would indeed be very interesting and even informative to investigate thoroughly the ideas of someone born blind, and to hear how he would describe shapes. For he could achieve that, and could even understand optical theory in so far as it rests on distinct mathematical ideas, though he would not be able to achieve a conception of the *vivid-confused,* i.e. of the image of light and colours. That is why one man born blind, who had heard lessons in optics and appeared to understand them quite well, when he was asked what he believed light was, replied that he supposed it must be something pleasant like sugar. Similarly, it would be very important to investigate the ideas which a man born deaf and dumb can have about things without shapes: we ordinarily have the description of such things in words, but he would have to have it in an entirely different manner—though it might be equivalent to ours, just as Chinese writing produces an effect equivalent to that of our alphabet although it is utterly different from it and might appear to have been invented by a deaf man. I am indebted to a great Prince for the report of a man in Paris who was born deaf and dumb and whose ears have finally begun to perform their function. He has now learned the French language (the report came from the French court, not long ago), and will be able to tell very interesting things about his conceptions during his previous state and about how his ideas have 138 changed since beginning to exercise his sense of hearing. Men born deaf and dumb can accomplish more than one might think. There was one at Oldenburg, during the time of the last Count, who had become a good painter and also proved himself to be a very intelligent man. A most learned Breton has told me that around 1690 in Blain—a town belonging to the Duke de Rohan, ten leagues from Nantes—there was a poor man, born deaf and dumb, who lived in a hut near the chateau, outside the town; he would carry letters and so on to the town, and would be guided to the right houses by certain signs made to him by people who were used to employing him. Eventually the poor man became blind as well, yet he still made himself useful taking letters to the town, wherever was indicated to him by touch. He had a board in his hut, running from the door to the spot where his feet rested, and the movements of this would announce to him when someone was coming in. Men are very remiss in not informing themselves accurately about how such people think. If he is no longer alive there is likely to be someone on the spot who could still give us some information about him and explain how people indicated to him the tasks he was to carry out.

But to return to the man born blind who begins to see, and to what he would judge about the sphere and the cube when he saw but did not touch them: as I said a moment ago, I reply that he will know which is which if he is told that, of the two appearances or perceptions he has of them, one belongs to the sphere and the other to the cube. But if he is not thus instructed in advance, I grant that it will not at once occur to him that these paintings of them (as it were) that he forms at the back of his eyes, which could come from a flat painting on the table, represent bodies. That will occur to him only when he becomes convinced of it by the sense of touch or when he comes, through applying principles of optics to the light rays, to understand from the evidence of the lights and shadows that there is something blocking the rays and that it must be precisely the same thing that resists his touch. He will eventually come to understand this when he sees the sphere and cube rolling, with consequent changes in their appearances and in the shadows they cast; or when, with the two bodies remaining still, the source of the light falling on them is moved or the position of his eyes changes. For these are pretty much the means that we do have for distinguishing at a distance between a picture or perspective representing an object and the real object.

Phil. §11. Let us return to perception in general. It "puts the distinction betwixt the animal kingdom, and the inferior" beings.

139　　*Theo.* The great analogy which exists between plants and animals inclines me to believe that there is some perception and appetite even in plants; and if there is a vegetative soul, as is generally thought, then it must have perception. All the same, I attribute to mechanism everything which takes place in the bodies of plants and animals except their initial formation. Thus I agree that the movements of what are called "sensitive" plants result from mechanism,[18] and I do not approve of bringing in the soul when plant and animal phenomena have to be explained in detail.

Phil. §§13–14. Indeed, "I cannot but think, there is some small dull perception" even in such animals as oysters and cockles. For "quickness of

sensation [would only] be an inconvenience to an animal, that must lie still, where chance has once placed it; and there receive the afflux of colder or warmer, clean or foul water, as it happens to come to it."

Theo. Very good, and I believe that almost the same could be said about plants. In man's case, however, perceptions are accompanied by the power to reflect, which turns into actual reflection when there are the means for it. But when a man is reduced to a state where it is as though he were in a coma, and where he has almost no feeling, he does lose reflection and awareness, and gives no thought to general truths. Nevertheless, his faculties and dispositions, both innate and acquired, and even the impressions which he receives in this state of confusion, still continue: they are not obliterated though they are forgotten. Some day their turn will come to contribute to some noticeable result; for nothing in nature is useless, all confusion must be resolved, and even the animals, which have sunk into a condition of stupidity, must return at last to perceptions of a higher degree. Since simple substances endure for ever it is wrong to judge of eternity from a few years.

Chapter x　　　　　140

"Of Retention"

Philalethes. §1. "The next faculty of the mind, whereby it makes a farther progress towards knowledge [of things than it does through simple perception],[19] is that which I call retention," or the preserving of those items of knowledge[20] which the mind has received through the senses or through reflection. This is done in two ways: by keeping the idea actually in view, which is called contemplation; and §2. by keeping the power to bring ideas back before the mind, which is what is called memory.

Theophilus. We also retain and contemplate innate knowledge, and very often we cannot distinguish the innate from the acquired. There is also perception of images, both those we have had for some time and those which have newly come into being in us.

Phil. But it is believed by our party that these images or ideas "cease to be any thing, when there is no perception of them, [and that] this laying up of . . . ideas in the repository of the memory, signifies no more but this, that the [soul] has a power, in many cases, to revive perceptions, which it has once had," accompanied by a feeling which convinces it that it has had these sorts of perceptions before.[21]

Theo. If ideas were only the forms or manners of thoughts, they would cease with them; but you yourself have acknowledged, sir, that they are the inner objects of thoughts, and as such they can persist. I am surprised that you can constantly rest content with bare "powers" and "faculties," which you would apparently not accept from the scholastic philosophers. What is needed is a somewhat clearer explanation of what this faculty consists in and how it is exercised: that would show that there are dispositions which are the remains of past impressions, in the soul as well as in the body, but which we are unaware of except when the memory has a use for them. If nothing were left of past thoughts the moment we ceased to think of them, it would be impossible to explain how we could keep the memory of them; to resort to a bare faculty to do the work is to talk unintelligibly.

141

Chapter xi

Of Discerning, or the Faculty of Distinguishing Ideas.[22]

Philalethes. **§1.** On the faculty of "discerning" ideas "depends the evidence and certainty" of various propositions which are taken to be innate truths.

Theophilus. I grant that it requires discernment to think of these innate ideas and to sort them out, but they are no less innate on that account.

Phil. **§2.** Quickness of wit[23] consists in the ready recall of ideas, but there is judgment in setting them out precisely and separating them accurately.

Theo. It may be that each of those is quickness of imagination, and that judgment consists in the scrutiny of propositions in accordance with reason.

Phil. I pretty much agree with this distinction between wit and judgment. And sometimes there is judgment in not over-using judgment. For instance, "it is a kind of an affront [to a witty re-

mark] to go about to examine it, by the severe rules of truth, and good reason."

Theo. That is a good point. Witty thoughts must at least appear to be grounded in reason, but they should not be scrutinized too minutely, just as we ought not to look at a painting from too close. It seems to me that Father Bouhours, in his *Right Thinking in the Exercise of Wit,* has gone wrong on this count more than once; for instance in his scorn for Lucan's epigram: "The winning cause pleased the Gods, but the losing one pleased Cato."

Phil. **§4.** "The comparing them one with another, in respect of extent, degrees, time, place, or any other circumstances, is another operation of the mind about its ideas, and is that upon which depends all that large tribe of ideas, comprehended under relation."

Theo. I take relation to be more general than   142
comparison. Relations divide into those of *comparison* and those of *concurrence.* The former concern *agreement* and *disagreement* (using these terms in a narrower sense), and include resemblance, equality, inequality etc. The latter involve some *connection,* such as that of cause and effect, whole and parts, position and order etc.

Phil. **§6.** The "composition" of simple ideas to make complex ones is another operation of our mind. This may be taken to cover the faculty of "enlarging" ideas by putting together several of the same kind, as in forming a dozen out of several units.

Theo. No doubt one is as much composition as the other, but the composition of like ideas is simpler than that of different ideas.

Phil. **§7.** "A bitch will nurse, play with, and be fond of young foxes, as much as . . . of her puppies, if you can but get them once to suck her so long, that her milk may go through them. And those animals, which have a numerous brood of young ones at once, appear not to have any knowledge of their number."

Theo. The affection of animals arises from a pleasure which is increased by familiarity. But as for precise numbers, even human beings can know the numbers of things only by means of some artifice, such as using numerals for counting, or arranging things in patterns so that it can be seen at a glance, without counting, if one is missing.

Phil. **§10.** The beasts do not make abstractions either.

Theo. That is my view too. They apparently recognize whiteness, and observe it in chalk as in snow; but this does not amount to abstraction, which requires attention to the general apart from the particular, and consequently involves knowledge of universal truths, which beasts do not possess. It is also very well said that beasts which talk do not use speech to express general ideas, and that men who are incapable of speech and of words still make other general signs.[24] I am delighted to see you so well aware, here and elsewhere, of the privileges of human nature.

Phil. **§11.** However, if beasts "have any ideas at all, and are not bare machines (as some would have them) we cannot deny them to have [a certain degree of] reason. It seems as evident to me, that the . . .[25] reason, as that they have sense; but it is only in particular ideas, just as they received them from their senses."

Theo. Beasts pass from one imagining to another by means of a link between them which they have previously experienced. For instance, when his master picks up a stick the dog anticipates being beaten. In many cases children, and for that matter grown men, move from thought to thought in no other way but that. This could be called "inference" or "reasoning" in a very broad sense. But I prefer to keep to accepted usage, reserving these words for men and restricting them to the knowledge of some *reason* for perceptions' being linked together. Mere sensations cannot provide this: all they do is to cause one naturally to expect once more that same linking which has been observed previously, even though the reasons may no longer be the same. Hence those who are guided only by their senses are frequently disappointed.

Phil. **§13.** Imbeciles[26] are lacking in "quickness, activity, and motion, in the intellectual faculties, whereby they are deprived of reason: whereas mad men, . . . seem to suffer by the other extreme. For they do not appear to me to have lost the faculty of reasoning: but having joined together some ideas very wrongly, they mistake them for truths; and they err as men do, that argue right from wrong principles. . . . Thus you shall find a distracted man fancying himself a king, with a right inference, require suitable attendance, respect, and obedience."

Theo. Imbeciles don't exercise reason at all. They differ from the stupid, whose judgment is sound but who are looked down on and are a nuisance because they are so slow to grasp things—as someone would be who insisted on playing cards with important people and then spent too long, too often, deciding how to play his hand. I recall that an able man who had lost his memory through using certain drugs was reduced to that condition, but his judgment continued to be evident. A complete madman lacks judgment in almost every situation, yet the quickness of his imagination can make him entertaining. But there are people who are selectively mad: they acquire a false conviction about some important aspect of their lives and then reason correctly from it, as you have rightly pointed out. A man of this kind is well known at a certain court; he believes that he is destined to re-establish the Protestants and to put France to rights, and that to this end God has caused the most eminent personages to pass through his body in order to ennoble it. He seeks to marry all the marriageable princesses that he meets, but only after having sanctified them, in order to establish a holy lineage to govern the earth. He blames all the miseries of the war on the lack of respect paid to his counsels. When he speaks to a sovereign he takes all necessary measures to preserve his dignity. And when anyone engages in reasoning with him he defends himself so skillfully that more than once I have suspected that he is only feigning madness, since he does very well out of it. However, those who know him more intimately assure me that it is quite genuine.

Phil. **§17.** "The understanding is not much unlike a closet wholly shut from light, with only some little openings left, to let in external visible [images];[27] would the [images][28] coming into such a dark room but stay there, and lie so orderly as to be found upon occasion, it would very much resemble the understanding of a man."

Theo. To increase the resemblance we should have to postulate that there is a screen in this dark room to receive the species,[29] and that it is not uniform but is diversified by folds representing items of innate knowledge; and, what is more, that this screen or membrane, being under tension, has a kind of elasticity or active force, and indeed that it acts (or reacts) in ways which are adapted both to past folds and to new ones coming from impressions of the species. This action would consist in certain vibrations or oscillations, like those we see when a cord under tension is plucked and gives off something of a musical sound. For not only do we receive images and traces in the brain, but we form new ones from them when we bring "complex ideas" to mind; and so the screen which represents our brain must be active and elastic. This analogy would explain reasonably well what goes on in the brain. As for the soul, which is a simple substance or 'monad': without being extended it represents these various extended masses and has perceptions of them.

NOTES

1. "*excite ou détermine plutôt.*"
2. Locke: 'Preserver of things, who never'. Coste's expansion.
3. Locke: "sensible of it." Coste's change.
4. Added by Leibniz.
5. Locke: 'is'. Coste's change.
6. Added by Leibniz.
7. Added by Leibniz.
8. Locke: "complex." Coste's change.
9. Locke: "idea."
10. Leibniz's "*répugnance*" could mean either "reluctance" or "logical impossibility," but the latter does not fit the context. There are other indications, too, that Leibniz wants this passage to have an anthropomorphic tone.
11. Added by Leibniz, as is the following parenthetical phrase.
12. Added by Leibniz.
13. Locke: "which convey themselves into."
14. The content of this paragraph was dropped after the third edition of the *Essay,* but retained by Coste.

15. This refers to Locke's §16.
16. Locke: "it takes no notice." Coste: "*il ne s'aperçoit en aucune manière.*"
17. Locke: "the judgment . . . alters the appearances into their causes." Coste: "*nous mettons . . . à la place de ce qui nous paraît, la cause même de l'image . . . joignant à la vision un jugement que nous confondons avec elle.*" The clause "*joignant . . . elle,*" which may be based on Locke's §9, is contracted by Leibniz to "*et confondons le jugement avec la vision.*"
18. Locke says this in § 11.
19. Added by Coste.
20. Locke: "those simple ideas."
21. Locke: "with this additional perception annexed to them, that it has had them before." Coste's change.
22. Locke: "Of discerning, and other operations of the mind."
23. "*esprit,*" which means both "wit" and "mind." Locke in §2 is contrasting "judgment" with "wit."
24. Presumably referring to Locke's §11, though that speaks of beasts which can "pronounce words distinctly enough," not of ones which can "talk."
25. Locke: "do some of them in certain instances." Coste's omission.
26. Locke uses the now obsolete word "naturals."
27. Locke: "resemblances." Coste's change.
28. Locke: "pictures." Coste's change.
29. "*espèces*"—i.e. the "sensible species" which Leibniz declares to be tolerable when understood as here.

9

DAVID HUME

David Hume (1711–1776) set himself the unreasonable goal of producing for philosophy what Sir Issac Newton had articulated for physics—a clear, unifying set of laws with predictive power. *A Treatise of Human Nature,* the product of a four-year retreat in France following college at the University of Edinburgh, was not well received; so Hume needed to find an alternative source of funds. He was considered for a position in moral philosophy at Edinburgh, but the skepticism about God in his *Treatise* made Hume an unacceptable and unsuccessful candidate. Following a series of odd jobs appropriate for the younger son of a Scottish laird, Hume traveled with General James St. Clair to the courts of Vienna and Turin during 1748–49. In 1752, he accepted the position of keeper of the Advocates' Library in his beloved Edinburgh. Hume's access to this amazing collection of documents culminated in his *History of England,* an immense chronicle of detailed narrative from Caesar to 1688, in six volumes. In addition to the scale and scope of this work, Hume had written a substantially more readable history than any preceding author, which led to fame, fortune, and the Roman Catholic Church placing all his writings on its *Index* of forbidden books in 1761. In 1763, Hume joined the British embassy in Paris and found, to his surprise, acceptance by the elite and enjoyment in Parisian society and salons. He returned to Edinburgh in 1769 and spent his time in conversation with friends, including economist Adam Smith, author of *The Wealth of Nations,* and revising his various texts. There he died after a long, debilitating illness, but to the final moments of his life, he remained the decent, caring, cheerful, and profoundly skeptical man admired and loved by many.

AN INQUIRY CONCERNING HUMAN UNDERSTANDING

SECTION II

Of the Origin of Ideas

Everyone will readily allow that there is a considerable difference between the perceptions of the mind when a man feels the pain of excessive heat or the pleasure of moderate warmth, and when he afterwards recalls to his memory this sensation or anticipates it by his imagination. These faculties may mimic or copy the perceptions of the senses, but they never can entirely reach the force and vivacity of the original sentiment. The utmost we say of them, even when they operate with greatest vigor, is that they represent their object in so lively a manner that we could *almost* say we feel or see it. But, except the mind be disordered by disease or madness, they never can arrive at such a pitch of vivacity as to render these perceptions altogether undistinguishable. All the colors of poetry, however splendid, can never paint natural objects in such a manner as to make the description be taken for a real landscape. The most lively thought is still inferior to the dullest sensation.

We may observe a like distinction to run through all the other perceptions of the mind. A man in a fit of anger is actuated in a very different manner from one who only thinks of that emotion. If you tell me that any person is in love, I easily understand your meaning and

form a just conception of his situation, but never can mistake that conception for the real disorders and agitations of the passion. When we reflect on our past sentiments and affections, our thought is a faithful mirror and copies its objects truly, but the colors which it employs are faint and dull in comparison of those in which our original perceptions were clothed. It requires no nice discernment or metaphysical head to mark the distinction between them.

Here, therefore, we may divide all the perceptions of the mind into two classes or species, which are distinguished by their different degrees of force and vivacity. The less forcible and lively are commonly denominated "thoughts" or "ideas." The other species want a name in our language, and in most others; I suppose, because it was not requisite for any but philosophical purposes to rank them under a general term or appellation. Let us, therefore, use a little freedom and call them "impressions," employing that word in a sense somewhat different from the usual. By the term "impression," then, I mean all our more lively perceptions, when we hear, or see, or feel, or love, or hate, or desire, or will. And impressions are distinguished from ideas, which are the less lively perceptions of which we are conscious when we reflect on any of those sensations or movements above mentioned.

Nothing, at first view, may seem more unbounded

From David Hume, "Of the Origin of Ideas. Of the Association of Ideas. Of the Idea of Necessary Connection." In C. W. Hendel (Ed.), *An Inquiry Concerning Human Understanding* (pp. 26–39, 72–89). New York: Macmillan, 1987. (Original work published 1748) than the thought of man, which not only escapes all human power and authority, but is not even restrained within the limits of nature and reality. To form monsters and join incongruous shapes and appearances costs the imagination no more trouble than to conceive the most natural and familiar objects. And while the body is confined to one planet, along which it creeps with pain and difficulty, the thought can in an instant transport us into the most distant regions of the universe, or even beyond the universe into the unbounded chaos where nature is supposed to lie in total confusion. What never was seen or heard of, may yet be conceived, nor is anything beyond the power of thought except what implies an absolute contradiction.

But though our thought seems to possess this unbounded liberty, we shall find upon a nearer examination that it is really confined within very narrow limits, and that all this creative power of the mind amounts to no more than the faculty of compounding, transposing, augmenting, or diminishing the materials afforded us by the senses and experience. When we think of a golden mountain, we only join two consistent ideas, "gold" and "mountain," with which we were formerly acquainted. A virtuous horse we can conceive, because, from our own feeling, we can conceive virtue; and this we may unite to the figure and shape of a horse, which is an animal familiar to us. In short, all the materials of thinking are derived either from our outward or inward sentiment; the mixture and composition of these belongs alone to the mind and will, or, to express myself in philosophical language, all our ideas or more feeble perceptions are copies of our impressions or more lively ones.

To prove this, the two following arguments will, I hope, be sufficient. *First,* when we analyze our thoughts or ideas, however compounded or sublime, we always find that they resolve themselves into such simple ideas as were copied from a precedent feeling or sentiment. Even those ideas which at first view seem the most wide of this origin are found, upon a nearer scrutiny, to be derived from it. The idea of God, as meaning an infinitely intelligent, wise, and good Being, arises from reflecting on the operations of our own mind and augmenting, without limit, those qualities of goodness and wisdom. We may prosecute this inquiry to what length we please; where we shall always find that every idea which we examine is copied from a similar impression. Those who would assert that this position is not universally true, nor without exception, have only one, and that an easy, method of refuting it by producing that idea which, in their opinion, is not derived from this source. It will then

be incumbent on us, if we would maintain our doctrine, to produce the impression or lively perception which corresponds to it.

Secondly, if it happen, from a defect of the organ, that a man is not susceptible of any species of sensation, we always find that he is as little susceptible of the correspondent idea. A blind man can form no notion of colors, a deaf man of sounds. Restore either of them that sense in which he is deficient by opening this new inlet for his sensations, you also open an inlet for the ideas, and he finds no difficulty in conceiving these objects. The case is the same if the object proper for exciting any sensation has never been applied to the organ. A Laplander or Negro has no notion of the relish of wine. And though there are few or no instances of a like deficiency in the mind where a person has never felt or is wholly incapable of a sentiment or passion that belongs to his species, yet we find the same observation to take place in a less degree. A man of mild manners can form no idea of inveterate revenge or cruelty, nor can a selfish heart easily conceive the heights of friendship and generosity. It is readily allowed that other beings may possess many senses of which we can have no conception, because the ideas of them have never been introduced to us in the only manner by which an idea can have access to the mind, to wit, by the actual feeling and sensation.

There is, however, one contradictory phenomenon which may prove that it is not absolutely impossible for ideas to arise independent of their correspondent impressions. I believe it will readily be allowed that the several distinct ideas of color, which enter by the eye, or those of sound, which are conveyed by the ear, are really different from each other, though at the same time resembling. Now, if this be true of different colors, it must be no less so of the different shades of the same color; and each shade produces a distinct idea, independent of the rest. For if this should be denied, it is possible, by the continual gradation of shades, to run a color insensibly into what is most remote from it; and if you will not allow any of the means to be different, you cannot, without absurdity, deny the extremes to be the same. Suppose, therefore, a person to have enjoyed his sight for thirty years and to have become perfectly acquainted with colors of all kinds, except one particular shade of blue, for instance, which it never has been his fortune to meet with; let all the different shades of that color, except that single one, be placed before him, descending gradually from the deepest to the lightest, it is plain that he will perceive a blank where that shade is wanting, and will be sensible that there is a greater distance in that place between the contiguous colors than in any other. Now I ask whether it be possible for him, from his own imagination, to supply this deficiency and raise up to himself the idea of that particular shade, though it had never been conveyed to him by his senses? I believe there are few but will be of opinion that he can; and this may serve as a proof that the simple ideas are not always, in every instance, derived from the correspondent impressions, though this instance is so singular that it is scarcely worth our observing, and does not merit that for it alone we should alter our general maxim.

Here, therefore, is a proposition which not only seems in itself simple and intelligible, but, if a proper use were made of it, might render every dispute equally intelligible, and banish all that jargon which has so long taken possession of metaphysical reasonings and drawn disgrace upon them. All ideas, especially abstract ones, are naturally faint and obscure. The mind has but a slender hold of them. They are apt to be confounded with other resembling ideas; and when we have often employed any term, though without a distinct meaning, we are apt to imagine it has a determinate idea annexed to it. On the contrary, all impressions, that is, all sensations either outward or inward, are strong and vivid. The limits between them are more exactly determined, nor is it easy to fall into any error or mistake with regard to them. When we entertain, therefore, any suspicion that a philosophical term is employed without any meaning or idea (as is but too frequent), we need but inquire, *from what impression is that supposed idea derived?* And if it be impossible to assign any, this will serve to confirm our suspicion. By bringing ideas in so clear a light, we may reasonably hope to remove all dispute which may arise concerning their nature and reality.[1]

SECTION III

Of the Association[2] of Ideas

It is evident that there is a principle of connection between the different thoughts or ideas of the mind, and that, in their appearance to the memory or imagination, they introduce each other with a certain degree of method and regularity. In our more serious thinking or discourse this is so observable that any particular thought which breaks in upon the regular tract or chain of ideas is immediately remarked and rejected. And even in our wildest and most wandering reveries, nay, in our very dreams, we shall find, if we reflect, that the imagination ran not altogether at adventures, but that there was still a connection upheld among the different ideas which succeeded each other. Were the loosest and freest conversation to be transcribed, there would immediately be observed something which connected it in all its transitions. Or where this is wanting, the person who broke the thread of discourse might still inform you that there had secretly revolved in his mind a succession of thought which had gradually led him from the subject of conversation. Among different languages, even when we cannot suspect the least connection or communication, it is found that the words expressive of ideas the most compounded do yet nearly correspond to each other—a certain proof that the simple ideas comprehended in the compound ones were bound together by some universal principle which had an equal influence on all mankind.

Though it be too obvious to escape observation that different ideas are connected together, I do not find that any philosopher has attempted to enumerate or class all the principles of association—a subject, however, that seems worthy of curiosity. To me there appear to be only three principles of connection among ideas, namely, *Resemblance, Contiguity* in time or place, and *Cause* or *Effect.*

That these principles serve to connect ideas will not, I believe, be much doubted. A picture naturally leads our thoughts to the original.[3] The mention of one apartment in a building naturally introduces an inquiry or discourse concerning the others;[4] and if we think of a wound, we can scarcely forbear reflecting on the pain which follows it.[5] But that this enumeration is complete, and that there are no other principles of association except these, may be difficult to prove to the satisfaction of the reader or even to a man's own satisfaction. All we can do, in such cases, is to run over several instances and examine carefully the principle which binds the different thoughts to each other, never stopping till we render the principle as general as possible.[6] The more instances we examine and the more care we employ, the more assurance shall we acquire that the enumeration which we form from the whole is complete and entire.

This Section, as it stands in Editions K, L, and N, thus continues:

Instead of entering into a detail of this kind, which would lead us into many useless subtilties, we shall consider some of the effects of this connection upon the passions and imagination; where we may open up a field of speculation more entertaining, and perhaps more instructive, than the other.

As man is a reasonable being and is continually in pursuit of happiness, which he hopes to find in the gratification of some passion or affection, he seldom acts or speaks or thinks without a purpose and intention. He has still some object in view; and however improper the means may sometimes be which he chooses for the attainment of his end, he never loses view of an end, nor will he so much as throw away his thoughts or reflections where he hopes not to reap any satisfaction from them.

In all compositions of genius, therefore, it is requisite that the writer have some plan or object; and though he may be hurried from this plan by the vehemence of thought, as in an ode, or drop it carelessly, as in an epistle or essay, there must appear some aim or intention in his first setting out, if not in the composition of the whole work. A production without a design would resemble more the ravings of a madman than the sober efforts of genius and learning.

As this rule admits of no exception, it follows that in narrative compositions the events or actions which the writer relates must be connected together by some bond or tie: They must be related to each other in the imagination, and form a kind of *unity* which may bring them under one plan or view, and which may be the object or end of the writer in his first undertaking.

This connecting principle among the several events which form the subject of a poem or history may be very different according to the different designs of the poet or historian. Ovid has formed his plan upon the connecting principle of resemblance. Every fabulous transformation produced by the miraculous power of the gods falls within the compass of his work. There needs but this one circumstance, in any event, to bring it under his original plan or intention.

An annalist or historian who should undertake to write the history of Europe during any century would be influenced by the connection of contiguity in time or place. All events which happen in that portion of space and period of time are comprehended in his design, though in other respects different and unconnected. They have still a species of unity amidst all their diversity.

But the most usual species of connection among the different events which enter into any narrative composition is that of cause and effect; while the historian traces the series of actions according to their natural order, remounts to their secret springs and principles, and delineates their most remote consequences. He chooses for his subject a certain portion of that great chain of events which compose the history of mankind: each link in this chain he endeavors to touch in his narration; sometimes unavoidable ignorance renders all his attempts fruitless; sometimes he supplies by conjecture what is wanting in

knowledge; and always he is sensible that the more unbroken the chain is which he presents to his readers, the more perfect is his production. He sees that the knowledge of causes is not only the most satisfactory, this relation or connection being the strongest of all others, but also the most instructive; since it is by this knowledge alone we are enabled to control events and govern futurity.

Here, therefore, we may attain some notion of that *unity* of *action* about which all critics after Aristotle have talked so much, perhaps to little purpose, while they directed not their taste or sentiment by the accuracy of philosophy. It appears that in all productions, as well as in the epic and tragic, there is a certain unity required, and that on no occasion our thoughts can be allowed to run at adventures if we would produce a work that will give any lasting entertainment to mankind. It appears, also, that even a biographer who should write the life of Achilles would connect the events by showing their mutual dependence and relation, as much as a poet who should make the anger of that hero the subject of his narration.[7] Not only in any limited portion of life a man's actions have a dependence on each other, but also during the whole period of his duration from the cradle to the grave; nor is it possible to strike off one link, however minute, in this regular chain without affecting the whole series of events which follow. The unity of action, therefore, which is to be found in biography or history differs from that of epic poetry, not in kind, but in degree. In epic poetry, the connection among the events is more close and sensible; the narration is not carried on through such a length of time; and the actors hasten to some remarkable period which satisfies the curiosity of the reader. This conduct of the epic poet depends on that particular situation of the imagination and of the passions which is supposed in that production. The imagination both of writer and reader is more enlivened, and the passions more inflamed than in history, biography, or any species of narration that confine themselves to strict truth and reality. Let us consider the effect of these two circumstances of an enlivened imagination and inflamed passions which belong to poetry, especially the epic kind, above any other species of composition; and let us see for what reason they require a stricter and closer unity in the fable.

First, all poetry, being a species of painting, approaches us nearer to the objects than any other species of narration, throws a stronger light upon them, and delineates more distinctly those minute circumstances which, though to the historian they seem superfluous, serve mightily to enliven the imagery and gratify the fancy. If it be not necessary, as in the *Iliad,* to inform us each time the hero buckles his shoes and ties his garters, it will be requisite, perhaps, to enter into a greater detail than in the *Henriade,* where the events are run over with such rapidity that we scarce have leisure to become acquainted with the scene or action. Were a poet, therefore, to comprehend in his subject any great compass of time or series of events, and trace up the death of Hector to its remote causes in the rape of Helen or the judgment of Paris, he must draw out his poem to an immeasurable length in order to fill this large canvas with just painting and imagery. The reader's imagination, inflamed with such a series of poetical descriptions, and his passions, agitated by a continual sympathy with the actors, must flag long before the period of narration and must sink into lassitude and disgust from the repeated violence of the same movements.

Secondly, that an epic poet must not trace the causes to any great distance will further appear if we consider another reason, which is drawn from a property of the passions still more remarkable and singular. It is evident that in a just composition all the affections excited by the different events described and represented add mutual force to each other; and that, while the heroes are all engaged in one common scene, and each action is strongly connected with the whole, the concern is continually awake, and the passions make an easy transition from one object to another. The strong connection of the events, as it facilitates the passage of the thought or imagination from one to another, facilitates also the transfusion of the passions and preserves the affection still in the same channel and direction. Our sympathy and concern for Eve prepares the way for a like sympathy with Adam: the affection is preserved almost entire in the transition, and the mind seizes immediately the new object as strongly related to that which formerly engaged its attention. But were the poet to make a total digression from his subject and introduce a new actor no way connected with the personages, the imagination, feeling a breach in the transition, would enter coldly into the new scene; would kindle by slow degrees; and in returning to the main subject of the poem would pass, as it were, upon foreign ground and have its concern to excite anew in order to take party with the principal actors. The same inconvenience follows in a lesser degree where the poet traces his events to too great a distance and binds together actions which, though not altogether disjoined, have not so strong a connection as is requisite to forward the transition of the passions. Hence arises the artifice of oblique narration employed in the *Odyssey* and *Æneid*—where the hero is introduced, at first,

near the period of his designs, and afterwards shows us, as it were in perspective, the more distant events and causes. By this means, the reader's curiosity is immediately excited; the events follow with rapidity, and in a very close connection; and the concern is preserved alive, and continually increases by means of the near relation of the objects, from the beginning to the end of the narration.

The same rule takes place in dramatic poetry; nor is it ever permitted in a regular composition to introduce an actor who has no connection, or but a small one, with the principal personages of the fable. The spectator's concern must not be diverted by any scenes disjoined and separated from the rest. This breaks the course of the passions, and prevents that communication of the several emotions by which one scene adds force to another, and transfuses the pity and terror which it excites upon each succeeding scene until the whole produces that rapidity of movement which is peculiar to the theater. How must it extinguish this warmth of affection to be entertained on a sudden with a new action and new personages no way related to the former; to find so sensible a breach or vacuity in the course of the passions, by means of this breach in the connection of ideas; and instead of carrying the sympathy of one scene into the following, to be obliged every moment to excite a new concern, and take party in a new scene of action?

But though this rule of unity of action be common to dramatic and epic poetry, we may still observe a difference betwixt them which may, perhaps, deserve our attention. In both these species of composition it is requisite the action be one and simple, in order to preserve the concern or sympathy entire and undiverted: but in epic or narrative poetry, this rule is also established upon another foundation, viz., the necessity that is incumbent on every writer to form some plan or design before he enter on any discourse or narration, and to comprehend his subject in some general aspect or united view which may be the constant object of his attention. As the author is entirely lost in dramatic compositions, and the spectator supposes himself to be really present at the actions represented, this reason has no place with regard to the stage; but any dialogue or conversation may be introduced which, without improbability, might have passed in that determinate portion of space represented by the theater. Hence, in all our English comedies, even those of Congreve, the unity of action is never strictly observed; but the poet thinks it sufficient if his personages be any way related to each other by blood, or by living in the same family; and he afterwards introduces them in particular scenes, where they display their humors and characters without much forwarding the main action. The double plots of Terence are licenses of the same kind, but in a lesser degree. And though this conduct be not perfectly regular, it is not wholly unsuitable to the nature of comedy, where the movements and passions are not raised to such a height as in tragedy; at the same time that the fiction or representation palliates, in some degree, such licenses. In a narrative poem, the first proposition or design confines the author to one subject; and any digressions of this nature would, at first view, be rejected as absurd and monstrous. Neither Boccace, La Fontaine, nor any author of that kind, though pleasantry be their chief object, have ever indulged them.

To return to the comparison of history and epic poetry, we may conclude from the foregoing reasonings that as a certain unity is requisite in all productions, it cannot be wanting to history more than to any other; that in history the connection among the several events which unites them into one body is the relation of cause and effect, the same which takes place in epic poetry; and that, in the latter composition, this connection is only required to be closer and more sensible on account of the lively imagination and strong passions which must be touched by the poet in his narration. The Peloponnesian war is a proper subject for history, the siege of Athens for an epic poem, and the death of Alcibiades for a tragedy.

As the difference, therefore, betwixt history and epic poetry consists only in the degrees of connection which bind together those several events of which their subject is composed, it will be difficult, if not impossible, by words to determine exactly the bounds which separate them from each other. That is a matter of taste more than of reasoning; and perhaps this unity may often be discovered in a subject where, at first view, and from an abstract consideration, we should least expect to find it.

It is evident that Homer, in the course of his narration, exceeds the first proposition of his subject; and that the anger of Achilles, which caused the death of Hector, is not the same with that which produced so many ills to the Greeks. But the strong connection betwixt these two movements, the quick transition from one to the other, the contrast betwixt the effects of concord and discord amongst the princes, and the natural curiosity we have to see Achilles in action after so long repose—all these causes carry on the reader, and produce a sufficient unity in the subject.

It may be objected to Milton that he has traced up his causes to too great a distance, and that the rebellion of the angels produces the fall of man by a train of events which is both very long and very casual. Not to mention that the creation of the world, which he has related at

length, is no more the cause of that catastrophe than of the battle of Pharsalia, or any other event that has ever happened. But if we consider, on the other hand, that all these events, the rebellion of the angels, the creation of the world, and the fall of man, *resemble* each other in being miraculous, and out of the common course of nature; that they are supposed to be *contiguous* in time; and that, being detached from all other events, and being the only original facts which revelation discovers, they strike the eye at once, and naturally recall each other to the thought or imagination—if we consider all these circumstances, I say, we shall find that these parts of the action have a sufficient unity to make them be comprehended in one fable or narration. To which we may add that the rebellion of the angels and the fall of man have a peculiar resemblance, as being counterparts to each other, and presenting to the reader the same moral of obedience to our Creator.

These loose hints I have thrown together in order to excite the curiosity of philosophers, and beget a suspicion at least if not a full persuasion that this subject is very copious, and that many operations of the human mind depend on the connection or association of ideas which is here explained. Particularly, the sympathy betwixt the passions and imagination will, perhaps, appear remarkable; while we observe that the affections, excited by one object, pass easily to another connected with it, but transfuse themselves with difficulty, or not at all, along different objects which have no manner of connection together. By introducing into any composition personages and actions foreign to each other, an injudicious author loses that communication of emotions by which alone he can interest the heart and raise the passions to their proper height and period. The full explication of this principle and all its consequences would lead us into reasonings too profound and too copious for these Essays. It is sufficient for us, at present, to have established this conclusion, that the three connecting principles of all ideas are the relations of *resemblance, contiguity,* and *causation.*

SECTION VII

Of the Idea of Necessary Connection[8]

Part I

The great advantage of the mathematical sciences above the moral consists in this, that the ideas of the former, being sensible, are always clear and determinate, the smallest distinction between them is immediately perceptible, and the same terms are still expressive of the same ideas without ambiguity or variation. An oval is never mistaken for a circle, nor a hyperbola for an ellipsis. The isosceles and scalenum are distinguished by boundaries more exact than vice and virtue, right and wrong. If any term be defined in geometry, the mind readily, of itself, substitutes on all occasions the definition for the term defined, or, even when no definition is employed, the object itself may be presented to the senses and by that means be steadily and clearly apprehended. But the finer sentiments of the mind, the operations of the understanding, the various agitations of the passions, though really in themselves distinct, easily escape us when surveyed by reflection, nor is it in our power to recall the original object as often as we have occasion to contemplate it. Ambiguity, by this means, is gradually introduced into our reasonings: similar objects are readily taken to be the same, and the conclusion becomes at last very wide of the premises.

One may safely, however, affirm that if we consider these sciences in a proper light, their advantages and disadvantages nearly compensate each other and reduce both of them to a state of equality. If the mind, with greater facility, retains the ideas of geometry clear and determinate, it must carry on a much longer and more intricate chain of reasoning and compare ideas much wider of each other in order to reach the abstruser truths of that science. And if moral ideas are apt, without extreme care, to fall into obscurity and confusion, the inferences are always much shorter in these disquisitions, and the intermediate steps which lead to the conclusion much fewer than in the sciences which treat of quantity and number. In reality, there is scarcely a proposition in Euclid so simple as not to consist of more parts than are to be found in any moral reasoning which runs not into chimera and conceit. Where we trace the principles of the human mind through a few steps, we may be very well satisfied with our progress, considering how soon nature throws a bar to all our inquiries concerning causes and reduces us to an acknowledgment of our ignorance. The chief obstacle, therefore, to our improvement in the moral or metaphysical sciences is the obscurity of the ideas and ambiguity of the terms. The principal difficulty in the mathematics is the length of inferences and compass of thought requisite to the forming of any conclusion. And, perhaps, our progress in natural philosophy is chiefly retarded by the want of proper experiments and phenomena, which are often discovered by chance and cannot always be found when requisite, even by the most diligent and prudent inquiry. As moral

philosophy seems hitherto to have received less improvement than either geometry or physics, we may conclude that if there be any difference in this respect among these sciences, the difficulties which obstruct the progress of the former require superior care and capacity to be surmounted.

There are no ideas which occur in metaphysics more obscure and uncertain than those of "power," "force," "energy," or "necessary connection," of which it is every moment necessary for us to treat in all our disquisitions. We shall, therefore, endeavor in this Section to fix, if possible, the precise meaning of these terms and thereby remove some part of that obscurity which is so much complained of in this species of philosophy.

It seems a proposition which will not admit of much dispute that all our ideas are nothing but copies of our impressions, or, in other words, that it is impossible for us to *think* of anything which we have not antecedently *felt,* either by our external or internal senses. I have endeavored[9] to explain and prove this proposition, and have expressed my hopes that by a proper application of it men may reach a greater clearness and precision in philosophical reasonings than what they have hitherto been able to attain. Complex ideas may, perhaps, be well known by definition, which is nothing but an enumeration of those parts or simple ideas that compose them. But when we have pushed up definitions to the most simple ideas and find still some ambiguity and obscurity, what resources are we then possessed of? By what invention can we throw light upon these ideas and render them altogether precise and determinate to our intellectual view? Produce the impressions or original sentiments from which the ideas are copied. These impressions are all strong and sensible. They admit not of ambiguity. They are not only placed in a full light themselves, but may throw light on their correspondent ideas, which lie in obscurity. And by this means we may perhaps obtain a new microscope or species of optics by which, in the moral sciences, the most minute and most simple ideas may be so enlarged as to fall readily under our apprehension and be equally known with the grossest and most sensible ideas that can be the object of our inquiry.

To be fully acquainted, therefore, with the idea of power or necessary connection, let us examine its impression and, in order to find the impression with greater certainty, let us search for it in all the sources from which it may possibly be derived.

When we look about us toward external objects and consider the operation of causes, we are never able, in a single instance, to discover any power or necessary connection, any quality which binds the effect to the cause and renders the one an infallible consequence of the other. We only find that the one does actually in fact follow the other. The impulse of one billiard ball is attended with motion in the second. This is the whole that appears to the *outward* senses. The mind feels no sentiment or *inward* impression from this succession of objects; consequently, there is not, in any single particular instance of cause and effect, anything which can suggest the idea of power or necessary connection.

From the first appearance of an object we never can conjecture what effect will result from it. But were the power or energy of any cause discoverable by the mind, we could foresee the effect, even without experience, and might, at first, pronounce with certainty concerning it by the mere dint of thought and reasoning.

In reality, there is no part of matter that does ever, by its sensible qualities, discover any power or energy, or give us ground to imagine that it could produce anything, or be followed by any other object, which we could denominate its effect. Solidity, extension, motion—these qualities are all complete in themselves and never point out any other event which may result from them. The scenes of the universe are continually shifting, and one object follows another in an uninterrupted succession; but the power or force which actuates the whole machine is entirely concealed from us and never discovers itself in any of the sensible qualities of body. We know that, in fact, heat is a constant attendant of flame; but what is the connection between them we have no room so much as to conjecture or imagine. It is impossible, therefore, that the idea of power can be derived from the contemplation of bodies in single instances of their operation, because no bodies ever discover any power which can be the original of this idea.[10]

Since, therefore, external objects as they appear to the senses give us no idea of power or necessary connection by their operation in particular instances, let us see whether this idea be derived from reflection on the operations of our own minds and be copied from any internal impression. It may be said that we are every moment conscious of internal power while we feel that, by the simple command of our will, we can move the organs of our body or direct the faculties of our mind. An act of volition produces motion in our limbs or raises a new idea in our imagination. This influence of the will we know by consciousness. Hence we acquire the idea of power or energy, and are certain that we ourselves and all other intelligent beings are possessed of power.[11] This idea, then, is an idea of reflection since it arises from reflecting on the operations of our own mind and

on the command which is exercised by will both over the organs of the body and faculties of the soul.[12]

We shall proceed to examine this pretension[13] and, first, with regard to the influence of volition over the organs of the body. This influence, we may observe, is a fact which, like all other natural events, can be known only by experience, and can never be foreseen from any apparent energy or power in the cause which connects it with the effect and renders the one an infallible consequence of the other. The motion of our body follows upon the command of our will. Of this we are every moment conscious. But the means by which this is effected, the energy by which the will performs so extraordinary an operation—of this we are so far from being immediately conscious that it must forever escape our most diligent inquiry.

For, *first,* is there any principle in all nature more mysterious than the union of soul with body, by which a supposed spiritual substance acquires such an influence over a material one that the most refined thought is able to actuate the grossest matter? Were we empowered by a secret wish to remove mountains or control the planets in their orbit, this extensive authority would not be more extraordinary, nor more beyond our comprehension. But if, by consciousness, we perceived any power or energy in the will, we must know this power; we must know its connection with the effect; we must know the secret union of soul and body, and the nature of both these substances by which the one is able to operate in so many instances upon the other.

Secondly, we are not able to move all the organs of the body with a like authority, though we cannot assign any reason, besides experience, for so remarkable a difference between one and the other. Why has the will an influence over the tongue and fingers, not over the heart or liver? This question would never embarrass us were we conscious of a power in the former case, not in the latter. We should then perceive, independent of experience, why the authority of the will over the organs of the body is circumscribed within such particular limits. Being in that case fully acquainted with the power or force by which it operates, we should also know why its influence reaches precisely to such boundaries, and no further.

A man suddenly struck with a palsy in the leg or arm, or who had newly lost those members, frequently endeavors, at first, to move them and employ them in their usual offices. Here he is as much conscious of power to command such limbs as a man in perfect health is conscious of power to actuate any member which remains in its natural state and condition. But consciousness never deceives. Consequently, neither in the one case nor in the other are we ever conscious of any power. We learn the influence of our will from experience alone. And experience only teaches us how one event constantly follows another, without instructing us in the secret connection which binds them together and renders them inseparable.

Thirdly, we learn from anatomy that the immediate object of power in voluntary motion is not the member itself which is moved, but certain muscles and nerves and animal spirits, and, perhaps, something still more minute and more unknown, through which the motion is successively propagated ere it reach the member itself whose motion is the immediate object of volition. Can there be a more certain proof that the power by which this whole operation is performed, so far from being directly and fully known by an inward sentiment or consciousness, is to the last degree mysterious and unintelligible? Here the mind wills a certain event; immediately another event, unknown to ourselves and totally different from the one intended, is produced. This event produces another, equally unknown, till, at last, through a long succession the desired event is produced. But if the original power were felt, it must be known; were it known, its effect must also be known, since all power is relative to its effect. And, *vice versa,* if the effect be not known, the power cannot be known nor felt. How indeed can we be conscious of a power to move our limbs when we have no such power, but only that to move certain animal spirits which, though they produce at last the motion of our limbs, yet operate in such a manner as is wholly beyond our comprehension?

We may therefore conclude from the whole, I hope, without any temerity, though with assurance, that our idea of power is not copied from any sentiment or consciousness of power within ourselves when we give rise to animal motion or apply our limbs to their proper use and office. That their motion follows the command of the will is a matter of common experience, like other natural events; but the power or energy by which this is effected, like that in other natural events, is unknown and inconceivable.[14]

Shall we then assert that we are conscious of a power or energy in our own minds when, by an act or command of our will, we raise up a new idea, fix the mind to the contemplation of it, turn it on all sides, and at last dismiss it for some other idea when we think that we have surveyed it with sufficient accuracy? I believe the same arguments will prove that even this command of the will gives us no real idea of force or energy.

First, it must be allowed that when we know a power, we know that very circumstance in the cause by which it is enabled to produce the effect, for these are supposed to be synonymous. We must, therefore, know both the cause and effect and the relation between them. But do we pretend to be acquainted with the nature of the human soul and the nature of an idea, or the aptitude of the one to produce the other? This is a real creation, a production of something out of nothing, which implies a power so great that it may seem, at first sight, beyond the reach of any being less than infinite. At least it must be owned that such a power is not felt, nor known, nor even conceivable by the mind. We only feel the event, namely, the existence of an idea consequent to a command of the will; but the manner in which this operation is performed, the power by which it is produced, is entirely beyond our comprehension.

Secondly, the command of the mind over itself is limited, as well as its command over the body; and these limits are not known by reason or any acquaintance with the nature of cause and effect, but only by experience and observation, as in all other natural events and in the operation of external objects. Our authority over our sentiments and passions is much weaker than that over our ideas; and even the latter authority is circumscribed within very narrow boundaries. Will anyone pretend to assign the ultimate reason of these boundaries, or show why the power is deficient in one case, not in another?

Thirdly, this self-command is very different at different times. A man in health possesses more of it than one languishing with sickness. We are more master of our thoughts in the morning than in the evening; fasting, than after a full meal. Can we give any reason for these variations except experience? Where then is the power of which we pretend to be conscious? Is there not here, either in a spiritual or material substance, or both, some secret mechanism or structure of parts upon which the effect depends, and which, being entirely unknown to us, renders the power or energy of the will equally unknown and incomprehensible?

Volition is surely an act of the mind with which we are sufficiently acquainted. Reflect upon it. Consider it on all sides. Do you find anything in it like this creative power by which it raises from nothing a new idea and, with a kind of *fiat,* imitates the omnipotence of its Maker, if I may be allowed so to speak, who called forth into existence all the various scenes of nature? So far from being conscious of this energy in the will, it requires as certain experience as that of which we are possessed to convince us that such extraordinary effects do ever result from a simple act of volition.

The generality of mankind never find any difficulty

in accounting for the more common and familiar operations of nature, such as the descent of heavy bodies, the growth of plants, the generation of animals, or the nourishment of bodies by food; but suppose that in all these cases they perceive the very force or energy of the cause by which it is connected with its effect, and is forever infallible in its operation. They acquire, by long habit, such a turn of mind that upon the appearance of the cause they immediately expect, with assurance, its usual attendant, and hardly conceive it possible that any other event could result from it. It is only on the discovery of extraordinary phenomena, such as earthquakes, pestilence, and prodigies of any kind, that they find themselves at a loss to assign a proper cause and to explain the manner in which the effect is produced by it. It is usual for men, in such difficulties, to have recourse to some invisible intelligent principle[15] as the immediate cause of that event which surprises them, and which they think cannot be accounted for from the common powers of nature. But philosophers, who carry their scrutiny a little further, immediately perceive that, even in the most familiar events, the energy of the cause is as unintelligible as in the most unusual, and that we only learn by experience the frequent conjunction of objects, without being ever able to comprehend anything like connection between them. Here, then, many philosophers think themselves obliged by reason to have recourse, on all occasions, to the same principle which the vulgar never appeal to but in cases that appear miraculous and supernatural. They acknowledge mind and intelligence to be, not only the ultimate and original cause of all things, but the immediate and sole cause of every event which appears in nature. They pretend that those objects which are commonly denominated "causes" are in reality nothing but "occasions," and that the true and direct principle of every effect is not any power or force in nature, but a volition of the Supreme Being, who wills that such particular objects should forever be conjoined with each other. Instead of saying that one billiard ball moves another by a force which it has derived from the author of nature, it is the Deity himself, they say, who, by a particular volition, moves the second ball, being determined to this operation by the impulse of the first ball, in consequence of those general laws which he has laid down to himself in the government of the universe. But philosophers, advancing still in their inquiries, discover that as we are totally ignorant of the power on which depends the mutual operation of bodies, we are no less ignorant of that power on which depends the operation of mind on body, or of body on mind; nor are we able, either from our senses or con-

sciousness, to assign the ultimate principle in the one case more than in the other. The same ignorance, therefore, reduces them to the same conclusion. They assert that the Deity is the immediate cause of the union between soul and body, and that they are not the organs of sense which, being agitated by external objects, produce sensations in the mind; but that it is a particular volition of our omnipotent Maker which excites such a sensation in consequence of such a motion in the organ. In like manner, it is not any energy in the will that produces local motion in our members: It is God himself, who is pleased to second our will, in itself impotent, and to command that motion which we erroneously attribute to our own power and efficacy. Nor do philosophers stop at this conclusion. They sometimes extend the same inference to the mind itself in its internal operations. Our mental vision or conception of ideas is nothing but a revelation made to us by our Maker. When we voluntarily turn our thoughts to any object and raise up its image in the fancy, it is not the will which creates that idea, it is the universal Creator who discovers it to the mind and renders it present to us.[16]

Thus, according to these philosophers, everything is full of God. Not content with the principle that nothing exists but by his will, that nothing possesses any power but by his concession, they rob nature and all created beings of every power in order to render their dependence on the Deity still more sensible and immediate. They consider not that by this theory they diminish, instead of magnifying, the grandeur of those attributes which they affect so much to celebrate. It argues, surely, more power in the Deity to delegate a certain degree of power to inferior creatures than to produce everything by his own immediate volition. It argues more wisdom to contrive at first the fabric of the world with such perfect foresight that of itself, and by its proper operation, it may serve all the purposes of Providence than if the great Creator were obliged every moment to adjust its parts and animate by his breath all the wheels of that stupendous machine.

But if we would have a more philosophical confutation of this theory, perhaps the two following reflections may suffice:

First, it seems to me that this theory of the universal energy and operation of the Supreme Being is too bold ever to carry conviction with it to a man sufficiently apprised of the weakness of human reason and the narrow limits to which it is confined in all its operations. Though the chain of arguments which conduct to it were ever so logical, there must arise a strong suspicion, if not an absolute assurance, that it has carried us quite beyond the reach of our faculties when it leads to conclusions so extraordinary and so remote from common life and experience. We are got into fairyland long ere we have reached the last steps of our theory; and *there* we have no reason to trust our common methods of argument or to think that our usual analogies and probabilities have any authority. Our line is too short to fathom such immense abysses. And however we may flatter ourselves that we are guided, in every step which we take, by a kind of verisimilitude and experience, we may be assured that this fancied experience has no authority when we thus apply it to subjects that lie entirely out of the sphere of experience. But on this we shall have occasion to touch afterwards.[17]

Secondly, I cannot perceive any force in the arguments on which this theory is founded. We are ignorant, it is true, of the manner in which bodies operate on each other. Their force or energy is entirely incomprehensible. But are we not equally ignorant of the manner or force by which a mind, even the Supreme Mind, operates, either on itself or on body? Whence, I beseech you, do we acquire any idea of it? We have no sentiment or consciousness of this power in ourselves. We have no idea of the Supreme Being but what we learn from reflection on our own faculties. Were our ignorance, therefore, a good reason for rejecting anything, we should be led into that principle of denying all energy in the Supreme Being, as much as in the grossest matter. We surely comprehend as little the operations of the one as of the other. Is it more difficult to conceive that motion may arise from impulse than that it may arise from volition? All we know is our profound ignorance in both cases.[18]

Part II

But to hasten to a conclusion of this argument, which is already drawn out to too great a length: We have sought in vain for an idea of power or necessary connection in all the sources from which we would suppose it to be derived. It appears that in single instances of the operation of bodies we never can, by our utmost scrutiny, discover anything but one event following another, without being able to comprehend any force or power by which the cause operates or any connection between it and its supposed effect. The same difficulty occurs in contemplating the operations of mind on body, where we observe the motion of the latter to follow upon the volition of the former, but are not able to observe or conceive the tie which binds together the motion and volition, or the energy, by which the mind produces this effect. The au-

thority of the will over its own faculties and ideas is not a whit more comprehensible, so that, upon the whole, there appears not, throughout all nature, any one instance of connection which is conceivable by us. All events seem entirely loose and separate. One event follows another, but we never can observe any tie between them. They seem *conjoined,* but never *connected.* But as we can have no idea of anything which never appeared to our outward sense or inward sentiment, the necessary conclusion *seems* to be that we have no idea of connection or power at all, and that these words are absolutely without any meaning when employed either in philosophical reasonings or common life.

But there still remains one method of avoiding this conclusion, and one source which we have not yet examined. When any natural object or event is presented, it is impossible for us, by any sagacity or penetration, to discover, or even conjecture, without experience, what event will result from it, or to carry our foresight beyond that object which is immediately present to the memory and senses. Even after one instance or experiment where we have observed a particular event to follow upon another, we are not entitled to form a general rule or foretell what will happen in like cases, it being justly esteemed an unpardonable temerity to judge of the whole course of nature from one single experiment, however accurate or certain. But when one particular species of events has always, in all instances, been conjoined with another, we make no longer any scruple of foretelling one upon the appearance of the other, and of employing that reasoning which can alone assure us of any matter of fact or existence. We then call the one object "cause," the other "effect." We suppose that there is some connection between them, some power in the one by which it infallibly produces the other and operates with the greatest certainty and strongest necessity.

It appears, then, that this idea of a necessary connection among events arises from a number of similar instances which occur, of the constant conjunction of these events; nor can that idea ever be suggested by any one of these instances surveyed in all possible lights and positions. But there is nothing in a number of instances, different from every single instance, which is supposed to be exactly similar, except only that after a repetition of similar instances the mind is carried by habit, upon the appearance of one event, to expect its usual attendant and to believe that it will exist. This connection, therefore, which we *feel* in the mind, this customary transition of the imagination from one object to its usual attendant, is the sentiment or impression from which we form the idea of power or necessary connection.

Nothing further is in the case. Contemplate the subjects on all sides, you will never find any other origin of that idea. This is the sole difference between one instance, from which we can never receive the idea of connection, and a number of similar instances by which it is suggested. The first time a man saw the communication of motion by impulse, as by the shock of two billiard balls, he could not pronounce that the one event was *connected,* but only that it was *conjoined* with the other. After he has observed several instances of this nature, he then pronounces them to be *connected.* What alteration has happened to give rise to this new idea of *connection?* Nothing but that he now *feels* these events to be *connected* in his imagination, and can readily foretell the existence of one from the appearance of the other. When we say, therefore, that one object is connected with another, we mean only that they have acquired a connection in our thought and gave rise to this inference by which they become proofs of each other's existence—a conclusion which is somewhat extraordinary, but which seems founded on sufficient evidence. Nor will its evidence be weakened by any general diffidence of the understanding or skeptical suspicion concerning every conclusion which is new and extraordinary. No conclusions can be more agreeable to skepticism than such as make discoveries concerning the weakness and narrow limits of human reason and capacity.

And what stronger instance can be produced of the surprising ignorance and weakness of the understanding than the present? For surely, if there be any relation among objects which it imports us to know perfectly, it is that of cause and effect. On this are founded all our reasonings concerning matter of fact or existence. By means of it alone we attain any assurance concerning objects which are removed from the present testimony of our memory and senses. The only immediate utility of all sciences is to teach us how to control and regulate future events by their causes. Our thoughts and inquiries are, therefore, every moment employed about this relation; yet so imperfect are the ideas which we form concerning it that it is impossible to give any just definition of cause, except what is drawn from something extraneous and foreign to it. Similar objects are always conjoined with similar. Of this we have experience. Suitably to this experience, therefore, we may define a cause to be *an object followed by another, and where all the objects, similar to the first, are followed by objects similar to the second.* Or, in other words, *where, if the first object had not been, the second never had existed.* The appearance of a cause always conveys the mind, by a customary transition, to the idea of the effect. Of this

also we have experience. We may, therefore, suitably to this experience, form another definition of cause and call it *an object followed by another, and whose appearance always conveys the thought to that other.* But though both these definitions be drawn from circumstances foreign to the cause, we cannot remedy this inconvenience or attain any more perfect definition which may point out that circumstance in the cause which gives it a connection with its effect. We have no idea of this connection, nor even any distinct notion what it is we desire to know when we endeavor at a conception of it. We say, for instance, that the vibration of this string is the cause of this particular sound. But what do we mean by that affirmation? We either mean *that this vibration is followed by this sound, and that all similar vibrations have been followed by similar sounds; or, that this vibration is followed by this sound, and that, upon the appearance of one, the mind anticipates the senses and forms immediately an idea of the other.* We may consider the relation of cause and effect in either of these two lights; but beyond these we have no idea of it.[19]

To recapitulate, therefore, the reasonings of this Section:

Every idea is copied from some preceding impression or sentiment; and where we cannot find any impression, we may be certain that there is no idea. In all single instances of the operation of bodies or minds there is nothing that produces any impression, nor consequently can suggest any idea, of power or necessary connection. But when many uniform instances appear, and the same object is always followed by the same event, we then begin to entertain the notion of cause and connection. We then *feel* a new sentiment or impression, to wit, a customary connection in the thought or imagination between one object and its usual attendant; and this sentiment is the original of that idea which we seek for. For as this idea arises from a number of similar instances, and not from any single instance, it must arise from that circumstance in which the number of instances differ from every individual instance. But this customary connection or transition of the imagination is the only circumstance in which they differ. In every other particular they are alike. The first instance which we saw of motion, communicated by the shock of two billiard balls (to return to this obvious illustration), is exactly similar to any instance that may at present occur to us, except only that we could not at first *infer* one event from the other, which we are enabled to do at present, after so long a course of uniform experience. I know not whether the reader will readily apprehend this reasoning. I am afraid that, should I multiply words about it or throw it into a greater variety of lights, it would only become more obscure and intricate. In all abstract reasonings there is one point of view which, if we can happily hit, we shall go further toward illustrating the subject than by all the eloquence and copious expression in the world. This point of view we should endeavor to reach, and reserve the flowers of rhetoric for subjects which are more adapted to them.

NOTES

1. It is probable that no more was meant by those who denied innate ideas than that all ideas were copies of our impressions, though it must be confessed that the terms which they employed were not chosen with such caution, nor so exactly defined, as to prevent all mistakes about their doctrine. For what is meant by "innate"? If "innate" be equivalent to "natural," then all the perceptions and ideas of the mind must be allowed to be innate or natural, in whatever sense we take the latter word, whether in opposition to what is uncommon, artificial, or miraculous. If by innate be meant contemporary to our birth, the dispute seems to be frivolous, nor is it worth while to inquire at what time thinking begins, whether before, at, or after our birth. Again, the word "idea" seems to be commonly taken in a very loose sense by Locke and others, as standing for any of our perceptions, our sensations and passions, as well as thoughts. Now, in this sense, I should desire to know what can be meant by asserting that self-love, or resentment of injuries, or the passion between the sexes is not innate?

But admitting these terms "impressions" and "ideas" in the sense above explained, and understanding by "innate" what is original or copied from no precedent perception, then may we assert that all our impressions are innate, and our ideas not innate.

To be ingenuous, I must own it to be my opinion that Locke was betrayed into this question by the schoolmen, who, making use of undefined terms, draw out their disputes to a tedious length without ever touching the point in question. A like ambiguity and circumlocution seem to run through that philosopher's reasonings, on this as well as most other subjects.

2. [Editions K and L: "Connection of Ideas."]
3. Resemblance.
4. Contiguity.
5. Cause and Effect.
6. For instance, *Contrast* or *Contrariety* is also a connection among ideas, but it may perhaps be considered as a mixture of *Causation* and *Resemblance*. Where two objects are contrary, the one destroys the other; that is, the cause of

its annihilation, and the idea of the annihilation of an object, implies the idea of its former existence.

7. Contrary to Aristotle [cf. 1450a].
8. [Entitled in Editions K and L: "Of the Idea of Power, or Necessary Connexion."]
9. Section II.
10. Mr. Locke, in his chapter of Power, says that, finding from experience that there are several new productions in matter, and concluding that there must somewhere be a power capable of producing them, we arrive at last by this reasoning at the idea of power. But no reasoning can ever give us a new, original, simple idea, as this philosopher himself confesses. This, therefore, can never be the origin of that idea.
11. [Editions K and L add: "The operations and mutual influence of bodies are perhaps sufficient to prove that they also are possessed of it."]
12. [Editions K to N: "of the mind."]
13. [Editions K and L read: "We shall proceed to examine this pretension, and shall endeavor to avoid, as far as we are able, all jargon and confusion in treating of such subtile and such profound subjects.

"I assert then, in the first place, that the influence of volition over the organs of the body is a fact, etc."]
14. It may be pretended, that the resistance which we meet with in bodies, obliging us frequently to exert our force and call up all our power, this gives us the idea of force and power. It is this *nisus* or strong endeavor of which we are conscious, that is the original impression from which this idea is copied. But, *first,* we attribute power to a vast number of objects where we never can suppose this resistance or exertion of force to take place: to the Supreme Being, who never meets with any resistance; to the mind in its command over its ideas and limbs, in common thinking and motion, where the effect follows immediately upon the will, without any exertion or summoning up of force; to inanimate matter, which is not capable of this sentiment. *Secondly,* this sentiment of an endeavor to overcome resistance has no known connection with any event: What follows it we know by experience, but could not know it *a priori.* It must, however, be confessed that the animal *nisus* which we experience, though it can afford no accurate precise idea of power, enters very much into that vulgar, inaccurate idea which is formed of it. The last sentence is not in Editions K and L.
15. Θεὸς ἀπὸ μηχανῆς. [Edition K reads: "*Quasi deus ex machina.*" Edition L adds the reference: "Cicero *de Natura deorum.*"]
16. [Hume refers here to the French philosopher, Nicolas de Malebranche (1638–1715), and his major work, *De la Recherche de la vérité* (1674).—Ed.]

17. Section XII.

18. I need not examine at length the *vis inertiae* which is so much talked of in the new philosophy, and which is ascribed to matter. We find by experience that a body at rest or in motion continues forever in its present state, till put from it by some new cause; and that a body impelled takes as much motion from the impelling body as it acquires itself. These are facts. When we call this a *vis inertiae,* we only mark these facts, without pretending to have any idea of the inert power, in the same manner as, when we talk of gravity, we mean certain effects without comprehending that active power. (Editions K and L: "matter.") It was never the meaning of Sir Isaac Newton to rob second causes of all force or energy, though some of his followers have endeavored to establish that theory upon his authority. On the contrary, that great philosopher had recourse to an ethereal active fluid to explain his universal attraction, though he was so cautious and modest as to allow that it was a mere hypothesis not to be insisted on without more experiments. I must confess that there is something in the fate of opinions a little extraordinary. Descartes insinuated that doctrine of the universal and sole efficacy of the Deity, without insisting on it. Malebranche and other Cartesians made it the foundation of all their philosophy. It had, however, no authority in England. Locke, Clarke, and Cudworth never so much as take notice of it, but suppose all along that matter has a real, though subordinate and derived, power. By what means has it become so prevalent among our modern metaphysicians?

19. According to these explications and definitions, the idea of *power* is relative as much as that of *cause;* and both have a reference to an effect, or some other event constantly conjoined with the former. When we consider the *unknown* circumstance of an object by which the degree or quantity of its effect is fixed and determined, we call that its power. And accordingly, it is allowed by all philosophers that the effect is the measure of the power. But if they had any idea of power as it is in itself, why could they not measure it in itself? The dispute, whether the force of a body in motion be as its velocity, or the square of its velocity; this dispute, I say, needed not be decided by comparing its effects in equal or unequal times, but by a direct mensuration and comparison. (This note was first introduced in Edition L.)

As to the frequent use of the words "force," "power," "energy," etc., which everywhere occur in common conversation as well as in philosophy, that is no proof that we are acquainted, in any instance, with the connecting principle between cause and effect, or can account ultimately for the production of one thing by another. These words, as commonly used, have very loose meanings annexed to them, and their ideas are very uncertain and confused. No animal can put external bodies in motion without the sentiment of a *nisus* or endeavor; and every animal has a sentiment or feeling from the stroke or blow of an external object that is in motion. These sensations, which are merely animal, and from which we can *a priori* draw no inference, we are apt to transfer to inanimate objects, and to suppose that they have some such feelings whenever they transfer or receive motion. With regard to energies, which are exerted without our annexing to them any idea of communicated motion, we consider only the constant experienced conjunction of the events; and as we *feel* a customary connection between the ideas, we transfer that feeling to the objects, as nothing is more usual than to apply to external bodies every internal sensation which they occasion. Instead of this concluding passage there stood in Edition L: "A *cause* is different from a *sign,* as it implies precedence and contiguity in time and place, as well as constant conjunction. A *sign* is nothing but a correlative effect from the same cause."

10

IMMANUEL KANT

Immanuel Kant (1724–1804) did not present an imposing or impressive figure in the lecture hall, with his deformed chest, small stature, and generally poor health. His speech, however, was phenomenal—complex points made clear with humor, examples from classical and popular literature, and discussion of the latest scientific findings. Starting in

1755, upon receiving his degree from the University of Königsburg, Kant began to develop a stunning reputation as a teacher and writer. In addition to being offered a chair in poetry at the University of Berlin, for 30 years he taught a popular summer lecture series on physical geography. In 1770, after many years of lecturing on subjects ranging from physics to anthropology, Kant became a professor of logic and metaphysics at the University of Königsburg. The son of devout Lutherans, Kant was educated at the school of his pastor and grew particularly fond of the poetry of Lucretius. He began at Königsburg in 1740 as a theology student, but found the work of Sir Issac Newton more compelling. In 1746, straitened financial circumstances led Kant to become a private tutor. Finally, in 1755 he was able to finish his degree at Königsburg and become a *Privatdocent,* or lecturer. His philosophical writings became famous during his lifetime, transforming Königsburg into a philosophical Mecca, complete with philosophical pilgrims.

ANTHROPOLOGY FROM A PRAGMATIC POINT OF VIEW

FIRST BOOK

On the Cognitive Faculty

On Being Conscious of One's Self

§1. The fact that man is aware of an ego-concept raises him infinitely above all other creatures living on earth. Because of this, he is a person; and by virtue of this oneness of consciousness, he remains one and the same person despite all the vicissitudes which may befall him. He is a being who, by reason of his preeminence and dignity, is wholly different from *things,* such as the irrational animals whom he can master and rule at will. He enjoys this superiority even when he cannot yet give utterance to his ego, although it is already present in his thought, just as all languages must think it when they speak in the first person, even if the language lacks a specific word to refer to this ego-concept. This faculty (to think) is understanding.

It is noteworthy, however, that the child who already speaks fairly well begins to use the pronoun *I* rather late (perhaps after a year), in the meantime speaking of himself in the third person ("Carl wants to eat, go, . . ." etc.). A light seems to dawn upon him when he begins speaking in the first person. From that day on he will never again revert to the third person. At first the child merely *felt* himself, now he *thinks* himself. The explanation of this phenomenon might be rather difficult for the anthropologist.

The observation that a child does neither weep nor smile until after it is three months old appears to be based on the development of certain notions of offense and injustice, which point toward reason. In this period, when his eyes begin to follow bright objects which are held before him, we have the crude beginnings of a process of broadening perceptions (the apprehensions of sensory awareness) into a recognition of objects of the senses, that is, of experience.

When the child tries to talk, his mangling of words makes him so lovable to mother and nurse, and makes both of them so well-disposed that they hug and kiss him continually. They also thoroughly spoil the little tyrant by catering to his every wish and desire. That the little creature is lovable in the period of the development of his human nature must be credited to his innocence and the candor of his still stumbling utterances which are free from guilt or deceit. Yet the child's charm must also be credited to the natural inclination of nurses to care for a creature that flatteringly submits itself completely to the will of someone else. The child does so because he knows that a playtime, the best time of all, will be granted, and in this way the teacher, who now becomes a child again, enjoys once more the pleasures of childhood.

The teacher's memory of his own childhood does, however, not reach back to that time, since the time of early childhood is not a time of experiences but rather a time of mere sporadic perceptions which have not yet been unified by any real concept of an object.

From Immanuel Kant, "On the Cognitive Faculty." In V. L. Dowdell (Ed.), *Anthropology from a Pragmatic Point of View,* (pp. 9–41, 90). Carbondale: Southern Illinois University Press, 1978. (Original work published 1798)

On Egoism

§2. From the day that man begins to speak in the first person, he brings his beloved self to light wherever he can, and his egoism advances unrestrained. If he does not do so openly (for then the egoism of others may oppose him), his egoism expresses itself covertly and with seeming self-abnegation and pretended modesty in order to ensure for himself a superior value in the judgment of others.

Egoism may be thought of as containing three presumptions: that of reason, that of taste, and that of practical interest, that is, it may be logical, aesthetic, or practical.

The logical egoist considers it unnecessary to test his judgment by the reason of others, as if he had no need of a touchstone (*criterium veritatis externum*). However, it is so certain that we cannot dispense with this means of ensuring ourselves of the truth of our judgment, that this is perhaps the most important reason why learned people insist so emphatically on the freedom of writing. If this freedom is denied, we are deprived of an effective means of testing the correctness of our judgment, and we expose ourselves to error. It should not even be said that a mathematician is privileged to make judgments on his own authority, for if the perceived and verified agreement between the judgments of one geometer and those of all others who devote themselves with talent and industry to the same subject did not prevail, then even mathematics would not be free from having somewhere fallen into error. There are also certain cases where we do not trust solely in the judgment of our own senses, where we find it necessary to inquire of other people if they seem to have had the same *impression* as ours, for example, whether the ringing of a bell was real or only in our ears. And although, when philosophizing, we are not even permitted to appeal to the judgments of others for establishing our own (as the jurists do in appealing to those well-versed in law), every writer who finds that no one agrees with his clearly expressed and important views is suspected by the public of being in error.

Therefore, it is a risk to hold a view which conflicts with public opinion, even if it is deemed to be reasonable. Such a display of egoism is called paradoxical. Boldness does not lie in running the risk that the view is untrue, but rather in the risk that the view might be accepted by only a few. Preference for the paradoxical is logical obstinacy in which a man does not want to be an imitator of others, but rather prefers to appear as an unusual human being. Instead of accomplishing his purpose, such a man frequently succeeds only in being odd. But, because everyone must have and maintain his own intelligence (*Si omnes patres sic, at ego non sic.—* ABAILARD), the reproach of being paradoxical, when it is not based on vanity or the desire to be different, carries no bad connotations. Opposite to the paradoxical is the commonplace, which sides with the general opinion. But with the commonplace there is as little safety, if not less, because it lulls the mind to sleep, whereas the paradox awakens the mind to attention and investigation, which often lead to discoveries.

The aesthetic egoist is satisfied with his own taste, even though others may dislike, criticize, or even ridicule his verse, his painting, or his music. He deprives himself of the progress toward improvement when he isolates himself and his own judgment; he applauds himself, and he seeks art's touchstone of beauty only in himself.

Finally, the moral egoist limits all purposes to himself; as a eudaemonist, he concentrates the highest motives of his will merely on profit and his own happiness, but not on the concept of duty. Because every other person has a different concept of what he counts as happiness, it is exactly egoism which causes him to have no touchstone of a genuine concept of duty which truly must be a universally valid principle. All eudaemonists are consequently egoists.

Egoism can only be contrasted with pluralism, which is a frame of mind in which the self, instead of being enwrapped in itself as if it were the whole world, understands and behaves itself as a mere citizen of the world. The above is all that belongs to anthropology. The consideration of the contrast between egoism and pluralism from a metaphysical perspective lies beyond the scope of the science with which we are dealing here. If the question were only whether I, as a thinking being, have any reason to assume that beside my existence there exists a totality of other beings (called the world) with whom I am in relation, then it is not an anthropological but merely a metaphysical question.

NOTE ON THE FORMALITY OF EGOISTIC LANGUAGE. The language used by the head of state, when speaking of himself to the people, is nowadays in the plural (We, King by the Grace of God . . .). The question arises whether the meaning of this is not rather egoistic, that is, indicative of the speaker's own authority; the same meaning is expressed by the King of Spain when he refers to himself as *Io, el Rey* (I, the King). It appears to be a fact, however, that such formality in speaking about the highest authority was originally to indicate condescension (We, the King and his Counsel, or Estates). But how does it happen that the reciprocal form of address, which was formerly expressed in the old classical languages by the familiar Thou in the singular, should later be indicated by the formal You in the plural when spoken by various (chiefly German) peoples? For the sake of giving greater distinction to the person addressed, the German language uses two distinctive expressions, namely *he* and *they* (as if it were not a form of address at all, but a story about someone absent, be it one person or more). This has finally led, to complete the absurdity, to the use of such expressions as Your Grace, Right Honorable, Right Noble, High-and-Noble, in which the speaker, rather than pretending to humble himself before the person addressed, shows deference instead to the abstract quality of his station. Probably all this is the result of feudalism which saw to it that the degree of respect due the socially more distinguished not be violated in a hierarchy extending from the royal dignity down through all the stages until even human dignity itself ceases and only man remains, that is, down to the position of serfdom, where a man is addressed by his superiors as *you,* or down to the position of a child who is not allowed to have its own way.

On Being Arbitrarily Conscious of One's Ideas

§3. The effort to become conscious of one's sense impressions [ideas] is either the perception (*attentio*) or the abstraction (*abstractio*) of a sense impression of which I am conscious within myself. Abstraction is not just a neglect and cessation of perception (since that would be distraction [*distractio*]), but rather it is a considered act of the faculty of cognition; it is a sense impression of which I am inwardly conscious, keeping it separate from other sense impressions in my consciousness. Therefore, one does not speak of abstracting (separating) something, but of abstracting from something, that is, abstracting a definition from the object of my sense impression, whereby the definition preserves the universality of a concept, and is thus taken into the understanding.

For a man to be able to make an abstraction from a sense impression, even when the sense impression forces itself on his senses, is proof of a far greater faculty than just paying attention, because it gives evidence of a freedom of the faculty of thought and sovereignty of the mind in having the condition of one's sense impressions under one's control (*animus sui compos*). In this respect the faculty of abstraction is much more difficult, but also more important than the faculty of perception when it encounters sense impressions.

Many people are unhappy because they cannot engage in abstraction. Many a suitor could make a good marriage if he could only shut his eyes to a wart on his sweetheart's face or to a gap where teeth are missing. But it is a peculiarly bad habit of our faculty of perception to observe too closely, even involuntarily, what is faulty in other people. Likewise, it is bad manners to fix one's eyes on the spot where a button is missing from the coat of a man who is directly in front of us, or upon a missing-tooth gap, or to call attention to a habitual speech defect, or to make the other person feel uneasy by staring at him and thus ruining any possibility of personal relations with him. If the essentials are good, it is not only fair but wise to shut one's eyes to the shortcomings of others, as well as to our own good fortune. The capacity to abstract, however, is a power of mind which can only be acquired by exercising it.

On Self-Observation

§4. Noticing (*animadvertere*) oneself is not the same thing as observing (*observare*) oneself. Observation is a methodical compilation of perceptions which we have experienced. Such perceptions furnish material for the diary of an *observer of the self* and they may easily lead to wild imaginings and insanity.

The perception (*attentio*) of oneself when dealing with others is necessary, but it must not be obvious in daily intercourse; if it is noticeable, it makes conversation awkward (a hindrance) or affected (a mockery). The opposite of both is a free and easy manner (*air dégagé*), the self-confidence that one's behavior is not going to be criticized unfavorably by others. He who pretends to judge himself as if he were standing in front of a mirror, and he who speaks as if he heard himself speak (and not simply as if someone else heard him), is a kind of actor. He wishes to appear as someone, and so he feigns a semblance of his own person. However, on this account, he suffers in the estimation of other persons who perceive his attempt because it arouses the suspicion that he intends to deceive. Candid behavior (a manner which causes no such suspicion) is called natural behavior (although it does not exclude all fine art and the cultivation of taste). Such behavior pleases because of its simple *truth* in expression. But when sincerity appears to proceed from simplicity, that is, because a mode of perception has been neglected which has already been established as a rule, then simplicity is called naïveté.

The naïve manner of revealing one's self as evidenced when a girl is approached by a man for the first time, or when a peasant, unfamiliar with urbane manners, entering the city for the first time, provokes, because of the person's innocence and simplicity (caused by the lack of the art of pretense), a benevolent smile from those who are already well versed and adept in this art. Such a smile is not a condemnation, since honesty and sincerity are still respected; it is a good-natured and kindly ridicule at inexperience based on the evil art of pretense, indicative of our already corrupted human nature. It is an art which should be lamented rather than ridiculed, especially if one compared it with the idea of a still uncorrupted human nature[1]. It is a momentary joy, as when a cloudy sky breaks open for an instant and lets a sunbeam through, only to close up at once as if to avoid hurting the purblind eyes of egoism.

But the real purpose of this section is the previous warning against engaging in deliberate observation and studied compilation of an inner history of the involuntary course of our thoughts and feelings. The warning is given because deliberate observation is the most direct path to illuminism and terrorism in the confused belief that we are open to higher inspiration and, without our help, who knows why, are subject to unknown interior forces. In such a situation, without noticing it, we make pretended discoveries of what we ourselves have introduced into our own minds, like a Bourignon, with flattery, or a Pascal, with terrifying and frightful implications, or as was the case with Albrecht Haller, an otherwise splendid mind, who while writing the extensive and much-interrupted diary of his spiritual life, finally came to the point of asking a famous theologian, his former academic colleague Doctor Less, whether in his extensive store of divine learning he could not find any consolation for his anguished soul.

To scrutinize the various acts of the imagination within me, when I call them forth, is indeed worth reflection, as well as necessary and useful for logic and metaphysics. But to wish to play the spy upon one's self, when those acts come to mind unsummoned and of their own accord (which happens through the play of the unpremeditatedly creative imagination), is to reverse the natural order of the cognitive powers, since then the rational elements do not take the lead (as they should) but instead follow behind. This desire for self-investigation is either already a disease of the mind (hypochondria), or will lead to such a disease and ultimately to the madhouse. He who has a great deal to tell of inner experiences (for example, of grace, of temptations, etc.) may, in the course of his voyage to self-discovery, have made his first landing only at Anticyra. Inner experiences are not like external experiences of objects in space, wherein the objects appear side by side and permanently fixed.

The inner sense sees the conditions for its definition only in Time and, consequently, in a state of flux, which is without that permanence of observation necessary for experience.[2]

On the Ideas We Have Without Being Aware of Them

§5. To have ideas and still not to be conscious of them seems to be a contradiction; for how can we know that we have them unless we are conscious of them? This objection has already been raised by Locke, who on that account rejected the existence of such a type of ideas. Nevertheless, we can be indirectly conscious of having an idea, although we are not directly conscious of it. Such ideas are called obscure, the others are clear, and when their clarity extends to the components of the whole idea and their combination, then they are called distinct ideas either of thought or of perception.

Whenever I am conscious of seeing a person in the distant meadow, though I am not aware of seeing his eyes, nose, mouth, and so forth, then I really only conclude that this thing is a person. If I were to say that I did not have any idea at all of these perceptions (simply because I was not conscious of perceiving these and other parts of the person), then I would not be able to say that I saw a person. It is these partial ideas that contribute to the entirety of the head or of the person.

Sense perceptions and sensations of which we are not aware but whose existence we can undoubtedly infer, that is, obscure ideas in both man and animals, constitute an immeasurable field. The clear ideas, on the other hand, contain infinitely few instances of sense perceptions and sensations which reveal themselves to consciousness. It is as if just a few places on the vast map of our mind were illuminated. This can inspire wonder at our own being; for a higher power would need only cry, "Let there be light" and then, without further action (if, for instance, we take an author and find out all that he has stored in his mind), there would be laid open before the eyes half a universe. Everything that the eye reveals when strengthened by the telescope (perhaps directed toward the moon) or by the microscope (directed upon infusoria) is perceived by the naked eye, for these optical instruments do not bring more rays of light and subsequently more pictures into the eye. The pictures reflect themselves upon the retina without such ingenious instruments. They simply enlarge the images so that we become conscious of them. The same thing is true of the sensation of hearing, when the musician plays a phantasy on the organ with his ten fingers and two feet, while at the same time he is speaking to someone standing beside him. Within a few seconds a host of ideas is awakened in his soul, and every idea requires special judgment as to its appropriateness, since a single stroke of the finger, not fitted to the harmony, would immediately be heard as a discord. Yet the whole comes out so well that the improvisator must often wish to have preserved in a score many a passage which he has performed in this happy fashion, but which he could not have performed so well with real diligence and attention.

Because obscure ideas can only be perceived by man passively as a play of sensations, their theory does not belong to pragmatic anthropology but to physiological anthropology with which we are not properly concerned.

We often play with obscure ideas, and we have an interest in removing objects that are liked or disliked by the imagination. But still more often we ourselves become an object of obscure ideas, and our understanding is unable to rescue itself from absurdities which were caused by those ideas, although we recognize them as an illusion.

Such is the case with sexual love where no benevolence is intended but only the enjoyment of its object. How much cleverness has been wasted in throwing a delicate veil over man's desires, but revealing still enough of man's close relation to the animal kingdom so that bashfulness results. Blunt expressions are replaced by euphemisms in polite society even though they are transparent enough to inspire a smile. Here the imagination may well walk in obscurity, and it requires an uncommon skill if, in order to avoid cynicism, one does not risk falling into absurd purism.

On the other hand, we are often enough the victims of obscure ideas which are reluctant to vanish even when understanding has thrown light upon them. To arrange for his grave in his garden or under a shady tree, in a field or in a dry plot of ground, is often a very important affair to a dying man, even though he knows that if he chooses the one, he has no reason to hope for a nice view; and if he chooses the other, he has no reason to worry about catching a cold.

The saying, "Clothes make the man," holds true in a certain measure even for an intelligent man. The Russian proverb says: "One receives a guest according to his clothes, and accompanies him according to his understanding." But understanding cannot prevent the obscure impression that a well-dressed person is a person of a certain importance, but the preliminary judgment may be revised later.

Even studied obscurity is often used purposely to re-

flect profundity and thoroughness in much the same way as objects seen at dusk or in a fog always appear to be larger than they actually are.[3] Skotison (make it obscure) is the catchword of all mystics in order to lure with fictitious obscurity those who dig for the hidden treasures of wisdom. But generally the reader welcomes a certain degree of mystery in a manuscript, because he thereby becomes aware of his own intellectual power in resolving the obscure into clear thoughts.

On Distinctness and Indistinctness in Relation to the Consciousness of One's Ideas

§6. The awareness of one's ideas, sufficient for distinguishing one object from another, is clearness. Awareness which makes the composition of ideas clear is called distinctness. Distinctness alone makes it possible for an aggregate of ideas to become cognition, whereby order is established from manifold ideas, because every conscious combination presupposes a unity of awareness which in turn supplies the rule for the unity. One cannot contrast clear ideas with confused ones (*perceptio confusa*); rather, they must be contrasted with the indistinct (*mere clara*) ideas. Whatever is confused must be compounded, for within the simple there is neither order nor confusion. Confusion is the cause of indistinctness, not its definition. In every complex idea (*perceptio complexa*), and thus in every cognition (which requires both perception and concept), we see that distinctness depends upon the order according to which contributory ideas are combined (merely considering form) which order gives rise either to a logical division into primary or secondary (*perceptio primaria et secundaria*) ideas or a real division into principal and accessory ideas (*perceptio principalis et adhaerens*). Distinct cognition results from order. One can see that if the faculty of cognition is to be called understanding (in the most general sense of the word), it must contain the faculty of apprehending (*attentio*) given ideas in order to produce perception; furthermore, it must contain the power of separating what is common to more than one object (*abstractio*); in order to produce the concept, it also must contain the faculty of deliberation (*reflexio*), in order to produce cognition of an object.

We say that he who possesses these powers to a superior degree has a head; and he who has a small measure of these faculties is called a simpleton, because he always allows himself to be guided by other persons. But we call him a genius who makes use of originality and produces out of himself what must ordinarily be learned under the guidance of others.

He who has learned nothing of what must be taught

in order to be knowledgeable is called an ignoramus, if he has been expected to know because of his claim to be a man of learning. Without such a claim he may still be a genius. He who cannot think for himself, though he can learn much, is limited (warped). One can be a person of vast learning (a machine for the instruction of others, teaching what one has once been taught) and still be limited in reference to the rational use of his actual knowledge. The pedant is the one whose conversation on what he has learned betrays academic constraint and consequently a lack of independent thought. This is so whether he is a scholar, a soldier, or even a courtier. Of all kinds of pedants the most tolerable is the learned pedant, because we can still learn from him. On the other hand, in a courtier scrupulousness in formalities (pedantries) is not merely useless, but, in view of the pride inevitably exhibited by the pedant, also ridiculous since it is the pride of an ignoramus.

The art, or rather the skill, of speaking in the socially proper tone, and appearing up-to-date, especially when the conversation is about science, is falsely called popularity, but should rather be called polished superficiality because it frequently cloaks the paltriness of a narrow-minded person. Only children can be fooled by this. Addison had the Quaker say to the constantly talking officer who was traveling with him in the coach: "Thy drum is a symbol of thee, it soundeth because it is empty."

In order to judge men according to their cognitive faculty (according to their understanding as such) we make a division into two classes: those to whom must be attributed common sense (*sensus communis*), which certainly is not common (*sensus vulgaris*), and men of science. People with common sense are familiar with the principles relating to practical application (*in concerto*). Scientific people are familiar with the principles themselves prior to their application (*in abstracto*). The understanding, which belongs to the first cognitive capacity, is sometimes called horse sense (*bon sens*), whereas the understanding belonging to the second cognitive faculty we call perspicuity (*ingenium perspicax*). It is noteworthy that we interpret horse sense, which is generally considered only as practical cognition, not just as an understanding which can exist without cultivation, but rather as an understanding to which cultivation can be a hindrance if it is not conscientiously followed through. Some praise this understanding fanatically and represent it as a storehouse of treasures hidden in the depths of the mind. Sometimes we even interpret the dictum of horse sense as an oracle (the genius of Socrates) which is more accurate than anything that erudite wisdom has to offer. So much is certain, that, when-ever the answer to a question rests upon general and innate rules of the understanding (the possession of which is called native intelligence), we may be sure that seeking for studied and artificially established principles (school learning), and forming a conclusion accordingly, is less reliable than gradually coming to a conclusion from the grounds of judgment which lie in the dark recesses of the mind. This may be called logical tact, in which reflection looks at the object from many angles and produces the correct result without being aware of the acts occurring within the mind during this process.

Horse sense, however, can demonstrate this superiority only with regard to an object of experience. In this way it not only grows in knowledge but even extends experience itself; not, however, in a speculative, but only in an empirico-practical respect. For in the speculative employment of understanding, scientific principles a priori are required, while in the empirico-practical employment of understanding it is possible to have experiences, that is, judgments, which are continually confirmed by experiment and result.

On Sensibility in Contrast to Understanding

§7. With respect to the state of its ideas, my mind is either active, and shows a capacity (*facultas*) for accomplishment, or it is passive, and continues in a receptive capacity (*receptivitas*). Cognition contains a union of both states of ideas. The possibility of having such a cognition bears the name of cognitive faculty, a term derived from its most important part, namely, the activity of the mind in combining or separating ideas.

Ideas with respect to which the mind is passive, and by which the subject is therefore affected (whether it affects itself or is affected by an object), belong to the sensual cognitive faculty. But ideas which involve a pure activity (that is, thinking) belong to the intellectual cognitive faculty. The first is called the lower; the other, the higher cognitive faculty.[4] The sensual cognition has the character of passivity toward the inner sense of awareness, while intellectual cognition has the character of spontaneity of apperception, that is, of the pure consciousness of the act which constitutes thought and appertains to logic (a system of the rules of the understanding). Passivity, in turn, belongs to the field of psychology (a summary of all inner perceptions under the laws of nature). Psychology is the foundation of inner experience.

REMARK. The object of an idea, which comprises only the manner in which I am affected by the object, can be recognized by me only as it appears to me. All experience (empirical cognition), the inner not less than the outer, is nothing but the cognition of objects as they appear to us, not as they are (when considered by themselves). Not only the quality of the idea, but also the quality of the subject and its susceptibility is important in determining the kind of sensual perception on which the thought process concerning the object (the concept of the object) bases itself. The formal character of this receptivity cannot be borrowed from the senses; it must be given a priori, that is, it must be a sense perception which remains after everything empirical (the content of sense perception) is taken away; in inner experiences, this formal factor of intuition is Time.

Experience is empirical cognition, but cognition (dependent as it is on judgments) requires reflection (*reflexio*), and consequently consciousness of activity in arranging the multitude of ideas according to a rule of unity, that is, a concept; and, finally, it requires thought as such (which makes it different from sense perception). On this account consciousness is divided into the discursive (which, being logical, must take the lead because it provides the rule) and intuitive consciousness. Discursive consciousness (the pure apperception of its mental activity) is simple. The "I" of reflection contains no manifold within itself, and is always one and the same in every judgment, because it contains merely the formal part of consciousness. On the other hand, inner experience contains the material of itself as well as a manifold of the [142] empirical, inner perception, that is, the "I" of apprehension (hence an empirical apperception).

I, as a thinking being and as a being endowed with senses, am one and the same subject. However, as an object of inner empirical intuition, so far as I am inwardly affected by temporal sensations (simultaneous or successive), I cognize myself only as I appear to myself, not as a thing-in-itself. Such cognition depends on a temporal condition which is no concept of the understanding (hence not mere spontaneity), and hence is a condition in regard to which my faculty of ideas is passive. It is a condition that belongs to receptivity. Therefore, through inner experience I always know myself only as I appear to myself. This axiom has frequently been distorted to read: It only *seems* to me (*mihi videri*) that I have definite ideas and sensations, and that, indeed, I only appear to exist. This illusion is the basis of erroneous judgment emanating from subjective causes falsely treated as objective. Appearance, however, is no judgment, but merely empirical intuition which, through reflection and concept of the understanding resulting

therefrom, becomes inner experience and consequently truth.

The cause of these errors lies in the fact that the terms *inner sense* and *apperception* are generally considered synonymous by psychologists, although inner sense should designate only psychological (applied) consciousness, while apperception should designate logical (pure) consciousness. From this it is evident that the only perception we have of ourselves by means of the inner sense is of how we appear to ourselves, because apprehension (*apprehensio*) of impressions of the inner sense presupposes a formal condition of the inner perception of a subject. The condition is Time, which certainly is not a concept of the understanding. It is merely a subjective condition by which inner sensations are given to us in consequence of the nature of the human soul. Thus it is not without our power to know what an object is in itself.

This note does not really belong to anthropology. In anthropology, experiences are appearances united according to the laws (rules) of the understanding, and no question is asked concerning the manner of representing things as they are apart from their relation to the senses (as they are in themselves). This investigation belongs to metaphysics which has to do with the possibility of knowledge a priori. Nevertheless, it was necessary to go back as far as we did just to avoid the mistakes of the speculative mind with regard to this question. On the whole, knowledge of man through inner experience, according to which he judges others, is of great importance and perhaps even more difficult to achieve than the ability to judge others correctly, in that the one who investigates his inner consciousness easily carries many things into his own self-consciousness instead of simply observing what is there. On this account it is advisable and even necessary to begin with observed phenomena within oneself before proceeding to make exact statements concerning man's nature, that is, before proceeding to the study of inner experience.

Apology for Sensibility

§8. Understanding is highly esteemed by everyone. Its very definition as the higher cognitive faculty only goes to show that whoever ventures to praise it would be sent away with the same ridicule earned by an orator praising virtue: *Stulte! quis unquam vituperavit.* Sensibility, on the other hand, is in bad repute. We say uncomplimentary things, such as (1) that it confuses the power of imagination; (2) that it boasts, and is like a sovereign mistress, stubborn and hard to subdue, whereas it ought to be only the handmaid of the understanding; (3) that it is even deceptive, so that we cannot be sufficiently on our guard where it is concerned. Yet sensibility is not without praise, especially among poets and people of good taste. They highly esteem the figurative representation of ideas not only as a gain, but because in this way concepts need not be analyzed into their constituent parts with painstaking care to express the full meaning of a thought or the emphasis (the force) of speech and the self-evidence (the clarity in consciousness) of sensibility. They declare that understanding without adornment is a deficiency.[5] We do not need panegyrists here, but only someone to act as a defender of sensibility against the accuser.

The passive element in sensibility, which we cannot ignore, is really the cause of all the difficulties we ascribe to it. The inner perfection of man consists in having the power to use all his faculties, a power to subject their use to his own free volition. For this, it is necessary that the understanding should rule without weakening sensibility (which in itself is like a mob of people since it does not think) because without sensibility no material would be provided for the use of the law-giving understanding.

JUSTIFICATION OF SENSIBILITY AGAINST THE FIRST INDICTMENT

§9. *The senses do not confuse.* We cannot say of a person who grasps, but has not yet ordered, a given manifold, that he confuses it. Perceptions of the senses (empirical ideas with consciousness) can only be called inner phenomena. Only the understanding, which joins perceptions and combines them under a rule of thought, by introducing order into the manifold, establishes them as empirical cognition, that is, experience. The understanding is, therefore, neglecting its duty if it judges rashly, without having arranged sense impressions according to concepts, and then later complains of their state of confusion, which it blames on man's sensual nature. This reproach applies equally to the unfounded complaint concerning the confusion of outer as well as inner perceptions through sensibility.

Sense perceptions certainly precede perceptions of the understanding and display themselves en masse. Yet the harvest [*Ertrag*] is more abundant when the understanding with its order and intellectual form is added. The same is true when, for example, the understanding brings into consciousness significant expressions for the concept, emphatic perceptions for the feeling, and interesting perceptions for the determination of the will. The riches, which rhetoric and poetry place before the understanding all at once (en masse) often embarrass the understanding if it tries to clarify and explain all the acts of reflection which it performs, even obscurely, in such a process. Sensibility, however, is not to blame. On the contrary, it is to be esteemed for having presented abundant material to the understanding, in comparison with which its abstract concepts are often very paltry indeed.

JUSTIFICATION OF SENSIBILITY AGAINST THE SECOND INDICTMENT

§10. *The senses do not control the understanding.* They, on the contrary, offer themselves to the understanding only for the sake of being put to work in its service. That the senses do not wish to have their significance misunderstood, a significance which belongs to them specifically in what we call the common sense of human intelligence (*sensus communis*), is a fact that cannot be interpreted as an arrogant intention to dominate the understanding. There are judgments which, in view of the fact that they are not brought formally to the tribunal of the understanding for final decision, appear to be dictated directly by sense. They are embodied in so-called mottoes or oracular outbursts (such as those to whose utterance Socrates ascribed his own genius). It is thereby supposed that our first judgment about that which is wise and just to do on a particular occasion is generally the correct one and that pondering over it will only lead to something artificial. These judgments, however, do not actually come from the senses; instead, they proceed from real, though obscure, deliberations of the understanding. The senses make no claim in this respect; they are like the common people, though not like the rabble *(ignobile vulgus),* who are happily willing to subordinate themselves to their superior, the understanding, as long as they are listened to. However, if certain judgments and insights are regarded as proceeding directly from the inner sense, without the mediation of understanding, and if these are further regarded as governing themselves so that sensations are passed off as judgments, we have nothing but that fanaticism which is akin to insanity.

JUSTIFICATION OF SENSIBILITY AGAINST THE THIRD INDICTMENT

§11. *The senses do not deceive.* This statement is the rejection of the most important, as well as, strictly speaking, the emptiest reproach which can be directed against the senses; not because they do not judge correctly, but because they do not judge at all. For this reason error must always be charged to the understanding. Sensible appearances (*species, apparentia*), however, turn to the understanding, if not for justification, at least for vindication. Thus man often mistakes the subjective for the objective. (He thinks a distant tower is round if he sees no corners on it. He believes the sea to be higher than its shore [*altum mare*] when the distant water meets the eye through rays of light more sharply bent. The full moon seems to be farther away and therefore larger when he sees it ascend at the horizon through a hazy atmosphere than when it is high in the heavens, although he catches sight of it from the same visual angle.) Thus man takes appearance for experience. In this way man errs, not through any shortcoming of his senses, but through a failure of his understanding.

Logic charges sensibility with the flaw that cognition, as it is advanced by logic, is associated with shallowness (individually and limitation to the particular), whereas understanding which tends toward the universal, and therefore has to accommodate itself with abstractions, is associated with denseness. The aesthetic treatment, whose first claim is popularity, follows a course on which both fallacies can be avoided.

On the Potentiality of the Cognitive Faculty

§12. The preceding section, which dealt with the faculty of appearance, concentrated on aspects which no man can control. It leads us to a discussion of the concepts of the easy [*leicht*] and the difficult [*schwer*], which literally signify in German only material conditions and powers. But in Latin (*leve et grave*), by an exact analogy, they should signify that which can be done (*facile*) and that which, relatively speaking, cannot be done (*difficile*). What is scarcely possible of being done is regarded as subjectively impracticable by a creature who doubts whether he has the necessary ability to perform in certain situations and relationships.

Facility in doing something (*promptitudo*) must not be confused with readiness in such actions (*habitus*). Facility signifies a certain degree of mechanical ability, the "I can if I want to" indicating a subjective possibility. Readiness signifies subjective-practical necessity, that is, habit, which signifies a positive degree of the will acquired through the oft-repeated use of one's faculty, "I want to because duty asks me to." We cannot explain virtue by saying that it is readiness for free and lawful actions, because virtue would then be a mere mechanism of applying power. Virtue, on the contrary, is moral strength in pursuit of one's duty, a duty which should never be a matter of habit, but should always proceed, fresh and original, from one's mode of thought.

The easy is contrasted with the difficult, but many times it is contrasted with the burdensome as well.

Whatever requires for its accomplishment a great deal less power of application than a subject has at his command is regarded by him as easy. What is easier than going through the formalities of social visits, of congratulations, and of condolences? But what is more demanding for a busy man? They are friendship's vexations (drudgeries) from which everyone heartily wishes to be free. And yet everyone has scruples against violating such social customs.

What vexations there are in the external customs which are thought to belong to religion, but which in reality are related to ecclesiastical form! The merits of piety have been set up in such a way that the ritual is of no use at all except for the simple submission of the believers to ceremonies and observances, expiations and mortifications (the more the better). But such compulsory services, which are mechanically easy (because no vicious inclination is thus sacrificed), must be found morally very difficult and burdensome to the rational man. When, therefore, the great moral teacher said, "My commandments are not difficult," he did not mean that they require only limited exercise of strength in order to be fulfilled. As a matter of fact, as commandments which require pure dispositions of the heart, they are the hardest that can be given. Yet, for a rational man, they are nevertheless infinitely easier to keep than the commandments involving activity which accomplishes nothing (*gratis anhelare, multa agendo nihil agere*), like those upon which Judaism is built. Even the mechanically easy feels like lifting hundredweights to the rational man when he sees that all the energy spent is wasted.

To make the difficult easy is meritorious. To depict what is difficult as easy, although one is not able to accomplish it himself, is deception. There is no merit in doing what is easy. Methods and machines, and among these the division of labor among various craftsmen, make many things easy which would be hard to do with one's hands without other tools.

To point out difficulties before one gives the order to go ahead with the task (as for example, in metaphysical investigations) may have the effect of a deterrent, but it is better than concealing the difficulties. He who regards everything he wants to do as easy is reckless; he who performs everything he does with ease is adept; while he whose work shows signs of great labor is awkward. The social exchange of ideas (conversation) is merely a game wherein everything has to be easy and has to appear easy. Ceremonious (stiff) conversation, for example, the pompous "good-bye" when one makes a departure after a banquet, should be abolished as something antiquated.

According to the difference in temperament, the mental disposition of people differs when they are faced with a business undertaking. Some begin with difficulties and fears (the melancholic), while others (the sanguine) are at once inspired by the hope and assumed easiness of completing the job.

But what shall we say of the vainglorious boaster, whose claim is not founded on mere temperament—"What man wants to do, he can do?" This is just a high-sounding tautology. What he wants to do upon the command of his morally commanding reason is exactly what he ought to do. Consequently, it is what he can do (since reason would not command him to do the impossible). Yet, a few years ago, there were such fools who extolled this high-sounding tautology even in a physical sense, announcing themselves as world-assailants, but this breed has long since disappeared.

Habit (*consuetudo*) finally makes the endurance of evil easy (which, under the name of patience, is falsely honored as a virtue), because sensations of the same type, when continued without alteration for a long time, draw our attention away from the senses so that we are scarcely conscious of them at all. On the other hand, habit also makes the consciousness and the remembrance of good that has been received more difficult, which then gradually leads to ingratitude (a real vice).

Customary habit (*assuetudo*), however, is a physical and inner compulsion to proceed farther in the very same way in which we have been traveling. Acquired habit deprives good actions of their moral value because it undermines mental freedom and, moreover, it leads to thoughtless repetitions of the same acts (monotony), and thus becomes ridiculous. Customary expletives (clichés used merely to stuff the emptiness of thoughts) make the listener apprehensive that he will have to hear these favorite expressions over and over, and they make the orator into a talking-machine. The reason for being disgusted with someone's acquired habits lies in the fact that the animal here predominates over the man, so that instinctively, according to the rule of acquired habit, that person is categorized as another nature, a nonhuman nature, so that he runs the risk of falling into the same class with the beast. Nevertheless, certain continued practices may be started intentionally and kept up when Nature refuses help to the free will; for example, to become accustomed in old age to the time of eating and sleeping, or to the quality and quantity of food, or sleep, thus making it gradually mechanical. But this is the exception to the rule, and it occurs only in a case of necessity. Generally, all acquired habits are objectionable.

On the Artificial Games Played with Sensory Perceptions

§13. Delusion (*praestigiae*), to which the understanding is subjected by sense perception, may be either natural or artificial; it is either illusion (*illusio*) or deception (*fraus*). The delusion whereby we are forced to accept as real, by the evidence of our eyes, something which we declare to be impossible through the use of our understanding, is called optical delusion (*praestigiae*).

Illusion is that visual error which persists although we know at the same time that the supposed object is not real. This caprice of the mind is very agreeable to the senses and is amusing when, for example, we look at the perspective drawings of the interior of a temple, or as Raphael Mengs says about the painting from the school of the Peripatetics (I think he refers to Correggio): "If we look at them long enough, the people seem to walk;" or, we are tempted to try to mount the painted steps through the half-open door in Amsterdam's town hall.

Deception of the senses exists when the appearance vanishes as soon as we know the nature of the object. It is the same with all kinds of sleight of hand. Clothing whose color attractively sets off one's complexion constitutes an illusion, while makeup is a deception; we are misled by the former and mocked by the latter. Thus it happens that we do not like statues of men or animals which have been painted in natural colors, because we are constantly deceived into treating them as living, whenever we come upon them unexpectedly.

Fascination (*fascinatio*) in an otherwise sound mental state is a delusion of the senses about which it is said that the senses are not dealing with natural things. The senses seem to contradict each other because the judgment that an object (or a characteristic of it) exists is irresistibly changed after closer attention to the judgment that the object does not exist (or if, then in a different shape). It is like a bird that flits against a mirror in which he sees himself, sometimes thinking that the reflection is another bird, sometimes that it is not. Such games, in which men do not trust their own senses, occur especially in those who are intensely dominated by passion. There is the case of the lover who (according to Helvétius) saw his beloved in the arms of another. The beloved, who plainly deceived him, was able to say: "You faithless one, you do not love me any more. You believe what you see, instead of what I tell you!" More insolent, at least more injurious, has been the deception practiced by ventriloquists, gassnerists, mesmerists, and other pretended necromancers. In olden times ignorant women who pretended to do something supernatural were believed to be witches; and even in this century belief in witchcraft has not been fully rooted out.[6] It seems that the feeling of wonder at something unprecedented has in itself much that is alluring to weak minds. This is not because new prospects are suddenly opened to him, but because the weak person is seduced by them into escaping from the tiresome work of understanding and into making others as ignorant as himself.

On the Admissible Moral Perception

§14. Collectively, the more civilized men are, the more they are actors. They assume the appearance of attachment, of esteem for others, of modesty, and of disinterestedness, without ever deceiving anyone, because everyone understands that nothing sincere is meant. Persons are familiar with this, and it is even a good thing that this is so in this world, for when men play these roles, virtues are gradually established, whose appearance had up until now only been affected. These virtues ultimately will become part of the actor's disposition. To deceive the deceiver in ourselves, or the tendency to deceive, is a fresh return to obedience under the law of virtue. It is not a deception, but rather a blameless deluding of ourselves.

There is a disgust of one's own existence, which arises from the emptiness of mind toward the sensations for which the mind continually strives, that is caused by boredom. One grows weary of inactivity, that is, the weariness of all occupation that could be called work, and which could drive away that disgust because it is associated with hardship, a highly contrary feeling, whose original cause is none other than a natural inclination toward being at ease (rest without preceding fatigue). This inclination, however, is deceptive even with regard to the purpose which the human reason ordains for man, namely, self-contentment, when he does nothing at all (when he vegetates without purpose), because he assumes that he can do nothing evil in this state. This inclination toward further self-deception (which can be achieved by concentrating one's attention on the fine arts or, more effectively, through social activities) is called passing the time (*tempus fallere*). Here, indeed, the expression signifies the intention, which is really an inclination to self-deception through lazy inactivity, when the mind amuses itself by dallying with the fine arts, or when at least a mental cultivation is effected by a peaceful effort, which is pointless in itself; otherwise it would be called killing time. Force accomplishes nothing in the struggle against sensuality in the inclinations; instead we must outwit these inclinations, and, as Swift says, in order to save the ship, we must fling an empty tub to a whale, so that he can play with it.

Nature has wisely implanted in man the propensity to easy self-deception in order to save, or at least lead man to, virtue. Good and honorable formal behavior is an external appearance which instills respect in others (an appearance which does not demean). Womankind is not at all satisfied when the male sex does not appear to admire her charms. Modesty (*pudicitia*), however, is self-constraint which conceals passion; nevertheless, as an illusion it is beneficial, for it creates the necessary distance between the sexes so that we do not degrade the one as a mere instrument of pleasure for the other. In general, everything that we call decency (*decorum*) is of the same sort; it is just a beautiful illusion.

Politeness (*politesse*) is an appearance of affability which instills affection. Bowing and scraping (compliments) and all courtly gallantry, together with the warmest verbal assurances of friendship, are not always completely truthful. "My dear friends," says Aristotle, "there is no friend." But these demonstrations of politeness do not deceive because everyone knows how they should be taken, especially because signs of well-wishing and respect, though originally empty, gradually lead to genuine dispositions of this sort.

Every human virtue in circulation is small change; only a child takes it for real gold. Nevertheless, it is better to circulate pocket pieces than nothing at all. In the end, they can be converted into genuine gold coin, though at a considerable discount. To pass them off as nothing but counters which have no value, to say with the sarcastic Swift that "Honesty [is] a pair of Shoes worn out in the Dirt," and so forth, or to slander even a Socrates (as the preacher Hofstede did in his attack on Marmontel's *Belisar*), for the sake of preventing anyone from believing in virtue, all this is high treason perpetrated upon humanity. Even the appearance of the good in others must have value for us, because in the long run something serious can come from such a play with pretenses which gain respect even if they do not deserve to. Only the illusion of the good inside ourselves must be wiped out, and the veil, with which self-love conceals our moral infirmity, must be torn away. The appearance is deceptive if one pretends that one's guilt can be erased, simply cast off, by doing something that is without moral value, or one can convince oneself of being in no way in the wrong. Good examples of repentance of sins at the end of life are represented as actual improvement, or willful transgression is represented as human weakness.

On the Five Senses

§15. Sensibility in the cognitive faculty sense and imagination. Sense is the faculty of intuition in the presence of an object. Imagination is intuition without the presence of the object. The senses, however, are in turn divided into outer and inner (*sensus internus*). The outer sense is where the human body is affected by physical things. The inner sense is where the human body is affected by the mind. It should be noticed that this inner sense, as a bare faculty of perception (of the empirical intuition), must be regarded as differing from the feeling of pleasure and pain, that is, from the susceptibility of the subject to be determined through certain ideas for the conservation or rejection of the condition of these ideas, which might be called the interior sense (*sensus interior*). An idea that comes through the senses, and of which one is conscious as it arises, is specifically called sensation, when at the same time the perception centers our attention on the state of the subject.

§16. To begin with, we can divide the senses of physical sensation into those of the sensation of vitality (*sensus vagus*), and those of organic sensation (*sensus fixus*), and, since they are met with only where there are nerves, into those which affect the whole system of nerves, and those which affect only those nerves which belong to a certain member of the body. The sensations of warmth and cold, even those which are aroused by the mind (for example, through quickly rising hope or fear), belong to the vital sense. The shudder which seizes men even at the idea of something sublime, and the terror, with which nurses' tales drive children to bed late at night, belong to the latter type. They penetrate the body to the center of life.

The organic senses, however, so far as they relate to external sensation, we can conveniently reckon as five, no more and no less.

Three of them are more objective than subjective, that is, they contribute, as empirical intuition, more to the cognition of the exterior object, than they arouse the consciousness of the affected organ. Two, however, are more subjective than objective, that is, the idea obtained from them is more an idea of enjoyment, rather than the cognition of the external object. Consequently, we can easily agree with others in respect to the three objective senses. But with respect to the other two, the manner in which the subject responds can be quite different from whatever the external empirical perception and designation of the object might have been.

The senses of the first class are (*1*) touch (*tactus*), (*2*) sight (*visus*), (*3*) hearing (*auditus*). Of the latter class are (A) taste (*gustus*), (B) smell (*olfactus*). All together they are senses of organic sensation which correspond in number to the inlets from the outside, provided by na-ture so that the creature is able to distinguish between objects.

On the Faculty of Cognition as Far as It Is Based on Understanding

§40. Understanding as the faculty of thinking (representing something by means of concepts), is called the higher cognitive faculty (as distinguished from sensuousness, which is the lower), because the faculty of perceptions (pure or empirical) contains nothing but the particulars of objects, whereas the faculty of concepts contains the universals of the ideas of the objects, that is, the rule to which the multitude of sensuous perceptions must be subordinated, so that unity in the cognition of the object can be achieved. Certainly understanding is of higher rank than sensibility. Irrational animals can get along with sensibility alone following their implanted instincts, like a nation without a head of state. However, a head of state without a nation (like understanding without sensibility) has no power at all. Between the two, moreover, there is no actual dispute about rank, though one is considered higher and the other lower.

The word understanding is, however, also taken in a particular sense if it is subordinated to understanding in a general sense as one member of classification, together with two other faculties; and then the higher cognitive faculty (materially, that is, considered not by itself, but rather in relation to the cognition of objects), consists of understanding, judgment, and Reason. Let us now observe how one man differs from another in this mental faculty, or how his customary use or misuse is distinguished, first in a healthy mind, and then also in mental illness.

NOTES

1. In reference to this, the familiar verse of Persius can be parodied as follows: *Naturam videant ingemiscantque relicta.* [That they may look on Nature, and sigh because they have lost her—Dowdell.]

2. If we consciously imagine for ourselves the inner action (spontaneity), whereby a concept (a thought) becomes possible, we engage in reflection; if we consciously imagine for ourselves the susceptibility (receptivity), whereby a perception (*perceptio*), i.e., empirical observation, becomes possible, we engage in apprehension; however, if we consciously imagine both acts, then consciousness of one's self (*apperceptio*) can be divided into that of reflection and that of apprehension. Reflection is a consciousness of the

understanding, while apprehension is a consciousness of the inner sense; reflection is pure apperception, and apprehension is empirical apperception; consequently, the former is falsely referred to as the inner sense. In psychology we investigate ourselves according to our perceptions of the inner sense; but in logic we make the investigation on the grounds of what the intellectual consciousness supplies us with. Here the self appears to us as twofold (which would be contradictory): (1) the self, as the subject of thinking (in logic), which means pure apperception (the merely reflecting self) of which nothing more can be said, except that it is an entirely simple perception. (2) The self, as the object of the perception, consequently also part of the inner sense, contains a multiplicity of definitions which make inner experience possible.

To ask whether or not a man conscious of different inner mental changes (either of his thoughts or of fundamental principles assumed by him) can say that he is the self-same man, is an absurd question. For he can be conscious of these changes in the first place only on condition that he represents himself, in the different situations, as one and the same subject. The human ego is indeed twofold as regards its form (manner of representation), but not with respect to its matter (content).

3. But in looking at an object in daylight, it is apparent that what seems lighter than surrounding objects also seems larger, e.g., white stockings display fuller calves than black ones. A fire in the night, burning on a high mountain, appears to be larger than one actually finds it to be upon inspection. Perhaps we can also explain in this way the apparently larger size of the moon [MS and Cassirer; B: the apparent size of the moon—Dowdell] as well as the apparently greater distance between stars close to the horizon. In both cases shining objects appear to us as being high in the sky. They are objects close to the horizon seen through an obscuring layer of air; and what is dark is judged smaller because of the light which surrounds it. In target practice, therefore, a dark target with a white circle in the center would be more advantageous for shooting than a white target with a dark center.

4. To posit sensibility only in the obscurity of ideas, and intellectuality in distinctness, and thereby merely positing a formal (logical) distinction of cognition instead of a real (psychological) distinction, which not only refers to the form, but also to the content of thinking, has been a great mistake of the Leibniz-Wolff school. The error consisted in attributing a deficiency (as to clarity and constituent ideas) to sensibility and thus associating it with indistinctness, whereas the nature of rational ideas was understood to be distinct on the grounds that sensibility is something very positive and an indispensable ingredient of rational ideas for the process of producing cognition. Leibniz is really the one to blame. As a Platonist, he posited innate, pure perceptions of understanding, called ideas, which are encountered, though only obscurely, in the human mind. By applying our intellectual awareness to the analysis and elucidation of Platonic ideas, we are said to arrive at the cognition of objects as they really are.

5. Since we are speaking here only of the cognitive faculty, and, therefore, of ideas (not of the feeling of pleasure or displeasure), sensibility will mean nothing more than sense perception (empirical perception [MS: sense-*perception*—Dowdell]) in distinction to concepts (pertaining to thoughts) as well as pure perception (pertaining to the perception of Space and Time).

6. In this very century a Protestant clergyman testifying in Scotland as a witness in such a case, said to the judge: "Your Honor, I assure you on my priestly word that this woman is a witch." The judge replied: "And I assure you on my judicial word that you are no magician yourself." The word *Hexe* (witch) has now become a German word. It derives from the first words of the Mass formula used at the Consecration of the Host which the faithful behold with bodily eyes as a small disc of bread. After the formula has been pronounced, however, the faithful must look upon the bread with spiritual eyes as the body of a man. The words *hoc est* have been associated with the word *corpus;* thus *hoc est corpus* was changed to *hocus-pocus.* I suppose this resulted from pious reticence at saying and profaning the actual words, just as the superstitious are accustomed to do in the face of supernatural objects, in order to avoid sacrilege. [The etymology of *Hexe* (witch) today is assumed to derive from *Hag* (fence, hedge, little forest). Therefore *Hexe* is a demonic woman inhabiting such an area—Dowdell]

GUSTAV THEODOR FECHNER

Gustav Theodor Fechner (1801–1887) found only two of his courses as a university student interesting: Ernst Heinrich Weber's physiology course and Karl Brandan Mollweide's algebra course—understandable favorites for the future psychophysicist. Fechner earned a medical degree from the University of Leipzig, but never practiced—probably a blessing for potential patients, since he writes that he "had not learned to tie an artery, to apply the simplest bandage, or to perform the simplest operation connected with childbirth" for lack of interest in the practical side of medicine. Fechner's father, a Lutheran minister, did have a practical side, installing a lightning rod on his church steeple and admonishing his congregation to honor the laws of physics as well as the laws of God. Writing to earn money, Fechner not only published a series of satiric articles as Dr. Mises, including "Proof that the Moon is Made of Iodine" and "On the Comparative Anatomy of Angels," but also translated a number of French texts on physics and chemistry. Appointed to a lectureship in physics at the University of Leipzig in 1824, Fechner continued to support himself with translations, publishing his first original physics research in 1828. After he advanced to the rank of full professor, extremely poor health led to his resignation in 1840. Following a long recovery process, Fechner explored a wide variety of metaphysical, esthetic, and parapsychological issues, and on October 22, 1850, reported that while lying in bed he realized how to connect the physical, measurable world to the psychological experience via a proportion. Fechner's psychophysics was recognized by many established scientists, including Hermann von Helmholtz (p. 154) and Ernst Mach, as critical to establishing psychology as a scientific discipline unique from philosophy and physiology.

ELEMENTS OF PSYCHOPHYSICS

INTRODUCTION

I.

General Considerations on the Relation of Body and Mind

While knowledge of the material world has blossomed in the great development of the various branches of natural science and has benefited from exact principles and methods that assure it of successful progress, and while knowledge of the mind has, at least up to a certain point, established for itself a solid basis in psychology and logic, knowledge of the relation of mind and matter, of body and soul, has up to now remained merely a field for philosophical argument without solid foundation and without sure principles and methods for the progress of inquiry.

The immediate cause of this less favorable condition is, in my opinion, to be sought in the following factual circumstances, which admittedly only make us seek their more remote origins. The relationships of the material world itself we can pursue directly and in accord with experience, as no less the relationships of the inner or mental world. Knowledge of the former, of course, is limited by the reach of our senses and their amplifications, and of the latter by the limitations of everyone's

From Gustav Fechner, "Introduction. Outer Psychophysics." In T. B. H. E. Adler, D. H. Howes, & E. G. Boring (Eds.), *Elements of Psychophysics* (pp. 1–18, 38–45). New York: Holt, Rinehart & Winston, 1966. (Original work published 1860)

mind; still, these researches go on in such a way that we are able to find basic facts, basic laws, and basic relationships in each of the fields, information which can serve us as a secure foundation and starting point for inference and further progress. The situation is not the same in relating the material and mental worlds, since each of these two inextricably associated fields enters into immediate experience only one at a time, while the other remains hidden. At the moment when we are conscious of our feelings and thoughts, we are unable to perceive the activity of the brain that is associated with them and with which they are in turn associated—the material side is then hidden by the mental. Similarly, although we are able to examine the bodies of other people, animals, and the whole of nature directly in anatomical, physiological, physical, and chemical terms, we are not able to know anything directly about the minds that belong to the former nor of God who belongs to the latter,[1] for the spiritual side is here hidden by the material. There thus remains great latitude for hypothesis and disbelief. Is there really anything revealed, we may ask, once the covers are lifted, and if so, what?

The uncertainty, the vacillation, the argument over these factual issues has so far not allowed us to gain a solid foothold or to find a point of attack for a theory of these relationships, whose factual basis is still in dispute.

And what can be the reason for this singular condition, in which body and mind can be observed, each for itself but never together, in spite of the fact that they belong to each other? Usually we can best observe things which belong together when they occur together. The inviolability of this aspect of the relationship between the mental and material worlds makes us suspect that it is fundamental, that it is rooted in their basic natures. Is there nothing similar that can at least illustrate these facts even though it cannot get to the root of the matter?

Admittedly, we can point to one thing or another. For example, when standing inside a circle, its convex side is hidden, covered by the concave side; conversely, when outside, the concave side is covered by the convex. Both sides belong together as indivisibly as do the mental and material sides of man and can be looked upon as analogous to his inner and outer sides. It is just as impossible, standing in the plane of a circle, to see both sides of the circle simultaneously as it is to see both sides of man from the plane of human existence. Only when we change our standpoint is the side of the circle we view changed, so that we now see the hidden side behind the one we had seen before. The circle is, however, only a metaphor and what counts is a question of fact.

Now, it is not the task or the intention of this work to enter into deep or penetrating discussions on the basic question of the relationship of body and mind. Let everyone seek to solve this puzzle—insofar as it appears to him as such—in his own way. It will therefore be without prejudice for what follows, if I state my opinion here in a few words, in order not to leave unanswered some possible questions about the general beliefs that formed the starting point of this inquiry and that for me, at least, still form the background. At the same time I am providing something to go by in this field of fluctuating ideas for those who are still seeking a point of view rather than believing that they have found one, even though what I say will not contain anything essential for further progress of this work. In view of the great temptation in starting a work such as this to lose oneself in voluminous and extensive discussions of this sort, and of the difficulty, by no means slight, of avoiding them completely, I hope that I will be forgiven if I limit myself here to the following brief exposition of my position.

To begin with, however, let me add a second illustrative example to the first. The solar system offers quite different aspects as seen from the sun and as observed from the earth. One is the world of Copernicus, the other the world of Ptolemy. It will always be impossible for the same observer to perceive both world systems simultaneously, in spite of the fact that both belong quite indivisibly together and, just like the concave and convex sides of the circle, are basically only two different modes of appearance of the same matter from different standpoints. Here again one needs but to change the point of view in order to make evident the one world rather than the other.

The whole world is full of such examples, which prove to us that what is in fact one thing will appear as two from two points of view; one cannot expect to find things the same from one standpoint and from the other. Who would not admit that it is always thus and cannot be otherwise? Only with respect to the greatest and most decisive example does one deny it or fail to think of it. That is the relationship of the mental and material worlds.

What will appear to you as your mind from the internal standpoint, where you yourself are this mind, will, on the other hand, appear from the outside point of view as the material basis of this mind. There is a difference whether one thinks with the brain or examines the brain of a thinking person.[2] These activities appear to be quite different, but the standpoint is quite different too, for here one is an inner, the other an outer point of view. The views are even more completely different than were the previous examples, and for that reason the differences between the modes of their appearance are immensely greater. For the twofold mode of appearance of the circle or the planetary system was after all basically gained by taking two different external standpoints; whether within the circle or on the sun, the observer remained outside the sweep of the circles outside the planets. The appearance of the mind to itself, on the other hand, is gained from the truly inner point of view of the underlying being regarding itself, as in coincidence with itself, whereas the appearance of the material state belonging to it derives from a standpoint that is truly external, and not in coincidence.

Now it becomes obvious why no one can ever observe mind and body simultaneously even though they are inextricably united, for it is impossible for anyone to be inside and outside the same thing at one time.

Here lies also the reason why one mind cannot perceive another mind as such, even though one might believe it would be easiest to become aware of the same kind of entity. One mind, insofar as it does not coincide with the other, becomes aware only of the other's material manifestations. A mind can, therefore, gain awareness of another only through the aid of its corporeality, for the mind's exterior appearance is no more than its material nature.

For this reason, too, the mind appears always as unitary, because there exists only the one inner standpoint, whereas every body appears different according to the multitude of external standpoints and the differences among those occupying them.

The present way of looking at these phenomena thus covers the most fundamental relationships between body and mind, as any basic point of view should seek to do.

One more item: body and mind parallel each other; changes in one correspond to changes in the other. Why? Leibniz says: one can hold different opinions. Two clocks mounted on the same board adjust their movement to each other by means of their common attachment (if they do not vary too much from each other); this is the usual dualistic notion of the mind-body relation. It could also be that someone moves the hands of both clocks so that they keep in harmony; this view is occasionalism, according to which God creates the mental changes appropriate to the bodily changes and vice versa, in constant harmony. The clocks could also be adjusted so perfectly from the beginning that they keep perfect time, without ever needing adjustment; that is the notion of prestabilized harmony. Leibniz has left out one point of view—the most simple possible. They can keep time harmoniously—indeed never differ—because they are not really two different clocks. Therewith

we can dispense with the common board, the constant adjustment, the artificiality of the original setting. What appears to the external observer as the organic clock with its movement and its works of organic wheels and levers (or as its most important and essential part), appears to the clock itself quite differently, as its own mind with its works of feelings, drives, and thoughts. No insult is meant, if man here be called a clock. If he is called that in one respect, yet he will not be so called in every respect.

The difference of appearance depends not only on the difference of standpoint, but also on the differences among those that occupy it. A blind person does not see any of the exterior world from an external standpoint, though his position is just as favorable as that of a seeing person; and a nonliving clock does not see its interior in spite of its standpoint of coincidence, which is just as favorable as that of a brain. A clock can exist only as external appearance.

The natural sciences employ consistently the external standpoint in their considerations, the humanities the internal. The common opinions of everyday life are based on changes of the standpoints, and natural philosophy on the identity of what appears double from two standpoints. A theory of the relationship of mind and body will have to trace the relationship of the two modes of appearance of a single thing that is a unity.

These are my fundamental opinions. They will not clear up the ultimate nature of body and mind, but I do seek by means of them to unify the most general factual relationships between them under a single point of view.

However, as I mentioned before, it remains open to everyone to seek to effect the same end by another approach, or not to seek to accomplish it at all. Everyone's chosen approach will depend on the context of his other opinions. By arguing backwards, he will have to determine the possibility or impossibility of finding a suitable general relationship himself. At this point it is not important whether he wants to consider body and mind as only two different modes of appearance of the same entity or as two entities brought together externally, or to consider the soul as a point in a nexus of other points of essentially the same or of a different nature, or to dispense entirely with a fundamentally unitary approach. Insofar as an empirical relationship between body and mind is acknowledged and its empirical pursuit is allowed, there is no objection to trying even the most complicated kind of representation. In what follows we shall base our inquiry only on the empirical relationships of body and mind, and in addition adopt for use the most common expressions for the designation of these facts, though they are expressed more in the terms of a dualistic approach than my own monistic one. Translation from one to the other is easy.

This does not mean, however, that the theory which will be developed here will be altogether indifferent to the points of view on the basic relationships of body and mind and without influence upon them, for the contrary is true. Still, one must not confuse the effects that this theory may have some day—and that are partially beginning to take form even now—with the basis of this theory. This basis is indeed purely empirical and every assumption is to be rejected from the start.

One may well ask whether the possibility of such a basis does not directly contradict the fact, with which we started, that the relationships of body and mind are outside the realm of experience. They are not, however, beyond experience altogether, for only the immediate relationships are beyond immediate experience. Our own interpretation of the general relation of body and mind already has had the support of common experiences with these relationships, even if they do not strike everyone who comes to this work with preconceived notions as necessary. What follows will show how we can draw quite as much on special experiences, which can serve us partly to orient ourselves in the area of mediated relationships and partly to provide a foundation for deductions regarding immediate relationships.

Indeed, we could not rest content with this general point of view, even if it were generally accepted. The proof, the fertility, and the depth of a universal law do not depend on the general principles but on the elementary facts. The law of gravitation and the molecular laws (which undoubtedly include the former) are elementary laws; were they thoroughly known and the whole range of their implications exhausted, we would have a theory of the material world in its most general form. Similarly we must seek to form elementary laws of the relationship of the material and the mental world in order to gain a durable and developed theory instead of a general opinion, and we will only be able to do this, here as elsewhere, by building on a foundation of elementary facts.

Psychophysics is a theory that must be based on this point of view. More details follow in the next chapter.

II.

The Concept and the Task of Psychophysics

Psychophysics should be understood here as an exact theory of the functionally dependent relations of body

and soul or, more generally, of the material and the mental, of the physical and the psychological worlds.

We count as mental, psychological, or belonging to the soul, all that can be grasped by introspective observation or that can be abstracted from it; as bodily, corporeal, physical, or material, all that can be grasped by observation from the outside or abstracted from it. These designations refer only to those aspects of the world of appearance, with whose relationships psychophysics will have to occupy itself, provided that one understands inner and outer observation in the sense of everyday language to refer to the activities through which alone existence becomes apparent.

In any case, all discussions and investigations of psychophysics relate only to the apparent phenomena of the material and mental worlds, to a world that either appears directly through introspection or through outside observation, or that can be deduced from its appearance or grasped as a phenomenological relationship, category, association, deduction, or law. Briefly, psychophysics refers to the *physical* in the sense of physics and chemistry, to the *psychical* in the sense of experiential psychology, without referring back in any way to the nature of the body or of the soul beyond the phenomenal in the metaphysical sense.

In general, we call the psychic a dependent function of the physical, and vice versa, insofar as there exists between them such a constant or lawful relationship that, from the presence and changes of one, we can deduce those of the other.

The existence of a functional relationship between body and mind is, in general, not denied; nevertheless, there exists a still unresolved dispute over the reasons for this fact, and the interpretation and extent of it.

With no regard to the metaphysical points of this argument (points which concern rather more the so-called essence than the appearance), psychophysics undertakes to determine the actual functional relationships between the modes of appearance of body and mind as exactly as possible.

What things belong together quantitatively and qualitatively, distant and close, in the material and in the mental world? What are the laws governing their changes in the same or in opposite directions? These are the questions in general that psychophysics asks and tries to answer with exactitude.

In other words, but still with the same meaning: what belong together in the inner and outer modes of appearance of things, and what laws exist regarding their respective changes?

Insofar as a functional relationship linking body and

mind exists, there is actually nothing to prevent us from looking at it and pursuing it from the one direction rather than from the other. One can illustrate this relationship suitably by means of a mathematical function, an equation between the variables x and y, where each variable can be looked upon at will as a function of the other, and where each is dependent upon the changes of the other. There is a reason, however, why psychophysics prefers to make the approach from the side of the dependence of the mind on the body rather than the contrary, for it is only the physical that is immediately open to measurement, whereas the measurement of the psychical can be obtained only as dependent on the physical—as we shall see later. This reason is decisive; it determines the direction of approach in what follows.

The materialistic reasons for such a preference we need not discuss, nor are they meaningful in psychophysics, and the dispute between materialism and idealism over the essential nature of the dependency of one on the other remains alien and immaterial to psychophysics, since it concerns itself only with the phenomenal relationships.

One can distinguish immediate and mediated relationships of dependency or direct and indirect functions relating body and mind. Sensations are in a directly dependent relationship to certain processes in our brains as far as the one is determined by the other or has the other as its immediate consequence; but sensations are merely in a mediated relationship to the external stimulus, which initiates these processes only via the intervention of a neural conductor. All our mental activity has dependent upon it an immediate activity in our brain, or is accompanied immediately by brain activity, or else directly causes the activity, of which the effects then are transmitted to the external world via the medium of our neural and effector organs.

The mediated functional relationships of body and mind fulfill completely the concept of a functional relationship only under the supposition that the mediation enters into the relationship, since omission of the mediation leads to the absence of the constancy or lawfulness of the relationship of body and mind, which exists by virtue of this mediation. A stimulus then releases proper sensations only when a living brain does not lack the living nerves to transmit the effect of the stimulus to the brain.

As far as the psychic is to be considered a direct function of the physical, the physical can be called the carrier, the factor underlying the psychical. Physical processes that accompany or underlie psychical func-

tions, and consequently stand in a direct functional relationship to them, we shall call psychophysical.

Without making any assumptions about the nature of psychophysical processes, the question of their substrate and form we may leave undecided from the start. There is a twofold reason why we may dispense with this question right away: first, because the determination of the general principles of psychophysics will involve the handling only of quantitative relations, just as in physics, where qualitative depend on earlier quantitative relationships; and second, because we will have to give no special consideration to psychophysical processes in the first part, under the plan of work which follows immediately.

By its nature, psychophysics may be divided into an outer and an inner part, depending on whether consideration is focused on the relationship of the psychical to the body's external aspects, or on those internal functions with which the psychic are closely related. In other words, the division is between the mediated and the immediate functional relationships of mind and body.

The truly basic empirical evidence for the whole of psychophysics can be sought only in the realm of outer psychophysics, inasmuch as it is only this part that is available to immediate experience. Our point of departure therefore has to be taken from outer psychophysics. However, there can be no development of outer psychophysics without constant regard to inner psychophysics, in view of the fact that the body's external world is functionally related to the mind only by the mediation of the body's internal world.

Moreover, while we are considering the regular relations of external stimulus and sensation, we must not forget that the stimulus, after all, does not awaken our sensations directly, but only via the awakening of those bodily processes within us that stand in direct relation to sensation. Their nature may still be quite unknown, the inquiry regarding their nature may be neglected for the present (as already stated), but the fact that they do exist must be affirmed and referred to often, whenever it comes to the point of taking dead aim and following up those lawful relationships which are our immediate concern in outer psychophysics. Similarly, even though the body's activities, which are directly subject to the activity of our will and obey it, are still totally unknown, we should not forget that the effect of the will on the outer world can only be achieved via just such activities. We thus have implicitly to interpolate everywhere the unknown intermediate link that is necessary to complete the chain of effects.

Psychophysics, already related to psychology and physics by name, must on the one hand be based on psychology, and on the other hand promises to give psychology a mathematical foundation. From physics outer psychophysics borrows aids and methodology; inner psychophysics leans more to physiology and anatomy, particularly of the nervous system, with which a certain acquaintance is presupposed. Unfortunately, however, inner psychophysics has not profited so far from recent pains-taking, exact, and valuable investigations in this field to the extent it should. Inner psychophysics undoubtedly will do this one day, once these investigations (and those from the different kind of attack on which this work is based) have succeeded to the point of reaching a common meeting ground, where they will be able to cross-fertilize each other. That this is not yet the case to any extent indicates only the incomplete state in which our theory finds itself.

The point of view from which we plan to attack our task is as follows:

Even before the means are available to discover the nature of the processes of the body that stand in direct relation to our mental activities, we will nevertheless be able to determine to a certain degree the quantitative relationship between them. Sensation depends on stimulation; a stronger sensation depends on a stronger stimulus; the stimulus, however, causes sensation only via the intermediate action of some internal process of the body. To the extent that lawful relationships between sensation and stimulus can be found, they must include lawful relationships between the stimulus and this inner physical activity, which obey the same general laws of interaction of bodily processes and thereby give us a basis for drawing general conclusions about the nature of this inner activity. Indeed, later discussion will show that, in spite of all our ignorance of the detailed nature of psychophysical processes there exists, for those aspects which are concerned with the more important relationships of ordinary mental life, a basis which within limits already allows us to form certain and sufficient conceptions of the fundamental facts and laws which define the connection of outer to inner psychophysics.

Quite apart from their import for inner psychophysics, these lawful relationships, which may be ascertained in the area of outer psychophysics, have their own importance. Based on them, as we shall see, physical measurement yields a psychic measurement, on which we can base arguments that in their turn are of importance and interest.

III.

A Preliminary Question

For the present the discussion of all obscure and controversial questions of inner psychophysics and almost the whole of inner psychophysics at this time consists of such questions will be postponed along with the discussion of inner psychophysics itself. Later experience will provide us with the means for the answers. Nevertheless, one of these questions will at least have to be touched upon briefly at the start. This point, which concerns the future of the whole of psychophysics, we take up now in order to answer it to the extent that it can be answered in general, leaving everything else for later discussion.

If we classify thinking, willing, and the finer esthetic feelings as higher mental activities, and sensations and drives as lower mental activities, then, at least in this world leaving the question of the next world quite open the higher mental activities can go on no less than the lower without involving physical processes or being tied to psychophysical processes. No one could think with a frozen brain. There can be just as little doubt that a specific visual sensation or auditory sensation can only come about because of specific activities of our nervous system. No one questions this. The idea of the sensory side of the mind is actually based on the conception that there exists an exact connection between it and corporeality. Great doubt exists, however, as to whether each specific thought is tied to just as specific a process in the brain and, if not, whether brain activity as a whole suffices for thinking and the higher mental activities in general, without the necessity for a special type or direction of physiological process in the brain in order for these processes to take place in a specific way and direction. Indeed, it seems that the essential difference between the higher and lower mental spheres (distinguished by some as soul and mind in their narrower senses) is sought precisely in this point.

If we now assume that the higher mental activities are really exempt from a specific relationship to physical processes, there would still be their general relationship, which may be granted to be real, and which would be subject to the consideration and investigation of inner psychophysics. This general relationship will, in any case, be subject to general laws, including common principles, still to be discovered. Indeed, their discovery should always remain the most important of the tasks of inner psychophysics. One of the next chapters (Chapter

V) will lead us to a consideration of just such conditions.

A metaphor: thought may be regarded as part of the stream of bodily processes itself, and may be real only in terms of these processes, or it may need this stream only for steering as an oarsman steers his boat, raising only some incidental ripples with his oar. The conditions and laws of the river must be taken into account in both instances when the flow or progress of thought is concerned, though in each case from a quite different point of view, to be sure. Even the freest navigation[3] is subject to laws, as to the nature of the elements and the means that serve it. Similarly, psychophysics will find it necessary, in any case, to deal with the relationship of higher mental activity to its physical base. From what point of view, however, and to what extent, psychophysics will one day have itself to decide.

For the time being everyone should try to confine the conception and the scope of inner psychophysics as much as he can until the force and limitations of facts compel him to abandon the attempt. In my opinion, which as of now has to be considered as a mere opinion, there are no boundaries in this respect.

Indeed, I feel that the experience of harmony and melody, which undoubtedly have a higher character than single tones, is based on the ratios of the vibrations that themselves underlie the separate sensations, and that these ratios can change only in exact relationship to the manner in which the single tones are sounded together or follow one another. Thus, harmony and melody suggest to me only a higher relation, and not one lacking a special relationship of dependency between the higher mental sphere and its physical basis. Indeed everything seems to agree with this suggestion so easily pursued and extended. However, neither the pursuit nor even the assertion of this matter is relevant here at the start.

IV.

Concepts Concerning Sensation and Stimulus

In the present incomplete state of psychophysical investigations, there would be little profit in an enumeration, definition, and classification of all the psychological conditions that could at some time form their subject matter. At first we shall occupy ourselves mainly with sensory experiences in the common meaning of the word experience, making use of the following distinctions in nomenclature.

I intend to distinguish between intensive and extensive sensations, depending on whether they concern the sensory perception of something whose magnitude can be judged intensively or extensively. For example, I shall include as an intensive sensation the sensation of brightness, as an extensive sensation the perception of a spatial extent by sight or touch; and accordingly I shall distinguish between the intensive and extensive magnitude of a sensation. When one object appears to us brighter than another, we call the sensation it arouses intensively greater; when it appears larger than another we call it extensively greater. This is merely a matter of definition and implies, as generally understood, no specific measure of sensation.

With every sensation whatsoever, intensive as well as extensive, magnitude and form may be distinguished, although in the case of intensive sensations magnitude is often called strength and form quality. With sounds, the pitch, even though it is a quality of the sound, has also a quantitative aspect insofar as we can distinguish a higher from a lower pitch.

E. H. Weber—and undoubtedly quite to the point— calls the spatial sense, or the capacity or sense whereby we arrive at extensive sensations (as the term is used here), a general sense. Those senses that give rise to intensive sensations he calls special senses. The former sensations cannot, like the latter, arise from the impression of single independent nerve fibers or their respective ramifications (sensory circles), but can do so only by a coordination of the impressions of several fibers, wherein the strength and quality of the impression as well as the number and arrangement of the nerve centers are essential to fix the size and form of the extensive sensation. His discussions of this matter[4] are very apt contributions to the clarification of the general relationship of the senses. At present it suffices to have pointed out the foregoing difference in the circumstances on which intensive and extensive sensations depend. In fact, these brief preliminary discussions are intended only to introduce the discussion of appropriate measures of sensitivity and sensation, and therefore do not enter into the theory of sensations to any greater extent than this purpose warrants.

Because of their different natures and the different conditions upon which they depend, it is necessary to make a special examination of the laws governing extensive and intensive sensations. One might think that the magnitude of extensive sensations, or the extensive size of sensations, depended on the number of sensory circles stimulated, according to the same laws and corresponding to the way in which the magnitude of intensive sensations depends on the intensity of stimulation;

but this is both incorrect to assume a priori and impossible to prove as yet. Our future investigations will preferably concern themselves, though not exclusively, with the intensive sensations, and in the main are so to be understood, unless the contrary is apparent from the added adjective *extensive* or from the context.

Next to the distinction between extensive and intensive sensations we may consider the distinctions between objective and common sensations and between the so-called positive and negative sensations. Objective sensations, such as sensations of light and sound, are those that can be referred to the presence of a source external to the sensory organ. Changes of the common sensations, such as pain, pleasure, hunger, and thirst, can, however, be felt only as conditions of our own bodies. For this relationship the reader is also referred to Weber's classic work in his treatise on touch and common sensations.[5]

As positive and negative sensations it is usual to contrast such sensations as warmth and cold, pleasure and pain, which share the characteristic that the manner of their arousal or the relation to that which gives rise to them includes an antithesis. For example, the sensation of cold originates and increases through the withdrawal of heat, whereas warmth arises through the addition of heat. The sensation of pleasure is connected with a seeking of the cause of its arousal, just as dislike is connected with the opposite tendency.

While such designations as positive and negative sensations may be allowed in the usage of common language, one should not fail to note that the so-called negative sensations have nothing negative about them psychologically. They do not represent a lack, a lessening, a removal of sensations. On the contrary, they may be as violent, or even more so, than the so-called positive sensations, and are able to manifest themselves or give rise to just as strong positive effects on the body. For example, the sensation of freezing can cause a shaking of the whole body, and that of pain can cause crying besides other vigorous movements of the body.

The term *stimulus,* in its narrow sense, refers only to means of arousing the body, the excitation of intensive sensations. To the extent that stimuli belong to the outside world, they are external stimuli; insofar as they belong to the internal world of the body, they are internal stimuli. The former concept can be explained factually by recording external stimuli, such as light and sound; the latter concept will first need closer examination and may then perhaps be at least partially eliminated. A murmuring in our ears can start through the external influences of oscillations of the air, which a waterfall

sends to our ears. A similar murmur can originate without outside influence through causes within our body. These are in general unknown: yet insofar as they produce the equivalent of the effect of an outside stimulus, they must be considered its equivalent. From this point of view it will often suit us to treat these unknown, but admittedly (according to their effects) factual, internal bodily sources of sensations under the same concepts, standpoints, and formulas as the external sources.

If the mind were affected only by external and internal excitations to the extent that their effects reach a specific part of the body, then all sensations would, as far as we grant their dependence on the body, be only results of activities of the body. Thus even the innermost conditions of the body would fall under the concept of stimuli. If, on the other hand, it is essentially the case that sensations are only accompanied by bodily activities in a functional relationship, it would not be proper to include such simultaneously conditioned sensations with directly determined sensations. Only those stimuli that serve to cause sensations should be included, if one does not wish to mix two different kinds of things. In the meanwhile we do not immediately have to come to a decision. These diverse opinions have no influence on our factual observations, as long as we consider the existence and magnitude of internal stimuli only according to their equivalent effects as compared to external stimuli and take them into account as such. At this time internal stimuli are an unknown x as to their location and quality, although they enter despite this limitation into the phenomenal sphere with a quantitative effect that is comparable to that of an external stimulus. The internal stimulus derives its name and value from this effect.

Some things, like weights, to which one would hesitate to give the meaning of stimulus in everyday life, will be classed as such without misgivings, as far as they give rise to tactile pressure, or weight, when lifted. On the other hand, a generalization of the word stimulus to the causes by which extensive sensations are evoked in us has its drawbacks, especially inasmuch as little clarity exists so far about these causes. We perceive, with our eyes closed, a black visual field of a certain extent, even without the addition of external causes, and, by specially focusing our attention, we can become conscious of a certain extent of our body surface, even without being touched by calipers or other instruments. Added outside stimulation partially sets the boundaries of these natural sensation fields, partially determines their form, and partially provides a basis for judging relative size and distance, without, however, giving rise to the sensation of space. This sensation seems to be rooted in the inborn coordination and organic connections of active nerves, or of their central endings although nothing certain has been decided about the matter so far. If it is still possible to talk of a stimulus in this connection, we could do so only with respect to the coordination of the internal excitation of these nerves. Since these, however, are probably conditions that occur simultaneously with the sensation, this expression [the sensation of space] would again become unsuitable. Experience can also, aided by movements, take part in the judging of extents—as some like to emphasize. This is not the place, however, to go any deeper into this still rather obscure matter, where only the definitions of words are concerned.

One can say, disregarding this obscurity and the question of the extent to which the term *stimulus* is appropriate, that the magnitude of the stimulus in intensive sensations is replaced in the extensive case by the number of active sensory circles insofar as the perceived extension decreases or increases as a dependent function. Thus, in relation to quantitatively dependent relationships, this number can be brought under a common, though rather general, point of view. One cannot assert in this way, however, that the law by which they are dependent is the same in both cases, or that the magnitude of the extensive sensation does not depend on other circumstances besides that number. Indeed, these points are themselves the object of important psychophysical investigations.

Under the application of most outer forces on which sensations are dependent, the sensation increases, after it once becomes noticeable, as the force acting on it is increased continually and in the same direction, and decreases with the lessening of the force continually until unnoticeable. With regard to some sensations, however, such as warmth and pressure on the skin, the organism is so constituted that a sensation arises only by reason of a difference from a given average or normal influence, such as the normal skin temperature or normal air pressure. This sensation then increases in both directions but with different characteristics, as a sensation of warmth or cold, pressure or tension, depending on whether one increases the influence above this point or reduces it below this point. In this case one would correctly regard as the stimulus, not the absolute magnitude of the acting force, but its positive or negative deviation from the point that divides the sensations of contrasting character, the point at which no sensation exists. We could call the former a positive, the latter a negative stimulus.

As far as the interrelationship of stimulus and sensation is to be considered, stimuli are always assumed to be effective under comparable circumstances, unless the contrary is expressly mentioned or can be seen from the context. This comparability can, however, be nullified by a different mode of stimulation, as well as by a differing condition of the subject or the organ at the time the stimulus impinges. The concept of differential sensitivity relates to this condition, a concept and its measurement that will be discussed in detail in Chapter VI.

For the sake of brevity one says of a stimulus which evokes a sensation, as well as of a stimulus difference which is accompanied by a difference in sensations, that they are felt more strongly or weakly, according to whether the sensation or difference in sensations is stronger or weaker. This is also an expression that must be allowed to serve us without giving rise to misunderstanding.

OUTER PSYCHOPHYSICS: THE PRINCIPLE OF PSYCHOPHYSICAL MEASUREMENT

VI.

The Principle of Measurement of Sensitivity

Even when applied in the same way, one and the same stimulus may be perceived as stronger or weaker by one subject or organ than by another, or by the same subject or organ at one time as stronger or weaker than at another. Conversely, stimuli of different magnitudes may be perceived as equally strong under certain circumstances. Accordingly we ascribe to the subject or organ at one time or other a greater or lesser sensitivity.

When the sense organs are paralyzed, even the strongest stimuli are no longer felt their sensitivity is nil. On the other hand, in some conditions of excitation of the eye or ear even the weakest light or sound stimulus brings about a vivid, even annoying, sensation—the sensitivity of the organ is tremendously increased. Between these extremes exist all possible gradations of sensitivity. There is, therefore, sufficient reason to distinguish and to compare degrees of sensitivity. The question is: how can that be done precisely, how can a real measurement be made?

The following matter should be considered. Generally the measurement of a quantity consists of ascertaining how often a unit quantity of the same kind is contained in it. In this definition, sensitivity is an abstract capacity and as little a measure as is abstract energy. But instead of measuring it by itself, one can measure something related to it, something of which it is a function, which in accord with this concept increases and decreases with sensitivity—or conversely with which sensitivity increases and decreases—and thus we obtain an indirect measure in the same way as we do with energy. Instead of measuring energy itself we measure related or dependent velocities that bodies of the same mass can acquire, or the masses that can be given the same velocities. Thus we can also try to measure either the intensity of sensations that are produced by stimuli of equal magnitude, or the magnitude of stimuli that cause sensations of equal intensity. In the first case we could say sensitivity is twice as much, if the identical stimulus produces twice the intensity of sensation; in the second case, it is twice as much if a stimulus half as strong now causes just as intense a sensation.

The first course cannot, however, be taken, because we do not as yet have a measure of sensation, and, as we shall show later, such a measure itself rests on a differently derived measure of sensitivity. On the other hand, there is nothing to prevent us from taking the second course. The magnitude of stimuli can be approached by exact measurement, and the equality of sensation may well be found by taking the necessary steps, which we will discuss later in detail. We therefore take stimulus sensitivity as inversely proportional, or, in short, as reciprocal, to the magnitude of stimuli that cause equally intense sensations, or (more generally and in order to include extensive sensations) that cause equally large sensations.

One has to admit that it is ultimately only a matter of definition if we call sensitivity exactly twice as great when only half the simulus produces the same sensation. If sensitivity were measurable on its own, we could take no such liberties, but the proportional increase would have to be determined by experience or deduction. Such, however, is not the case. Interpretation is arbitrary, and the simplest possible interpretation is preferable, as it allows the least complex application.

So considered, this measure will be an aid and should be taken to have no further significance than its usefulness in orienting ourselves in the sphere of the factual relationships of stimulus and sensation and in making it possible to relate them mathematically. It neither can nor should enable us to make any statement at all in the abstract about the magnitude of our capacity for sensations. What always remains certain is that, for any one subject at any one time, it takes twice the stimulus to cause an identical sensation as it does for another subject at another time. Instead of saying this in many words, we may express ourselves briefly with but a few: in one case sensitivity for the stimulus is half as great as

in the other case. Every other numerical quantity refers to a different factual relationship in this respect and should mean no more than that.

The strength or vigor of the physical activities that the stimulus starts within us, and on which the sensation directly depends—in short, the psychophysical processes—are not involved in this measure which belongs to outer psychophysics. The question as to whether these activities are proportional to the intensity of stimuli or not is immaterial for this concept and its applications. For as a measure of stimulus sensitivity it is, after all, only applicable to a relationship of sensations and stimuli, and not to the processes that stimuli initiate within us. The question should undoubtedly be raised, but can only be decided on the basis of facts that presuppose this measure.

But it is important to avoid the following fallacy. When with twice the sensitivity for a given stimulus a half-strength stimulus is sufficient to cause a sensation of equal intensity, we cannot conclude that the same stimulus would then evoke twice the sensation. At present we cannot judge, for we do not have a measure of sensation, and later, when we do, we shall find that this relationship is by no means true.

It is important to differentiate the sensitivity for stimulus change and stimulus difference from stimulus sensitivity. These measurements, however, are subject to the same approach, except that stimulus change and stimulus difference take the place of the stimulus.

Indeed, just as a stimulus of the same, double, or treble the strength may be required to evoke sensations of equal intensities, so may the same, double, or treble the stimulus change, or the same, double, or treble the difference between stimuli, be required in order to evoke the same degree of change of sensation, or the same difference between two sensations. Stimulus change, as a stimulus difference in temporal sequence, can therefore be subsumed under the same point of view and name as the difference between two simultaneously occurring stimuli. We shall in general use this terminology from now on. This does not, of course, imply that it is immaterial whether one takes the components of a difference simultaneously or successively. By "components" we shall understand, here as well as in the future, the stimuli between which the difference exists, as shown by the corresponding sensations.

On superficial examination one might be inclined to regard measures of stimulus sensitivity, and those of stimulus difference, as reducible to each other. Given two tones of different physical intensities, we can imagine a third, of a loudness equal to the difference in loudness of the first two, and one could think for example, that the least loud tone which can just be heard and the least possible difference which can still be noticed between two tones have generally the same magnitude; but this is in fact not correct. Rather, casual observations teach us (and later, exact proof will be given) that the difference between two physical tones, lights, and so forth, in order, still to be noticeable, must be all the larger, the greater their absolute intensity, while the absolute intensity that is still just perceptible remains the same.

This fact makes it necessary, it can be seen, to differentiate between stimuli and stimulus differences with regard to sensitivity and the measure of sensitivity.

To the extent that the same stimulus difference is perceived more or less readily, depending on whether it is between weaker or stronger pairs of stimuli, differential sensitivity will in general vary not only with the state of the individual, but also with the intensity of the stimulus, usually being less for stronger than for weaker stimulation. Indeed, as later investigations show, the magnitude of a difference sensation evoked by a stimulus difference depends mainly on the ratio of the stimulus differences to the stimuli and the consequent ratio of the stimuli to each other. The inquiry into the law according to which sensation differences depend on stimulus intensity—that is to say, the law according to which the degree of stimulus difference that produces a uniformly distinct difference of sensation changes with stimulus intensity—is one of the most important tasks of outer psychophysics.

The following inquiries into the various sense domains will show that, at least within certain limits, a difference between given stimuli is always equally noticeable, if it increases and decreases proportionally to its components. By this statement we mean that the relative stimulus difference and the stimulus ratio for it stay the same, however the absolute magnitude of the stimulus differences and of the stimuli may be changed.

By relative stimulus difference we are to understand in general the difference of stimuli in relation to their sum, to their average, or to one or the other of them, for it does not matter which, inasmuch as by the constancy of one ratio the constancy of the other is determined automatically. In fact, relative stimulus difference and stimulus ratio always remain so closely linked that it does not matter whether one refers to the constancy of one or of the other.

If, for example, the components 5 and 3 are both doubled, the ratio of the two remains $^5/_3$ and the relative difference between them is unchanged, whether

one sets the latter at $(5 - 3)/(5 + 3) = {}^2/_8$ or as $(5 - 3)/5 = {}^2/_5$ or as $(5 - 3)/3 = {}^2/_3$, in that after doubling it becomes respectively $^4/_{16}$, $^4/_{10}$, and $^4/_6$, fractions which correspond with the above.

On the other hand, if the stimulus ratio is changed, the stimulus difference necessarily is changed in the same direction, but not proportionally. If, for example, the ratio $^5/_3$ of the components 5 and 3 becomes $^6/_3$ in that the component 5 is changed without the 3 being changed, the relative stimulus difference $(5 - 3)/(5 + 3) = {}^2/_8$ changes to $(6 - 3)/(6 + 3) = {}^3/_9$ or from $^1/_4$ to $^1/_3$, which is a change from a ratio of 5:6 to 3:4.

Now, as far as the law holds that a difference is equally noticeable, if it increases or decreases in proportion to its components (that is to say, if the relative stimulus difference and the stimulus ratio remain the same), one will have to say that differential sensitivity is reciprocal to the magnitude of the stimuli, since with double the stimulation the difference must be doubled in order to yield the same sensation of difference.

It may accordingly seem appropriate to express the sensitivity for differences immediately as a proportion, that is to say, to consider it equal not insofar as the same absolute stimulus difference evokes the same difference of sensation, but insofar as the same relative stimulus difference or stimulus ratio does so, and thus to express it as a reciprocal of the one or the other. Which one is used is again only a matter of definition and has no influence on the results when a measure of sensitivity is used, as long as one continues to use the measure according to its definition. It will be shown in the context of further work that for formal reasons it will be more appropriate to measure changes in the differential sensitivity, if taken as proportions of the reciprocal of the stimulus ratio rather than of the relative stimulus difference at which the sensation of difference remains the same. On the other hand, the equality of relative sensitivity can always be referred to the constancy of either the relative stimulus difference or the stimulus ratio.

To sum up: we must always make a twofold distinction with regard to sensitivity. (1) We must distinguish sensitivity for absolute stimulus intensities and for stimulus differences; in short, absolute sensitivity and differential sensitivity, of which the first is measured by the reciprocal of the absolute stimulus magnitudes that produce sensations of equal intensity. (2) The second, however, is usually understood to be measured in one of the following two ways: in the case of differential sensitivity, we have to distinguish between an absolute and a proportional, or relative, differential sensitivity, depending on whether the reciprocal of absolute difference of the ratio of stimulus intensities is used as our measure. The first of these we will usually call the simple differential sensitivity, the latter the relative differential sensitivity.

These distinctions may appear at this point as trivial and idle, but it will be shown later that they are by no means that. Indeed the clarity of conception of the most important factual relationships depends on this distinction, and, at least partially, the lack of lucidity that has continually plagued the theory of irritability is due to the lack, so far, of a clear distinction between them.

In general, the term *sensitivity* means no more than what is otherwise referred to by the terms *irritability, excitability,* or *sensibility.* It is only that these terms are generally used to refer not only to the evocation of sensations, but also to the activities of outer and inner stimuli. However, insofar as all sensations depend on inner processes, one could well relate the term sensitivity to its underlying psychophysical process instead of to sensation. One could then say of absolute sensitivity, for example, that it is equally large, twice as large, or three times as large, according to whether an equally strong, half or twice as strong an outer or inner stimulus is needed to evoke the same psychophysical process.[6] But this way of thinking is not practical, because the psychophysical process is not accessible to observation.

In other places the terms irritability and excitability are used partly as synonyms, partly as arbitrary distinctions, without these distinctions being based on a clearly defined, factual relationship. It will be convenient, however, after clarifying the concept of the different sensitivities, to introduce a distinctive usage, and I will therefore use irritability in the future solely for the absolute, and excitability for the relative differential sensitivity, with the former referring to sensations and the latter to perceived differences.

In our definitions, so far, we have focused our attention primarily on the intensive sensations, to which, strictly speaking, the concept of stimulus alone refers. Nevertheless, the measurement of sensitivity is transferable from the sphere of intensive sensations to that of extensive sensations, as is consistent with the following facts.

As is well known, E. H. Weber's experiments show that it takes a certain spread of the sharp points of calipers placed on the skin to make the distance between them just noticeable. There is nothing to stop us by using a modification of his procedure (of which I will have to say more later) from determining apparently equally large distances on different places of the skin, by means of which it can be shown that the real distance which is just noticeable (or, more generally, appears equally large) is very different at different places on the skin. It can be proven just as well, by methods to be given later, that the differences between distances which can still be noticed on different parts of the skin are of different size. Differences in the perception of spatial magnitudes and of differences in magnitude that are analogous to those between diverse parts of the skin can be found between various regions of the retina, especially between the more central and peripheral parts. One can, therefore, speak of differential sensitivity in the perception of extensive size as one can in the perception of intensive size, and distinguish them briefly as extensive and intensive sensitivity.

The absolute measure and the differential measure of the extensive sensitivity of the different places on the skin and retina will then also have to be sought in the reciprocal of equally large-appearing extents, differences in extent, or ratios of extents, just as the measure of intensive sensitivity was sought in intensities appearing equally strong in intensity differences, or in ratios of intensity. For example, one place on the skin may have twice the extensive sensitivity as another, taken absolutely, if half the distance between the caliper points appears on it as equally large.

Notwithstanding the fact that the extensive sensitivity of the parts under discussion undeniably stands in some kind of dependent relationship to the number of so-called sensory circles[7] contained in a given area, it would still be just as invalid to relate the measure of extensive sensitivity to this unknown number of sensory circles, as it would be to relate the measure of intensive sensitivity to the unknown magnitude of psychophysical processes. Undeniably a given area of the back contains many fewer of these circles than do the finger tips, and the lesser extensive sensitivity of the back compared to that of the finger is based just on this fact. However, the concept of extensive sensitivity also takes account of the fact that due to its biological arrangement and state, one organ may in this respect be constituted differently from another. Were one to reduce all measurement of sensitivity to the different numbers of sensory circles, this concept of differential sensitivity would probably fall by the wayside. In any case one would have no data available, and thus the whole measure would remain pure speculation, even though undeniably there exists a generally valid, if as yet unknown, relationship of dependency in this respect, which might in all cases lead to the same value. As of now, it must be admitted that measured data of the extensive sensitivity, as well as those of the intensive, when taken according to the principle provided here, have only the value of observational data, which by themselves do not provide insight into the basic relationships of sensations to their physical basis, but which, together with other data, may yet serve to contribute to the establishment of this relationship, if one consistently takes and uses them as purely observational data.

One might entertain doubts from the start—considering the great variability of sensitivity due to individual differences, time, and innumerable internal and external conditions—that it would be of any use to strive for a measure for either form of sensitivity. For one thing, something that is constantly varying is not amenable to exact measurement; for another, results do not show constancy, and therefore are valueless, since results observed with certain individuals, at a certain time and under certain circumstances, are not found again at other times and circumstances.

Indeed, it cannot be denied that in this respect there do exist difficulties of measurement in our psychophysical domain, difficulties which do not exist in purely physical or astronomical areas. But instead of the measure or the possibility of obtaining fruitful results by its means being destroyed thereby, this difference only means that the sphere of inquiry must be widened, and considerations introduced which do not exist in the other areas.

Insofar as sensitivity is a variable, we should not seek for a constant as its measure. We may, however, look for (1) its limits and (2) its mean values; we may also investigate (3) how its variations depend on conditions; finally we may seek (4) lawful relations that remain constant during variation; the last are the most important. The methods for measuring sensitivity that will be discussed will provide not only sufficient means, but

also sufficient precision, for research and investigations into all these matters.

A thorough investigation under these circumstances is necessarily more complex than it would be for a single, constant, unchanging subject, for it cannot be accomplished for one person alone and it has as yet not been carried out adequately for a single sense domain. In this respect, rather, there opens up a rich field for future research, especially for the younger generation, by means of the methods that we will now discuss. This research is by itself not difficult, yet it demands patience, attention, endurance, and faithfulness.

NOTES

1. Trans. Note: A typical Fechner notion. God is the soul of the universe.

2. Examination in this case is equivalent to forming, from deductions based on external observations, an adequate concept of how the internal condition would appear upon removal of barriers to direct examination.

3. Trans. Note: A reference to free navigation as a political problem—for example, free navigation on the Rhine.

4. *Berichte der sächs. Soc.* 1853, p. 83; abstracted in *Fechner's Centralblatt für Naturwissenschaften und Anthropologie.* 1853, No. 31.

5. Ed. Note: E. H. Weber, *Der Tastsinn und das Gmeingefühl. R. Wagner's Handwörterbuch der Physiologie.* 1846, III, ii, 481–588.

6. Trans. Note: Fechner undoubtedly meant one third, rather than twice as strong a stimulus, for three times the sensitivity.

7. Ed. Note: This sensory circle is a translation of E. H. Weber's *Empfindungskreis.*

12

HERMANN VON HELMHOLTZ

Hermann Ludwig Ferdinand von Helmholtz (1821–1894) writes in his autobiography that he had trouble as a child in school because he "had a bad memory for disconnected things." He did find, however, that he enjoyed memorizing poetry of the highest sort—including some books of the *Odyssey* and Horace's *Odes.* He found his true subject following the discovery of some old physics textbooks of his high school–teaching father. He writes, "Physics was at that time looked upon as an art by which a living could not be made," so his only opportunity for advanced education involved trading eight years of army service as a surgeon for training in medicine, a scholarship program sponsored by the Prussian government. During the course of his studies, Helmholtz began working with physiologist Johannes Müller and was able to apply certain concepts of physics to physiological problems. Following some brilliant work concerning force and the conservation of energy accomplished in a laboratory he built in the barracks, the Prussian army released Helmholtz from part of his service obligation. He was subsequently appointed as a lecturer on anatomy at Berlin's Academy of the Arts in 1848, moving the next year to the university at Königsberg as a professor of physiology. He eventually became a professor of physics at the University of Berlin in 1871, but not before making major contributions to both physiology and psychology.

THE FACTS OF PERCEPTION

Honored Assembly!

Today we celebrate our university's commemoration holiday on the day of our founder's birth, the much-tested King Frederick William III. The year of this founding, 1811, came at the time of our State's greatest foreign troubles: a considerable amount of territory was lost, and the country was fully exhausted by the preceding war and hostile occupation. The warlike pride that had remained from the days of the great Electors and the Great King was deeply humiliated. And yet, when we look back, that very same time now seems to us so rich in goods of a spiritual kind—in inspiration, energy, ideal hopes, and creative thoughts—that, notwithstanding the relatively brilliant foreign situation in which the State and Nation now find themselves, we want to look back on that period almost with envy. That the King thought of founding the University during this distressing situation before attending to other material demands, and that he risked the throne and his life in order to entrust himself to the Nation's resolute inspiration in the struggle against the conqueror—this shows how deeply he too, a man who was disinclined to simple, spirited expressions of feeling, won the trust of his people's spiritual forces.

At the time, Germany had a stately series of praiseworthy names for display in both art and science, names whose bearers are partly to be counted among the first rank of all times and peoples in the history of human cultural education.

Goethe and Beethoven lived then; Schiller, Kant, Herder, and Haydn had yet to experience the century's first years. Wilhelm von Humboldt outlined the new science of comparative linguistics; Niebuhr, Fr. Aug. Wolf, and Savigny taught ancient history, poetry, and law with a penetrating, lively understanding; Schleiermacher sought seriously to comprehend the intellectual content of religion; and Joh. Gottlieb Fichte, our University's second rector and the powerful, fearless speaker, swept his listeners away with the stream of his moral inspiration and the bold intellectual flight of his Idealism.

Even the aberrations of this way of thinking, which expressed itself in the weaknesses of Romanticism that are so readily seen, have something attractive compared to dry, calculating egoism. One admired oneself in the beautiful feelings in which one knew to revel; one sought to cultivate the art of having such feelings; one believed that the more fantasy freed itself from the rules of the understanding, the more one had to admire it as a creative force. Therein resided much vanity—yet it was a vanity that reveled in high ideals.

The older ones among us still knew the men of that period: men who had entered into the army as the first volunteers; who were always ready to immerse themselves in the discussion of metaphysical problems; who

From Hermann von Helmholtz, "The Facts of Perception." In D. Cahan (Ed.), *Science and Culture* (pp. 342–366). Chicago: University of Chicago Press, 1995. (Original work Published 1878)

were well read in the works of Germany's great poets; and who still burned with anger when Napoleon I, inspiration and pride, and the acts of the War of Liberation were discussed.

How things have changed! We cry out with astonishment in an age in which cynical contempt for all the human race's ideal goods has spread into the streets and the press, and has culminated in two abominable crimes which chose our Emperor's head as their object simply because his person united all that humanity to date had considered worthy of honor and gratitude.

It almost requires an effort for us to remember that only eight years have passed since the great moment when all classes of our people, full of joyful sacrifice and inspired by love of the Fatherland, unhesitatingly rose to the call of that same monarch and engaged in a dangerous war against an opponent whose power and bravery was not unknown to us. And it almost requires an effort for us to recall the broad scope that political and humane efforts have taken in the activities and thoughts of the educated classes, not least to give the poorer classes of our people a more carefree and humane existence, to think of how very much their lot has really improved in material and legal relations.

It seems to be humanity's nature that, along with much light, there is also found much shadow: political freedom at first gives the baser motives greater license to manifest themselves and mutually to encourage one another—so long as an armed public opinion does not confront them in energetic opposition. Even in the years prior to the War of Liberation, when Fichte held penitential sermons, these elements were not lacking. He describes governing conditions and convictions that remind us of the worst of our time. "In its fundamental principle, the present age arrogantly looks down upon those who, by some dream of virtue, allow themselves to be extricated from pleasures; and it is glad that it may be beyond such things, and in this way allows nothing to be imposed upon itself." He refers to the only pleasure—beyond the purely sensual—with which the era's representatives are acquainted as "comfort in their own cunning." Nonetheless, a powerful impetus belonging to our history's most glorious events prepared itself in this very same era.

If we need not, therefore, think of our era as hopelessly lost, we should also not too easily calm ourselves with the consolation that it was not better in other times than it is now. It is, nonetheless, advisable that in such serious circumstances each person be watchful in the circle in which he works and which he knows, as to how the work of humanity's immortal goals is proceeding, that they are being kept in view, whether we may have

drawn nearer to them. During our University's youth, science was also youthfully bold and filled with hope: its eye was turned chiefly to the highest goals. If these goals were not as easily reached as that generation had hoped, and if it also became clear that detailed individual investigations had to prepare the way—and thus, by the very nature of the tasks themselves, at first another type of work, one less enthusiastic and less directly, aimed at the ideal goals was needed—it would, for all that, doubtless be damaging if our generation should, thanks to secondary and practically useful tasks, lose sight of humanity's eternal ideals.

Epistemology was at that time the fundamental problem posited at the start of all science: "What is truth in our intuitions and thought? and in what sense do our ideas correspond to reality?" Philosophy and natural science approached this problem from two opposite sides; it is a common task of both. The first, which considers the intellectual side, seeks to exclude from our knowledge and ideas that which originates from the influences of the corporeal world in order to be able to state that which belongs to the mind's own activity. Natural science, by contrast, seeks to divide off that which is definition, designation, form of representation, and hypothesis in order to retain as pure residue that which belongs to the world of reality, whose laws it seeks. Both seek to accomplish the same division, even if each is interested in another part of the divide. Even the natural scientist cannot avoid these questions in the theory of sense perceptions and in the investigations on the fundamental principles of geometry, mechanics, and physics. Since my own work has often concerned both fields, I shall try to give you an overview (from the side of natural science) of what has been done in this direction. The laws of thought in men who pursue natural science are, of course, ultimately no different than in those who do philosophy. In all cases where the facts of daily experience—whose abundance is indeed already very large—suffice to give a rigorous thinker with an unprejudiced feel for the truth enough material to reach a correct judgment, the natural researcher must be content to acknowledge that the methodical and complete collection of the facts of experience simply confirms results previously gained. However, opposite cases also occur. This is an apology—if apology it must be—that in what follows not all answers are new, but are, for the most part, long-known answers to the relevant questions. Often enough, even an older concept, when compared with new facts, takes on a livelier coloration and new authority.

Shortly before the start of the new century, Kant had developed the theory of what is given prior to all experience, or, as he called it, "transcendental" forms of intuitions and thought, wherein all the content of our representations must necessarily be received if it should become an idea. For the qualities of sensation, Locke had already considered the contribution which our corporeal and intellectual organization make to how things appear to us. In this way, the investigations in sensory physiology—that (above all) Johannes Müller completed, critically envisioned, and then summarized in the law of specific energies of sensory nerves—have now brought the fullest confirmation—one can almost say to a degree unexpected—and thereby at once presented and made evident the nature and meaning of one such *a priori,* subjective form of sensation in a very decisive and tangible way. This theme has already often been reviewed; hence I need discuss it only briefly today.

Among the different kinds of sense perceptions there occur two different types of distinction. The most fundamental is the distinction among sensations that belong to the different senses, as among blue, sweet, warm, and high-pitched. I have permitted myself to call this a distinction in the modality of sensation. It is so fundamental that it excludes any transition from one to the other, from any relation of greater or lesser similarity. For example, it simply cannot be an issue as to whether sweet may be similar to blue or red. By contrast, the second type of distinction, which is less fundamental, is that among different sensations of the same sense. To it I restrict the designation of a difference in quality. Fichte summarized these qualities of each sense as a circle of qualities, and calls what I called difference in modality a difference in the circle of qualities. A transition and comparison is possible within each such circle. We can move from blue through violet and carmine red into scarlet red; and, for example, assert that yellow may be more similar to orange red than to blue. Now physiological investigations teach that that fundamental distinction does not completely depend on the type of external impression by which the sensation is stimulated; rather, it is determined completely, solely, and exclusively by the sensory nerve that has been affected by the impression. Stimulation of the optic nerve produces only sensations of light, no matter whether it is struck by objective light—that is, by vibrations of the aether—or by electric currents which are conducted through the eye, or by pressure on the eyeball, or by stretching the nerve endings during a rapid change of view. The sensation that originates with the latter effects is so similar to that of objective light that one had long believed in an actual development of light in the eye. Johannes Müller showed that such a development definitely does not oc-

cur and that the sensation of light is most certainly only there because the optic nerve is stimulated.

On the one hand, just as each sensory nerve, stimulated by the most manifold influences, always gives sensations only from its particular circle of qualities, so, on the other hand, do the same external influences produce, when they meet different sensory nerves, the most different types of sensations, and these latter are always taken from the circle of qualities of the nerves in question. The same aether vibrations which the eye feels as light, the skin feels as heat. The same aerial vibrations which the skin feels as whirring motions, the ear feels as sound. Here, once again, the impression's heterogeneity is so great that physicists were first assuaged with the idea that agents like light and radiating heat, which appear so different, may be of the same kind and partly identical, after the complete homogeneity of their physical behavior was determined in every way by laborious experimental investigations.

Yet the most unexpected incongruencies also occur within the circle of qualities of each individual sense, where the type of effective object at least co-determines the quality of the sensation produced. In this regard, the comparison of eye and ear is instructive, since the objects of both—light and sound—are vibrating motions, which, depending on the speed of their vibrations, stimulate different sensations of different colors in the eye, of different pitches in the ear. If, for greater clarity, we may designate the light's vibrational relations with the names of musical intervals formed by the corresponding sound vibrations, then the following occurs: The ear senses about 10 octaves of different tones, the eye only a sixth, although the vibrations lying beyond these limits occur in sound, as in light, and can be demonstrated physically. The eye (in its short scale) has only three sensations fundamentally different from one another, by which all its qualities are composed through addition: namely, red, green, and blue-violet. These mix together in the sensation without disturbing one another. The ear, by contrast, distinguishes an enormous number of sounds of different levels. No chord sounds like any other chord which is composed of different sounds, while in the eye precisely the analogue is the case: for a similar shade of white can be produced by red and green-blue of the spectrum; by yellow and ultramarine blue; by green-yellow and violet; by green, red, and violet; or, in any case, by two, three or all of these mixtures together. Were the relations in the ear similar, then the chords C and F would be equal-sounding with D and G, with E and A, or with C, D, E, F, G, A, etc. Moreover, concerning the objective meaning of color it is noteworthy that, apart from the effect on the eye, no single physical relation has been found in which similarly appearing light may be regularly equivalent. Finally, the entire foundation of the musical effect of consonance and dissonance depends on the characteristic phenomenon of beats. These are based on a rapid change in the intensity of sound from which thereby arises that two nearly equal high sounds cooperate in exchanging the same and opposite phases, and, accordingly, stimulate first strong, then weak vibrations of co-vibrating bodies. The physical phenomenon could occur quite similarly in the cooperation of two light-wave impulses, as it recurs in the cooperation of two sound-wave impulses. However, the nerve must first be able to be affected by both wave impulses; and second, it must be able to follow rapidly enough the change of stronger and weaker intensity. In the latter relation, the auditory nerve is far superior to the optic nerve. At the same time, each fibre of the auditory nerve is sensitive only to sounds from a narrow interval of the scale, so that only sounds situated very closely to one another can, in general, work together in it, while those situated far apart from one another cannot or cannot directly do so. If they do so, then this arises from accompanying upper harmonics or combination tones. Hence, the distinction of humming and non-humming intervals occurs in the ear, that is, of consonance and dissonance. By contrast, each optic nerve fibre senses throughout the entire spectrum, although it does so with different strengths in different parts. If the optic nerve could in general follow the tremendously rapid beats of light oscillations in the sensation, then each color mixture would operate as dissonance.

You see how all these distinctions as to the manner in which light and sound produce effects are conditioned by the type, by how the nerve apparatus reacts to them.

Our sensations are precisely effects produced by external causes in our organs, and the manner in which one such effect expresses itself depends, of course, essentially on the type of apparatus which is affected. Insofar as the quality of our sensation gives us information about the peculiarity of the external influence stimulating it, it can pass for a sign—but not for an image. For one requires from an image some sort of similarity with the object imaged: from a statue, similarity of form; from a drawing, equality of perspectival projection in the visual field; and from a painting, similarity of colors. A sign, however, need not have any type of similarity with what it is a sign for. The relations between the two are so restricted that the same object, taking effect under equal circumstances, produces the same sign, and hence unequal signs always correspond to unequal effects.

Compared to popular opinion, which in good faith assumes the complete truth of images that give us our sense of things, this residue of similarity which we acknowledge may seem very limited. In truth, it is not; for with it something of the very greatest significance can still be accomplished: namely, the imaging of the lawlike in the processes of the real world. Each natural law says that, given preconditions which are alike in certain respects, consequences which are alike in certain other respects will always follow. Since likeness in our world of sensation is shown by like signs, then there will also correspond to the natural-law consequence of like effects upon like causes a regular consequence in the field of our sensations.

If a certain type of berry developes (at maturity) both red pigment and sugar, then red color and sweet taste will always be found together in our sensation of berries of this type.

Hence, even though our sensations are, in their quality, only signs whose special type depends completely on our organization, they are nonetheless certainly not to be dismissed as empty appearance; rather, they are precisely signs of something, be it something enduring or occurring, and, what is most important, they can delineate for us the law of this occurring.

Hence, physiology also recognizes the qualities of sensation as a mere form of intuition. Kant, however, went further. He addressed not only the qualities of sense perception as given by the characteristics of our intuitive capability, but also space and time, since we can perceive nothing in the external world without it occurring at a definite time and in a definite place; determination in time may also be attributed, moreover, to each internal perception. He thus designates time as the given and necessary transcendental form of inner intuition, and space as the corresponding form of outer intuition. Kant thus considered spatial determinations as little belonging to the real world, "to the thing in itself," as the colors which we see belong to bodies in themselves, and which are rather brought into them through our eye. Even here the natural scientific view can, up to a certain point, go along. Namely, if we ask whether there is a marker which is common and perceptible by direct sensation, through which every perception relating to objects in space is characterized, then we find, in fact, one such marker in the circumstance that the movement of our body places us in other spatial relationships to perceived objects and thereby also changes the impression which they make on us. However, the impulse to movement that we give through innervation of our motor nerves, is something directly perceivable. We feel that we do something when we give one such impulse. We do not know directly what we do. Physiology only teaches us that we displace or innervate the motor nerves into a stimulated state; that its stimulation is conducted to the muscles; and that this contracts as a consequence and moves the limbs. Again however, without any scientific study we also know which perceptible effect follows from each different innervation that we can induce. It is demonstrable in a large number of cases that we learn this by frequently repeated experiments and observations. We can still learn in adulthood to locate the innervations necessary to enunciate letters of a foreign language or to produce a special type of voice in singing; we can learn innervations to move the ears, to squint with the eyes inward or outward, even upwards and downwards, etc. The difficulty in executing these consists only in that we must try to find by experiments the still-unknown innervations needed for such previously unexecuted movements. Moreover, we ourselves know these impulses under no other form and by no other definable feature than that they induce precisely the intended observable effect; this alone thus serves to distinguish different impulses in our own representation.

If we now make such types of impulses—take a look, move the hands, go back and forth—then we find that the sensations belonging to certain quality circles—namely, those with respect to spatial objects—can be changed; while other mental states of which we are conscious—memories, intentions, wishes, moods—cannot at all. A decisive distinction between the former and the latter is thus posited in direct perception. If we then want to call "spatial" the relation which we change directly by our will's impulse but whose type may still be quite unknown to us, then the perceptions of psychic activities do not at all enter into any such relation. All sensations of the external senses must, however, proceed through some type of innervation, that is, be spatially determined. Accordingly, space will also seem physical to us, laden with the qualities of our perceptions of movement, as that through which we move ourselves, through which we are able to look. In this sense spatial intuition would thus be a subjective form of intuition, like the sensory qualities red, sweet, and cold. Naturally it would mean just as little for the former as for the latter, that the location of a certain individual object might be a mere appearance.

However, from this point of view space would appear as the necessary form of outer intuition, since we understand as the external world precisely what we perceive as spatially determined. That which has no perceptible spatial relation, we conceive as the world of inner intuition, as the world of the self-conscious.

And space would be an innate form of intuition prior to all experience insofar as its perception would be tied to the possibility of the will's motoric impulses, and for which the mental and corporeal ability must be given us through our organization before we can have spatial intuition.

Moreover, there will certainly be little doubt that the marker noted by us of the change in movement belongs to all spatial objects and perceptions, respectively. On the other hand, the question remains to be answered as to whether all particular determinations of our spatial intuition are to be derived from this source. Toward that end we must consider what can be attained with the means of perception considered so far.

Let us try to put ourselves in the position of a person without any experience. In order to begin without any spatial intuition, we must assume that such a human being also knows no more about the effects of his innervations beyond that by which he may have learned by putting himself in the initial state (from which he withdrew through the first impulse) through the reduction of an initial innervation or by the carrying through of a second, opposing impulse. Since this mutual self-neutralization of different innervations is completely independent of what is perceived, the observer can discover how he has to do that without having previously reached any kind of understanding of the external world.

Let such an observer at first find himself facing an environment of objects at rest. This will initially allow itself to be recognized by him that, as long as he emits no motoric impulses, his sensations will remain unchanged. If he gives one such impulse—for example, if he moves his eyes or his hands, or if he steps forward—then the sensations change. If he returns to the previous condition through relaxation or through the appropriate counterimpulse, then all sensations again become the previous ones.

Let us call the entire group of aggregate sensations induced during the said period of time by a certain definite and finite group of the will's impulses the "current presentables"; by contrast, let us call "present" the aggregate of sensations from this group which is just coming to perception. Our observer is now bound to a certain circle of presentables from which, however, he can make each individual presentable present to himself at any moment through execution of the relevant movement. In this way it seems to him that each individual from this group of presentables exists at each moment during this period of time. He observed it in every individual instant that he chose to. The claim that he would also have been able to observe it in every other intervening moment (when he would have wanted it), is to be considered as an inductive conclusion simply drawn from each moment of a successful attempt at each moment of the concerned period of time. Thus the idea of a simultaneous and continuous existence of different things alongside one another will be achieved. "Coexistence" is a spatial designation; it is, however, justified because we have defined as "spatial" that relation changed by the will's impulses. One still does not need to think of that which is here said to coexist as substantive things. "It is bright on the right, it is dark on the left"; "resistance is ahead, behind it is not," could, for example, be said at this level of knowledge, whereby right and left are only names for definite eye movements, ahead and behind for definite hand movements.

At other times the circle of presentables becomes another circle for the same group of the will's impulses. This circle thereby confronts us with its individual contents as a given, as an "object." Those changes which can bring forth and annul by conscious impulses of the will are to be distinguished from those which are not consequences of the will's impulses and cannot be overcome by such. The latter finding is negative. Fichte's appropriate expression for it is that a *Non-ego* forces recognition of itself vis-à-vis the *Ego*.

If we inquire about the empirical conditions under which spatial intuition develops, then we mainly have to take into consideration the sense of touch, since blind people can fully form spatial intuition without help from vision. Even though the filling of space with objects for them will be sparser and less fine than for the seeing, it nonetheless seems in the highest degree improbable that the foundations of spatial intuition in both classes of persons should be completely different. Let us try to observe in the dark or with the eyes closed by touch: then we can touch very well with a finger, even with a pencil held in the hand, like a surgeon with a probe, and determine quite precisely and certainly the bodily shape of the object before us. When we want to find our way around in the dark, we usually touch larger objects with five or ten fingertips at once. We then get five to ten times as much information in the same amount of time as with one finger alone. And we also need the fingers to measure, as the tips of an open compass do, the sizes of objects. Anyway, in the case of touch the circumstance that there is a stretched-out, sensing skin surface with many sensory points retreats into the background. What we can determine by the skin's feel with a hand laid still upon an object, for example on a medal's impressions,

is extraordinarily dull and poor in comparison with what we discover by feeling obtained through a motion, even if only with a pencil tip. With the sense of sight this procedure becomes much more complex in that—alongside the retina's most sensitive point, its central cavity, which in the act of seeing is simultaneously led around by the retinal image—a large quantity of still other, more sensitive points cooperate simultaneously in a much more productive manner than is the case with the sense of touch.

It is easy to appreciate that by moving the touching finger along the objects, the sequence in which the impressions of the object are presented becomes known; that this sequence shows itself to be independent of whether one feels with this or with that finger; that, furthermore, it is not a single-channelled, determined series, whose elements one must again and again traverse forward or backward in the same order so as to go from one to another—and thus is no linear series, but rather a surface-like coexistence, or, in Riemann's terminology, a manifold of the second order. The touching finger can, of course, go from one point to another of the tangible surface by means of motoric impulses other than those which displace it along the tangible surface, and different tangible surfaces require different motions in order to glide along them. A higher manifold is then required for the space in which the touching moves than in that for the tangible surface: it will have to add a third dimension. This suffices, however, for all experiences being considered; for a closed surface fully divides the space which we know. Also, liquids and gases which are not limited to the form of human capacities for representation, cannot escape through a surface closed all the way round. And as only a surface, not a space—thus a spatial formation of two, not of three dimensions—is bounded by a closed line, so can only a space of three dimensions, not one of four, be completed by a surface.

In such a way may knowledge of the spatial ordering of things existing beside one another be acquired. Comparisons of size would be added to this by observation of the congruence of a touching hand with parts or points of body surfaces, or of retinal congruence with parts and points of the retinal image.

Hence, in the completed representation of the experienced observer it remains, finally, a wonderful consequence that this observed spatial order of things originally derives from the sequence in which the qualities of the sensation present themselves to the moved sensory organ: namely, the objects at hand in space seem to us clothed with the qualities of our sensations. They appear to us as red or green, cold or warm, to have smell or taste, etc., although these qualities of sensation belong to our nervous system alone and do not at all reach beyond into external space. Yet even when we know this, the appearance does not end, because this appearance is, in fact, the original truth; they are precisely the sensations which initially present themselves to us in the spatial order.

You see that in this way the most essential characteristics of spatial intuition can be derived. However, an intuition seems to the popular consciousness to be something simply given, that comes about without reflection and seeking, and in general is unresolvable into other mental processes. Some students of physiological optics, and also strictly observant Kantians, agree with this popular opinion, at least as far as it concerns spatial intuition. It is well known that already Kant assumed not only that the general form of spatial intuition may be transcendentally given, but that the very same form also contains from the very beginning and before all possible experience certain more specific determinations, as they are expressed in the axioms of geometry. These can be reduced to the following theorems:

1. Between two points there is only one possible shortest line. We call such a line "straight."
2. Through any three points a plane can be placed. A plane is a surface which completely includes any straight line if it coincides with any two of its points.
3. Through any point, only one line parallel to a given straight line is possible. Two straight lines are parallel if they lie in the same plane and do not intersect with one another within any finite distance.

Indeed, Kant uses the supposed fact that these geometrical theorems seem to us as necessarily correct and that we cannot even imagine any spatially deviating behavior, precisely as proof for it, that they had to be given prior to all experience and that, therefore, spatial intuition may also contain in them a transcendental form of intuition independent of experience.

I would like to emphasize at this point, on account of the controversies which have taken place in recent years concerning the issue as to whether geometrical axioms are transcendental or principles of experience, that this question is completely separate from the first question discussed (whether space in general may or may not be a transcendental form of intuition).

Our eye sees all that it sees as an aggregate of color surfaces in the visual field: that is its form of intuition.

Which special color appears by this or that opportunity, in which context, and in which order, is a result of external influences and is determined by no organizational law. Nothing about the facts expressed in the axioms follows from the thought that space may be a form of intuition. If such theorems should not be theorems of experience, but rather should belong to the necessary form of intuition, then this is a further special determination of the general form of space, and therefore those reasons which permit us to conclude that the form of spatial intuition may be transcendental still do not necessarily also suffice to prove that the axioms may be of transcendental origin.

Kant was influenced in his claim that spatial relations which might contradict Euclid's axioms cannot even be imagined—just as he was in his overall view of intuition as a simple, not further reducible mental process—by the then current state of mathematics and sensory physiology.

If one wants to try to imagine something never before seen, then one has to know how to imagine the series of sense impressions that would have to come about according to the known laws of the same if one observed that object and its gradual changes one after another from each point of view and with all the senses. At the same time, these impressions must be of the kind that every other interpretation is excluded. If this series of sense impressions can be given completely and clearly, then in my opinion one has to understand the object as intuitively imaginable. Since by the initial assumption the thing has never been observed, no previous experience can come to our aid and guide our fantasy in discovering the required series of impressions; rather, this can only happen through the concept of the object or relation to be imagined. Such a concept is first to be elaborated and specialized so far as is required for the given purpose. The concept of spatial structures, which should not correspond to the usual intuition, can only be confidently developed by calculations using analytical geometry. For the present problem, Gauss had first (in 1828) given the analytical tool in his treatise on the curvature of surfaces, and Riemann applied this toward the invention of logically possible and consistent systems of geometry. One has not unfittingly designated these investigations as metamathematical. Moreover, it is to be noted that already in 1829 and 1840 Lobachevsky had developed a geometry without the parallel axiom in the usual, synthetic intuitive way, one which is in complete agreement with the corresponding part of the newer analytical investigations. Finally, Beltrami has given a method of modelling metamathematical spaces in part of Euclidean space, by which the determination of their manner of appearance in perspectival vision is made fairly easy. Lipschitz has proven the transformability of the general principles of mechanics to such spaces, so that the series of sense impressions which would occur in them can be given completely, whereby the intuitability of such spaces is proven in the sense of the previously given definition of this concept.

Now, however, comes the contradiction. For proof of intuitability, I require only that for each path of observation the originating sense impressions be definitely and unambiguously indicated, if necessary by the use of the scientific knowledge of their laws, from which—at least for one who knows these laws—would result that the thing in question or the relation intuited may actually be at hand. The task of imagining the spatial relations in metamathematical spaces requires, in fact, some exercise in the understanding of analytical methods, perspective constructions, and optical phenomena.

This, however, contradicts the older concept of intuition, which only recognizes that as given by intuition whose representation comes to consciousness immediately with the sense impression and without recollection and effort. Our experiments for imagining mathematical spaces do not, in fact, have this case, rapidity, and lightning-like self-evidence with which we perceive, for example, the shape of a room that we enter for the first time, the order and shape of the objects contained therein, the matter of which they consist, and much else. If this type of evidence were an originally given, necessary characteristic of all intuition, then we could not maintain as yet the intuitability of such spaces.

Now, upon further consideration there occurs to us a number of cases which show that certainty and rapidity of appearance of certain ideas in the case of certain impressions can also be achieved, even where nothing concerning such a connection is given by nature. One of the most striking examples of this sort is the understanding of our mother-tongue. The words are arbitrarily or accidentally chosen signs; each different language has different signs. Its understanding is not inherited: for a German child who has grown up among Frenchmen and who has never heard German spoken, German is a foreign language. The child becomes acquainted with the meaning of words and sentences only through examples of their use, whereby, prior to understanding the language, the child cannot even make comprehensible to itself that the sounds which it hears are signs which have a meaning. The child ultimately, when grown up, understands these words and sentences without recollection, without effort, without knowing when, where, and

through which examples it has learned them; it understands the most refined changes of meaning, often such whose attempts at logical definition lag behind quite clumsily.

It will not be necessary for me to pile up examples of such processes: daily life is rich enough with them. Art—most obviously poetry and the fine arts—is virtually grounded therein. The highest type of intuition, as we find it in the vision of the artist, is such a registering of a new type of resting or moving appearance of men and nature. If the similar traces, which are often left behind in our memories by repeated perceptions, increase, then it is precisely the law-like that repeats itself most regularly in a similar manner, while fortuitous change is eliminated. By this means there develops in the loving and attentive observer an intuitive image of the typical behavior of the objects which interest him, of which he subsequently knows just as little as to how it came about as a child knows by which examples he has learnt the meaning of words. That the artist has beheld the real may be concluded from the fact that when he brings before us an example cleansed of accidental disturbances it again fills us with the conviction of truth. He is, however, superior to us in that he knew how to sift out everything accidental and confusing of the doings of the world.

So much just in order to remember how this mental process is effective from the lowest to the highest stages of development of our mental life. In my earlier works I have referred to the connection of ideas herein entering as unconscious inferences—unconscious insofar as the major premise is formed from a series of experiences which have individually disappeared from memory and have also entered into our consciousness only in the form of sentient observations, not necessarily conceived as sentences in words. In present perception, the newly appearing sense impression forms the minor premise to which is applied the rule imprinted through earlier observations. I later avoided the name of unconscious inference so as to circumvent confusion with—so it seems to me—the completely unclear and unjustified idea which Schopenhauer and his followers designate by this name. However, we are here obviously concerned with an elementary process which underlies all actual, so-called thinking, even if the critical sighting and completeness of the individual steps which enter into the scientific formation of concepts and conclusions is still also missing.

Hence, as concerns, first of all, the question as to the origin of geometrical axioms: the lack of ease of representation of metamathematical spatial relations because of insufficient experience cannot be validly used as a reason against their intuitability. Moreover, the latter is completely provable. Kant's proof of the transcendental nature of geometrical axioms is thus untenable. On the other hand, the investigation of the facts of experience shows that the geometrical axioms, taken in that sense as they alone may be applied to the real world, can be tested, proven, and also eventually refuted by experience.

The memory traces of earlier experiences still play an additional and highly influential role in the observation of our visual field.

An observer who is no longer completely inexperienced also receives—be it by momentary illumination through an electric discharge, be it by intentional, rigid fixation—without any eye movement a relatively rich image of the objects found before him. Yet even an adult easily convinces himself that this image becomes much richer—and, namely, much more exact—when he sweeps his gaze around the visual field, and thus applies that very type of spatial observation that I have previously described as fundamental. We are, in fact, so very much accustomed to allowing the sight of the objects we are considering to wander, that it requires a good deal of practice before we succeed in holding it steady at a certain point for a longer time while doing experiments in physiological optics. In my studies on physiological optics I have sought to analyze how our knowledge of the visual field can be acquired through observation of images during eye movements, when only some sort of perceptible difference exists between otherwise qualitatively similar retinal sensations corresponding to the distinction of different places on the retina. According to Lotze's terminology, one may call one such distinction a local sign; only, that this sign may be a local sign—that is, correspond to a difference of place—and need not be known beforehand. More recent observations have again confirmed that persons who were blind from youth onwards, but subsequently regained sight through an operation, could at first not even distinguish by the eye such simple shapes as a circle and a square before they had touched them. Furthermore, physiological investigation teaches that we can perform relatively exact and certain comparisons, by means of a naked-eye estimate exclusively at such lines and angles in the visual field that allow imaging through normal eye movements occurring in rapid succession on the same place of the retina. We can even estimate much more certainly the true sizes and distances of spatial objects that are not too distant than we can estimate the perspectival sizes and distances which vary with the

point of view in the observer's visual field, although the former task of three-dimensional space is much more involved than the latter, which concerns only an image's surface. It is well known that one of the greatest difficulties in drawing is to free oneself from the involuntary influence exercised by the idea of the true size of an object seen. It is exactly such relations which we have to expect when we have acquired understanding of the local signs first through experience. For that which remains objectively constant, we can become well acquainted with the changing physical signs much more easily than for that which changes with each motion of our body as perspectival images do.

Moreover, for a large number of physiologists, whose opinion we can call the nativistic, in contrast to the empiricist, which I myself have sought to defend, this idea of acquired knowledge of the visual field seems unacceptable because they themselves have not clarified what is to be found so clearly in the example of language: how much accumulated memory impressions accomplish. Thus, a number of different attempts have been made to reduce at least a certain share of knowledge to an innate mechanism in the sense that certain sense impressions would cause certain, completed spatial representations. I have proven in detail that until now all proposed hypotheses of this type are inadequate because ultimately one always discovers cases where our visual perception finds itself in more exact agreement with reality than those assumptions would yield. One is then forced to the additional hypothesis that the experience gained in the movements can ultimately overcome the innate intuition, and so, contrary to the latter, accomplishes what one would, following the empiricist hypothesis, accomplish without any such impediment.

Hence, the nativistic hypotheses explain, in the first place, nothing. Rather, they only assume the very fact to be explained, in that they simultaneously reject the possible reduction of the fact to the safely established mental processes, but to which they are then anyway forced to refer in other cases. Second, the assumption of all nativistic theories that complete ideas of objects are produced by the organic mechanism seems much more audacious and dubious than the assumption of the empiricist theory, that only the uncomprehended material of sensations derives from external influences, while all ideas are formed out of it according to the laws of thought.

Third, the nativist assumptions are unnecessary. The sole objection which can be brought against the empiricist explanation is the assured motion of many newborns or even of animals hatched from eggs. The less mentally endowed they are, the more quickly do they learn what they are in general capable of learning. The narrower are the paths which their thoughts must travel, the easier do they find them. The new-born human child is extremely unskilled at seeing; it requires several days before it learns to judge the direction of the visual image towards which it must turn its head so as to reach the mother's breast. To be sure, young animals are much more independent of individual experience. What, however, is this instinct which directs it? Is direct inheritance of the parents' circles of representation possible? Does it concern only pleasure or displeasure, or a motoric drive, which attach themselves to certain aggregates of sensations? About all that we know as good as nothing. Plainly recognizable residues of the these phenomena still occur in humans. In this area, clean and critically conducted observations are highly desirable.

For facilitating the discovery of the first law-like relations the arrangements presumed by the nativist hypothesis can at best claim a certain pedagogical value. The empiricist view would also be compatible with presumptions tending in that direction: for example, that the local signs of neighboring points on the retina are as similar to one another as the more distant ones are, that corresponding positions of both retinae are more similar than disparate, etc. For our present investigation it suffices to know that spatial intuition can also originate completely in blind individuals, and that in those who can see—even if the nativist hypotheses are partially correct—the final and most precise determination of spatial relations is certainly conditioned by observations made in movement.

I return now to discussing the elementary, original facts of our perception. As we have seen, we not only have changing sense impressions which come over us without our doing anything; we also observe during our own continuing activity—and thereby attain knowledge of the existence of a lawful relationship between our innervations and the becoming present of the different impressions from the circle of the current presentables. Each of our voluntary motions by which we modify the manner of appearance of objects, is to be considered as an experiment by which we test whether we have correctly conceived the lawful behavior of the phenomenon in question, that is, its presumed existence in a definite spatial order.

The convincing force of every experiment is, however, in general so much greater than that of the observation of a process occurring without our involvement, because in the experiment the causal chain runs

throughout our self-consciousness. We know one member of these causes—our will's impulse—from inner intuition, and know the motive by which it has occurred. The chain of physical causes which transpires in the course of the experiment has its initial effect from it, as from one initial member known to us and to one point in time known to us. However, an essential assumption for the conviction to be achieved is that our will's impulse has neither already been influenced by physical causes, which simultaneously determine the physical process, nor itself psychically influenced the succeeding perceptions.

In particular, this last doubt can come into consideration of our theme. The will's impulse for a definite motion is a mental act, and, so too, is the related perceived change in sensation. Now, cannot the first act bring about the second through a purely mental agency? It is not impossible. Something like this happens when we dream. Dreaming, we believe we execute a movement, and we then dream further that the very thing happens that should be its natural consequence. We dream that we climb into a canoe, push it off from the shore, slide it out onto the water, see it displace the objects lying around it, etc. Here the dreamer's expectation, that he will see the consequences of his actions occur, seems to bring about the dreamed perception in purely mental ways. Who can say how long and finely spun out, how logically executed any such dream can be? If everything therein may occur in the highest degree in a law-like manner, following the order of nature, then no other distinction from the waking state would exist than that of the possibility of awakening, the interruption of the dreamt series of intuitions.

I do not see how one could refute a system of even the most extremely subjective idealism that wanted to view life as a dream. One could explain it as so improbable, as so dissatisfying as possible—in which regard I would agree with the harshest expressions of rejection—but it may be logically feasible; and it seems to me to be very important to keep this in mind. It is well known how ingeniously Calderon developed this theme in *Life a Dream*.

Fichte, too, assumes that the Ego posits for itself the Non-Ego, i.e., the world of appearance, because it needs to develop its thinking activity. However, his idealism distinguishes itself from that just designated in that he conceives other individual human beings not as phantoms but, on the basis of the assertion of moral law, as being the same nature as his own Ego. Since, however, their images in which they imagine the Non-Ego must all harmonize again, he therefore conceived all the individual Egos as parts or emanations of the absolute Ego. The world in which those Egos then found themselves was the world of ideas, which the World Spirit posits for itself, and could again assume the concept of reality, as occurred with Hegel.

By contrast, the realistic hypothesis trusts the assertions of the normal self-observation, according to which the changes of perception following an action are in no way in any mental connection with the previously occurring impulses of the will. It regards as existing independently of our ideas, that which seems to endure in daily perception, the material world external to us. The realistic hypothesis is doubtless the simplest that we can form; tested and confirmed in extraordinarily wide circles of application; sharply defined in all individual features, and thus extraordinarily useful and fruitful as the foundation for action. We would, even from an idealistic viewpoint, hardly know how else to express the law-like in our sensations than when we say: "The acts of consciousness occurring with the character of perception take their course as if the world of material things assumed by the realistic hypothesis may really exist." However, we do not overcome this "as if"; we cannot recognize the realistic opinion as more than a superbly useful and precise hypothesis; we may not ascribe necessary truth to it, since in addition to it still other, irrefutable idealistic hypotheses are possible.

It is always good to keep this in mind so as not to conclude more from the facts than is warranted. The different shadings of idealistic and realistic opinions are metaphysical hypotheses which, so long as they are recognized as such, and however injurious they may become when represented as dogma or as supposed necessities of thought, are completely justified scientifically. Science must discuss all admissible hypotheses in order to retain a full overview of all possible attempts at explanation. Still more necessary are hypotheses for practical action, since one cannot always wait until a certain scientific decision has been reached, but instead must make a decision, be it according to probability or to aesthetic or moral feeling. In this sense, too, there is nothing objectionable in metaphysical hypotheses. It is, however, unworthy of a thinker wanting to be scientific if he forgets the hypothetical origin of his principles. The arrogance and the passion with which such hidden hypotheses are defended are the usual consequence of the dissatisfied feeling that its defender harbors in the hidden depth of his conscience about the correctness of his cause.

Yet what we find unambiguously and factually, without any hypothetical imputation, is the law-like in the phenomenon. From the first step on, where we perceive the abiding objects distributed before us in space, this perception is the recognition of a law-like connection between our movements and the sensations appearing therefrom. Thus the first elementary ideas already contain in themselves a thought and proceed according to the laws of thought. If we take a sufficiently broad concept of thought, as we did above, then everything that is added in the intuition to the raw material of sensations can be resolved in thought.

For if "conceive" means to form concepts, and if we try to summarize in the concept of a class of objects their similar characteristics, then it follows completely analogously that the concept must try to summarize a changing series of phenomena over time, one which remains the same in all its stages. The wise man, as Schiller expresses it:

Seeks the trusting law in Chance's horrifying wonders,
Seeks the resting pole in Phenomena's flight.

We call substance that which, without dependence on other things, remains the same over time; and we call the constant relationship between changeable quantities the law that binds them. It is only the latter that we perceive directly. The concept of substance can only be attained through exhaustive testing, and it always remains problematic insofar as further testing is always held in reserve. In previous times, light and heat were thought to be substances, until it later turned out that they may be transient forms of motion. Moreover, we must always be prepared for new decompositions of what are today considered to be chemical elements. The first product of the reflective understanding of a phenomenon is the law-like. If we have so far quite excluded it, so completely and certainly delimited its conditions, and, at the same time, so generally conceived it that the outcome for all possibly occurring cases that may occur is unambiguously determined, and if at the same time we become convinced that it may have maintained itself and will maintain itself in all times and in all cases, then we recognize it as something existing independently of our ideas, and we call it the cause, i.e., that which, behind the change, is the originally abiding and existing. In my opinion, in this sense alone is the use of the word justified, even if common linguistic usage generally uses it in a very vague way as antecedent or cause. Insofar, then, as we recognize the law as directing our perception and natural processes, as a power equivalent to our will, we call it "force." This concept of a power opposing us is directly conditioned by the ways and means that our simplest perceptions occur. From the very start, the changes which we ourselves make by our acts of will are separated off from those which are not made by our will and which cannot be overcome by our will. It is, namely, pain which gives us the most penetrating instruction about the power of reality. The emphasis here falls on the facts of observation, that the perceived circle of presentables is not determined by a conscious act of our idea or will. Fichte's Non-Ego is here exactly the right negative expression. To the dreamer, too, it seems that what he believes to see and feel is not produced by his will or by the conscious linking of his ideas, even if unconsciously the latter is in reality often enough the case; to him, too, it is a Non-Ego. So, too, with the idealist who looks at it as the world of ideas of the World Spirit.

We have in our language a very fortunate designation for that which, behind the change of phenomena permanently influences us, namely the "real." Herein only the effect is expressed; it lacks the additional connection to the existent as substance, which the concept of the real, i.e., the material, includes. On the other hand, the concept of the finished image of an object largely inserts itself into the concept of the objective, which does not fit into most original perceptions. We also have to designate as effective and real in the dreamer's logic those spiritual conditions or motives which, at the time, foist on him the law-like sensations corresponding to the present state of his dreamt world. On the other hand, it is clear that a separation of thought and reality first becomes possible after we know how to complete the separation of that which the Ego can and cannot change. This, however, only becomes possible after we recognize which law-like consequences the will's impulses have at that time. The law-like is thus the essential presumption for the character of the real.

I need not explain to you that it may be a contradiction in terms to want to represent the real or Kant's "thing-in-itself" through positive determinations without admitting it into the form of our representation. That has often been discussed. However, what we can attain is knowledge of the law-like order in the realm of the real; to be sure, this can only be presented in the sign system of our sense impressions.

All things transitory
But as images are sent.

I consider it a good sign that here and elsewhere we find Goethe along with us on the same road. Where it concerns a broad outlook, we can well trust his clear and unprejudiced gaze for the truth. He demanded of science

that it should only be an artistic ordering of facts and that beyond that it should form no abstract concepts which, to him, seem to be but empty names that only cloud the facts. In roughly the same sense, Gustav Kirchhoff has recently designated this as the task of the most abstract field among the natural sciences, mechanics, which in the completest and simplest way describes the movements occurring in nature. Concerning the "clouding," this in fact occurs when we remain in the realm of abstract concepts and do not analyze their factual sense, i.e., clarify to ourselves which observable, new, and law-like relations between the phenomena follow therefrom. Each properly developed hypothesis yields, depending on its factual sense, a more general law of phenomena than we have previously observed directly; it is an attempt to ascend to an ever-more-general and comprehensive lawfulness. Those new things that it maintains in the way of facts, must be tested and confirmed by observation and experiment. Hypotheses which do not have such a factual sense, or in general do not give clear and certain statements of the facts falling under them, are to be considered only as valueless phrases.

Every reduction of the phenomena to the underlying substances and forces claims to have found something unchangeable and definitive. We are never justified in making an unconditional claim of this type; for it grants neither the fragmentary nature of our knowledge nor the nature of inductive conclusions, upon which rests, from the first step on, all our perception of the real.

Every conclusion by induction is based upon trust that a previously observed law-like behavior will maintain itself in all cases which have yet to come under observation. It is a trust in the law-likeness of all that occurs. Law-likeness is, however, the condition of conceivability. Trust in law-likeness is thus simultaneously trust in the conceivability of natural phenomena. If we assume, however, that the conceptualization will be brought to completion, that we will be able to establish a final unchangeable something as the cause of the observed changes, then we call the regulative principle of our thinking, that which impels us, the causal law. We can say that it expresses the trust in the complete conceivability of the world. Conceiving, in the sense that I have described it, is the method by means of which our thinking subordinates itself to the world, orders the facts, predetermines the future. It is its right and its duty to expand the application of this method to all that occurs, and by this means it has already harvested truly great results. Still, for the causal law's applicability we have no additional security than its success. We could live in a world in which each atom might be different from every other atom, and where nothing may be at rest. There would thus be no way to discover conformity to law, and our thinking activity would have to cease.

The causal law is really an *a priori* given, a transcendental law. It is not possible to prove it by experience because, as we have seen, not even the first steps of experience are possible without the application of inductive conclusions, i.e., without the causal law; and from the completed experience, when it too taught that everything observed so far has proceeded in a law-like manner—which we are assuredly far from being justified in claiming—would always only be able to follow by an inductive conclusion, i.e., under the assumption of the causal law, that now the causal law would also be valid in the future. Only one piece of advice is valid here: trust and act!

> *Earth's insufficiency*
> *Here grows to Event.*

This would be the response that we would have to offer to the question: what is truth in our representation? In that which has always seemed to me to constitute the most essential progress in Kant's philosophy, we still stand on the ground of his system. In this sense I too have frequently emphasized in my previous works the agreement of modern sensory physiology with Kant's theories. To be sure, I did not, however, also thereby mean to have sworn to the master's words in all subsidiary points. I believe that one must view the modern era's most essential progress as the resolution of the concept of intuition into the elementary processes of thought, which is still lacking in Kant; this, then, also conditions his view of geometrical axioms as transcendental theorems. It was the physiological investigations on sense perception, which led us to the final elementary processes in knowledge and which were still not comprehensible in words, remained unknown and inaccessible to philosophy so long as it only investigated such knowledge that finds its expression in language.

To be sure, that which we have considered as a noteworthy deficiency, as one of the unsatisfactory developments of the specialized sciences of Kant's day, appears to those philosophers who have retained the tendency to metaphysical speculation precisely that which is most essential in Kant's philosophy. In fact, Kant's proof of the possibility of a metaphysics—about which alleged science he himself did indeed not know how to discover anything further—is based entirely on the opinion that the geometrical axioms and the applied principles of mechanics may be transcendental, *a priori* given theo-

rems. Moreover, his entire system actually contradicts the existence of metaphysics and the obscure points of his epistemology—about whose interpretation so much has been disputed—derive from this root.

Considering all that, natural science may have its secure, well-established ground on which it can seek the laws of the real, a wonderfully rich and fruitful field of activity. So long as it limits itself to this activity, it will not be confronted by idealistic doubts. In comparison to the high-flying plans of the metaphysicians, such work may seem modest.

> *For never against*
> *The immortals, a mortal*
> *May measure himself,*
> *Upwards aspiring,*
> *He toucheth the stars with his forehead,*
> *Then do his insecure feet*
> *Stumble and totter and reel;*
> *Then do the cloud and the tempest*
> *Make him their pastime and sport.*
>
> *Let him with sturdy,*
> *Sinewy limbs,*
> *Tread the enduring*
> *Firm-seated earth;*
> *Aiming no further, than*
> *The oak or the vine to compare!*

Nonetheless, the example of the one who said this may teach us how a mortal—who had indeed learned to stand even if he touched the stars with his forehead—still kept a clear eye for truth and reality. The true researcher must always have something of the artist's insight, of the insight which led Goethe, and Leonardo da Vinci, too, to great scientific thoughts. Both artist and researcher strive—even if in different ways—towards the same goal: to discover new lawfulness. One must not, however, want to propagate idle daydreams and crazy fantasies for artistic insight. Both the true artist and the true researcher know how to work properly and how to give to their work a stable form and convincing similitude.

Time and again, moreover, reality has so far revealed itself much more nobly and in a much richer way to the investigating science true to its laws than the most extreme efforts of mythical fantasy and metaphysical speculation knew how to portray them. What have all the monstrous products of Indian daydreaming, the accumulations of vast dimensions and numbers got to say in comparison to the reality of the world structure, and in comparison to the space of time into which the sun and earth formed themselves, into which life developed during geological history in ever more complete forms, adjusting itself to the quieter physical conditions of our planet?

Which metaphysics has concepts armed with effects, like those that magnets and current electricity exert upon one another—concerning whose reduction to well-determined elementary effects contemporary physics is still struggling—without yet having arrived at a clear conclusion? Even light, too, already seems to be nothing more than a form of motion of those two agents, and the space-filling aether, as a magnetizable and electrifiable medium, contains completely new characteristic properties.

And into which scheme of scholastic concepts should we classify this supply of effect-producing energy, whose constancy is expressed in the law of the conservation of force, which, like a substance, is indestructible and unincreasable, and which is active as a motive power in each motion of inorganic and organic matter, a Proteus clothing himself in ever-new forms, operating through infinite space, and yet not without remainder divisible by space, the operative in each effect, the mover in each motion, and yet neither spirit nor matter?—Has the Poet intuited it?

In the tides of Life, in Action's storm,
A fluctuant wave,
A shuttle free,
Birth and the Grave,
An eternal sea,
A weaving, flowing
Life, all-glowing,
Thus at Time's humming loom 'tis my hand prepares
The garment of Life which the Deity wears!

We: bits of dust on the surface of our planet, itself hardly worth calling a grain of sand in the universe's infinite space; we: the most recent race among the living on earth, according to geological chronology barely out of the cradle, still in the learning stage, barely half-educated, declared of age only out of mutual respect, and yet already, through the more powerful force of the causal law, grown beyond all our fellow creatures and vanquishing them in the struggle for existence; we truly have reason enough to be proud that "the inconceivably sublime work" has been given to us to learn to understand slowly through constant work. And we need not feel in the least ashamed if this does not at once succeed in the first assault of a flight of Icarus.

13
~

HERMANN EBBINGHAUS

Hermann Ebbinghaus (1850–1909), like all well-educated individuals, had certainly read Immanuel Kant's (p. 127) philosophical works and his statements concerning the impossibility of studying cognitive phenomena experimentally, but wisely chose to ignore that stricture. The son of a wealthy textile and paper merchant, Ebbinghaus studied at a variety of schools and received his Ph.D. in philosophy from the University of Bonn in 1873. He stumbled upon Gustav T. Fechner's (p. 142) *Elements of Psychophysics* while touring England and France and began the first experimental study of memory in 1878. For stimuli, he drew on his earlier interest in philology and heroically studied his own memory. Lecturing at the University of Berlin, he conducted additional memory experiments from 1883 to 1884, publishing the combined work in 1885. Ebbinghaus was broadly interested in psychology, with published work that includes topics ranging from color vision to intelligence testing of children, which used a word-completion technique he developed. In 1890, Ebbinghaus, Carl Stumpf, Hermann von Helmholtz (p. 154), and other experimentalists established *Zeitschrift für Psychologie und Physiologie der Sinnesorgane* (*Journal of the Psychology and Physiology of the Sense Organs*), the second experimental psychology journal. That year, Ebbinghaus turned down a position at Cornell University—a position that E. B. Titchener (p. 324) accepted a few years later. Ebbinghaus became a full professor at the University of Breslau in 1894 and moved to the University of Halle in 1905.

MEMORY: A CONTRIBUTION TO EXPERIMENTAL PSYCHOLOGY

MEMORY

Chapter I

Our Knowledge Concerning Memory

SECTION I. MEMORY IN ITS EFFECTS. The language of life as well as of science in attributing a memory to the mind attempts to point out the facts and their interpretation somewhat as follows:

Mental states of every kind,—sensations, feelings, ideas,—which were at one time present in consciousness and then have disappeared from it, have not with their disappearance absolutely ceased to exist. Although the inwardly-turned look may no longer be able to find them, nevertheless they have not been utterly destroyed and annulled, but in a certain manner they continue to exist, stored up, so to speak, in the memory. We cannot, of course, directly observe their present existence, but it is revealed by the effects which come to our knowledge with a certainty like that with which we infer the existence of the stars below the horizon. These effects are of different kinds.

In a first group of cases we can call back into consciousness by an exertion of the will directed to this purpose the seemingly lost states (or, indeed, in case these consisted in immediate sense-perceptions, we can recall their true memory images): that is, we can reproduce them *voluntarily*. During attempts of this sort,—that is, attempts to recollect—all sorts of images toward which our aim was not directed, accompany the desired images to the light of consciousness. Often, indeed, the latter entirely miss the goal, but as a general thing among the representations is found the one which we sought, and it is immediately recognised as something formerly experienced. It would be absurd to suppose that our will has created it anew and, as it were, out of nothing; it must have been present somehow or somewhere. The will, so to speak, has only discovered it and brought it to us again.

In a second group of cases this survival is even more striking. Often, even after years, mental states once present in consciousness return to it with apparent spontaneity and without any act of the will; that is, they are reproduced *involuntarily*. Here, also, in the majority of cases we at once recognise the returned mental state as one that has already been experienced; that is, we remember it. Under certain conditions, however, this accompanying consciousness is lacking, and we know only indirectly that the "now" must be identical with the "then"; yet we receive in this way a no less valid proof for its existence during the intervening time. As more exact observation teaches us, the occurrence of these involuntary reproductions is not an entirely random and accidental one. On the contrary they are brought about through the instrumentality of other, immediately present mental images. Moreover they occur in certain regular ways which in general terms are described under the so-called 'laws of association.'

Finally there is a third and large group to be reckoned with here. The vanished mental states give indubitable proof of their continuing existence even if they themselves do not return to consciousness at all, or at least not exactly at the given time. Employment of a certain range of thought facilitates under certain conditions the employment of a similar range of thought, even if the former does not come before the mind directly either in its methods or in its results. The boundless domain of the effect of accumulated experiences belongs here. This effect results from the frequent conscious occurrence of any condition or process, and consists in facilitating the occurrence and progress of similar processes. This effect is not fettered by the condition that the factors constituting the experience shall return *in toto* to consciousness. This may incidentally be the case with a part of them; it must not happen to a too great extent and with too great clearness, otherwise the course of the present process will immediately be disturbed. Most of these experiences remain concealed from consciousness and yet produce an effect which is significant and which authenticates their previous existence.

From Hermann Ebbinghaus, "Our Knowledge Concerning Memory" and "The Method of Investigation." In H.A. Ruger and C. E. Bussenius (Translators) *Memory: A Contribution to Experimental Psychology* (pp. 1–6, 19–33). New York: Dover Publications 1964. (Original work published 1885)

SECTION 2. MEMORY IN ITS DEPENDENCE. Along with this bare knowledge of the existence of memory and its *effects,* there is abundant knowledge concerning the *conditions* upon which depend the vitality of that inner survival as well as the fidelity and promptness of the reproduction.

How differently do different *individuals* behave in this respect! One retains and reproduces well; another, poorly. And not only does this comparison hold good when different individuals are compared with each other, but also when different phases of the existence of the same individual are compared: morning and evening, youth and old age, find him different in this respect.

Differences in the *content* of the thing to be reproduced are of great influence. Melodies may become a source of torment by the undesired persistency of their return. Forms and colors are not so importunate; and if they do return, it is with noticeable loss of clearness and certainty. The musician writes for the orchestra what his inner voice sings to him; the painter rarely relies without disadvantage solely upon the images which his inner eye presents to him; nature gives him his forms, study governs his combinations of them. It is with something of a struggle that past states of feeling are realized; when realized, and this is often only through the instrumentality of the movements which accompanied them, they are but pale shadows of themselves. Emotionally true singing is rarer than technically correct singing.

If the two foregoing points of view are taken together—differences in individuals and differences in content—an endless number of differences come to light. One individual overflows with poetical reminiscences, another directs symphonies from memory, while numbers and formulae, which come to a third without effort, slip away from the other two as from a polished stone.

Very great is the dependence of retention and reproduction upon the intensity of the *attention* and *interest* which were attached to the mental states the first time they were present. The burnt child shuns the fire, and the dog which has been beaten runs from the whip, after a single vivid experience. People in whom we are interested we may see daily and yet not be able to recall the color of their hair or of their eyes.

Under ordinary circumstances, indeed, frequent repetitions are indispensable in order to make possible the reproduction of a given content. Vocabularies, discourses, and poems of any length cannot be learned by a single repetition even with the greatest concentration of attention on the part of an individual of very great ability. By a sufficient number of repetitions their final mastery is ensured, and by additional later reproductions gain in assurance and ease is secured.

Left to itself every mental content gradually loses its capacity for being revived, or at least suffers loss in this regard under the influence of time. Facts crammed at examination time soon vanish, if they were not sufficiently grounded by other study and later subjected to a sufficient review. But even a thing so early and deeply founded as one's mother tongue is noticeably impaired if not used for several years.

SECTION 3. DEFICIENCIES IN OUR KNOWLEDGE CONCERNING MEMORY. The foregoing sketch of our knowledge concerning memory makes no claim to completeness. To it might be added such a series of propositions known to psychology as the following: "He who learns quickly also forgets quickly," "Relatively long series of ideas are retained better than relatively short ones," "Old people forget most quickly the things they learned last," and the like. Psychology is wont to make the picture rich with anecdote and illustration. But—and this is the main point—even if we particularise our knowledge by a most extended use of illustrative material, everything that we can say retains the indefinite, general, and comparative character of the propositions quoted above. Our information comes almost exclusively from the observation of extreme and especially striking cases. We are able to describe these quite correctly in a general way and in vague expressions of more or less. We suppose, again quite correctly, that the same influences exert themselves, although in a less degree, in the case of the inconspicuous, but a thousand-fold more frequent, daily activities of memory. But if our curiosity carries us further and we crave more specific and detailed information concerning these dependencies and inter-dependencies, both those already mentioned and others,—if we put questions, so to speak, concerning their inner structure—our answer is silence. How does the disappearance of the ability to reproduce, forgetfulness, depend upon the length of time during which no repetitions have taken place? What proportion does the increase in the certainty of reproduction bear to the number of repetitions? How do these relations vary with the greater or less intensity of the interest in the thing to be reproduced? These and similar questions no one can answer.

This inability does not arise from a chance neglect of investigation of these relations. We cannot say that to-morrow, or whenever we wish to take time, we can investigate these problems. On the contrary this inability is inherent in the nature of the questions themselves. Although the conceptions in question—namely, degrees of forgetfulness, of certainty and interest—are quite correct, we have no means for establishing such degrees in our experience except at the extremes, and even then we cannot accurately limit those extremes. We feel therefore that we are not at all in a condition to undertake the investigation. We form certain conceptions during striking experiences, but we cannot find any realisation of them in the similar but less striking experiences of everyday life. *Vice versa* there are probably many conceptions which we have not as yet formed which would be serviceable and indispensable for a clear understanding of the facts, and their theoretical mastery.

The amount of detailed information which an individual has at his command and his theoretical elaborations of the same are mutually dependent; they grow in and through each other. It is because of the indefinite and little specialised character of our knowledge that the theories concerning the processes of memory, reproduction, and association have been up to the present time of so little value for a proper comprehension of those processes. For example, to express our ideas concerning their physical basis we use different metaphors—stored up ideas, engraved images, well-beaten paths. There is only one thing certain about these figures of speech and that is that they are not suitable.

Of course the existence of all these deficiencies has its perfectly sufficient basis in the extraordinary difficulty and complexity of the matter. It remains to be proved whether, in spite of the clearest insight into the inadequacy of our knowledge, we shall ever make any actual progress. Perhaps we shall always have to be resigned to this. But a somewhat greater accessibility than has so far been realised in this field cannot be denied to it, as I hope to prove presently. If by any chance a way to a deeper penetration into this matter should present itself, surely, considering the significance of memory for all mental phenomena, it should be our wish to enter that path at once. For at the very worst we should prefer to see resignation arise from the failure of earnest investigations rather than from persistent, helpless astonishment in the face of their difficulties.

SECTION 9. RESUMÉ. Two fundamental difficulties arise in the way of the application of the so-called Natural Science Method to the examination of psychical processes:

(1) The constant flux and caprice of mental events do not admit of the establishment of stable experimental conditions.

(2) Psychical processes offer no means for measurement or enumeration.

In the case of the special field of memory (learning, retention, reproduction) the second difficulty may be overcome to a certain extent. Among the external conditions of these processes some are directly accessible to measurement (the time, the number of repetitions). They may be employed in getting numerical values indirectly where that would not have been possible directly. We must not wait until the series of ideas committed to memory return to consciousness of themselves, but we must meet them halfway and renew them to such an extent that they may just be reproduced without error. The work requisite for this under certain conditions I take experimentally as a measure of the influence of these conditions; the differences in the work which appear with a change of conditions I interpret as a measure of the influence of that change.

Whether the first difficulty, the establishment of stable experimental conditions, may also be overcome satisfactorily cannot be decided *a priori*. Experiments must be made under conditions as far as possible the same, to see whether the results, which will probably deviate from one another when taken separately, will furnish constant mean values when collected to form larger groups. However, taken by itself, this is not sufficient to enable us to utilise such numerical results for the establishment of numerical relations of dependence in the natural science sense. Statistics is concerned with a great mass of constant mean values that do not at all arise from the frequent repetition of an ideally frequent occurrence and therefore cannot favor further insight into it. Such is the great complexity of our mental life that it is not possible to deny that constant mean values, when obtained, are of the nature of such statistical constants. To test that, I examine the distribution of the separate numbers represented in an average value. If it corresponds to the distribution found everywhere in natural science, where repeated observation of the same occurrence furnishes different separate values, I suppose—tentatively again—that the repeatedly examined psychical process in question occurred each time under conditions sufficiently similar for our purposes. This supposition is not compulsory, but is very probable. If it is wrong, the continuation of experimentation will presumably teach this by itself: the questions put from different points of view will lead to contradictory results.

SECTION 10. THE PROBABLE ERROR. The quantity which measures the compactness of the observed values obtained in any given case and which makes the formula which represents their distribution a definite one may, as has already been stated, be chosen differently. I use the so-called "probable error" (P.E.)—*i.e.,* that deviation above and below the mean value which is just as often exceeded by the separate values as not reached by them, and which, therefore, between its positive and negative limits, includes just half of all the observational results symmetrically arranged around the mean value. As is evident from the definition these values can be obtained from the results by simple enumeration; it is done more accurately by a theoretically based calculation.

If now this calculation is tried out tentatively for any group of observations, a grouping of these values according to the "law of errors" is recognised by the fact that between the submultiples and the multiples of the empirically calculated probable error there are obtained as many separate measures symmetrically arranged about a central value as the theory requires.

According to this out of 1,000 observations there should be:

Within the limits	Number of separate measures
$\pm\ \frac{1}{10}$ P.E.	54
$\pm\ \frac{1}{6}$ P.E.	89.5
$\pm\ \frac{1}{4}$ P.E.	134
$\pm\ \frac{1}{2}$ P.E.	264
$\pm$ P.E.	500
$\pm\ 1\frac{1}{2}$ P.E.	688
$\pm\ 2$ P.E.	823
$\pm\ 2\frac{1}{2}$ P.E.	908
$\pm\ 3$ P.E.	957
$\pm\ 4$ P.E.	993

If this conformity exists in a sufficient degree, then the mere statement of the probable error suffices to characterise the arrangement of all the observed values, and at the same time its quantity gives a serviceable measure for the compactness of the distribution around the central value—*i.e.,* for its exactness and trustworthiness.

As we have spoken of the probable error of the separate observations, (P.E.$_\text{o}$), so can we also speak of the probable error of the measures of the central tendency, or mean values, (P.E.$_\text{m}$). This describes in similar fashion the grouping which would arise for the separate mean values if the observation of the same phenomenon were repeated very many times and each time an equally great number of observations were combined into a central value. It furnishes a brief but sufficient characterisation of the fluctuations of the mean values resulting from repeated observations, and along with it a mea-

sure of the security and the trustworthiness of the results already found.

The P.E.$_\text{m}$ is accordingly in general included in what follows. How it is found by calculation, again, cannot be explained here; suffice it that what it means be clear. It tells us, then, that, on the basis of the character of the total observations from which a mean value has just been obtained, it may be expected with a probability of 1 to 1 that the latter value departs from the presumably correct average by not more at the most than the amount of its probable error. By the presumably correct average we mean that one which would have been obtained if the observations had been indefinitely repeated. A larger deviation than this becomes improbable in the mathematical sense—*i.e.,* there is a greater probability against it than for it. And, as a glance at the accompanying table shows us, the improbability of larger deviations increases with extreme rapidity as their size increases. The probability that the obtained average should deviate from the true one by more than $2\frac{1}{2}$ times the probable error is only 92 to 908, therefore about 1/10; the probability for its exceeding four times the probable error is very slight, 7 to 993 (1 to 142).

Chapter III

The Method of Investigation

SECTION II. SERIES OF NONSENSE SYLLABLES. In order to test practically, although only for a limited field, a way of penetrating more deeply into memory processes—and it is to these that the preceding considerations have been directed—I have hit upon the following method.

Out of the simple consonants of the alphabet and our eleven vowels and diphthongs all possible syllables of a certain sort were constructed, a vowel sound being placed between two consonants.[1]

These syllables, about 2,300 in number, were mixed together and then drawn out by chance and used to construct series of different lengths, several of which each time formed the material for a test.[2]

At the beginning a few rules were observed to prevent, in the construction of the syllables, too immediate repetition of similar sounds, but these were not strictly adhered to. Later they were abandoned and the matter left to chance. The syllables used each time were carefully laid aside till the whole number had been used, then they were mixed together and used again.

The aim of the tests carried on with these syllable series was, by means of repeated audible perusal of the separate series, to so impress them that immediately afterwards they could voluntarily just be reproduced. This aim was considered attained when, the initial syllable being given, a series could be recited at the first attempt, without hesitation, at a certain rate, and with the consciousness of being correct.

SECTION 12. ADVANTAGES OF THE MATERIAL. The nonsense material, just described, offers many advantages, in part because of this very lack of meaning. First of all, it is relatively simple and relatively homogeneous. In the case of the material nearest at hand, namely poetry or prose, the content is now narrative in style, now descriptive, or now reflective; it contains now a phrase that is pathetic, now one that is humorous; its metaphors are sometimes beautiful, sometimes harsh; its rhythm is sometimes smooth and sometimes rough. There is thus brought into play a multiplicity of influences which change without regularity and are therefore disturbing. Such are associations which dart here and there, different degrees of interest, lines of verse recalled because of their striking quality or their beauty, and the like. All this is avoided with our syllables. Among many thousand combinations there occur scarcely a few dozen that have a meaning and among these there are again only a few whose meaning was realised while they were being memorised.

However, the simplicity and homogeneity of the material must not be overestimated. It is still far from ideal. The learning of the syllables calls into play the three sensory fields, sight, hearing and the muscle sense of the organs of speech. And although the part that each of these senses plays is well limited and always similar in kind, a certain complication of the results must still be anticipated because of their combined action. Again, to particularise, the homogeneity of the series of syllables falls considerably short of what might be expected of it. These series exhibit very important and almost incomprehensible variations as to the ease or difficulty with which they are learned. It even appears from this point of view as if the differences between sense and nonsense material were not nearly so great as one would be inclined *a priori* to imagine. At least I found in the case of learning by heart a few cantos from Byron's "Don Juan" no greater range of distribution of the separate numerical measures than in the case of a series of nonsense syllables in the learning of which an approximately equal time had been spent. In the former case the innumerable disturbing influences mentioned above seem to have compensated each other in producing a certain intermediate effect; whereas in the latter case the

predisposition, due to the influence of the mother tongue, for certain combinations of letters and syllables must be a very heterogeneous one.

More indubitable are the advantages of our material in two other respects. In the first place it permits an inexhaustible amount of new combinations of quite homogeneous character, while different poems, different prose pieces always have something incomparable. It also makes possible a quantitative variation which is adequate and certain; whereas to break off before the end or to begin in the middle of the verse or the sentence leads to new complications because of various and unavoidable disturbances of the meaning.

Series of numbers, which I also tried, appeared impracticable for the more thorough tests. Their fundamental elements were too small in number and therefore too easily exhausted.

SECTION 13. ESTABLISHMENT OF THE MOST CONSTANT EXPERIMENTAL CONDITIONS POSSIBLE. The following rules were made for the process of memorising.

1. The separate series were always read through completely from beginning to end; they were not learned in separate parts which were then joined together; neither were especially difficult parts detached and repeated more frequently. There was a perfectly free interchange between the reading and the occasionally necessary tests of the capacity to reproduce by heart. For the latter there was an important rule to the effect that upon hesitation the rest of the series was to be read through to the end before beginning it again.

2. The reading and the recitation of the series took place at a constant rate, that of 150 strokes per minute. A clockwork metronome placed at some distance was at first used to regulate the rate; but very soon the ticking of a watch was substituted, that being much simpler and less disturbing to the attention. The mechanism of escapement of most watches swings 300 times per minute.

3. Since it is practically impossible to speak continuously without variation of accent, the following method was adopted to avoid irregular variations: either three or four syllables were united into a measure, and thus either the 1st, 4th, 7th, or the 1st, 5th, 9th . . . syllables were pronounced with a slight accent. Stressing of the voice was otherwise, as far as possible, avoided.

4. After the learning of each separate series a pause of 15 seconds was made, and used for the tabulation of results. Then the following series of the same test was immediately taken up.

5. During the process of learning, the purpose of reaching the desired goal as soon as possible was kept in mind as much as was feasible. Thus, to the limited degree to which conscious resolve is of influence here, the attempt was made to keep the attention concentrated on the tiresome task and its purpose. It goes without saying that care was taken to keep away all outer disturbances in order to make possible the attainment of this aim. The smaller distractions caused by carrying on the test in various surroundings were also avoided as far as that could be done.

6. There was no attempt to connect the nonsense syllables by the invention of special associations of the mnemotechnik type; learning was carried on solely by the influence of the mere repetitions upon the natural memory. As I do not possess the least practical knowledge of the mnemotechnical devices, the fulfillment of this condition offered no difficulty to me.

7. Finally and chiefly, care was taken that the objective conditions of life during the period of the tests were so controlled as to eliminate too great changes or irregularities. Of course, since the tests extended over many months, this was possible only to a limited extent. But, even so, the attempt was made to conduct, under as similar conditions of life as possible, those tests the results of which were to be directly compared. In particular the activity immediately preceding the test was kept as constant in character as was possible. Since the mental as well as the physical condition of man is subject to an evident periodicity of 24 hours, it was taken for granted that like experimental conditions are obtainable only at like times of day. However, in order to carry out more than one test in a given day, different experiments were occasionally carried on together at different times of day. When too great changes in the outer and inner life occurred, the tests were discontinued for a length of time. Their resumption was preceded by some days of renewed training varying according to the length of the interruption.

SECTION 14. SOURCES OF ERROR. The guiding point of view in the selection of material and in determining the rules for its employment was, as is evident, the attempt to simplify as far as possible, and to keep as constant as possible, the conditions under which the activity to be observed, that of memory, came into play. Naturally the better one succeeds in this attempt the more does he withdraw from the complicated and changing conditions under which this activity takes place in ordinary life and under which it is of importance to us. But that is no objection to the method. The freely falling

body and the frictionless machine, etc., with which physics deals, are also only abstractions when compared with the actual happenings in nature which are of import to us. We can almost nowhere get a direct knowledge of the complicated and the real, but must get at them in roundabout ways by successive combinations of experiences, each of which is obtained in artificial, experimental cases, rarely or never furnished in this form by nature.

Meanwhile the fact that the connection with the activity of memory in ordinary life is for the moment lost is of less importance than the reverse, namely, that this connection with the complications and fluctuations of life is necessarily still a too close one. The struggle to attain the most simple and uniform conditions possible at numerous points naturally encounters obstacles that are rooted in the nature of the case and which thwart the attempt. The unavoidable dissimilarity of the material and the equally unavoidable irregularity of the external conditions have already been touched upon. I pass next to two other unsurmountable sources of difficulty.

By means of the successive repetitions the series are, so to speak, raised to ever higher levels. The natural assumption would be that at the moment when they could for the first time be reproduced by heart the level thus attained would always be the same. If only this were the case, i.e., if this characteristic first reproduction were everywhere an invariable objective sign of an equally invariable fixedness of the series, it would be of real value to us. This, however, is not actually the case. The inner conditions of the separate series at the moment of the first possible reproduction are not always the same, and the most that can be assumed is that in the case of these different series these conditions always oscillate about the same degree of inner surety. This is clearly seen if the learning and repeating of the series is continued after that first spontaneous reproduction of the series has been attained. As a general thing the capacity for voluntary reproduction persists after it has once been reached. In numerous cases, however, it disappears immediately after its first appearance, and is regained only after several further repetitions. This proves that the predisposition for memorising the series, irrespective of their differences of a larger sort according to the time of day, to the objective and subjective conditions, etc., is subject to small variations of short duration, whether they be called oscillations of attention or something else. If, at the very instant when the material to be memorised has almost reached the desired degree of surety, a chance moment of especial mental clearness occurs, then the series is caught on the wing as it were, often to the learner's surprise; but the series cannot long be re-

tained. By the occurrence of a moment of special dull-
ness, on the other hand, the first errorless reproduction
is postponed for a while, although the learner feels that
he really is master of the thing and wonders at the constantly recurring hesitations. In the former case, in spite
of the homogeneity of the external conditions, the first
errorless reproduction is reached at a point a little below
the level of retention normally connected with it. In the
latter case it is reached at a point a little above that level.
As was said before, the most plausible conjecture to
make in this connection is that these deviations will
compensate each other in the case of large groups.

Of the other source of error, I can only say that it
may occur and that, when it does, it is a source of great
danger. I mean the secret influence of theories and opinions which are in the process of formation. An investigation usually starts out with definite presuppositions as
to what the results will be. But if this is not the case at
the start, such presuppositions form gradually in case
the experimenter is obliged to work alone. For it is impossible to carry on the investigations for any length of
time without taking notice of the results. The experimenter must know whether the problem has been properly formulated or whether it needs completion or correction. The fluctuations of the results must be
controlled in order that the separate observations may
be continued long enough to give to the mean value the
certainty necessary for the purpose in hand. Consequently it is unavoidable that, after the observation of
the numerical results, suppositions should arise as to
general principles which are concealed in them and
which occasionally give hints as to their presence. As
the investigations are carried further, these suppositions,
as well as those present at the beginning, constitute a
complicating factor which probably has a definite influence upon the subsequent results. It goes without saying
that what I have in mind is not any consciously recognised influence but something similar to that which
takes place when one tries to be very unprejudiced or to
rid one's self of a thought and by that very attempt fos-
ters that thought or prejudice. The results are met half
way with an anticipatory knowledge, with a kind of expectation. Simply for the experimenter to say to himself
that such anticipations must not be allowed to alter the
impartial character of the investigation will not by itself
bring about that result. On the contrary, they do remain
and play a rôle in determining the whole inner attitude.
According as the subject notices that these anticipations
are confirmed or not confirmed (and in general he notices this during the learning), he will feel, if only in a
slight degree, a sort of pleasure or surprise. And would

you not expect that, in spite of the greatest conscien-
tiousness, the surprise felt by the subject over especially
startling deviations, whether positive or negative, would
result, without any volition on his part, in a slight
change of attitude? Would he not be likely to exert himself a little more here and to relax a little more there
than would have been the case had he had no knowledge
or presupposition concerning the probable numerical
value of the results? I cannot assert that this is always or
even frequently the case, since we are not here concerned with things that can be directly observed, and
since numerous results in which such secret warping of
the truth might be expected show evident independence
of it. All I can say is, we must expect something of the
sort from our general knowledge of human nature, and
in any investigations in which the inner attitude is of
very great importance, as for example in experiments on
sense perception, we must give special heed to its misleading influence.

It is evident how this influence in general makes itself felt. With average values it would tend to level the
extremes; where especially large or small numbers are
expected it would tend to further increase or decrease
the values. This influence can only be avoided with certainty when the tests are made by two persons working
together, one of whom acts as subject for a certain time
without raising any questions concerning the purpose or
the result of the investigations. Otherwise help can be
obtained only by roundabout methods, and then, probably, only to a limited extent. The subject, as I myself always did, can conceal from himself as long as possible
the exact results. The investigation can be extended in
such a way that the upper limits of the variables in question are attained. In this way, whatever warping of the
truth takes place becomes relatively more difficult and
unimportant. Finally, the subject can propose many
problems which will appear to be independent of each
other in the hope that, as a result, the true relation of the
interconnected mental processes will break its way
through.

To what extent the sources of error mentioned have
affected the results given below naturally cannot be exactly determined. The absolute value of the numbers
will doubtless be frequently influenced by them, but as
the purpose of the tests could never have been the precise determination of absolute values, but rather the attainment of comparative results (especially in the numerical sense) and relatively still more general results,
there is no reason for too great anxiety. In one important
case (§ 38) I could directly convince myself that the exclusion of all knowledge concerning the character of the

results brought about no change; in another case where I myself could not eliminate a doubt I called especial attention to it. In any case he who is inclined *a priori* to estimate very highly the unconscious influence of secret wishes on the total mental attitude will also have to take into consideration that the secret wish to find objective truth and not with disproportionate toil to place the creation of his own fancy upon feet of clay—that this wish, I say, may also claim a place in the complicated mechanism of these possible influences.

SECTION 15. MEASUREMENT OF WORK RE-QUIRED. The number of repetitions which were necessary for memorising a series up to the first possible reproduction was not originally determined by counting, but indirectly by measuring in seconds the time that was required to memorise it. My purpose was in this way to avoid the distraction necessarily connected with counting; and I could assume that there was a proportional relation existing between the times and the number of repetitions occurring at any time in a definite rhythm. We could scarcely expect this proportionality to be perfect, since, when only the time is measured, the moments of hesitation and reflection are included, which is not true when the repetitions are counted. Difficult series in which hesitation will occur relatively more frequently, will, by the method of time measurement, get comparatively greater numbers, the easier series will get comparatively smaller numbers than when the repetitions are counted. But with larger groups of series a tolerably equal distribution of difficult and equal series may be taken for granted. Consequently the deviations from proportionality will compensate themselves in a similar manner in the case of each group.

When, for certain tests, the direct counting of the repetitions became necessary, I proceeded in the following manner. Little wooden buttons measuring about 14 mms. in diameter and 4 mms. at their greatest thickness were strung on a cord which would permit of easy displacement and yet heavy enough to prevent accidental slipping. Each tenth piece was black; the others had their natural color. During the memorisation the cord was held in the hand and at each new repetition a piece was displaced some centimeters from left to right. When the series could be recited, a glance at the cord, since it was divided into tens, was enough to ascertain the number of repetitions that had been necessary. The manipulation required so little attention that in the mean values of the time used (which was always tabulated at the same time) no lengthening could be noted as compared with earlier tests.

By means of this simultaneous measurement of time and repetitions incidental opportunity was afforded for verifying and more accurately defining that which had been foreseen and which has just been explained with regard to their interrelation. When the prescribed rhythm of 150 strokes per minute was precisely maintained, each syllable would take 0.4 second; and when the simple reading of the series was interrupted by attempts to recite it by heart, the unavoidable hesitations would lengthen the time by small but fairly uniform amounts. This, however, did not hold true with any exactness; on the contrary, the following modifications appeared.

When the direct reading of the series predominated, a certain forcing, an acceleration of the rhythm, occurred which, without coming to consciousness, on the whole lowered the time for each syllable below the standard of 0.4 sec.

When there was interchange between reading and reciting, however, the lengthening of the time was not in general constant, but was greater with the longer series. In this case, since the difficulty increases very rapidly with increasing length of the series, there occurs a slowing of the tempo, again involuntary and not directly noticeable. Both are illustrated by the following table.

Series of 16 syllables, for the most part read	Each syllable required the average time of	Number of series	Number of syllables
8 times	0.398 sec.	60	960
16 "	0.399 "	108	1728

Series of X syllables	Were in part read, in part recited on an average Y times	Each syllable required an average time of Z secs.	Number of series	Number of syllables
X=	Y=	Z=		
12	18	0.416	63	756
16	31	0.427	252	4032
24	45	0.438	21	504
36	56	0.459	14	504

As soon as this direction of deviation from exact proportionality was noticed there appeared in the learning a certain conscious reaction against it.

Finally, it appeared that the probable error of the time measurements was somewhat larger than that of the repetitions. This relation is quite intelligible in the light of the explanations given above. In the case of the time measurements the larger values, which naturally occurred with the more difficult series, were relatively somewhat greater than in the case of the number of repetitions, because relatively they were for the most part lengthened by the hesitations; conversely, the smaller times were necessarily somewhat smaller relatively than the number of repetitions, because in general they corresponded to the easier series. The distribution of the values in the case of the times is therefore greater than that of the values in the case of the repetitions.

The differences between the two methods of reckoning are, as is readily seen, sufficiently large to lead to different results in the case of investigations seeking a high degree of exactness. That is not the case with the results as yet obtained; it is therefore immaterial whether the number of seconds is used or that of the repetitions.

Decision cannot be given *a priori* as to which method of measurement is more correct—*i.e.,* is the more adequate measure of the mental work expended. It can be said that the impressions are due entirely to the repetitions, they are the thing that counts; it can be said that a hesitating repetition is just as good as a simple fluent reproduction of the line, and that both are to be counted equally. But on the other hand it may be doubted that the moments of recollection are merely a loss. In any case a certain display of energy takes place in them: on the one hand, a very rapid additional recollection of the immediately preceding words occurs, a new start, so to speak, to get over the period of hesitation; on the other hand, there is heightened attention to the passages following. If with this, as is probable, a firmer memorisation of the series takes place, then these moments have a claim upon consideration which can only be given to them through the measurement of the times.

Only when a considerable difference in the results of the two kinds of tabulation appears will it be possible to give one the preference over the other. That one will then be chosen which gives the simpler formulation of the results in question.

SECTION 16. PERIODS OF THE TESTS. The tests were made in two periods, in the years 1879–80 and 1883–84, and extended each over more than a year. During a long time preliminary experiments of a similar nature had preceded the definite tests of the first period, so that, for all results communicated, the time of increasing skill may be considered as past. At the beginning of the second period I was careful to give myself renewed training. This temporal distribution of the tests with a separating interval of more than three years gives the desired possibility of a certain mutual control of most of the results. Frankly, the tests of the two periods are not strictly comparable. In the case of the tests of the first period, in order to limit the significance of the first fleeting grasp[3] of the series in moments of special concentration, it was decided to study the series until two successive faultless reproductions were possible. Later I abandoned this method, which only incompletely accomplished its purpose, and kept to the first fluent reproduction. The earlier method evidently in many cases resulted in a somewhat longer period of learning. In addition there was a difference in the hours of the day appointed for the tests. Those of the later period all occurred in the afternoon hours between one and three o'clock; those of the earlier period were unequally divided between the hours of 10–11 A.M., 11–12 A.M., and 6–8 P.M., which for the sake of brevity I shall designate A, B, and C.

NOTES

1. The vowel sounds employed were a, e, i, o, u, ä, ö, ü, au, ei, eu. For the beginning of the syllables the following consonants were employed: b, d, f, g, h, j, k, l, m, n, p, r, s, (= sz), t, w and in addition ch, sch, soft s, and the French j (19 altogether); for the end of the syllables f, k, l, m, n, p, r, s, (= sz) t, ch, sch (11 altogether). For the final sound fewer consonants were employed than for the initial sound, because a German tongue even after several years practise in foreign languages does not quite accustom itself to the correct pronunciation of the mediae at the end. For the same reason I refrained from the use of other foreign sounds although I tried at first to use them for the sake of enriching the material.

2. I shall retain in what follows the designations employed above and call a group of several syllable series or a single series a "test." A number of "tests" I shall speak of as a "test series" or a "group of tests."

3. Described in § 14.

14

IVAN PAVLOV

Ivan Petrovich Pavlov (1849–1936) valued discipline and order within his laboratory but was notoriously absent-minded at home. He felt successful and happy at work and at home, writing in his autobiography "I dreamed of finding happiness in intellectual work, in science—and I found it. I wanted to have a kind person as a companion in life and I found this companion in my wife Sara Vasilievna." Initially enrolled at the Ryazan Ecclesiastical Seminary, Pavlov was encouraged by the priests to read widely, which led him to works by Charles Darwin (p. 188) and Ivan Sechenov, the Russian physiologist who wrote *Reflexes of the Brain*. He transferred to the University of St. Petersburg to pursue a scientific career, continuing upon graduation in 1875 to the Military-Medical Academy, and received his medical degree in 1883. Pavlov developed incredible surgical techniques and collaborated with Heidenhain of Germany to perfect a method for isolating part of a dog's stomach, keeping the nerve and blood supply intact and attaching an external fistula to collect samples, thus allowing study of the various gastric acids during different phases of digestion. His own research began in earnest in 1890, when he became a professor of pharmacology (he switched to a chair of physiology in 1895). Pavlov was openly critical of the Bolsheviks, but both the revolutionaries of October 1917 and the later Soviet government heaped honor and privilege upon the internationally renowned scientist, providing generous support for his professional activities and even extending double rations to his immediate family.

CONDITIONAL REFLEXES: AN INVESTIGATION OF THE PHYSIOLOGICAL ACTIVITY OF THE CEREBRAL CORTEX

LECTURES ON THE WORK OF THE CEREBRAL HEMISPHERES

The substantiation and the history of the fundamental methods employed in the investigation of the activity of the cerebral hemispheres. The concept of the reflex. The variety of reflexes. Signalling activity as the most general physiological characteristic of the cerebral hemispheres.

Gentlemen,

One cannot but be struck by a comparison of the following facts. First, the cerebral hemispheres, the higher part of the central nervous system, is a rather impressive organ. In structure it is exceedingly complex, compris-ing millions and millions (in man—even billions) of cells, i.e., centres or foci of nervous activity. These cells vary in size, shape and arrangement and are connected with each other by countless branches. Such structural complexity naturally suggests a very high degree of functional complexity. Consequently, it would seem that a boundless field of investigation is offered here for the physiologist. Secondly, take the dog, man's companion and friend since prehistoric times, in its various roles as hunter, sentinel, etc. We know that this complex behaviour of the dog, its higher nervous activity (since no one will dispute that this is higher nervous activity), is chiefly associated with the cerebral hemispheres. If we remove the cerebral hemispheres in the dog (Goltz and others), it becomes incapable of performing not only the

From Ivan Pavlov, "Lectures on the Work of the Cerebral Hemispheres." In *Experimental Psychology and Other Essays* (pp. 171–187). New York: Philosophical Library, 1957. (Original work published 1926)

roles mentioned above, but even of looking after itself. It becomes profoundly disabled and will die unless well cared for. This implies that both in respect of structure and function, the cerebral hemispheres perform considerable physiological work.

Let us turn now to man. His entire higher nervous activity is also dependent on the normal structure and functioning of the cerebral hemispheres. The moment the complex structure of his hemispheres is damaged or disturbed in one way or another, he also becomes an invalid; he can no longer freely associate with his fellows as an equal and must be isolated.

In amazing contrast to this boundless activity of the cerebral hemispheres is the scant content of the present-day physiology of these hemispheres. Up to 1870 there was no physiology of the cerebral hemispheres at all; they seemed inaccessible to the physiologist. It was in that year that Fritsch and Hitzig first successfully applied the ordinary physiological methods of stimulation and destruction to their study. Stimulation of certain parts of the cerebral cortex regularly evoked contractions in definite groups of the skeletal muscles (the cortical motor region). Extirpation of these parts led to certain disturbances in the normal activity of the corresponding groups of muscles.

Shortly afterwards H. Munk, Ferrier and others demonstrated that other regions of the cortex, seemingly not susceptible to artificial stimulation, are also functionally differentiated. Removal of these parts leads to defects in the activity of certain receptor organs—the eye, the ear and the skin.

Many researchers have been thoroughly investigating these phenomena. More precision and more details have been obtained, especially as regards the motor region, and this knowledge has even found practical application in medicine; however, investigation as yet has not gone far beyond the initial point. The essential fact is that the entire higher and complex behaviour of the animal, which is dependent on the cerebral hemispheres, as shown by the previously mentioned experiment by Goltz with the extirpation of the hemispheres in a dog, has hardly been touched upon in these investigations and is not included even in the programme of current physiological research. What do the facts relating to the cerebral hemispheres, which are now at the disposal of the physiologist, explain with regard to the behaviour of the higher animals? Is there a general scheme of the higher nervous activity? What kind of general rules govern this activity? The contemporary physiologist finds himself truly empty-handed when he has to answer these lawful questions. While the object of investigation is highly

complex in relation to structure, and extremely rich in function, research in this sphere remains, as it were, in a blind alley, unable to open up before the physiologist the boundless vistas which might have been expected.

Why is this so? The reason is clear: the work of the cerebral hemispheres has never been regarded from the same point of view as that of other organs of the body, or even other parts of the central nervous system. It has been described as special *psychical* activity which we feel and apprehend in ourselves and which we suppose exists in animals by analogy with human beings. Hence the highly peculiar and difficult position of the physiologist. On the one hand, the study of the cerebral hemispheres, as of all other parts of the organism, seems to come within the scope of physiology, but on the other hand, it is an object of study by a special branch of science—psychology. What, then, should be the attitude of the physiologist? Should he first acquire psychological methods and knowledge and only then begin to study the activity of the cerebral hemispheres? But there is a real complication here. It is quite natural that physiology, in analysing living matter, should always base itself on the more exact and advanced sciences—mechanics, physics and chemistry. But here we are dealing with an altogether different matter, since in this particular case we should have to rely on a science which has no claim to exactness as compared with physiology. Until recently discussion revolved even around the question whether psychology should be considered a natural science or a science at all. Without going deeply into this question, I should like to cite some facts which, although crude and superficial, seem to me very convincing. Even the psychologists themselves do not regard their science as being exact. Not so long ago James, an outstanding American psychologist, called psychology not a science, but a "hope for science." Another striking illustration has been provided by Wundt, formerly a physiologist, who became a celebrated psychologist and philosopher and even the founder of the so-called experimental psychology. Prior to the war, in 1913, a discussion took place in Germany as to the advisability of separating the psychological branch of science from the philosophical in the universities, i.e., of having two separate chairs instead of one. Wundt opposed separation, one of his arguments being the impossibility of establishing a common and obligatory examination programme in psychology, since each professor had his own ideas of the essence of psychology. Is it not clear, then, that psychology has not yet reached the stage of an exact science?

This being the case, there is no need for the physiologist to have recourse to psychology. In view of the steadily developing natural science it would be more logical to expect that not psychology should render assistance to the physiology of the cerebral hemispheres, but, on the contrary, physiological investigation of the activity of this organ in animals should lay the foundation for the exact scientific analysis of the human subjective world. Consequently, physiology must follow its own path—the path blazed for it long ago. Taking as his starting-point the assumption that the functioning of the animal's organism, unlike that of the human being, is similar to the work of a machine, Descartes three hundred years ago evolved the idea of the reflex as the basic activity of the nervous system. Descartes regarded every activity of the organism as a natural response to certain external agents and believed that the connection between the active organ and the given agent, that is, between cause and effect, is achieved through a definite nervous path. In this way the study of the activity of the animal nervous system was placed on the firm basis of natural science. In the eighteenth, nineteenth and twentieth centuries the idea of the reflex had been extensively used by physiologists, but only in their work on the lower parts of the central nervous system; gradually, however, they began to study its higher parts, until finally, after Sherrington's classical works on spinal reflexes, Magnus, his successor, established the reflex nature of all the basic locomotor activities of the organism. And so experiment fully justified the idea of the reflex which, thereafter, was used in the study of the central nervous system almost up to the cerebral hemispheres. It is to be hoped that the more complex activities of the organism, including the basic locomotor reflexes—states so far referred to in psychology as anger, fear, playfulness, etc.—will soon be related to the simple reflex activity of the subcortical parts of the brain.

A bold attempt to apply the idea of the reflex to the cerebral hemispheres not only of animals but also of man, was made by I. M. Sechenov, the Russian physiologist, on the basis of the contemporary physiology of the nervous system. In a paper published in Russian in 1863 and entitled *Reflexes of the Brain* Sechenov characterized the activity of the cerebral hemispheres as reflex, i.e., determined activity. He regarded thoughts as reflexes in which the effector end is inhibited, and affects as exaggerated reflexes with a wide irradiation of excitation. A like attempt has been made in our time by Ch. Richet who introduced the concept of the psychical reflex in which the reaction to a given stimulus is determined by its union with the traces left in the cerebral hemispheres by previous stimuli. Generally, the recent

physiology of the higher nervous activity related to the cerebral hemispheres tends to associate acting stimulations with traces left by previous ones (associative memory—according to J. Loeb; training, education by experience—according to other physiologists). But this was mere theorizing. The time had come for a transition to the experimental analysis of the subject, and from the objective external aspect, as is the case with any other branch of natural science. This transition was determined by comparative physiology which had just made its appearance as a result of the influence of the theory of evolution. Now that it had turned its attention to the entire animal kingdom, physiology, in dealing with its lower representatives, was forced, of necessity, to abandon the anthropomorphic concept and concentrate on the scientific elucidation of the relations between the external agents influencing the animal and the responsive external activity, the locomotor reaction of the latter. This gave birth to J. Loeb's doctrine of animal tropisms; to the suggestion by Beer, Bethe and Uexküll of an objective terminology for designating the animal reactions; and finally, to the investigation by zoologists of the behaviour of the lower representatives of the animal world, by means of purely objective methods, by comparing the effect of external influences on the animal with its responsive external activity—as for example in the classical work of Jennings, etc.

Influenced by this new tendency in biology and having a practical cast of mind, American psychologists who also became interested in comparative psychology displayed a tendency to subject the external activity of animals to experimental analysis under deliberately induced conditions. Thorndike's *Animal Intelligence* (1898) must be regarded as the starting-point for investigations of this kind. In these investigations the animal was kept in a box and food placed outside, within sight. The animal, naturally, tried to reach the food, but to do so it had to open the door which in the different experiments was fastened in a different way. Tables and charts registered the speed and the manner in which the animal solved this problem. The entire process was interpreted as the formation of an association, connection between the visual and the tactile stimulation and the locomotor activity. Afterwards by means of this method, and by modifications of it, researchers studied numerous questions relating to the associative ability of various animals. Almost simultaneously with the above-mentioned work by Thorndike, of which I was not then aware, I too had arrived at the idea of the need for a similar attitude to the subject. The following episode, which occurred in my laboratory, gave birth to the idea.

While making a detailed investigation of the digestive glands I had to busy myself also with the so-called psychical stimulation of the glands. When, together with one of my collaborators, I attempted a deeper analysis of this fact, at first in the generally accepted way, i.e., psychologically, visualizing the probable thoughts and feelings of the animal, I stumbled on a fact unusual in laboratory practice. I found myself unable to agree with my colleague; each of us stuck to his point of view, and we were unable to convince each other by certain experiments. This made me definitely reject any further psychological discussion of the subject, and I decided to investigate it in a purely objective way, externally, i.e., strictly recording all stimuli reaching the animal at the given moment and observing its corresponding responses either in the form of movements or in the form of salivation (as occurred in this particular case).

This was the beginning of the investigations that I have carried on now for the past twenty-five years with the participation of numerous colleagues who joined hand and brain with me in this work and to whom I am deeply grateful. We have, of course, passed through different stages, and the subject has been advanced only gradually. At first we had but a few separate facts at our disposal, but today so much material has been accumulated by us that we can make an attempt to present it in a more or less systematized form. I am now in a position to place before you a physiological theory of the activity of the cerebral hemispheres which at any rate conforms much more to the structural and functional complexity of this organ than the theory which until now has been based on a few fragmentary, though very important, facts of modern physiology.

Thus, research along these new lines of strictly objective investigation of the higher nervous activity has been carried out mainly in my laboratories (with the participation of a hundred colleagues); work along the same lines has been carried out also by American psychologists. As for other physiological laboratories, so far only a few have begun, starting somewhat later, to investigate this subject, but in most cases their work is still in the initial stage. So far there has been one essential point of difference in the research of the Americans and in ours. Since in the case of the Americans the objective investigation is being conducted by psychologists, this means that, although psychologists study the facts from the purely external aspect, nevertheless, in posing the problems, in analysing and formulating the results, they tend to think more in terms of psychology. The result is that with the exception of the group of "behaviourists" their work does not bear a purely physio-

logical character. Whereas, we, having started from physiology, invariably and strictly adhere to the physiological point of view, and we are investigating and systematizing the whole subject solely in a physiological way.

I shall now pass to an exposition of our material, but before doing so I should like to touch on the concept of the reflex in general, on reflexes in physiology and the so-called instincts.

In the main we base ourselves on Descartes' concept of the reflex. Of course, this is a genuinely scientific concept, since the phenomenon implied by it can be strictly determined. It means that a certain agent of the external world, or of the organism's internal medium produces a certain effect in one or other nervous receptor, which is transformed into a nervous process, into nervous excitation. The excitation is transmitted along certain nerve fibres, as if along an electric cable, to the central nervous system; thence, thanks to the established nervous connections, it passes along other nerve fibres to the working organ, where it in its turn is transformed into a special activity of the cells of this organ. Thus, the stimulating agent proves to be indispensably connected with the definite activity of the organism, as cause and effect.

It is quite obvious that the entire activity of the organism is governed by definite laws. If the animal were not (in the biological sense) strictly adapted to the surrounding world, it would, sooner or later, cease to exist. If instead of being attracted by food, the animal turned away from it, or instead of avoiding fire threw itself into it, and so on, it would perish. The animal *must* so react to the environment that all its responsive activity ensures its existence. The same is true if we think of life in terms of mechanics, physics and chemistry. Every material system can exist as an entity only so long as its internal forces of attraction, cohesion, etc., are equilibrated with the external forces influencing it. This applies in equal measure to such a simple object as a stone and to the most complex chemical substance, and it also holds good for the organism. As a definite material system complete in itself, the organism can exist only so long as it is in equilibrium with the environment; the moment this equilibrium is seriously disturbed, the organism ceases to exist as a particular system. Reflexes are the elements of this constant adaptation or equilibration. Physiologists have studied and are studying numerous reflexes, these indispensable, machine-like reactions of the organism, which at the same time are inborn, i.e., determined by the peculiar organization of the given nervous system. Reflexes, like the belts of machines made by human hands, are of two kinds: the positive and the negative inhibitory, in other words, those which excite certain activities and those which inhibit them. Although investigation of these reflexes by physiologists has been under way for a long time, it is, of course, a long way from being finished. More and more new reflexes are being discovered; the properties of the receptor organs, in which the external and especially the internal stimuli produce certain impulses, still remain in many cases unexplored. The paths along which nervous excitation is conducted within the central nervous system are often little known or not known at all. The central mechanism of inhibitory reflexes, excluding those which manifest themselves along the inhibitory efferent nerves, is quite obscure; the combination and interaction of the various reflexes have not yet been sufficiently elucidated. Nevertheless, physiologists are penetrating deeper and deeper into the mechanism of this machine-like functioning of the organism, and have every reason for believing that sooner or later they will elucidate it in full measure and exercise complete control over it.

Akin to the usual reflexes that have long been the object of physiological investigation in the laboratory and which concern mainly the functions of separate organs, are other inborn reactions; these reactions also take place in the nervous system, and are governed by definite laws, i.e., they are strictly determined by definite conditions. They are the reactions of different animals in relation to the functioning of the organism as a whole, manifested in the general behaviour of the animals and designated by the special term "instincts." Since full agreement has not yet been attained with regard to the essential similarity of these reactions to reflexes, I shall dwell on this question somewhat longer.

Physiology owes to Herbert Spenser, the English philosopher, the first suggestion that instinctive reactions are reflexes too. Afterwards zoologists, physiologists and comparative psychologists produced numerous facts in support of this suggestion. I shall try to systematize the various arguments to the effect that there is not a single essential feature distinguishing reflexes from instincts. First of all there are numerous, imperceptible stages of transition from the usual reflexes to instincts. Take, for example, a newly hatched chick; it reacts by pecking movements to any stimulus in the field of its vision, be it a tiny object or a stain on the surface on which it is walking. In what way does it differ, say, from inclining the head and closing the lids when something flashes near the eye? We should call the latter a defensive reflex, and the first an alimentary instinct,

although in the case of the pecking, if it is caused by the sight of a stain, nothing but inclining the head and a movement of the beak occurs.

Further, it has been noted that instincts are more complex than reflexes. But there are exceedingly complex reflexes which no one designates as instincts. Take, for example, vomiting. This is a highly complex action and one that involves extraordinary co-ordination of a large number of muscles, both striated and smooth, usually employed in other functions of the organism and spread over a large area. It also involves the secretion of various glands which normally participate in quite different activities of the organism.

The fact that instincts involve a long chain of successive actions, while reflexes are, so to speak, one-storeyed, has also been regarded as a point of distinction between them. By way of example let us take the building of a nest, or of animal dwellings in general. Here, of course, we have a long chain of actions: the animal must search for the material, bring it to the site and put it together and secure it. If we regard this as a reflex, we must assume that the ending of one reflex excites a new one, or, in other words, that these are chain-reflexes. But such chain activities are by no means peculiar to instincts alone. We are familiar with many reflexes which are also interlocked. Here is an instance. When we stimulate an afferent nerve, for example, the n. ischiadicus, there takes place a reflex rise of blood pressure. This is the first reflex. The high pressure in the left ventricle of the heart and in the first part of the aorta acts as a stimulus to another reflex: it stimulates the endings of the n. depressoris cordis which evokes a depressor reflex moderating the effect of the first reflex. Let us take the chain-reflex recently established by Magnus. A cat, even deprived of the cerebral hemispheres will in most cases fall on its feet when thrown from a height. How does this occur? The change in the spatial position of the otolithic organ of the ear causes a certain reflex contraction of the muscles in the neck, which restores the animal's head to a normal position in relation to the horizon. This is the first reflex. The end of this reflex—the contraction of the muscles in the neck and the righting of the head in general—stimulates a fresh reflex on certain muscles of the trunk and limbs which come into action and, in the end, restore the animal's proper standing posture.

Yet another difference between reflexes and instincts has been assumed, namely, that instincts often depend on the internal state or condition of the organism. For instance, a bird builds its nest only in the mating season. Or, to take a simpler example, when the animal is sated, it is no longer attracted by food and stops eating. The same applies to the sexual instinct, which is connected with the age of the organism, as well as with the state of the reproductive glands. In general the hormones, products of the glands of internal secretion, are of considerable importance in this respect. But this, too, is not a peculiar property of the instincts alone. The intensity of any reflex, as well as its presence of absence, directly depends on the state of excitability of the reflex centres which in turn always depends on the chemical and physical properties of the blood (automatic stimulation of the centres) and on the interaction of different reflexes.

Finally, importance is sometimes attached to the fact that reflexes are related to the activity of separate organs, whereas instincts involve the activity of the organism as a whole, i.e., actually the whole skeleto-muscular system. However, we know from the works of Magnus and de Kleyn that standing, walking, and bodily balance in general, are reflexes.

Thus, reflexes and instincts alike are natural reactions of the organism to certain stimulating agents, and consequently there is no need to designate them by different terms. The term "reflex" is preferable, since a strictly scientific sense has been imparted to it from the very outset.

The aggregate of these reflexes constitutes the foundation of the nervous activity both in men and animals. Consequently, thorough study of all these fundamental nervous reactions of the organism is, of course, a matter of great importance. Unfortunately, as already mentioned, this is a long way from having been accomplished, especially in the case of those reflexes which are called instincts. Our knowledge of these instincts is very limited and fragmentary. We have but a rough classification of them—alimentary, self-defensive, sexual, parental and social. But almost each of these groups often includes numerous separate reflexes, some of which have not been even identified by us, while some are confused with others or, at least, they are not fully appreciated by us as to their vital importance. To what extent this subject remains unelucidated and how full it is still of gaps can be demonstrated by this example from my own experience.

Once, in the course of our experimental work which I shall describe presently, we were puzzled by the peculiar behaviour of our animal. This was a tractable dog with which we were on very friendly terms. The dog was given a rather easy assignment. It was placed in the stand and had its movements restricted only by soft loops fastened round its legs (to which at first it did not react at all). Nothing else was done except to feed it re-

peatedly at intervals of several minutes. At first the dog was quiet and ate willingly, but as time went on it became more and more excited: it began to struggle against the surrounding objects, tried to break loose, pawing at the floor, gnawing the supports of the stand, etc. This ceaseless muscular exertion brought on dyspnoea and a continuous secretion of saliva; this persisted for weeks, becoming worse and worse, with the result that the dog was no longer fit for our experimental work. This phenomenon puzzled us for a long time. We advanced many hypotheses as to the possible reason for this unusual behaviour, and although we had by then acquired sufficient knowledge of the behaviour of dogs, our efforts were in vain until it occurred to us that it might be interpreted quite simply—as the manifestation of a freedom reflex, and that the dog would not remain quiet so long as its movements were constrained. We overcame this reflex by means of another—a food reflex. We began to feed the dog only in the stand. At first it ate sparingly and steadily lost weight, but gradually it began to eat more—until it consumed the whole of its daily ration. At the same time it became quiet during the experiments; the freedom reflex was thus inhibited. It is obvious that the freedom reflex is one of the most important reflexes, or, to use a more general term, reactions of any living being. But this reflex is seldom referred to, as if it were not finally recognized. James does not enumerate it even among the special human reflexes (instincts). Without a reflex protest against restriction of an animal's movements any insignificant obstacle in its way would interfere with the performance of certain of its important functions. As we know, in some animals the freedom reflex is so strong that when placed in captivity they reject food, pine away and die.

Let us turn to another example. There is a reflex which is still insufficiently appreciated and which can be termed the investigatory reflex. I sometimes call it the "What-is-it?" reflex. It also belongs to the fundamental reflexes and is responsible for the fact that given the slightest change in the surrounding world both man and animals immediately orientate their respective receptor organs towards the agent evoking the change. The biological significance of this reflex is enormous. If the animal were not provided with this reaction, its life, one may say, would always hang by a thread. In man this reflex is highly developed, manifesting itself in the form of an inquisitiveness which gives birth to scientific thought, ensuring for us a most reliable and unrestricted orientation in the surrounding world. Still less elucidated and differentiated is the category of negative, inhibitory reflexes (instincts) induced by any strong stimuli, or even by weak but unusual stimuli. So-called animal hypnotism belongs, of course, to this category.

Thus, the fundamental nervous reactions both of man and animals are inborn in the form of reflexes. And I repeat once more that it is highly important to have a complete list of these reflexes and properly to classify them, since, as we shall see later, all the remaining nervous activity of the organism is based on these reflexes.

However, although the reflexes just described constitute the fundamental condition for the safety of the organism in the surrounding nature, they in themselves are not sufficient to ensure a lasting, stable and normal existence for the organism. This is proved by the following experiment, carried out on a dog in which the cerebral hemispheres have been extirpated. Besides the internal reflexes, such a dog retains the fundamental external reflexes. It is attracted by food; it keeps away from destructive stimuli; it displays the investigatory reflex pricking up its ears and lifting its head to sound. It possesses the freedom reflex as well, and strongly resists any attempt at capture. Nevertheless, it is an invalid and would not survive without care. Evidently something vital is missing in its nervous activity. But what? It is impossible not to see that the number of stimulating agents evoking reflex reactions in this dog has decreased considerably, that the stimuli act at a very short distance and are of a very elementary and very general character, being undifferentiated. Hence, the equilibrium of this higher organism with the environment in a wide sphere of its life has also become very elementary, limited and obviously inadequate.

Let us now revert to the simple example with which we began our investigations. When food or some unpalatable substance gets into the mouth of the animal, it evokes a secretion of saliva which moistens, dissolves and chemically alters the food, or in the case of disagreeable substances removes them and cleanses the mouth. This reflex is caused by the physical and chemical properties of the above-mentioned substances when they come in contact with the mucous membrane of the oral cavity. However, a similar secretory reaction is produced by the same substances when placed at a distance from the dog and act on it only by appearance and smell. Moreover, even the sight of the vessel from which the dog is fed suffices to evoke salivation, and what is more, this reaction can be produced by the sight of the person who usually brings the food, even by the sound of his footsteps in the next room. All these numerous, distant, complex and delicately differentiated stimuli lose their effect irretrievably when the dog is deprived of the cere-

bral hemispheres; only the physical and chemical properties of substances, when they come in contact with the mucous membrane of the mouth, retain their effect. Meanwhile, the processing significance of the lost stimuli is, in normal conditions, very great. Dry food immediately encounters plenty of the required liquid; unpalatable substances, which often destroy the mucous membrane of the mouth, are removed from it by a layer of saliva rapidly diluted and so on. But their significance is still greater when they bring into action the motor component of the alimentary reflex, i.e., when the seeking of food is effected.

Here is another important example of the defensive reflex. The strong animals prey on those smaller and weaker, and the latter must inevitably perish if they begin to defend themselves only when the fangs and claws of the enemy are already in their flesh. But the situation is quite different when the defensive reaction arises at the sight and sound of the approaching foe. The weak animal has a chance of escaping by seeking cover or in flight.

What, then, would be our general summing up of this difference in attitude of the normal and of the decorticated animal to the external world? What is the general mechanism of this distinction and what is its basic principle?

It is not difficult to see that in normal conditions the reactions of the organism are evoked not only by those agents of the external world that are essential for the organism, i.e., the agents that bring direct benefit or harm to the organism, but by other countless agents which are merely signals of the first agents, as demonstrated above. It is not the sight and sound of the strong animal which destroy the smaller and weaker animal, but its fangs and its claws. However, the signalling, or to use Sherrington's term, the distant stimuli, although comparatively limited in number, play a part in the aforementioned reflexes. The essential feature of the higher nervous activity, with which we shall be concerned and which in the higher animal is probably inherent in the cerebral hemispheres alone, is not only the action of countless signalling stimuli, rather it is the important fact that in certain conditions their physiological action changes.

In the above-mentioned salivary reaction now one particular vessel acted as a signal, now another, now one man, now another—strictly depending on the vessel that contained the food or the unpalatable substances before they were introduced in the dog's mouth, and which person brought and gave them to the dog. This, clearly, makes the machine-like activity of the organism still more precise and perfect. The environment of the animal is so infinitely complex and is so continuously in a state of flux, that the intricate and complete system of the organism has the chance of becoming equilibrated with the environment only if it is also in a corresponding state of constant flux.

Hence, the fundamental and most general activity of the cerebral hemispheres is signalling, the number of signals being infinite and the signalization variable.

PART 4

EMOTION AND INSTINCT IN ANIMALS AND HUMANS

15

CHARLES DARWIN

Charles Robert Darwin (1809–1882) was generally regarded as a pleasant and congenial fellow, with a particularly enthusiastic penchant for collecting samples. A selection from his autobiography reveals his passion: "One day, on tearing off some old bark, I saw two rare beetles and seized one in each hand; then I saw a third and new kind, which I could not bear to lose, so that I popped the one which I held in my right hand into my mouth. Alas it ejected some intensely acrid fluid, which burnt my tongue so that I was forced to spit the beetle out, which was lost, as well as the third one." Darwin's family tree is remarkable, rooted with two famous grandfathers: Erasmus Darwin, a poet-scientist who proposed an early theory of evolution, and Josiah Wedgwood, who revolutionized the pottery industry with streamlined factory procedures and new marketing techniques for his Jasper wares. Charles Darwin initially tried to study medicine at the University of Edinburgh, but found witnessing surgery nauseating and so turned to theology at Cambridge University, with plans to combine a country parsonage with an avocation for natural history. However, thanks to his rambles with Anglican clergyman and botanist John Stevens Henslow, Darwin was offered the opportunity to buy a berth on HMS *Beagle* to study and collect specimens from around the world. His father eventually agreed to pay his son's expenses, and Darwin began reading on geology, geography, and biology and collecting and observing with an incredible eye for detail. Though a variety of publications resulted from his travels, Darwin hesitated to publish his theory of natural selection without sufficient supporting evidence, realizing that evolution might seem at odds with a literal interpretation of the biblical story of creation in Genesis. He summarized his notion privately in 1842 and 1844, circulating his work among a few close correspondents. Finally, in 1856, Darwin began to draft a book with the proper volume of evidence, a tome he expected to be 3,000 pages. Before the manuscript was completed, however, Alfred Russel Wallace sent him a brief outline of a new theory of evolution. Wallace had independently, with far less evidence, developed the same theory and was asking Darwin, known for his congeniality and expertise as a naturalist, for a critique. It was arranged that both men would be credited with the first public announcement of the theory, and excerpts from each work were read at the next meeting of the Linnean Society in July 1858, to little notice by the public. Darwin wrote a 490-page abridgement of his planned book, and *Origin of Species* appeared in 1859; this time the public noticed. The quantity and quality of Darwin's data are often not appropriately highlighted, though its seemingly outlandish predictions have time and again been demonstrated true. For example, in 1861, just after a particularly public debate between Thomas Henry "Darwin's Bulldog" Huxley and Bishop Samuel Wilberforce, the first fossil remains of archaeopteryx, the oldest bird, were unearthed. Darwin had suggested that birds evolved from lizards, and archaeopteryx, with feathers on its wings but the fingers and vertebrae of a reptile, provides, from beyond antiquity, the necessary transitional form.

From Charles Darwin, "General Principles of Expression." In *Expression of the Emotions in Man and Animals* (pp. 27–65). New York: D. Appleton, 1873.

EXPRESSION OF THE EMOTIONS IN MAN AND ANIMALS

CHAPTER 1

General Principles of Expression

The three chief principles stated—The first principle—Serviceable actions become habitual in association with certain states of the mind, and are performed whether or not of service in each particular case—The force of habit—Inheritance—Associated habitual movements in man—Reflex actions—Passage of habits into reflex actions—Associated habitual movements in the lower animals—Concluding remarks.

I WILL begin by giving the three Principles, which appear to me to account for most of the expressions and gestures involuntarily used by man and the lower animals, under the influence of various emotions and sensations.[1] I arrived, however, at these three Principles only at the close of my observations. They will be discussed in the present and two following chapters in a general manner. Facts observed both with man and the lower animals will here be made use of; but the latter facts are preferable, as less likely to deceive us. In the fourth and fifth chapters, I will describe the special expressions of some of the lower animals; and in the succeeding chapters those of man. Everyone will thus be able to judge for himself, how far my three principles throw light on the theory of the subject. It appears to me that so many expressions are thus explained in a fairly satisfactory manner, that probably all will hereafter be found to come under the same or closely analogous heads. I need hardly premise that movements or changes in any part of the body,—as the wagging of a dog's tail, the drawing back of a horse's ears, the shrugging of a man's shoulders, or the dilatation of the capillary vessels of the skin,—may all equally well serve for expression. The three Principles are as follows.

I. *The principle of serviceable associated Habits.*—Certain complex actions are of direct or indirect service under certain states of the mind, in order to relieve or gratify certain sensations, desires, &c.; and whenever the same state of mind is induced, however feebly, there is a tendency through the force of habit and association for the same movements to be performed, though they may not then be of the least use. Some actions ordinarily associated through habit with certain states of the

mind may be partially repressed through the will, and in such cases the muscles which are least under the separate control of the will are the most liable still to act, causing movements which we recognise as expressive. In certain other cases the checking of one habitual movement requires other slight movements; and these are likewise expressive.

II. *The principle of Antithesis.*—Certain states of the mind lead to certain habitual actions, which are of service, as under our first principle. Now when a directly opposite state of mind is induced, there is a strong and involuntary tendency to the performance of movements of a directly opposite nature, though these are of no use; and such movements are in some cases highly expressive.

III. *The principle of actions due to the constitution of the Nervous System, independently from the first of the Will, and independently to a certain extent of Habit.*—When the sensorium is strongly excited, nerve-force is generated in excess, and is transmitted in certain definite directions, depending on the connection of the nerve-cells, and partly on habit: or the supply of nerve-force may, as it appears, be interrupted. Effects are thus produced which we recognise as expressive. This third principle may, for the sake of brevity, be called that of the direct action of the nervous system.

With respect to our *first Principle,* it is notorious how powerful is the force of habit. The most complex and difficult movements can in time be performed without the least effort or consciousness. It is not positively known how it comes that habit is so efficient in facilitating complex movements; but physiologists admit[2] "that the conducting power of the nervous fibres increases with the frequency of their excitement." This applies to the nerves of motion and sensation, as well as to those connected with the act of thinking. That some physical change is produced in the nerve-cells or nerves which are habitually used can hardly be doubted, for otherwise it is impossible to understand how the tendency to certain acquired movements is inherited. That they are inherited we see with horses in certain transmitted paces, such as cantering and ambling, which are not natural to them,—in the pointing of young pointers and the setting of young setters—in the peculiar manner of flight of certain breeds of the pigeon, &c. We have analogous cases with mankind in the inheritance of tricks or unusual gestures, to which we shall presently recur. To those who admit the gradual evolution of species, a most striking instance of the perfection with which the most difficult consensual movements can be transmitted, is afforded by the humming-bird Sphinx-moth (*Macroglossa*); for this moth, shortly after its emergence from the cocoon, as shown by the bloom on its unruffled scales, may be seen poised stationary in the air, with its long hair-like proboscis uncurled and inserted into the minute orifices of flowers; and no one, I believe, has ever seen this moth learning to perform its difficult task, which requires such unerring aim.

When there exists an inherited or instinctive tendency to the performance of an action, or an inherited taste for certain kinds of food, some degree of habit in the individual is often or generally requisite. We find this in the paces of the horse, and to a certain extent in the pointing of dogs; although some young dogs point excellently the first time they are taken out, yet they often associate the proper inherited attitude with a wrong odour, and even with eyesight. I have heard it asserted that if a calf be allowed to suck its mother only once, it is much more difficult afterwards to rear it by hand.[3] Caterpillars which have been fed on the leaves of one kind of tree, have been known to perish from hunger rather than to eat the leaves of another tree, although this afforded them their proper food, under a state of nature;[4] and so it is in many other cases.

The power of Association is admitted by everyone. Mr. Bain remarks, that "actions, sensations, and states of feeling, occurring together or in close succession, tend to grow together, or cohere, in such a way that when any one of them is afterwards presented to the mind, the others are apt to be brought up in idea."[5] It is so important for our purpose fully to recognise that actions readily become associated with other actions and with various states of the mind, that I will give a good many instances, in the first place relating to man, and afterwards to the lower animals. Some of the instances are of a very trifling nature, but they are as good for our purpose as more important habits. It is known to everyone how difficult, or even impossible it is, without repeated trials, to move the limbs in certain opposed directions which have never been practised. Analogous cases occur with sensations, as in the common experiment of rolling a marble beneath the tips of two crossed fingers, when it feels exactly like two marbles. Everyone protects himself when falling to the ground by extending his arms, and as Professor Alison has remarked, few can resist acting thus, when voluntarily falling on a soft bed. A man when going out of doors puts on his gloves quite unconsciously; and this may seem an ex-

tremely simple operation, but he who has taught a child to put on gloves, knows that this is by no means the case.

When our minds are much affected, so are the movements of our bodies; but here another principle besides habit, namely the undirected overflow of nerve-force, partially comes into play. Norfolk, in speaking of Cardinal Wolsey, says—

"Some strange commotion
  Is in his brain; he bites his lip and starts;
  Stops on a sudden, looks upon the ground,
  Then, lays his finger on his temple: straight,
  Springs out into fast gait; then, stops again,
  Strikes his breast hard; and anon, he casts
  His eye against the moon: in most strange postures
  We have seen him set himself."   (*Hen. VIII.*, act 3, sc. 2.)

A vulgar man often scratches his head when perplexed in mind; and I believe that he acts thus from habit, as if he experienced a slightly uncomfortable bodily sensation, namely, the itching of his head, to which he is particularly liable, and which he thus relieves. Another man rubs his eyes when perplexed, or gives a little cough when embarrassed, acting in either case as if he felt a slightly uncomfortable sensation in his eyes or windpipe.[6]

From the continued use of the eyes, these organs are especially liable to be acted on through association under various states of the mind, although there is manifestly nothing to be seen. A man, as Gratiolet remarks, who vehemently rejects a proposition, will almost certainly shut his eyes or turn away his face; but if he accepts the proposition, he will nod his head in affirmation and open his eyes widely. The man acts in this latter case as if he clearly saw the thing, and in the former case as if he did not or would not see it. I have noticed that persons in describing a horrid sight often shut their eyes momentarily and firmly, or shake their heads, as if not to see or to drive away something disagreeable; and I have caught myself, when thinking in the dark of a horrid spectacle, closing my eyes firmly. In looking suddenly at any object, or in looking all around, everyone raises his eyebrows, so that the eyes may be quickly and widely opened; and Duchenne remarks that[7] a person in trying to remember something often raises his eyebrows, as if to see it. A Hindoo gentleman made exactly the same remark to Mr. Erskine in regard to his countrymen. I noticed a young lady earnestly trying to recollect a painter's name, and she first looked to one corner of the ceiling and then to the opposite corner, arching the one eyebrow on that side; although, of course, there was nothing to be seen there.

In most of the foregoing cases, we can understand how the associated movements were acquired through habit; but with some individuals, certain strange gestures or tricks have arisen in association with certain states of the mind, owing to wholly inexplicable causes, and are undoubtedly inherited. I have elsewhere given one instance from my own observation of an extraordinary and complex gesture, associated with pleasurable feelings, which was transmitted from a father to his daughter, as well as some other analogous facts.[8] Another curious instance of an odd inherited movement, associated with the wish to obtain an object, will be given in the course of this volume.

There are other actions which are commonly performed under certain circumstances, independently of habit, and which seem to be due to imitation or some sort of sympathy. Thus persons cutting anything with a pair of scissors may be seen to move their jaws simultaneously with the blades of the scissors. Children learning to write often twist about their tongues as their fingers move, in a ridiculous fashion. When a public singer suddenly becomes a little hoarse, many of those present may be heard, as I have been assured by a gentleman on whom I can rely, to clear their throats; but here habit probably comes into play, as we clear our own throats under similar circumstances. I have also been told that at leaping matches, as the performer makes his spring, many of the spectators, generally men and boys, move their feet; but here again habit probably comes into play, for it is very doubtful whether women would thus act.

Reflex actions.—Reflex actions, in the strict sense of the term are due to the excitement of a peripheral nerve, which transmits its influence to certain nerve-cells, and these in their turn excite certain muscles or glands into action; and all this may take place without any sensation or consciousness on our part, though often thus accompanied. As many reflex actions are highly expressive, the subject must here be noticed at some little length. We shall also see that some of them graduate into, and can hardly be distinguished from actions which have arisen through habit.[9] Coughing and sneezing are familiar instances of reflex actions. With infants the first act of respiration is often a sneeze, although this requires the co-ordinated movement of numerous muscles. Respiration is partly voluntary, but mainly reflex, and is performed in the most natural and best manner without the interference of the will. A vast number of complex

movements are reflex. As good an instance as can be given is the often-quoted one of a decapitated frog, which cannot of course feel, and cannot consciously perform, any movement. Yet if a drop of acid be placed on the lower surface of the thigh of a frog in this state, it will rub off the drop with the upper surface of the foot of the same leg. If this foot be cut off, it cannot thus act. "After some fruitless efforts, therefore, it gives up trying in that way, seems restless, as though, says Pflüger, it was seeking some other way, and at last it makes use of the foot of the other leg and succeeds in rubbing off the acid. Notably we have here not merely contractions of muscles, but combined and harmonized contractions in due sequence for a special purpose. These are actions that have all the appearance of being guided by intelligence and instigated by will in an animal, the recognized organ of whose intelligence and will has been removed."[10]

We see the difference between reflex and voluntary movements in very young children not being able to perform, as I am informed by Sir Henry Holland, certain acts somewhat analogous to those of sneezing and coughing, namely, in their not being able to blow their noses (*i. e.* to compress the nose and blow violently through the passage), and in their not being able to clear their throats of phlegm. They have to learn to perform these acts, yet they are performed by us, when a little older, almost as easily as reflex actions. Sneezing and coughing, however, can be controlled by the will only partially or not at all; whilst the clearing the throat and blowing the nose are completely under our command.

When we are conscious of the presence of an irritating particle in our nostrils or windpipe—that is, when the same sensory nerve-cells are excited, as in the case of sneezing and coughing—we can voluntarily expel the particle by forcibly driving air through these passages; but we cannot do this with nearly the same force, rapidity, and precision, as by a reflex action. In this latter case the sensory nerve-cells apparently excite the motor nerve-cells without any waste of power by first communicating with the cerebral hemispheres—the seat of our consciousness and volition. In all cases there seems to exist a profound antagonism between the same movements, as directed by the will and by a reflex stimulant, in the force with which they are performed and in the facility with which they are excited. As Claude Bernard asserts, "L'influence du cerveau tend done à entraver les mouvements réflexes, à limiter leur force et leur étendue."[11]

The conscious wish to perform a reflex action sometimes stops or interrupts its performance, though the proper sensory nerves may be stimulated. For instance, many years ago I laid a small wager with a dozen young men that they would not sneeze if they took snuff, although they all declared that they invariably did so; accordingly they all took a pinch, but from wishing much to succeed, not one sneezed, though their eyes watered, and all, without exception, had to pay me the wager. Sir H. Holland remarks[12] that attention paid to the act of swallowing interferes with the proper movements; from which it probably follows, at least in part, that some persons find it so difficult to swallow a pill.

Another familiar instance of a reflex action is the involuntary closing of the eyelids when the surface of the eye is touched. A similar winking movement is caused when a blow is directed towards the face; but this is an habitual and not a strictly reflex action, as the stimulus is conveyed through the mind and not by the excitement of a peripheral nerve. The whole body and head are generally at the same time drawn suddenly backwards. These latter movements, however, can be prevented, if the danger does not appear to the imagination imminent; but our reason telling us that there is no danger does not suffice. I may mention a trifling fact, illustrating this point, and which at the time amused me. I put my face close to the thick glassplate in front of a puff-adder in the Zoological Gardens, with the firm determination of not starting back if the snake struck at me; but, as soon as the blow was struck, my resolution went for nothing, and I jumped a yard or two backwards with astonishing rapidity. My will and reason were powerless against the imagination of a danger which had never been experienced.

The violence of a start seems to depend partly on the vividness of the imagination, and partly on the condition, either habitual or temporary, of the nervous system. He who will attend to the starting of his horse, when tired and fresh, will perceive how perfect is the gradation from a mere glance at some unexpected object, with a momentary doubt whether it is dangerous, to a jump so rapid and violent, that the animal probably could not voluntarily whirl round in so rapid a manner. The nervous system of a fresh and highly-fed horse sends its order to the motory system so quickly, that no time is allowed for him to consider whether or not the danger is real. After one violent start, when he is excited and the blood flows freely through his brain, he is very apt to start again; and so it is, as I have noticed, with young infants.

A start from a sudden noise, when the stimulus is conveyed through the auditory nerves, is always accompanied in grown-up persons by the winking of the eyelids.[13] I observed, however, that though my infants started at sudden sounds, when under a fortnight old, they certainly did not always wink their eyes, and I believe never did so. The start of an older infant apparently represents a vague catching hold of something to prevent falling. I shook a pasteboard box close before the eyes of one of my infants, when 114 days old, and it did not in the least wink; but when I put a few comfits into the box, holding it in the same position as before, and rattled them, the child blinked its eyes violently every time, and started a little. It was obviously impossible that a carefully-guarded infant could have learnt by experience that a rattling sound near its eyes indicated danger to them. But such experience will have been slowly gained at a later age during a long series of generations; and from what we know of inheritance, there is nothing improbable in the transmission of a habit to the offspring at an earlier age than that at which it was first acquired by the parents.

From the foregoing remarks it seems probable that some actions, which were at first performed consciously, have become through habit and association converted into reflex actions, and are now so firmly fixed and inherited, that they are performed, even when not of the least use,[14] as often as the same causes arise, which originally excited them in us through the volition. In such cases the sensory nerve-cells excite the motor cells, without first communicating with those cells on which our consciousness and volition depend. It is probable that sneezing and coughing were originally acquired by the habit of expelling, as violently as possible, any irritating particle from the sensitive air-passages. As far as time is concerned, there has been more than enough for these habits to have become innate or converted into reflex actions; for they are common to most or all of the higher quadrupeds, and must therefore have been first acquired at a very remote period. Why the act of clearing the throat is not a reflex action, and has to be learnt by our children, I cannot pretend to say; but we can see why blowing the nose on a handkerchief has to be learnt.

It is scarcely credible that the movements of a headless frog, when it wipes off a drop of acid or other object from its thigh, and which movements are so well coordinated for a special purpose, were not at first performed voluntarily, being afterwards rendered easy through long-continued habit so as at last to be performed unconsciously, or independently of the cerebral hemispheres.

So again it appears probable that starting was originally acquired by the habit of jumping away as quickly as possible from danger, whenever any of our senses gave us warning. Starting, as we have seen, is accompanied by the blinking of the eyelids so as to protect the eyes, the most tender and sensitive organs of the body; and it is, I believe, always accompanied by a sudden and forcible inspiration, which is the natural preparation for any violent effort. But when a man or horse starts, his heart beats wildly against his ribs, and here it may be truly said we have an organ which has never been under the control of the will, partaking in the general reflex movements of the body. To this point, however, I shall return in a future chapter.

The contraction of the iris, when the retina is stimulated by a bright light, is another instance of a movement, which it appears cannot possibly have been at first voluntarily performed and then fixed by habit; for the iris is not known to be under the conscious control of the will in any animal. In such cases some explanation, quite distinct from habit, will have to be discovered. The radiation of nerve-force from strongly-excited nerve-cells to other connected cells, as in the case of a bright light on the retina causing a sneeze, may perhaps aid us in understanding how some reflex actions originated. A radiation of nerve-force of this kind, if it caused a movement tending to lessen the primary irritation, as in the case of the contraction of the iris preventing too much light from falling on the retina, might afterwards have been taken advantage of and modified for this special purpose.

It further deserves notice that reflex actions are in all probability liable to slight variations, as are all corporeal structures and instincts; and any variations which were beneficial and of sufficient importance, would tend to be preserved and inherited. Thus reflex actions, when once gained for one purpose, might afterwards be modified independently of the will or habit, so as to serve for some distinct purpose. Such cases would be parallel with those which, as we have every reason to believe, have occurred with many instincts; for although some instincts have been developed simply through long-continued and inherited habit, other highly complex ones have been developed through the preservation of variations of pre-existing instincts—that is, through natural selection.

I have discussed at some little length, though as I am well aware, in a very imperfect manner, the acquirement of reflex actions, because they are often brought into play in connection with movements expressive of our emotions; and it was necessary to show that at least some of them might have been first acquired through the will in order to satisfy a desire, or to relieve a disagreeable sensation.

Associated habitual movements in the lower animals.—I have already given in the case of Man several instances of movements, associated with various states of the mind or body, which are now purposeless, but which were originally of use, and are still of use under certain circumstances. As this subject is very important for us, I will here give a considerable number of analogous facts, with reference to animals; although many of them are of a very trifling nature. My object is to show that certain movements were originally performed for a definite end, and that, under nearly the same circumstances, they are still pertinaciously performed through habit when not of the least use. That the tendency in most of the following cases is inherited, we may infer from such actions being performed in the same manner by all the individuals, young and old, of the same species. We shall also see that they are excited by the most diversified, often circuitous, and sometimes mistaken associations.

Dogs, when they wish to go to sleep on a carpet or other hard surface, generally turn round and round and scratch the ground with their fore-paws in a senseless manner, as if they intended to trample down the grass and scoop out a hollow, as no doubt their wild parents did, when they lived on open grassy plains or in the woods. Jackals, fennecs, and other allied animals in the Zoological Gardens, treat their straw in this manner; but it is a rather odd circumstance that the keepers, after observing for some months, have never seen the wolves thus behave. A semi-idiotic dog—and an animal in this condition would be particularly liable to follow a senseless habit—was observed by a friend to turn completely round on a carpet thirteen times before going to sleep.

Many carnivorous animals, as they crawl towards their prey and prepare to rush or spring on it, lower their heads and crouch, partly, as it would appear, to hide themselves, and partly to get ready for their rush; and this habit in an exaggerated form has become hereditary in our pointers and setters. Now I have noticed scores of times that when two strange dogs meet on an open road, the one which first sees the other, though at the distance of one or two hundred yards, after the first glance always lowers its head, generally crouches a little, or even lies down; that is, he takes the proper attitude for concealing himself and for making a rush or spring, although the road is quite open and the distance great. Again, dogs of all kinds when intently watching and slowly approaching their prey, frequently keep one of their fore-legs doubled up for a long time, ready for the next cautious step; and this is eminently characteristic of the pointer. But from habit they behave in exactly the same manner whenever their attention is aroused (fig. 15.1). I have seen a dog at the foot of a high wall, listening attentively to a sound on the opposite side, with one leg doubled up; and in this case there could have been no intention of making a cautious approach.

Dogs after voiding their excrement often make with all four feet a few scratches backwards, even on a bare stone pavement, as if for the purpose of covering up their excrement with earth, in nearly the same manner as do cats. Wolves and jackals behave in the Zoological Gardens in exactly the same manner, yet, as I am assured by the keepers, neither wolves, jackals, nor foxes, when they have the means of doing so, ever cover up their excrement, any more than do dogs. All these animals, however, bury superfluous food. Hence, if we rightly understand the meaning of the above cat-like habit, of which there can be little doubt, we have a purposeless remnant of an habitual movement, which was originally followed by some remote progenitor of the dog-genus for a definite purpose, and which has been retained for a prodigious length of time.

Dogs and jackals[15] take much pleasure in rolling and rubbing their necks and backs on carrion. The odour seems delightful to them, though dogs at least do not eat carrion. Mr. Bartlett has observed wolves for me, and has given them carrion, but has never seen them roll on it. I have heard it remarked, and I believe it to be true, that the larger dogs, which are probably descended from wolves, do not so often roll in carrion as do smaller dogs, which are probably descended from jackals. When a piece of brown biscuit is offered to a terrier of mine and she is not hungry (and I have heard of similar instances), she first tosses it about and worries it, as if it were a rat or other prey; she then repeatedly rolls on it precisely as if it were a piece of carrion, and at last eats it. It would appear that an imaginary relish has to be given to the distasteful morsel; and to effect this the dog acts in his habitual manner, as if the biscuit was a live

FIGURE 15.1   Small dog watching a cat on a table. From a photograph taken by Mr. Bejiander.

animal or smelt like carrion, though he knows better than we do that this is not the case. I have seen this same terrier act in the same manner after killing a little bird or mouse.

Dogs scratch themselves by a rapid movement of one of their hind feet; and when their backs are rubbed with a stick, so strong is the habit, that they cannot help rapidly scratching the air or the ground in a useless and ludicrous manner. The terrier just alluded to, when thus scratched with a stick, will sometimes show her delight by another habitual movement, namely, by licking the air as if it were my hand.

Horses scratch themselves by nibbling those parts of their bodies which they can reach with their teeth; but more commonly one horse shows another where he wants to be scratched, and they then nibble each other. A friend whose attention I had called to the subject, observed that when he rubbed his horse's neck, the animal protruded his head, uncovered his teeth, and moved his jaws, exactly as if nibbling another horse's neck, for he could never have nibbled his own neck. If a horse is much tickled, as when curry-combed, his wish to bite something becomes so intolerably strong, that he will clatter his teeth together, and though not vicious, bite his groom. At the same time from habit he closely depresses his ears, so as to protect them from being bitten, as if he were fighting with another horse.

A horse when eager to start on a journey makes the nearest approach which he can to the habitual movement of progression by pawing the ground. Now when horses in their stalls are about to be fed and are eager for their corn, they paw the pavement or the straw. Two of my horses thus behave when they see or hear the corn given to their neighbours. But here we have what may almost be called a true expression, as pawing the ground is universally recognized as a sign of eagerness.

Cats cover up their excrements of both kinds with earth; and my grandfather[16] saw a kitten scraping ashes over a spoonful of pure water spilt on the hearth; so that here an habitual or instinctive action was falsely excited, not by a previous act or by odour, but by eyesight. It is well known that cats dislike wetting their feet, owing, it is probable, to their having aboriginally inhabited the dry country of Egypt; and when they wet their feet they shake them violently. My daughter poured some water into a glass close to the head of a kitten; and it immediately shook its feet in the usual manner; so that here we have an habitual movement falsely excited by an associated sound instead of by the sense of touch.

Kittens, puppies, young pigs and probably many other young animals, alternately push with their fore-feet against the mammary glands of their mothers, to excite a freer secretion of milk, or to make it flow. Now it is very common with young cats, and not at all rare with old cats of the common and Persian breeds (believed by some naturalists to be specifically extinct), when comfortably lying on a warm shawl or other soft substance, to pound it quietly and alternately with their fore-feet; their toes being spread out and claws slightly protruded, precisely as when sucking their mother. That it is the same movement is clearly shown by their often at the same time taking a bit of the shawl into their mouths and sucking it; generally closing their eyes and purring from delight. This curious movement is commonly excited only in association with the sensation of a warm soft surface; but I have seen an old cat, when pleased by having its back scratched, pounding the air with its feet in the same manner; so that this action has almost become the expression of a pleasurable sensation.

Having referred to the act of sucking, I may add that this complex movement, as well as the alternate protrusion of the fore-feet, are reflex actions; for they are performed if a finger moistened with milk is placed in the mouth of a puppy, the front part of whose brain has been removed.[17] It has recently been stated in France, that the action of sucking is excited solely through the sense of smell, so that if the olfactory nerves of a puppy are destroyed, it never sucks. In like manner the wonderful power which a chicken possesses only a few hours after being hatched, of picking up small particles of food, seems to be started into action through the sense of hearing; for with chickens hatched by artificial heat, a good observer found that "making a noise with the finger-nail against a board, in imitation of the hen-mother, first taught them to peck at their meat."[18]

I will give only one other instance of an habitual and purposeless movement. The Sheldrake (*Tadorna*) feeds on the sands left uncovered by the tide, and when a worm-cast is discovered, "it begins patting the ground with its feet, dancing as it were, over the hole;" and this makes the worm come to the surface. Now Mr. St. John says, that when his tame Sheldrakes "came to ask for food, they patted the ground in an impatient and rapid manner."[19] This therefore may almost be considered as their expression of hunger. Mr. Bartlett informs me that the Flamingo and the Kagu (*Rhinochetus jubatus*) when anxious to be fed, beat the ground with their feet in the same odd manner. So again Kingfishers, when they catch a fish, always beat it until it is killed; and in the Zoological Gardens they always beat the raw meat, with which they are sometimes fed, before devouring it.

We have now, I think, sufficiently shown the truth of our first Principle, namely, that when any sensation, desire, dislike, &c., has led during a long series of generations to some voluntary movement, then a tendency to the performance of a similar movement will almost certainly be excited, whenever the same, or any analogous or associated sensation &c., although very weak, is experienced; notwithstanding that the movement in this case may not be of the least use. Such habitual movements are often, or generally inherited; and they then differ but little from reflex actions. When we treat of the special expressions of man, the latter part of our first Principle, as given at the commencement of this chapter, will be seen to hold good; namely, that when movements, associated through habit with certain states of the mind, are partially repressed by the will, the strictly involuntary muscles, as well as those which are least under the separate control of the will, are liable still to act; and their action is often highly expressive. Conversely, when the will is temporarily or permanently weakened, the voluntary muscles fail before the involuntary. It is a fact familiar to pathologists, as Sir C. Bell remarks,[20] "that when debility arises from affection of the brain, the influence is greatest on those muscles which are, in their natural condition, most under the command of the will." We shall, also, in our future chapters, consider another proposition included in our first Principle; namely, that the checking of one habitual movement sometimes requires other slight movements; these latter serving as a means of expression.

CHAPTER II

General Principles of Expression—*continued.*

The Principle of Antithesis—Instances in the dog and cat—Origin of the principle—Conventional signs—The principle of antithesis has not arisen from opposite actions being consciously performed under opposite impulses.

WE will now consider our second Principle, that of Antithesis. Certain states of the mind lead, as we have seen in the last chapter, to certain habitual movements which were primarily, or may still be, of service; and we shall find that when a directly opposite state of mind is induced, there is a strong and involuntary tendency to the performance of movements of a directly opposite nature, though these have never been of any service. A few striking instances of antithesis will be given, when we treat of the special expressions of man; but as, in these cases, we are particularly liable to confound conventional or artificial gestures and expressions with those which are innate or universal, and which alone deserve to rank as true expressions, I will in the present chapter almost confine myself to the lower animals.

When a dog approaches a strange dog or man in a savage or hostile frame of mind he walks upright and very stiffly; his head is slightly raised, or not much lowered; the tail is held erect and quite rigid; the hairs bristle, especially along the neck and back; the pricked ears are directed forwards, and the eyes have a fixed stare: (see figs. 15.2 and 15.4). These actions, as will hereafter be explained, follow from the dog's intention to attack his enemy, and are thus to a large extent intelligible. As he prepares to spring with a savage growl on his enemy, the canine teeth are uncovered, and the ears are pressed close backwards on the head; but with these latter actions, we are not here concerned. Let us now suppose that the dog suddenly discovers that the man whom he is approaching, is not a stranger, but his master; and let it be observed how completely and instantaneously his whole bearing is reversed. Instead of walking upright, the body sinks downwards or even crouches, and is thrown into flexuous movements; his tail, instead of being held stiff and upright, is lowered and wagged from side to side; his hair instantly becomes smooth; his ears

are depressed and drawn backwards, but not closely to the head; and his lips hang loosely. From the drawing back of the ears, the eyelids become elongated, and the eyes no longer appear round and staring. It should be added that the animal is at such times in an excited condition from joy; and nerve-force will be generated in excess, which naturally leads to action of some kind. Not one of the above movements, so clearly expressive of affection, are of the least direct service to the animal. They are explicable, as far as I can see, solely from being in complete opposition or antithesis to the attitude and movements which, from intelligible causes, are assumed when a dog intends to fight, and which consequently are expressive of anger. I request the reader to look at the four accompanying sketches, which have been given in order to recall vividly the appearance of a dog under these two states of mind. It is, however, not a little difficult to represent affection in a dog, whilst caressing his master and wagging his tail, as the essence of the expression lies in the continuous flexuous movements.

We will now turn to the cat. When this animal is threatened by a dog, it arches its back in a surprising manner, erects its hair, opens its mouth and spits. But we are not here concerned with this well-known attitude, expressive of terror combined with anger; we are

FIGURE 15.2   Dog approaching another dog with hostile intentions. By Mr. Riviere.

FIGURE 15.3   The same in a humble and affectionate frame of mind. By Mr. Riviere.

concerned only with that of rage or anger. This is not often seen, but may be observed when two cats are fighting together; and I have seen it well exhibited by a savage cat whilst plagued by a boy. The attitude is almost exactly the same as that of a tiger disturbed and growling over its food, which every one must have beheld in menageries. The animal assumes a crouching position, with the body extended; and the whole tail, or the tip alone, is lashed or curled from side to side. The hair is not in the least erect. Thus far, the attitude and movements are nearly the same as when the animal is prepared to spring on its prey, and when, no doubt, it feels savage. But when preparing to fight, there is this difference, that the ears are closely pressed backwards; the mouth is partially opened, showing the teeth; the fore feet are occasionally struck out with protruded claws; and the animal occasionally utters a fierce growl. (See figs. 15.6 and 15.7.) All, or almost all, these actions naturally follow (as hereafter to be explained), from the cat's manner and intention of attacking its enemy.

Let us now look at a cat in a directly opposite frame of mind, whilst feeling affectionate and caressing her master; and mark how opposite is her attitude in every respect. She now stands upright with her back slightly arched, which makes the hair appear rather rough, but it does not bristle; her tail, instead of being extended and lashed from side to side, is held quite stiff and perpendicularly upwards; her ears are erect and pointed; her mouth is closed; and she rubs against her master with a purr instead of a growl. Let is further be observed how widely different is the whole bearing of an affectionate cat from that of a dog, when with his body crouching and flexuous, his tail lowered and wagging, and ears depressed, he caresses his master. This contrast in the attitudes and movements of these two carnivorous animals, under the same pleased and affectionate frame of mind, can be explained, as it appears to me, solely by their movements standing in complete antithesis to those which are naturally assumed, when these animals feel savage and are prepared either to fight or to seize their prey.

In these cases of the dog and cat, there is every reason to believe that the gestures both of hostility and affection are innate or inherited; for they are almost identically the same in the different races of the species, and in all the individuals of the same race, both young and old.

I will here give one other instance of antithesis in expression. I formerly possessed a large dog, who, like every other dog, was much pleased to go out walking. He showed his pleasure by trotting gravely before me with high steps, head much raised, moderately erected ears, and tail carried aloft but not stiffly. Not far from my house a path branches off to the right, leading to the hot-house, which I used often to visit for a few moments, to look at my experimental plants. This was al-

FIGURE 15.4   Half-bred Shepherd Dog in the same state as in Fig. 15.2. By Mr. A. May.

ways a great disappointment to the dog, as he did not know whether I should continue my walk; and the instantaneous and complete change of expression which came over him, as soon as my body swerved in the least towards the path (and I sometimes tried this as an experiment) was laughable. His look of dejection was known to every member of the family, and was called his *hot-house face.* This consisted in the head drooping much, the whole body sinking a little and remaining motionless; the ears and tail falling suddenly down, but the tail was by no means wagged. With the falling of the ears and of his great chaps, the eyes became much changed in appearance, and I fancied that they looked less bright. His aspect was that of piteous, hopeless dejection; and it was, as I have said, laughable, as the cause was so slight. Every detail in his attitude was in complete opposition to his former joyful yet dignified bearing; and can be explained, as it appears to me, in no other way, except through the principle of antithesis. Had not the change been so instantaneous, I should have attributed it to his lowered spirits affecting, as in the case of man, the nervous system and circulation, and consequently the tone of his whole muscular frame; and this may have been in part the cause.

We will now consider how the principle of antithesis

in expression has arisen. With social animals, the power of intercommunication between the members of the same community,—and with other species, between the opposite sexes, as well as between the young and the old,—is of the highest importance to them. This is generally effected by means of the voice, but it is certain that gestures and expressions are to a certain extent mutually intelligible. Man not only uses inarticulate cries, gestures, and expressions, but has invented articulate language; if, indeed, the word *invented* can be applied to a process, completed by innumerable steps, half-consciously made. Any one who has watched monkeys will not doubt that they perfectly understand each other's gestures and expression, and to a large extent, as Rengger asserts,[21] those of man. An animal when going to attack another, or when afraid of another, often makes itself appear terrible, by erecting its hair, thus increasing the apparent bulk of its body, by showing its teeth, or brandishing its horns, or by uttering fierce sounds.

As the power of intercommunication is certainly of high service to many animals, there is no *à priori* improbability in the supposition, that gestures manifestly of an opposite nature to those by which certain feelings are already expressed, should at first have been voluntarily employed under the influence of an opposite state

FIGURE 15.5 The same caressing his master. By Mr. A. May.

of feeling. The fact of the gestures being now innate, would be no valid objection to the belief that they were at first intentional; for if practised during many generations, they would probably at last be inherited. Nevertheless it is more than doubtful, as we shall immediately see, whether any of the cases which come under our present head of antithesis, have thus originated.

With conventional signs which are not innate, such as those used by the deaf and dumb and by savages, the principle of opposition or antithesis has been partially brought into play. The Cistercian monks thought it sinful to speak, and as they could not avoid holding some communication, they invented a gesture language, in which the principle of opposition seems to have been employed.[22] Dr. Scott, of the Exeter Deaf and Dumb Institution, writes to me that "opposites are greatly used in teaching the deaf and dumb, who have a lively sense of

them." Nevertheless I have been surprised how few unequivocal instances can be adduced. This depends partly on all the signs having commonly had some natural origin; and partly on the practice of the deaf and dumb and of savages to contract their signs as much as possible for the sake of rapidity.[23] Hence their natural source or origin often becomes doubtful or is completely lost; as is likewise the case with articulate language.

Many signs, moreover, which plainly stand in opposition to each other, appear to have had on both sides a significant origin. This seems to hold good with the signs used by the deaf and dumb for light and darkness, for strength and weakness, &c. In a future chapter I shall endeavour to show that the opposite gestures of affirmation and negation, namely, vertically nodding and laterally shaking the head, have both probably had a natural beginning. The waving of the hand from right to left, which is used as a negative by some savages, may have been invented in imitation of shaking the head; but whether the opposite movement of waving the hand in a straight line from the face, which is used in affirmation, has arisen through antithesis or in some quite distinct manner, is doubtful.

If we now turn to the gestures which are innate or common to all the individuals of the same species, and which come under the present head of antithesis, it is extremely doubtful, whether any of them were at first deliberately invented and consciously performed. With mankind the best instance of a gesture standing in direct opposition to other movements, naturally assumed under an opposite frame of mind, is that of shrugging the shoulders. This expresses impotence or an apology,—something which cannot be done, or cannot be avoided. The gesture is sometimes used consciously and voluntarily, but it is extremely improbable that it was at first deliberately invented, and afterwards fixed by habit; for not only do young children sometimes shrug their shoulders under the above states of mind, but the movement is accompanied, as will be shown in a future chapter, by various subordinate movements, which not one man in a thousand is aware of, unless he has specially attended to the subject.

Dogs when approaching a strange dog, may find it useful to show by their movements that they are friendly, and do not wish to fight. When two young dogs in play are growling and biting each other's faces and legs, it is obvious that they mutually understand each other's gestures and manners. There seems, indeed, some degree of instinctive knowledge in puppies and kittens, that they must not use their sharp little teeth or claws too freely in their play, though this sometimes

FIGURE 15.6   Cat, savage, and prepared to fight, drawn from life by Mr. Wood.

happens and a squeal is the result; otherwise they would often injure each other's eyes. When my terrier bites my hand in play, often snarling at the same time, if he bites too hard and I say *gently, gently,* he goes on biting, but answers me by a few wags of the tail, which seems to say "Never mind, it is all fun." Although dogs do thus express, and may wish to express, to other dogs and to man, that they are in a friendly state of mind, it is incredible that they could ever have deliberately thought of drawing back and depressing their ears, instead of holding them erect,—of lowering and wagging their tails, instead of keeping them stiff and upright, &c., because they knew that these movements stood in direct opposition to those assumed under an opposite and savage frame of mind.

Again, when a cat, or rather when some early progenitor of the species, from feeling affectionate first slightly arched its back, held its tail perpendicularly upwards and pricked its ears, can it be believed that the animal consciously wished thus to show that its frame of mind was directly the reverse of that, when from being ready to fight or to spring on its prey, it assumed a crouching attitude, curled its tail from side to side and depressed its ears? Even still less can I believe that my dog voluntarily put on his dejected attitude and "*hot-house face,*" which formed so complete a contrast to his

previous cheerful attitude and whole bearing. It cannot be supposed that he knew that I should understand his expression, and that he could thus soften my heart and make me give up visiting the hot-house.

Hence for the development of the movements which come under the present head, some other principle, distinct from the will and consciousness, must have intervened. This principle appears to be that every movement which we have voluntarily performed throughout our lives has required the action of certain muscles; and when we have performed a directly opposite movement, an opposite set of muscles has been habitually brought into play,—as in turning to the right or to the left, in pushing away or pulling an object towards us, and in lifting or lowering a weight. So strongly are our intentions and movements associated together, that if we eagerly wish an object to move in any direction, we can hardly avoid moving our bodies in the same direction, although we may be perfectly aware that this can have no influence. A good illustration of this fact has already been given in the Introduction, namely, in the grotesque movements of a young and eager billiard-player, whilst watching the course of his ball. A man or child in a passion, if he tells any one in a loud voice to begone, generally moves his arm as if to push him away, although the offender may not be standing near, and although there

FIGURE 15.7   Cat in an affectionate frame of mind, by
Mr. Wood.

may be not the least need to explain by a gesture what is
meant. On the other hand, if we eagerly desire some one
to approach us closely, we act as if pulling him towards
us; and so in innumerable other instances.

As the performance of ordinary movements of an
opposite kind, under opposite impulses of the will, has
become habitual in us and in the lower animals, so
when actions of one kind have become firmly associated with any sensation or emotion, it appears natural that
actions of a directly opposite kind, though of no use,
should be unconsciously performed through habit and
association, under the influence of a directly opposite
sensation or emotion. On this principle alone can I understand how the gestures and expressions which come
under the present head of antithesis have originated. If
indeed they are serviceable to man or to any other ani-

mal, in aid of inarticulate cries or language, they will
likewise be voluntarily employed, and the habit will
thus be strengthened. But whether or not of service as a
means of communication, the tendency to perform opposite movements under opposite sensations or emotions would, if we may judge by analogy, become
hereditary through long practice; and there cannot be a
doubt that several expressive movements due to the
principle of antithesis are inherited.

NOTES

1. Mr. Herbert Spencer ("Essays," Second Series,
1863, p. 138) has drawn a clear distinction between emotions and sensations, the latter being "generated in our corporeal framework." He classes as Feelings both emotions
and sensations.

2. Müller, "Elements of Physiology," Eng. translat. vol.
ii. p. 939. See also Mr. H. Spencer's interesting speculations on the same subject, and on the genesis of nerves, in
his "Principles of Biology," vol. ii. p. 346; and in Lis "Principles of Psychology," 2nd edit. pp. 511–557.

3. A remark to much the same effect was made long
ago by Hippocrates and by the illustrious Harvey; for both
assert that a young animal forgets in the course of a few
days the art of sucking, and cannot without some difficulty
again acquire it. I give these assertions on the authority of
Dr. Darwin, "Zoonomia," 1794, vol. i. p. 140.

4. See for my authorities, and for various analogous
facts, "The Variation of Animals and Plants under Domestication," 1868, vol. ii. p. 304.

5. "The Senses and the Intellect," 2nd edit. 1864, p.
332. Prof. Huxley remarks ("Elementary Lessons in Physiology," 5th edit. 1872, p. 306), "It may be laid down as a
rule, that, if any two mental states be called up together, or
in succession, with due frequency and vividness, the subsequent production of the one of them will suffice to call up
the other, and that whether we desire it or not."

6. Gratiolet ("De la Physionomie," p. 324), in his discussion on this subject, gives many analogous instances.
See p. 42, on the opening and shutting of the eyes. Engel is
quoted (p. 323) on the changed paces of a man, as his
thoughts change.

7. "Méeanisme de la Physiouomie Humaine," 1862, p.
17.

8. "The Variation of Animals and Plants under Domestication," vol. ii. p. 6. The inheritance of habitual gestures is
so important for us, that I gladly avail myself of Mr. F. Galton's permission to give in his own words the following remarkable case:—"The following account of a habit occur-

ring in individuals of three consecutive generations is of peculiar interest, because it occurs only during sound sleep, and therefore cannot be due to imitation, but must be altogether natural. The particulars are perfectly trustworthy, for I have enquired fully into them, and speak from abundant and independent evidence. A gentleman of considerable position was found by his wife to have the curious trick, when he lay fast asleep on his back in bed, of raising his right arm slowly in front of his face, up to his forehead, and then dropping it with a jerk, so that the wrist fell heavily on the bridge of his nose. The trick did not occur every night, but occasionally, and was independent of any ascertained cause. Sometimes it was repeated incessantly for an hour or more. The gentleman's nose was prominent, and its bridge often became sore from the blows which it received. At one time an awkward sore was produced, that was long in healing, on account of the recurrence, night after night, of the blows which first caused it. His wife had to remove the button from the wrist of his night-gown as it made severe scratches, and some means were attempted of tying his arm."

"Many years after his death, his son married a lady who had never heard of the family incident. She, however, observed precisely the same peculiarity in her husband; but his nose, from not being particularly prominent, has never as yet suffered from the blows. The trick does not occur when he is half-asleep, as, for example, when dozing in his arm-chair, but the moment he is fast asleep it is apt to begin. It is, as with his father, intermittent; sometimes ceasing for many nights, and sometimes almost incessant during a part of every night. It is performed, as it was by his father, with his right hand."

"One of his children, a girl, has inherited the same trick. She performs it, likewise, with the right hand, but in a slightly modified form; for, after raising the arm, she does not allow the wrist to drop upon the bridge of the nose, but the palm of the half-closed hand falls over and down the nose, striking it rather rapidly. It is also very intermittent with this child, not occurring for periods of some months, but sometimes occurring almost incessantly."

9. Prof. Huxley remarks ("Elementary Physiology," 5th edit. p. 305) that reflex actions proper to the spinal cord are *natural;* but, by the help of the brain, that is through habit, an infinity of *artificial* reflex actions may be acquired. Vir-

chow admits ("Sammlung wissenschaft. Vorträge," &c., "Ueber das Rückenmark," 1871, ss. 24, 31) that some reflex actions can hardly be distinguished from instincts; and, of the latter, it may be added, some cannot be distinguished from inherited habits.

10. Dr. Maudsley, "Body and Mind," 1870, p. 8.

11. See the very interesting discussion on the whole subject by Claude Bernard, "Tissus Vivants," 1866, pp. 353–356.

12. "Chapters on Mental Physiology," 1858, p. 85.

13. Müller remarks ("Elements of Physiology," Eng. tr. vol. ii. p. 1311) on starting being always accompanied by the closure of the eyelids.

14. Dr. Maudsley remarks ("Body and Mind," p. 10) that "reflex movements which commonly effect a useful end may, under the changed circumstances of disease, do great mischief, becoming even the occasion of violent suffering and of a most painful death."

15. See Mr. F. H. Salvin's account of a tame jackal in "Land and Water," October, 1869.

16. Dr. Darwin, "Zoonomia," 1794, vol. i. p. 160. I find that the fact of cats protruding their feet when pleased is also noticed (p. 151) in this work.

17. Carpenter, "Principles of Comparative Physiology," 1854, p. 690 and Müller's "Elements of Physiology," Eng. translat. vol. ii. p. 936.

18. Mowbray on "Poultry," 6th edit. 1830, p. 54.

19. See the account given by this excellent observer in "Wild Sports of the Highlands," 1846, p. 142.

20. "Philosophical Translations," 1823; p. 182.

21. 'Naturgeschichte der Säugethiere von Paraguay,' 1830, s. 55.

22. Mr. Tylor gives an account of the Cistercian gesture-language in his 'Early History of Mankind' (2nd edit. 1870, p. 40), and makes some remarks on the principle of opposition in gestures.

23. See on this subject Dr. W. R. Scott's interesting work. "The Deaf and Dumb," 2nd edit. 1870, p. 12. He says, "This contracting of natural gestures into much shorter gestures than the natural expression requires, is very common amongst the deaf and dumb. This contracted gesture is frequently so shortened as nearly to lose all semblance of the natural one, but to the deaf and dumb who use it, it still has the force of the original expression."

16

MARGARET FLOY WASHBURN

Margaret Floy Washburn (1871–1939) found herself at Vassar College in 1891 with "two dominant intellectual interests, science and philosophy. They seemed to be combined in what I heard of the wonderful new science of experimental psychology." An only child with parents who were continuously supportive of her scholarly interests, Washburn spent her early life in Harlem, then an isolated residential suburb of New York City. Following college, she arranged immediately to study with James McKeen Cattell at Columbia University, but could not formally enroll because of the Trustees' restrictions barring women. Cattell, whom Washburn found very supportive, suggested that she consider Cornell University, which offered women the full range of graduate study and degree candidacy. Awarded a prestigious scholarship, Washburn was one of the first students of E. B. Titchener (p. 324), recently arrived from Wilhelm Wundt's (p. 296) Leipzig laboratory to begin an experimental psychology program at Cornell. Washburn earned her Ph.D. in 1894, the first woman to receive the degree in psychology, and was elected to membership in the American Psychological Association the same year. She eventually returned to Vassar as an associate professor of philosophy, developing a remarkable body of research without some of the advantages available to her colleagues at research institutions or inclusion in Titchener's elite "Experimentalists" club, a vibrant discussion group of top North American psychologists. Washburn combined teaching and research by designing a variety of experiments for senior students to conduct and interpret. Fifty-seven times Washburn and her students found significant new results, which she published, with her respective student coauthors, as the series "Studies from the Psychological Laboratory of Vassar College" in the *American Journal of Psychology.* Washburn's professional activities extended well beyond Vassar and mark her as one of a growing number of college professors who were beginning to consider their careers in terms of their academic disciplines, as opposed to a particular loyalty to their current institution. In addition to serving in a variety of leadership roles, including president of the American Psychological Association and editor of the *American Journal of Psychology,* Washburn was elected to the National Academy of Sciences in 1931.

THE ANIMAL MIND

CHAPTER I

The Difficulties and Methods of Comparative Psychology

§ 1.   *Difficulties*

THAT the mind of each human being forms a region inaccessible to all save its possessor, is one of the commonplaces of reflection. His neighbor's knowledge of each person's mind must always be indirect, a matter of inference. How wide of the truth this inference may be, even under the most favorable circumstances, is also an affair of everyday experience: each of us can judge his fellow-men only on the basis of his own thoughts and feelings in similar circumstances, and the individual peculiarities of different members of the human species

From Margaret Floy Washburn, "The Difficulties and Methods of Comparative Psychology," and "The Evidence of Mind." In *The Animal Mind* (pp. 1–32). New York: Macmillan. 1907.

are of necessity very imperfectly comprehended by others. The science of human psychology has to reckon with this unbridgeable gap between minds as its chief difficulty. The psychologist may look into his own mind and study its workings with impartial insight, yet he can never be sure that the laws which he derives from such a study are not distorted by some personal twist or bias. For example, it has been suggested that the philosopher Hume was influenced by his tendency toward a visual type of imagination in his discussion of the nature of ideas, which to him were evidently visual images. As is well known, the experimental method in psychology has aimed to minimize the danger of confusing individual peculiarities with general mental laws. In a psychological experiment, an unbiased observer is asked to study his own experience under certain definite conditions, and to put it into words so that the experimenter may know what the contents of another mind are like in the circumstances. Thus language is an essential apparatus in experimental psychology; language with all its defects, its ambiguity, its substitution of crystallized concepts for the protean flux of actually lived experience, its lack of terms to express those parts of experience which are of small practical importance in everyday life, but which may be of the highest importance to mental science. Outside of the psychological laboratory language is not always the best guide to the contents of other minds, because it is not always the expression of a genuine wish to communicate thought. "Actions speak louder than words," the proverb says; but when words are backed by good faith they furnish by far the safest indication of the thought of others. Whether, however, our inferences are made on the basis of words or of actions, they are all necessarily made on the hypothesis that human minds are built on the same pattern, that what a given word or action would mean for my mind, this it means also for my neighbor's mind.

If this hypothesis be uncertain when applied to our fellow human beings, it fails us utterly when we turn to the lower animals. If my neighbor's mind is a mystery to me, how great is the mystery which looks out of the eyes of a dog, and how insoluble the problem presented by the mind of an invertebrate animal, an ant or a spider! We know that such minds must differ from ours not only in certain individual peculiarities, but in ways at whose nature we can only guess. The nervous systems of many animals vary widely from our own. We have, perhaps, too little knowledge about the functions of our own to conjecture with any certainty what difference this must make in the conscious life of such animals; but when we find sense-organs, such as the compound eyes of insects

or crustaceans, constructed on a plan wholly diverse from that of ours; when we find organs apparently sensory in function, but so unlike our own that we cannot tell what purpose they serve,—we are baffled in our attempt to construct the mental life of the animals possessing them, for lack of power to supply the sensation elements of that life. "It is not," said Locke, "in the power of the most exalted wit or enlarged understanding, by any quickness or variety of thought, to invent or frame one new simple idea in the mind" (869, Bk. II, ch. 2); we cannot imagine a color or a sound or a smell that we have never experienced; how much less the sensations of a sense radically different from any that we possess! Again, a bodily structure entirely unlike our own must create a background of organic sensation which renders the whole mental life of an animal foreign and unfamiliar to us. We speak, for example, of an "angry" wasp. Anger, in our own experience, is largely composed of sensations of quickened heart beat, of altered breathing, of muscular tension, of increased blood pressure in the head and face. The circulation of a wasp is fundamentally different from that of any vertebrate. The wasp does not breathe through lungs, it wears its skeleton on the outside, and it has the muscles attached to the inside of the skeleton. What is anger like in the wasp's consciousness? We can form no adequate idea of it.

To this fundamental difficulty of the dissimilarity between animal minds and ours is added, of course, the obstacle that animals have no language in which to describe their experience to us. Where this unlikeness is greatest, as in the case of invertebrate animals, language would be of little use since we could not interpret it from our experience; but the higher vertebrates could give us much insight into their minds if they could only speak. We are, however, restricted to the inferences we can draw from movements and sounds that are made for the most part without the intention of communicating anything to us. One happy consequence of this fact, which to a slight extent balances its disadvantages, is that we have not to contend with self-consciousness and posing, which often invalidate human reports of introspection.

From these general considerations we can understand something of the special difficulties that beset the path of the comparative psychologist, who desires to know the contents of minds below the human level. Knowledge regarding the animal mind, like knowledge of human minds other than our own, must come by way of inference from behavior. Two fundamental questions then confront the comparative psychologist. First, by what method shall he find out how an animal behaves?

Second, how shall he interpret the conscious aspect of that behavior?

§ 2.   Methods of Obtaining Facts: The Method of Anecdote

The reading of such a book as Romanes's "Animal Intelligence," or of the letters about animal behavior in the London *Spectator,* will reveal one method of gathering information about what animals do. This has been termed the Method of Anecdote. It consists essentially in taking the report of another person regarding the action of an animal, observed most commonly by accident, and attracting attention because of its unusual character. In certain cases the observer while engaged in some other pursuit happens to notice the singular behavior of an animal, and at his leisure writes out an account of it. In others, the animal is a pet, in whose high intellectual powers its master takes pride. It is safe to say that this method of collecting information always labors under at least one, and frequently under several, of the following disadvantages:—

1. The observer is not scientifically trained to distinguish what he sees from what he infers.
2. He is not intimately acquainted with the habits of the species to which the animal belongs.
3. He is not acquainted with the past experience of the individual animal concerned.
4. He has a personal affection for the animal concerned, and a desire to show its superior intelligence.
5. He has the desire, common to all humanity, to tell a good story.

Some of these tendencies to error it is unnecessary to illustrate. A good example of the dangers of lack of acquaintance with the habits of the species, is given by Mr. and Mrs. Peckham. They quote the following anecdote reported by no less eminent and trained an observer than Wundt. "I had made myself," says that psychologist, "as a boy, a fly-trap like a pigeon cote. The flies were attracted by scattering sugar and caught as soon as they had entered the cage. Behind the trap was a second box separated from it by a sliding door, which could be opened or shut at pleasure. In this I had put a large garden spider. Cage and box were provided with glass windows on the top, so that I could quite well observe anything that was going on inside. . . . When some flies had been caught, and the slide was drawn out, the spider of course rushed upon her prey and devoured them. . . . This went on for some time. The spider was sometimes

let into the cage, sometimes confined to her own box. But one day I made a notable discovery. During an absence the slide had been accidentally left open for some little while. When I came to shut it, I found that there was an unusual resistance. As I looked more closely, I found that the spider had drawn a large number of thick threads directly under the lifted door, and that these were preventing my closing it. . . ."

"What was going on in the spider's mind?" Wundt asks, and points out that it is unnecessary to assume that she understood and reasoned out the mechanical requirements of the situation. The whole matter can be explained, he thinks, in a simpler way. "I imagine that as the days went by there had been formed in the mind of the spider a determinate association on the one hand between free entry into the cage and the pleasurable feeling attending satisfaction of the nutritive impulse, and on the other between the closed slide and the unpleasant feeling of hunger and inhibited impulse. Now in her free life the spider had always employed her web in the service of the nutritive impulse. Associations had therefore grown up between the definite positions of her web and definite peculiarities of the objects to which it was attached, as well as changes which it produced in the positions of certain of these objects,—leaves, small twigs, etc. The impression of the falling slide, that is, called up by association the idea of other objects similarly moved which had been held in their places by threads properly spun; and finally there were connected with this association the other two of pleasure and raising, unpleasantness and closing, of the door."

The Peckhams remark in criticism of this observation: "Had Wundt been familiar with the habits of spiders, he would have known that whenever they are confined they walk around and around the cage, leaving behind them lines of web. Of course many lines passed under his little sliding door, and when he came to close it there was a slight resistance. These are the facts. His inference that there was even a remotest intention on the part of his prisoner to hinder the movement of the door is entirely gratuitous. Even the simpler mental states that are supposed to have passed through the mind of the spider were the products of Wundt's own imagination." The fact that the anecdote was a recollection of childhood, so that it would probably be impossible to bring any evidence from the character of the web or other circumstance against the suggestion of Mr. and Mrs. Peckham, is a further instance of the unscientific use of anecdotal testimony.

An illustration of the third objection mentioned above, the disadvantage of ignorance of the animal's individual history, is furnished by Lloyd Morgan. In describing his futile efforts to teach a fox terrier the best way to pull a crooked stick through a fence, he says that the dog showed no sign "of perceiving that by pushing the stick and freeing the crook he could pull the stick through. Each time the crook caught he pulled with all his strength, seizing the stick now at the end, now in the middle, and now near the crook. At length he seized the crook itself and with a wrench broke it off. A man who was passing . . . said, 'Clever dog that, sir; he knows where the hitch do lie.' The remark was the characteristic outcome of two minutes' chance observation." How many anecdotes of animals are based on similar accidents?

It will be seen that in both the cases just criticized the error lies in the interpretation of the animal's behavior. Indeed, a root of evil in the method of anecdote consists in the fact that observation in this form is imperfectly divorced from interpretation. The maker of an anecdote is seldom content with merely telling one what the animal did and leaving future investigation and the comparative study of many facts to decide what the animal's conscious experience in doing it was like. The point of the anecdote usually consists in showing that a human interpretation of the animal's behavior is possible. Here is shown the desire to tell a good story, which we mentioned among the pitfalls of the anecdotal method; the wish to report something unusual, not to get a just conception of the normal behavior of an animal. As Thorndike forcibly put it: "Dogs get lost hundreds of times and no one ever notices it or sends an account of it to a scientific magazine. But let one find his way from Brooklyn to Yonkers and the fact immediately becomes a circulating anecdote. Thousands of cats on thousands of occasions sit helplessly yowling, and no one takes thought of it or writes to his friend the professor; but let one cat claw at the knob of a door supposedly as a signal to be let out, and straightway this cat becomes the representative of the cat-mind in all the books."

All this is not to deny that much of the testimony to be found in Romanes's "Animal Intelligence" and Darwin's "Descent of Man" is the trustworthy report of trained observers; but it is difficult to separate the grain from the chaff, and one feels toward many of the anecdotes the attitude of scepticism produced, for example, by this tale which an Australian lady reported to the Linnæan Society. The burial of some deceased comrades was accomplished, she says, by a nest of "soldier ants" near Sydney, in the following fashion. "All fell into rank walking regularly and slowly two by two, until they arrived at the spot where lay the dead bodies. . . . Two of the ants advanced and took up the dead body of one of their comrades; then two others, and so on until all were ready to march. First walked two ants bearing a body, then two without a burden; then two others with another dead ant, and so on, until the line was extended to about forty pairs, and the procession now moved slowly onward, followed by an irregular body of about two hundred ants. Occasionally the two laden ants stopped, and laying down the dead ant, it was taken up by the two walking unburdened behind them, and thus, by occasionally relieving each other, they arrived at a sandy spot near the sea." A separate grave was then dug for each dead ant. "Some six or seven of the ants had attempted to run off without performing their share of the task of digging; these were caught and brought back, when they were at once attacked by the body of ants and killed upon the spot. A single grave was quickly dug and they were all dropped into it." No funeral procession for them! Of this story Romanes says, "The observation seems to have been one about which there could scarcely have been a mistake." One is inclined to think it just possible that there was.

§ 3. Methods of Obtaining Facts: The Method of Experiment

Diametrically opposed to the Method of Anecdote and its unscientific character is the Method of Experiment. An experiment, properly conducted, always implies that the conditions are controlled, or at least known; whereas ignorance of the conditions is, as we have seen, a common feature of anecdote. The experimenter is impartial; he has no desire to bring about any particular result. The teller of an anecdote wishes to prove animal intelligence. The experimenter is willing to report the facts precisely as he observes them, and is in no haste to make them prove anything. The conduct of an experiment upon an animal will, of course, vary according to the problem to be solved. If the object is to test some innate reaction on the animal's part, such as its ordinary responses to stimulation or its instincts, one need merely place the animal under favorable conditions for observation, make sure that it is not frightened or in an abnormal state, supply the appropriate stimulus unmixed with others, and watch the result. If it is desired to study the process by which an animal learns to adapt itself to a new situation, one must, of course, make sure in addition that the situation really is new to the animal, and yet that it makes sufficient appeal to some instinctive tendency to supply a motive for the learning process.

As one might expect, among the earliest experiments upon animals were those made by physiologists with a view to determining the functions of sense-organs. The experimental movement in psychology was slow in extending itself into the field of the animal mind.

Romanes, whose adherence to the anecdotal method we have noted, made in 1881, rather as a physiologist than as a psychologist, a number of exact and highly valued experiments on cœlenterates and echinoderms, which were summarized in his book entitled "Jelly-Fish, Star-Fish, and Sea-Urchins," published in 1885. He also recorded some rather informal experiments on the keenness of smell in dogs. Sir John Lubbock, in 1883, reported the results of some experiments on the color sense of the small crustacean Daphnia, and his book on "Ants, Bees, and Wasps," containing an account of experimental tests of the senses and "intelligence" of these insects, appeared in the same year. A German entomologist, Vitus Graber, experimented very extensively at about this period on the senses of sight and smell in many animals. Preyer, the authority on child psychology, published in 1886 an experimental study of the behavior of the starfish. Loeb's work on the reactions of animals to stimulation began to appear in 1888. Max Verworn, the physiologist, published in 1889 an exhaustive experimental study of the behavior of single-celled animals. With the exception of Preyer and Romanes, all these men had but a secondary interest in comparative psychology. Lloyd Morgan, who has written instructively on comparative psychology, makes but a limited use of the experimental method. Wesley Mills, professor of physiology in McGill University, studied very carefully the mental development of young animals such as cats and dogs, but was inclined to criticize the use of experiment in observing animals. The work of E. L. Thorndike, whose "Animal Intelligence" appeared in 1898, represents, perhaps, the first definite effect of the modern experimental movement in psychology upon the study of the animal mind. Thorndike's aim in this research was to place his animals (chicks, cats, and dogs) under the most rigidly controlled experimental conditions. The cats and dogs, reduced by fasting to a state of "utter hunger," were placed in boxes, with food outside, and the process whereby they learned to work the various mechanisms which let them out was carefully observed. Since the appearance of Thorndike's work the performance of experiments upon animals has played much part in the work of American psychological laboratories. It has been extensively undertaken also in those of Europe, but this is one experimental field in which America can claim priority of entry.

Despite the obvious advantages of experiment as a method for the study of animal behavior, it is not with-

out its dangers. These were clearly stated by Wesley Mills in a criticism of Thorndike's "Animal Intelligence." They may be summed up by saying that there is a risk of placing the animal experimented upon under abnormal conditions in the attempt to make them definite and controllable. Did not, for example, the extreme hunger to which Thorndike's cats and dogs were reduced, while it simplified the conditions in one sense by making the strength of the motive to escape as nearly as possible equal for all the animals, complicate matters in another sense by diminishing their capacity to learn? Were the animals perhaps frightened and distracted by the unusual character of their surroundings. Thorndike thinks not; but whether or no he succeeded in averting these dangers, it is clear that they are real. It is also obvious that they are the more threatening, the higher the animal with which one has to deal. Fright, bewilderment, loneliness, are conditions more apt to be met with among the higher vertebrates than lower down in the scale, and the utmost care should be taken to make sure that animals likely to be affected by them are thoroughly trained and at home in their surroundings before the experimenter records results.

<h2>§ 4.   Methods of Obtaining Facts: The Ideal Method</h2>

The ideal method for the study of a higher animal involves patient observation upon a specimen known from birth, watched in its ordinary behavior and environment, and occasionally experimented upon with proper control of the conditions and without frightening it or otherwise rendering it abnormal. The observer should acquaint himself with the individual peculiarities of each animal studied, for there is no doubt that striking differences in mental capacity occur among the individuals of a single species. At the same time that he obtains the confidence of each individual animal, he should be able to hold in check the tendency to humanize it and to take a personal pleasure in its achievements if it be unusually endowed. This is, to say the least, not easy. Absolute indifference to the animals studied, if not so dangerous as doting affection, is yet to be avoided.

<h2>§ 5.   Methods of Interpreting Facts</h2>

We may now turn from the problem of discovering the facts about animal behavior to the problem of interpreting them. If an animal behaves in a certain manner, what may we conclude the consciousness accompanying its behavior to be like? As we have seen, the interpretation is often confused with the observation, especially in the making of anecdotes; but theoretically the two problems are distinct. And at the outset of our discussion of the former, we are obliged to acknowledge that *all psychic interpretation of animal behavior must be on the analogy of human experience.* We do not know the meaning of such terms as perception, pleasure, fear, anger, visual sensation, etc., except as these processes form a part of the content of our own minds. Whether we will or no, we must be anthropomorphic in the notions we form of what takes place in the mind of an animal. Accepting this fundamental proposition, the students of animals have yet differed widely in the conclusions they have drawn from it. Some have gone to the extreme of declaring that comparative psychology is therefore impossible. Others have joyfully hastened to make animals as human as they could. Still others have occupied an intermediate position.

Descartes and Montaigne are the two writers antedating the modern period who are most frequently quoted in this connection. The latter had evidently a natural sympathy with animals. In that delightful twelfth chapter of the second book of Essays, "An Apology of Raymond Sebonde," he gives free rein to the inclination to humanize them. I quote Florio's translation: "The Swallowes which at the approach of spring time we see to pry, to search and ferret all the corners of our houses; is it without judgment they seeke, or without discretion they chuse from out a thousand places, that which is fittest for them, to build their nests and lodging? . . . Would they (suppose you) first take water and then clay, unlesse they guessed that the hardnesse of the one is softened by the moistnesse of the other? . . . Why doth the spider spin her artificiall web thicke in one place and thin in another? And now useth one, and then another knot, except she had an imaginary kind of deliberation, forethought, and conclusion?" To ascribe such behavior to the working of mere instinct, "with a kinde of unknowne, naturall and servile inclination," is unreasonable. "The Fox, which the inhabitants of Thrace use" to test the ice on a river before crossing, which listens to the roaring of the water underneath and so judges whether the ice is safe or not; "might not we lawfully judge that the same discourse possesseth her head as in like case it would ours? And that it is a kinde of debating reason and consequence, drawne from natural sense? 'Whatsoever maketh a noyse moveth, whatsoever moveth, is not frozen, whatsoever is not frozen, is liquid; whatsoever is liquid, yields under any weight?'"

Descartes, on the other hand, writing some sixty years later, takes, as is well known, the opposite ground. He says in a letter to the Marquis of Newcastle, "As for

the understanding or thought attributed by Montaigne and others to brutes, I cannot hold their opinion." While animals surpass us in certain actions, it is, he holds, only in those "which are not directed by thought. . . . They act by force of nature and by springs, like a clock, which tells better what the hour is than our judgment can inform us. And doubtless when swallows come in the spring, they act in that like clocks. All that honey bees do is of the same nature." The statement of Descartes, contained in the letter to Mersenne of July 30, 1640, that animals are automata, is often misunderstood. Descartes does not assert that animals are unconscious in the sense which that term would carry to-day, but only that they are without thought. Sensations, feelings, passions, he is willing to ascribe to them, in so far as these do no involve thought. "It must however, be observed that I speak of thought, not of life, nor of sensation," he says in the letter to Henry More, 1649; "I do not refuse to them feeling . . . in so far as it depends only on the bodily organs." In this he does not go so far as some modern writers, who decline to assert the presence of any psychic process in the lower forms of animal life.

Turning to recent times, we find arguments very like those of Montaigne used by the earlier evolutionary writers. Darwin, for instance, says in "Descent of Man," "As dogs, cats, horses, and probably all the higher animals, even birds, have vivid dreams, and this is shown by their movements and the sounds uttered, we must admit that they possess some power of imagination." "Even brute beasts," says Montaigne, ". . . are seen to be subject to the power of imagination; witnesse some Dogs . . . whom we ordinarily see to startle and barke in their sleep." "Only a few persons," Darwin continues, "now dispute that animals possess some power of reasoning. Animals may constantly be seen to pause, deliberate, and resolve." And he states that his object in the third chapter of the work quoted is "to show that there is no fundamental difference between man and the higher mammals in their mental faculties." Romanes is evidently guided by the same desire to humanize animals.

Now these writers were not led to take such an attitude merely out of general sympathy with the brute creation, like Montaigne; they had an ulterior motive; namely, to meet the objection raised in their time against the doctrine of evolution, based on the supposed fact of a great mental and moral gulf between man and the lower animals. They wished to show, as Darwin clearly states, that this gulf is not absolute but may conceivably have been bridged by intermediate stages of mental and moral development. While this argument against evolution was being pressed, the evolutionary writers were very unsafe guides in the field of animal psychology, for they distinctly "held a brief for animal intelligence," to use Thorndike's phrase. In more recent times interest in both the positive and the negative sides of the objection drawn from man's superiority has died out, and such special pleading has become unnecessary.

On the other hand, the fact that the greater part of the experiments on animals were until the last twenty-five years performed by physiologists has given rise to an opposite tendency in interpreting the animal mind: the tendency to make purely biological concepts suffice as far as possible for the explanation of animal behavior and to assume the presence even of consciousness in animals only when it is absolutely necessary to do so. Loeb in 1890 suggested the theory which he has since elaborated, that the responses of animals to stimulation, instead of being signs of "sensation," are in every way analogous to the reactions of plants to such forces as light and gravity; hence unconscious "tropisms." Bethe in 1898 attempted to explain all the complicated behavior of ants and bees, which the humanizing writers had compared with our own civilization, as a result of reflex responses, chiefly to chemical stimulation, unaccompanied by any consciousness whatever. This revival, in an altered form, of the Cartesian doctrine has met with energetic opposition, especially from writers having philosophical interests. When the first edition of the present work appeared, the parties in the controversy could be divided into three groups: those who believed that consciousness should be ascribed to all animals; those who believed that it should be ascribed only to those animals whose behavior presents certain peculiarities regarded as evidence of mind; and those who held that we have no trustworthy evidence of mind in any animal, and should therefore abandon comparative psychology and use only physiological terms. Of recent years, the tendency has been towards the survival only of the two extreme parties: it has been more and more recognized that there exists no evidence of mind which is not either equally bad or equally good in the case of all animals.

Among the authorities who would ascribe mind to all animals belong Claparède of Geneva, the Swiss naturalist Forel, and the Jesuit Wasmann. They maintained this position from widely different philosophical points of view. The first-named is what is called a parallelist; that is, he believes that mental processes and bodily processes are not causally related, but form two parallel and non-interfering series of events. In the study of animals, both the physical and the psychical series should, he thinks, be investigated. Biology should use two parallel methods, the one ascending, attempting to explain ani-

mal behavior by physical and chemical laws; the other descending, giving an account of the mental processes of animals. Ultimately, it may be hoped, according to Claparède, that both methods will be applied throughout the whole range of animal life. At present the ascending method is most successful with the lowest forms, the descending method with the highest forms. We cannot afford to abandon the psychological study of animals, for our knowledge of the nervous processes underlying the higher mental activities is very slight; physiology here fails us, and psychology must be left in command of the field. The danger besetting the attempt at a purely physical explanation of animal behavior is that the facts shall be unduly simplified to fit the theory. Thus Bethe's effort at explaining the way in which bees find their way back to the hive as a reflex response, or tropism, produced by "an unknown force," is highly questionable; the facts seem to point toward the exercise of some sort of memory by the bees. It is always possible, further, that the tropism is accompanied by consciousness. A physiologist from Saturn might reduce all human activities to tropisms, says Claparède in a striking passage. "The youth who feels himself drawn to medical studies, or he who is attracted to botany, can no more account for his profoundest aspirations than the beetle which runs to the odor of a dead animal or the butterfly invited by the flowers; and if the first shows a certain feeling corresponding to these secret states of the organism (a feeling of 'predilection' for such a career, etc.), how can we dare to deny to the second analogous states of consciousness?" If it is argued that we have no direct, but only an inferential, knowledge of the processes in an animal's mind, the argument is equally valid against human psychology, for the psychologist has only an inferential knowledge of his neighbor's mind.

Wasmann defends the animal mind from a different position. For one thing, he believes that mental processes may act causally upon bodily states. He accepts, in other words, what is called interactionism, as opposed to parallelism. Further, although he strongly opposes the doctrine that the reactions of animals are unconscious tropisms and constantly emphasizes their variability and modifiability through experience, he nevertheless believes that a gulf separates the human from the animal mind. The term "intelligence" which most writers use to designate merely the power of learning by individual experience, Wasmann would reserve for the power of deducing and understanding relations, and would assign only to human beings. Although animals have their instincts modified by sense experience, man "stands through his reason and freedom immeasurably high above the irrational animal that follows, and must follow, its sensuous impulse without deliberation."

Forel, in the third place, is what is called a monist in metaphysics. That is, he does not believe either that mind and body are parallel, or that they interact causally, but that they are two aspects of the same reality. "Every psychic phenomenon is the same real thing as the molecular or neurocymic activity of the brain-cortex coinciding with it." The psychic and the physical, on this theory, should be coextensive; not merely should consciousness in some form belong to all living things, but every atom of matter should have its psychic aspect. On such a basis, Forel takes highly optimistic views of the animal mind. In insects, of which he has made a special study, it is, he thinks, "possible to demonstrate the existence of memory, associations of sensory images, perceptions, attention, habits, simple powers of inference from analogy, the utilization of individual experience, and hence distinct, though feeble, plastic individual deliberations or adaptations."

A peculiar position on the problem of mind in animals is occupied by the "vitalists," of whom Driesch is the foremost representative. They regard the reactions of organisms as requiring the operation of psychic forces or "entelechies"; they hold that as physical phenomena such reactions cannot be explained save through the working of these psychic forces. A living being is forever distinguished from a lifeless creature by the presence of such entelechies. Thus the vitalist is an interactionist and a dualist: the worlds of the lifeless and the living are to him forever distinct. The vitalistic position in comparative psychology is defended by W. McDougall. It involves abandoning all attempts to explain the mind of animals by reference to underlying physiological processes; maintaining that conscious purpose is involved in instinctive as well as in intelligent action, and assuming, as a result of this belief, that a bird, for example, building its first nest, is guided by an innate idea of the pattern.

The opposite camp is represented by Bethe, Beer, von Uexküll, Loeb, and other physiologists, as well as by Watson.

The eminent neurologist Bethe, in his study of the behavior of ants and bees, refuses to allow these animals any "psychic qualities" whatever, and suggests the term "chemo-reception" instead of "smell," to designate the influence which directs most of their reactions,—"smell" implying a psychic quality (89). In a footnote to a later article he says: "Psychic qualities cannot be demonstrated. Even what we call sensation is known to each man only in himself, since it is something subjec-

tive. We possess the capacity of modifying our behavior [*i.e.*, of learning], and every one knows from his own experience that psychic qualities play a part connected with this modifying process. Every statement that another being possesses psychic qualities is a conclusion from analogy, not a certainty; it is a matter of faith. If one wishes to draw this analogical inference, it should be made where the capacity for modification can be shown. When this is lacking, there is not the slightest scientific justification for assuming psychic qualities. They *may* exist, but there is no probability of it, and hence science should deny them. Hence if one ventures to speak of a Psyche in animals at all, one should give the preference to those which can modify their behavior." But that Bethe himself prefers not to make the venture is evident from statements in the text of the same article. The psychic or subjective, he says, is unknowable, and the only thing we may hope to know anything about is the chemical and the physiological processes involved. "These chemo-physical processes and their consequences, that is, the objective aspect of psychic phenomena, and these alone, should be the object of scientific investigation."

Together with Beer and von Uexküll, Bethe shortly afterward published "Proposals for an Objectifying Nomenclature in the Physiology of the Nervous System." The main purpose of this paper was to suggest that all terms having a psychological implication, such as sight, smell, sense-organ, memory, learning, and the like, be carefully excluded from discussions of animal reactions to stimulation and animal behavior generally. In their stead the authors propose such expressions as the following: for responses to stimulation where no nervous system exists, the term *antitypes;* for those involving a nervous system, *antikineses;* the latter are divided into *reflexes,* where the response is uniform, and *antiklises,* where the response is modifiable. A sense-organ becomes a *reception-organ,* sensory nerves are *receptory-nerves,* and we have *phono-reception, stibo-reception, photo-reception,* instead of hearing, smell, and sight. The after-effect of a stimulus upon later ones is the *resonance* of the stimulus.

Loeb agrees with Bethe that physico-chemical processes and not states of consciousness are the proper objects of investigation for the psychologist. These men evidently regard the universe as essentially uniform throughout—there exists for them no gulf between living and lifeless things; the behavior of living beings will be reduced to a series of chemical reactions as soon as science has progressed sufficiently far. They are "mechanists." It is, however, perfectly possible to be a mechanist so far as the explanation of animal behavior is concerned, and still admit that animals have consciousness and that their behavior is accompanied by inner, mental states which it is the business of the psychologist to investigate. One does not have to be a vitalist to believe that animals have minds: one may hold that every action of an animal will some day be explained as the result of physico-chemical processes, and yet maintain that the actions of animals are conscious. The consciousness would be an accompaniment, an inner aspect, of the physico-chemical processes.

The views of Loeb and Bethe gained much ground among certain American psychologists, notably Watson. The position of these "behaviorists" seems not to have been fully thought out in its philosophical aspects, but is somewhat as follows. The difficulties of interpreting an animal's mind from its behavior are so great that such inferences have no scientific value. We may therefore proceed as if animals had no minds; or rather, as if mind were a kind of behavior, observable by outside means. Since it is obvious that the difficulty of interpreting an animal's mind from its behavior is only greater in degree than, not unlike in kind, the difficulty of interpreting other human minds from behavior, human psychology also should confine itself to the observation merely of the actions of other persons, and permit no inferences as to the inner aspect of such actions. In fact, there is no inner aspect to such actions—thoughts and feelings, human as well as animal, are only behavior, and if we have at present no instruments for inspecting and measuring the movements which are thoughts and feelings, such instruments will in time be discovered.

In opposition to these views, we shall in this book maintain the following position. There exists an inner aspect to behavior, the realm of sensations, feelings, and thoughts, which is not itself identical with behavior or with any form of movement. Thoughts probably always have as their accompaniment bodily movements, but the thought is not identical with the movement. If a physiologist perfected an instrument by which he could observe the nervous process in my cortex that occurs when I am conscious of the sensation red, he would see nothing red about it; if he could watch the bodily movements that result from this stimulation, say, for instance, the slight contraction of the articulatory muscles that occurs when I say "red" to myself, he would not see them as red. The red is in my consciousness, and no devices for observing and registering my movements will ever observe the red, though they may easily lead to the inference that it exists in my consciousness. And precisely the same is true of all my sensations, thoughts, and feelings.

Since an inner world of experience exists, we may legitimately try to investigate it. For this purpose we possess a method, which is called introspection. We can, that is, attentively and, if we have had practice, dispassionately and scientifically, observe what goes on in our own consciousness when we receive certain stimuli and make certain movements. Further, we can by the use of the same kind of inference from one case to another similar case, upon which all scientific generalization is based, infer that when a being whose structure resembles ours receives the same stimulus that affects us and moves in the same way as a result, he has an inner experience which resembles our own. Finally, we may extend this inference to the lower animals, with proper safeguards, just as far as they present resemblances in structure and behavior to ourselves. One main object in this book will be the interpretation of the inner aspect of the behavior of animals; we shall be interested in what animals do largely as it throws light upon what they feel. To the true psychologist, no challenge is so enticing as that presented by the problem of how it feels to be another person or another animal; and although we must sometimes give up the problem in despair, yet we have also our successes. We have wonderfully advanced, within the last twenty-five years, in knowledge as to how the world looks from the point of view of our brother animals.

We may now note briefly some of the special precautions that must be observed in interpreting the conscious aspect of animal behavior. First, there is no doubt that great caution should be used in regarding the quality of a human conscious process as identical with the quality of the corresponding process in the animal mind. For example, we might say with a fair degree of assurance that an animal consciously discriminates between light and darkness; that is, receives conscious impressions of different quality from the two, yet the mental impression produced by white light upon the animal may be very different from the sensation of white as we know it, and the impression produced by the absence of light very different from our sensation of black. Black and white may, for all we know, depend for their quality upon some substance existing only in the human retina. Yet where there is resemblance both in sense-organ structure and in discriminative behavior, the possibility of unlikeness in sensation quality becomes too remote to be interesting.

A second precaution concerns the simplicity or complexity of the interpretation put upon animal behavior. Lloyd Morgan, in his "Introduction to Comparative Psychology," formulated a conservative principle of interpretation which has often been quoted as "Lloyd Morgan's Canon." The principle is as follows: "In no case may we interpret an action as the outcome of the exercise of a higher psychical faculty, if it can be interpreted as the outcome of the exercise of one which stands lower in the psychological scale." In other words, when in doubt take the simpler interpretation. For example, a dog detected in a theft cowers and whines. One possible mental accompaniment of this behavior is remorse; the dog is conscious that he has fallen below a moral standard, and grieved or offended his master. A second is the anticipation of punishment; the dog has a mental representation of the consequences of his action upon former occasions, and imagining himself likely to experience them anew, is terrified at the prospect. A third possibility is that the dog's previous experience of punishment, instead of being revived in the form of definite images, makes itself effective merely in his feelings and behavior; he is uncomfortable and frightened, he knows not definitely why. It is evident that these three possibilities represent three different grades of complexity of mental process, the first being by far the highest. Lloyd Morgan's canon enjoins upon us in such a case to prefer the third alternative, provided that it will really account for the dog's behavior.

Now why should the simplest interpretation be preferred? We must not forget that the more complex ones remain in the field of possibility. Dogmatic assertions have no place in comparative psychology. We cannot say that the simplicity of an hypothesis is sufficient warrant of its truth, for nature does not always proceed by the paths which seem to us least complicated. The fact is that Lloyd Morgan's principle serves to counterbalance our most important source of error in interpreting animal behavior. It is like tipping a boat in one direction to compensate for the fact that some one is pulling the opposite gunwale. We must interpret the animal mind humanly if we are to interpret it at all. Yet we know that it differs from the human mind, and that the difference is partly a matter of complexity. Let us therefore take the least complex interpretation that the facts of animal behavior will admit, always remembering that we may be wrong in so doing, but resting assured that we are, upon the whole, on the safer side. The social consciousness of man is very strong, and his tendency to think of other creatures, even of inanimate nature, as sharing his own thoughts and feelings, has shown itself in his past to be almost irresistible. Lloyd Morgan's canon offers the best safeguard against this natural inclination, short of abandoning all attempt to study the mental life of the lower animals.

CHAPTER II

The Evidence of Mind

§ 6.   *Inferring Mind from Behavior*

In this chapter we shall try to show that there exists no evidence for denying mind to any animals, if we do not deny it to all; in other words, that there is no such thing as an objective proof of the presence of mind, whose absence may be regarded as proof of the absence of mind.

To begin with, can it be said that when an animal makes a movement in response to a certain stimulus, there is an accompanying consciousness of the stimulus, and that when it fails to move, there is no consciousness? Is *response to stimulation* evidence of consciousness? In the case of man, we know that absence of visible response does not prove that the stimulus has not been sensed; while it is probable that some effect upon motor channels always occurs when consciousness accompanies stimulation, the effect may not be apparent to an outside observer. On the other hand, if movement in response to the impact of a physical force is evidence of consciousness, then the ball which falls under the influence of gravity and rebounds on striking the floor is conscious. Nor is the case improved if we point out that the movements which animals make in response to stimulation are not the equivalent in energy of the stimulus applied, but involve the setting free of energy stored in the animal as well. True, when a microscopic animal meets an obstacle in its swimming, and darts backward, the movement is not a mere rebound; it implies energy contributed by the animal's own body. But just so an explosion of gunpowder is not the equivalent in energy of the heat of the match, the stimulus. Similarly it is possible to think of the response made by animals to external stimuli as involving nothing more than certain physical and chemical processes identical with those existing in inanimate nature.

If we find that the movements made by an animal as a result of external stimulation regularly involve withdrawal from certain stimuli and acceptance of others, it is natural to use the term "*choice*" in describing such behavior. But if consciousness is supposed to accompany the exercise of choice in this sense, then consciousness must be assumed to accompany the behavior of ions in chemical combinations. When hydrochloric acid is added to a solution of silver nitrate, the ions of chlorine and those of silver find each other by an unerring "instinct" and combine into the white precipitate of silver chloride, while the hydrogen and the nitric acid similarly "choose" each other. Nor can the fact that behavior in animals is adapted to an end be used as evidence of mind; for "purposive" reactions, which contribute to the welfare of an organism, are themselves selective. The search for food, the care for the young, and the complex activities which further welfare, are made up of reactions involving "choice" between stimuli; and if the simple "choice" reaction is on a par with the behavior of chemical ions, so far as proof of consciousness goes, then *adaptation to an end,* apparent purposiveness, is in a similar position.

Thus the mere fact that an animal reacts to stimulation, even selectively and for its own best interests, offers no evidence for the existence of mind that does not apply equally well to particles of inanimate matter. Moreover, there is some ground for holding that the reactions of the lowest animals are unconscious. This ground consists in the apparent lack of variability which characterizes such reactions. In our own case, we know that certain bodily movements, those of digestion and circulation, for example, are normally carried on without accompanying consciousness, and that in other cases where there is consciousness of the stimulus, as in the reflex knee-jerk, it occurs after the movement is initiated, so that the nervous process underlying the sensation would seem to be immaterial to the performance of the movement. These unconscious reactions in human beings are characterized by their relative uniformity, by the absence of variation in their performance. Moreover, when an action originally accompanied by consciousness is often repeated, it tends, by what is apparently one and the same process, to become unconscious and to become uniform. There is consequently reason for believing that when the behavior of lower animals displays perfect uniformity, consciousness is not present. On the other hand, an important reservation must be made in the use of this negative test. It is by no means easy to be sure that an animal's reactions are uniform. The more carefully the complexer ones are studied, the more are variability and difference brought to light where superficial observation had revealed a mechanical and automatic regularity. It is quite possible that even in the simple, apparently fixed response of microscopic animals to stimulation, better facilities for observation might show variations that do not now appear.

This matter of uniformity *versus* variability suggests a further step in our search for a satisfactory test of the presence of mind. Is mere *variability* in behavior, mere irregularity in response, to be taken as such a test? Not if we argue from our own experience. While that portion of our own behavior which involves consciousness shows more irregularity than the portion which does not, yet the causes of the irregularity are often clearly to be found in physiological conditions with which consciousness has nothing to do. There are days when we can think clearly and recall easily, and days when obscurities refuse to vanish and the right word refuses to come; days when we are irritable and days when we are sluggish. Yet since we can find nothing in our mental processes to account for this variability, it would be absurd to take analogous fluctuations in animal behavior as evidence of mind. So complicated a machine as an animal organism, even if it be nothing more than a machine, must show irregularities in its working.

Behavior, then, must be variable, but not merely variable, to give evidence of mind. The criterion most frequently applied to determine the presence or absence of the psychic is *a variation in behavior that shows definitely the result of previous individual experience.* "Does the organism," says Romanes, "learn to make new adjustments, or to modify old ones, in accordance with the results of its own individual experience?" Loeb declared that "the fundamental process which occurs in all psychic phenomena as the elemental component" is "the activity of the associative memory, or of association," and defines associative memory as "that mechanism by which a stimulus brings about not only the effects which its nature and the specific structure of the irritable organ call for, but by which it brings about also the effects of other stimuli which formerly acted upon the organism almost or quite simultaneously with the stimulus in question." "If an animal can be trained," he continued, "if it can learn, it possesses associative memory," and therefore mind. The psychologist finds the term "associative memory" hardly satisfactory, and objects to the confusion between mental and physical concepts which renders it possible to speak of a "mechanism" as forming an "elemental component" in "psychic phenomena," but these points may be passed over. The power to learn by individual experience is the evidence which Romanes, Morgan, and Loeb will accept as demonstrating the presence of mind in an animal.

Does the absence of proof that an animal learns by experience show that the animal is unconscious? Romanes is careful to answer this question in the negative. "Because a lowly organized animal," he says, "does *not* learn by its own individual experience, we may not therefore conclude that in performing its natural or ancestral adaptations to appropriate stimuli, consciousness, or the mind element, is wholly absent; we can only say that this element, if present, reveals no evidence of the fact." Loeb, on the other hand, wrote as if absence of proof for consciousness amounted to disproof, evidently relying on the principle of parsimony, that no unnecessary assumptions should be admitted. "Our criterion," he remarked, "puts an end to the metaphysical ideas that all matter, and hence the whole animal world, possesses consciousness." If learning by experience be really a satisfactory proof of mind, then its absence in certain animals would indeed prevent the positive assertion that all animals are conscious; but it could not abolish the possibility that they might be. Such a possibility might, however, be of no more scientific interest than any one of a million wild possibilities that science cannot spare time to disprove. But we shall find that learning by experience, taken by itself, is too indefinite a concept to be of much service, and that when defined, it is inadequate to bear the whole weight of proving consciousness in animals. Such being the case, the possibility that animals which have not been shown to learn may yet be conscious, acquires the right to be reckoned with.

The first point that strikes us in examining the proposed test is that the learning by experience must not be too slow, or we can find parallels for it in the inanimate world. An animal may be said to have learned by experience if it behaves differently to a stimulus because of preceding stimuli. But it is one thing to have behavior altered by a single preceding stimulus, and another to have it altered by two hundred repetitions of a stimulus. The wood of a violin reacts differently to the vibrations of the strings after it has "experienced" them for ten years; the molecules of the wood have gradually taken on an altered arrangement. A steel rail reacts differently to the pounding of wheels after that process has been long continued; it may snap under the strain. Shall we say that the violin and the rail have learned by individual experience? If the obvious retort be made that it is only in living creatures that learning by experience should be taken as evidence of mind, let us take an example from living creatures. When a blacksmith has been practising his trade for a year, the reactions of his muscles are different from what they were at the outset. But this difference is not merely a matter of more accurate sense-discrimination, a better "placing" of attention and the like; there have been going on within the structure of his muscles changes which have increased their efficiency, and with which consciousness has had nothing to do. These changes have been extremely slow compared to the learning which does involve consciousness. In one or two lessons the apprentice learned what he was to do; but only very gradually have his muscles acquired the strength to do it as it should be done. Now

among the lower animal forms we sometimes meet with learning by experience that is very slow; that requires a hundred or more repetitions of the stimulus before the new reaction is acquired. In such a case we can find analogical reasons for suspecting that a gradual change in the tissues of the body has taken place, of the sort which, like the attuning of the violin wood or the slow development of a muscle, have no conscious accompaniment.

We must then ask the question: *What kind of learning by experience never,* so far as we know, *occurs unconsciously?* Suppose a human being shut up in a room from which he can escape only by working a combination lock. As we shall see later, this is one of the methods by which the learning power of animals has been tested. The man, after prolonged investigation, hits upon the right combination and gets out. Suppose that he later finds himself again in the same predicament, and that without hesitation or fumbling he opens the lock at once, and performs the feat again and again, to show that it was not a lucky accident. But one interpretation of such behavior is possible. We know from our own experience that the man could not have worked the lock the second time he saw it, unless he consciously remembered the movements he made the first time; that is, unless he had in mind some kind of idea as a guide. Here, at least, there can have been no change in the structure of the muscles, for such changes are gradual; the change must have taken place in the most easily alterable portion of the organism, the nervous system; and further, it must have taken place in the most unstable and variable part of the nervous system, the higher cortical centres whose activity is accompanied by consciousness. In other words, we may be practically assured that consciousness accompanies learning only when the learning is so rapid as to show that the effects of previous experience are recalled in the guise of an idea or mental image of some sort. But does even the most rapid learning possible assure us of the presence of an idea in the mind of a lower animal? Where the motive, the beneficial or harmful consequence of action, is very strong, may not a single experience suffice to modify action without being revived in idea? Moreover, animals as high in the scale as dogs and cats learn to solve problems analogous to that of the combination lock so slowly that we cannot infer the presence of ideas. Are we then to conclude that these animals are unconscious, or that there is absolutely no reason for supposing them possessed of consciousness? Yerkes has criticized the "learning by experience" criterion by pointing out that "no organism . . . has thus far been proved incapable of profiting by experience." It is a question rather of the rapidity and of the kind of learning involved. "The fact that the crayfish needs a hundred or more experiences for the learning of a type of reaction that the frog would learn with twenty experiences, the dog with five, say, and the human subject with perhaps a single experience, is indicative of the fundamental difficulty in the use of this sign." Nagel has pointed out that Loeb, in asserting "associative memory" as the criterion of consciousness, offers no evidence for his statement. The fact is that while proof of the existence of mind can be derived from animal learning by experience only if the learning is very rapid, other evidence, equally valid on the principle of analogy, makes it *highly improbable that all animals which learn too slowly to evince the presence of ideas are therefore unconscious.* This evidence is of a *morphological* character.

§7. INFERRING MIND FROM STRUCTURE. Both Yerkes and Lukas urge that the resemblance of an animal's nervous system and sense-organs to those of human beings ought to be taken into consideration in deciding whether the animal is conscious or not. Lukas suggested that the criteria of consciousness should be grouped under three heads: morphological, including the structure of the brain and sense-organs, physiological, and teleological. Under the second rubric he maintained that "individual purposiveness" is characteristic of the movements from which consciousness may be inferred; that individual purposiveness pertains only to voluntary acts, and that voluntary acts are acts "which are preceded by the intention to perform a definite movement, hence by the idea of this movement." We have reached the same conclusion in the preceding paragraph. The third test of the presence of consciousness, the teleological test, rests on the consideration: "What significance for the organism may be possessed by the production of a conscious effect by certain stimuli?" This test, however, being of a purely *a priori* character, would seem to be distinctly less valuable than the others.

Yerkes proposed "the following six criteria in what seems to me in general the order of increasing importance. The functional signs are of greater value as a rule than the structural; and within each of the categories the particular sign is usually of more value than the general. In certain cases, however, it might be maintained that neural specialization is of greater importance than modifiability.

> "I. Structural Criteria.
>   1. General form of organism (Organization).
>   2. Nervous system (Neural organization).
>   3. Specialization in the nervous system (Neural specialization).
> II. Functional Criteria.
>   1. General form of reaction (Discrimination).
>   2. Modifiability of reaction (Docility).
>   3. Variability of reaction (Initiative)."

The terms "discrimination," "docility," and "initiative" in this connection are borrowed from Royce's "Outlines of Psychology."

If resemblance of nervous and sense-organ structure to the human type is to be taken along with rapid learning as co-ordinate evidence of consciousness, it is clear that here also we have to deal with a matter of degree. The structure of the lower animals differs increasingly from our own as we go down the scale. At what degree of difference shall we draw the line and say that the animals above it may be conscious, but that those below it cannot be? No one could possibly establish such a line. The truth of the whole matter seems to be this: *We can say neither what amount of resemblance in structure to human beings, nor what speed of learning, constitutes a definite mark distinguishing animals with minds from those without minds, unless we are prepared to assert that only animals which learn so fast that they must have memory ideas possess mind at all.* And this would conflict with the argument from structure. For example, there was until recently no good experimental evidence that cats possess ideas, yet there was enough analogy between their nervous systems and our own to make it improbable that consciousness, so complex and highly developed in us, was in them wholly lacking. We know not where consciousness begins in the animal world. We know where it surely resides—in ourselves; we know where it exists beyond a reasonable doubt—in those animals of structure resembling ours which rapidly adapt themselves to the lessons of experience. Beyond this point, for all we know, it may exist in simpler and simpler forms until we reach the very lowest of living beings.

17
~

WILLIAM JAMES

William James (1842–1910) taught the first American course on the new scientific psychology and introduced generations of students to the subject through his popular, but lengthy, *Principles of Psychology*. Though he eventually developed into an extraordinary teacher and prolific, stylish writer, James struggled to find his vocation, perhaps because he was so broadly interested in physiology, psychology, and philosophy, and perhaps because of his extended bouts of depression. James spent his childhood traveling throughout Europe and America with his family, including his younger brother Henry James of later literary fame. In 1861, James entered the Lawrence Scientific School at Harvard University to study chemistry, but withdrew for most of a year following a dramatic sophomore slump. Returning with a new interest in comparative anatomy, James left school again to join Harvard zoologist and geologist Louis Agassiz, a particular critic of Charles Darwin's (p. 188) recent *Origin of Species,* on an expedition to Brazil in 1864. Several years later, after a trip or two to Germany, during which he attended some particularly intriguing lectures on physiology by Emil du Bois-Reymond, James was offered a temporary position at Harvard to teach a course on comparative anatomy. A year later, following a final trip to Europe, James returned to Harvard and began a productive career that included contributions to psychology, philosophy, and religious studies.

PSYCHOLOGY: A BRIEFER COURSE

EMOTION

Emotions Compared with Instincts

An emotion is a tendency to feel, and an instinct is a tendency to act, characteristically, when in presence of a certain object in the environment. But the emotions also have their bodily "expression," which may involve strong muscular activity (as in fear or anger, for example); and it becomes a little hard in many cases to separate the description of the "emotional" condition from that of the "instinctive" reaction which one and the same object may provoke. Shall *fear* be described in the chapter on Instincts or in that on Emotions? Where shall one describe *curiosity, emulation,* and the like? The answer is quite arbitrary from the scientific point of view, and practical convenience may decide. As inner mental conditions, emotions are quite indescribable. Description,

moreover, would be superfluous, for the reader knows already how they feel. Their relations to the objects which prompt them and to the reactions which they provoke are all that one can put down in a book.

Every object that excites an instinct excites an emotion as well. The only distinction one may draw is that the reaction called emotional terminates in the subject's own body, whilst the reaction called instinctive is apt to go farther and enter into practical relations with the exciting object. In both instinct and emotion the mere memory or imagination of the object may suffice to liberate the excitement. One may even get angrier in thinking over one's insult than one was in receiving it; and melt more over a mother who is dead than one ever did when she was living. In the rest of the chapter I shall use the word *object* of emotion indifferently to mean one which is physically present or one which is merely thought of.

From William James, "Emotion" and "Instinct." In *Psychology: A Briefer Course* (pp. 324–357). Cambridge, MA: Harvard University Press, 1984. (Original work published 1892)

The Varieties of Emotion Are Innumerable

Anger, fear, love, hate, joy, grief, shame, pride, and their varieties, may be called the *coarser* emotions, being coupled as they are with relatively strong bodily reverberations. The *subtler* emotions are the moral, intellectual, and æsthetic feelings, and their bodily reaction is usually much less strong. The mere description of the objects, circumstances, and varieties of the different species of emotion may go to any length. Their internal shadings merge endlessly into each other, and have been partly commemorated in language, as, for example, by such synonyms as hatred, antipathy, animosity, resentment, dislike, aversion, malice, spite, revenge, abhorrence, etc., etc. Dictionaries of synonyms have discriminated them, as well as text-books of psychology—in fact, many German psychological text-books *are* nothing but dictionaries of synonyms when it comes to the chapter on Emotion. But there are limits to the profitable elaboration of the obvious, and the result of all this flux is that the merely descriptive literature of the subject, from Descartes downwards, is one of the most tedious parts of psychology. And not only is it tedious, but you feel that its subdivisions are to a great extent either fictitious or unimportant, and that its pretences to accuracy are a sham. But unfortunately there is little psychological writing about the emotions which is not merely descriptive. As emotions are described in novels, they interest us, for we are made to share them. We have grown acquainted with the concrete objects and emergencies which call them forth, and any knowing touch of introspection which may grace the page meets with a quick and feeling response. Confessedly literary works of aphoristic philosophy also flash lights into our emotional life, and give us a fitful delight. But as far as the "scientific psychology" of the emotions goes, I may have been surfeited by too much reading of classic works on the subject, but I should as lief read verbal descriptions of the shapes of the rocks on a New Hampshire farm as toil through them again. They give one nowhere a central point of view, or a deductive or generative principle. They distinguish and refine and specify *in infinitum* without ever getting on to another logical level. Whereas the beauty of all truly scientific work is to get to ever deeper levels. Is there no way out from this level of individual description in the case of the emotions? I believe there is a way out, if one will only take it.

The Cause of Their Varieties

The trouble with the emotions in psychology is that they are regarded too much as absolutely individual things.

So long as they are set down as so many eternal and sacred psychic entities, like the old immutable species in natural history, so long all that *can* be done with them is reverently to catalogue their separate characters, points, and effects. But if we regard them as products of more general causes (as "species" are now regarded as products of heredity and variation), the mere distinguishing and cataloguing becomes of subsidiary importance. Having the goose which lays the golden eggs, the description of each egg already laid is a minor matter. I will devote the next few pages to setting forth one very general cause of our emotional feeling, limiting myself in the first instance to what may be called the *coarser* emotions.

The Feeling, in the Coarser Emotions, Results from the Bodily Expression

Our natural way of thinking about these coarser emotions is that the mental perception of some fact excites the mental affection called the emotion, and that this latter state of mind gives rise to the bodily expression. My theory, on the contrary, is that *the bodily changes follow directly the perception of the exciting fact, and that our feeling of the same changes as they occur* IS *the emotion.* Common-sense says, we lose our fortune, are sorry and weep; we meet a bear, are frightened and run: we are insulted by a rival, are angry and strike. The hypothesis here to be defended says that this order of sequence is incorrect, that the one mental state is not immediately induced by the other, that the bodily manifestations must first be interposed between, and that the more rational statement is that we feel sorry because we cry, angry because we strike, afraid because we tremble, and not that we cry, strike, or tremble because we are sorry, angry, or fearful, as the case may be. Without the bodily states following on the perception, the latter would be purely cognitive in form, pale, colorless, destitute of emotional warmth. We might then see the bear and judge it best to run, receive the insult and deem it right to strike, but we should not actually *feel* afraid or angry.

Stated in this crude way, the hypothesis is pretty sure to meet with immediate disbelief. And yet neither many nor far-fetched considerations are required to mitigate its paradoxical character, and possibly to produce conviction of its truth.

To begin with, *particular perceptions certainly do produce wide-spread bodily effects by a sort of immediate physical influence, antecedent to the arousal of an emotion or emotional idea.* In listening to poetry, drama, or heroic narrative we are often surprised at the cutaneous shiver which like a sudden wave flows over us, and at the heart-swelling and the lachrymal effusion that unexpectedly catch us at intervals. In hearing music the same is even more strikingly true. If we abruptly see a dark moving form in the woods, our heart stops beating, and we catch our breath instantly and before any articulate idea of danger can arise. If our friend goes near to the edge of a precipice, we get the well-known feeling of "all-overishness," and we shrink back, although we positively *know* him to be safe, and have no distinct imagination of his fall. The writer well remembers his astonishment, when a boy of seven or eight, at fainting when he saw a horse bled. The blood was in a bucket, with a stick in it, and, if memory does not deceive him, he stirred it round and saw it drip from the stick with no feeling save that of childish curiosity. Suddenly the world grew black before his eyes, his ears began to buzz, and he knew no more. He had never heard of the sight of blood producing faintness or sickness, and he had so little repugnance to it, and so little apprehension of any other sort of danger from it, that even at that tender age, as he well remembers, he could not help wondering how the mere physical presence of a pailful of crimson fluid could occasion in him such formidable bodily effects.

The best proof that the immediate cause of emotion is a physical effect on the nerves is furnished by *those pathological cases in which the emotion is objectless.* One of the chief merits, in fact, of the view which I propose seems to be that we can so easily formulate by its means pathological cases and normal cases under a common scheme. In every asylum we find examples of absolutely unmotived fear, anger, melancholy, or conceit; and others of an equally unmotived apathy which persists in spite of the best of outward reasons why it should give way. In the former cases we must suppose the nervous machinery to be so "labile" in some one emotional direction that almost every stimulus (however inappropriate) causes it to upset in that way, and to engender the particular complex of feelings of which the psychic body of the emotion consists. Thus, to take one special instance, if inability to draw deep breath, fluttering of the heart, and that peculiar epigastric change felt as "precordial anxiety," with an irresistible tendency to take a somewhat crouching attitude and to sit still, and with perhaps other visceral processes not now known, all spontaneously occur together in a certain person, his feeling of their combination *is* the emotion of dread, and he is the victim of what is known as morbid fear. A friend who has had occasional attacks of this most evil of all maladies tells me that in his case the whole drama seems to centre about the region of the heart and respiratory apparatus, that his main effort during the attacks is to get control of his inspirations and to slow his heart, and that the moment he attains to breathing deeply and to holding himself erect, the dread, *ipso facto,* seems to depart.

The emotion here is nothing but the feeling of a bodily state, and it has a purely bodily cause.

The next thing to be noticed is this, that *every one of the bodily changes, whatsoever it be, is* FELT, *acutely or obscurely, the moment it occurs.* If the reader has never paid attention to this matter, he will be both interested and astonished to learn how many different local bodily feelings he can detect in himself as characteristic of his various emotional moods. It would be perhaps too much to expect him to arrest the tide of any strong gust of passion for the sake of any such curious analysis as this; but he can observe more tranquil states, and that may be assumed here to be true of the greater which is shown to be true of the less. Our whole cubic capacity is sensibly alive; and each morsel of it contributes its pulsations of feeling, dim or sharp, pleasant, painful, or dubious, to that sense of personality that every one of us unfailingly carries with him. It is surprising what little items give accent to these complexes of sensibility. When worried by any slight trouble, one may find that the focus of one's bodily consciousness is the contraction, often quite inconsiderable, of the eyes and brows. When momentarily embarrassed, it is something in the pharynx that compels either a swallow, a clearing of the throat, or a slight cough; and so on for as many more instances as might be named. The various permutations of which these organic changes are susceptible make it abstractly possible that no shade of emotion should be without a bodily reverberation as unique, when taken in its totality, as is the mental mood itself. The immense number of parts modified is what makes it so difficult for us to reproduce in cold blood the total and integral expression of any one emotion. We may catch the trick with the voluntary muscles, but fail with the skin, glands, heart, and other viscera. Just as an artificially imitated sneeze lacks something of the reality, so the attempt to imitate grief or enthusiasm in the absence of its normal instigating cause is apt to be rather "hollow."

I now proceed to urge the vital point of my whole theory, which is this: *If we fancy some strong emotion, and then try to abstract from our consciousness of it all the feelings of its bodily symptoms, we find we have nothing left behind,* no "mind-stuff" out of which the emotion can be constituted, and that a cold and neutral state of intellectual perception is all that remains. It is true that, although most people, when asked, say that their introspection verifies this statement, some persist in saying theirs does not. Many cannot be made to understand the question. When you beg them to imagine away every feeling of laughter and of tendency to laugh from their consciousness of the ludicrousness of an object, and then to tell you what the feeling of its ludicrousness would be like, whether it be anything more than the perception that the object belongs to the class "funny," they persist in replying that the thing proposed is a physical impossibility, and that they always *must* laugh if they see a funny object. Of course the task proposed is not the practical one of seeing a ludicrous object and annihilating one's tendency to laugh. It is the purely speculative one of subtracting certain elements of feeling from an emotional state supposed to exist in its fulness, and saying what the residual elements are. I cannot help thinking that all who rightly apprehend this problem will agree with the proposition above laid down. What kind of an emotion of fear would be left if the feeling neither of quickened heart-beats nor of shallow breathing, neither of trembling lips nor of weakened limbs, neither of goose-flesh nor of visceral stirrings, were present, it is quite impossible for me to think. Can one fancy the state of rage and picture no ebullition in the chest, no flushing of the face, no dilatation of the nostrils, no clenching of the teeth, no impulse to vigorous action, but in their stead limp muscles, calm breathing, and a placid face? The present writer, for one, certainly cannot. The rage is as completely evaporated as the sensation of its so-called manifestations, and the only thing that can possibly be supposed to take its place is some cold-blooded and dispassionate judicial sentence, confined entirely to the intellectual realm, to the effect that a certain person or persons merit chastisement for their sins. In like manner of grief: what would it be without its tears, its sobs, its suffocation of the heart, its pang in the breast-bone? A feelingless cognition that certain circumstances are deplorable, and nothing more. Every passion in turn tells the same story. A disembodied human emotion is a sheer nonentity. I do not say that it is a contradiction in the nature of things, or that pure spirits are necessarily condemned to cold intellectual lives; but I say that for *us* emotion dissociated from all bodily feeling is inconceivable. The more closely I scrutinize my states, the more persuaded I become that whatever "coarse" affections and passions I have are in very truth constituted by, and made up of, those bodily changes which we ordinarily call their expression or consequence; and the more it seems to me that if I were to become corporeally anæsthetic, I should be excluded from the life of the affections, harsh and tender alike, and drag out an existence of merely cognitive or intellectual form. Such an existence, although it seems to have been the ideal of ancient sages, is too apathetic to be keenly sought after by those born after the revival of the worship of sensibility, a few generations ago.

Let Not This View Be Called Materialistic

It is neither more nor less materialistic than any other view which says that our emotions are conditioned by nervous processes. No reader of this book is likely to rebel against such a saying so long as it is expressed in general terms; and if anyone still finds materialism in the thesis now defended, that must be because of the special processes invoked. They are *sensational* processes, processes due to inward currents set up by physical happenings. Such processes have, it is true, always been regarded by the platonizers in psychology as having something peculiarly base about them. But our emotions must always be *inwardly* what they are, whatever be the physiological ground of their apparition. If they are deep pure worthy spiritual facts on any conceivable theory of their physiological source, they remain no less deep pure spiritual and worthy of regard on this present sensational theory. They carry their own inner measure of worth with them; and it is just as logical to use the present theory of the emotions for proving that sensational processes need not be vile and material, as to use their vileness and materiality as a proof that such a theory cannot be true.

This View Explains the Great Variability of Emotion

If such a theory is true, then each emotion is the resultant of a sum of elements, and each element is caused by a physiological process of a sort already well known. The elements are all organic changes, and each of them is the reflex effect of the exciting object. Definite questions now immediately arise—questions very different from those which were the only possible ones without this view. Those were questions of classification: "Which are the proper genera of emotion, and which the species under each?"—or of description: "By what expression is each emotion characterized?" The questions now are *causal:* "Just what changes does this object and what changes does that object excite?" and "How come they to excite these particular changes and not others?" We step from a superficial to a deep order of inquiry. Classification and description are the lowest stage of science. They sink into the background the moment questions of causation are formulated, and remain important only so far as they facilitate our answering these.

Now the moment an emotion is causally accounted for, as the arousal by an object of a lot of reflex acts which are forthwith felt, *we immediately see why there is no limit to the number of possible different emotions which may exist, and why the emotions of different individuals may vary indefinitely,* both as to their constitution and as to the objects which call them forth. For there is nothing sacramental or eternally fixed in reflex action. Any sort of reflex effect is possible, and reflexes actually vary indefinitely, as we know.

In short, *any classification of the emotions is seen to be as true and as "natural" as any other,* if it only serves some purpose; and such a question as "What is the 'real' or 'typical' expression of anger, or fear?" is seen to have no objective meaning at all. Instead of it we now have the question as to how any given "expression" of anger or fear may have come to exist; and that is a real question of physiological mechanics on the one hand, and of history on the other, which (like all real questions) is in essence answerable, although the answer may be hard to find. On a later page I shall mention the attempts to answer it which have been made.

A Corollary Verified

If our theory be true, a necessary corollary of it ought to be this: that any voluntary and cold-blooded arousal of the so-called manifestations of a special emotion should give us the emotion itself. Now within the limits in which it can be verified, experience corroborates rather than disproves this inference. Everyone knows how panic is increased by flight, and how the giving way to the symptoms of grief or anger increases those passions themselves. Each fit of sobbing makes the sorrow more acute, and calls forth another fit stronger still, until at last repose only ensues with lassitude and with the apparent exhaustion of the machinery. In rage, it is notorious how we "work ourselves up" to a climax by repeated outbreaks of expression. Refuse to express a passion, and it dies. Count ten before venting your anger, and its occasion seems ridiculous. Whistling to keep up courage is no mere figure of speech. On the other hand, sit all day in a moping posture, sigh, and reply to everything with a dismal voice, and your melancholy lingers. There is no more valuable precept in moral education than this, as all who have experience know: if we wish to conquer undesirable emotional tendencies in ourselves, we must assiduously, and in the first instance cold-bloodedly, go through the *outward movements* of those contrary dispositions which we prefer to cultivate. The reward of persistency will infallibly come, in the fading out of the sullenness or depression, and the advent of real cheerfulness and kindliness in their stead. Smooth the brow, brighten the eye, contract the dorsal rather than the ventral aspect of the frame, and speak in a major key, pass the genial compliment, and your heart must be frigid indeed if it do not gradually thaw!

Against this it is to be said that many actors who perfectly mimic the outward appearances of emotion in face, gait, and voice declare that they feel no emotion at all. Others, however, according to Mr. William Archer, who has made a very instructive statistical inquiry among them, say that the emotion of the part masters them whenever they play it well. The explanation for the discrepancy amongst actors is probably simple. The *visceral and organic* part of the expression can be suppressed in some men, but not in others, and on this it must be that the chief part of the felt emotion depends. Those actors who feel the emotion are probably unable, those who are inwardly cold are probably able, to affect the dissociation in a complete way.

An Objection Replied To

It may be objected to the general theory which I maintain that stopping the expression of an emotion often makes it worse. The funniness becomes quite excruciating when we are forbidden by the situation to laugh, and anger pent in by fear turns into tenfold hate. Expressing either emotion freely, however, gives relief.

This objection is more specious than real. *During* the expression the emotion is always felt. *After* it, the centres having normally discharged themselves, we feel it no more. But where the facial part of the discharge is suppressed the thoracic and visceral may be all the more violent and persistent, as in suppressed laughter; or the original emotion may be changed, by the combination of the provoking object with the restraining pressure, into *another emotion altogether,* in which different and possibly profounder organic disturbance occurs. If I would kill my enemy but dare not, my emotion is surely altogether other than that which would possess me if I let my anger explode.—On the whole, therefore this objection has no weight.

The Subtler Emotions

In the æsthetic emotions the bodily reverberation and the feeling may both be faint. A connoisseur is apt to judge a work of art dryly and intellectually, and with no bodily thrill. On the other hand, works of art may arouse intense emotion; and whenever they do so, the experience is completely covered by the terms of our theory. Our theory requires that *incoming currents* be the basis of emotion. But, whether secondary organic reverberations be or be not aroused by it, the perception of a work of art (music, decoration, etc.) is always in the first instance at any rate an affair of incoming currents. The work itself is an object of sensation; and, the perception of an object of sensation being a "coarse" or vivid experience, what pleasure goes with it will partake of the "coarse" or vivid form.

That there may be subtle pleasure too, I do not deny. In other words, there may be purely cerebral emotion, independent of all currents from outside. Such feelings as moral satisfaction, thankfulness, curiosity, relief at getting a problem solved, may be of this sort. But the thinness and paleness of these feelings, when unmixed with bodily effects, is in very striking contrast to the coarser emotions. In all sentimental and impressionable people the bodily effects mix in: the voice breaks and the eyes moisten when the moral truth is felt, etc. Wherever there is anything like *rapture,* however intellectual its ground, we find these secondary processes ensue. Unless we actually laugh at the neatness of the demonstration or witticism; unless we thrill at the case of justice, or tingle at the act of magnanimity, our state of mind can hardly be called emotional at all. It is in fact a mere intellectual perception of how certain things are to be called—neat, right, witty, generous, and the like. Such a judicial state of mind as this is to be classed among cognitive rather than among emotional acts.

Description of Fear

For the reasons given on p. 217, I will append no inventory or classification of emotions or description of their symptoms. The reader has practically almost all the facts in his own hand. As an example, however, of the best sort of descriptive work on the symptoms, I will quote Darwin's account of them in fear.

"Fear is often preceded by astonishment, and is so far akin to it, that both lead to the senses of sight and hearing being instantly aroused. In both cases the eyes and mouth are widely opened, and the eyebrows raised. The frightened man at first stands like a statue motionless and breathless, or crouches down as if instinctively to escape observation. The heart beats quickly and violently, so that it palpitates or knocks against the ribs; but it is very doubtful whether it then works more efficiently than usual, so as to send a greater supply of blood to all parts of the body; for the skin instantly becomes pale, as during incipient faintness. This paleness of the surface, however, is probably in large part, or exclusively, due to the vaso-motor centre being affected in such a manner as to cause the contraction of the small arteries of the skin. That the skin is much affected under the sense of great fear, we see in the marvellous manner in which perspiration immediately exudes from it. This exudation is all the more remarkable, as the surface is then cold, and hence the term a cold sweat; whereas, the sudorific glands are properly excited into action when the surface is heated. The hairs also on the skin stand erect; and the superficial muscles shiver. In connection with the disturbed action of the heart, the breathing is hurried. The salivary glands act imperfectly; the mouth becomes dry, and is often opened and shut. I have also noticed that under slight fear there is a strong tendency to yawn. One of the best-marked symptoms is the trembling of all the muscles of the body: and this is often first seen in the lips. From this cause, and from the dryness of the mouth, the voice becomes husky or indistinct, or may altogether fail. 'Obstupui, steteruntque comæ, et vox faucibus hæsit.' . . . As fear increases into an agony of terror, we behold, as under all violent emotions, diversified results. The heart beats wildly, or may fail to act and faintness ensue; there is a death-like pallor; the breathing is laboured; the wings of the nostrils are widely dilated; 'there is a gasping and convulsive motion of the lips, a tremor on the hollow cheek, a gulping and catching of the throat'; the uncovered and protruding eyeballs are fixed on the object of terror; or they may roll restlessly from side to side, *huc illuc volvens oculos totunque pererrat.* The pupils are said to be enormously dilated. All the muscles of the body may become rigid, or may be thrown into convulsive movements. The hands are alternately clenched and opened, often with a twitching movement. The arms may be protruded, as if to avert some dreadful danger, or may be thrown wildly over the head. The Rev. Mr. Hagenauer has seen this latter action in a terrified Australian. In other cases there is a sudden and uncontrollable tendency to headlong flight; and so strong is this, that the boldest soldiers may be seized with a sudden panic."[1]

Genesis of the Emotional Reactions

How come the various objects which excite emotion to produce such special and different bodily effects? This question was not asked till quite recently, but already some interesting suggestions towards answering it have been made.

Some movements of expression can be accounted for

as *weakened repetitions of movements which formerly* (when they were stronger) *were of utility to the subject.* Others are similarly weakened repetitions of movements which under other conditions were *physiologically necessary concomitants of the useful movements.* Of the latter reactions the respiratory disturbances in anger and fear might be taken as examples—organic reminiscences, as it were, reverberations in imagination of the blowings of the man making a series of combative efforts, of the pantings of one in precipitate flight. Such at least is a suggestion made by Mr. Spencer which has found approval. And he also was the first, so far as I know, to suggest that other movements in anger and fear could be explained by the nascent excitation of formerly useful acts.

"To have in a slight degree," he says, "such psychical states as accompany the reception of wounds, and are experienced during flight, is to be in a state of what we call fear. And to have in a slight degree such psychical states as the processes of catching, killing, and eating imply, is to have the desires to catch, kill, and eat. That the propensities to the acts are nothing else than nascent excitations of the psychical state involved in the acts, is proved by the natural language of the propensities. Fear, when strong, expresses itself in cries, in efforts to escape, in palpitations, in tremblings; and these are just the manifestations that go along with an actual suffering of the evil feared. The destructive passion is shown in a general tension of the muscular system, in gnashing of teeth and protrusion of the claws, in dilated eyes and nostrils, in growls; and these are weaker forms of the actions that accompany the killing of prey. To such objective evidences, every one can add subjective evidences. Every one can testify that the psychical state called fear, consists of mental representations of certain painful results; and that the one called anger, consists of mental representations of the actions and impressions which would occur while inflicting some kind of pain."

The principle of *revival, in weakened form, of reactions useful in more violent dealings with the object inspiring the emotion,* has found many applications. So slight a symptom as the snarl or sneer, the one-sided uncovering of the upper teeth, is accounted for by Darwin as a survival from the time when our ancestors had large canines, and unfleshed them (as dogs now do) for attack. Similarly the raising of the eyebrows in outward attention, the opening of the mouth in astonishment, come, according to the same author, from the utility of these movements in extreme cases. The raising of the eyebrows goes with the opening of the eye for better vi-

sion; the opening of the mouth with the intensest listening, and with the rapid catching of the breath which precedes muscular effort. The distention of the nostrils in anger is interpreted by Spencer as an echo of the way in which our ancestors had to breathe when, during combat, their "mouth was filled up by a part of an antagonist's body that had been seized" (!). The trembling of fear is supposed by Mantegazza to be for the sake of warming the blood (!). The reddening of the face and neck is called by Wundt a compensatory arrangement for relieving the brain of the blood-pressure which the simultaneous excitement of the heart brings with it. The effusion of tears is explained both by this author and by Darwin to be a blood-withdrawing agency of a similar sort. The contraction of the muscles around the eyes, of which the primitive use is to protect those organs from being too much gorged with blood during the screaming fits of infancy, survives in adult life in the shape of the frown, which instantly comes over the brow when anything difficult or displeasing presents itself either to thought or action.

"As the habit of contracting the brows has been followed by infants during innumerable generations, at the commencement of every crying or screaming fit," says Darwin, "it has become firmly associated with the incipient sense of something distressing or disagreeable. Hence under similar circumstances it would be apt to be continued during maturity, although never then developed into a crying-fit. Screaming or weeping begins to be voluntarily restrained at an early period of life, whereas frowning is hardly ever restrained at any age."

Another principle, to which Darwin perhaps hardly does sufficient justice, may be called the principle of *reacting similarly to analogous-feeling stimuli.* There is a whole vocabulary of descriptive adjectives common to impressions belonging to different sensible spheres—experiences of all classes are *sweet,* impressions of all classes *rich* or *solid,* sensations of all classes *sharp.* Wundt and Piderit accordingly explain many of our most expressive reactions upon moral causes as symbolic gustatory movements. As soon as any experience arises which has an affinity with the feeling of sweet, or bitter, or sour, the same movements are executed which would result from the taste in point. "All the states of mind which language designates by the metaphors bitter, harsh, sweet, combine themselves, therefore, with the corresponding mimetic movements of the mouth." Certainly the emotions of disgust and satisfaction do express themselves in this mimetic way. Disgust is an incipient regurgitation or retching, limiting its expression often to the grimace of the lips and nose; satisfaction goes with a sucking smile, or tasting motion of the lips. The ordinary gesture of negation—among us, moving the head about its axis from side to side—is a reaction originally used by babies to keep disagreeables from getting into their mouth, and may be observed in perfection in any nursery. It is now evoked where the stimulus is only an unwelcome idea. Similarly the nod forwards in affirmation is after the analogy of taking food into the mouth. The connection of the expression of moral or social disdain or dislike, especially in women, with movements having a perfectly definite original olfactory function, is too obvious for comment. Winking is the effect of any threatening surprise, not only of what puts the eyes in danger; and a momentary aversion of the eyes is very apt to be one's first symptom of response to an unexpectedly unwelcome proposition.—These may suffice as examples of movements expressive from analogy.

But if certain of our emotional reactions can be explained by the two principles invoked—and the reader will himself have felt how conjectural and fallible in some of the instances the explanation is—there remain many reactions which cannot so be explained at all, and these we must write down for the present as purely idiopathic effects of the stimulus. Amongst them are the effects on the viscera and internal glands, the dryness of the mouth and diarrhœa and nausea of fear, the liver-disturbances which sometimes produce jaundice after excessive rage, the urinary secretion of sanguine excitement, and the bladder-contraction of apprehension, the gaping of expectancy, the "lump in the throat" of grief, the tickling there and the swallowing of embarrassment, the "precordial anxiety" of dread, the changes in the pupil, the various sweatings of the skin, cold or hot, local or general, and its flushings, together with other symptoms which probably exist but are too hidden to have been noticed or named. Trembling, which is found in many excitements besides that of terror, is, *pace* Mr. Spencer and Sig. Mantegazza, quite pathological. So are terror's other strong symptoms: they are harmful to the creature who presents them. In an organism as complex as the nervous system there must be many *incidental* reactions which would never themselves have been evolved independently, for any utility they might possess. Sea-sickness, ticklishness, shyness, the love of music, of the various intoxicants, nay, the entire æsthetic life of man, must be traced to this accidental origin. It would be foolish to suppose that none of the reactions called emotional could have arisen in this *quasi*-accidental way.

INSTINCT

Its Definition

Instinct is usually defined as the faculty of acting in such a way as to produce certain ends, without foresight of the ends, and without previous education in the performance. Instincts are the functional correlatives of structure. With the presence of a certain organ goes, one may say, almost always a native aptitude for its use.

The actions we call instinctive all conform to the general reflex type; they are called forth by determinate sensory stimuli in contact with the animal's body, or at a distance in his environment. The cat runs after the mouse, runs or shows fight before the dog, avoids falling from walls and trees, shuns fire and water, etc., not because he has any notion either of life or of death, or of self, or of preservation. He has probably attained to no one of these conceptions in such a way as to react definitely upon it. He acts in each case separately, and simply because he cannot help it; being so framed that when that particular running thing called a mouse appears in his field of vision he *must* pursue; that when that particular barking and obstreperous thing called a dog appears there he *must* retire, if at a distance, and scratch if close by; that he *must* withdraw his feet from water and his face from flame, etc. His nervous system is to a great extent a preorganized bundle of such reactions—they are as fatal as sneezing, and as exactly correlated to their special excitants as it is to its own. Although the naturalist may, for his own convenience, class these reactions under general heads, he must not forget that in the animal it is a particular sensation or perception or image which calls them forth.

At first this view astounds us by the enormous number of special adjustments it supposes animals to possess ready-made in anticipation of the outer things among which they are to dwell. *Can* mutual dependence be so intricate and go so far? Is each thing born fitted to particular other things, and to them exclusively, as locks are fitted to their keys? Undoubtedly this must be believed to be so. Each nook and cranny of creation, down to our very skin and entrails, has its living inhabitants, with organs suited to the place, to devour and digest the food it harbors and to meet the dangers it conceals; and the minuteness of adaptation thus shown in the way of *structure* knows no bounds. Even so are there no bounds to the minuteness of adaptation in the way of *conduct* which the several inhabitants display.

The older writings on instinct are ineffectual wastes of words, because their authors never came down to this

definite and simple point of view, but smothered everything in vague wonder at the clairvoyant and prophetic
power of the animals—so superior to anything in man—
and at the beneficence of God in endowing them with
such a gift. But God's beneficence endows them, first of
all, with a nervous system; and, turning our attention to
this, makes instinct immediately appear neither more
nor less wonderful than all the other facts of life.

Every Instinct Is an Impulse

Whether we shall call such impulses as blushing, sneezing, coughing, smiling, or dodging, or keeping time to
music, instincts or not, is a mere matter of terminology.
The process is the same throughout. In his delightfully
fresh and interesting work, *Der thierische Wille,* Herr
G. H. Schneider subdivides impulses (*Triebe*) into sen-
sation-impulses, perception-impulses, and idea-impuls-
es. To crouch from cold is a sensation-impulse; to turn
and follow, if we see people running one way, is a per-
ception-impulse; to cast about for cover, if it begins to
blow and rain, is an imagination-impulse. A single complex instinctive action may involve successively the
awakening of impulses of all three classes. Thus a hungry lion starts to *seek* prey by the awakening in him of
imagination coupled with desire; he begins to *stalk* it
when, on eye, ear, or nostril, he gets an impression of its
presence at a certain distance; he *springs* upon it, either
when the booty takes alarm and flees, or when the distance is sufficiently reduced; he proceeds to *tear* and *devour* it the moment he gets a sensation of its contact
with his claws and fangs. Seeking, stalking, springing,
and devouring are just so many different kinds of muscular contraction, and neither kind is called forth by the
stimulus appropriate to the other.

*Now, why do the various animals do what seem to us
such strange things,* in the presence of such outlandish
stimuli? Why does the hen, for example, submit herself
to the tedium of incubating such a fearfully uninteresting set of objects as a nestful of eggs, unless she have
some sort of a prophetic inkling of the result? The only
answer is *ad hominem.* We can only interpret the instincts of brutes by what we know of instincts in ourselves. Why do men always lie down, when they can, on
soft beds rather than on hard floors? Why do they sit
round the stove on a cold day? Why, in a room, do they
place themselves, ninety-nine times out of a hundred,
with their faces towards its middle rather than to the
wall? Why do they prefer saddle of mutton and champagne to hard-tack and pond-water? Why does the
maiden interest the youth so that everything about her
seems more important and significant than anything else

in the world? Nothing more can be said than that these
are human ways, and that every creature *likes* its own
ways, and takes to the following them as a matter of
course. Science may come and consider these ways, and
find that most of them are useful. But it is not for the
sake of their utility that they are followed, but because at
the moment of following them we feel that that is the
only appropriate and natural thing to do. Not one man in
a billion, when taking his dinner, ever thinks of utility.
He eats because the food tastes good and makes him
want more. If you ask him *why* he should want to eat
more of what tastes like that, instead of revering you as
a philosopher he will probably laugh at you for a fool.
The connection between the savory sensation and the
act it awakens is for him absolute and *selbstverständ-
lich,* an "*a priori* synthesis" of the most perfect sort,
needing no proof but its own evidence. It takes, in short,
what Berkeley calls a mind debauched by learning to
carry the process of making the natural seem strange, so
far as to ask for the *why* of any instinctive human act. To
the metaphysician alone can such questions occur as:
Why do we smile, when pleased, and not scowl? Why
are we unable to talk to a crowd as we talk to a single
friend? Why does a particular maiden turn our wits so
upside-down? The common man can only say, "*Of
course* we smile, *of course* our heart palpitates at the
sight of the crowd, *of course* we love the maiden, that
beautiful soul clad in that perfect form, so palpably and
flagrantly made from all eternity to be loved!"

And so, probably, does each animal feel about the
particular things it tends to do in presence of particular
objects. They, too, are *a priori* syntheses. To the lion it is
the lioness which is made to be loved; to the bear, the
she-bear. To the broody hen the notion would probably
seem monstrous that there should be a creature in the
world to whom a nestful of eggs was not the utterly fascinating and precious and never-to-be-too-much-sat-
upon object which it is to her.

Thus we may be sure that, however mysterious some
animals' instincts may appear to us, our instincts will appear no less mysterious to them. And we may conclude
that, to the animal which obeys it, every impulse and
every step of every instinct shines with its own sufficient
light, and seems at the moment the only eternally right
and proper thing to do. It is done for its own sake exclusively. What voluptuous thrill may not shake a fly, when
she at last discovers the one particular leaf, or carrion, or
bit of dung, that out of all the world can stimulate her
ovipositor to its discharge? Does not the discharge then
seem to her the only fitting thing? And need she care or
know anything about the future maggot and its food?

Instincts Are Not Always Blind or Invariable

Nothing is commoner than the remark that man differs from lower creatures by the almost total absence of instincts, and the assumption of their work in him by "reason." A fruitless discussion might be waged on this point by two theorizers who were careful not to define their terms. We must of course avoid a quarrel about words, and the facts of the case are really tolerably plain. Man has a far greater variety of *impulses* than any lower animal: and any one of these impulses, taken in itself, is as "blind" as the lowest instinct can be; but, owing to man's memory, power of reflection, and power of inference, they come each one to be felt by him, after he has once yielded to them and experienced their results, in connection with a *foresight* of those results. In this condition an impulse acted out may be said to be acted out, in part at least, *for the sake* of its results. It is obvious that *every instinctive act, in an animal with memory, must cease to be "blind" after being once repeated,* and must be accompanied with foresight of its "end" just so far as that end may have fallen under the animal's cognizance. An insect that lays her eggs in a place where she never sees them hatch must always do so "blindly"; but a hen who has already hatched a brood can hardly be assumed to sit with perfect "blindness" on her second nest. Some expectation of consequences must in every case like this be aroused; and this expectation, according as it is that of something desired or of something disliked, must necessarily either re-enforce or inhibit the mere impulse. The hen's idea of the chickens would probably encourage her to sit; a rat's memory, on the other hand, of a former escape from a trap would neutralize his impulse to take bait from anything that reminded him of that trap. If a boy sees a fat hopping-toad, he probably has incontinently an impulse (especially if with other boys) to smash the creature with a stone, which impulse we may suppose him blindly to obey. But something in the expression of the dying toad's clasped hands suggests the meanness of the act, or reminds him of sayings he has heard about the sufferings of animals being like his own; so that, when next he is tempted by a toad, an idea arises which, far from spurring him again to the torment, prompts kindly actions, and may even make him the toad's champion against less reflecting boys.

It is plain, then, that, *no matter how well endowed an animal may originally be in the way of instincts, his resultant actions will be much modified if the instincts combine with experience,* if in addition to impulses he have memories, associations, inferences, and expectations, on any considerable scale. An object O, on which

he has an instinctive impulse to react in the manner A, would *directly* provoke him to that reaction. But O has meantime become for him a *sign* of the nearness of P, on which he has an equally strong impulse to react in the manner B, quite unlike A. So that when he meets O, the immediate impulse A and the remote impulse B struggle in his breast for the mastery. The fatality and uniformity said to be characteristic of instinctive actions will be so little manifest that one might be tempted to deny to him altogether the possession of any instinct about the object O. Yet how false this judgment would be! The instinct about O is there; only by the complication of the associative machinery it has come into conflict with another instinct about P.

Here we immediately reap the good fruits of our simple physiological conception of what an instinct is. If it be a mere excitomotor impulse, due to the preëxistence of a certain "reflex arc" in the nerve-centres of the creature, of course it must follow the law of all such reflex arcs. One liability of such arcs is to have their activity "inhibited" by other processes going on at the same time. It makes no difference whether the arc be organized at birth, or ripen spontaneously later, or be due to acquired habit; it must take its chances with all the other arcs, and sometimes succeed, and sometimes fail, in drafting off the currents through itself. The mystical view of an instinct would make it invariable. The physiological view would require it to show occasional irregularities in any animal in whom the number of separate instincts, and the possible entrance of the same stimulus into several of them, were great. And such irregularities are what every superior animal's instincts do show in abundance.

Wherever the mind is elevated enough to discriminate; wherever several distinct sensory elements must combine to discharge the reflex arc; wherever, instead of plumping into action instantly at the first rough intimation of what *sort* of a thing is there, the agent waits to see which *one* of its kind it is and what the *circumstances* are of its appearance; wherever different individuals and different circumstances can impel him in different ways; wherever these are the conditions—we have a masking of the elementary constitution of the instinctive life. The whole story of our dealings with the lower wild animals is the history of our taking advantage of the way in which they judge of everything by its mere label, as it were, so as to ensnare or kill them. Nature, in them, has left matters in this rough way, and made them act *always* in the manner which would be *oftenest* right. There are more worms unattached to hooks than impaled upon them; therefore, on the whole, says

Nature to her fishy children, bite at *every* worm and take your chances. But as her children get higher, and their lives more precious, she reduces the risks. Since what seems to be the same object may be now a genuine food and now a bait; since in gregarious species each individual may prove to be either the friend or the rival, according to the circumstances, of another; since any entirely unknown object may be fraught with weal or woe, *Nature implants contrary impulses to act on many classes of things,* and leaves it to slight alterations in the conditions of the individual case to decide which impulse shall carry the day. Thus, greediness and suspicion, curiosity and timidity, coyness and desire, bashfulness and vanity, sociability and pugnacity, seem to shoot over into each other as quickly, and to remain in as unstable an equilibrium, in the higher birds and mammals as in man. All are impulses, congenital, blind at first, and productive of motor reactions of a rigorously determinate sort. *Each one of them then is an instinct,* as instincts are commonly defined. *But they contradict each other—* "experience" in each particular opportunity of application usually deciding the issue. *The animal that exhibits them loses the "instinctive" demeanor* and appears to lead a life of hesitation and choice, an intellectual life; *not, however, because he has no instincts—rather because he has so many that they block each other's path.*

Thus we may confidently say that however uncertain man's reactions upon his environment may sometimes seem in comparison with those of lower mammals, the uncertainty is probably not due to their possession of any principles of action which he lacks. *On the contrary, man possesses all the impulses that they have, and a great many more besides.* In other words, there is no material antagonism between instinct and reason. Reason, *per se,* can inhibit no impulses; the only thing that can neutralize an impulse is an impulse the other way. Reason may, however, make an *inference which will excite the imagination so as to let loose* the impulse the other way; and thus though the animal richest in reason is also the animal richest in instinctive impulses too, he never seems the fatal automaton which a *merely* instinctive animal must be.

Two Principles of Non-uniformity

Instincts may be masked in the mature animal's life by two other causes. These are:

a. The *inhibition of instincts by habits;* and
b. The *transitoriness of instincts.*

a. The law of **inhibition of instincts by habits** is this: *When objects of a certain class elicit from an animal a certain sort of reaction, it often happens that the animal becomes partial to the first specimen of the class on which it has reacted, and will not afterwards react on any other specimen.*

The selection of a particular hole to live in, of a particular mate, of a particular feeding-ground, a particular variety of diet, a particular anything, in short, out of a possible multitude, is a very wide-spread tendency among animals, even those low down in the scale. The limpet will return to the same sticking-place in its rock, and the lobster to its favorite nook on the sea-bottom. The rabbit will deposit its dung in the same corner; the bird makes its nest on the same bough. But each of these preferences carries with it an insensibility to *other* opportunities and occasions—an insensibility which can only be described physiologically as an inhibition of new impulses by the habit of old ones already formed. The possession of homes and wives of our own makes us strangely insensible to the charms of those of other people. Few of us are adventurous in the matter of food; in fact, most of us think there is something disgusting in a bill of fare to which we are unused. Strangers, we are apt to think, cannot be worth knowing, especially if they come from distant cities, etc. The original impulse which got us homes, wives, dietaries, and friends at all, seems to exhaust itself in its first achievements and to leave no surplus energy for reacting on new cases. And so it comes about that, witnessing this torpor, an observer of mankind might say that no *instinctive* propensity towards certain objects existed at all. It existed, but it existed *miscellaneously,* or as an instinct pure and simple, only before habit was formed. A habit, once grafted on an instinctive tendency, restricts the range of the tendency itself, and keeps us from reacting on any but the habitual object, although other objects might just as well have been chosen had they been the first-comers.

Another sort of arrest of instinct by habit is where the same class of objects awakens contrary instinctive impulses. Here the impulse first followed towards a given individual of the class is apt to keep him from ever awakening the opposite impulse in us. In fact, the whole class may be protected by this individual specimen from the application to it of the other impulse. Animals, for example, awaken in a child the opposite impulses of fearing and fondling. But if a child, in his first attempts to pat a dog, gets snapped at or bitten, so that the impulse of fear is strongly aroused, it may be that for years to come no dog will excite in him the impulse to fondle again. On the other hand, the greatest natural enemies, if carefully introduced to each other when young and guided at the outset by superior authority, settle down into those "happy families" of friends which we see in our menageries. Young animals, immediately after birth, have no instinct of fear, but show their dependence by allowing themselves to be freely handled. Later, however, they grow "wild," and, if left to themselves, will not let man approach them. I am told by farmers in the Adirondack wilderness that it is a very serious matter if a cow wanders off and calves in the woods and is not found for a week or more. The calf, by that time, is as wild and almost as fleet as a deer, and hard to capture without violence. But calves rarely show any wildness to the men who have been in contact with them during the first days of their life, when the instinct to attach themselves is uppermost, nor do they dread strangers as they would if brought up wild.

Chickens give a curious illustration of the same law. Mr. Spalding's wonderful article on instinct shall supply us with the facts. These little creatures show opposite instincts of attachment and fear, either of which may be aroused by the same object, man. If a chick is born in the absence of the hen, it "will follow any moving object. And, when guided by sight alone, they seem to have no more disposition to follow a hen than to follow a duck, or a human being. Unreflecting on-lookers, when they saw chickens a day old running after me," says Mr. Spalding, "and older ones following me miles and answering to my whistle, imagined that I must have some occult power over the creatures, whereas I simply allowed them to follow me from the first. There is the instinct to follow; and . . . their ear prior to experience attaches them to the right object."[2]

But if a man presents himself for the first time when the instinct of *fear* is strong, the phenomena are altogether reversed. Mr. Spalding kept three chickens hooded until they were nearly four days old, and thus describes their behavior:

"Each of these on being unhooded evinced the greatest terror of me, dashing off in the opposite direction whenever I sought to approach it. The table on which they were unhooded stood before a window, and each in its turn beat against the glass like a wild bird. One of them darted behind some books, and squeezing itself into a corner, remained cowering for a length of time. We might guess at the meaning of this strange and exceptional wildness; but the odd fact is enough for my present purpose. Whatever might have been the meaning of this marked change in their mental constitution— had they been unhooded on the previous day they would have run to me instead of from me—it could not have

been the effect of experience; it must have resulted wholly from changes in their own organization."[3]

Their case was precisely analogous to that of the Adirondack calves. The two opposite instincts relative to the same object ripen in succession. If the first one engenders a habit, that habit will inhibit the application of the second instinct to that object. All animals are tame during the earliest phase of their infancy. Habits formed then limit the effects of whatever instincts of wildness may later be evolved.

b. This leads us to the **law of transitoriness,** which is this: *Many instincts ripen at a certain age and then fade away.* A consequence of this law is that if, during the time of such an instinct's vivacity, objects adequate to arouse it are met with, a *habit* of acting on them is formed, which remains when the original instinct has passed away; but that if no such objects are met with, then no habit will be formed; and, later on in life, when the animal meets the objects, he will altogether fail to react, as at the earlier epoch he would instinctively have done.

No doubt such a law is restricted. Some instincts are far less transient than others—those connected with feeding and "self-preservation" may hardly be transient at all—and some, after fading out for a time, recur as strong as ever; e.g., the instincts of pairing and rearing young. The law, however, though not absolute, is certainly very widespread, and a few examples will illustrate just what it means.

In the chickens and calves above mentioned it is obvious that the instinct to follow and become attached fades out after a few days, and that the instinct of flight then takes its place, the conduct of the creature towards man being decided by the formation or non-formation of a certain habit during those days. The transiency of the chicken's instinct to follow is also proved by its conduct towards the hen. Mr. Spalding kept some chickens shut up till they were comparatively old, and, speaking of these, he says:

"A chicken that has not heard the call of the mother until eight or ten days old then hears it as if it heard it not. I regret to find that on this point my notes are not so full as I could wish, or as they might have been. There is, however, an account of one chicken that could not be returned to the mother when ten days old. The hen followed it, and tried to entice it in every way; still it continually left her and ran to the house or to any person of whom it caught sight. This is persisted in doing, though beaten back with a small branch dozens of times, and indeed cruelly maltreated. It was also placed under the mother at night, but it again left her in the morning."

The instinct of sucking is ripe in all mammals at birth, and leads to that habit of taking the breast which, in the human infant, may be prolonged by daily exercise long beyond its usual term of a year or a year and a half. But the instinct itself is transient, in the sense that if, for any reason, the child be fed by spoon during the first few days of its life and not put to the breast, it may be no easy matter after that to make it suck at all. So of calves. If their mother die, or be dry, or refuse to let them suck for a day or two, so that they are fed by hand, it becomes hard to get them to suck at all when a new nurse is provided. The ease with which sucking creatures are weaned, by simply breaking the habit and giving them food in a new way, shows that the instinct, purely as such, must be entirely extinct.

Assuredly the simple fact that instincts are transient, and that the effect of later ones may be altered by the habits which earlier ones have left behind, is a far more philosophical explanation than the notion of an instinctive constitution vaguely "deranged" or "thrown out of gear."

I have observed a Scotch terrier, born on the floor of a stable in December, and transferred six weeks later to a carpeted house, make, when he was less than four months old, a very elaborate pretence of burying things, such as gloves, etc., with which he had played till he was tired. He scratched the carpet with his fore-feet, dropped the object from his mouth upon the spot, then scratched all about it, and finally went away and let it lie. Of course, the act was entirely useless. I saw him perform it at that age some four or five times, and never again in his life. The conditions were not present to fix a habit which should last when the prompting instinct died away. But suppose meat instead of a glove, earth instead of a carpet, hunger-pangs instead of a fresh supper a few hours later, and it is easy to see how this dog might have got into a habit of burying superfluous food, which might have lasted all his life. Who can swear that the strictly instinctive part of the food-burying propensity in the wild *Canidæ* may not be as short-lived as it was in this terrier?

Leaving lower animals aside, and turning to human instincts, we see the law of transiency corroborated on the widest scale by the alternation of different interests and passions as human life goes on. With the child, life is all play and fairy-tales and learning the external properties of "things"; with the youth, it is bodily exercises of a more systematic sort, novels of the real world, boon-fellowship and song, friendship and love, nature, travel and adventure, science and philosophy; with the man, ambition and policy, acquisitiveness, responsibility to others, and the selfish zest of the battle of life. If a boy grows up alone at the age of games and sports, and learns neither to play ball, nor row, nor sail, nor ride, nor skate, nor fish, nor shoot, probably he will be sedentary to the end of his days; and, though the best of opportunities be afforded him for learning these things later, it is a hundred to one but he will pass them by and shrink back from the effort of taking those necessary first steps the prospect of which, at an earlier age, would have filled him with eager delight. The sexual passion expires after a protracted reign; but it is well known that its peculiar manifestations in a given individual depend almost entirely on the habits he may form during the early period of its activity. Exposure to bad company then makes him a loose liver all his days; chastity kept at first makes the same easy later on. In all pedagogy the great thing is to strike the iron while hot, and to seize the wave of the pupil's interest in each successive subject before its ebb has come, so that knowledge may be got and a habit of skill acquired—a headway of interest, in short, secured, on which afterwards the individual may float. There is a happy moment for fixing skill in drawing, for making boys collectors in natural history, and presently dissectors and botanists; then for initiating them into the harmonies of mechanics and the wonders of physical and chemical law. Later, introspective psychology and the metaphysical and religious mysteries take their turn; and, last of all, the drama of human affairs and worldly wisdom in the widest sense of the term. In each of us a saturation-point is soon reached in all these things; the impetus of our purely intellectual zeal expires, and unless the topic be one associated with some urgent personal need that keeps our wits constantly whetted about it, we settle into an equilibrium, and live on what we learned when our interest was fresh and instinctive, without adding to the store. Outside of their own business, the ideas gained by men before they are twenty-five are practically the only ideas they shall have in their lives. They *cannot* get anything new. Disinterested curiosity is past, the mental grooves and channels set, the power of assimilation gone. If by chance we ever do learn anything about some entirely new topic, we are afflicted with a strange sense of insecurity, and we fear to advance a resolute opinion. But with things learned in the plastic days of instinctive curiosity we never lose entirely our sense of being at home. There remains a kinship, a sentiment of intimate acquaintance, which, even when we know we have failed to keep abreast of the subject, flatters us with a sense of power over it, and makes us feel not altogether out of the pale.

Whatever individual exceptions to this might be cited are of the sort that "prove the rule."

To detect the moment of the instinctive readiness for the subject is, then, the first duty of every educator. As for the pupils, it would probably lead to a more earnest temper on the part of college students if they had less belief in their unlimited future intellectual potentialities, and could be brought to realize that whatever physics and political economy and philosophy they are now acquiring are, for better or worse, the physics and political economy and philosophy that will have to serve them to the end.

Enumeration of Instincts in Man

Professor Preyer, in his careful little work, *Die Seele des Kindes,* says "instinctive acts are in man few in number, and, apart from those connected with the sexual passion, difficult to recognize after early youth is past." And he adds, "so much the more attention should we pay to the instinctive movements of new-born babies, sucklings, and small children." That instinctive acts should be easiest *recognized* in childhood would be a very natural effect of our principles of transitoriness, and of the restrictive influence of habits once acquired; but they are far indeed from being "few in number" in man. Professor Preyer divides the movements of infants into *impulsive, reflex,* and *instinctive.* By impulsive movements he means *random* movements of limbs, body, and voice, with no aim, and before perception is aroused. Among the first reflex movements are crying on contact with the air, *sneezing, snuffing, snoring, coughing, sighing, sobbing, gagging, vomiting, hiccuping, starting, moving the limbs when touched,* and *sucking.* To these may now be added *hanging by the hands* (see *Nineteenth Century,* Nov. 1891). Later on come *biting, clasping objects,* and *carrying them to the mouth, sitting up, standing, creeping,* and *walking.* It is probable that the centres for executing these three latter acts ripen spontaneously, just as those for flight have been proved to do in birds, and that the appearance of *learning* to stand and walk, by trial and failure, is due to the exercise beginning in most children before the centres are ripe. Children vary enormously in the rate and manner in which they learn to walk. With the first impulses to *imitation,* those to significant *vocalization* are born. *Emulation* rapidly ensues, with *pugnacity* in its train. *Fear* of definite objects comes in early, *sympathy* much later, though on the instinct (or emotion?—see p. 216) of sympathy so much in human life depends. *Shyness* and *sociability, play, curiosity, acquisitiveness,* all begin very early in life. The *hunting instinct, modesty, love,* the *parental instinct,* etc., come later. By the age of 15 or 16 the whole array of human instincts is complete. It will be observed that *no other mammal, not even the monkey, shows so large a list.* In a perfectly-rounded development every one of these instincts would start a habit towards certain objects and inhibit a habit towards certain others. Usually this is the case; but, in the one-sided development of civilized life, it happens that the timely age goes by in a sort of starvation of objects, and the individual then grows up with gaps in his psychic constitution which future experiences can never fill. Compare the accomplished gentleman with the poor artisan or tradesman of a city: during the adolescence of the former, objects appropriate to his growing interests, bodily and mental, were offered as fast as the interests awoke, and, as a consequence, he is armed and equipped at every angle to meet the world. Sport came to the rescue and completed his education where real things were lacking. He has tasted of the essence of every side of human life, being sailor, hunter, athlete, scholar, fighter, talker, dandy, man of affairs, etc., all in one. Over the city poor boy's youth no such golden opportunities were hung, and in his manhood no desires for most of them exist. Fortunate it is for him if gaps are the only anomalies his instinctive life presents; perversions are too often the fruit of his unnatural bringing-up.

Description of Fear

In order to treat at least one instinct at greater length, I will take the instance of *fear.*

Fear is a reaction aroused by the same objects that arouse ferocity. The antagonism of the two is an interesting study in instinctive dynamics. We both fear, and wish to kill, anything that may kill us; and the question which of the two impulses we shall follow is usually decided by some one of those collateral circumstances of the particular case, to be moved by which is the mark of superior mental natures. Of course this introduces uncertainty into the reaction; but it is an uncertainty found in the higher brutes as well as in men, and ought not to be taken as proof that we are less instinctive than they. Fear has bodily expressions of an extremely energetic kind, and stands, beside lust and anger, as one of the three most exciting emotions of which our nature is susceptible. The progress from brute to man is characterized by nothing so much as by the decrease in frequency of proper occasions for fear. In civilized life, in particular, it has at last become possible for large numbers of people to pass from the cradle to the grave without ever having had a pang of genuine fear. Many of us need an attack of mental disease to teach us the meaning of the

word. Hence the possibility of so much blindly optimistic philosophy and religion. The atrocities of life become "like a tale of little meaning tho' the words are
strong"; we doubt if anything like *us* ever really was
within the tiger's jaws, and conclude that the horrors we
hear of are but a sort of painted tapestry for the chambers in which we lie so comfortably at peace with ourselves and with the world.

Be this as it may, fear is a genuine instinct, and one
of the earliest shown by the human child. *Noises* seem
especially to call it forth. Most noises from the outer
world, to a child bred in the house, have no exact significance. They are simply startling. To quote a good observer, M. Perez:

"Children between three and ten months are less often alarmed by visual than by auditory impressions. In
cats, from the fifteenth day, the contrary is the case. A
child, three and a half months old, in the midst of the
turmoil of a conflagration, in presence of the devouring
flames and ruined walls, showed neither astonishment
nor fear, but smiled at the woman who was taking care
of him, while his parents were busy. The noise, however, of the trumpet of the firemen, who were approaching,
and that of the wheels of the engine, made him start and
cry. At this age I have never yet seen an infant startled at
a flash of lightning, even when intense; but I have seen
many of them alarmed at the voice of the thunder. . . .
Thus fear comes rather by the ears than by the eyes, to
the child without experience."[4]

The effect of noise in heightening any terror we may
feel in adult years is very marked. The *howling* of the
storm, whether on sea or land, is a principal cause of our
anxiety when exposed to it. The writer has been interested in noticing in his own person, while lying in bed, and
kept awake by the wind outside, how invariably each
loud gust of it arrested momentarily his heart. A dog attacking us is much more dreadful by reason of the noises he makes.

Strange men, and *strange animals,* either large or
small, excite fear, but especially men or animals advancing towards us in a threatening way. This is entirely instinctive and antecedent to experience. Some children
will cry with terror at their very first sight of a cat or
dog, and it will often be impossible for weeks to make
them touch it. Others will wish to fondle it almost immediately. Certain kinds of "vermin," especially spiders
and snakes, seem to excite a fear unusually difficult to
overcome. It is impossible to say how much of this difference is instinctive and how much the result of stories
heard about these creatures. That the fear of "vermin"
ripens gradually seemed to me to be proved in a child of

my own to whom I gave a live frog once, at the age of
six to eight months, and again when he was a year and a
half old. The first time, he seized it promptly, and holding it in spite of its struggling, at last got its head into his
mouth. He then let it crawl up his breast, and get upon
his face, without showing alarm. But the second time,
although he had seen no frog and heard no story about a
frog between-whiles, it was almost impossible to induce
him to touch it. Another child, a year old, eagerly took
some very large spiders into his hand. At present he is
afraid, but has been exposed meanwhile to the teachings
of the nursery. One of my children from her birth upwards saw daily the pet pug-dog of the house, and never
betrayed the slightest fear until she was (if I recollect
rightly) about eight months old. Then the instinct suddenly seemed to develop, and with such intensity that
familiarity had no mitigating effect. She screamed
whenever the dog entered the room, and for many
months remained afraid to touch him. It is needless to
say that no change in the pug's unfailingly friendly conduct had anything to do with this change of feeling in
the child. Two of my children were afraid, when babies,
of *fur:* Richet reports a similar observation.

Preyer tells of a young child screaming with fear on
being carried near to the *sea.* The great source of terror
to infancy is solitude. The teleology of this is obvious,
as is also that of the infant's expression of dismay—the
never-failing cry—on waking up and finding himself
alone.

Black things, and especially *dark places,* holes, caverns, etc., arouse a peculiarly gruesome fear. This fear,
as well as that of solitude, of being "lost," are explained
after a fashion by ancestral experience. Says Schneider:

"It is a fact that men, especially in childhood, fear to
go into a dark cavern or a gloomy wood. This feeling of
fear arises, to be sure, partly from the fact that we easily
suspect that dangerous beasts may lurk in these localities—a suspicion due to stories we have heard and read.
But, on the other hand, it is quite sure that this fear at a
certain perception is also directly inherited. Children
who have been carefully guarded from all ghost-stories
are nevertheless terrified and cry if led into a dark place,
especially if sounds are made there. Even an adult can
easily observe that an uncomfortable timidity steals
over him in a lonely wood at night, although he may
have the fixed conviction that not the slightest danger is
near.

"This feeling of fear occurs in many men even in
their own house after dark, although it is much stronger
in a dark cavern or forest. The fact of such instinctive
fear is easily explicable when we consider that our sav-

age ancestors through innumerable generations were accustomed to meet with dangerous beasts in caverns, especially bears, and were for the most part attacked by such beasts during the night and in the woods, and that thus an inseparable association between the perceptions of darkness, caverns, woods, and fear took place, and was inherited."[5]

High places cause fear of a peculiarly sickening sort, though here, again, individuals differ enormously. The utterly blind instinctive character of the motor impulses here is shown by the fact that they are almost always entirely unreasonable, but that reason is powerless to suppress them. That they are a mere incidental peculiarity of the nervous system, like liability to sea-sickness, or love of music, with no teleological significance, seems more than probable. The fear in question varies so much from one person to another, and its detrimental effects are so much more obvious than its uses, that it is hard to see how it could be a selected instinct. Man is anatomically one of the best fitted of animals for climbing about high places. The best psychical complement to this equipment would seem to be a "level head" when there, not a dread of going there at all. In fact, the teleology of fear, beyond a certain point, is more than dubious. A certain amount of timidity obviously adapts us to the world we live in, but the *fear-paroxysm* is surely altogether harmful to him who is its prey.

Fear of the supernatural is one variety of fear. It is difficult to assign any normal object for this fear, unless it were a genuine ghost. But, in spite of psychical-research societies, science has not yet adopted ghosts; so we can only say that certain *ideas* of supernatural agency, associated with real circumstances, produce a peculiar kind of horror. This horror is probably explicable as the result of a combination of simpler horrors. To bring the ghostly terror to its maximum, many usual elements of the dreadful must combine, such as loneliness, darkness, inexplicable sounds, especially of a dismal character, moving figures half discerned (or, if discerned, of dreadful aspect), and a vertiginous baffling of the expectation. This last element, which is *intellectual,* is very important. It produces a strange emotional "curdle" in our blood to see a process with which we are familiar deliberately taking an unwonted course. Anyone's heart would stop beating if he perceived his chair sliding unassisted across the floor. The lower animals appear to be sensitive to the mysteriously exceptional as well as ourselves. My friend Professor W. K. Brooks told me of his large and noble dog being frightened into a sort of epileptic fit by a bone being drawn across the floor by a thread which the dog did not see. Darwin and

Romanes have given similar experiences. The idea of the supernatural involves that the usual should be set at naught. In the witch and hobgoblin supernatural, other elements still of fear are brought in—caverns, slime and ooze, vermin, corpses, and the like. A human corpse seems normally to produce an instinctive dread, which is no doubt somewhat due to its mysteriousness, and which familiarity rapidly dispels. But, in view of the fact that cadaveric, reptilian, and underground horrors play so specific and constant a part in many nightmares and forms of delirium, it seems not altogether unwise to ask whether these forms of dreadful circumstance may not at a former period have been more normal objects of the environment than now. The ordinary cock-sure evolutionist ought to have no difficulty in explaining these terrors, and the scenery that provokes them, as relapses into the consciousness of the cave-men, a consciousness usually overlaid in us by experiences of more recent date.

There are certain other pathological fears, and certain peculiarities in the expression of ordinary fear, which might receive an explanatory light from ancestral conditions, even infra-human ones. In ordinary fear, one may either run, or remain semi-paralyzed. The latter condition reminds us of the so-called death-shamming instinct shown by many animals. Dr. Lindsay, in his work *Mind in Animals,* says this must require great self-command in those that practise it. But it is really no feigning of death at all, and requires no self-command. It is simply a terror-paralysis which has been so useful as to become hereditary. The beast of prey does not think the motionless bird, insect, or crustacean dead. He simply fails to notice them at all; because his senses, like ours, are much more strongly excited by a moving object than by a still one. It is the same instinct which leads a boy playing "I spy" to hold his very breath when the seeker is near, and which makes the beast of prey himself in many cases motionlessly lie in wait for his victim or silently "stalk" it, by stealthy advances alternated with periods of immobility. It is the opposite of the instinct which makes us jump up and down and move our arms when we wish to attract the notice of someone passing far away, and makes the shipwrecked sailor upon the raft where he is floating frantically wave a cloth when a distant sail appears. Now, may not the statue-like, crouching immobility of some melancholiacs, insane with general anxiety and fear of everything, be in some way connected with this old instinct? They can give no *reason* for their fear to move; but immobility makes them feel safer and more comfortable. Is not this the mental state of the "feigning" animal?

Again, take the strange symptom which has been described of late years by the rather absurd name of *agoraphobia*. The patient is seized with palpitation and terror at the sight of any open place or broad street which he has to cross alone. He trembles, his knees bend, he may even faint at the idea. Where he has sufficient self-command he sometimes accomplishes the object by keeping safe under the lee of a vehicle going across, or joining himself to a knot of other people. But usually he slinks round the sides of the square, hugging the houses as closely as he can. This emotion has no utility in a civilized man, but when we notice the chronic agoraphobia of our domestic cats, and see the tenacious way in which many wild animals, especially rodents, cling to cover, and only venture on a dash across the open as a desperate measure—even then making for every stone or bunch of weeds which

may give a momentary shelter—when we see this we are strongly tempted to ask whether such an odd kind of fear in us be not due to the accidental resurrection, through disease, of a sort of instinct which may in some of our remote ancestors have had a permanent and on the whole a useful part to play?

NOTES

1. *The Expression of the Emotions in Man and Animals* (N.Y. ed.), p. 290.
2. Spalding: *Macmillan's Magazine*, Feb. 1873, p. 287.
3. *Ibid.*, p. 289.
4. *Psychologie de l'enfant*, p. 72.
5. *Der menschliche Wille*, p. 224.

18
~

FRANCIS GALTON

Francis Galton (1822–1911) loved to measure things. Over his lifetime, he tabulated and analyzed data involving high- and low-pressure fronts as he developed the first weather maps, charted southwest Africa (today's Namibia), and tried to quantify everything from a woman's beauty to a man's intellectual talents and proclivities to various degrees of boredom of attendees at scientific lectures. Galton was born into a wealthy family, his father was a banker, and his mother was the eldest daughter of Erasmus Darwin, perhaps the most famous physician and philosopher of the previous generation. As the youngest child, Galton enjoyed the doting attention of his mother and older sisters. Indeed, as the result of sororal tutoring, Galton was reading as a toddler and enjoyed Shakespeare at the age of 7. He found boarding school abhorrent and later said that his classical education, focused on Latin and Greek prose, did not contribute to his eventual scientific interests. Galton attended a number of colleges, studying medicine at Birmingham General Hospital; anatomy and chemistry at Kings College; and mathematics, which he particularly enjoyed, at Cambridge University, where he received his degree in 1843. Like his cousin, Charles Darwin (p. 188), Galton found witnessing surgery repellent but eventually learned to detach the agonizing screams of the patients (who then underwent surgery without anesthesia) from the mechanics of the operation. When, with the death of his father, he came into his inheritance, Galton traveled to Egypt, the Sudan, and the Middle East, returning with such a variety of experiences that he was asked to instruct British soldiers in the camping techniques. He wrote a popular book, *The Art of Travel, Or, Shifts and Contrivances Available in Wild Countries,* for the tourist seeking exotic adventure. The publication of Darwin's (p. 188) *The Origin of Species* inspired Galton to start exploring human behavior and inheritance. Several publications followed, including the 1888 article, "Co-Relations and Their

Measurement, Chiefly from Anthropometric Data," which introduced the concepts of correlation, regression to the mean, and the median, thus earning Galton a special place in the heart of all statistics students.

INQUIRIES INTO HUMAN FACULTY AND ITS DEVELOPMENT

HISTORY OF TWINS

The exceedingly close resemblance attributed to twins has been the subject of many novels and plays, and most persons have felt a desire to know upon what basis of truth those works of fiction may rest. But twins have a special claim upon our attention; it is, that their history affords means of distinguishing between the effects of tendencies received at birth, and of those that were imposed by the special circumstances of their after lives. The objection to statistical evidence in proof of the inheritance of peculiar faculties has always been: "The persons whom you compare may have lived under similar social conditions and have had similar advantages of education, but such prominent conditions are only a small part of those that determine the future of each man's life. It is to trifling accidental circumstances that the bent of his disposition and his success are mainly due, and these you leave wholly out of account—in fact, they do not admit of being tabulated, and therefore your statistics, however plausible at first sight, are really of very little use." No method of inquiry which I had previously been able to carry out—and I have tried many methods—is wholly free from this objection. I have therefore attacked the problem from the opposite side, seeking for some new method by which it would be possible to weigh in just scales the effects of Nature and Nurture, and to ascertain their respective shares in framing the disposition and intellectual ability of men. The life-history of twins supplies what I wanted. We may begin by inquiring about twins who were closely alike in boyhood and youth, and who were educated together for many years, and learn whether they subsequently grew unlike, and, if so, what the main causes were which, in the opinion of the family, produced the dissimilarity. In this way we can obtain direct evidence of the kind we want. Again, we may obtain yet more valuable evidence by a converse method. We can inquire into the history of twins who were exceedingly unlike in childhood, and learn how far their characters became assimilated under

the influence of identical nurture, isasmush as they had the same home, the same teachers, the same associates, and in every other respect the same surroundings.

My materials were obtained by sending circulars of inquiry to persons who were either twins themselves or near relations of twins. The printed questions were in thirteen groups; the last of them asked for the addresses of other twins known to the recipient, who might be likely to respond if I wrote to them. This happily led to a continually widening circle of correspondence, which I pursued until enough material was accumulated for a general reconnaisance of the subject.

There is a large literature relating to twins in their purely surgical and physiological aspect. The reader interested in this should consult *Die Lehre von den Zwillingen,* von L. Kleinwächter, Prag. 1871. It is full of references, but it is also unhappily disfigured by a number of numerical misprints, especially in page 26. I have not found any book that treats of twins from my present point of view.

The reader will easily understand that the word "twins" is a vague expression, which covers two very dissimilar events—the one corresponding to the progeny of animals that usually bear more than one at a birth, each of the progeny being derived from a separate ovum, while the other event is due to the development of two germinal spots in the same ovum. In the latter case they are enveloped in the same membrane, and all such twins are found invariably to be of the same sex. The consequence of this is, that I find a curious discontinuity in my results. One would have expected that twins would commonly be found to possess a certain average likeness to one another; that a few would greatly exceed that average likeness, and a few would greatly fall short of it. But this is not at all the case. Extreme similarity and extreme dissimilarity between twins of the same sex are nearly as common as moderate resemblance. When the twins are a boy and a girl, they are never closely alike; in fact, their origin is never due to the development of two germinal spots in the same ovum.

From Francis Galton, "The History of Twins," "Selection and Race," "Influence of Man Upon Race," and "Conclusion." In *Inquiries into Human Faculty and its Development* (pp. 155–173, 198–207, 216–220). New York: E. P. Dutton 1907.

I received about eighty returns of cases of close similarity, thirty-five of which entered into many instructive details. In a few of these not a single point of difference could be specified. In the remainder, the colour of the hair and eyes were almost always identical; the height, weight, and strength were nearly so. Nevertheless, I have a few cases of a notable difference in height, weight, and strength, although the resemblance was otherwise very near. The manner and personal address of the thirty-five pairs of twins are usually described as very similar, but accompanied by a slight difference of expression, familiar to near relatives, though unperceived by strangers. The intonation of the voice when speaking is commonly the same, but it frequently happens that the twins sing in different keys. Most singularly, the one point in which similarity is rare is the hand writing. I cannot account for this, considering how strongly handwriting runs in families, but I am sure of the fact. I have only one case in which nobody, not even the twins themselves, could distinguish their own notes of lectures, etc.; barely two or three in which the handwriting was undistinguishable by others, and only a few in which it was described as closely alike. On the other hand, I have many in which it is stated to be unlike, and some in which it is alluded to as the only point of difference. It would appear that the handwriting is a very delicate test of difference in organisation—a conclusion which I commend to the notice of enthusiasts in the art of discovering character by the handwriting.

One of my inquiries was for anecdotes regarding mistakes made between the twins by their near relatives. The replies are numerous, but not very varied in character. When the twins are children, they are usually distinguished by ribbons tied round the wrist or neck; nevertheless the one is sometimes fed, physicked, and whipped by mistake for the other, and the description of these little domestic catastrophes was usually given by the mother, in a phraseology that is somewhat touching by reason of its seriousness. I have one case in which a doubt remains whether the children were not changed in their bath, and the presumed A is not really B, and *vice versâ*. In another case, an artist was engaged on the portraits of twins who were between three and four years of age; he had to lay aside his work for three weeks, and, on resuming it, could not tell to which child the respective likenesses he had in hand belonged. The mistakes become less numerous on the part of the mother during the boyhood and girlhood of the twins, but are almost as frequent as before on the part of strangers. I have many instances of tutors being unable to distinguish their twin pupils. Two girls used regularly to impose on their mu-

sic teacher when one of them wanted a whole holiday; they had their lessons at separate hours, and the one girl sacrificed herself to receive two lessons on the same day, while the other one enjoyed herself from morning to evening. Here is a brief and comprehensive account:—

"Exactly alike in all, their schoolmasters never could tell them apart; at dancing parties they constantly changed partners without discovery; their close resemblance is scarcely diminished by age."

The following is a typical schoolboy anecdote:—

"Two twins were fond of playing tricks, and complaints were frequently made; but the boys would never own which was the guilty one, and the complainants were never certain which of the two he was. One head master used to say he would never flog the innocent for the guilty, and another used to flog both."

No less than nine anecdotes have reached me of a twin seeing his or her reflection in a looking-glass, and addressing it in the belief it was the other twin in person.

I have many anecdotes of mistakes when the twins were nearly grown up. Thus:—

"Amusing scenes occurred at college when one twin came to visit the other; the porter on one occasion refusing to let the visitor out of the college gates, for, though they stood side by side, he professed ignorance as to which he ought to allow to depart."

Children are usually quick in distinguishing between their parent and his or her twin; but I have two cases to the contrary. Thus, the daughter of a twin says:—

"Such was the marvellous similarity of their features, voice, manner, etc., that I remember, as a child, being very much puzzled, and I think, had my aunt lived much with us, I should have ended by thinking I had two mothers."

In the other case, a father who was a twin, remarks of himself and his brother:—

"We were extremely alike, and are so at this moment, so much so that our children up to five and six years old did not know us apart."

I have four or five instances of doubt during an engagement of marriage. Thus:—

"A married first, but both twins met the lady together for the first time, and fell in love with her there and then. A managed to see her home and to gain her affection, though B went sometimes courting in his place, and neither the lady nor her parents could tell which was which."

I have also a German letter, written in quaint terms, about twin brothers who married sisters, but could not easily be distinguished by them.[1] In the well-known novel by Mr. Wilkie Collins of *Poor Miss Finch,* the blind girl distinguishes the twin she loves by the touch of his hand, which gives her a thrill that the touch of the other brother does not. Philosophers have not, I believe, as yet investigated the conditions of such thrills; but I have a case in which Miss Finch's test would have failed. Two persons, both friends of a certain twin lady, told me that she had frequently remarked to them that "kissing her twin sister was not like kissing her other sisters, but like kissing herself—her own hand, for example."

It would be an interesting experiment for twins who were closely alike to try how far dogs could distinguish them by scent.

I have a few anecdotes of strange mistakes made between twins in adult life. Thus, an officer writes:—

"On one occasion when I returned from foreign service my father turned to me and said, 'I thought you were in London,' thinking I was my brother—yet he had not seen me for nearly four years—our resemblance was so great."

The next and last anecdote I shall give is, perhaps, the most remarkable of those I have; it was sent me by the brother of the twins, who were in middle life at the time of its occurrence:—

"A was again coming home from India, on leave; the ship did not arrive for some days after it was due; the twin brother B had come up from his quarters to receive A, and their old mother was very nervous. One morning A rushed in saying, 'Oh, mother, how are you?' Her answer was, 'No, B, it's a bad joke; you know how anxious I am!' and it was a little time before A could persuade her that he was the real man."

Enough has been said to prove that an extremely close personal resemblance frequently exists between twins of the same sex; and that, although the resemblance usually diminishes as they grow into manhood and womanhood, some cases occur in which the diminution of resemblance is hardly perceptible. It must be borne in mind that it is not necessary to ascribe the divergence of development, when it occurs, to the effect of different nurtures, but it is quite possible that it may be due to the late appearance of qualities inherited at birth, though dormant in early life, like gout. To this I shall recur.

There is a curious feature in the character of the resemblance between twins, which has been alluded to by a few correspondents; it is well illustrated by the following quotations. A mother of twins says:—

"There seemed to be a sort of interchangeable likeness in expression, that often gave to each the effect of being more like his brother than himself."

Again, two twin brothers, writing to me, after analysing their points of resemblance, which are close and numerous, and pointing out certain shades of difference, add—

"These seem to have marked us through life, though for a while, when we were first separated, the one to go to business, and the other to college, our respective characters were inverted; we both think that at that time we each ran into the character of the other. The proof of this consists in our own recollections, in our correspondence by letter, and in the views which we then took of matters in which we were interested."

In explanation of this apparent interchangeableness, we must recollect that no character is simple, and that in twins who strongly resemble each other, every expression in the one may be matched by a corresponding expression in the other, but it does not follow that the same expression should be the prevalent one in both cases. Now it is by their prevalent expression: that we should distinguish between the twins; consequently when one twin has temporarily the expression which is the prevalent one in his brother, he is apt to be mistaken for him. There are also cases where the development of the two twins is not strictly *pari passu;* they reach the same goal at the same time, but not by identical stages. Thus: A is born the larger, then B overtakes and surpasses A, and is in his turn overtaken by A, the end being that the twins, on reaching adult life, are of the same size. This process would aid in giving an interchangeable likeness at certain periods of their growth, and is undoubtedly due to nature more frequently than to nurture.

Among my thirty-five detailed cases of close similarity, there are no less than seven in which both twins suffered from some special ailment or had some exceptional peculiarity. One twin writes that she and her sister "have both the defect of not being able to come downstairs quickly, which, however, was not born with them, but came on at the age of twenty." Three pairs of twins have peculiarities in their fingers; in one case it consists in a slight congenital flexure of one of the joints of the little finger; it was inherited from a grandmother, but neither parents, nor brothers, nor sisters show the least trace of it. In another case the twins have a peculiar way of bending the fingers, and there was a faint tendency to the same peculiarity in the mother, but in her alone of all the family. In a third case, about which I made a few inquiries, which is given by Mr. Darwin, but is not included in my returns, there was no known family tendency to the peculiarity which was observed in the twins of having a crooked little finger. In another pair of twins, one was born ruptured, and the other became so at six months old. Two twins at the age of twenty-three were attacked by toothache, and the same tooth had to be extracted in each case. There are curious and close correspondences mentioned in the falling off of the hair. Two cases are mentioned of death from the same disease; one of which is very affecting. The outline of the story was that the twins were closely alike and singularly attached, and had identical tastes; they both obtained Government clerkships, and kept house together, when one sickened and died of Bright's disease, and the other also sickened of the same disease and died seven months later.

Both twins were apt to sicken at the same time in no less than nine out of the thirty-five cases. Either their illnesses, to which I refer, were non-contagious, or, if contagious, the twins caught them simultaneously; they did not catch them the one from the other. This implies so intimate a constitutional resemblance, that it is proper to give some quotations in evidence. Thus, the father of two twins says:—

"Their general health is closely alike; whenever one of them has an illness, the other invariably has the same within a day or two, and they usually recover in the same order. Such has been the case with whooping-cough, chicken-pox, and measles; also with slight bilious attacks, which they have successively. Latterly, they had a feverish attack at the same time."

Another parent of twins says:—

"If anything ails one of them, identical symptoms *nearly always* appear in the other; this has been singularly visible in two instances during the last two months. Thus, when in London, one fell ill with a violent attack of dysentery, and within twenty-four hours the other had precisely the same symptoms."

A medical man writes of twins with whom he is well acquainted:—

"Whilst I knew them, for a period of two years, there was not the slightest tendency towards a difference in body or mind; external influences seemed powerless to produce any dissimilarity."

The mother of two other twins, after describing how they were ill simultaneously up to the age of fifteen, adds, that they shed their first milk-teeth within a few hours of each other.

Trousseau has a very remarkable case (in the chapter on Asthma) in his important work *Clinique Médicale*. (In the edition of 1873 it is in vol. ii. p. 473.) It was quoted at length in the original French, in Mr. Darwin's *Variation under Domestication*, vol. ii. p. 252. The following is a translation:—

"I attended twin brothers so extraordinarily alike, that it was impossible for me to tell which was which, without seeing them side by side. But their physical likeness extended still deeper, for they had, so to speak, a yet more remarkable pathological resemblance. Thus, one of them, whom I saw at the Néothermes at Paris, suffering from rheumatic ophthalmia, said to me, 'At this instant my brother must be having an ophthalmia like mine;' and, as I had exclaimed against such an assertion, he showed me a few days afterwards a letter just received by him from his brother, who was at that time at Vienna, and who expressed himself in these words—'I have my ophthalmia; you must be having yours.' However singular this story may appear, the fact is none the less exact; it has not been told to me by others, but I have seen it myself; and I have seen other analogous cases in my practice. These twins were also asthmatic, and asthmatic to a frightful degree. Though born in Marseilles, they were never able to stay in that town, where their business affairs required them to go, without having an attack. Still more strange, it was sufficient for them to get away only as far as

Toulon in order to be cured of the attack caught at Marseilles. They travelled continually, and in all countries, on business affairs, and they remarked that certain localities were extremely hurtful to them, and that in others they were free from all asthmatic symptoms."

I do not like to pass over here a most dramatic tale in the *Psychologie Morbide* of Dr. J. Moreau (de Tours), Médecin de l'Hospice de Bicêtre. Paris, 1859, p. 172. He speaks "of two twin brothers who had been confined, on account of monomania, at Bicêtre":—

"Physically the two young men are so nearly alike that the one is easily mistaken for the other. Morally, their resemblance is no less complete, and is most remarkable in its details. Thus, their dominant ideas are absolutely the same. They both consider themselves subject to imaginary persecutions; the same enemies have sworn their destruction, and employ the same means to effect it. Both have hallucinations of hearing. They are both of them melancholy and morose; they never address a word to anybody, and will hardly answer the questions that others address to them. They always keep apart, and never communicate with one another. An extremely curious fact which has been frequently noted by the superintendents of their section of the hospital, and by myself, is this: From time to time, at very irregular intervals of two, three, and many months, without appreciable cause, and by the purely spontaneous effect of their illness, a very marked change takes place in the condition of the two brothers. Both of them, at the same time, and often on the same day, rouse themselves from their habitual stupor and prostration; they make the same complaints, and they come of their own accord to the physician, with an urgent request to be liberated. I have seen this strange thing occur, even when they were some miles apart, the one being at Bicêtre, and the other living at Saint-Anne."

I sent a copy of this passage to the principal authorities among the physicians to the insane in England, asking if they had ever witnessed any similar case. In reply, I have received three noteworthy instances, but none to be compared in their exact parallelism with that just given. The details of these three cases are painful, and it is not necessary to my general purpose that I should further allude to them.

There is another curious French case of insanity in twins, which was pointed out to me by Sir James Paget, described by Dr. Baume in the *Annales Médico-Psychologiques,* 4 série, vol. i., 1863, p. 312, of which the following is an abstract. The original contains a few more details, but is too long to quote: François and Martin, fifty years of age, worked as railroad contractors between Quimper and Châteaulin. Martin had twice slight attacks of insanity. On January 15 a box was robbed in which the twins had deposited their savings. On the night of January 23–24 both François (who lodged at Quimper) and Martin (who lived with his wife and children at St. Lorette, two leagues from Quimper) had the same dream at the same hour, three a.m., and both awoke with a violent start, calling out, "I have caught the thief! I have caught the thief! they are doing mischief to my brother!" They were both of them extremely agitated, and gave way to similar extravagances, dancing and leaping. Martin sprang on his grandchild, declaring that he was the thief, and would have strangled him if he had not been prevented; he then became steadily worse, complained of violent pains in his head, went out of doors on some excuse, and tried to drown himself in the river Steir, but was forcibly stopped by his son, who had watched and followed him. He was then taken to an asylum by gendarmes, where he died in three hours. François, on his part, calmed down on the morning of the 24th, and employed the day in inquiring about the robbery. By a strange chance, he crossed his brother's path at the moment when the latter was struggling with the gendarmes; then he himself became maddened, giving way to extravagant gestures and using incoherent language (similar to that of his brother). He then asked to be bled, which was done, and afterwards, declaring himself to be better, went out on the pretext of executing some commission, but really to drown himself in the River Steir, which he actually did, at the very spot where Martin had attempted to do the same thing a few hours previously.

The next point which I shall mention in illustration of the extremely close resemblance between certain twins is the similarity in the association of their ideas. No less than eleven out of the thirty-five cases testify to this. They make the same remarks on the same occasion, begin singing the same song at the same moment, and so on; or one would commence a sentence, and the other would finish it. An observant friend graphically described to me the effect produced on her by two such twins whom she had met casually. She said: "Their teeth grew alike, they spoke alike and together, and said the same things, and seemed just like one person." One of the most curious anecdotes that I have received concerning this similarity of ideas was that one twin, A, who happened to be at a town in Scotland, bought a set of champagne glasses which caught his attention, as a surprise for his brother B; while, at the same time, B, being in England, bought a similar set of precisely the same pattern as a surprise for A. Other anecdotes of a like kind have reached me about these twins.

The last point to which I shall allude regards the tastes and dispositions of the thirty-five pairs of twins. In sixteen cases—that is, in nearly one-half of them—these were described as closely similar; in the remaining nineteen they were much alike, but subject to certain named differences. These differences belonged almost wholly to such groups of qualities as these: The one was the more vigorous, fearless, energetic; the other was gentle, clinging, and timid; or the one was more ardent, the other more calm and placid; or again, the one was the more independent, original, and self-contained; the other the more generous, hasty, and vivacious. In short, the difference was that of intensity or energy in one or other of its protean forms; it did not extend more deeply into the structure of the characters. The more vivacious might be subdued by ill health, until he assumed the character of the other; or the latter might be raised by excellent health to that of the former. The difference was in the key-note, not in the melody.

It follows from what has been said concerning the similar dispositions of the twins, the similarity in the associations of their ideas, of their special ailments, and of their illnesses generally, that the resemblances are not superficial, but extremely intimate. I have only two cases of a strong bodily resemblance being accompanied by mental diversity, and one case only of the converse kind. It must be remembered that the conditions which govern extreme likeness between twins are not the same as those between ordinary brothers and sisters, and that it would be incorrect to conclude from what has just been said about the twins that mental and bodily likeness are invariably co-ordinate, such being by no means the case.

We are now in a position to understand that the phrase "close similarity" is no exaggeration, and to realise the value of the evidence I am about to adduce. Here are thirty-five cases of twins who were "closely alike" in body and mind when they were young, and who have been reared exactly alike up to their early manhood and womanhood. Since then the conditions of their lives have changed; what change of Nurture has produced the most variation?

It was with no little interest that I searched the records of the thirty-five cases for an answer; and they gave an answer that was not altogether direct, but it was distinct, and not at all what I had expected. They showed me that in some cases the resemblance of body and mind had continued unaltered up to old age, notwithstanding very different conditions of life; and they showed in the other cases that the parents ascribed such dissimilarity as there was, wholly or almost wholly to some form of illness. In four cases it was scarlet fever; in a fifth, typhus; in a sixth, a slight effect was ascribed to a nervous fever; in a seventh it was the effect of an Indian climate; in an eighth, an illness (unnamed) of nine months' duration; in a ninth, varicose veins; in a tenth, a bad fracture of the leg, which prevented all active exercise afterwards; and there were three additional instances of undefined forms of ill health. It will be sufficient to quote one of the returns; in this the father writes:

"At birth they were *exactly* alike, except that one was born with a bad varicose affection, the effect of which had been to prevent any violent exercise, such as dancing or running, and, as she has grown older, to make her more serious and thoughtful. Had it not been for this infirmity, I think the two would have been as exactly alike as it is possible for two women to be, both mentally and physically; even now they are constantly mistaken for one another."

In only a very few cases is some allusion made to the dissimilarity being partly due to the combined action of many small influences, and in none of the thirty-five cases is it largely, much less wholly, ascribed to that cause. In not a single instance have I met with a word about the growing dissimilarity being due to the action of the firm free-will of one or both of the twins, which had triumphed over natural tendencies; and yet a large proportion of my correspondents happen to be clergymen, whose bent of mind is opposed, as I feel assured from the tone of their letters, to a necessitarian view of life.

It has been remarked that a growing diversity between twins may be ascribed to the tardy development of naturally diverse qualities; but we have a right, upon the evidence I have received, to go farther than this. We have seen that a few twins retain their close resemblance through life; in other words, instances do exist of an apparently thorough similarity of nature, in which such difference of external circumstances as may be consistent with the ordinary conditions of the same social rank and country do not create dissimilarity. Positive evidence, such as this, cannot be outweighed by any amount of negative evidence. Therefore, in those cases where there is a growing diversity, and where no external cause can be assigned either by the twins themselves or by their family for it, we may feel sure that it must be chiefly or altogether due to a want of thorough similarity in their nature. Nay, further, in some cases it is distinctly affirmed that the growing dissimilarity can be accounted for in no other way. We may, therefore, broadly conclude that the only circumstance, within the range of those by which persons of similar conditions of life are affected, that is capable of producing a marked effect on the character of adults, is illness or some accident which causes physical infirmity. The twins who closely resembled each other in childhood and early youth, and were reared under not very dissimilar conditions, either grow unlike through the development of natural characteristics which had lain dormant at first, or else they continue their lives, keeping time like two watches, hardly to be thrown out of accord except by some physical jar. Nature is far stronger than Nurture within the limited range that I have been careful to assign to the latter.

The effect of illness, as shown by these replies, is great, and well deserves further consideration. It appears that the constitution of youth is not so elastic as we are apt to think, but that an attack, say of scarlet fever, leaves a permanent mark, easily to be measured by the present method of comparison. This recalls an impression made strongly on my mind several years ago, by the sight of some curves drawn by a mathematical friend. He took monthly measurements of the circumference of his children's heads during the first few years of their lives, and he laid down the successive measurements on the successive lines of a piece of ruled paper, by taking the edge of the paper as a base. He then joined the free ends of the lines, and so obtained a curve of growth. These curves had, on the whole, that regularity of sweep that might have been expected, but each of them showed occasional halts, like the landing-places on a long flight of stairs. The development had been arrested by something, and was not made up for by after growth. Now, on the same piece of paper my friend had also registered the various infantine illnesses of the children, and corresponding to each illness was one of these halts. There remained no doubt in my mind that, if these illnesses had been warded off, the development of the children would have been increased by almost the precise amount lost in these halts. In other words, the disease had drawn largely upon the capital, and not only on the income, of their constitutions. I hope these remarks may induce some men of science to repeat similar experiments on their children of the future. They may compress two years of a child's history on one side of a ruled half-sheet of foolscap paper, if

they cause each successive line to stand for a successive month, beginning from the birth of the child; and if they economise space by laying, not the 0-inch division of the tape against the edge of the pages, but, say, the 10-inch division.

The steady and pitiless march of the hidden weaknesses in our constitutions, through illness to death, is painfully revealed by these histories of twins. We are too apt to look upon illness and death as capricious events, and there are some who ascribe them to the direct effect of supernatural interference, whereas the fact of the maladies of two twins being continually alike shows that illness and death are necessary incidents in a regular sequence of constitutional changes beginning at birth, and upon which external circumstances have, on the whole, very small effect. In cases where the maladies of the twins are continually alike, the clocks of their two lives move regularly on at the same rate, governed by their internal mechanism. When the hands approach the hour, there are sudden clicks, followed by a whirring of wheels; the moment that they touch it, the strokes fall. Necessitarians may derive new arguments from the life-histories of twins.

We will now consider the converse side of our subject, which appears to me even the more important of the two. Hitherto we have investigated cases where the similarity at first was close, but afterwards became less; now we will examine those in which there was great dissimilarity at first, and will see how far an identity of nurture in childhood and youth tended to assimilate them. As has been already mentioned, there is a large proportion of cases of sharply-contrasted characteristics, both of body and mind, among twins I have twenty such cases, given with much detail. It is a fact that extreme dissimilarity, such as existed between Esau and Jacob, is a no less marked peculiarity in twins of the same sex than extreme similarity. On this curious point, and on much else in the history of twins, I have many remarks to make, but this is not the place to make them.

The evidence given by the twenty cases above mentioned is absolutely accordant, so that the character of the whole may be exactly conveyed by a few quotations.

(1) One parent says:—"They have had *exactly the same nurture* from their birth up to the present time; they are both perfectly healthy and strong, yet they are otherwise as dissimilar as two boys could be, physically, mentally, and in their emotional nature."

(2) "I can answer most decidedly that the twins have been perfectly dissimilar in character,

habits, and likeness from the moment of their birth to the present time, though they were nursed by the same woman, went to school together, and were never separated till the age of fifteen."

(3) "They have never been separated, never the least differently treated in food, clothing, or education; both teethed at the same time, both had measles, whooping-cough, and scarlatina at the same time, and neither had had any other serious illness. Both are and have been exceedingly healthy, and have good abilities, yet they differ as much from each other in mental cast as any one of my family differs from another."

(4) "Very dissimilar in body and mind: the one is quiet, retiring, and slow but sure; good-tempered, but disposed to be sulky when provoked;—the other is quick, vivacious, forward, acquiring easily and forgetting soon; quick-tempered and choleric, but quickly forgiving and forgetting. They have been educated together and never separated."

(5) "They were never alike either in body or mind, and their dissimilarity increases daily. The external influences have been identical; they have never been separated."

(6) "The two sisters are very different in ability and disposition. The one is retiring, but firm and determined; she has no taste for music or drawing. The other is of an active, excitable temperament: she displays an unusual amount of quickness and talent, and is passionately fond of music and drawing. From infancy, they have been rarely separated even at school, and as children visiting their friends, they always went together."

(7) "They have been treated exactly alike; both were brought up by hand; they have been under the same nurse and governess from their birth, and they are very fond of each other. Their increasing dissimilarity must be ascribed to a natural difference of mind and character, as there has been nothing in their treatment to account for it."

(8) "They are as different as possible. [A minute and unsparing analysis of the characters of the two twins is given by their father, most instructive to read, but impossible to publish without the certainty of wounding the feelings of one of the twins, if these pages should chance to fall under his eyes.] They were brought up entirely by hand, that is, on cow's milk, and treated by one nurse in precisely the same manner."

(9) "The home-training and influence were precisely the same, and therefore I consider the dissimilarity to be accounted for almost entirely by innate disposition and by causes over which we have no control."

(10) "This case is, I should think, somewhat remarkable for dissimilarity in physique as well as for strong contrast in character. They have been unlike in body and mind throughout their lives. Both were reared in a country house, and both were at the same schools till æt. 16."

(11) "Singularly unlike in body and mind from babyhood; in looks, dispositions, and tastes they are quite different. I think I may say the dissimilarity was innate, and developed more by time than circumstance."

(12) "We were never in the least degree alike. I should say my sister's and my own character are diametrically opposed, and have been utterly different from our birth, though a very strong affection subsists between us."

(13) The father remarks:—"They were curiously different in body and mind from their birth."

The surviving twin (a senior wrangler of Cambridge) adds:—"A fact struck all our school contemporaries, that my brother and I were complementary, so to speak, in point of ability and disposition. He was contemplative, poetical, and literary to a remarkable degree, showing great power in that line. I was practical, mathematical, and linguistic. Between us we should have made a very decent sort of a man."

I could quote others just as strong as these, in some of which the above phrase "complementary" also appears, while I have not a single case in which my correspondents speak of originally dissimilar characters having become assimilated through identity of nurture. However, a somewhat exaggerated estimate of dissimilarity may be due to the tendency of relatives to dwell unconsciously on distinctive peculiarities, and to disregard the far more numerous points of likeness that would first attract the notice of a stranger. Thus in case 11 I find the remark, "Strangers see a strong likeness between them, but none who knows them well can perceive it." Instances are common of slight acquaintances mistaking members, and especially daughters of a family, for one another, between whom intimate friends can barely discover a resemblance. Still, making reasonable allowance for unintentional exaggeration, the impression that all this evidence leaves on the mind is one of some wonder whether nurture can do anything at all, beyond giving instruction and professional training. It emphatically corroborates and goes far beyond the conclusions to which we had already been driven by the cases of similarity. In those, the causes of divergence began to act about the period of adult life, when the characters had become somewhat fixed; but here the causes conducive to assimilation began to act from the earliest moment of the existence of the twins, when the disposition was most pliant, and they were continuous until the period of adult life. There is no escape from the conclusion that nature prevails enormously over nurture when the differences of nurture do not exceed what is commonly to be found among persons of the same rank of society and in the same country. My fear is, that my evidence may seem to prove too much, and be discredited on that account, as it appears contrary to all experience that nurture should go for so little. But experience is often fallacious in ascribing great effects to trifling circumstances. Many a person has amused himself with throwing bits of stick into a tiny brook and watching their progress; how they are arrested, first by one chance obstacle, then by another; and again, how their onward course is facilitated by a combination of circumstances. He might ascribe much importance to each of these events, and think how largely the destiny of the stick had been governed by a series of trifling accidents. Nevertheless all the sticks succeed in passing down the current, and in the long-run, they travel at nearly the same rate. So it is with life, in respect to the several accidents which seem to have had a great effect upon our careers. The one element, that varies in different individuals, but is constant in each of them, is the natural tendency; it corresponds to the current in the stream, and inevitably asserts itself.

Much stress is laid on the persistence of moral impressions made in childhood, and the conclusion is drawn, that the effects of early teaching must be important in a corresponding degree. I acknowledge the fact, so far as has been explained in the chapter on Early Sentiments, but there is a considerable set-off on the other side. Those teachings that conform to the natural aptitudes of the child leave much more enduring marks than others. Now both the teachings and the natural aptitudes of the child are usually derived from its parents. They are able to understand the ways of one another more intimately than is possible to persons not of the same blood, and the child instinctively assimilates the habits and ways of thought of its parents. Its disposition is "educated" by them, in the true sense of the word; that is to say, it is evoked, not formed by them. On these grounds I ascribe the persistence of many habits that date from early home education, to the peculiarities of the instructors rather than to the period when the instruction was given. The marks left on the memory by the instructions of a foster-mother are soon sponged clean away. Consider the history of the cuckoo, which is reared exclusively by foster-mothers. It is probable that nearly every young cuckoo, during a series of many hundred generations, has been brought up in a family whose language is a chirp and a twitter. But the cuckoo cannot or will not adopt that language, or any other of the habits of its foster-parents. It leaves its birthplace as soon as it is able, and finds out its own kith and kin, and identifies itself henceforth with them. So utterly are its earliest instructions in an alien bird-language neglected, and so completely is its new education successful, that the note of the cuckoo tribe is singularly correct.

SELECTION AND RACE

The fact of an individual being naturally gifted with high qualities, may be due either to his being an exceptionally good specimen of a poor race, or an average specimen of a high one. The difference of origin would betray itself in his descendants; they would revert towards the typical centre of their race, deteriorating in the first case but not in the second. The two cases, though theoretically distinct, are confused in reality, owing to the frequency with which exceptional personal qualities connote the departure of the entire nature of the individual from his ancestral type, and the formation of a new strain having its own typical centre. It is hardly necessary to add that it is in this indirect way that natural selection improves a race. The two events of selection and difference of race ought, however, to be carefully distinguished in broad practical considerations, while the frequency of their concurrence is borne in mind and allowed for.

So long as the race remains radically the same, the stringent selection of the best specimens to rear and breed from, can never lead to any permanent result. The attempt to raise the standard of such a race is like the labour of Sisyphus in rolling his stone uphill; let the effort be relaxed for a moment, and the stone will roll back. Whenever a new typical centre appears, it is as though there was a facet upon the lower surface of the stone, on which it is capable of resting without rolling back. It affords a temporary sticking-point in the forward progress of evolution.

The causes that check the unlimited improvement of

highly-bred animals, so long as the race remains unchanged, are many and absolute.

In the first place there is an increasing delicacy of constitution; the growing fineness of limb and structure end, after a few generations, in fragility. Overbred animals have little stamina; they resemble in this respect the "weedy" colts so often reared from first-class racers. One can perhaps see in a general way why this should be so. Each individual is the outcome of a vast number of organic elements of the most various species, just as some nation might be the outcome of a vast number of castes of individuals, each caste monopolising a special pursuit. Banish a number of the humbler castes—the bakers, the bricklayers, and the smiths, and the nation would soon come to grief. This is what is done in high breeding; certain qualities are bred for, and the rest are diminished as far as possible, but they cannot be dispensed with entirely.

The next difficulty lies in the diminished fertility of highly-bred animals. It is not improbable that its cause is of the same character as that of the delicacy of their constitution. Together with infertility is combined some degree of sexual indifference, or when passion is shown, it is not unfrequently for some specimen of a coarser type. This is certainly the case with horses and with dogs.

It will be easily understood that these difficulties, which are so formidable in the case of plants and animals, which we can mate as we please and destroy when we please, would make the maintenance of a highly-selected breed of men an impossibility.

Whenever a low race is preserved under conditions of life that exact a high level of efficiency, it must be subjected to rigorous selection. The few best specimens of that race can alone be allowed to become parents, and not many of their descendants can be allowed to live. On the other hand, if a higher race be substituted for the low one, all this terrible misery disappears. The most merciful form of what I ventured to call "eugenics" would consist in watching for the indications of superior strains or races, and in so favouring them that their progeny shall outnumber and gradually replace that of the old one. Such strains are of no infrequent occurrence. It is easy to specify families who are characterised by strong resemblances, and whose features and character are usually prepotent over those of their wives or husbands in their joint offspring, and who are at the same time as prolific as the average of their class. These strains can be conveniently studied in the families of exiles, which, for obvious reasons, are easy to trace in their various branches.

The debt that most countries owe to the race of men whom they received from one another as immigrants, whether leaving their native country of their own free will, or as exiles on political or religious grounds, has been often pointed out, and may, I think, be accounted for as follows:—The fact of a man leaving his compatriots, or so irritating them that they compel him to go, is fair evidence that either he or they, or both, feel that his character is alien to theirs. Exiles are also on the whole men of considerable force of character; a quiet man would endure and succumb, he would not have energy to transplant himself or to become so conspicuous as to be an object of general attack. We may justly infer from this, that exiles are on the whole men of exceptional and energetic natures, and it is especially from such men as these that new strains of race are likely to proceed.

INFLUENCE OF MAN UPON RACE

The influence of man upon the nature of his own race has already been very large, but it has not been intelligently directed, and has in many instances done great harm. Its action has been by invasions and migration of races, by war and massacre, by wholesale deportation of population, by emigration, and by many social customs which have a silent but widespread effect.

There exists a sentiment, for the most part quite unreasonable, against the gradual extinction of an inferior race. It rests on some confusion between the race and the individual, as if the destruction of a race was equivalent to the destruction of a large number of men. It is nothing of the kind when the process of extinction works silently and slowly through the earlier marriage of members of the superior race, through their greater vitality under equal stress, through their better chances of getting a livelihood, or through their prepotency in mixed marriages. That the members of an inferior class should dislike being elbowed out of the way is another matter; but it may be somewhat brutally argued that whenever two individuals struggle for a single place, one must yield, and that there will be no more unhappiness on the whole, if the inferior yield to the superior than conversely, whereas the world will be permanently enriched by the success of the superior. The conditions of happiness are, however, too complex to be disposed of by *à priori* argument; it is safest to appeal to observation. I think it could be easily shown that when the differences between the races is not so great as to divide them into obviously different classes, and where their language, education, and general interests are the same, the substitution may take place gradually without any unhappiness. Thus the movements of commerce have introduced fresh and vigorous blood into various parts of England: the new-comers have intermarried with the residents, and their characteristics have been prepotent in the descendants of the mixed marriages. I have referred in the earlier part of the book to the changes of type in the English nature that have occurred during the last few hundred years. These have been effected so silently that we only know of them by the results.

One of the most misleading of words is that of "aborigines." Its use dates from the time when the cosmogony was thought to be young and life to be of very recent appearance. Its usual meaning seems to be derived from the supposition that nations disseminated themselves like colonists from a common centre about four thousand years, say 120 generations ago, and thence-forward occupied their lands undisturbed until the very recent historic period with which the narrator deals, when some invading host drove out the "aborigines." This idyllic view of the march of events is contradicted by ancient sepulchral remains, by language, and by the habits of those modern barbarians whose history we know. There are probably hardly any spots on the earth that have not, within the last few thousand years, been tenanted by very different races; none hardly that have not been tenanted by very different tribes having the character of at least subraces.

The absence of a criterion to distinguish between races and sub-races, and our ethnological ignorance generally, makes it impossible to offer more than a very off-hand estimate of the average variety of races in the different countries of the world. I have, however, endeavoured to form one, which I give with much hesitation, knowing how very little it is worth. I registered the usually recognised races inhabiting each of upwards of twenty countries, and who at the same time formed at least half per cent of the population. It was, I am perfectly aware, a very rough proceeding, so rough that for the United Kingdom I ignored the prehistoric types and accepted only the three headings of British, Low Dutch, and Norman-French. Again, as regards India I registered as follows:—Forest tribes (numerous), Dravidian (three principal divisions), Early Arian, Tartar (numerous, including Afghans), Arab, and lastly European, on account of their political importance, notwithstanding the fewness of their numbers. Proceeding in this off-hand way, and after considering the results, the broad conclusion to which I arrived was that on the average at least three different recognised races were to be found in every moderately-sized district on the earth's surface. The materials were far too scanty to enable any idea to be formed of the rate of change in the relative numbers

of the constituent races in each country, and still less to estimate the secular changes of type in those races.

It may be well to take one or two examples of intermixture. Spain was occupied in the earliest historic times by at least two races, of whom we know very little; it was afterwards colonised here and there by Phœnicians in its southern ports, and by Greeks in its eastern. In the third century B.C. it was invaded by the Carthaginians, who conquered and held a large part of it, but were afterwards supplanted by the Romans, who ruled it more or less completely for 700 years. It was invaded in the fifth century A.D. by a succession of German tribes, and was finally completely overrun by the Visigoths, who ruled it for more than 200 years. Then came the invasion of the Moors, who rapidly conquered the whole of the Peninsula up to the mountains of Asturias, where the Goths still held their own, and whence they issued from time to time and ultimately recovered the country. The present population consists of the remnants of one or more tribes of ancient Iberians, of the still more ancient Basques, and of relics of all the invaders who have just been named. There is, besides, a notable proportion of Gypsies and not a few Jews.

This is obviously a most heterogeneous mixture, but to fully appreciate the diversity of its origin the several elements should be traced farther back towards their sources. Thus, the Moors are principally descendants of Arabs, who flooded the northern provinces of Africa in successive waves of emigration eastwards, both before and after the Hegira, partly combining with the Berbers as they went, and partly displacing them from the littoral districts and driving them to the oases of the Sahara, whence they in their turn displaced the Negro population, whom they drove down to the Soudan. The Gypsies, according to Sir Henry Rawlinson,[2] came from the Indo-Scythic tribes who inhabited the mouths of the Indus, and began to migrate northward, from the fourth century onward. They settled in the Chaldean marshes, assumed independence and defied the caliph. In A.D. 831 the grandson of Haroun al-Raschid sent a large expedition against them, which, after slaughtering ten thousand, deported the whole of the remainder first to Baghdad and thence onwards to Persia. They continued unmanageable in their new home, and were finally transplanted to the Cilician frontier in Asia Minor, and established there as a military colony to guard the passes of the Taurus. In A.D. 962 the Greeks, having obtained some temporary successes, drove the Gypsies back more into the interior, whence they gradually moved towards the Hellespont under the pressure of the advancing Seljukians, during the twelfth and thirteenth centuries. They then crossed over to Europe and gradually overspread it, where they are now estimated to number more than three millions.

It must not be supposed that emigration on a large scale implies even a moderate degree of civilisation among those who emigrate, because the process has been frequently traced among the more barbarous tribes, to say nothing of the evidence largely derived from ancient burial-places. My own impression of the races in South Africa was one of a continual state of ferment and change, of the rapid development of some clan here and of the complete or almost complete suppression of another clan there. The well-known history of the rise of the Zulus and the destruction of their neighbours is a case in point. In the country with which I myself was familiar the changes had been numerous and rapid in the preceding few years, and there were undoubted signs of much more important substitutions of race in bygone times. The facts were briefly these: Damara Land was inhabited by pastoral tribes of the brown Bantu race who were in continual war with various alternations of fortune, and the several tribes had special characteristics that were readily appreciated by themselves. On the tops of the escarped hills lived a fugitive black people speaking a vile dialect of Hottentot, and families of yellow Bushmen were found in the lowlands wherever the country was unsuited for the pastoral Damaras. Lastly, the steadily encroaching Namaquas, a superior Hottentot race, lived on the edge of the district. They had very much more civilisation than the Bushmen, and more than the Damaras, and they contained a large infusion of Dutch blood.

The interpretation of all this was obviously that the land had been tenanted a long time ago by Negroes, that an invasion of Bushmen drove the Negroes to the hills, and that the supremacy of these lasted so long that the Negroes lost their own language and acquired that of the Bushmen. Then an invasion of a tribe of Bantu race supplanted the Bushmen, and the Bantus, after endless struggles among themselves, were being pushed aside at the time I visited them by the incoming Namaquas, who themselves are a mixed race. This is merely a sample of Africa; everywhere there are evidences of changing races.

The last 300 or 400 years, say the last ten generations of mankind, have witnessed changes of population on the largest scale, by the extension of races long resident in Europe to the temperate regions of Asia, Africa, America, and Australasia.

Siberia was barely known to the Russians of nine generations ago, but since that time it has been continuously overspread by their colonists, soldiers, political exiles, and transported criminals; already some two-thirds of its population are Sclaves.

In South Africa the settlement at the Cape of Good Hope is barely six generations old, yet during that time a curious and continuous series of changes has taken place, resulting in the substitution of an alien population for the Hottentots in the south and the Bantus in the north. One-third of it is white, consisting of Dutch, English, descendants of French Huguenot refugees, some Germans and Portuguese, and the remainder is a strange medley of Hottentot, Bantu, Malay, and Negro elements. In North Africa Egypt has become infiltrated with Greeks, Italians, Frenchmen, and Englishmen during the last two generations, and Algeria with Frenchmen.

In North America the change has been most striking, from a sparse Indian population of hunters into that of the present inhabitants of the United States and Canada; the former of these, with its total of fifty millions inhabitants, already contains more than forty-three millions of whites, chiefly of English origin; that is more of European blood than is to be found in any one of the five great European kingdoms of England, France, Italy, Germany, and Austria, and less than that of Russia alone. The remainder are chiefly black, the descendants of slaves imported from Africa. In the Dominion of Canada, with its much smaller population of four millions, there has been a less, but still a complete, swamping of the previous Indian element by incoming whites.

In South America, and thence upwards to Mexico inclusive, the population has been infiltrated in some parts and transformed in others, by Spanish blood and by that of the Negroes whom they introduced, so that not one half of its population can be reckoned as of pure Indian descent.

The West Indian Islands have had their population absolutely swept away since the time of the Spanish Conquest, except in a few rare instances, and African Negroes have been substituted for them.

Australia and New Zealand tell much the same tale as Canada. A native population has been almost extinguished in the former and is swamped in the latter, under the pressure of an immigrant population of Europeans, which is now twelve times as numerous as the Maories. The time during which this great change has been effected is less than that covered by three generations.

To this brief sketch of changes of population in very recent periods, I might add the wave of Arab admixture that has extended from Egypt and the northern provinces of Africa into the Soudan, and that of the yellow races of China, who have already made their industrial and social influence felt in many distant regions, and who bid fair hereafter, when certain of their peculiar religious fancies shall have fallen into decay, to become one of the most effective of the colonising nations, and who may, as I trust, extrude hereafter the coarse and lazy Negro from at least the metaliferous regions of tropical Africa.

It is clear from what has been said, that men of former generations have exercised enormous influence over the human stock of the present day, and that the average humanity of the world now and in future years is and will be very different to what it would have been if the action of our forefathers had been different. The power in man of varying the future human stock vests a great responsibility in the hands of each fresh generation, which has not yet been recognised at its just importance, nor deliberately employed. It is foolish to fold the hands and to say that nothing can be done, inasmuch as social forces and self-interests are too strong to be resisted. They need not be resisted; they can be guided. It is one thing to check the course of a huge steam vessel by the shock of a sudden encounter when she is going at full speed in the wrong direction, and another to cause her to change her course slowly and gently by a slight turn of the helm. Nay, a ship may be made to describe a half circle, and to end by following a course exactly opposite to the first, without attracting the notice of the passengers.

CONCLUSION

It remains to sketch in outline the principal conclusions to which we seem to be driven by the results of the various inquiries contained in this volume, and by what we know on allied topics from the works of others.

We cannot but recognise the vast variety of natural faculty, useful and harmful, in members of the same race, and much more in the human family at large, all of which tend to be transmitted by inheritance. Neither can we fail to observe that the faculties of men generally, are unequal to the requirements of a high and growing civilisation. This is principally owing to their entire ancestry having lived up to recent times under very uncivilised conditions, and to the somewhat capricious distribution in late times of inherited wealth, which affords various degrees of immunity from the usual selective agencies.

In solution of the question whether a continual improvement in education might not compensate for a sta-

tionary or even retrograde condition of natural gifts, I made inquiry into the life history of twins, which resulted in proving the vastly preponderating effects of nature over nurture.

The fact that the very foundation and outcome of the human mind is dependent on race, and that the qualities of races vary, and therefore that humanity taken as a whole is not fixed but variable, compels us to reconsider what may be the true place and function of man in the order of the world. I have examined this question freely from many points of view, because whatever may be the vehemence with which particular opinions are insisted upon, its solution is unquestionably doubtful. There is a wide and growing conviction among truth-seeking, earnest, humble-minded, and thoughtful men, both in this country and abroad, that our cosmic relations are by no means so clear and simple as they are popularly supposed to be, while the worthy and intelligent teachers of various creeds, who have strong persuasions on the character of those relations, do not concur in their several views.

The results of the inquiries I have made into certain alleged forms of our relations with the unseen world do not, so far as they go, confirm the common doctrines. One, for example, on the objective efficacy of prayer[3] was decidedly negative. It showed that while contradicting the commonly expressed doctrine, it concurred with the almost universal practical opinion of the present day. Another inquiry into visions showed that, however ill explained they may still be, they belong for the most part, if not altogether, to an order of phenomena which no one dreams in other cases of calling supernatural. Many investigations concur in showing the vast multiplicity of mental operations that are in simultaneous action, of which only a minute part falls within the ken of consciousness, and suggest that much of what passes for supernatural is due to one portion of our mind being contemplated by another portion of it, as if it had been that of another person. The term "individuality" is in fact a most misleading word.

I do not for a moment wish to imply that the few inquiries published in this volume exhaust the list of those that might be made, for I distinctly hold the contrary, but I refer to them in corroboration of the previous assertion that our relations with the unseen world are different to those we are commonly taught to believe.

In our doubt as to the character of our mysterious relations with the unseen ocean of actual and potential life by which we are surrounded, the generally accepted fact of the solidarity of the universe—that is, of the intimate connections between distant parts that bind it together as a whole—justifies us, I think, in looking upon ourselves as members of a vast system which in one of its aspects resembles a cosmic republic.

On the one hand, we know that evolution has proceeded during an enormous time on this earth, under, so far as we can gather, a system of rigorous causation, with no economy of time or of instruments, and with no show of special ruth for those who may in pure ignorance have violated the conditions of life.

On the other hand, while recognising the awful mystery of conscious existence and the inscrutable background of evolution, we find that as the foremost outcome of many and long birth-throes, intelligent and kindly man finds himself in being. He knows how petty he is, but he also perceives that he stands here on this particular earth, at this particular time, as the heir of untold ages and in the van of circumstance. He ought therefore, I think, to be less diffident than he is usually instructed to be, and to rise to the conception that he has a considerable function to perform in the order of events, and that his exertions are needed. It seems to me that he should look upon himself more as a freeman, with power of shaping the course of future humanity, and that he should look upon himself less as the subject of a despotic government, in which case it would be his chief merit to depend wholly upon what had been regulated for him, and to render abject obedience.

The question then arises as to the way in which man can assist in the order of events. I reply, by furthering the course of evolution. He may use his intelligence to discover and expedite the changes that are necessary to adapt circumstance to race and race to circumstance, and his kindly sympathy will urge him to effect them mercifully.

When we begin to inquire, with some misgiving perhaps, as to the evidence that man has present power to influence the quality of future humanity, we soon discover that his past influence in that direction has been very large indeed. It has been exerted hitherto for other ends than that which is now contemplated, such as for conquest or emigration, also through social conditions whose effects upon race were imperfectly foreseen. There can be no doubt that the hitherto unused means of his influence are also numerous and great. I have not cared to go much into detail concerning these, but restricted myself to a few broad considerations, as by showing how largely the balance of population becomes affected by the earlier marriages of some of its classes, and by pointing out the great influence that endowments have had in checking the marriage of monks and scholars, and therefore the yet larger influence they might be

expected to have if they were directed not to thwart but to harmonise with natural inclination, by promoting early marriages in the classes to be favoured. I also showed that a powerful influence might flow from a public recognition in early life of the true value of the probability of future performance, as based on the past performance of the ancestors of the child. It is an element of forecast, in addition to that of present personal merit, which has yet to be appraised and recognised. Its recognition would attract assistance in various ways, impossible now to specify, to the young families of those who were most likely to stock the world with healthy, moral, intelligent, and fair-natured citizens. The stream of charity is not unlimited, and it is requisite for the speedier evolution of a more perfect humanity that it should be so distributed as to favour the best-adapted races. I have not spoken of the repression of the rest, believing that it would ensue indirectly as a matter of course; but I may add that few would deserve better of their country than those who determine to live celibate lives, through a reasonable conviction that their issue would probably be less fitted than the generality to play their part as citizens.

It would be easy to add to the number of possible agencies by which the evolution of a higher humanity might be furthered, but it is premature to do so until the importance of attending to the improvement of our race shall have been so well established in the popular mind that a discussion of them would be likely to receive serious consideration.

It is hardly necessary to insist on the certainty that our present imperfect knowledge of the limitations and conditions of hereditary transmission will be steadily added to; but I would call attention again to the serious want of adequate materials for study in the form of life-histories. It is fortunately the case that many of the rising medical practitioners of the foremost rank are become strongly impressed with the necessity of possessing them, not only for the better knowledge of the theory of disease, but for the personal advantage of their patients, whom they now have to treat less appropriately than they otherwise would, through ignorance of their hereditary tendencies and of their illnesses in past years, the medical details of which are rarely remembered by the patient, even if he ever knew them. With the help of so powerful a personal motive for keeping life-histories, and of so influential a body as the medical profession to advocate its being done,[4] and to show how to do it, there is considerable hope that the want of materials to which I have alluded will gradually be supplied.

To sum up in a few words. The chief result of these

Inquiries has been to elicit the religious significance of the doctrine of evolution. It suggests an alteration in our mental attitude, and imposes a new moral duty. The new mental attitude is one of a greater sense of moral freedom, responsibility, and opportunity; the new duty which is supposed to be exercised concurrently with, and not in opposition to the old ones upon which the social fabric depends, is an endeavour to further evolution, especially that of the human race.

NOTES

1. I take this opportunity of withdrawing an anecdote, happily of no great importance, published in *Men of Science,* p. 14, about a man personating his twin brother for a joke at supper, and not being discovered by his wife. It was told me on good authority; but I have reason to doubt the fact, as the story is not known to the son of one of the twins. However, the twins in question were extraordinarily alike, and I have many anecdotes about them sent me by the latter gentleman.

2. *Proceedings of the Royal Geographical Society,* vol. i. This account of the routes of the Gypsies is by no means universally accepted, nor, indeed, was offered as a complete solution of the problem of their migration, but it will serve to show how complex that problem is.

3. Not reprinted in this edition.

4. See an address on the Collective Investigation of Disease, by Sir William Gull, *British Medical Journal,* January 27, 1883, p. 143; also the following address by Sir James Paget, p. 144.

Human Development

19

MILICENT W. SHINN

Milicent Washburn Shinn (1858–1940) lived among meadowlarks and wildflowers on the family ranch in California for most her life. Attending the University of California in 1874, the second year it began admitting women, she thoroughly enjoyed her time as a student and scholarly pursuits. She then returned home to care for her parents and tutor her younger brother, choosing the ranch over an offer to attend the Harvard Annex, a newly constituted but unofficial series of private courses that allowed women access to graduate studies in Cambridge. In 1882, Shinn began editing a local literary magazine, *Overland Monthly*, motivated, in part, by a desire to encourage fellow Californians to take up the literary life, which she thought might improve society and the basic moral fiber of the youth. Ruth, Shinn's niece and the subject of her book *The Biography of a Baby*, was born in 1890, the center of doting attention for the entire family. Shinn was fascinated by the child, but, unlike most aunts, had what she described as, "the notebook habit from college and editorial days, and jotted things down as I watched, till quite unexpectedly I found myself in possession of a large mass of data." Shinn was eventually convinced of the value of her notes, begun as a private project, and returned for graduate study at Berkeley in 1894. Her various publications, including the popular *Biography*, were greeted with wild enthusiasm by scholars, both in America and abroad. After becoming the first woman to receive a Ph.D. from the University of California at Berkeley, Shinn returned to the family to care for her aging parents, a responsibility she refused to share with her two brothers or sister-in-law. Her sense of family responsibility extended to tutoring her brother's four children, as she had tutored that brother in his youth, and maintaining copious correspondence with the extended family.

THE BIOGRAPHY OF A BABY

I

Baby Biographies in General

"IT is a well recognized fact in the history of science that the very subjects which concern our dearest interests, which lie nearest our hearts, are exactly those which are the last to submit to scientific methods, to be reduced to scientific law. Thus it has come to pass that while babies are born and grow up in every household, and while the gradual unfolding of their faculties has been watched with the keenest interest and intensest joy by intelligent and even scientific fathers and mothers from time immemorial, yet very little has yet been done in the scientific study of this most important of all possible subjects—the ontogenetic evolution of the faculties of the human mind.

"Only in the last few years has scientific attention been drawn to the subject at all. Its transcendent importance has already enlisted many observers, but on account of the great complexity of the phenomena, and still more the intrinsic difficulty of their interpretation, scientific progress has scarcely yet commenced.

"What is wanted most of all in this, as in every sci-

From Milicent W. Shinn, "Baby Biographies in General," and "The Dawn of Intelligence." In *The Biography of a Baby* (pp. 1–19, 161–181). New York: Houghton Mifflin, 1900.

ence, is *a body of carefully observed facts.* But to be an accomplished investigator in this field requires a rare combination of qualities. There must be a wide intelligence combined with patience in observing and honesty in recording. There must be also an earnest scientific spirit, a loving sympathy with the subject of investigation, yet under watchful restraint, lest it cloud the judgment; keenness of intuitive perception, yet soberness of judgment in interpretation."

I have appropriated these words of Dr. Joseph Le Conte because the general reader is not likely to see them where they were originally printed, in a little university study, and it is a pity to let the general reader miss so good an introduction to the subject. Not all learned men rate baby biography as highly as Dr. Le Conte does; but probably all biologists do, and those psychologists who are most strongly impressed with the evolutionary interpretation of life.

It is easy to see why one's views of evolution affect the matter. In botany, for instance, we do not think that we can understand the mature plant by studying it alone, without knowledge of its germinating period. If we omitted all study of radicle and plumule and cotyledon, we should not only lose an interesting chapter from the science, but even the part we kept, the classification and morphology and physiology of the grown plant itself, would be seriously misunderstood in some ways. So in other sciences: it is necessary to understand how things came to be what they are, to study the *process of becoming,* so to speak, before the completed result can be understood. This is what we mean by "the genetic method" of studying a subject.

Now, in proportion as one believes that the faculties of the human mind unfold by evolutionary law, like a plant from the germ, he will feel the need of studying these also genetically. As we find them in our grown selves, they are often perplexing. What seems a single complete, inborn faculty may really be made up of simpler ones, so fused together by long practice that they cannot be discerned. We know that this is the case with seeing. For instance, we give a glance at a ball, and see its form with a single act of mind. Yet that act became possible only after long drill in putting simpler perceptions together. Many a test of form, turning objects over and over, passing the hands round and round them, learning the absence of corners, the equality of diameters, did we go through in babyhood, many an inspection by eye, many an exercise of memory, connecting the peculiar arrangement of light and shade with the form as felt, before we could "see" a ball. Had this been understood in Froebel's time, it would have made a ma-

terial difference in his suggestions as to sense training in earliest infancy. So other powers that seem simple and inborn may perhaps be detected in the act of forming themselves out of simpler ones, if we watch babies closely enough, and it may lead us to revise some of our theories about education.

There are enthusiasts, indeed, who would have us believe that child study is going to revolutionize all our educational methods, but those who are surest of these wonderful results, and readiest to tell mothers and teachers what is the truly scientific thing to do with their children, are not the ones who have done the most serious first hand study of children. From indications so far, it is likely that the outcome of such study will oftener be to confirm some good old-fashioned ways of training (showing that they rested unconsciously on a sound psychological basis) than to discover new ways. No substitute has yet been found by scientific pedagogy for motherly good sense and devotion.

Yet the direct study of child minds does bring out some new suggestions of educational value, does give a verdict sometimes between old conflicting theories, and always makes us understand more clearly what we are doing with children. And on the purely scientific side there is one aspect of especial interest in genetic studies. That is, the possible light we may get on the past of the human race.

It has long been observed that there are curious resemblances between babies and monkeys, between boys and barbaric tribes. Schoolboys administer law among themselves much as a tribal court does; babies sit like monkeys, with the soles of their little feet facing each other. Such resemblances led, long before the age of Darwin, to the speculation that children in developing passed through stages similar to those the race had passed through; and the speculation has become an accepted doctrine since embryology has shown how each individual before birth passes in successive stages through the lower forms of life.

This series of changes in the individual is called by evolutionists the Ontogenic Series; and the similar series through which the race has passed in the myriads of ages of its evolution is called the Phylogenic.

Now, of these two versions of the great world history, the phylogenic is a worn and ancient volume, mutilated in many places, and often illegible. The most interesting chapter of all is torn out—that which records the passing over of man from brute to human, the beginning of true human reason, speech, and skill. The lowest living races are far beyond the transition line; the remains of the past can never tell us how it was crossed, for before man could leave anything more than bones—any products of his art, such as weapons, or signs of fire—he had traveled a long way from his first human condition.

But from the ontogenic record no chapter can be torn out: a fresh copy of the whole history, from alpha to omega, is written out every time an infant is conceived, and born, and grows to manhood. And somewhere on the way between the first cell of the embryo and maturity each one must repeat in his own life that wonderful transition into human intelligence. If we can thoroughly decipher this ontogenic record, then, what may we not hope to learn of the road by which we human beings came?

We must not forget that the correspondence between these life books is only a rough one. They are versions of the same world story, but they have traveled far from their common origin, and have become widely unlike in details. The baby has to take many short cuts, and condense and omit inconceivably, to get through in a few brief years a development that the race took ages for. Even the order of development gets disarranged sometimes. For instance, primitive man probably reached a higher development before he could talk than babies have to now, after ages of talking ancestry: we must not look to a child just learning to talk, to get an idea of what the minds of men were like when *they* were just learning to talk. Again, the human child is carrying on under the influence of adults an evolution that primitive man worked out without help or hindrance from any one wiser than himself; and that makes a great difference in the way he does it.

The moral of all this is that people should be very cautious indeed in drawing parallels between the child and the race, and especially in basing educational theories on them. But if one is cautious enough and patient enough, there are many hints about our race history to be found in every nursery. Some of these I shall relate in the following chapters.

Most studies of children deal with later childhood, the school years; and these are almost always statistical in their method, taking the individual child very little into account. My own study has been of babyhood, and its method has been biographical. It is hard to get statistics about babies, scattered as they are, one by one, in different homes, not massed in schoolrooms. Now and then a doctor has found material for good comparative investigations, and much effort has been spent in trying to gather up measurements of babies' growth; but on the whole the most fruitful method so far has been the biographical one—that of watching one baby's development, day by day, and recording it.

I am often asked if the results one gets in this way are not misleading, since each child might differ greatly from others. One must, of course, use great caution in drawing general conclusions from a single child, but in many things all babies are alike, and one learns to perceive pretty well which are the things. Babyhood is mainly taken up with the development of the large, general racial powers; individual differences are less important than in later childhood. And the biographical method of child study has the inestimable advantage of showing the process of evolution going on, the actual unfolding of one stage out of another, and the steps by which the changes come about. No amount of comparative statistics could give this. If I should find out that a thousand babies learned to stand at an average age of forty-six weeks and two days, I should not know as much that is important about standing, as a stage in human progress, as I should after watching a single baby carefully through the whole process of achieving balance on his little soles.

Yet there are not many baby biographies in existence. There are scarcely half a dozen records that are full and consecutive enough to be at all entitled to the name, and even of more fragmentary ones the number in print as separate essays is scarcely larger. A good many more, however, have been available in manuscript to students, and many mothers no doubt keep such little notebooks. These notes are often highly exact and intelligent, as far as they go (I have found this especially true of the notebooks of members of the Association of Collegiate Alumnæ), and afford important corroborations here and there to more continuous records.

It was the Germans who first thought baby life worth recording, and the most complete and scientific of all the records is a German one. The first record known was published in the last century by a Professor Tiedemann—a mere slip of an essay, long completely forgotten, but resuscitated about the middle of this century, translated into French (and lately into English), and used by all students of the subject. Some of its observations we must, with our present knowledge, set down as erroneous; but it is on the whole exact and valuable, and a remarkable thing for a man to have done more than a hundred years ago.

Perhaps Darwin, in 1840, was the next person to take notes of an infant's development; but they were taken only incidentally to another study, and were not published for more than thirty years (partly in "The Expression of the Emotions in Man and Animals," 1873, partly in a magazine article in 1877). They are scanty but important. In the interval before they were published two or three small records had been published in Germany, and at least one paper, that of M. Taine, in France.

In 1881, the first edition of Professor Preyer's "model record" was published, and before his death, in 1897, it had reached its third edition in Germany, and had been widely circulated in America in Mr. Brown's excellent translation, "The Senses and the Will," and "The Development of the Intellect." It did more to stimulate and direct the study of infancy than any other publication. It has, however, the limitations that were to be expected from Professor Preyer's special training as a physiologist, and is meagre on the side of mental, moral, and emotional development. Professor Sully's "Extracts from a Father's Diary," published in part in 1881 and 1884 and fully in 1896, is richer on these sides, and also more readable.

Within the present decade, it is worth observing, the principal records have been American, not German, and have been written by women. Outside of America, only men, usually university professors, have made extended records. Professor Preyer and Professor Sully have both appealed in vain to their countrywomen to keep such records, holding up American women for emulation. My "Notes on the Development of a Child" were published in 1893 and 1899. In 1896 appeared Mrs. Hall's "The First 500 Days of a Child's Life," a brief record, and confined to a short period, but a very good one, and perhaps the best for use as a guide by any one who wishes to keep a record and finds Preyer too technical. Mrs. Moore's "Mental Development of a Child" is quite as much a psychological study as a record, but is based on full biographical notes; it will be more used by students than general readers. Mrs. Hogan's "A Study of a Child," 1898, is less scholarly than the others, but has a great deal of useful material; it does not begin at birth, however, but with the fourteenth month.

Perhaps I should say a word here as to the way in which I came to make a baby biography, for I am often asked how one should go to work at it. It was not done in my case for any scientific purpose, for I did not feel competent to make observations of scientific value. But I had for years desired an opportunity to see the wonderful unfolding of human powers out of the limp helplessness of the new-born baby; to watch this fascinating drama of evolution daily, minutely, and with an effort to understand it as far as I could, for my own pleasure and information. I scarcely know whence the suggestion had come; probably almost by inheritance, for my mother and grandmother had both been in somewhat notable degree observers of the development of babies' minds. But, unlike them, I had the notebook habit from college

and editorial days, and jotted things down as I watched, till quite unexpectedly I found myself in possession of a large mass of data.

A few days after my own notes began I obtained Professor Preyer's record, and without it I should have found the earliest weeks quite unintelligible. For some months my notes were largely memoranda of the likenesses and differences between my niece's development and that of Preyer's boy, and I still think this is the best way for a new observer to get started. As time went on, I departed more and more from the lines of Preyer's observations, and after the first year was little influenced by them. Later, I devoted a good deal of study to the notes, and tried to analyze their scientific results.

There is one question that I have been asked a hundred times about baby biography: "Doesn't it do the children some harm? Doesn't it make them nervous? Doesn't it make them self-conscious?" At first this seemed to me an odd misapprehension—as if people supposed observing children meant doing something to them. But I have no doubt it could be so foolishly managed as to harm the child. There are thousands of parents who tell anecdotes about children before their faces every day in the year, and if such a parent turns child student it is hard to say what he may not do in the way of dissecting a child's mind openly, questioning the little one about himself, and experimenting with his thoughts and feelings. But such observing is as worthless scientifically as it is bad for the child: the whole value of an observation is gone as soon as the phenomena observed lose simplicity and spontaneity. It should be unnecessary to say that no competent observer tampers with the child in any way. If Professor Preyer, observing the baby as he first grasps at objects, notes down the way in which he misdirects his inexpert little hands; if Mrs. Barus keeps record of her boy's favorite playthings; if I sit by the window and catch with my pencil my niece's prattle as she plays about below—and if these babies afterward turn out spoiled, the mischief must be credited to some other agency than the silent notebook.

Even direct experimenting on a child is not so bad as it sounds. When you show a baby his father's photograph to see if he recognizes it, you are experimenting on him. The only difference between the child student's experimenting and that which all the members of the family are doing all day with the baby, is that the student knows better what he is trying to find out, and that he writes it down.

Probably women are more skillful than men in quietly following the course of the child's mind, even leading him to reveal himself without at all meddling with him or marring his simplicity. It has been so in a marked degree in the cases I have seen. But no one who has good judgment will allow himself to spoil both the child and his own observation; and any one who has not good judgment will find plenty of ways to spoil a child more potent than observing him.

IX

The Dawn of Intelligence

THE sixth month, though it lay between two great development periods,—that of learning to use the senses, and that of learning to carry the body,—was not in itself a period of suspended development. It is true that its progress, being more purely mental, could not be so continuously traced as that which came before and after, but rather cropped up to the surface every now and then in a more or less broken way; still, no doubt, it really went on in the same gradual method, one thread and another knitting together into the fabric of new powers.

It was to this month, as I said in closing the last chapter, that the beginnings of adaptive intelligence belonged; and this alone marks it a great epoch.

There is a great deal of discussion about the use of the words "intelligence," "reason," "instinct," "judgment," "inference," and the like: what these faculties and acts really are, how they come about, where the line is to be drawn between their manifestations (in the minds of animals and of man, for instance), and many other problems. But I think that all agree upon recognizing two types of action that come under the discussion: one, that which shows merely the ability to adapt means to ends, to use one's own wit in novel circumstances; the other, that which rests on the higher, abstract reasoning power, such as is hardly possible without carrying on a train of thought in words. Whether these two types are to be called intelligence and reason, as Professor Lloyd Morgan calls them, or whether both come under the head of reason, lower and higher, we need not trouble to decide. If we call them adaptive intelligence and higher or abstract reason, we are safe enough.

Even if it be true that any glimmer of the higher reason penetrates back into the grades of life below the attainment of speech, it must be only into those just below, and is not to be looked for in our baby for a long time yet. But the mere practical intelligence that I am now speaking of seems to appear in babies close on the completion of a fair mastery of their senses, about the

middle of the first year, and it goes pretty far down in the animal kingdom. Darwin thought the lowest example of it he knew was in the crab, who would remove shells that were thrown near the mouth of his burrow, apparently realizing that they might fall in.

Recent psychologists have shown strong reason for thinking that such acts as this are at bottom only the same old hit and miss trick that we have seen from the first, of repeating lucky movements; only in a higher stage, as the associations that guide the movements become more delicate and complicated, and memory and imagination enter in. However this may be as a matter of theoretic analysis, there is in practice a clear test of difference between the unintelligent earlier type of actions and those that all agree in calling intelligent: I have indicated it above, in saying that in intelligent action one's own wit must be used "in novel circumstances." The case must be such that one cannot fall back on race instinct nor on his own previous habit.

Our baby, for instance, first used her intelligence to steer her toe into her mouth, and the way she did it, compared with the way she slowly settled on the proper movements for getting her rattle into her mouth, shows clearly the practical difference between unintelligent and intelligent action, even if both are at bottom made of the same psychological stuff.

It was just before the sixth month began that the baby accomplished this feat, but it belongs with the developments of that month. She was already fond of playing with her toes; and sitting unclad that evening in her mother's lap, she first tried to pull them straight to her mouth. This was, of course, the mere repetition of a frequent movement, learned by simple association. But when it failed—for the toes would kick away, just as her arms used to do, carrying the thumb from her lips—the little one put her mind on corralling them. She took them in one hand, clasped the other hand about her instep, and so brought the foot safely up. Still it escaped, and at last she clasped ankle and heel firmly, one with each hand, and after several attempts brought the elusive toe triumphantly into her mouth. It is true that by looking up to us for sympathy in her success, and relaxing attention, she promptly lost it once more; but she recaptured it, and from this time on, for weeks, had immense satisfaction in it every time she was undressed.

There may have been a certain element of instinct in this—getting the toe to the mouth is so persistent a habit with babies that it seems as if there must be some inheritance about it; but inheritance could hardly have given the special devices for managing the insubordinate foot; there was clearly some use of individual intelligence. All through the process of learning to manage the body, the baby showed instinct and intelligence most intricately mingled; and, indeed, we do so ourselves our lives long.

Of all a baby's doings this toe business is the one that people find it most impossible to regard with scientific seriousness. But its indirect usefulness is considerable. The cooperation of different parts of the body that it teaches is remarkable; and it must have great influence in extending the sense of self to the legs and feet, where it has hitherto seemed but weakly developed. This is important in getting the body ready for standing and walking.

The baby now showed intelligence in her actions in several little ways, such as tugging with impatient cries at her mother's dress when she wanted her dinner, and leaning over to pluck at the carriage blanket, under which her mother had laid some flowers to keep them from her. She slipped a long-handled spoon farther down in her hand to get the end of the handle into her mouth (almost exactly the same act as the one that Darwin thought first showed "a sort of practical reflection" in his child at about the same age: the boy slipped his hand down his father's finger, in order to get the finger tip into his mouth). In the second week of the month she began to watch things as they fell, and then to throw them down purposely, to watch them falling.

I have already mentioned certain doubtful imitations in the fourth month, and a clearer one in the fifth. Now the baby began to imitate unmistakably. Her uncle had a fashion of slapping his hand down on the table by way of a salutation to her, and one day (when she had passed a week of her sixth month) she slapped down her little hand in return. The next day as soon as her uncle came in, she began to slap her hand down, watching him, delighted to repeat the movement back and forth, as long as he would keep it up. She would imitate me also when I did it; and in the course of the month several other little imitations occurred.

I have already spoken of the great importance psychologists attach to imitation. Professor Baldwin makes it the great principle of development in child and race— all evolution one long history of its workings; but he uses the word in a far wider sense than the ordinary one, tracing "imitation" from the mechanical repetition of life-preserving motions by the lowest living things, up to the spiritual effort of men and women to live up to their own highest ideals. Even using the word in its ordinary sense, we know what a potent force in the little one's education imitation is. The age, however, at which it is most efficient is considerably later than the sixth month, and it did not count for much yet with our baby.

Her sounds had been more various and expressive from the first days of the month. She had taken up a curious puppy-like whine of desire or complaint, and a funny little ecstatic sniffing and catching her breath, to express some shades of delight; and she had also begun to pour out long, varied successions of babbling sounds, which expressed content, interest, or complaint very clearly. She would "talk to" any interesting object (a hedge in gorgeous bloom, for instance) with this expressive babble, sometimes holding out her arms to it at the same time. But now, in the second week of the month, the day after the first decisive imitation, a surprising advance beyond these means of communication took place.

I must explain that the wise grandma, who believed in encouraging babies to creep, as the best possible preparation for standing and walking, had begun to set the little one on her hands and knees on the big dining-table, putting a hand against her feet as a brace in case she should be moved to struggle forward. The baby had a habit of pushing with her feet when she felt anything against her soles; and pushing thus, thrust herself forward; and as the table-cover slid with her movement, she would half slide with it, half shove herself, across the table, grunting with exertion, and highly pleased.

On the day in question I was sitting with her by this table, and she pulled at the table-cover, as she was wont to pull and handle anything she could reach. Suddenly she threw herself back on my arm, and looked earnestly in my face; sat up and pulled at the cover again, then threw herself back and looked at me again.

"What does she want?" I said, surprised, and hardly able to think that the little thing could really be trying to say something to me. But grandma interpreted easily, and when I put the baby on the table accordingly, to make her sliding sprawl across the surface, she was satisfied.

This remarkable advance in sign language comes well under our definition of intelligent action: it was not a stereotyped sign, already fixed in her mind in association with a certain wish, like holding out her arms to be taken, but a device of her own, to meet the special occasion.

Her increased power of communication was not the only way in which her mind showed itself more wide awake to other people. A rather uncomfortable phase of this development was timidity. In the first week of the month, she was frightened by some one who came in suddenly between her and her mother, in a strange house, and spoke abruptly, in a deep, unfamiliar voice; and after that she often cried or became uneasy when strange men took her, or came near her, especially if they were abrupt. She drew distinct lines, according to some principle of her own, and certain people were affably accepted at once, while others, no more terrific that we could see, made the little lip quiver every time they came near. This timidity toward people was not at all deeply fixed in her temperament, and though it lasted all this month, it was never very marked afterward.

Some indications of the dawn of affection also appeared now. The baby's desire to touch our faces with her mouth and hands seemed to have a certain element of attachment in it. The touches were often soft and caressing, and they were bestowed only on her especial friends, or on one or two strangers that she had taken at once into notable favor. Once she leaned out of her baby carriage, calling and reaching to me, as if she wished to be taken; but when I came to her, she wanted only to get hold of me, to put her hands and mouth softly on my face.

Up to about the middle of the month, in spite of her daily exercises with her toe, the baby had not altogether annexed her legs to her conscious self and brought them under her orders. She still had to hold the foot forcibly with her hands all the time her toe was in her mouth, or it would have kicked away from her as if it was none of hers. It is likely, too, that she had scarcely any idea of those parts of her body which she could not see and did not often touch. Indeed, the psychologists tell us that we ourselves have a decidedly inferior bodily consciousness in such parts—say between the shoulder blades. Even her own head must have been mainly unknown territory to the baby still, in spite of the curiosity she had felt about it the month before. But now she discovered by a chance touch that she could investigate it with her hands, and proceeded at once to do so, with a serious face.

In the latter half of the month, she went a good deal farther toward getting a roughly complete knowledge and control of her body. She investigated her ear, her cheek, and the back and sides of her head, from time to time. She became quite expert in using legs and hands, head and mouth, together, in getting hold of her toe. She sat alone longer and longer, and by the end of the month could have done so by the half hour, if she had not always upset herself in five minutes or so by turning and reaching about. She had become very free in bending, squirming, and changing her position when she lay on the floor, and early in the third week of the month she had turned clear over, from back to stomach, in reaching after something. She followed up the lesson at once, and soon was rolling over whenever she wished—at first having much ado to get her arm disentangled from under her, but managing it nicely before long.

It is possible she would have begun creeping at this time but for the impediment of her clothes. She did stumble once upon almost the right movement, in trying to get forward to something she wanted; but her feet and knees became entangled in her skirts, and she gave it up. A week later, she was put into short skirts, but by that time the ability to roll over had diverted her mind from creeping.

Babies must lose a great deal of their normal activity through clothes. They are retracing a stage of human history in which clothes had no part, and this new element must hamper the repetition immensely. Clothes they must wear—they do not live in tropic forests nor own hair coverings; but we ought to leave the little limbs as free as we can without risk from cold. A chance to roll about nude in a room that is safely warm is a great thing for a baby.

She did not again use any sign language as advanced as when she had asked to be put on the table; that incident was a sort of herald of a later stage of development. But in the latter part of the month her regular means of communication were decidedly better developed than in the first part. She would coax for a frolic by leaning forward with an urgent "Oo! oo!" and expressive movements of her body; but if she was asking instead for an object she wished, or to be taken into her mother's arms, there were small but quite definite differences in tone, expression, and movement, so that we usually knew at once which she meant.

About a week before the end of the month a great step toward intercommunication by speech took place. We began to suspect that the baby knew her own name, she turned to look so often just after it had been spoken. To test it I stood behind her, and in an ordinary tone accosted her as Bobby, Tom, Kitten, Mary, Jacob, Baby, and all sorts of other names. Whenever I said Ruth, Toodles, or Toots, she turned and looked expectantly at me, but not at any other name. Now, Ruth is our baby's proper name; so it was evident that she really did have some inkling of the sound that meant her.

Not that she could rise yet to any such abstract conception as that of a person or of a name. But she had learned that this sound was connected with interesting experiences—with frolics, and caresses, and trips outdoors, with relief from discomforts, with dinners, and all the other things that happened when people were attending to her. It was out of such a beginning as this that full understanding of articulate speech, in all its logical intricacy, was to develop.

One of the most marked traits of the latter weeks of this month was the surprising rapidity with which things were grouping themselves in the baby's mind by association, in a way that came nearer and nearer to definite memory. She coaxed for a spoon, and when she got it was still discontented, till we found that she wished it to have milk in, as she knew befitted a spoon—though for the milk itself she did not care at all. She understood what particular frolic was to be expected from each of us. She turned, when she saw reflections, to look for the real object. She made demonstrations of joy when she saw her baby carriage, knowing well what it portended.

In two or three cases, there was at last unmistakable evidence of true memory, for at least a few minutes. For instance, in the last week of the month, sitting on her mother's lap, the baby caught sight of a knot of loops that adorned the centre of an ottoman close by, and reached her arms for it. By way of a joke on her, her mother set her on the ottoman. It was quite beyond the baby's sense of locality to divine what had become of the knot, and she looked all about her diligently to find it, leaning this way and that. By and by her mother took her back into her arms to nurse; but all the time she was nursing, she would stop now and then, sit up, and lean over to look for the lost knot.

At another time, when her mother came into the room with a new hat on, she reached out her hands for it with delight; her mother retreated at once, and put the hat safely out of sight, but when some minutes later the baby saw her again, her first look was at the top of her head, and seeing it now bare of lace and buttercups, she broke into a disappointed whimper.

All this time practice in her earlier attainments went vigorously on. She was watching, handling, reaching after things, all day long. Especially she watched all the movements of people; often, now, as they went in and out of doors, as they were seen through windows, came into sight or disappeared around corners. She must have been getting thus some idea of the way walls acted in shutting out her view, and of the relation of visible and invisible positions.

She had perhaps more troubles in this month than even before, what with some fear of people, and the discomforts connected with her first pair of teeth, and also with the beginning of the weaning period. There were a number of days when her health and spirits were considerably depressed, and there was a good deal of fretting. When the teeth were fairly through, and the insufficient food supplemented, her spirits came up with a bound, and she was more joyous than ever.

She had her first skin pain in this month—a scratched finger from a clasp on my shoulder—and wailed with vigor; yet it was forgotten in a few moments, and never thought of again. It was evident that skin sensitiveness was still low, and that hurts left no after soreness.

It was about ten days before the end of the month that she first showed a decided emotional dependence on her mother. She had been separated from her for some time (by a tedious dentist's engagement), had become hungry and sleepy, and had been frightened by an abrupt stranger. At last she settled into a pitiful, steady crying—stopping at every angle in the corridor where I walked with her, and watching eagerly till it was turned, then breaking out anew when her mother did not prove to be around the corner. This tragic experience left a much deeper mark than the physical woes, and for some days the baby watched her mother rather anxiously, as if she feared she might lose her again unless she kept her eyes constantly upon her.

And so she was come to the end of her first half year. The breathing automaton had become an eager and joyous little being, seeing and hearing and feeling much as we do, knowing her own body somewhat, and controlling it throughout to a certain extent, laughing and frolicking, enjoying the vision of the world with a delicious zest, clinging to us not so much for physical protection as for human companionship, beginning to show a glimmer of intelligence, and to cross over with sign and sound the abyss between spirit and spirit.

20

SIGMUND FREUD

Sigmund Freud (1856–1939) enjoyed school and was a star pupil; his interest in history and humanities seemed a perfect match for his planned study of the law, but he became intrigued by science and so enrolled in the University of Vienna's medical school instead. Working with the physiologist Ernst Brucke, Freud developed an appreciation for mechanistic explanations and published articles in neuroanatomy as a student. Employment as a researcher seemed unlikely—not only were such positions rare, but Freud's Jewish heritage would be held against him. A desire to marry prompted a reassessment of his financial opportunities, and Freud began a training program at Vienna's General Hospital. In 1885, Freud won a travel grant to study with the French doctor Jean-Martin Charcot, the leading authority on the treatment of patients with various forms of hysteria. Returning to Vienna, Freud entered private practice, initially treating ordinary neurological cases, but he began accepting patients with hysteria to address his financial concerns. When he experienced difficulties with Charcot's hypnosis treatment, Freud developed alternative procedures that eventually led to his psychoanalytic theory of mind and psychotherapy. Throughout the 1930s, the climate was becoming increasingly hostile for Jews in Vienna, so Freud took his family to London in 1938. Tragically, his sisters were not granted exit visas and were among over 5 million Jews led to Nazi gas chambers.

THE ORIGIN AND DEVELOPMENT OF PSYCHOANALYSIS

THIRD LECTURE

Ladies and Gentlemen: It is not always easy to tell the truth, especially when one must be brief, and so to-day I must correct an incorrect statement that I made in my last lecture.

I told you how when I gave up using hypnosis I pressed my patients to tell me what came into their minds that had to do with the problem we were working on, I told them that they would remember what they had apparently forgotten, and that the thought which irrupted into consciousness (*Einfall*) would surely embody the memory for which we were seeking. I claimed that I substantiated the fact that the first idea of my patients brought the right clue and could be shown to be the forgotten continuation of the memory. Now this is not always so; I represented it as being so simple only for purposes of abbreviation. In fact, it would only happen the

first times that the right forgotten material would emerge through simple pressure on my part. If the experience was continued, ideas emerged in every case which could not be the right ones, for they were not to the purpose, and the patients themselves rejected them as incorrect. Pressure was of no further service here, and one could only regret again having given up hypnosis. In this state of perplexity I clung to a prejudice which years later was proved by my friend C. G. Jung of the University of Zürich, and his pupils to have a scientific justification. I must confess that it is often of great advantage to have prejudices. I put a high value on the strength of the determination of mental processes, and I could not believe that any idea which occurred to the patient, which originated in a state of concentrated attention, could be quite arbitrary and out of all relation to the forgotten idea that we were seeking. That it was not identical with the latter, could be satisfactorily ex-

From Sigmund Freud, "The Origin and Development of Psychoanalysis (Third, Fourth and Fifth Lectures)." *American Journal of Psychology* 21 (1910): 196–218.

plained by the hypothetical psychological situation. In the patients whom I treated there were two opposing forces: on the one hand the conscious striving to drag up into consciousness the forgotten experience which was present in the unconscious; and on the other hand the resistance which we have seen, which set itself against the emergence of the suppressed idea or its associates into consciousness. In case this resistance was nonexistent or very slight, the forgotten material could become conscious without disguise (*Entstellung*). It was then a natural supposition that the disguise would be the more complete, the greater the resistance to the emergence of the idea. Thoughts which broke into the patient's consciousness instead of the ideas sought for, were accordingly made up just like symptoms; they were new, artificial, ephemeral surrogates for the repressed ideas, and differed from these just in proportion as they had been more completely disguised under the influence of the resistances. These surrogates must, however, show a certain similarity with the ideas which are the object of our search, by virtue of their nature as symptoms; and when the resistance is not too intensive it is possible from the nature of these irruptions to discover the hidden object of our search. This must be related to the repressed thought as a sort of allusion, as a statement of the same thing in *indirect* terms.

We know cases in normal psychology in which analogous situations to the one which we have assumed give rise to similar experiences. Such a case is that of wit. By my study of psychoanalytic technique I was necessarily led to a consideration of the problem of the nature of wit. I will give one example of this sort, which, too, is a story that originally appeared in English.

The anecdote runs: [1]Two unscrupulous business men had succeeded by fortunate speculations in accumulating a large fortune, and then directed their efforts to breaking into good society. Among other means they thought it would be of advantage to be painted by the most famous and expensive artist of the city, a man whose paintings were considered as events. The costly paintings were first shown at a great soirée and both hosts led the most influential connoisseur and art critic to the wall of the salon on which the portraits were hung, to elicit his admiring judgment. The artist looked for a long time, looked about as though in search of something, and then merely asked, pointing out the vacant space between the two pictures; "And where is the Saviour?"

I see that you are all laughing over this good example of wit, which we will now attempt to analyse. We understand that the critic means to say; "You are a couple of

malefactors, like those between whom the Saviour was crucified." But he does not say this, he expresses himself instead in a way that at first seems not to the purpose and not related to the matter in hand, but which at the next moment we recognize as an *allusion* to the insult at which he aims, and as a perfect surrogate for it. We cannot expect to find in the case of wit all those relations that our theory supposes for the origin of the irruptive ideas of our patients, but it is my desire to lay stress on the similar motivation of wit and irruptive idea. Why does not the critic say directly what he has to say to the two rogues? Because, in addition to his desire to say it straight out, he is actuated by strong opposite motives. It is a proceeding which is liable to be dangerous to offend people who are one's hosts, and who can call to their aid the strong arms of numerous servants. One might easily suffer the same fate that I used in the previous lecture to illustrate repression. On this ground, the critic does not express the particular insult directly, but in a disguised form, as an allusion with omission. The same constellation comes into play, according to our hypothesis, when our patient produces the irruptive idea as a surrogate for the forgotten idea which is the object of the quest.

Ladies and gentlemen, it is very useful to designate a group of ideas which belong together and have a common emotive tone, according to the custom of the Zürich school (Bleuler, Jung and others), as a "complex." So we can say that if we set out from the last memories of the patient to look for a repressed complex, that we have every prospect of discovering it, if only the patient will communicate to us a sufficient number of the ideas which come into his head. So we let the patient speak along any line that he desires, and cling to the hypothesis that nothing can occur to him except what has some indirect bearing on the complex that we are seeking. If this method of discovering the repressed complexes seems too circumstantial, I can at least assure you that it is the only available one.

In practicing this technique, one is further bothered by the fact that the patient often stops, is at a stand-still, and considers that he has nothing to say; nothing occurs to him. If this were really the case and the patient were right, our procedure would again be proven inapplicable. Closer observation shows that such an absence of ideas never really occurs, and that it only appears to when the patient holds back or rejects the idea which he perceives, under the influence of the resistance, which disguises itself as critical judgment of the value of the idea. The patient can be protected from this if he is warned in advance of this circumstance, and told to take no account of the critical attitude. He must say anything that comes into his mind, fully laying aside such critical choice, even though he may think it unessential, irrelevant, nonsensical, especially when the idea is one which is unpleasant to dwell on. By following this prescription we secure the material which sets us on the track of the repressed complex.

These irruptive ideas, which the patient himself values little, if he is under the influence of the resistance and not that of the physician, are for the psychologist like the ore, which by simple methods of interpretation he reduces from its crude state to valuable metal. If one desires to gain in a short time a preliminary knowledge of the patient's repressed complexes, without going into the question of their arrangement and associations, this examination may be conducted with the help of the association experiments, as Jung[2] and his pupils have perfected them. This procedure is to the psychologist what qualitative analysis to the chemist; it may be dispensed with in the therapy of neurotic patients, but is indispensable in the investigations of the psychoses, which have been begun by the Zürich school with such valuable results.

This method of work with whatever comes into the patient's head when he submits to psychoanalytic treatment, is not the only technical means at our disposal for the widening of consciousness. Two other methods of procedure serve the same purpose, the interpretation of his dreams and the evaluation of acts which he bungles or does without intending to (*Fehl-und Zufallshandlungen*).

I might say, esteemed hearers, that for a long time I hesitated whether instead of this hurried survey of the whole field of psychoanalysis, I should not rather offer you a thorough consideration of the analysis of dreams; a purely subjective and apparently secondary motive decided me against this. It seemed rather an impropriety that in this country, so devoted to practical pursuits, I should pose as "interpreter of dreams," before you had a chance to discover what significance the old and despised art can claim.

Interpretation of dreams is in fact the *via regia* to the interpretation of the unconscious, the surest ground of psychoanalysis and a field in which every worker must win his convictions and gain his education. If I were asked how one could become a psychoanalist, I should answer, through the study of his own dreams. With great tact all opponents of the psychoanalytic theory have so far either evaded any criticism of the "*Traumdeutung*"[3] or have attempted to pass over it with the most superficial objections. If, on the contrary, you will undertake

the solution of the problems of dream life, the novelties which psychoanalysis present to your thoughts will no longer be difficulties.

You must remember that our nightly dream productions show the greatest outer similarity and inner relationship to the creations of the insane, but on the other hand are compatible with full health during waking life. It does not sound at all absurd to say that whoever regards these normal sense illusions, these delusions and alterations of character as matter for amazement instead of understanding, has not the least prospect of understanding the abnormal creations of diseased mental states in any other than the lay sense. You may with confidence place in this lay group all the psychiatrists of today. Follow me now on a brief excursion through the field of dream problems.

In our waking state we usually treat dreams with as little consideration as the patient treats the irruptive ideas which the psychoanalyst demands from him. It is evident that we reject them, for we forget them quickly and completely. The slight valuation which we place on them is based, with those dreams that are not confused and nonsensical, on the feeling that they are foreign to our personality, and, with other dreams, on their evident absurdity and senselessness. Our rejection derives support from the unrestrained shamelessness and the immoral longings which are obvious in many dreams. Antiquity, as we know, did not share this light valuation of dreams. The lower classes of our people to-day stick close to the value which they set on dreams; they, however, expect from them, as did the ancients, the revelation of the future. I confess that I see no need to adopt mystical hypotheses to fill out the gaps in our present knowledge, and so I have never been able to find anything that supported the hypothesis of the prophetic nature of dreams. Many other things, which are wonderful enough, can be said about them.

And first, not all dreams are so foreign to the character of the dreamer, are incomprehensible and confused. If you will undertake to consider the dreams of young children from the age of a year and a half on, you will find them quite simple and easy to interpret. The young child always dreams of the fulfillment of wishes which were aroused in him the day before and were not satisfied. You need no art of interpretation to discover this simple solution, you only need to inquire into the experiences of the child on the day before (the "dream day"). Now it would certainly be a most satisfactory solution of the dream-riddle, if the dreams of adults, too, were the same as those of children, fulfillments of wishes which had been aroused in them during the dream day.

This is actually the fact; the difficulties which stand in the way of this solution can be removed step by step by a thorough analysis of the dream.

There is, first of all, the most weighty objection, that the dreams of adults generally have an incomprehensible content, which shows wish-fulfillment least of anything. The answer is this: these dreams have undergone a process of disguise, the psychic content which underlies them was originally meant for quite different verbal expression. You must differentiate between the *manifest dream-content,* which we remember in the morning only confusedly, and with difficulty clothe in words which seem arbitrary, and the *latent dream-thoughts,* whose presence in the unconscious we must assume. This distortion of the dream (*Traumentstellung*) is the same process which has been revealed to you in the investigations of the creations (*symptoms*) of hysterical subjects; it points to the fact that the same opposition of psychic forces has its share in the creation of dreams as in the creation of symptoms.

The manifest dream-content is the disguised surrogate for the unconscious dream thoughts, and this disguising is the work of the defensive forces of the ego, of the resistances. These prevent the repressed wishes from entering consciousness during the waking life, and even in the relaxation of sleep they are still strong enough to force them to hide themselves by a sort of masquerading. The dreamer, then, knows just as little the sense of his dream as the hysterical knows the relation and significance of his symptoms. That there are latent dream-thoughts and that between them and the manifest dream-content there exists the relation just described— of this you may convince yourselves by the analysis of dreams, a procedure the technique of which is exactly that of psychoanalysis. You must abstract entirely from the apparent connection of the elements in the manifest dream and seek for the irruptive ideas which arise through free association, according to the psychoanalytic laws, from each separate dream element. From this material the latent dream thoughts may be discovered, exactly as one divines the concealed complexes of the patient from the fancies connected with his symptoms and memories. From the latent dream thoughts which you will find in this way, you will see at once how thoroughly justified one is in interpreting the dreams of adults by the same rubrics as those of children. What is now substituted for the manifest dream-content is the real sense of the dream, is always clearly comprehensible, associated with the impressions of the day before, and appears as the fulfilling of an unsatisfied wish. The manifest dream, which we remember after waking, may

then be described as a *disguised* fulfillment of *repressed* wishes.

It is also possible by a sort of synthesis to get some insight into the process which has brought about the disguise of the unconscious dream thoughts as the manifest dream-content. We call this process "dream-work" (*Traumarbeit*). This deserves our fullest theoretical interest, since here as nowhere else we can study the unsuspected psychic processes which are existent in the unconscious, or, to express it more exactly, *between* two such separate systems as the conscious and the unconscious. Among these newly discovered psychic processes, two, condensation (*Verdichtung*) and displacement or transvaluation, change of psychic accent (*Verschiebung*), stand out most prominently. Dream work is a special case of the reaction of different mental groupings on each other, and as such is the consequence of psychic fission. In all essential points it seems identical with the work of disguise, which changes the repressed complex in the case of failing repression into symptoms.

You will furthermore discover by the analysis of dreams, most convincingly your own, the unsuspected importance of the rôle which impressions and experiences from early childhood exert on the development of men. In the dream life the child, as it were, continues his existence in the man, with a retention of all his traits and wishes, including those which he was obliged to allow to fall into disuse in his later years. With irresistible might it will be impressed on you by what processes of development, of repression, sublimation and reaction there arises out of the child, with its peculiar gifts and tendencies, the so-called normal man, the bearer and partly the victim of our painfully acquired civilization. I will also direct your attention to the fact that we have discovered from the analysis of dreams that the unconscious makes use of a sort of symbolism, especially in the presentation of sexual complexes. This symbolism in part varies with the individual, but in part is of a typical nature, and seems to be identical with the symbolism which we suppose to lie behind our myths and legends. It is not impossible that these latter creations of the people may find their explanation from the study of dreams.

Finally, I must remind you that you must not be led astray by the objection that the occurrence of anxiety-dreams (*Angsttraüme*), contradicts our idea of the dream as a wish-fulfillment. Apart from the consideration that anxiety-dreams also require interpretation before judgment can be passed on them, one can say quite generally that the anxiety does not depend in such a simple way on the dream content as one might suppose without more knowledge of the facts, and more attention to the conditions of neurotic anxiety. Anxiety is one of the ways in which the ego relieves itself of repressed wishes which have become too strong, and so is easy to explain in the dream, if the dream has gone too far towards the fulfilling of the objectionable wish.

You see that the investigation of dreams was justified by the conclusions which it has given us concerning things otherwise hard to understand. But we came to it in connection with the psychoanalytic treatment of neurotics. From what has been said you can easily understand how the interpretation of dreams, if it is not made too difficult by the resistance of the patient, can lead to a knowledge of the patient's concealed and repressed wishes and the complexes which he is nourishing. I may now pass to that group of everyday mental phenomena whose study has become a technical help for psychoanalysis.

These are the bungling of acts (*Fehlhandlungen*) among normal men as well as among neurotics, to which no significance is ordinarily attached; the forgetting of things which one is supposed to know and at other times really does know (for example the temporary forgetting of proper names); mistakes in speaking (*Versprechen*), which occur so frequently; analogous mistakes in writing (*Verschreiben*) and in reading (*Verlesen*), the automatic execution of purposive acts in wrong situations (*Vergreifen*) and the loss or breaking of objects, etc. These are trifles, for which no one has ever sought a psychological determination, which have passed unchallenged as chance experiences, as consequences of absent-mindedness, inattention and similar conditions. Here, too, are included the acts and gestures executed without being noticed by the subject, to say nothing of the fact that he attaches no psychic importance to them; as playing and trifling with objects, humming melodies, handling one's person and clothing and the like.[4]

These little things, the bungling of acts, like the symptomatic and chance acts (*Symptom- und Zufallshandlungen*) are not so entirely without meaning as is generally supposed by a sort of tacit agreement. They have a meaning, generally easy and sure to interpret from the situation in which they occur, and it can be demonstrated that they either express impulses and purposes which are repressed, hidden if possible from the consciousness of the individual, or that they spring from exactly the same sort of repressed wishes and complexes which we have learned to know already as the creators of symptoms and dreams.

It follows that they deserve the rank of symptoms, and their observation, like that of dreams, can lead to the discovery of the hidden complexes of the psychic life. With their help one will usually betray the most intimate of his secrets. If these occur so easily and commonly among people in health, with whom repression has on the whole succeeded fairly well, this is due to their insignificance and their inconspicuous nature. But they can lay claim to high theoretic value, for they prove the existence of repression and surrogate creations even under the conditions of health. You have already noticed that the psychoanalyst is distinguished by an especially strong belief in the determination of the psychic life. For him there is in the expressions of the psyche nothing trifling, nothing arbitrary and lawless, he expects everywhere a widespread motivation, where customarily such claims are not made; more than that, he is even prepared to find a manifold motivation of these psychic expressions, while our supposedly inborn causal need is satisfied with a single psychic cause.

Now keeping in mind the means which we possess for the discovery of the hidden, forgotten, repressed things in the soul life: the study of the irruptive ideas called up by free association, the patient's dreams, and his bungled and symptomatic acts; and adding to these the evaluation of other phenomena which emerge during the psychoanalytic treatment, on which I shall later make a few remarks under the heading of "transfer" (*Uebertragung*), you will come with me to the conclusion that our technique is already sufficiently efficacious for the solution of the problem of how to introduce the pathogenic psychic material into consciousness, and so to do away with the suffering brought on by the creation of surrogate symptoms.

The fact that by such therapeutic endeavors our knowledge of the mental life of the normal and the abnormal is widened and deepened, can of course only be regarded as an especial attraction and superiority of this method.

I do not know whether you have gained the impression that the technique through whose arsenal I have led you is a peculiarly difficult one. I consider that on the contrary, for one who has mastered it, it is quite adapted for use. But so much is sure, that it is not obvious, that it must be learned no less than the histological or the surgical technique.

You may be surprised to learn that in Europe we have heard very frequently judgments passed on psychoanalysis by persons who knew nothing of its technique and had never practised it, but who demanded scornfully that we show the correctness of our results. There are among these people some who are not in other things unacquainted with scientific methods of thought, who for example would not reject the result of a microscopical research because it cannot be confirmed with the naked eye in anatomical preparations, and who would not pass judgment until they had used the microscope. But in matters of psychoanalysis circumstances are really more unfavorable for gaining recognition. Psychoanalysis will bring the repressed in mental life to conscious acknowledgment, and every one who judges it is himself a man who has such repressions, perhaps only maintained with difficulty. It will consequently call forth the same resistances from him as from the patient, and this resistance can easily succeed in disguising itself as intellectual rejection, and bring forward arguments similar to those from which we protect our patients by the basic principles of psychoanalysis. It is not difficult to substantiate in our opponents the same impairment of intelligence produced by emotivity which we may observe every day with our patients. The arrogance of consciousness which for example rejects dreams so lightly, belongs—quite generally—to the strongest protective apparatus which guards us against the breaking through of the unconscious complexes, and as a result it is hard to convince people of the reality of the unconscious, and to teach them anew, what their conscious knowledge contradicts.

FOURTH LECTURE

Ladies and Gentlemen: At this point you will be asking what the technique which I have described has taught us of the nature of the pathogenic complexes and repressed wishes of neurotics.

One thing in particular: psychoanalytic investigations trace back the symptoms of disease with really surprising regularity to impressions from the sexual life, show us that the pathogenic wishes are of the nature of erotic impulse-components (*Trieb-komponente*), and necessitate the assumption that to disturbances of the erotic sphere must be ascribed the greatest significance among the etiological factors of the disease. This holds of both sexes.

I know that this assertion will not willingly be credited. Even those investigators who gladly follow my psychological labors, are inclined to think that I overestimate the etiological share of the sexual moments. They ask me why other mental excitations should not lead to the phenomena of repression and surrogate-creation which I have described. I can give them this answer; that I do not know why they should not do this, I have no objection to their doing it, but experience shows that they

do not possess such a significance, and that they merely support the effect of the sexual moments, without being able to supplant them. This conclusion was not a theoretical postulate; in the *Studien über Hysterie*, published in 1895 with Dr. Breuer, I did not stand on this ground. I was converted to it when my experience was richer and had led me deeper into the nature of the case. Gentlemen, there are among you some of my closest friends and adherents, who have travelled to Worcester with me. Ask them, and they will tell you that they all were at first completely sceptical of the assertion of the determinative significance of the sexual etiology, until they were compelled by their own analytic labors to come to the same conclusion.

The conduct of the patients does not make it any easier to convince one's self of the correctness of the view which I have expressed. Instead of willingly giving us information concerning their sexual life, they try to conceal it by every means in their power. Men generally are not candid in sexual matters. They do not show their sexuality freely, but they wear a thick overcoat—a fabric of lies—to conceal it, as though it were bad weather in the world of sex. And they are not wrong; sun and wind are not favorable in our civilized society to any demonstration of sex life. In truth no one can freely disclose his erotic life to his neighbor. But when your patients see that in your treatment they may disregard the conventional restraints, they lay aside this veil of lies, and then only are you in a position to formulate a judgment on the question in dispute. Unfortunately physicians are not favored above the rest of the children of men in their personal relationship to the questions of the sex life. Many of them are under the ban of that mixture of prudery and lasciviousness which determines the behaviour of most *Kulturmenschen* in affairs of sex.

Now to proceed with the communication of our results. It is true that in another series of cases psychoanalysis at first traces the symptoms back not to the sexual, but to banal traumatic experiences. But the distinction loses its significance through other circumstances. The work of analysis which is necessary for the thorough explanation and complete cure of a case of sickness does not stop in any case with the experience of the time of onset of the disease, but in every case it goes back to the adolescence and the early childhood of the patient. Here only do we hit upon the impressions and circumstances which determine the later sickness. Only the childhood experiences can give the explanation for the sensitivity to later traumata and only when these memory traces, which almost always are forgotten, are discovered and made conscious, is the power developed to banish the symptoms. We arrive here at the same conclusion as in the investigation of dreams—that it is the incompatible, repressed wishes of childhood which lend their power to the creation of symptoms. Without these the reactions upon later traumata discharge normally. But we must consider these mighty wishes of childhood very generally as sexual in nature.

Now I can at any rate be sure of your astonishment. Is there an infantile sexuality? you will ask. Is childhood not rather that period of life which is distinguished by the lack of the sexual impulse? No, gentlemen, it is not at all true that the sexual impulse enters into the child at puberty, as the devils in the gospel entered into the swine. The child has his sexual impulses and activities from the beginning, he brings them with him into the world, and from these the so-called normal sexuality of adults emerges by a significant development through manifold stages. It is not very difficult to observe the expressions of this childish sexual activity; it needs rather a certain art to overlook them or to fail to interpret them.[5]

As fate would have it, I am in a position to call a witness for my assertions from your own midst. I show you here the work of one Dr. Sanford Bell, published in 1902 in the *American Journal of Psychology*. The author was a fellow of Clark University, the same institution within whose walls we now stand. In this thesis, entitled "A Preliminary Study of the Emotion of Love between the Sexes," which appeared three years before my "Drei Abhandlungen zur Sexualtheorie," the author says just what I have been saying to you: "The emotion of sex love . . . does not make its appearance for the first time at the period of adolescence as has been thought." He has, as we should say in Europe, worked by the American method, and has gathered not less than 2,500 positive observations in the course of fifteen years, among them 800 of his own. He says of the signs by which this amorous condition manifests itself: "The unprejudiced mind, in observing these manifestations in hundreds of couples of children, cannot escape referring them to sex origin. The most exacting mind is satisfied when to these observations are added the confessions of those who have as children experienced the emotion to a marked degree of intensity, and whose memories of childhood are relatively distinct." Those of you who are unwilling to believe in infantile sexuality will be most astonished to hear that among those children who fell in love so early not a few are of the tender ages of three, four, and five years.

It would not be surprising if you should believe the observations of a fellow-countryman rather than my

own. Fortunately a short time ago from the analysis of a five-year-old boy who was suffering from anxiety, an analysis undertaken with correct technique by his own father,[6] I succeeded in getting a fairly complete picture of the bodily expressions of the impulse and the mental productions of an early stage of childish sexual life. And I must remind you that my friend, Dr. C. G. Jung, read you a few hours ago in this room an observation on a still younger girl who from the same cause as my patient—the birth of a little child in the family—betrayed certainly almost the same secret excitement, wish and complex-creation. Accordingly I am not without hope that you may feel friendly toward this idea of infantile sexuality that was so strange at first. I might also quote the remarkable example of the Zürich psychiatrist, E. Bleuler, who said a few years ago openly that he faced my sexual theories incredulous and bewildered, and since that time by his own observations had substantiated them in their whole scope.[7] If it is true that most men, medical observers and others, do not want to know anything about the sexual life of the child, the fact is capable of explanation only too easily. They have forgotten their own infantile sexual activity under the pressure of education for civilization and do not care to be reminded now of the repressed material. You will be convinced otherwise if you begin the investigation by a self-analysis, by an interpretation of your own childhood memories.

Lay aside your doubts and let us evaluate the infantile sexuality of the earliest years.[8] The sexual impulse of the child manifests itself as a very complex one, it permits of an analysis into many components, which spring from different sources. It is entirely disconnected from the function of reproduction which it is later to serve. It permits the child to gain different sorts of pleasure sensations, which we include, by the analogues and connections which they show, under the term sexual pleasures. The great source of infantile sexual pleasure is the auto-excitation of certain particularly sensitive parts of the body; besides the genitals are included the rectum and the opening of the urinary canal, and also the skin and other sensory surfaces. Since in this first phase of child sexual life the satisfaction is found on the child's own body and has nothing to do with any other object, we call this phase after a word coined by Havelock Ellis, that of "auto-erotism." The parts of the body significant in giving sexual pleasure we call "erogenous zones." The thumb-sucking (*Ludeln*) or passionate sucking (*Wonnesaugen*) of very young children is a good example of such an auto-erotic satisfaction of an erogenous zone. The first scientific observer of this phenomenon, a specialist in children's diseases in Budapest by the name of Lindner, interpreted these rightly as sexual satisfaction and described exhaustively their transformation into other and higher forms of sexual gratification.[9] Another sexual satisfaction of this time of life is the excitation of the genitals by masturbation, which has such a great significance for later life and, in the case of many individuals, is never fully overcome. Besides this and other auto-erotic manifestations we see very early in the child the impulse-components of *sexual pleasure,* or, as we may say, of the *libido,* which presupposes a second person as its object. These impulses appear in opposed pairs, as active and passive. The most important representatives of this group are the pleasure in inflicting pain (sadism) with its passive opposite (masochism) and active and passive exhibition-pleasure (*Schaulust*). From the first of these later pairs splits off the curiosity for knowledge, as from the latter the impulse toward artistic and theatrical representation. Other sexual manifestations of the child can already be regarded from the view-point of object-choice, in which the second person plays the prominent part. The significance of this was primarily based upon motives of the impulse of self-preservation. The difference between the sexes plays, however, in the child no very great rôle. One may attribute to every child, without wronging him, a bit of the homosexual disposition.

The sexual life of the child, rich, but dissociated, in which each single impulse goes about the business of arousing pleasure independently of every other, is later correlated and organized in two general directions, so that by the close of puberty the definite sexual character of the individual is practically finally determined. The single impulses subordinate themselves to the overlordship of the genital zone, so that the whole sexual life is taken over into the service of procreation, and their gratification is now significant only so far as they help to prepare and promote the true sexual act. On the other hand, object-choice prevails over auto-erotism, so that now in the sexual life all components of the sexual impulse are satisfied in the loved person. But not all the original impulse-components are given a share in the final shaping of the sexual life. Even before the advent of puberty certain impulses have undergone the most energetic repression under the impulse of education, and mental forces like shame, disgust and morality are developed, which, like sentinels, keep the repressed wishes in subjection. When there comes, in puberty, the high tide of sexual desire it finds dams in this creation of reactions and resistances. These guide the outflow into the so-called normal channels, and make it impossible to revivify the impulses which have undergone repression.

The most important of these repressed impulses are koprophilism, that is, the pleasure in children connected with the excrements; and, further, the tendencies attaching themselves to the persons of the primitive object-choice.

Gentlemen, a sentence of general pathology says that every process of development brings with it the germ of pathological dispositions in so far as it may be inhibited, delayed, or incompletely carried out. This holds for the development of the sexual function, with its many complications. It is not smoothly completed in all individuals, and may leave behind either abnormalities or disposition to later diseases by the way of later falling back or *regression.* It may happen that not all the partial impulses subordinate themselves to the rule of the genital zone. Such an impulse which has remained disconnected brings about what we call a perversion, which may replace the normal sexual goal by one of its own. It may happen, as has been said before, that the auto-erotism is not fully overcome, as many sorts of disturbances testify. The originally equal value of both sexes as sexual objects may be maintained and an inclination to homosexual activities in adult life result from this, which, under suitable conditions, rises to the level of exclusive homosexuality. This series of disturbances corresponds to the direct inhibition of development of the sexual function, it includes the perversions and the general *infantilism* of the sex life that are not seldom met with.

The disposition to neuroses is to be derived in another way from an injury to the development of the sex life. The neuroses are related to the perversions as the negative to the positive; in them we find the same impulse-components as in perversions, as bearers of the complexes and as creators of the symptoms; but here they work from out the unconscious. They have undergone a repression, but in spite of this they maintain themselves in the unconscious. Psychoanalysis teaches us that over-strong expression of the impulse in very early life leads to a sort of fixation (*Fixirung*), which then offers a weak point in the articulation of the sexual function. If the exercise of the normal sexual function meets with hindrances in later life, this repression, dating from the time of development, is broken through at just that point at which the infantile fixation took place.

You will now perhaps make the objection: "But all that is not sexuality." I have used the word in a very much wider sense than you are accustomed to understand it. This I willingly concede. But it is a question whether you do not rather use the word in much too narrow a sense when you restrict it to the realm of procreation. You sacrifice by that the understanding of perversions; of the connection between perversion, neurosis and normal sexual life; and have no means of recognizing, in its true significance, the easily observable beginning of the somatic and mental sexual life of the child. But however you decide about the use of the word, remember that the psychoanalyst understands sexuality in that full sense to which he is led by the evaluation of infantile sexuality.

Now we turn again to the sexual development of the child. We still have much to say here, since we have given more attention to the somatic than to the mental expressions of the sexual life. The primitive object-choice of the child, which is derived from his need of help, demands our further interest. It first attaches to all persons to whom he is accustomed, but soon these give way in favor of his parents. The relation of the child to his parents is, as both direct observation of the child and later analytic investigation of adults agree, not at all free from elements of sexual accessory-excitation (*Miterregung*). The child takes both parents, and especially one, as an object of his erotic wishes. Usually he follows in this the stimulus given by his parents, whose tenderness has very clearly the character of a sex manifestation, though inhibited so far as its goal is concerned. As a rule, the father prefers the daughter, the mother the son; the child reacts to this situation, since, as son, he wishes himself in the place of his father, as daughter, in the place of the mother. The feelings awakened in these relations between parents and children, and, as a resultant of them, those among the children in relation to each other, are not only positively of a tender, but negatively of an inimical sort. The complex built up in this way is destined to quick repression, but it still exerts a great and lasting effect from the unconscious. We must express the opinion that this with its ramifications presents the *nuclear complex* of every neurosis, and so we are prepared to meet with it in a not less effectual way in the other fields of mental life. The myth of King Œdipus, who kills his father and wins his mother as a wife is only the slightly altered presentation of the infantile wish, rejected later by the opposing barriers of incest. Shakespeare's tale of Hamlet rests on the same basis of an incest complex, though better concealed. At the time when the child is still ruled by the still unrepressed nuclear complex, there begins a very significant part of his mental activity which serves sexual interest. He begins to investigate the question of where children come from and guesses more than adults imagine of the true relations by deduction from the signs which he sees. Usually his interest in this investigation is awakened by the threat to his welfare through the birth of another child in the family, in whom at first he sees only a rival. Under the influence of the partial impulses which are active in him he arrives at a number of "infantile sexual theories," as that the same male genitals belong to both sexes, that children are conceived by eating and born through the opening of the intestine, and that sexual intercourse is to be regarded as an inimical act, a sort of overpowering.

But just the unfinished nature of his sexual constitution and the gaps in his knowledge brought about by the hidden condition of the feminine sexual canal, cause the infant investigator to discontinue his work as a failure. The facts of this childish investigation itself as well as the infant sex theories created by it are of determinative significance in the building of the child's character, and in the content of his later neuroses.

It is unavoidable and quite normal that the child should make his parents the objects of his first object-choice. But his *libido* must not remain fixed on these first chosen objects, but must take them merely as a prototype and transfer from these to other persons in the time of definite object-choice. The breaking loose (*Ablösung*) of the child from his parents is thus a problem impossible to escape if the social virtue of the young individual is not to be impaired. During the time that the repressive activity is making its choice among the partial sexual impulses and later, when the influence of the parents, which in the most essential way has furnished the material for these repressions, is lessened, great problems fall to the work of education, which at present certainly does not always solve them in the most intelligent and economic way.

Gentlemen, do not think that with these explanations of the sexual life and the sexual development of the child we have too far departed from psychoanalysis and the cure of neurotic disturbances. If you like, you may regard the psychoanalytic treatment only as a continued education for the overcoming of childhood-remnants (*Kindheitsresten*).

FIFTH LECTURE

Ladies and Gentlemen: With the discovery of infantile sexuality and the tracing back of the neurotic symptoms to erotic impulse-components we have arrived at several unexpected formulæ for expressing the nature and tendencies of neurotic diseases. We see that the individual falls ill when in consequence of outer hindrances or inner lack of adaptability the satisfaction of the erotic needs in the sphere of reality is denied. We see that he then flees to sickness, in order to find with its help a surrogate satisfaction for that denied him. We recognize that the symptoms of illness contain fractions of the sexual activity of the individual, or his whole sexual life, and we find in the turning away from reality the chief tendency and also the chief injury of the sickness. We may guess that the resistance of our patients against the cure is not a simple one, but is composed of many motives. Not only does the ego of the patient strive against the giving up of the repressions by which it has changed itself from its original constitution into its present form, but also the sexual impulses may not renounce their surrogate satisfaction so long as it is not certain that they can be offered anything better in the sphere of reality.

The flight from the unsatisfying reality into what we call, on account of its biologically injurious nature, disease, but which is never without an individual gain in pleasure for the patient, takes place over the path of regression, the return to earlier phases of the sexual life, when satisfaction was not lacking. This regression is seemingly a twofold one, a *temporal,* in so far as the *libido* or erotic need falls back to a temporally earlier stage of development, and a *formal,* since the original and primitive psychic 'means of expression are applied to the expression of this need. Both sorts of regression focus in childhood and have their common point in the production of an infantile condition of sexual life.

The deeper you penetrate into the pathogenesis of neurotic diseases, the more the connection of neuroses with other products of human mentality, even the most valuable, will be revealed to you. You will be reminded that we men, with the high claims of our civilization and under the pressure of our repressions, find reality generally quite unsatisfactory and so keep up a life of fancy in which we love to compensate for what is lacking in the sphere of reality by the production of wish-fulfillments. In these phantasies is often contained very much of the particular constitutional essence of personality and of its tendencies, repressed in real life. The energetic and successful man is he who succeeds by dint of labor in transforming his wish fancies into reality. Where this is not successful in consequence of the resistance of the outer world and the weakness of the individual, there begins the turning away from reality. The individual takes refuge in his satisfying world of fancy. Under certain favorable conditions it still remains possible for him to find another connecting link between these fancies and reality, instead of permanently becoming a stranger to it through the regression into the infantile. If the individual who is displeased with reality is in possession of that *artistic talent* which is still a psychological riddle, he can transform his fancies into artistic creations. So he

escapes the fate of a neurosis and wins back his connection with reality by this round-about way.[10] Where this opposition to the real world exists, but this valuable talent fails or proves insufficient, it is unavoidable that the *libido,* following the origin of the fancies, succeeds by means of regression in revivifying the infantile wishes and so producing a neurosis. The neurosis takes, in our time, the place of the cloister, in which were accustomed to take refuge all those whom life had undeceived or who felt themselves too weak for life. Let me give at this point the main result at which we have arrived by the psychoanalytic investigation of neurotics, namely, that neuroses have no peculiar psychic content of their own, which is not also to be found in healthy states; or, as C. G. Jung has expressed it, neurotics fall ill of the same complexes with which we sound people struggle. It depends on quantitative relationships, on the relations of the forces wrestling with each other, whether the struggle leads to health, to a neurosis, or to compensatory over-functioning (*Ueberleistung*).

Ladies and gentlemen, I have still withheld from you the most remarkable experience which corroborates our assumptions of the sexual impulse-forces of neurotics. Every time that we treat a neurotic psychoanalytically, there occurs in him the so-called phenomenon of *transfer* (Uebertragung), that is, he applies to the person of the physician a great amount of tender emotion, often mixed with enmity, which has no foundation in any real relation, and must be derived in every respect from the old wish-fancies of the patient which have become unconscious. Every fragment of his emotive life, which can no longer be called back into memory, is accordingly lived over by the patient in his relations to the physician, and only by such a living of them over in the "transfer" is he convinced of the existence and the power of these unconscious sexual excitations. The symptoms, which, to use a simile from chemistry, are the precipitates of earlier love experiences (in the widest sense), can only be dissolved in the higher temperature of the experience of transfer and transformed into other psychic products. The physician plays in this reaction, to use an excellent expression of S. Ferenczi,[11] the rôle of a *catalytic ferment,* which temporarily attracts to itself the affect which has become free in the course of the process.

The study of transfer can also give you the key to the understanding of hypnotic suggestion, which we at first used with our patients as a technical means of investigation of the unconscious. Hypnosis showed itself at that time to be a therapeutic help, but a hindrance to the scientific knowledge of the real nature of the case, since it cleared away the psychic resistances from a certain field, only to pile them up in an unscalable wall at the boundaries of this field. You must not think that the phenomenon of transfer, about which I can unfortunately say only too little here, is created by the influence of the psychoanalytic treatment. The transfer arises spontaneously in all human relations and in the relations of the patient to the physician; it is everywhere the especial bearer of therapeutic influences, and it works the stronger the less one knows of its presence. Accordingly psychoanalysis does not create it, it merely discloses it to consciousness, and avails itself of it, in order to direct the psychic processes to the wished for goal. But I cannot leave the theme of transfer without stressing the fact that this phenomenon is of decisive importance to convince not only the patient, but also the physician. I know that all my adherents were first convinced of the correctness of my views through their experience with transfer, and I can very well conceive that one may not win such a surety of judgment so long as he makes no psychoanalysis, and so has not himself observed the effects of transfer.

Ladies and gentlemen, I am of the opinion that there are, on the intellectual side, two hindrances to acknowledging the value of the psychoanalytic view-point: first, the fact that we are not accustomed to reckon with a strict determination of mental life, which holds without exception, and second, the lack of knowledge of the peculiarities through which unconscious mental processes differ from those conscious ones with which we are familiar. One of the most widespread resistances against the work of psychoanalysis with patients as with persons in health reduces to the latter of the two moments. One is afraid of doing harm by psychoanalysis, one is anxious about calling up into consciousness the repressed sexual impulses of the patient, as though there were danger that they could overpower the higher ethical strivings and rob him of his cultural acquisitions. One can see that the patient has sore places in his soul life, but one is afraid to touch them, lest his suffering be increased. We may use this analogy. It is, of course, better not to touch diseased places when one can only cause pain. But we know that the surgeon does not refrain from the investigation and reinvestigation of the seat of illness, if his invasion has as its aim the restoration of lasting health. Nobody thinks of blaming him for the unavoidable difficulties of the investigation or the phenomena of reaction from the operation, if these only accomplish their purpose, and gain for the patient a final cure by temporarily making his condition worse. The case is similar in psychoanalysis; it can lay claim to the same things as surgery; the increase of pain which takes place in the patient during the treatment is very much less than that which the surgeon imposes upon him, and especially negligible in comparison with the pains of serious illness. But the consequence which is feared, that of a disturbance of the cultural character by the impulse which has been freed from repression, is wholly impossible. In relation to this anxiety we must consider what our experiences have taught us with certainty, that the somatic and mental power of a wish, if once its repression has not succeeded, is incomparably stronger when it is unconscious than when it is conscious, so that by being made conscious it can only be weakened. The unconscious wish cannot be influenced, is free from all strivings in the contrary direction, while the conscious is inhibited by those wishes which are also conscious and which strive against it. The work of psychoanalysis accordingly presents a better substitute, in the service of the highest and most valuable cultural strivings, for the repression which has failed.

Now what is the fate of the wishes which have become free by psychoanalysis, by what means shall they be made harmless for the life of the individual? There are several ways. The general consequence is, that the wish is consumed during the work by the correct mental activity of those better tendencies which are opposed to it. The repression is supplanted by a condemnation carried through with the best means at one's disposal. This is possible, since for the most part we have to abolish only the effects of earlier developmental stages of the ego. The individual for his part only repressed the useless impulse, because at that time he was himself still incompletely organized and weak; in his present maturity and strength he can, perhaps, conquer without injury to himself that which is inimical to him. A second issue of the work of psychoanalysis may be that the revealed unconscious impulses can now arrive at those useful applications which, in the case of undisturbed development, they would have found earlier. The extirpation of the infantile wishes is not at all the ideal aim of development. The neurotic has lost, by his repressions, many sources of mental energy whose contingents would have been very valuable for his character building and his life activities. We know a far more purposive process of development, the so-called *sublimation (Sublimirung)*, by which the energy of infantile wish-excitations is not secluded, but remains capable of application, while for the particular excitations, instead of becoming useless, a higher, eventually no longer sexual, goal is set up. The components of the sexual instinct are especially distinguished by such a capacity for the sublimation and exchange of their sexual goal for one more remote and socially more valuable. To the contributions of the energy won in such a way for the functions of our mental life we probably owe the highest cultural consequences. A repression taking place at an early period excludes the sublimation of the repressed impulse; after the removal of the repression the way to sublimation is again free.

We must not neglect, also, to glance at the third of the possible issues. A certain part of the suppressed libidinous excitation has a right to direct satisfaction and ought to find it in life. The claims of our civilization make life too hard for the greater part of humanity, and so further the aversion to reality and the origin of neuroses, without producing an excess of cultural gain by this excess of sexual repression. We ought not to go so far as to fully neglect the original animal part of our nature, we ought not to forget that the happiness of individuals cannot be dispensed with as one of the aims of our culture. The plasticity of the sexual-components, manifest in their capacity for sublimation, may cause a great temptation to accomplish greater culture-effects by a more and more far reaching sublimation. But just as little as with our machines we expect to change more than a certain fraction of the applied heat into useful mechanical work, just as little ought we to strive to separate the sexual impulse in its whole extent of energy from its peculiar goal. This cannot succeed, and if the narrowing of sexuality is pushed too far it will have all the evil effects of a robbery.

I do not know whether you will regard the exhortation with which I close as a presumptuous one. I only venture the indirect presentation of my conviction, if I relate an old tale, whose application you may make yourselves. German literature knows a town called Schilda, to whose inhabitants were attributed all sorts of clever pranks. The wiseacres, so the story goes, had a horse, with whose powers of work they were well satisfied, and against whom they had only one grudge, that he consumed so much expensive oats. They concluded that by good management they would break him of this

bad habit, by cutting down his rations by several stalks each day, until he had learned to do without them altogether. Things went finely for a while, the horse was weaned to one stalk a day, and on the next day he would at last work without fodder. On the morning of this day the malicious horse was found dead; the citizens of Schilda could not understand why he had died. We should be inclined to believe that the horse had starved, and that without a certain ration of oats no work could be expected from an animal.

I thank you for calling me here to speak, and for the attention which you have given me.

NOTES

1. Der Witz und seine Beziehung zum Unbewussten. Deuticke, Vienna, 1905, p. 59.

2. C. G. Jung: Diagnostische Assoziationsstudien, B. 1, 1906.

3. Die Traumdeutung: 2d edition. Deuticke, Vienna, 1909.

4. Zur Psychopathologie des Alltagslebens. 3d edition, 1910. S. Kargar, Berlin.

5. Drei Abhandlungen zur Sexualtheorie. Wien, F. Deuticke, 1908, 2d ed.

6. Analyse der Phobie eines 5-jährigen Knaben. Jahrbuch f. Psychoanalytische u. psychopathologische Forschungen. B. 1, H. 1., 1909.

7. Bleuler: Sexuelle Abnormitäten der Kinder. Jahrbuch der schweizer, Gesellschaft für Schulgesundheitspflege. IX, 1908.

8. Drei Abhandlungen zur Sexualtheorie, Vienna, 1910, 2d ed.

9. Jahrbuch f. Kinderheilkunde, 1879.

10. Compare, Rank, Otto: Der Künstler, Ansätze zu einer Sexual-Psychologie. 56 p. Heller & Co., Wien, 1907.

11. *S. Ferenczi:* Introduction und Uebertragung. Jahrbuch f. psychoanal. u. psychopath. Forschungen, Bd. I, H. 2., 1909.

21

ALFRED BINET AND THEODORE SIMON

Alfred Binet (1857–1911) noticed that his daughters thought about the world differently, each with a distinct style. Madeleine, whom he called *l'observateur,* was cautious and careful, with observations that were detailed and precise. Alice, on the other hand, was his *l'imaginitif*—seeing drama and adventure in the simplest things. His parents had also been quite different: his mother an amateur artist, and his father a stern medical doctor who was physically and emotionally distant. These family experiences underscored for Binet that people are individuals and that observers are not readily dispassionate. Never formally trained in psychology, Binet had some unfortunate public humiliations regarding his research method. In 1880, an enthusiastic Binet published his first paper, but his work on the sensation of touch was flawed methodologically: he had failed to conduct a thorough literature review, and his "new" idea was already in print. He then volunteered as a research assistant at Paris's Salpêtrière Hospital to learn from Jean-Martin Charcot, the leading authority on hypnosis and a proponent of a particular theory regarding hysteria, but not a careful experimentalist. In 1891, Binet volunteered for the new Laboratory for Physiological Psychology at the Sorbonne, Paris, and developed a wide array of projects. The quality and variety were sufficient to convince the laboratory's director, Henri Beaunis, that a new journal was warranted, so *L'Année Psychologique* went to press in 1895. Though he was unable to offer academic credit or degrees, Binet's work attracted a number of students. Theodore Simon (1873–1961), a physician with interests in mentally delayed children, arrived in Paris in 1899 to learn from Binet. In addition to his psychological writings, Binet coauthored lurid plays with the "Prince of Terror," André de Lorde, which featured tormented and murderous characters.

NEW METHODS FOR THE DIAGNOSIS OF THE INTELLECTUAL LEVEL OF SUBNORMALS

Before explaining these methods let us recall exactly the conditions of the problem which we are attempting to solve. Our purpose is to be able to measure the intellectual capacity of a child who is brought to us in order to know whether he is normal or retarded. We should therefore, study his condition at the time and that only. We have nothing to do either with his past history or with his future; consequently we shall neglect his etiology, and we shall make no attempt to distinguish between acquired and congenital idiocy; for a stronger reason we shall set aside all consideration of pathological anatomy which might explain his intellectual deficiency. So much for his past. As to that which concerns his future, we shall exercise the same abstinence; we do not attempt to establish or prepare a prognosis and we leave unanswered the question of whether this retardation is curable, or even improvable. We shall limit ourselves to ascertaining the truth in regard to his present mental state.

Furthermore, in the definition of this state, we should

From Alfred Binet and Theodore Simon. "New Methods for the Diagnosis of the Intellectual Level of Subnormals." *L'Annee Psychologique* 12 (1905): 191–244. Reprinted in E. Kite (Trans.) *The Development of Intelligence in Children* (pp. 37–75 Nashville, TN: Williams Printing Co., 1980) make some restrictions. Most subnormal children, especially those in the schools, are habitually grouped in two categories, those of backward intelligence, and those who are unstable. This latter class, which certain alienists call moral imbeciles, do not necessarily manifest inferiority of intelligence; they are turbulent, vicious, rebellious to all discipline; they lack sequence of ideas, and probably power of attention. It is a matter of great delicacy to make the distinction between children who are unstable, and those who have rebellious dispositions. Elsewhere we have insisted upon the necessity of instructors not treating as unstable, that is as pathological cases, those children whose character is not sympathetic with their own. It would necessitate a long study, and probably a very difficult one, to establish the distinctive signs which separate the unstable from the undisciplined. For the present we shall not take up this study. We shall set the unstable aside, and shall consider only that which bears upon those who are backward in intelligence.

This is not, however, to be the only limitation of our subject because backward states of intelligence present several different types. There is the insane type—or the type of intellectual decay—which consists in a progressive loss of former acquired intelligence. Many epileptics, who suffer from frequent attacks, progress toward insanity. It would be possible and probably very important, to be able to make the distinction between those with decaying intelligence on the one hand, and those of inferior intelligence on the other. But as we have determined to limit on this side also, the domain of our study, we shall rigorously exclude all forms of insanity and decay. Moreover we believe that these are rarely present in the schools, and need not be taken into consideration in the operation of new classes for subnormals.

Another distinction is made between those of inferior intelligence and degenerates. The latter are subjects in whom occur clearly defined, episodical phenomena, such as impulsions, obsessions, deliriums. We shall eliminate the degenerates as well as the insane.

Lastly, we should say a word upon our manner of studying those whom most alienists call idiots but whom we here call of inferior intelligence. The exact nature of this inferiority is not known; and today without other proof, one very prudently refuses to liken this state to that of an arrest of normal development. It certainly seems that the intelligence of these beings has undergone a certain arrest; but it does not follow that the disproportion between the degree of intelligence and the age is the only characteristic of their condition. There is also in many cases, most probably a deviation in the de-

velopment, a perversion. The idiot of fifteen years, who, like a baby of three, is making his first verbal attempts, can not be completely likened to a three-year old child, because the latter is normal, but the idiot is not. There exists therefore between them, necessarily, differences either apparent or hidden. The careful study of idiots shows, among some of them at least, that whereas certain faculties are almost wanting, others are better developed. They have therefore certain aptitudes. Some have a good auditory or musical memory, and a whole repertoire of songs; others have mechanical ability. If all were carefully examined, many examples of these partial aptitudes would probably be found.

Our purpose is in no wise to study, analyze, or set forth the aptitudes of those of inferior intelligence. That will be the object of a later work. Here we shall limit ourselves to the measuring of their general intelligence. We shall determine their intellectual level, and, in order the better to appreciate this level, we shall compare it with that of normal children of the same age or of an analogous level. The reservations previously made as to the true conception of arrested development, will not prevent our finding great advantage in a methodical comparison between those of inferior and those of normal intelligence.

To what method should we have recourse in making our diagnosis of the intellectual level? No one method exists, but there are a number of different ones which should be used cumulatively, because the question is a very difficult one to solve, and demands rather a collaboration of methods. It is important that the practitioner be equipped in such a manner that he shall use, only as accessory, the information given by the parents of the child, so that he may always be able to verify this information, or, when necessary, dispense with it. In actual practice quite the opposite occurs. When the child is taken to the clinic the physician listens a great deal to the parents and questions the child very little, in fact scarcely looks at him, allowing himself to be influenced by a very strong presumption that the child is intellectually inferior. If, by a chance not likely to occur, but which would be most interesting some time to bring about, the physician were submitted to the test of selecting the subnormals from a mixed group of children, he would certainly find himself in the midst of grave difficulties, and would commit many errors especially in cases of slight defect.

The organization of methods is especially important because, as soon as the schools for subnormals are in operation, one must be on his guard against the attitude of the parents. Their sincerity will be worth very little when it is in conflict with their interests. If the parents wish the child to remain in the regular school, they will not be silent concerning his intelligence. "My child understands everything," they will say, and they will be very careful not to give any significant information in regard to him. If, on the contrary, they wish him to be admitted into an institution where gratuitous board and lodging are furnished, they will change completely. They will be capable even of teaching him how to simulate mental debility. One should, therefore, be on his guard against all possible frauds.

In order to recognize the inferior states of intelligence we believe that three different methods should be employed. We have arrived at this synthetic view only after many years of research, but we are now certain that each of these methods renders some service. These methods are:

1. *The medical method,* which aims to appreciate the anatomical, physiological, and pathological signs of inferior intelligence.

2. *The pedagogical method,* which aims to judge of the intelligence according to the sum of acquired knowledge.

3. *The psychological method,* which makes direct observations and measurements of the degree of intelligence.

From what has gone before it is easy to see the value of each of these methods. The medical method is indirect because it conjectures the mental from the physical. The pedagogical method is more direct; but the psychological is the most direct of all because it aims to measure the state of the intelligence as it is at the present moment. It does this by experiments which oblige the subject to make an effort which shows his capability in the way of comprehension, judgment, reasoning, and invention.

I.   The Psychological Method

The fundamental idea of this method is the establishment of what we shall call a measuring scale of intelligence. This scale is composed of a series of tests of increasing difficulty, starting from the lowest intellectual level that can be observed, and ending with that of average normal intelligence. Each group in the series corresponds to a different mental level.

This scale properly speaking does not permit the measure of the intelligence,[1] because intellectual qualities are not superposable, and therefore cannot be measured as linear surfaces are measured, but are on the contrary, a classification, a hierarchy among diverse in-

telligences and for the necessities of practice this classification is equivalent to a measure. We shall therefore be able to know, after studying two individuals, if one rises above the other and to how many degrees, if one rises above the average level of other individuals considered as normal, or if he remains below. Understanding the normal progress of intellectual development among normals, we shall be able to determine how many years such an individual is advanced or retarded. In a word we shall be able to determine to what degrees of the scale idiocy, imbecility, and moronity[2] correspond.

The scale that we shall describe is not a theoretical work; it is the result of long investigations, first at the Salpêtrière, and afterwards in the primary schools of Paris, with both normal and subnormal children. These short psychological questions have been given the name of tests. The use of tests is today very common, and there are even contemporary authors who have made a specialty of organizing new tests according to theoretical views, but who have made no effort to patiently try them out in the schools. Theirs is an amusing occupation, comparable to a person's making a colonizing expedition into Algeria, advancing always only upon the map, without taking off his dressing gown. We place but slight confidence in the tests invented by these authors and we have borrowed nothing from them. All the tests which we propose have been repeatedly tried, and have been retained from among many, which after trial have been discarded. We can certify that those which are here presented have proved themselves valuable.

We have aimed to make all our tests simple, rapid, convenient, precise, heterogeneous, holding the subject in continued contact with the experimenter, and bearing principally upon the faculty of judgment. Rapidity is necessary for this sort of examination. It is impossible to prolong it beyond twenty minutes without fatiguing the subject. During this maximum of twenty minutes, it must be turned and turned about in every sense, and at least ten tests must be executed, so that not more than about two minutes can be given to each. In spite of their interest, we were obliged to proscribe long exercises. For example, it would be very instructive to know how a subject learns by heart a series of sentences. We have often tested the advantage of leaving a person by himself with a lesson of prose or verse after having said to him, "Try to learn as much as you can of this in five minutes." Five minutes is too long for our test, because during that time the subject escapes us; it may be that he becomes distracted or thinks of other things; the test loses its clinical character and becomes too scholastic. We have therefore reluctantly been obliged to renounce testing the rapidity and extent of the memory by this method. Several other equivalent examples of elimination could be cited. In order to cover rapidly a wide field of observation, it goes without saying that the tests should be heterogeneous.

Another consideration. Our purpose is to evaluate a level of intelligence. It is understood that we here separate natural intelligence and instruction. It is the intelligence alone that we seek to measure, by disregarding in so far as possible, the degree of instruction which the subject possesses. He should, indeed, be considered by the examiner as a complete ignoramus knowing neither how to read nor write. This necessity forces us to forego a great many exercises having a verbal, literary or scholastic character. These belong to a pedagogical examination. We believe that we have succeeded in completely disregarding the acquired information of the subject. We give him nothing to read, nothing to write, and submit him to no test in which he might succeed by means of rote learning. In fact we do not even notice his inability to read if a case occurs. It is simply the level of his natural intelligence that is taken into account.

But here we must come to an understanding of what meaning to give to that word so vague and so comprehensive, "the intelligence." Nearly all the phenomena with which psychology concerns itself are phenomena of intelligence; sensation, perception, are intellectual manifestations as much as reasoning. Should we therefore bring into our examination the measure of sensation after the manner of the psycho-physicists? Should we put to the test all of his psychological processes? A slight reflection has shown us that this would indeed be wasted time.

It seems to us that in intelligence there is a fundamental faculty, the alteration or the lack of which, is of the utmost importance for practical life. This faculty is judgment, otherwise called good sense, practical sense, initiative, the faculty of adapting one's self to circumstances. To judge well, to comprehend well, to reason well, these are the essential activities of intelligence. A person may be a moron or an imbecile if he is lacking in judgment; but with good judgment he can never be either. Indeed the rest of the intellectual faculties seem of little importance in comparison with judgment. What does it matter, for example, whether the organs of sense function normally? Of what import that certain ones are hyperesthetic, or that others are anesthetic or are weakened? Laura Bridgman, Helen Keller and their fellow-unfortunates were blind as well as deaf, but this did not prevent them from being very intelligent. Certainly this is demonstrative proof that the total or even partial in-

tegrity of the senses does not form a mental factor equal to judgment. We may measure the acuteness of the sensibility of subjects; nothing could be easier. But we should do this, not so much to find out the state of their sensibility as to learn the exactitude of their judgment.

The same remark holds good for the study of the memory. At first glance, memory being a psychological phenomenon of capital importance, one would be tempted to give it a very conspicuous part in an examination of intelligence. But memory is distinct from and independent of judgment. One may have good sense and lack memory. The reverse is also common. Just at the present time we are observing a backward girl who is developing before our astonished eyes a memory very much greater than our own. We have measured that memory and we are not deceived regarding it. Nevertheless that girl presents a most beautifully classic type of imbecility.

As a result of all this investigation, in the scale which we present we accord the first place to judgment; that which is of importance to us is not certain errors which the subject commits, but absurd errors, which prove that he lacks judgment. We have even made special provision to encourage people to make absurd replies. In spite of the accuracy of this directing idea, it will be easily understood that it has been impossible to permit of its regulating exclusively our examinations. For example, one can not make tests of judgment on children of less than two years when one begins to watch their first gleams of intelligence. Much is gained when one can discern in them traces of coördination, the first delineation of attention and memory. We shall therefore bring out in our lists some tests of memory; but so far as we are able, we shall give these tests such a turn as to invite the subject to make absurd replies, and thus under cover of a test of memory, we shall have an appreciation of their judgment.

Measuring Scale of Intelligence

General recommendations. The examination should take place in a quiet room, quite isolated, and the child should be called in alone without other children. It is important that when a child sees the experimenter for the first time, he should be reassured by the presence of someone he knows, a relative, an attendant, or a school superintendent. The witness should be instructed to remain passive and mute, and not to intervene in the examination either by word or gesture.

The experimenter should receive each child with a friendly familiarity to dispel the timidity of early years. Greet him the moment he enters, shake hands with him and seat him comfortably. If he is intelligent enough to understand certain words, awaken his curiosity, his pride. If he refuses to reply to a test, pass to the next one, or perhaps offer him a piece of candy; if his silence continues, send him away until another time. These are little incidents that frequently occur in an examination of the mental state, because in its last analysis, an examination of this kind is based upon the good will of the subject.

We here give the technique of each question. It will not suffice simply to read what we have written in order to be able to conduct examinations. A good experimenter can be produced only by example and imitation, and nothing equals the lesson gained from the thing itself. Every person who wishes to familiarize himself with our method of examination should come to our school. Theoretical instruction is valuable only when it merges into practical experience. Having made these reservations, let us point out the principal errors likely to be committed by inexperienced persons. There are two: the first consists in recording the gross results without making psychological observations, without noticing such little facts as permit one to give to the gross results their true value. The second error, equally frequent, is that of making suggestions. An inexperienced examiner has no idea of the influence of words; he talks too much, he aids his subject, he puts him on the track, unconscious of the help he is thus giving. He plays the part of pedagogue, when he should remain psychologist. Thus his examination is vitiated. It is a difficult art to be able to encourage a subject, to hold his attention, to make him do his best without giving aid in any form by an unskillful suggestion.[3]

The Series of Tests

1. "LE REGARD."[4] In this test the examiner seeks to discover if there exists that coördination in the movement of the head and the eyes which is associated with the act of vision. If such coördination does exist it proves that the subject not only sees but more than that he "regards" (that is he is able to follow with his eyes a moving object).

Procedure. A lighted match is slowly moved before the eyes of the subject in such a way as to provoke a movement of the head or of the eyes to follow the flame. If a first attempt does not succeed the experiment should be tried again after a little while. It is preferable to operate in a quiet place where no kind of distraction is likely to occur. It is not important that the subject follow the movements of the match constantly for any length of time or persistently. The least sign of coördination of the movements of vision is sufficient, if it leaves no doubt in the mind of the examiner.

Additional remarks. The observation of a few spontaneous phenomena may well be noted. Thus it is possible sometimes for the examiner, by fixing his gaze steadily upon the child, to satisfy himself that the child really coördinates for a moment. If the subject is afflicted with or suspected of blindness, the visual stimulus may be replaced by an auditory stimulus. For example, call him loudly, or better, ring a little bell behind his head and notice if he turns his head toward the sound, or if he has any peculiar facial expression which would indicate that he hears. The reaction of attention to sound seems to develop later than the reaction to light. We have observed children who, when a bell was rung behind the head, would not make a single movement in order to hear better, and yet would follow with their eyes the lighted match. It is scarcely necessary to add that the child who hides his face behind his hand when questioned, or who replies to your smile by a smile, or who walks about the room without knocking against obstacles, stove, chairs, wall, table, proves by his behavior that he coördinates the movements of vision, and thus he has passed the first test.

2. PREHENSION PROVOKED BY A TACTILE STIMULUS. Here the purpose is to discover whether the coördination exists between a tactile stimulus of the hand, and the movement of seizing and carrying to the mouth.

Procedure. A small object, easily handled, for example a piece of wood, is placed in contact with the hand of the child in order to determine if he succeeds in seizing the object, holding it in his hand without letting it fall, and carrying it to his mouth. It is well to stimulate the contact either on the back of the hand or on the palm, and note the results. It is possible that the subject, after having taken the little object, loosens his fingers and lets it fall. It is necessary in that case to try again with a little patience, in order to learn if the letting go came of a chance distraction, or if the subject is not capable of performing the muscular act which would consist in carrying it to his mouth.

3. PREHENSION PROVOKED BY A VISUAL PERCEPTION. Here the purpose is to find whether coördination exists between the sight of an object and its prehension, when the object is not placed in contact with the hand of the subject.

Procedure. The object is presented to his view and

within reach of his hand, in a manner to provoke an intentional movement of his hand to take it. This third test is passed when the subject, following a visual perception of the object, makes a movement of the hand towards the object, reaches, seizes and carries it to his mouth. A small cube of white wood, easy to handle is used. In these presentations it is not forbidden to speak and hence the object is offered to the child as follows: "Here is a little object, take it, it is for you—Come now, pay attention, etc." If the subject understands, so much the better for him; if he does not understand the sound of these words has the advantage of attracting his attention. Moreover the examiner makes gestures and makes them more naturally if he talks at the same time.

4. RECOGNITION OF FOOD.

Here the purpose is to discover whether the subject can make the distinction by sight between familiar food and what can not be eaten.

Procedure. A piece of chocolate (half a bar) and a little cube of white wood of similar dimensions are successively presented. The test is to see if the subject, by sight alone, makes the distinction between the two objects before carrying them to his mouth. Does he carry only the chocolate to his mouth and begin to eat it? Does he refuse to take the piece of wood, or having taken it does he push it away, or again does he hold it in his hand without putting it to his mouth?

Tests 3 and 4 can be made rapidly as a single experiment. A piece of chocolate is first shown to the child and his attention is drawn to it. Note whether he tries to take it or not. If he makes no effort to attain it, and is not distracted by anything, place the chocolate in the palm of his hand, and note what happens. If on the contrary he takes the chocolate which is shown him and carries it to his mouth, the chocolate is taken from him, and the piece of wood put in its place, to see if he carries this new object also to his mouth.

Although these tests succeed with very many children by appealing to their greediness, it often happens that a willful child, or one frightened by the sight of the examiner whom he does not know, turns away from him and refuses to look at what is shown him. These movements of defense indicate already a mentality that corresponds most likely to the fourth degree. The experimenter must be armed with patience and gentleness. He may have a relative, an attendant, or any other person who knows the child, present the chocolate, but he must carefully note the behavior of the child throughout the operation. If the attack of anger, or tears, or fear lasts too long, the examination is necessarily suspended to be taken up at a more favorable time. These are the disappointments to which alienists are accustomed.

5. QUEST OF FOOD COMPLICATED BY A SLIGHT MECHANICAL DIFFICULTY.

This test is designed to bring into play a rudiment of memory, an effort of will, and a coördination of movements.

Procedure. First be sure that the child recognizes the candy or bonbon to be used in this experiment. Then while he is watching you, wrap the bonbon in a piece of paper. Present it to him and carefully note his movements. Does he remember that the paper contains a bonbon? Does he reject it as a useless object, or does he try to pull it apart? Does he carry the covered morsel to his mouth? Does he eat the paper or does he make some effort to unfold it? Does he completely succeed in unfolding it, or does he seem satisfied with one attempt? Does he present the covered morsel to some one else as if to ask his aid?

6. EXECUTION OF SIMPLE COMMANDS AND IMITATION OF SIMPLE GESTURES.

This test involves various motor coördinations, and associations between certain movements, and the understanding of the significance of certain gestures. In these tests the subject enters for the first time into social relations with the experimenter and it is therefore necessary that he understand the will and desires of the latter. It is the beginning of inter-psychology.

Procedure. As soon as the subject enters the room say good morning to him with expression, give him your hand with accentuated gesture to see if he understands the salutation and if he knows how to shake hands. In cases where the subject walks in, ask him to be seated; this permits one to see whether he understands the meaning of the invitation and if he knows the use of a chair. Throw some object on the floor and request him by gestures as well as by speech to pick it up and give it back. Make him get up, shut the door, send him away, call him back. So much for commands. Imitation of simple gestures is accomplished by fixing his attention by repeating several times, "Look at me carefully," and when his attention is gained, by saying "Do as I do." The examiner then claps his hands together, puts them in the air, on the shoulders, behind the back; he turns the thumbs one about the other, raises the foot, etc. All this mimicry must be conducted gaily with the air of play. It is sufficient if a single well marked imitation is provoked; the rest is unnecessary. Do not confound the inaptitude for imitation, with bad humor, ill-will, or timidity.

7. VERBAL KNOWLEDGE OF OBJECTS. The object of this test is to discover if associations exist between things and their names. Comprehension and the first possibilities of language are here studied. This test is a continuation of the previous one and represents the second degree of communication between individuals; the first degree is made through imitation, the second through words.

Procedure. This test is composed of two parts. In the first place the examiner names a part of the body and asks the child to point to it. The questions may relate to the head, the hair, the eyes, the feet, the hands, the nose, the ears, the mouth. Ask the child with a smile "Where is your head?" If he seems embarrassed or timid, encourage him by aiding him a little. "There is your head," pointing it out and touching it if the child does not seem to understand what is wanted of him. On the other hand if he replies by a correct designation to the first question go no further, because if he knows where his head is he should know equally well where are his ears and his mouth. Give him therefore some more difficult questions, for example, his cheek, his eyebrow, his heart.

The second part of the experiment consists in making him designate familiar objects, a string, a cup, a key. Bring the child to the table and by means of gestures indicate the objects and turn his attention to them. When his attention is fixed upon the objects tell him to give you the one you name. "Give me the cup. Give me the key, etc." The cup, the key, the string are the three objects asked for. It is of little importance that he shows awkwardness in taking and presenting them. The essential is that by the play of the countenance and gestures, he indicates clearly that he distinguishes these objects by their names. It is preferable to keep these three objects, others less familiar should be rejected, as for instance a box of matches, a cork, etc. The test is made with three objects in order to avoid the right designation by simple chance. With backward children the following facts may present themselves. They do not know the name of the object presented to them, but having understood that they are to designate an object, they point to anything that is on the table. This is a manner of reacting very common among idiots and imbeciles. They make mistakes but they do not realize it, being in fact very well satisfied with their achievements. Here is another source of error to be avoided. In consequence of their extreme docility, many backward children may be bewildered by the least contradiction. When they have handed you a cup, if you ask them "Isn't this a key?" some might make a sign of acquiescence. This is a test of suggestibility of which more will be said further on.

To a blind child, give objects to be recognized by the sense of touch.

8. VERBAL KNOWLEDGE OF PICTURES. This exercise is the same as the preceding one with this difference only, that the objects are replaced by pictures which, in consequence of the diminished size and the reduction to a plane surface, are a little more difficult to recognize than in nature, and more than this in a picture the objects must be sought for.

Procedure. We make use of a print borrowed from the picture-book of Inspector Lacabe and Mlle. Goergin. This print in colors represents a complex family scene. We show the print to the child and ask him to designate successively the following objects: the window, mamma, big sister, little sister, little girl, cat, broom, basket, bouquet, duster, coffee-mill. The questions are asked in this way: "Where is the window?" or "Tell me where the window is." or "Show me the window," or "Put your finger on the window."

The last suggestion is generally unnecessary because the child has a tendency to place his forefinger, generally a dirty one, upon the detail which is named for him. If he makes an error in designation be careful not to correct it, but make a note of it. In a psychological examination of this kind, one must never point out to a child the errors which he makes. The examiner is not a pedagogue. It is rare that those who take an interest in the picture can not designate the principal details named to them. The incapable ones give no attention to the picture and do not seem to comprehend what is wanted of them. It is interesting to study the attitude of a child during this test. There are two acts to be accomplished, one a search for the object, the other the recognition of the object. At once in the search the aptitudes or inaptitudes betray themselves. Many defective persons show an excess of eagerness to designate the object, which in itself is a sign of faulty attention. They point out at once without waiting to comprehend. They sometimes point out before one has finished the sentence. "Where is the—," said with a suspension in the voice, and already their finger is placed haphazard upon the picture. Such as these do not hunt with care and are incapable of suspending their judgment. This is, it seems to us, a striking characteristic of a weak mind. The child must be closely studied in order to find if, in spite of this special manner, he really knows the names of the objects. A reprimand gently given will sometimes put him on his guard, "No, no, pay attention, you go too fast," and if the question is repeated he will often give a correct answer.

In other cases, errors are sometimes made through

suggestibility. The subject seems to imagine that he will commit a fault if he does not designate some object when the question is asked, and out of compliance or of timidity, he makes an erroneous designation for an object whose name he does not know, or which he does not succeed in finding. Notice again, the more reasonable attitude of those who, not knowing the name of the object, refrain from pointing it out but continue the search or reply distinctly, "I do not know." It is rare that an imbecile uses that little phrase. The avowal of ignorance is a proof of judgment and is always a good indication.

9. NAMING OF DESIGNATED OBJECTS. This test is the opposite of the preceding one. It shows the passing from the thing to the word. It also is executed by the use of pictures.

Procedure. Here we make use of another colored print borrowed from the same collection as the preceding. We place it before the eyes of the child and designate with a pencil different objects while asking each time, "What is this?" The objects upon which we place the pencil are the little girl, the dog, the boy, the father, the lamp-lighter, the sky, the advertisement. For the lamp-lighter we ask what he does. Here as elsewhere it is unnecessary to exhaust the complete series of questions unless the subject fails. One or two positive replies are sufficient to satisfy the requirements of the test. This test permits us to know the vocabulary and the pronunciation of the child. Defects of pronunciation, so frequent in the young, are a serious source of embarrassment. It often requires a very indulgent ear to recognize the right word in an indistinct and very brief murmur, and in a case of this sort the examiner will do well to use an interrogation point. Added to the difficulties which proceed from faulty pronunciation, are those brought about by a special vocabulary. Many little children though normal use a vocabulary invented or deformed by them, which is understood only by themselves and their parents.

Additional remarks. Tests 7, 8, and 9 do not constitute differing degrees in the rigorous sense of the word, that is to say they are not tests corresponding to different levels of intelligence. We have ascertained that generally with subnormals those who can pass test 7, pass 8 and also 9. These would therefore be tests of equal rank. We have kept them, however, because these tests occupy an important place in our measuring scale of intelligence, as they constitute a borderline test between imbecility and idiocy. It is useful to have this borderline solidly placed and all these tests will serve as buttresses.

Observations, such as one may make every day on those afflicted with general paralysis, aphasia, or simply people very much fatigued, show that it is much more difficult to pass from the object to the word than it is to pass from the word to the object, or we may say, that one recognizes a word more easily than one finds it. It does not seem clear up to the present that this observation is also applicable to inferior states of intelligence.

10. IMMEDIATE COMPARISON OF TWO LINES OF UNEQUAL LENGTHS. As we enter the field of what may properly be called psychological experimentation, we shall find it difficult to define which mental functions are being exercised because they are very numerous. Here the child must understand that it is a question of comparison, that the comparison is between two lines that are shown to him; he must understand the meaning of the words, "Show me the longer." He must be capable of comparing, that is of bringing together a conception and an image, and of turning his mind in the direction of searching for a difference. We often have illusions as to the simplicity of psychical processes, because we judge them in relation to others, still more complex. In fact here is a test which will seem to show but little mentality in those who are able to execute it; nevertheless when analyzed it reveals a great complexity.

Procedure. The subject is presented successively with three pieces of paper upon each of which two lines, drawn in ink, are to be compared. Each piece of paper measures 15 by 20 cm.; the lines are drawn lengthwise of the paper, on the same level, and separated by a space of 5 mm. The lines are respectively 4 and 3 cm. in length and one-half of a millimeter in width. On the first sheet the longer line is at the right and on the other two at the left. Each sheet is shown to the subject while saying to him, "Which is the longer line?" Note if his reply is correct but do not tell him. In order to eliminate haphazard replies, it is well to repeat the whole series at least twice. The end is not to discover just how far the accuracy of the child's glance may go, but simply to find if he is capable of making a correct comparison between two lines. Many subnormals are incapable of this; but they act as though they were capable; they seem to understand what is said to them and each time put the finger upon one of the lines saying, "This one." It is necessary to recognize those subjects whose errors are not, strictly speaking, faults of comparison but absence of comparison. It often happens that the subject constantly chooses the line on the same side for the longer, for example always the one on the right side. This manner of reacting would be a sign of defect were it not that one encounters the same thing with some normals.

11. REPETITION OF THREE FIGURES. This is a test of immediate memory and voluntary attention.

Procedure. Looking the subject squarely in the eye to be sure his attention is fixed, one pronounces three figures, after having told him to repeat them. Choose figures that do not follow each other, as for instance 3, 0, 8, or 5, 9, 7, Pronounce the three figures in the same voice without accentuating one more than the others and without rhythm, but with a certain energy. The rapidity to be observed is two figures per second. Listen carefully and record the repetition which is made. Often the first attempt is unsuccessful because the subject has not clearly understood and commences to repeat the first figure the moment he hears it; he must be made to be quiet, renew the explanation and commence the pronunciation of another series of figures. There are certain subjects who can not repeat a single figure; in general these are the ones whose mental condition is such that they have not understood anything at all of what is asked of them. Others repeat only a single figure, the first or the last; others pronounce more than three. Special attention must be given to those whose error consists in pronouncing a greater number of figures than that which is said, or in pronouncing a series of figures in their natural order. An individual who, when asked to repeat 3, 0, 8, replies 2, 3, 4, 5, commits a serious error, which would cause one to suspect mental debility. But on the other hand it is true that all feeble-minded and all imbeciles do not commit this error, and that many young normals may commit it. Be careful to notice also if the subject seems satisfied with his reply when this is obviously and grossly false; this indicates an absence of judgment which constitutes an aggravated condition.

Let us say, apropos of this test, that it is important to make a distinction between errors of attention and adaptation on the one hand, and errors of judgment on the other. When a failure is produced by distraction it is not very important. Thus it may happen that a subject does not repeat the three figures the first time. Begin again and if he succeeds the second time in retaining them he should be considered as having passed the test. A little farther on we shall have to deal with tests of judgment properly so-called, and three or four difficulties will be presented for solution. In this last case, failure will be much more serious, because it can not be due to inattention and the test cannot be considered as passed unless the solutions are given complete.

12. COMPARISON OF TWO WEIGHTS. This is a test of attention, of comparison and of the muscular sense.

Procedure. Place side by side on the table before the subject two small cubical boxes having the same dimensions, (23 mm. on a side) and the same color, but of different weights. The boxes, weighted by grains of lead rolled in cotton and not perceptible by shaking, weigh 3 grams and 12 grams respectively. The subject is asked to find out which is the heavier. The operation terminated, two other cubes of 6 and 15 grams respectively are given him to compare, and again 3 grams and 15 grams. If the subject hesitates or seems to be going haphazard, start over again mixing the cubes in order to be sure that he really compares the weights.

At the injunction, "See the two boxes, now tell me which is the heavier," many young subjects designate haphazard one of the two boxes without testing the weights. This error, all the more naïve since the two are exactly alike in appearance, does not prove that the subject is incapable of weighing them in his hand and of judging of the weights while exercising muscular sense. One must then order him to take the boxes in his hand and weigh them. Some are very awkward, and put the two boxes into one hand at the same time to weigh them. One must again interfere and teach him how to put a box in each hand and weigh the two simultaneously.

Additional remarks. Following this weighing of two boxes of different weight and equal volume, one can propose to weigh two boxes of equal weight but different volume. The illusion which is produced under these circumstances is well known. With the weights equal, the larger box will appear lighter; and the apparent difference of weight increases with the difference of volume. Investigations have been made to determine whether this illusion takes place with backward children, and it has been observed by Demoor that there are certain ones who are not affected by it, something which we ourselves have recently verified. We put before the defective children long boxes of white wood, of the same weight, the largest one $24 \times 4 \times 4$ cm., the smallest $12 \times 2 \times 2$ cm., the medium one $18 \times 3 \times 3$ cm. Like many normal children our subnormals, when given two for comparison and asked "Which is the heavier," pointed out the larger. The first naïve response has but little significance. If one insists, if one tells the subject to weigh them in his hand, it sometimes happens that subnormals either cling to their first designation, or abandon it altogether and find the smaller one the heavier; in the latter case they are sensitive to the illusion. It seems to us that before declaring that a subnormal is not sensitive, one must first find if he can compare two weights, and whether he is able to judge which is the heavier of two weights having the same volume. Having made this preliminary test, one will perceive that very many subnormals are insensible to the illusion because they are incapable of comparing weights. What they lack therefore is a more elementary aptitude.

13. SUGGESTIBILITY. Suggestibility is by no means a test of intelligence, because very many persons of superior intelligence are susceptible to suggestion, through distraction, timidity, fear of doing wrong, or some preconceived idea. Suggestion produces effects which from certain points of view closely resemble the natural manifestations of feeble-mindedness; in fact suggestion disturbs the judgment, paralyzes the critical sense, and forces us to attempt unreasonable or unfitting acts worthy of a defective. It is therefore necessary, when examining a child suspected of retardation, not to give a suggestion unconsciously, for thus artificial debility is produced which might make the diagnosis deceptive. If a person is forced to give an absurd reply by making use of an alternative pronounced in an authoritative voice, it does not in the least prove that he is lacking in judgment. But this source of error being once recognized and set aside, it is none the less interesting to bring into the examination a precise attempt at suggestion, and note what happens. It is a means of testing the force of judgment of a subject and his power of resistance.[5]

Procedure. The proof of suggestibility which we have devised does not give rise to a special experiment: it complicates by a slight addition other exercises which we have already described.

(a) *Designation of objects named by the experimenter.* When we ask the child (test 7) to show us the thread, the cup, the thimble, we add, "Show me the button." On the empty table there is no button, there are only the three preceding objects and yet by gesture and look we invite the subject to search for the button on the table. It is a suggestion by personal action, developing obedience. Certain ones obey quickly and easily, presenting to us again the cup or no matter what other objects. Their suggestibility is complete. Others resist a little, pout, while feigning to hunt for it on the table, or in the cup; they do not reply, but cover their embarrassment by a search which they continue indefinitely if not interrupted. One should consider this attitude as a sufficient expression of resistance, and go no further. It would be unnecessary as we are not seeking a victory over them. Lastly, those least affected by suggestion, reply clearly, "I do not know," or "There is no button." Some laugh.

(b) *Designation of parts of a picture named by the*

experimenter. When the child has looked at the picture and we have asked him to point out the window, etc., at the very last say, "Where is the patapoum?" and then "Where is the nitchevo?" words that have no sense for him. These demands are made in the same manner as the preceding ones. Here again we find the three types, children who docilely designate any object whatever, others who search indefinitely without finding anything, and again others who declare, "There is none."

(c) *Snare of lines.* Following the three pairs of unequal lines, which serve to show the correctness of comparison, we place before the subject three other similar sheets each containing two equal lines. We present them saying, "And here?" Led on by the former replies he has a tendency, an acquired force, for again finding one line longer than the other. Some succumb to the snare completely. Others stop at the first pair and declare, "They are equal," but at the second and third they say one of the lines is longer than the other. Others find them all equal but hesitate. Others again fall into the snare without a shadow of hesitation.

14. VERBAL DEFINITION OF KNOWN OBJECTS. Vocabulary, some general notions, ability to put a simple idea into words, are all brought to light by means of this test.

Procedure. Ask the child what is a house, a horse, a fork, a mamma. This is the conversation that takes place: "Do you know what a——is?" If the child answers yes then ask him: "Very well, then tell me what it is." Try to overcome his silence a little and his timidity. Aid him, only when necessary, by giving him an example: "A dog, it barks," and then see if the child understands and approves that definition.

Very young normal children of two or three years, reply to questions of this kind with enthusiasm. They ordinarily reply in terms of use, "A fork is to eat with." This is typical. Record the answer verbatim. Some will keep silent, some give absurd, incomprehensible replies, or again will repeat the word, "A house, it is a house."

15. REPETITION OF SENTENCES OF FIFTEEN WORDS.[6] This is a test of immediate memory, so far as it concerns the recollection of words; a proof of voluntary attention, naturally because voluntary attention must accompany all psychological experiments; lastly it is a test of language.

Procedure. First be sure that the child is listening carefully, then, after having warned him that he will have to repeat what is said to him, pronounce slowly, intelligibly, the following sentence: *I get up in the morn-*

ing, I dine at noon, I go to bed at night. Then make a sign for him to repeat. Often the child, still not very well adapted, has not fully understood. Never repeat a sentence but go on to another. When the subject repeats it write down verbatim what he says. Many even among normals make absurd repetitions, for example: "I go to bed at noon." Often the child replaces the cultured expression "I dine" for a more familiar form, "I eat." The fact of being able to repeat the sentence correctly after the first hearing is a good sign. The second sentence is easier than the first, *In the summer the weather is beautiful; in winter snow falls.* Here is the third, *Germaine has been bad, she has not worked, she will be scolded.* Now we give five sentences quite difficult to understand:

> The horse-chestnut tree in the garden throws upon the ground the faint shade of its new young leaves.
> The horse draws the carriage, the road is steep and the carriage is heavy.
> It is one o'clock in the afternoon, the house is silent, the cat sleeps in the shade.
> One should not say all that he thinks, but he must think all that he says.
> The spirit of criticism must not be confounded with the spirit of contradiction.

16. COMPARISON OF KNOWN OBJECTS FROM MEMORY. This is an exercise in ideation, in the notion of differences, and somewhat in powers of observation.

Procedure. One asks what difference there is between paper and cardboard, between a fly and a butterfly, between a piece of wood and a piece of glass. First be sure that the subject knows these objects. Ask him, "Have you seen paper?" "Do you know what cardboard is?" Thus ask him about all the objects before drawing his attention to the difference between them. It may happen that little Parisians, even though normal, and eight or nine years old, have never seen a butterfly. These are examples of astounding ignorance, but we have found, what is still more extraordinary, Parisians of ten years who have never seen the Seine.

After being assured that the two objects to be compared are known, demand their difference. If the word is not understood, take notice and afterward choose more familiar language. "In what are they not alike? How are they not alike?" Three classes of replies may be expected. First, that of the children who have no comprehension of what is desired of them. When asked the difference between cardboard and paper, they reply, "The cardboard." When one has provoked replies of this kind,

the explanation must be renewed with patience to see if there is not some means of making oneself understood. Second, the absurd replies, such as, "The fly is larger than the butterfly." "The wood is thicker than the glass," or "The butterfly flies and so does the fly." Third, the correct reply.

17. EXERCISE OF MEMORY ON PICTURES. This is a test of attention and visual memory.

Procedure. The subject is told that several pictures will be shown to him, which he will be allowed to look at for thirty seconds, and that he must then repeat the names of the objects seen, from memory. There are thirteen pictures, each 6 by 6 centimeters, representing the following objects: clock, key, nail, omnibus, barrel, bed, cherry, rose, mouth of a beast, nose, head of a child, eggs, landscape. These pictures are pasted on two cardboards and are shown simultaneously. Measure the time of exposure with the second hand of the watch. In order that the subject shall not become absorbed in one picture, say to him, "Make haste. Look at all." The thirty seconds passed, the examiner writes from dictation the names of the pictures the subject recalls.

This test does indeed give an idea of the memory of a person, but two subjects may have very unequal memories of the same picture; one of them may recall only one detail while another recalls the whole. Moreover there is a weak point in this test in that it may be affected by failure of attention. It is sufficient that a fly should alight, a door should open, a cock should crow, or for the subject to have a desire to use his handkerchief during the thirty seconds, to disturb the work of memorizing. If the result is altogether lacking, the test should be repeated with another collection of pictures to find whether the first error was the result of distraction.

18. DRAWING A DESIGN FROM MEMORY. This is a test of attention, visual memory, and a little analysis.

Procedure. The subject is told that two designs will be shown to him, which he will be allowed to look at for ten seconds, and which he must then draw from memo-

 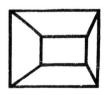

FIGURE 21.1 Design to Be Drawn from Memory After Being Studied 10 Seconds

ry. Excite his emulation. The two designs which we re-produce here, are shown to him and left exposed for ten seconds. (Regulate the time by the second hand of a watch; the time must be exact within one or two seconds.) Then see that the subject commences the reproduction of the design without loss of time.

Marking the results of this test, that is the errors committed, is a delicate operation. Simply note if the reproduction is absolutely correct; or if without being correct it resembles the model; or if, on the contrary, it bears no resemblance whatever to it.

19. IMMEDIATE REPETITION OF FIGURES. This is a test of immediate memory and immediate attention

Procedure. This is the same as for the three figures, see above. Here the errors noted for the three figures take on greater proportions. One must be on the watch for errors of judgment. A normal may fail but the manner is different.

20. RESEMBLANCES OF SEVERAL KNOWN OBJECTS GIVEN FROM MEMORY. This is a test of memory, conscious recognition of resemblances, power of observation.

Procedure. This test closely resembles test 16, except that here resemblances are to be indicated instead of differences. It may be surprising to learn that children have a good deal of trouble noting resemblances; they much more willingly find differences in the objects given them to compare. One must insist a good deal and show them that although unlike two objects may be somewhat similar. Here are the questions to be asked:

In what are a poppy and blood alike?
How are a fly, an ant, a butterfly, a flea alike?
In what way are a newspaper, a label, a picture alike?

Under test 16 we have indicated the precautions that must be taken, notably that of assuring oneself that the child knows the objects to be compared. There are little Parisians who have never seen poppies or ants.

21. COMPARISON OF LENGTHS. This is a test in exactness of glance in rapid comparison.

Procedure. In this test one presents a series of pairs of lines. One line of each pair is 30 mm. long and the other varies from 31 to 35 mm. These lines are drawn on the pages of a blank book, 15 by 30 cm.; there are only two lines on a page. They extend in the same direction, end to end, separated by 5 mm. The longer occupies first the right then the left of the page. There are fifteen pairs.

After placing them in order one begins by showing the pair where the difference is greatest. The subject is asked to point out the longer of the two lines.

We then present, in another blank book, a series of pairs of lines very much more difficult to estimate. The pages of this book are 20 by 30 cm.; the constant line is 100 mm. long, the variable ranging from 101 to 103 mm. The exact comparison of such long lines is beyond the ability of many adults. The number of pairs is twelve.

22. FIVE WEIGHTS TO BE PLACED IN ORDER. This test requires a direct concentration of attention, an appreciation of weight, and the memory of judgment.

Procedure. Five little boxes of the same color and volume are placed in a group on the table. They weigh respectively 3, 6, 9, 12, and 15 grams. They are shown to the subject while saying to him: "Look at these little boxes, they have not the same weight; you are going to arrange them here in their right order. Here to the left first the heaviest weight; next, the one a little less heavy; here one a little less heavy; here one a little less heavy, and here the lightest one." This explanation is difficult to give in childish terms. It must be attempted, however, and repeated if one perceives that it is not understood.

The explanation terminated, one must observe with attention the attitude of the child. One child does not understand, puts nothing in order; another arranges the weights very well but does not compare them; he takes one at random and puts it at the left as the heaviest, without comparing it with the others, and places those remaining without weighing them. A third tries them a little, but noticeably goes at it blindly. The reading of the weights which is inscribed on each, shows us the errors.

There are three classes to distinguish. First, the subject who goes at random without comparing, often committing a serious error, four degrees for example. Second, the subject who compares, but makes a slight error of one or two degrees. Third, the one who has the order exact. We propose to estimate the errors in this test by taking account of the displacement that must be made to re-establish the correct order. Thus in the following example: 12, 9, 6; 3, 15,—15 is not in its place, and the error is of four degrees because it must make four moves to find the place where it belongs. All the others must be changed one degree. The sum of the changes indicates the total error which is of eight degrees. It is necessary to make a distinction between those who commit slight errors of inattention, and those who by the enormity of an error of 6 or 8 prove that they act at random.

23. GAP IN WEIGHTS. As soon as the subject has correctly arranged the weights and only then, tell him that one of the weights is to be taken away while he closes his eyes, and that he is to discover which has been taken away by weighing them in his hand. The operation demanded of him is delicate. One must note that he does not cheat by reading the marking on the box. If there is any fear of this, wrap the boxes in paper.

24. EXERCISE UPON RHYMES. This exercise requires an ample vocabulary, suppleness of mind, spontaneity, intellectual activity.

Procedure. Begin by asking the subject if he knows what a rhyme is. Then explain by means of examples: "Rhymes are words that end in the same way. Thus 'grenouille' rhymes with 'citrouille,' because it is the same sound 'ouille.' 'Compote' rhymes with 'carotte,' they both end with 'ote,' 'Baton' rhymes with 'macaron,' and with 'citron.' Here the rhyme is on 'on.'[7] Do you now understand what a rhyme is? Very well, you must find all the rhymes you can. The word with which you must find rhymes is 'obéissance.'[8] Come, begin, find some." In order to accomplish this test, the subject must not only find rhymes, which is partly a matter of imagination, but he must understand the preceding explanation, which is a matter of judgment. There are subjects who remain silent who either have not understood or are unable to find rhymes. Others are more loquacious but the false rhymes they cite prove that they have not comprehended. The minute having elapsed, renew the explanation and try the test again.

25. VERBAL GAPS TO BE FILLED. This test thought out and proposed by Professor Ebbinghaus of Berlin, varies in significance according to its mode of use. It consists essentially in this: a word of a text is omitted and the subject is asked to replace it. The nature of the intellectual work by which the gap is filled, varies according to the case. This may be a test of memory, a test of style, or a test of judgment. In the sentence: "Louis IX was born in ——" the gap is filled by memory. "The crow —— his feathers with his beak;" in this the idea of the suppressed word is not at all obscure, and the task consists in finding the proper word. We may say in passing, that according to the opinion of several teachers before whom we have tried it, this kind of exercise furnishes excellent scholastic training. Lastly, in sentences of the nature of those we have chosen, the filling of the gaps requires an attentive examination and an appreciation of the facts set forth by the sentence. It is therefore an exercise of judgment.

Procedure. We have simplified it by suppressing all explanations. The words forming the gap are intentionally placed at the end of the sentence. It is sufficient to read the text with expression, then suspend the voice with the tone of interrogation when one arrives at the gap. The subject naturally fills in the gap. If he does not do so spontaneously, urge him a little by saying, "Finish. What must one say?" Once the operation is set going it continues easily.

The operator knows the true words of the text which have been suppressed. He should not yield to the temptation of considering those the only correct ones. He must examine and weigh with care all the words that are given him. Some are good, others altogether bad, nonsensical or absurd. There will be all degrees.

Here is the text with the gaps. The words to be suppressed are in italics.

The weather is clear, the sky is (1) *blue.* The sun has quickly dried the linen which the women have spread on the line. The cloth, white as snow, dazzles the (2) *eyes.* The women gather up the large sheets which are as stiff as though they had been (3) *starched.* They shake them and hold them by the four (4) *corners.* Then they snap the sheets with a (5) *noise.* Meanwhile the housewife irons the fine linen. She takes the irons one after the other and places them on the (6) *stove.* Little Mary who is dressing her doll would like to do some (7) *ironing,* but she has not had permission to touch the (8) *irons.*

26. SYNTHESIS OF THREE WORDS IN ONE SENTENCE. This exercise is a test in spontaneity, facility of invention and combination, aptitude to construct sentences.

Procedure. Three words are proposed: Paris, river, fortune. Ask that a sentence be made using those three words. It is necessary to be very clear, and to explain to those who may not chance to know what a sentence is. Many subjects remain powerless before this difficulty, which is beyond their capacity. Others can make a sentence with a given word but they can not attain to the putting of three words in a single sentence.

27. REPLY TO AN ABSTRACT QUESTION. This test is one of the most important of all, for the diagnosis of mental debility. It is rapid, easily given, sufficiently precise. It consists in placing the subject in a situation presenting a difficulty of an abstract nature. Any mind which is not apt in abstraction succumbs here.

Procedure. This consists in reading the beginning of

a sentence and suspending the voice when one arrives at the point, and repeating, "What ought one to do?" The sentences are constructed in such a manner that the slight difficulty of comprehension which they present, comes from the ideas rather than from the words. The child who does not understand, is hindered less by his ignorance of the language than by his lack of ability to seize an abstract idea. There are twenty-five questions. The first are very easy and tend to put the subject at his ease. We do not reproduce them here as they will be found farther on with the results. Here are only four of the sentences. They are among those of medium difficulty.

1. When one has need of good advice—what must one do?
2. Before making a decision about a very important affair— what must one do?
3. When anyone has offended you and asks you to excuse him—what ought you to do?
4. When one asks your opinion of someone whom you know only a little—what ought you to say?

It is often a delicate matter to estimate the value of a reply. Sometimes the subject does not gather all the shades of the question and the reply is too simple, not absolutely adequate to the demand. Nevertheless one must be satisfied if it expresses sense, if it proves that the general bearing of the question has been grasped.

In other cases the reply is equivocal; it would be excellent if it came from a dilettante, or a decadent, because of the double meaning which is ironically evoked. It is of no value in the mouth of a school child. Thus to the first question, "When one has need of good advice—" a child replied, "one says nothing." We suppose he has not understood but if this had been an ironical reply, one might have found in it a curious meaning. As a matter of fact, these uncertainties, which are truly matters of conscience with the examiner, present themselves but rarely. Ordinarily the interpretation is easy because one knows already about what to expect from his subject.

28. REVERSAL OF THE HANDS OF A CLOCK. This is a test of reasoning, attention, visual imagery.

Procedure. First ask the subject if he knows how to tell time. In case his answer is in the affirmative, put him to the test because it is not best to trust his word. There are imbeciles who say they know how to tell time and give extravagant answers when a watch is given them to read. It is important to note this error in judgment. Having found that the subject knows how to tell time, re-

mind him that the long hand indicates the minutes and the short hand the hours. Then say to him, "Suppose that it is a quarter of three, do you clearly see where the long hand is, and the short hand? Very well, now suppose the long hand is changed to the place where the short hand is, and the short hand to the place of the long, what time is it?" Reverse the hands for the following hours: twenty minutes past six; four minutes of three. The correct solutions are, half past four, and a quarter past eleven.

The subject must not see the face of a watch, nor make the design upon paper, or his cuff or his nail to aid his imagination. As the experiment is made individually, supervision is easy.

When the subject gives the two solutions correctly, one can push him a little further, imposing a question much more difficult. Say to him, "For each of the hours that you have indicated, the reversal of the hands brings about the result that you have found; nevertheless this result is not altogether correct. The transposition indicated is not altogether possible. By analyzing the case with care, tell me why."

This test permits of varying degrees of accuracy in the replies. First, certain ones are not able to make any transposition; they give no solution, or else it is absolutely incorrect. Others who come nearer the truth give a solution which is partially correct; for example, only one of the hands is rightly placed, or perhaps an error of symmetry has been committed, one has put to the right what ought to have been at the left or inversely. The third category is that of subjects who give correct solutions. Finally the fourth is composed of those who give a correct solution and are capable of criticizing the slight inaccuracies.

29. PAPER CUTTING. This exercise calls for voluntary attention, reasoning, visual imagery, but not for vocabulary.

Procedure. Take two sheets of white paper of the same dimensions. Call the attention of the subject to their equality. "You see they are alike." Lay the first one on the table, fold the other into two equal parts slowly before the subject, then fold again into two equal parts at right angles to the first fold. The sheet is now folded in four equal divisions. On the edge that presents a single fold, cut out with the scissors, a triangle. Take away the triangular piece of paper without allowing the subject to study it, but show him the folded paper, and say to him: "The sheet of paper is now cut. If I were to open it, it would no longer resemble the first sheet of paper here on the table; there will be a hole in it. Draw on this first sheet of paper what I shall see when I unfold this one." It is important that the experimenter say neither more nor less than our text, and that he compel himself to employ the words chosen by us although scarcely exact and accurate. The subject now draws upon the first sheet the result of the cutting which he has just witnessed. He should not be allowed to handle the perforated sheet. Some subjects look a little at the perforation, others rely upon their imagination and begin at once to draw. The less intelligent simply draw an angle placed no matter where on the white page, or perhaps a triangle whose form and dimensions are not those of the cut. A little closer observation causes some to consider the form and dimensions. Somewhat better is the triangle replaced by a diamond drawn in the center of the page. Although better, it is still not the correct result, for to be correct two diamonds must be drawn, one in the center of each half of the paper. This test interests everybody. It requires no development of style. It has nothing literary, and rests upon entirely different faculties than those required by preceding tests. Moreover the correctness of the result is easy to grade.

30. DEFINITIONS OF ABSTRACT TERMS. This test resembles closely those which consist in replying to an abstract question. It differs especially in that it requires a knowledge of vocabulary.

Procedure. Without preliminaries, one asks of the subject, "What difference is there between esteem and affection? What difference is there between weariness and sadness?" Often the subject does not reply. He sometimes gives an absurd or nonsensical answer.

We conclude here the list of tests we have used. It would have been easy to continue them by rendering them more complicated, if one had wished to form a hierarchy among normal children. One could even extend the scale up to the adult normal, the average intelligent, the very intelligent, the hyper-intelligent and measure, or try to measure, talent and genius. We shall postpone for another time this difficult study.

When a subnormal, or a child suspected of being such, is questioned, it is not necessary to follow the exact order of tests. A little practice enables one to cut short, and put the finger upon the decisive test.

The solutions given by the subjects can be put into four categories:

1. *Absence of solution.* This is either a case of mutism, or refraining from making an attempt, or an error so great that there is nothing satisfactory in the result. We indicate the absence of result by the algebraic sign minus (−).
2. *Partial solutions.* A part of the truth has been dis-

covered. The reply is passable. This is indicated by a fraction; the fraction in use is $\frac{1}{2}$. When the test permits several degrees one can have $\frac{1}{4}$, or $\frac{3}{4}$, etc.
3. *Complete solution.* This does not admit of definition. It is indicated by the algebraic sign plus (+).
4. *Absurdities.* We have cited a great number of examples and insist upon their importance; they are indicated by the exclamation sign (!).

The cause for certain defective replies can sometimes be grasped with sufficient clearness to admit of classification.

Besides the failure to comprehend the tests as a whole, we encounter:

1. Ignorance; the subject does not know the sense of a word or has never seen the object of which one speaks. Thus a child does not know a poppy. We write an I.
2. Resistance to the examination because of bad humor, unwillingness, state of nerves, etc. We write an R.
3. Accentuated timidity. We write a T.
4. The failure of attention, distraction. We write a D. The distraction may be of different kinds. There is an accidental distraction, produced by an exterior excitant or an occasional cause. For example, the case of a normal who spoils a memory test because he must use his handkerchief. There is constitutional distraction frequent among subnormals. We have ascertained among them the following types: Distraction from scattered perceptions. Distraction from preoccupation. Distraction from inability to fix the attention.

II. Pedagogical Method

The pedagogical method consists in making an inventory of the total knowledge of a subject, in comparing this total with that of a normal subject, in measuring the difference, and in finding if the difference in the knowledge of a subject is explained by the insufficiency of scholastic training.

The first idea of this method was suggested to us by reading the pamphlets in which Dr. Demoor and his colleagues explain the function of the special school at Brussels. To this school are admitted all children "pedagogically retarded." The pedagogically retarded are those whose instruction puts them two years behind normal children of the same age.

In France, our ministerial commission estimated that these pedagogically retarded, or to speak more accurately, these children lacking education, do not need to be sent to a special class; being normal they ought to remain in the ordinary schools, there to make up their instruction. We have thought that since it is of practical value to make a distinction between the normal who is lacking in school training and the subnormals, this distinction could be made in the type of scholastic knowledge beneficial to each of these classes.

The normal retarded child is one who is not at the level of his comrades of the same age, for causes that have no relation to his intelligence; he has missed school, or he has not attended regularly, or he has had mediocre teachers, who have made him lose time, etc. The subnormal ignoramus is one whose ignorance comes from a personal cause; he does not learn as quickly as his comrades, he comprehends less clearly, in a word, he is more or less impervious to the usual methods of instruction. We now have a method of recognizing subnormal ignoramuses; this consists in estimating at the same time their degree of instruction and their knowledge. Thus the idea of the pedagogical method originated.

Having acknowledged what we owe to Dr. Demoor and to his colleagues, we must nevertheless add that these authors do not seem to appreciate the need of precise methods of evaluating even among normals the amount of retardation in instruction. It is probable that in their practice the amount of this retardation is taken into account. Teachers do not hesitate, however, to make estimates of this nature. They will say without hesitation that such a child is two years or three years retarded. The value of these estimates is as yet undetermined.

We have found the following direction of great value to teachers who are attempting to designate the subnormals in their school. "Any child is subnormal who, in spite of regular or sufficient schooling, is two years behind children of the same age." This criterion fixes the ideas and evades some uncertainties. But even though it constitutes a great improvement over subjective appreciation, which has no guide, it has still the fault of lacking precision. It remains to be seen what is acquired from school instruction by normal children of different ages; one must to some extent make a barometer of instruction. On the other hand there remains to be organized rapid methods which permit one to tell with precision the degree of instruction which a candidate has attained. These two lines of research can scarcely be followed out except by persons belonging to the teaching profession. We have succeeded in interesting different distinguished persons. M. Lacabe, primary inspector in Paris, has consented to confide to the instructors of his staff the preparation of a work designed to measure the knowledge of his pupils in grammar. M. Behr, primary inspector of Fontainebleau, has undertaken to determine the scholastic attainments of the average child, ideally average, of neither over nor under intelligence, of average health, and who has had professors of average merit. The idea is original, the attempt promises to be interesting; it will be laborious. Another work,[9] entirely different in idea, is due to M. Vaney, school director of Paris. It is devoted to the measuring of proficiency acquired in mathematics.

In considering the question as a whole, it is clear that the pedagogical or instruction method, divides into two very distinct categories:

1. The methods permitting one to evaluate scholastic knowledge including arithmetic, grammar, history, geography—in a word, all that figures in the curriculums and can be easily measured.
2. The investigation of knowledge acquired outside the schools.

It is upon this last point that we invite the attention of our colleagues, the teachers. There is a mass of information that a child acquires outside of school, which figures on no program. It is acquired by conversation, reading the paper, observation of all that goes on in the street, in the house, everywhere. It is pre-eminently practical knowledge, part of it is useless, much is very important, quite as important surely as that which has a scholastic character.

We have ourselves recently begun a quest upon this side of the question. We have made collective tests in the school, asking the children to reply in writing to certain questions concerning practical life. More than this, we have asked teachers to put questions individually to the children upon points that we have designated to them. Here is a little sample of the nature of the information which every child is to furnish of himself without the aid of anyone.

1. What is your name? What is your first name?
2. What is your age?
3. What is the exact date of your birth?
4. How long have you attended school?
5. What day is today?
6. What month is it?
7. What year is it?
8. What day of the month is it?
9. What hour is it?

10. Is it morning or afternoon?
11. What is the address of your parents (street, number, apartment)?
12. What is your father's trade, your mother's trade?
13. What are the names of your mother, brothers and sisters if you have any?
14. Which are younger, which are older than you?
15. Count this money. How much is it? (Show 12 sous in 2-sou pieces—1 fr. 80 centimes, one piece of 1 franc; 1 piece of 50 centimes, and the remainder four single sous and a 2-sou piece).
16. Name the colors. (Squares of colored paper, vivid red, pink, light yellow, deep yellow, orange, green, light blue, deep blue, violet, white, grey, black.)
17. Do you read the paper? Which one?
18. Have you learned to ride a bicycle?
19. What is a "correspondence d'omnibus" and what is its use?[10]
20. What stamps must one put on a letter sent from Paris to Geneva?
21. How much does a loaf of bread cost?
22. Describe how to fry an egg.
23. How much does a sack of charcoal cost?
24. What do you think is the age of your principal?
25. Did you ever see a cow milked?
26. How much does a street car conductor get a day?
27. Have you ever seen a goat? a frog? a rat? an elephant?
28. Did you ever light a fire?
29. Do you ever do several errands at a time?
30. What is a janitor?
31. What is meant by "le term?" (Obscure for an American but not so for a French child.)

Sommer, the German alienist, well known for his work of pathological psychology, has indicated in a special book the utility of these investigations in determining what he calls orientation in time and space. We do not know what advantages he has been able to draw from them; we are also ignorant of whether or not he has taken the elementary precaution, nearly always neglected, of first establishing how a normal child replies. Here are several examples of the information which we have gathered in the primary schools, upon the extra-scholastic knowledge of normals.

"*Correspondence d'Omnibus.*" In the first class (from 11 to 15 years) there were 16 boys who replied correctly—11 did not know, and 2 replied ambiguously. In the third class (from 9 to 14 years) 4 boys knew, 28 did not know. In the fifth class (from 7 to 12 years) 1 boy knew, 41 did not know. In the sixth class (6 to 9 years) 42 boys did not know. Here is a test that is good for the higher grade because the number of correct replies is proportional to the age.

Frying an egg. In the first class, 15 children described very well the manner, and 15 did not know. In the sixth class 10 described it well, 28 did not know, and 4 had doubtful replies.

Price of a sack of charcoal. In the first class 22 gave a reasonable price (2 fr. 50 to 5 fr.); 3 gave unreasonable prices (25 fr., 50 fr., etc.); 4 did not know. In the sixth class, 7 gave a reasonable price (2 fr., to 5 fr.); 5 gave prices too high (10 fr., 50 fr., 70 fr., etc.); 11 gave too low a price (10 centimes, 1 fr. 80) and 18 did not know.

Know how to ride a bicycle. In the first class 15 knew and 15 did not know. In the sixth class 13 knew, and 29 did not know.

Have you ever seen a goat? a frog? a rat? an elephant? In the first class, all had seen the animals. In the sixth class of 42 pupils, 2 had not seen a goat, 9 had never seen a frog, 8 had never seen a rat and 3 had never seen an elephant. It is curious that the frog should be less known than the elephant.

What is meant by "le terme?" In the first class, 14 knew, and 16 gave ambiguous replies. In the sixth class 3 knew, 3 gave doubtful answers, and 36 did not know.

We hope soon to be able to make out a complete list of items of extra-scholastic knowledge. This is only a sample. It will be necessary to give by ages the percentage of correct replies.

The question is still open as to what extent extra-scholastic knowledge is foreign to subnormals. We can at present only make conjectures on this point. It is probable that the slightly subnormal possess many of these notions of practical life; perhaps their defect manifests itself especially in an inability to assimilate that which is properly scholastic, and on the other hand these may be quite apt in the more concrete facts of every-day life. The absence of this knowledge characterizes especially true imbeciles, those who are more seriously affected. Not to know either the number or names of one's brother or sisters, to be unable to distinguish one's given name and one's family name, ignorance of the address of one's parents, would constitute then a sufficiently serious sign of intellectual inferiority, if this manner of looking at the matter is right, and if there are not extenuating circumstances connected with this ignorance.

To sum up, the pedagogical method is two fold. It consists in establishing as it were the balance sheet of the scholastic knowledge acquired by the child; on the other hand it consists in establishing the balance sheet of extra-scholastic knowledge. The general result will be found, not by a complete inventory—that would take too long—but by tests bearing upon a small number of questions judged to be representative of the whole.

The pedagogical method is somewhat indirect in its manner of arriving at the state and degree of the intelligence; it grasps the intelligence through the memory only. One who is rich in memory may be poor in judgment. One even finds imbeciles who have an amazing memory. It is right to add that in spite of this, these imbeciles are but little instructed, which proves to us that instruction, although it depends principally upon memory, demands also other intellectual faculties, especially judgment. One must not therefore exaggerate the bearing of this theoretic criticism which we here make upon the pedagogical method.

The disadvantages which our use of the method permits us already to suspect, are the following: in the first place it cannot be applied to very young children, of from 3 to 6 years, and it is especially important to point out mental debility at that age; in the second place it requires that one should know the scholastic attainments of each child. It is not always easy to see clearly into the past life of a child. Did he miss his class three years ago? If he followed the class, had he in his temperament, his state of health, his habits, special reasons for relaxation? Was his master a poor one, did he fail to understand the child? The quest may find itself face to face with facts, which from their remoteness and their nature, are very difficult to evaluate. These doubtful cases will not be in the majority, let us hope; but they will present themselves in abundance. M. Vaney has noted several in a statistical study, which is restricted, however. Dr. Demoor finds 50 doubtful in a total of 246 retarded and subnormal children; that is approximately one-fifth doubtful. These facts show that the pedagogical method has its imperfections. It should not be employed exclusively.

NOTES

1. One of us (Binet) has elsewhere insisted that a distinction be made between the measure and the classification. See "Suggestibilite," p. 103, Vol. 11, *L'Année Psychologique.*

2. *Kite's note:* Binet's classification of defectives is idiot, imbecile, and "débile." This seems to correspond closely to our American terminology of idiot, imbecile, and moron. We have accordingly translated "débile" as moron and "débilité" as moronity.

3. One of us (Binet) has been for some years the president of "Société libre pour l'étude de l'enfant," and he has striven to spread among his colleagues, mostly teachers, the taste for scientific research. He has found that the two errors mentioned in the text are those which appear most frequently among beginners.

4. *Kite's note:* We have here retained the word used by Binet, because in the English there is no one word exactly synonymous with it. The word literally translated means "the ability to follow with the eyes a moving object."

5. In a book specially devoted to *Suggestibility* (Paris, Schleicher, 1900) one of us (Binet) has described several methods of testing for suggestibility which are valuable for application in the schools.

6. *Kite's note:* Binet's sentences vary in length from thirteen to eighteen words. He has corrected this discrepancy in the 1908 edition by counting the number of syllables given in this and kindred tests. A literal translation of his sentences obviously may not contain the same number of words in English as in French.

7. *Kite's note:* We have here retained the French words because it is obvious that the English equivalents would not rhyme. In using the test one must of course use suitable English rhymes.

8. *Kite's note:* There are many words in the French which rhyme with "obéissance" and which are perfectly familiar to a French child. This is not true of its English equivalent. One would not think of asking a child to make rhymes with "obedience."

9. See *L'Année Psychologique,* Vol. II, p. 146–162.

10. *Kite's note:* "Correspondance d'omnibus" cannot be translated into English because the system has no counterpart in this country. But experience would soon teach a resident of Paris the use of this term.

22

HUGO MÜNSTERBERG

Hugo Münsterberg (1863–1916) created quite a sensation in Chicago at the World's Columbian Exhibition of 1893 when he introduced the American public to the new science of experimental psychology with a display of the shiny brass and polished mahogany instruments used in Germany to measure the mind. Born to a wealthy family in Danzig, Prussia (now Gdansk, Poland), Münsterberg studied at the University of Leipzig under Wilhelm Wundt (p. 296) and received his Ph.D. in 1885. He earned a medical degree from the University of Heidelberg in 1887 and began as a *Privatdocent,* or lecturer, at the University of Freiburg. In 1889, William James (p. 216) arranged to meet Münsterberg at the first International Congress of Psychology in Paris upon reading his book, *Voluntary Action,* a work James found brilliant but that Wundt thought ridiculous. James successfully recruited Münsterberg to the faculty of Harvard University in 1892, but Münsterberg remained equivocal about leaving Germany. He returned to the University of Freiburg in 1895, but no academic jobs were forthcoming in Germany, so Münsterberg settled permanently at Harvard in 1897. The application of psychology intrigued Münsterberg, and he wrote several popular books detailing the practical nature of psychology, including *On the Witness Stand* (1908); *Psychology and the Teacher* (1910); and *The Photoplay* (1916), a work on the psychology of movies. An ardent and vocal German patriot, Münsterberg opposed the United States' entrance into World War I, a stance that led to isolation from his Harvard colleagues and vilification by the public.

PSYCHOLOGY AND INDUSTRIAL EFFICIENCY

INTRODUCTION

I

Applied Psychology

OUR aim is to sketch the outlines of a new science which is to intermediate between the modern laboratory psychology and the problems of economics: the psychological experiment is systematically to be placed at the service of commerce and industry. So far we have only scattered beginnings of the new doctrine, only tentative efforts and disconnected attempts which have started, sometimes in economic, and sometimes in psychological, quarters. The time when an exact psychology of business life will be presented as a closed and perfected system lies very far distant. But the earlier the attention

of wider circles is directed to its beginnings and to the importance and bearings of its tasks, the quicker and the more sound will be the development of this young science. What is most needed to-day at the beginning of the new movement are clear, concrete illustrations which demonstrate the possibilities of the new method. In the following pages, accordingly, it will be my aim to analyze the results of experiments which have actually been carried out, experiments belonging to many different spheres of economic life. But these detached experiments ought always at least to point to a connected whole; the single experiments will, therefore, always need a general discussion of the principles as a background. In the interest of such a wider perspective we may at first enter into some preparatory questions of theory. They may serve as an introduction which is to

From Hugo Münsterberg, "Applied Psychology," "Means and Ends," and "Vocation and Fitness." In *Psychology and Industrial Efficiency* (pp. 3–10, 17–36). New York: Houghton Mifflin 1913.

lead us to the actual economic life and the present achievements of experimental psychology.

It is well known that the modern psychologists only slowly and very reluctantly approached the apparently natural task of rendering useful service to practical life. As long as the study of the mind was entirely dependent upon philosophical or theological speculation, no help could be expected from such endeavors to assist in the daily walks of life. But half a century has passed since the study of consciousness was switched into the tracks of exact scientific investigation. Five decades ago the psychologists began to devote themselves to the most minute description of the mental experiences and to explain the mental life in a way which was modeled after the pattern of exact natural sciences. Their aim was no longer to speculate about the soul, but to find the psychical elements and the constant laws which control their connections. Psychology became experimental and physiological. For more than thirty years the psychologists have also had their workshops. Laboratories for experimental psychology have grown up in all civilized countries, and the new method has been applied to one group of mental traits after another. And yet we stand before the surprising fact that all the manifold results of the new science have remained book knowledge, detached from any practical interests. Only in the last ten years do we find systematic efforts to apply the experimental results of psychology to the needs of society.

It is clear that the reason for this late beginning is not an unwillingness of the last century to make theoretical knowledge serviceable to the demands of life. Every one knows, on the contrary, that the glorious advance of the natural sciences became at the same time a triumphal march of technique. Whatever was brought to light in the laboratories of the physicists and chemists, of the physiologists and pathologists, was quickly transformed into achievements of physical and chemical industry, of medicine and hygiene, of agriculture and mining and transportation. No realm of the external social life remained untouched. The scientists, on the other hand, felt that the far-reaching practical effect which came from their discoveries exerted a stimulating influence on the theoretical researches themselves. The pure search for truth and knowledge was not lowered when the electrical waves were harnessed for wireless telegraphy, or the Roentgen rays were forced into the service of surgery. The knowledge of nature and the mastery of nature have always belonged together.

The persistent hesitation of the psychologists to make similar practical use of their experimental results has therefore come from different causes. The students

of mental life evidently had the feeling that quiet, undisturbed research was needed for the new science of psychology in order that a certain maturity might be reached before a contact with the turmoil of practical life would be advisable. The sciences themselves cannot escape injury if their results are forced into the rush of the day before the fundamental ideas have been cleared up, the methods of investigation really tried, and an ample supply of facts collected. But this very justified reluctance becomes a real danger if it grows into an instinctive fear of coming into contact at all with practical life. To be sure, in any single case there may be a difference of opinion as to when the right time has come and when the inner consolidation of a new science is sufficiently advanced for the technical service, but it ought to be clear that it is not wise to wait until the scientists have settled all the theoretical problems involved. True progress in every scientific field means that the problems become multiplied and that ever new questions keep coming to the surface. If the psychologists were to refrain from practical application until the theoretical results of their laboratories need no supplement, the time for applied psychology would never come. Whoever looks without prejudice on the development of modern psychology ought to acknowledge that the hesitancy which was justified in the beginning would to-day be inexcusable lack of initiative. For the sciences of the mind, too, the time has come when theory and practice must support each other. An exceedingly large mass of facts has been gathered, the methods have become refined and differentiated, and however much may still be under discussion, the ground common to all is ample enough to build upon.

Another important reason for the slowness of practical progress was probably this. When the psychologists began to work with the new experimental methods, their most immediate concern was to get rid of mere speculation and to take hold of actual facts. Hence they regarded the natural sciences as their model, and, together with the experimental method which distinguishes scientific work, the characteristic goal of the sciences was accepted too. This scientific goal is always the attainment of general laws; and so it happened that in the first decades after the foundation of psychological laboratories the general laws of the mind absorbed the entire attention and interest of the investigators. The result of such an attitude was, that we learned to understand the working of the typical mind, but that all the individual variations were almost neglected. When the various individuals differed in their mental behavior, these differences appeared almost as disturbances which the psychologists had to eliminate in order to find the general laws which hold for every mind. The studies were accordingly confined to the general averages of mental experience, while the variations from such averages were hardly included in the scientific account. In earlier centuries, to be sure, the interest of the psychological observers had been given almost entirely to the rich manifoldness of human characters and intelligences and talents. In the new period of experimental work, this interest was taken as an indication of the unscientific fancies of the earlier age, in which the curious and the anecdotal attracted the view. The new science which was to seek the laws was to overcome such popular curiosity. In this sign experimental psychology has conquered. The fundamental laws of the ideas and of the attention, of the memory and of the will, of the feeling and of the emotions, have been elaborated. Yet it slowly became evident that such one-sidedness, however necessary it may have been at the beginning, would make any practical application impossible. In practical life we never have to do with what is common to all human beings, even when we are to influence large masses; we have to deal with personalities whose mental life is characterized by particular traits of nationality, or race, or vocation, or sex, or age, or special interests, or other features by which they differ from the average mind which the theoretical psychologist may construct as a type. Still more frequently we have to act with reference to smaller groups or to single individuals whose mental physiognomy demands careful consideration. As long as experimental psychology remained essentially a science of the mental laws, common to all human beings, an adjustment to the practical demands of daily life could hardly come in question. With such general laws we could never have mastered the concrete situations of society, because we should have had to leave out of view the fact that there are gifted and ungifted, intelligent and stupid, sensitive and obtuse, quick and slow, energetic and weak individuals.

But in recent years a complete change can be traced in our science. Experiments which refer to these individual differences themselves have been carried on by means of the psychological laboratory, at first reluctantly and in tentative forms, but within the last ten years the movement has made rapid progress. To-day we have a psychology of individual variations from the point of view of the psychological laboratory. This development of schemes to compare the differences between the individuals by the methods of experimental science was after all the most important advance toward the practical application of psychology. The study of the individual

differences itself is not applied psychology, but it is the presupposition without which applied psychology would have remained a phantom.

III

Means and Ends

Applied psychology is evidently to be classed with the technical sciences. It may be considered as psychotechnics, since we must recognize any science as technical if it teaches us to apply theoretical knowledge for the furtherance of human purposes. Like all technical sciences, applied psychology tells us what we ought to do if we want to reach certain ends; but we ought to realize at the threshold where the limits of such a technical science lie, as they are easily overlooked, with resulting confusion. We must understand that every technical science says only: you must make use of this means, if you wish to reach this or that particular end. But no technical science can decide within its limits whether the end itself is really a desirable one. The technical specialist knows how he ought to build a bridge or how he ought to pierce a tunnel, presupposing that the bridge or the tunnel is desired. But whether they are desirable or not is a question which does not concern the technical scientist, but which must be considered from economic or political or other points of view. Everywhere the engineer must know how to reach an end, and must leave it to others to settle whether the end is in itself desirable. Often the end may be a matter of course for every reasonable being. The extreme case is presented by the applied science of medicine, where the physician subordinates all his technique to the end of curing the patient. Yet if we are consistent we must acknowledge that all his medical knowledge can prescribe to him only that he proceed in a certain way if the long life of the patient is acknowledged as a desirable end. The application of anatomy, physiology, and pathology may just as well be used for the opposite end of killing a man. Whether it is wise to work toward long life, or whether it is better to kill people, is again a problem which lies outside the sphere of the applied sciences. Ethics or social philosophy or religion have to solve these preliminary questions. The physician as such has only to deal with the means which lead toward that goal.

We must make the same discrimination in the psychotechnical field. The psychologist may point out the methods by which an involuntary confession can be secured from a defendant, but whether it is justifiable to extort involuntary confessions is a problem which does not concern the psychologist. The lawyers or the legislators must decide as to the right or wrong, the legality or illegality, of forcing a man to show his hidden ideas. If such an end is desirable, the psychotechnical student can determine the right means, and that is the limit of his office. We ought to keep in mind that the same holds true for the application of psychology in economic life. Economic psychotechnics may serve certain ends of commerce and industry, but whether these ends are the best ones is not a care with which the psychologist has to be burdened. For instance, the end may be the selection of the most efficient laborers for particular industries. The psychologist may develop methods in his laboratory by which this purpose can be fulfilled. But if some mills prefer another goal,—for instance, to have not the most efficient but the cheapest possible laborers,—entirely different means for the selection are necessary. The psychologist is, therefore, not entangled in the economic discussions of the day; it is not his concern to decide whether the policy of the trusts or the policy of the trade-unions or any other policy for the selection of laborers is the ideal one. He is confined to the statement: if you wish this end, then you must proceed in this way; but it is left to you to express your preference among the ends. Applied psychology can, therefore, speak the language of an exact science in its own field, independent of economic opinions and debatable partisan interests. This is a necessary limitation, but in this limitation lies the strength of the new science. The psychologist may show how a special commodity can be advertised; but whether from a social point of view it is desirable to reinforce the sale of these goods is no problem for psychotechnics. If a sociologist insists that it would be better if not so many useless goods were bought, and that the aim ought rather to be to protect the buyer than to help the seller, the psychologist would not object. His interest would only be to find the right psychological means to lead to this other social end. He is partisan neither of the salesman nor of the customer, neither of the capitalist nor of the laborer, he is neither Socialist nor anti-Socialist, neither high-tariff man nor free-trader. Here, too, of course, there are certain goals which are acknowledged on all sides, and which therefore hardly need any discussion, just as in the case of the physician, where the prolongation of life is practically acknowledged as a desirable end by every one. But everywhere where the aim is not perfectly a matter of course, the psychotechnical specialist fulfills his task only when he is satisfied with demonstrating that certain psychical means serve a certain end, and that they ought to be applied as soon as that end is accepted.

The whole system of psychotechnical knowledge might be subdivided under either of the two aspects. Either we might start from the various mental processes and ask for what end each mental factor can be practically useful and important, or we can begin with studying what significant ends are acknowledged in our society and then we can seek the various psychological facts which are needed as means for the realization of these ends. The first way offers many conveniences. There we should begin with the mental states of attention, memory, feeling, and so on, and should study how the psychological knowledge of every one of these mental states can render service in many different practical fields. The attention, for instance, is important in the classroom when the teacher tries to secure the attention of the pupils, but the judge expects the same attention from the jurymen in the courtroom, the artist seeks to stir up the attention of the spectator, the advertiser demands the attention of the newspaper readers. Whoever studies the characteristics of the mental process of attention may then be able to indicate how in every one of these unlike cases the attention can be stimulated and retained. Nevertheless the opposite way which starts from the tasks to be fulfilled seems more helpful and more fundamentally significant. The question, then, is what mental processes become important for the tasks of education, what for the purposes of the courtroom, what for the hospital, what for the church, what for politics, and so on.

As this whole essay is to be devoted exclusively to the economic problems, we are obliged to choose the second way; that is, to arrange applied psychology with reference to its chief ends and not with reference to the various means. But the same question comes up in the further subdivision of the material. In the field of economic psychology, too, we might ask how far the study of attention, or of perception, or of feeling, or of will, or of memory, and so on, can be useful for the purposes of the business man. Or here, too, we might begin with the consideration of the various ends and purposes. The ends of commerce are different from those of industry, those of publishing different from those of transportation, those of agriculture different from those of mining; or, in the field of commerce, the purposes of the retailer are different from those of the wholesale merchant. There can be no limit to such subdivisions; each particular industry has its own aims, and in the same industry a large variety of tasks are united. We should accordingly be led to an ample classification of special economic ends with pigeonholes for every possible kind of business and of labor. The psychologist would have to find for every one of these ends the right mental means. This would be the ideal system of economic psychology.

But we are still endlessly far from such a perfect system. Modern educational psychology and medical psychology have reached a stage at which an effort for such a complete system might be realized, but economic psychology is still at too early a stage of development. It would be entirely artificial to-day to aim at such ideal completeness. If we were to construct such a complete system of questions, we should have no answers. In the present stage nothing can be seriously proposed but the selection of a few central purposes which occur in every department of business life, and a study of the means to reach these special ends by the discussion of some typical cases which may clearly illustrate the methods involved.

From this point of view we select three chief purposes of business life, purposes which are important in commerce and industry and every economic endeavor. We ask how we can find the men whose mental qualities make them best fitted for the work which they have to do; secondly, under what psychological conditions we can secure the greatest and most satisfactory output of work from every man; and finally, how we can produce most completely the influences on human minds which are desired in the interest of business. In other words, we ask how to find the best possible man, how to produce the best possible work, and how to secure the best possible effects.

THE BEST POSSIBLE MAN

IV

Vocation and Fitness

Instead of lingering over theoretical discussions, we will move straight on toward our first practical problem. The economic task, with reference to which we want to demonstrate the new psychotechnic method, is the selection of those personalities which by their mental qualities are especially fit for a particular kind of economic work. This problem is especially useful to show what the new method can do and what it cannot do. Whether the method is sufficiently developed to secure full results to-day, or whether they will come to-morrow, is unimportant. It is clear that the success of to-morrow is to be hoped for, only if understanding and interest in the problem is already alive to-day.

When we inquire into the qualities of men, we use the word here in its widest meaning. It covers, on the one side, the mental dispositions which may still be quite undeveloped and which may unfold only under the influence of special conditions in the surroundings; but, on the other side, it covers the habitual traits of the personality, the features of the individual temperament and character, of the intelligence and of the ability, of the collected knowledge and of the acquired experience. All variations of will and feeling, of perception and thought, of attention and emotion, of memory and imagination, are included here. From a purely psychological standpoint, quite incomparable contents and functions and dispositions of the personality are thus thrown together, but in practical life we are accustomed to proceed after this fashion: If a man applies for a position, he is considered with regard to the totality of his qualities, and at first nobody cares whether the particular feature is inherited or acquired, whether it is an individual chance variation or whether it is common to a larger group, perhaps to all members of a certain nationality or race. We simply start from the clear fact that the personalities which enter into the world of affairs present an unlimited manifoldness of talents and abilities and functions of the mind. From this manifoldness, it necessarily follows that some are more, some less, fit for the particular economic task. In view of the far-reaching division of labor in our modern economic life, it is impossible to avoid the question how we can select the fit personalities and reject the unfit ones.

How has modern society prepared itself to settle this social demand? In case that certain knowledge is indispensable for the work or that technical abilities must have been acquired, the vocation is surrounded by examinations. This is true of the lower as well as of the higher activities. The direct examination is everywhere supplemented by testimonials covering the previous achievements, by certificates referring to the previous education, and in frequent cases by the endeavor to gain a personal impression from the applicant. But if we take all this together, the total result remains a social machinery by which perhaps the elimination of the entirely unfit can be secured. But no one could speak of a really satisfactory adaptation of the manifold personalities to the economic vocational tasks. All those examinations and tests and certificates refer essentially to what can be learned from without, and not to the true qualities of the mind and the deeper traits. The so-called impressions, too, are determined by the most secondary and external factors. Society relies instinctively on the hope that the natural wishes and interests will push every one to the place for which his dispositions, talents, and psychophysical gifts prepare him.

In reality this confidence is entirely unfounded. A threefold difficulty exists. In the first place, young people know very little about themselves and their abilities. When the day comes on which they discover their real strong points and their weaknesses, it is often too late. They have usually been drawn into the current of a particular vocation, and have given too much energy to the preparation for a specific achievement to change the whole life-plan once more. The entire scheme of education gives to the individual little chance to find himself. A mere interest for one or another subject in school is influenced by many accidental circumstances, by the personality of the teacher or the methods of instruction, by suggestions of the surroundings and by home traditions, and accordingly even such a preference gives rather a slight final indication of the individual mental qualities. Moreover, such mere inclinations and interests cannot determine the true psychological fitness for a vocation. To choose a crude illustration, a boy may think with passion of the vocation of a sailor, and yet may be entirely unfit for it, because his mind lacks the ability to discriminate red and green. He himself may never have discovered that he is color-blind, but when he is ready to turn to the sailor's calling, the examination of his color-sensitiveness which is demanded may have shown the disturbing mental deficiency. Similar defects may exist in a boy's attention or memory, judgment or feeling, thought or imagination, suggestibility or emotion, and they may remain just as undiscovered as the defect of color-blindness, which is characteristic of four per cent of the male population. All such deficiencies may be dangerous in particular callings. But while the vocation of the ship officer is fortunately protected nowadays by such a special psychological examination, most other vocations are unguarded against the entrance of the mentally unfit individuals.

As the boys and girls grow up without recognizing their psychical weaknesses, the exceptional strength of one or another mental function too often remains unnoticed by them as well. They may find out when they are favored with a special talent for art or music or scholarship, but they hardly ever know that their attention, or their memory, or their will, or their intellectual apprehension, or their sensory perceptions, are unusually developed in a particular direction; yet such an exceptional mental disposition might be the cause of special success in certain vocations. But we may abstract from the extremes of abnormal deficiency and abnormal overdevelopment in particular functions. Between them we find the broad region of the average minds with their numberless variations, and these variations are usually quite unknown to their possessors. It is often surprising to see how the most manifest differences of psychical

organization remain unnoticed by the individuals themselves. Men with a pronounced visual type of memory and men with a marked acoustical type may live together without the slightest idea that their contents of consciousness are fundamentally different from each other. Neither the children nor their parents nor their teachers burden themselves with the careful analysis of such actual mental qualities when the choice of a vocation is before them. They know that a boy who is completely unmusical must not become a musician, and that the child who cannot draw at all must not become a painter, just as on physical grounds a boy with very weak muscles is not fit to become a blacksmith. But as soon as the subtler differentiation is needed, the judgment of all concerned seems helpless and the psychical characteristics remain disregarded.

A further reason for the lack of adaptation, and surely a most important one, lies in the fact that the individual usually knows only the most external conditions of the vocations from which he chooses. The most essential requisite for a truly perfect adaptation, namely, a real analysis of the vocational demands with reference to the desirable personal qualities, is so far not in existence. The young people generally see some superficial traits of the careers which seem to stand open, and, besides, perhaps they notice the great rewards of the most successful. The inner labor, the inner values, and the inner difficulties and frictions are too often unknown to those who decide for a vocation, and they are unable to correlate those essential factors of the life-calling with all that nature by inheritance, and society by surroundings and training, have planted and developed in their minds.

In addition to this ignorance as to one's own mental disposition and to the lack of understanding of the true mental requirements of the various social tasks comes finally the abundance of trivial chance influences which become decisive in the choice of a vocation. Vocation and marriage are the two most consequential decisions in life. In the selection of a husband or wife, too, the decision is very frequently made dependent upon the most superficial and trivial motives. Yet the social philosopher may content himself with the belief that even in the fugitive love desire a deeper instinct of nature is expressed, which may at least serve the biological tasks of married life. In the choice of a vocation, even such a belief in a biological instinct is impossible. The choice of a vocation, determined by fugitive whims and chance fancies, by mere imitation, by a hope for quick earnings, by irresponsible recommendation, or by mere laziness, has no internal reason or excuse. Illusory ideas as to the prospects of a career, moreover, often falsify the whole vista; and if we consider all this, we can hardly be surprised that our total result is in many respects hardly better than if everything were left entirely to accident. Even on the height of a mental training to the end of adolescence, we see how the college graduates are too often led by accidental motives to the decision whether they shall become lawyers or physicians or business men, but this superficiality of choice of course appears much more strongly where the lifework is to be built upon the basis of a mere elementary or high school education.

The final result corresponds exactly to these conditions. Everywhere, in all countries and in all vocations, but especially in the economic careers, we hear the complaint that there is lack of really good men. Everywhere places are waiting for the right man, while at the same time we find everywhere an oversupply of mediocre aspirants. This, however, does not in the least imply that there really are not enough personalities who might be perfectly fit even for the highest demands of the vocations; it means only that as a matter of course the result in the filling of positions cannot be satisfactory, if the placing of the individuals is carried on without serious regard for the personal mental qualities. The complaint that there is lack of fit human material would probably never entirely disappear, as with a better adjustment of the material, the demands would steadily increase; but it could at least be predicted with high probability that this lack of really fit material would not be felt so keenly everywhere if the really decisive factor for the adjustment of personality and vocation, namely, the dispositions of the mind, were not so carelessly ignored.

Society, to be sure, has a convenient means of correction. The individual tries, and when he is doing his work too badly, he loses his job, he is pushed out from the career which he has chosen, with the great probability that he will be crushed by the wheels of social life. It is a rare occurrence for the man who is a failure in his chosen vocation, and who has been thrown out of it, to happen to come into the career in which he can make a success. Social statistics show with an appalling clearness what a burden and what a danger to the social body is growing from the masses of those who do not succeed and who by their lack of success become discouraged and embittered. The social psychologist cannot resist the conviction that every single one could have found a place in which he could have achieved something of value for the commonwealth. The laborer, who in spite of his best efforts shows himself useless and clumsy before one machine, might perhaps have done satisfactory work in the next mill where the machines demand another type of mental reaction. His psychical rhythm and his inner functions would be able to adjust themselves to the requirements of the one kind of labor and not to those of the other. Truly the whole social body has had to pay a heavy penalty for not making even the faintest effort to settle systematically the fundamental problem of vocational choice, the problem of the psychical adaptation of the individuality. An improvement would lie equally in the interest of those who seek positions and those who have positions to offer. The employers can hope that in all departments better work will be done as soon as better adapted individuals can be obtained; and, on the other hand, those who are anxious to make their working energies effective may expect that the careful selection of individual mental characters for the various tasks of the world will insure not only greater success and gain, but above all greater joy in the work, deeper satisfaction, and more harmonious unfolding of the personality.

WHAT IS THE GOAL OF PSYCHOLOGY?

23

WILHELM WUNDT

Wilhelm Maximilian Wundt (1832–1920) dreamed of becoming a famous scholar as an author of important works in comparative religion, much to the detriment of his early academic career. His daydreaming caused his parents to despair and wonder if they should even bother sending him, their second son, to the university. Fortunately, Wundt did attend the University of Tubingen to study medicine, where he became enchanted by the study of physiology, beginning with his uncle Friedrich Arnold's brain anatomy course. Wundt finished his training at the University of Heidelberg, becoming fascinated by experimental research. Before heading his own program, Wundt worked with a number of famous scientists, including the chemist Robert Bunsen, inventor of the Bunsen burner, and physiologists Johannes Müller and Emile du Bois-Reymond, and spent 13 years assisting Hermann von Helmholtz (p. 154). A prolific writer, Wundt eventually earned an excellent reputation and became a professor of philosophy at the University of Leipzig. When he first arrived in 1875, his plans of teaching experimental, or physiological, psychology were thwarted by the lack of adequate space for his equipment. Finally, in 1879, proper space was arranged—and this date is often given as the year the first laboratory conducting psychological research opened. Wundt's program was so popular that his laboratory was expanded in 1888, 1892, and 1897. During his first years at Leipzig, Wundt attended a seance and wrote a critique of the performance, entitled "Spiritualism as a Scientific Question," that challenged the event's realism and suggested that magicians, or those who study how to fool the senses, would be better critics than would scientists. The breadth of Wundt's writings and his emphasis on the experimental method have not always been apparent, in part because one of his famous American students, E. B. Titchener (p. 324), provided what was for many years the only English translation of his work and focused only on those aspects of Wundt's research and philosophy that Titchener found supportive of his own program. Wundt continued teaching until the age of 85 and writing until his death, leaving a legacy of 60,000 pages of published material.

LECTURES ON HUMAN AND ANIMAL PSYCHOLOGY

LECTURE I

§ I. Philosophical Anticipations of Psychology. § II. Spiritualism and Materialism. § III. Methods and Aids of Psychological Investigation.

§ I

Psychology, even in our own day, shows more clearly than any other experiential science traces of the conflict of philosophical systems. We may regret this influence in the interest of psychological investigation, because it has been the chief obstacle in the way of an impartial examination of mental life. But in the light of history we see that it was inevitable. Natural science has gradually taken shape from a natural philosophy which paved the way for it, and the effects of which may still be recognised in current scientific theory. That these effects are more fundamental and more permanent in the case of psychology

From Wilhelm Wundt, "Lectures 1 and 30." In J. E. Creighton and E. B. Titchener (Eds.), *Lectures on Human and Animal Psychology* (pp. 1–11, 437–454). New York: Macmillan, 1894.

is intelligible when we consider the problem which is set before it. Psychology has to investigate that which we call internal experience,—*i.e.,* our own sensation and feeling, our thought and volition,—in contradistinction to the objects of external experience, which form the subject matter of natural science. Man himself, not as he appears from without, but as he is in his own immediate experience, is the real problem of psychology. Whatever else is included in the circle of psychological discussion,—the mental life of animals, the common ideas and actions of mankind which spring from similarity of mental nature, and the mental achievements of the individual or of society,—all this has reference to the one original problem, however much our understanding of mental life be widened and deepened by the consideration of it. But the questions with which psychology thus comes into contact are at the same time problems for philosophy. And philosophy had made various attempts to solve them long before psychology as an experiential science had come into being.

The psychology of to-day, then, neither wishes to deny to philosophy its right to occupy itself with these matters, nor is able to dispute the close connection of philosophical and psychological problems. But in one respect it has undergone a radical change of standpoint. It refuses to regard psychological investigation as in any sense dependent upon foregone metaphysical conclusions. It would rather reverse the relation of psychology to philosophy, just as empirical natural science long ago reversed its relation to natural philosophy,—in so far, that is, as it rejected all philosophic speculations which were not based upon experience. Instead of a psychology founded upon philosophical presuppositions, we require a philosophy to whose speculations value is ascribed only so long as they pay regard at every step to the facts of psychological, as well as to those of scientific, experience.

It will, therefore, be a matter of principle for us in these lectures to stand apart from the strife of philosophic systems. But since the thought of to-day is subjected on all sides to the influence of a philosophic past which counts its years by thousands, and since the concepts and general notions under which an undifferentiated philosophy arranged the facts of mental life have become part of the general educated consciousness, and have never ceased to hinder the unprejudiced consideration of things as they are, it is our bounden duty to characterise and justify the standpoint which we propose to adopt. We will, therefore, first of all glance for a moment at the history of philosophy before the appearance of psychology.

In the beginnings of reflective thought, the perception of the external world preponderates over the internal experience of idea and thought, of feeling and will. The earliest psychology is therefore Materialism: the mind is air, or fire, or ether,—always some form of matter, however attenuated this matter may become in the effort to dematerialise it. Plato was the first among the Greeks to separate mind from body. Mind he regarded as the ruling principle of the body. And this separation paved the way for the future one-sided dualism which considered sensible existence as the obscuring and debasing of an ideal, purely mental being. Aristotle, who combined with the gift of speculation a marvellous keenness of observation, attempted to harmonise these opposites by regarding mind as the principle which vitalises and informs matter. He saw the direct operation of mental powers in the forms of animals, in the expression of the human figure at rest and in movement, even in the processes of growth and nutrition. And he generalised all this in his conclusion that mind is the creator of all organic form, working upon matter as the sculptor works on marble. Life and mentality were for him identical terms; even the vegetable world was on his theory endowed with mind. But, apart from this, Aristotle penetrated more deeply than any of his predecessors into the facts of mental experience. In his work upon the mind, the first in which psychology was ever treated as an independent science, he sharply separates from one another the fundamental mental activities; and, so far as the knowledge of his time allowed, sets forth their causal connections.

The Middle Ages were wholly dominated by the Aristotelian psychology, and more especially by its basal proposition that mind is the principle of life. But with the dawn of the modern period begins in psychology, as elsewhere, the return to Platonism. Another influence combined with this to displace Aristotelianism; namely, the development of modern natural science and the mechanical metaphysics which this development brought with it. The result of these influences was the origin of two psychological schools, which have disputed with one another down to the present day,—Spiritualism and Materialism. It is a curious fact that the thought of a single man has been of primary importance in the development of both these standpoints. Descartes, the mathematician and philosopher, had defined mind, in opposition to Aristotle, as exclusively thinking substance; and following Plato, he ascribed to it an original existence apart from the body, whence it has received in permanent possession all those ideas which transcend the bounds of sensible experience. This mind, in itself unspatial, he connected with the body at one point in the brain, where it was affected by processes in the external world, and in its turn exercised influence upon the body.

Later Spiritualism has not extended its views far beyond these limits. It is true that Leibniz, whose doctrine of monads regarded all existence as an ascending series of mental forces, attempted to substitute for the Cartesian mind-substance a more general principle, approximating once more to the Aristotelian concept of mind. But his successor Christian Wolff returned to the Cartesian dualism. Wolff is the originator of the so-called theory of mental faculties, which has influenced psychology down to the present day. This theory, based upon a superficial classification of mental processes, was couched in terms of a number of general notions,—memory, imagination, sensibility, understanding, etc.,—which it regarded as simple and fundamental forces of mind. It was left for Herbart, one of the acutest thinkers of our century, to give a convincing proof of the utter emptiness of this 'theory.' Herbart is at the same time the last great representative of that modern Spiritualism which began with Descartes. For the works of Kant and of the other philosophers who came after him,—Fichte, Schelling, and Hegel,—belong to a different sphere. In Herbart we still find the concept of a simple mind-substance, which Descartes introduced into modern philosophy, but pushed to its extreme logical conclusion, and at the same time modified by the first principles of Leibniz' monadology. And the consistency of this final representative of speculative psychology makes it all the more plain that any attempt to derive the facts of mental life from the notion of a simple mind and its relation to other existences different from or similar to itself must be vain and fruitless. Think what lasting service Herbart might have done psychology, endowed as he was in exceptional measure with the power of analysing subjective perception, had he not expended the best part of his ingenuity in the elaboration of that wholly imaginary mechanics of ideation, to which his metaphysical presuppositions led him. Still, just because he carried the concept of a simple mind-substance to its logical conclusion, we may perhaps ascribe to his psychology, besides its positive merits, this negative value,—that it showed as clearly as could be the barrenness of Spiritualism. All that is permanent in Herbart's psychological works we owe to his capacity of accurate observation of mental fact; all that is untenable and mistaken proceeds from his metaphysical concept of mind and the secondary hypotheses which it compelled him to set up. So that the achievements of this great Spiritualist show most plainly that the path which he travelled, apart from all

the contradictions into which it led him, cannot ever be the right road for psychology. This notion of a simple mental substance was not reached by analysis of mental phenomena, but was superimposed upon them from without. To assure the pre-existence and immortality of the soul, and (secondarily) to conform in the most direct way with the logical principle that the complex presupposes the simple, it seemed necessary to posit an indestructible and therefore absolutely simple and unalterable mind-atom. It was then the business of psychological experience to reconcile itself with this idea as best it might.

§ II

When Descartes denied mind to animals, on the ground that the essence of mind consists in thought, and man is the only thinking being, he could have little imagined that this proposition would do as much as the strictly mechanical views which he represented in natural philosophy to further the doctrines which are the direct opposite of the Spiritualism which he taught,—the doctrines of modern Materialism. If animals are natural automata, and if all the phenomena which general belief refers to sensation, feeling, and will are the result of purely mechanical conditions, why should not the same explanation hold of man? This was the obvious inference which the Materialism of the seventeenth and eighteenth centuries drew from Descartes' principles.

The naïve Materialism with which philosophy began had simply ascribed some kind of corporeality to mental existence. But this modern Materialism took as its first principles physiological hypotheses; thought, sense, and idea are physiological functions of certain organs within the nervous system. Observation of the facts of consciousness is of no avail until these are derived from chemical and physical processes. Thought is simply a result of brain activity. Since this activity ceases when circulation is arrested and life departs, thought is nothing more than a function of the substances of which the brain is composed.

More particularly were the scientific investigators and physicians of the time inclined, by the character of their pursuits, to accept this explanation of mental life in terms of what seemed to them intelligible scientific facts. The Materialism of to-day has made no great advance in this or in any other direction upon the views promulgated in the last century, *e.g.* by de la Mettrie, and developed by Helvétius, Holbach, and others. But this equating of mental process and brain function, which makes psychology a department of cerebral physiology, and therefore a part of a general atomic mechanics, sins against the very first rule of scientific logic,—that only those connections of facts may be regarded as causal which obtain between generically similar phenomena. Our feelings, thoughts, and volitions cannot be made objects of sensible perception. We can hear the word which expresses the thought, we can see the man who has thought it, we can dissect the brain in which it arose; but the word, the man, and the brain are not the thought. And the blood which circulates in the brain, the chemical changes which take place there, are wholly different from the act of thought itself.

Materialism, it is true, does not assert that these *are* the thought, but that they *form* it. As the liver secretes bile, as the muscle exerts motor force, so do blood and brain, heat and electrolysis, produce idea and thought. But surely there is no small difference between the two cases. We can prove that bile arises in the liver by chemical processes which we are able, in part at least, to follow out in detail. We can show, too, that movement is produced in muscles by definite processes, which are again the immediate result of chemical transformation. But cerebral processes give us no shadow of indication as to how our mental life comes into being. For the two series of phenomena are not comparable. We can conceive how one motion may be transformed into another, perhaps also how one sensation or feeling is transformed into a second. But no system of cosmic mechanics can make plain to us how a motion can pass over into a sensation or feeling.

At the same time modern Materialism pointed out a more legitimate method of research. There are numerous experiences which put beyond all doubt the connection of physiological cerebral function on the one hand and of mental activity on the other. And to investigate this connection by means of experiment and observation is assuredly a task worth undertaking. But we do not find that Materialism, even in this connection, has made a single noteworthy contribution to our positive knowledge. It has been content to set up baseless hypotheses regarding the dependence of mental function upon physical process; or it has been concerned to refer the nature of mental forces to some known physical agency. No analogy has been too halting, no hypothesis too visionary, for its purpose. It was for some time a matter of dispute whether the mental force had more resemblance to light or to electricity. Only on one point was there general agreement,—that it was not ponderable.

In our day the conflict between Materialism and Spiritualism, which was raging in the middle of the century, has almost worn itself out. It has left behind it nothing of value for science; and that will not surprise

any one who is acquainted with its details. For the clash of opinion was centred once more round the old point: in the questions concerning mind, the seat of mind, and its connection with body. Materialism had made the very same mistake which we have charged to the spiritualistic philosophy. Instead of plunging boldly into the phenomena which are presented to our observation and investigating the uniformities of their relation, it busied itself with metaphysical questions, an answer to which, if we may expect it at all, can only be based upon an absolutely impartial consideration of experience, which refuses to be bound at the outset by any metaphysical hypothesis.

§ III

We find, then, that Materialism and Spiritualism, which set out from such different postulates, converge in their final result. The most obvious reason of this is their common methodological error. The belief that it was possible to establish a science of mental experience in terms of speculation, and the thought that a chemical and physical investigation of the brain must be the first step towards a scientific psychology led alike to mistakes in method. The doctrine of mind must be primarily regarded as an experiential science. Were this otherwise, we should not be able so much as to state a psychological problem. The standpoint of exclusive speculation is, therefore, as unjustifiable in psychology as it is in any science. But more than this, so soon as we take our stand upon the ground of experience, we have to begin our science, not with the investigation of those experiences which refer primarily only to objects more or less closely connected with mind, but with the direct examination of mind itself,—that is, of the phenomena from which its existence was long ago inferred, and which formed the original incentive to psychological study. The history of the science shows us that mind and the principal mental functions were distinguished before there was any idea that these functions were connected with the brain. It was not any doubt as to the purpose of this organ which led to the abstraction which lies at the foundation of the doctrine of mind, but simply observation of mental phenomena. Sense, feeling, idea, and will seemed to be related activities; and they appeared, further, to be bound together by the unity of self-consciousness. The mental processes began, therefore, to be looked upon as the actions of a single being. But since these actions were found again to be intimately connected with bodily functions, there necessarily arose the question of assigning to mind a seat within the body, whether in the heart, or the brain, or any other organ. It was reserved for later investigation to show that the brain is the sole organ which really stands in close connection with the mental life.

But if it be sensation, feeling, idea, and will which led in the first instance to the assumption of mind, the only natural method of psychological investigation will be that which begins with just these facts. First of all we must understand their empirical nature, and then go on to reflect upon them. For it is experience and reflection which constitute each and every science. Experience comes first; it gives us our bricks: reflection is the mortar, which holds the bricks together. We cannot build without both. Reflection apart from experience and experience without reflection are alike powerless. It is therefore essential for scientific progress that the sphere of experience be enlarged, and new instruments of reflection from time to time invented.

But how is it possible to extend our experience of sensations, feelings, and thoughts? Did not mankind feel and think thousands of years ago, as it feels and thinks to-day? It does, indeed, seem as though our observation of what goes on in the mind could never extend beyond the circle to which our own consciousness confines it. But appearances are deceptive. Long ago the step was taken which raised the science of psychology above the level of this its first beginning, and extended its horizon almost indefinitely. History, dealing with the experience of all times, has furnished us with a picture in the large of the character, the impulses, and the passions of mankind. More especially is it the study of language and linguistic development, of mythology and the history of religion and custom, which has approached more and more closely, as historical knowledge has increased, to the standpoint of psychological inquiry.

The belief that our observation is confined to the brief span of our individual life, with its scanty experience, was one of the greatest obstacles to psychological progress in the days of the earlier empiricism. And the opening up of the rich mines of experience to which social psychology gives us access, for the extension of our own subjective perceptions, is an event of importance and of promise for the whole circle of the mental sciences. Nor is that all. A second fact, of still greater import for the solution of the simplest and therefore, most general psychological problems, is the attempt that has been made to discover new methods of observation. One new method has been found; it is that of experiment, which, though it revolutionized the natural sciences, had not up to quite recent times found application in psychology. When the scientific investigator is inquiring into the causes of a phenomenon, he does not confine himself to the investigation of things as they are given in ordinary perception. That would never take him to his goal, though he had at his command the experiences of all time. Thunderstorms have been recorded, indeed carefully described, since the first beginnings of history; but what a storm was could not be explained until the phenomena of electricity had become familiar, until electrical machines had been constructed and experiments made with them. Then the matter was easy. For when once the effects of a storm had been observed and compared with the effect of an electric spark, the inference was plain that the discharge of the machine was simply a storm in miniature. What the observation of a thousand years had left unexplained was understood in the light of a single experiment. Even astronomy, a science which we might think must of its very nature be confined to observation, is in its more recent development founded in a certain sense upon experiment. So long as mere observations were taken, the general opinion that the earth was fixed, and that the sun and stars moved round it, could not be overthrown. It is true that there were many phenomena which made against this belief; but simple observation could not furnish means for the attainment of a better explanation. Then came Copernicus, with the thought: "Suppose I stand upon the sun!" and henceforth it was the earth that moved, and not the sun; the contradictions of the old theory disappeared, and the new system of the universe had come into being. But it was an experiment that had led to this, though an experiment of thought. Observation still tells us that the earth is fixed, and the sun moving; and if the opposite view is to become clear, we must just repeat the Copernican experiment, and take our stand upon the sun.

It is experiment, then, that has been the source of the decided advance in natural science, and brought about such revolutions in our scientific views. Let us now apply experiment to the science of mind. We must remember that in every department of investigation the experimental method takes on an especial form, according to the nature of the facts investigated. In psychology we find that only those mental phenomena which are directly accessible to physical influences can be made the subject matter of experiment. We cannot experiment upon mind itself, but only upon its outworks, the organs of sense and movement which are functionally related to mental processes. So that every psychological experiment is at the same time physiological, just as there are physical processes corresponding to the mental processes of sensation, idea, and will. This is, of course, no reason for denying to experiment the character of a psychological method. It is simply due to the general conditions of our mental life, one aspect of which is its constant connection with the body.

The following lectures are intended as an introduction to psychology. They do not attempt any exhaustive exposition of the methods and results of experimental psychological investigation. That would have to assume previous knowledge which cannot here be presupposed. Neither shall we include in the range of our discussion the facts of social psychology, whose contents is extensive enough to demand an independent treatise. We shall confine ourselves to the mental life of the individual; and within those limits it will be the human mind to which we shall for the most part devote ourselves. At the same time it appears desirable, for the right understanding of individual mental development, that we should now and again institute a brief comparison with the mental life of animals.

LECTURE XXX

§ I. Concluding Remarks; the Question of Immortality. § II. The Principle of Psychophysical Parallelism. § III. Old and New Phrenology. § IV. The Empirical Significance of the Principle of Parallelism. § V. The Nature of Mind.

§ I

At the beginning of these lectures upon the mental life of man and the animals we declined to base our considerations from the outset upon any hard and fast conception of the nature of mind, and to force the facts of experience into agreement with that conception, in the way of the metaphysical psychologists. On the contrary, we regarded it as our primary duty to acquaint ourselves with the facts, and then, without the aid of any other assumptions than those suggested by introspection and supported by experimentation and objective observation, to try and establish laws under which the phenomena of mind might be subsumed.

But, now that we have come to the end of our task, it becomes imperative for us to cast a glance over the body of facts that we have collected, and to consider what answer is to be given to the ultimate questions of psychology. The path that we have travelled was not lighted by any metaphysical guiding star. What is the result? Do these questions refuse to be answered? do they transcend the limits of human knowledge? Or has experimental psychology something to say about them, something which may be believed and accepted as the issue of an unprejudiced appeal to experience?

There is, indeed, one problem of speculative psychology which we must exclude from the first as insoluble. Not only does it transcend the limits of the empirical doctrine of mind: it does not stand upon the plane of scientific knowledge at all. It is the question of the condition of the mind before or after this conscious life of ours, a question which has really as little place in psychology as that of the 'creation' of the world has in physics or astronomy. The hope of constructing from the materials of our knowledge of the universe a conceptual edifice in which the objects of a supersensuous world are transformed into objects of knowledge,—that hope has always and again proved to be one of those fatal illusions from which neither belief nor knowledge has anything to gain.

If you need confirmation of this, look for a moment at the question of immortality, one of the principal problems of metaphysical psychology. It was necessary to put the imperishability of the individual mind beyond all doubt. That necessitated the continual emphasising of its substantial simplicity. And that led in the last instance to the logical extreme of the Herbartian metaphysic, in which we have a mental atom of simple quality with an unalterable content comparable,—these are Herbart's own words,—to a simple sensational quality, like 'blue' or 'red.' How does the imperishability of this mind-substance differ from, say, the imperishability of a material atom? Is it anything better?

The one aim of empirical psychology is to explain the interconnection of the phenomena of our mental life. It must decline once and for all to furnish any information regarding a supersensuous mental existence. At the same time, the question may with some right be raised whether it is not at least indirectly concerned in this problem. We cannot deny to *philosophy* either the privilege or the duty of passing beyond the mere explanation of facts of actual life, on the basis of the total sum of knowledge amassed by the several sciences. The actual character of the world-process renders it inevitable that the solution of this our first problem should be followed by the presentation of a second. Facts are given us in the form of continuous developmental series which in experience terminate at this point or that. Philosophy must go beyond experience, and strive to attain the ideal goal of all science,—a coherent theory of the universe. Now our mental life in particular is presented in the form of a whole number of developmental series, all directly or indirectly interconnected and all together tending towards the same end, which, indeed, is inaccessible to our immediate experience, but the nature of which we may infer, if we are allowed to assume that the developments beginning in experience are continued on the same lines beyond the bounds of experience. It is the aim of philosophy to *supplement* the world of experience in this way. In doing so she is only carrying to its logical conclusion a method of procedure which is begun in every one of the separate sciences, and which is rendered necessary both by the character of the experiential developments and the impulse to fill out incomplete systems of knowledge. Now the mental life of the individual stands at the centre of this plurality of mental developments. The individual, with all his actions and impulses, is placed in mental communities of wide and of narrow radius. As a member of such communities, he contributes his share in the last resort to the sum of the achievements and creations of the human mind. What is the ultimate goal of all this mighty current of mental development? Experience alone cannot answer; while the ideal completion of experience, which philosophy tries to discover, can have no other foundations than the developments given in experience. It is here that psychology finds a place; it is one of the first witnesses called upon by philosophy for information which shall aid in her ideal construction. And this must never be opposed at any point to established psychological fact.

Now, if we recognise the existence of this problem of an ideal completion of reality, we have also recognised a *continuance of mentality* in the widest sense,—*i.e.,* a persistence of the mental developments beyond every experiential limit wherever and whenever attained. For the hypothesis that mental development might somewhere come to an end, to be replaced by simply nothing, would, of course, imply a recognition of the invalidity of any ideal completion. More than that, the whole of the mental content of the universe would cease to have any significance. For what meaning could we read into mental life in general other than that of a great and lamentable illusion, the growing store of man's mental possessions confirming him more and more strongly in his justifiable expectation of further development, while the end of all things should still be nothingness?

There can be no doubt that it was this philosophical notion of purposiveness, and not any particular speculation as to the nature of the individual mind, which ultimately gave rise to the idea of immortality, and has empowered it to resist throughout all times the attacks of philosophic doubt and the force of opposing philosophic argument. But mankind inclines to look at things *sub specie individualitatis* rather than *sub specie æternitatis,*

and has therefore transformed this general conviction of the imperishability of mental development into a belief in the imperishability of each individual mind, with all its sensuous contents,—a contents that could only have been acquired under the special conditions of this present sensuous life.

Psychology proves that not only our sense-perceptions, but the memorial images that renew them, depend for their origin upon the functioning of the organs of sense and movement, of the nervous system, and ultimately of the total mechanism of the living body. A continuance of this sensuous consciousness must appear to her irreconcilable with the facts of her own experience. And surely we may well doubt whether such a continuance is an ethical requisite: more, whether the fulfilment of a wish for it, if possible, were not an intolerable destiny. But when we turn away from this, the idea of immortality in a bygone mythology, and return to its true philosophic foundation, empirical psychology has nothing to urge against it. For the mental development of the individual is a necessary constituent of the development of the universal mind, and points not less unequivocally than this to something lying beyond it.

§ II

Besides this first question, which has taken us from psychology into philosophy, and into the most difficult and uncertain part of philosophy, there are two others of general import to which we may be required to give a final answer on the basis of the facts which we have been discussing. The first is that of the *relation of mental to bodily processes;* the second, that of the *nature of mind,* as inferable from our survey of the whole range of mental experience. Our only way to furnish an answer to either is, of course, to put together the results of our various investigations.

We emphasised the fact, at the very beginning of these lectures, that mental phenomena could not be referred to bodily as effect to cause. It is an inevitable presupposition of the natural sciences that the processes of nature constitute a straitly closed circle of movements of unchangeable elements, governed by the general laws of mechanics. Nothing can ever be derived from motion except another motion. In other words, the circle of these natural processes which are presented to our objective observation can never lead to anything beyond itself Recognising this, we recognised the necessity of deriving every mental process from some other, the more complicated from the simpler, and of making it our business as psychologists to discover the mental laws of this interconnection. And at every stage upon the road which we have travelled we have found confirmation of this general position. Every well-established case of a connexion of mental phenomena has proved capable of a psychological interpretation; more, we have always seen that no other interpretatory method could throw light on the specifically psychological character of the process under investigation. Thus the fundamental law of the doctrine of sensation, Weber's law, was shown to be a mathematical expression of the principle of relativity of mental states. And the different modes of ideational connection in sense-perception and in the temporal and spatial combinations of memorial images were referable to the laws of association, which themselves, when analysed into the two elementary processes of connexion by likeness and connexion by contiguity, appeared as directly dependent upon psychological conditions. Further, the laws of apperception, with their corollaries of the composition and disintegration of general ideas which underlie the intellectual processes, are only capable of psychological interpretation. Finally, the feelings, with their classification,—again, only psychologically intelligible,—as pleasurable and unpleasurable mental reactions, and the excitations of volition, took their places as terms in a developmental series, extending from the simplest forms of impulse to the most complicated expressions of self-initiated, voluntary activity. It may very well be that we have not yet discovered the simplest and best formulation for many of these causal connexions; and it cannot be doubted that many important laws of mental life still await discovery. But neither does it admit of any doubt that psychical can only be adequately explained from psychical, just as motion can only be derived from motion, and never from a mental process, of whatever kind.

At the same time, we found it to be a truth of equal universality that mental processes are connected with definite physical processes within the body, and especially in the brain; there is a uniform co-ordination of the two. How are we to conceive of this connexion, if, as we have stated to be the case, it is not to be thought as that of cause and effect? The answer to this question has been given in detail in the preceding pages of the book. The connexion can only be regarded as a *parallelism* of two causal series existing side by side, but never directly interfering with each other in virtue of the incomparability of their terms. Wherever we have met with this principle, we have named it that of *psychophysical parallelism.* Its validity cannot be doubted even by those who may be of the opinion that there may still perhaps be some metaphysical bridge to take them from physical to psychical, or *vice versâ.* Even they must admit that it

is the most obvious empirical expression of the connexion which we actually found to obtain between the bodily and mental series of vital processes. But the question of the extent of the validity of the principle is a different matter. It requires further consideration; and only at the conclusion of this shall we be able to hazard a conjecture as to whether we are dealing with an ultimate principle of dualistic metaphysics, beyond which our knowledge cannot go, or whether the psychophysical facts which we have co-ordinated tend at all to justify the philosophical attempt to fuse these two parallel and independent causal series in the last resort in a higher metaphysical unity.

The question of the extent of the validity of this principle of psychophysical parallelism can be approached either from the physical or mental side. From the former point of view, our direct experience of the parallelism tells us in plain terms enough that its range is exceedingly limited. Of the whole number of physical processes, which constitute the course of the material universe, vital phenomena form but a narrow and circumscribed part; and of vital phenomena themselves there are again but few in which mental processes can either be perceived or inferred from objective observation. This is undoubtedly one of the principal reasons upon which is based the materialistic view that psychophysical parallelism itself formulates a causal dependence of the mental upon the physical. Regarded as systems of processes in nature, the physical is wider than the psychical; mind is bound up with certain definite connexions and attributes of matter. And so it seems an obvious assumption that mental activities are functions of certain highly organised substances. But such statements do not meet the requirements of a really causal explanation. It is surely inadmissible to suppose that mental existence suddenly appeared at some definite point in the developmental chronology of life. It is a far more justifiable hypothesis that that point merely serves to mark in a general way the limen of a more clearly conscious mental life. An isolated sensation, out of all connexion with other sensations or ideas, could not make itself known to us, whether subjectively or objectively, by any symptoms of consciousness. But since our analysis of ideas takes us back to sensations as their ultimate elements, we have every right to assume that primitive mentality was a state of simple feeling and sensing; while the possibility that this state accompanies every material movement-process,—that is to say, that the principle of psychological parallelism, even when regarded from the physical side, is of universal validity,—though, like every ultimate assumption, incapable of proof, is still certainly not to be denied. At least, it looks very much more probable than the materialistic function-hypothesis, if we accept the dictum "Ex nihilo nihil fit." That the beginnings of mental life are to be found in the vegetable kingdom, and particularly in the protozoa, whose life represents the earliest stages of development both of plants and animals, is a theory, it is true; but it is the only theory which can explain the phenomena of movement displayed by these primitive creatures.

If, on the other hand, we prefer to consider the principle of psychophysical parallelism from its second or mental side, we again find ourselves in some doubt as to the extent of the connexion between mind and body. The older spiritualistic psychology was inclined upon the whole to restrict it to senseperceptions and external voluntary actions,—processes whose relation to physiological conditions could not well be overlooked. But in more recent times there has sprung up a tendency both in physiology and in psychology to look upon a considerable extension of the sphere of psychophysics as right and necessary. Every conscious content which possesses sensible attributes of whatever kind,—i.e., which is to some extent constituted by sensations, however slight their intensity,—must be recognised at once as a psychical content with a physical substrate. There is, as you know, no certain characteristic by which to discriminate the sensational content of a memorial or fancy image from that of a sense-perception. The ordinary one, that of the different intensity of the sensations, does not furnish a valid criterion; for the intensity of a peripherally stimulated sensation may be just as near the limen of noticeability as that of a memorial image, while the strength of the latter, when it takes the form of a hallucination or an illusion, may rival that of any externally excited sensation. Since, moreover, as we have seen, the intensity of sensation stands in a uniform relation to the intensity of the physical excitation, there is not the slightest reason to suppose that the difference between memory-image and sense-perception consists on the physiological side in anything more than a difference in the intensity of the underlying excitation-processes.

But if all the mental processes whose contents involves the presence of sensation in any form may be thus subsumed to the principle of psychophysical parallelism, it becomes impossible to make an exception in favour of the intellectual processes. Every concept requires an idea to serve as its symbol in consciousness; and an idea without sensational contents is an absurdity. Conceptual thought will, therefore, be accompanied by an excitation-process in certain sensory centres. If thought is engaged upon the composition or analysis of concepts, there will always be effected an alteration in the contents of these, i.e., in the sensational contents of their representative ideas. Corresponding to every process of thought there will be some physical excitation, varying with the variation of sensational elements. And we can go even farther. The apperception of an idea, the strain of attention upon an idea, is always attended by changes in the sensational content of that idea. Sharp as is the general distinction between the clearness or obscurity of an idea on the one hand and its strength or weakness on the other, still both alike depend upon the greater or less noticeability of its sensational constituents and attributes. So that if sensations themselves are accompanied by physical processes, the alterations in ideas connected with alterations in certain of their constituent sensations will also be accompanied by them. In the case of strained attention we must add to these alterations the associated muscle-sensations, which must, of course, follow the rule governing sensation in general. And, finally, if the apperception of ideas can be subsumed to the parallelistic principle, we must recognise that its intimate relation to volition cannot but involve the internal impulses of will in the same fate. Every volition as well implies an alteration in the ideational,—i.e., also in the sensational,—contents of consciousness. So that the physical processes which attend the external voluntary movement are only a further expression of a relation in which the will has stood from the time of its very first beginnings.

§ III

The result of all these considerations, then, is to make it exceedingly probable that no mental process which contains sensational elements of any kind can occur without there being at the same time set up corresponding physical processes. The universal validity of the principle of psychophysical parallelism is given with the sensible nature of the foundations upon which our whole mental life rests. There is no concept so abstract, no notion so remote from the world of sense, that it must not be represented in thought by some kind of sensible idea. But it would for this very reason be wrong to regard this parallelism as though it implied an equivalence of the two series of processes. Physical and psychical are, as you know, wholly incomparable. And they differ more especially in this point,—that the criterion of *value* which is the ultimate standard of reference both for those of our conscious activities which affect the world outside us, and even to a greater degree for our appreciation of the phenomena of consciousness itself, is wholly inapplicable to physical processes, or, at least, can only be applied where they can be derived from some mental purpose, *i.e.,* are subsumed to the psychological point of view. Regarded as such, considered simply from the standpoint of natural science, every physical process is a link in the unbroken chain of movement-processes, of as much or as little value as any other link. A memorial image may hurry through consciousness as the transient reproduction of some past experience to which we are utterly indifferent; or it may serve as a vicarious idea to embody a concept which expresses an important result of logical reflection. Within the circle of physical processes there will occur in both cases the same weak sense-excitation, connected, if you will, with very different antecedent and consequent motions, but giving not the least sign of the difference in mental value which attaches to it. If we could see every wheel in the physical mechanism whose working the mental processes are accompanying, we should still find no more than a chain of movements showing no trace whatsoever of their significance for mind. So that, despite the universality of the parallelistic principle, all that is valuable in our mental life still falls to the psychical side. And the fact of parallelism can affect this value just as little as the necessity of embodying an idea in a word or some other sensible symbol, if it is to be a permanent property of thought, or even thought at all, affects the value of the idea itself. The value of a work of art of imperishable beauty does not depend upon the material of which it is made. The material only becomes valuable because capable of giving expression to the conception of the artist. And it is only carrying this relation of mental conception to its objective realisation one step farther back to apply it to the less durable, but therefore all the more plastic, material of ideation, upon the varying content of which consciousness has to work. The artist could not call his thought to life in stone or bronze, in word or picture, if it had not already gained the potentiality of that life in his own mind as a work of the constructive imagination from the sensible material of ideas.

It need now hardly be said, that psychophysical parallelism is a principle whose application extends only to the elementary mental processes, to which definite movement-processes run parallel, not to the more complicated products of our mental life, the sensible material of which has been formed and shaped in consciousness, nor to the general intellectual powers which are the necessary presupposition of those products. Phrenology, as you may know, localised memory, imagination, understanding, and even such narrowly defined faculties as memory for things or words, sense of colour, love of children, and so forth, in particular parts

of the brain. It assumed that the physical processes in those parts,—and it left their physiological character altogether undetermined,—run parallel to these complicated mental capacities and activities. These are the ideas of the crudest forms of materialism, and render any psychological understanding of our mental life altogether impossible.

The absurdity of the phrenological hypothesis is not greatly diminished in the more modern form of it. Starting out from the facts of cerebral localisation, it assumes that each single idea is deposited in some particular nerve-cell; so that the excitation of this cell is synchronous with the appearance of its special idea. We can only account for such notions by supposing that observers who had absorbed the false doctrines of the older phrenology, when they came into contact with the modern discoveries of the histology and minute anatomy of the brain, felt it their duty to transfer the phrenological functions of lobe and convolution to the more elemental cell. To do this, it was necessary to get rid of memory, imagination, linguistic talent, etc., and to endow the morphological units with the separate ideas of which the complex mental faculties are constituted. Now we have seen how complicated, as a rule, those mental processes are which terminate in the formation of an idea, how many sensations taken from the most various departments of sense may be involved in them. It is impossible to suppose that the structural elements of the brain can be related to mental processes in any way differently from the structural elements of the external sense-organs. Each such element is adequate only to a very simple function; but it can play a part in the most diverse and complicated functions. A single cell from the visual area of the cortex can no more be the seat of a definite idea,—say, of a house or of the face of a friend,—than can a single retinal rod or *opticus* fibril. The phrenological view has only to be carried to its logical extreme for its impossibility to become manifest. Suppose that we are in daily intercourse with a friend; that we have seen him in numberless situations. We must assume that he takes up not one cell, but a whole number of cells, in our brain. If our next meeting with him takes place under ordinary circumstances, we can use one of our stock of ideas; if not,—if he has a new hat on, perhaps,—this new idea will have to be stored away in some cell that happens to be empty at the time. Or suppose that we have learned a word of a foreign language. It is deposited in some cell of the central organ of speech. If we hear the same word with some slight change of pronunciation, this modified form must be laid up in a second cell, and so *ad infinitum.* It is evident at the first glance that the hypothesis of idea-cells gives no account of the manifold forms of ideational and sensational connexion. It would fall to pieces at the first attempt from the inherent impossibility of its effort. For, as a matter of fact, it is never ready-made and isolated ideas that combine, but ideational elements, or, better, elementary ideational processes, as we saw when analysing out the simple associative processes underlying the cognition and recognition of an object. The radical error of the phrenological hypothesis is, that it substitutes an *anatomical* for a *physiological* parallelism. It is a true scion of the old-time phrenological doctrines in this as well as in its extraordinarily naïve notions about psychology in general.[1]

§ IV

The principle of psychophysical parallelism, then, refers always to a parallelism of elementary physical and psychical processes, and not to any parallelism of complex activities on either side or of mental function and bodily structure. But this suggests a further question,—whether a principle which after all includes two utterly disparate principles, disparate and yet never out of relation to each other, can properly be regarded as an ultimate psychological postulate. Is not a dualistic principle like this in opposition to our justifiable endeavour after a monistic world-theory? And if we cannot doubt its validity, since psychological and physiological facts alike attest it, should we not still, perhaps, look upon it as provisional only?

Certainly we have reached the point where psychological assistance can avail us no more, and where we must appeal to metaphysics for an answer. It is, or it should be, the aim of metaphysics to satisfy this craving of the reason for final unification. The results gained in the separate spheres of scientific investigation are unable to do this. If, then, there is anything at all for metaphysics to do, it is to furnish the ultimate explanation of this parallelism, which physiology and psychology accept as bare fact. Physiology cannot be called on for this explanation. It restricts itself to the explanation of the physical manifestations of life; and though often and again it comes upon the signs of mental function, it is obliged to consider this as a department of knowledge with which it has no concern. The problem of psychology, again, is the explanation of the interconnection of the psychical manifestations of life, which form another and a separate causal series. But the two sciences supplement each other; where certain links are wanting in the causal nexus of the one side, they may be given in that of the other. In these cases, of course, physiology

must have recourse to psychological, psychology to physiological, connecting terms. But it is always understood that the interpolation does not carry with it any real completion of the broken chain of connected processes; it is simply the substitution for a term of one series of the parallel term of the other. We may speak in such instances, perhaps, of the influence of mind upon body, or *vice versa.* But we always mean, if we do not say, that the word "influence" is not to be taken *sensu stricto:* that, for instance, a direct causal influence cannot be exerted by psychical term upon physical, but only upon the psychical process which this physical represents by parallelism. Thus an external voluntary movement is not produced by the internal act of will, but by the cerebral processes correlated with it; an idea does not follow from the physiological excitations of the sensory centre, but from the processes, sensational and associative, which run parallel to them. We must even suppose, continuing this train of reasoning, that it is not the physical stimulus which occasions the sensation; but that this latter arises from some elementary psychical processes, lying below the limen of consciousness and connecting our mental life with some more general complex of elementary psychical processes in the world outside us. But since we are utterly ignorant of all that belongs to these, we have no choice: at the beginning of the development of the empirical mental life, we must substitute a physiological first term for the psychological. But is psychology here so much worse off than physiology? Will it ever be able to demonstrate the physiological processes which correspond to the highest productions of psychical life?

In all its empirical investigations, then, psychology is obliged to take up the same position as regards the links in the chain of physiological causality as physiology must assume with regard to psychological phenomena. The severance of the spheres of the two sciences must, to be fruitful, go hand in hand with mutual recognition of these spheres. The only views of the nature of the bodily processes which are possible for psychology are, therefore, those current in physiology and the other natural sciences: it must assume an actually presented, absolutely constant, material substrate, unalterable save as regards the movements of its parts. Over against this stands the circle of the psychical phenomena of life, an equally independent sphere of investigation, not admitting of causal explanation in terms of the connection of motions of matter. So for psychology, as for physiology, the principle of psycho-physical parallelism turns out to be an ultimate postulate, behind which it cannot go.

The attitude of metaphysics in this matter is, of

course, a quite different one. The very nature of the objects with which psychology and natural science alike begin their analysis furnishes it with a sufficient reason for the inquiry after a higher unity in which the dualism of the parallelistic principle may be resolved. All that we know of the phenomena of nature comes to us in the form of ideas. The distinction of idea and object, upon which the division of the experiential sciences into those of nature and mind depends, is simply a result of the analytic activity of thought. In itself the idea is at the same time object; there are no objects which are not also ideas, or which must not be thought of in accordance with the laws governing the formation of ideas. But if it is thought which, by abstracting and distinguishing, has broken up the original unity of the worlds without and within, you can easily understand the mind's persistent impulse to restore that unity as the final act of its own development. Nay more, you will recognise the endeavour as just, and its fulfilment as a task for science. To point out means to this end is the business not of psychology, but of philosophy. Psychology can only indicate the path which leads to territories beyond her own, ruled by other laws than those to which her realm is subject.

§ V

These considerations have brought us to the last task which remains to be performed. We have learned all that we could of the interconnection of mental phenomena. What now is the *nature of mind?* The real answer to this question is contained in all that has been said before. Our mind is nothing else than the sum of our inner experiences, than our ideation, feeling, and willing collected together to a unity in consciousness, and rising in a series of developmental stages to culminate in self-conscious thought and a will that is morally free. At no point in our explanation of the interconnection of these inner experiences have we found occasion to apply this attribute of mentality to anything else than the concrete complex of idea, feeling, and will. The fiction of a transcendental substance, of which actual mental content is only the outward manifestation, a fleeting shadow-picture thrown by the still unknown reality of the mind,—such a theory misses the essential difference between the inner and the outer experience, and threatens to turn to mere empty show all that lends solid value and real significance to our mental life. Conscious experience is immediate experience. Being immediate, it can never require that distinction of a substrate, existing independently of our subjective appreciation, which is rendered necessary in natural science by its conception of nature as a sum-total of real things presented to us and

persisting independently of us. Our mental experiences are as they are presented to us. The distinction between appearance and reality necessary for the apprehension of the world without, and culminating in the concept of a material substance as a secondary conceptual hypothesis which so far seems to do justice to the facts of experience, ceases to have any meaning when applied to the apprehension of the thinking subject by himself. You can understand, therefore, that when we are analysing our internal experiences we are never met by the contradictions between particular phenomena which in natural science furnish both incentive and means to the gradual developing and perfecting of the concept of matter, a concept which, destined as it is to remain for ever a hypothesis, can still hope to approximate to the truth by an infinite number of efforts towards it.

There is just one single group of empirical facts which have with some show of reason been adduced to prove the necessity of assuming a mental substrate analogous to material substance,—the facts of the *revival of previous experiences.* If we can call up some past idea, it is urged, it surely follows that some trace of that idea has remained in the mind during the meantime, else its reproduction would not be possible. Now we have seen, of course, that no idea, that no mental process whatsoever, can be called up again unchanged. Every remembered idea is really a new formation, composed of numerous elements of various past ideas. Nevertheless, it might be supposed that these very elements were the ideational traces left behind in the mind. But it is evident that even in this form the theory has presuppositions due simply to a transference of the permanent effects observed in the case of physical processes to the hypothetical mental substrate, in other words to an unconscious intermixture of materialistic views. A physical influence acting upon a body produces some more or less permanent alterations in it. Thus we have every right to suppose that a nervous excitation leaves an after-effect in the nervous organs, which is of significance for the physiology of the processes of practice and revival. Now in the theory of 'traces' these physical analogies are applied without more ado to the mind. Mind is conceived either as identical with brain, or as a substance localised somewhere in the brain, resembling it and other material substances in every essential attribute. But the physical excitation-process can only leave its after-effect upon the nerve, because it is itself a process of movement in or with a permanent substrate. And if mental processes are not phenomena, but actual immediate experiences, it is very hard to see how their after-effects can be psychologically conceived, except also in the form of directly presented mental processes. If we try to imagine an idea as persisting beneath the limen of consciousness, we can as a matter of fact only think of it as still an idea, *i.e.,* as the same process as that which it was so long as we were conscious of it, with the single difference that it is now no longer conscious. But this implies that psychological explanation has here reached a limit similar to that which confronts it in the question as to the ultimate origin of sensations. It is the limit beyond which one of the two causal series,—the physical,—can be continued, but where the other,—the psychical,—must end; and where the attempt to push this latter farther must inevitably lead to the thinking of the psychical in physical,—*i.e.,* material,—terms.

We conclude, then, that the assumption of a mental substance different from the various manifestations of mental life involves the unjustifiable transference of a mode of thought necessary for the investigation of external nature to a sphere in which it is wholly inapplicable; it implies a kind of unconscious materialism. The consequences of this transference follow at once from its nature; the true value of our mental life is in jeopardy. For this value attaches simply and solely to the actual and concrete processes in mind. What can this "substance" do for us, a substance devoid of will, of feeling, and of thought, and having no part in the constitution of our personality? If you answer, as is sometimes done, that it is these very operations of mind that go to make up its nature, and that therefore mind cannot be thought

or conceived without them, why, then the position is granted: the real nature of mind consists in nothing else than our mental life itself. The notion of "operation" as applied to it can only mean, if it has any admissible meaning at all, that we are able to demonstrate how certain mental manifestations follow from, are the effects of the operation of certain other mental manifestations. Physical causality and psychical causality are polar opposites: the former implies always the postulate of a material substance; the latter never transcends the limits of what is immediately given in mental experience. "Substance" is a metaphysical surplusage for which psychology has no use. And this accords with the fundamental character of mental life, which I would have you always bear in mind. It does not consist in the connexion of unalterable objects and varying conditions: in all its phases it is *process;* an *active,* not a passive, existence; *development,* not stagnation. The understanding of the basal laws of this development is the final goal of psychology.

NOTES

1. For other proofs of the untenable character of the neo-phrenological localisation-hypothesis, drawn chiefly from the phenomena of normal and pathological disturbances of memory, I may refer the reader to my *Essays,* pp. 109 ff. (Leipzig, 1885).

24
~

MAX WERTHEIMER

Max Wertheimer (1880–1943) left his chair in philosophy and psychology at the University of Frankfurt in 1933, one of many European scholars who were forced to flee their homelands with Hitler's rise to power. Wertheimer attended Charles University in his native city of Prague, where he became intrigued by Christian von Ehrenfel's critique of Wilhelm Wundt's (p. 296) elemental approach to perceptual experience. Wertheimer continued at the University of Berlin and received his Ph.D. in 1904 from the University of Wurzburg. He conducted graduate work with Oswald Kulpe and Karl Marbe on the use of word-association tasks to detect criminal guilt or innocence. Wertheimer was involved with a number of different laboratories over the next several years, supported by his father, a college administrator in Prague, and his mother an accomplished violinist who also enjoyed literature and art. Using borrowed laboratory space, Wertheimer began a systematic study of apparent motion in 1910 with Kurt Koffka and Wolfgang Kohler as his experimental observers. This work eventually led to his position at the University of Frankfurt in 1929. His appointment to the New School's University in Exile, in New York City, aided his family's departure from Germany, made necessary by Wertheimer's Jewish heritage.

GESTALT THEORY (ADDRESS BEFORE THE KANT SOCIETY, 1924)

39 What is Gestalt theory and what does it intend? Gestalt theory was the outcome of concrete investigations in psychology, logic, and epistemology. The prevailing situation at the time of its origin may be briefly sketched as follows. We go from the world of everyday events to that of science, and not unnaturally assume that in making this transition we shall gain a deeper and more precise understanding of essentials. The transition *should* mark an advance. And yet, though one may have learned a great deal, one is poorer than before. It is the same in psychology. Here too we find science intent upon a systematic collection of data, yet often excluding through that very activity precisely *that* which is most vivid and real in the living phenomena it studies. Somehow the thing that matters has eluded us.

40 What happens when a problem is solved, when one suddenly "sees the point"? Common as this experience is, we seek in vain for it in the textbooks of psychology. Of things arid, poor, and inessential there is an abundance, but that which really matters is missing. Instead we are told of formation of concepts, of abstraction and generalization, of class concepts and judgments, perhaps of associations, creative phantasy, intuitions, talents—anything but an answer to our original problem. And what are these last words but *names* for the problem? Where are the penetrating answers? Psychology is replete with terms of great potentiality—personality, essence, intuition, and the rest. But when one seeks to grasp their concrete content, such terms fail.

This is the situation and it is characteristic of modern science that the same problem should appear everywhere. Several attempts have been made to remedy the matter. One was a frank defeatism preaching the severance of science and

life: there are regions which are inaccessible to science. Other theories established a sharp distinction between the natural and moral sciences: the exactitude and precision of chemistry and physics are characteristic of natural science, but "scientific" accuracy has no place in a study of the mind and its ways. This must be renounced in favour of *other* categories.

Without pausing for further examples, let us consider rather a question naturally underlying the whole discussion: Is "*science*" really the kind of thing we have implied? The word science has often suggested a certain outlook, certain fundamental assumptions, certain procedures and attitudes—but do these imply that this is the only possibility of scientific method? Perhaps science already embodies methods leading in an entirely different direction, methods which have been continually stifled by the seemingly necessary, dominant ones. It is conceivable, for instance, that a host of facts and problems have been concealed rather than illuminated by the prevailing scientific tradition. Even though the traditional methods of science are undoubtedly adequate in many cases, there may be others where they lead us astray. Perhaps something in the very nature of the traditional outlook may have led its exponents at times to ignore precisely that which is truly essential.

Gestalt theory will not be satisfied with sham solutions suggested by a simple dichotomy of science and life. Instead, Gestalt theory is resolved to penetrate the *problem* itself by examining the fundamental assumptions of science. It has long seemed obvious—and is, in fact, the characteristic tone of European science—that "science" means breaking up complexes into their component elements. Isolate the elements, discover their laws, then reassemble them, and the problem is solved.

41

42

From Max Wertheimer, "Gestalt Theory" and "Laws of Organization in Perceptual Forms." In W. D. Ellis (Ed.), *A Source Book of Gestalt Psychology* (pp. 1–11, 71–88). New York: Humanities Press, 1955. (Original work published 1925)

All wholes are reduced to pieces and piecewise relations between pieces.

43 The fundamental "formula" of Gestalt theory might be expressed in this way:[1] There are wholes, the behaviour of which is not determined by that of their individual elements, but where the part-processes are themselves determined by the intrinsic nature of the whole. It is the hope of Gestalt theory to determine the nature of such wholes.

With a formula such as this, one might close, for Gestalt theory is neither more nor less than this. It is not interested in puzzling out philosophic questions which such a formula might suggest. Gestalt theory has to do with concrete research; it is not only an *outcome* but a *device:* not only a theory *about* results but a means toward further discoveries. This is not merely the proposal of one or more problems but an attempt to *see* what is really taking place in science. This problem cannot be solved by listing possibilities for systematization, classification, and arrangement. If it is to be attacked at all, we must be guided by the spirit of the new method and by the concrete nature of the things themselves which we are studying, and set ourselves to penetrate to that which is really given by nature.

44 There is another difficulty that may be illustrated by the following example. Suppose a mathematician shows you a proposition and you begin to "classify" it. This proposition, you say, is of such and such type, belongs in this or that historical category, and so on. Is that how the mathematician works?

"Why, you haven't grasped the thing at all," the mathematician will exclaim. "See here, this formula is not an independent, closed fact that can be dealt with for itself alone. You must see its dynamic *functional* relationship to the whole from which it was lifted or you will never understand it."

What holds for the mathematical formula applies also to the "formula" of Gestalt theory. The attempt of Gestalt theory to disclose the functional meaning of its own formula is no less strict than is the mathematician's. The attempt to explain Gestalt theory in a short essay is the more difficult because of the terms which are used: part, whole, intrinsic determination. All of them have in the past been the topic of endless discussions where each disputant has understood them differently. And even worse has been the cataloguing attitude adopted toward them. What they *lacked* has been actual research. Like many another "philosophic" problem they have been withheld from contact with reality and scientific work.

45 About all I can hope for in so short a discussion is to suggest a few of the problems which at present occupy the attention of Gestalt theory and something of the way they are being attacked.

To repeat: the *problem* has not merely to do with scientific work—it is a fundamental problem of our times. Gestalt theory is not something suddenly and unexpectedly dropped upon us from above; it is, rather, a palpable convergence of problems ranging throughout the sciences and the various philosophic standpoints of modern times.

Let us take, for example, an event in the history of psychology. One turned from a living experience to science and asked what it had to say about this experience, and one found an assortment of elements, sensations, images, feelings, acts of will and laws governing these elements—and was told, "Take your choice, reconstruct from them the experience you had." Such procedure led to difficulties in concrete psychological research and to the emergence of problems which defied solution by the traditional analytic methods. Historically the most important impulse came from v. Ehrenfels who raised the following problem. Psychology had said that experience is a compound of elements: we hear a melody and then, upon hearing it again, memory enables us to recognize it. But what is it that enables us to recognize the melody when it is played in a new key? The sum of the elements is different, yet the melody is the same; indeed, one is often not even aware that a transposition has been made.

46 When in retrospect we consider the prevailing situation we are struck by two aspects of v. Ehrenfels's thesis; on the one hand one is surprised at the essentially summative character of his theory, on the other one admires his courage in propounding and defending his proposition. Strictly interpreted, v. Ehrenfels's position was this: I play a familiar melody of six tones and employ six *new* tones, yet you recognize the melody despite the change. There must be a something *more* than the sum of six tones, viz. a seventh something, which is the form-quality, the *Gestaltqualität,* of the original six. It is this *seventh* factor or element which enabled you to recognize the melody despite its transposition.

However strange this view may seem, it shares with many another subsequently abandoned hypothesis the honour of having clearly seen and emphasized a fundamental problem.

47 But other explanations were also proposed. One maintained that in addition to the six tones there were intervals—relations—and that *these* were what remained constant. In other words we are asked to assume not only elements but "relations-between-elements" as additional components of the total complex. But this view failed to account for the phenomenon because in some cases the relations *too* may be altered without destroying the original melody.

Another type of explanation, also designed to bolster the elementaristic hypothesis, was that *to* this total of six or more tones there come certain "higher processes" which operate upon the given material to "*produce*" unity.

This was the situation until Gestalt theory raised the radical question: Is it really true that when I hear a melody I have a *sum* of individual tones (pieces) which constitute the primary foundation of my experience? Is not perhaps the reverse of this true? What I really have, what I hear of each individual note, what I experience at each place in the melody is a *part* which is itself determined by the character of the whole. What is given me by the melody does not arise (through the agency of any auxiliary factor) as a *secondary* process from the sum of the pieces as such. Instead, what takes place in each single part already depends upon what the whole is. The flesh and blood of a tone depends from the start upon its role in the melody: a *b* as leading tone to *c* is something radically different from the *b* as tonic. It belongs to the flesh and blood of the things given in experience [*Gegebenheiten*], how, in what role, in what function they are in their whole.

48 Let us leave the melody example and turn to another field. Take the case of threshold phenomena. It has long been held that a certain stimulus necessarily produces a certain sensation. Thus, when two stimuli are sufficiently different, the sensations also will be different. Psychology is filled with careful inquiries regarding threshold phenomena. To account for the difficulties constantly being encountered it was assumed that these phenomena must be influenced by higher mental functions, judgments, illusions, attention, etc. And this continued until the radical question was raised: Is

it really true that a specific stimulus *always* gives rise to the same sensation? Perhaps the prevailing whole-conditions will themselves determine the effect of stimulation? This kind of formulation leads to experimentation, and experiments show, for example, that when I see two colours the sensations I have are determined by the whole-conditions of the entire stimulus situation. Thus, also, the same local *physical* stimulus pattern can give rise to either a unitary and homogeneous figure, or to an articulated figure with different parts, all depending upon the whole-conditions which may favour either unity or articulation. Obviously the task, then, is to investigate these "whole-conditions" and discover what influences they exert upon experience.

49 Advancing another step we come to the question whether perhaps any part depends upon the particular whole in which it occurs. Experiments, largely on vision, have answered this question in the affirmative. Among other things they demand that the traditional theory of visual contrast be replaced by a theory which takes account of whole-part conditions.

50 Our next point is that my field comprises also my Ego. There is not from the beginning an Ego over-against others, but the genesis of an Ego offers one of the most fascinating problems, the solution of which seems to lie in Gestalt principles. However, once constituted, the Ego is a functional part of the total field. Proceeding as before we may therefore ask: What happens to the Ego as a part of the field? Is the resulting behaviour the piecewise sort of thing associationism, experience theory, and the like, would have us believe? Experimental results contradict this interpretation and again we often find that the laws of whole-processes operative in such a field tend toward a meaningful behaviour of its parts.

This field is not a summation of sense data and no description of it which considers such separate pieces to be *primary* will be correct. If it were, then for children, primitive peoples and animals experience would be nothing but piece-sensations. The next most developed creatures would have, in addition to independent sensations, something higher, and so on. But this whole picture is the opposite of what actual inquiry has disclosed. We have learned to recognize the "sensations" of our textbooks as products of a late culture utterly different from the experiences of more primitive stages. Who experiences the sensation of a specific red in that sense? What the man of the streets, children, or primitive men normally react to is something coloured but at the same time exciting, gay, strong, or affecting—*not* "sensations."

The programme to treat the organism as a part in a larger field necessitates the reformulation of the problem as to the relation between organism and environment. The stimulus-sensation connection must be replaced by a connection between alteration in the field conditions, the vital situation, and the total reaction of the organism by a change in its attitude, striving, and feeling.

There is, however, another step to be considered. A man is not only a part of his field, he is also one among other men. When a group of people work together it rarely occurs, and then only under very special conditions, that they constitute a mere sum of independent Egos. Instead the common enterprise often becomes their mutual concern and each works *as* a meaningfully functioning part of the whole. Consider a group of South Sea Islanders engaged in some community occupation, or a group of children playing together. Only under very special circumstances does an "I" stand out alone. Then the balance which obtained during harmonious and systematic occupation may be upset and give way to a surrogate (under certain conditions, pathological) *new* balance.[4]

Further discussion of this point would carry us into the work of social and cultural science which cannot be followed here. Instead let us consider certain other illustrations. What was said above of stimulus and sensation is applicable to physiology and the biological sciences no less than to psychology. It has been tried, for example, by postulating sums of more and more special apparatus, to account for meaningful or, as it is often called, purposive behaviour. Once more we find meaninglessly combined reflexes taken for granted although it is probable that even with minute organisms it is not true that a piece-stimulus automatically bring about its corresponding piece-effect.

Opposing this view is *vitalism* which, however, as it appears to Gestalt theory, also errs in its efforts to solve the problem, for it, too, begins with the assumption that natural occurrences are themselves essentially blind and haphazard—and *adds* a mystical something over and above them

which imposes order. Vitalism fails to inquire of physical events whether a genuine order might not already prevail amongst them. And yet nature *does* exhibit numerous instances of physical wholes in which part events are determined by the inner structure of the whole.

These brief references to biology will suffice to remind us that whole-phenomena are not "merely" psychological, but appear in other sciences as well. Obviously, therefore, the problem is not solved by separating off various provinces of science and classifying whole-phenomena as something peculiar to psychology.

The fundamental question can be very simply stated: Are the parts of a given whole determined by the inner structure of that whole, or are the events such that, as independent, piecemeal, fortuitous and blind the total activity is a sum of the part-activities? Human beings can, of course, *devise* a kind of physics of their own—e.g. a sequence of machines—exemplifying the latter half of our question, but this does not signify that *all natural* phenomena are of this type. Here is a place where Gestalt theory is least easily understood and this because of the great number of prejudices about nature which have accumulated during the centuries. Nature is thought of as something essentially blind in its laws, where whatever takes place in the whole is purely a sum of individual occurrences. This view was the natural result of the struggle which physics has always had to purge itself of teleology. To-day it can be seen that we are obliged to traverse other routes than those suggested by this kind of purposivism.

Let us proceed another step and ask: How does all this stand with regard to the problem of body and mind? What does my knowledge of another's mental experiences amount to and how do I obtain it? There are, of course, old and established dogmas on these points: The mental and physical are wholly heterogeneous: there obtains between them an absolute dichotomy. (From this point of departure philosophers have drawn an array of metaphysical deductions so as to attribute all the good qualities to mind while reserving for nature the odious.) As regards the second question, my discerning mental phenomena in others is traditionally explained as inference by analogy. Strictly interpreted the principle here is that something mental is meaninglessly coupled with something physical. I observe the physical and infer the mental from it more or less according to the following scheme: I see someone press a button on the wall and infer that he wants the light to go on. There *may be* couplings of this sort. However, many scientists have been disturbed by this dualism and have tried to save themselves by recourse to very curious hypotheses. Indeed, the ordinary person would violently refuse to believe that when he sees his companion startled, frightened, or angry he is seeing only certain physical occurrences which themselves have nothing to do (in their inner nature) with the mental, being only superficially coupled with it: you have frequently seen this and this combined . . . etc. There have been many attempts to surmount this problem. One speaks, for example, of *intuition* and says there can be no other possibility, for I *see* my companion's fear. It is not true, argue the intuitionists, that I see only the bare bodily activities meaninglessly coupled with other and invisible activities. However inadmissible it may otherwise be, an intuition theory does have at least this in its favour, it shows a suspicion that the traditional procedure might be successfully reversed. But the word intuition is at best only a *naming* of that which we must strive to lay hold of.

This and other hypotheses, apprehended as they now are, will not advance scientific pursuit, for science demands fruitful penetration, not mere cataloguing and systematization. But the question is, How does the matter really stand? Looking more closely we find a third assumption, namely that a process such as fear is a matter of consciousness. Is this true? Suppose you see a person who is kindly or benevolent. Does anyone suppose that this person is feeling mawkish? No one could possibly believe that. The characteristic feature of such behaviour has very little to do with consciousness. It has been one of the easiest contrivances of philosophy to identify a man's real behaviour and the direction of his mind with his consciousness. Parenthetically, in the opinion of many people the distinction between idealism and materialism implies that between the noble and the ignoble. Yet does one really mean by this to contrast consciousness with the blithesome budding of trees? Indeed, what is there so repugnant about the materialistic and mechanical? What is so attractive about the idealistic? Does it come from the *material* qualities of the connected pieces? Broadly speaking most psychological the-

56

ories and textbooks, despite their continued emphasis upon consciousness, are far more "materialistic," arid, and spiritless than a living tree—which probably has no consciousness at all. The point is not what the material pieces are, but what *kind* of whole it is. Proceeding in terms of specific problems one soon realizes how many bodily activities there are which give no hint of a separation between body and mind. Imagine a dance, a dance full of grace and joy. What is the situation in such a dance? Do we have a summation of *physical* limb movements and a *psychical* consciousness? No. Obviously this answer does not solve the problem; we have to start anew—and it seems to me that a proper and fruitful point of attack has been discovered. One finds many processes which, in their dynamical form, are identical regardless of variations in the material character of their elements. When a man is timid, afraid or energetic, happy or sad, it can often be shown that the course of his physical processes is Gestalt-identical with the course pursued by the mental processes.

Again I can only indicate the direction of thought. I have touched on the question of body and mind merely to show that the problem we are discussing also has its philosophic aspects. To strengthen the import of the foregoing suggestions let us consider the fields of epistemology and logic. For centuries the assumption has prevailed that our world is essentially a summation of elements. For Hume and largely also for Kant the world is like a bundle of fragments, and the dogma of meaningless summations continues to play its part. As for logic, it supplies: *concepts,* which when rigorously viewed are but sums of properties; *classes,* which upon closer inspection prove to be mere catchalls; *syllogisms,* devised by arbitrarily lumping together any two propositions having the character that . . . etc. When one considers what a concept *is* in living thought, what it really means to grasp a conclusion; when one considers what the crucial thing *is* about a mathematical proof and the concrete interrelationships it involves, one sees that the categories of traditional logic have accomplished nothing in this direction.

It is our task to inquire whether a logic is possible which is *not* piecemeal. Indeed the same question arises in mathematics also. Is it *necessary* that all mathematics be established upon a

57

58

piecewise basis? What sort of mathematical system would it be in which this were *not* the case? There have been attempts to answer the latter question but almost always they have fallen back in the end upon the old procedures. This fate has overtaken many, for the result of training in piecewise thinking is extraordinarily tenacious. It is not enough and certainly does not constitute a solution of the principal problem if one shows that the axioms of mathematics are both piecemeal and at the same time evince something of the opposite character. The problem has been scientifically grasped only when an attack specifically designed to yield positive results has been launched. Just how this attack is to be made seems to many mathematicians a colossal problem, but perhaps the quantum theory will force the mathematicians to attack it.

59   This brings us to the close of an attempt to present a view of the problem as illustrated by its specific appearances in various fields. In concluding I may suggest a certain unification of these illustrations somewhat as follows. I consider the situation from the point of view of a theory of aggregates and say: How should a world be where science, concepts, inquiry, investigation, and comprehension of inner unities were impossible? The answer is obvious. This world would be a manifold of disparate pieces. Secondly, what kind of world would there have to be in which a piecewise science would apply? The answer is again quite simple, for here one needs only a system of recurrent couplings that are blind and piecewise

in character, whereupon everything is available for a pursuit of the traditional piecewise methods of logic, mathematics, and science generally in so far as these presuppose this kind of world. But there is a third kind of aggregate which has been but cursorily investigated. These are the aggregates in which a manifold is not compounded from adjacently situated pieces but rather such that a term at its place in that aggregate is determined by the whole-laws of the aggregate itself.

Pictorially: suppose the world were a vast plateau upon which were many musicians. I walk about listening and watching the players. First suppose that the world is a meaningless plurality. Everyone does as he will, each for himself. What happens together when I hear ten players might be the basis for my guessing as to what they all are doing, but this is merely a matter of chance and probability much as in the kinetics of gas molecules.—A second possibility would be that each time one musician played *c*, another played *f* so and so many seconds later. I work out a theory of blind couplings but the playing as a whole remains meaningless. This is what many people think physics does, but the real work of physics belies this.—The third possibility is, say, a Beethoven symphony where it would be possible for one to select one part of the whole and work from that towards an idea of the structural principle motivating and determining the whole. Here the fundamental laws are not those of fortuitous pieces, but concern the very character of the event.

Laws of Organization in Perceptual Forms (from Psychologische Forschung, 1923)

301   I stand at the window and see a house, trees, sky.

Theoretically I might say there were 327 brightnesses and nuances of colour. Do I *have* "327"? No. I have sky, house, and trees. It is im-

possible to achieve "327" as such. And yet even though such droll calculation were possible—and implied, say, for the house 120, the trees 90, the sky 117—I should at least have *this* arrangement and division of the total, and not, say, 127 and 100 and 100; or 150 and 177.

The concrete division which I *see* is not determined by some arbitrary mode of organization ly-

Grateful acknowledgment is hereby made to *Julius Springer, Verlagsbuchhandlung,* Berlin, for permission to reproduce the illustrations used in this Selection.

ing solely within my own pleasure; instead I see the arrangement and division which is given there before me. And what a remarkable process it is when some other mode of apprehension *does* succeed! I gaze for a long time from my window, adopt after some effort the most unreal attitude possible. And I *discover* that part of a window sash and part of a bare branch together compose an *N*.

Or, I look at a picture. Two faces cheek to cheek. I see one (with its, if you will, "57" brightness) and the other ("49" brightness). I do not see an arrangement of 66 plus 40 nor of 6 plus 100. There *have* been theories which would require that I see "106". In reality I see two faces!

Or, I hear a melody (17 tones) with its accompaniment (32 tones). I hear the melody and accompaniment, not simply "49"—and certainly not 20 plus 29. And the same is true even in cases where there is no stimulus continuum. I hear the melody and its accompaniment even when they are played by an old-fashioned clock where each tone is separate from the others. Or, one sees a series of discontinuous dots upon a homogeneous ground not as a sum of dots, but as figures. Even though there may here be a greater latitude of possible arrangements, the dots usually combine in some "spontaneous," "natural" articulation—and any other arrangement, even if it can be achieved, is artificial and difficult to maintain.

When we are presented with a number of stimuli we do not as a rule experience "a number" of individual things, this one and that and that. Instead larger wholes separated from and related to one another are given in experience; their arrangement and division are concrete and definite.

Do such arrangements and divisions follow definite principles? When the stimuli *abcde* appear together what are the principles according to which *abc/de* and not *ab/cde* is experienced? It is the purpose of this paper to examine this problem, and we shall therefore begin with cases of discontinuous stimulus constellations.

304 *I.* A row of dots is presented upon a homogeneous ground. The alternate intervals are 3 mm. and 12 mm.

(i)

Normally this row will be seen as *ab/cd,* not as *a/bc/de.* As a matter of fact it is for most people impossible to see the whole series simultaneously in the latter grouping.

We are interested here in what is actually *seen.* The following will make this clear. One sees a row of groups obliquely tilted from lower left to upper right (*ab/cd/ef*). The arrangement *a/bc/de* is extremely difficult to achieve. Even when it can be seen, such an arrangement is far less certain than the other and is quite likely to be upset by eye-movements or variations of attention.

(ii)

This is even more clear in (iii).

(iii)

I.e.:—   c   f   i   l   o
          b   e   h   k   n   etc.
          a   d   g   j   m

Quite obviously the arrangement *abc/def/ghi* is greatly superior to *ceg/fhj/ikm.*

Another, still clearer example of spontaneous arrangement is that given in (iv). The natural grouping is, of course, *a/bcd/efghi,* etc.

(iv)

Resembling (i) but still more compelling is the row of three-dot groupings given in (v). One sees *abc/def,* and not some other (theoretically possible) arrangement.

(v)

Another example of seeing what the objective arrangement dictates is contained in (vi) for vertical, and in (vii) for horizontal groupings.

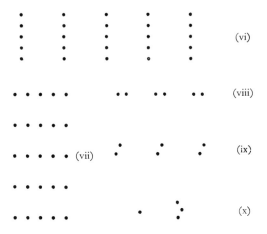

(vi)

(viii)

(vii)   (ix)

(x)

an identical proximity throughout but vary the colour of the dots themselves:—

○ ○ • • ○ ○ • • ○ ○ • • ○ ○ • • ○ ○ • •   (xi)

Or, again:—   309

○ • ○ • ○ • ○ • ○ • ○ •
○ • ○ • ○ • ○ • ○ • ○ •
○ • ○ • ○ • ○ • ○ • ○ •
○ • ○ • ○ • ○ • ○ • ○ •
○ • ○ • ○ • ○ • ○ • ○ •
○ • ○ • ○ • ○ • ○ • ○ •   (xii)
○ • ○ • ○ • ○ • ○ • ○ •
○ • ○ • ○ • ○ • ○ • ○ •
○ • ○ • ○ • ○ • ○ • ○ •
○ • ○ • ○ • ○ • ○ • ○ •

○ ○ ○ ○ ○ ○ ○ ○ ○ ○ ○ ○
• • • • • • • • • • • •
○ ○ ○ ○ ○ ○ ○ ○ ○ ○ ○ ○
• • • • • • • • • • • •
○ ○ ○ ○ ○ ○ ○ ○ ○ ○ ○ ○   (xiii)
• • • • • • • • • • • •
○ ○ ○ ○ ○ ○ ○ ○ ○ ○ ○ ○
• • • • • • • • • • • •
○ ○ ○ ○ ○ ○ ○ ○ ○ ○ ○ ○
• • • • • • • • • • • •

Or, to repeat (v) but with uniform proximity:—

○ ○ ○ • • • ○ ○ ○ • • • ○ ○ ○ • • • ○ ○ ○ • • •   (xiv)

In all the foregoing cases we have used a relatively large number of dots for each figure. Using fewer we find that the arrangement is not so imperatively dictated as before, and reversing the more obvious grouping is comparatively easy. Examples: (viii)–(x).

307   It would be false to assume that (viii)–(x) lend themselves more readily to reversal because fewer stimulus points (dots) are involved. Such incorrect reasoning would be based upon the proposition: "The more dots, the more difficult it will be to unite them into groups." Actually it is only the unnatural, artificial arrangement which is rendered more difficult by a larger number of points. The natural grouping (cf., e.g., (i), (ii), etc.) is not at all impeded by increasing the number of dots. It never occurs, for example, that with a long row of such dots the process of "uniting" them into pairs is abandoned and individual points seen instead. It is not true that fewer stimulus points "obviously" yield simpler, surer, more elementary results.

308   In each of the above cases that form of grouping is most natural which involves the smallest interval. They all show, that is to say, the predominant influence of what we may call *The Factor of Proximity*. Here is the first of the principles which we undertook to discover. That the principle holds also for auditory organization can readily be seen by substituting tap-tap, pause, tap-tap, pause, etc. for (i), and so on for the others.

II. Proximity is not, however, the only factor involved in natural groupings. This is apparent from the following examples. We shall maintain

Thus we are led to the discovery of a second principle—viz. the tendency of like parts to band together—which we may call *The Factor of Similarity*. And again it should be remarked that this principle applies also to auditory experience. Maintaining a constant interval, the beats may be soft and loud (analogous to (xi)) thus: . . ! ! . . ! ! etc. Even when the attempt to hear some other arrangement succeeds, this cannot be maintained for long. The natural grouping soon returns as an overpowering "upset" of the artificial arrangement.

In (xi)–(xiv) there is, however, the possibility   310 of another arrangement which should not be overlooked. We have treated these sequences in terms of a *constant* direction from left to right. But it is also true that a continual *change* of direction is taking place between the groups themselves: viz. the transition from group one to group two (soft-to-loud), the transition from group two to group three (loud-to-soft), and so on. This naturally involves a special factor. To retain a constant direction it would be necessary to make each succeeding pair louder than the last. Schematically this can be represented as:—

(xv)

Or, in the same way:—

(xvi)

This retention of constant direction could also be demonstrated with achromatic colours (green background) thus: white, light grey, medium grey, dark grey, black. A musical reproduction of (xv) would be *C, C, E, E, F#, F#, A, A, C, C, . . .* ; and similarly for (xvi): *C, C, C, E, E, E, F#, F#, F#, A, A, A, C, C, C, . . .*

Thus far we have dealt merely with a special case of the general law. Not only similarity and dissimilarity, but *more and less dissimilarity* operate to determine experienced arrangement. With tones, for example, *C, C#, E, F, G#, A, C, C# . . .* will be heard in the grouping *ab/cd . . .* and *C, C#, D, E, F, F#, G#, A, A#, C, C#, D . . .* in the grouping *abc/def . . .* Or, again using achromatic colours, we might present these same relationships in the manner suggested (schematically) by (xvii) and (xviii).

(xvii)

(xviii)

(It is apparent from the foregoing that quantitative comparisons can be made regarding the application of the same laws in regions—form, colour, sound—heretofore treated as psychologically separate and heterogeneous.)

III. What will happen when *two* such factors appear in the same constellation? They may be made to co-operate; or, they can be set in opposition—as, for example, when *one* operates to favour *ab/cd* while the *other* favours */bc/de*. By appropriate variations, either factor may be weakened or strengthened. As an example, consider this arrangement:—   312

(xix)

where both similarity and proximity are employed. An illustration of opposition in which similarity is victorious despite the preferential status given to proximity is this:—   313

(xx)

A less decided victory by similarity:—

(xxi)

Functioning together towards the same end, similarity and proximity greatly strengthen the prominence here of verticality:—

(xxii)

Where, in cases such as these, *proximity* is the predominant factor, a gradual increase of interval will eventually introduce a point at which *similarity* is predominant. In this way it is possible to test the strength of these Factors.

IV. A row of dots is presented:—   315

• • •   • • •   • • •   • • •
a b c d e f g h i j k l

and then, without the subject's expecting it, but before his eyes, a sudden, slight shift upward is given, say, to d, e, f or to d, e, f and j, k, l together. *This* shift is "pro-structural", since it involves an entire group of naturally related dots. A shift upward of, say, c, d, e or of c, d, e and i, j, k would be "contra-structural" because the common fate (i.e. the shift) to which these dots are subjected does *not* conform with their natural groupings.

316   Shifts of the latter kind are far less "smooth" than those of the former type. The former often call forth from the subject no more than bare recognition that a change has occurred; not so with the latter type. Here it is as if some particular "opposition" to the change had been encountered. The result is confusing and discomforting. Sometimes a revolt against the originally dominant Factor of Proximity will occur and the shifted dots themselves thereupon constitute a new grouping whose common fate it has been to be shifted above the original row. The principle involved here may be designated *The Factor of Uniform Destiny* (or of "*Common Fate*").

     V. Imagine a sequence of rows of which this would be the first:—

Row A.   • •   • •   • •   • •   • •
              a b c d e f g h i j

     The intervals between a-b, c-d, etc. (designated hereafter as S_1) are in this row 2 mm.; those between b-c, d-e, etc. (S_2) are 20 mm. We shall hold $a, c, e, g,$ and i constant while varying the horizontal position of $b, d, f, h,$ and j thus:—

		$S_1 + S_2 = 22$	
317	Row A	$S_1 = 2$ mm.	$S_2 = 20$ mm.
	B	5	17
	C	8	14
	D	11	11
	E	14	8
	F	17	5
	G	20	2

Experimentally we now present these rows *separately.*[2] It will be found that there are three major constellations: The dominant impression in Row A is *ab/cd*, and in Row G it is */bc/de*. But in the middle row (represented in our schema by D) the predominant impression is that of uniformity. These three constellations thus constitute "unique regions" and it will be found that intervening rows are more indefinite in character and their arrangement less striking; indeed they are often most easily seen in the sense of the nearest major constellation. Example: intermediate rows in the vicinity of D will be seen *as* "not quite equally spaced" (even when the difference between intervals S_1 and S_2 is clearly supraliminal).

318   Or to take another example. Suppose one side of an angle is held horizontal and the other passes through an arc from 30° to 150°. No more here than in the preceding case is *each* degree of equal value psychologically. Instead there are three principal stages: acute, right, and obtuse. The "right angle," for example, has a certain region such that an angle of 93° appears *as* a (more or less inadequate) right angle. Stages intermediate between the major ones have the character of indefiniteness about them and are readily seen in the sense of one *or* the other adjacent *Prägnanzstufen*.[3] This can be very clearly demonstrated by tachistoscopic presentations, for in this case the observer frequently *sees* a right angle even when objectively a more acute or more obtuse angle is being presented. Although the observer may report that it was "not quite correct", "somehow wrong," etc., he is usually unable to say in which direction the "error" lies.

319   In general we may say, as in the case above where the location of b between a and c was varied, that our impressions are not psychologically equivalent for all positions of b. Instead there are certain *Prägnanzstufen* with their appropriate realms or regions, and intermediate stages typically appear "in the sense of" one of these characteristic regions.

     VI. Suppose now that the variations from A to G are carried out before the observer's eyes. This procedure leads to a discovery of *The Factor of Objective Set* [*Einstellung*]. As one proceeds from A towards G or from G towards A the *original* grouping in each case (i.e. *ab/cd* in the former, */bc/de* in the latter) tends to maintain itself even beyond the middle row. Then there occurs an upset and the opposite grouping becomes dominant. The constellation of Row C, for example, will be different when preceded by A and B from what it would be when preceded by G, F, E. This means that the row is *a part in a sequence* and the law of its arrangement is such that the constellation resulting from *one* form of sequence will be different from that given by some *other* sequence. Or, again, a certain (objectively) ambiguous arrangement will be perfectly definite and unequivocal when given as a part in a sequence. (In view of its great strength this Factor must in all cases be considered with much care.)

Parenthetically: it is customary to attribute influences such as these to purely subjective (meaning by this "purely arbitrary") conditions. But our examples refer only to *objective* factors: the presence or absence of a certain row of dots in a sequence is determined solely by objective conditions. It is objectively quite different whether a Row M is presented after Row L or after Row N; or, whether the presentations follow one another

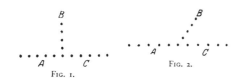

FIG. 1.

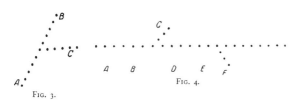

FIG. 3.   FIG. 4.

immediately or occur on different days. When several rows are simultaneously presented it is of course possible to select one row or another quite according to one's (subjective) fancy; or any certain row may be compared with another just above or below it. But this special case is not what we are here concerned with. Such subjectively determined arrangements are possible *only* if the rows of dots permit of two or more modes of apprehension. Curiously enough, however, it has been just this special case (where objective conditions do not themselves compel us to see one arrangement rather than another) which has usually been thought of as *the* fundamental relationship. As a matter of fact we shall see below how

even purely subjective factors are by no means as arbitrary in their operations as one might suppose.

VII. That spatial proximity will not alone account for organization can be shown by an example such as Fig. 1. Taken individually the points in B are in closer proximity to the individual points of A (or C) than the points of A and C are to each oth-

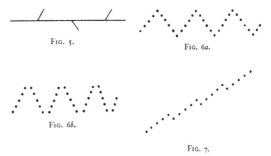

FIG. 5.

FIG. 6a.

FIG. 6b.

FIG. 7.

er. Nevertheless the perceived grouping is not AB/C or BC/A, but, quite clearly "a horizontal line and a vertical line"—i.e. AC/B. In Fig. 2 the spatial proximity of B and C is even greater, yet the result is still AC/B—i.e. horizontal-oblique. The same is true of the relationship AB/C in Fig. 3. As Figs. 4–7 also show we are dealing now with a new principle which we may call *The Factor of Direction.* That direction may still be unequivocally given even when curved lines are used is of course obvious (cf. Figs. 8–12). The dominance of this Factor in

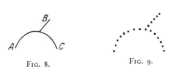

FIG. 8.   FIG. 9.

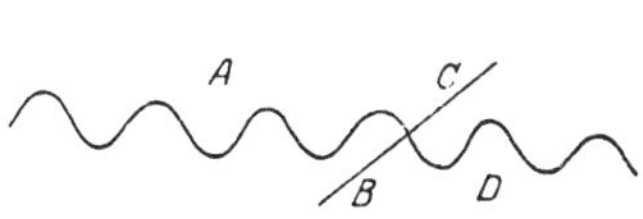

FIG. 10.

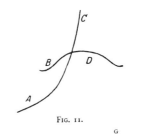

FIG. 11.

G

certain cases will be especially clear if one attempts to see Fig. 13 as (*abefil* . . .) (*cdghkm* . . .) instead of (*acegik* . . .) (*bdfhlm* . . .).

Suppose in Fig. 8 we had only the part designated as *A*, and suppose any two other lines were to be added. Which of the additional ones would join *A* as its continuation and which would appear as an

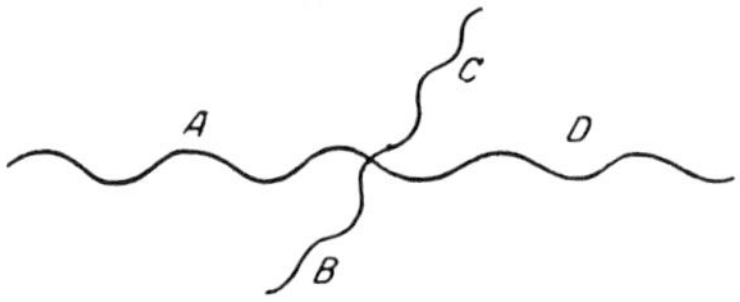

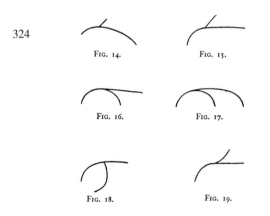

FIG. 12.

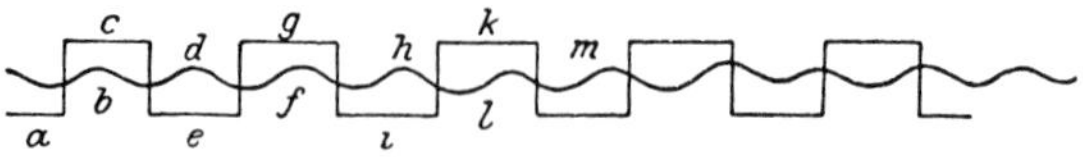

FIG. 13.

appendage? As it is now drawn *AC* constitutes the continuity, *B* the appendage. Figs. 14–19 represent a few such variations. Thus, for example, we see that *AC/B* is still the dominant organization even in Fig. 15 (where *C* is tangent to the circle implied by *A*). But in Fig. 16, when *B* is tangent to *A*, we still

324

FIG. 14. FIG. 15.

FIG. 16. FIG. 17.

FIG. 18. FIG. 19.

have *AC/B*. Naturally, however, the length of *B* and *C* is an important consideration. In all such cases there arise the same questions as those suggested above in our discussion of *Prägnanzstufen*. Certain arrangements are stronger than others, and seem to "triumph"; intermediate arrangements are less distinctive, more equivocal.

On the whole the reader should find no difficulty in *seeing* what is meant here. In designing a pattern, for example, one has a feeling how successive parts should follow one another; one knows what a "good" continuation is, how "inner coherence" is to be achieved, etc.; one recognizes a resultant "good Gestalt" simply by its own "inner necessity." A more detailed study at this juncture would require consideration of the following: Additions to an incomplete object (e.g. the segment of a 325 curve) may proceed in a direction opposed to that of the original, or they may *carry on* the principle

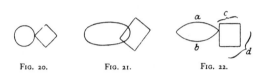

FIG. 20. FIG. 21. FIG. 22.

"logically demanded" by the original. It is in the latter case that "unity" will result. This does not mean, however, that "simplicity" will result from an addition which is (piecewise considered) "simple." Indeed even a very "complicated" addition may promote unity of the resultant whole. "Simplicity" does not refer to the properties of individual parts; simplicity is a property of wholes. Finally, the addition must be viewed also in terms of such characteristic "whole properties" as closure, equilibrium, and symmetry.[4]

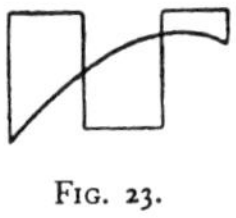

FIG. 23.

From an inspection of Figs. 20–22 we are led to the discovery of still another principle: *The Factor of Closure*. If *A*, *B*, *C*, *D* are given and *AB/CD* constitute two self-enclosed units, then *this* arrangement rather than *AC/BD* will be appre- 326 hended. It is not true, however, that closure is necessarily the dominant Factor in all cases which satisfy these conditions. In Fig. 23, for example, it is not three self-enclosed areas but rather *The Factor of the "Good Curve"* which predominates.

It is instructive in this connection to determine the conditions under which two figures will appear as *two* independent figures, and those under

327 which they will combine to yield an entirely different (single) figure. (Examples: Figs. 24–27.) And this applies also to surfaces. The reader may test the influence of surface wholeness by attempting to see Fig. 24 as three separate, closed figures. With coloured areas the unity of naturally
328 coherent parts may be enhanced still more. Fig.

FIGURE 24.    FIGURE 25. 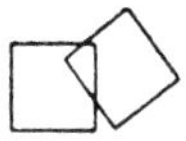   FIGURE 26. 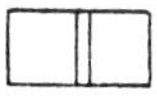 FIGURE 27.

28 is most readily seen as an oblique deltoid (*bc*) within a rectangle (*ad*). Try now to see on the left side a hexagon whose lower right-hand corner is shaded, and on the right side another hexagon whose upper left-hand corner is shaded [viz. Figs. 28*a* and 28*b*].

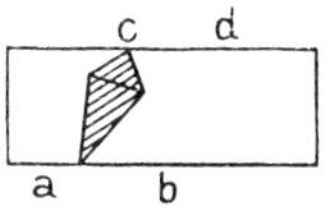

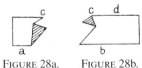

FIGURE 28.

Once more we observe (as with the curves of Figs. 9–12) the influence of a tendency towards the "good" Gestalt, and in the present case it is probably easier than before to grasp the meaning of this expression. Here it is clearly evident that a unitary colour tends to bring about uniformity of colouring within the given surface.

FIGURE 28a.   FIGURE 28b.

Taking any figure (e.g. Fig. 29) it is instructive to raise such questions as the following: By means of what additions can one so alter the figure that a spontaneous apprehension of the original would
329 be impossible? (Figs. 30–32 are examples.) An excellent method of achieving this result is to complete certain "good subsidiaries" in a manner which is "contra-structural" relative to the original. (But notice that not all additions to the original will have this effect. Figs. 33–34, for example,

represent additions which we may call "indifferent" since they are neither "pro-structural" nor "contra-structural.")

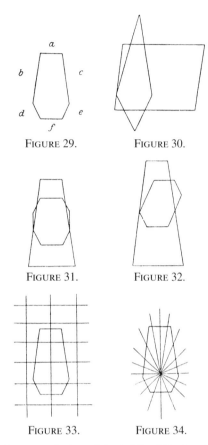

FIGURE 29.   FIGURE 30.

FIGURE 31.   FIGURE 32.

FIGURE 33.   FIGURE 34.

Let us call the original (Fig. 29) *O* and any contra-structural addition *C*, while any pro-structural addition we shall call *P*. For our purposes, then, *O* is to be thought of as a subsidiary of some more inclusive whole. Now *O* whether taken alone or as part of *OP* is different from what it would be in *OC*. It is of the first importance for *O* in *which* constellation it appears. (In this way a person thoroughly familiar with *O* can be made quite blind to its existence. This applies not only to recognition but to perception in general.)

VIII. Another Factor is that of past experience 331 or habit. Its principle is that if *AB* and *C* but not *BC* have become habitual (or "associated") there is then a tendency for *ABC* to appear as *AB/C*. Unlike the other principles with which we have been dealing, it is characteristic of this one that the *con-*

tents A, B, C are assumed to be independent of the constellation in which they appear. Their arrangement is on principle determined merely by extrinsic circumstances (e.g. drill).

332   There can be no doubt that some of our apprehensions are determined in this way.[6] Often arbitrary material can be arranged in arbitrary form and, after a sufficient drill, made habitual. The difficulty is, however, that many people are inclined to attribute to this principle the fundamental structure of *all* apprehension. The situation in § VII, they would say, simply involves the prominence of habitual complexes. Straight lines, right angles, the arcs of circles, squares—all are familiar from everyday experience. And so it is also with the intervals between parts (e.g. the spaces between written words), and with uniformity of coloured surfaces. Experience supplies a constant drill in such matters.

And yet, despite its plausibility, the doctrine of past experience brushes aside the real problems of apprehension much too easily. Its duty should be to demonstrate in each of the foregoing cases (1) that the dominant apprehension was due to earlier experience (and to nothing else); (2) that non-
333   dominant apprehensions in each instance had *not* been previously experienced; and, in general, (3) that in the *amassing* of experience none but adventitious factors need ever be involved. It should be clear from our earlier discussions and examples that this programme could not succeed. A single example will suffice to show this. Right angles surround us from childhood (table, cupboard, window, corners of rooms, houses). At first this seems quite self-evident. But does the child's environment consist of nothing but man-made objects? Are there not in nature (e.g. the branches of trees) fully as many obtuse and acute angles? But far more important than these is the following consideration. Is it *true* that cupboards, tables, etc., actually present right angles to the child's eye? If we consider the literal reception of stimuli upon the retina, how often are *right angles* as such involved? Certainly less often than the *perception* of right angles. As a matter of fact the conditions necessary for a literal "right angle" stimulation are realized but rarely in everyday life (viz. *only* when the table or other object appears in a frontal parallel plane). Hence the argument from experience is referring not to repetition of literal stimulus conditions, but to repetition of phenomenal

experience—and the problem therefore simply repeats itself.

Regardless of whether or not one believes that the relationships discussed in § VII depend upon past experience, the question remains in either

FIGURE 35.   FIGURE 36.

case: Do these relationships exhibit the operations of intrinsic laws or not, and if so, which laws? Such a question requires experimental inquiry and cannot be answered by the mere expression "past experience." Let us take two arrangements which have been habitually experienced in the forms *abc* and *def* many thousands of times. I place them to-
334   gether and present *abcdef*. Is the result sure to be *abc/def?* Fig. 35, which is merely the combination of a W and an M, may be taken as an example. One ordinarily sees not the familiar letters W and M, but a sinuation between two symmetrically curved uprights. If we designate parts of the W from left to right as *abc* and those of the M as *def,* the figure may be described as *ad/be/cf* (or as */be/* between */ad/* and */cf/*); *not,* however, as *abc/def.*

335   But the objection might be raised that while we are familiar enough with W and M, we are not accustomed to seeing them in *this* way (one above the other) and that this is why the other arrangement is dominant. It would certainly be false, however, to consider this an "explanation". At best this mode of approach could show only why the arrangement W-M is *not* seen; the positive side would still be untouched. But apart from this, the objection is rendered impotent when we arrange *abc* and *def* one above the other (Fig. 36) in a fashion quite as unusual as that given in Fig. 35. Nor is the argument admissible that the arrangements */ad/* and */be/* and */cf/* in Fig. 35 are themselves familiar from past experience. It simply is not true that as much experience has been had with */be/* as with the *b* in *abc* and the *e* in *def.*

348   *IX.* When an object appears upon a homogeneous field there must be stimulus differentiation (inhomogeneity) in order that the object may be perceived. A perfectly homogeneous field appears as a total field [*Ganzfeld*] opposing subdivision, disintegration, etc. To effect a segregation within

this field requires relatively strong differentiation between the object and its background. And this holds not only for ideally homogeneous fields but also for fields in which, e.g., a symmetrical brightness distribution obtains, or in which the "homogeneity" consists in a uniform dappled effect. The best case for the resulting of a figure in such a field is when in the total field a closed surface of simple form is different in colour from the remaining field. Such a surface figure is not one member of a duo (of which the total field or "ground" would be the other member); its contours serve as boundary lines only for *this* figure. The background is not limited by the figure, but usually seems to continue unbroken beneath that figure.

349   *Within* this figure there may be then further subdivision resulting in subsidiary wholes. The procedure here as before is in the direction "from above downward" and it will be found that the Factors discussed in § VII are crucial for these subdivisions.[7] As regards attention, fixation, etc., it follows that they are *secondarily* determined relative to the natural relations already given by whole-constellations as such. Consider, e.g., the difference between some artificially determined concentration of attention and that spontaneously resulting from the pro-structural emphasis given by a figure itself. For an approach "from above downward," i.e. from whole-properties downward towards subsidiary wholes and parts, individual parts ("elements") are not primary, not pieces to be combined in and-summations, but are *parts of wholes.*

bei denen nicht, was im Ganzen geschieht, sich daraus herleitet, wie die einzelne Stücke sind und sich zusammensetzen, sondern umgekehrt, wo—im prägnanten Fall—sich *das, was an einem Teil dieses Ganzen geschicht, bestimmt von inneren Strukturgesetzen dieses seines Ganzen.*"

2. The above classification of but 7 rows is intended merely as a schema. In actual experimentation many more than 7 (with correspondingly more minute variations of intervals) are needed.

3. ["*Stufen*" = steps or stages; the term "*Prägnanz*" cannot be translated. In the present usage "*Prägnanzstufen*" means *regions* of figural stability in a sense which should be clear from the text.]

4. Symmetry signifies far more than mere similarity of parts; it refers rather to the logical correctness of a part considered relative to the whole in which that part occurs.

5. The Factor of similarity can thus be seen as a special instance of *The Factor of the Good Gestalt.*

6. Example: 314 cm. is apprehended as *abc/de,* not as *ab/cde*—i.e. as 314 cm., not 31/4 cm. nor as 314c/m.

7. Epistemologically this distinction between "above" and "below" is of great importance. The mind and the psychophysiological reception of stimuli do *not* respond after the manner of a mirror or photographic apparatus receiving individual "stimuli" *qua* individual units and working them up "from below" into the objects of experience. Instead response is made to articulation as a whole—and this after the manner suggested by the Factors of § VII. It follows that the apparatus of reception cannot be described as a piecewise sort of mechanism. It must be of such a nature as to be able *to grasp the inner necessity* of articulated wholes. When we consider the problem in this light it becomes apparent that pieces are not even experienced as such but that apprehension itself is characteristically "from above."

NOTES

1. "Man könnte das Grundproblem der Gestalttheorie etwa so zu formulieren suchen: Es gibt Zusammenhänge,

25

E. B. TITCHENER

Edward Bradford Titchener (1867–1927), a formal and frank Englishman with an imposing beard, arrived at Cornell University in 1892 having just received his Ph.D. from the University of Leipzig. A fine musician, Titchener provided music instruction at Cornell until a formal music department was established, presenting weekly concerts at his home followed by casual conversation. In the course of developing one of the largest psychology programs in the United States, he maintained a firm, some say iron-fisted, understanding of what ought to considered psychology. Titchener deplored the inclusion of applied fields, arguing that the application of psychology would be best accomplished by separate disciplines (e.g., that educational psychology should be under the education department). Titchener became intrigued with experimental psychology while a student at Oxford University, translating Wilhelm Wundt's (p. 296) *Principles of Physiological Psychology* from the original German before traveling to Leipzig to study with Wundt. In an era when the Trustees of both Harvard University and Columbia University refused to allow women access to graduate study, Cornell's doors were open to any who sought instruction. In fact, Titchener's first graduate student was Margaret Floy Washburn (p. 203), who wrote that he had two great gifts, "his comprehensive scholarship . . . and his genius as a lecturer," but an unfortunate tendency to isolate himself from his surroundings. Titchener was a product of his times and felt that while women could be trained, and ought to be hired, as scientists, it was personally inconceivable to have truly collegial relations with them. In 1904, he organized the "Experimentalists" as an annual meeting for the critical presentation and open discussion of experimental psychology. The guest list included the heads of all the prestigious psychological laboratories in North America and their male junior colleagues and graduate students. This forum provided invaluable exposure and contacts, but Titchener did not allow women in the group, despite a handful of obviously qualified and interested women—he felt their presence would diminish frank criticism and place restrictions on smoking. Women, even active scientists, in his mind, were simply incapable of engaging in open, critical discussion. He was not alone in this opinion, and despite some spirited protests by Christine Ladd-Franklin, an incredibly active researcher with part-time lecturing positions at Johns Hopkins University and Columbia University, women were not invited until the group reorganized two years after Titchener's death in 1927.

From E.B. Titchener, "Ideational Type and the Association of Ideas." In *Experimental Psychology: A Manual of Laboratory Practice* (pp. 195–206). New York: Macmillan 1927.

EXPERIMENTAL PSYCHOLOGY: A MANUAL OF LABORATORY PRACTICE

IDEATIONAL TYPE AND THE ASSOCIATION OF IDEAS

Experiment XXXVI

§ 51. *Ideational Types*

Our own mind is so much a matter of course to us, and we are so ready to "judge other people by ourselves," that the *differences* between mind and mind are likely to escape notice. We know that so-and-so is "imaginative," that so-and-so has "a tremendous memory," and that so-and-so "seems to take it all in, when we can't make head or tail of it"; and we sometimes make, in the course of conversation, a surprised remark about these differences. Nevertheless, we soon slip back into our self-complacency, into the idea that our own mind is the typical human mind.

This error has, of course, a good deal of truth in it. If minds were not fundamentally alike, there could not be the intercourse in the world that there actually is. There could be no high development of commerce, or literature, or science; no settled condition of society. Our mistake is confirmed, then, on the practical side, by the constant observation that one man *is* like another, that the one can treat the other as if he were a second self. But the mistake is also strengthened by the science of mind itself. It is the uniformities of mind that psychology emphasises. We take it for granted, after a few preliminary tests for colour blindness and what not, that the workers in a psychological laboratory have all a like outfit of sensations and feelings, a similar capacity of attention, and so on. The elementary processes and the basal functions of mind are the same in all "normal" individuals.

Yet our first idea is erroneous. Though the elementary processes of every normal mind are the same, yet the parts played by the various groups of processes differ very greatly in different consciousnesses. And though the basal functions of all normal minds are the same, yet the mechanism of these functions differs very greatly from mind to mind. One man, we say, is "eye minded," another is "ear minded." The phrases do not mean that the one man has more visual and fewer auditory sensations than the other, and *vice versa;* it means (*a*) that in the one case the average consciousness is composed for the most part of visual, in the other of au-

ditory material; and (*b*) that in the one case the great functions of attending, willing, acting, remembering, imagining, are set going by visual cues and discharged in visual terms, while in the other the vehicle of these same functions is auditory mind-stuff.

In the present experiment, we are to change our standpoint, and examine into the characteristic differences of the average mind. The results cannot be foreseen. *E* may find that the *O* with whom he has been working is of like constitution with himself, thinking as he thinks and speaking as he speaks. On the other hand, he may find that though the trains of ideas in both minds "shoot to the same conclusion," so that "the thinkers have had substantially the same thought," yet the "scenery" of the one mind differs astonishingly from the scenery of the other (James).

Let us see what the possibilities are; and let us take the universal function of *memory* as our point of departure. How may one remember?

One may remember an event (*a*) in terms of sight. The purely eye-minded man would recognise persons, things and places by their look, and would recall events as a panorama of views. Or one may remember (*b*) in terms of hearing. The purely ear-minded man would recognise persons, things and places by the sounds connected with them, and would recall events as a succession of sounds. Plainly, his "reading" of a situation would be very different from that of his eye-minded friend, and the available ideas of his memory very different from the ideas of the other. One may remember (*c*) in terms of touch. The tactual or motor type of mind recognises and recalls in terms of strains and pressures, the sensations set up by movements and attitudes. One may remember (*d*) in terms of organic sensations. The organic type of mind is emotional; when it recognises and recalls, it revives the organic accompaniments of first (or previous) acquaintance, the quivers and chokings and flutterings and sinkings that form the proper basis of the sense-feelings. One may remember (*e*) in terms of taste and smell. Images from these sense-departments seem, however, to be less common than the rest. And lastly, one may—as, probably, everybody does—remember (*f*) in mixed terms: some one kind of image predominating, while other kinds form a "halo" or "fringe" about the nuclear complex.

Consider, again, the universal function of *speech.* One may recall words (conversation, statements in the literature of one's science, poetry, lectures) in terms (*a*) of the written or printed symbols. The visual-verbal mind reads from a memory manuscript or printed page, lying open before the mind's eye. Or one may remember words (*b*) in terms of their sound. One may remember them (*c*) in terms of their "feel" in the throat, or perhaps of the "feel" of the hand that writes them. And, of course, one may remember them (*d*) in a mixed fashion. More than this: when one speaks,—answers or asks a question, delivers a lecture, recites a lesson,—the words are released or touched off by a sense cue derived from one or more of these sources. The visual-verbal mind sees, the auditory-verbal hears, the tactual-verbal "feels," what words are coming.

Verbal ideas play a very important part in the educated mind. They offer a common language, into which all other ideas and perceptions may be translated; they furnish a common denominator, to which all the rest may be reduced. Hence it is not surprising that some consciousnesses should be almost, if not entirely, verbal, and that we have to distinguish verbal sub-types alongside of our main ideational types.

The method that has been most largely employed for the determination of ideational type is that of the *questionary*. The questionary or "questionnaire" is a series of questions bearing upon the matter to be investigated, and submitted to a large number of persons for introspective answer. It is assumed that, although the answers returned by any given person may be of little psychological value, yet the intercomparison of a long list of such answers by a trained psychologist will yield results of real scientific import.

QUESTION (I). What are the characteristics of a good questionary? In what fields of psychology does the method promise to be of value?

Questionary Upon Ideational Type
Read the whole questionary twice through before you begin to write your answers.

1. Think of a bunch of white rose-buds, lying among fern leaves in a florist's box.

(*a*) Are the colours—the creamy white, the green, the shiny white—quite distinct and natural?

(*b*) Do you see the flowers in a good light? Is the image as bright as the objects would be if they lay on the table before you?

(*c*) Are the flowers and leaves and box well-defined and clear-cut? Can you see the whole group of objects together, or is one part distinctly outlined while the others are blurred?

(*d*) Can you call up the scent of the rose-buds? Of the moist ferns? Of the damp paste-board?

(*e*) Can you feel the softness of the rose petals? The roughness of the ferns? The stiffness of the box?

(*f*) Can you feel the coldness of the buds as you lay them against your check?

(*g*) Can you feel the prick of a thorn? Can you see the drop of blood welling-out upon your finger? Can you feel the smart and soreness of the wound?

(*h*) Can you call up the taste of candied rose leaves? Of candied violets? Salt? Sugar? Lemon juice? Quinine?

2. Think of some person who is well known to you, but whom you have not seen for some little time.

(*a*) Can you see the features distinctly? The outline of the figure? The colours of the clothes?

(*b*) Can you hear the person's voice? Can you recognise your friends by their voices? Can you call up the note of a musical instrument in its appropriate clang-tint: piano, harp, organ, bassoon, flute, trumpet? Can you hear, in imagination, a note that is too high for you to sing? Think of the playing of an orchestra. Can you hear two different instruments playing together? More than two? Do the tones ring out in their natural loudness? Do they come to you from their natural places in the orchestra?

(*c*) Can you hear, in memory, the beat of rain against the window panes; the crack of a whip; a church bell; the hum of bees; the clinking of teaspoons in their saucers; the slam of a door?

(*d*) Can you see the person in familiar surroundings? Can you see more of these surroundings (*e.g.,* a room) than could be taken in by any single glance of the eyes? Can you mentally see more than three faces of a die, or more than one hemisphere of a globe, at the same instant of time?

(*e*) Do you possess accurate mental pictures of places that you have visited? Do you see the scenes and incidents described in novels and books of travel?

(*f*) Are numerals, dates, particular words or phrases, invariably associated in your mind with peculiar mental imagery (diagrams, colours)? Are certain sounds always connected with certain colours? Have you any other constant associations from different sense-departments? Have you a special gift or liking for mental arithmetic or mechanics? Can you lay a plane through a cube in such a way that the exposed surface shall be a regular hexagon? Through an octahedron? Have you ever played chess blindfold? Explain fully how far your procedure in these cases depends on the use of visual images.

3. Think of the national anthem.

(*a*) Can you see the words printed? Can you hear yourself say or sing them? Can you hear a company singing them? Can you feel yourself forming the words in your throat, and with your lips and tongue? Can you hear the organ playing the air?

(*b*) Do you recall music easily? Do you "make up tunes in your head" when you are thinking steadily or in reverie? Does imagined music take any considerable part in your mental life: *i.e.,* do airs and motives and snatches of music play or sing themselves to you during the various occupations of the day? Have you an "absolute" memory for music: *i.e.,* can you identify a note that is struck upon the piano keyboard, or tell the pitch of a creaking door?

(*c*) Partly open your mouth, and think of words that contain labials or dentals: "bubble," "toddle," "putty," "thumping." Is the word-image distinct? Can you think of a number of soldiers marching, without there being any sympathetic movement or movement-feel in your own legs? Think of getting up from your seat to close the door. Can you feel all the movements? As intensively as if they were really made?

(*d*) Are you stirred and moved as you think of the words or music of the anthem? Are you affected in this way at the theatre, or when reading novels? Do you choke and cry (or feel like crying) as you read, *e.g.,* of Colonel Newcome's death? When you think of your childish terrors, or of your childhood's injustices, do you feel over again the fear and resentment?

(*e*) If you see an accident—the crushing of a limb or the catching of a finger in the door—do you yourself feel the blow and the bruise? Does the sight make you shiver, give you "goose flesh"? Do you pant or hold your breath as you watch a difficult feat of climbing or trapeze-work? Can you, in general, call up organic sensations: hunger, thirst, fatigue, feverishness, drowsiness, the stuffiness of a bad cold?

4. Arrange the following 20 experiences in groups, according to the clearness, vividness and distinctness with which you can remember or imagine them.

(*a*) A gloomy, clouded sky; a sheet of yellow paper; a black circle on a white ground.

(*b*) The feel of velvet; of dough; of a crisp dead leaf.

(*c*) The smell of tar; of a fur coat; of an oil-lamp just blown out.

(*d*) The taste of chocolate; of olives; of pastry.

(*e*) The warmth of a hot-water bag at your feet; the cold of a piercing wind that cuts through your clothing.

(*f*) Singing in the ear; the buzz of an induction-coil vibrator; the preliminary a^1 of the violin.

(*g*) Nausea; tooth-ache; pins and needles.

5. Give any supplementary information that occurs to you on the topics of this questionary. Do you recollect what your powers of visualising, etc., were in childhood? Have they varied much within your recollection?—What difference do you find between a very vivid mental picture called up in the dark, and a real scene? Have you ever mistaken a mental image for a reality when in health and wide awake?—Are the characteristics of your mental imagery repeated in the other members of your family?—Have you a good command of your images? Etc., etc.

RESULTS. Enter your own answers in your note-book, and hand the original sheet to the Instructor. He will presently inform you of your position on the scale of imagery in the different sense-departments. Consult with him as to the advisability of practising one or other of your partial memories. If possible, secure the answers of an *O* whose "type" is radically different from your own and enter these too in your note-book.

QUESTIONS (2). Can you devise any experimental method for the determination of ideational type? If you can, ask the Instructor whether it is practicable. Work with the questionary should always be supplemented by work with some experimental method.

(3) Is the distinction of "types" applicable to other mental processes than ideas?

Experiment XXXVII

§ 52.   *The Association of Ideas*

It is one of the fundamental laws of our mental life that all the connections set up between sensations, by their welding together into perceptions and ideas, tend to persist, even when the original conditions of connection are no longer fulfilled. This law we term, in conformity with historical usage, the law of the association of ideas. The phrase is, however, to be accepted with great caution, and with two qualifications. In the first place, it is not ideas that associate, but the elementary processes of which the ideas are composed; and, secondly, the connection is not an 'association,' if we mean by association a mere juxtaposition, an unchanged togetherness. It would be more correct to speak, in non-committal language, of the law of temporal and spatial connection of the conscious elements. On its physiological side, the law then reduces to a law of habit. "When two elementary brain-processes have been active together or in immediate succession, one of them, on reoccurring, tends to propagate its excitement into the other" (James).

Both of the above formulæ employ the word "tend." The connections "tend" to persist; the brain activities "tend" to discharge. The question arises: under what conditions is the tendency realised? Suppose that the complex ab is given. The part-process b has been in connection with $c,d,e, \ldots z$. Will the association-consciousness have the form abc, or abd, or abz? This is a question which experimental psychology is called upon to answer. It is, also, a question to which a fairly complete answer can be returned.

The conditions under which a given connection—abc or abz—is realised may be summed up as follows.

A. If the consciousness of the moment is an attentive consciousness, the appearance of c or z depends upon

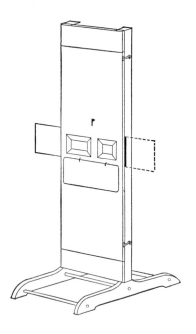

FIGURE 25.1

(*a*) the *frequency* of connection with b,
(*b*) the *recency* of connection,
(*c*) the relative *vividness* (intensity, extent, etc.) of c and z, and
(*d*) the relative *position* (primacy) of c and z in a definite series of processes.

B. If the consciousness of the moment is an inattentive consciousness, the appearance of c or z depends upon

(*e*) the relative power of c and z to attract the attention (see p. 116, above).

All five of these rules are to be subjected to experimental test

A. I. SUCCESSIVE METHOD. VISUAL STIMULI

Materials.—Memory Apparatus. [This apparatus consists of a black upright screen, 82 by 21 cm., at the centre of which is an oblong window, 15 cm. broad and 3 cm. high. A flap of japanned tin, hinged below, can be turned up to cover the window. Behind the window slides a horizontal strip of japanned tin, having two openings, of 6 by 2.5 and 2 by 2.5 cm. respectively. The card holder, 40 by 18 cm., runs in grooves behind the screen. To its back is nailed a strip of gutta percha, cut out step-fashion in such a way that each turn of a lever to right or left drops the card holder through 2.5 cm. The card is covered with letters, numerals, bands of colour, etc. It is possible, if the card holder starts at its full height, to expose 14 successive stimuli behind each of the openings in the horizontal strip of tin.]

Stimulus cards. Test cards. [These are prepared by E under the Instructor's directions, and are not seen by O.] Stopwatch.

Experiment (1). Frequency.—The apparatus is set up, in a good light, at a convenient distance from O. The horizontal strip is so placed that its larger opening fills the centre of the oblong window. It is well to stand screens of black cardboard to right and left, so that E shall be entirely concealed from view. E selects a stimulus card, with its corresponding test card, and slides the former into the card holder. The stop-watch lies on the table by his side.

E takes the string of the shutter in his left, and the lever in his right hand. At a "Now!" O fixates the centre of the shutter. Some 1.5 sec. later, E drops the shutter, and O sees a coloured strip in the opening. This remains in sight for 2 sec. Then, without pause, the card holder is dropped a step, and a number appears. This remains for 2 sec. The shutter is then raised, and nothing is shown for 4 sec. During this interval, *O* should count aloud *a, b, c, d, . . .* Before the 4 sec. are over, *E* has dropped the card holder another step. On the falling of the shutter, a new colour is seen; it remains for 2 sec.; then comes a number for 2 sec.; then the shutter for 4 sec., with the speaking of the alphabet by *O*. We thus have a series of 14 2-sec. exposures, each pair of which is separated by an alphabet-interval of 4 sec.

At the end of the series, *E* slips the lever, draws out the card holder, quickly substitutes the test card for the stimulus card, and replaces the holder. With practice, these operations should not take more than 10 sec.; but 15 or 20 sec. may be allowed, if the Instructor thinks fit. The experiment is then resumed. Each colour is exposed for 4 sec., and there are no intervals. *O* is required to write down, as the colour appears, the number (if there be any) with which it is associated. At the end of the series, *O* adds such introspective remarks as occur to him, noting with especial care cases in which the connection of colour and number corresponded to a preformed association.

At least 20 series should be taken.

Experiments (2), (3), (4).—The experiment is performed in the same way, except that "recency," "vividness" and "primacy cards" are substituted for the "frequency cards."

Results.—*E* has the cards, and *O*'s lists of associated numbers. His task is, to estimate the importance of frequency, etc., as conditions of connection.

(1) The first thing to do is to rule out all cases in which a connection between colour and number already existed. If the connection is found at a critical point of the series,—if, *i.e.,* it obtains between the frequent, recent, etc., colour and number,—the whole series is rejected; if it occur at any other point, only the single term of the series need be sacrificed.

(2) *E* must then calculate the relation of actual to possible "correct associations" in the full 80 series,—critical combinations being omitted. In other words, he answers the question: What proportion of the ordinary combinations, in an experiment of this kind, is remembered by *O?* The experiment is reduced to a simple test of memory, and a percentage is obtained which serves as a basis of comparison for the special percentages which are now to be worked out.

(3) Four Tables are to be made out, one for each of the sets of 20 series, showing (*a*) the percentage of cases in which both numbers—the critical and the normal—were associated, (*b*) the percentage in which only the normal number was recalled, and (*c*) the percentage in which only the critical number was recalled. Cases in which one digit of the number was correctly associated are termed "half cases," and counted as half correct.

The following Questions arise.

E(1) What is the relative importance of the four conditions studied in these experiments?

E and *O* (2) Do you regard these results as generally valid, or as valid only under the special conditions of the experiments?

O (3) You have probably found, in the course of the experiments, combinations of colour and number which were already associated in your mind. Can you account for these preëxisting connections? Are they referrible to any one of the four conditions under investigation?

II. SIMULTANEOUS METHOD. VISUAL STIMULI

Experiments (5)–(8).—These experiments are performed in the same manner as the preceding, except that both openings in the horizontal strip fall within the oblong window, that the 12-term simultaneous cards are substituted for the 7-term successive cards, and that the paired stimuli are shown for 3 sec. Ten series are to be taken under each of the four rubrics, and the results worked out as before.

E and *O* Question (4) Can you suggest experiments, similar to exps. (1)–(8), with auditory in place of visual stimuli? Can you propose other modifications of these experiments?

B. The investigation of the conditions summed up under (*e*) is more difficult than that of conditions (*a*) to (*d*). For we cannot secure in *O* a state of "voluntary inattention," in order to subject him to attention-compelling stimuli. We can, however, employ an indirect method to show the extreme importance, for associative supplementing, of what is, in adult life, one of the chief determinants of attention.

Materials.—The apparatus is that of Exp. XXV. (4). The object cards are prepared by *E* as directed by the Instructor.

Experiment (9).—The apparatus is set up with an exposure sector of 3.6°, and a rate of revolution of 1 per second. *E* pronounces two words, which give a certain "trend" to *O*'s consciousness, or 'prepare' it for the arousal of a certain class of ideas. As soon as he has heard the words, *O* looks through the tube; sees, first, the accommodation A; and, at the next revolution of the disc, reads the word shown upon the object card. He writes an account of what he has seen.

Results.—*E* has his own record of stimuli, and *O*'s descriptions. The following Questions arise.

E (5) What is the general conclusion to be drawn from this experiment? What is the 'determinant of attention,' referred to above?

O and *E* (6) Can you suggest a similar experiment with auditory stimuli?

O and *E* (7) Is this "indirect method" adequate to our problem? Criticise it in detail.

C. THE TRAIN OF IDEAS.—In the last experiment we have been dealing with "associative supplementing," one of the forms of simultaneous association. The counterpart of associative supplementing, on the successive side, is the "train of ideas." A consciousness is set up, and allowed to work itself out, idea following idea along the line of least mental resistance, until the "stream of thought" runs dry. The train of ideas is historically interesting, as the form of association discussed and illustrated by the older psychologists under the general title "association of ideas."

Materials.—Speaking-tube, leading from the dark room to an adjoining room. Stop-watch.

Experiment (10).—*O* sits comfortably in the dark room, his ear to the speaking-tube. His mood should be as passive and receptive as possible. After a signal (the stroke of an electric bell, or a "Now!" called through the tube), he listens attentively for *E*'s voice. *E* speaks a sentence, or asks a question, through the tube. The sentence or question must be concrete, pictorial,—one that can

hardly be apperceived or answered simply in terms of words. *O* gives free rein to the series of ideas aroused by the stimulus. As situation follows situation in his consciousness, he calls catch-words through the tube: *E* writes these down, and notes the time of their utterance. At the end of the experiment, when the train of ideas is exhausted, *O* goes over the catch-words with *E*, in introspective review, and so reconstructs, as accurately as may be, the whole association consciousness.

The principal points to note in the reconstruction are (*a*) the number and order of the situations (constellations of ideas); (*b*) the quality of consciousness—visual, auditory, etc.—at each situation; (*c*) the affective colouring of each situation; (*d*) the form of connection (association "by contiguity" or "by similarity"); (*e*) the richness, fulness, clearness, of the part-consciousnesses (the processes composing a situation or constellation); and (*f*) the points of departure of the various constellations. Under (*e*), for instance, *O* notes the relative expansion or contraction of consciousness, whether it is made up of a single strand or of several interwoven strands; under (*f*), he draws a diagram, showing where the associative train is continuous, *a* giving rise to *b,b* to *c,c* to *d,* and so on,—and where there is a hark-back to a former situation, *a* giving rise to *b,b* to *c,* and then *a* coming into play again as the source of *d.*

Results.—*E* has the full verbal record of *O*'s associations. He has, further, a Table of seven columns, showing respectively the times, situations, qualities, affective concomitants, modes of connection, richness, and points of departure of these associations. Six experiments should be made. The records will present a fair picture of *O*'s consciousness during the 'train of ideas.'

E and *O* Question (8) Define the terms "association by similarity" and "association by contiguity." Give instances. How do you reconcile the existence of two distinct forms of association with the preliminary statements on pp. 200 f.?

LEARNING

26

JOHN B. WATSON

John Broadus Watson (1878–1958) was named for a nationally prominent Baptist minister from Greenville, South Carolina; his devout mother hoped he would consider the ministry, but Watson had other interests. While Watson was a student at Furman University, his philosophy and psychology professor Gordon Moore warned that any student turning in a paper "backwards" would immediately flunk. This was a challenge Watson could not ignore, so the honor student spent a fifth year at Furman, though he did earn a master's, rather than a bachelor's, degree during that final year. With Moore's recommendation and support, Watson went to the University of Chicago's joint philosophy and psychology department and earned his Ph.D. in 1903, working under James Rowland Angell and Henry H. Donaldson. Watson remained at Chicago until 1908, when he joined the faculty at Johns Hopkins University. Watson inherited editorship of the *Psychological Review* within months of arriving at Hopkins, the result of a newspaper exposé involving his senior colleague and a bordello. In 1915, Watson helped found the *Journal of Experimental Psychology*, was president of the American Psychological Association, and introduced the work of Ivan Pavlov (p. 178) to American psychology. Watson's academic career came to an abrupt halt in 1920 when he agreed to resign from Johns Hopkins—a request made by the administration when Watson married his graduate student on the heels of a highly publicized and scandalous divorce from his first wife. He eventually rose to the top of his new career in advertising and provided articles for popular magazines, but wrote no more articles, popular or scientific, on psychology.

PSYCHOLOGY AS THE BEHAVIORIST VIEWS IT

Psychology as the behaviorist views it is a purely objective experimental branch of natural science. Its theoretical goal is the prediction and control of behavior. Introspection forms no essential part of its methods, nor is the scientific value of its data dependent upon the readiness with which they lend themselves to interpretation in terms of consciousness. The behaviorist, in his efforts to get a unitary scheme of animal response, recognizes no dividing line between man and brute. The behavior of man, with all of its refinement and complexity, forms only a part of the behaviorist's total scheme of investigation.

It has been maintained by its followers generally that psychology is a study of the science of the phenomena of consciousness. It has taken as its problem, on the one hand, the analysis of complex mental states (or processes) into simple elementary constituents, and on the other the construction of complex states when the elementary constituents are given. The world of physical objects (stimuli, including here anything which may excite activity in a receptor), which forms the total phenomena of the natural scientist, is looked upon merely as means to an end. That end is the production of mental states that may be "inspected" or "observed." The psychological object of observation in the case of an emotion, for example, is the mental state itself. The problem in emotion is the determination of the number and kind of elementary constituents present, their loci, intensity, order of appearance, etc. It is agreed that introspection is the method *par excellence* by means of which mental

From John B. Watson, "Psychology as a Behaviorist Views It." *Psychological Review* 20 (1913):158–177.

states may be manipulated for purposes of psychology. On this assumption, behavior data (including under this term everything which goes under the name of comparative psychology) have no value *per se*. They possess significance only in so far as they may throw light upon conscious states.[1] Such data must have at least an analogical or indirect reference to belong to the realm of psychology.

Indeed, at times, one finds psychologists who are sceptical of even this analogical reference. Such scepticism is often shown by the question which is put to the student of behavior, "what is the bearing of animal work upon human psychology?" I used to have to study over this question. Indeed it always embarrassed me somewhat. I was interested in my own work and felt that it was important, and yet I could not trace any close connection between it and psychology as my questioner understood psychology. I hope that such a confession will clear the atmosphere to such an extent that we will no longer have to work under false pretences. We must frankly admit that the facts so important to us which we have been able to glean from extended work upon the senses of animals by the behavior method have contributed only in a fragmentary way to the general theory of human sense organ processes, nor have they suggested new points of experimental attack. The enormous number of experiments which we have carried out upon learning have likewise contributed little to human psychology. It seems reasonably clear that some kind of compromise must be effected: either psychology must change its viewpoint so as to take in facts of behavior, whether or not they have bearings upon the problems of "consciousness"; or else behavior must stand alone as a wholly separate and independent science. Should human psychologists fail to look with favor upon our overtures and refuse to modify their position, the behaviorists will be driven to using human beings as subjects and to employ methods of investigation which are exactly comparable to those now employed in the animal work.

Any other hypothesis than that which admits the independent value of behavior material, regardless of any bearing such material may have upon consciousness, will inevitably force us to the absurd position of attempting to *construct* the conscious content of the animal whose behavior we have been studying. On this view, after having determined our animal's ability to learn, the simplicity or complexity of its methods of learning, the effect of past habit upon present response, the range of stimuli to which it ordinarily responds, the widened range to which it can respond under experimental conditions,—in more general terms, its various

problems and its various ways of solving them,—we should still feel that the task is unfinished and that the results are worthless, until we can interpret them by analogy in the light of consciousness. Although we have solved our problem we feel uneasy and unrestful because of our definition of psychology: we feel forced to say something about the possible mental processes of our animal. We say that, having no eyes, its stream of consciousness cannot contain brightness and color sensations as we know them,—having no taste buds this stream can contain no sensations of sweet, sour, salt and bitter. But on the other hand, since it does respond to thermal, tactual and organic stimuli, its conscious content must be made up largely of these sensations; and we usually add, to protect ourselves against the reproach of being anthropomorphic, "if it has any consciousness." Surely this doctrine which calls for an analogical interpretation of all behavior data may be shown to be false: the position that the standing of an observation upon behavior is determined by its fruitfulness in yielding results which are interpretable only in the narrow realm of (really human) consciousness.

This emphasis upon analogy in psychology has led the behaviorist somewhat afield. Not being willing to throw off the yoke of consciousness he feels impelled to make a place in the scheme of behavior where the rise of consciousness can be determined. This point has been a shifting one. A few years ago certain animals were supposed to possess "associative memory," while certain others were supposed to lack it. One meets this search for the origin of consciousness under a good many disguises. Some of our texts state that consciousness arises at the moment when reflex and instinctive activities fail properly to conserve the organism. A perfectly adjusted organism would be lacking in consciousness. On the other hand whenever we find the presence of diffuse activity which results in habit formation, we are justified in assuming consciousness. I must confess that these arguments had weight with me when I began the study of behavior. I fear that a good many of us are still viewing behavior problems with something like this in mind. More than one student in behavior has attempted to frame criteria of the psychic—to devise a set of objective, structural and functional criteria which, when applied in the particular instance, will enable us to decide whether such and such responses are positively conscious, merely indicative of consciousness, or whether they are purely "physiological." Such problems as these can no longer satisfy behavior men. It would be better to give up the province altogether and admit frankly that the study of the behavior of animals has no justification, than to admit that our search is of such a "will o' the wisp" character. One can assume either the presence or the absence of consciousness anywhere in the phylogenetic scale without affecting the problems of behavior by one jot or one tittle; and without influencing in any way the mode of experimental attack upon them. On the other hand, I cannot for one moment assume that the paramecium responds to light; that the rat learns a problem more quickly by working at the task five times a day than once a day, or that the human child exhibits plateaux in his learning curves. These are questions which vitally concern behavior and which must be decided by direct observation under experimental conditions.

This attempt to reason by analogy from human conscious processes to the conscious processes in animals, and *vice versa:* to make consciousness, as the human being knows it, the center of reference of all behavior, forces us into a situation similar to that which existed in biology in Darwin's time. The whole Darwinian movement was judged by the bearing it had upon the origin and development of the human race. Expeditions were undertaken to collect material which would establish the position that the rise of the human race was a perfectly natural phenomenon and not an act of special creation. Variations were carefully sought along with the evidence for the heaping up effect and the weeding out effect of selection; for in these and the other Darwinian mechanisms were to be found factors sufficiently complex to account for the origin and race differentiation of man. The wealth of material collected at this time was considered valuable largely in so far as it tended to develop the concept of evolution in man. It is strange that this situation should have remained the dominant one in biology for so many years. The moment zoölogy undertook the experimental study of evolution and descent, the situation immediately changed. Man ceased to be the center of reference. I doubt if any experimental biologist today, unless actually engaged in the problem of race differentiation in man, tries to interpret his findings in terms of human evolution, or ever refers to it in his thinking. He gathers his data from the study of many species of plants and animals and tries to work out the laws of inheritance in the particular type upon which he is conducting experiments. Naturally, he follows the progress of the work upon race differentiation in man and in the descent of man, but he looks upon these as special topics, equal in importance with his own yet ones in which his interests will never be vitally engaged. It is not fair to say that all of his work is directed toward human evolution or that it must be interpreted in terms of human evolution. He does not have to dismiss certain of his facts on the inheritance of coat color in mice because, forsooth, they have little bearing upon the differentiation of the *genus homo* into separate races, or upon the descent of the *genus homo* from some more primitive stock.

In psychology we are still in that stage of development where we feel that we must select our material. We have a general place of discard for processes, which we anathematize so far as their value for psychology is concerned by saying, "this is a reflex"; "that is a purely physiological fact which has nothing to do with psychology." We are not interested (as psychologists) in getting all of the processes of adjustment which the animal as a whole employs, and in finding how these various responses are associated, and how they fall apart, thus working out a systematic scheme for the prediction and control of response in general. Unless our observed facts are indicative of consciousness, we have no use for them, and unless our apparatus and method are designed to throw such facts into relief, they are thought of in just as disparaging a way. I shall always remember the remark one distinguished psychologist made as he looked over the color apparatus designed for testing the responses of animals to monochromatic light in the attic at Johns Hopkins. It was this: "And they call this psychology!"

I do not wish unduly to criticize psychology. It has failed signally, I believe, during the fifty-odd years of its existence as an experimental discipline to make its place in the world as an undisputed natural science. Psychology, as it is generally thought of, has something esoteric in its methods. If you fail to reproduce my findings, it is not due to some fault in your apparatus or in the control of your stimulus, but it is due to the fact that your introspection is untrained.[2] The attack is made upon the observer and not upon the experimental setting. In physics and in chemistry the attack is made upon the experimental conditions. The apparatus was not sensitive enough, impure chemicals were used, etc. In these sciences a better technique will give reproducible results. Psychology is otherwise. If you can't observe 3–9 states of clearness in attention, your introspection is poor. If, on the other hand, a feeling seems reasonably clear to you, your introspection is again faulty. You are seeing too much. Feelings are never clear.

The time seems to have come when psychology must discard all reference to consciousness; when it need no longer delude itself into thinking that it is making mental states the object of observation. We have become so enmeshed in speculative questions concerning the elements of mind, the nature of conscious content (for example, imageless thought, attitudes, and Bewusseinslage, etc.) that I, as an experimental student, feel that something is wrong with our premises and the types of problems which develop from them. There is no longer any guarantee that we all mean the same thing when we use the terms now current in psychology. Take the case of sensation. A sensation is defined in terms of its attributes. One psychologist will state with readiness that the attributes of a visual sensation are *quality, extension, duration,* and *intensity.* Another will add *clearness.* Still another that of *order.* I doubt if any one psychologist can draw up a set of statements describing what he means by sensation which will be agreed to by three other psychologists of different training. Turn for a moment to the question of the number of isolable sensations. Is there an extremely large number of color sensations—or only four, red, green, yellow and blue? Again, yellow, while psychologically simple, can be obtained by superimposing red and green spectral rays upon the same diffusing surface! If, on the other hand, we say that every just noticeable difference in the spectrum is a simple sensation, and that every just noticeable increase in the white value of a given color gives simple sensations, we are forced to admit that the number is so large and the conditions for obtaining them so complex that the concept of sensation is unusable, either for the purpose of analysis or that of synthesis. Titchener, who has fought the most valiant fight in this country for a psychology based upon introspection, feels that these differences of opinion as to the number of sensations and their attributes; as to whether there are relations (in the sense of elements) and on the many others which seem to be fundamental in every attempt at analysis, are perfectly natural in the present undeveloped state of psychology. While it is admitted that every growing science is full of unanswered questions, surely only those who are wedded to the system as we now have it, who have fought and suffered for it, can confidently believe that there will ever be any greater uniformity than there is now in the answers we have to such questions. I firmly believe that two hundred years from now, unless the introspective method is discarded, psychology will still be divided on the question as to whether auditory sensations have the quality of "extension," whether intensity is an attribute which can be applied to color, whether there is a difference in "texture" between image and sensation and upon many hundreds of others of like character.

The condition in regard to other mental processes is just as chaotic. Can image type be experimentally tested and verified? Are recondite thought processes dependent mechanically upon imagery at all? Are psychologists agreed upon what feeling is? One states that feelings are attitudes. Another finds them to be groups of organic sensations possessing a certain solidarity. Still another and larger group finds them to be new elements correlative with and ranking equally with sensations.

My psychological quarrel is not with the systematic and structural psychologist alone. The last fifteen years have seen the growth of what is called functional psychology. This type of psychology decries the use of elements in the static sense of the structuralists. It throws emphasis upon the biological significance of conscious processes instead of upon the analysis of conscious states into introspectively isolable elements. I have done my best to understand the difference between functional psychology and structural psychology. Instead of clarity, confusion grows upon me. The terms sensation, perception, affection, emotion, volition are used as much by the functionalist as by the structuralist. The addition of the word "process" ("mental act as a whole," and like terms are frequently met) after each serves in some way to remove the corpse of "content" and to leave "function" in its stead. Surely if these concepts are elusive when looked at from a content standpoint, they are still more deceptive when viewed from the angle of function, and especially so when function is obtained by the introspection method. It is rather interesting that no functional psychologist has carefully distinguished between "perception" (and this is true of the other psychological terms as well) as employed by the systematist, and "perceptual process" as used in functional psychology. It seems illogical and hardly fair to criticize the psychology which the systematist gives us, and then to utilize his terms without carefully showing the changes in meaning which are to be attached to them. I was greatly surprised some time ago when I opened Pillsbury's book and saw psychology defined as the "science of behavior." A still more recent text states that psychology is the "science of mental behavior." When I saw these promising statements I thought, now surely we will have texts based upon different lines. After a few pages the science of behavior is dropped and one finds the conventional treatment of sensation, perception, imagery, etc., along with certain shifts in emphasis and additional facts which serve to give the author's personal imprint.

One of the difficulties in the way of a consistent functional psychology is the parallelistic hypothesis. If the functionalist attempts to express his formulations in terms which make mental states really appear to function, to play some active rôle in the world of adjustment, he almost inevitably lapses into terms which are connotative of interaction. When taxed with this he replies that it is more convenient to do so and that he does it to avoid the circumlocution and clumsiness which are inherent in any thoroughgoing parallelism.[3] As a matter of fact I believe the functionalist actually thinks in terms of interaction and resorts to parallelism only when forced to give expression to his views. I feel that *behaviorism* is the only consistent and logical functionalism. In it one avoids both the Scylla of parallelism and the Charybdis of interaction. Those time-honored relics of philosophical speculation need trouble the student of behavior as little as they trouble the student of physics. The consideration of the mind-body problem affects neither the type of problem selected nor the formulation of the solution of that problem. I can state my position here no better than by saying that I should like to bring my students up in the same ignorance of such hypotheses as one finds among the students of other branches of science.

This leads me to the point where I should like to make the argument constructive. I believe we can write a psychology, define it as Pillsbury, and never go back upon our definition: never use the terms consciousness, mental states, mind, content, introspectively verifiable, imagery, and the like. I believe that we can do it in a few years without running into the absurd terminology of Beer, Bethe, Von Uexküll, Nuel, and that of the so-called objective schools generally. It can be done in terms of stimulus and response, in terms of habit formation, habit integrations and the like. Furthermore, I believe that it is really worth while to make this attempt now.

The psychology which I should attempt to build up would take as a starting point, first, the observable fact that organisms, man and animal alike, do adjust themselves to their environment by means of hereditary and habit equipments. These adjustments may be very adequate or they may be so inadequate that the organism barely maintains its existence; secondly, that certain stimuli lead the organisms to make the responses. In a system of psychology completely worked out, given the response the stimuli can be predicted; given the stimuli the response can be predicted. Such a set of statements is crass and raw in the extreme, as all such generalizations must be. Yet they are hardly more raw and less realizable than the ones which appear in the psychology texts of the day, I possibly might illustrate my point better by choosing an everyday problem which anyone is likely to meet in the course of his work. Some time ago I was called upon to make a study of certain species of birds. Until I went to Tortugas I had never seen these birds alive. When I reached there I found the animals doing certain things: some of the acts seemed to work peculiarly well in such an environment, while others seemed to be unsuited to their type of life. I first studied the responses of the group as a whole and later those of

individuals. In order to understand more thoroughly the relation between what was habit and what was hereditary in these responses, I took the young birds and reared them. In this way I was able to study the order of appearance of hereditary adjustments and their complexity, and later the beginnings of habit formation. My efforts in determining the stimuli which called forth such adjustments were crude indeed. Consequently my attempts to control behavior and to produce responses at will did not meet with much success. Their food and water, sex and other social relations, light and temperature conditions were all beyond control in a field study. I did find it possible to control their reactions in a measure by using the nest and egg (or young) as stimuli. It is not necessary in this paper to develop further how such a study should be carried out and how work of this kind must be supplemented by carefully controlled laboratory experiments. Had I been called upon to examine the natives of some of the Australian tribes, I should have gone about my task in the same way. I should have found the problem more difficult: the types of responses called forth by physical stimuli would have been more varied, and the number of effective stimuli larger. I should have had to determine the social setting of their lives in a far more careful way. These savages would be more influenced by the responses of each other than was the case with the birds. Furthermore, habits would have been more complex and the influences of past habits upon the present responses would have appeared more clearly. Finally, if I had been called upon to work out the psychology of the educated European, my problem would have required several lifetimes. But in the one I have at my disposal I should have followed the same general line of attack. In the main, my desire in all such work is to gain an accurate knowledge of adjustments and the stimuli calling them forth. My final reason for this is to learn general and particular methods by which I may control behavior. My goal is not "the description and explanation of states of consciousness as such," nor that of obtaining such proficiency in mental gymnastics that I can immediately lay hold of a state of consciousness and say, "this, as a whole, consists of gray sensation number 350, of such and such extent, occurring in conjunction with the sensation of cold of a certain intensity; one of pressure of a certain intensity and extent," and so on *ad infinitum*. If psychology would follow the plan I suggest, the educator, the physician, the jurist and the business man could utilize our data in a practical way, as soon as we are able, experimentally, to obtain them. Those who have occasion to apply psychological principles practically would find no need to complain as they do at the present time. Ask any physician or jurist today whether scientific psychology plays a practical part in his daily routine and you will hear him deny that the psychology of the laboratories finds a place in his scheme of work. I think the criticism is extremely just. One of the earliest conditions which made me dissatisfied with psychology was the feeling that there was no realm of application for the principles which were being worked out in content terms.

What gives me hope that the behaviorist's position is a defensible one is the fact that those branches of psychology which have already partially withdrawn from the parent, experimental psychology, and which are consequently less dependent upon introspection are today in a most flourishing condition. Experimental pedagogy, the psychology of drugs, the psychology of advertising, legal psychology, the psychology of tests, and psychopathology are all vigorous growths. These are sometimes wrongly called "practical" or "applied" psychology. Surely there was never a worse misnomer. In the future there may grow up vocational bureaus which really apply psychology. At present these fields are truly scientific and are in search of broad generalizations which will lead to the control of human behavior. For example, we find out by experimentation whether a series of stanzas may be acquired more readily if the whole is learned at once, or whether it is more advantageous to learn each stanza separately and then pass to the succeeding. We do not attempt to apply our findings. The application of this principle is purely voluntary on the part of the teacher. In the psychology of drugs we may show the effect upon behavior of certain doses of caffeine. We may reach the conclusion that caffeine has a good effect upon the speed and accuracy of work. But these are general principles. We leave it to the individual as to whether the results of our tests shall be applied or not. Again, in legal testimony, we test the effects of recency upon the reliability of a witness's report. We test the accuracy of the report with respect to moving objects, stationary objects, color, etc. It depends upon the judicial machinery of the country to decide whether these facts are ever to be applied. For a "pure" psychologist to say that he is not interested in the questions raised in these divisions of the science because they relate indirectly to the application of psychology shows, in the first place, that he fails to understand the scientific aim in such problems, and secondly, that he is not interested in a psychology which concerns itself with human life. The only fault I have to find with these disciplines is that much of their material is stated in terms of introspection, whereas a statement in terms of

objective results would be far more valuable. There is no reason why appeal should ever be made to consciousness in any of them. Or why introspective data should ever be sought during the experimentation, or published in the results. In experimental pedagogy especially one can see the desirability of keeping all of the results on a purely objective plane. If this is done, work there on the human being will be comparable directly with the work upon animals. For example, at Hopkins, Mr. Ulrich has obtained certain results upon the distribution of effort in learning—using rats as subjects. He is prepared to give comparative results upon the effect of having an animal work at the problem once per day, three times per day, and five times per day. Whether it is advisable to have the animal learn only one problem at a time or to learn three abreast. We need to have similar experiments made upon man, but we care as little about his "conscious processes" during the conduct of the experiment as we care about such processes in the rats.

I am more interested at the present moment in trying to show the necessity for maintaining uniformity in experimental procedure and in the method of stating results in both human and animal work, than in developing any ideas I may have upon the changes which are certain to come in the scope of human psychology. Let us consider for a moment the subject of the range of stimuli to which animals respond. I shall speak first of the work upon vision in animals. We put our animal in a situation where he will respond (or learn to respond) to one of two monochromatic lights. We feed him at the one (positive) and punish him at the other (negative). In a short time the animal learns to go to the light at which he is fed. At this point questions arise which I may phrase in two ways: I may choose the psychological way and say "does the animal see these two lights as I do, *i. e.,* as two distinct colors, or does he see them as two grays differing in brightness, as does the totally color blind?" Phrased by the behaviorist, it would read as follows: "Is my animal responding upon the basis of the difference in intensity between the two stimuli, or upon the difference in wave-lengths?" He nowhere thinks of the animal's response in terms of his own experiences of colors and grays. He wishes to establish the fact whether wave-length is a factor in that animal's adjustment.[4] If so, what wave-lengths are effective and what differences in wave-length must be maintained in the different regions to afford bases for differential responses? If wave-length is not a factor in adjustment he wishes to know what difference in intensity will serve as a basis for response, and whether that same difference will suffice throughout the spectrum. Furthermore, he wishes to test whether the animal can respond to wave-lengths which do not affect the human eye. He is as much interested in comparing the rat's spectrum with that of the chick as in comparing it with man's. The point of view when the various sets of comparisons are made does not change in the slightest.

However we phrase the question to ourselves, we take our animal after the association has been formed and then introduce certain control experiments which enable us to return answers to the questions just raised. But there is just as keen a desire on our part to test man under the same conditions, and to state the results in both cases in common terms.

The man and the animal should be placed as nearly as possible under the same experimental conditions. Instead of feeding or punishing the human subject, we should ask him to respond by setting a second apparatus until standard and control offered no basis for a differential response. Do I lay myself open to the charge here that I am using introspection? My reply is not at all; that while I might very well feed my human subject for a right choice and punish him for a wrong one and thus produce the response if the subject could give it, there is no need of going to extremes even on the platform I suggest. But be it understood that I am merely using this second method as an abridged behavior method.[5] We can go just as far and reach just as dependable results by the longer method as by the abridged. In many cases the direct and typically human method cannot be safely used. Suppose, for example, that I doubt the accuracy of the setting of the control instrument, in the above experiment, as I am very likely to do if I suspect a defect in vision? It is hopeless for me to get his introspective report. He will say: "There is no difference in sensation, both are reds, identical in quality." But suppose I confront him with the standard and the control and so arrange conditions that he is punished if he responds to the 'control' but not with the standard. I interchange the positions of the standard and the control at will and force him to attempt to differentiate the one from the other. If he can learn to make the adjustment even after a large number of trials it is evident that the two stimuli do afford the basis for a differential response. Such a method may sound nonsensical, but I firmly believe we will have to resort increasingly to just such method where we have reason to distrust the language method.

There is hardly a problem in human vision which is not also a problem in animal vision: I mention the limits of the spectrum, threshold values, absolute and relative, flicker, Talbot's law, Weber's law, field of vision, the Purkinje phenomenon, etc. Every one is capable of be-

ing worked out by behavior methods. Many of them are being worked out at the present time.

I feel that all the work upon the senses can be consistently carried forward along the lines I have suggested here for vision. Our results will, in the end, give an excellent picture of what each organ stands for in the way of function. The anatomist and the physiologist may take our data and show, on the one hand, the structures which are responsible for these responses, and, on the other, the physico-chemical relations which are necessarily involved (physiological chemistry of nerve and muscle) in these and other reactions.

The situation in regard to the study of memory is hardly different. Nearly all of the memory methods in actual use in the laboratory today yield the type of results I am arguing for. A certain series of nonsense syllables or other material is presented to the human subject. What should receive the emphasis are the rapidity of the habit formation, the errors, peculiarities in the form of the curve, the persistence of the habit so formed, the relation of such habits to those formed when more complex material is used, etc. Now such results are taken down with the subject's introspection. The experiments are made for the purpose of discussing the mental machinery[6] involved in learning, in recall, recollection and forgetting, and not for the purpose of seeking the human being's way of shaping his responses to meet the problems in the terribly complex environment into which he is thrown, nor for that of showing the similarities and differences between man's methods and those of other animals.

The situation is somewhat different when we come to a study of the more complex forms of behavior, such as imagination, judgment, reasoning, and conception. At present the only statements we have of them are in content terms.[7] Our minds have been so warped by the fifty-odd years which have been devoted to the study of states of consciousness that we can envisage these problems only in one way. We should meet the situation squarely and say that we are not able to carry forward investigations along all of these lines by the behavior methods which are in use at the present time. In extenuation I should like to call attention to the paragraph above where I made the point that the introspective method itself has reached a *cul-de-sac* with respect to them. The topics have become so threadbare from much handling that they may well be put away for a time. As our methods become better developed it will be possible to undertake investigations of more and more complex forms of behavior. Problems which are now laid aside will again become imperative, but they can be viewed as they arise from a new angle and in more concrete settings.

Will there be left over in psychology a world of pure psychics, to use Yerkes' term? I confess I do not know. The plans which I most favor for psychology lead practically to the ignoring of consciousness in the sense that that term is used by psychologists today. I have virtually denied that this realm of psychics is open to experimental investigation. I don't wish to go further into the problem at present because it leads inevitably over into metaphysics. If you will grant the behaviorist the right to use consciousness in the same way that other natural scientists employ it—that is, without making consciousness a special object of observation—you have granted all that my thesis requires.

In concluding, I suppose I must confess to a deep bias on these questions. I have devoted nearly twelve years to experimentation on animals. It is natural that such a one should drift into a theoretical position which is in harmony with his experimental work. Possibly I have put up a straw man and have been fighting that. There may be no absolute lack of harmony between the position outlined here and that of functional psychology. I am inclined to think, however, that the two positions cannot be easily harmonized. Certainly the position I advocate is weak enough at present and can be attacked from many standpoints. Yet when all this is admitted I still feel that the considerations which I have urged should have a wide influence upon the type of psychology which is to be developed in the future. What we need to do is to start work upon psychology, making *behavior,* not *consciousness,* the objective point of our attack. Certainly there are enough problems in the control of behavior to keep us all working many lifetimes without ever allowing us time to think of consciousness *an sich.* Once launched in the undertaking, we will find ourselves in a short time as far divorced from an introspective psychology as the psychology of the present time is divorced from faculty psychology.

SUMMARY

1. Human psychology has failed to make good its claim as a natural science. Due to a mistaken notion that its fields of facts are conscious phenomena and that introspection is the only direct method of ascertaining these facts, it has enmeshed itself in a series of speculative questions which, while fundamental to its present tenets, are not open to experimental treatment. In the pursuit of answers to these questions, it has become further and further divorced from contact with problems which vitally concern human interest.

2. Psychology, as the behaviorist views it, is a purely objective, experimental branch of natural science which needs introspection as little as do the sciences of chemistry and physics. It is granted that the behavior of animals can be investigated without appeal to consciousness. Heretofore the viewpoint has been that such data have value only in so far as they can be interpreted by analogy in terms of consciousness. The position is taken here that the behavior of man and the behavior of animals must be considered on the same plane; as being equally essential to a general understanding of behavior. It can dispense with consciousness in a psychological sense. The separate observation of 'states of consciousness' is, on this assumption, no more a part of the task of the psychologist than of the physicist. We might call this the return to a non-reflective and naïve use of consciousness. In this sense consciousness may be said to be the instrument or tool with which all scientists work. Whether or not the tool is properly used at present by scientists is a problem for philosophy and not for psychology.

3. From the viewpoint here suggested the facts on the behavior of amœbæ have value in and for themselves without reference to the behavior of man. In biology studies on race differentiation and inheritance in amœbæ form a separate division of study which must be evaluated in terms of the laws found there. The conclusions so reached may not hold in any other form. Regardless of the possible lack of generality, such studies must be made if evolution as a whole is ever to be regulated and controlled. Similarly the laws of behavior in amœbæ, the range of responses, and the determination of effective stimuli, of habit formation, persistency of habits, interference and reinforcement of habits, must be determined and evaluated in and for themselves, regardless of their generality, or of their bearing upon such laws in other forms, if the phenomena of behavior are ever to be brought within the sphere of scientific control.

4. This suggested elimination of states of consciousness as proper objects of investigation in themselves will remove the barrier from psychology which exists between it and the other sciences. The findings of psychology become the functional correlates of structure and lend themselves to explanation in physico-chemical terms.

5. Psychology as behavior will, after all, have to neglect but few of the really essential problems with which psychology as an introspective science now concerns itself. In all probability even this residue of problems may be phrased in such a way that refined methods

in behavior (which certainly must come) will lead to their solution.

NOTES

1. That is, either directly upon the conscious state of the observer or indirectly upon the conscious state of the experimenter.

2. In this connection I call attention to the controversy now on between the adherents and the opposers of image-less thought. The "types of reactors" (sensory and motor) were also matters of bitter dispute. The complication experiment was the source of another war of words concerning the accuracy of the opponents' introspection.

3. My colleague, Professor H. C. Warren, by whose advice this article was offered to the REVIEW, believes that the parallelist can avoid the interaction terminology completely by exercising a little care.

4. He would have exactly the same attitude as if he were conducting an experiment to show whether an ant would crawl over a pencil laid across the trail or go round it.

5. I should prefer to look upon this abbreviated method, where the human subject is told in words, for example, to equate two stimuli; or to state in words whether a given stimulus is present or absent, etc., as the *language method* in behavior. It is no way changes the status of experimentation. The method becomes possible merely by virtue of the fact that in the particular case the experimenter and his animal have systems of abbreviations or shorthand behavior signs (language), any one of which may stand for a habit belonging to the repertoire both of the experimenter and his subject. To make the data obtained by the language method virtually the whole of behavior—or to attempt to mould all of the data obtained by other methods in terms of the one which has by all odds the most limited range—is putting the cart before the horse with a vengeance.

6. They are often undertaken apparently for the purpose of making crude pictures of what must or must not go on in the nervous system.

7. There is need of questioning more and more the existence of what psychology calls imagery. Until a few years ago I thought that centrally aroused visual sensations were as clear as those peripherally aroused. I had never accredited myself with any other kind. However, closer examination leads me to deny in my own case the presence of imagery in the Galtonian sense. The whole doctrine of the centrally aroused image is, I believe, at present, on a very insecure foundation. Angell as well as Fernald reach the conclusion that an objective determination of image type is impossible. It would be an interesting confirmation of their experimental work if we should find by degrees that we have been mistaken in building up this enormous structure of the centrally aroused sensation (or image).

The hypothesis that all of the so-called "higher thought" processes go on in terms of faint reinstatements of the original muscular act (including speech here) and that these are integrated into systems which respond in serial order (associative mechanisms) is, I believe, a tenable one. It makes reflective processes as mechanical as habit. The scheme of habit which James long ago described—where each return or afferent current releases the next appropriate motor discharge—is as true for "thought processes" as for overt muscular acts. Paucity of "imagery" would be the rule. In other words, wherever there are thought processes there are faint contractions of the systems of musculature involved in the overt exercise of the customary act, and especially in the still finer systems of musculature involved in speech. If this is true, and I do not see how it can be gainsaid, imagery becomes a mental luxury (even if it really exists) without any functional significance whatever. If experimental procedure justifies this hypothesis, we shall have at hand tangible phenomena which may be studied as behavior material. I should say that the day when we can study reflective processes by such methods is about as far off as the day when we can tell by physico-chemical methods the difference in the structure and arrangement of molecules between living protoplasm and inorganic substances. The solutions of both problems await the advent of methods and apparatus.

[After writing this paper I heard the addresses of Professors Thorndike and Angell, at the Cleveland meeting of the American Psychological Association. I hope to have the opportunity to discuss them at another time. I must even here attempt to answer one question raised by Thorndike.

Thorndike (see this issue) casts suspicions upon ideo-motor action. If by ideo-motor action he means just that and would not include sensori-motor action in his general denunciation, I heartily agree with him. I should throw out imagery altogether and attempt to show that practically all natural thought goes on in terms of sensori-motor processes in the larynx (but not in terms of "imageless thought") which rarely come to consciousness in any person who has not groped for imagery in the psychological laboratory. This easily explains why so many of the well-educated laity know nothing of imagery. I doubt if Thorndike conceives of the matter in this way. He and Woodworth seem to have neglected the speech mechanisms.

It has been shown that improvement in habit comes unconsciously. The first we know of it is when it is achieved—when it becomes an object. I believe that "consciousness" has just as little to do with *improvement* in thought processes. Since, according to my view, thought processes are really motor habits in the larynx, improvements, short cuts, changes, etc., in these habits are brought about in the same way that such changes are produced in other motor habits. This view carries with it the implication that there are no reflective processes (centrally initiated processes): The individual is always *examining objects*, in the one case objects in the now accepted sense, in the other their substitutes, viz., the movements in the speech musculature. From this it follows that there is no theoretical limitation of the behavior method. There remains, to be sure, the practical difficulty, which may never be overcome, of examining speech movements in the way that general bodily behavior may be examined.]

27
~

EDWARD C. TOLMAN

Edward Chace Tolman (1886–1959) and his brother, Richard, were expected to follow in their father's footsteps, and while they each did attend the Massachusetts Institute of Technology, as their father had before them, neither went into the family business. Richard continued in chemistry and physics, demonstrating that it is the electron that carries the charge in the flow of electricity. Edward found philosophy and psychology more intriguing, following summer courses at Harvard from Robert Yerkes. He enrolled at Harvard and worked with Hugo Munsterberg (p. 288), earning his Ph.D. in 1915. His first job was as an instructor at Northwestern University, where he found the classroom intimidating. In 1918, Tolman lost his job, ostensibly because of his lack of classroom prowess; however, the publication date of an essay articulating his pacifist position and the entry of the United States into World War I complicates the tale. He was then offered a job at the University of California at Berkeley. During World War II, Tolman served in the Office of Strategic Services, the precursor to today's Central Intelligence Agency. In 1949, Berkeley asked its faculty to sign a loyalty oath, an idea made popular by Senator Joseph R. McCarthy's unsubstantiated claims of communist infiltration of the U.S. government. Tolman refused to sign and encouraged other senior faculty to protest, since they were ones for whom such actions would involve less personal and financial risk. He was suspended from his duties at Berkeley but was invited to teach at Harvard University and the University of Chicago. Later Berkeley reinstated Tolman after admitting he had been correct to reject the loyalty oath and awarded him an honorary doctorate in 1959. Just before his death, Tolman wrote, "I have liked to think about psychology in ways that have proved congenial to me. . . . In the end, the only sure criterion is to have fun. And I have had fun."

COGNITIVE MAPS IN RATS AND MEN[1]

I shall devote the body of this paper to a description of experiments with rats. But I shall also attempt in a few words at the close to indicate the significance of these findings on rats for the clinical behavior of men. Most of the rat investigations, which I shall report, were carried out in the Berkeley laboratory. But I shall also include,

From Edward C. Tolman, "Cognitive Maps in Rats and Men." *Psychological Review* 55 (1948):189–208.

occasionally, accounts of the behavior of non-Berkeley rats who obviously have misspent their lives in out-of-State laboratories. Furthermore, in reporting our Berkeley experiments I shall have to omit a very great many. The ones I *shall* talk about were carried out by graduate students (or underpaid research assistants) who, supposedly, got some of their ideas from me. And a few, though a very few, were even carried out by me myself.

Let me begin by presenting diagrams for a couple of typical mazes, an alley maze and an elevated maze. In the typical experiment a hungry rat is put at the entrance of the maze (alley or elevated), and wanders about through the various true path segments and blind alleys until he finally comes to the food box and eats. This is repeated (again in the typical experiment) one trial every 24 hours and the animal tends to make fewer and fewer errors (that is, blind-alley entrances) and to take less and less time between start and goal-box until finally he is entering no blinds at all and running in a very few seconds from start to goal. The results are usually presented in the form of average curves of blind-entrances, or of seconds from start to finish, for groups of rats.

All students agree as to the facts. They disagree, however, on theory and explanation.

(1) First, there is a school of animal psychologists which believes that the maze behavior of rats is a matter of mere simple stimulus-response connections. Learning, according to them, consists in the strengthening of some of these connections and in the weakening of others. According to this "stimulus-response" school the rat in progressing down the maze is helplessly responding to a succession of external stimuli—sights, sounds, smells, pressures, etc. impinging upon his external sense organs—plus internal stimuli coming from the viscera and from the skeletal muscles. These external and internal stimuli call out the walkings, runnings, turnings, retracings, smellings, rearings, and the like which appear. The rat's central nervous system, according to this view, may be likened to a complicated telephone switchboard. There are the incoming calls from sense-organs and there are the outgoing messages to muscles. Before the learning of a specific maze, the connecting switches (synapses according to the physiologist) are closed in one set of ways and produce the primarily exploratory responses which appear in the early trials. *Learning,* according to this view, consists in the respective strengthening and weakening of various of these connections; those connections which result in the animal's going down the true path become relatively

more open to the passage of nervous impulses, whereas those which lead him into the blinds become relatively less open.

It must be noted in addition, however, that this stimulus-response school divides further into two subgroups.

(a) There is a subgroup which holds that the mere mechanics involved in the running of a maze is such that the crucial stimuli from the maze get presented simultaneously with the correct responses more frequently than they do with any of the incorrect responses. Hence, just on a basis of this greater frequency, the neural connections between the crucial stimuli and the correct responses will tend, it is said, to get strengthened at the expense of the incorrect connections.

(b) There is a second subgroup in this stimulus-response school which holds that the reason the appropriate connections get strengthened relatively to the inappropriate ones is, rather, the fact that the responses resulting from the correct connections are followed more closely in time by need-reductions. Thus a hungry rat in a maze tends to get to food and have his hunger reduced *sooner* as a result of the true path responses than as a result of the blind alley responses. And such immediately following need-reductions or, to use another term, such "positive reinforcements" tend somehow, it is said, to strengthen the connections which have most closely preceded them. Thus it is as if—although this is certainly not the way this subgroup would themselves state it—the satisfaction-receiving part of the rat telephoned back to Central and said to the girl: "Hold that connection; it was good; and see to it that you blankety-blank well use it again the next time these same stimuli come in." These theorists also assume (at least some of them do some of the time) that, if bad results—"annoyances," "negative reinforcements"—follow, then this same satisfaction-and-annoyance-receiving part of the rat will telephone back and say, "Break that connection and don't you dare use it next time either."

So much for a brief summary of the two subvarieties of the "stimulus-response," or telephone switchboard school.

(2) Let us turn now to the second main school. This group (and I belong to them) may be called the field theorists. We believe that in the course of learning something like a field map of the environment gets established in the rat's brain. We agree with the other school that the rat in running a maze is exposed to stimuli and is finally led as a result of these stimuli to the responses which ac-

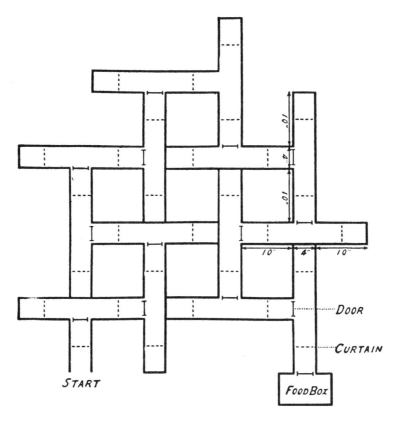

FIGURE 27.1   Plan of maze, 14-Unit T-Alley Maze (From M. H. Elliott, The effect of change of reward on the maze performance of rats. *Univ. Calif. Publ. Psychol.,* 1928, 4, p. 20.)

tually occur. We feel, however, that the intervening brain processes are more complicated, more patterned and often, pragmatically speaking, more autonomous than do the stimulus-response psychologists. Although we admit that the rat is bombarded by stimuli, we hold that his nervous system is surprisingly selective as to which of these stimuli it will let in at any given time.

Secondly, we assert that the central office itself is far more like a map control room than it is like an old-fashioned telephone exchange. The stimuli, which are allowed in, are not connected by just simple one-to-one switches to the outgoing responses. Rather, the incoming impulses are usually worked over and elaborated in the central control room into a tentative, cognitive-like map of the environment. And it is this tentative map, indicating routes and paths and environmental relationships, which finally determines what responses, if any, the animal will finally release.

Finally, I, personally, would hold further that it is

also important to discover in how far these maps are relatively narrow and strip-like or relatively broad and comprehensive. Both strip-maps and comprehensive-maps may be either correct or incorrect in the sense that they may (or may not), when acted upon, lead successfully to the animal's goal. The differences between such strip maps and such comprehensive maps will appear only when the rat is later presented with some change within the given environment. Then, the narrower and more strip-like the original map, the less will it carry over successfully to the new problem; whereas, the wider and the more comprehensive it was, the more adequately it will serve in the new set-up. In a strip-map the given position of the animal is connected by only a relatively simple and single path to the position of the goal. In a comprehensive-map a wider arc of the environment is represented, so that, if the starting position of the animal be changed or variations in the specific routes be introduced, this wider map will allow the ani-

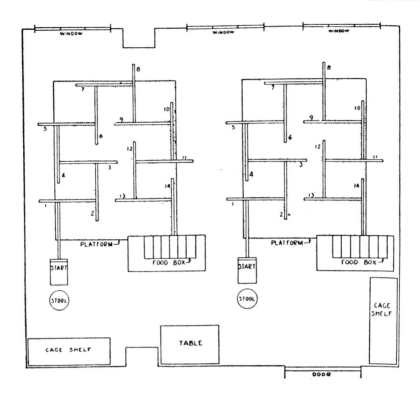

FIGURE 27.2   14-Unit T-Elevated Mazes (From C. H. Honzik, The sensory basis of maze learning in rats. *Compar. Psychol. Monogr.*, 1936, 13, No. 4, p. 4. These were two identical mazes placed side by side in the same room.)

mal still to behave relatively correctly and to choose the appropriate new route.

But let us turn, now, to the actual experiments. The ones, out of many, which I have selected to report are simply ones which seem especially important in reinforcing the theoretical position I have been presenting. This position, I repeat, contains two assumptions: First, that learning consists not in stimulus-response connections but in the building up in the nervous system of sets which function like cognitive maps, and second, that such cognitive maps may be usefully characterized as varying from a narrow strip variety to a broader comprehensive variety.

The experiments fall under five heads: (1) "latent learning," (2) "vicarious trial and error" or "VTE," (3) "searching for the stimulus," (4) "hypotheses" and (5) "spatial orientation."

(1) *"Latent Learning" Experiments.* The first of the latent learning experiments was performed at Berkeley by Blodgett. It was published in 1929. Blodgett not only

performed the experiments, he also originated the concept. He ran three groups of rats through a six-unit alley maze, shown in Fig. 27.4. He had a control group and two experimental groups. The error curves for these groups appear in Fig. 27.5. The solid line shows the error curve for Group I, the control group. These animals were run in orthodox fashion. That is, they were run one trial a day and found food in the goal-box at the end of each trial. Groups II and III were the experimental groups. The animals of Group II, the dash line, were not fed in the maze for the first six days but only in their home cages some two hours later. On the seventh day (indicated by the small cross) the rats found food at the end of the maze for the first time and continued to find it on subsequent days. The animals of Group III were treated similarly except that they first found food at the end of the maze on the third day and continued to find it there on subsequent days. It will be observed that the experimental groups as long as they were not finding food did not appear to learn much. (Their error curves did not drop.) But on the days immediately succeeding

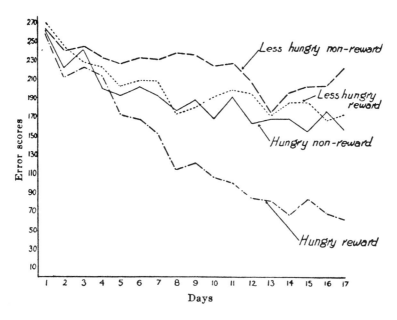

FIGURE 27.3   Error curves for four groups, 36 rats (From E. C. Tolman and C. H. Honzik, Degrees of hunger, reward and nonreward, and maze learning in rats. *Univ. Calif. Publ. Psychol.,* 1930, 4, No. 16, p. 246. A maze identical with the alley maze shown in Fig. 1 was used.)

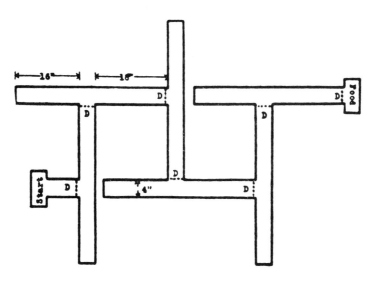

FIGURE 27.4   6-Unit Alley T-Maze (From H. C. Blodgett, The effect of the introduction of reward upon the maze performance of rats. *Univ. Calif. Publ. Psychol.,* 1929, 4, No. 8, p. 117.)

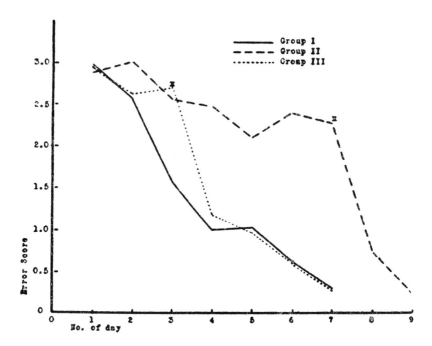

FIGURE 27.5   (From H. C. Blodgett, The effect of the introduction of reward upon the maze performance of rats. *Univ. Calif. Publ. Psychol.*, 1929, 4, No. 8, p. 120.)

their first finding of the food their error curves did drop astoundingly. It appeared, in short, that during the non-rewarded trials these animals had been learning much more than they had exhibited. This learning, which did not manifest itself until after the food had been introduced, Blodgett called "latent learning." Interpreting these results anthropomorphically, we would say that as long as the animals were not getting any food at the end of the maze they continued to take their time in going through it—they continued to enter many blinds. Once, however, they knew they were to get food, they demonstrated that during these preceding non-rewarded trials they had learned where many of the blinds were. They had been building up a 'map,' and could utilize the latter as soon as they were motivated to do so.

Honzik and myself repeated the experiments (or rather he did and I got some of the credit) with the 14-unit T-mazes shown in Fig. 27.1, and with larger groups of animals, and got similar results. The resulting curves are shown in Fig. 27.6. We used two control groups—one that never found food in the maze (HNR) and one that found it throughout (HR). The experimental group (HNR-R) found food at the end of the maze from the 11th day on and showed the same sort of a sudden drop.

But probably the best experiment demonstrating latent learning was, unfortunately, done not in Berkeley but at the University of Iowa, by Spence and Lippitt. Only an abstract of this experiment has as yet been published. However, Spence has sent a preliminary manuscript from which the following account is summarized. A simple Y-maze (see Fig. 27.7) with two goal-boxes was used. Water was at the end of the right arm of the Y and food at the end of the left arm. During the training period the rats were run neither hungry nor thirsty. They were satiated for both food and water before each day's trials. However, they were willing to run because after each run they were taken out of whichever end box they had got to and put into a living cage, with other animals in it. They were given four trials a day in this fashion for seven days, two trials to the right and two to the left.

In the crucial test the animals were divided into two subgroups one made solely hungry and one solely thirsty. It was then found that on the first trial the hungry group went at once to the left, where the food had been, statistically more frequently than to the right; and the thirsty group went to the right, where the water had been, statistically more frequently than to the left. These results indicated that under the previous non-differential

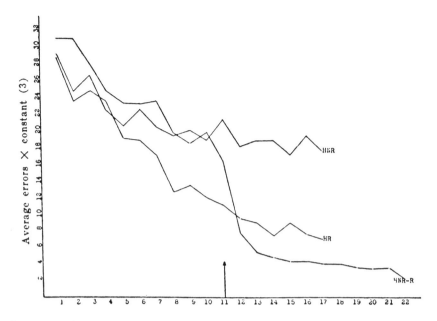

FIGURE 27.6   Error curves for HR, HNR, and HNR-R (From E. C. Tolman and C. H. Honzik, Introduction and removal of reward, and maze performance in rats. *Univ. Calif. Publ. Psychol.,* 1930, 4, No. 19, p. 267.)

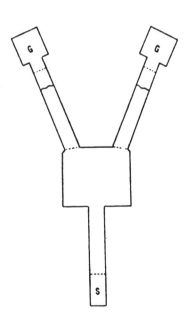

FIGURE 27.7   Ground plan of the apparatus (Taken from K. W. Spence and R. Lippitt, An experimental test of the sign-gestalt theory of trial and error learning. *J. exper. Psychol.,* 1946, 36, p. 494. In this article they were describing another experiment but used the same maze.)

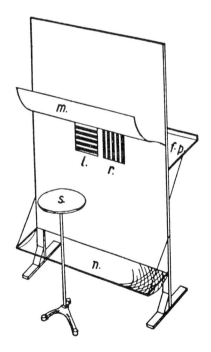

FIGURE 27.8   Apparatus used for testing discrimination of visual patterns (From K. S. Lashley, The mechanism of vision. I. A method for rapid analyses of pattern-vision in the rat. *J. genet. Psychol.,* 1930, 37, p. 454.)

and very mild rewarding conditions of merely being returned to the home cages the animals had nevertheless
been learning where the water was and where the food
was. In short, they had acquired a cognitive map to the
effect that food was to the left and water to the right, although during the acquisition of this map they had not
exhibited any stimulus-response propensities to go more
to the side which became later the side of the appropriate goal.

There have been numerous other latent learning experiments done in the Berkeley laboratory and elsewhere. In general, they have for the most part all confirmed the above sort of findings.

Let us turn now to the second group of experiments.

(2) *"Vicarious Trial and Error" or "VTE."* The term
Vicarious Trial and Error (abbreviated as VTE) was invented by Prof. Muenzinger at Colorado[2] to designate
the hesitating, looking-back-and-forth, sort of behavior
which rats can often be observed to indulge in at a
choice-point before actually going one way or the other.

Quite a number of experiments upon VTEing have
been carried out in our laboratory. I shall report only a
few. In most of them what is called a discrimination set-
up has been used. In one characteristic type of visual
discrimination apparatus designed by Lashley (shown in
Fig. 27.8) the animal is put on a jumping stand and
faced with two doors which differ in some visual property say, as here shown, vertical stripes vs. horizontal
stripes.

One of each such pair of visual stimuli is made always correct and the other wrong; and the two are inter-
changed from side to side in random fashion. The animal is required to learn, say, that the vertically striped
door is always the correct one. If he jumps to it, the door
falls open and he gets to food on a platform behind. If,
on the other hand, he jumps incorrectly, he finds the
door locked and falls into a net some two feet below
from which he is picked up and started over again.

Using a similar set-up (see Fig. 27.9), but with landing platforms in front of the doors so that if the rat chose
incorrectly he could jump back again and start over, I
found that when the choice was an easy one, say between a white door and a black door, the animals not
only learned sooner but also did more VTEing than
when the choice was difficult, say between a white door
and a gray door (see Fig. 27.10). It appeared further (see
Fig. 27.11) that the VTEing began to appear just as (or

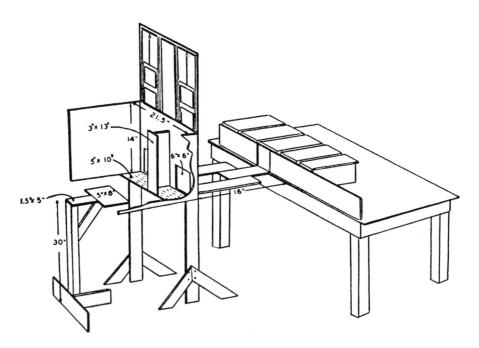

FIGURE 27.9   (From E. C. Tolman, Prediction of vicarious trial and error by means of the schematic sow-bug. PSYCHOL.
REV., 1939, 46, p. 319.)

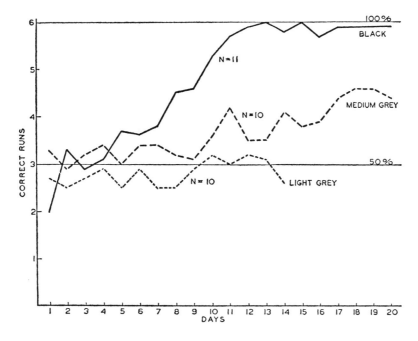

FIGURE 27.10   (From E. C. Tolman, Prediction of vicarious trial and error by means of the schematic sow-bug. PSYCHOL. REV., 1939, 46, p. 319.)

just before) the rats began to learn. After the learning had become established, however, the VTE's began to go down. Further, in a study of individual differences by myself, Geier and Levin[3] (actually done by Geier and Levin) using this same visual discrimination apparatus, it was found that with one and the same difficulty of problem the smarter animal did the more VTEing.

To sum up, in *visual discrimination* experiments the better the learning, the more the VTE's. But this seems contrary to what we would perhaps have expected. We ourselves would expect to do more VTEing, more sampling of the two stimuli, when it is difficult to choose between them than when it is easy.

What is the explanation? The answer lies, I believe, in the fact that the manner in which we set the visual discrimination problems for the rats and the manner in which we set similar problems for ourselves are different. *We* already have our "instructions." We know beforehand what it is we are to do. We are told, or we tell ourselves that it is the lighter of the two grays, the heavier of the two weights, or the like, which is to be chosen. In such a setting we do more sampling, more VTEing, when the stimulus-difference is small. But for the rats the usual problem in a discrimination apparatus is quite different. They do not know what is wanted of them.

The major part of their learning in most such experiments seems to consist in their discovering the instructions. The rats have to discover that it is the differences in visual brightness, not the differences between left and right, which they are to pay attention to. Their VTEing appears when they begin to "catch on." The greater the difference between the two stimuli the more the animals are attracted by this difference. Hence the sooner they catch on, and during this catching on, the more they VTE.

That this is a reasonable interpretation appeared further, from an experiment by myself and Minium (the actual work done, of course, by Minium) in which a group of six rats was first taught a white vs. black discrimination, then two successively more difficult gray vs. black discriminations. For each difficulty the rats were given a long series of further trials beyond the points at which they had learned. Comparing the beginning of each of these three difficulties the results were that the rats did more VTEing for the easy discriminations than for the more difficult ones. When, however, it came to a comparison of amounts of VTEing during the final performance after each learning had reached a plateau, the opposite results were obtained. In other words, after the rats had finally divined their instructions, then they, like

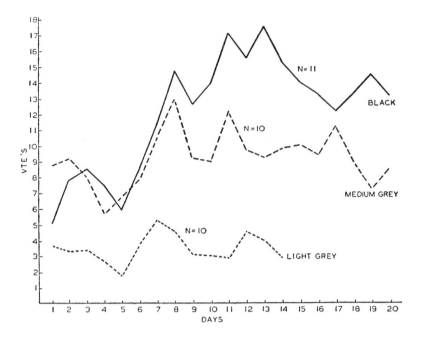

FIGURE 27.11   (From E. C. Tolman, Prediction of vicarious trial and error by means of the schematic sow-bug.
PSYCHOL. REV., 1939, 46, p. 320.)

human beings, did more VTEing, more sampling, the more difficult the discrimination.

Finally, now let us note that it was also found at Berkeley by Jackson[4] that in a maze the difficult maze units produce more VTEing and also that the more stupid rats do the more VTEing. The explanation, as I see it, is that, in the case of mazes, rats know their instructions. For them it is natural to expect that the same spatial path will always lead to the same outcome. Rats in mazes don't have to be told.

But what, now, is the final significance of all this VTEing? How do these facts about VTEing affect our theoretical argument? My answer is that these facts lend further support to the doctrine of a building up of maps. VTEing, as I see it, is evidence that in the critical stages—whether in the first picking up of the instructions or in the later making sure of which stimulus is which—the animal's activity is not just one of responding passively to discrete stimuli, but rather one of the active selecting and comparing of stimuli. This brings me then to the third type of experiment.

(3) *"Searching for the Stimulus."* I refer to a recent, and it seems to me extremely important experiment,

done for a Ph.D. dissertation by Hudson. Hudson was first interested in the question of whether or not rats could learn an avoidance reaction in one trial. His animals were tested one at a time in a living cage (see Fig. 27.13) with a small striped visual pattern at the end, on which was mounted a food cup. The hungry rat approached this food cup and ate. An electrical arrangement was provided so that when the rat touched the cup he could be given an electric shock. And one such shock did appear to be enough. For when the rat was replaced in this same cage days or even weeks afterwards, he usually demonstrated immediately strong avoidance reactions to the visual pattern. The animal withdrew from that end of the cage, or piled up sawdust and covered the pattern, or showed various other amusing responses all of which were in the nature of withdrawing from the pattern or making it disappear.

But the particular finding which I am interested in now appeared as a result of a modification of this standard procedure. Hudson noticed that the animals, anthropomorphically speaking, often seemed to look around *after* the shock to see what it was that had hit them. Hence it occurred to him that, if the pattern were made to disappear the instant the shock occurred, the

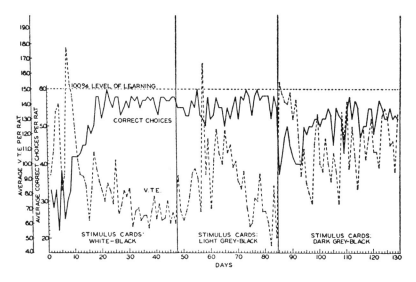

FIGURE 27.12   (From E. C. Tolman and E. Minium, VTE in rats: overlearning and difficulty of discrimination. *J. comp. Psychol.*, 1942, 34, p. 303.)

rats might not establish the association. And this indeed is what happened in the case of many individuals. Hudson added further electrical connections so that when the shock was received during the eating, the lights went out, the pattern and the food cup dropped out of sight, and the lights came on again all within the matter of a second. When such animals were again put in the cage 24 hours later, a large percentage showed no avoidance of the pattern. Or to quote Hudson's own words:

> "Learning what object to avoid . . . may occur exclusively during the period *after* the shock. For if the object from which the shock was actually received is removed at the moment of the shock, a significant number of animals fail to learn to avoid it, some selecting other features in the environment for avoidance, and others avoiding nothing."

In other words, I feel that this experiment reinforces the notion of the largely active selective character in the rat's building up of his cognitive map. He often has to look actively for the significant stimuli in order to form his map and does not merely passively receive and react to all the stimuli which are physically present.

Turn now to the fourth type of experiment.

(4) *The "Hypothesis" Experiments.* Both the notion of hypotheses in rats and the design of the experiments

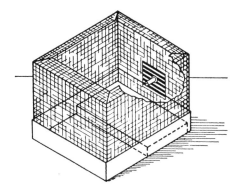

FIGURE 27.13   (From Bradford Hudson. Ph.D. Thesis: "One trial learning: A study of the avoidance behavior of the rat." On deposit in the Library of the University of California, Berkeley, California.)

to demonstrate such hypotheses are to be credited to Krech. Krech used a four-compartment discrimination-box. In such a four-choice box the correct door at each choice-point may be determined by the experimenter in terms of its being lighted or dark, left or right, or various combinations of these. If all possibilities are randomized for the 40 choices made in 10 runs of each day's test, the problem could be made insoluble.

When this was done, Krech found that the individual

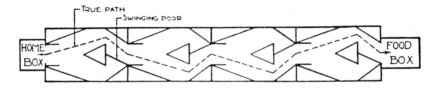

FIGURE 27.14   (From I. Krechevsky (Now D. Krech), The genesis of "hypotheses" in rats. *Univ. Calif. Publ. Psychol.,*
1932, 6, No. 4, p. 46.)

rat went through a succession of systematic choices. That is, the individual animal might perhaps begin by choosing practically all right-hand doors, then he might give this up for choosing practically all left-hand doors, and then, for choosing all dark doors, and so on. These relatively persistent, and well-above-chance systematic types of choice Krech called "hypotheses." In using this term he obviously did not mean to imply verbal processes in the rat but merely referred to what I have been call-

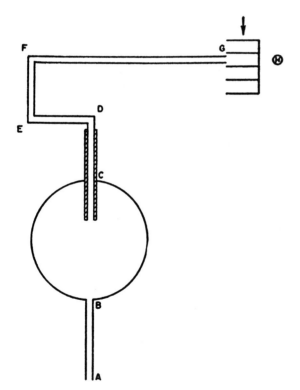

FIGURE 27.15   (From E. C. Tolman, B. F. Ritchie and D. Kalish, Studies in spatial learning. I. Orientation and the short-cut. *J. exp. Psychol.,* 1946, 36, p. 16.)

ing cognitive maps which, it appears from his experiments, get set up in a tentative fashion to be tried out first one and then another until, if possible, one is found which works.

Finally, it is to be noted that these hypothesis experiments, like the latent learning, VTE, and "looking for the stimulus" experiments, do not, as such, throw light upon the widths of the maps which are picked up but do indicate the generally map-like and self-initiated character of learning.

For the beginning of an attack upon the problem of the width of the maps let me turn to the last group of experiments.

(5) *"Spatial Orientation" Experiments.* As early as 1929, Lashley reported incidentally the case of a couple of his rats who, after having learned an alley maze, pushed back the cover near the starting box, climbed out and ran directly across the top to the goal-box where they climbed down in again and ate. Other investigators have reported related findings. All such observations suggest that rats really develop wider spatial maps which include more than the mere trained-on specific paths. In the experiments now to be reported this possibility has been subjected to further examination.

In the first experiment, Tolman, Ritchie and Kalish (actually Ritchie and Kalish) used the set-up shown in Fig. 27.15.

This was an elevated maze. The animals ran from A across the open circular table through CD (which had alley walls) and finally to G, the food box. H was a light which shone directly down the path from G to F. After four nights, three trials per night, in which the rats learned to run directly and without hesitation from A to G, the apparatus was changed to the sun-burst shown in Fig. 27.16. The starting path and the table remained the same but a series of radiating paths was added.

The animals were again started at A and ran across the circular table into the alley and found themselves blocked. They then returned onto the table and began

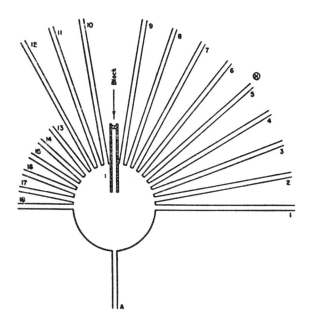

FIGURE 27.16   Apparatus used in the test trial (From E. C. Tolman, B. F. Ritchie and D. Kalish, Studies in spatial learning. I. Orientation and short-cut. *J. exp. Psychol.,* 1946, 36, p. 17.)

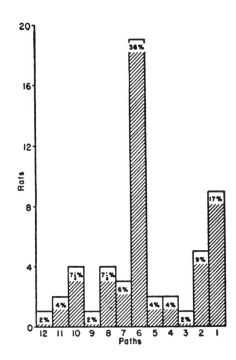

FIGURE 27.17   Numbers of rats which chose each of the paths (From E. C. Tolman, B. F. Ritchie and D. Kalish, Studies in spatial learning. I. Orientation and the short-cut. *J. exp. Psychol.,* 1946, 36, p. 19.)

exploring practically all the radiating paths. After going out a few inches only on any one path, each rat finally chose to run all the way out on one. The percentages of rats finally choosing each of the long paths from 1 to 12 are shown in Fig. 27.17. It appears that there was a preponderant tendency to choose path No. 6 which ran to a point some four inches in front of where the entrance to the food-box had been. The only other path chosen with any appreciable frequency was No. 1—that is, the path which pointed perpendicularly to the food-side of the room.

These results seem to indicate that the rats in this experiment had learned not only to run rapidly down the original roundabout route but also, when this was blocked and radiating paths presented, to select one pointing rather directly towards the point where the food had been or else at least to select a path running perpendicularly to the food-side of the room.

As a result of their original training, the rats had, it would seem, acquired not merely a strip-map to the effect that the original specifically trained-on path led to food but, rather, a wider comprehensive map to the effect that food was located in such and such a direction in the room.

Consider now a further experiment done by Ritchie

alone. This experiment tested still further the breadth of the spatial map which is acquired. In this further experiment the rats were again run across the table—this time to the arms of a simple T. (See Fig. 27.18.)

Twenty-five animals were trained for seven days, 20 trials in all, to find food at F_1; and twenty-five animals were trained to find it at F_2. The L's in the diagram indicate lights. On the eighth day the starting path and table top were rotated through 180 degrees so that they were now in the position shown in Fig. 27.19. The dotted lines represent the old position. And a series of radiating paths was added. What happened? Again the rats ran across the table into the central alley. When, however, they found themselves blocked, they turned back onto the table and this time also spent many seconds touching and trying out for only a few steps practically all the paths. Finally, however, within seven minutes, 42 of the 50 rats chose one path and ran all the way out on it. The paths finally chosen by the 19 of these animals that had been fed at F_1 and by the 23 that had been fed at F_2 are shown in Fig. 27.20.

This time the rats tended to choose, not the paths which pointed directly to the spots where the food had

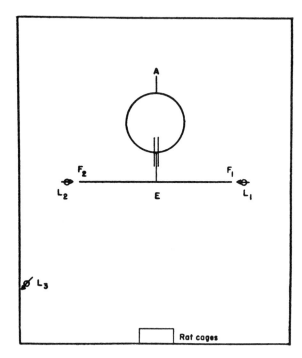

FIGURE 27.18   (From B. F. Ritchie. Ph.D. Thesis: "Spatial learning in rats." On deposit in the Library of the University of California, Berkeley, California.)

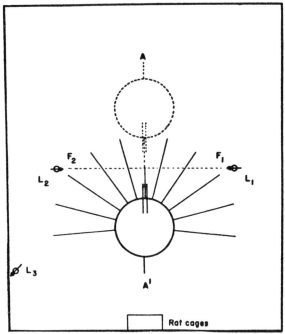

FIGURE 27.19   (From B. F. Ritchie. Ph.D. Thesis: "Spatial learning in rats." On deposit in the Library of the University of California, Berkeley, California.)

been, but rather paths which ran perpendicularly to the corresponding sides of the room. The spatial maps of these rats, when the animals were started from the opposite side of the room, were thus not completely adequate to the precise goal positions but were adequate as to the correct sides of the room. The maps of these animals were, in short, not altogether strip-like and narrow.

This completes my report of experiments. There were the *latent learning experiments,* the *VTE experiments,* the *searching for the stimulus experiment,* the *hypothesis experiments,* and these last *spatial orientation experiments.*

And now, at last, I come to the humanly significant and exciting problem: namely, what are the conditions which favor narrow strip-maps and what are those which tend to favor broad comprehensive maps not only in rats but also in men?

There is considerable evidence scattered throughout the literature bearing on this question both for rats and for men. Some of this evidence was obtained in Berkeley and some of it elsewhere. I have not time to present it in any detail. I can merely summarize it by saying that

narrow strip maps rather than broad comprehensive maps seem to be induced: (1) by a damaged brain, (2) by an inadequate array of environmentally presented cues, (3) by an overdose of repetitions on the original trained-on path and (4) by the presence of too strongly motivational or of too strongly frustrating conditions.

It is this fourth factor which I wish to elaborate upon briefly in my concluding remarks. For it is going to be my contention that some, at least, of the so-called "psychological mechanisms" which the clinical psychologists and the other students of personality have uncovered as the devils underlying many of our individual and social maladjustments can be interpreted as narrowings of our cognitive maps due to too strong motivations or to too intense frustration.

My argument will be brief, cavalier, and dogmatic. For I am not myself a clinician or a social psychologist. What I am going to say must be considered, therefore, simply as in the nature of a *rat* psychologist's *rat*iocinations offered free.

By way of illustration, let me suggest that at least the three dynamisms called, respectively, "regression," "fix-

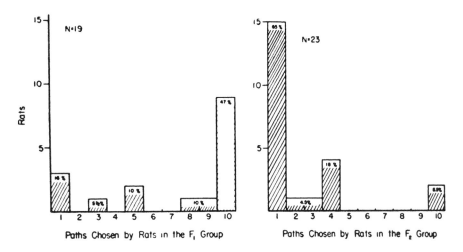

N•19

N•23

Rats

Paths Chosen by Rats in the F₁ Group

Paths Chosen by Rats in the F₂ Group

FIGURE 27.20   (From B. F. Ritchie. Ph.D. Thesis: "Spatial learning in rats." On deposit in the Library of the University of California, Berkeley, California.)

ation," and "displacement of aggression onto out-groups" are expressions of cognitive maps which are too narrow and which get built up in us as a result of too violent motivation or of too intense frustration.

(a) Consider *regression.* This is the term used for those cases in which an individual, in the face of too difficult a problem, returns to earlier more childish ways of behaving. Thus, to take an example, the overprotected middle-aged woman (reported a couple of years ago in *Time Magazine*) who, after losing her husband, regressed (much to the distress of her growing daughters) into dressing in too youthful a fashion and into competing for their beaux and then finally into behaving like a child requiring continuous care, would be an illustration of regression. I would not wish you to put too much confidence in the reportorial accuracy of *Time,* but such an extreme case is not too different from many actually to be found in our mental hospitals or even sometimes in ourselves. In all such instances my argument would be (1) that such regression results from too strong a present emotional situation and (2) that it consists in going back to too narrow an earlier map, itself due to too much frustration or motivation in early childhood. *Time's* middle-aged woman was presented by too frustrating an emotional situation at her husband's death and she regressed, I would wager, to too narrow adolescent and childhood maps since these latter had been originally excessively impressed because of over-stressful experiences at the time she was growing up.

(b) Consider *fixation.* Regression and fixation tend to go hand in hand. For another way of stating the fact of the undue persistence of early maps is to say that they were fixated. This has even been demonstrated in rats. If rats are too strongly motivated in their original learning, they find it very difficult to relearn when the original path is no longer correct. Also after they have relearned, if they are given an electric shock they, like *Time's* woman, tend to regress back again to choosing the earlier path.

(c) Finally, consider the "*displacement of aggressions onto outgroups.*" Adherence to one's own group is an ever-present tendency among primates. It is found in chimpanzees and monkeys as strongly as in men. We primates operate in groups. And each individual in such a group tends to identify with his whole group in the sense that the group's goals become his goals, the group's life and immortality, his life and immortality. Furthermore, each individual soon learns that, when as an individual he is frustrated, he must not take out his aggressions on the other members of his own group. He learns instead to displace his aggressions onto out-groups. Such a displacement of aggression I would claim is also a narrowing of the cognitive map. The individual comes no longer to distinguish the true locus of the cause of his frustration. The poor Southern whites, who take it out on the Negroes, are displacing their aggressions from the landlords, the southern economic system, the northern capitalists, or wherever the true cause of their frustration may lie, onto a mere convenient outgroup. The physicists on the Faculty who criticize the humanities, or we psychologists who criticize all the other departments, or the University as a whole which criticizes the Secondary School system or, vice versa, the Secondary School system which criticizes the University—or, on a still larger and far more dangerous scene—we Americans who criticize the Russians and the Russians who criticize us, are also engaging, at least in part, in nothing more than such irrational displacements of our aggressions onto outgroups.

I do not mean to imply that there may not be some true interferences by the one group with the goals of the other and hence that the aggressions of the members of the one group against the members of the other are necessarily *wholly* and *merely* displaced aggressions. But I do assert that often and in large part they are such mere displacements.

Over and over again men are blinded by too violent motivations and too intense frustrations into blind and unintelligent and in the end desperately dangerous hates of outsiders. And the expression of these their displaced hates ranges all the way from discrimination against minorities to world conflagrations.

What in the name of Heaven and Psychology can we do about it? My only answer is to preach again the virtues of reason—of, that is, broad cognitive maps. And to suggest that the child-trainers and the world-planners of the future can only, if at all, bring about the presence of the required rationality (*i.e.,* comprehensive maps) if they see to it that nobody's children are too over-motivated or too frustrated. Only then can these children learn to look before and after, learn to see that there are often round-about and safer paths to their quite proper goals—learn, that is, to realize that the well-beings of White and of Negro, of Catholic and of Protestant, of Christian and of Jew, of American and of Russian (and even of males and females) are mutually interdependent.

We dare not let ourselves or others become so overemotional, so hungry, so ill-clad, so over-motivated that only narrow strip-maps will be developed. All of us in Europe as well as in America, in the Orient as well as in the Occident, must be made calm enough and well-fed enough to be able to develop truly comprehensive maps, or, as Freud would have put it, to be able to learn to live according to the Reality Principle rather than according to the too narrow and too immediate Pleasure Principle.

We must, in short, subject our children and ourselves (as the kindly experimenter would his rats) to the optimal conditions of moderate motivation and of an absence of unnecessary frustrations, whenever we put them and ourselves before that great God-given maze which is our human world. I cannot predict whether or not we will be able, or be allowed, to do this; but I *can* say that, only insofar as we *are* able and *are* allowed, have we cause for hope.

NOTES

1. 34th Annual Faculty Research Lecture, delivered at the University of California, Berkeley, March 17, 1947. Presented also on March 26, 1947 as one in a series of lectures in Dynamic Psychology sponsored by the division of psychology of Western Reserve University, Cleveland, Ohio.

2. *Vide:* K. F. Muenzinger, Vicarious trial and error at a point of choice: I. A general survey of its relation to learning efficiency. *J. genet. Psychol.,* 1938, 53, 75–86.

3. F. M. Geier, M. Levin & E. C. Tolman, Individual differences in emotionality, hypothesis formation, vicarious trial and error and visual discrimination learning in rats. *Compar. Psychol. Monogr.,* 1941, 17, No. 3.

4. L. L. Jackson, V. T. E. on an elevated maze. *J. comp. Psychol.,* 1943, 36, 99–107.

28

D. O. HEBB

Donald Olding Hebb (1904–1985) became intrigued with psychology through the writings of Sigmund Freud (p. 258), which convinced him there was room for a more rigorous approach. This insight came while spending some nine years teaching school in Quebec following his graduation from Dalhousie University in 1925. Curious about psychology, Hebb arranged to attend McGill University as a part-time student, and was introduced to the more precise methods of Ivan Pavlov (p. 178) by Boris P. Babkin and Leonid Andreyev. Hebb went on to work with two brain pioneers: Karl S. Lashley and Wilder Penfield. He worked with Lashley at Harvard, receiving his Ph.D. in 1936, and again in 1942 when Lashley was appointed director of the Yerkes Laboratory of Primate Biology in Orange Park, Florida. During the intervening years, Hebb enjoyed a fellowship at the Montreal Neurological Institute with Penfield and taught at Queens University in Ontario. He took all his teaching responsibilities seriously, from his days as an elementary school principal and high school teacher to the training of graduate students at McGill, where he returned as a professor in 1946. His approach was unique—he sent misbehaving elementary school children out to play and had graduate students audit courses, rather taking them for credit—each mechanism designed to develop and motivate better learning.

THE ORGANIZATION OF BEHAVIOR: A NEUROPSYCHOLOGICAL THEORY

4. THE FIRST STAGE OF PERCEPTION: GROWTH OF THE ASSEMBLY

This chapter and the next develop a schema of neural action to show how a rapprochement can be made between (1) perceptual generalization, (2) the permanence of learning, and (3) attention, determining tendency, or the like. It is proposed first that a repeated stimulation of specific receptors will lead slowly to the formation of an "assembly" of association-area cells which can act briefly as a closed system after stimulation has ceased; this prolongs the time during which the structural changes of learning can occur and constitutes the simplest instance of a representative process (image or idea). The way in which this cell-assembly might be established, and its characteristics, are the subject matter of the present chapter. In the following chapter the interrelationships between cell-assemblies are dealt with; these are the basis of temporal organization in central processes (attention, attitude, thought, and so on). The two chapters (4 and 5) construct the conceptual tools with which, in the following chapters, the problems of behavior are to be attacked.

The first step in this neural schematizing is a bald assumption about the structural changes that make lasting memory possible. The assumption has repeatedly been made before, in one way or another, and repeatedly found unsatisfactory by the critics of learning theory. I believe it is still necessary. As a result, I must show that in another context, of added anatomical and physiological knowledge, it becomes more defensible and more fertile than in the past.

The assumption, in brief, is that a growth process accompanying synaptic activity makes the synapse more

From D. O. Hebb, "The First Stage of Perception: Growth of the Assembly." In *The Organization of Behavior: A Neuropsychological Theory* (pp. 60–79). New York: John Wiley & Sons, 1949.

readily traversed. This hypothesis of synaptic resistances, however, is different from earlier ones in the following respects: (1) structural connections are postulated between single cells, but single cells are not effective units of transmission and such connections would be only one factor determining the direction of transmission; (2) no direct sensori-motor connections are supposed to be established in this way, in the adult animal; and (3) an intimate relationship is postulated between reverberatory action and structural changes at the synapse, implying a dual trace mechanism.

The Possibility of a Dual Trace Mechanism

Hilgard and Marquis (1940) have shown how a reverberatory, transient trace mechanism might be proposed on the basis of Lorente de Nó's conclusions, that a cell is fired only by the simultaneous activity of two or more afferent fibers, and that internuncial fibers are arranged in closed (potentially self-exciting) circuits. Their diagram is arranged to show how a reverberatory circuit might establish a sensori-motor connection between receptor cells and the effectors which carry out a conditioned response. There is of course a good deal of psychological evidence which is opposed to such an oversimplified hypothesis, and Hilgard and Marquis do not put weight on it. At the same time, it is important to see that something of the kind is not merely a possible but a necessary inference from certain neurological ideas. To the extent that anatomical and physiological observations establish the possibility of reverberatory after-effects of a sensory event, it is established that such a process would be the physiological basis of a transient "memory" of the stimulus. There may, then, be a memory trace that is wholly a function of a pattern of neural activity, independent of any structural change.

Hilgard and Marquis go on to point out that such a trace would be quite unstable. A reverberatory activity would be subject to the development of refractory states in the cells of the circuit in which it occurs, and external events could readily interrupt it. We have already seen (in Chapter 1) that an "activity" trace can hardly account for the permanence of early learning, but at the same time one may regard reverberatory activity as the explanation of other phenomena.

There are memories which are instantaneously established, and as evanescent as they are immediate. In the repetition of digits, for example, an interval of a few seconds is enough to prevent any interference from one series on the next. Also, some memories are both instantaneously established and permanent. To account for the permanence, some structural change seems necessary, but a structural growth presumably would require an appreciable time. If some way can be found of supposing that a reverberatory trace might cooperate with the structural change, and *carry the memory until the growth change is made,* we should be able to recognize the theoretical value of the trace which is an activity only, without having to ascribe all memory to it. The conception of a transient, unstable reverberatory trace is therefore useful, if it is possible to suppose also that some more permanent structural change reinforces it. There is no reason to think that a choice must be made between the two conceptions; there may be traces of both kinds, and memories which are dependent on both.

A Neurophysiological Postulate

Let us assume then that the persistence or repetition of a reverberatory activity (or "trace") tends to induce lasting cellular changes that add to its stability. The assumption can be precisely stated as follows: *When an axon of cell* A *is near enough to excite a cell* B *and repeatedly or persistently takes part in firing it, some growth process or metabolic change takes place in one or both cells such that* A*'s efficiency, as one of the cells firing* B, *is increased.*

The most obvious and I believe much the most probable suggestion concerning the way in which one cell could become more capable of firing another is that synaptic knobs develop and increase the area of contact between the afferent axon and efferent soma. ("Soma" refers to dendrites and body, or all of the cell except its axon.) There is certainly no direct evidence that this is so, and the postulated change if it exists may be metabolic, affecting cellular rhythmicity and limen; or there might be both metabolic and structural changes, including a limited neurobiotaxis. There are several considerations, however, that make the growth of synaptic knobs a plausible conception. The assumption stated above can be put more definitely, as follows:

When one cell repeatedly assists in firing another, the axon of the first cell develops synaptic knobs (or enlarges them if they already exist) in contact with the soma of the second cell. This seems to me the most likely mechanism of a lasting effect of reverberatory action, but I wish to make it clear that the subsequent discussion depends only on the more generally stated proposition italicized above.

It is wise to be explicit on another point also. The proposition does not require action at any great distance, and certainly is not the same as Kappers' (Kappers, Hu-

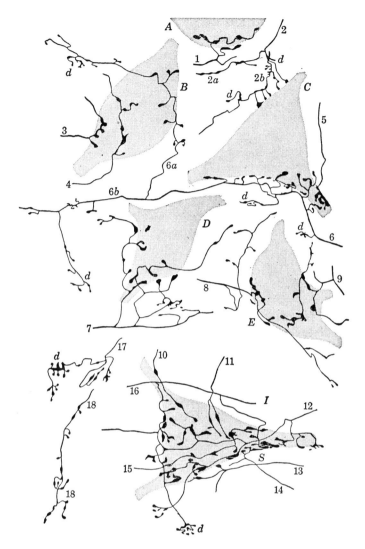

FIGURE 28.1   Relationships between synaptic knobs and the cell body. From Lorente de Nó, 1938a. Courtesy of Charles C Thomas and of the author.

ber, and Crosby, 1936) conception of the way in which neurobiotaxis controls axonal and dendritic outgrowth. But my assumption is evidently related to Kappers' ideas, and not inconsistent with them. The theory of neurobiotaxis has been severely criticized, and clearly it does not do all it was once thought to do. On the other hand, neurobiotaxis may still be one factor determining the connections made by neural cells. If so, it would co-operate very neatly with the knob formation postulated above. Criticism has been directed at the idea that neu-

robiotaxis directs axonal growth throughout its whole course, and that the process sufficiently accounts for all neural connections. The idea is not tenable, particularly in view of such work as that of Weiss (1941b) and Sperry (1943).

But none of this has shown that neurobiotaxis has *no* influence in neural growth; its operation, within ranges of a centimeter or so, is still plausible. Thus, in figure 28.1 (Lorente de Nó, 1938a), the multiple synaptic knobs of fiber 2 on cell *C* might be outgrowths from a fiber passing the cell at a distance, and determined by the fact of repeated simultaneous excitations in the two. Again, the course followed by fiber 7 in the neighborhood of cell *D* may include deflections from the original course of the fiber, determined in the same way.

The details of these histological speculations are not important except to show what some of the possibilities of change at the synapse might be and to show that the mechanism of learning discussed in this chapter is not wholly out of touch with what is known about the neural cell. The changed facilitation that constitutes learning might occur in other ways without affecting the rest of the theory. To make it more specific, I have chosen to assume that the growth of synaptic knobs, with or without neurobiotaxis, is the basis of the change of facilitation from one cell on another, and this is not altogether implausible. It has been demonstrated by Arvanitaki (1942) that a contiguity alone will permit the excitation aroused in one cell to be transmitted to another. There are also earlier experiments, reviewed by Arvanitaki, with the same implication. Even more important, perhaps, is Erlanger's (1939) demonstration of impulse transmission across an artificial "synapse," a blocked segment of nerve more than a millimeter in extent. Consequently, in the intact nervous system, an axon that passes close to the dendrites or body of a second cell would be capable of *helping* to fire it, when the second cell is also exposed to other stimulation at the same point. The probability that such closely timed coincidental excitations would occur is not considered for the moment but will be returned to. When the coincidence does occur, and the active fiber, which is merely close to the soma of another cell, adds to a local excitation in it, I assume that the joint action tends to produce a thickening of the fiber—forming a synaptic knob—or adds to a thickening already present.

Lorente de Nó (1938a) has shown that the synaptic knob is usually not a terminal structure (thus the term "end foot" or "end button" is misleading), nor always separated by a stalk from the axon or axon collateral. If it were, of course, some action at a distance would be inevitably suggested, if such connections are formed in learning. The knob instead is often a rather irregular thickening in the unmyelinated part of an axon near its ending, where it is threading its way through a thicket of dendrites and cell bodies. The point in the axon where the thickening occurs does not appear to be determined by the structure of the cell of which it is a part but by something external to the cell and related to the presence of a second cell. The number and size of the knobs formed by one cell in contact with a second cell vary

also. In the light of these facts it is not implausible to suppose that the extent of the contact established is a function of joint cellular activity, given propinquity of the two cells.

Also, if a synapse is crossed only by the action of two or more afferent cells, the implication is that the greater the area of contact the greater the likelihood that action in one cell will be *decisive* in firing another.[1] Thus three afferent fibers with extensive knob contact could fire a cell that otherwise might be fired only by four or more fibers; or fired sooner with knobs than without.

In short, it is feasible to assume that synaptic knobs develop with neural activity and represent a lowered synaptic resistance. It is implied that the knobs appear in the course of learning, but this does not give us a means of testing the assumption. There is apparently no good evidence concerning the relative frequency of knobs in infant and adult brains, and the assumption does *not* imply that there should be none in the newborn infant. The learning referred to is learning in a very general sense, which must certainly have begun long before birth.

Conduction from Area 17

In order to apply this idea (of a structural reinforcement of synaptic transmission) to visual perception, it is necessary first to examine the known properties of conduction from the visual cortex, area 17, to areas 18, 19, and 20. (In view of the criticisms of architectonic theory by Lashley and Clark [1946], it may be said that Brodmann's areas are referred to here as a convenient designation of relative cortical position, without supposing that the areas are necessarily functional entities or always histologically distinctive.)

It has already been seen that there is a topological reproduction of retinal activities in area 17, but that conduction from 17 to 18 is diffuse. Von Bonin, Garol, and McCulloch (1942) have found that a localized excitation in 17 is conducted to a large part of 18, a band lying along the margins of 17. There is no point-to-point correspondence of 17 and 18. Excitation from 18 is conducted back to the nearest border region of 17; to all parts of area 18 itself; and to all parts of the contralateral 18, of area 19 (lying anterior to 18), and of area 20 (in the lower part of the temporal lobe).

The diffusity of conduction from area 17 is illustrated by the diagram of figure 28.2. Cells lying in the same part of 17 may conduct to different points in 18. The cells in 18, thus stimulated, also lead to points in 18 it-

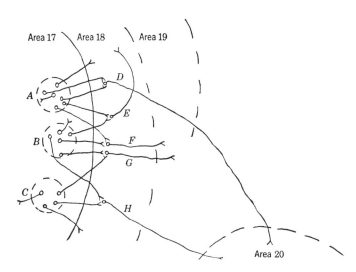

FIGURE 28.2   Illustrating convergence of cells in Brodmann's area 17 upon cells in area 18, these cells in turn leading to other areas. *A, B, C,* three grossly distinct regions in area 17; *D, E, F, G, H,* cells in area 18. See text.

self which are widely separated; to any part of the ipsilateral areas 19 and 20; and, through one synapse, to any part of the contralateral 19 and 20. Conversely, *cells lying in different parts of* 17 *or* 18 *may have connections with the same point in* 18 *or* 20.

Thus there is convergence as well as spread of excitation. The second point illustrated by figure 28.2 is a selective action in 18, depending on the convergence of fibers from 17. In the figure, *F* and *G* are two cells in area 18 connecting the same macroscopic areas. *F,* however, is one that happens to be exposed to excitations from both *A* and *B* (two different regions in area 17). When an area-17 excitation includes both *A* and *B, F* is much more likely to be fired than *G.* The figure does not show the short, closed, multiple chains which are found in all parts of the cortex and whose facilitating activity would often make it possible for a single fiber from *B* to fire *G.* But the same sort of local bombardment would also aid in firing *F;* and the cell which receives excitations from two area-17 fibers simultaneously would be more likely to fire than that which receives excitation from only one.

On the other hand, when *B* and *C* (instead of *A* and *B*) are excited simultaneously, *G* would be more likely to fire than *F.* Any specific region of activity in area 17 would tend to excite specific cells in area 18 which would tend not to be fired by the excitation of another region in 17. These specific cells in 18 would be diffusely arranged, as far as we know at random. They would be usually at some distance from one another and would always be intermingled with others which are not fired

by the same afferent stimulation, but because of their lasting structural connections would tend always to be selectively excited, in the same combination, whenever the same excitation recurs in area 17. This of course would apply also in areas 19 and 20. Since a single point in 18 fires to many points throughout 19 and 20, excitation of any large number of area-18 cells means that convergence in 19 and 20 must be expected. How often it would happen is a statistical question, which will be deferred to a later section.

The tissues made active beyond area 17, by two different visual stimuli, would thus be (1) grossly the same, (2) histologically distinct. A difference of stimulating pattern would not mean any gross difference in the part of the brain which mediates perception (except in the afferent structures up to and including area 17, the visual cortex). Even a completely unilateral activity, it should be noted, would have diffuse effects throughout areas 18, 19, and 20 not only on one side of the brain but on both. At the same time, a difference of locus or pattern of stimulation would mean a difference in the particular cells in these areas that are consistently or maximally fired.

Mode of Perceptual Integration: The Cell-Assembly

In the last chapter it was shown that there are important properties of perception which cannot be ascribed to events in area 17, and that these are properties which seem particularly dependent on learning. That "identity" is not due to what happens in 17 is strongly implied by the distortions that occur in the projection of a retinal excitation to the cortex. When the facts of hemianopic completion are also considered, the conclusion appears inescapable. Perception must depend on other structures besides area 17.

But we now find, at the level of area 18 and beyond, that all topographical organization in the visual process seems to have disappeared. All that is left is activity in an irregular arrangement of cells, which are intertangled with others that have nothing to do with the perception of the moment. We know of course that perception of simple objects is unified and determinate, a well-organized process. What basis can be found for an integration of action, in cells that are anatomically so disorganized?

An answer to this question is provided by the structural change at the synapse which has been assumed to take place in learning. The answer is not simple; perceptual integration would not be accomplished directly, but only as a slow development, and, for the purposes of exposition, at least, would involve several distinct stages, with the first of which we shall now be concerned.

The general idea is an old one, that any two cells or systems of cells that are repeatedly active at the same time will tend to become "associated," so that activity in one facilitates activity in the other. The details of speculation that follow are intended to show how this old idea might be put to work again, with the equally old idea of a lowered synaptic "resistance," under the eye of a different neurophysiology from that which engendered them. (It is perhaps worth while to note that the two ideas have most often been combined only in the special case in which one cell is associated with another, of a

higher level or order in transmission, which it fires; what I am proposing is a possible basis of association of two afferent fibers of the same order—in principle, a sensori-sensory association,[2] in addition to the linear association of conditioning theory.)

The proposal is most simply illustrated by cells A, B, and C in figure 28.3. A and B, visual-area cells, are simultaneously active. The cell A synapses, of course, with a large number of cells in 18, and C is supposed to be one that happens to lead back into 17. Cells such as C would be those that produce the local wedge-shaped area of firing in 17 when a point in 18 is strychninized (von Bonin, Garol, and McCulloch, 1942). The cells in the region of 17 to which C leads are being fired by the same massive sensory excitation that fires A, and C would almost necessarily make contact with some cell B that also fires into 18, or communicate with B at one step removed, through a short-axon circuit. With repetition of the same massive excitation in 17 the same firing relations would recur and, according to the assumption made, growth changes would take place at synapses AC and CB. This means that A and B, both afferent neurons of the same order, would no longer act independently of each other.

At the same time, in the conditions of stimulation that are diagrammed in figure 28.3. A would also be likely to synapse (directly, or via a short closed link) with a cell D which leads back into an unexcited part of 17, and there synapses with still another cell E of the same order as A and B. The synapse DE, however, would be unlikely to be traversed, since it is not like CB exposed to concentrated afferent bombardment. Upon

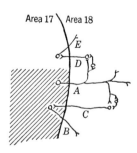

FIGURE 28.3   Cells A and B lie in a region of area 17 (shown by hatching) which is massively excited by an afferent stimulation. C is a cell in area 18 which leads back into 17. E is in area 17 but lies outside the region of activity. See text.

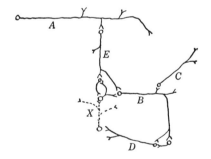

FIGURE 28.4   A, B, and C are cells in area 18 which are excited by converging fibers (not shown) leading from a specific pattern of activity in area 17. D, E, and X are, among the many cells with which A, B, and C have connections, ones which would contribute to an integration of their activity. See text.

frequent repetition of the particular excitation in area 17, a functional relationship of activity in *A* and *B* would increase much more than a relationship of *A* to *E*.

The same considerations can be applied to the activity of the enormous number of individual cells in 18, 19, and 20 that are simultaneously aroused by an extensive activity in 17. Here, it should be observed, the evidence of neuronography implies that there are anatomical connections of every point with every other point, within a few millimeters, and that there is no orderly arrangement of the cells concerned.

Figure 28.4 diagrams three cells, *A, B,* and *C,* that are effectively fired in 18 by a particular visual stimulation, frequently repeated (by fixation, for example, on some point in a constant distant environment). *D, E,* and *X* represent possible connections which might be found between such cells, directly or with intervening links. Supposing that time relations in the firing of these cells make it possible, activity in *A* would contribute to the firing of *E,* and that in *B* to firing *C* and *D.* Growth changes at the synapses *AE, BC, BD,* and so on, would be a beginning of integration and would increase the probability of coordinated activity in each pair of neurons.

The fundamental meaning of the assumption of growth at the synapse is in the effect this would have on the timing of action by the efferent cell. The increased area of contact means that firing by the efferent cell is more likely to follow the lead of the afferent cell. A fiber of order *n* thus gains increased control over a fiber *n* + 1, making the firing of *n* + 1 more predictable or determinate. The control cannot be absolute, but "optional" (Lorente de Nó, 1939), and depends also on other events in the system. In the present case, however, the massive excitation in 17 would tend to establish constant conditions throughout the system during the brief period of a single visual fixation; and the postulated synaptic changes would also increase the degree of this constancy. *A* would acquire an increasing control of *E,* and *E,* with each repetition of the visual stimulus, would fire more consistently at the same time that *B* is firing (*B,* it will be recalled, is directly controlled by the area-17 action). Synaptic changes *EB* would therefore result. Similarly, *B* acquires an increasing control of *D;* and whenever a cell such as *D* happens to be one that connects again with *B,* through *X,* a closed cycle (*BDXB*) is set up.

It is, however, misleading to put emphasis on the coincidences necessary for the occurrence of such a simple closed circuit. Instead of a ring or hoop, the best analogy to the sort of structure which would be set up or "assembled" is a closed solid cage-work, or three-

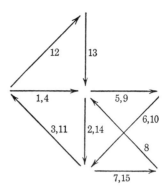

FIGURE 28.5 Arrows represent a simple "assembly" of neural pathways or open multiple chains firing according to the numbers on each (the pathway "1, 4" fires first and fourth, and so on), illustrating the possibility of an "alternating" reverberation which would not extinguish as readily as that in a simple closed circuit.

dimensional lattice, with no regular structure, and with connections possible from any one intersection to any other. Let me say explicitly, again, that the *specificity of such an assembly of cells in* 18 *or* 20, *to a particular excitation in* 17, *depends on convergences.* Whenever two cells, directly or indirectly controlled by that excitation, converge on another cell (as *E* and *X* converge on *B* in figure 28.4) the essential condition of the present schematizing is fulfilled; the two converging cells need not have any simple anatomical or physiological relation to one another, and physiological integration would not be supposed to consist of independent closed chains.

This has an important consequence. Lorente de Nó (1938*b*) has put stress on the fact that activity in a short closed circuit must be rapidly extinguished, and could hardly persist as long as a hundredth of a second. It is hard, on the other hand, to see how a long, many-linked chain, capable of longer reverberation, would get established as a functional unit. But look now at figure 28.5, which diagrams a different sort of possibility. Arrows represent not neurons, but multiple pathways, of whatever complexity is necessary so that each arrow stands for a functional unit. These units fire in the order 1, 2, 3, ... 15. The pathway labeled (1, 4) is the first to fire, and also the fourth; (2, 14) fires second and fourteenth; and so on. The activity 1-2-3-4 is in a relatively simple closed circuit. At this point the next unit (2, 14) may be refractory, which would effectively extinguish reverberation in that simple circuit. But at this point, also, another pathway (5, 9) may be excitable and permit activity in the larger system to continue in some way as that suggested by the numbers in the figure. The sort of irregular three-dimensional net which might be the anatomical basis of perceptual integration in the association areas would be infinitely more complex than anything one could show with a diagram and would provide a large number of the multiple parallel (or alternate) units which are suggested by figure 28.5. If so, an indefinite reverberation in the structure might be possible, so long as the background activity in other cells in the same gross region remained the same. It would not of course remain the same for long, especially with changes of visual fixation; but such considerations make it possible to conceive of "alternating" reverberation which might frequently last for periods of time as great as half a second or a second.

(What I have in mind, in emphasizing half a second or so as the duration of a reverberatory activity, is the observed duration of a single content in perception [Pillsbury, 1913; Boring, 1933]. Attention wanders, and the best estimate one can make of the duration of a single "conscious content" is of this time-order.)

This then is the cell-assembly. Some of its characteristics have been defined only by implication, and these are to be developed elsewhere, particularly in the remainder of this chapter, in the following chapter, and in Chapter 8. The assembly is thought of as a system inherently involving some equipotentiality, in the presence of alternate pathways each having the same function, so that brain damage might remove some pathways without preventing the system from functioning, particularly if the system has been long established, with well-developed synaptic knobs which decrease the number of fibers that must be active at once to traverse a synapse.

Statistical Considerations

It must have appeared to the reader who examined figures 28.3 and 28.4 carefully that there was something unlikely about its being arranged at the Creation to have such neat connections exactly where they were most needed for my hypothesis of perceptual integration. The answer of course is statistical: the neurons diagrammed were those which happen to have such connections, and, given a large enough population of connecting fibers distributed at random, the improbable connection must become quite frequent, in absolute numbers. The next task is to assess the statistical element in these calculations, and show that probability is not stretched too far.

The diagrams and discussion of the preceding sec-

tion require the frequent existence of two kinds of coincidence: (1) synchronization of firing in two or more converging axons, and (2) the anatomical fact of convergence in fibers which are, so far as we know, arranged at random. The necessity of these coincidences sets a limit to postulating functional connections *ad lib.* as the basis of integration. But this is not really a difficulty, since the psychological evidence (as we shall see) also implies that there are limits to perceptual integration.

Consider first the enormous frequency and complexity of the actual neural connections that have been demonstrated histologically and physiologically. One is apt to think of the neural cell as having perhaps two or three or half a dozen connections with other cells, and as leading from one minute point in the central nervous system to one other minute point. This impression is far from the truth and no doubt is due to the difficulty of representing the true state of affairs in a printed drawing.

Forbes (1939) mentions for example an estimate of 1300 synaptic knobs on a single anterior horn cell. Lorente de Nó's drawings (1943, figures 71–73, 75) show a complexity, in the ramification of axon and dendrite, that simply has no relation whatever to diagrams (such as mine) showing a cell with one or two connections. The gross extent of the volume of cortex infiltrated by the collaterals of the axon of a single neuron is measured in millimeters, not in microns; it certainly is not a single point, microscopic in size. In area 18, the strychnine method demonstrates that each tiny area of cortex has connections with the whole region. (These areas are about as small as 1 sq. mm., according to McCulloch, 1944b.) It puts no great strain on probabilities to suppose that there would be, in area 18, some anatomical connection of any one cell, excited by a particular visual stimulation, with a number of others excited in the same way.

There is, therefore, the *anatomical* basis of a great number of convergences among the multitude of cortical cells directly or indirectly excited by any massive retinal activity. This is to be kept in mind as one approaches the physiological question of synchronization in the converging fibers. In the tridimensional, lattice-like assembly of cells that I have supposed to be the basis of perceptual integration, those interconnecting neurons which synapse with the same cell would be functionally in parallel. Figure 28.5 illustrates this. The pathways labeled (1, 4), (8), and (13), converging on one synapse, must have the same function in the system; or the two-link pathway (5, 9)–(6, 10) the same function as the single link (2, 14). When impulses in one such path are not effective, those in another, arriving at a different time, could be.

Once more, the oversimplification of such diagrams is highly misleading. At each synapse there must be a considerable dispersion in the time of arrival of impulses, and in each individual fiber a constant variation of responsiveness; and one could never predicate a determinate pattern of action in any small segment of the system. In the larger system, however, a statistical constancy might be quite predictable.

It is not necessary, and not possible, to define the cell-assembly underlying a perception as being made up of neurons all of which are active when the proper visual stimulation occurs. One can suppose that there would always be activity in some of the group of elements which are in functional parallel (they are not of course geometrically parallel). When for example excitation can be conducted to a particular point in the system from five different directions, the activity characteristic of the system as a whole might be maintained by excitation in any three of the five pathways, and no one fiber would have to be synchronized with any other one fiber.

There would still be some necessity of synchronization, and this has another aspect. In the integration which has been hypothesized, depending on the development of synaptic knobs and an increasing probability of control by afferent over efferent fibers, there would necessarily be a gradual change of the frequency characteristics of the system. The consequence would be a sort of fractionation and recruitment, and some change in the neurons making up the system. That is, some units, capable at first of synchronizing with others in the system, would no longer be able to do so and would drop out: "fractionation." Others, at first incompatible, would be recruited. *With perceptual development there would thus be a slow growth in the assembly,* understanding by "growth" not necessarily an increase in the number of constituent cells, but a change. How great the change would be there is no way of telling, but it is a change that may have importance for psychological problems when some of the phenomena of association are considered.

This then is the statistical approach to the problem. It is directly implied that an "association" of two cells in the same region, or of two systems of cells, would vary, in the probability of its occurrence, over a wide range. If one chose such pairs at random one would find some between which no association was possible, some in which association was promptly and easily established when the two were simultaneously active, and a large proportion making up a gradation from one of these extremes to the other. The larger the system with a determinate general pattern of action, the more readily an association could be formed with another system. On a statistical basis, the more points at which a chance anatomical convergence could occur, the greater the frequency of effective interfacilitation between the two assemblies.

Psychologically, these ideas mean (1) that there is a prolonged period of integration of the individual perception, apart from associating the perception with anything else; (2) that an association between two perceptions is likely to be possible only after each one has independently been organized, or integrated; (3) that, even between two integrated perceptions, there may be a considerable variation in the ease with which association can occur. Finally, (4) the apparent necessity of supposing that there would be a "growth," or fractionation and recruitment, in the cell-assembly underlying perception means that there might be significant differences in the properties of perception at different stages of integration. One cannot guess how great the changes of growth would be; but it is conceivable, even probable, that if one knew where to look for the evidence one would find marked differences of identity in the perceptions of child and adult.

The psychological implications of my schematizing, as far as it has gone, have been made explicit in order to show briefly that they are not contrary to fact. We are not used to thinking of a simple perception as slowly and painfully learned, as the present chapter would suggest; but it has already been seen, in the discussion of the vision of the congenitally blind after operation, that it actually is. The slowness of learning, and the frequent instances of total failure to learn at all in periods as great as a year following operation (Senden, 1932), are extraordinary and incredible (if it were not for the full confirmation by Riesen, 1947). The principles of learning to be found in psychological textbooks are derived from the behavior of the half-grown or adult animal. Our ideas as to the readiness with which association is set up apply to the behavior of the developed organism, as Boring (1946) has noted; there is no evidence whatever to show that a similarly prompt association of separate perceptions can occur at birth—that it is independent of a slow process in which the perceptions to be associated must first be integrated.

As to the wide range in difficulty of associating two ideas or perceptions, even for the adult, this is psychologically a matter of common experience. Who has not had trouble remembering, in spite of repeated efforts, the spelling or pronunciation of some word, or the name of some acquaintance? The fact of the unequal difficulty of associations is not stressed in the literature, probably because it does not fit into conditioned-reflex theory; but it is a fact. My speculations concerning the nature of the trace and the aboriginal development of perception thus are not obviously opposed to the psychological evidence. Further evaluation can be postponed until the speculations have been fully developed.

NOTES

1. One point should perhaps be made explicit. Following Lorente de Nó, two afferent cells are considered to be effective at the synapse, when one is not, only because their contacts with the efferent cell are close together so their action summates. When both are active, they create a larger region of *local* disturbance in the efferent soma. The larger the knobs in a given cluster, therefore, the smaller the number that might activate the cell on which they are located. On occasion, a single afferent cell must be effective in transmission. It is worth pointing this out, also, because it might appear to the reader otherwise that there is something mysterious about emphasis on the necessity of activity in two or more cells to activate the synapse. All that has really been shown is that in some circumstances two or more afferent cells are necessary. However, this inevitably implies that an increase in the number of afferent cells simultaneously active must increase the reliability with which the synapse is traversed.

2. It should be observed, however, that some theorists have continued to maintain that "S-S" (sensori-sensory) associations are formed in the learning process, and have provided experimental evidence that seems to establish the fact. See, *e.g.,* Brogden, *J. Exp. Psychol.,* 1947, 37, 527–539, and earlier papers cited therein.

29

JEAN PIAGET

Jean Piaget (1896–1980) began his career classifying not the intellectual development of children, but the shells of mollusks. Fascinated by nature as a child, he spent hours observing the fauna of Neuchâtel, Switzerland, where his father was a professor of medieval literature at the university. Not content with observation, Piaget wrote volumes and at age 10 enjoyed his first publication: a paragraph in a local amateur naturalists journal describing a rare albino sparrow he had seen in a nearby park. The director of the natural history museum specialized in malacology, and Piaget learned about clams and snails as his volunteer assistant, publishing 21 additional articles before he attended the University of Neuchâtel. In 1915, Piaget finished college, having enjoyed his studies in logic, epistemology, and religion, though he blamed some of his readings in philosophy for ill health that required a year's recuperation in the mountains. He returned to graduate studies at the University of Neuchâtel, and though he was interested in psychology, no courses were offered, so he completed his doctorate in natural history, with a thesis on mollusks. Piaget attended Carl Jung's lectures in Zurich, but then traveled to Paris for a more experimental approach to psychology. Theodore Simon (p. 270) had retained control of Alfred Binet's (p. 270) Parisian laboratory following Binet's death and was interested in standardizing a French translation of a new reasoning test. Impressed with Piaget, Simon offered him the job, but Piaget quickly became frustrated with what seemed like endless repetition necessary for standardization and so began to interview the children, following the psychiatric tradition. In 1921, Piaget moved to Geneva to be the director of research at the Jean-Jacques Rousseau Institute, where he remained, holding a number of different positions. Using observations that began with his nephew Gérard and daughter Jacqueline, Piaget published his first five books from 1923 to 1932. During the 1920s and 1930s, Piaget's work was highly regarded in the United States, and he received an honorary doctorate from Harvard University in 1936. Piaget continued to develop and enhance his theories regarding the development of knowledge throughout his life, publishing over 60,000 pages.

THE LANGUAGE AND THOUGHT OF THE CHILD

CHAPTER 1

The Functions of Language in Two Children of Six[1]

The question which we shall attempt to answer in this book may be stated as follows: What are the needs which a child tends to satisfy when he talks? This problem is, strictly speaking, neither linguistic nor logical; it belongs to functional psychology, but it should serve nevertheless as a fitting prelude to any study of child logic.

At first sight the question may strike one as curious, for with the child, as with us, language would seem to enable the individual to communicate his thoughts to others. But the matter is not so simple. In the first place,

From Jean Piaget, "The Functions of Language in Two Children of Six. In *The Language and Thought of the Child* (3rd ed., pp. 1–49; Marjorie and Ruth Gabain, (Trans.). London: Routledge & Kegan Paul, 1959. (Original work published 1923)

the adult conveys different modes of thought by means of speech. At times, his language serves only to assert, words state objective facts, they convey information, and are closely bound up with cognition. "The weather is changing for the worse," "Bodies fall to the ground." At times, on the other hand, language expresses commands or desires, and serves to criticize or to threaten, in a word to arouse feelings and provoke action— "Let's go," "How horrible!" etc. If we knew approximately in the case of each individual the proportion of one type of speech to another, we should be in possession of psychological data of great interest. But another point arises. Is it certain that even adults always use language to communicate thoughts? To say nothing of internal speech, a large number of people, whether from the working classes or the more absent-minded of the *intelligentsia,* are in the habit of talking to themselves, of keeping up an audible soliloquy. This phenomenon points perhaps to a preparation for social language. The solitary talker invokes imaginary listeners, just as the child invokes imaginary playfellows. This is perhaps an example of that return shock of social habits which has been described by Baldwin; the individual repeats in relation to himself a form of behaviour which he originally adopted only in relation to others. In this case he would talk to himself in order to make himself work, simply because he has formed the habit of talking to others in order to work on them. Whichever explanation is adopted, it would seem that language has been side-tracked from its supposed function, for in talking to himself, the individual experiences sufficient pleasure and excitement to divert him from the desire to communicate his thoughts to other people. Finally, if the function of language were merely to "communicate," the phenomenon of verbalism would hardly admit of explanation. How could words, confined as they are by usage to certain precise meanings (precise, because their object is to be understood), eventually come to veil the confusion of thought, even to create obscurity by the multiplication of verbal entities, and actually to prevent thought from being communicable? This is not the place to raise the vexed question of the relation between thought and language, but we may note in passing that the very existence of such questions shows how complex are the functions of language, and how futile the attempt to reduce them all to one—that of communicating thought.

The functional problem therefore exists for the adult. How much more urgently will it present itself in the case of defective persons, primitive races and young children. Janet, Freud, Ferenczi, Jones, Spielrein, etc., have brought forward various theories on the language of savages, imbeciles, and young children, all of which are of the utmost significance for an investigation such as we propose to make of the child mind from the age of six.

M. Janet, for example, considers that the earliest words are derived from cries with which animals and even savages accompany their action—threats, cries of anger in the fight, etc. In the earliest forms of social activity, for instance, the cry uttered by the chief as he enters into battle becomes the signal to attack. Hence the earliest words of all, which are words of command. Thus the word, originally bound up with the act of which it is an element, at a later stage suffices alone to release the act.[2] The psycho-analysts have given an analogous explanation of word magic. The word, they say, having originally formed part of the act, is able to evoke all the concrete emotional contents of the act. Love cries, for instance, which lead up to the sexual act are obviously among the most primitive words; henceforward these and all other words alluding to the act retain a definite emotional charge. Such facts as these explain the very wide-spread tendency of primitive thought to look upon the names of persons and objects, and upon the designation of events as pregnant with the qualities of these objects and events. Hence the belief that it is possible to work upon them by the mere evocation of words, the word being no longer a mere label, but a formidable reality partaking of the nature of the named object.[3] Mme Spielrein[4] has endeavoured to find the same phenomena in an analysis of the very earliest stages of child language. She has tried to prove that the baby syllables, *mama,* uttered in so many tongues to call the mother, are formed by labial sounds which indicate nothing more than a prolongation of the act of sucking. "Mama" would therefore be a cry of desire, and then a command given to the only being capable of satisfying this desire. But on the other hand, the mere cry of "mama" has in it a soothing element; in so far as it is the continuation of the act of sucking, it produces a kind of hallucinatory satisfaction. Command and immediate satisfaction are in this case therefore almost indistinguishable, and so intermingled are these two factors that one cannot tell when the word is being used as a real command and when it is playing its almost magical role.

Meumann and Stern have shown that the earliest substantives of child language are very far from denoting concepts, but rather express commands or desires; and there are strong reasons for presuming that primitive child language fulfils far more complicated functions than would at first appear to be the case. Even when due allowance is made for these theories in all their details, the fact remains that many expressions which for us have a purely conceptual meaning, retain for many years in the child mind a significance that is not only affective but also well-nigh magical, or at least connected with peculiar modes of behaviour which should be studied for themselves and quite apart from adult mentality.

It may therefore be of interest to state the functional problem in connexion with older children, and this is what we intend to do as an introduction to the study of child logic, since logic and language are obviously interdependent. We may not find any traces of "primitive" phenomena. At any rate, we shall be very far removed from the common-sense view that the child makes use of language to communicate his thoughts.

We need not apologize for the introductory character of the questions dealt with in this work. We have simply thrown out certain feelers. We have aimed first and foremost at creating a method which could be applied to fresh observations and lead to a comparison of results. This method, which it was our only object to obtain, has already enabled us to establish certain facts. But as we have only worked on two children of six years old, and as we have taken down their talk—in its entirety, it is true—only for a month and during certain hours of the day, we advance our conclusions provisionally, pending their confirmation in the later chapters of the book.

I. The Material

The method we have adopted is as follows. Two of us followed each a child (a boy) for about a month at the morning class at the *Maison des Petits de l'Institut Rousseau,* taking down in minute detail and in its context everything that was said by the child. In the class where our two subjects were observed the scholars draw or make whatever they like; they model and play at games of arithmetic and reading, etc. These activities take place in complete freedom; no check is put upon any desire that may manifest itself to talk or play together; no intervention takes place unless it is asked for. The children work individually or in groups, as they choose; the groups are formed and then break up again without any interference on the part of the adult; the children go from one room to another (modelling room, drawing room, etc.) just as they please without being asked to do any continuous work so long as they do not themselves feel any desire for it. In short, these school-rooms supply a first-class field of observation for everything connected with the study of the social life and of the language of childhood.[5]

We must anticipate at once any objection that may be advanced on the plea that since these children were used as subjects they were not observed in natural conditions. In the first place, the children, when they are in the play-room with their friends, talk just as much as they would at home, since they are allowed to talk all day long at school, and do not feel censured or constrained in any way whatsoever. In the second place, they do not talk any more at school than they would at home, since observation shows that up to a certain age, varying between 5 and $7\frac{1}{2}$, children generally prefer to work individually rather than in groups even of two. Moreover, as we have taken down in its entirety the context of our two subjects' conversations, especially when it was addressed to an adult, it will be quite easy to eliminate from our statistics all that is not spontaneous talk on the part of the children, *i.e.,* all that may have been said in answer to questions that were put to them.

Once the material was collected, we utilized it as follows. We began by numbering all the subjects' sentences. As a rule the child speaks in short sentences interspersed with long silences or with the talk of other children. Each sentence is numbered separately. Where the talk is a little prolonged, the reader must not be afraid of reckoning several consecutive sentences to one number, so long as to each sentence containing a definite idea only one number is affixed. In such cases, which are rare enough, the division is necessarily arbitrary, but this is of no importance for statistics dealing with hundreds of sentences.

Once the talk has been portioned out into numbered sentences, we endeavour to classify these into elementary functional categories. It is this method of classification which we are now about to study.

§ 1. AN EXAMPLE OF THE TALK TAKEN DOWN. Let us first of all give one complete example of the documents collected in this way, and let us examine it in all its complexity:

23. Pie (to Ez who is drawing a tram-car with carriages in tow): *But the trams that are hooked on behind don't have any flags.* (No answer.)

24. (Talking about his tram). *They don't have any carriages hooked on . . .* (He was addressing no one in particular. No one answers him.)

25. (To Béa), *'T'sa tram that hasn't got no carriages.* (No answer.)

26. (To Hei), *This tram hasn't got no carriages, Hei, look, it isn't red, d'you see . . .* (No answer.)

27. (Lev says out loud, "A funny gentleman" from a certain distance, and without addressing him-

self to Pie or to anyone else). Pie: *A funny gentle-man!* (Goes on drawing his tram.)

28. *I'm leaving the tram white.*

29. (Ez who is drawing next to him says, "I'm doing it yellow"), *No, you mustn't do it all yellow.*

30. *I'm doing the stair-case, look.* (Béa answers, "I can't come this afternoon, I've got a Eurhythmic class.")

31. *What did you say?* (Béa repeats the same sentence.)

32. *What did you say?* (Béa does not answer. She has forgotten what she said, and gives Ro a push.)

33. (To Béa), *Leave him alone.*

34. (Mlle B. asks Ez if he would like to come with her), *Come here Ez, it isn't finished.* 34 bis. *Please teacher, Ez hasn't finished.*

35. (Without addressing himself to anyone,) *I'm doing some black stones. . . .*

36. (Id), *Pretty . . . these stones.*

37. (To Ez), *Better than you, eh?* (No answer. Ez had not heard the previous remark.)

We have chosen this example from Pie ($6\frac{1}{2}$ years) because it is taken during the most sociable activity of which this child is capable: he is drawing at the same table as his bosom friend, Ez, and is talking to him the whole time. It would therefore be natural in a case of this kind if the sole function of speech were to communicate thought. But let us examine the matter a little more closely. It will be seen that from the social point of view the significance of these sentences or fragments of sentences is extremely varied. When Pie says: *"They don't have . . .* etc." (24), or *"I'm doing . . . etc."* (35) he is not speaking to anyone. He is thinking aloud over his own drawing, just as people of the working classes mutter to themselves over their work. Here, then, is a first category which should be singled out, and which in future we shall designate as *monologue.* When Pie says to Hei or to Béa: *"'T'sa tram . . . etc."* (25) or *"This tram . . . etc."* (26) he seems on this occasion to want to make himself understood; but on closer examination it will be seen that he cares very little who is listening to him (he turns from Béa to Hei to say exactly the same thing) and, furthermore, that he does not care whether the person he addresses has really heard him or not. He believes that someone is listening to him; that is all he wants. Similarly, when Béa gives him an answer devoid of any connexion with what he has just been saying (30), it is obvious that he does not seek to understand his friend's observation nor to make his own remark any clearer. Each one sticks to his own idea and is perfectly satisfied (30–32).

The audience is there simply as a stimulus. Pie talks about himself just as he does when he soliloquizes, but with the added pleasure of feeling himself an object of interest to other people. Here then is a new category which we shall call the *collective monologue.* It is to be distinguished from the preceding category and also from those in which thoughts are actually exchanged or information given. This last case constitutes a separate category which we shall call *adapted information,* and to which we can relegate sentences 23 and 34 *b.* In this case the child talks, not at random, but to specified persons, and with the object of making them listen and understand. In addition to these practical and objective forms of information, we can distinguish others of a more subjective character consisting of commands (33), expressions of derision or criticism, or assertions of personal superiority, etc. (37). Finally, we may distinguish mere senseless repetitions, questions and answers.

Let us now establish the criteria of these various categories.

§ 2. THE FUNCTIONS OF CHILD LANGUAGE CLASSIFIED. The talk of our two subjects may be divided into two large groups—the *ego-centric* and the *socialized.* When a child utters phrases belonging to the first group, he does not bother to know to whom he is speaking nor whether he is being listened to. He talks either for himself or for the pleasure of associating anyone who happens to be there with the activity of the moment. This talk is ego-centric, partly because the child speaks only about himself, but chiefly because he does not attempt to place himself at the point of view of his hearer. Anyone who happens to be there will serve as an audience. The child asks for no more than an apparent interest, though he has the illusion (except perhaps in pure soliloquy if even then) of being heard and understood. He feels no desire to influence his hearer nor to tell him anything; not unlike a certain type of drawing-room conversation where every one talks about himself and no one listens.

Ego-centric speech may be divided into three categories:

1° *Repetition* (*echolalia*): We shall deal only with the repetition of words and syllables. The child repeats them for the pleasure of talking, with no thought of talking to anyone, nor even at times of saying words that will make sense. This is a remnant of baby prattle, obviously devoid of any social character.

2° *Monologue:* The child talks to himself as though he were thinking aloud. He does not address anyone.

3° *Dual or collective monologue:* The contradiction contained in the phrase recalls the paradox of those conversations between children which we were discussing, where an outsider is always associated with the action or thought of the moment, but is expected neither to attend nor to understand. The point of view of the other person is never taken into account; his presence serves only as a stimulus.

In *Socialized speech* we can distinguish:

4° *Adapted information:* Here the child really exchanges his thoughts with others, either by telling his hearer something that will interest him and influence his actions, or by an actual interchange of ideas by argument or even by collaboration in pursuit of a common aim.

Adapted information takes place when the child adopts the point of view of his hearer, and when the latter is not chosen at random. Collective monologues, on the other hand, take place when the child talks only about himself, regardless of his hearers' point of view, and very often without making sure whether he is being attended to or understood. We shall examine this criterion in more detail later on.

5° *Criticism:* This group includes all remarks made about the work or behaviour of others, but having the same character as adapted information; in other words, remarks specified in relation to a given audience. But these are more affective than intellectual, *i.e.,* they assert the superiority of the self and depreciate others. One might be tempted in view of this to place this group among the ego-centric categories. But "ego-centric" is to be taken in an intellectual, not in an ethical sense, and there can be no doubt that in the cases under consideration one child acts upon another in a way that may give rise to arguments, quarrels, and emulation, whereas the utterances of the collective monologue are without any effect upon the person to whom they are addressed. The shades of distinction, moreover, between adapted information and criticism are often extremely subtle and can only be established by the context.

6° *Commands, requests* and *threats:* In all of these there is definite interaction between one child and another.

7° *Questions:* Most questions asked by children among themselves call for an answer and can therefore be classed as socialized speech, with certain reservations to which we shall draw attention later on.

8° *Answers:* By these are meant answers to real questions (with interrogation mark) and to commands.

They are not to be compared to those answers given in the course of conversation (categ. 4), to remarks which are not questions but belong to "information."

These, then, are the eight fundamental categories of speech. It goes without saying that this classification, like any other, is open to the charge of artificiality. What is more important, however, is that it should stand the test of practical application, *i.e.,* that any reader who has made himself familiar with our criteria should place the same phrases more or less in the same categories. Four people have been engaged in classifying the material in hand, including that which is dealt with in the next chapter, and the results of their respective enquiries were found to coincide within 2 or 3 per cent.

Let us now return to one of these categories in order to establish the constants of our statistical results.

§ 3. REPETITION (ECHOLALIA). Everyone knows how, in the first years of his life, a child loves to repeat the words he hears, to imitate syllables and sounds, even those of which he hardly understands the meaning. It is not easy to define the function of this imitation in a single formula. From the point of view of behaviour, imitation is, according to Claparède, an ideomotor adaptation by means of which the child reproduces and then simulates the movements and ideas of those around him. But from the point of view of personality and from the social point of view, imitation would seem to be, as Janet and Baldwin maintain, a confusion between the I and the not-I, between the activity of one's own body and that of other people's bodies. At his most imitative stage, the child mimics with his whole being, identifying himself with his model. But this game, though it seems to imply an essentially social attitude, really indicates one that is essentially ego-centric. The copied movements and behaviour have nothing in them to interest the child, there is no adaptation of the I to anyone else; there is a confusion by which the child does not know that he is imitating, but plays his game as though it were his own creation. This is why children up to the age of 6 or 7, when they have had something explained to them and are asked to do it immediately afterwards, invariably imagine that they have discovered by themselves what in reality they are only repeating from a model. In such cases imitation is completely unconscious, as we have often had occasion to observe.

This mental disposition constitutes a fringe on the child's activity, which persists throughout different ages, changing in contents but always identical in function. At the ages of our two children, many of the remarks collected partake of the nature of pure repetition or echolalia. The part played by this echolalia is simply that of a game; the child enjoys repeating the words for their own sake, for the pleasure they give him, without any external adaptation and without an audience. Here are a few typical examples:

> (Mlle E. teaches My the word "celluloid") Lev, busy with his drawing at another table: "*Luloïd . . . le le loid . . .*" etc.
>
> (Before an aquarium Pie stands outside the group and takes no interest in what is being shown. Somebody says the word "triton"). Pie: "*Triton . . . triton.*" Lev (after hearing the clock strike "coucou"): "*Coucou . . . coucou.*"

These pure repetitions, rare enough at the age of Pie and Lev, have no interest for us. Their sudden appearance in the midst of ordinary conversation is more illuminating.

> Jac says to Ez: "Look, Ez, your pants are showing." Pie, who is in another part of the room immediately repeats: "*Look, my pants are showing, and my shirt, too.*"

Now there is not a word of truth in all this. It is simply the joy of repeating for its own sake that makes Pie talk in this way, *i.e.,* the pleasure of using words not for the sake of adapting oneself to the conversation, but for the sake of playing with them.

> We have seen on page 7 the example of Pie hearing Lev say: "A funny gentleman," and repeating this remark for his own amusement although he is busy drawing a tram-car (27). This shows how little repetition distracts Pie from his class-work. (Ez. says: "I want to ride on the train up there"), Pie: "*I want to ride on the train up there.*"

There is no need to multiply examples. The process is always the same. The children are occupied with drawing or playing; they all talk intermittently without listening very much to each other; but words thrown out are caught on the bounce, like balls. Sometimes they are repeated as they are, like the remarks of the present category, sometimes they set in action those dual monologues of which we shall speak later on.

The frequency of repetition is about 2% and 1% for Pie and Lev respectively. If the talk be divided into sections of 100 sentences, then in each hundred will be found repetitions in the proportion of 1%, 4%, 0%, 5%, 3%, etc.

§ 4. MONOLOGUE. Janet and the psycho-analysts have shown us how close in their opinion is the bond which originally connected word and action, words being so packed with concrete significance that the mere fact of uttering them, even without any reference to action, could be looked upon as the factor in initiating the action in question.

Now, independently of the question of origins, it is a matter of common observation that for the child words are much nearer to action and movement than for us. This leads us to two results which are of considerable importance in the study of child language in general and of the monologue in particular. 1° The child is impelled, even when he is alone, to speak as he acts, to accompany his movements with a play of shouts and words. True, there are silences, and very curious ones at that, when children work together as in the *Maison des Petits*. But, alongside of these silences, how many a soliloquy must take place when a child is alone in a room, or when children speak without addressing themselves to anyone. 2° If the child talks even when he is alone as an accompaniment to his action, he can reverse the process and use words to bring about what the action of itself is powerless to do. Hence the habit of romancing or inventing, which consists in creating reality by words and magical language, in working on things by means of words alone, apart from any contact either with them or with persons.

These two varieties belong to the same category, that of the monologue. It is worth noting that the monologue still plays an important part between the ages of 6 and 7. At this age the child soliloquizes even in the society of other children, as in the class-rooms where our work has been carried on. We have sometimes seen as many as ten children seated at separate tables or in groups of two or three, each talking to himself without taking any notice of his neighbour.

Here are a few examples of simple monologue (the first variety) where the child simply accompanies his action with sentences spoken aloud.

> Lev sits down at his table alone: "*I want to do that drawing, there . . . I want to draw something, I do. I shall need a big piece of paper to do that.*"
>
> Lev knocks over a game: "*There! everything's fallen down.*"
>
> Lev has just finished his drawing: "*Now I want to do something else.*"

Lev is a little fellow who is very much wrapped up in himself. He is always telling every one else what he is doing at the moment. In his case, therefore, monologue tends in the direction of collective monologue, where every one talks about himself without listening to the others. All the same, when he is alone he goes on announcing what he is going to do, with no other audience than himself. It is in these circumstances that we have the true monologue.

In the case of Pie, the monologue is rarer, but more true to type; the child will often talk with the sole aim of marking the rhythm of his action, without exhibiting a shade of self-satisfaction in the process. Here is one of Pie's conversations with context, where monologue is interspersed with other forms of talk:

53. Pie takes his arithmetic copy-book and turns the pages: "*1, 2 . . . 3, 4, 5, 6, 7 . . . 8 . . . 8, 8, 8, 8 and 8 . . . 9. Number 9, number 9, number 9* (singing) *I want number 9.* (This is the number he is going to represent by a drawing).

54. (Looking at Béa who is standing by the counting-frame but without speaking to him): *Now I'm going to do 9, 9, I'm doing 9, I'm doing 9.* (He draws).

55. (Mlle. L. passes by his table without saying anything). *Look, teacher, 9, 9, 9 . . . number 9.*

56. (He goes to the frame to see what colour to choose for his number so that it should correspond to the 9th row in the frame). *Pink chalk, it will have to be 9.* (He sings).

57. (To Ez as he passes): *I'm doing 9, I am—*(Ez) What are you going to do?—*Little rounds.*

58. (Accident to the pencil) *Ow, ow!*

59. *Now I've got to 9.*"

The whole of this monologue has no further aim than to accompany the action as it takes place. There are only two diversions. Pie would like to inform someone about his plans (sentences 55 and 57). But in spite of this the monologue runs on uninterrupted as though Pie were alone in the room. Speech in this case functions only as a stimulus, and in nowise as a means of communication. Pie no doubt enjoys the feeling of being in a room full of people, but if he were alone, his remarks would be substantially the same.

At the same time it is obvious that this stimulus contains a certain danger. Although in some cases it accelerates action, it also runs the risk of supplanting it. "When the distance between two points has to be traversed, a man can actually walk it with his legs, but he

can also stand still and shout: 'On, on! . . .' like an opera singer."[6] Hence the second variety of child soliloquy where speech serves not so much to accompany and accelerate action as to replace it by an illusory satisfaction. To this last group belong certain cases of word magic; but these, frequent as they are, occur only in the strictest solitude.[7] What is more usual is that the child takes so much pleasure in soliloquizing that he forgets his activity and does nothing but talk. The word then becomes a command to the external world. Here is an example of pure and of collective monologue (cf. next chapter) where the child gradually works himself up into issuing a command to physical objects and to animals:

"*Now then, it's coming* (a tortoise). *It's coming, it's coming, its coming. Get out of the way, Da, it's coming, it's coming, it's coming. . . . Come along, tortoise!*"

A little later, after having watched the aquarium, soliloquizing all the time: "*Oh, isn't it* (a salamander) *surprised at the great big giant* (a fish)," he exclaims, "*Salamander, you must eat up the fishes!*"

In short we have here the mechanism of solitary games, where, after thinking out his action aloud, the child, under the influence of verbal excitement as much as of any voluntary illusion, comes to command both animate and inanimate beings.

In conclusion, the general characteristic of monologues of this category is that the words have no social function. In such cases speech does not communicate the thoughts of the speaker, it serves to accompany, to reinforce, or to supplement his action. It may be said that this is simply a side-tracking of the original function of language, and that the child commands himself and external things just as he has learned to command and speak to others. There can be no doubt that without originally imitating others and without the desire to call his parents and to influence them, the child would probably never learn to talk; in a sense, then, the monologue is due only to a return shock of words acquired in relation to other people. It should be remembered, however, that throughout the time when he is learning to speak, the child is constantly the victim of a confusion between his own point of view and that of other people. For one thing, he does not know that he is imitating. For another, he talks as much to himself as to others, as much for the pleasure of prattling or of perpetuating some past state of being as for the sake of giving orders. It is therefore impossible to say that the monologue is either prior to or later than the more socialized forms of language; both spring from that undifferentiated state where cries and words accompany action, and then tend to prolong it; and both react one upon the other at the very outset of their development.

But as we pass from early childhood to the adult stage, we shall naturally see the gradual disappearance of the monologue, for it is a primitive and infantile function of language. It is remarkable in this connexion that in the cases of Pie and Lev this form should still constitute about 5% and 15% respectively of their total conversation. This percentage is considerable when the conditions in which the material was collected are taken into account. The difference in the percentages, however, corresponds to a marked difference in temperament, Pie being of a more practical disposition than Lev, better adapted to reality and therefore to the society of other children. When he speaks, it is therefore generally in order to make himself heard. It is true, as we saw, that when Pie does talk to himself his monologue is on the whole more genuine than Lev's, but Pie does not produce in such abundance those rather self-satisfied remarks in which a child is continually announcing his plans to himself, and which are the obvious sign of a certain imaginative exuberance.

§ 5. Collective Monologue

This form is the most social of the ego-centric varieties of child language, since to the pleasure of talking it adds that of soliloquizing before others and of interesting, or thinking to interest, them in one's own action and one's own thoughts. But as we have already pointed out, the child who acts in this manner does not succeed in making his audience listen, because, as a matter of fact, he is not really addressing himself to it. He is not speaking to anyone. He talks aloud to himself in front of others. This way of behaving reappears in certain men and women of a puerile disposition (certain hysterical subjects, if hysteria be described as the survival of infantile characteristics) who are in the habit of thinking aloud as though they were talking to themselves, but are also conscious of their audience. Suppress the slightly theatrical element in this attitude, and you have the equivalent of the collective monologue in normal children.

The examples of § 1 should now be re-read if we wish to realize how socially ineffectual is this form of language, *i.e.,* how little impression it makes upon the person spoken to. Pie makes the same remark to two different persons (25 and 26), and is in nowise astonished when he is neither listened to nor answered by either of them. Later on he asks Béa twice, "What did you say?" (31 and 32), but without listening to her. He busies himself with his own idea and his own drawing, and talks only about himself.

Here are a few more examples which show how little a child is concerned with speaking to anyone in particular, or even with making himself heard:

Mlle L. tells a group of children that owls cannot see by day. Lev: "*Well, I know quite well that it can't.*"

Lev (at a table where a group is at work): "*I've already done 'moon' so I'll have to change it.*"

Lev picks up some barley-sugar crumbs: "*I say, I've got a lovely pile of eye-glasses.*"

Lev: "*I say, I've got a gun to kill him with. I say, I am the captain on horseback. I say, I've got a horse and a gun as well.*"

The opening phrase, "I say, I" which occurs in most of these sentences is significant. Every one is supposed to be listening. This is what distinguishes this type of remark from pure monologue. But with regard to its contents it is the exact equivalent of the monologue. The child is simply thinking out his actions aloud, with no desire to give anyone any information about it.

We shall find in the next chapter examples of collective monologues no longer isolated or chosen from the talk of two children only, but taken down verbatim from all-round conversations. This particular category need not therefore occupy us any longer.

The collective monologue represents about 23% of Lev's and 30% of Pie's entire conversation. But we have seen that it is harder to distinguish the pure from the collective monologue in Lev's case than in Pie's. Taking therefore the two types of monologue together, we may say that with Lev they represent 38%, and with Pie 35% of the subject's sum of conversation.

§ 6. ADAPTED INFORMATION. The criterion of adapted information, as opposed to the pseudo-information contained in the collective monologue, is that it is successful. The child actually makes his hearer listen, and contrives to influence him, *i.e.,* to tell him something. This time the child speaks from the point of view of his audience. The function of language is no longer merely to excite the speaker to action, but actually to communicate his thoughts to other people. These criteria, however, are difficult of application, and we shall try to discover some that admit of greater precision.

It is adapted information, moreover, that gives rise to dialogue. The dialogues of children deserve to be made the object of a special and very searching investigation, for it is probably through the habit of arguing that, as

Janet and Baldwin have insisted, we first become conscious of the rules of logic and the forms of deductive reasoning. We shall therefore attempt in the next chapter to give a rough outline of the different stages of conversation as it takes place between children. In the meantime we shall content ourselves with examining adapted information (whether it takes place in dialogue or not) in relation to the main body of talk indulged in by our two subjects, and with noting how small is the part played by this form of language in comparison to the ego-centric forms and those socialized forms of speech such as commands, threats, criticisms, etc., which are not connected with mere statement of fact.

The form in which adapted information first presents itself to us, is that of simple information. Here are a few clear examples:

> Lev is helping Geo to play Lotto: *"I think that goes here."* Geo points to a duplicate card. Lev: *"If you lose one, there will still be one left."* Then: *"You've got three of the same,"* or: *"You all see what you have to do."*
>
> Mlle R. calls Ar "Roger." Pie: *"He isn't called Roger."*

Such remarks as these are clearly very different from dual monologues. The child's object is definitely to convey something to his hearer. It is from the latter's point of view that the subject speaks, and no longer from his own. Henceforward the child lays claim to be understood, and presses his claim if he does not gain his point; whereas in the collective monologue words were thrown out at random, and it little mattered where they fell.

In adapted information the child can naturally talk about himself as about any other subject of conversation. All that is needed is that his remarks should be "adapted" as in the following examples:

> Ez and Pie: "I shall have one to-morrow (a season-ticket on the tramway)—*I shall have mine this afternoon.*"
>
> Ez and Pie are building a church with bricks: *"We could do that with parallels too. I want to put the parallels on."*

We are now in a position to define more closely the distinction between the collective monologue and adapted information. The collective monologue takes place whenever the child talks about himself, except in those cases where he does so during collaboration with his hearer (as in the example just given of the church building game), and except in cases of dialogue. Dialogue, in our view, occurs when the child who has been spoken to in a proposition, answers by talking about something that was treated of in this proposition (as in the example of the tramway season-ticket), and does not start off on some cock-and-bull story as so often happens in collective monologue.[8]

In conclusion, as soon as the child informs his hearer about anything but himself, or as soon as in speaking of himself, he enters into collaboration or simply into dialogue with his hearer, there is adapted information. So long as the child talks about himself without collaborating with his audience or without evoking a dialogue, there is only collective monologue.

These definitions and the inability of collective monologue to draw others into the speakers sphere of action render it all the more remarkable that with Pie and Lev adapted information numbers only half as many remarks as collective monologue. Before establishing the exact proportion we must find out what sort of things our two subjects tell each other, and what they argue about on those rare occasions when we can talk of arguments taking place between children.

On the first point we may note the complete absence between the children of anything in the nature of explanation, if by this word we mean causal explanation, *i.e.,* an answer of the form "for such a reason" to the question "why?" All the observed cases of information which might be thought to resemble explanation are statements of fact or descriptions, and are free from any desire to explain the causes of phenomena.

Here are examples of information which simply state or describe:

> Lev and Pie: "That's 420." "It isn't 10 o'clock." "A roof doesn't look like that" (talking of a drawing). "This is a village, a great big village," etc.

Even when they talk about natural phenomena, the information they give each other never touches on causality.

> Lev: "Thunder rolls—*No, it doesn't roll*—It's water—*No it doesn't roll*—What is thunder?—*Thunder is . . .*" (He doesn't go on.)

This absence of causal explanations is remarkable, especially in the case of machines, motors, bicycles, etc., which the subjects occasionally discuss, but always from what we may call the factual point of view.

Lev: *"It's on the same rail. Funny sort of cart, a motor cart—A bicycle for two men."*

Now each of these children taken separately is able to explain the mechanism of a bicycle. Pie does so imperfectly, but Lev does so quite well. Each has a number of ideas on mechanics, but they never discuss them together. Causal relations remain unexpressed and are thought about only by the individual, probably because, to the child mind they are represented by images rather than by words. Only the underlying factual element finds expression

This peculiarity comes out very clearly when children collaborate in a game.

Here for instance are Pie and Ez occupied in drawing a house together. Pie: *"You must have a little button there for the light, a little button for the light ... Now I'm doing the 'lectric light ... There are two 'lectric lights. Look we'll have two 'lectric lights. These are all squares of 'lectric lights."*

We shall have occasion in later chapters to confirm our hypothesis that the causal "why" hardly enters into child conversation. We shall see, particularly in Chapter III, that the explanations elicited from one child by another between the ages of 6 and 8 are for the most part imperfectly understood in so far as they seem to express any sort of causal relation. Questions of causality are therefore confined to conversations between children and adults, or to those between younger and older children. Which is the same thing as saying that most of these questions are kept hidden away by the child in the fastness of his intimate and unformulated thought.

Here are those of the remarks exchanged by Lev and Pie which approach most nearly to causal explanation. It will be seen that they are almost entirely descriptive:

Lev: *"We ought to have a little water. This green paint is so very hard, most awfully hard"* ... *"In cardboard, don't you know? You don't know how to, but it is rather difficult for you, it is for every one."*

Childish arguments, it is curious to note, present exactly the same features. Just as our two subjects never communicate their thoughts on the why and wherefore of phenomena, so in arguing they never support their statements with the "because" and "since" of logic. For them, with two exceptions only, arguing consists simply in a clash of affirmations, without any attempt at logical justification. It belongs to the type which we shall denote as "primitive argument" in our essay in the following chapter on the different stages of child conversation, and which we shall characterize by just this lack of motivation.

The example given on page 376 (the argument between Lev and a child of the same age about thunder) proves this very clearly. Here are three more examples, the first two quite definite, the third of a more intermediate character.

Ez to Pie: *"You're going to marry me—Pie: No, I won't marry you—Oh yes you'll marry me—No—Yes . . . etc."*

"Look how lovely my 6 is going to be—Lev: Yes it's a 6 but really and truly it's a 9—No, it's a 6, Nought—You said nought, and it's not true, it's a 9. Really it is—No—Yes—It was done like that already—Oh no, that's a lie. You silly."

Lev looks to see what Hei is doing: *"Two moons—No, two suns.—Suns aren't like that, with a mouth. They're like this, suns up there—They're round—Yes they're quite round, but they haven't got eyes and a mouth.—Yes they have, they can see—No they can't. It's only God who can see."*

In the first two examples the argument is simply a clash of contrary affirmations, without mutual concessions and without motivation. The last is more complex. When Lev says *"It's only God who can see ..."* or *"They are like this,"* he does seem at the first glance to be justifying his remarks, to be doing something more than merely stating facts. But there is no explicit justification, no attempt to demonstrate. Hei asserts and Lev denies. Hei makes no effort to give any reasons for believing that the sun has eyes, he does not say that he has seen pictures which have led him to such an idea, etc. Lev for his part does not attempt to get at Hei's point of view, and gives no explicit reason for defending his own. In the main then there is still only a clash of assertions, different enough from the two following little arguments, one of which, by the way, takes place between a child and an adult.

These indeed are the only examples we have found where the child tries to prove his assertions. They should be carefully examined, considering how seldom the fact occurs before the age of 7 or 8.

Lev talking to Mlle G.: *"You've been eating paint—No, I haven't, which?—White paint—No—Oh, yes you have 'cos there's some on your mouth."*

The reader will note the correct use made of "because" at the age of $6\frac{1}{2}$. In the three lists of complete vocabularies given by Mlle Descœudres[9] "because" is used by the seven-year-old but not by the five-year-old child.

Here is another instance, again of Lev: *"That is 420—But it's not the number of the house—Why not?—The number of the house is on the door."*

Note here the use of "why" in the sense of "for what reason" (*cf.* Chapter V). The reader will see how superior these two arguments are to the preceding examples.

We can draw the following conclusions from these various facts:

1° Adapted information, together with most of the questions and answers which we shall examine later, constitute the only categories of child language whose function, in contrast to the divers functions of the egocentric categories, is to communicate intellectual processes.

2° The frequency of adapted information is only 13% for Lev and 14% for Pie, a remarkable fact, and one which shows how little the intellectual enquiry of a child can be said to be social. These figures are all the more striking when we remember that collective monologue constitutes respectively 23% and 30% of the sum of the remarks made by the same subjects.

3° These informations conveyed from one child to another are factual in the sense that they do not point to any causal relations, even when they deal with the material used by the children in their work and with the numerous objects, natural or artificial, which they like to draw or build (animals, stars, motor-cars, bicycles, etc.).

4° The arguments between the two children are, with two exceptions only, of a low type, inasmuch as they consist merely of a clash of contrary assertions without any explicit demonstration.

§ 7. CRITICISM AND DERISION. If we set aside questions and answers, the socialized language of the child in its non-intellectual aspect may be divided into two easily distinguishable categories: on the one hand commands, on the other criticism and derision. There is nothing peculiar about these categories in children; only their percentage is interesting.

Here are a few examples of criticisms, taunts, *Schadenfreude,* etc., which at the first glance one might be tempted to place under information and dialogue, but which it will perhaps be found useful to class apart. Their function is not to convey thoughts, but to satisfy non-intellectual instincts such as pugnacity, pride, emulation, etc.:

Lev: *"You're not putting it in the middle"* (a plate on the table). *"That's not fair." "Pooh! that's no good." "We made that house, it isn't theirs." "That's not like an owl. Look, Pie, what he's done." "Well, I know that he can't." "It's much prettier than ours." "I've got a much bigger pencil than you." "Well, I'm the strongest all the same,"* etc.

All these remarks have this in common with adapted information that they are addressed to a specified person whom they influence, rouse to emulation and provoke to retort and even to quarrelling. This is what obliges us to class as socialized language such remarks as those towards the end, beginning: "Well, I," which in other respects resemble collective monologue. What, on the other hand, distinguishes these phrases from information proper, is that with the child even apparently objective criticisms contain judgments of value which retain a strongly subjective flavour. They are not mere statements of fact. They contain elements of derision, of combativeness, and of the desire to assert personal superiority. They therefore justify the creation of a separate category.

The percentage of this group is low: 3% for Lev, and 7% for Pie. This may be a question of individual types, and if this category is too weakly represented in subsequent research, we may have to assimilate it to one of the preceding ones.

§ 8. COMMANDS, REQUESTS, THREATS. Why is the ratio of adapted information so low in comparison to that of the ego-centric forms of speech, particularly in comparison to collective monologue? The reason is quite simple. The child does not in the first instance communicate with his fellow-beings in order to share thoughts and reflexions; he does so in order to play. The result is that the part played by intellectual interchange is reduced to the strictly necessary minimum. The rest of language will only assist action, and will consist of commands, etc.

Commands and threats, then, like criticisms, deserve a category to themselves. They are, moreover, very easy to recognize:

Lev (outside a shop): *"Mustn't come in here without paying. I shall tell Gé"* (if you come). *"Come here Mr Passport." "Give me the blue one." "You must make a flag." "Come along, Ro. Look . . . you shall be the cart,"* etc.

Pie: *"Ez, come and see the salamander." "Get out of the way, I shan't be able to see,"* etc. (About a roof): *"No, take it away, take it away 'cos I want to put on mine,"* etc.

We need not labour the point. The only distinction calling for delicate discrimination is that between requests which tend imperceptibly to become commands, and questions which contain an implicit request. All requests which are not expressed in interrogative form we shall agree to call 'entreaties,' and shall include in the present category; while for interrogative requests a place will be reserved in our next category. Here are some examples of entreaty:

Lev: *"The yellow paint, please." "I should like some water,"* etc.

Pie: *"The india-rubber, teacher, I want the india-rubber."*

Under requests, on the other hand, we shall classify such sentences as: "Ez, do you mind helping me?" "May I look at it?" etc. This distinction is certainly artificial. But between an interrogative request and a question bearing on immediate action there are many intermediate types. And since it is desirable to distinguish between questions and commands, we must not be afraid of facing the artificiality of our classification. So long as we are agreed upon the conventions adopted, and do not take the statistics too literally, the rest need not detain us. It is not, moreover, the ratio of commands to orders that will be of most use to us, but the ratio of the bulk of socialized language to the bulk of ego-centric language. It is easy enough to agree upon these fundamental distinctions.

The percentage of the present category is 10% for Lev and 15% for Pie. Dialogue and information were for the same subjects respectively, 12% and 14%.

§ 9. QUESTIONS AND ANSWERS. A preliminary difficulty presents itself in connexion with these two categories which we propose to treat of together: do they both belong to socialized language? As far as answers are concerned, we need be in no doubt. Indeed, we shall describe as an 'answer' the adapted words used by the person spoken to, after he has heard and understood a question. For instance:

"What colour is that?—(Lev) *Brownish yellow."*
"What are you doing, Lev?—*The boat,"* etc.

To answers we shall assimilate refusals and acceptances, which are answers given not to questions of fact but to commands and requests:

"Will you give it back to me? (the ticket).—*No, I don't need it. I'm in the boat"* (Lev).

These two groups, which together constitute answers, obviously belong to socialized language. If we place them in a separate category instead of assimilating them to adapted information, it is chiefly because answers do not belong to the spontaneous speech of the child. It would be sufficient for his neighbours to interrupt him and for adults to question him all the time, to raise a child's socialized language to a much higher percentage. We shall therefore eliminate answers from our calculations in the following paragraph. All remarks provoked by adults will thus be done away with. Answers, moreover, constitute only 18% of Lev's language and 14% of Pie's.

The psychological contents of answers are highly interesting, and would alone suffice to render the category distinct from information. It is of course closely connected to the contents of the question, and we shall therefore deal simultaneously with the two problems.

And the questions which children ask one another—do they too belong to socialized language? Curiously enough the point is one that can be raised, for many remarks are made by children in an interrogative form without being in any way questions addressed to anyone. The proof of this is that the child does not listen to the answer, and does not even expect it. He supplies it himself. This happens frequently between the ages of 3 and 5. At the age of our two subjects it is rarer. When such pseudo-questions do occur, we have classed them as monologue or information (*e.g. "Please teacher is half right? Yes, look"* Lev). For the present we shall therefore deal only with questions proper.

Questions make up 17% of Lev's language and 13% of Pie's. Their importance is therefore equal and even superior to that of information, and since a question is a spontaneous search for information, we shall now be able to check the accuracy of our assertions concerning this last category. Two of its characteristics were particularly striking: the absence of intellectual intercourse among the children on the subject of causality, and the absence of proof and logical justification in their discussions. If we jump to the conclusion that children keep such thoughts to themselves and do not socialize them, we may be met with the counter assertion that children simply do not have such thoughts, in which case there would be no question of their socializing them! This is partly the case as regards logical demonstration. With regard to causal explanation, however—and by this we mean not only the appeal to mechanical causality such as is made only after the ages of 7 or 8, but also the appeal to final, or as we shall call it, to pre-causality, *i.e.*, that which is invoked in the child's "whys" between the ages of 3 and 7 to 8—as regards this type of explanation, then, there are two things to be noted. In the first place, the children of the *Maison des Petits* deal in their drawings and free compositions with animals, physical objects (stars, sky, rain, etc.), with machines and manufactured objects (trains, motors, boats, houses, bicycles, etc.). These might therefore give rise to questions of origin and causality. In the second place, "whys" play an important part in all questions asked of grown-ups by children under 7 (out of three groups of 250 spontaneous questions we noted respectively 91, 53 and 41 "whys"). Now among these "whys" a large number are "whys of explanation," meaning "for what reason" or "for what object." Explanation supplies about 18% of the subject-matter dealt with in the questions of the child of 6 or 7, such as we shall study it in Chapter V. If, therefore, there are few questions of explanation in the talk of our two present subjects, this is strongly in favour of the interpretation we have given of information and dialogue between children in general. Intellectual intercourse between children is still factual or descriptive, *i.e.*, little concerned with causality, which remains the subject of conversation between children and adults or of the child's own solitary reflexion.

The facts seem to bear this out. Only 3 out of Pie's 173 questions are "whys." Out of Lev's 224 questions only 10 are "whys." Of these, only two "whys" of Lev's are "whys of explanation."[10]

"*Why has he turned round?*" (a stuffed owl which Lev believes to be alive), and "*Why has he turned round a little?*" (the same).

The rest are "whys" not of causal but of psychological explanation, "intentions" as we shall call them,[11] which is quite another matter:

"*Why did he say: 'Hullo Lev'?*" "*Why was Rey crying?*" "*Why has he gone away?*" etc.

In addition to these we have one "logical why" from Lev, that which we dealt with in connexion with the discussion on page 378. It is clear how rarely children ask each other "why?," and how little such questions have to do with causality.

Thus out of the 224 questions asked by Lev and the 173 asked by Pie only two are about explanation, and those two both come from Lev. All the rest can be divided as follows. First of all, we have 141 questions of Lev's and 78 of Pie's about children's activities as such, about "actions and intentions":[12]

Lev: "*And my scissors, can you see them?*" "*Are we going to play at Indians?*" "*I'm working, are you?*" "*I didn't hurt you, did I?*" "*Do you know that gentleman?*" "*How shall I paint the house?*" "*How does this go?*" (a ball in the counting-frame).
   Pie: "*Are you coming this afternoon, Béa?*" "*I say, have you finished yet?*" etc.

This enormous numerical difference between the questions bearing upon children's activity as such, and those dealing with causal explanation is very remarkable. It proves how individualistic the child of 6 still shows himself to be in his intellectual activity, and how restricted in consequence is the interchange of ideas that takes place between children.

A second category of questions, made up of 27 of Lev's and 41 of Pie's, deals with facts and events, time and place (questions of "reality" treated of in Chapter V).

Facts: "*Is your drum closed?*" "*Is there some paper, too?*" "*Are there snails in there?*" (Pie.)
   Place: "*Where is the blue, Ez?*" "*Where is she?*" (the tortoise).
   Time: "*Please teacher, is it late?*" "*How old are you?*" (Pie.)

It will be seen that these questions do not touch upon causality, but are all about matters of fact. Questions of place predominate in this category, 29 for Pie and 13 for Lev.

Another numerous category (51 for Pie, 48 for Lev) is made up of questions purely concerning matters of fact, questions of nomenclature, classification and evaluation.

Nomenclature: *"What does 'behind' mean?" "What is he called?"* (a cook) (Lev).

Classification: *"What ever is that?" "Is that yellow?"* (Lev).

Evaluation: *"Is it pretty?"* (Lev, Pie).

We may add a few questions about number (5 by Lev, 1 by Pie):

"Isn't all that enough for 2fr.50?" "And how much for 11?" (Lev).

Finally, mention should be made of two questions by Pie and one by Lev about rules (writing, etc.).

"You put it on this side, don't you?" (the figure 3) (Lev).

The following table completely summarizes the questions asked by Lev and Pie, including their "whys."

	LEV		**PIE**	
Questions of causal explanation	2		0	
	—	2	—	0
Questions of Reality { Facts and events	7		8	
Time	7		4	
Place	13		29	
	—	27	—	41
Actions and intentions	. . .	141	. . .	78
Rules	. . .	1	. . .	2
Questions of Classification { Nomenclature	7		0	
Classification and evaluation	41		51	
	—	48	—	51
Number	. . .	5	. . .	7
TOTAL		224		173

We shall not dwell upon the criteria of the different categories nor upon their functional interest; these problems form the subject-matter of a later chapter on "A child's questions" (Chapter V). It will be enough if we conclude from this table that questions from one child to another (questions from children to adults play only a negligible part in this group), bear first and foremost upon actual psychological activity (actions and intentions). Otherwise, when they concern objects and not persons, they bear upon the factual aspect of reality, and not upon causal relations. These conclusions are markedly different from the results supplied by Del (Chapter V: Questions of a child to an adult). Before

drawing any conclusions, however, from the difference between questions from child to child and questions from child to adult, we should have to solve a big preliminary problem: how far do the questions which Lev and Pie ask adults out of school hours resemble those of Del (whys of explanation, etc.)? At the first glance, Del, although he has worked like the others during school hours, seems to approximate much more closely to what we know of the ordinary questioning child of 6. But Lev and Pie are perhaps special types, more prone to statement and less to explanation. All we can do, therefore, is to extend the work of research as carried out in this chapter and in Chapter V.

II.   Conclusions

Having defined, so far as was possible the various categories of the language used by our two children, it now remains for us to see whether it is not possible to establish certain numerical constants from the material before us. We wish to emphasize at the very outset the artificial character of such abstractions. The number of unclassifiable remarks, indeed, weighs heavily in the statistics. In any case, a perusal of the list of Lev's first 50 remarks, which we shall give as an example for those who wish to make use of our method, should give a fair idea of the degree of objectivity belonging to our classification.[13] But these difficulties are immaterial. If among our results some are definitely more constant than others, then we shall feel justified in attributing to these a certain objective value.

§ 10. THE MEASURE OF EGO-CENTRISM. Among the data we have obtained there is one, incidentally of the greatest interest for the study of child logic, which seems to supply the necessary guarantee of objectivity: we mean the proportion of ego-centric language to the sum of the child's spontaneous conversation. Ego-centric language is, as we have seen, the group made up by the first three of the categories we have enumerated—*repetition, monologue* and *collective monologue*. All three have this in common that they consist of remarks that are not addressed to anyone, or not to anyone in particular, and that they evoke no reaction adapted to them on the part of anyone to whom they may chance to be addressed. Spontaneous language is therefore made up of the first seven categories, *i.e.,* of all except *answers*. It is therefore the sum total of all remarks, *minus* those which are made as an answer to a question asked by an adult or a child. We have eliminated this heading as being subject to chance circumstances; it is sufficient for a child to have come in contact with many adults or with some talkative companion, to undergo a marked change in the percentage of his answers. Answers given, not to definite questions (with interrogation mark) or commands, but in the course of the dialogue, *i.e.,* propositions answering to other propositions, have naturally been classed under the heading *information and dialogue,* so that there is nothing artificial about the omission of questions from the statistics which we shall give. The child's language *minus* his answers constitutes a complete whole in which intelligence is represented at every stage of its development.

The proportion of ego-centric to other spontaneous forms of language is represented by the following fractions:

$$\frac{Eg.\ L}{Sp.\ L} = 0.47 \text{ for Lev}, \quad \frac{Eg.\ L}{Sp.\ L} = 0.43 \text{ for Pie}.$$

(The proportion of ego-centric language to the sum total of the subject's speech, including answers, is 39% for Lev and 37% for Pie.) The similarity of result for Lev and Pie is a propitious sign, especially as what difference there is corresponds to a marked difference of temperament. (Lev is certainly more ego-centric than Pie.) But the value of the result is vouched for in yet another way.

If we divide the 1400 remarks made by Lev during the month in which his talk was being studied into sections of 100 sentences, and seek to establish for each section the ratio *Eg. L./Sp. L.,* the fraction will be found to vary only from 0.40 to 0.57, which indicates only a small maximum deviation. On the contrary, the *mean variation, i.e.,* the average of the deviations between each value and the arithmetical average of these values, is only 0.04, which is really very little.

If Pie's 1500 remarks are submitted to the same treatment, the proportions will be found to vary between 0.31 and 0.59, with an average variation of 0.06. This greater variability is just what we should expect from what we know of Pie's character, which at first sight seems more practical, better adapted than Lev's, more inclined to collaboration (particularly with his bosom friend Ez). But Pie every now and then indulges in fantasies which isolate him for several hours, and during which he soliloquizes without ceasing.

We shall see in the next chapter, moreover, that these two coefficients do actually represent the average for children between the ages of 7 and 8. The same calculation based on some 1500 remarks in quite another class room yielded the result of 0.45 (a. v. = 0.05).

This constancy in the proportion of ego-centric language is the more remarkable in view of the fact that we have found nothing of the kind in connexion with the other coefficients which we have sought to establish. We have, it is true, determined the proportion of socialized factual language (*information* and *questions*) to socialized non-factual language (*criticism, commands,* and *requests*). But this proportion fluctuates from 0.72 to 2.23 with a mean variation 0.71 for Lev (as compared with 0.04 and 0.06 as the coefficients of ego-centrism), and between 0.43 and 2.33 with a mean variation of 0.42 for Pie. Similarly, the relation of ego-centric to socialized factual language yields no coefficient of any constancy.

Of all this calculation let us bear only this in mind, that our two subjects of $6\frac{1}{2}$ have each an ego-centric language which amounts to nearly half of their total spontaneous speech.

The following table summarizes the functions of the language used by both these children:

		Pie	Lev
1	Repetition	2	1
2	Monologue	5	15
3	Collective Monologue	30	23
4	Adapted Information	14	13
5	Criticism	7	3
6	Commands	15	10
7	Requests	13	17
8	Answers	14	18
	Ego-centric Language	37	39
	Spontaneous Socialized language	49	43
	Sum of Socialized language	63	61
	Coefficient of Ego-centrism	0.43 ∓ 0.06	0.47 ∓ 0.04

We must once more emphasize the fact that in all these calculations the number of remarks made by children to adults is negligible. By omitting them we raise the coefficient of ego-centrism to about 0.02, which is within the allowed limits of deviation. In future, however, we shall have completely to eliminate such remarks from our calculations, even if it means making a separate class for them. We shall, moreover, observe this rule in the next chapter where the coefficient of ego-centrism has been calculated solely on the basis of remarks made between children.

§ II. CONCLUSION. What are the conclusions we can draw from these facts? It would seem that up to a certain age we may safely admit that children think and act more ego-centrically than adults, that they share each other's intellectual life less than we do. True, when they are together they seem to talk to each other a great deal more than we do about what they are doing, but for the most part they are only talking to themselves. We, on the contrary, keep silent far longer about our action, but our talk is almost always socialized.

Such assertions may seem paradoxical. In observing children between the ages of 4 and 7 at work together in the classes of the *Maison des Petits,* one is certainly struck by silences, which are, we repeat, in no way imposed nor even suggested by the adults. One would expect, not indeed the formation of working groups, since children are slow to awake to social life, but a hubbub caused by all the children talking at once. This is not what happens. All the same, it is obvious that a child between the ages of 4 and 7, placed in the conditions of spontaneous work provided by the educational games of the *Maison des Petits,* breaks silence far oftener than does the adult at work, and seems at first sight to be continuously communicating his thoughts to those around him.

Ego-centrism must not be confused with secrecy. Reflexion in the child does not admit of privacy. Apart from thinking by images or autistic symbols which cannot be directly communicated, the child up to an age, as yet undetermined but probably somewhere about seven, is incapable of keeping to himself the thoughts which enter his mind. He says everything. He has no verbal continence. Does this mean that he socializes his thought more than we do? That is the whole question, and it is for us to see to whom the child really speaks. It may be to others. We think on the contrary that, as the preceding study shows, it is first and foremost to himself, and that speech, before it can be used to socialize thought, serves to accompany and reinforce individual activity. Let us try to examine more closely the difference between thought which is socialized but capable of secrecy, and infantile thought which is ego-centric but incapable of secrecy.

The adult, even in his most personal and private occupation, even when he is engaged on an enquiry which is incomprehensible to his fellow-beings, thinks socially, has continually in his mind's eye his collaborators or opponents, actual or eventual, at any rate members of his own profession to whom sooner or later he will announce the result of his labours. This mental picture pursues him throughout his task. The task itself is henceforth socialized at almost every stage of its development. Invention eludes this process, but the need for checking and demonstrating calls into being an inner speech addressed throughout to a hypothetical opponent, whom the imagination often pictures as one of flesh and blood. When, therefore, the adult is brought

face to face with his fellow-beings, what he announces to them is something already socially elaborated and therefore roughly adapted to his audience, *i.e.,* it is comprehensible. Indeed, the further a man has advanced in his own line of thought, the better able is he to see things from the point of view of others and to make himself understood by them.

The child, on the other hand, placed in the conditions which we have described, seems to talk far more than the adult. Almost everything he does is to the tune of remarks such as "I'm drawing a hat," "I'm doing it better than you," etc. Child thought, therefore, seems more social, less capable of sustained and solitary research. This is so only in appearance. The child has less verbal continence simply because he does not know what it is to keep a thing to himself. Although he talks almost incessantly to his neighbours, he rarely places himself at their point of view. He speaks to them for the most part as if he were alone, and as if he were thinking aloud. He speaks, therefore, in a language which disregards the precise shade of meaning in things and ignores the particular angle from which they are viewed, and which above all is always making assertions, even in argument, instead of justifying them. Nothing could be harder to understand than the note-books which we have filled with the conversation of Pie and Lev. Without full commentaries, taken down at the same time as the children's remarks, they would be incomprehensible. Everything is indicated by allusion, by pronouns and demonstrative articles—"he, she, the, mine, him, etc."—which can mean anything in turn, regardless of the demands of clarity or even of intelligibility. (The examination of this style must not detain us now; it will appear again in Chapter III in connexion with verbal explanation between one child and another.) In a word, the child hardly ever even asks himself whether he has been understood. For him, that goes without saying, for he does not think about others when he talks. He utters a "collective monologue." His language only begins to resemble that of adults when he is directly interested in making himself understood; when he gives orders or asks questions. To put it quite simply, we may say that the adult thinks socially, even when he is alone, and that the child under 7 thinks ego-centrically, even in the society of others.

What is the reason for this? It is, in our opinion, twofold. It is due, in the first place, to the absence of any sustained social intercourse between the children of less than 7 or 8, and in the second place to the fact that the language used in the fundamental activity of the child—play—is one of gestures, movement and mimicry as much as of words. There is, as we have said, no real social life between children of less than 7 or 8 years. The type of children's society represented in a class-room of the *Maison des Petits* is obviously of a fragmentary character, in which consequently there is neither division of work, centralization of effort, nor unity of conversation. We may go further, and say that it is a society in which, strictly speaking, individual and social life are not differentiated. An adult is at once far more highly individualized and far more highly socialized than a child forming part of such a society. He is more individualized, since he can work in private without perpetually announcing what he is doing, and without imitating his neighbours. He is more socialized for the reasons which have just given. The child is neither individualized, since he cannot keep a single thought secret, and since everything done by one member of the group is repeated through a sort of imitative repercussion by almost every other member, nor is he socialized, since this imitation is not accompanied by what may properly be called an interchange of thought, about half the remarks made by children being ego-centric in character. If, as Baldwin and Janet maintain, imitation is accompanied by a sort of confusion between one's own action and that of others, then we may find in this fragmentary type of society based on imitation some sort of explanation of the paradoxical character of the conversation of children who, while they are continually announcing their doings, yet talk only for themselves, without listening to anyone else.

Social life at the *Maison des Petits* passes, according to the observations of Mlles Audemars and Lafendel, through three stages. Up till the age of about 5, the child almost always works alone. From 5 to about $7\frac{1}{2}$, little groups of two are formed, like that of Pie and Ez (*cf.* the remarks taken down under the heading "adapted information.") These groups are transitory and irregular. Finally, between 7 and 8 the desire manifests itself to work with others. Now it is in our opinion just at this age that ego-centric talk loses some of its importance, and it is at this age, as we shall see in the next chapter, that we shall place the higher stages of conversation properly so-called as it takes place between children. It is also at this age, (*cf.* Chapter III) that children begin to understand each other in spoken explanations, as opposed to explanations in which gestures play as important a part as words.

A simple way of verifying these hypotheses is to re-examine children between 7 and 8 whose ego-centrism at an earlier stage has been ascertained. This is the task which Mlle. Berguer undertook with Lev. She took down under the same conditions as previously some 600

remarks made by Lev at the age of 7 and a few months. The co-efficient of ego-centricism was reduced to 0.27.[14]

These stages of social development naturally concern only the child's intellectual activity (drawings, constructive games, arithmetic, etc.). It goes without saying that in outdoor games the problem is a completely different one; but these games touch only on a tiny portion of the thought and language of the child.

If language in the child of about $6\frac{1}{2}$ is still so far from being socialized, and if the part played in it by the ego-centric forms is so considerable in comparison to information and dialogue etc., the reason for this lies in the fact that childish language includes two distinct varieties, one made up of gestures, movements, mimicry etc., which accompany or even completely supplant the use of words, and the other consisting solely of the spoken word. Now, gesture cannot express everything. Intellectual processes, therefore, will remain ego-centric, whereas commands etc., all the language that is bound up with action, with handicraft, and especially with play, will tend to become more socialized. We shall come across this essential distinction again in Chapter III. It will then be seen that verbal understanding between children is less adequate than between adults, but this does not mean that in their games and in their manual occupations they do not understand each other fairly well; this understanding, however, is not yet altogether verbal.

§ 12. RESULTS AND HYPOTHESES. Psycho-analysts have been led to distinguish two fundamentally different modes of thinking: *directed* or *intelligent thought,* and *undirected* or, as Bleuler proposes to call it, *autistic thought.* Directed thought is conscious, *i.e.,* it pursues an aim which is present to the mind of the thinker; it is intelligent, which means that it is adapted to reality and tries to influence it; it admits of being true or false (empirically or logically true), and it can be communicated by language. Autistic thought is subconscious, which means that the aims it pursues and the problems it tries to solve are not present in consciousness; it is not adapted to reality, but creates for itself a dream world of imagination; it tends, not to establish truths, but so to satisfy desires, and it remains strictly individual and incommunicable as such by means of language. On the contrary, it works chiefly by images, and in order to express itself, has recourse to indirect methods, evoking by means of symbols and myths the feeling by which it is led.

Here, then, are two fundamental modes of thought

which, though separated neither at their origin nor in the course of their functioning are subject, nevertheless, to two diverging sets of logical laws.[15] Directed thought, as it develops, is controlled more and more by the laws of experience and of logic in the stricter sense. Autistic thought, on the other hand, obeys a whole system of special laws (laws of symbolism and of immediate satisfaction) which we need not elaborate here. Let us consider, for instance, the completely different lines of thought pursued from the point of view of intelligence and from that of autism when we think of such an object as, say, water.

To intelligence, water is a natural substance whose origin we know, or whose formation we can at least empirically observe; its behaviour and motions are subject to certain laws which can be studied, and it has from the dawn of history been the object of technical experiment (for purposes of irrigation, etc.). To the autistic attitude, on the other hand, water is interesting only in connexion with the satisfaction of organic wants. It can be drunk. But as such, as well as simply in virtue of its external appearance, it has come to represent in folk and child fantasies, and in those of adult subconsciousness, themes of a purely organic character. It has in fact been identified with the liquid substances which issue from the human body, and has come, in this way, to symbolize birth itself, as is proved by so many myths (birth of Aphrodite, etc.), rites (baptism the symbol of a new birth), dreams[16] and stories told by children.[17] Thus in the one case thought adapts itself to water as part of the external world, in the other, thought uses the idea of water not in order to adapt itself to it, but in order to assimilate it to those more or less conscious images connected with fecundation and the idea of birth.

Now these two forms of thought, whose characteristics diverge so profoundly, differ chiefly as to their origin, the one being socialized and guided by the increasing adaptation of individuals one to another, whereas the other remains individual and uncommunicated. Furthermore—and this is of the very first importance for the understanding of child thought—this divergence is due in large part to the following fact. Intelligence, just because it undergoes a gradual process of socialization, is enabled through the bond established by language between thoughts and words to make an increasing use of concepts; whereas autism, just because it remains individual, is still tied to imagery, to organic activity, and even to organic movements. The mere fact, then, of telling one's thought, of telling it to others, or of keeping silence and telling it only to oneself must be of enormous importance to the fundamental structure and func-

tioning of thought in general, and of child logic in particular. Now between autism and intelligence there are many degrees, varying with their capacity for being communicated. These intermediate varieties must therefore be subject to a special logic, intermediate too between the logic of autism and that of intelligence. The chief of those intermediate forms, *i.e.,* the type of thought which like that exhibited by our children seeks to adapt itself to reality, but does not communicate itself as such, we propose to call *Ego-centric thought.* This gives us the following table:

	Non-communicable thought	**Communicable thought**
Undirected thought	*Autistic thought*	(*Mythological thought*)
Directed thought	*Ego-centric thought*	*Communicated intelligence*

We shall quickly realize the full importance of ego-centrism if we consider a certain familiar experience of daily life. We are looking, say, for the solution of some problem, when suddenly everything seems quite clear; we have understood, and we experience that *sui generis* feeling of intellectual satisfaction. But as soon as we try to explain to others what it is we have understood, difficulties come thick and fast. These difficulties do not arise merely because of the effort of attention needed to hold in a single grasp the links in the chain of argument; they are attributable also to our judging faculty itself. Conclusions which we deemed positive no longer seem so; between certain propositions whole series of intermediate links are now seen to be lacking in order to fill the gaps of which we were previously not even conscious; arguments which seemed convincing because they were connected with some schema of visual imagery or based on some sort of analogy, lose all their potency from the moment we feel the need to appeal to these schemas, and find that they are incommunicable; doubt is cast on propositions connected with judgments of value, as soon as we realize the personal nature of such judgments. If such, then, is the difference between personal understanding and spoken explanation, how much more marked will be the characteristics of personal understanding when the individual has for a long time been bottling up his own thoughts, when he has not even formed the habit of thinking in terms of other people, and of communicating his thoughts to them. We need only recall the inextricable chaos of adolescent thought to realize the truth of this distinction.

Ego-centric thought and intelligence therefore represent two different forms of reasoning, and we may even say, without paradox, two different logics. By logic is meant here the sum of the habits which the mind adopts in the general conduct of its operations—in the general conduct of a game of chess, in contrast, as Poincaré says, to the special rules which govern each separate proposition, each particular move in the game. Ego-centric logic and communicable logic will therefore differ less in their conclusions (except with the child where ego-centric logic often functions) than in the way they work. The points of divergence are as follows:

1° Ego-centric logic is more intuitive, more "syncretistic" than deductive, *i.e.,* its reasoning is not made explicit. The mind leaps from premise to conclusion at a single bound, without stopping on the way. 2° Little value is attached to proving, or even checking propositions. The vision of the whole brings about a state of belief and a feeling of security far more rapidly than if each step in the argument were made explicit. 3° Personal schemas of analogy are made use of, likewise memories of earlier reasoning, which control the present course of reasoning without openly manifesting their influence. 4° Visual schemas also play an important part, and can even take the place of proof in supporting the deduction that is made. 5° Finally, judgments of value have far more influence on ego centric than on communicable thought.

In communicated intelligence, on the other hand, we find 1° far more deduction, more of an attempt to render explicit the relations between propositions by such expressions as *therefore, if . . . then,* etc. 2° Greater emphasis is laid on proof. Indeed, the whole exposition is framed in view of the proof, *i.e.,* in view of the necessity of convincing someone else, and (as a corollary) of convincing oneself whenever one's personal certainty may have been shaken by the process of deductive reasoning. 3° Schemas of analogy tend to be eliminated, and to be replaced by deduction proper. 4° Visual schemas are also done away with, first as incommunicable, and later as useless for purposes of demonstration. 5° Finally personal judgments of value are eliminated in favour of collective judgments of value, these being more in keeping with ordinary reason.

If then the difference between thought that can be communicated and what remains of ego-centric thought in the adult or the adolescent is such as we have described it, how much more emphasis shall we be justified in laying on the ego-centric nature of thought in the child. It is chiefly in connexion with children between 3 to 7 and, to a lesser degree, with those between 7 to 11

that we have endeavoured to distinguish ego-centric thought. In the child between 3 and 7 the five characteristics which have just been enumerated actually go to make up a kind of special logic which we shall have occasion to mention throughout this volume and the next. Between 7 and 11 this ego-centric logic no longer influences what Binet and Simon call the "perceptual intelligence" of the child, but it is found in its entirety in his "verbal intelligence." In the following chapters we shall study a large number of phenomena due to ego-centrism, which, after having influenced the perceptual intelligence of children between the ages of 3 and 7, influence their verbal intelligence between the ages of 7 and 11. We are now therefore in a position to realize that the fact of being or of not being communicable is not an attribute which can be added to thought from the outside, but is a constitutive feature of profound significance for the shape and structure which reasoning may assume.

The question of communicability has thus proved itself to be one of those preliminary problems which must be solved as an introduction to the study of child logic. There are other such problems, all of which can be classed under two main headings.

A. *Communicability:* (1) To what extent do children of the same age think by themselves, and to what extent do they communicate with each other? (2) Same question as between older and younger children, (a) of the same family; (b) of different families. (3) Same question as between children and parents.

B. *Understanding:* (1) To what extent do children of the same age understand each other? (2) Same question as between older and younger children (of the same and of different families). (3) Same question as between children and parents.

The problems of the second group will be dealt with in a subsequent chapter. As to group A, we think that we have supplied a partial solution to the first of its problems. If it be granted that the first three categories of child language as we have laid them down are egocentric, then the thought of the child of $6\frac{1}{2}$ is in its spoken manifestation ego-centric in the proportion of 44 to 47%. What is socialized by language, moreover, belongs only to the factual categories of thought. At this age, causality and the faculty for explanation are still unexpressed. Does the period between 6 and 7 mark a turning point in this respect? We still lack the material to make a sufficient number of comparisons, but judging from what seems to be the rule at the *Maison des Petits,* we believe that the age at which the child begins to communicate his thought (the age when ego-centric language is 25%) is probably somewhere between 7 and 8. This does not mean that from the age of 7 or 8 children can immediately understand each other—we shall see later on that this is far from being the case—it simply means that from this age onwards they try to improve upon their methods of interchanging ideas and upon their mutual understanding of one another.

NOTES

1. With the collaboration of Mlle Germaine Guex and of Mlle Hilda de Meyenburg.

2. *British Journ. of Psych.* (Med. Sect.), Vol. I, Part 2, 1921, p. 151.

3. See Jones, E, "A Linguistic Factor in English Characterology," *Intern. Journal of Psycho-Anal.*, Vol. I, Part 3, p. 256 (see quotations from Ferenczi and Freud, p. 257).

4. See *Intern. Zeitschrift f. Psychoanal.*, Vol. VI, p. 401 (a report of the proceedings of the Psycho-analytical Conference at the Hague).

5. Our grateful thanks are due to the ladies in charge of the *Maison des Petits*, Mlles Audemars and Lafandel, who gave us full freedom to work in their classes.

6. P. Janet, *loc. cit.,* p. 150.

7. These cases will be dealt with elsewhere.

8. For such cock-and-bull stories, see p. 371, sentence 30.

9. A. Descœudres, "Le developpement de l'enfant de deux à sept ans," *Coll. Actual. Ped.,* 1922, p. 190.

10. For the definition of this term, see Chapter V.

11. *Id.*

12. See Chapter V.

13. See Appendix.

14. We are at the moment collecting similar data from various children between the ages of 3 and 7, in such a way as to establish a graph of development. These results will probably appear in the *Archives de Psychologie.*

15. There is interaction between these two modes of thought. Autism undoubtedly calls into being and enriches many inventions which are subsequently clarified and demonstrated by intelligence.

16. See Flournoy, H. "Quelques rêves au sujet de la signification symbolique de l'eau et du feu." *Intern. Zeitschr. f. Psychoan.*, Vol. VI. p. 398 (*cf.* pp. 329 and 330).

17. We have published the case of Vo of a child of 9, who regards humanity as descended from a baby who issued from a worm which came out of the sea. *Cf.* Piaget, "La pensée symbolique et la pensée de l'enfant." *Arch. Psych.,* Vol. XVIII, 1923.

30
~

L. S. VYGOTSKI

Lev Semyonovich Vygotski (1896–1934) was fascinated by history and literature, but his parents persuaded him that medicine was a more practical career. Having graduated with honors and a gold medal from high school, it seemed likely that he would be accepted to the Medical School at Moscow University, but in 1913 it was determined that the 3 percent quota allowed for Jews would be filled by randomly selecting applicants. To Vygotski's surprise, he was accepted, though his foray into medicine did not last through the first semester, and he transferred to the law school. During the 1910s in Moscow, many of the leading faculty had left Moscow University for Shaniavsky University to protest various oppressive acts by the minister of education. Consequently, Vygotski enrolled there as well and majored in philosophy and history. During the October Revolution of 1917, the recent graduate Vygotski was at his parents' new home in Gomel. He remained in Gomel and taught literature in a local school but developed a fascination with works like William James's (p. 216) *The Varieties of Religious Experience,* and Sigmund Freud's (p. 258) *Psychopathology of Everyday Life.* In 1924 at the Second Psychoneurological Congress in

Leningrad, Vygotski delivered a talk that challenged the position of the leading Soviet behavioral scientists by insisting that psychology must consider consciousness, not treat it as a superstitious notion. While most remained unconvinced, Vygotski did garner the attention of Alexander Luria, who convinced the Moscow Institute of Psychology to offer Vygotsky a research position. In 1925, Vygotski submitted to the institute his manuscript, *The Psychology of Art,* begun during his years in Gomel, and received his Ph.D. He continued to develop his theories and attracted loyal students, though the 1930s brought deteriorating health and an increasingly hostile political climate. When Stalin declared that all psychological theories and categories must derive from Engels, Lenin, and Marx, Vygotski's work, which drew on concepts from a variety of schools, including psychoanalysis and Gestalt theory, was soon declared erroneous and irrelevant. Vygotski died of tuberculosis in 1934, and his work was not widely published, in Russia or abroad, until the 1960s.

MIND IN SOCIETY

THOUGHT AND WORD

The word I forgot
Which once I wished to say
And voiceless thought
Returns to shadows' chamber.   Osip Mandelstam

I

We began our study with an attempt to discover the relation between thought and speech at the earliest stages of phylogenetic and ontogenetic development. We found no specific interdependence between the genetic roots of thought and word. It became plain that the inner relations we were looking for was not a prerequisite for, but rather a product of, the historical development of human consciousness.

In animals, even in anthropoids whose speech is phonetically like human speech and whose intellect is akin to man's, speech and thinking are not interrelated. A prelinguistic period in thought and a preintellectual period in speech undoubtedly exist also in the development of the child. Thought and word are not connected by a primary bond. A connection originates, changes, and grows in the course of the evolution of thinking and speech.

It would be wrong, however, to regard thought and speech as two unrelated processes, either parallel or crossing at certain points and mechanically influencing each other. The absence of a primary bond does not mean that a connection between them can be formed only in a mechanical way. The futility of most of the

earlier investigations was largely due to the assumption that thought and word were isolated, independent elements, and verbal thought the fruit of their external union.

The method of analysis based on this conception was bound to fail. It sought to explain the properties of verbal thought by breaking it up into its component elements, thought and word, neither of which, taken separately, possesses the properties of the whole. This method is not true analysis, helpful in solving concrete problems. It leads, rather, to generalization. We compared it to the analysis of water into hydrogen and oxygen—which can result only in findings applicable to all water existing in nature, from the Pacific Ocean to a raindrop. Similarly, the statement that verbal thought is composed of intellectual processes and speech functions proper applies to all verbal thought and all its manifestations and explains none of the specific problems facing the student of verbal thought.

We tried a new approach and replaced analysis into elements [*elementy*] by analysis into units [*edinitsy*]. Units are products of analysis that correspond to specific aspects of the phenomena under investigation. At the same time, unlike elements, units are capable of retaining and expressing the essence of that whole being analyzed. The unit of our analysis will thus contain in the most fundamental and elementary form those properties that belong to verbal thinking as a whole.

We found this unit of verbal thought in word meaning. Word meaning is an elementary "cell" that cannot be further analyzed and that represents the most elementary form of the unity between thought and word.

From L. S. Vygotski, "Thought and Word." In A. Kozulin (Trans. and Ed.) *Thought and Language* (pp. 210–214, 217–235, 249–256). Cambridge: MIT Press, 1987. (Original work published 1934)

The meaning of a word represents such a close amalgam of thought and language that it is hard to tell whether it is a phenomenon of speech or a phenomenon of thought. A word without meaning is an empty sound; meaning, therefore, is a criterion of "word," its indispensable component. It would seem, then, that it may be regarded as a phenomenon of speech. But from the point of view of psychology, the meaning of every word is a generalization or a concept. And since generalizations and concepts are undeniably acts of thought, we may regard meaning as a phenomenon of thinking. It does not follow, however, that meaning formally belongs in two different spheres of psychic life. Word meaning is a phenomenon of thought only insofar as thought is embodied in speech, and of speech only insofar as speech is connected with thought and illuminated by it. It is a phenomenon of verbal thought, or meaningful speech—a union of word and thought.

Our experimental investigations fully confirm this basic thesis. They not only proved that the concrete study of the development of verbal thought is made possible by the use of word meaning as the analytical unit, but they also led to a further thesis, which we consider the major result of our study and which issues directly from the first: the thesis that word meanings develop. This insight must replace the postulate of the immutability of word meanings.

From the point of view of the old schools of psychology, the bond between word and meaning is an associative bond, established through the repeated simultaneous perception of a certain sound and a certain object. A word calls to mind its content as the overcoat of a friend reminds us of that friend, or a house of its inhabitants. The association between word and meaning may grow stronger or weaker, be enriched by linkage with other objects of a similar kind, spread over a wider field, or become more limited (i.e., it may undergo quantitative and external changes), but it cannot change its psychological nature. To do that, it would have to cease being an association. From that point of view, any development in word meanings is inexplicable and impossible—an implication that handicapped linguistics as well as psychology. Once having committed itself to the association theory, semantics persisted in treating word meaning as an association between a word's sound and its content. All words, from the most concrete to the most abstract, appeared to be formed in the same manner in regard to meaning, and to contain nothing peculiar to speech as such; a word made us think of its meaning just as any object might remind us of another. It is hardly surprising that semantics did not even pose the larger question of the development of word meanings. Development was reduced to changes in the associative connections between single words and single objects: A word might denote at first one object and then become associated with another, just as an overcoat, having changed owners, might remind us first of one person and later of another. Linguistics did not realize that in the historical evolution of language the very structure of meaning and its psychological nature also change. From primitive generalizations, verbal thought rises to the most abstract concepts. It is not merely the content of a word that changes, but the way in which reality is generalized and reflected in a word.

Association theory is equally inadequate in explaining the development of word meanings in childhood. Here, too, it can account only for the purely external, quantitative changes in the bonds uniting word and meaning, for their enrichment and strengthening, but not for the fundamental structural and psychological changes that can and do occur in the development of language in children. . . .

This critical survey may be summed up as follows: All the psychological schools and trends overlook the cardinal point that every thought is a generalization; and they all study word and meaning without any reference to development. As long as these two conditions persist in the successive trends, there cannot be much difference in the treatment of the problem.

II

The discovery that word meanings evolve leads the study of thought and speech out of a blind alley. Word meanings are dynamic rather than static formations. They change as the child develops; they change also with the various ways in which thought functions.

If word meanings change in their inner nature, then the relation of thought to word also changes. To understand the dynamics of that relation, we must supplement the genetic approach of our main study by functional analysis and examine the role of word meaning in the process of thought.

Let us consider the process of verbal thinking from the first dim stirring of a thought to its formulation. What we want to show now is not how meanings develop over long periods of time, but the way they function in the live process of verbal thought. On the basis of such a functional analysis, we shall be able to show also that each stage in the development of word meaning has its own particular relation between thought and speech. Since functional problems are most readily solved by examining the highest form of a given activity, we shall, for a while, put aside the problem of development and consider the relations between thought and word in the mature mind.

As soon as we start approaching these relations, the most complex and grand panorama opens before our eyes. Its intricate architectonics surpasses the richest imagination of research schemas. The words of Lev Tolstoy proved to be correct: "The relation of word to thought, and the creation of new concepts is a complex, delicate, and enigmatic process unfolding in our soul."

The leading idea in the following discussion can be reduced to this formula: The relation of thought to word is not a thing but a process, a continual movement back and forth from thought to word and from word to thought. In that process, the relation of thought to word undergoes changes that themselves may be regarded as development in the functional sense. Thought is not merely expressed in words; it comes into existence through them. Every thought tends to connect something with something else, to establish a relation between things. Every thought moves, grows and develops, fulfills a function, solves a problem. This flow of thought occurs as an inner movement through a series of planes. An analysis of the interaction of thought and word must begin with an investigation of the different phases and planes a thought traverses before it is embodied in words.

The first thing such a study reveals is the need to distinguish between two planes of speech. Both the inner, meaningful, semantic aspect of speech and the external, phonetic aspect, though forming a true unity, have their own laws of movement. The unity of speech is a complex, not a homogeneous, unity. A number of facts in the linguistic development of the child indicate independent movement in the phonetic and the semantic spheres. We shall point out two of the most important of these facts.

In mastering external speech, the child starts from one word, then connects two or three words; a little later, he advances from simple sentences to more complicated ones, and finally to coherent speech made up of series of such sentences; in other words, he proceeds from a part to the whole. In regard to meaning, on the other hand, the first word of the child is a whole sentence. Semantically, the child starts from the whole, from a meaningful complex, and only later begins to master the separate semantic units, the meanings of words, and to divide his formerly undifferentiated thought into those units. The external and the semantic aspects of speech develop in opposite directions—one from the particular to the whole, from word to sentence,

and the other from the whole to the particular, from sentence to word.

This in itself suffices to show how important it is to distinguish between the vocal and the semantic aspects of speech. Since they move in opposite directions, their development does not coincide; but that does not mean that they are independent of each other. On the contrary, their difference is the first stage of a close union. In fact, our example reveals their inner relatedness as clearly as it does their distinction. A child's thought, precisely because it is born as a dim, amorphous whole, must find expression in a single word. As his thought becomes more differentiated, the child is less apt to express it in single words, but constructs a composite whole. Conversely, progress in speech to the differentiated whole of a sentence helps the child's thoughts to progress from a homogeneous whole to well-defined parts. Thought and word are not cut from one pattern. In a sense, there are more differences than likenesses between them. The structure of speech does not simply mirror the structure of thought; that is why words cannot be put on by thought like a ready-made garment. Thought undergoes many changes as it turns into speech. It does not merely find expression in speech; it finds its reality and form. The semantic and the phonetic developmental processes are essentially one, precisely because of their opposite directions.

The second, equally important, fact emerges at a later period of development. Piaget demonstrated that the child uses subordinate clauses with *because, although,* etc., long before he grasps the structures of meaning corresponding to these syntactic forms. Grammar precedes logic. Here, too, as in our previous example, the discrepancy does not exclude union, but is, in fact, necessary for union.

In adults, the divergence between the semantic and the phonetic aspects of speech is even more striking. Modern, psychologically oriented linguistics is familiar with this phenomenon, especially in regard to grammatical and psychological subject and predicate. For example, in the sentence "The clock fell," emphasis and meaning may change in different situations. Suppose I notice that the clock has stopped and ask how this happened. The answer is, "The clock fell." Grammatical and psychological subject coincide: "The clock" is the first idea in my consciousness; "fell" is what is said about the clock. But if I hear a crash in the next room and inquire what happened, and get the same answer, subject and predicate are psychologically reversed. I knew something had fallen—that is what we are talking about. "The clock" completes the idea. The sentence could be changed to "What has fallen is the clock"; then the grammatical and the psychological subjects would coincide. In the prologue to his play *Duke Ernst von Schwaben,* Uhland says, "Grim scenes will pass before you." Psychologically, "will pass" is the subject. The spectator knows he will see events unfold; the additional idea, the predicate, is "grim scenes." Uhland meant, "What will pass before your eyes is a tragedy."

Analysis shows that any part of a sentence may become a psychological predicate, the carrier of topical emphasis. The grammatical category, according to Hermann Paul, is a petrified form of the psychological one. To revive it, one makes a logical emphasis that reveals its semantic meaning. Paul shows that entirely different meanings may lie hidden behind one and the same grammatical structure. Accord between syntactical organization and psychological organization is not as prevalent as we tend to assume—rather, it is a requirement that is seldom met. Not only the subject and predicate, but grammatical gender, number, case, tense, degree, etc., have their psychological doubles. A spontaneous utterance, wrong from the point of view of grammar, may have charm and esthetic value. Alexander Pushkin's lines

> As rose lips without a smile,
> Without error in the grammar
> I Russian language will despise. . . .

bear a more serious message than is usually assumed. Absolute correctness is achieved only in mathematics. It seems that Descartes was the first who recognized in mathematics a form of thought that, although originating in language, goes beyond it. Our daily speech constantly fluctuates between the ideals of mathematical harmony and imaginative harmony.

We shall illustrate the interdependence of the semantic and the grammatical aspects of language by citing two examples that show that changes in formal structure can entail far-reaching changes in meaning.

In translating the fable "The Grasshopper and the Ant," Krylov substituted a dragonfly for La Fontaine's grasshopper. In French, *grasshopper* is feminine and therefore well suited to symbolize a lighthearted, carefree attitude. The nuance would be lost in a literal translation, since in Russian *grasshopper* is masculine. When he settled for *dragonfly,* which is feminine in Russian, Krylov disregarded the literal meaning in favor of the grammatical form required to render La Fontaine's thought.

Tiutchev did the same in his translation of Heine's poem about a fir and a palm. In German *fir* is masculine and *palm* feminine, and the poem suggests the love of a man for a woman. In Russian, both trees are feminine. To retain the implication, Tiutchev replaced the fir by a masculine cedar. Lermontov, in his more literal translation of the same poem, deprived it of these poetic overtones and gave it an essentially different meaning, more abstract and generalized. One grammatical detail may, on occasion, change the whole purport of what is said.

Behind words, there is the independent grammar of thought, the syntax of word meanings. The simplest utterance, far from reflecting a constant, rigid correspondence between sound and meaning, is really a process. Verbal expressions cannot emerge fully formed, but must develop gradually. This complex process of transition from meaning to sound must itself be developed and perfected. The child must learn to distinguish between semantics and phonetics and understand the nature of the difference. At first, he uses verbal forms and meanings without being conscious of them as separate. The word, to the child, is an integral part of the object it denotes. Such a conception seems to be characteristic of primitive linguistic consciousness. Wilhelm von Humboldt retells the anecdotal story about the rustic who said he wasn't surprised that savants with all their instruments could figure out the size of stars and their course—what baffled him was how they found out their names. Simple experiments show that preschool children "explain" the names of objects by their attributes. According to them, an animal is called "cow" because it has horns, "calf" because its horns are still small, "dog" because it is small and has no horns; an object is called "car" because it is not an animal. When asked whether one could interchange the names of objects, for instance, call a cow "ink," and ink "cow," children will answer no, "because ink is used for writing, and the cow gives milk." An exchange of names would mean an exchange of characteristic features, so inseparable is the connection between them in the child's mind. In one experiment, the children were told that in a game a dog would be called "cow." Here is a typical sample of questions and answers:

> "Does a cow have horns?"
> "Yes."
> "But don't you remember that the cow is really a dog? Come now, does a dog have horns?"
> "Sure, if it is a cow, if it's called cow, it has horns. That kind of dog has got to have little horns."

We can see how difficult it is for children to separate

the name of an object from its attributes, which cling to the name when it is transferred like possessions following their owner.

The fusion of the two planes of speech, semantic and vocal, begins to break down as the child grows older, and the distance between them gradually increases. Each stage in the development of word meanings has its own specific interrelation of the two planes. A child's ability to communicate through language is directly related to the differentiation of word meanings in his speech and consciousness.

To understand this, we must remember a basic characteristic of the structure of word meanings. In the semantic structure of a word, we distinguish between referent and meaning; correspondingly, we distinguish a word's nominative function from its significative function. When we compare these structural and functional relations at the earliest, middle, and advanced stages of development, we find the following genetic regularity: In the beginning, only the nominative function exists; and semantically, only the objective reference; signification independent of naming, and meaning independent of reference, appear later and develop along the paths we have attempted to trace and describe.

Only when this development is completed does the child become fully able to formulate his own thought and to understand the speech of others. Until then, his usuage of words coincides with that of adults in its objective reference, but not in its meaning.

III

We must probe still deeper and explore the plane of inner speech lying beyond the semantic plane. We shall discuss here some of the data of the special investigation we have made of it. The relation of thought and word cannot be understood in all its complexity without a clear understanding of the psychological nature of inner speech. Yet, of all the problems connected with thought and language, this is perhaps the most complicated, beset as it is with terminology and other misunderstandings.

The term *inner speech,* or *endophasy,* has been applied to various phenomena, and authors argue about different things that they call by the same name. Originally, inner speech seems to have been understood as verbal memory. An example would be the silent recital of a poem known by heart. In that case, inner speech differs from vocal speech only as the idea or image of an object differs from the real object. It was in this sense that inner speech was understood by the French authors who tried to find out how words were reproduced in memory—whether as auditory, visual, motor, or synthetic images. We shall see that word memory is indeed one of the constituent elements of inner speech, but not all of it.

In a second interpretation, inner speech is seen as truncated external speech—as "speech minus sound" (Müller) or "subvocal speech" (Watson). Ivan Sechenov called it a reflex arrested after it traveled two-thirds of its way. Vladimir Bekhterev defined it as a speech reflex inhibited in its motor part. All these definitions may serve as subordinate moments in the scientific interpretation of inner speech, but taken in themselves they are grossly inadequate.

The third definition is, on the contrary, too broad. To Kurt Goldstein, the term covers everything that precedes the motor act of speaking, including Wundt's "motives of speech" and the indefinable, nonsensory and nonmotor specific speech experience—i.e., the whole interior aspect of any speech activity. It is hard to accept the equation of inner speech with an inarticulate inner experience in which the separate identifiable structural planes are dissolved without trace. This central experience is common to all linguistic activity, and for this reason alone Goldstein's interpretation does not fit that specific, unique function that alone deserves the name of inner speech. Logically developed, Goldstein's view must lead to the thesis that inner speech is not speech at all, but rather an intellectual and affective-volitional activity, since it includes the motives of speech and the thought that is expressed in words.

To get a true picture of inner speech, one must start from the assumption that it is a specific formation, with its own laws and complex relations to the other forms of speech activity. Before we can study its relation to thought, on the one hand, and to speech, on the other hand, we must determine its special characteristics and function.

Inner speech is speech for oneself; external speech is for others. It would be surprising indeed if such a basic difference in function did not affect the structure of the two kinds of speech. That is why Jackson and Head were most probably wrong when they claimed that the difference between these two kinds of speech is just in degree but not in nature. Absence of vocalization per se is only a consequence of the specific character of inner speech, which is neither an antecedent of external speech nor its reproduction in memory, but is, in a sense, the opposite of external speech. The latter is the turning of thoughts into words, their materialization and objectification. With inner speech, the process is reversed, going from outside to inside. Overt speech sublimates into thoughts. Consequently, the structures of these two kinds of speech must differ.

The area of inner speech is one of the most difficult to investigate. It remained almost inaccessible to experiments until ways were found to apply the genetic method of experimentation. Piaget was the first to pay attention to the child's egocentric speech and to see its theoretical significance, but he remained blind to the most important trait of egocentric speech—its genetic connection with inner speech—and this warped his interpretation of its function and structure. We made that relation the central problem of our study, and thus were able to investigate the nature of inner speech with unusual completeness. A number of considerations and observations led us to conclude that egocentric speech is a stage of development preceding inner speech: Both fulfill intellectual functions; their structures are similar; egocentric speech disappears at school age, when inner speech begins to develop. From all this we infer that one changes into the other.

If this transformation does take place, then egocentric speech provides the key to the study of inner speech. One advantage of approaching inner speech through egocentric speech is its accessibility to experimentation and observation. It is still vocalized, audible speech, i.e., external in its mode of expression, but at the same time it is inner speech in function and structure. To study an internal process, it is necessary to externalize it experimentally, by connecting it with some outer activity; only then is objective functional analysis possible. Egocentric speech is, in fact, a natural experiment of this type.

This method has another great advantage: Since egocentric speech can be studied at the time when some of its characteristics are waning and new ones forming, we are able to judge which traits are essential to inner speech and which are only temporary, and thus to determine the goal of this movement from egocentric speech to inner speech—i.e., the nature of inner speech.

Before we go on to the results obtained by this method, we shall briefly discuss the nature of egocentric speech, stressing the differences between our theory and Piaget's. Piaget contends that the child's egocentric speech is a direct expression of the egocentrism of his thought, which in turn is a compromise between the primary autism of his thinking and its gradual socialization. As the child grows older, autism recedes and socialization progresses, leading to the waning of egocentrism in his thinking and speech.

In Piaget's conception, the child in his egocentric speech does not adapt himself to the thinking of adults. His thought remains entirely egocentric; this makes his talk incomprehensible to others. Egocentric speech has no function in the child's realistic thinking or activity—it merely accompanies them. And since it is an expression of egocentric thought, it disappears together with the child's egocentrism. From its climax at the beginning of the child's development, egocentric speech drops to zero on the threshold of school age. Its history is one of involution rather than evolution. One may say about egocentric speech what Ferenz List said about the infant prodigy, that his entire future lies in the past.

In our conception, egocentric speech is a phenomenon of the transition from interpsychic to intrapsychic functioning, i.e., from the social, collective activity of the child to his more individualized activity—a pattern of development common to all the higher psychological functions. Speech for oneself originates through differentiation from speech for others. Since the main course of the child's development is one of gradual individualization, this tendency is reflected in the function and structure of his speech.

Our experimental results indicate that the function of egocentric speech is similar to that of inner speech: It does not merely accompany the child's activity; it serves mental orientation, conscious understanding; it helps in overcoming difficulties; it is speech for oneself, intimately and usefully connected with the child's thinking. Its fate is very different from that described by Piaget. Egocentric speech develops along a rising, not a declining, curve; it goes through an evolution, not an involution. In the end, it becomes inner speech.

Our hypothesis has several advantages over Piaget's: It explains the function and development of egocentric speech and, in particular, its sudden increase when the child faces difficulties that demand consciousness and reflection—a fact uncovered by our experiments and that Piaget's theory cannot explain. But the greatest advantage of our theory is that it supplies a satisfying answer to a paradoxical situation described by Piaget himself. To Piaget, the quantitative drop in egocentric speech as the child grows older means the withering of that form of speech. If that were so, its structural peculiarities might also be expected to decline; it is hard to believe that the process would affect only its quantity, and not its inner structure. The child's thought becomes infinitely less egocentric between the ages of three and seven. If the characteristics of egocentric speech that make it incomprehensible to others are indeed rooted in egocentrism, they should become less apparent as that form of speech becomes less frequent; egocentric speech should approach social speech and become more and more intelligible. Yet what are the facts? Is the talk of a three-year-old harder to follow than that of a seven-year-old? Our investigation established that the traits of egocentric speech that make for inscrutability are at their lowest point at three and at their peak at seven. They develop in a direction opposite to the frequency of egocentric speech. While the latter keeps falling and reaches zero at school age, the structural characteristics become more and more pronounced.

This throws a new light on the quantitative decrease in egocentric speech, which is the cornerstone of Piaget's thesis.

What does this decrease mean? The structural peculiarities of speech for oneself and its differentiation from external speech increase with age. What is it, then, that diminishes? Only one of its aspects: vocalization. Does this mean that egocentric speech as a whole is dying out? We believe that it does not, for how then could we explain the growth of the functional and structural traits of egocentric speech? On the other hand, their growth is perfectly compatible with the decrease of vocalization—indeed, clarifies its meaning. Its rapid dwindling and the equally rapid growth of the other characteristics are contradictory in appearance only.

To explain this, let us start from an undeniable, experimentally established fact. The structural and functional qualities of egocentric speech become more marked as the child develops. At three, the difference between egocentric speech and social speech equals zero; at seven, we have speech that in structure and function is totally unlike social speech. A differentiation of the two speech functions has taken place. This is a fact—and facts are notoriously hard to refute.

Once we accept this, everything else falls into place. If the developing structural and functional peculiarities of egocentric speech progressively isolate it from external speech, then its vocal aspect must fade away; and this is exactly what happens between three and seven years. With the progressive isolation of speech for oneself, its vocalization becomes unnecessary and meaningless and, because of its growing structural peculiarities, also impossible. Speech for oneself cannot find expression in external speech. The more independent and autonomous egocentric speech becomes, the poorer it grows in its external manifestations. In the end, it separates itself entirely from speech for others, ceases to be vocalized, and thus appears to die out.

But this is only an illusion. To interpret the sinking coefficient of egocentric speech as an indication that this kind of speech is dying out is like saying that the child stops counting when he ceases to use his fingers and starts adding in his head. In reality, behind the symptoms of dissolution lies a progressive development, the birth of a new speech form.

The decreasing vocalization of egocentric speech denotes a developing abstraction from sound, the child's new faculty to "think words" instead of pronouncing them. This is the positive meaning of the sinking coefficient of egocentric speech. The downward curve indicates development toward inner speech.

We can see that all the known facts about the functional, structural, and genetic characteristics of egocentric speech point to one thing: It develops in the direction of inner speech. Its developmental history can be understood only as a gradual unfolding of the traits of inner speech.

We believe that this corroborates our hypothesis about the origin and nature of egocentric speech. To turn our hypothesis into a certainty, we must devise an experiment capable of showing which of the two interpretations is correct. What are the data for this critical experiment?

Let us restate the theories between which we must decide. Piaget believes that egocentric speech stems from the insufficient socialization of speech and that its only development is decrease and eventual death. Its culmination lies in the past. Inner speech is something new brought in from the outside along with socialization. We believe that egocentric speech stems from the insufficient individualization of primary social speech. Its culmination lies in the future. It develops into inner speech.

To obtain evidence for one or the other view, we must place the child alternately in experimental situations encouraging social speech and in situations discouraging it, and see how these changes affect egocentric speech. We consider this an *experimentum crucis* for the following reasons.

If the child's egocentric talk results from the egocentrism of his thinking and its insufficient socialization, then any weakening of the social elements in the experimental setup, any factor contributing to the child's isolation from the group, must lead to a sudden increase in egocentric speech. But if the latter results from an insufficient differentiation of speech for oneself from speech for others, then the same changes must cause it to decrease.

We took as the starting point of our experiment three of Piaget's own observations: (1) Egocentric speech occurs only in the presence of other children engaged in the same activity, and not when the child is alone; i.e., it is a collective monologue. (2) The child is under the illusion that his egocentric talk, directed to nobody, is understood by those who surround him. (3) Egocentric speech has the character of external speech: It is not inaudible or whispered. These are certainly not chance peculiarities. From the child's own point of view, egocentric speech is not yet separated from social speech. It occurs under the subjective and objective conditions of social speech and may be considered a correlate of the insufficient isolation of the child's individual consciousness from the social whole.

Our position regarding these observations of Piaget can hardly be called biased, for Abraham Grünbaum came to the same conclusion as we do, making no counterexperiments, but just interpreting Piaget's own data.

For a superficial observer—explains Grünbaum—the child appears to be deep in his thoughts, but this is an erroneous impression, stemming from an erroneous expectation. Three-year-olds do not have a logical outlook, and this absence of a logical attitude is incorrectly taken as a sign of the child's egocentrism. Three- to five-year-olds while playing together often speak only to themselves. What looks like a conversation turns out to be a collective monologue. But even such a monologue, being the most spectacular example of child "egocentrism," actually reveals the social engagement of the child's psyche. A collective monologue does not require either a purposive isolation or autism. Children who are participants of the collective monologue do believe that they communicate with each other. They believe that their thoughts, even those that are poorly expressed or unarticulated, belong to all participants. This, according to Grünbaum, points to the insufficient separation of the child's individual psyche from the social whole.

And yet it is experiment, and not interpretations, that can resolve the problem of inner speech and egocentrism. In our first series of experiments, we tried to destroy the illusion of being understood. After measuring the child's coefficient of egocentric speech in a situation similar to that of Piaget's experiments, we put him into a new situation: either with deaf-mute children or with children speaking a foreign language. In all other respects the setup remained the same. The coefficient of egocentric speech dropped to zero in the majority of cases, and in the rest to one-eighth of the previous figure, on the average. This proves that the illusion of being understood is not a mere epiphenomenon of egocentric speech, but is functionally connected with it. Our results must seem paradoxical from the point of view of Piaget's theory: The weaker the child's contact is with the group—the less the social situation forces him to adjust his thoughts to others and to use social speech—the more freely should the egocentrism of his thinking and speech manifest itself. But from the point of view of our hypothesis, the meaning of these findings is clear: Egocentric speech, springing from the lack of differentiation of speech for oneself from speech for others, disappears when the feeling of being understood, essential for social speech, is absent.

In the second series of experiments, the variable factor was the possibility of collective monologue. Having measured the child's coefficient of egocentric speech in a situation permitting collective monologue, we put him into a situation excluding it—in a group of children who were strangers to him or by himself at a separate table in a corner of the room; or working quite alone (even the experimenter left the room). The results of this series agreed with the first results. The exclusion of the group monologue caused a drop in the coefficient of egocentric speech, though not such a striking one as in the first case—seldom to zero, and, on the average, to one-sixth of the original figure. The different methods of precluding collective monologue were not equally effective in reducing the coefficient of egocentric speech. The trend, however, was obvious in all the variations of the experiment. The exclusion of the collective factor, instead of giving full freedom to egocentric speech, depressed it. Our hypothesis was once more confirmed.

In the third series of experiments, the variable factor was the vocal quality of egocentric speech. Just outside the laboratory where the experiment was in progress, an orchestra played so loudly, or so much noise was made, that it drowned out not only the voices of others but the child's own; in a variant of the experiment, the child was expressly forbidden to talk loudly and allowed to talk only in whispers. Once again the coefficient of egocentric speech went down, the relation to the original figure being 5:1. Again the different methods were not equally effective, but the basic trend was invariably present.

The purpose of all three series of experiments was to eliminate those characteristics of egocentric speech that bring it close to social speech. We found that this always led to the dwindling of egocentric speech. It is logical, then, to assume that egocentric speech is a form developing out of social speech and not yet separated from it in its manifestation, though already distinct in function and structure.

The disagreement between us and Piaget on this point will be made quite clear by the following example: I am sitting at my desk talking to a person who is behind me and whom I cannot see; he leaves the room without my noticing it, and I continue to talk, under the illusion that he listens and understands. Outwardly, I am talking with myself and for myself, but psychologically my speech is social. From the point of view of Piaget's theory, the opposite happens in the case of the child: His egocentric talk is for and with himself; it only has the appearance of social speech, just as my speech gave the false impression of being egocentric. From our point of view, the whole situation is much more complicated than that: Subjectively, the child's egocentric speech already has its own peculiar function—to that extent, it is independent from social speech; yet its independence is not complete because it is not felt as inner speech and is not distinguished by the child from speech for others. Objectively, also, it is different from social speech, but again not entirely, because it functions only within social situations. Both subjectively and objectively, egocentric speech represents a transition from speech for others to speech for oneself. It already has the function of inner speech, but remains similar to social speech in its expression.

The investigation of egocentric speech has paved the way to the understanding of inner speech, which we shall examine next.

VI

We can now return to the definition of inner speech that we proposed before presenting our analysis. Inner speech is not the interior aspect of external speech—it is a function in itself. It still remains speech, i.e., thought connected with words. But while in external speech thought is embodied in words, in inner speech words die as they bring forth thought. Inner speech is to a large extent thinking in pure meanings. It is a dynamic, shifting, unstable thing, fluttering between word and thought, the two more or less stable, more or less firmly delineated components of verbal thought. Its true nature and place can be understood only after examining the next plane of verbal thought, the one still more inward than inner speech.

That plane is thought itself. As we have said, every thought creates a connection, fulfills a function, solves a problem. The flow of thought is not accompanied by a simultaneous unfolding of speech. The two processes are not identical, and there is no rigid correspondence between the units of thought and speech. This is especially obvious when a thought process miscarries—when, as Dostoevsky put it, a thought "will not enter words."

Here one literary example will be appropriate. Gleb Uspensky's character, a poor peasant, who must address an official with some life-important issue, cannot put his thoughts into words. Embarrassed by his failure, he re-

treats and prays, asking the Lord "to give him a concept." This scene leaves the reader disturbed and depressed. But in its essence, the problem facing this poor and illiterate peasant is of the same kind constantly hounding thinkers and writers: How to put thoughts into words. Sometimes even the speech of Uspensky's character starts to resemble that of a poet: "I would tell you all of this, my friend, concealing nothing . . . but, you know, folks of my kind cannot talk. . . . It is as if they are all here, in my head, but cannot slip from the tongue. That is our, fools', sorrow."

In this fragment the watershed between thoughts and words becomes highly visible. If thoughts were identical in structure and development with speech, the case described by Uspensky would be impossible.

Thought has its own structure, and the transition from it to speech is no easy matter. The theater faced the problem of the thought behind the words before psychology did. In teaching his system of acting, Konstantin Stanislavsky required the actors to uncover the "subtext" of their lines in a play. In Griboedov's comedy *Woe from Wit,* the hero, Chatsky, says to the heroine, who maintains that she has never stopped thinking of him, "Thrice blessed who believes. Believing warms the heart." Stanislavsky interpreted this as "Let us stop this talk"; but it could just as well be interpreted as "I do not believe you. You say it to comfort me," or as "Don't you see how you torment me? I wish I could believe you. That would be bliss." Every sentence that we say in real life has some kind of subtext, a thought hidden behind it. In the examples we gave earlier of the lack of coincidence between grammatical and psychological subject and predicate, we did not pursue our analysis to the end. Just as one sentence may express different thoughts, one thought may be expressed in different sentences. For instance, "The clock fell," in answer to the question "Why did the clock stop?" could mean, "It is not my fault that the clock is out of order; it fell." The same thought, self-justification, could take, among others, the form "It is not my habit to touch other people's things. I was just dusting here."

Thought, unlike speech, does not consist of separate units. When I wish to communicate the thought that today I saw a barefoot boy in a blue shirt running down the street, I do not see every item separately: the boy, the shirt, its blue color, his running, the absence of shoes. I conceive of all this in one thought, but I put it into separate words. A speaker often takes several minutes to disclose one thought. In his mind the whole thought is present at once, but in speech it has to be developed successively. A thought may be compared to a cloud shedding a shower of words. Precisely because thought does not have its automatic counterpart in words, the transition from thought to word leads through meaning. In our speech, there is always the hidden thought, the subtext. Because a direct transition from thought to word is impossible, there have always been laments about the inexpressibility of thought:

> How shall the heart express itself?
> How shall another understand?
> F. Tiutchev

or

> If only soul might speak without words!
> A. Fet

To overcome this problem, new paths from thought to word leading through new word meanings must be cut. Velemir Khlebnikov compared his futuristic poetry with the construction of roads connecting one valley to another.

Experience teaches us that thought does not express itself in words, but rather realizes itself in them. Sometimes such realization cannot be accomplished, as in the case of Uspensky's character. We must ask, Does this character know what he is going to think about? Yes, but he does it as one who wants to remember something but is unable to. Does he start thinking? Yes, but again he does it as one who is absorbed by remembering. Does he succeed in turning his thought into a process? No. The problem is that thought is mediated by signs externally, but it also is mediated internally, this time by word meanings. Direct communication between minds is impossible, not only physically but psychologically. Communication can be achieved only in a roundabout way. Thought must first pass through meanings and only then through words.

We come now to the last step in our analysis of inner planes of verbal thought. Thought is not the superior authority in this process. Thought is not begotten by thought; it is engendered by motivation, i.e., by our desires and needs, our interests and emotions. Behind every thought there is an affective-volitional tendency, which holds the answer to the last "why" in the analysis of thinking. A true and full understanding of another's thought is possible only when we understand its affective-volitional basis. We shall illustrate this by an example already used: the interpretation of parts in a play. Stanislavsky, in his instructions to actors, listed the motives behind the words of their parts for A. Griboedov's *Woe from Wit,* act I:

Text of the Play	Parallel Motives
SOPHYA:	
O, Chatsky, but I am glad you've come	Tries to hide her confusion.
CHATSKY:	
You are glad, that's very nice; But gladness such as yours not easily one tells. It rather seems to me, all told, That making man and horse catch cold I've pleased myself and no one else	Tries to make her feel guilty by teasing her. Aren't you ashamed of yourself! Tries to force her to be frank.
LIZA:	
There, sir, and if you'd stood on the same landing here Five minutes, no, not five ago You'd heard your name clear as clear. You say, Miss! Tell him it was so.	Tries to calm him. Tries to help Sophya in a difficult situation.
SOPHYA:	
And always so, no less, no more. No, as to that, I'm sure you can't reproach me.	Tries to reassure Chatsky. I am not guilty of anything!
CHATSKY:	
Well, let's suppose it's so. Thrice blessed who believes. Believing warms the heart.	Let us stop this conversation; etc.

To understand another's speech, it is not sufficient to understand his words—we must understand his thought. But even that is not enough—we must also know its motivation. No psychological analysis of an utterance is complete until that plane is reached.

We have come to the end of our analysis; let us survey its results. Verbal thought appeared as a complex, dynamic entity, and the relation of thought and word within it as a movement through a series of planes. Our analysis followed the process from the outermost plane to the innermost plane. In reality, the development of verbal thought takes the opposite course: from the motive that engenders a thought to the shaping of the thought, first in inner speech, then in meanings of words, and finally in words. It would be a mistake, however, to imagine that this is the only road from thought to word. The development may stop at any point in its complicated course: an infinite variety of movements to and fro, of ways still unknown to us, is possible. A study of these manifold variations lies beyond the scope of our present task.

Our investigation followed a rather unusual path. We wished to study the inner workings of thought and speech, hidden from direct observation. Meaning and the whole inward aspect of language, the side turned toward the person, not toward the outer world, have been so far an almost unknown territory. No matter how they were interpreted, the relations between thought and word were always considered constant, established forever. Our investigation has shown that they are, on the contrary, delicate, changeable relations between processes, which arise during the development of verbal thought. We did not intend to, and could not, exhaust the subject of verbal thought. We tried only to give a general conception of the infinite complexity of this dynamic structure—a conception starting from experimentally documented facts.

To association psychology, thought and word were united by external bonds, similar to the bonds between two nonsense syllables. Gestalt psychology introduced the concept of structural bonds, but, like the older theory, did not account for the specific relations between thought and word. All the other theories grouped themselves around two poles—either the behaviorist concept of thought as speech minus sound or the idealistic view, held by the Würzburg school and Bergson, that thought could be "pure," unrelated to language, and that it was distorted by words. Tiutchev's "A thought once uttered is a lie" could well serve as an epigraph for the latter group. Whether inclining toward pure naturalism or extreme idealism, all these theories have one trait in common— their antihistorical bias. They study thought and speech without any reference to their developmental history.

Only a historical theory of inner speech can deal with this immense and complex problem. The relation between thought and word is a living process; thought is born through words. A word devoid of thought is a dead thing:

> . . . and like bees in the deserted hive
> The dead words have a rotten smell.
> N. Gumilev

But thought that fails to realize itself in words also remains a "Stygian shadow" [O. Mandelstam]. Hegel con-

sidered word as a Being animated by thought. This Being is absolutely essential for our thinking.

The connection between thought and word, however, is neither preformed nor constant. It emerges in the course of development, and itself evolves. To the biblical "In the beginning was the Word," Goethe makes Faust reply, "In the beginning was the deed." The intent here is to detract from the value of the word, but we can accept this version if we emphasize it differently: In the *beginning* was the deed. The word was not the beginning—action was there first; it is the end of development, crowning the deed.

We cannot close our study without mentioning the perspectives that our investigation opens up. This is even more momentous a problem than that of thinking; what I mean is the problem of consciousness. We studied the inward aspects of speech, which were as unknown to science as the other side of the moon. We tried to establish the connection between word and object, word and reality. We attempted to study experimentally the dialectics of transition from perception to thinking, and to show that a generalized reflection of reality is the basic characteristic of words. This aspect of the word brings us to the threshold of a wider and deeper subject, i.e., the problem of the relation between word and consciousness. If perceptive consciousness and intellectual consciousness reflect reality differently, then we have two different forms of consciousness. *Thought and speech turn out to be the key to the nature of human consciousness.*

If language is as old as consciousness itself, and if language is a practical consciousness-for-others and, consequently, consciousness-for-myself, then not only one particular thought but all consciousness is connected with the development of the word. The word is a thing in our consciousness, as Ludwig Feuerbach put it, that is absolutely impossible for one person, but that becomes a reality for two. The word is a direct expression of the historical nature of human consciousness.

Consciousness is reflected in a word as the sun in a drop of water. A word relates to consciousness as a living cell relates to a whole organism, as an atom relates to the universe. A word is a microcosm of human consciousness.

31

B. F. SKINNER

Burrhus Frederic Skinner (1904–1990), a boy who enjoyed tinkering, built a wide variety of gadgets and models while growing up in Susquehanna, Pennsylvania. This facility with his hands presaged his various inventions that reshaped the study of behavior. As a student at Hamilton College, Skinner wrote for a range of college publications, including humorous tracts by "Sir Burrhus de Beerus." Graduating in 1926 with a bachelor's degree in English literature, Skinner returned home with dreams of becoming a professional writer but instead found loneliness, depression, and writer's block in the remodeled family attic. Skinner first encountered behaviorism through a critique by philosopher Bertrand Russell of John B. Watson's (p. 332) book *Behaviorism*. Further reading, including Ivan Pavlov's (p. 178) recently translated works, led Skinner to realize that he "was interested in human behavior, but had been investigating it the wrong way." Following graduate school at Harvard University, Skinner taught at the University of Minnesota, where he started to examine behavior with pigeons. Later he worked at Indiana University and then returned to Harvard, first as a William James lecturer and the next year as a professor. His focus on the control of behavior from environmental contingencies led him to question the validity of an individual's experience of freewill, which garnered him some unpleasant publicity. Given this dry perspective on human existence, some may find it odd that Skinner enjoyed music—particularly the romantic composers Gustav Mahler and Anton Bruckner.

VERBAL BEHAVIOR

CHAPTER 3

The Mand

In a given verbal community, certain responses are characteristically followed by certain consequences. *Wait!* is followed by someone's waiting and *Sh-h!* by silence. Much of the verbal behavior of young children is of this sort. *Candy!* is characteristically followed by the receipt of candy and *Out!* by the opening of a door. These effects are not inevitable, but we can usually find one consequence of each response which is commoner than any other. There are nonverbal parallels. *Out!*, as we have seen, has the same ultimate effect as turning a knob and pushing against a door. Both forms of behavior become part of the repertoire of the organism through operant conditioning. When a response is characteristically rein-

forced in a given way, its likelihood of appearing in the behavior of the speaker is a function of the deprivation associated with that reinforcement. The response *Candy!* will be more likely to occur after a period of candy deprivation, and least likely after candy satiation. The response *Quiet!* is reinforced through the reduction of an aversive condition, and we can increase the probability of its occurrence by creating such a condition—that is, by making a noise.

It will be convenient to have a name for the type of verbal operant in which a response of given form is characteristically followed by a given consequence in a verbal community. The basic relationship has been recognized in syntactic and grammatical analyses (expressions such as the "imperative mood" and "commands and entreaties" suggest themselves), but no traditional term can safely be used here. The term "mand" has a

From B. F. Skinner, "The Mand." In *Verbal Behavior* (pp. 35–51). New York: Appleton-Century-Crofts, 1957.

certain mnemonic value derived from "command," "demand," "countermand," and so on, and is conveniently brief. A "mand," then, may be defined as a verbal operant in which the response is reinforced by a characteristic consequence and is therefore under the functional control of relevant conditions of deprivation or aversive stimulation. Adjectival and verbal uses of the term are self-explanatory. In particular, and in contrast with other types of verbal operants to be discussed later, the response has no specified relation to a prior stimulus.

A mand is characterized by the unique relationship between the form of the response and the reinforcement characteristically received in a given verbal community. It is sometimes convenient to refer to this relation by saying that a mand "specifies" its reinforcement. *Listen!, Look!, Run!, Stop!,* and *Say yes!* specify the behavior of a listener; but when a hungry diner calls *Bread!,* or *More soup!,* he is specifying the ultimate reinforcement. Frequently both the behavior of the listener and the ultimate reinforcement are specified. The mand *Pass the salt!* specifies an action (*pass*) and an ultimate reinforcement (*the salt*).

A mand is a type of verbal operant singled out by its controlling variables. It is not a formal unit of analysis. No response can be said to be a mand from its form alone. As a general rule, in order to identify any type of verbal operant we need to know the kind of variables of which the response is a function. In a given verbal community, however, certain formal properties may be so closely associated with specific kinds of variables that the latter may often be safely inferred. In the present case, we may say that some responses, simply because of formal properties, are very probably mands.

The pattern of response which characteristically achieves the given reinforcement depends, of course, upon the "language"—that is, upon the reinforcing practices of the verbal community. But we have to explain not only the relationships between patterns of response and reinforcements, but the maintenance of the behavior of the *listener.* When we come to consider other types of verbal operants, we shall find that the behavior functions mainly for the benefit of the listener, and in that case his behavior is not difficult to explain. The mand, however, works primarily for the benefit of the speaker; why should the listener perform the necessary mediation of reinforcement?

What needs to be explained, in other words, is the total speech episode. This can be done by listing all relevant events in the behavior of both speaker and listener in their proper temporal order. The deprivation or aversive stimulation responsible for the strength of each

must be specified, and the reinforcing contingencies must explain the origin and continued maintenance of the behavior. Several interchanges between the two organisms frequently occur.

Figure 31.1 represents an episode in which one person asks another for bread. The problem of motivation is disposed of by assuming a hungry speaker and a listener already predisposed to reinforce him with bread. The first physical interchange takes place when the mere presence of the listener provides the occasion $(S^D)^1$ for the speaker's mand *Bread, please!* The speaker does not ordinarily emit the response when no one is present, but when a listener appears, the probability of response is increased (Chapter 7). The visual and other stimulation supplied by the listener is indicated by the first ↑ in the diagram. The speaker's response (*Bread, please*) produces a verbal stimulus for the listener. The interchange here (the first ⇊) is in the form of auditory stimulation which supplies the occasion (S^{DV}) for the nonverbal response of passing the bread. Though we have assumed a listener predisposed to give bread to the speaker, the behavior does not appear indiscriminately. The speaker's mand (*Bread, please*) establishes an occasion upon which the listener can, so to speak, successfully give bread. The interchange of the bread is indicated by the second ↑ The effect upon the speaker is to reinforce the mand by the presentation of bread, and this completes the account so far as the speaker is concerned. It is characteristic of many cultures, however, that the successful reinforcement of a mand is followed by another verbal response, designed to assure similar behavior of the listener in the future. In the diagram, this is indicated by the verbal response *Thank you.* This response is under the control of the stimulation provided by the preceding parts of the episode indicated in the diagram as the second S^D. The auditory stimulation (the second ⇊) supplies a reinforcing stimulus for the listener, which accounts to some extent for the behavior of passing the bread. This verbal stimulus may also contribute to the occasion for a verbal response on the part of the listener (*You're welcome*) which, when heard by the speaker, reinforces the response *Thank you.* These last two interchanges are not an integral part of the speech episode containing a mand; they supplement our assumptions respecting the motivation of the two individuals. (The effect of a verbal response in serving as a reinforcement is further discussed in Chapter 6.)

Kinds of Mands

The mand represented in Figure 31.1, in which the listener is independently motivated to reinforce the speak-

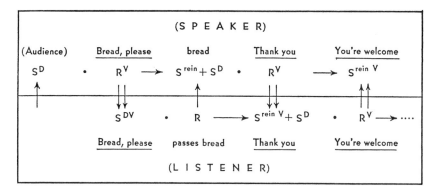

FIGURE 31.1

er, is commonly called a *request*. The response serves merely to indicate that the speaker will accept what the listener is already disposed to give. It is, to repeat, an occasion for successful giving. Often, however, the speaker's response, in addition to specifying a reinforcement, may need to establish an aversive situation from which the listener can escape only by providing the appropriate mediation. When the listener's behavior is thus reinforced by reducing a threat, the speaker's response is called a *command. Hands up!* not only specifies a form of action, it constitutes a threat from which the victim can escape only by holding up his hands. The threat may be carried by a characteristic intonation or may be made explicit, as in *Your money or your life!*, where the first two words specify the reinforcement and the last two the aversive consequences with which the listener is threatened. Military commands are obeyed because of a sort of standing threat.

A paradigm showing the interaction of speaker and listener in a command is shown in Figure 31.2. Here again the first interchange is from listener to speaker. The presence of the listener constitutes the occasion for verbal behavior (S^D) and also in this instance an aversive stimulus (S^{nV}) from which the speaker's response will bring escape. Let us say that the listener is in the speaker's way. The response *Step aside!* specifies an action on the part of the listener and its intonation constitutes a threat. Heard by the listener (at ⇊), these evoke the appropriate response of stepping aside which, in clearing the way for the speaker, reinforces his mand. The reinforcement is also the occasion for a change in his behavior, possibly quite conspicuous, by virtue of which the threat is withdrawn. This change reinforces the listener for stepping aside (at ↓).

There are other ways in which the speaker may alter the probability that the listener will respond in an appropriate fashion. A mand which promotes reinforcement by generating an emotional disposition is commonly called a *prayer* or *entreaty*. A *question* is a mand which specifies verbal action, and the behavior of the listener

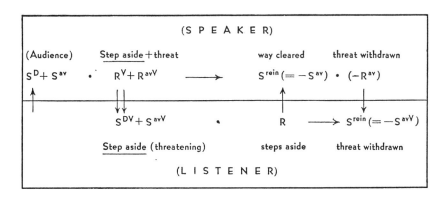

FIGURE 31.2

permits us to classify it as a request, a command, or a prayer, as the case may be. In Figure 31.3 we assume that the listener not only provides an audience for the speaker but creates a situation in which the speaker will be reinforced by being told the listener's name. The speaker's mand *What's your name?* becomes (at the first ⇊) a verbal stimulus for the listener who replies either because of a standing tendency to respond to the speaker or an implied threat in the speaker's response, or because the speaker has emotionally predisposed him to reply. His reply at ⇈ completes the paradigm for the speaker, but it also serves as the occasion for the response *Thank you,* which completes the paradigm for the listener if that is necessary. If the speaker has controlled the listener mainly through aversive stimulation, *Thank you* may be replaced by some visible relaxation of a threat.

(An analysis of this sort seems to do violence to the temporal dimensions of behavior. All of the events represented in one of these paradigms might take place in two or three seconds. The events described, however, *can* occur within a brief period, and we can demonstrate the reality of such a linkage by interrupting the chain at any point. The function of the interlocking paradigm is to check the completeness of our account of verbal behavior. Have the behaviors of both speaker and listener been fully accounted for? Have we identified appropriate states of deprivation or aversive stimulation in all cases? Have we correctly represented the actual physical interchange between the two organisms? In this account of the speech episode, it should be noted that nothing is appealed to beyond the separate behaviors of speaker and listener. By assuming the conditions supplied by a listener, we analyze the behavior of a speaker, and vice versa. By putting the two cases together we construct the total episode and show how it naturally arises and completes itself.)

Several other classes of mands may be distinguished in terms of the behavior of the listener. In mediating the reinforcement of the speaker, the listener will occasionally enjoy consequences in which the speaker does not otherwise participate but which are nevertheless reinforcing. When these consist of positive reinforcement, we call the mand *advice (Go west!).* When by carrying out the behavior specified by the speaker the listener escapes from aversive stimulation, we call the mand a *warning (Look out!).* When the listener is already inclined to act in a given way but is restrained by, for example, a threat, the mand which cancels the threat is commonly called *permission (Go ahead!).* When gratuitous reinforcement of the behavior of the listener is extended by the speaker, the mand is called an *offer (Take one free!).* When the speaker characteristically goes on to emit other behavior which may serve as reinforcement for the listener, the mand is a *call*—either a call to attention or the "vocative" call-by-name.

Classifying the behavior of the speaker in terms of the characteristics of the mediating behavior of the listener may be distinguished from the traditional practice of defining requests, commands, prayers, advice, warnings, permission, offers, and calls in terms of "the intention" of the speaker. In general, intention may be reduced to contingencies of reinforcement. In the present case the conspicuous differences lie in the behavior of the listener and the conditions which control it. But these result in different contingencies of reinforcement for the speaker, which yield different dynamic properties, different interrelationships among responses, different intonations, and so on.

Since verbal behavior in the form of the mand oper-

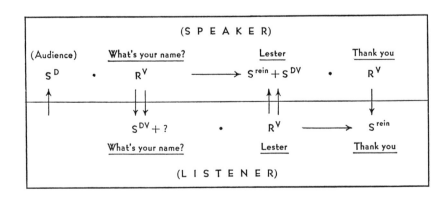

FIGURE 31.3

ates primarily for the benefit of the speaker, repeated mands are likely to move the listener to revolt. It is customary to soften or conceal the mand character. The response *Water!* is not so likely to be successful as *I'm thirsty,* the form of which is characteristic of a type of verbal operant to be described in Chapter 5, or *May I have some water?,* which appears to specify only the less burdensome act of saying *Yes.* (The pretense is exposed if the listener simply says *Yes.*) *Would you mind getting me a drink?* also specifies merely a verbal response *(No, not at all),* but the implied mand may be effective because of the suggested deference to the inclination of the listener. Explicit deference appears in tags such as *if you don't mind, if you please,* or simply *please.* When emphasized, these may convert a mere request into the stronger entreaty.

The inclination of the listener to respond may be heightened by flattery or praise, as in *Get me a drink, my good fellow.* The Lord's Prayer is a mixture of mands and praise following this pattern. The praise may be made conditional upon the execution of the reinforcement, as in *Be a good fellow and get me a drink,* which may be translated *Only if you get me a drink will I call you a good fellow.* Gratitude may be withheld until the listener responds, as in *I'll thank you to get me a drink.* Open bargaining is sometimes resorted to, as in *Give me a drink and I'll tell you all about it.* The abundance of such supplementary techniques merely emphasizes the precariousness of the reinforcement of the mand.

Any response used in conjunction with different mands specifying different reinforcements comes under the control of different deprivations and acquires certain general properties. *Please* is the best known example. It is strengthened by almost any state of deprivation, and is often emitted without further specification of the behavior of the reinforcer. Mands of lesser generality include the emphatic forms *So!, Now!, Now, then!,* and *Here!* where the common consequence is the response of the listener in paying attention. Since the listener's subsequent behavior may be relevant to many states of deprivation, these responses come under a rather broad control. Generalized mands reinforced by the attention of the listener are often used in conjunction with other types of verbal behavior to be considered later.

The mand relation is clearest when it is in exclusive control of a response, but it is also effective in combination with other kinds of variables. A hungry man may show a high frequency of responses which, if they were mands, would be said to specify food, even though they appear under circumstances which more clearly suggest other types of verbal operants to be described below.

Such "multiple causation" of a single response is treated in Chapter 9.

Dynamic Properties of the Mand

The energy level of the mand may vary from very faint to very loud, and the speed with which it is emitted when the occasion arises may vary from very fast to very slow. If the pattern is of substantial length, it may be executed slowly or rapidly. If the reinforcement is not immediately forthcoming, the response may be emitted only once or may be repeated. These properties vary as the result of many conditions in the past and present history of the speaker. Particularly relevant are level of deprivation and intensity of aversive stimulation and the extent to which a given listener or someone like him has reinforced similar responses in the past (or has refused to do so). Such conditions have a relatively greater effect upon the mand than upon the other types of verbal behavior to be discussed in later chapters. The wide range of dynamic properties which result makes the mand a very expressive type of operant.

The probability and intensity of the listener's behavior may also vary over a wide range. If the listener is not already predisposed to act, the probability of his mediating a reinforcement may depend upon the effectiveness of the aversive stimulation supplied by the speaker. Some listeners are accustomed to taking orders—they have felt the unconditioned aversive consequences of not doing so—and respond appropriately to simple mands. Others are more likely to react to softened forms. The intonation, loudness, or other indication that the speaker will supply aversive consequences has an appropriate effect. A hesitant or weak request or command is least likely to be reinforced. A loud and threatening response is likely to be reinforced subject only to the relative strength of listener and speaker. It is to be noted that mands are characteristic of most hypnotic instructions, and the extent to which the subject co-operates or obliges the hypnotist will depend upon the kinds of variables here being considered. These variables enter into what is called the authority or prestige of the speaker.

The net result of a long history of responding to mands is a general tendency no longer easily traced to any form of deprivation or aversive stimulation. The listener obliges and may not even be aware (see Chapter 5) that he is doing so. A classroom experiment designed by F. S. Keller illustrates this point. The instructor says, "Before *summing up* these influences, there is an *additional* one that should be mentioned. I can illustrate this best with an example." At this point he turns to the blackboard and writes

5
<u>4</u>
DO IT ON PAPER

The instructor then continues, "What you did was the result of the 'set' or 'attitude' that you had at the moment you were presented with this stimulus situation. Examples of this are *multiple* and you could supply them from your own experience by the hour. Usually no one is aware of the *times* when they occur in everyday life, but our generalization is the *product* of laboratory experimentation and can readily be checked." He then puts on the board

4
<u>3</u>
DO IT ON PAPER

When the number of those who multiplied in the first instance is compared with the number who multiplied in the second, there is almost always more multiplying in the second case. The underlined words, which of course are not emphasized in the instructions, exert some control over the listener's behavior.

Traditional Treatment

In the traditional treatment of verbal behavior, the "meaning" of a mand is presumably the reinforcement which characteristically follows it. The meaning of *Candy!* is the kind of object frequently produced by that response. But "what is communicated" would appear to be "the speaker's need for candy," which refers to the controlling state of deprivation. The concept of the mand, or of the verbal operant in general, explicitly recognizes both contingency of reinforcement and deprivation or aversive stimulation and is free to deal with these variables in appropriate fashion without trying to identify a relation of reference or a process of communication.

Apart from these questions of semantics, the formulation carries some of the burden of grammar and syntax in dealing with the dynamic properties of verbal behavior. The mand obviously suggests the *imperative* mood, but *interrogatives* are also mands, as are most *interjections* and *vocatives,* and some *subjunctives* and *optatives.* The traditional classifications suffer from a mixture of levels of analysis. In particular they show the influence of formal descriptive systems in which sentences are classified with little or no reference to the behavior of the speaker. It is here that the shortcomings of grammar and syntax in a causal analysis are most obvi-

ous. Appropriate techniques are lacking. As Epictetus said, "When you are to write to your friend, grammar will tell you how to write; but whether you are to write to your friend at all, grammar will not tell you." The use of the mand as a unit of analysis does not mean that the work of linguistic analysis can be avoided, but it simplifies our task by isolating the behavior of the individual speaker as an object of study and by making appropriate techniques available.

In choosing between descriptive systems on the basis of simplicity and effectiveness, the greater familiarity of the classical approach should not be put into the balance. Consider, for example, the following quotation:

In many countries it has been observed that very early a child uses a long *m* (without a vowel) as a sign that it wants something, but we can hardly be right in supposing that the sound is originally meant by children in this sense. They do not use it consciously until they see that grown-up people, on hearing the sound, come up and find out what the child wants.[2]

Although this passage may be said to make an intelligible point in connection with an episode which is intelligibly reported, much is left to be done. It is not the most advantageous account *for all concerned,* for the psychological terms it contains raise many problems.

How would the point be made in the present terms? The expression "uses a long *m* as a sign that it wants something" becomes "emits the sound *m* in a given state of deprivation or aversive stimulation." The expression "the sound is not originally meant in this sense" becomes "the relation between the sound and the state of deprivation or aversive stimulation is innate, or at least of some earlier origin, and the response is not verbal according to our definition." "They do not use it consciously . . ." becomes "It is not conditioned as a verbal response. . . ." And " . . . until they see that grown-up people, on hearing the sound, come up and find out what the child wants" becomes " . . . until the emission of the sound leads listeners to supply reinforcements appropriate to a particular deprivation." The whole passage might be translated:

It has been observed that very early a child emits the sound *m* in certain states of deprivation or aversive stimulation, but we can hardly be right in calling the response verbal at this stage. It is conditioned as a verbal operant only when people, upon hearing the sound, come up and supply appropriate reinforcement.

The distinction between learned and unlearned response is much easier to make in terms of a history of reinforcement than in terms of meaning and conscious use. An important example is crying. Vocal behavior of this sort is clearly an unconditioned response in the newborn infant. For some time it is a function of various states of deprivation and aversive stimulation. But when crying is characteristically followed by parental attentions which are reinforcing, it may become verbal according to our definition. It has become a different behavioral unit because it is now under the control of different variables. It has also probably acquired different properties, for parents are likely to react differently to different intonations or intensities of crying.

The simplicity of such a translation is very different from the simplicity of the original account. The translation is simple because its terms can be defined with respect to experimental operations and because it is consistent with other statements about verbal and nonverbal behavior. The original account is simple because it is familiar and appropriate for casual discourse. It is the difference between the systematic simplicity of science and the ready comprehensibility of the layman's account. Newton's *Principia* was not simple to the man in the street, but in one sense it was simpler than everything which the man in the street had to say about the same subject.

The Extended Mand

A mand assumes a given form because of contingencies of reinforcement maintained by the listener or by the verbal community as a whole. The stimulating conditions which prevail when such a response is emitted and reinforced do not enter into the definition of the unit. When a mand is reinforced by a reduction in unconditioned or conditioned aversive stimuli, stimuli occurring prior to the response must, of course, be taken into account, but these serve a different function from the stimuli being considered here. Stimuli affecting the speaker prior to the emission of verbal behavior are often important and are never wholly irrelevant, as we shall see in the following chapters. The probability of emission of a response is greatest when the stimulating conditions closely resemble those which have previously prevailed before reinforcement. But past and present circumstances need not be identical; indeed, any aspect or feature of the present situation which resembles the situation at the time of reinforcement may be supposed to make some contribution to the probability of response.

An example of extended stimulus control is seen when people mand the behavior of dolls, small babies,

and untrained animals. These "listeners" cannot possibly reinforce the behavior in characteristic fashion. Nevertheless, they have enough in common with listeners who have previously provided reinforcement to control the response, at least when it shows appreciable strength. The fact that reinforcement is unlikely or impossible may affect the dynamic properties. The response may be weak, or emitted in a whimsical fashion, or accompanied by suitable comment (Chapter 12). On the other hand, such behavior often occurs when its "irrational" aspects are not seen by the speaker. We acquire and retain the response *Stop!* because many listeners stop whatever they are doing when we emit it, but as a result we may say *Stop!* to a car with faulty brakes or to a cue ball which threatens to drop into a pocket of the pool table.

The same process leads in the extreme case to the emission of mands in the absence of any listener whatsoever. The lone man dying of thirst gasps *Water!* An unattended king calls *A horse, a horse, my kingdom for a horse!* These responses are "unreasonable" in the sense that they can have no possible effect upon the momentary environment, but the underlying process is lawful. Through a process of stimulus induction situations which are similar to earlier situations come to control the behavior, and in the extreme case a very strong response is emitted when no comparable stimulus can be detected.

There are many familiar nonverbal instances of stimulus induction. It may be true that one cannot open a door without a door or eat a meal without a meal, but in a state of great strength parts of even the most practical behavior occur in the absence of the stimulation required for proper execution. A baseball player who has dropped the ball at a crucial moment may pantomime the correct throw with an empty hand. A thirsty person may "pretend" to drink from an empty glass. Many gestures appear to have originated as "irrational" extension of practical responses. The traffic officer extends his hand, palm outward, toward an oncoming car, as if to bring the car to a stop by physical means. The gesture functions as a verbal response, but it exemplifies the extension of a practical response through stimulus induction to a situation in which normal reinforcement is impossible. Verbal behavior may more easily break free from stimulus control, because by its very nature it does not require environmental support—that is, no stimuli need be present to direct it or to form important links in chaining responses.

SUPERSTITIOUS MANDS. There are mands which cannot be explained by arguing that responses of the same form have been reinforced under similar circumstances. The dice player exclaims *Come seven!*, for example, even though he has not asked for and got sevens anywhere. Accidental reinforcement of the response appears to be the explanation. The experimental study of nonverbal behavior has shown that merely intermittent reinforcement, such as that provided by chance throws of seven, is sufficient to maintain a response in strength. The player may readily admit that there is no mechanical connection between his response and the behavior of the dice, but he retains the response in some strength and continues to utter it, either whimsically or seriously under sufficient stress, because of its occasional "consequences." Mands which specify the behavior of inanimate objects often receive some reinforcement in this sense. The response *Blow, blow, thou winter wind,* for example, is usually uttered when the wind is already blowing, and the correlation between behavior and effect, though spurious, may work a change in operant strength.

Other "unreasonable" mands owe their strength to collateral effects not strictly specified in the form of the response. Many responses mand emotional behavior even though, because of the special ways in which such behavior is conditioned, true emotional responses on the part of the listener cannot be carried out to order. The mand *O dry your tears* has no effect upon lacrimal secretion. We cannot write a paradigm similar to that of Figure 31.1 in which the mand has the form *Weep, please!* because we cannot complete the account of the listener. A verbal response may be part of a larger pattern, however, which produces tears in the sensitive listener or reader for other reasons. Intonation and other properties are important in eliciting emotional behavior, and an emotional speaker will supplement his responses with very generous sound effects. We do not say *Cheer up!* in a dull tone, for we cannot leave the effect upon the listener to the mand alone. Properly pronounced, however, such a response may have an effect. The general process is not characteristic of the mand, and the same result is frequently (and probably more easily) obtained without the mand form.

THE MAGICAL MAND. There are mands which cannot be accounted for by showing that they have ever had the effect specified or any similar effect upon similar occasions. The speaker appears to create new mands on the analogy of old ones. Having effectively manded bread and butter, he goes on to mand the jam, even though he has never obtained jam before in this way. The poet exclaims *Milton, thou shouldst be living in this hour!*, al-

though he has never successfully addressed Milton before nor brought anyone to life with a similar response. The special relation between response and consequence exemplified by the mand establishes a general pattern of control over the environment. In moments of sufficient stress, the speaker simply describes the reinforcement appropriate to a given state of deprivation or aversive stimulation. The response must, of course, already be part of his verbal repertoire as some other type of verbal operant (Chapters 4 and 5).

This sort of extended operant may be called a magical mand. It does not exhaust the field of verbal magic, but it is the commonest example. Flushed with our success under favorable reinforcing circumstances, we set out to change the world without benefit of listener. Unable to imagine how the universe could have been created out of nothing, we conjecture that it was done with a verbal response. It was only necessary to say, with sufficient authority, *Let there be light!* The form *Let* is taken from situations in which it has been effective *(Let me go, Let him have it),* but we do not specify the listener who will make this instance effective.

Wishing frequently takes the mand form and must be classified as a magical mand if the consequences specified have never actually occurred as the result of similar verbal behavior. The speaker may specify some reinforcing state of affairs either for himself *(O to be in England, now that April's there!)* or for others *(Happy birthday!).* In *cursing,* the mand specifies punishing circumstances. The curse is more clearly a mand when it enjoins the listener to arrange his own punishment; *Oh, go jump in the lake!* is somewhat more explicit as to the modus operandi than *Bad luck to you!*

The form *may* is associated with mands in many ways. *You may go* is permission (as contrasted with *You can go*) and, as we have seen, permission is a type of mand. *May I go?* is a mand for verbal action which is to have the form of permission. In *I may (possibly) go* or *Maybe I'll go, may* is an example of a kind of verbal behavior (to be discussed in Chapter 12) which is close to the mand. In *May you always be happy* or *May you suffer the torments of Job* the form is a sort of generalized mand *(cf. Please).* In the expanded form *I wish that* (or *My wish is that) you may always be happy,* the *may* keeps the same "optative" function. *Would* is another common generalized mand *(Would God I were a tender apple blossom). O* serves something of the same function *(cf.* Browning's wish to be in England in April), but also serves to point up the mand character of vocatives *(O Captain, my Captain!)* and questions *(O what can ail thee, knight-at-arms).* When the accompanying response is not in the form of a mand (*O, Brignall banks are wild and fair*), *O* may be regarded as manding the attention of the listener or reader. This is evidently its function in such an example as *O, what a beautiful morning!,* in which case it functions very much like the more specific mand *Look,* noted below.

THE MAND IN LITERATURE. As several of these examples suggest, certain forms of literary behavior are rich in mands. Some of these are vocatives (*Reader, I married him*), some mand verbal behavior (*Call me Ishmael*), and some mand the attention of the reader (*Listen, my children, and you shall hear . . .*). Because of the tenuous relation between writer and reader, many of these are necessarily magical. Lyric poems in particular are rich in literary mands. Of the first lines of English lyric poems in a number of anthologies about 40 per cent were found to be of a form most characteristic of mands. Fifteen per cent of these specify the behavior of the reader: he is to pay attention, with both eyes and ears. The poet is affected here by the reinforcements which are responsible for the vulgar forms *Look, See,* and *Listen*—forms which mainly call attention to the speaker (*Listen, have you seen George?, Look, can you give me some help?* or *See here, what are you up to?*). *See* is also used to mand attention to something being described (*There he stood, see, and I said to him . . .*). The poetic variant of *See* is *Behold.* The poet mands the listener to see someone sitting upon a grassy green and to hark, not only to his words, but to the lark. He also mands him to speak up (*Tell me, where is fancy bred?*), to be quiet (*Oh, never say that I was false of heart*), and to co-operate in various practical affairs related to the poet's deprivation: *Come, let us kiss, Come live with me and be my love, Take, O take those lips away,* or *Drink to me only with thine eyes.* These are not always *magical* mands—though an appropriate reinforcement would possibly come as a surprise—but other examples seem to be necessarily so (*Go and catch a falling star*). When the reader is manded to alter or control his emotions

(*Then hate me when thou wilt, Weep with me, Love me no more*), these specifications cannot be followed to the letter, as we have seen, but collateral results may not be inappropriate.

In another 15 per cent of the first lines, the poet begins by addressing someone or something besides the reader. Crimson roses are asked to speak, spotted snakes with double tongues are asked to vanish, and Ulysses, worthy Greek, is asked to appear. The remaining 10 per cent of probable mands are plain statements of wishes (*A book of verses underneath the bough . . .*) or statements prefixed with *Let, May, O,* or *Would.*

The richness of these examples from literature exemplifies a general principle which will be confirmed again in later chapters. "Poetic license" is not an empty term. Literature is the product of a special verbal practice which brings out behavior which would otherwise remain latent in the repertoires of most speakers (see Chapter 16). Among other things the tradition and practice of lyric poetry encourage the emission of behavior under the control of strong deprivations—in other words, responses in the form of mands. Evidently the lyric poet needs many things and needs them badly. He needs a reader and a reader's attention and participation. After that he needs to have someone or something brought to him or taken away. Verbal behavior strengthened as the result of these various deprivations is emitted, in spite of its manifest ineffectiveness or weakness, because of the poetic practice. The lyric form warrants or permits "unreasonable" behavior, and in so doing it supplies the student of verbal behavior with especially useful material.

NOTES

1. S = stimulus, R = response. The superscript V identifies verbal terms. S^D is technically a *discriminative* stimulus, i.e., not an eliciting stimulus.

2. Jesperson, O., *Language* (New York, 1922), p. 157.

32

NOAM CHOMSKY

Avram Noam Chomsky (1928–) was first exposed to linguistics by his father, a scholar who examined the historical linguistics of Hebrew. Chomsky received his B.A. (1949), M.A. (1951), and Ph.D. (1955) from the University of Pennsylvania, where he worked with Zellig S. Harris. He accepted a job at the Massachusetts Institute of Technology in 1955, becoming a full professor in 1961 and the Ferrari P. Ward professor of foreign languages and linguistics in 1966. In addition to his numerous books and articles on linguistics, Chomsky writes books critical of American foreign policy and mass media, including *Necessary Illusions: Thought Control in Democratic Societies* (1989) and *A New Generation Draws the Line: Kosovo, East Timor and the Standards of the West* (2001).

REVIEW OF VERBAL BEHAVIOR BY B. F. SKINNER

1. A great many linguists and philosophers concerned with language have expressed the hope that their studies might ultimately be embedded in a framework provided by behaviorist psychology, and that refractory areas of investigation, particularly those in which meaning is involved, will in this way be opened up to fruitful exploration. Since this volume is the first large-scale attempt to incorporate the major aspects of linguistic behavior within a behaviorist framework, it merits and will undoubtedly receive careful attention. Skinner is noted for his contributions to the study of animal behavior. The book under review is the product of study of linguistic behavior extending over more than twenty years. Earlier versions of it have been fairly widely circulated, and there are quite a few references in the psychological literature to its major ideas.

The problem to which this book is addressed is that of giving a "functional analysis" of verbal behavior. By functional analysis, Skinner means identification of the variables that control this behavior and specification of how they interact to determine a particular verbal response. Furthermore, the controlling variables are to be described completely in terms of such notions as stimulus, reinforcement, deprivation, which have been given a reasonably clear meaning in animal experimentation. In other words, the goal of the book is to provide a way to predict and control verbal behavior by observing and manipulating the physical environment of the speaker.

Skinner feels that recent advances in the laboratory study of animal behavior permit us to approach this problem with a certain optimism, since "the basic processes and relations which give verbal behavior its special characteristics are now fairly well understood . . . the results [of this experimental work] have been surprisingly free of species restrictions. Recent work has shown that the methods can be extended to human behavior without serious modification" (3).[1]

It is important to see clearly just what it is in Skinner's program and claims that makes them appear so bold and remarkable. It is not primarily the fact that he has set functional analysis as his problem, or that he limits himself to study of "observables," i.e. input-output relations. What is so surprising is the particular limitations he has imposed on the way in which the observables of behavior are to be studied, and, above all, the particularly simple nature of the "function" which, he claims, describes the causation of behavior. One would naturally expect that prediction of the behavior of a complex organism (or machine) would require, in addition to information about external stimulation, knowledge of the internal structure of the organism, the ways in which it processes input information and organizes its

From Noam Chomsky, "Verbal Behavior, Review." *Language* 35 (1959):26–58.

own behavior. These characteristics of the organism are in general a complicated product of inborn structure, the genetically determined course of maturation, and past experience. Insofar as independent neurophysiological evidence is not available, it is obvious that inferences concerning the structure of the organism are based on observation of behavior and outside events. Nevertheless, one's estimate of the relative importance of external factors and internal structure in the determination of behavior will have an important effect on the direction of research on linguistic (or any other) behavior, and on the kinds of analogies from animal behavior studies that will be considered relevant or suggestive.

Putting it differently, anyone who sets himself the problem of analyzing the causation of behavior will (in the absence of independent neurophysiological evidence) concern himself with the only data available, namely the record of inputs to the organism and the organism's present response, and will try to describe the function specifying the response in terms of the history of inputs. This is nothing more than the definition of his problem. There are no possible grounds for argument here, if one accepts the problem as legitimate, though Skinner has often advanced and defended this definition of a problem as if it were a thesis which other investigators reject. The differences that arise between those who affirm and those who deny the importance of the specific "contribution of the organism" to learning and performance concern the particular character and complexity of this function, and the kinds of observations and research necessary for arriving at a precise specification of it. If the contribution of the organism is complex, the only hope of predicting behavior even in a gross way will be through a very indirect program of research that begins by studying the detailed character of the behavior itself and the particular capacities of the organism involved.

Skinner's thesis is that external factors consisting of present stimulation and the history of reinforcement (in particular the frequency, arrangement, and withholding of reinforcing stimuli) are of overwhelming importance, and that the general principles revealed in laboratory studies of these phenomena provide the basis for understanding the complexities of verbal behavior. He confidently and repeatedly voices his claim to have demonstrated that the contribution of the speaker is quite trivial and elementary, and that precise prediction of verbal behavior involves only specification of the few external factors that he has isolated experimentally with lower organisms.

Careful study of this book (and of the research on

which it draws) reveals, however, that these astonishing claims are far from justified. It indicates, furthermore, that the insights that have been achieved in the laboratories of the reinforcement theorist, though quite genuine, can be applied to complex human behavior only in the most gross and superficial way, and that speculative attempts to discuss linguistic behavior in these terms alone omit from consideration factors of fundamental importance that are, no doubt, amenable to scientific study, although their specific character cannot at present be precisely formulated. Since Skinner's work is the most extensive attempt to accommodate human behavior involving higher mental faculties within a strict behaviorist schema of the type that has attracted many linguists and philosophers, as well as psychologists, a detailed documentation is of independent interest. The magnitude of the failure of this attempt to account for verbal behavior serves as a kind of measure of the importance of the factors omitted from consideration, and an indication of how little is really known about this remarkably complex phenomenon.

The force of Skinner's argument lies in the enormous wealth and range of examples for which he proposes a functional analysis. The only way to evaluate the success of his program and the correctness of his basic assumptions about verbal behavior is to review these examples in detail and to determine the precise character of the concepts in terms of which the functional analysis is presented. §2 of this review describes the experimental context with respect to which these concepts are originally defined. §§3–4 deal with the basic concepts "stimulus," "response," and "reinforcement," §§6–10 with the new descriptive machinery developed specifically for the description of verbal behavior. In §5 we consider the status of the fundamental claim, drawn from the laboratory, which serves as the basis for the analogic guesses about human behavior that have been proposed by many psychologists. The final section (§11) will consider some ways in which further linguistic work may play a part in clarifying some of these problems.

2. Although this book makes no direct reference to experimental work, it can be understood only in terms of the general framework that Skinner has developed for the description of behavior. Skinner divides the responses of the animal into two main categories. *Respondents* are purely reflex responses elicited by particular stimuli. *Operants* are emitted responses, for which no obvious stimulus can be discovered. Skinner has been concerned primarily with operant behavior. The experimental arrangement that he introduced consists basically of a box with a bar attached to one wall in such a way that

when the bar is pressed, a food pellet is dropped into a tray (and the bar press is recorded). A rat placed in the box will soon press the bar, releasing a pellet into the tray. This state of affairs, resulting from the bar press, increases the *strength* of the bar-pressing operant. The food pellet is called a *reinforcer;* the event, a reinforcing event. The strength of an operant is defined by Skinner in terms of the rate of response during extinction (i.e., after the last reinforcement and before return to the pre-conditioning rate).

Suppose that release of the pellet is conditional on the flashing of a light. Then the rat will come to press the bar only when the light flashes. This is called *stimulus discrimination.* The response is called a *discriminated operant* and the light is called the *occasion* for its emission; this is to be distinguished from elicitation of a response by a stimulus in the case of the respondent.[2] Suppose that the apparatus is so arranged that bar-pressing of only a certain character (e.g., duration) will release the pellet. The rat will then come to press the bar in the required way. This process is called *response differentiation.* By successive slight changes in the conditions under which the response will be reinforced it is possible to shape the response of a rat or a pigeon in very surprising ways in a very short time, so that rather complex behavior can be produced by a process of successive approximation.

A stimulus can become reinforcing by repeated association with an already reinforcing stimulus. Such a stimulus is called a *secondary reinforcer.* Like many contemporary behaviorists, Skinner considers money, approval, and the like to be secondary reinforcers which have become reinforcing because of their association with food etc.[3] Secondary reinforcers can be *generalized* by associating them with a variety of different primary reinforcers.

Another variable that can affect the rate of the bar-pressing operant is drive, which Skinner defines operationally in terms of hours of deprivation. His major scientific book, *Behavior of organisms,* is a study of the effects of food-deprivation and conditioning on the strength of the bar-pressing response of healthy mature rats. Probably Skinner's most original contribution to animal behavior studies has been his investigation of the effects of intermittent reinforcement, arranged in various different ways, presented in *Behavior of organisms* and extended (with pecking of pigeons as the operant under investigation) in the recent *Schedules of reinforcement* by Ferster and Skinner (1957). It is apparently these studies that Skinner has in mind when he refers to the recent advances in the study of animal behavior.[4]

The notions "stimulus," "response," "reinforcement" are relatively well defined with respect to the bar-pressing experiments and others similarly restricted. Before we can extend them to real-life behavior, however, certain difficulties must be faced. We must decide, first of all, whether any physical event to which the organism is capable of reacting is to be called a stimulus on a given occasion, or only one to which the organism in fact reacts; and correspondingly, we must decide whether any part of behavior is to be called a response, or only one connected with stimuli in lawful ways. Questions of this sort pose something of a dilemma for the experimental psychologist. If he accepts the broad definitions, characterizing any physical event impinging on the organism as a stimulus and any part of the organism's behavior as a response, he must conclude that behavior has not been demonstrated to be lawful. In the present state of our knowledge, we must attribute an overwhelming influence on actual behavior to ill-defined factors of attention, set, volition, and caprice. If we accept the narrower definitions, then behavior is lawful by definition (if it consists of responses); but this fact is of limited significance, since most of what the animal does will simply not be considered behavior. Hence the psychologist either must admit that behavior is not lawful (or that he cannot at present show that it is—not at all a damaging admission for a developing science), or must restrict his attention to those highly limited areas in which it is lawful (e.g. with adequate controls, bar-pressing in rats; lawfulness of the observed behavior provides, for Skinner, an implicit definition of a good experiment).

Skinner does not consistently adopt either course. He utilizes the experimental results as evidence for the scientific character of his system of behavior, and analogic guesses (formulated in terms of a metaphoric extension of the technical vocabulary of the laboratory) as evidence for its scope. This creates the illusion of a rigorous scientific theory with a very broad scope, although in fact the terms used in the description of real-life and of laboratory behavior may be mere homonyms, with at most a vague similarity of meaning. To substantiate this evaluation, a critical account of his book must show that with a literal reading (where the terms of the descriptive system have something like the technical meanings given in Skinner's definitions) the book covers almost no aspect of linguistic behavior, and that with a metaphoric reading, it is no more scientific than the traditional approaches to this subject matter, and rarely as clear and careful.[5]

3. Consider first Skinner's use of the notions "stimulus" and "response." In *Behavior of organisms* (9) he

commits himself to the narrow definitions for these terms. A part of the environment and a part of behavior are called stimulus (eliciting, discriminated, or reinforcing) and response, respectively, only if they are lawfully related; that is, if the "dynamic laws" relating them show smooth and reproducible curves. Evidently stimuli and responses, so defined, have not been shown to figure very widely in ordinary human behavior.[6] We can, in the face of presently available evidence, continue to maintain the lawfulness of the relation between stimulus and response only by depriving them of their objective character. A typical example of "stimulus control" for Skinner would be the response to a piece of music with the utterance *Mozart* or to a painting with the response *Dutch.* These responses are asserted to be "under the control of extremely subtle properties" of the physical object or event (108). Suppose instead of saying *Dutch* we had said *Clashes with the wallpaper, I thought you liked abstract work, Never saw it before, Tilted, Hanging too low, Beautiful, Hideous, Remember our camping trip last summer?,* or whatever else might come into our minds when looking at a picture (in Skinnerian translation, whatever other responses exist in sufficient strength). Skinner could only say that each of these responses is under the control of some other stimulus property of the physical object. If we look at a red chair and say *red,* the response is under the control of the stimulus "redness"; if we say *chair,* it is under the control of the collection of properties (for Skinner, the object) "chairness" (110), and similarly for any other response. This device is as simple as it is empty. Since properties are free for the asking (we have as many of them as we have nonsynonymous descriptive expressions in our language, whatever this means exactly), we can account for a wide class of responses in terms of Skinnerian functional analysis by identifying the "controlling stimuli." But the word "stimulus" has lost all objectivity in this usage. Stimuli are no longer part of the outside physical world; they are driven back into the organism. We identify the stimulus when we hear the response. It is clear from such examples, which abound, that the talk of "stimulus control" simply disguises a complete retreat to mentalistic psychology. We cannot predict verbal behavior in terms of the stimuli in the speaker's environment, since we do not know what the current stimuli are until he responds. Furthermore, since we cannot control the property of a physical object to which an individual will respond, except in highly artificial cases, Skinner's claim that his system, as opposed to the traditional one, permits the practical control of verbal behavior[7] is quite false.

Other examples of "stimulus control" merely add to the general mystification. Thus a proper noun is held to be a response "under the control of a specific person or thing" (as controlling stimulus, 113). I have often used the words *Eisenhower* and *Moscow,* which I presume are proper nouns if anything is, but have never been "stimulated" by the corresponding objects. How can this fact be made compatible with this definition? Suppose that I use the name of a friend who is not present. Is this an instance of a proper noun under the control of the friend as stimulus? Elsewhere it is asserted that a stimulus controls a response in the sense that presence of the stimulus increases the probability of the response. But it is obviously untrue that the probability that a speaker will produce a full name is increased when its bearer faces the speaker. Furthermore, how can one's own name be a proper noun in this sense? A multitude of similar questions arise immediately. It appears that the word "control" here is merely a misleading paraphrase for the traditional "denote" or "refer." The assertion (115) that so far as the speaker is concerned, the relation of reference is "simply the probability that the speaker will emit a response of a given form in the presence of a stimulus having specified properties" is surely incorrect if we take the words "presence," "stimulus," and "probability" in their literal sense. That they are not intended to be taken literally is indicated by many examples, as when a response is said to be "controlled" by a situation or state of affairs as "stimulus." Thus, the expression *a needle in a haystack* "may be controlled as a unit by a particular type of situation" (116); the words in a single part of speech, e.g. all adjectives, are under the control of a single set of subtle properties of stimuli (121); "the sentence *The boy runs a store* is under the control of an extremely complex stimulus situation" (335); "*He is not at all well* may function as a standard response under the control of a state of affairs which might also control *He is ailing*" (325); when an envoy observes events in a foreign country and reports upon his return, his report is under "remote stimulus control" (416); the statement *This is war* may be a response to a "confusing international situation" (441); the suffix-*ed* is controlled by that "subtle property of stimuli which we speak of as action-in-the-past" (121) just as the -*s* in *The boy runs* is under the control of such specific features of the situation as its "currency" (332). No characterization of the notion "stimulus control" that is remotely related to the bar-pressing experiment (or that preserves the faintest objectivity) can be made to cover a set of examples like these, in which, for example, the "controlling stimulus" need not even impinge on the responding organism.

Consider now Skinner's use of the notion "response." The problem of identifying units in verbal behavior has of course been a primary concern of linguists, and it seems very likely that experimental psychologists should be able to provide much-needed assistance in clearing up the many remaining difficulties in systematic identification. Skinner recognizes (20) the fundamental character of the problem of identification of a unit of verbal behavior, but is satisfied with an answer so vague and subjective that it does not really contribute to its solution. The unit of verbal behavior—the verbal operant—is defined as a class of responses of identifiable form functionally related to one or more controlling variables. No method is suggested for determining in a particular instance what are the controlling variables, how many such units have occurred, or where their boundaries are in the total response. Nor is any attempt made to specify how much or what kind of similarity in form or "control" is required for two physical events to be considered instances of the same operant. In short, no answers are suggested for the most elementary questions that must be asked of anyone proposing a method for description of behavior. Skinner is content with what he calls an "extrapolation" of the concept of operant developed in the laboratory to the verbal field. In the typical Skinnerian experiment, the problem of identifying the unit of behavior is not too crucial. It is defined, by fiat, as a recorded peck or bar-press, and systematic variations in the rate of this operant and its resistance to extinction are studied as a function of deprivation and scheduling of reinforcement (pellets). The operant is thus defined with respect to a particular experimental procedure. This is perfectly reasonable, and has led to many interesting results. It is, however, completely meaningless to speak of extrapolating this concept of operant to ordinary verbal behavior. Such "extrapolation" leaves us with no way of justifying one or another decision about the units in the "verbal repertoire."

Skinner specifies "response strength" as the basic datum, the basic dependent variable in his functional analysis. In the bar-pressing experiment, response strength is defined in terms of rate of emission during extinction. Skinner has argued[8] that this is "the only datum that varies significantly and in the expected direction under conditions which are relevant to the 'learning process.'" In the book under review, response strength is defined as "probability of emission" (22). This definition provides a comforting impression of objectivity, which, however, is quickly dispelled when we look into the matter more closely. The term "probability" has some rather obscure meaning for Skinner in this book.[9] We are told, on the one hand, that "our evidence for the contribution of each variable [to response strength] is based on observation of frequencies alone" (28). At the same time, it appears that frequency is a very misleading measure of strength, since, for example, the frequency of a response may be "primarily attributable to the frequency of occurrence of controlling variables" (27). It is not clear how the frequency of a response can be attributable to anything BUT the frequency of occurrence of its controlling variables if we accept Skinner's view that the behavior occurring in a given situation is "fully determined" by the relevant controlling variables (175, 228). Furthermore, although the evidence for the contribution of each variable to response strength is based on observation of frequencies alone, it turns out that "we base the notion of strength upon several kinds of evidence" (22), in particular (22-8): emission of the response (particularly in unusual circumstances), energy level (stress), pitch level, speed and delay of emission, size of letters etc. in writing, immediate repetition, and—a final factor, relevant but misleading—over-all frequency.

Of course, Skinner recognizes that these measures do not co-vary, because (among other reasons) pitch, stress, quantity, and reduplication may have internal linguistic functions.[10] However, he does not hold these conflicts to be very important, since the proposed factors indicative of strength are "fully understood by everyone" in the culture (27). For example, "if we are shown a prized work of art and exclaim *Beautiful!*, the speed and energy of the response will not be lost on the owner." It does not appear totally obvious that in this case the way to impress the owner is to shriek *Beautiful* in a loud, high-pitched voice, repeatedly, and with no delay (high response strength). It may be equally effective to look at the picture silently (long delay), and then to murmur *Beautiful* in a soft, low-pitched voice (by definition, very low response strength).

It is not unfair, I believe, to conclude from Skinner's discussion of response strength, the "basic datum" in functional analysis, that his "extrapolation" of the notion of probability can best be interpreted as, in effect, nothing more than a decision to use the word "probability," with its favorable connotations of objectivity, as a cover term to paraphrase such low-status words as "interest," "intention," "belief," and the like. This interpretation is fully justified by the way in which Skinner uses the terms "probability" and "strength." To cite just one example, Skinner defines the process of confirming an assertion in science as one of "generating additional variables to increase its probability" (425), and more generally, its strength (425–9). If we take this suggestion quite literally, the degree of confirmation of a scientific assertion can be measured as a simple function of the loudness, pitch, and frequency with which it is proclaimed, and a general procedure for increasing its degree of confirmation would be, for instance, to train machine guns on large crowds of people who have been instructed to shout it. A better indication of what Skinner probably has in mind here is given by his description of how the theory of evolution, as an example, is confirmed. This "single set of verbal responses . . . is made more plausible—is strengthened—by several types of construction based upon verbal responses in geology, paleontology, genetics, and so on" (427). We are no doubt to interpret the terms "strength" and "probability" in this context as paraphrases of more familiar locutions such as "justified belief" or "warranted assertability," or something of the sort. Similar latitude of interpretation is presumably expected when we read that "frequency of effective action accounts in turn for what we may call the listener's 'belief'" (88) or that "our belief in what someone tells us is similarly a function of, or identical with, our tendency to act upon the verbal stimuli which he provides" (160).[11]

I think it is evident, then, that Skinner's use of the terms "stimulus," "control," "response," and "strength" justify the general conclusion stated in the last paragraph of §2 above. The way in which these terms are brought to bear on the actual data indicates that we must interpret them as mere paraphrases for the popular vocabulary commonly used to describe behavior, and as having no particular connection with the homonymous expressions used in the description of laboratory experiments. Naturally, this terminological revision adds no objectivity to the familiar "mentalistic" mode of description.

4. The other fundamental notion borrowed from the description of barpressing experiments is "reinforcement." It raises problems which are similar, and even more serious. In *Behavior of organisms,* "the operation of reinforcement is defined as the presentation of a certain kind of stimulus in a temporal relation with either a stimulus or response. A reinforcing stimulus is defined as such by its power to produce the resulting change [in strength]. There is no circularity about this: some stimuli are found to produce the change, others not, and they are classified as reinforcing and non-reinforcing accordingly" (62). This is a perfectly appropriate definition[12] for the study of schedules of reinforcement. It is perfectly useless, however, in the discussion of real-life behav-

ior, unless we can somehow characterize the stimuli which are reinforcing (and the situations and conditions under which they are reinforcing). Consider first of all the status of the basic principle that Skinner calls the "law of conditioning" (law of effect). It reads: "if the occurrence of an operant is followed by presence of a reinforcing stimulus, the strength is increased" (*Behavior of organisms* 21). As "reinforcement" was defined, this law becomes a tautology.[13] For Skinner, learning is just change in response strength.[14] Although the statement that presence of reinforcement is a sufficient condition for learning and maintenance of behavior is vacuous, the claim that it is a necessary condition may have some content, depending on how the class of reinforcers (and appropriate situations) is characterized. Skinner does make it very clear that in his view reinforcement is a necessary condition for language learning and for the continued availability of linguistic responses in the adult.[15] However, the looseness of the term "reinforcement" as Skinner uses it in the book under review makes it entirely pointless to inquire into the truth or falsity of this claim. Examining the instances of what Skinner calls "reinforcement," we find that not even the requirement that a reinforcer be an identifiable stimulus is taken seriously. In fact, the term is used in such a way that the assertion that reinforcement is necessary for learning and continued availability of behavior is likewise empty.

To show this, we consider some example of "reinforcement." First of all, we find a heavy appeal to automatic self-reinforcement. Thus, "a man talks to himself . . . because of the reinforcement he receives" (163); "the child is reinforced automatically when he duplicates the sounds of airplanes, streetcars . . ." (164); "the young child alone in the nursery may automatically reinforce his own exploratory verbal behavior when he produces sounds which he has heard in the speech of others" (58); "the speaker who is also an accomplished listener 'knows when he has correctly echoed a response' and is reinforced thereby" (68); thinking is "behaving which automatically affects the behaver and is reinforcing because it does so" (438; cutting one's finger should thus be reinforcing, and an example of thinking); "the verbal fantasy, whether overt or covert, is automatically reinforcing to the speaker as listener. Just as the musician plays or composes what he is reinforced by hearing, or as the artist paints what reinforces him visually, so the speaker engaged in verbal fantasy says what he is reinforced by hearing or writes what he is reinforced by reading" (439); similarly, care in problem solving, and rationalization, are automatically self-reinforcing (442–3). We can also reinforce someone by emitting verbal behavior as such (since this rules out a class of aversive stimulations, 167), by not emitting verbal behavior (keeping silent and paying attention, 199), or by acting appropriately on some future occasion (152: "the strength of [the speaker's] behavior is determined mainly by the behavior which the listener will exhibit with respect to a given state of affairs"; this Skinner considers the general case of "communication" or "letting the listener know"). In most such cases, of course, the speaker is not present at the time when the reinforcement takes place, as when "the artist . . . is reinforced by the effects his works have upon . . . others" (224), or when the writer is reinforced by the fact that his "verbal behavior may reach over centuries or to thousands of listeners or readers at the same time. The writer may not be reinforced often or immediately, but his net reinforcement may be great" (206; this accounts for the great "strength" of his behavior). An individual may also find it reinforcing to injure someone by criticism or by bringing bad news, or to publish an experimental result which upsets the theory of a rival (154), to describe circumstances which would be reinforcing if they were to occur (165), to avoid repetition (222), to "hear" his own name though in fact it was not mentioned or to hear nonexistent words in his child's babbling (259), to clarify or otherwise intensify the effect of a stimulus which serves an important discriminative function (416), etc.

From this sample, it can be seen that the notion of reinforcement has totally lost whatever objective meaning it may ever have had. Running through these examples, we see that a person can be reinforced though he emits no response at all, and that the reinforcing "stimulus" need not impinge on the "reinforced person" or need not even exist (it is sufficient that it be imagined or hoped for). When we read that a person plays what music he likes (165), says what he likes (165), thinks what he likes (438 9), reads what books he likes (163), etc., BECAUSE he finds it reinforcing to do so, or that we write books or inform others of facts BECAUSE we are reinforced by what we hope will be the ultimate behavior of reader or listener, we can only conclude that the term "reinforcement" has a purely ritual function. The phrase "X is reinforced by Y (stimulus, state of affairs, event, etc.)" is being used as a cover term for "X wants Y," "X likes Y," "X wishes that Y were the case," etc. Invoking the term "reinforcement" has no explanatory force, and any idea that this paraphrase introduces any new clarity or objectivity into the description of wishing, liking, etc., is a serious delusion. The only effect is to obscure

the important differences among the notions being paraphrased. Once we recognize the latitude with which the term "reinforcement" is being used, many rather startling comments lose their initial effect—for instance, that the behavior of the creative artist is "controlled entirely by the contingencies of reinforcement" (150). What has been hoped for from the psychologist is some indication how the casual and informal description of everyday behavior in the popular vocabulary can be explained or clarified in terms of the notions developed in careful experiment and observation, or perhaps replaced in terms of a better scheme. A mere terminological revision, in which a term borrowed from the laboratory is used with the full vagueness of the ordinary vocabulary, is of no conceivable interest.

It seems that Skinner's claim that all verbal behavior is acquired and maintained in "strength" through reinforcement is quite empty, because his notion of reinforcement has no clear content, functioning only as a cover term for any factor, detectable or not, related to acquisition or maintenance of verbal behavior.[16] Skinner's use of the term "conditioning" suffers from a similar difficulty. Pavlovian and operant conditioning are processes about which psychologists have developed real understanding. Instruction of human beings is not. The claim that instruction and imparting of information are simply matters of conditioning (357 66) is pointless. The claim is true, if we extend the term "conditioning" to cover these processes, but we know no more about them after having revised this term in such a way as to deprive it of its relatively clear and objective character. It is, as far as we know, quite false, if we use "conditioning" in its literal sense. Similarly, when we say that "it is the function of predication to facilitate the transfer of response from one term to another or from one object to another" (361), we have said nothing of any significance. In what sense is this true of the predication *Whales are mammals?* Or, to take Skinner's example, what point is there in saying that the effect of *The telephone is out of order* on the listener is to bring behavior formerly controlled by the stimulus *out of order* under control of the stimulus *telephone* (or the telephone itself) by a process of simple conditioning (362)? What laws of conditioning hold in this case? Furthermore, what behavior is "controlled" by the stimulus *out of order,* in the abstract? Depending on the object of which this is predicated, the present state of motivation of the listener, etc., the behavior may vary from rage to pleasure, from fixing the object to throwing it out, from simply not using it to trying to use it in the normal way (e.g. to see if it is really out of order), and so on. To speak of "conditioning" or "bringing previously available behavior under control of a new stimulus" in such a case is just a kind of play-acting at science. Cf. also footnote 43.

5. The claim that careful arrangement of contingencies of reinforcement by the verbal community is a necessary condition for language learning has appeared, in one form or another, in many places.[17] Since it is based not on actual observation, but on analogies to laboratory study of lower organisms, it is important to determine the status of the underlying assertion within experimental psychology proper. The most common characterization of reinforcement (one which Skinner explicitly rejects, incidentally) is in terms of drive reduction. This characterization can be given substance by defining drives in some way independently of what in fact is learned. If a drive is postulated on the basis of the fact that learning takes place, the claim that reinforcement is necessary for learning will again become as empty as it is in the Skinnerian framework. There is an extensive literature on the question of whether there can be learning with out drive-reduction (latent learning). The "classical" experiment of Blodgett indicated that rats who had explored a maze without reward showed a marked drop in number of errors (as compared to a control group which had not explored the maze) upon introduction of a food reward, indicating that the rat had learned the structure of the maze without reduction of the hunger drive. Drive-reduction theorists countered with an exploratory drive which was reduced during the prereward learning, and claimed that a slight decrement in errors could be noted before food reward. A wide variety of experiments, with somewhat conflicting results, have been carried out with a similar design.[18] Few investigators still doubt the existence of the phenomenon. Hilgard, in his general review of learning theory,[19] concludes that "there is no longer any doubt but that, under appropriate circumstances, latent learning is demonstrable."

More recent work has shown that novelty and variety of stimulus are sufficient to arouse curiosity in the rat and to motivate it to explore (visually), and in fact, to learn (since on a presentation of two stimuli, one novel, one repeated, the rat will attend to the novel one);[20] that rats will learn to choose the arm of a single-choice maze that leads to a complex maze, running through this being their only "reward";[21] that monkeys can learn object discriminations and maintain their performance at a high level of efficiency with visual exploration (looking out of a window for 30 seconds) as the only reward;[22] and, perhaps most strikingly of all, that monkeys and apes will solve rather complex manipulation problems that are simply placed in their cages, and will solve discrimination problems with only exploration and manipulation as incentives.[23] In these cases, solving the problem is apparently its own "reward." Results of this kind can be handled by reinforcement theorists only if they are willing to set up curiosity, exploration, and manipulation drives, or to speculate somehow about acquired drives[24] for which there is no evidence outside of the fact that learning takes place in these cases.

There is a variety of other kinds of evidence that has been offered to challenge the view that drive-reduction is necessary for learning. Results on sensory-sensory conditioning have been interpreted as demonstrating learning without drive-reduction.[25] Olds has reported reinforcement by direct stimulation of the brain, from which he concludes that reward need not satisfy a physiological need or withdraw a drive stimulus.[26] The phenomenon of imprinting, long observed by zoologists, is of particular interest in this connection. Some of the most complex patterns of behavior of birds, in particular, are directed towards objects and animals of the type to which they have been exposed at certain critical early periods of life.[27] Imprinting is the most striking evidence for the innate disposition of the animal to learn in a certain direction, and to react appropriately to patterns and objects of certain restricted types, often only long after the original learning has taken place. It is, consequently, unrewarded learning, though the resulting patterns of behavior may be refined through reinforcement. Acquisition of the typical songs of song birds is, in some cases, a type of imprinting. Thorpe reports studies that show "that some characteristics of the normal song have been learnt in the earliest youth, before the bird itself is able to produce any kind of full song."[28] The phenomenon of imprinting has recently been investigated under laboratory conditions and controls with positive results.[29]

Phenomena of this general type are certainly familiar from everyday experience. We recognize people and places to which we have given no particular attention. We can look up something in a book and learn it perfectly well with no other motive than to confute reinforcement theory, or out of boredom, or idle curiosity. Everyone engaged in research must have had the experience of working with feverish and prolonged intensity to write a paper which no one else will read or to solve a problem which no one else thinks important and which will bring no conceivable reward—which may only confirm a general opinion that the researcher is wasting his time on irrelevancies. The fact that rats and monkeys do likewise is interesting, and important to show in careful experiment. In fact, studies of behavior of the type mentioned above have an independent and positive significance that far outweighs their incidental importance in bringing into question the claim that learning is impossible without drive-reduction. It is not at all unlikely that insights arising from animal behavior studies with this broadened scope may have the kind of relevance to such complex activities as verbal behavior that reinforcement theory has, so far, failed to exhibit. In any event, in the light of presently available evidence, it is difficult to see how anyone can be willing to claim that reinforcement is necessary for learning, if reinforcement is taken seriously as something identifiable independently of the resulting change in behavior.

Similarly, it seems quite beyond question that children acquire a good deal of their verbal and nonverbal behavior by casual observation and imitation of adults and other children.[30] It is simply not true that children can learn language only through "meticulous care" on the part of adults who shape their verbal repertoire through careful differential reinforcement, though it may be that such care is often the custom in academic families. It is a common observation that a young child of immigrant parents may learn a second language in the streets, from other children, with amazing rapidity, and that his speech may be completely fluent and correct to the last allophone, while the subtleties that become second nature to the child may elude his parents despite high motivation and continued practice. A child may pick up a large part of his vocabulary and "feel" for sentence structure from television, from reading, from listening to adults, etc. Even a very young child who has not yet acquired a minimal repertoire from which to form new utterances may imitate a word quite well on an early try, with no attempt on the part of his parents to teach it to him. It is also perfectly obvious that, at a later stage, a child will be able to construct and understand utterances which are quite new, and are, at the same time, acceptable sentences in his language. Every time an adult reads a newspaper, he undoubtedly comes upon countless new sentences which are not at all similar, in a simple, physical sense, to any that he has heard before, and which he will recognize as sentences and understand; he will also be able to detect slight distortions or misprints. Talk of "stimulus generalization" in such a case simply perpetuates the mystery under a new title. These abilities indicate that there must be fundamental processes at work quite independently of "feedback" from the environment. I have been able to find no support whatsoever for the doctrine of Skinner and others that slow and careful shaping of verbal behavior through

differential reinforcement is an absolute necessity. If reinforcement theory really requires the assumption that there be such meticulous care, it seems best to regard this simply as a reductio ad absurdum argument against this approach. It is also not easy to find any basis (or, for that matter, to attach very much content) to the claim that reinforcing contingencies set up by the verbal community are the single factor responsible for maintaining the strength of verbal behavior. The sources of the "strength" of this behavior are almost a total mystery at present. Reinforcement undoubtedly plays a significant role, but so do a variety of motivational factors about which nothing serious is known in the case of human beings.

As far as acquisition of language is concerned, it seems clear that reinforcement, casual observation, and natural inquisitiveness (coupled with a strong tendency to imitate) are important factors, as is the remarkable capacity of the child to generalize, hypothesize, and "process information" in a variety of very special and apparently highly complex ways which we cannot yet describe or begin to understand, and which may be largely innate, or may develop through some sort of learning or through maturation of the nervous system. The manner in which such factors operate and interact in language acquisition is completely unknown. It is clear that what is necessary in such a case is research, not dogmatic and perfectly arbitrary claims, based on analogies to that small part of the experimental literature in which one happens to be interested.

The pointlessness of these claims becomes clear when we consider the well-known difficulties in determining to what extent inborn structure, maturation, and learning are responsible for the particular form of a skilled or complex performance.[31] To take just one example,[32] the gaping response of a nestling thrush is at first released by jarring of the nest, and, at a later stage, by a moving object of specific size, shape, and position relative to the nestling. At this later stage the response is directed towards the part of the stimulus object corresponding to the parent's head, and characterized by a complex configuration of stimuli that can be precisely described. Knowing just this, it would be possible to construct a speculative, learning-theoretic account of how this sequence of behavior patterns might have developed through a process of differential reinforcement, and it would no doubt be possible to train rats to do something similar. However, there appears to be good evidence that these responses to fairly complex "sign stimuli" are genetically determined and mature without learning. Clearly, the possibility cannot be discounted.

Consider now the comparable case of a child imitating new words. At an early stage we may find rather gross correspondence. At a later stage, we find that repetition is of course far from exact (i.e. it is not mimicry, a fact which itself is interesting), but that it reproduces the highly complex configuration of sound features that constitute the phonological structure of the language in question. Again, we can propose a speculative account of how this result might have been obtained through elaborate arrangement of reinforcing contingencies. Here too, however, it is possible that ability to select out of the complex auditory input those features that are phonologically relevant may develop largely independently of reinforcement, through genetically determined maturation. To the extent that this is true, an account of the development and causation of behavior that fails to consider the structure of the organism will provide no understanding of the real processes involved.

It is often argued that experience, rather than innate capacity to handle information in certain specific ways, must be the factor of overwhelming dominance in determining the specific character of language acquisition, since a child speaks the language of the group in which he lives. But this is a superficial argument. As long as we are speculating, we may consider the possibility that the brain has evolved to the point where, given an input of observed Chinese sentences, it produces (by an "induction" of apparently fantastic complexity and suddenness) the "rules" of Chinese grammar, and given an input of observed English sentences, it produces (by, perhaps, exactly the same process of induction) the rules of English grammar; or that given an observed application of a term to certain instances it automatically predicts the extension to a class of complexly related instances. If clearly recognized as such, this speculation is neither unreasonable nor fantastic; nor, for that matter, is it beyond the bounds of possible study. There is of course no known neural structure capable of performing this task in the specific ways that observation of the resulting behavior might lead us to postulate; but for that matter, the structures capable of accounting for even the simplest kinds of learning have similarly defied detection.[33]

Summarizing this brief discussion, it seems that there is neither empirical evidence nor any known argument to support any SPECIFIC claim about the relative importance of "feedback" from the environment and the "independent contribution of the organism" in the process of language acquisition.

6. We now turn to the system that Skinner develops specifically for the description of verbal behavior. Since this system is based on the notions "stimulus," "re-

sponse," and "reinforcement," we can conclude from the preceding sections that it will be vague and arbitrary. For reasons noted in §1, however, I think it is important to see in detail how far from the mark any analysis phrased solely in these terms must be and how completely this system fails to account for the facts of verbal behavior.

Consider first the term "verbal behavior" itself. This is defined as "behavior reinforced through the mediation of other persons" (2). The definition is clearly much too broad. It would include as "verbal behavior," for example, a rat pressing the bar in a Skinner-box, a child brushing his teeth, a boxer retreating before an opponent, and a mechanic repairing an automobile. Exactly how much of ordinary linguistic behavior is "verbal" in this sense, however, is something of a question: perhaps, as I have pointed out above, a fairly small fraction of it, if any substantive meaning is assigned to the term "reinforced." This definition is subsequently refined by the additional provision that the mediating response of the reinforcing person (the "listener") must itself "have been conditioned *precisely in order to reinforce* the behavior of the speaker" (225, italics his). This still covers the examples given above, if we can assume that the "reinforcing" behavior of the psychologist, the parent, the opposing boxer, and the paying customer are the result of appropriate training, which is perhaps not unreasonable. A significant part of the fragment of linguistic behavior covered by the earlier definition will no doubt be excluded by the refinement, however. Suppose, for example, that while crossing the street I hear someone shout *Watch out for the car* and jump out of the way. It can hardly be proposed that my jumping (the mediating, reinforcing response in Skinner's usage) was conditioned (that is, I was trained to jump) precisely in order to reinforce the behavior of the speaker. Similarly for a wide class of cases. Skinner's assertion that with this refined definition "we narrow our subject to what is traditionally recognized as the verbal field" (225) appears to be grossly in error.

7. Verbal operants are classified by Skinner in terms of their "functional" relation to discriminated stimulus, reinforcement, and other verbal responses. A *mand* is defined as "a verbal operant in which the response is reinforced by a characteristic consequence and is therefore under the functional control of relevant conditions of deprivation or aversive stimulation" (35). This is meant to include questions, commands, etc. Each of the terms in this definition raises a host of problems. A mand such as *Pass the salt* is a class of responses. We cannot tell by observing the form of a response whether

it belongs to this class (Skinner is very clear about this), but only by identifying the controlling variables. This is generally impossible. Deprivation is defined in the bar-pressing experiment in terms of length of time that the animal has not been fed or permitted to drink. In the present context, however, it is quite a mysterious notion. No attempt is made here to describe a method for determining "relevant conditions of deprivation" independently of the "controlled" response. It is of no help at all to be told (32) that it can be characterized in terms of the operations of the experimenter. If we define deprivation in terms of elapsed time, then at any moment a person is in countless states of deprivation.[34] It appears that we must decide that the relevant condition of deprivation was (say) salt-deprivation, on the basis of the fact that the speaker asked for salt (the reinforcing community which "sets up" the mand is in a similar predicament). In this case, the assertion that a mand is under the control of relevant deprivation is empty, and we are (contrary to Skinner's intention) identifying the response as a mand completely in terms of form. The word "relevant" in the definition above conceals some rather serious complications.

In the case of the mand *Pass the salt,* the word "deprivation" is not out of place, though it appears to be of little use for functional analysis. Suppose however that the speaker says *Give me the book, Take me for a ride,* or *Let me fix it.* What kinds of deprivation can be associated with these mands? How do we determine or measure the relevant deprivation? I think we must conclude in this case, as before, either that the notion "deprivation" is relevant at most to a minute fragment of verbal behavior, or else that the statement "X is under Y-deprivation" is just an odd paraphrase for "X wants Y," bearing a misleading and unjustifiable connotation of objectivity.

The notion "aversive control" is just as confused. This is intended to cover threats, beating, and the like (33). The manner in which aversive stimulation functions is simply described. If a speaker has had a history of appropriate reinforcement (e.g. if a certain response was followed by "cessation of the threat of such injury of events which have previously been followed by such injury and which are therefore conditioned aversive stimuli") then he will tend to give the proper response when the threat which had previously been followed by the injury is presented. It would appear to follow from this description that a speaker will not respond properly to the mand *Your money or your life* (38) unless he has a past history of being killed. But even if the difficulties in describing the mechanism of aversive

control are somehow removed by a more careful analysis, it will be of little use for identifying operants for reasons similar to those mentioned in the case of deprivation.

It seems, then, that in Skinner's terms there is in most cases no way to decide whether a given response is an instance of a particular mand. Hence it is meaningless, within the terms of his system, to speak of the *characteristic* consequences of a mand, as in the definition above. Furthermore, even if we extend the system so that mands can somehow be identified, we will have to face the obvious fact that most of us are not fortunate enough to have our requests, commands, advice, and so on characteristically reinforced (they may nevertheless exist in considerable "strength"). These responses could therefore not be considered mands by Skinner. In fact, Skinner sets up a category of "magical mands" (48–9) to cover the case of 'mands which cannot be accounted for by showing that they have ever had the effect specified or any similar effect upon similar occasions' (the word "ever" in this statement should be replaced by "characteristically"). In these pseudo mands, "the speaker simply describes the reinforcement appropriate to a given state of deprivation or aversive stimulation." In other words, given the meaning that we have been led to assign to "reinforcement" and "deprivation," the speaker asks for what he wants. The remark that "a speaker appears to create new mands on the analogy of old ones" is also not very helpful.

Skinner's claim that his new descriptive system is superior to the traditional one "because its terms can be defined with respect to experimental operations" (45) is, we see once again, an illusion. The statement "X wants Y" is not clarified by pointing out a relation between rate of bar-pressing and hours of food-deprivation; replacing "X wants Y" by "X is deprived of Y" adds no new objectivity to the description of behavior. His further claim for the superiority of the new analysis of mands is that it provides an objective basis for the traditional classification into requests, commands, etc. (38–41). The traditional classification is in terms of the intention of the speaker. But intention, Skinner holds, can be reduced to contingencies of reinforcement, and, correspondingly, we can explain the traditional classification in terms of the reinforcing behavior of the listener. Thus a question is a mand which "specifies verbal action, and the behavior of the listener permits us to classify it as a request, a command, or a prayer" (39). It is a request if "the listener is independently motivated to reinforce the speaker"; a command if "the listener's behavior is . . . reinforced by reducing a threat"; a prayer if the mand "promotes reinforcement by generating an emotional disposition." The mand is advice if the listener is positively reinforced by the consequences of mediating the reinforcement of the speaker; it is a warning if "by carrying out the behavior specified by the speaker the listener escapes from aversive stimulation"; and so on. All this is obviously wrong if Skinner is using the words "request," "command," etc., in anything like the sense of the corresponding English words. The word "question" does not cover commands. *Please pass the salt* is a request (but not a question), whether or not the listener happens to be motivated to fulfill it; not everyone to whom a request is addressed is favorably disposed. A response does not cease to be a command if it is not followed; nor does a question become a command if the speaker answers it because of an implied or imagined threat. Not all advice is good advice, and a response does not cease to be advice if it is not followed. Similarly, a warning may be misguided; heeding it may cause aversive stimulation, and ignoring it might be positively reinforcing. In short, the entire classification is beside the point. A moment's thought is sufficient to demonstrate the impossibility of distinguishing between requests, commands, advice, etc., on the basis of the behavior or disposition of the particular listener. Nor can we do this on the basis of the typical behavior of all listeners. Some advice is never taken, is always bad, etc., and similarly with other kinds of mands. Skinner's evident satisfaction with this analysis of the traditional classification is extremely puzzling.

8. Mands are operants with no specified relation to a prior stimulus. A *tact,* on the other hand, is defined as "a verbal operant in which a response of given form is evoked (or at least strengthened) by a particular object or event or property of an object or event" (81). The examples quoted in the discussion of stimulus control (§3) are all tacts. The obscurity of the notion "stimulus control" makes the concept of the tact rather mystical. Since, however, the tact is "the most important of verbal operants," it is important to investigate the development of this concept in more detail.

We first ask why the verbal community "sets up" tacts in the child—that is, how the parent is reinforced by setting up the tact. The basic explanation for this behavior of the parent (85–6) is the reinforcement he obtains by the fact that his contact with the environment is extended; to use Skinner's example, the child may later be able to call him to the telephone. (It is difficult to see, then, how first children acquire tacts, since the parent does not have the appropriate history of reinforcement). Reasoning in the same way, we may conclude that the

parent induces the child to walk so that he can make some money delivering newspapers. Similarly, the parent sets up an "echoic repertoire" (e.g. a phonemic system) in the child because this makes it easier to teach him new vocabulary, and extending the child's vocabulary is ultimately useful to the parent. "In all these cases we explain the behavior of the reinforcing listener by pointing to an improvement in the possibility of controlling the speaker whom he reinforces" (56). Perhaps this provides the explanation for the behavior of the parent in inducing the child to walk: the parent is reinforced by the improvement in his control of the child when the child's mobility increases. Underlying these modes of explanation is a curious view that it is somehow more scientific to attribute to a parent a desire to control the child or enhance his own possibilities for action than a desire to see the child develop and extend his capacities. Needless to say, no evidence is offered to support this contention.

Consider now the problem of explaining the response of the listener to a tact. Suppose, for example, that B hears A say *fox* and reacts appropriately, looks around, runs away, aims his rifle, etc. How can we explain B's behavior? Skinner rightly rejects analyses of this offered by Watson and Bertrand Russell. His own equally inadequate analysis proceeds as follows (87–8). We assume (1) "that in the history of [B] the stimulus *fox* has been an occasion upon which looking around has been followed by seeing a fox" and (2) "that the listener has some current 'interest in seeing foxes'—that behavior which depends upon a seen fox for its execution is strong, and that the stimulus supplied by a fox is therefore reinforcing." B carries out the appropriate behavior, then, because "the heard stimulus *fox* is the occasion upon which turning and looking about is frequently followed by the reinforcement of seeing a fox"; i.e. his behavior is a discriminated operant. This explanation is unconvincing. B may never have seen a fox and may have no current interest in seeing one, and yet may react appropriately to the stimulus *fox*.[35] Since exactly the same behavior may take place when neither of the assumptions is fulfilled, some other mechanism must be operative here.

Skinner remarks several times that his analysis of the tact in terms of stimulus control is an improvement over the traditional formulations in terms of reference and meaning. This is simply not true. His analysis is fundamentally the same as the traditional one, though much less carefully phrased. In particular, it differs only by indiscriminate paraphrase of such notions as denotation (reference) and connotation (meaning), which have been kept clearly apart in traditional formulations, in terms of the vague concept "stimulus control." In one traditional formulation a descriptive term is said to denote a set of entities and to connote or designate a certain property or condition that an entity must possess or fulfil if the term is to apply to it.[36] Thus the term *vertebrate* refers to (denotes, is true of) vertebrates and connotes the property "having a spine" or something of the sort. This connoted defining property is called the meaning of the term. Two terms may have the same reference but different meanings. Thus it is apparently true that the creatures with hearts are all and only the vertebrates. If so, then the term *creature with a heart* refers to vertebrates and designates the property "having a heart." This is presumably a different property (a different general condition) from having a spine; hence the terms *vertebrate* and *creature with a heart* are said to have different meanings. This analysis is not incorrect (for at least one sense of meaning), but its many limitations have frequently been pointed out.[37] The major problem is that there is no good way to decide whether two descriptive terms designate the same property.[38] As we have just seen, it is not sufficient that they refer to the same objects. *Vertebrate* and *creature with a spine* would be said to designate the same property (distinct from that designated by *creature with a heart*). If we ask why this is so, the only answer appears to be that the terms are synonymous. The notion "property" thus seems somehow language-bound, and appeal to "defining properties" sheds little light on questions of meaning and synonymy.

Skinner accepts the traditional account in toto, as can be seen from his definition of a tact as a response under control of a property (stimulus) of some physical object or event. We have found that the notion "control" has no real substance, and is perhaps best understood as a paraphrase of "denote" or "connote" or, ambiguously, both. The only consequence of adopting the new term "stimulus control" is that the important differences between reference and meaning are obscured. It provides no new objectivity. The stimulus controlling the response is determined by the response itself; there is no independent and objective method of identification (see §3 above). Consequently, when Skinner defines "synonymy" as the case in which "the same stimulus leads to quite different responses" (118), we can have no objection. The responses *chair* and *red* made alternatively to the same object are not synonymous, because the stimuli are called different. The responses *vertebrate* and *creature with a spine* would be considered synonymous because they are controlled by the same property of the object under investigation; in more traditional and no less scientific terms, they evoke the same concept. Similarly, when metaphorical extension is explained as due to "the control exercised by properties of the stimulus which, though present at reinforcement, do not enter into the contingency respected by the verbal community" (92; traditionally, accidental properties), no objection can be raised which has not already been levelled against the traditional account. Just as we could "explain" the response *Mozart* to a piece of music in terms of subtle properties of the controlling stimuli, we can, with equal facility, explain the appearance of the response *sun* when no sun is present, as in *Juliet is [like] the sun.* "We do so by noting that Juliet and the sun have common properties, at least in their effect on the speaker" (93). Since any two objects have indefinitely many properties in common, we can be certain that we will never be at a loss to explain a response of the form *A is like B,* for arbitrary A and B. It is clear, however, that Skinner's recurrent claim that his formulation is simpler and more scientific than the traditional account has no basis in fact.

Tacts under the control of private stimuli (Bloomfield's "displaced speech") form a large and important class (130–46), including not only such responses as *familiar* and *beautiful,* but also verbal responses referring to past, potential, or future events or behavior. For example, the response *There was an elephant at the zoo* "must be understood as a response to current stimuli, including events within the speaker himself" (143).[39] If we now ask ourselves what proportion of the tacts in actual life are responses to (descriptions of) actual current outside stimulation, we can see just how large a role must be attributed to private stimuli. A minute amount of verbal behavior, outside the nursery, consists of such remarks as *This is red* and *There is a man.* The fact that "functional analysis" must make such a heavy appeal to obscure internal stimuli is again a measure of its actual advance over traditional formulations.

9. Responses under the control of prior verbal stimuli are considered under a different heading from the tact. An *echoic operant* is a response which "generates a sound pattern similar to that of the stimulus" (55). It covers only cases of immediate imitation.[40] No attempt is made to define the sense in which a child's echoic response is "similar" to the stimulus spoken in the father's bass voice; it seems, though there are no clear statements about this, that Skinner would not accept the account of the phonologist in this respect, but nothing else is offered. The development of an echoic repertoire is attributed completely to differential reinforcement. Since the speaker will do no more, according to Skinner,

than what is demanded of him by the verbal community, the degree of accuracy insisted on by this community will determine the elements of the repertoire, whatever these may be (not necessarily phonemes). "In a verbal community which does not insist on a precise correspondence, an echoic repertoire may remain slack and will be less successfully applied to novel patterns." There is no discussion of such familiar phenomena as the accuracy with which a child will pick up a second language or a local dialect in the course of playing with other children, which seem sharply in conflict with these assertions. No anthropological evidence is cited to support the claim that an effective phonemic system does not develop (this is the substance of the quoted remark) in communities that do not insist on precise correspondence.

A verbal response to a written stimulus (reading) is called "textual behavior."

Other verbal responses to verbal stimuli are called "intraverbal operants." Paradigm instances are the response *four* to the stimulus *two plus two* or the response *Paris* to the stimulus *capital of France*. Simple conditioning may be sufficient to account for the response *four* to *two plus two*,[41] but the notion of intraverbal response loses all meaning when we find it extended to cover most of the facts of history and many of the facts of science (72, 129); all word association and "flight of ideas" (73-6); all translations and paraphrase (77); reports of things seen, heard, or remembered (315); and, in general, large segments of scientific, mathematical, and literary discourse. Obviously the kind of explanation that might be proposed for a student's ability to respond with *Paris* to *capital of France,* after suitable practice, can hardly be seriously offered to account for his ability to make a judicious guess in answering the questions (to him new) *What is the seat of the French government?,* . . . *the source of the literary dialect?,* . . . *the chief target of the German blitzkrieg?,* etc., or his ability to prove a new theorem, translate a new passage, or paraphrase a remark for the first time or in a new way.

The process of "getting someone to see a point," to see something your way, or to understand a complex state of affairs (e.g. a difficult political situation or a mathematical proof) is, for Skinner, simply a matter of increasing the strength of the listener's already available behavior.[42] Since "the process is often exemplified by relatively intellectual scientific or philosophical discourse," Skinner considers it "all the more surprising that it may be reduced to echoic, textual, or intraverbal supplementation" (269). Again, it is only the vagueness and latitude with which the notions "strength" and "in-

traverbal response" are used that save this from absurdity. If we use these terms in their literal sense, it is clear that understanding a statement cannot be equated to shouting it frequently in a high-pitched voice (high response strength), and a clever and convincing argument cannot be accounted for on the basis of a history of pairings of verbal responses.[43]

10. A final class of operants, called *autoclitics,* includes those that are involved in assertion, negation, quantification, qualification of responses, construction of sentences, and the "highly complex manipulations of verbal thinking." All these acts are to be explained "in terms of behavior which is evoked by or acts upon other behavior of the speaker" (313). Autoclitics are, then, responses to already given responses, or rather, as we find in reading through this section, they are responses to covert or incipient or potential verbal behavior. Among the autoclitics are listed such expressions as *I recall, I imagine, for example, assume, let X equal* . . . , the terms of negation, the *is* of predication and assertion, *all, some, if, then,* and, in general, all morphemes other than nouns, verbs, and adjectives, as well as grammatical processes of ordering and arrangement. Hardly a remark in this section can be accepted without serious qualification. To take just one example, consider Skinner's account of the autoclitic *all* in *All swans are white* (329). Obviously we cannot assume that this is a tact to all swans as stimulus. It is suggested, therefore, that we take *all* to be an autoclitic modifying the whole sentence *Swans are white. All* can then be taken as equivalent to *always,* or *always it is possible to say.* Notice, however, that the modified sentence *Swans are white* is just as general as *All swans are white.* Furthermore, the proposed translation of *all* is incorrect if taken literally. It is just as possible to say *Swans are green* as to say *Swans are white.* It is not always possible to say either (e.g. while you are saying something else or sleeping). Probably what Skinner means is that the sentence can be paraphrased "*X is white* is true, for each swan X." But this paraphrase cannot be given within his system, which has no place for *true.*

Skinner's account of grammar and syntax as autoclitic processes (Chapter 13) differs from a familiar traditional account mainly in the use of the pseudoscientific terms "control" or "evoke" in place of the traditional "refer." Thus in *The boy runs,* the final *s* of *runs* is a tact under control of such "subtle properties of a situation" as "the nature of running as an *activity* rather than an object or property of an object."[44] (Presumably, then, in *The attempt fails, The difficulty remains, His anxiety increases,* etc., we must also say that the *s* indicates that the object described as the attempt is carrying out the activity of failing, etc.) In *the boy's gun,* however, the *s* denotes possession (as, presumably, in *the boy's arrival, . . . story, . . . age,* etc.) and is under the control of this "relational aspect of the situation" (336). The "relational autoclitic of order" (whatever it may mean to call the order of a set of responses a response to them) in *The boy runs the store* is under the control of an "extremely complex stimulus situation," namely, that the boy is running the store (335). *And* in *the hat and the shoe* is under the control of the property "pair." *Through* in *the dog went through the hedge* is under the control of the "relation between the going dog and the hedge" (342). In general, nouns are evoked by objects, verbs by actions, and so on.

Skinner considers a sentence to be a set of key responses (nouns, verbs, adjectives) on a skeletal frame (346). If we are concerned with the fact that Sam rented a leaky boat, the raw responses to the situation are *rent, boat, leak,* and *Sam.* Autoclitics (including order) which qualify these responses, express relations between them, and the like, are then added by a process called "composition" and the result is a grammatical sentence, one of many alternatives among which selection is rather arbitrary. The idea that sentences consist of lexical items placed in a grammatical frame is of course a traditional one, within both philosophy and linguistics. Skinner adds to it only the very implausible speculation that in the internal process of composition, the nouns, verbs, and adjectives are chosen first and then are arranged, qualified, etc., by autoclitic responses to these internal activities.[45]

This view of sentence structure, whether phrased in terms of autoclitics, syncategorematic expressions, or grammatical and lexical morphemes, is inadequate. *Sheep provide wool* has no (physical) frame at all, but no other arrangement of these words is an English sentence. The sequences *furiously sleep ideas green colorless* and *friendly young dogs seem harmless* have the same frames, but only one is a sentence of English (similarly, only one of the sequences formed by reading these from back to front). *Struggling artists can be a nuisance* has the same frame as *marking papers can be a nuisance,* but is quite different in sentence structure, as can be seen by replacing *can be* by *is* or *are* in both cases. There are many other similar and equally simple examples. It is evident that more is involved in sentence structure than insertion of lexical items in grammatical frames; no approach to language that fails to take these deeper processes into account can possibly achieve much success in accounting for actual linguistic behavior.

11. The preceding discussion covers all the major notions that Skinner introduces in his descriptive system. My purpose in discussing the concepts one by one was to show that in each case, if we take his terms in their literal meaning, the description covers almost no aspect of verbal behavior, and if we take them metaphorically, the description offers no improvement over various traditional formulations. The terms borrowed from experimental psychology simply lose their objective meaning with this extension, and take over the full vagueness of ordinary language. Since Skinner limits himself to such a small set of terms for paraphrase, many important distinctions are obscured. I think that this analysis supports the view expressed in §1 above, that elimination of the independent contribution of the speaker and learner (a result which Skinner considers of great importance, cf. 311–2) can be achieved only at the cost of eliminating all significance from the descriptive system, which then operates at a level so gross and crude that no answers are suggested to the most elementary questions.[46] The questions to which Skinner has addressed his speculations are hopelessly premature. It is futile to inquire into the causation of verbal behavior until much more is known about the specific character of this behavior; and there is little point in speculating about the process of acquisition without much better understanding of what is acquired.

Anyone who seriously approaches the study of linguistic behavior, whether linguist, psychologist, or philosopher, must quickly become aware of the enormous difficulty of stating a problem which will define the area of his investigations, and which will not be either completely trivial or hopelessly beyond the range of present-day understanding and technique. In selecting functional analysis as his problem, Skinner has set himself a task of the latter type. In an extremely interesting and insightful paper,[47] K. S. Lashley has implicitly delimited a class of problems which can be approached in a fruitful way by the linguist and psychologist, and which are clearly preliminary to those with which Skinner is concerned. Lashley recognizes, as anyone must who seriously considers the data, that the composition and production of an utterance is not simply a matter of stringing together a sequence of responses under the control of outside stimulation and intraverbal association, and that the syntactic organization of an utterance is not something directly represented in any simple way in the physical structure of the utterance itself. A variety of observations lead him to conclude that syntactic structure is "a generalized pattern imposed on the specific acts as they occur," and that "a consideration of the structure of the sentence and other motor sequences will show . . . that there are, behind the overtly expressed sequences, a multiplicity of integrative processes which can only be inferred from the final results of their activity." He also comments on the great difficulty of determining the "selective mechanisms" used in the actual construction of a particular utterance.

Although present-day linguistics cannot provide a precise account of these integrative processes, imposed patterns, and selective mechanisms, it can at least set itself the problem of characterizing these completely. It is reasonable to regard the grammar of a language L ideally as a mechanism that provides an enumeration of the sentences of L in something like the way in which a deductive theory gives an enumeration of a set of theorems. ("Grammar," in this sense of the word, includes phonology.) Furthermore, the theory of language can be regarded as a study of the formal properties of such grammars, and, with a precise enough formulation, this general theory can provide a uniform method for determining, from the process of generation of a given sentence, a structural description which can give a good deal of insight into how this sentence is used and understood. In short, it should be possible to derive from a properly formulated grammar a statement of the integrative processes and generalized patterns imposed on the specific acts that constitute an utterance. The rules of a grammar of the appropriate form can be subdivided into the two types, optional and obligatory; only the latter must be applied in generating an utterance. The optional rules of the grammar can be viewed, then, as the selective mechanisms involved in the production of a particular utterance. The problem of specifying these integrative processes and selective mechanisms is nontrivial and not beyond the range of possible investigation. The results of such a study might, as Lashley suggests, be of independent interest for psychology and neurology (and conversely). Although such a study, even if successful, would by no means answer the major problems involved in the investigation of meaning and the causation of behavior, it surely will not be unrelated to these. It is at least possible, furthermore, that such notions as "semantic generalization," to which such heavy appeal is made in all approaches to language in use, conceal complexities and specific structure of inference not far different from those that can be studied and exhibited in the case of syntax, and that consequently the general character of the results of syntactic investigations may be a corrective to oversimplified approaches to the theory of meaning.

The behavior of the speaker, listener, and learner of language constitutes, of course, the actual data for any study of language. The construction of a grammar which enumerates sentences in such a way that a meaningful structural description can be determined for each sentence does not in itself provide an account of this actual behavior. It merely characterizes abstractly the ability of one who has mastered the language to distinguish sentences from nonsentences, to understand new sentences (in part), to note certain ambiguities, etc. These are very remarkable abilities. We constantly read and hear new sequences of words, recognize them as sentences, and understand them. It is easy to show that the new events that we accept and understand as sentences are not related to those with which we are familiar by any simple notion of formal (or semantic or statistical) similarity or identity of grammatical frame. Talk of generalization in this case is entirely pointless and empty. It appears that we recognize a new item as a sentence not because it matches some familiar item in any simple way, but because it is generated by the grammar that each individual has somehow and in some form internalized. And we understand a new sentence, in part, because we are somehow capable of determining the process by which this sentence is derived in this grammar.

Suppose that we manage to construct grammars having the properties outlined above. We can then attempt to describe and study the achievement of the speaker, listener, and learner. The speaker and the listener, we must assume, have already acquired the capacities characterized abstractly by the grammar. The speaker's task is to select a particular compatible set of optional rules. If we know, from grammatical study, what choices are available to him and what conditions of compatibility the choices must meet, we can proceed meaningfully to investigate the factors that lead him to make one or another choice. The listener (or reader) must determine, from an exhibited utterance, what optional rules were chosen in the construction of the utterance. It must be admitted that the ability of a human being to do this far surpasses our present understanding. The child who learns a language has in some sense constructed the grammar for himself on the basis of his observation of sentences and nonsentences (i.e. corrections by the verbal community). Study of the actual observed ability of a speaker to distinguish sentences from nonsentences, detect ambiguities, etc., apparently forces us to the conclusion that this grammar is of an extremely complex and abstract character, and that the young child has succeeded in carrying out what from the formal point of view, at least, seems to be a remarkable type of theory construction. Furthermore, this task is accomplished in an astonishingly short time, to a large extent independently of intelligence, and in a comparable way by all children. Any theory of learning must cope with these facts.

It is not easy to accept the view that a child is capable of constructing an extremely complex mechanism for generating a set of sentences, some of which he has heard, or that an adult can instantaneously determine whether (and if so, how) a particular item is generated by this mechanism, which has many of the properties of an abstract deductive theory. Yet this appears to be a fair description of the performance of the speaker, listener, and learner. If this is correct, we can predict that a direct attempt to account for the actual behavior of speaker, listener, and learner, not based on a prior understanding of the structure of grammars, will achieve very limited success. The grammar must be regraded as a component in the behavior of the speaker and listener which can only be inferred, as Lashley has put it, from the resulting physical acts. The fact that all normal children acquire essentially comparable grammars of great complexity with remarkable rapidity suggests that human beings are somehow specially designed to do this, with data-handling or "hypothesis-formulating" ability of unknown character and complexity.[48] The study of linguistic structure may ultimately lead to some significant insights into this matter. At the moment the question cannot be seriously posed, but in principle it may be possible to study the problem of determining what the built-in structure of an information-processing (hypothesis-forming) system must be to enable it to arrive at the grammar of a language from the available data in the available time. At any rate, just as the attempt to eliminate the contribution of the speaker leads to a "mentalistic" descriptive system that succeeds only in blurring important traditional distinctions, a refusal to study the contribution of the child to language learning permits only a superficial account of language acquisition, with a vast and unanalyzed contribution attributed to a step called "generalization" which in fact includes just about everything of interest in this process. If the study of language is limited in these ways, it seems inevitable that major aspects of verbal behavior will remain a mystery.

NOTES

1. Skinner's confidence in recent achievements in the study of animal behavior and their applicability to complex human behavior does not appear to be widely shared. In many recent publications of confirmed behaviorists there is a prevailing note of skepticism with regard to the scope of these achievements. For representative comments, see the contributions to *Modern learning theory* (by Estes et al.; New York, 1954); Bugelski, *Psychology of learning* (New York, 1956); Koch, in *Nebraska symposium on motivation* 58 (Lincoln, 1956); Verplanck, Learned and innate behavior, *Psych. rev.* 52.139 (1955). Perhaps the strongest view is that of Harlow, who has asserted (Mice, monkeys, men, and motives, *Psych. rev.* 60.23–32 [1953]) that "a strong case can be made for the proposition that the importance of the psychological problems studied during the last 15 years has decreased as a negatively accelerated function approaching an asymptote of complete indifference." Tinbergen, a leading representative of a different approach to animal behavior studies (comparative ethology), concludes a discussion of "functional analysis" with the comment that "we may now draw the conclusion that the causation of behavior is immensely more complex than was assumed in the generalizations of the past. A number of internal and external factors act upon complex central nervous structures. Second, it will be obvious that the facts at our disposal are very fragmentary indeed"—*The study of instinct* 74 (Oxford, 1951).

2. In *Behavior of organisms* (New York, 1938), Skinner remarks that "although a conditioned operant is the result of the correlation of the response with a particular reinforcement, a relation between it and a discriminative stimulus acting prior to the response is the almost universal rule" (178–9). Even emitted behavior is held to be produced by some sort of "originating force" (51) which, in the case of operant behavior is not under experimental control. The distinction between eliciting stimuli, discriminated stimuli, and "originating forces" has never been adequately clarified, and becomes even more confusing when private internal events are considered to be discriminated stimuli (see below).

3. In a famous experiment, chimpanzees were taught to perform complex tasks to receive tokens which had become secondary reinforcers because of association with food. The idea that money, approval, prestige, etc. actually acquire their motivating effects on human behavior according to this paradigm is unproved, and not particularly plausible. Many psychologists within the behaviorist movement are quite skeptical about this (cf. fn. 23). As in the case of most aspects of human behavior, the evidence about secondary reinforcement is so fragmentary, conflicting, and complex that almost any view can find some support.

4. Skinner's remark quoted above about the generality of his basic results must be understood in the light of the experimental limitations he has imposed. If it were true in any deep sense that the basic processes in language are well understood and free of species restrictions, it would be ex-

tremely odd that language is limited to man. With the exception of a few scattered observations (cf. his article, A case history in scientific method, *The American psychologist* 11.221–33 [1956]), Skinner is apparently basing this claim on the fact that qualitatively similar results are obtained with bar-pressing of rats and pecking of pigeons under special conditions of deprivation and various schedules of reinforcement. One immediately questions how much can be based on these facts, which are in part at least an artifact traceable to experimental design and the definition of "stimulus" and "response" in terms of "smooth dynamic curves" (see below). The dangers inherent in any attempt to "extrapolate" to complex behavior from the study of such simple responses as bar-pressing should be obvious, and have often been commented on (cf. e.g. Harlow, op.cit.). The generality of even the simplest results is open to serious question. Cf. in this connection Bitterman, Wodinsky, and Candland, Some comparative psychology, *Am. jour. of psych.* 71.94–110 (1958), where it is shown that there are important qualitative differences in solution of comparable elementary problems by rats and fish.

5. An analogous argument, in connection with a different aspect of Skinner's thinking, is given by Seriven in *A study of radical behaviorism = Univ. of Minn. studies in philosophy of science,* Vol. 1. Cf. Verplanck's contribution to *Modern learning theory* (283–8) for more general discussion of the difficulties in formulating an adequate definition of "stimulus" and "response." He concludes, quite correctly, that in Skinner's sense of the word, stimuli are not objectively identifiable independently of the resulting behavior, nor are they manipulable. Verplanck presents a clear discussion of many other aspects of Skinner's system, commenting on the untestability of many of the so called "laws of behavior" and the limited scope of many of the others, and the arbitrary and obscure character of Skinner's notion of "lawful relation"; and, at the same time, noting the importance of the experimental data that Skinner has accumulated.

6. In *Behavior of organisms,* Skinner apparently was willing to accept this consequence. He insists (41–2) that the terms of casual description in the popular vocabulary are not validly descriptive until the defining properties of stimulus and response are specified, the correlation is demonstrated experimentally, and the dynamic changes in it are shown to be lawful. Thus, in describing a child as hiding from a dog, "it will not be enough to dignify the popular vocabulary by appealing to essential properties of 'dogness' or 'hidingness' and to suppose them intuitively known." But this is exactly what Skinner does in the book under review, as we will see directly.

7. 253 f. and elsewhere, repeatedly. As an example of how well we can control behavior using the notions developed in this book, Skinner shows here how he would go about evoking the response *pencil*. The most effective way, he suggests, is to say to the subject "Please say *pencil*" (our chances would, presumably, be even further improved by use of "aversive stimulation," e.g. holding a gun to his head). We can also "make sure that no pencil or writing instrument is available, then hand our subject a pad of paper appropriate to pencil sketching, and offer him a handsome reward for a recognizable picture of a cat." It would also be useful to have voices saying *pencil* or *pen and . . .* in the background; signs reading *pencil* or *pen and . . .*; or to place a "large and unusual pencil in an unusual place clearly in sight." "Under such circumstances, it is highly probable that our subject will say *pencil*." "The available techniques are all illustrated in this sample." These contributions of behavior theory to the practical control of human behavior are amply illustrated elsewhere in the book, as when Skinner shows (113–4) how we can evoke the response *red* (the device suggested is to hold a red object before the subject and say "Tell me what color this is").

In fairness, it must be mentioned that there are certain nontrivial applications of 'operant conditioning' to the control of human behavior. A wide variety of experiments have shown that the number of plural nouns (for example) produced by a subject will increase if the experimenter says "right" or "good" when one is produced (similarly, positive attitudes on a certain issue, stories with particular content, etc.; cf. Krasner, Studies of the conditioning of verbal behavior, *Psych. bull.,* Vol. 55 [1958], for a survey of several dozen experiments of this kind, mostly with positive results). It is of some interest that the subject is usually unaware of the process. Just what insight this gives into normal verbal behavior is not obvious. Nevertheless, it is an example of positive and not totally expected results using the Skinnerian paradigm.

8. Are theories of learning necessary?, *Psych. rev.* 57.193–216 (1950).

9. And elsewhere. In his paper Are theories of learning necessary?, Skinner considers the problem how to extend his analysis of behavior to experimental situations in which it is impossible to observe frequencies, rate of response being the only valid datum. His answer is that "the notion of probability is usually extrapolated to cases in which a frequency analysis cannot be carried out. In the field of behavior we arrange a situation in which frequencies are available as data, but we use the notion of probability in analyzing or formulating instances of even types of behavior which are not susceptible to this analysis" (199). There are, of course, conceptions of probability not based directly on frequency, but I do not see how any of these apply to the

cases that Skinner has in mind. I see no way of interpreting
the quoted passage other than as signifying an intention to
use the word "probability" in describing behavior quite independently of whether the notion of probability is at all
relevant.

10. Fortunately, "In English this presents no great difficulty" since, for example, "relative pitch levels . . . are not
. . . important" (25). No reference is made to the numerous
studies of the function of relative pitch levels and other in-
tonational features in English.

11. The vagueness of the word "tendency," as opposed
to "frequency," saves the latter quotation from the obvious
incorrectness of the former. Nevertheless, a good deal of
stretching is necessary. If "tendency" has anything like its
ordinary meaning, the remark is clearly false. One may believe strongly the assertion that Jupiter has four moons, that
many of Sophocles' plays have been irretrievably lost, that
the earth will burn to a crisp in ten million years, etc., without experiencing the slightest tendency to act upon these
verbal stimuli. We may, of course, turn Skinner's assertion
into a very unilluminating truth by defining "tendency to
act" to include tendencies to answer questions in certain
ways, under motivation to say what one believes is true.

12. One should add, however, that it is in general not
the stimulus as such that is reinforcing, but the stimulus in
a particular situational context. Depending on experimental
arrangement, a particular physical event or object may be
reinforcing, punishing, or unnoticed. Because Skinner limits himself to a particular, very simple experimental
arrangement, it is not necessary for him to add this qualification, which would not be at all easy to formulate precisely. But it is of course necessary if he expects to extend his
descriptive system to behavior in general.

13. This has been frequently noted.

14. See, for example, Are theories of learning necessary? 199. Elsewhere, he suggests that the term "learning"
be restricted to complex situations, but these are not characterized.

15. "A child acquires verbal behavior when relatively
unpatterned vocalizations, selectively reinforced, gradually
assume forms which produce appropriate consequences in
a given verbal community" (31). "Differential reinforcement shapes up all verbal forms, and when a prior stimulus
enters into the contingency, reinforcement is responsible
for its resulting control . . . The availability of behavior, its
probability or strength, depends on whether reinforcements
continue in effect and according to what schedules"
(203–4). Elsewhere, frequently.

16. Talk of schedules of reinforcement here is entirely
pointless. How are we to decide, for example, according to
what schedules covert reinforcement is "arranged," as in

thinking or verbal fantasy, or what the scheduling is of such
factors as silence, speech, and appropriate future reactions
to communicated information?

17. See, for example, Miller and Dollard, *Social learning and imitation* 82-3 (New York, 1941), for a discussion
of the "meticulous training" that they seem to consider necessary for a child to learn the meanings of words and syntactic patterns. The same notion is implicit in Mowrer's
speculative account of how language might be acquired, in
Learning theory and personality dynamics, Chapter 23
(New York, 1950). Actually, the view appears to be quite
general.

18. For a general review and analysis of this literature,
see Thistlethwaite, A critical review of latent learning and
related experiments, *Psych. bull.* 48.97–129 (1951). Mac-
Corquodale and Meehl, in their contribution to *Modern
learning theory,* carry out a serious and considered attempt
to handle the latent learning material from the standpoint of
drive-reduction theory, with (as they point out) not entirely
satisfactory results. Thorpe reviews the literature from the
standpoint of the ethologist, adding also material on hom-
ing and topographical orientation (*Learning and instinct in
animals* [Cambridge, 1956]).

19. *Theories of learning* 214 (1956).

20. Berlyne, Novelty and curiosity as determinants of
exploratory behavior, *Brit. jour. of psych.* 41.68 80 (1950);
id., Perceptual curiosity in the rat, *Jour. of comp. physiol.
psych.* 48.238 46 (1955); Thompson and Solomon, Spontaneous pattern discrimination in the rat, ibid. 47.104 7
(1951).

21. Montgomery, The role of the exploratory drive in
learning, ibid. 60–3. Many other papers in the same journal
are designed to show that exploratory behavior is a relatively independent primary "drive" aroused by novel external
stimulation.

22. Butler, Discrimination learning by Rhesus monkeys to visual exploration motivation, ibid. 46.95 8 (1953).
Later experiments showed that this "drive" is highly persistent, as opposed to derived drives which rapidly extinguish.

23. Harlow, Harlow, and Meyer, Learning motivated by
a manipulation drive, *Jour. exp. psych.* 40.228 34 (1950),
and later investigations initiated by Harlow. Harlow has
been particularly insistent on maintaining the inadequacy
of physiologically based drives and homeostatic need states
for explaining the persistence of motivation and rapidity of
learning in primates. He points out, in many papers, that
curiosity, play, exploration, and manipulation are, for primates, often more potent drives than hunger and the like,
and that they show none of the characteristics of acquired
drives. Hebb also presents behavioral and supporting neurological evidence in support of the view that in higher an-

imals there is a positive attraction in work, risk, puzzle, intellectual activity, mild fear and frustration, etc. (Drives and the CNS, *Psych. rev.* 62.243–54 [1955]). He concludes that "we need not work out tortuous and improbable ways to explain why men work for money, why children learn without, pain, why people dislike doing nothing."

In a brief note (Early recognition of the manipulative drive in monkeys, *British journal of animal behaviour* 3.71–2 [1955]), W. Dennis calls attention to the fact that early investigators (Romanes, 1882; Thorndike, 1901), whose "perception was relatively unaffected by learning theory, did note the intrinsically motivated behavior of monkeys," although, he asserts, no similar observations on monkeys have been made until Harlow's experiments. He quotes Romanes (*Animal intelligence* [1882]) as saying that "much the most striking feature in the psychology of this animal, and the one which is least like anything met with in other animals, was the tireless spirit of investigation." Analogous developments, in which genuine discoveries have blinded systematic investigators to the important insights of earlier work, are easily found within recent structural linguistics as well.

24. Thus J. S. Brown, in commenting on a paper of Harlow's in *Current theory and research in motivation* (Lincoln, 1953), argues that "in probably every instance [of the experiments cited by Harlow] an ingenious drive reduction theorist could find some fragment of fear, insecurity, frustration, or whatever, that he could insist was reduced and hence was reinforcing"(53). The same sort of thing could be said for the ingenious phlogiston or ether theorist.

25. Cf. Birch and Bitterman, Reinforcement and learning: The process of sensory integration, *Psych. rev.* 56.292–308 (1949).

26. See, for example, his paper A physiological study of reward in McClelland (ed.), *Studies in motivation* 134 43 (New York, 1955).

27. See Thorpe, op.cit., particularly 115–8 and 337–76, for an excellent discussion of this phenomenon, which has been brought to prominence particularly by the work of K. Lorenz (cf. Der Kumpan in der Umwelt des Vogels, parts of which are reprinted in English translation in Schiller (ed.), *Instinctive behavior* 83–128 (New York, 1957).

28. Op.cit. 372.

29. See e.g. Jaynes, Imprinting: Interaction of learned and innate behavior, *Jour. of comp. physiol. psych.* 49.201–6 (1956), where the conclusion is reached that 'the experiments prove that without any observable reward young birds of this species follow a moving stimulus object and very rapidly come to prefer that object to others.'

30. Of course it is perfectly possible to incorporate this fact within the Skinnerian frame work. If, for example, a

child watches an adult using a comb and then, with no instruction tries to comb his own hair, we can explain this act by saying that he performs it because he finds it reinforcing to do so, or because of the reinforcement provided by behaving like a person who is "reinforcing" (cf. 164). Similarly, an automatic explanation is available for any other behavior. It seems strange at first that Skinner pays so little attention to the literature on latent learning and related topics, considering the tremendous reliance that he places on the notion of reinforcement; I have seen no reference to it in his writings. Similarly, Keller and Schoenfeld, in what appears to be the only text written under predominantly Skinnerian influence, *Principles of psychology* (New York, 1950), dismiss the latent learning literature in one sentence as "beside the point," serving only "to obscure, rather than clarify, a fundamental principle" (the law of effect, 41). However, this neglect is perfectly appropriate in Skinner's case. To the drive-reductionist, or anyone else for whom the notion "reinforcement" has some substantive meaning, these experiments and observations are important (and often embarrassing). But in the Skinnerian sense of the word, neither these results nor any conceivable others can cast any doubt on the claim that reinforcement is essential for the acquisition and maintenance of behavior. Behavior certainly has some concomitant circumstances, and whatever they are, we can call them "reinforcement."

31. Tinbergen (op.cit., Chapter VI) reviews some aspects of this problem, discussing the primary role of maturation in the development of many complex motor patterns (e.g. flying, swimming) in lower organisms, and the effect of an "innate disposition to learn" in certain specific ways and at certain specific times. Cf. also Schiller, *Instinctive behavior* 265–88, for a discussion of the role of maturing motor patterns in apparently insightful behavior in the chimpanzee.

Lenneberg (*Language, evolution, and purposive behavior,* unpublished) presents a very interesting discussion of the part that biological structure may play in the acquisition of language, and the dangers in neglecting this possibility.

32. From among many cited by Tinbergen, op.cit. (this on page 85).

33. Cf. Lasbley, In search of the engram, *Symposium of the Society for Experimental Biology* 4.454–82 (1950). Sperry, On the neural basis of the conditioned response, *British journal of animal behaviour* 3.41–4 (1955), argues that to account for the experimental results of Lashley and others, and for other facts that he cites, it is necessary to assume that high level cerebral activity of the type of insight, expectancy, etc. is involved even in simple conditioning. He states that "we still lack today a satisfactory picture of the underlying neural mechanism" of the conditioned response.

34. Furthermore, the motivation of the speaker does not, except in the simplest cases, correspond in intensity to the duration of deprivation. An obvious counter-example is what Hebb has called the "salted-nut phenomenon" (*Organization of behavior* 199 [New York, 1949]). The difficulty is of course even more serious when we consider "deprivations" not related to physiological drives.

35. Just as he may have the appropriate reaction, both emotional and behavioral, to such utterances as *The volcano is erupting* or *There's a homicidal maniac in the next room* without any previous pairing of the verbal and the physical stimulus. Skinner's discussion of Pavlovian conditioning in language (154) is similarly unconvincing.

36. Mill, *A system of logic* (1843). Carnap gives a recent reformulation in Meaning and synonymy in natural languages, *Phil. studies* 6.33-47 (1955), defining the meaning (intension) of a predicate "Q" for a speaker X as "the general condition which an object y must fulfill in order for X to be willing to ascribe the predicate 'Q' to y." The connotation of an expression is often said to constitute its "cognitive meaning" as opposed to its "emotive meaning," which is, essentially, the emotional reaction to the expression.

Whether or not this is the best way to approach meaning, it is clear that denotation, cognitive meaning, and emotive meaning are quite different things. The differences are often obscured in empirical studies of meaning, with much consequent confusion. Thus Osgood has set himself the task of accounting for the fact that a stimulus comes to be a sign for another stimulus (a buzzer becomes a sign for food, a word for a things etc.). This is clearly (for linguistic signs) a problem of denotation. The method that he actually develops for quantifying and measuring meaning (cf. Osgood, Suci, Tannenbaum, *The measurement of meaning* [Urbana, 1957]) applies, however, only to emotive meaning. Suppose, for example, that A hates both Hitler and science intensely, and considers both highly potent and "active," while B, agreeing with A about Hitler, likes science very much, although he considers it rather ineffective and not too important. Then A may assign to "Hitler" and "science" the same position on the semantic differential, while B will assign "Hitler" the same position as A did, but "science" a totally different position. Yet A does not think that "Hitler" and "science" are synonymous or that they have the same reference, and A and B may agree precisely on the cognitive meaning of "science." Clearly it is the attitude toward the things (the emotive meaning of the words) that is being measured here. There is a gradual shift in Osgood's account from denotation to cognitive meaning to emotive meaning. The confusion is caused, no doubt, by the fact that the term "meaning" is used in all three senses (and oth-

ers). [See Carroll's review of the book by Osgood, Suci, and Tannenbaum in this number of LANGUAGE.]

37. Most clearly by Quine. See *From a logical point of view* (Cambridge, 1953), especially Chapters 2, 3, and 7.

38. A method for characterizing synonymy in terms of reference is suggested by Goodman, On likeness of meaning, *Analysis* 10.1-7 (1949). Difficulties are discussed by Goodman, On some differences about meaning, ibid. 13.90-6 (1953). Carnap (op.cit.) presents a very similar idea (§6), but somewhat misleadingly phrased, since he does not bring out the fact that only extensional (referential) notions are being used.

39. In general, the examples discussed here are badly handled, and the success of the proposed analyses is overstated. In each case, it is easy to see that the proposed analysis, which usually has an air of objectivity, is not equivalent to the analyzed expression. To take just one example, the response *I am looking for my glasses* is certainly not equivalent to the proposed paraphrases: "When I have behaved in this way in the past, I have found my glasses and have then stopped behaving in this way," or "Circumstances have arisen in which I am inclined to emit any behavior which in the past has led to the discovery of my glasses; such behavior includes the behavior of looking in which I am now engaged." One may look for one's glasses for the first time; or one may emit the same behavior in looking for one's glasses as in looking for one's watch, in which case *I am looking for my glasses* and *I am looking for my watch* are equivalent, under the Skinnerian paraphrase. The difficult questions of purposiveness cannot be handled in this superficial manner.

40. Skinner takes great pains, however, to deny the existence in human beings (or parrots) of any innate faculty or tendency to imitate. His only argument is that no one would suggest an innate tendency to read, yet reading and echoic behavior have similar "dynamic properties." This similarity, however, simply indicates the grossness of his descriptive categories.

In the case of parrots, Skinner claims that they have no instinctive capacity to imitate, but only to be reinforced by successful imitation (59). Given Skinner's use of the word "reinforcement," it is difficult to perceive any distinction here, since exactly the same thing could be said of any other instinctive behavior. For example, where another scientist would say that a certain bird instinctively builds a nest in a certain way, we could say in Skinner's terminology (equivalently) that the bird is instinctively reinforced by building the nest in this way. One is therefore inclined to dismiss this claim as another ritual introduction of the word "reinforce." Though there may, under some suitable clarification, be some truth in it, it is difficult to see how many of the cases reported by competent observers can be handled if "reinforcement" is given some substantive meaning. Cf. Thorpe, op.cit. 353 f.; Lorenz, *King Solomon's ring* 85–8 (New York, 1952); even Mowrer, who tries to show how imitation might develop through secondary reinforcement, cites a case, op.cit. 694, which he apparently believes, but where this could hardly be true. In young children, it seems most implausible to explain imitation in terms of secondary reinforcement.

41. Though even this possibility is limited. If we were to take these paradigm instances seriously, it should follow that a child who knows how to count from one to 100 could learn an arbitrary 10×10 matrix with these numbers as entries as readily as the multiplication table.

42. Similarly, "the universality of a literary work refers to the number of potential readers inclined to say the same thing" (275; i.e. the most "universal" work is a dictionary of clichés and greetings); a speaker is "stimulating" if he says what we are about to say ourselves (272); etc.

43. Similarly, consider Skinner's contention (362–5) that communication of knowledge or facts is just the process of making a new response available to the speaker. Here the analogy to animal experiments is particularly weak. When we train a rat to carry out some peculiar act, it makes sense to consider this a matter of adding a response to his repertoire. In the case of human communication, however, it is very difficult to attach any meaning to this terminology. If A imparts to B the information (new to B) that the railroads face collapse, in what sense can the response *The railroads face collapse* be said to be now, but not previously, available to B? Surely B could have said it before (not knowing whether it was true), and known that it was a sentence (as opposed to *Collapse face railroads the*). Nor is there any reason to assume that the response has increased in strength, whatever this means exactly (e.g. B may have no interest in the fact, or he may want it suppressed). It is not clear how we can characterize this notion of "making a response available" without reducing Skinner's account of "imparting knowledge" to a triviality.

44. 332. On the next page, however, the *s* in the same example indicates that "the object described as *the boy* possesses the property of running." The difficulty of even maintaining consistency with a conceptual scheme like this is easy to appreciate.

45. One might just as well argue that exactly the opposite is true. The study of hesitation pauses has shown that these tend to occur before the large categories—noun, verb, adjective; this finding is usually described by the statement that the pauses occur where there is maximum uncertainty or information. Insofar as hesitation indicates on-going composition (if it does at all), it would appear that the "key

responses" are chosen only after the "grammatical frame." Cf. C. E. Osgood, unpublished paper; Goldman-Eisler, Speech analysis and mental processes, *Language and speech* 1.67 (1958).

46. E.g. what are in fact the actual units of verbal behavior? Under what conditions will a physical event capture the attention (be a stimulus) or be a reinforcer? How do we decide what stimuli are in "control" in a specific case? When are stimuli "similar"? And so on. (It is not interesting to be told e.g. that we say *Stop* to an automobile or billiard ball because they are sufficiently similar to reinforcing people [46].)

The use of unanalyzed notions like "similar" and "generalization" is particularly disturbing, since it indicates an apparent lack of interest in every significant aspect of the learning or the use of language in new situations. No one has ever doubted that in some sense, language is learned by generalization, or that novel utterances and situations are in some way similar to familiar ones. The only matter of serious interest is the specific "similarity." Skinner has, apparently, no interest in this. Keller and Schoenfeld (op. cit.) proceed to incorporate these notions (which they identify) into their Skinnerian "modern objective psychology" by defining two stimuli to be similar when "we make the same sort of *response* to them" (124; but when are responses of the "same sort"?). They do not seem to notice that this definition converts their "principle of generalization" (116), under any reasonable interpretation of this, into a tautology. It is obvious that such a definition will not be of much help in the study of language learning or construction of new responses in appropriate situations.

47. The problem of serial order in behavior, in Jeffress (ed.), *Hixon symposium on cerebral mechanisms in behavior* (New York, 1951).

48. There is nothing essentially mysterious about this. Complex innate behavior patterns and innate "tendencies to learn in specific ways" have been carefully studied in lower organisms. Many psychologists have been inclined to believe that such biological structure will not have an important effect on acquisition of complex behavior in higher organisms, but I have not been able to find any serious justification for this attitude. Some recent studies have stressed the necessity for carefully analyzing the strategies available to the organism, regarded as a complex "information-processing system" (cf. Bruner, Goodnow, and Austin, *A study of thinking* [New York, 1956]; Newell, Shaw, and Simon, Elements of a theory of human problem solving, *Psych. rev.* 65.151–66 [1958]), if anything significant is to be said about the character of human learning. These may be largely innate, or developed by early learning processes about which very little is yet known. (But see Harlow, The

formation of learning sets, *Psych. rev.* 56.51–65 (1949), and many later papers, where striking shifts in the character of learning are shown as a result of early training; also Hebb, *Organization of behavior* 109 ff.) They are undoubt-

edly quite complex. Cf. Lenneberg, op.cit., and Lees, review of Chomsky's *Syntactic structures* in *Lg.* 33.4406 f. (1957), for discussion of the topics mentioned in this section.

33
~

SIR FREDERIC C. BARTLETT

Sir Frederic Charles Bartlett (1886–1969) discovered psychology through his philosophical interests, but once he had been introduced to the field, he repeatedly traveled 18 miles to the nearest public library to read the *Encyclopedia Britannica* article on psychology. He earned an M.A. in sociology and ethics from London University and continued at St. John's College, Cambridge, with plans to study anthropology. To prepare for anthropological fieldwork, Bartlett decided to study moral science and found the required and dreaded work of four hours a week in the psychology laboratory quite interesting. He graduated with a degree in moral science and accepted a position in the Cambridge Psychological Laboratory in 1922, and a new chair in experimental psychology in 1931. During World War II, he worked on a variety of applied problems for the Royal Air Force, for which he was knighted in 1948. Experimental psychology and ergonomics fascinated him throughout his career. In his autobiography he wrote: "I will finish with the sort of remark that ought to be perfectly obvious. A psychologist who thinks that his work is done, that all that is now needed is the application of a final scheme to new instances, is dead. Psychology will go and leave him lamenting. Like the reactions it studies, psychology is living and oriented forward: there can be no end to its achievements."

REMEMBERING: A STUDY IN EXPERIMENTAL AND SOCIAL PSYCHOLOGY

CHAPTER V

Experiments on Remembering
(b) The Method of Repeated Reproduction

1. Description of the Method

The *Method of Repeated Reproduction* follows almost exactly the plan of investigation adopted by Philippe in his experiments *Sur les transformations de nos images mentales,*[1] except that the material used was different

and the experiments themselves were continued for a much longer period. A subject was given a story, or an argumentative prose passage, or a simple drawing to study under prescribed conditions. He attempted a first reproduction usually after an interval of 15 minutes, and thereafter gave further reproductions at intervals of increasing length. By using this method I hoped to find something about the common types of change introduced by normal individuals into remembered material with increasing lapse of time. Obviously the nature of

From Sir Frederic C. Bartlett, "The Method of Repeated Production." In *Remembering: A Study in Experimental and Social Psychology* (pp. 63–94). Cambridge: Cambridge University Press, 1932.

the experiment renders it rather hazardous to speculate as to the exact conditions of change, but it is fairly easy to keep a check on the progressive nature of such transformations as actually occur.

There is one difficulty which is particularly acute. I hoped to continue to get reproductions until the particular material concerned had reached a stereotyped form. If reproductions are effected frequently, however, the form tends to become fixed very rapidly, while if long intervals are allowed to elapse between successive reproductions the process of gradual transformation may go on almost indefinitely. Consequently, the results of the experiment as they are here described no doubt represent a section only of an incomplete process of transformation.

Further, it is certain that in the transformations of material which, for example, produce the popular legend, or which develop current rumours, social influences play a very great part. These cannot be fully studied by *The Method of Repeated Reproduction,* though they are present in varying degrees. The method needs in this respect to be supplemented by others, and as will be seen I made an attempt to develop in this direction later.[2]

The material used in *The Method of Repeated Reproduction* belonged to two groups, and was either (*a*) verbal, or (*b*) graphic. All verbal material was written by the subject at the time of recall, and all graphic material reproduced by drawings. In this chapter I shall not present any of the data gained from the use of the graphical material. Practically all of the points which they brought out were repeatedly illustrated in a yet more striking way, in methods to be described and discussed later, and will be more conveniently considered then.[3]

Moreover, it would be impossible to present more than a very small part of the data obtained from verbal material without prolonging the discussion to an intolerable length. I shall therefore confine all detailed illustrations to a study of some of the repeated reproductions of a single story, though I shall have in mind throughout a mass of corroborative detail which cannot be presented here.

2. *The Material used and the Method of Presenting Results*

I have selected for special consideration a story which was adapted from a translation by Dr Franz Boas[4] of a North American folk-tale. Several reasons prompted the use of this story.

First, the story as presented belonged to a level of culture and a social environment exceedingly different from those of my subjects. Hence it seemed likely to af-

ford good material for persistent transformation. I had also in mind the general problem of what actually happens when a popular story travels about from one social group to another, and thought that possibly the use of this story might throw some light upon the general conditions of transformation under such circumstances. It may fairly be said that this hope was at least to some extent realised.

Secondly, the incidents described in some of the cases had no very manifest interconnexion, and I wished particularly to see how educated and rather sophisticated subjects would deal with this lack of obvious rational order.

Thirdly, the dramatic character of some of the events recorded seemed likely to arouse fairly vivid visual imagery in suitable subjects, and I thought perhaps further light might be thrown on some of the suggestions regarding the conditions and functions of imaging arising from the use of *The Method of Description.*

Fourthly, the conclusion of the story might easily be regarded as introducing a supernatural element, and I desired to see how this would be dealt with.

The original story was as follows:

The War of the Ghosts

One night two young men from Egulac went down to the river to hunt seals, and while they were there it became foggy and calm. Then they heard war-cries, and they thought: "Maybe this is a war-party." They escaped to the shore, and hid behind a log. Now canoes came up, and they heard the noise of paddles, and saw one canoe coming up to them. There were five men in the canoe, and they said:

"What do you think? We wish to take you along. We are going up the river to make war on the people."

One of the young men said: "I have no arrows."

"Arrows are in the canoe," they said.

"I will not go along. I might be killed. My relatives do not know where I have gone. But you," he said, turning to the other, "may go with them."

So one of the young men went, but the other returned home.

And the warriors went on up the river to a town on the other side of Kalama. The people came down to the water, and they began to fight, and many were killed. But presently the young man heard one of the warriors say: "Quick, let us go home: that Indian has been hit." Now he thought: "Oh, they are ghosts." He did not feel sick, but they said he had been shot.

So the canoes went back to Egulac, and the young

man went ashore to his house, and made a fire. And he told everybody and said: "Behold I accompanied the ghosts, and we went to fight. Many of our fellows were killed, and many of those who attacked us were killed. They said I was hit, and I did not feel sick."

He told it all, and then he became quiet. When the sun rose he fell down. Something black came out of his mouth. His face became contorted. The people jumped up and cried.

He was dead.

Each subject read the story through to himself twice, at his normal reading rate. Except in the case which will be indicated later, the first reproduction was made 15 minutes after this reading. Other reproductions were effected at intervals as opportunity offered. No attempt was made to secure uniformity in the length of interval for all subjects; obviously equalising intervals of any length in no way equalises the effective conditions of reproduction in the case of different subjects. No subject knew the aim of the experiment. All who were interested in this were allowed to think that the test was merely one for accuracy of recall.

I shall analyse the results obtained in three ways:

First, a number of reproductions will be given in full, together with some comments;

Secondly, special details of interest in this particular story will be considered;

Thirdly, certain general or common tendencies in the successive remembering of the story will be stated and discussed more fully.

3.   Some Complete Reproductions together with Comments

(a) After an interval of 20 hours subject H produced the following first reproduction:

The War of the Ghosts
Two men from Edulae went fishing. While thus occupied by the river they heard a noise in the distance.

"It sounds like a cry," said one, and presently there appeared some men in canoes who invited them to join the party on their adventure. One of the young men refused to go, on the ground of family ties, but the other offered to go.

"But there are no arrows," he said.

"The arrows are in the boat," was the reply.

He thereupon took his place, while his friend returned home. The party paddled up the river to Kalo-

ma, and began to land on the banks of the river. The enemy came rushing upon them, and some sharp fighting ensued. Presently some one was injured, and the cry was raised that the enemy were ghosts.

The party returned down the stream, and the young man arrived home feeling none the worse for his experience. The next morning at dawn he endeavoured to recount his adventures. While he was talking something black issued from his mouth. Suddenly he uttered a cry and fell down. His friends gathered round him.

But he was dead.

In general form (i) the story is considerably shortened, mainly by omissions; (ii) the phraseology becomes more modern, more "journalistic," e.g. "refused, on the ground of family ties"; "sharp fighting ensued"; "feeling none the worse for his experience"; "endeavoured to recount his adventures"; "something black issued from his mouth"; (iii) the story has already become somewhat more coherent and consequential than in its original form.

In matter there are numerous omissions and some transformations. The more familiar "boat" once replaces "canoe"; hunting seals becomes merely "fishing"; Egulac becomes Edulac, while Kalama changes to Kaloma. The main point about the ghosts is entirely misunderstood. The two excuses made by the man who did not wish to join the war-party change places; that "he refused on the ground of family ties" becomes the only excuse explicitly offered.

Eight days later this subject remembered the story as follows:

The War of the Ghosts
Two young men from Edulac went fishing. While thus engaged they heard a noise in the distance. "That sounds like a war-cry," said one, "there is going to be some fighting." Presently there appeared some warriors who invited them to join an expedition up the river.

One of the young men excused himself on the ground of family ties. "I cannot come," he said, "as I might get killed." So he returned home. The other man, however, joined the party, and they proceeded on canoes up the river. While landing on the banks the enemy appeared and were running down to meet them. Soon someone was wounded, and the party discovered that they were fighting against ghosts. The young man and his companion returned to the boats, and went back to their homes.

The next morning at dawn he was describing his adventures to his friends, who had gathered round him. Suddenly something black issued from his mouth, and he fell down uttering a cry. His friends closed around him, but found that he was dead.

All the tendencies to change manifested in the first reproduction now seem to be more marked. The story has become still more concise, still more coherent. The proper name Kaloma has disappeared, and the lack of arrows, put into the second place a week earlier, has now dropped out completely. On the other hand a part of the other excuse: "I might get killed," now comes back into the story, though it found no place in the first version. It is perhaps odd that the friend, after having returned home, seems suddenly to come back into the story again when the young man is wounded. But this kind of confusion of connected incidents is a common characteristic of remembering.

(b) Subject N first dealt with the story in this way:

The Ghosts

There were two men on the banks of the river near Egulac. They heard the sound of paddles, and a canoe with five men in it appeared, who called to them, saying: "We are going to fight the people. Will you come with us?"

One of the two men answered, saying: "Our relations do not know where we are, and we have not got any arrows."

They answered: "There are arrows in the canoe."

So the man went, and they fought the people, and then he heard them saying: "An Indian is killed, let us return."

So he returned to Egulac, and told them he knew they were Ghosts.

He spoke to the people of Egulac, and told them that he had fought with the Ghosts, and many men were killed on both sides, and that he was wounded, but felt nothing. He lay down and became calmer, and in the night he was convulsed, and something black came out of his mouth.

The people said:

"He is dead."

Leaving aside smaller details, much the most interesting feature of this reproduction is the attempt made to deal with the ghosts. The subject volunteered an account of his procedure. "When I read the story," he said, "I thought that the main point was the reference to the

Ghosts who went off to fight the people farther on. I then had images, in visual form, of a wide river, of trees on each side of it, and of men on the banks and in canoes. The second time I read through the story, I readily visualised the whole thing. The images of the last part were confused. The people left the wounded man, and went into the bush. Then I saw the man telling his tale to the villagers. He was pleased and proud because the Ghosts belonged to a higher class than he did himself. He was jumping about all the time. Then he went into convulsions, and a clot of blood came from his mouth. The people realised that he was dead and made a fuss about him.

"I wrote out the story mainly by following my own images. I had a vague feeling of the style. There was a sort of rhythm about it which I tried to imitate.

"I can't understand the contradiction about somebody being killed, and the man's being wounded, but feeling nothing.

"At first I thought there was something supernatural about the story. Then I saw that Ghosts must be a class, or a clan name. That made the whole thing more comprehensible."

In fact this subject has clearly missed the real point about the ghosts from the outset, although he makes them central in his version of the story. The reproduction is a beautiful illustration of a strong tendency to rationalise, common to all of my subjects. Whenever anything appeared incomprehensible, or "queer," it was either omitted or explained. Rather rarely this rationalisation was the effect of a conscious effort. More often it was effected apparently unwittingly, the subject transforming his original without suspecting what he was doing. Just as in all the other experimental series so far described, there may be prepotency of certain detail, without any explicit analysis. In this case, for example, the ghosts were the central part of the story. They alone remained in the title. They were always written with a capital initial letter—a true case of unwitting transformation which solved a special problem. Then came the specific explanation: "Ghosts" are a clan name; and the whole difficulty disappeared. This subject was extremely well satisfied with his version, just as the visualisers in the earlier experiments seemed to be contented with their work. The satisfaction persisted, and a fortnight later the "Ghosts" had become more prominent still. The story was remembered thus:

The Ghosts

There were two men on the banks of a river near the village of Etishu (?). They heard the sound of paddles coming from up-stream, and shortly a canoe appeared. The men in the canoe spoke, saying: "We are going to fight the people: will you come with us?"

One of the young men answered, saying: "Our relations do not know where we are; but my companion may go with you. Besides, we have no arrows."

So the young man went with them, and they fought the people, and many were killed on both sides. And then he heard shouting: "The Indian is wounded; let us return." And he heard the people say: "They are the Ghosts." He did not know he was wounded, and returned to Etishu (?). The people collected round him and bathed his wounds, and he said he had fought with the Ghosts. Then he became quiet. But in the night he was convulsed, and something black came out of his mouth.

And the people cried:

"He is dead."

By now the antagonists of the young man up the river are definitely made to say that the people he is helping are "the Ghosts" (*i.e.* members of the Ghost clan). The Indian becomes more of a hero and is a centre of interest at the end, when, for the first time, his wounds are "bathed." The Indian's ignorance of his wound, a point which had worried this subject a fortnight earlier, comes back into the main body of the story, but appears to be attributed to mere general excitement. In fact the supernatural element is practically entirely dropped out.

This ingenious rationalisation of the "Ghosts" was a clear instance of how potent may be a special interest in producing an unrealised distortion in remembered material. The subject was a keen student of Anthropology who, later, carried out much important field-work, particularly in regard to the topics of kinship names and clan systems. This subject also first dropped the "arrow" excuse to the second place, and later regarded it as probably an invention on his part. The reference to relatives persisted. Proper names again presented special difficulty.

(*c*) It is interesting to consider a case of rationalisation which was complete, and at the same time almost entirely unwitting. Subject L's first reproduction was:

War Ghost Story

Two young men from Egulac went out to hunt seals. They thought they heard war-cries, and a little later they heard the noise of the paddling of canoes. One of these canoes, in which there were five na-

tives, came forward towards them. One of the natives shouted out: "Come with us: we are going to make war on some natives up the river." The two young men answered: "We have no arrows." "There are arrows in our canoes," came the reply. One of the young men then said: "My folk will not know where I have gone"; but, turning to the other, he said: "But you could go." So the one returned whilst the other joined the natives.

The party went up the river as far as a town opposite Kalama, where they got on land. The natives of that part came down to the river to meet them. There was some severe fighting, and many on both sides were slain. Then one of the natives that had made the expedition up the river shouted: "Let us return: the Indian has fallen." Then they endeavoured to persuade the young man to return, telling him that he was sick, but he did not feel as if he were. Then he thought he saw ghosts all round him.

When they returned, the young man told all his friends of what had happened. He described how many had been slain on both sides.

It was nearly dawn when the young man became very ill; and at sunrise a black substance rushed out of his mouth, and the natives said one to another: "He is dead."

This version shows the usual tendency towards increasing conventionalisation of language, a little increased dramatisation at the end, a few abbreviations, and the common difficulty about the ghosts. This last difficulty is here solved in a novel manner. Apart from these points the reproduction is on the whole accurate and full. Nearly four months later the subject tried to remember the story once more, and he dictated it to me as follows:

I have no idea of the title.

There were two men in a boat, sailing towards an island. When they approached the island, some natives came running towards them, and informed them that there was fighting going on on the island, and invited them to join. One said to the other: "You had better go. I cannot very well, because I have relatives expecting me, and they will not know what has become of me. But you have no one to expect you." So one accompanied the natives, but the other returned.

Here there is a part that I can't remember. What I don't know is how the man got to the fight. However, anyhow the man was in the midst of the fighting, and was wounded. The natives endeavoured to persuade the man to return, but he assured them that he had not been wounded.

I have an idea that his fighting won the admiration of the natives.

The wounded man ultimately fell unconscious. He was taken from the fighting by the natives.

Then, I think it is, the natives describe what happened, and they seem to have imagined seeing a ghost coming out of his mouth. Really it was a kind of materialisation of his breath. I know this *phrase* was not in the story, but that is the idea I have. Ultimately the man died at dawn the next day.

"First," said this subject, "my remembrance was in visual terms of a man approaching an island, and also of breath somehow materialising into a ghost. But perhaps this may belong to another story."

The two most incomprehensible parts of the original story, to all my subjects, were the ghosts and the final death of the Indian. In the first of these two reproductions the ghosts play a little and a very simple part: they are merely imagined by the Indian when he is wounded. But apparently they are not to be so simply disposed of, and in the later version, by a single stroke of condensation, and by a rationalisation which the subject certainly did not set himself consciously to carry through, both the difficulties are rendered manageable. This is only one of several versions in which the original "something black" became "escaping breath."

Once more, of the Indian's two excuses the one based on the probable anxiety of relatives gets increasing emphasis, and the other, in this case, disappears altogether. Title and proper names are forgotten.

The fact of rationalisation was illustrated in practically every reproduction or series of reproductions, but, as would be expected, the way in which it was effected varied greatly from case to case. For the particular form adopted is due directly to the functioning of individual special interests, as in the "Ghost clan" instance, or to some fact of personal experience, or to some peculiarity of individual attitude which determines the salience or potency of the details in the whole material dealt with.

Here is another version, for example, of *The War of the Ghosts,* as it was recalled by one subject six months after the original reading:

(No title was given.) Four men came down to the water. They were told to get into a boat and to take arms with them. They inquired "What arms?" and were answered "Arms for battle." When they came

to the battle-field they heard a great noise and shouting, and a voice said: "The black man is dead." And he was brought to the place where they were, and laid on the ground. And he foamed at the mouth.

From this short version, all unusual terms, all proper names, all mention of a supernatural element have disappeared. But the most interesting point is the treatment of the troublesome "something black" which concludes the original story. "Black" was transferred to the man and so rendered perfectly natural, while "foamed at the mouth" is as much a rationalisation of the original statement as was the materialisation of the dying man's breath introduced by subject L. Why the one subject should use one phrase or notion and the other a different one is no doubt a matter of individual psychology; both served the same general rationalising tendency.

(*d*) Each illustration so far given shows a tendency to abbreviate and simplify both the story as a whole and also all the details that are reported. More rarely some incident was elaborated, usually with some dramatic flourish and at the expense of other incidents belonging to the story. A longer series of successive versions by subject P will illustrate this. The first reproduction was:

The War of the Ghosts

Two youths were standing by a river about to start seal-catching, when a boat appeared with five men in it. They were all armed for war.

The youths were at first frightened, but they were asked by the men to come and help them fight some enemies on the other bank. One youth said he could not come as his relations would be anxious about him; the other said he would go, and entered the boat.

In the evening he returned to his hut, and told his friends that he had been in a battle. A great many had been slain, and he had been wounded by an arrow; he had not felt any pain, he said. They told him that he must have been fighting in a battle of ghosts. Then he remembered that it had been queer and he was very excited.

In the morning, however, he became ill, and his friends gathered round; he fell down and his face became very pale. Then he writhed and shrieked and his friends were filled with terror. At last he became calm. Something hard and black came out of his mouth, and he lay contorted and dead.

The subject who produced this version is a painter. He definitely visualised the whole scene and drew for me a plan of his imagery on paper. The middle part of the story escaped him completely, but, as will be seen, the final part was elaborated with increased dramatisation. "The story," he remarked, "first recalled a missionary story, and then took on a character of its own. It also vaguely recalled something about Egyptians who, I think, imagined that peoples' souls came out of their mouths when they died."

A fortnight later came the second attempt:

The War of the Ghosts

There were two young men who once went out in the afternoon to catch seals. They were about to begin when a boat appeared on the river and in it were five warriors. These looked so fierce that the men thought they were going to attack them. But they were reassured when they asked the youths to enter the boat and help them to fight some enemies.

The elder said he would not come because his relations might be anxious about him. But the other said he would go and went off.

He returned in the evening tired and excited, and he told his friends that he had been fighting in a great battle. "Many of us and many of the foe were slain," he said. "I was wounded, but did not feel sick."

Later in the evening he retired quietly to bed, after lighting a fire. The next morning, however, when the neighbours came to see him, he said that he must have been fighting in a battle of ghosts.

Then he fell down and writhed in agony. Something black jumped out of his mouth. All the neighbours held up their hands and shrieked with terror, and when they examined the youth they found that he was dead.

There are a few more omissions in this version, but both the beginning and the end of the story tend to become more elaborate, and more dramatic. The "fright" of the youths at the beginning is exaggerated, and it is now the "elder" of the two who says that he will not go. As usual the sole remaining alleged excuse is the anxiety of relatives. Direct speech is introduced at the end, and the "fire" of the original, having been omitted from the first version, returns to the story. As before, the subject pursued a definitely visualising method of recall.

A further month passed by, and the subject now remembered the story as follows:

The War of the Ghosts

Two youths went down to the river to fish for seals. They perceived, soon, coming down the river,

a canoe with five warriors in it, and they were alarmed. But the warriors said: "We are friends. Come with us, for we are going to fight a battle."

The elder youth would not go, because he thought his relations would be anxious about him. The younger, however, went.

In the evening he returned from the battle, and he said that he had been wounded, but that he had felt no pain.

There had been a great fight and many had been slain on either side. He lit a fire and retired to rest in his hut. The next morning, when the neighbours came round to see how he was, they found him in a fever. And when he came out into the open at sunrise he fell down. The neighbours shrieked. He became livid and writhed upon the ground. Something black came out of his mouth, and he died. So the neighbours decided that he must have been to war with the ghosts.

Again the end part of the story gains additional detail. It is the neighbours who now decide, in a more or less reasonable fashion, that the young man must have been fighting with ghosts. In some respects, *e.g.* in the mention of sunrise, the version is nearer to the original form than those given earlier. "The whole of my imagery," he remarked, "has grown very dim. Details of the story seem mostly to have vanished. There was no difficulty in remembering as much as was written, but I have also disjointed ideas about the early part of the story, of *arrows* and a *rock,* which I cannot fit in. My memory seems to depend on visual images,[5] and it may really consist of them; and I can't set down any more."

Another two months elapsed, and the subject, at my request, remembered the story again, not having thought of it in the interval, he asserted. The "rock," already foreshadowed in his earlier comments, is now fitted into its setting, and is, in fact, put exactly into the place of the original "log."

The War of the Ghosts

Two youths went down to the river to hunt for seals. They were hiding behind a rock when a boat with some warriors in it came up to them. The warriors, however, said they were friends, and invited them to help them to fight an enemy over the river. The elder one said he could not go because his relations would be so anxious if he did not return home. So the younger one went with the warriors in the boat.

In the evening he returned and told his friends

that he had been fighting in a great battle, and that many were slain on both sides.

After lighting a fire he retired to sleep. In the morning, when the sun rose, he fell ill, and his neighbours came to see him. He had told them that he had been wounded in the battle but had felt no pain then. But soon he became worse. He writhed and shrieked and fell to the ground dead. Something black came out of his mouth.

The neighbours said he must have been at war with the ghosts.

There is still some further elaboration in the early part of the story, but beyond that very little change. In its general form, and in several of the expressions used, the story seems now to be at least temporarily stereotyped. The ghosts have definitely taken up their position at the end of the narrative, and the whole thing has become more connected and coherent than at the beginning. With repetitions at fairly frequent intervals, as a rule the form of a story soon became fairly fixed, though some of the details suffered progressive change.

But what of the long interval? Two years and six months later, the subject not having seen or, according to his own statement, thought of the story in the meantime, he agreed to attempt a further reproduction and wrote:

Some warriors went to wage war against the ghosts. They fought all day and one of their number was wounded.

They returned home in the evening, bearing their sick comrade. As the day drew to a close, he became rapidly worse and the villagers came round him. At sunset he sighed: something black came out of his mouth. He was dead.

In bare outline the story remains. The ghosts, who seemed to have settled down at the end, now have moved up to the beginning of the narrative. All tendency to elaboration has disappeared, perhaps as a result of the almost complete disappearance of visualisation as the method of recall. "There was something," said the subject, "about a canoe, but I can't fit it in. I suppose it was his soul that came out of his mouth when he died." Thus it looks as though the rationalisation indicated in this subject's comment of nearly two years and nine months before, but never actually expressed in any of his reproductions, has yet somehow persisted. Now for the first time, in this series, the wounded man dies at sunset. This was a change several times introduced, probably

unwittingly, in conformity with a common popular view that a man frequently dies as the sun goes down. The subject thought that there was certainly more to be said at the end, as if his earlier elaborations were still having some effect.

(*e*) The preceding reproductions may be compared with a short series obtained from a native of Northern India, subject R, who was on a very different educational plane from that of the rest of my subjects. He was a man of considerable intelligence, but ill-trained, from the point of view of an English University, and ill-adapted to the environment in which he was living. He was impressionable, imaginative, and, using the word in its ordinary conventional sense, nervous to a high degree. He first reproduced the story as follows:

Story

There were two young men, and they went on the river side. They heard war cries, and said: "There is a war of the ghosts." They had no arrows. They saw a canoe, and there were five men in it. They said: "The arrows are in the canoe." The war of the ghosts begins. Many were killed. There was one young man who was hit, but did not become sick. He heard that the Indian was wounded. He came back to his village in the canoe. In the morning he was sick, and his face contracted. Something black came out of his mouth, and they cried: "He was dead."

The subject appeared very excited. He said that he clearly visualised the whole scene, and that especially vivid were some Red Indians with feathers on their heads. The story is greatly abbreviated and is very jerky and inconsequential in style. "Ghosts" made a tremendous impression on this subject, and are introduced at the very beginning of the story, though it may be that this is partly on account of the omission of the title.

A fortnight later the following version was obtained:

Story

There were two ghosts. They went on a river. There was a canoe on the river with five men in it. There occurred a war of ghosts. One of the ghosts asked: "Where are the arrows?" The other said: "In the canoe." They started the war and several were wounded, and some killed. One ghost was wounded but did not feel sick. He went back to the village in the canoe. The next morning he was sick and something black came out of his mouth, and they cried: "He is dead."

The ghosts appear to have strengthened their hold on the story during the interval, and have entirely displaced the two young men. If anything the narrative has become even less coherent.

After another month the subject tried again, and produced:

Story

There were ghosts. There took place a fight between them. One of them asked: "Where are the arrows?" The other said: "They are in the canoe." A good many of the combatants were wounded or killed. One of them was wounded, but did not feel sick. They carried him to his village some miles away by rowing in the canoe. The next day something black came out of his mouth and they cried: "He is dead."

The first part of the story has completely disappeared, and the whole is now entirely a matter of a fight between ghosts. The dominant detail seems to have suppressed or overmastered nearly all the rest. To the subject himself the tale seemed clear enough, but as compared with most of the preceding versions it appears very jerky and disconnected.

(*f*) Finally I will choose two of a number of long distance memories. They represent utterly different methods and processes. Each, in its own way, raises attractive problems.

The following version was obtained six and a half years after the original reading. The subject (W) had previously given only the one "immediate" reproduction. This offered the usual features: some abbreviation, a little modernisation of the phraseology and a comment, made at the end, after the reproduction, to the effect that the "something black" must have been the man's soul, after the "ancient Egyptian belief." At the end of six and a half years I unexpectedly met this man again and he volunteered to try to remember the story. He recalled it in steps, with some pondering and hesitation, but on the whole with surprising ease. I will give his version exactly as he wrote it:

1. Brothers.
2. Canoe.
3. Something black from mouth.
4. Totem.
5. One of the brothers died.
6. Cannot remember whether one slew the other or was helping the other.
7. Were going on journey, but why I cannot remember.
8. Party in war canoe.
9. Was the journey a pilgrimage for filial or religious reasons?
10. Am now *sure* it was a pilgrimage.
11. Purpose had something to do with totem.
12. Was it on a pilgrimage that they met a hostile party and one brother was slain?
13. I think there was some reference to a dark forest.
14. Two brothers were on a pilgrimage, having something to do with a totem, in a canoe, up a river flowing through a dark forest. While on their pilgrimage they met a hostile party of Indians in a war canoe. In the fight one brother was slain, and something black came from his mouth.
15. Am not confident about the way brother died. May have been something sacrificial in the manner of his death.
16. The cause of the journey had *both* something to do with a totem, and with filial piety.
17. The totem was the patron god of the family and so was connected with filial piety.

This is a brilliant example of obviously constructive remembering. The subject was very pleased and satisfied with the result of his effort, and indeed, considering the length of the interval involved, he is remarkably accurate and detailed. There is a good deal of invention, and it was precisely concerning his inventions that the subject was most pleased and most certain. The totem, the filial piety, the pilgrimage—these were what he regarded as his most brilliant re-captures, and he was almost equally sure of the dark forest, once it had come in. It looks very much as if the "ghost" element of the original, connected by this subject with Egyptian beliefs, and now apparently dropped out completely, is still somehow active, and helping to produce elaborations which take the forms of the totem, filial piety, a mysterious forest, and a sacrificial death. It will be noticed that the story as he constructed it is full of rationalisations and explanations, and most of the running comments of the subject concerned the interconnexion of the various events and were directed to making the whole narration appear as coherent as possible.

This constructive method, and its elaborate result, must now be compared with a very different case. The interval here was longer still, one of almost exactly ten years. The subject (C) read the story in the spring of 1917. In 1919 she unexpectedly saw me pass her on a bicycle and immediately afterwards found herself murmuring "Egulac," "Kalama." She then recognised me, and remembered reading the story, and that these names were a part of the story. In the summer of 1927 she agreed to try definitely to remember the tale. She wrote down at once "Egulac" and "Calama," but then stopped and said that she could do no more. Then she said that she had a visual image of a sandy bank and of two men going down a river in a boat. There, however, she stopped.

In both of these cases certain dominant detail remains, apparently, and is readily remembered. But in the one case these details are made a basis which the subject builds together, and upon which he constructs new detail, so that in the end he achieves a fairly complete structure. In the other case the dominant details remain relatively isolated. Almost certainly, with some encouragement, the second subject could have been induced to put her few details together and perhaps to amplify them. But I thought it best, for the purposes of these experiments, to try to influence the subjects' procedure as little as possible.

4.   Certain Particular Points of Interest in The War of the Ghosts

(A) A POSSIBLE CASE OF AFFECTIVE DETERMINATION. Twenty subjects were given *The War of the Ghosts* in this experiment, seven being women and the rest men. If we take the two excuses given by the young men for not joining the war-party and see how they were dealt with, we find that the "we have no arrows" plea was omitted by half the subjects, either in their first reproduction or in subsequent versions. Of the ten subjects who continued to include the reference to arrows six were women. On the other hand, except in long-distance reproductions, only two subjects—one man and one woman—omitted the reference to relatives. Four men who gave the arrow excuse correctly on their first attempt relegated it to the second place and then omitted it from subsequent versions. *The Method of Description* has already shown that the positional factor, which gives an advantage in memory processes to material presented early in a series, can easily be disturbed. Nearly all the men who reproduced this story had been to the War or were faced with the probability that they would soon have to go, or thought that they ought to go. I think it not fanciful to say that this story reminded them of their situation, and in fact some of them admitted that it did. The reference to relatives had a personal application in most of the cases, and it is more than likely that it was this that made the reference a dominant detail in remembering. In all

the later versions this excuse also disappeared. The anxiety about relatives, on which, if I am right, its preservation was based, was only a fleeting one, and with its passing the material which it had dealt with went too.

(B) "SYMPATHETIC" WEATHER. My next point may at first appear to be distinctly fantastic. Throughout the whole of these experiments, however, I had in mind the connexion between memory processes and the growth of all kinds of conventions and conventional modes of representation. Now an exceedingly common feature in popular fiction is what may be called "sympathetic weather"; storms blow up before the moment of tragedy, a peaceful sky presages a happy ending, and so on. I wondered how my subjects would deal, in the case of *The War of the Ghosts,* with the "calm and foggy night." Only eight ever reproduced it, and five of these speedily dropped it from their later versions. As a matter of fact, "sympathetic weather" seems to belong to a class of features which are very effective in setting up a sort of vague atmosphere of attitude, but do not provide outstanding detail, as a rule. Thus a subject who failed to record the weather in his first version said nevertheless: "I formed some sort of association, I do not know what, in connexion with the thick, still evening on the river. I think it recalled something I had seen before, but I cannot exactly remember the circumstances." A fortnight later there appeared in his remembered version of the story: "The evening was misty down by the river, and for a time they were conscious only of their own presence." This seems to give us another case of the delayed appearance of material in a reproduction.

Even when the weather was recorded it was often given inaccurately. "Two Indians," said a subject, "went down to the marsh on the side of a lake in order to fish. However, the dampness of the air and the calmness of the sea were disadvantageous to their sport." In his second attempt he made the weather "calm" and the sea "hazy," and finally, much later, asserted: "the day was damp and misty." Another subject reported: "the night was cold and foggy"; and another: "while they were there darkness and mist gathered." Perhaps what is evoked in all such cases is, in fact, merely a "weather scheme" which is consonant with a given mood, but no detailed weather characteristics.

(C) THE ORDER OF EVENTS. If the suggestion made on the basis of the results from *The Method of Description* is right, the order of events in a story ought to be fairly well preserved in repeated reproduction. For it appeared probable that words are fit or apt material for dealing with order. And on the whole this was borne out very definitely in the present series of experiments, and the order of events was well preserved. But when any incident called out unusual interest, that incident tended to displace events which occurred earlier in the original version. As we have seen repeatedly, from the very beginning of this experimental work, salient features are a characteristic of practically every act of observation; however incapable of analysis both the act and its object may appear. Thus the two excuses of the young Indians were consistently transposed when one was not lost altogether. The ghosts, again and again, with greater emphasis as time elapsed, tended to be pushed up towards the beginning of the story. But the subject who was preoccupied with the mysterious death of the Indian, and to whom the ghosts, merely regarded as ghosts, were secondary, unwittingly let them drop down to the last place in the story. It also appeared as if the tendency to place striking units early was a special characteristic of the visualising subject; but the evidence on this point cannot yet be regarded as very definite.

(D) THE REPRODUCTION OF STYLE. The style, rhythm or construction of a prose or verse narrative is perhaps in some ways analogous to the "rule of structure" of a regular figure. And as there are some people who are particularly sensitive to the latter, so in many cases the former may make an early and a lasting impression. Nearly all of my subjects who made any comments on *The War of the Ghosts* described it as "terse," "disjointed," "Biblical," "inconsequential," and so on. However, style seems to be one of those factors which are extremely readily responded to, but extremely rarely reproduced with any fidelity. Thus we may react to a narrative or an argument largely because of its formal character, may even remember it largely on this account, and yet the form may be singularly ineffective in shaping any subsequent reproduction. Completely satisfactory comprehension does not necessarily lead to complete fidelity of reproduction; the good auditor may be a bad mimic, the good reader a bad writer. Transformations of form and style are excessively likely to appear quickly. In this case it might happen that a subject, trying to retain the style of the original, as he thought, would merely use rather out-of-date or unusual phrases: the young man "drew in" towards the bank, taking refuge behind a "prone log"; the warriors, seeing many people, "accordingly touched in towards the bank of the river." One subject having produced an extremely matter-of-fact version, said: "I tried to reproduce the original story in all its terseness." Obviously, ability to respond to form does not of necessity carry with it ability to reproduce, or even to remember, form. Nevertheless, the form itself may well be an important factor in what makes remembering possible.

(E) THE COMMONEST OMISSIONS AND TRANSPOSITIONS. To work completely through the whole list of omissions and transpositions in the case of *The War of the Ghosts* would be a fruitlessly long and weary task. The commonest of these concerned (1) the title; (2) proper names; (3) definite numbers; (4) the precise significance of the "ghosts," and (5) canoes.

The title was speedily omitted by seven of the twenty subjects and transformed by ten of the others. Variants were: "The two young men of Egulack"; "War-Ghost story"; "The Ghosts"; "The story of the Ghosts," and so on. It would, I think, be a matter of some interest to try to discover how far titles of stories in general, headlines in newspapers, and, in fact, all such general initial labels influence perceiving and remembering. Some unpublished experiments, carried out in Cambridge by the late Prof. Bernard Muscio, suggested strongly that their importance is commonly greatly exaggerated, and my own results, for what they are worth, point in the same direction.

Sooner or later, the proper names dropped out of all the reproductions, with the single exception of the one in which they seemed, after ten years, to be the only readily accessible detail. As a rule, before they entirely disappeared, they suffered change. Egulac became Emlac, Eggulick, Edulac, Egulick; and Kalama became Kalamata, Kuluma, Karnac, to give only a few of the variations.

No subject retained for more than one reproduction the point about the ghosts as it was related in the original.

Every subject, at some point in the story, introduced "boats" for canoes. Some retained "canoes" as well. With the change to "boat," as a rule "paddling" was transformed into "rowing."

There were, of course, numerous other omissions from the various reproductions, and also a considerable number of inventions. In general character they were much the same as those which marked the course of *Serial Reproduction,* and may be better discussed in that connexion.

5. *Some General Points Arising from the use of the Method of Repeated Reproduction*

Although all the illustrations given in the present chapter have, so far, been concerned with *The War of the*

Ghosts, every one of the points raised could equally well have been illustrated from the repeated reproduction of other material. In all, I have used eight different stories, several descriptive and argumentative passages, and a considerable amount of graphic material. With some variations for the differing types of material, the general method of work and the main trend of the results were constant. Different subjects took part in the experiment and material was employed having a wide range of subject-matter and style, but this also, certain specifically individual points aside, made no essential difference. In attempting to discuss generally some of the wider conclusions which may be tentatively drawn at this stage, I shall have the whole of the work in mind.

(A) PERSISTENCE OF 'FORM' IN REPRODUC-
TION. The most general characteristic of the whole of this group of experiments was the persistence, for any given subject, of the "form" of his first reproduction. With the single but probably significant exception of a few subjects of strongly visualising type, the great majority of the changes introduced into a story—save after a lapse of very long intervals indeed—were effected in the early stages of the experiment. In fact, response to a general scheme, form, order and arrangement of material seems to be dominant, both in initial reception and in subsequent remembering. The "rule of structure" operated frequently in the perceiving experiments; the "general outline" played a great part in the setting up of image responses; in the description of faces "general impression" was extremely important, and here again, no sooner was a story presented than it was labelled, said to be of this or of that type, and in addition to possess a few outstanding details. The type gave the form of the story, and as a rule one or two striking details seemed to recur with as little change as the form itself. The other details were omitted, rearranged, or transformed—rearrangements and transformations being generally effected very rapidly, and omissions continuing for almost indefinite periods. However, although the general form, or scheme, or plan of a prose passage thus persisted with relatively little change, once the reproduction had been effected, as I have already shown, the actual style of the original was nearly always rapidly and unwittingly transformed.

This persistence of form was most of all marked in such instances as those of the well-known "cumulative" type of story, and perhaps has something to do with the fact that stories of this type are more widely distributed than any others in the popular tales of various social groups. The two stories of this form of construction

which I used were almost always greeted with the remark: "Yes, that's a story of the 'House that Jack Built' type."

The form, plan, type, or scheme of a story seems, in fact, for the ordinary, educated adult to be the most dominant and persistent factor in this kind of material. It ought to be possible experimentally to follow the development of the response to form, and to determine its relative importance in individuals of different ages and different intellectual status. Possibly, once the response to the form factor is established, its stability and effectiveness may be due to its possessing a marked affective character. This point, and also the study of the mechanisms by which transformations of detail are produced, are best pursued by a consideration of the parts played by the process of rationalisation in the course of repeated reproduction.

(B) THE PROCESSES OF RATIONALISATION. There is a marked and well-known distinction, both in perceiving and in remembering, between direct reaction to what is literally present and reaction under the guidance of some tendency which gives to what is presented a setting and an explanation. The latter tendency is present to some extent in all perceiving and in all remembering, but may vary greatly in importance and in prominence from case to case. Sometimes, in these experiments, reasons were definitely and explicitly formulated and introduced into reproductions to account for material which had been presented without explanation. Sometimes, without any definite formulation of reasons, the material was so changed that it could be accepted by the observer without question and with satisfaction. The first process appears to be a special instance of the second. Both have the same general function in mental life, and I shall discuss both under the head of rationalisation.

In these experiments rationalisation was applied sometimes to the stories as a whole and sometimes to particular details. In the first case, the process expressed the need, felt by practically every educated observer, that a story should have a general setting. Hardly ever, at the outset, was there an attitude of simple acceptance. Every story presented had to be connected, certainly as a whole, and, if possible, as regards its details also, with something else. This is, of course, the factor which I have already called "effort after meaning" coming again into play. It could be said that there is a constant effort to get the maximum possible of meaning into the material presented. So long as maximum of meaning is understood to imply an effort to find that connexion which puts a subject most at his ease in reference to a given story, the statement is true. The meaning, in this sense, however, may be of a very tenuous and undetermined nature, and apparently may even be mainly negative.

A very common remark made about the folk-stories used, for example, was: "That is not an English tale." Sometimes the narrative was rendered satisfactory by being called a "dream." "This," said one observer, "is very clearly a murder concealment dream." She proceeded to an interpretation along the lines of modern symbolism, and the story was, with no further trouble, comfortably accepted.

In fact, all incoming material, if it is to be accepted and dealt with in any manner, must be somehow labelled. A negative label is often enough. When an Englishman calls a tale "not English" he can at once proceed to accept odd, out of the way, and perhaps even inconsistent material, with very little resistance. How these labels are developed and in what ways they are taken over ready-made from society are matters of some interest, not out of the reach of experimental study.

The rationalisation which stops short at finding a label is interesting in two ways. Firstly, the process is emphatically not merely a question of relating the newly presented material to old acquirements of knowledge. Primarily, it depends upon the active bias, or special reaction tendencies, that are awakened in the observer by the new material, and it is these tendencies which then set the new into relation to the old. To speak as if what is accepted and given a place in mental life is always simply a question of what fits into already formed apperception systems is to miss the obvious point that the process of fitting is an active process, depending directly upon the pre-formed tendencies and bias which the subject brings to his task. The second point is that this process of rationalisation is only partially—it might be said only lazily—an intellectual process. No doubt the attempt, however little defined, to seek out the connexions of things is always to some degree intellectual. But here the effort stops when it produces an attitude best described as "the attitude in which no further questions are asked." The end state is primarily affective. Once reached, and it is generally reached very quickly, it recurs very readily, and it is this, more than anything else, which accounts for the persistent sameness of repeated reproduction.

The rationalisation which gives to material as a whole its appropriate frame is only a part of the total process. Details also must be dealt with, and every chain of reproductions illustrated how the rationalising process was applied to particular items.

The most direct method is to provide definite, stated links of connexion between parts of material which are

prima facie disconnected. The current versions of most folk-stories appear jerky, perhaps incoherent in parts, and very badly strung together. This is because of their strong social setting, which makes it possible for narrators and hearers to take much for granted that is not expressed. If reproductions are obtained in a social community different from that in which the original version was developed, the subject, acting almost always unwittingly, supplies connecting links. In *The War of the Ghosts* events follow one another, but their connexion is not, as a rule, actually stated. The situation is like that which would confront the spectator of one of the earlier cinematograph films with the usual explanatory connecting tags omitted. The subjects, in the experiments, supplied the tags, but without realising what they were doing: "they (*i.e.* the young men) heard some canoes approaching them, *and so hid* . . ."; "one said he would not go *as* his relations did not know where he was"; "he heard the Indians cry: 'Let us go home, *as* the man of Egulack is wounded'"; "the young man did not feel sick (i.e. *wounded*), *but nevertheless* they proceeded home (*evidently the opposing forces were quite willing to stop fighting*)"; "when he got back the young man lit a fire (*probably to cook his breakfast*)"—all of these explanatory particles and phrases come from the version of one subject, and similar illustrations could be given in nearly all cases. The net result is that before long the story tends to be robbed of all its surprising, jerky and apparently inconsequential form, and reduced to an orderly narration. It is denuded of all the elements that left the reader puzzled and uneasy, or it has been given specific associative links which, in the original form, were assumed as immediately understood.

Suppose the very same observers, however, are presented with well-ordered argumentative passages, and are required to make repeated reproductions of these. It does not follow that the bonds of connexion which are now supplied will be retained and will reappear. They fulfil their function by making the material appear coherent. The form of whatever is presented may produce its effect, even though the elements of which the form is constructed are given but scanty notice. Any normal, educated observer strives after associative links, but whether the mode of connexion or the matter of such links, when they are supplied, is faithfully reproduced is another question altogether.

Rationalisation in regard to form found its main expression in the linking together of events within the stories; rationalisation as concerned with the details of material was usually carried out by connecting the given items with something outside the story and supplied by the observer himself. This is analogous to what I have called "importation" in *The Method of Description:* it was of three main types.

First there was the process, in all instances witting during its early stages, but later producing unwitting transformations, by which presented material was connected with other matter outside the story, but having the same general nature. For example, in *The War of the Ghosts* the "something black" was frequently interpreted as a materialisation of the dying man's breath. Again, an instance telling how a raven's beak turned into a knife was accepted and persistently preserved by being treated as a symbol in a murder dream. To call these cases "witting" is perhaps not strictly accurate. Usually there is some delay before the actual explanation is formulated, and in all such cases the material which is rationalised is first treated as symbolic. With repeated reproduction the symbolised materials or facts eventually replace completely that by which in the original they were symbolised. Perhaps, psychologically, all processes of symbolisation fall into place as subordinate to a wider process of rationalisation, and, in the complete process of symbolisation, the final stage is the obliteration of the symbol.[6]

The second process of rationalisation, as it here occurred, was unwitting from start to finish. The transformation of "something black" into "foamed at the mouth" was a case in point. So was the introduction of an "island" into *The War of the Ghosts* by several subjects. Probably the changing of an apparently irrelevant remark at the end of one of the tales: "And so the sparrow never got home," into: "And so the sparrow got home at last, and here ends my story" belonged to the same class. No symbolisation, in the proper sense of the word, was involved in this type of rationalisation. At no stage of the transformation had the material employed a double signification, so far, at any rate, as could be ascertained.

This is the type of rationalisation in which individual interests and peculiarities come most clearly into play. In the first type that part of the process which is witting tends to follow the lines of current belief, or of the modes of language expression which have been built into the general communication habits of a community. Thus it is likely to manifest the same development in different members of the same social group. In the third type, as I shall go on to show, although the process is unwitting, the results are extremely likely to display the same character throughout a given community. It is in the second type that individual bias and interest most directly determine the transformations effected.

For example, a long series of reproductions was obtained of a Provençal story which may be called *The Citizens and the Plague.* The last paragraph of this story in the original was:

> This city is like unto the world, for the world is filled with mad folk. Is not the greatest wisdom a man can have to love God and obey His will? But now this wisdom is lost, and covetousness and blindness have fallen like rain upon the earth. And if one man escapes this rain, his fellows account him mad. They have lost the wisdom of God, so they say that he is mad who has lost the wisdom of the world.

In a series of successive reproductions this moral was progressively elaborated and emphasised. The subject was all the time unwittingly satisfying a well-developed interest in moralising. His version remained extremely accurate, but the final paragraph was somewhat lengthened, as compared with the rest of the story, and was given a more definitely religious tone:

> This great city is like the world. For in the world are many people, and upon them at times come plagues from heaven, and none know how they come. For it is well that men should live simply, and love God, and do His will. But men turn aside and go about after wisdom and the prizes of the world, nor pay heed to the high and simple life. And so it is that those few who seek to serve God and to live simply, as He desires, are despised by the rest, and being alone in their right thinking, are yet accounted mad by the madmen.

In this there is not much transformation, but considerable increase of emphasis. An original rationalising element in the story has been seized upon, and so developed that it plays a greater part in the whole. This development was directly the work of a marked individual interest, though the subject was utterly unaware at the time that the interest was coming into operation.

The third type of rationalisation is very closely related to the second. It is the case in which some particular, and maybe isolated detail, is transformed immediately into a more familiar character. Thus "canoe" rapidly became "boat"; "paddling" became "rowing"; a "peanut" became an "acorn"; a "bush-cat" became an ordinary "cat"; "Kashim" (a proper name for a shelter) became "cabin"; and so on in a very large number of different cases.

Both the second and the third types of rationalisation are unwitting; neither results in the explicit provision of definite reasons, and both consist in changing the relatively unfamiliar into the relatively familiar. But the second is characteristically individual, so that an incident is likely to be transformed or developed differently as it is dealt with by different observers, while the third type is apt to exhibit the same results so long as the observers are drawn from the same social class or group. Changes of this type, which nearly all concern the names of common objects, or special phrases, or the like, may therefore be of particular importance when any attempt is being made to trace the line of passage of material from one social group to another.

The general function of rationalisation is in all the instances the same. It is to render material acceptable, understandable, comfortable, straightforward; to rob it of all puzzling elements. As such it is a powerful factor in all perceptual and in all reproductive processes. The forms it takes are often directly social in significance.

(C) THE DETERMINATION OF OUTSTANDING DETAIL. In all perceiving and remembering we have to take account both of a general setting and of outstanding detail. At first glance the problems set by the persistence of these appear to be different. Sometimes the setting seems to persist while the detail dwindles almost to nothing; or perhaps the setting vanishes, and only a few outstanding details are remembered. More commonly both remain to some degree.

In the determination of outstanding detail there are apparently four common groups of cases:

1. There is a strong presumption, most definitely increasing as the observer approximates to a true vocalising type, that words or phrases popular at the time of the experiment, in the group to which the observer belongs, will stand out prominently from their background, and be reproduced without change as to form, though possibly with change of position.

2. Any word, or combination of words, or any event which appears comic, is almost certain to be reproduced so long as the comic significance is retained. Nevertheless, the comic is extremely liable to change, for what appears comic varies within wide limits from person to person. Proper names, for example, which have a peculiar liability to produce laughter, are the more likely to reappear in proportion as they do this, but are at the same time excessively likely to be transformed.

3. Material which is a direct or an indirect stimulus to pre-formed interests is sure to reappear. Probably the affective tone accompanying the arousal of such interests is an important factor here. The affect is certainly not always pleasing. On the whole, the results indicate

that, if the interesting material is pleasing, the change is in the direction of elaboration and development; if the affect is displeasing, distortions are most likely to occur. Persistence of material, in these cases, seems to be due rather to the interest or bias evoked than directly to the feeling itself. But the evidence of other methods ought to be called in at this point.

4. There is a puzzling class of material which appears striking by reason of its triviality. Much further analysis is doubtless called for in order to determine why and when material is treated as trivial. But when all has been said that may be, it remains that the trivial is in fact often striking, and that as such it is likely to be retained.

Most of these points can be more forcibly illustrated from the results of *The Method of Serial Reproduction.*[7]

(D) INVENTIONS OR IMPORTATIONS. I have already discussed importation, or invention, in relation to *The Method of Description.* Little additional evidence can be gathered from the results of *The Method of Repeated Reproduction,* but what there is goes to confirm our earlier conclusions. Most of the importations concerned late stages in the reproductions, and they were often to be traced to a play of visual imagery. Two factors were important. First, the subject's attitude or point of view in relation to a particular story; and, secondly, the utilisation of any vividly presented material which seemed fit or appropriate to this point of view. In many cases of long-distance remembering, in particular, this attitude, or point of view, was by far the leading factor. Apparently in some way tied up with the attitude may go material belonging to very varied settings. If, at the time of reproduction, any of this material came vividly before the mind, as with the case of the particular and clear-cut visual image, it was apt to get incorporated in the story. This is how the "totem" came into *The War of the Ghosts.* The "pilgrimage," and "filial piety," each having a concrete visual symbol, had the same explanation. However, I must confess to some disappointment that this series of experiments should have given only scanty evidence of importation.

One thing did definitely emerge. Cumulative stories, of *The House that Jack Built* or *The Old Woman who Went to Market* type, definitely favoured invention. I shall illustrate this in dealing with the results of *The Method of Serial Reproduction.*[8]

(E) DELAY IN MANIFEST CHANGE. I have already indicated that changes were sometimes foreshadowed before they were given a manifest place in the reproductions.[9]

For example, an observer who had completed one of his reproductions casually remarked: "I've a sort of feeling that there was something about a rock, but I can't fit it in." He gave the matter slight consideration and finally rejected the notion. Two months later, without a word of comment or of explanation, the rock took its place in the story. There was no rock in the original.

All the various transformations or importations that occurred in an observer's reproductions were apt to get connected together in the course of successive reproduction; and also, in a number of cases, tales reverted to their original form after an interval during which deviations from the original had occurred. Thus it appears that influences may be at work tending to settle the eventual form of material recalled which fail to find immediate expression.

Such delay—and we get numerous illustrations in everyday experience—raises difficult problems. For one thing, it seems to mean that when an attempt is being made to establish causal relations between psychical processes, direct temporal sequence may sometimes have comparatively little significance. We cannot look with certainty, for the leading conditions of a particular response, to other reactions immediately preceding the one which we are trying to explain.

A particular stimulus, or feature of a situation, gives rise to a tendency to respond in a specific manner. At first the tendency is held in check and produces slight or perhaps no manifest results. As time elapses, apparently the unexpressed tendency may gain strength, and so manifestly affect the response; or other tendencies simultaneously excited may lose strength, and in this way also a new manifest change of response may appear.

Can we understand how an unexpressed tendency may gain strength? There appears to be little real ground for holding, as some do, that the mere checking, suppression, or damming up of any tendency is able to add strength to that tendency. But perhaps we may hold that a weaker tendency may gain in strength by being associated with a stronger one. Many of the manifest changes, when they appeared, did so in close relation to other transformations which were actually made earlier in the series of reproductions. For example, one subject, in dealing with *The War of the Ghosts,* first said that the war-party were "heard to advance": three months later "they marched forward." He first made the only canoe mentioned the property of the young man who accompanied the party, and later described the warriors definitely as "a land force." In his later versions both young

men were unwillingly forced upon the expedition, for they were both together hiding behind a log, a detail which made a marked impression upon this subject at the beginning of the experiment. In his first reproduction the Indian was "shot," later he was "struck by a bullet." Thereupon he "shouted: 'These are ghosts that we fight with'"; but at first he had not shouted this but only "thought" it. Very probably some of the delay in manifest change is due to the linking together of tendencies which are initially weak with others stronger than themselves. There is, however, no real evidence to show how, if at all, this takes place.

On the other hand, such transformations as that of the mention of a rock six weeks after the first reproduction of a story, and its definite introduction two months later, seems rather to be a case of the weakening of certain tendencies and the consequent relative strengthening of others. For the manifest change, when it appears, does not seem to be specifically connected with any preceding change. Whether, and in what precise sense, this view can be maintained, must depend upon definite experimental evidence as to the effect upon different, and particularly upon competing, tendencies of the mere lapse of time. For, on the face of it, there is little or no more reason for assuming that tendencies weaken with lapse of time than that they are strengthened by being merely denied immediate expression.

Finally, the whole notion of an unexpressed tendency, continuing for long periods to have the capacity of coming into operation, while to all outward appearance, and to inward observation also, it is wholly in abeyance, is not easy to understand. The notion seems to be demanded by many of the facts of mental life, but it clearly calls for a very critical consideration.

6. *A Summary of the main Conclusions drawn from The Method of Repeated Reproduction*

1. It again appears that accuracy of reproduction, in a literal sense, is the rare exception and not the rule.

2. In a chain of reproductions obtained from a single individual, the general form, or outline, is remarkably persistent, once the first version has been given.

3. At the same time, style, rhythm, precise mode of construction, while they are apt to be immediately reacted to, are very rarely faithfully reproduced.

4. With frequent reproduction the form and items of remembered detail very quickly become stereotyped and thereafter suffer little change.

5. With infrequent reproduction, omission of detail, simplification of events and structure, and transformation of items into more familiar detail, may go on almost indefinitely, or so long as unaided recall is possible.

6. At the same time, in long-distance remembering, elaboration becomes rather more common in some cases; and there may be increasing importation, or invention, aided, as in *The Method of Description,* by the use of visual images.

7. Long-distance remembering is of two types at least:
    (*a*) The general setting, as expressed mainly through the subject's attitude to the material, continues to function, as also does outstanding detail. The actual memory process is strongly and evidently constructive, and there is much use of inference.
    (*b*) All that appears to function are one or two isolated but striking details.

8. Detail is outstanding when it fits in with a subject's pre-formed interests and tendencies. It is then remembered, though often transformed, and it tends to take a progressively earlier place in successive reproductions.

9. There is some indication, as with *The Method of Description,* that, in some cases, the influence of affective attitude may be intensified with lapse of time.

10. In all successive remembering, rationalisation, the reduction of material to a form that can be readily and "satisfyingly" dealt with is very prominent.

11. It is this process, itself often based upon an affective attitude, which gives the whole dealt with that specific ground, frame, or setting, without which it will not be persistently remembered.

12. Or, again, rationalisation may deal with details, explicitly linking them together and so rendering them apparently coherent, or linking given detail with other detail not actually present in the original setting.

13. In the latter case rationalisation has three main forms:
    (*a*) The given material is initially connected with something else—usually with some definitely formulated explanation—and treated as a symbol of that other material. Eventually it tends to be unwittingly replaced by that which it has symbolised.
    (*b*) The whole rationalising process is unwitting and involves no symbolisation. It then tends to possess characteristics peculiar to the work of the individual who effects it and due directly to his particular temperament and character.
    (*c*) Names, phrases and events are immediately changed so that they appear in forms current within the social group to which the subject belongs.

14. There is evidence of delay in manifest change, transformations being foreshadowed weeks, or perhaps months, before they actually appear.

NOTES

1. *Rev. Phil.* 1897, XLII, 481–93. My attention was drawn to Philippe's most interesting work by the late Prof. James Ward.

2. Cf. chs. VII and VIII.

3. See ch. VIII.

4. See *Ann. Rep. Bur. of Amer. Ethnol.* Bull. 26, pp. 184–5.

5. He means, of course, his memory processes in general. But though he says that his specific imagery in this case has become dim, the version does not appear much less detailed or definite than his earlier attempts.

6. Cf. F. C. Bartlett, "Symbolism in Folk Lore," *Seventh International Congress of Psychology,* Cambridge 1924, pp. 278–89.

7. See ch. VII.

8. See pp. 129–46.

9. See pp. 72–5.

34

ULRIC NEISSER

Ulric Richard Gustav Neisser (1928–) began his undergraduate studies at Harvard interested in physics, but shifted to psychology and earned his B.A. in 1950. He studied with Wolfgang Kölher at Swarthmore and received an M.A. before returning to Harvard where he earned his Ph.D. in 1956. He taught at Brandeis University and Emory University and is currently a professor in the Cognitive Studies Program at Cornell University. Neisser remains interested in memory, intelligence, and self-concepts, with recently coauthored articles including "Language-dependent Recall of Autobiographical Memories" (*Journal of Experimental Psychology* 129:361–368) and "Are Young Infants Sensitive to Interpersonal Contingency?" (*Infant Behavior and Development,* 21:355–366).

COGNITIVE PSYCHOLOGY

CHAPTER 1

The Cognitive Approach

It has been said that beauty is in the eye of the beholder. As a hypothesis about localization of function, the statement is not quite right—the brain and not the eye is surely the most important organ involved. Nevertheless it points clearly enough toward the central problem of cognition. Whether beautiful or ugly or just conveniently at hand, the world of experience is produced by the man who experiences it.

This is not the attitude of a skeptic, only of a psychologist. There certainly is a real world of trees and people and cars and even books, and it has a great deal to do with our experiences of these objects. However, we have no direct, *im*mediate access to the world, nor to any of its properties. The ancient theory of *eidola*, which supposed that faint copies of objects can enter the mind directly, must be rejected. Whatever we know about reality has been *mediated*, not only by the organs of sense but by complex systems which interpret and reinterpret sensory information. The activity of the cognitive systems results in—and is integrated with—the activity of muscles and glands that we call "behavior." It is also partially—very partially—reflected in those private experiences of seeing, hearing, imagining, and thinking to which verbal descriptions never do full justice.

Physically, this page is an array of small mounds of ink, lying in certain positions on the more highly reflective surface of the paper. It is this physical page which Koffka (1935) and others would have called the "distal stimulus," and from which the reader is hopefully acquiring some information. But the sensory input is not the page itself; it is a pattern of light rays, originating in the sun or in some artificial source, that are reflected from the page and happen to reach the eye. Suitably focused by the lens and other ocular apparatus, the rays fall on the sensitive retina, where they can initiate the neural processes that eventually lead to seeing and reading and remembering. These patterns of light at the retina are the so-called "proximal stimuli." They are not the least bit like *eidola*. One-sided in their perspective, shifting radically several times each second, unique and novel at every moment, the proximal stimuli bear little resemblance to either the real object that gave rise to them or to the object of experience that the perceiver will construct as a result.

Visual cognition, then, deals with the processes by

From Ulric Neisser, "The Cognitive Approach" and "A Cognitive Approach to Memory and Thought." In *Cognitive Psychology* (pp. 3–11, 279–305). New York: Meredith 1967.

which a perceived, remembered, and thought-about world is brought into being from as unpromising a beginning as the retinal patterns. Similarly, auditory cognition is concerned with transformation of the fluctuating pressure-pattern at the ear into the sounds and the speech and music that we hear. The problem of understanding these transformations may usefully be compared to a very different question, that arises in another psychological context. One of Freud's papers on human motivation is entitled "Instincts and their Vicissitudes" (1915). The title reflects a basic axiom of psychoanalysis: that man's fundamental motives suffer an intricate series of transformations, reformulations, and changes before they appear in either consciousness or action. Borrowing Freud's phrase—without intending any commitment to his theory of motivation—a book like this one might be called "Stimulus Information and its Vicissitudes." As used here, the term "cognition" refers to all the processes by which the sensory input is transformed, reduced, elaborated, stored, recovered, and used. It is concerned with these processes even when they operate in the absence of relevant stimulation, as in images and hallucinations. Such terms as *sensation, perception, imagery, retention, recall, problem-solving,* and *thinking,* among many others, refer to hypothetical stages or aspects of cognition.

Given such a sweeping definition, it is apparent that cognition is involved in everything a human being might possibly do; that every psychological phenomenon is a cognitive phenomenon. But although cognitive psychology is concerned with all human activity rather than some fraction of it, the concern is from a particular point of view. Other viewpoints are equally legitimate and necessary. Dynamic psychology, which begins with motives rather than with sensory input, is a case in point. Instead of asking how a man's actions and experiences result from what he saw, remembered, or believed, the dynamic psychologist asks how they follow from the subject's goals, needs, or instincts. Both questions can be asked about any activity, whether it be normal or abnormal, spontaneous or induced, overt or covert, waking or dreaming. Asked why I did a certain thing, I may answer in dynamic terms, "Because I wanted . . . ," or, from the cognitive point of view, "Because it seemed to me . . ."

In attempting to trace the fate of the input, our task is both easier and harder than that of dynamic psychology. It is easier because we have a tangible starting point. The pattern of stimulation that reaches the eye or the ear can be directly observed; the beginning of the cognitive transformations is open to inspection. The student of

motivation does not have this advantage, except when he deals with the physical-deprivation motives like hunger and thirst. This forces him to rely rather more on speculation and less on observation than the cognitive theorist. But by the same token, the latter has an additional set of responsibilities. He cannot make assumptions casually, for they must conform to the results of 100 years of experimentation.

Recognition of the difference between cognitive and dynamic theory does not mean that we can afford to ignore motivation in a book like this one. Many cognitive phenomena are incomprehensible unless one takes some account of what the subject is trying to do. However, his purposes are treated here primarily as independent variables: we will note that they can affect one or another cognitive mechanism without inquiring closely into their origin. This strategy will break down in the final chapter; remembering and thinking are too "inner-directed" to be treated in such a fashion. As a consequence, the last chapter has a different format, and even a different purpose, from the others.

The cognitive and the dynamic viewpoints are by no means the only possible approaches to psychology. Behaviorism, for example, represents a very different tradition, which is essentially incompatible with both. From Watson (1913) to Skinner (1963), radical behaviorists have maintained that man's actions should be explained only in terms of observable variables, without any inner vicissitudes at all. The appeal to hypothetical mechanisms is said to be speculative at best, and deceptive at worst. For them, it is legitimate to speak of stimuli, responses, reinforcements, and hours of deprivation, but not of categories or images or ideas. A generation ago, a book like this one would have needed at least a chapter of self-defense against the behaviorist position. Today, happily, the climate of opinion has changed, and little or no defense is necessary. Indeed, stimulus-response theorists themselves are inventing hypothetical mechanisms with vigor and enthusiasm and only faint twinges of conscience. The basic reason for studying cognitive processes has become as clear as the reason for studying anything else: because they are there. Our knowledge of the world *must* be somehow developed from the stimulus input; the theory of *eidola* is false. Cognitive processes surely exist, so it can hardly be unscientific to study them.

Another approach to psychological questions, a world apart from behaviorism, is that of the physiologist. Cognition, like other psychological processes, can validly be studied in terms of the underlying neural events. For my part, I do not doubt that human behavior and consciousness depend entirely on the activity of the brain, in interaction with other physical systems. Most readers of this book will probably have the same prejudice. Nevertheless, there is very little of physiology or biochemistry in the chapters ahead. At a time when these fields are making impressive advances, such an omission may seem strange. An example may help to justify it. For this purpose, let us consider recent work on the physical basis of memory.

No one would dispute that human beings store a great deal of information about their past experiences, and it seems obvious that this information must be physically embodied somewhere in the brain. Recent discoveries in biochemistry have opened up a promising possibility. Some experimental findings have hinted that the complex molecules of DNA and RNA, known to be involved in the transmission of inherited traits, may be the substrate of memory as well. Although the supporting evidence so far is shaky, this hypothesis has already gained many adherents. But psychology is not just something "to do until the biochemist comes" (as I have recently heard psychiatry described); the truth or falsity of this new hypothesis is only marginally relevant to psychological questions. A pair of analogies will show why this is so.

First, let us consider the familiar parallel between man and computer. Although it is an inadequate analogy in many ways, it may suffice for this purpose. The task of a psychologist trying to understand human cognition is analogous to that of a man trying to discover how a computer has been programmed. In particular, if the program seems to store and reuse information, he would like to know by what "routines" or "procedures" this is done. Given this purpose, he will not care much whether his particular computer stores information in magnetic cores or in thin films; he wants to understand the program, not the "hardware." By the same token, it would not help the psychologist to know that memory is carried by RNA as opposed to some other medium. He wants to understand its utilization, not its incarnation.

Perhaps this overstates the case a little. The hardware of a computer may have some indirect effects on programming, and likewise the physical substrate may impose some limitations on the organization of mental events. This is particularly likely where peripheral (sensory and motor) processes are concerned, just as the input-output routines of a program will be most affected by the specific properties of the computer being used. Indeed, a few fragments of peripheral physiology will be considered in later chapters. Nevertheless they remain, in the familiar phrase, of only "peripheral interest."

The same point can be illustrated with quite a different analogy, hat between psychology and economics. The economist wishes to understand, say, the flow of capital. The object of his study must have some tangible representation, in the form of checks, gold, paper money, and so on, but these objects are not what he really cares about. The physical properties of money, its location in banks, its movement in armored cars, are of little interest to him. To be sure, the remarkable permanence of gold has some economic importance. The flow of capital would be markedly different if every medium of exchange were subject to rapid corrosion. Nevertheless, such matters are not the main concern of the economist, and knowledge of them does not much simplify economic theory.

Psychology, like economics, is a science concerned with the interdependence among certain events rather than with their physical nature. Although there are many disciplines of this sort (classical genetics is another good example), the most prominent ones today are probably the so-called "information sciences," which include the mathematical theory of communication, computer programming, systems analysis, and related fields. It seems obvious that these must be relevant to cognitive psychology, which is itself much concerned with information. However, their importance for psychologists has often been misunderstood, and deserves careful consideration.

Information, in the sense first clearly defined by Shannon (1948), is essentially *choice,* the narrowing down of alternatives. He developed the mathematical theory of communication in order to deal quantitatively with the transmission of messages over "channels." A channel, like a telephone line, transmits information to the extent that the choices made at one end determine those made at the other. The words of the speaker are regarded as successive selections from among all the possible words of English. Ideally, the transmitted message will enable the listener to choose the same ones; that is, to identify each correctly. For practical purposes, it is important to measure the *amount* of information that a system can transmit, and early applications of information theory were much concerned with measurement. As is now well known, amounts of information are measured in units called "bits," or binary digits, where one "bit" is represented by a choice between two equally probable alternatives.

Early attempts to apply information theory to psychology were very much in this spirit (e.g., Miller, 1953; Quastler, 1955), and even today many psychologists continue to theorize and to report data in terms of "bits" (e.g., Garner, 1962; Posner, 1964a, 1966). I do not believe, however, that this approach was or is a fruitful one. Attempts to quantify psychological processes in informational terms have usually led, after much effort, to the conclusion that the "bit rate" is not a relevant variable after all. Such promising topics as reaction time, memory span, and language have all failed to sustain early estimates of the usefulness of information measurement. With the advantage of hindsight, we can see why this might have been expected. The "bit" was developed to describe the performance of rather unselective systems: a telephone cannot decide which portions of the incoming message are important. We shall see throughout this book that human beings behave very differently, and are by no means neutral or passive toward the incoming information. Instead, they select some parts for attention at the expense of others, recording and reformulating them in complex ways.

Although information measurement may be of little value to the cognitive psychologist, another branch of the information sciences, computer *programming,* has much more to offer. A program is not a device for measuring information, but a recipe for selecting, storing, recovering, combining, outputting, and generally manipulating it. As pointed out by Newell, Shaw, and Simon (1958), this means that programs have much in common with theories of cognition. Both are descriptions of the vicissitudes of input information.

We must be careful not to confuse the program with the computer that it controls. Any single general-purpose computer can be "loaded" with an essentially infinite number of different programs. On the other hand, most programs can be run, with minor modifications, on many physically different kinds of computers. A program is not a machine; it is a series of instructions for dealing with symbols: "If the input has certain characteristics . . . then carry out certain procedures . . . otherwise other procedures . . . combine their results in various ways . . . store or retrieve various items . . . depending on prior results . . . use them in further specified ways . . . etc." The cognitive psychologist would like to give a similar account of the way information is processed by men.

This way of defining the cognitive problem is not really a new one. We are still asking "how the mind works." However, the "program analogy" (which may be a better term than "computer analogy") has several advantages over earlier conceptions. Most important is the philosophical reassurance which it provides. Although a program is nothing but a flow of symbols, it has reality enough to control the operation of very tangible machinery that executes very physical operations. A man who seeks to discover the program of a computer is surely not doing anything self-contradictory!

There were cognitive theorists long before the advent of the computer. Bartlett, whose influence on my own thinking will become obvious in later chapters, is a case in point. But, in the eyes of many psychologists, a theory which dealt with cognitive transformations, memory schemata, and the like was not *about* anything. One could understand theories that dealt with overt movements, or with physiology; one could even understand (and deplore) theories which dealt with the content of consciousness; but what kind of a thing is a schema? If memory consists of transformations, what is transformed? So long as cognitive psychology literally did not know what it was talking about, there was always a danger that it was talking about nothing at all. This is no longer a serious risk. *Information* is what is transformed, and the structured pattern of its transformations is what we want to understand.

A second advantage of the "program analogy" is that, like other analogies, it is a fruitful source of hypotheses. A field which is directly concerned with information processing should be at least as rich in ideas for psychology as other fields of science have been before. Just as we have borrowed atomic units, energy distributions, hydraulic pressures, and mechanical linkages from physics and engineering, so may we choose to adopt certain concepts from programming today. This will be done rather freely in some of the following chapters. Such notions as "parallel processing," "feature extraction," "analysis-by-synthesis," and "executive routine" have been borrowed from programmers, in the hope that they will prove theoretically useful. The test of their value, of course, is strictly psychological. We will have to see how well they fit the data.

The occasional and analogic use of programming concepts does not imply a commitment to computer "simulation" of psychological processes. It is true that a number of researchers, not content with noting that computer programs are *like* cognitive theories, have tried to write programs which *are* cognitive theories. The "Logic Theorist," a program developed by Newell, Shaw, and Simon (1958), does more than find proofs for logical theorems: it is intended as a theory of how human beings find such proofs. There has been a great deal of work in this vein recently. It has been lucidly reviewed, and sympathetically criticized, by Reitman (1965). However, such models will not be discussed here except in passing. In my opinion, none of them does even remote justice to the complexity of human mental processes. Unlike men, "artificially intelligent" programs tend to be single-minded, undistractable, and unemotional. Moreover, they are generally equipped from the beginning of each problem with all the cognitive resources necessary to solve it. These criticisms have already been presented elsewhere (Neisser, 1963c), and there is no need to elaborate them now. In a sense, the rest of this book can be construed as an extensive argument against models of this kind, and also against other simplistic theories of the cognitive processes. If the account of cognition given here is even roughly accurate, it will not be "simulated" for a long time to come.

The present volume is meant to serve a double purpose. On the one hand, I hope to provide a useful and current account of the existing "state of the art." In discussing any particular phenomenon—immediate memory, or understanding sentences, or subception, or selective listening—an attempt is made to cover the significant experiments, and to discuss the major theories. On the other hand, it must be admitted that few of these discussions are neutral. When the weight of the evidence points overwhelmingly in one direction rather than another, I prefer to say so frankly. This is especially because in most cases the indicated direction seems (to me) to be consistent with a particular view of the cognitive processes. Some of the chapters only hint at this theory, while in others it emerges explicitly. When it does, the first person singular is used rather freely, to help the reader distinguish between the facts and my interpretation of them. In the end, I hope to have presented not only a survey of cognitive psychology but the beginnings of an integration.

The title of this book involves a certain deliberate ambiguity. In one sense, "cognitive psychology" refers generally to the study of the cognitive mechanisms, quite apart from the interpretations put forward here. In another sense, "cognitive psychology" is a particular theory to which I have a specific personal commitment. By Chapter 11, it will have become so specific that Rock and Ceraso's (1964) "Cognitive Theory of Associative Learning" will be rejected as not cognitive enough! If the reader finds this dual usage confusing, I can only say that it seems unavoidable. Such double meanings are very common in psychology. Surely "Behavior Theory" is only one of many approaches to the study of behavior, just as "Gestalt Psychology" is not the only possible theory of visual figures (Gestalten), and "Psychoanalysis" is only one of many hypothetical analyses of psychological structure.

The present approach is more closely related to that of Bartlett (1932, 1958) than to any other contemporary

psychologist, while its roots are at least as old as the "act psychology" of the nineteenth century. The central assertion is that seeing, hearing, and remembering are all acts of *construction,* which may make more or less use of stimulus information depending on circumstances. The constructive processes are assumed to have two stages, of which the first is fast, crude, wholistic, and parallel while the second is deliberate, attentive, detailed, and sequential.

The model is first elaborated here in five chapters on visual processes. These chapters include an account of the very temporary, "iconic" memory which stores the output of the first stage of construction; a review of various theories of pattern recognition together with relevant data; a specific presentation of the constructive theory as applied to visual recognition; a survey of reading and tachistoscopic word-perception insofar as they are understood; and a discussion of visual memory, imagery, and hallucination. Four subsequent chapters on hearing[1] cover the perception of words, considered in terms of both acoustics and linguistics; various theories of auditory attention, including one which interprets it as a constructive process; the classical "immediate memory" for strings of words; and an account of linguistic structure together with its implications for psychology.

The final chapter on memory and thought is essentially an epilogue, different in structure from the rest of the book. Because of the tremendous scope of these higher mental processes, no attempt is made to cover the relevant data, or to refute competing theories, and the views put forward are quite tentative. Nevertheless, the reader of a book called *Cognitive Psychology* has a right to expect some discussion of thinking, concept-formation, remembering, problem-solving, and the like; they have traditionally been part of the field. If they take up only a tenth of these pages, it is because I believe there is still relatively little to say about them, even after 100 years of psychological research.

There is another respect in which this book may seem incomplete. The cognitive processes under discussion are primarily those of the American adult, or at least of the college student who is so frequently the subject of psychological experiments. Although there will be occasional references to the developmental psychology of cognition, it will not be reviewed systematically. In part, this is because the course of cognitive growth is so little understood. However, even in areas where development is being actively studied, such as concept formation and psycholinguistics, I have not felt qualified to review it.

One last word of explanation is necessary, before

concluding an introduction that is already overlong. Many topics that the reader may have expected to find have now been set aside. We will consider neither physiological mechanisms nor information measurement nor computer simulation nor developmental psychology; even remembering and thought are to receive short shrift. Despite these omissions, it must not be thought that the field which remains to be explored is a narrow one. Although the core of the material presented here is taken from within experimental psychology itself, there is extensive use of data and concepts from other fields, including psychiatry and clinical psychology (especially in connection with hallucinations); hypnosis; the social psychology of the psychological experiment; the physiology and psychology of sleep; the study of reading, which too often has been relegated to educational psychology; computer programming; linguistics and psycholinguistics. The reader may hesitate to follow along a path that seems so full of side alleys, and perhaps blind ones at that. I can only hope he will not be altogether discouraged. No shorter route seems to do justice to the vicissitudes of the input, and to the continuously creative processes by which the world of experience is constructed.

CHAPTER 11

A Cognitive Approach to Memory and Thought

It is assumed that remembering and thinking are analogous to adaptive movement and motor skill; they also resemble the synthetic processes of visual memory and speech perception. Stored information consists of traces of earlier constructive acts, organized in ways that correspond to the structure of those acts. However, the "traces" are not dormant copies of earlier experiences, somehow aroused into consciousness from time to time. Stored information is never aroused, it is only used, just as stimulus information is used in the act of perception.

The processes of remembering are themselves organized in two stages, analogous to the preattentive and attentive processes of perception. The products of the crude, wholistic, and parallel "primary processes" are usually elaborated by the "secondary processes," which include deliberate manipulation of information by an active agent. An analogy to the "executive routines" of computer programs shows that an agent need not be a *homunculus.* However, it is clear that motivation enters at several points in

these processes to determine their outcome. Thus, an integration of cognitive and dynamic psychology is necessary to the understanding of the higher mental processes.

This chapter will be concerned with relatively *delayed* vicissitudes of sensory information—with remembering events that happened more than a few seconds ago, or solving problems that require some use of stored information. The "constructive" view of these processes, which is to be presented here, has a long history. Bartlett, who demonstrated long ago that reorganization and change are the rule rather than the exception in memory, has been its outstanding advocate. At the end of *Remembering,* for example, he remarks:

> . . . the description of memories as "fixed and lifeless" is merely an unpleasant fiction . . . memory is itself constructive. . . . I have regarded it rather as one achievement in the line of the ceaseless struggle to master and enjoy a world full of variety and rapid change. Memory, and all the life of images and words which goes with it, is one with the age-old acquisition of the distance senses, and with that development of constructive imagination and constructive thought wherein at length we find the most complete release from the narrowness of presented time and place (1932, pp. 311, 312, 314).

It is hard to disagree with these sentiments, especially after one has spent ten chapters expounding an active, constructive theory of the more immediate cognitive processes. Nevertheless, it must be admitted that this kind of theorizing deals at best with half the problem. Even if the constructive nature of memory is fully acknowledged, the fact remains that information about the past must be somehow stored and preserved for subsequent use. Today's experience must leave some sort of trace behind if it is to influence tomorrow's construction.

This problem was not central to earlier chapters of this book, because they dealt primarily with the cognitive transformations of *present* (or very recent) input. The question "what is being transformed" was easily answered in terms of stimulus information. Only in discussing imagery and hallucination (Chapter 6) did we consider processes that may be entirely "innerdirected." That argument attempted to show that visual memory is just as "constructive" as perception itself. However successful the attempt may have been, it left a whole series of questions rather awkwardly unanswered. If images are constructions, what is their raw material? How is this raw material organized? For that matter, how is the process of construction organized? What determines the particular image that is constructed; what purpose does it serve?

These questions do not apply to imagery alone but to all remembering, and to thinking and problem-solving as well. They can be answered only by an adequate theory of memory and thought. For various reasons—some of which will be discussed below—we are far from having such a theory today. The views to be presented here are not a theory either, and are offered only for their suggestive value. It is not even possible to review the experimental evidence that bears on them, in the manner of the earlier chapters, because there is far too much of it. The purpose of this epilogue is not so much to present a cognitive theory of the higher mental processes as to show that one is possible, consistent with the foregoing treatment of visual and auditory cognition.

The Reappearance Hypothesis

Given the fact that information about the past is somehow preserved, it is important to ask what aspects of experience are stored, how the stored information is organized, how and why it is recovered, and by whom. As noted in Chapter 1, we are not primarily interested in the way information is physically stored by the brain. Psychology deals with the organization and use of information, not with its representation in organic tissue. Our question is the one which has been addressed in the past with such concepts as *traces, ideas, associations, schemata, clusters, habit-family hierarchies,* and *response-strengths.*

Perhaps the simplest and the most influential account of memory is that given long ago by the English empiricist philosophers. Hobbes, Locke, Hume, and Mill all assumed that one retains "ideas," or "conceptions," which are nothing but slightly faded copies of sensory experiences. These ideas are linked to one another by bonds called "associations." Ideas become "associated" whenever the original experiences occur simultaneously or in rapid succession ("temporal contiguity"), and perhaps also if they are similar. A person's ideas are not all conscious at any given moment. Instead, they become aroused successively, so that only one or a few are active at once. The order in which they "come to mind" is governed by the associative links, and therefore by prior contiguity in time. As James Mill wrote in 1829, "Our ideas spring up, or exist, in the order in which the sensations existed, of which they are copies" (Dennis, 1948, p. 142).

In this view, mental processes are by no means "con-structive." Instead of the creation of something new in each act of remembering, there is only the arousal of something that already exists. The ideas lie dormant most of the time and spring to life intermittently when they are aroused or—as Freud put it—"cathected." Indeed, Freud's view of truly unconscious thinking, which he called the "primary process," resembled Mill's in many ways. He, too, supposed that ideas exist even when they are inactive, and that the flow of mental activity, or cathexis, tended to follow "association paths" (1900, p. 529). However, Freud did not leave this flow to its own devices as Mill had. Above it, he postulated elaborate subsystems like the ego, and executive functions like "censorship"; below, an internal source of excitation in the form of the sexual drive. Mill had resisted even this much inner-determination or spontaneity. Even where sex was concerned, he treated thinking as if it were entirely stimulus-bound: "The spot on which a tender maiden parted with her lover, when he embarked on the voyage from which he never returned, cannot afterwards be seen by her without an agony of grief" (Dennis, 1948, p. 145).

The notion that the stored information consists of ideas, suspended in a quiescent state from which they are occasionally aroused, has a very long history in psychology. It seems to me so important—and so misguided—that it deserves a special name. Here I will call it the "Reappearance Hypothesis," since it implies that the same "memory," image, or other cognitive unit can disappear and reappear over and over again. It has always had many supporters and a few beleaguered opponents, of whom William James is the most quoted: "A permanently existing 'idea' or 'Vorstellung' which makes its appearance before the foot-lights of consciousness at periodical intervals, is as mythological an entity as the Jack of Spades" (1890, Vol. 1, p. 236).

Despite James' opposition, the Reappearance Hypothesis has never stopped exerting a malevolent fascination over psychologists. It was adopted not only by associationism and psychoanalysis, but by behaviorism and even—as we shall see—by Gestalt psychology. The behaviorists introduced a new view of the elements involved—stimuli and responses were associated, rather than ideas—but they endowed the response with the same permanence that had once characterized the idea. Such terms as "habit strength" (which continues to exist even when the habit is dormant), "stimulus control" (of an independently existing response), and "stimulus generalization" (the response conditioned to one stimulus can also be elicited by another), all assume that something exists continuously and makes an occasional appearance "before the footlights." The stage on which it appears is observable behavior rather than consciousness, but the principle of Reappearance still applies.

This assumption is so ingrained in our thinking that we rarely notice how poorly it fits experience. If Reappearance were really the governing principle of mental life, repetition of earlier acts or thoughts should be the natural thing, and variation the exception. In fact, the opposite is true. Precise repetition of any movement, any spoken sentence, or any sequence of thought is extremely difficult to achieve. When repetition does occur, as in dramatic acting or nonsense-syllable learning or a compulsive sequence of actions, we ascribe it either to long, highly motivated practice or to neurotic defensiveness.

What *is* natural, on the contrary, is adaptive variation. We saw in Chapter 6 that visual images are not copies but suitably constructed originals, in Chapter 9 that verbal memory contains new rhythmic organizations rather than copies of stimuli, and in Chapters 7 and 10 that the words and sentences of normal speech are hardly ever duplicates of anything said earlier. The same generalization can be made about long-term memory, as Bartlett (1932) showed so vividly. Verbatim recall of a story occurs very rarely, while reorganization in line with the interests and values of the subject must be expected.

Even the simple conditioned response illustrates the weakness of the Reappearance Hypothesis. Although *theories* based on conditioning generally assume that "the response" is made conditional on a new stimulus through some form of reinforcement, no such "response" is observable. It is generally agreed that " . . . the CR and UCR are never strictly the same, and that the conditioned response is not simply a duplicate of the unconditioned one" (Kimble, 1961, p. 52).

Perhaps it is not surprising that behaviorists and psychoanalysts both continue to make Mill's Reappearance assumption; their historical roots in associationism are fairly clear. More striking is the degree to which their historical opponents, the Gestalt psychologists, adopted the same stance. In the Gestalt view, each perceptual experience lays down a "trace." Contiguous perceptions result in grouped *traces,* and associative recall consists of the rearousal of traces via these groups. To be sure, the aggregate, or "trace-field," was assumed to be active and self-organizing. Individual traces tend toward simpler forms, and groups like the successive nonsense syllables of a list form unified *structures,* which can submerge some of their parts (intraserial inhibition) and accentuate others (the isolation effect). Nevertheless, the Reappearance Hypothesis was not abandoned. Gestalt theory and its opponents agreed that stored in-

formation consists essentially of copies (traces) of earlier events (ideas, responses, perceptions). These copies are supposedly linked (associated) to form pairs or larger groups (complex ideas, response sequences), and they are aroused from time to time by means of these links. So great was the area of agreement that Osgood (1953) could find only a single testable difference between the Gestalt and the S-R theories of memory: the dubious hypothesis that memory traces change autonomously toward better form (see Riley, 1962, for a review of the inconclusive search for such changes).

In "Toward a Cognitive Theory of Associative Learning," Rock and Ceraso (1964) take a position very similar to that of Gestalt psychology. They advance forceful arguments against stimulus-response theory, pointing out that the very distinction between "stimulus" and "response" is artificial and confusing where verbal memory is concerned. However, they are unflinchingly loyal to the Reappearance Hypothesis.

A central feature of cognitive theory is the construct of a representational memory trace. This memory trace is conceived of as the product of learning, and serves as the basis of memory. The memory trace is taken to be representational in the sense that activation of a trace corresponding to a prior experience will give rise to a new experience similar to that prior experience (p. 112).

Although Rock and Ceraso choose to call their approach a "cognitive theory," it makes so little appeal to transformations and constructive processes that a better name might be "neo-associationism." They are not unaware of this:

Our intent in using the word "cognitive" is to do justice to the experiential aspects of learning and recall. If we do not give it any other surplus meaning (as, for example, notions about parts and wholes, emergentism, or the like) our meaning is approximately the same as that of classical association theory. Thinkers such as Locke, Hume, Titchener, and James were concerned with the association and recall of ideas. It is only the displacement of association theory by behavior theory that makes it necessary at this time to point up certain of its features that have been prematurely cast aside (p. 113). [They go on to say that their view differs from classical associationism in that certain perceptual organizing processes are assumed to precede the actual formation of the trace.]

The Reappearance Hypothesis has dominated not only theories about memory but also the experimental techniques used to investigate it. Studies of rote learning take for granted that the same nonsense-syllable response can be elicited over and over again, and ask only how its reappearance depends on certain variables. Similarly, studies of "concept formation" nearly always assume that the same classificatory response can occur repeatedly; the subject need only "attach" it to the proper stimuli. This theoretical commitment makes most of these studies difficult to interpret from a cognitive point of view. If "associations" (in the sense of connections between reappearing traces or responses) do not exist, it makes little sense to ask whether they are learned in a single trial, or more slowly in homogeneous lists, or more quickly with distributed practice. Experiments dealing with such questions have sometimes uncovered interesting phenomena, but they will not be reviewed here.

Of course, in an operational sense there is no doubt that responses *do* reappear. Subjects can be observed to press the same lever repeatedly, or to speak what sounds like the same syllable on many different trials. With prolonged practice, so much stereotypy may be created that the successive responses become indistinguishable in every respect, even in the subject's own awareness. But the fact that simple operations fail to distinguish between the complex problem-solving of the naive subject and the bored stereotypy of the sophisticated one does not make the distinction unimportant. Rather, it suggests that we should get better operations.

The Utilization Hypothesis

Is there an alternative to Reappearance? If the stored information does not consist of dormant ideas or images or responses, how are we to conceptualize it? Following Bartlett and Schachtel, we can agree that recall and thought are both constructive processes, but the metaphor of construction implies some raw material. Moreover, since repeated recalls of the "same event," or repeated appearances of the "same image" do have much in common, the raw material must exercise a good deal of control over the final product.

We have met this situation before. In fact, the same problem has arisen repeatedly throughout this book. Like recall, *attention* and *perception* are also constructive processes in which adaptive variation is the rule. Nevertheless, repeated perceptions of the "same event" may have much in common. This is easily explained by common properties of the *stimuli* in the two cases—properties which the mechanisms of cognition are pre-

pared to seize on and elaborate. Perception is constructive, but the input information often plays the largest single role in determining the constructive process. A very similar role, it seems to me, is played by the aggregate of information stored in long-term memory.

This is not to say that the stimuli themselves are copied and stored; far from it. The analogy being offered asserts only that the role which stored information plays in recall is like the role which stimulus information plays in perception. In neither case does it enter awareness directly, and in neither case can it be literally reproduced in behavior except after rather special training. The model of the paleontologist, which was applied to perception and focal attention in Chapter 4, applies also to memory: out of a few stored bone chips, we remember a dinosaur. To assert otherwise, to defend the Reappearance Hypothesis, would be to adopt an attitude reminiscent of naive realism in perception. It represents a fallacy in both contexts. One does not see objects simply "because they are there," but after an elaborate process of construction (which usually is designed to make use of relevant stimulus information). Similarly, one does not recall objects or responses simply because traces of them exist in the mind, but after an elaborate process of *re*construction, (which usually makes use of relevant stored information).

What is the information—the bone chips—on which reconstruction is based? The only plausible possibility is that it consists of traces of *prior processes of construction.* There are no stored copies of finished mental events, like images or sentences, but only traces of earlier constructive activity. In a sense, all learning is "response" learning; i.e., it is learning to carry out some coordinated series of acts. In the case of a motor skill like bicycling or speaking, the acts include overt movements. In visual memory the construction is largely internal, except when it spills over into the eye motions discussed in Chapter 6. Recall, by way of an image, takes place when a new construction is largely under the control of what remains from an earlier one. Recall in words, on the other hand, is a new verbal synthesis which may be based on information from a number of sources, including not only traces of earlier verbalizations, but perhaps visual images and other constructions as well.

The present proposal is, therefore, that we store traces of earlier cognitive acts, not of the products of those acts. The traces are not simply "revived" or "reactivated" in recall: instead, the stored fragments are used as information to support a new construction. It is as if the bone fragments used by the paleontologist did not appear in the model he builds at all—as indeed they need not, if it is to represent a fully fleshed-out, skin-covered dinosaur. The bones can be thought of, somewhat loosely, as remnants of the structure which created and supported the original dinosaur, and thus as sources of information about how to reconstruct it.

Cognitive Structures

When we first perceive or imagine something, the process of construction is not limited to the object itself. We generally build (or rebuild) a spatial, temporal, and conceptual framework as well. In previous chapters little has been said about this background; "construction" has meant construction in focal attention. But, when you see a friend across the street, you are not seeing only him. *He,* a person of a particular kind with a particular relevance to your life, is appearing *there,* a particular place in space, and *then,* at a certain point in time. Similarly, a spoken sentence is not just a string of words to be identified, but it has a particular meaning, is spoken by a particular person, at a particular time and place. These frames of reference can be thought of as a third level of cognitive construction. The preattentive processes delineate units, provide partial cues, and control simple responses; focal attention builds complexly structured objects or movements, one at a time, on the basis thus provided; the background processes build and maintain schemata to which these objects are referred.

Taken together, the activity of these background schemata creates what Shor (1959) has called the "generalized reality orientation." As he points out, it is not always with us, and its absence creates a rather peculiar state of consciousness.

> I had been asleep for a number of hours. My level of body tonus was fairly high and my mind clear of dream-images so that I believe I was not asleep but rather in some kind of trance-like state. At that time I was neither conscious of my personal identity, nor of prior experiences, nor of the external world. It was just that out of nowhere I was aware of my own thought processes. I did not know, however, that they were thought processes or who I was, or even that I was an *I*. There was sheer awareness in isolation from any experiential context. It was neither pleasant nor unpleasant, it was not goal directed, just sheer existing. After a time, "wondering" started to fill my awareness; that there was more than this, a gap, an emptiness. As soon as this "wondering" was set into motion there was immediately a change in my awareness. In an instant, as if in a flash, full

awareness of myself and reality expanded around me. To say that "I woke up" or that "I remembered," while perhaps correct, would miss the point of the experience entirely. The significant thing was that my mind changed fundamentally in that brief instant. In rediscovering myself and the world, something vital had happened; suddenly all the specifications of reality had become apparent to me. At one moment my awareness was devoid of all structure and in the next moment I was *myself* in a multivaried universe of time, space, motion, and desire (Shor, 1959, p. 586).

The "generalized reality orientation" described by Shor is only one example—though perhaps the most inclusive one—of the organized systems of stored information that we call "cognitive structures." In general, a cognitive structure may be defined as a nonspecific but organized representation of prior experiences. Our grasp of the surrounding geography, our understanding of American history, our "feel"for driving a car, our "intuitions" about linguistic form are all the result of a great number of individual experiences, but they do not reflect these experiences separately. One easily forgets the *occasions* on which one learned how the local streets are oriented, what the Civil War was about, how to shift gears, or how to speak grammatically, but they leave a residue behind. Because these residues are organized in the sense that their parts have regular and controlling interrelations, the term "cognitive structures" is appropriate for them. (This definition is meant to leave the question of empiricism and nativism open. It is very possible that the form and organization of at least some cognitive structures, especially those for space, time, and language, are determined genetically, or otherwise, before any experience has accumulated.)

Historically, a concern with these structures has been the distinguishing characteristic of "cognitive psychologists." The array of theorists who could be cited in this connection would have to include at least Bartlett, Piaget, Schachtel, Tolman, Lashley, Rapaport, and Bruner; many other names could be added as well. It is not possible to review all of their work here. The remainder of this section is only a commentary, from the viewpoint of the present author, on aspects of cognitive structure that have been treated far more extensively elsewhere.

Cognitive structures play a particularly interesting role in learning and remembering. In this connection, they are most frequently called "schemata," after Bartlett (1932). It is easy to see why the schemata control the fate of stored information; they are themselves information of a similar sort. The hypothesis of the present chapter is that cognition is constructive, and that the process of construction leaves traces behind. The schemata themselves are such constructions, elaborated at every moment in the course of attentive activity. Recall is organized in terms of these structures because the original experiences were elaborated in the same terms. It probably is unwise to think of them as filing systems into which specific memories can be put; they are integral parts of the memories themselves. In any case, it is easy to agree with Lashley's estimate of their importance:

 . . . every memory becomes part of a more or less extensive organization. When I read a scientific paper, the new facts presented become associated with the field of knowledge of which it is a part. Later availability of the specific items of the paper depends on a partial activation of the whole body of associations. If one has not thought of a topic for some time, it is difficult to recall details. With review or discussion of the subject, however, names, dates, references which seemed to be forgotten rapidly become available to memory. Head has given instances of such recall by multiple reinforcement in his studies of aphasia. Although there are no systematic experiments upon this "warming up" effect, it is a matter of common experience, and is evidence, I believe, that recall involves the subthreshold activation of a whole system of associations which exert some sort of mutual facilitation (1950, pp. 497–498).

Everyone recognizes the close relationship between interests and memory, which seems to result from the extensive schemata we build for material we care about. We have all known, or been, boys who could remember everything about baseball or fishing but not a bit of history. As adults, we can learn an endless variety of new facts that relate to our profession or our hobby, while everything else seems to go in one ear and out the other. In the same vein, Bartlett (1932) has described African herdsmen who were unable to give adequate testimony in a court of law, but could recall the details of cattle transactions for years with astonishing accuracy. The most important advice offered by the many practitioners of "memory improvement" systems (e.g., Furst, 1948) is to develop detailed and articulate schemata into which new material can be fitted.

If cognitive structures can facilitate recall, we should be able to work backwards from observations of recall to learn something about them. This aim has been exten-

sively pursued in recent studies of clustering and word-association. In a method devised by Bousfield (1953), for example, subjects are asked to memorize a list in which all the words belong to certain categories—animals, cities, weapons, or the like—but are presented in a randomized sequence. The order of recall is left to the subject's own discretion, and thus it can reveal a good deal about the "subjective organization" of the information involved. The typical subject recalls first a cluster of words from one category, then some from a second group, and so on. (As a matter of fact, idiosyncratic clusters appear in recall even when the material has not been specially designed to encourage them, but in such instances they are more difficult to detect—see Tulving, 1962.) One might regard these studies as the definitive refutation of James Mill: the order of ideas does *not* repeat the order of sensations by any means. Instead, it follows lines determined by cognitive structure.

Similar analyses can be made of data obtained with the method of word-association: "Say the first word that comes into your mind when I say *black*." Deese (1965) goes so far as to define an "associative structure" as a group of words that are likely to elicit the same associates. In such experiments, the subject is generally instructed to avoid any purposeful or directed thinking, so that a relatively unclouded view of the organization of memory may be obtained. However, some caution should be exercised in the use of the method, for this is a difficult instruction to follow. Many people have distinct notions about the kind of responses expected of them in such tasks, and behave accordingly. Like other performances, word-association depends not only on the organization of memory but on what the subject is trying to achieve.

While cognitive structures (or "coding systems," as they are called by Bruner, 1957a) make recall possible, they also have some negative effects. By necessity, they tend to introduce bias and distortion into both the initial construction and the later reconstruction. Documentation of these changes makes up the bulk of Bartlett's *Remembering* (1932). They have also been studied in more conventional experimental situations, notably by Postman (1954). However, there is no doubt that more experimental studies of these phenomena are needed. Replication of Bartlett's findings is not easy (but see Paul, 1959) and other kinds of mnemonic biasing seem to be even more tenuously established (see Waly & Cook, 1966).

It has been repeatedly emphasized that stored information is not revived, but simply used, in the constructive activity of recall. This applies to background schemata as well as to recall of specific figures or events. When I try to recall my first day at college, I do so by means of complex frames of reference, arrays of information, in which that day is included: college life as a whole, myself as a young man, the geography of the town, and so on. It is because these schemata are being used that I will go on to remember other, related facts which are not directly germane to the question. However, the critical frames of reference do not literally come to life again; if they did, I would be seventeen once more. (This is precisely the miracle claimed for so-called "hypnotic age regression." As we saw in Chapter 6, the age of miracles is over.) Instead, they are *used* by the present me, via the schemata which I am *now* capable of constructing.

For the attempted recall to succeed, the schemata I develop now, in the attempt to recall, must not be too different from those whose traces were established long ago. They can differ, but not so much that the present ones cannot incorporate the information stored earlier. Otherwise, the stored fragments of structure will be unusable, and recall will fail. This is what happens when an inappropriate "set" produces failures of memory, as in problem-solving experiments showing "functional fixedness," or in trick sentences like *Pas de la Rhone que nous.*

Of course, loss of a cognitive system can have much more serious consequences than this. Knowledge about oneself, one's own personal history, also comprises a rather tightly knit cognitive system. When it becomes unavailable we speak of "loss of memory," or more precisely of a "fugue." Rapaport (1957) gives a detailed account of a fugue, to illustrate the dramatic effects of cognitive structuring. In such states, the reason for the patient's inability to reconstruct his own past is generally a dynamic one: he does not *want* to use the schemata which concern himself. The result is not only a loss of memory but a badly weakened sense of present reality, as Shor's argument would have suggested.

Fugues are often reversible, especially with the aid of special techniques such as hypnosis. So are inappropriate sets, of course: one need only be told that *Pas de la Rhone que nous* is an English sentence beginning with *Paddle.* However, the rather similar state of *infantile amnesia*—inability to recall one's own early childhood—is not reversible to any substantial degree. The reason, as Schachtel (1947) saw clearly, is that adults cannot think as children do; they no longer carry out attentive constructions in the way they once did. As a result, they cannot make use of any fragments of infantile constructions that they may still retain. Elsewhere

(Neisser, 1962), I have considered this phenomenon in more detail.

A particularly important class of cognitive structures are those which represent arrangement in time. Except in unusual states of consciousness, adults—especially adults in our western, time-oriented culture—tend to construct the events of their experience in a temporal framework. I *am writing* these lines today (September 26, 1966), which is the day *before* I leave on a long-planned trip and several days *after* reorganizing this chapter into its present format. I *have been* at my office for several hours and *soon* it *will be* time to go to lunch. And, of course, the *I* to whom these experiences are referred is a temporally ordered entity, whose experiences are strung along a temporal line that begins hazily at about age five and continues without any serious disturbance of continuity far into the future. That (imagined) future is less definite than the (remembered) past, but the events foreseen in it—*next* Christmas, *next* summer—are for the most part in just as linear an array.

This temporal structuring is so pervasive for us that it has been given a central, primitive role in most theories of learning. The common assumption has been that the temporal succession of two stimuli, or of a stimulus and a response, automatically produces some inner representation in which their order is preserved. "Contiguity in time" has been taken as the basic principle of mental organization. In one sense, this is undeniable. Time must be important for the informational processes of cognition, as for any other processes in nature: whether and how two events interact depends in part on their temporal relations. But this does not mean that these temporal relations will be directly represented in recall or in performance. Conversely, the succession that *is* represented in recall need not result directly from the physical time-order of stimuli.

As an example of the first point, consider that I must have acquired my present vocabulary of English words in some order; in fact, the particular order was probably a factor in making some words easier to learn than others. However, this order of acquisition is not reflected in my current mental activity. It does not matter, nor do I know, which of the words "current," "mental," and "activity" I learned first. As an example of the second point, consider history. I know the sequence of American Presidents, or at least the first few, better than I know the sequence of my own grammar school teachers. This is not a matter of direct experience, nor even of having once changed "Washington, John Adams, Jefferson, . . ." in order. I also know the sequence of recent American Secretaries of State beginning with Cordell Hull, although I have surely never recited their names successively until today. Historical and personal facts each have their own representation in a *temporal structure.* Once such a structure exists, the real time-order of stimuli may help to determine their temporal representation, but other factors, including instruction and anticipation, can play an important role.

There are many experimental illustrations of the distinction between real temporal contiguity on the one hand and functional, experienced contiguity on the other. Perhaps the best is Thorndike's "belongingness" effect, discussed in Chapter 10, which shows that "associations" are formed only between words that have been incorporated into a single cognitive unit. For another example, consider the astonishing errors of sequence made by children, especially in their use of language, where inversions of words and syllables are common. This is not surprising if, as argued in Chapter 7, the order of linguistic units is recovered by constructing a larger pattern into which they fit. Because cognitive development is outside the scope of this book, this question will not be pursued further here. For those who are concerned with it, Piaget's account of the child's conception of time (see Flavell, 1963) is particularly relevant.

Space is another cognitive dimension which is important but not as "primitive" as is sometimes supposed. It is obvious enough that generally we conceive of ourselves and of the world in spatial terms. The words on the printed page have location as well as identity: left or right, top or bottom, near or far. Information about these spatial aspects of construction remains available to recall, so that we often know on what portion of the page a certain argument is to be found. (For a related phenomenon in rote learning, see Asch, Hay, and Diamond, 1960.) Again, it is important to note that this kind of spatiality does not simply reflect the raw spatial organization of the input. Position on the retina is an important source of stimulus information, but it is not directly represented by a position in cognitively elaborated space. As we have seen (Chapter 6), perceived space itself is the result of an integration of numerous retinal "snapshots." Moreover, one's "cognitive map" (Tolman, 1948) of the surrounding environment may easily include "contiguities" that have *never* been directly experienced. In imagining my own house, I am just as aware of the relationship between the dining room and the bedroom (which are above one another, and thus never experienced in immediate succession) as of that between the adjacent dining and living rooms. The extent to which this spatial organization exists fully articulated in the newborn infant (as opposed to developing through

commerce with the environment) is still a hotly disputed topic.

The Problem of the Executive

The cognitive approach to memory and thought emphasizes that recall and problem-solving are constructive acts, based on information remaining from earlier acts. That information, in turn, is organized according to the structure of those earlier acts, though its utilization depends also on present circumstances and present constructive skills. This suggests that the higher mental processes are closely related to skilled motor behavior—a relationship which Bartlett has explored and illustrated in two books, 26 years apart.

Suppose I am making a stroke in a quick game, such as tennis or cricket. How I make the stroke depends on the relating of certain new experiences, most of them visual, to other immediately preceding visual experiences and to my posture, or balance of postures, at the moment. The latter, balance of postures, is the result of a whole series of earlier movements, in which the last movement before the stroke is played has a predominant function. When I make the stroke I do not, as a matter of fact, produce something absolutely new, and I never merely repeat something old. The stroke is literally manufactured out of the living visual and postural "schemata" of the moment and their interrelations. I may say, I may think that I reproduce exactly a series of textbook movements, but demonstrably I do not; just as, under other circumstances, I may say and think that I reproduce exactly some isolated event which I want to remember, and again demonstrably I do not (*Remembering*, 1932, pp. 201–202).

. . . all skilled behaviour is set into a form of significant sequence within which it must be studied if understanding is to be reached . . . it submits to a control which lies outside itself and is appreciated, at the bodily level, by the receptor system . . . proper timing, the ways in which transition is made from one direction of move to another, "point of no return," and the character of direction and how it is appreciated are all critical features of skilled behaviour. From time to time, and in relation to all the kinds of thinking which I have discussed, I have returned particularly to those properties of skill, and it has seemed not only that thinking of all kinds possesses them, but also that their study does throw some real light upon the thinking processes themselves.

. . . thinking is an advanced form of skilled behaviour . . . it has grown out of earlier established forms of flexible adaptation to the environment . . . the characteristics which it possesses and the conditions to which it submits can best be studied as they are related to those of its own earlier forms (*Thinking,* 1958, pp. 198–199).

For many kinds of thinking, this is a convincing argument. Rational problem-solving and deliberate recall do seem like purposeful and skillful actions. However, there is a major difference between these activities and simple bodily skills, as Bartlett realized. Mental activities are far less dependent on the *immediate* past, on "the last movement before the stroke" than simple movements are. To account for our ability to use earlier experience selectively, he suggested that "An organism has somehow to acquire the ability to turn round upon its own 'schemata' and to construct them afresh" (1932, p. 206). Other theorists have dealt with the same issue by speaking of *searches through memory, strategies, censorship,* and even *covert trial and error.* All of these concepts, like *turning round,* raise a very serious question. Who does the turning, the trying, and the erring? Is there a little man in the head, a *homunculus,* who acts the part of the paleontologist vis-à-vis the dinosaur?

Unpalatable as such a notion may be, we can hardly avoid it altogether. If we do *not* postulate some agent who selects and uses the stored information, we must think of every thought and every response as just the momentary resultant of an interacting system, governed essentially by laissez-faire economics. Indeed, the notions of "habit strength" and "response competition" used by the behaviorists are based on exactly this model. However, it seems strained and uncomfortable where selective thought and action are involved. To see the problem, consider an experiment proposed by Yntema and Trask (1963), which highlights the need for some kind of active executive process in a theory of memory. Suppose we read a list of five words to a subject, and shortly thereafter read four of them again, in a scrambled order. He is to tell us which one was omitted on the second reading. People can easily do this, but Yntema and Trask point out that " . . . S does not respond with the missing item because it has been reinforced most often, or because it is in any conventional sense the strongest response. Thus, it seems reasonable, indeed almost necessary, to assume that some sort of data-processing mechanism can intervene between memory and overt response" (1963, p. 66).

There are many mechanisms which might successfully carry out this task, but it is hard to imagine any which do not distinguish between a *memory* in which

the first list is somehow stored, and an agent or *processor* which somehow makes use of it. Yntema and Trask suggest a number of alternative strategies; for example, the processor might check off each stored word as "repeated" when it appears in the second list, and subsequently skim through until it finds an unchecked item. Some kind of agent seems unavoidable here (as in Buschke's very similar "missing span" method, in which the subject must produce the digit that was *not* presented to him—see Chapter 9) simply because the correct response is not "in any conventional sense the strongest." This is true of many other situations as well. However, such responses are rarely thought to reflect only "memory." For the most part, experiments with this annoying property have been classed as studies of "thinking" or "problem-solving" or "reasoning" rather than "memory." This is virtually the definition of the "higher mental processes," as they appear in ordinary psychological texts. We credit a subject with something more than "remembering" when the response he makes is not the strongest in a conventional sense.

Most psychological theories are "conventional" in this respect. The notion of a separate processor, or *executive,* is rejected not only by classical association theory but by behaviorism, by the "trace theory" of Rock and Ceraso (1964), and by Gestalt psychology (except for a few cryptic passages in Koffka, 1935). It is also missing from Freud's notion of "primary-process thinking." Freud was quick to postulate executive processes of many kinds as well (e.g., the ego, the superego, the censorship) but he was usually more interested in what they suppressed than in what they produced.

A "conventional" theorist can deal with executive phenomena in two ways. First, he can classify them as "higher mental processes" and thus as outside his area of interest. Second, he can treat them directly, but this means that he must *reduce* them to conventional cases. He is obliged to argue that appearances are deceptive: what seems like an executive process is really the simple resultant of existing response strengths, and what seems like fresh and adaptive behavior is only the reappearance of previous elements. My own view is quite different. Appearances are indeed deceptive in many experiments, but they deceive at least as often in studies of "rote learning" as in work on thinking. What seems to be simple associative revival of earlier responses may actually be a complex process of search and construction; a subject instructed to memorize syllables by rote tends instead to construct complex rhythmic and semantic patterns which incorporate them. In this sense remembering is always a form of problem-solving, and therefore a higher mental process. That is why it is treated as one in this book. (A similar treatment appears in Miller, Galanter, and Pribram, 1960, Chapter 10.)

While there seems to be no justification for distinguishing remembering from other forms of thinking, there are certain problems of *retention* that must not be entirely overlooked. When information is stored over time, we have reason to ask a number of questions. For example, psychologists have long wondered whether long-term memory decays as a function of time alone ("simple forgetting"), or whether losses over time result only from interference by other material and other activities ("proactive inhibition" and "retroactive inhibition"). It has also been suggested that time can have a beneficial effect on stored information ("consolidation"), rendering it less vulnerable to such gross interventions as electroconvulsive shock. These are important issues, currently under intensive study. They will not be reviewed here, because (so far as I can presently judge) their resolution does not depend on the question of how memory is organized and used.

It is important to understand why the hypothesis of a separate executive process has always been rejected by the "conventional" theories. The most commonly cited ground is the law of parsimony, "Occam's Razor": constructs should not be elaborated more than is necessary. But this razor has two edges; Granit has remarked that ". . . the biologist's attitude should be humbler. His duty is to admit that he does not know nature well enough to understand her requirements or 'necessities.' That is why he experiments" (1955, p. 37).

In any case, the law of parsimony would hardly explain the very unparsimonious hypotheses erected by stimulus-response theorists to explain away what seem to be executive processes. Their real motive is a more serious one. They are afraid that a separate executive would return psychology to the soul, the will, and the *homunculus;* it would be equivalent to explaining behavior in terms of a "little man in the head." Such explanations seem to lead only to an infinite regress, which must bar further research and frustrate theory. If the actions of the executive account for behavior, what accounts for those actions in turn? Does the ego have an ego?

It now seems possible that there is an escape from the regress that formerly seemed infinite. As recently as a generation ago, processes of control had to be thought of as *homunculi,* because man was the only known model of an executive agent. Today, the stored-program computer has provided us with an alternative possibility, in the form of the *executive routine.* This is a concept which may be of considerable use to psychology.

Most computer programs consist of largely independent parts, or "subroutines." In complex sequential programs, the order in which the subroutines are applied will vary from one occasion to the next. In simple cases, a conditional decision can lead from one subroutine to the next appropriate one: "transfer control to register A if the computed number in register X is positive, but to register B if it is negative or zero." In other situations, however, the choice between register A and register B may depend on a more complicated set of conditions, which must be evaluated by a separate subroutine called "the executive." Common practice is to make all subroutines end by transferring control to the executive, which then decides what to do next in each case. One might well say that the executive "uses" the other routines, which are "subordinate" to it. Some programs may even have a hierarchical structure, in which routines at one level can call those which are "lower" and are themselves called by others which are "higher." However, the regress of control is not infinite: there is a "highest," or executive routine which is not used by anything else.

Note that the executive is in no sense a *programmulus,* or miniature of the entire program. It does not carry out the tests or the searches or the constructions which are the task of the subroutines, and it does not include the stored information which the subroutines use. Indeed, the executive may take only a small fraction of the computing time and space allotted to the program as a whole, and it need not contain any very sophisticated processes. Although there is a real sense in which it "uses" the rest of the program and the stored information, this creates no philosophical difficulties; it is not using itself. (As a matter of fact, some programs *do* have so-called recursive subroutines, which use themselves. An example is the "General Problem-Solver" of Newell and Simon, 1963, which Reitman, 1965, describes in some detail. However, we do not need to explore this possibility here.)

As noted in Chapter 1, the use of a concept borrowed from computer programming does not imply that existing "computer models" are satisfactory from a psychological point of view. In general, they are not. One of their most serious inadequacies becomes particularly apparent in the present context. The executive routine of a computer program must be established by the programmer from the beginning. Although artificially intelligent programs can easily "learn" (modify themselves as a result of experience), none so far can make major developmental changes in its own executive routine. In man, however, such functions as "turning round on one's own schemata" and "searching through memory" are themselves acquired through experience. We do not know much about this learning, but it poses no new problem in principle, if we already assume that human memory stores information about processes rather than about contents. Mental activities can be learned; perhaps they are the only things that are ever learned.

The Multiplicity of Thought

We were led to the notion of an executive by Bartlett's analogy between thought and purposeful action. It is time now to admit that this is not all of the story. Thought is by no means always coordinated toward a particular goal. We are not forever engaged in "filling up gaps in the evidence" (Bartlett, 1958, p. 20), nor in following out some strategic plan. It is true that I may construct an image in the course of directed train of thought, but more often the image just "comes by itself," as if "I," at least, had not constructed it. As we saw in Chapter 6, even the images that do accompany purposeful thinking tend to have only a tangential, symbolic relation to it. This is even more obvious in dreams and fantasy, which seem to represent a mode of thinking and remembering quite different from the step-by-step logic of reason.

Historically, psychology has long recognized the existence of two different forms of mental organization. The distinction has been given many names: "rational" vs. "intuitive," "constrained" vs. "creative," "logical" vs. "prelogical," "realistic" vs. "autistic," "secondary process" vs. "primary process." To list them together so casually may be misleading; the "autistic" thinking of schizophrenics, as described by Bleuler (1912), is surely not "creative." Nevertheless, a common thread runs through all the dichotomies. Some thinking and remembering is deliberate, efficient, and obviously goal-directed; it is usually experienced as self-controlled as well. Other mental activity is rich, chaotic, and inefficient; it tends to be experienced as involuntary, it just "happens." It often seems to be motivated, but not in the same way as directed thought; it seems not so much directed toward a goal as associated with an emotion.

The distinction between these two kinds of mental organization is reminiscent of the difference between *parallel* and *sequential* processing which is already familiar. We saw in Chapter 3 that a sequential program can be defined as one that "makes only those tests which are appropriate in the light of previous test outcomes." Viewed as a constructive process, it constructs only one thing at a time. The very definitions of "rational" and "logical" also suggest that each idea, image, or action is sensibly related to the preceding one, making an appearance only as it becomes necessary for the aim in view. A

parallel program, on the other hand, carries out many activities simultaneously, or at least independently. Their combined result may be useful, but then again it may not. This is just the chief characteristic of the "primary process," as it appears in dreams, slips of the tongue, "free association," and many forms of mental disorder. The very word "schizophrenia" refers to a state of mind in which ideas and trains of thought are *split* apart from one another, lacking any coherent sequence.

To call primary-process thought "parallel" may be misleading. The word tends to suggest straight lines that never meet, while the "wealth of trains of unconscious thought striving for expression in our minds" (Freud, 1900, p. 478) are not straight in any sense, and meet often. Selfridge's (1959) "Pandemonium" is tempting as an alternative term; Freud might not have objected to describing the primary process as a shouting horde of demons. This model, which was intended as an account of pattern recognition in the face of uncertainty and poor definition (see Chapter 3), has some merit as a description of uncertain and poorly defined thoughts also. Nevertheless, a less colorful term is desirable for everyday use. Elsewhere (Neisser, 1963a) I have suggested "multiple processing," as a phrase which seems appropriate to the ill-organized variety of dreamlike thoughts.

Multiple processing does not go on only in dreams, or in the minds of madmen. In waking life also, a hundred or a thousand "thoughts" appear briefly and are gone again even when we are primarily engaged in purposeful activity. The extent to which these fleeting thoughts are developed, and are permitted to interrupt the main direction of mental activity, varies from person to person and from time to time. For the most part, they are immediately forgotten, like the dreams they so strongly resemble. Occasionally they interrupt ongoing activity, and we recognize a "mental block," a "lapse of attention," or a "Freudian slip."

Without accepting Freud's claim that *all* such interruptions are the result of suppressed motives and ideas, we can acknowledge that at least some of them surely are. Freud's encounter with a young man on a train, reported in *The Psychopathology of Everyday Life* (Freud, 1904), provides a conveniently dramatic example. In the course of the conversation, the two travelers began to discuss, and to deplore, the difficult situation of European Jews. The young man concluded a particularly forceful statement with a Latin verse from the *Aeneid,* which expresses the hope that posterity will eventually right the wrongs of today. However, he cited the verse incorrectly, leaving out the single word *aliquis,* which Freud then supplied. Since he had heard of the psychoanalytic axiom that all errors are motivated, the young man immediately challenged Freud to explain his omission.

Freud accepted the challenge and encouraged his companion to free-associate to the word in question. After some associations like *liquid* and *fluid,* his thought turned to several Catholic Saints, including St. Simon (who was murdered as a child), St. Augustine (he had recently read an article entitled "What St. Augustine said concerning women"), and St. Januarius, whose blood was said to be preserved in a phial in Naples, and to liquefy miraculously each year on a certain holiday. Then he had a thought which at first he was reluctant to disclose; it turned out to be about a woman "from whom I could easily get a message that would be annoying to us both." To the young man's surprise, Freud immediately inferred the content of the feared message: that she had missed a menstrual period, i.e., was pregnant. He then pointed out that the first error and all the intervening associations had been related to this theme: the "liquid" in *aliquis;* the calendar-like names of two of the Saints; the child-murder of the other; the miracle of the blood. The original slip itself is also intelligible from this point of view. The Latin passage had expressed a wish for posterity, but the young man was not at all eager for any posterity that might arrive in nine months' time!

The thoughts involved here are evidently not sequential. They could have come in any order, and they lead nowhere in particular as far as the thinker is concerned. In short, they are multiple processes. To be sure, they are not truly simultaneous, at least as the young man describes them, but the definition of parallel or multiple processing does not require actual simultaneity so much as functional independence. Moreover, they may well have been simultaneous in fact, and only serialized for presentation aloud.

This example, in which every association is clearly related to a single theme, is an unusual one. Freud naturally used the best possible illustration of the point he wished to make: that even apparently undirected actions and thoughts are really drive-determined. The situation is not always so clear, and much primary-process thinking appears in such chaotic profusion that it can neither be adequately described nor easily accounted for. Nevertheless, it would be pointless to develop a theory of thought and memory that had no room for these phenomena.

Primary and Secondary Processes Reconsidered

We need a conception of the mind which allows for multiple activity at some levels, but also has a place for an executive process. Both kinds of operations seem to characterize human thinking. Moreover, neither one serves simply as a retrieval system, selecting and arousing particular "memory traces." Each is essentially constructive in nature, making use of stored information to build something new.

There are no adequate models of such processes among today's computer programs. Both parallel and sequential models have been proposed and programmed, as the examples of Pandemonium and EPAM illustrate, but none so far has done justice to the constructive character of thought. This critique applies even to an ingenious program which combines the two principles rather successfully: Reitman's "Argus" (Reitman, 1965, Chapter 8). Nevertheless, Argus is an interesting program, not so much because of what it can do (it solves analogies problems like *Hot is to Cold as Tall is to (Wall, Short, Wet, Hold)?*) as because of the way it is organized. Information is stored in the form of "semantic elements" like *Hot,* each represented by several lists of relevant data. The lists indicate the element's relations with other elements (Which one is its *opposite?* its *superordinate?*), its threshold, its state of arousal, and the time when it was last "fired." Elements can "fire" each other via their listed relations, so the aggregate is spontaneously active. Its activity is organized in parallel. In addition, Argus has an executive routine, which can carry out various sequential strategies. It may fire the alternative answers, examine the relationships among recently-fired elements, and so on. Thus both parallel and sequential organization contribute to the system's effectiveness.

Intriguing as Argus is, it seems far too heavily committed to the Reappearance Hypothesis. Only those elements can be aroused which already exist in a dormant state; only those relationships can be employed which have been explicitly entered by the programmer. This may be why, as Reitman himself notes (1965, Chapter 9), it cannot solve more challenging analogies *(Samson is to Hair as Achilles is to (Strength, Shield, Heel, Tent)?)* except in a very artificial way. The programmer can, of course, include a relationship like *point of susceptibility to major negative influence from the environment?* in the original semantic descriptions of Samson and Achilles. However, he would hardly do this except to anticipate the specific analogy in question, and such anticipations would make the program uninteresting. Human beings do not solve challenging problems by reviving relationships that already exist, but by constructing new ones, just as they construct new sentences, new images, new rhythms, and new movements to suit the needs of the moment.

It is fair to say that no contemporary psychological

theory and no existing program deals satisfactorily with the constructive nature of the higher mental processes. This deficiency will not be remedied here. As noted earlier, a serious theory of memory and thinking is beyond the scope of this book. I can, however, suggest an analogy which may be helpful. Like the Gestalt psychologists, though for different reasons, I believe that the processes of *visual cognition,* and perception in general, may serve as useful models for memory and thought.

To see why a perceptual analogy might be appropriate, let us briefly review the processing of visual information, especially in terms of the theory put forward in Chapter 4. The central distinction made there was between *focal attention* and the *preattentive processes.* There seem to be two distinguishable levels of visual activity. The first, preattentive stage is a parallel one. Stimulus information, arriving simultaneously all over the retina, is first used in the construction of separate visual figures, or objects. The processes involved are wholistic, both in terms of the stimulus information they use and of the properties of the constructed figures. This level of activity results in *iconic storage,* a transient persistence of the visual objects during which they are available for further analysis. If no additional processing takes place, only crude properties of the stimuli—movement, general location, brightness, etc.—can have any effect on behavior; often there is no effect at all. Like all parallel processes, preattentive activity is inherently "wasteful." Most of the visual figures thus formed never do receive additional processing, and disappear unnoticed.

The relationship of iconic memory to *consciousness* is particularly interesting. There is a sense in which we are aware of its contents, but the experience is a fleeting and tenuous one. After a tachistoscopic exposure in Sperling's (1960a) experiment, the subject feels that he "saw" all the letters, but he cannot remember most of them. The uncoded ones slip away even as he tries to grasp them, leaving no trace behind. Compared with the firm clarity of the few letters he really remembers, they have only a marginal claim to being called "conscious" at all.

A very different fate awaits that portion of the stimulus information which becomes the focus of attention. Attention is serial: only one object can be attended to at any given moment, and each attentive act takes an appreciable fraction of a second. Operating within the preattentively established boundaries, figural synthesis produces objects which may have considerable complexity, or be charged with considerable affect. The course of synthesis is partly determined by stimulus information, but it also depends on such factors as past experience, expectation, and preference. These nonstimulus variables

play a dual role, since they influence the choice of one figure rather than another for attention as well as the details of the construction which then takes place.

Although the constructive processes themselves never appear in consciousness, their products do: to construct something attentively is to see it clearly. Such objects can then be remembered; that is, they can be *re*constructed as visual images. In addition, they may achieve representation in other modalities if an appropriate coding system exists. Verbal recoding is particularly common and has the effect of re-storing relevant information in auditory memory, where it is more easily available for use in later descriptions. (For a demonstration that auditory and visual memory are functionally distinct, see Wallach and Averbach, 1955.)

This general description of the fate of sensory information seems to fit the higher mental processes as well. Perhaps the most striking analogy is between the preattentive processes and the multiple thinking that is so prominent in dreams and fantasy. Both produce only fleeting and evanescent objects of consciousness, crudely defined and hard to remember. If their products are not seized on and elaborated by an executive process of some kind, they have little effect on further thinking or behavior. Such effects as they do have reflect only crude and global properties of the objects involved. The "symbolism" of primary-process thinking is based on overall shapes, simple movements, and gross sound patterns: just the properties to which the preattentive processes of vision and hearing are sensitive.

The executive processes of thought, whose selective function is indispensable for rational problem-solving, share many of the properties of focal attention in vision and of analysis-by-synthesis in hearing. In thinking, we construct mental "objects" (and overt responses) of great complexity, selecting one or another of the crude products offered by the primary processes and elaborating it as necessary. The constructed mental objects may be invested with affect, or they may be emotionally neutral. They can even be recoded into other systems, as when we imagine a scene and then describe it. The course of construction is governed by motives and expectations as well as by the "input," which here is the aggregate of stored information about earlier constructions.

Whatever its defects, this analogy at least avoids the Reappearance Hypothesis—the unpalatable assumption that memory traces exist continuously and are occasionally aroused to action. Attentive synthesis does leave traces of a sort behind, but these are never subsequently "aroused," they are only used. I am proposing that their use requires a two-stage mechanism, analogous to those of vision and hearing. First, the so-called primary processes make an array of crudely defined "objects" or "ideas," along lines which tend to follow the structure of the "input," i.e., the information in memory. Then, in alert and waking subjects, the secondary processes of directed thought select among these objects and develop them further. In this interpretation, the primary and secondary processes are by no means as antagonistic as Freud believed. One is essential to the other. Rational thought is "secondary" in the sense that it works with objects already formed by a "primary" process. If these objects receive no secondary elaboration, as in some dreams and disorganized mental states, we experience them in the fleeting and imprecise way that characterizes the uncoded figures of iconic memory. However, the same multiple processes that produce these shadowy and impalpable experiences are also essential preliminaries to directed thinking.

These are not entirely new arguments. The notion that memory retains information about mental *acts* rather than copies of experiences is, as we have seen, closely related to Bartlett's views. It may also remind the reader of modern stimulus-response theory, in which internal or implicit "responses" play a major role. However, I am not simply saying that learning consists of the acquisition of (covert) responses. Indeed, *no* learning consists of responses in this sense. A movement-pattern, or the construction of an image, is not a series of responses which the subject will later tend to repeat. A new movement may be synthesized with the aid of information about an old one, but the two are rarely identical. Indeed, the whole conception of a structured synthesis is very different from that of a response sequence. As we saw in the case of rhythmic patterns and sentences, mental constructions are wholes, whose ends are prefigured in their beginnings. They are not organized as, nor do they stem from, chains of connected units.

The notion that the secondary process can serve to elaborate primary-process material is an old one. It has often been advanced in connection with the problem of "creativity" (e.g., Kris, 1950; Maslow, 1957). However, the present suggestion goes further. It seems to me that *all* directed thinking is an elaboration of this sort, just as *all* visual and auditory perception depends on prior wholistic construction of some kind of unit.

Also familiar is the idea that the primary process, as defined by Freud, has a perceptual function; it is often said to manifest itself in such phenomena as "subliminal perception" and "perceptual defense." Some have even supposed that the primary processes comprise a separate cognitive system with supersensitive capacities, able to detect and react to stimuli that are otherwise subthreshold. This hypothesis must be rejected; in previous chapters, we have repeatedly found contaminating artifacts in the experiments which seem to support it. I am making a different suggestion. There is indeed a stage of perception which corresponds to the primary processes of thought, but the relation between them is one of functional similarity, not identity. In remembering and thinking, as in perception, the secondary process further examines and further develops the objects made available to it by the primary one.

Another similarity between perception and memory is also worth remarking. Just as iconically present figures may go undeveloped by the visual attentive mechanisms, so may a tentatively formed idea receive no further elaboration by the secondary processes of thought. In vision, this can occur for many reasons—because of a certain strategy of search, because of competing interest in something else, or even by deliberate instruction (or self-instruction) as in the negative hallucinations discussed in Chapter 6. The same kinds of factors can prevent us from remembering or thinking about things, even when the necessary information was stored, and is being touched on by the primary processes. Again, the executive may be using an inappropriate strategy of search, may be concerned with some incompatible activity, or may be deliberately avoiding construction in certain areas. In this last case we usually speak of "repression," or perhaps of "censorship."

A Summing Up

At this point, it may be appropriate to review the speculative hypotheses that have been advanced. (1) Stored information consists of traces of previous constructive mental (or overt) actions. (2) The primary process is a multiple activity, somewhat analogous to parallel processing in computers, which constructs crudely formed "thoughts," or "ideas," on the basis of stored information. Its functions are similar to those of the pre-attentive processes in vision and hearing. Its products are only fleetingly conscious, unless they undergo elaboration by secondary processes. (3) The secondary processes of directed thought and deliberate recall are like focal attention in vision. They are serial in character, and construct ideas and images which are determined partly by stored information, partly by the preliminary organization of the primary processes, and partly by wishes and expectations. (4) The executive control of thinking in the secondary process is carried out by a system analogous to the executive routine of a computer program. It is not necessary to postulate a *homunculus* to account for the directed character of thought. (5) The secondary processes themselves are mostly acquired through experience, in the same way that all other memories—which also represent earlier *processes*—are acquired. (6) Failures to recall information which is actually in storage are like failures to notice something in the visual field, or failures to hear something that has been said. The executive processes of recall may be directed elsewhere, either deliberately or because of a misguided strategy of search; they may also lack the necessary constructive abilities altogether.

The reader who objects to the vague and speculative character of these hypotheses has good reason to do so. To be sure, he can be answered with the familiar excuse that psychology is a "young science," and that cognitive theory cannot be more explicitly formulated at the present time. But this reply may not satisfy him; he may legitimately ask why this should be the case. Why have the higher mental processes been so resistant to meaningful investigation? The earlier stages of cognition, which were the subject of the first ten chapters, made a different impression. The models proposed there were relatively specific; many pertinent experiments were considered; testable hypotheses were easy to formulate. What new difficulty appears in the study of thinking?

The problem can be phrased in terms of one particularly obvious weakness of the present approach. In accounting for the course of thought and action, there has been repeated reference to the subject's motives and expectations, and even to an "executive" that seems to have purposes of its own. We have seen that this leads to no logical impasse, to no *homunculus,* but it surely does raise a practical issue. If what the subject will remember depends in large part on what he is trying to accomplish, on his purposes, do not predictions become impossible and explanations *ad hoc?* If we give no further account of these purposes, how can we tell what he will think of next?

While this is indeed a weakness of the cognitive approach, it may be an inevitable one. In Chapter 1, the study of motives was assigned to dynamic rather than to cognitive psychology; thus, it could be conveniently set aside. This strategy worked well so long as we considered only the relatively "stimulus-bound" or "outer-directed" processes of perception and immediate memory. At those levels, motivation can select among a few alternative kinds of cognitive synthesis, but thereafter the constructive act is closely controlled by present or recent stimulus information. However, the course of thinking or of "inner-directed" activity is determined at every moment by what the subject is trying to do. Although we cannot always see only what we want to see, we can generally think what we like.

The classical procedures of experimental psychology attempt to avoid this problem by brute force. In an ordinary learning experiment, the subject is supposed to have only a single motive: he must get on with the experimental task, learn what he is told to learn, and solve what he is told to solve. If he has any other desires—to outwit the experimenter, to walk out, to ask what the answer is—he must do his best to act as if they did not exist. In this respect, experimental situations are very different from those of daily life. When I try to recall the name of the man who has just entered my office, it is for a number of partly independent reasons: I want to know who he is so I can have a meaningful relation with him; I don't want to offend him by having forgotten his name; I would prefer not to seem a fool, in his eyes or in my own. Moreover, one of my options would eliminate the necessity for remembering; I can ask him what his name is. Such multiplicity of motivation and flexibility of response are characteristic of ordinary life, but they are absent—or are assumed to be absent—from most experiments on the higher mental processes.

In itself, this is hardly a devastating criticism. Experiments need not imitate life. In fact, the art of experimentation is the creation of *new* situations, which catch the essence of some process without the circumstances that usually obscure it. The question in this case is whether the essence has truly been caught. The simplifications introduced by confining the subject to a single motive and a fixed set of alternative responses can be justified only if motivation and cognition are genuinely distinct. If—as I suppose—they are inseparable where remembering and thinking are concerned, the common experimental paradigms may pay too high a price for simplicity.

Thus, it is no accident that the cognitive approach gives us no way to know what the subject will think of next. We cannot possibly know this, unless we have a detailed understanding of what he is trying to do, and why. For this reason, a really satisfactory theory of the higher mental processes can only come into being when we also have theories of motivation, personality, and social interaction. The study of cognition is only one fraction of psychology, and it cannot stand alone.

NOTE

1. Sense modalities other than vision and hearing are largely ignored in this book, because so little is known about the cognitive processing involved.

CONSIDERATIONS OF CONTEXT

35

JAMES J. GIBSON

James J. Gibson (1904–1979) attended Princeton University interested in psychology's answer to the question, "What does it mean to be human?" He was exposed to a variety of psychological answers and methods by the Princeton faculty of the 1920s, themselves trained by German and American pioneers like Carl Stumpf and William James (p. 216). One of Gibson's first projects was to assist Leonard Carmichael, recently returned from Kurt Koffka's Berlin Institute, in building an apparatus to explore the apparent motion phenomena noted by Max Wertheimer (p. 308) and J. Ternus. Gibson received his Princeton Ph.D. in 1928 and began teaching at Smith College. During World War II, he studied the perceptual problems facing pilots, including how to land an airplane accurately on a short course. This altered the direction of Gibson's work because he became dissatisfied with the contemporary definition of "stimulus." He joined the Cornell University faculty in 1949 and wrote a great many articles and books, including the "Purple Perils"—short, controversial essays designed to spark discussion in his weekly seminar. Gibson became increasingly frustrated with psychology's orientation and direction: "It is time to stop pretending that scientific psychology is a well-founded discipline. We continue to do so by keeping silent about the contradictions at its foundations, and by glossing over the vagueness of its fundamental issues. . . . The student has the right to know what is really incoherent in the textbook, for part of his bewilderment is not the fault of his understanding, but of the subject-matter itself." Gibson's wife, Eleanor J. Gibson, professor emeritus of psychology at Cornell University, studies perceptual development in infants and is often mentioned in textbooks for her work on depth perception using the visual cliff.

THE ECOLOGICAL APPROACH TO VISUAL PERCEPTION

THE THEORY OF AFFORDANCES

I have described the environment as the surfaces that separate substances from the medium in which the animals live. But I have also described what the environment *affords* animals, mentioning the terrain, shelters, water, fire, objects, tools, other animals, and human displays. How do we go from surfaces to affordances? And if there is information in light for the perception of surfaces, is there information for the perception of what they afford? Perhaps the composition and layout of surfaces *constitute* what they afford. If so, to perceive them is to perceive what they afford.

This is a radical hypothesis, for it implies that the "values" and "meanings" of things in the environment can be directly perceived. Moreover, it would explain the sense in which values and meanings are external to the perceiver.

The *affordances* of the environment are what it *offers* the animal, what it *provides* or *furnishes*, either for good or ill. The verb to *afford* is found in the dictionary, but the noun *affordance* is not. I have made it up. I mean by it something that refers to both the environment and the animal in a way that no existing term does. It implies the complementarity of the animal and the environment. The antecedents of the term and the history of the con-

From James J. Gibson. "The Theory of Affordances." In *The Ecological Approach to Visual Perception,* (pp. 127–143). Hillsdale, NJ: Lawrence Erlbaum, 1979.

cept will be treated later; for the present, let us consider examples of an affordance.

If a terrestrial surface is nearly horizontal (instead of slanted), nearly flat (instead of convex or concave), and sufficiently extended (relative to the size of the animal) and if its substance is rigid (relative to the weight of the animal), then the surface *affords support*. It is a surface of support, and we call it a substratum, ground, or floor. It is stand-on-able, permitting an upright posture for quadrupeds and bipeds. It is therefore walk-on-able and run-over-able. It is not sink-into-able like a surface of water or a swamp, that is, not for heavy terrestrial animals. Support for water bugs is different.

Note that the four properties listed—horizontal, flat, extended, and rigid—would be *physical* properties of a surface if they were measured with the scales and standard units used in physics. As an affordance of support for a species of animal, however, they have to be measured *relative to the animal*. They are unique for that animal. They are not just abstract physical properties. They have unity relative to the posture and behavior of the animal being considered. So an affordance cannot be measured as we measure in physics.

Terrestrial surfaces, of course, are also climb-on-able or fall-off-able or get-under-neath-able or bump-into-able relative to the animal. Different layouts afford different behaviors for different animals, and different mechanical encounters. The human species in some cultures has the habit of sitting as distinguished from kneeling or squatting. If a surface of support with the four properties is also knee-high above the ground, it affords sitting on. We call it a *seat* in general, or a stool, bench, chair, and so on, in particular. It may be natural like a ledge or artificial like a couch. It may have various shapes, as long as its functional layout is that of a seat. The color and texture of the surface are irrelevant. Knee-high for a child is not the same as knee-high for an adult, so the affordance is relative to the size of the individual. But if a surface is horizontal, flat, extended, rigid, and knee-high relative to a perceiver, it can in fact be sat upon. If it can be discriminated as having just these properties, it should *look* sit-on-able. If it does, the affordance is perceived visually. If the surface properties are seen relative to the body surfaces, the self, they constitute a seat and have meaning.

There could be other examples. The different substances of the environment have different affordances for nutrition and for manufacture. The different objects of the environment have different affordances for manipulation. The other animals afford, above all, a rich and complex set of interactions, sexual, predatory, nur-

turing, fighting, playing, cooperating, and communicating. What other persons afford, comprises the whole realm of social significance for human beings. We pay the closest attention to the optical and acoustic information that specifies what the other person is, invites, threatens, and does.

The Niches of the Environment

Ecologists have the concept of a *niche*. A species of animal is said to utilize or occupy a certain niche in the environment. This is not quite the same as the *habitat* of the species; a niche refers more to *how* an animal lives than to *where* it lives. I suggest that a niche is a set of affordances.

The natural environment offers many ways of life, and different animals have different ways of life. The niche implies a kind of animal, and the animal implies a kind of niche. Note the complementarity of the two. But note also that the environment as a whole with its unlimited possibilities existed prior to animals. The physical, chemical, meteorological, and geological conditions of the surface of the earth and the pre-existence of plant life are what make animal life possible. They had to be invariant for animals to evolve.

There are all kinds of nutrients in the world and all sorts of ways of getting food; all sorts of shelters or hiding places, such as holes, crevices, and caves; all sorts of materials for *making* shelters, nests, mounds, huts; all kinds of locomotion that the environment makes possible, such as swimming, crawling, walking, climbing, flying. These offerings have been taken advantage of; the niches have been occupied. But, for all we know, there may be many offerings of the environment that have *not* been taken advantage of, that is, niches not yet occupied.

In architecture a niche is a place that is suitable for a piece of statuary, a place into which the object fits. In ecology a niche is a setting of environmental features that are suitable for an animal, into which it fits metaphorically.

An important fact about the affordances of the environment is that they are in a sense objective, real, and physical, unlike values and meanings, which are often supposed to be subjective, phenomenal, and mental. But, actually, an affordance is neither an objective property nor a subjective property; or it is both if you like. An affordance cuts across the dichotomy of subjective-objective and helps us to understand its inadequacy. It is equally a fact of the environment and a fact of behavior. It is both physical and psychical, yet neither. An affordance points both ways, to the environment and to the observer.

The niche for a certain species should not be confused with what some animal psychologists have called the *phenomenal environment* of the species. This can be taken erroneously to be the "private world" in which the species is supposed to live, the "subjective world," or the world of "consciousness." The behavior of observers depends on their perception of the environment, surely enough, but this does not mean that their behavior depends on a so-called private or subjective or conscious environment. The organism depends on its environment for its life, but the environment does not depend on the organism for its existence.

Man's Alteration of the Natural Environment

In the last few thousand years, as everybody now realizes, the very face of the earth has been modified by man. The layout of surfaces has been changed, by cutting, clearing, leveling, paving, and building. Natural deserts and mountains, swamps and rivers, forests and plains still exist, but they are being encroached upon and reshaped by man-made layouts. Moreover, the *substances* of the environment have been partly converted from the natural materials of the earth into various kinds of artificial materials such as bronze, iron, concrete, and bread. Even the *medium* of the environment—the air for us and the water for fish—is becoming slowly altered despite the restorative cycles that yielded a steady state for millions of years prior to man.

Why has man changed the shapes and substances of his environment? To change what it affords him. He has made more available what benefits him and less pressing what injures him. In making life easier for himself, of course, he has made life harder for most of the other animals. Over the millennia, he has made it easier for himself to get food, easier to keep warm, easier to see at night, easier to get about, and easier to train his offspring.

This is not a *new* environment—an artificial environment distinct from the natural environment—but the same old environment modified by man. It is a mistake to separate the natural from the artificial as if there were two environments; artifacts have to be manufactured from natural substances. It is also a mistake to separate the cultural environment from the natural environment, as if there were a world of mental products distinct from the world of material products. There is only one world, however diverse, and all animals live in it, although we human animals have altered it to suit ourselves. We have done so wastefully, thoughtlessly, and, if we do not mend our ways, fatally.

The fundamentals of the environment—the substances, the medium, and the surfaces—are the same for all animals. No matter how powerful men become they are not going to alter the fact of earth, air, and water—the lithosphere, the atmosphere, and the hydrosphere, together with the interfaces that separate them. For terrestrial animals like us, the earth and the sky are a basic structure on which all lesser structures depend. We cannot change it. We all fit into the substructures of the environment in our various ways, for we were all, in fact, formed by them. We were created by the world we live in.

Some Affordances of the Terrestrial Environment

Let us consider the affordances of the medium, of substances, of surfaces and their layout, of objects, of animals and persons, and finally a case of special interest for ecological optics, the affording of concealment by the occluding edges of the environment (Chapter 5).

The Medium

Air affords breathing, more exactly, respiration. It also affords unimpeded locomotion relative to the ground, which affords support. When illuminated and fog-free, it affords visual perception. It also affords the perception of vibratory events by means of sound fields and the perception of volatile sources by means of odor fields. The airspaces between obstacles and objects are the paths and the places where behavior occurs.

The optical information to specify air when it is clear and transparent is not obvious. The problem came up in Chapter 4, and the experimental evidence about the seeing of "nothing" will be described in the next chapter.

The Substances

Water is more substantial than air and always has a surface with air. It does not afford respiration for us. It affords drinking. Being fluid, it affords pouring from a container. Being a solvent, it affords washing and bathing. Its surface does not afford support for large animals with dense tissues. The optical information for water is well specified by the characteristics of its surface, especially the unique fluctuations caused by rippling (Chapter 5).

Solid substances, more substantial than water, have characteristic surfaces (Chapter 2). Depending on the animal species, some afford nutrition and some do not.

A few are toxic. Fruits and berries, for example, have more food value when they are ripe, and this is specified by the color of the surface. But the food values of substances are often misperceived.

Solids also afford various kinds of manufacture, depending on the kind of solid state. Some, such as flint, can be chipped; others, such as clay, can be molded; still others recover their original shape after deformation; and some resist deformation strongly. Note that manufacture, as the term implies, was originally a form of manual behavior like manipulation. Things were fabricated *by hand.* To identify the substance in such cases is to perceive what can be done with it, what it is good for, its utility; and the hands are involved.

The Surfaces and Their Layouts

I have already said that a horizontal, flat, extended, rigid surface affords support. It permits equilibrium and the maintaining of a posture with respect to gravity, this being a force perpendicular to the surface. The animal does not fall or slide as it would on a steep hillside. Equilibrium and posture are prerequisite to other behaviors, such as locomotion and manipulation. There will be more about this in Chapter 12, and more evidence about the perception of the ground in Chapter 9. The ground is quite literally the *basis* of the behavior of land animals. And it is also the basis of their visual perception, their so-called space perception. Geometry began with the study of the earth as abstracted by Euclid, not with the study of the axes of empty space as abstracted by Descartes. The affording of support and the geometry of a horizontal plane are therefore not in different realms of discourse; they are not as separate as we have supposed.

The flat earth, of course, lies *beneath* the attached and detached objects on it. The earth has "furniture," or as I have said, it is cluttered. The solid, level, flat surface extends behind the clutter and, in fact, extends all the way out to the horizon. This is not, of course, the earth of Copernicus; it is the earth at the scale of the human animal, and on that scale it is flat, not round. Wherever one goes, the earth is separated from the sky by a horizon that, although it may be hidden by the clutter, is always there. There will be evidence to show that the horizon can always be seen, in the sense that it can be visualized, and that it can always be felt, in the sense that any surface one touches is experienced in relation to the horizontal plane.

Of course, a horizontal, flat, extended surface that is *nonrigid,* a stream or lake, does not afford support for standing, or for walking and running. There is no footing, as we say. It may afford floating or swimming, but you have to be equipped for that, by nature or by learning.

A *vertical,* flat, extended, and rigid surface such as a wall or a cliff face is a barrier to pedestrian locomotion. Slopes between vertical and horizontal afford walking, if easy, but only climbing, if steep, and in the latter case the surface cannot be flat; there must be "holds" for the hands and feet. Similarly, a slope downward affords falling if steep; the brink of a cliff is a falling-off place. It is dangerous and looks dangerous. The affordance of a certain layout is perceived if the layout is perceived.

Civilized people have altered the steep slopes of their habitat by building stairways so as to afford ascent and descent. What we call the steps afford stepping, up or down, relative to the size of the person's legs. We are still capable of getting around in an arboreal layout of surfaces, tree branches, and we have ladders that afford this kind of locomotion, but most of us leave that to our children.

A cliff face, a wall, a chasm, and a stream are barriers; they do not afford pedestrian locomotion unless there is a door, a gate, or a bridge. A tree or a rock is an obstacle. Ordinarily, there are paths between obstacles, and these openings are visible. The progress of locomotion is guided by the perception of barriers and obstacles, that is, by the act of steering into the openings and away from the surfaces that afford injury. I have tried to describe the optical information for the control of locomotion (Gibson, 1958), and it will be further elaborated in Chapter 13. The *imminence* of collision with a surface during locomotion is specified in a particularly simple way, by an explosive rate of magnification of the optical texture. This has been called *looming* (e.g., Schiff, 1965). It should not be confused, however, with the magnification of an opening between obstacles, the opening up of a *vista* such as occurs in the approach to a doorway.

The Objects

The affordances of what we loosely call *objects* are extremely various. It will be recalled that my use of the terms is restricted and that I distinguish between *attached* objects and *detached* objects. We are not dealing with Newtonian objects in space, all of which are detached, but with the furniture of the earth, some items of which are attached to it and cannot be moved without breakage.

Detached objects must be comparable in size to the animal under consideration if they are to afford behavior. But those that are comparable afford an astonishing variety of behaviors, especially to animals with hands. Objects can be manufactured and manipulated. Some are portable in that they afford lifting and carrying, while others are not. Some are graspable and other not. To be graspable, an object must have opposite surfaces separated by a distance less than the span of the hand. A five-inch cube can be grasped, but a ten-inch cube cannot (Gibson, 1966*b*, p. 119). A large object needs a "handle" to afford grasping. Note that the size of an object that constitutes a graspable size is specified in the optic array. If this is true, it is *not* true that a tactual sensation of size has to become associated with the visual sensation of size in order for the affordance to be perceived.

Sheets, sticks, fibers, containers, clothing, and tools are detached objects that afford manipulation (Chapter 3). Additional examples are given below.

1. An elongated object of moderate size and weight affords wielding. If used to hit or strike, it is a *club* or *hammer.* If used by a chimpanzee behind bars to pull in a banana beyond its reach, it is a sort of *rake.* In either case, it is an extension of the arm. A rigid staff also affords leverage and in that use is a *lever.* A pointed elongated object affords piercing—if large it is a *spear,* if small a *needle* or *awl.*

2. A rigid object with a sharp dihedral angle, an edge, affords cutting and scraping; it is a *knife.* It may be designed for both striking and cutting, and then it is an *axe.*

3. A graspable rigid object of moderate size and weight affords throwing. It may be a *missile* or only an object for play, a *ball.* The launching of missiles by supplementary tools other than the hands alone—the sling, the bow, the catapult, the gun, and so on—is one of the behaviors that makes the human animal a nasty, dangerous species.

4. An elongated elastic object, such as a *fiber, thread, thong,* or *rope,* affords knotting, binding, lashing, knitting, and weaving. These are kinds of behavior where manipulation leads to manufacture.

5. A hand-held tool of enormous importance is one that, when applied to a surface, leaves traces and thus affords *trace-making.* The tool may be a *stylus, brush, crayon, pen,* or *pencil,* but if it marks the surface it can be used to depict and to write, to represent scenes and to specify words.

We have thousands of names for such objects, and we classify them in many ways: pliers and wrenches are tools; pots and pans are utensils; swords and pistols are weapons. They can all be said to have properties or qualities: color, texture, composition, size, shape and features of shape, mass, elasticity, rigidity, and mobility. Orthodox psychology asserts that *we perceive these objects insofar as we discriminate their properties or qualities.* Psychologists carry out elegant experiments in the laboratory to find out how and how well these qualities are discriminated. The psychologists assume that objects are *composed* of their qualities. But I now suggest that what we perceive when we look at objects are their affordances, not their qualities. We can discriminate the dimensions of difference if required to do so in an experiment, but what the object affords us is what we normally pay attention to. The special combination of qualities into which an object can be analyzed is ordinarily not noticed.

If this is true for the adult, what about the young child? There is much evidence to show that the infant does not begin by first discriminating the qualities of objects and then learning the combinations of qualities that specify them. Phenomenal objects are *not* built up of qualities; it is the other way around. The affordance of an object is what the infant begins by noticing. The meaning is observed before the substance and surface, the color and form, are seen as such. An affordance is an invariant combination of variables, and one might guess that it is easier to perceive such an invariant unit than it is to perceive all the variables separately. It is never necessary to distinguish *all* the features of an object and, in fact, it would be impossible to do so. Perception is economical. "Those features of a thing are noticed which distinguish it from other things that it is not—but not *all* the features that distinguish it from *everything* that it is not" (Gibson, 1966*b*, p. 286).

To Perceive an Affordance Is Not to Classify an Object

The fact that a stone is a missile does not imply that it cannot be other things as well. It can be a paperweight, a bookend, a hammer, or a pendulum bob. It can be piled on another rock to make a cairn or a stone wall. These affordances are all consistent with one another. The differences between them are not clear-cut, and the arbitrary names by which they are called do not count for perception. If you know what can be done with a graspable detached object, what it can be used for, you can call it whatever you please.

The theory of affordances rescues us from the philosophical muddle of assuming fixed classes of objects, each defined by its common features and then given a name. As Ludwig Wittgenstein knew, you *cannot* specify the necessary and sufficient features of the class of things to which a name is given. They have only a "family resemblance." But this does not mean you cannot learn how to use things and perceive their uses. You do not have to classify and label things in order to perceive what they afford.

Other Persons and Animals

The richest and most elaborate affordances of the environment are provided by other animals and, for us, other people. These are, of course, detached objects with topologically closed surfaces, but they change the shape of their surfaces while yet retaining the same fundamental shape. They move from place to place, changing the postures of their bodies, ingesting and emitting certain substances, and doing all this spontaneously, initiating their own movements, which is to say that their movements are *animate*. These bodies are subject to the laws of mechanics and yet *not* subject to the laws of mechanics, for they are not *governed* by these laws. They are so different from ordinary objects that infants learn almost immediately to distinguish them from plants and nonliving things. When touched they touch back, when struck they strike back; in short, they *interact* with the observer and with one another. Behavior affords behavior, and the whole subject matter of psychology and of the social sciences can be thought of as an elaboration of this basic fact. Sexual behavior, nurturing behavior, fighting behavior, cooperative behavior, economic behavior, political behavior—all depend on the perceiving of what another person or other persons afford, or sometimes on the misperceiving of it.

What the male affords the female is reciprocal to what the female affords the male; what the infant affords the mother is reciprocal to what the mother affords the infant; what the prey affords the predator goes along with what the predator affords the prey; what the buyer affords the seller cannot be separated from what the seller affords the buyer, and so on. The perceiving of these mutual affordances is enormously complex, but it is nonetheless lawful, and it is based on the pickup of the information in touch, sound, odor, taste, and ambient light. It is just as much based on stimulus information as is the simpler perception of the support that is offered by the ground under one's feet. For other animals and other persons can only give off information about themselves insofar as they are tangible, audible, odorous, tastable, or visible.

The other person, the generalized *other*, the *alter* as opposed to the *ego*, is an ecological object with a skin, even if clothed. It is an object, although it is not *merely* an object, and we do right to speak of *he* or *she* instead of *it*. But the other person has a surface that reflects light, and the information to specify what he or she is, invites, promises, threatens, or does can be found in the light.

Places and Hiding Places

The habitat of a given animal contains *places*. A place is not an object with definite boundaries but a region (Chapter 3). The different places of a habitat may have different affordances. Some are places where food is usually found and others where it is not. There are places of danger, such as the brink of a cliff and the regions where predators lurk. There are places of refuge from predators. Among these is the place where mate and young are, the home, which is usually a partial enclosure. Animals are skilled at what the psychologist calls place-learning. They can find their way to significant places.

An important kind of place, made intelligible by the ecological approach to visual perception, is a place that affords concealment, a *hiding place*. Note that it involves social perception and raises questions of epistemology. The concealing of oneself from other observers and the hiding of a detached object from other observers have different kinds of motivation. As every child discovers, a good hiding place for one's body is not necessarily a good hiding place for a treasure. A detached object can be concealed both from other observers and from the observer himself. The observer's body can be concealed from other observers but *not* from himself, as the last chapter emphasized. Animals as well as children hide themselves and also hide objects such as food.

One of the laws of the ambient optic array (Chapter 5) is that at any fixed point of observation some parts of the environment are revealed and the remaining parts are concealed. The reciprocal of this law is that the observer himself, his body considered as part of the environment, is revealed at some fixed points of observation and concealed at the remaining points. An observer can perceive not only that other observers are unhidden or hidden from him but also that he is hidden or unhidden from other observers. Surely, babies playing peek-a-boo and children playing hide-and-seek are practicing this kind of apprehension. To *hide* is to position one's body at a place that is concealed at the points of observation of other observers. A "good" hiding place is one that is concealed at nearly all points of observation.

All of these facts and many more depend on the principle of occluding edges at a point of observation, the law of reversible occlusion, and the facts of opaque and nonopaque substances. What we call privacy in the design of housing, for example, is the providing of opaque enclosures. A high degree of concealment is afforded by an enclosure, and complete concealment is afforded by a complete enclosure. But note that there are peepholes and screens that permit seeing without being seen. A transparent sheet of glass in a window transmits both illumination and information, whereas a *translucent* sheet transmits illumination but not information. There will be more of this in Chapter 11.

Note also that a glass wall affords seeing through but not walking through, whereas a cloth curtain affords going through but not seeing through. Architects and designers know such facts, but they lack a theory of affordances to encompass them in a system.

Summary: Positive and Negative Affordances

The foregoing examples of the affordances of the environment are enough to show how general and powerful the concept is. Substances have biochemical offerings and afford manufacture. Surfaces afford posture, locomotion, collision, manipulation, and in general behavior. Special forms of layout afford shelter and concealment. Fires afford warming and burning. Detached objects—tools, utensils, weapons—afford special types of behavior to primates and humans. The other animal and the other person provide mutual and reciprocal affordances at extremely high levels of behavioral complexity. At the highest level, when vocalization becomes speech and manufactured displays become images, pictures, and writing, the affordances of human behavior are staggering. No more of that will be considered at this stage except to point out that speech, pictures, and writing still have to be perceived.

At all these levels, we can now observe that some offerings of the environment are beneficial and some are injurious. These are slippery terms that should only be used with great care, but if their meanings are pinned down to biological and behavioral facts the danger of confusion can be minimized. First, consider substances that afford ingestion. Some afford nutrition for a given animal, some afford poisoning, and some are neutral. As I pointed out before, these facts are quite distinct from the affording of pleasure and displeasure in eating, for the experiences do not necessarily correlate with the biological effects. Second, consider the brink of a cliff. On the one side it affords walking along, locomotion, whereas on the other it affords falling off, injury. Third, consider a detached object with a sharp edge, a knife. It affords cutting if manipulated in one manner, but it affords being cut if manipulated in another manner. Simi-

larly, but at a different level of complexity, a middle-sized metallic object affords grasping, but if charged with current it affords electric shock. And fourth, consider the other person. The animate object can give caresses or blows, contact comfort or contact injury, reward or punishment, and it is not always easy to perceive which will be provided. Note that all these benefits and injuries, these safeties and dangers, these positive and negative affordances are properties of things *taken with reference to an observer* but not properties of the *experiences of the observer.* They are not subjective values; they are not feelings of pleasure or pain added to neutral perceptions.

There has been endless debate among philosophers and psychologists as to whether values are physical or phenomenal, in the world of matter or only in the world of mind. For affordances as distinguished from values, the debate does not apply. Affordances are neither in the one world or the other inasmuch as the theory of two worlds is rejected. There is only one environment, although it contains many observers with limitless opportunities for them to live in it.

The Origin of the Concept of Affordances: A Recent History

The gestalt psychologists recognized that the meaning or the value of a thing seems to be perceived just as immediately as its color. The value is clear *on the face of it,* as we say, and thus it has a *physiognomic* quality in the way that the emotions of a man appear *on his face.* To quote from the *Principles of Gestalt Psychology* (Koffka, 1935), "Each thing says what it is. . . . a fruit says 'Eat me'; water says 'Drink me'; thunder says 'Fear me'; and woman says 'Love me'" (p. 7). These values are vivid and essential features of the experience itself. Koffka did not believe that a meaning of this sort could be explained as a pale context of memory images or an unconscious set of response tendencies. The postbox "invites" the mailing of a letter, the handle "wants to be grasped," and things "tell us what to do with them" (p. 353). Hence, they have what Koffka called "demand character."

Kurt Lewin coined the term *Aufforderungscharakter,* which has been translated as *invitation character* (by J. F. Brown in 1929) and as *valence* (by D. K. Adams in 1931; cf. Marrow, 1969, p. 56, for the history of these translations). The latter term came into general use. *Valences* for Lewin had corresponding *vectors,* which could be represented as arrows pushing the observer toward or away from the object. What explanation could be given for these valences, the characters of objects that invited or demanded behavior? No one, not even the gestalt theorists, could think of them as physical and, indeed, they do not fall within the province of ordinary physics. They must therefore be phenomenal, given the assumption of dualism. If there were *two* objects, and if the valence could not belong to the physical object, it must belong to the phenomenal object—to what Koffka called the "behavioral" object but not to the "geographical" object. The valence of an object was bestowed upon it in experience, and bestowed by a need of the observer. Thus, Koffka argued that the postbox has a demand character only when the observer needs to mail a letter. He is attracted to it when he has a letter to post, not otherwise. The value of something was assumed to change as the need of the observer changed.

The concept of affordance is derived from these concepts of valence, invitation, and demand but with a crucial difference. The affordance of something does *not change* as the need of the observer changes. The observer may or may not perceive or attend to the affordance, according to his needs, but the affordance, being invariant, is always there to be perceived. An affordance is not bestowed upon an object by a need of an observer and his act of perceiving it. The object offers what it does because it is what it is. To be sure, we define *what it is* in terms of ecological physics instead of physical physics, and it therefore possesses meaning and value to begin with. But this is meaning and value of a new sort.

For Koffka it was the *phenomenal* postbox that invited letter-mailing, not the *physical* postbox. But this duality is pernicious. I prefer to say that the real postbox (the *only* one) affords letter-mailing to a letter-writing human in a community with a postal system. This fact is perceived when the postbox is identified as such, and it is apprehended whether the postbox is in sight or out of sight. To feel a special attraction to it when one has a letter to mail is not surprising, but the main fact is that it is perceived as part of the environment—as an item of the neighborhood in which we live. Everyone above the age of six knows what it is for and where the nearest one is. The perception of its affordance should therefore not be confused with the temporary special attraction it may have.

The gestalt psychologists explained the directness and immediacy of the experience of valences by postulating that the ego is an object in experience and that a "tension" may arise between a phenomenal object and the phenomenal ego. When the object is in "a dynamic relation with the ego" said Koffka, it has a demand character. Note that the "tension," the "relation," or the "vector" must arise in the "field," that is, in the field of phenomenal experience. Although many psychologists find this theory intelligible, I do not. There is an easier way of explaining why the values of things seem to be perceived immediately and directly. It is because the affordances of things for an observer are specified in stimulus information. They *seem* to be perceived directly because they *are* perceived directly.

The accepted theories of perception, to which the gestalt theorists were objecting, implied that *no* experiences were direct except sensations and that sensations mediated all other kinds of experience. Bare sensations had to be clothed with meaning. The seeming directness of meaningful perception was therefore an embarrassment to the orthodox theories, and the Gestaltists did right to emphasize it. They began to undermine the sensation-based theories. But their own explanations of

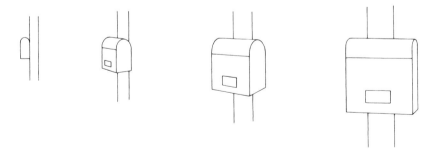

FIGURE 35.1   The changing perspective structure of a postbox during approach by an observer. As one reduces the distance to the object to one-third, the visual solid angle of the object increases three times. Actually this is only a detail near the center of an outflowing optic array. (From *The Perception of the Visual World* by James Jerome Gibson and used with the agreement of the reprint publisher, Greenwood Press, Inc.)

why it is that a fruit says "Eat me" and a woman says "Love me" are strained. The gestalt psychologists objected to the accepted theories of perception, but they never managed to go beyond them.

The Optical Information for Perceiving Affordances

The theory of affordances is a radical departure from existing theories of value and meaning. It begins with a new definition of what value and meaning *are*. The perceiving of an affordance is not a process of perceiving a value-free physical object to which meaning is somehow added in a way that no one has been able to agree upon; it is a process of perceiving a value-rich ecological object. Any substance, any surface, any layout has some affordance for benefit or injury to someone. Physics may be value-free, but ecology is not.

The central question for the theory of affordances is not whether they exist and are real but whether information is available in ambient light for perceiving them. The skeptic may now be convinced that there is information in light for some properties of a surface but not for such a property as being good to eat. The taste of a thing, he will say, is not specified in light; you can see its form and color and texture but not its palatability; you have to *taste* it for that. The skeptic understands the stimulus variables that specify the dimensions of visual sensation; he knows from psychophysics that brightness corresponds to intensity and color to wavelength of light. He may concede the invariants of structured stimulation that specify surfaces and how they are laid out and what they are made of. But he may boggle at invariant combinations of invariants that specify the affordances of the environment for an observer. The skeptic familiar with the experimental control of stimulus variables has enough trouble understanding the invariant variables I have been proposing without being asked to accept invariants of invariants.

Nevertheless, a unique combination of invariants, a *compound* invariant, is just another invariant. It is a unit, and the components do not *have* to be combined or associated. Only if percepts were combinations of sensations would they have to be associated. Even in the classical terminology, it could be argued that when a number of stimuli are completely covariant, when they *always* go together, they constitute a single "stimulus." If the visual system is capable of extracting invariants from a changing optic array, there is no reason why it should not extract invariants that seem to us highly complex.

The trouble with the assumption that high-order optical invariants specify high-order affordances is that experimenters, accustomed to working in the laboratory with low-order stimulus variables, cannot think of a way to *measure* them. How can they hope to isolate and control an invariant of optical structure so as to apply it to an observer if they cannot quantify it? The answer comes in two parts, I think. First, they should not hope to *apply* an invariant to an observer, only to make it available, for it is not a stimulus. And, second, they do not have to quantify an invariant, to apply numbers to it, but only to give it an exact mathematical description so that other experimenters can make it available to *their* observers. The virtue of the psychophysical experiment is simply that it is disciplined, not that it relates the psychical to the physical by a metric formula.

An affordance, as I said, points two ways, to the environment and to the observer. So does the information to specify an affordance. But this does not in the least imply separate realms of consciousness and matter, a psychophysical dualism. It says only that the information to specify the utilities of the environment is accompanied by information to specify the observer himself, his body, legs, hands, and mouth. This is only to reemphasize that exteroception is accompanied by proprioception—that to perceive the world is to coperceive oneself. This is wholly inconsistent with dualism in any form, either mind-matter dualism or mind-body dualism. The awareness of the world and of one's complementary relations to the world are not separable.

The child begins, no doubt, by perceiving the affordances of things for her, for her own personal behavior. She walks and sits and grasps relative to her own legs and body and hands. But she must learn to perceive the affordances of things for other observers as well as for herself. An affordance is often valid for all the animals of a species, as when it is part of a niche. I have described the invariants that enable a child to perceive the same solid shape at different points of observation and that likewise enable two or more children to perceive the same shape at different points of observation. These are the invariants that enable two children to perceive the common *affordance* of the solid shape despite the different perspectives, the affordance of a toy, for example. Only when each child perceives the values of things for others as well as for herself does she begin to be socialized.

Misinformation for Affordances

If there is information in the ambient light for the affordances of things, can there also be misinformation? According to the theory being developed, if information is picked up perception results; if misinformation is picked up misperception results.

The brink of a cliff affords falling off; it is in fact dangerous and it looks dangerous to us. It seems to look dangerous to many other terrestrial animals besides ourselves, including infant animals. Experimental studies have been made of this fact. If a sturdy sheet of plate glass is extended out over the edge it no longer affords falling and in fact is not dangerous, but it may still *look* dangerous. The optical information to specify depth-downward-at-an-edge is still present in the ambient light; for this reason the device was called a *visual cliff* by E. J. Gibson and R. D. Walk (1960). Haptic information was available to specify an adequate surface of support, but this was contradictory to the optical information. When human infants at the crawling stage of locomotion were tested with this apparatus, many of them would pat the glass with their hands but would not venture out on the surface. The babies misperceived the affordance of a transparent surface for support, and this result is not surprising.

Similarly, an adult can misperceive the affordance of a sheet of glass by mistaking a closed glass door for an open doorway and attempting to walk through it. He then crashes into the barrier and is injured. The affordance of collision was not specified by the outflow of optical texture in the array, or it was insufficiently specified. He mistook glass for air. The occluding edges of the doorway were specified and the empty visual solid angle opened up symmetrically in the normal manner as he approached, so his behavior was properly controlled, but the imminence of collision was not noticed. A little dirt on the surface, or highlights, would have saved him.

These two cases are instructive. In the first a surface of support was mistaken for air because the optic array specified air. In the second case a *barrier* was mistaken for air for the same reason. Air downward affords falling and is dangerous. Air forward affords passage and is safe. The mistaken perceptions led to inappropriate actions.

Things That Look Like What They Are

If the affordances of a thing are perceived correctly, we say that it looks like what it *is*. But we must, of course, *learn* to see what things really are—for example, that the innocent-looking leaf is really a nettle or that the helpful-sounding politician is really a demagogue. And this can be very difficult.

Errors in the perception of the surface of support are serious for a terrestrial animal. If quicksand is mistaken for sand, the perceiver is in deep trouble. If a covered pitfall is taken for solid ground, the animal is trapped. A danger is sometimes hidden—the shark under the calm water and the electric shock in the radio cabinet. In the natural environment, poison ivy is frequently mistaken for ivy. In the artificial environment, acid can be mistaken for water.

A wildcat may be hard to distinguish from a cat, and a thief may look like an honest person. When Koffka asserted that "each thing says what it is," he failed to mention that it may lie. More exactly, a thing may not look like what it is.

Nevertheless, however true all this may be, the basic affordances of the environment are perceivable and are usually perceivable directly, without an excessive amount of learning. The basic properties of the environment that make an affordance are specified in the structure of ambient light, and hence the affordance itself is specified in ambient light. Moreover, an invariant variable *that is commensurate with the body of the observer himself* is more easily picked up than one not commensurate with his body.

Summary

The medium, substances, surfaces, objects, places, and other animals have affordances for a given animal. They offer benefit or injury, life or death. This is why they need to be perceived.

The possibilities of the environment and the way of life of the animal go together inseparably. The environment constrains what the animal can do, and the concept of a niche in ecology reflects this fact. Within limits, the human animal can alter the affordances of the environment but is still the creature of his or her situation.

There is information in stimulation for the physical properties of things, and presumably there is information for the environmental properties. The doctrine that says we must distinguish among the variables of things before we can learn their meanings is questionable. Affordances are properties taken with reference to the observer. They are neither physical nor phenomenal.

The hypothesis of information in ambient light to specify affordances is the culmination of ecological optics. The notion of invariants that are related at one extreme to the motives and needs of an observer and at the other extreme to the substances and surfaces of a world provides a new approach to psychology.

36

JAMES L. McCLELLAND, DAVID E. RUMELHART, AND GEOFFREY E. HINTON

James L. McClelland (1948–) received his Ph.D. in cognitive psychology from the University of Pennsylvania in 1975. He was an assistant and associate professor at University of California, San Diego, before moving to his current positions as professor of psychology and computer science at Carnegie Mellon University, adjunct professor of neuroscience at the University of Pittsburgh, and codirector of the Center for Neural Basis of Cognition. His continued interest in cognitive neuroscience and computational models is apparent from recent coauthored publications, including "No Right to Speak? The Relationship Between Object Naming and Semantic Impairment: Neuropsychological Evidence and a Computational Model" (*Journal of Cognitive Neuroscience* 13:341–356). David E. Rumelhart did his undergraduate work at the University of South Dakota, majoring in psychology and mathematics. He went on to Stanford University and received his Ph.D. in mathematical psychology in 1967, at which point he joined the psychology faculty at the University of California, San Diego. He returned to Stanford as a professor in 1987 and retired in 1998. He has been diagnosed with Pick's disease, a neurodegenerative illness that involves the slow atrophy of frontal and temporal lobes with symptoms including agnosia, aphasia, and apraxia. Geoffrey E. Hinton is currently the director of the Gatsby Computational Neuroscience Unit at University College, London. He earned a B.A. in experimental psychology from Cambridge and a Ph.D. in artificial intelligence from Edinburgh. He worked at the University of California, San Diego, as a postdoctoral fellow before joining the computer science department of Carnegie Mellon University. Before he moved to London, he was professor of psychology, professor of computer science, and fellow at the Canadian Institute for Advanced Research in Toronto. He maintains a diverse array of research interests, and one of his many recent coauthored reports includes "A Mobile Robot that Learns Its Place" (*Neural Computation* 9:683–699).

PARALLEL DISTRIBUTED PROCESSING: EXPLORATIONS IN THE MICROSTRUCTURE OF COGNITION

THE APPEAL OF PARALLEL DISTRIBUTED PROCESSING

What makes people smarter than machines? They certainly are not quicker or more precise. Yet people are far better at perceiving objects in natural scenes and noting their relations, at understanding language and retrieving contextually appropriate information from memory, at making plans and carrying out contextually appropriate actions, and at a wide range of other natural cognitive tasks. People are also far better at learning to do these things more accurately and fluently through processing experience.

What is the basis for these differences? One answer,

From J. L. McClelland, D. E. Rumelhart, and G. E. Hinton, "The Appeal of Parallel Distributed Processing." In D. E. Rumelhart, J. L. McClelland, and the PDP Research Group, *Parallel Distributed Processing: Explorations in the Microstructure of Cognition* (pp. 3–13, 25–40). Cambridge: MIT Press, 1986.

perhaps the classic one we might expect from artificial intelligence, is "software." If we only had the right computer program, the argument goes, we might be able to capture the fluidity and adaptability of human information processing.

Certainly this answer is partially correct. There have been great breakthroughs in our understanding of cognition as a result of the development of expressive high-level computer languages and powerful algorithms. No doubt there will be more such breakthroughs in the future. However, we do not think that software is the whole story.

In our view, people are smarter than today's computers because the brain employs a basic computational architecture that is more suited to deal with a central aspect of the natural information processing tasks that people are so good at. In this chapter, we will show through examples that these tasks generally require the simultaneous consideration of many pieces of information or constraints. Each constraint may be imperfectly specified and ambiguous, yet each can play a potentially decisive role in determining the outcome of processing. After examining these points, we will introduce a computational framework for modeling cognitive processes that seems well suited to exploiting these constraints and that seems closer than other frameworks to the style of computation as it might be done by the brain. We will review several early examples of models developed in this framework, and we will show that the mechanisms these models employ can give rise to powerful emergent properties that begin to suggest attractive alternatives to traditional accounts of various aspects of cognition. We will also show that models of this class provide a basis for understanding how learning can occur spontaneously, as a by-product of processing activity.

Multiple Simultaneous Constraints

Reaching and Grasping

Hundreds of times each day we reach for things. We nearly never think about these acts of reaching. And yet, each time, a large number of different considerations appear to jointly determine exactly how we will reach for the object. The position of the object, our posture at the time, what else we may also be holding, the size, shape, and anticipated weight of the object, any obstacles that may be in the way—all of these factors jointly determine the exact method we will use for reaching and grasping.

Consider the situation shown in Figure 36.1. Figure 36.1A shows Jay McClelland's hand, in typing position

at his terminal. Figure 36.1B indicates the position his hand assumed in reaching for a small knob on the desk beside the terminal. We will let him describe what happened in the first person:

> On the desk next to my terminal are several objects—a chipped coffee mug, the end of a computer cable, a knob from a clock radio. I decide to pick the knob up. At first I hesitate, because it doesn't seem possible. Then I just reach for it, and find myself grasping the knob in what would normally be considered a very awkward position—but it solves all of the constraints. I'm not sure what all the details of the movement were, so I let myself try it a few times more. I observe that my right hand is carried up off the keyboard, bent at the elbow, until my forearm is at about a 30° angle to the desk top and parallel to the side of the terminal. The palm is facing downward through most of this. Then, my arm extends and lowers down more or less parallel to the edge of the desk and parallel to the side of the terminal and, as it drops, it turns about 90° so that the palm is facing the cup and the thumb and index finger are below. The turning motion occurs just in time, as my hand drops, to avoid hitting the coffee cup. My index finger and thumb close in on the knob and grasp it, with my hand completely upside down.

Though the details of what happened here might be quibbled with, the broad outlines are apparent. The shape of the knob and its position on the table; the starting position of the hand on the keyboard; the positions of the terminal, the cup, and the knob; and the constraints imposed by the structure of the arm and the musculature used to control it—all these things conspired to lead to a solution which exactly suits the problem. If any of these constraints had not been included, the movement would have failed. The hand would have hit the cup or the terminal—or it would have missed the knob.

The Mutual Influence of Syntax and Semantics

Multiple constraints operate just as strongly in language processing as they do in reaching and grasping. Rumelhart (1977) has documented many of these multiple constraints. Rather than catalog them here, we will use a few examples from language to illustrate the fact that the constraints tend to be reciprocal: The example shows that they do not run only from syntax to semantics—they also run the other way.

It is clear, of course, that syntax constrains the assignment of meaning. Without the syntactic rules of En-

A.

B.

FIGURE 36.1   *A:* An everyday situation in which it is necessary to take into account a large number of constraints to grasp a desired object. In this case the target object is the small knob to the left of the cup. *B:* The posture the arm arrives at in meeting these constraints.

glish to guide us, we cannot correctly understand who has done what to whom in the following sentence:

The boy the man chased kissed the girl.

But consider these examples (Rumelhart, 1977; Schank, 1973):

I saw the grand canyon flying to New York.
I saw the sheep grazing in the field.

Our knowledge of syntactic rules alone does not tell us what grammatical role is played by the prepositional phrases in these two cases. In the first, "flying to New York" is taken as describing the context in which the speaker saw the Grand Canyon—while he was flying to New York. In the second, "grazing in the field" could syntactically describe an analogous situation, in which the speaker is grazing in the field, but this possibility does not typically become available on first reading. Instead we assign "grazing in the field" as a modifier of the sheep (roughly, "who were grazing in the field"). The syntactic structure of each of these sentences, then, is determined in part by the semantic relations that the constituents of the sentence might plausibly bear to one another. Thus, the influences appear to run both ways, from the syntax to the semantics and from the semantics to the syntax.

In these examples, we see how syntactic considerations influence semantic ones and how semantic ones influence syntactic ones. We cannot say that one kind of constraint is primary.

Mutual constraints operate, not only between syntactic and semantic processing, but also within each of these domains as well. Here we consider an example from syntactic processing, namely, the assignment of words to syntactic categories. Consider the sentences:

I like the joke.
I like the drive.
I like to joke.
I like to drive.

In this case it looks as though the words *the* and *to* serve to determine whether the following word will be read as a noun or a verb. This, of course, is a very strong constraint in English and can serve to force a verb interpretation of a word that is not ordinarily used this way:

I like to mud.

On the other hand, if the information specifying whether the function word preceding the final word is *to* or *the* is ambiguous, then the typical reading of the word that follows it will determine which way the function word is heard. This was shown in an experiment by Isenberg, Walker, Ryder, and Schweikert (1980). They presented sounds halfway between *to* (actually /tˆ/) and *the* (actually /dˆ/) and found that words like *joke,* which we tend to think of first as nouns, made subjects hear the marginal stimuli as *the,* while words like *drive,* which we tend to think of first as verbs, made subjects hear the marginal stimuli as *to.* Generally, then, it would appear that each word can help constrain the syntactic role, and even the identity, of every other word.

Simultaneous Mutual Constraints in Word Recognition

Just as the syntactic role of one word can influence the role assigned to another in analyzing sentences, so the identity of one letter can influence the identity assigned to another in reading. A famous example of this, from Selfridge, is shown in Figure 36.2. Along with this is a second example in which none of the letters, considered separately, can be identified unambiguously, but in which the possibilities that the visual information leaves open for each so constrain the possible identities of the others that we are capable of identifying all of them.

FIGURE 36.2   Some ambiguous displays. The first one is from Selfridge, 1955. The second line shows that three ambiguous characters can each constrain the identity of the others. The third, fourth, and fifth lines show that these characters are indeed ambiguous in that they assume other identities in other contexts. (The ink-blot technique of making letters ambiguous is due to Lindsay and Norman, 1972).

At first glance, the situation here must seem paradoxical: The identity of each letter is constrained by the identities of each of the others. But since in general we cannot know the identities of any of the letters until we have established the identities of the others, how can we get the process started?

The resolution of the paradox, of course, is simple. One of the different possible letters in each position fits together with the others. It appears then that our perceptual system is capable of exploring all these possibilities without committing itself to one until all of the constraints are taken into account.

Understanding Through the Interplay of Multiple Sources of Knowledge

It is clear that we know a good deal about a large number of different standard situations. Several theorists have suggested that we store this knowledge in terms of structures called variously: *scripts* (Schank, 1976), *frames* (Minsky, 1975), or *schemata* (Norman & Bobrow, 1976; Rumelhart, 1975). Such knowledge structures are assumed to be the basis of comprehension. A great deal of progress has been made within the context of this view.

However, it is important to bear in mind that most everyday situations cannot be rigidly assigned to just a single script. They generally involve an interplay between a number of different sources of information. Consider, for example, a child's birthday party at a restaurant. We know things about birthday parties, and we know things about restaurants, but we would not want to assume that we have explicit knowledge (at least, not in advance of our first restaurant birthday party) about the conjunction of the two. Yet we can imagine what such a party might be like. The fact that the party was being held in a restaurant would modify certain aspects of our expectations for birthday parties (we would not expect a game of Pin-the-Tail-on-the-Donkey, for example), while the fact that the event was a birthday party would inform our expectations for what would be ordered and who would pay the bill.

Representations like scripts, frames, and schemata are useful structures for encoding knowledge, although we believe they only approximate the underlying structure of knowledge representation that emerges from the class of models we consider in this book, as explained in Chapter 14. Our main point here is that any theory that tries to account for human knowledge using script-like knowledge structures will have to allow them to interact with each other to capture the generative capacity of human understanding in novel situations. Achieving such interactions has been one of the greatest difficulties associated with implementing models that really think generatively using script- or frame-like representations.

Parallel Distributed Processing

In the examples we have considered, a number of different pieces of information must be kept in mind at once. Each plays a part, constraining others and being constrained by them. What kinds of mechanisms seem well suited to these task demands? Intuitively, these tasks seem to require mechanisms in which each aspect of the information in the situation can act on other aspects, simultaneously influencing other aspects and being influenced by them. To articulate these intuitions, we and others have turned to a class of models we call *Parallel Distributed Processing* (PDP) models. These models assume that information processing takes place through the interactions of a large number of simple processing elements called units, each sending excitatory and inhibitory signals to other units. In some cases, the units stand for possible hypotheses about such things as the letters in a particular display or the syntactic roles of the words in a particular sentence. In these cases, the activations stand roughly for the strengths associated with the different possible hypotheses, and the interconnections among the units stand for the constraints the system knows to exist between the hypotheses. In other cases, the units stand for possible goals and actions, such as the goal of typing a particular letter, or the action of moving the left index finger, and the connections relate goals to subgoals, subgoals to actions, and actions to muscle movements. In still other cases, units stand not for particular hypotheses or goals, but for aspects of these things. Thus a hypothesis about the identity of a word, for example, is itself distributed in the activations of a large number of units.

PDP Models: Cognitive Science or Neuroscience?

One reason for the appeal of PDP models is their obvious "physiological" flavor: They seem so much more closely tied to the physiology of the brain than are other kinds of information-processing models. The brain consists of a large number of highly interconnected elements which apparently send very simple excitatory and inhibitory messages to each other and update their excitations on the basis of these simple messages. The properties of the units in many of the PDP models we will be exploring were inspired by basic properties of the neural hardware. In a later section of this book, we will examine in some detail the relation between PDP models and the brain.

Though the appeal of PDP models is definitely enhanced by their physiological plausibility and neural inspiration, these are not the primary bases for their appeal to us. We are, after all, cognitive scientists, and PDP models appeal to us for psychological and computational reasons. They hold out the hope of offering computationally sufficient and psychologically accurate mechanistic accounts of the phenomena of human cognition which have eluded successful explication in conventional computational formalisms; and they have radically altered the way we think about the time-course of processing, the nature of representation, and the mechanisms of learning.

The Microstructure of Cognition

The process of human cognition, examined on a time scale of seconds and minutes, has a distinctly sequential character to it. Ideas come, seem promising, and then are rejected; leads in the solution to a problem are taken up, then abandoned and replaced with new ideas. Though the process may not be discrete, it has a decidedly sequential character, with transitions from state-to-state occurring, say, two or three times a second. Clearly, any useful description of the overall organization of this sequential flow of thought will necessarily describe a sequence of states.

But what is the internal structure of each of the states in the sequence, and how do they come about? Serious attempts to model even the simplest macrosteps of cognition—say, recognition of single words—require vast numbers of microsteps if they are implemented sequentially. As Feldman and Ballard (1982) have pointed out, the biological hardware is just too sluggish for sequential models of the microstructure to provide a plausible account, at least of the microstructure of *human* thought. And the time limitation only gets worse, not better, when sequential mechanisms try to take large numbers of constraints into account. Each additional constraint requires more time in a sequential machine, and, if the constraints are imprecise, the constraints can lead to a computational explosion. Yet people get faster, not slower, when they are able to exploit additional constraints.

Parallel distributed processing models offer alternatives to serial models of the microstructure of cognition. They do not deny that there is a macrostructure, just as the study of subatomic particles does not deny the existence of interactions between atoms. What PDP models do is describe the internal structure of the larger units, just as subatomic physics describes the internal structure of the atoms that form the constituents of larger units of chemical structure.

We shall show as we proceed through this book that the analysis of the microstructure of cognition has important implications for most of the central issues in cognitive science. In general, from the PDP point of view, the objects referred to in macrostructural models of cognitive processing are seen as approximate descriptions of emergent properties of the microstructure. Sometimes these approximate descriptions may be sufficiently accurate to capture a process or mechanism well enough; but many times, we will argue, they fail to provide sufficiently elegant or tractable accounts that capture the very flexibility and open-endedness of cognition that their inventors had originally intended to capture. We hope that our analysis of PDP models will show how an examination of the microstructure of cognition can lead us closer to an adequate description of the real extent of human processing and learning capacities.

The development of PDP models is still in its infancy. Thus far the models which have been proposed capture simplified versions of the kinds of phenomena we have been describing rather than the full elaboration that these phenomena display in real settings. But we think there have been enough steps forward in recent years to warrant a concerted effort at describing where the approach has gotten and where it is going now, and to point out some directions for the future.

The first section of the book represents an introductory course in parallel distributed processing. The rest of this chapter attempts to describe in informal terms a number of the models which have been proposed in previous work and to show that the approach is indeed a fruitful one. It also contains a brief description of the major sources of the inspiration we have obtained from the work of other researchers. This chapter is followed, in Chapter 2, by a description of the quantitative framework within which these models can be described and examined. Chapter 3 explicates one of the central concepts of the book: *distributed representation*. The final chapter in this section, Chapter 4, returns to the question of demonstrating the appeal of parallel distributed processing models and gives an overview of our explorations in the microstructure of cognition as they are laid out in the remainder of this book.

Examples of PDP Models

In what follows, we review a number of recent applications of PDP models to problems in motor control, perception, memory, and language. In many cases, as we shall see, parallel distributed processing mechanisms are used to provide natural accounts of the exploitation of multiple, simultaneous, and often mutual constraints. We will also see that these same mechanisms exhibit emergent properties which lead to novel interpretations of phenomena which have traditionally been interpreted in other ways.

Retrieving Information From Memory

CONTENT ADDRESSABILITY. One very prominent feature of human memory is that it is content addressable. It seems fairly clear that we can access information in memory based on nearly any attribute of the representation we are trying to retrieve.

Of course, some cues are much better than others. An attribute which is shared by a very large number of things we know about is not a very effective retrieval cue, since it does not accurately pick out a particular memory representation. But, several such cues, in conjunction, can do the job. Thus, if we ask a friend who goes out with several women, "Who was that woman I saw you with?", he may not know which one we mean—but if we specify something else about her—say the color of her hair, what she was wearing (in so far as he remembers this at all), where we saw him with her—he will likely be able to hit upon the right one.

It is, of course, possible to implement some kind of content addressability of memory on a standard computer in a variety of different ways. One way is to search sequentially, examining each memory in the system to find the memory or the set of memories which has the particular content specified in the cue. An alternative, somewhat more efficient, scheme involves some form of indexing—keeping a list, for every content a memory might have, of which memories have that content.

Such an indexing scheme can be made to work with error-free probes, but it will break down if there is an error in the specification of the retrieval cue. There are possible ways of recovering from such errors, but they lead to the kind of combinatorial explosions which plague this kind of computer implementation.

But suppose that we imagine that each memory is represented by a unit which has mutually excitatory interactions with units standing for each of its properties. Then, whenever any property of the memory became active, the memory would tend to be activated, and whenever the memory was activated, all of its contents would tend to become activated. Such a scheme would automatically produce content addressability for us. Though it would not be immune to errors, it would not be devastated by an error in the probe if the remaining properties specified the correct memory.

As described thus far, whenever a property that is a part of a number of different memories is activated, it will tend to activate all of the memories it is in. To keep these other activities from swamping the "correct" memory unit, we simply need to add initial inhibitory connections among the memory units. An additional desirable feature would be mutually inhibitory interactions among mutually incompatible property units. For example, a person cannot both be single and married at the same time, so the units for different marital states would be mutually inhibitory.

McClelland (1981) developed a simulation model that illustrates how a system with these properties would act as a content addressable memory. The model is obviously oversimplified, but it illustrates many of the characteristics of the more complex models that will be considered in later chapters.

Consider the information represented in Table 36.1, which lists a number of people we might meet if we went to live in an unsavory neighborhood, and some of their hypothetical characteristics. A subset of the units needed to represent this information is shown in Figure 36.3. In this network, there is an "instance unit" for each of the characters described in Table 36.1, and that unit is linked by mutually excitatory connections to all of the units for the fellow's properties. Note that we have included property units for the names of the characters, as well as units for their other properties.

Now, suppose we wish to retrieve the properties of a particular individual, say Lance. And suppose that we know Lance's name. Then we can probe the network by activating Lance's name unit, and we can see what pattern of activation arises as a result. Assuming that we know of no one else named Lance, we can expect the Lance name unit to be hooked up only to the instance unit for Lance. This will in turn activate the property units for Lance, thereby creating the pattern of activation corresponding to Lance. In effect, we have retrieved a representation of Lance. More will happen than just what we have described so far, but for the moment let us stop here.

Of course, sometimes we may wish to retrieve a name, given other information. In this case, we might start with some of Lance's properties, effectively asking the system, say "Who do you know who is a Shark and in his 20s?" by activating the Shark and 20s units. In this case it turns out that there is a single individual, Ken, who fits the description. So, when we activate these two properties, we will activate the instance unit for Ken, and this in turn will activate his name unit, and fill in his other properties as well.

The Jets and The Sharks

Name	Gang	Age	Edu	Mar	Occupation
Art	Jets	40's	J.H.	Sing.	Pusher
Al	Jets	30's	J.H.	Mar.	Burglar
Sam	Jets	20's	COL.	Sing.	Bookie
Clyde	Jets	40's	J.H.	Sing.	Bookie
Mike	Jets	30's	J.H.	Sing.	Bookie
Jim	Jets	20's	J.H.	Div.	Burglar
Greg	Jets	20's	H.S.	Mar.	Pusher
John	Jets	20's	J.H.	Mar.	Burglar
Doug	Jets	30's	H.S.	Sing.	Bookie
Lance	Jets	20's	J.H.	Mar.	Burglar
George	Jets	20's	J.H.	Div.	Burglar
Pete	Jets	20's	H.S.	Sing.	Bookie
Fred	Jets	20's	H.S.	Sing.	Pusher
Gene	Jets	20's	COL.	Sing.	Pusher
Ralph	Jets	30's	J.H.	Sing.	Pusher
Phil	Sharks	30's	COL.	Mar.	Pusher
Ike	Sharks	30's	J.H.	Sing.	Bookie
Nick	Sharks	30's	H.S.	Sing.	Pusher
Don	Sharks	30's	COL.	Mar.	Burglar
Ned	Sharks	30's	COL.	Mar.	Bookie
Karl	Sharks	40's	H.S.	Mar.	Bookie
Ken	Sharks	20's	H.S.	Sing.	Burglar
Earl	Sharks	40's	H.S.	Mar.	Burglar
Rick	Sharks	30's	H.S.	Div.	Burglar
Ol	Sharks	30's	COL.	Mar.	Pusher
Neal	Sharks	30's	H.S.	Sing.	Bookie
Dave	Sharks	30's	H.S.	Div.	Pusher

TABLE 36.1   Characteristics of a number of individuals belonging to two gangs, the Jets and the Sharks.

GRACEFUL DEGRADATION. A few of the desirable properties of this kind of model are visible from considering what happens as we vary the set of features we use to probe the memory in an attempt to retrieve a particular individual's name. Any set of features which is sufficient to uniquely characterize a particular item will activate the instance node for that item more strongly than any other instance node. A probe which contains misleading features will most strongly activate the node that it matches best. This will clearly be a poorer cue than one which contains no misleading information—but it will still be sufficient to activate the "right answer" more strongly than any other, as long as the introduction of misleading information does not make the probe closer to some other item. In general, though the degree of activation of a particular instance node and of the corresponding name nodes varies in this model as a function of the exact content of the probe, errors in the probe will not be fatal unless they make the probe point to the wrong memory. This kind of model's handling of incomplete or partial probes also requires no special error-recovery scheme to work—it is a natural by-product of the nature of the retrieval mechanism that it is capable of graceful degradation.

These aspects of the behavior of the Jets and Sharks model deserve more detailed consideration than the present space allows. One reason we do not go into them is that we view this model as a stepping stone in the development of other models, such as the models using more distributed representations, that occur in other parts of this book. We do, however, have more to say about this simple model, for like some of the other models we have already examined, this model exhibits some useful properties which emerge from the interactions of the processing units.

DEFAULT ASSIGNMENT. It probably will have occurred to the reader that in many of the situations we have been examining, there will be other activations occurring which may influence the pattern of activation which is retrieved. So, in the case where we retrieved the properties of Lance, those properties, once they become active, can begin to activate the units for other individuals with those same properties. The memory unit for Lance will be in competition with these units and will tend to keep their activation down, but to the extent that they do become active, they will tend to activate their own properties and therefore fill them in. In this way, the model can fill in properties of individuals based on what it knows about other, similar instances.

To illustrate how this might work we have simulated the case in which we do not know that Lance is a Burglar as opposed to a Bookie or a Pusher. It turns out that there are a group of individuals in the set who are very similar to Lance in many respects. When Lance's properties become activated, these other units become partially activated, and they start activating their properties. Since they all share the same "occupation," they work together to fill in that property for Lance. Of course, there is no reason why this should necessarily be the right answer, but generally speaking, the more similar two things are in respects that we know about, the more likely they are to be similar in respects that we do not, and the model implements this heuristic.

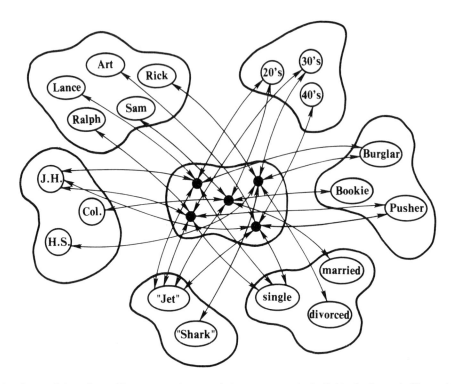

FIGURE 36.3   Some of the units and interconnections needed to represent the individuals shown in Figure 10. The units
connected with double-headed arrows are mutually excitatory. All the units within the same cloud are mutually
inhibitory. (From "Retrieving General and Specific Knowledge From Stored Knowledge of Specifics" by J. L.
McClelland, 1981, *Proceedings of the Third Annual Conference of the Cognitive Science Society,* Berkeley, CA.
Copyright 1981 by J. L. McClelland. Reprinted by permission.)

SPONTANEOUS GENERALIZATION. The model we
have been describing has another valuable property as
well—it tends to retrieve what is common to those memories which match a retrieval cue which is too general to
capture any one memory. Thus, for example, we could
probe the system by activating the unit corresponding to
membership in the Jets. This unit will partially activate
all the instances of the Jets, thereby causing each to send
activations to its properties. In this way the model can retrieve the typical values that the members of the Jets have
on each dimension—even though there is no one Jet that
has these typical values. In the example, 9 of 15 Jets are
single, 9 of 15 are in their 20s, and 9 of 15 have only a Junior High School education; when we probe by activating the Jet unit, all three of these properties dominate.
The Jets are evenly divided between the three occupations, so each of these units becomes partially activated.
Each has a different name, so that each name unit is very
weakly activated, nearly cancelling each other out.

In the example just given of spontaneous generalization, it would not be unreasonable to suppose that someone might have explicitly stored a generalization about
the members of a gang. The account just given would be
an alternative to "explicit storage" of the generalization.
It has two advantages, though, over such an account.
First, it does not require any special generalization formation mechanism. Second, it can provide us with generalizations on unanticipated lines, on demand. Thus, if
we want to know, for example, what people in their 20s
with a junior high school education are like, we can
probe the model by activating these two units. Since all
such people are Jets and Burglars, these two units are
strongly activated by the model in this case; two of them
are divorced and two are married, so both of these units
are partially activated.[1]

The sort of model we are considering, then, is considerably more than a content addressable memory. In
addition, it performs default assignment, and it can

spontaneously retrieve a general concept of the individuals that match any specifiable probe. These properties must be explicitly implemented as complicated computational extensions of other models of knowledge retrieval, but in PDP models they are natural by-products of the retrieval process itself.

Representation and Learning in PDP Models

In the Jets and Sharks model, we can speak of the model's *active representation* at a particular time, and associate this with the pattern of activation over the units in the system. We can also ask: What is the stored knowledge that gives rise to that pattern of activation? In considering this question, we see immediately an important difference between PDP models and other models of cognitive processes. In most models, knowledge is stored as a static copy of a pattern. Retrieval amounts to finding the pattern in long-term memory and copying it into a buffer or working memory. There is no real difference between the stored representation in long-term memory and the active representation in working memory. In PDP models, though, this is not the case. In these models, the patterns themselves are not stored. Rather, what is stored is the *connection strengths* between units that allow these patterns to be re-created. In the Jets and Sharks models, there is an instance unit assigned to each individual, but that unit does not contain a copy of the representation of that individual. Instead, it is simply the case that the connections between it and the other units in the system are such that activation of the unit will cause the pattern for the individual to be reinstated on the property units.

This difference between PDP models and conventional models has enormous implications, both for processing and for learning. We have already seen some of the implications for processing. The representation of the knowledge is set up in such a way that the knowledge necessarily influences the course of processing. Using knowledge in processing is no longer a matter of finding the relevant information in memory and bringing it to bear; it is part and parcel of the processing itself.

For learning, the implications are equally profound. For if the knowledge is the strengths of the connections, learning must be a matter of finding the right connection strengths so that the right patterns of activation will be produced under the right circumstances. This is an extremely important property of this class of models, for it opens up the possibility that an information processing mechanism could learn, as a result of tuning its connections, to capture the interdependencies between activations that it is exposed to in the course of processing.

In recent years, there has been quite a lot of interest in learning in cognitive science. Computational approaches to learning fall predominantly into what might be called the "explicit rule formulation" tradition, as represented by the work of Winston (1975), the suggestions of Chomsky, and the ACT* model of J. R. Anderson (1983). All of this work shares the assumption that the goal of learning is to formulate explicit rules (propositions, productions, etc.) which capture powerful generalizations in a succinct way. Fairly powerful mechanisms, usually with considerable innate knowledge about a domain, and/or some starting set of primitive propositional representations, then formulate hypothetical general rules, e.g., by comparing particular cases and formulating explicit generalizations.

The approach that we take in developing PDP models is completely different. First, we do not assume that the goal of learning is the formulation of explicit rules. Rather, we assume it is the acquisition of connection strengths which allow a network of simple units to act *as though* it knew the rules. Second, we do not attribute powerful computational capabilities to the learning mechanism. Rather, we assume very simple connection strength modulation mechanisms which adjust the strength of connections between units based on information locally available at the connection.

These issues will be addressed at length in later sections of this book. For now, our purpose is to give a simple, illustrative example of the connection strength modulation process, and how it can produce networks which exhibit some interesting behavior.

LOCAL VS. DISTRIBUTED REPRESENTATION. Before we turn to an explicit consideration of this issue, we raise a basic question about representation. Once we have achieved the insight that the knowledge is stored in the strengths of the interconnections between units, a question arises. Is there any reason to assign one unit to each pattern that we wish to learn? Another possibility—one that we explore extensively in this book—is the possibility that the knowledge about any individual pattern is not stored in the connections of a special unit reserved for that pattern, but is distributed over the connections among a large number of processing units. On this view, the Jets and Sharks model represents a special case in which separate units are reserved for each instance.

Models in which connection information is explicitly thought of as distributed have been proposed by a number of investigators. The units in these collections may themselves correspond to conceptual primitives, or they may have no particular meaning as individuals. In either case, the focus shifts to patterns of activation over these units and to mechanisms whose explicit purpose is to learn the right connection strengths to allow the right patterns of activation to become activated under the right circumstances.

In the rest of this section, we will give a simple example of a PDP model in which the knowledge is distributed. We will first explain how the model would work, given pre-existing connections, and we will then describe how it could come to acquire the right connection strengths through a very simple learning mechanism. A number of models which have taken this distributed approach have been discussed in this book's predecessor, Hinton and J. A. Anderson's (1981) *Parallel Models of Associative Memory*. We will consider a simple version of a common type of distributed model, a *pattern associator*.

Pattern associators are models in which a pattern of activation over one set of units can cause a pattern of activation over another set of units without any intervening units to stand for either pattern as a whole. Pattern associators would, for example, be capable of associat-

ing a pattern of activation on one set of units corresponding to the appearance of an object with a pattern on another set corresponding to the aroma of the object, so that, when an object is presented visually, causing its visual pattern to become active, the model produces the pattern corresponding to its aroma.

HOW A PATTERN ASSOCIATOR WORKS. For purposes of illustration, we present a very simple pattern associator in Figure 36.4. In this model, there are four units in each of two pools. The first pool, the A units, will be the pool in which patterns corresponding to the sight of various objects might be represented. The second pool, the B units, will be the pool in which the pattern corresponding to the aroma will be represented. We can pretend that alternative patterns of activation on the A units are produced upon viewing a rose or a grilled steak, and alternative patterns on the B units are produced upon sniffing the same objects. Figure 36.5 shows two pairs of patterns, as well as sets of interconnections necessary to allow the A member of each pair to reproduce the B member.

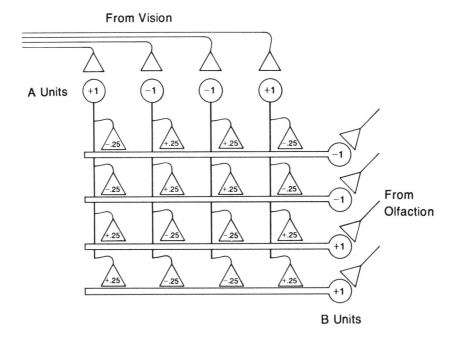

FIGURE 36.4   A simple pattern associator. The example assumes that patterns of activation in the A units can be produced by the visual system and patterns in the B units can be produced by the olfactory system. The synaptic connections allow the outputs of the A units to influence the activations of the B units. The synaptic weights linking the A units to the B units were selected so as to allow the pattern of activation shown on the A units to reproduce the pattern of activation shown on the B units without the need for any olfactory input.

The details of the behavior of the individual units vary among different versions of pattern associators. For present purposes, we'll assume that the units can take on positive or negative activation values, with 0 representing a kind of neutral intermediate value. The strengths of the interconnections between the units can be positive or negative real numbers.

The effect of an A unit on a B unit is determined by multiplying the activation of the A unit times the strength of its synaptic connection with the B unit. For example, if the connection from a particular A unit to a particular B unit has a positive sign, when the A unit is excited (activation greater than 0), it will excite the B unit. For this example, we'll simply assume that the activation of each unit is set to the sum of the excitatory and inhibitory effects operating on it. This is one of the simplest possible cases.

Suppose, now, that we have created on the A units the pattern corresponding to the first visual pattern shown in Figure 36.5, the rose. How should we arrange the strengths of the interconnections between the A units and the B units to reproduce the pattern corresponding to the aroma of a rose? We simply need to arrange for each A unit to tend to excite each B unit which has a positive activation in the aroma pattern and to inhibit each B unit which has a negative activation in the aroma pattern. It turns out that this goal is achieved by setting the strength of the connection between a given A unit and a given B unit to a value proportional to the product of the activation of the two units. In Figure 36.4, the weights on the connections were chosen to allow the A pattern illustrated there to produce the illustrated B pattern according to this principle. The actual strengths of the connections were set to ±.25, rather than ±1, so that the A pattern will produce the right magnitude, as well as the right sign, for the activations of the units in the B

pattern. The same connections are reproduced in matrix form in Figure 36.5.

Pattern associators like the one in Figure 36.4 have a number of nice properties. One is that they do not require a perfect copy of the input to produce the correct output, though its strength will be weaker in this case. For example, suppose that the associator shown in Figure 36.4 were presented with an A pattern of $(1,-1,0,1)$. This is the A pattern shown in the figure, with the activation of one of its elements set to 0. The B pattern produced in response will have the activations of all of the B units in the right direction; however, they will be somewhat weaker than they would be, had the complete A pattern been shown. Similar effects are produced if an element of the pattern is distorted—or if the model is damaged, either by removing whole units, or random sets of connections, etc. Thus, their pattern retrieval performance of the model degrades gracefully both under degraded input and under damage.

HOW A PATTERN ASSOCIATOR LEARNS. So far, we have seen how we as model builders can construct the right set of weights to allow one pattern to cause another. The interesting thing, though, is that we do not need to build these interconnection strengths in by hand. Instead, the pattern associator can teach itself the right set of interconnections through experience processing the patterns in conjunction with each other.

A number of different rules for adjusting connection strengths have been proposed. One of the first—and definitely the best known—is due to D. O. Hebb (1949). Hebb's actual proposal was not sufficiently quantitative to build into an explicit model. However, a number of different variants can trace their ancestry back to Hebb. Perhaps the simplest version is:

+1	−1	−1	+1				−1	+1	−1	+1		
−.25	+.25	+.25	−.25	−1			+.25	−.25	+.25	−.25	−1
−.25	+.25	+.25	−.25	−1			−.25	+.25	−.25	+.25	+1
+.25	−.25	−.25	+.25	+1			−.25	+.25	−.25	+.25	+1
+.25	−.25	−.25	+.25	+1			+.25	−.25	+.25	−.25	−1

FIGURE 36.5 Two simple associators represented as matrices. The weights in the first two matrices allow the A pattern shown above the matrix to produce the B pattern shown to the right of it. Note that the weights in the first matrix are the same as those shown in the diagram in Figure 36.4.

When unit A and unit B are simultaneously excited, increase the strength of the connection between them.

A natural extension of this rule to cover the positive and negative activation values allowed in our example is:

Adjust the strength of the connection between units A and B in proportion to the product of their simultaneous activation.

In this formulation, if the product is positive, the change makes the connection more excitatory, and if the product is negative, the change makes the connection more inhibitory. For simplicity of reference, we will call this the *Hebb rule*, although it is not exactly Hebb's original formulation.

With this simple learning rule, we could train a "blank copy" of the pattern associator shown in Figure 36.4 to produce the B pattern for rose when the A pattern is shown, simply by presenting the A and B patterns together and modulating the connection strengths according to the Hebb rule. The size of the change made on every trial would, of course, be a parameter. We generally assume that the changes made on each instance are rather small, and that connection strengths build up gradually. The values shown in Figure 36.5A, then, would be acquired as a result of a number of experiences with the A and B pattern pair.

It is very important to note that the information needed to use the Hebb rule to determine the value each connection should have is *locally available* at the connection. All a given connection needs to consider is the activation of the units on both sides of it. Thus, it would be possible to actually implement such a connection modulation scheme locally, in each connection, without requiring any programmer to reach into each connection and set it to just the right value.

It turns out that the Hebb rule as stated here has some serious limitations, and, to our knowledge, no theorists continue to use it in this simple form. More sophisticated connection modulation schemes have been proposed by other workers; most important among these are the delta rule, discussed extensively in Chapters 8 and 11; the competitive learning rule, discussed in Chapter 5; and the rules for learning in stochastic parallel models, described in Chapters 6 and 7. All of these learning rules have the property that they adjust the strengths of connections between units on the basis of information that can be assumed to be locally available to the unit. Learning, then, in all of these cases, amounts to a very simple process that can be implemented locally at each connection without the need for any overall supervision. Thus, models which incorporate these learning rules train themselves to have the right interconnections in the course of processing the members of an ensemble of patterns.

LEARNING MULTIPLE PATTERNS IN THE SAME SET OF INTERCONNECTIONS. Up to now, we have considered how we might teach our pattern associator to associate the visual pattern for one object with a pattern for the aroma of the same object. Obviously, different patterns of interconnections between the A and B units are appropriate for causing the visual pattern for a different object to give rise to the pattern for its aroma. The same principles apply, however, and if we presented our pattern associator with the A and B patterns for steak, it would learn the right set of interconnections for that case instead (these are shown in Figure 36.5B). In fact, it turns out that we can actually teach the same pattern associator a number of different associations. The matrix representing the set of interconnections that would be learned if we taught the same pattern associator both the rose association and the steak association is shown in Figure 36.6. The reader can verify this by adding the

$$
\begin{bmatrix}
- & + & + & - \\
- & + & + & - \\
+ & - & - & + \\
+ & - & - & +
\end{bmatrix}
+
\begin{bmatrix}
+ & - & + & - \\
- & + & - & + \\
- & + & - & + \\
+ & - & + & -
\end{bmatrix}
=
\begin{bmatrix}
 & & ++ & -- \\
-- & ++ & & \\
 & & -- & ++ \\
++ & -- & &
\end{bmatrix}
$$

FIGURE 36.6   The weights in the third matrix allow either A pattern shown in Figure 36.5 to recreate the corresponding B pattern. Each weight in this case is equal to the sum of the weight for the A pattern and the weight for the B pattern, as illustrated.

two matrices for the individual patterns together. The reader can also verify that this set of connections will allow the rose A pattern to produce the rose B pattern, and the steak A pattern to produce the steak B pattern: when either input pattern is presented, the correct corresponding output is produced.

The examples used here have the property that the two different visual patterns are completely uncorrelated with each other. This being the case, the rose pattern produces no effect when the interconnections for the steak have been established, and the steak pattern produces no effect when the interconnections for the rose association are in effect. For this reason, it is possible to add together the pattern of interconnections for the rose association and the pattern for the steak association, and still be able to associate the sight of the steak with the smell of a steak and the sight of a rose with the smell of a rose. The two sets of interconnections do not interact at all.

One of the limitations of the Hebbian learning rule is that it can learn the connection strengths appropriate to an entire ensemble of patterns only when all the patterns are completely uncorrelated. This restriction does not, however, apply to pattern associators which use more sophisticated learning schemes.

ATTRACTIVE PROPERTIES OF PATTERN ASSOCIATOR MODELS. Pattern associator models have the property that uncorrelated patterns do not interact with each other, but more similar ones do. Thus, to the extent that a new pattern of activation on the A units is similar to one of the old ones, it will tend to have similar effects. Furthermore, if we assume that learning the interconnections occurs in small increments, similar patterns will essentially reinforce the strengths of the links they share in common with other patterns. Thus, if we present the same pair of patterns over and over, but each time we add a little random noise to each element of each member of the pair, the system will automatically learn to associate the central tendency of the two patterns and will learn to ignore the noise. What will be stored will be an average of the similar patterns with the slight variations removed. On the other hand, when we present the system with completely uncorrelated patterns, they will not interact with each other in this way. Thus, the same pool of units can extract the central tendency of each of a number of pairs of unrelated patterns. This aspect of distributed models is exploited extensively in Chapters 17 and 25 on distributed memory and amnesia.

EXTRACTING THE STRUCTURE OF AN ENSEMBLE OF PATTERNS. The fact that similar patterns tend to

produce similar effects allows distributed models to exhibit a kind of spontaneous generalization, extending behavior appropriate for one pattern to other similar patterns. This property is shared by other PDP models, such as the word perception model and the Jets and Sharks model described above; the main difference here is in the existence of simple, local, learning mechanisms that can allow the acquisition of the connection strengths needed to produce these generalizations through experience with members of the ensemble of patterns. Distributed models have another interesting property as well: If there are regularities in the correspondences between pairs of patterns, the model will naturally extract these regularities. This property allows distributed models to acquire patterns of interconnections that lead them to behave in ways we ordinarily take as evidence for the use of linguistic rules.

A detailed example of such a model is described in Chapter 18. Here, we describe the model very briefly. The model is a mechanism that learns how to construct the past tenses of words from their root forms through repeated presentations of examples of root forms paired with the corresponding past-tense form. The model consists of two pools of units. In one pool, patterns of activation representing the phonological structure of the root form of the verb can be represented, and, in the other, patterns representing the phonological structure of the past tense can be represented. The goal of the model is simply to learn the right connection strengths between the root units and the past-tense units, so that whenever the root form of a verb is presented the model will construct the corresponding past-tense form. The model is trained by presenting the root form of the verb as a pattern of activation over the root units, and then using a simple, local, learning rule to adjust the connection strengths so that this root form will tend to produce the correct pattern of activation over the past-tense units. The model is tested by simply presenting the root form as a pattern of activation over the root units and examining the pattern of activation produced over the past-tense units.

The model is trained initially with a small number of verbs children learn early in the acquisition process. At this point in learning, it can only produce appropriate outputs for inputs that it has explicitly been shown. But as it learns more and more verbs, it exhibits two interesting behaviors. First, it produces the standard *ed* past tense when tested with pseudo-verbs or verbs it has never seen. Second, it "overregularizes" the past tense of irregular words it previously completed correctly. Often, the model will blend the irregular past tense of the word with the regular *ed* ending, and produce errors like *CAMED* as the past of *COME*. These phenomena mirror those observed in the early phases of acquisition of control over past tenses in young children.

The generativity of the child's responses—the creation of regular past tenses of new verbs and the over-regularization of the irregular verbs—has been taken as strong evidence that the child has induced the rule which states that the regular correspondence for the past tense in English is to add a final *ed* (Berko, 1958). On the evidence of its performance, then, the model can be said to have acquired the rule. However, no special rule-induction mechanism is used, and no special language-acquisition device is required. The model learns to behave in accordance with the rule, not by explicitly noting that most words take *ed* in the past tense in English and storing this rule away explicitly, but simply by building up a set of connections in a pattern associator through a long series of simple learning experiences. The same mechanisms of parallel distributed processing and connection modification which are used in a number of domains serve, in this case, to produce implicit knowledge tantamount to a linguistic rule. The model also provides a fairly detailed account of a number of the specific aspects of the error patterns children make in learning the rule. In this sense, it provides a richer and more detailed description of the acquisition process than any that falls out naturally from the assumption that the child is building up a repertoire of explicit but inaccessible rules.

There is a lot more to be said about distributed mod-els of learning, about their strengths and their weaknesses, than we have space for in this preliminary consideration. For now we hope mainly to have suggested that they provide dramatically different accounts of learning and acquisition than are offered by traditional models of these processes. We saw in earlier sections of this chapter that performance in accordance with rules can emerge from the interactions of simple, interconnected units. Now we can see how the acquisition of performance that conforms to linguistic rules can emerge from a simple, local, connection strength modulation process.

We have seen what the properties of PDP models are in informal terms, and we have seen how these properties operate to make the models do many of the kinds of things that they do. The business of the next chapter is to lay out these properties more formally, and to introduce some formal tools for their description and analysis. Before we turn to this, however, we wish to describe some of the major sources of inspiration for the PDP approach.

NOTE

1. In this and all other cases, there is a tendency for the pattern of activation to be influenced by partially activated, near neighbors, which do not quite match the probe. Thus, in this case, there is a Jet Al, who is a Married Burglar. The unit for Al gets slightly activated, giving Married a slight edge over Divorced in the simulation.

37

V. S. RAMACHANDRAN AND SANDRA BLAKESLEE

Vilayanur S. Ramachandran (1951–) received his medical degree from Stanley Medical College, Chennai, India, and his Ph.D. from Trinity College at the University of Cambridge. He is currently a professor of psychology, the neurosciences program, and the director of the Center for Brain and Cognition at the University of California, San Diego, and an adjunct professor of biology at the Salk Institute for Biological Studies in La Jolla, California. He has received numerous awards, including an honorary doctorate of science (D.Sc.) from Connecticut College. One example of his recent scholarship is the coauthored article "The Perception of Phantom Limbs: The D.O. Hebb Lecture" (*Brain*, 121, 1603–1630). Sandra Blakeslee (1943–) earned a B.S. in political science from University of California at

Berkeley. She is a regular contributor to the *New York Times* "Science Times" in addition to coauthoring books on women's health; family; marriage issues; and, most recently, *The Unexpected Legacy of Divorce: A 25-Year Landmark Study.*

DO MARTIANS SEE RED?

All of modern philosophy consists of unlocking, exhuming and recanting what has been said before. (—V.S. Ramachandran)

Why is thought, being a secretion of the brain, more wonderful than gravity, a property of matter? (—Charles Darwin)

In the first half of the next century, science will confront its greatest challenge in trying to answer a question that has been steeped in mysticism and metaphysics for millennia: What is the nature of the self? As someone who was born in India and raised in the Hindu tradition, I was taught that the concept of the self—the "I" within me that is aloof from the universe and engages in a lofty inspection of the world around me—is an illusion, a veil called *maya*. The search for enlightenment, I was told, consists of lifting this veil and realizing that you are really "One with the cosmos." Ironically, after extensive training in Western medicine and more than fifteen years of research on neurological patients and visual illusions, I have come to realize that there is much truth to this view—that the notion of a single unified self "inhabiting" the brain may indeed be an illusion. Everything I have learned from the intensive study of both normal people and patients who have sustained damage to various parts of their brains points to an unsettling notion: that you create your own "reality" from mere fragments of information, that what you "see" is a reliable—but not always accurate—representation of what exists in the world, that you are completely unaware of the vast majority of events going on in your brain. Indeed, most of your actions are carried out by a host of unconscious zombies who exist in peaceful harmony along with you (the "person") inside your body! I hope that the stories you have heard so far have helped convince you that the problem of self—far from being a metaphysical riddle—is now ripe for scientific inquiry.

Nevertheless, many people find it disturbing that all the richness of our mental life—all our thoughts, feelings, emotions, even what we regard as our intimate selves—arises entirely from the activity of little wisps of protoplasm in the brain. How is this possible? How could something as deeply mysterious as consciousness emerge from a chunk of meat inside the skull? The problem of mind and matter, substance and spirit, illusion and reality, has been a major preoccupation of both Eastern and Western philosophy for millennia, but very little of lasting value has emerged. As the British psychologist Stuart Sutherland has said, "Consciousness is a fascinating but elusive phenomenon: it is impossible to specify what it is, what it does, or why it evolved. Nothing worth reading has been written on it."

I won't pretend to have solved these mysteries,[1] but I do think there's a new way to study consciousness by treating it not as a philosophical, logical or conceptual issue, but rather as an empirical problem.

Except for a few eccentrics (called panpsychists) who believe everything in the universe is conscious, including things like anthills, thermostats, and Formica tabletops, most people now agree that consciousness arises in brains and not in spleens, livers, pancreases or any other organ. This is already a good start. But I will narrow the scope of inquiry even further and suggest that consciousness arises not from the whole brain but rather from certain specialized brain circuits that carry out a particular style of computation. To illustrate the nature of these circuits and the special computations they perform, I'll draw from the many examples in perceptual psychology and neurology that we have already considered in this book. These examples will show that the circuitry that embodies the vivid subjective quality of consciousness resides mainly in parts of the temporal lobes (such as the amygdala, septum, hypothalamus and insular cortex) and a single projection zone in the frontal lobes—the cingulate gyrus. And the activity of these structures must fulfill three important criteria, which I call (with apologies to Isaac Newton, who described the three basic laws of physics) the "three laws of qualia" ("qualia" simply means the raw feel of sensations such as the subjective quality of "pain" or "red" or "gnocchi with truffles"). My goal in identifying these

From V.S. Ramachandran and Sandra Blakeslee, "Do Martians See Red?" In *Phantoms in the Brain: Probing the Mysteries of the Human Mind* (pp. 227–257, 296–298). New York: Quill William Morrow, 1998.

three laws and the specialized structures embodying them is to stimulate further inquiry into the biological origin of consciousness.

The central mystery of the cosmos, as far as I'm concerned, is the following: Why are there always two parallel descriptions of the universe—the first-person account ("I see red") and the third-person account ("He says that he sees red when certain pathways in his brain encounter a wavelength of six hundred nanometers")? How can these two accounts be so utterly different yet complementary? Why isn't there only a third-person account, for according to the objective worldview of the physicist and neuroscientist, that's the only one that really exists? (Scientists who hold this view are called behaviorists.) Indeed, in their scheme of "objective science," the need for a first-person account doesn't even arise—implying that consciousness simply doesn't exist. But we all know perfectly well that can't be right. I'm reminded of the old quip about the behaviorist who, just having made passionate love, looks at his lover and says, "Obviously that was good for you, dear, but was it good for me?" This need to reconcile the first-person and third-person accounts of the universe (the "I" view versus the "he" or "it" view) is the single most important unsolved problem in science. Dissolve this barrier, say the Indian mystics and sages, and you will see that the separation between self and nonself is an illusion—that you are really One with the cosmos.

Philosophers call this conundrum the riddle of *qualia* or subjective sensation. How can the flux of ions and electrical currents in little specks of jelly—the neurons in my brain—generate the whole subjective world of sensations like red, warmth, cold or pain? By what magic is matter transmuted into the invisible fabric of feelings and sensations? This problem is so puzzling that not everyone agrees it is even a problem. I will illustrate this so-called qualia riddle with two simple thought experiments of the kind that philosophers love to make up. Such whimsical pretend experiments are virtually impossible to carry out in real life. My colleague Dr. Francis Crick is deeply suspicious of thought experiments, and I agree with him that they can be very misleading because they often contain hidden question-begging assumptions. But they can be used to clarify logical points, and I will use them here to introduce the problem of qualia in a colorful way.

First, imagine that you are a future superscientist with a complete knowledge of the workings of the human brain. Unfortunately you are also completely color-blind. You don't have any cone receptors (the structures in your retina that allow your eyes to discriminate the different colors), but you do have rods (for seeing black and white), and you also have the correct machinery for processing colors higher up inside your brain. If your eyes could distinguish colors, so could your brain.

Now suppose that you, the superscientist, study my brain. I am a normal color perceiver—I can see that the sky is blue, the grass is green and a banana is yellow—and you want to know what I mean by these color terms. When I look at objects and describe them as turquoise, chartreuse or vermilion, you don't have any idea what I'm talking about. To you, they all look like shades of gray.

But you are intensely curious about the phenomenon, so you point a spectrometer at the surface of a ripe red apple. It indicates that light with a wavelength of six hundred nanometers is emanating from the fruit. But you still have no idea what *color* this might correspond to because you can't experience it. Intrigued, you study the light-sensitive pigments of my eye and the color pathways in my brain until you eventually come up with a complete description of the laws of wavelength processing. Your theory allows you to trace the entire sequence of color perception, starting from the receptors in my eye and passing all the way into my brain, where you monitor the neural activity that generates the word "red." In short, you completely understand the laws of color vision (or more strictly, the laws of wavelength processing), and you can tell me in advance which word I will use to describe the color of an apple, orange or lemon. As a superscientist, *you have no reason to doubt the completeness of your account.*

Satisfied, you approach me with your flow diagram and say, "Ramachandran, this is what's going on in your brain!"

But I must protest. "Sure, that's what's going on. But I also *see* red. Where is the red in this diagram?"

"What is that?" you ask.

"That's part of the actual, ineffable experience of the color, which I can never seem to convey to you because you're totally color-blind."

This example leads to a definition of "qualia": they are aspects of my brain state that seem to make the scientific description incomplete—from my point of view.

As a second example, imagine a species of Amazonian electric fish that is very intelligent, in fact, as intelligent and sophisticated as you or I. But it has something we lack—namely, the ability to sense electrical fields using special organs in its skin. Like the superscientist in the previous example, you can study the neurophysiology of this fish and figure out how the electrical organs on the sides of its body transduce electrical current, how this information is conveyed to the brain, what part of the brain analyzes this information and how the fish uses this information to dodge predators, find prey and so on. If the fish could talk, however, it would say, "Fine, but you'll never know what it *feels* like to sense electricity."

These examples clearly state the problem of why qualia are thought to be essentially private. They also illustrate why the problem of qualia is not necessarily a scientific problem. Recall that your *scientific* description is complete. It's just that the your account is incomplete epistemologically because the actual experience of electric fields or redness is something you never will know. For you, it will forever remain a "third-person" account.

For centuries philosophers have assumed that this gap between brain and mind poses a deep epistemological problem—a barrier that simply cannot be crossed. But is this really true? I agree that the barrier hasn't yet been crossed, but does it follow that it can *never* be crossed? I'd like to argue that there is in fact no such barrier, no great vertical divide in nature between mind and matter, substance and spirit. Indeed, I believe that this barrier is only apparent and that it arises as a result of language. This sort of obstacle emerges when there is *any translation* from one language to another.[2]

How does this idea apply to the brain and the study of consciousness? I submit that we are dealing here with two mutually unintelligible languages. One is the language of nerve impulses—the spatial and temporal patterns of neuronal activity that allow us to see red, for example. The second language, the one that allows us to communicate what we are seeing to others, is a natural spoken tongue like English or German or Japanese—rarefied, compressed waves of air traveling between you and the listener. Both are languages in the strict technical sense, that is, they are information-rich messages that are intended to convey meaning, across synapses between different brain parts in one case and across the air between two people in the other.

The problem is that I can tell you, the color-blind superscientist, about my qualia (my experience of seeing red) only by using a spoken language. But the ineffable "experience" itself is lost in the translation. The actual "redness" of red will remain forever unavailable to you.

But what if I were to skip spoken language as a medium of communication and instead hook a cable of neural pathways (taken from tissue culture or from another person) from the color-processing areas in my brain directly into the color-processing regions of your brain (remember that your brain has the machinery to see color even though your eyes cannot discriminate wavelengths because they have no color receptors)? The cable allows the color information to go straight from my brain to neurons in your brain without intermediate translation. This is a farfetched scenario, but there is nothing logically impossible about it.

Earlier when I said "red," it didn't make any sense to you because the mere use of the word "red" already involves a translation. But if you skip the translation and use a cable, so that the nerve impulses themselves go directly to the color area, then perhaps you'll say, "Oh, my God, I see exactly what you mean. I'm having this wonderful new experience."[3]

This scenario demolishes the philosophers' argument that there is an insurmountable logical barrier to understanding qualia. In principle, you *can* experience another creature's qualia, even the electric fish's. If you could find out what the electroceptive part of the fish brain is doing and if you could somehow graft it onto the relevant parts of your brain with all the proper associated connections, then you would start experiencing the fish's electrical qualia. Now, we could get into a philosophical debate over whether you need to be a *fish* to experience it or whether as a human being you could experience it, but the debate is not relevant to my argument. The logical point I am making here pertains only to the electrical qualia—not to the whole experience of being a fish.

The key idea here is that the qualia problem is not unique to the mind-body problem. It is no different in kind from problems that arise from *any* translation, and thus there is no need to invoke a great division in nature between the world of qualia and the material world. There is only one world with lots of translation barriers. If you can overcome them, the problems vanish.

This may sound like an esoteric, theoretical debate, but let me give you a more realistic example—an experiment we are actually planning to do. In the seventeenth century the English astronomer William Molyneux posed a challenge (another thought experiment). What would happen, he asked, if a child were raised in complete darkness from birth to age twenty-one and were then suddenly allowed to see a cube? Would he recognize the cube? Indeed, what would happen if the child were suddenly allowed to see ordinary daylight? Would he experience the light, saying, "Aha! I now see what people mean by light!" or would he act utterly bewildered and continue to be blind? (For the sake of argument, the philosopher assumes that the child's visual pathways have not degenerated from the deprivation and that he has an intellectual concept of seeing, just as our superscientist had an intellectual concept of color before we used the cable.)

This turns out to be a thought experiment that can actually be answered empirically. Some unfortunate individuals are born with such serious damage to their eyes that they have never seen the world and are curious about what "seeing" really is: To them it's as puzzling as the fish's electroception is to you. It's now possible to stimulate small parts of their brains directly with a device called a transcranial magnetic stimulator—an extremely powerful, fluctuating magnet that activates neural tissue with some degree of precision. What if one were to stimulate the visual cortex of such a person with magnetic pulses, thereby bypassing the nonfunctional optics of the eye? I can imagine two possible outcomes. He might say, "Hey, I feel something funny zapping the back of my head," but nothing else. Or he might say, "Oh, my God, this is extraordinary! I now understand what all of you folks are talking about. I am finally experiencing this abstract thing called vision. So this is light, this is color, this is seeing!"

This experiment is logically equivalent to the neuron cable experiment we did on the superscientist because we are bypassing spoken language and directly hitting the blind person's brain. Now you may ask, If he does experience totally novel sensations (what you and I call seeing), how can we be sure that it is in fact true vision? One way would be to look for evidence of topography in his brain. I could stimulate different parts of his visual cortex and ask him to point to various regions of the outside world where he experiences these strange new sensations. This is akin to the way you might see stars "out there" in the world when I hit you on the head with a hammer; you don't experience the stars as being inside your skull. This exercise would provide convincing evidence that he was indeed experiencing for the first time something very close to our experience of seeing, although it might not be as discriminating or sophisticated as normal seeing.[4]

•

Why did qualia—subjective sensation—emerge in evolution? Why did some brain events come to have qualia? Is there a particular *style* of information processing that produces qualia, or are there some *types* of neurons exclusively associated with qualia? (The Spanish neurologist Ramón y Cajal calls these neurons the "psychic neurons.") Just as we know that only a tiny part of the cell, namely, the deoxyribonucleic acid (DNA) molecule, is directly involved in heredity and other parts

such as proteins are not, could it be that only some neural circuits are involved in qualia and others aren't? Francis Crick and Christof Koch have made the ingenious suggestion that qualia arise from a set of neurons in the lower layers of the primary sensory areas, because these are the ones that project to the frontal lobes where many so-called higher functions are carried out. Their theory has galvanized the entire scientific community and served as a catalyst for those seeking biological explanations for qualia. Others have suggested that the actual patterns of nerve impulses (spikes) from widely separated brain regions become "synchronized" when you pay attention to something and become aware of it.[5] In other words, it is the synchronization itself that leads to conscious awareness. There's no direct evidence for this yet, but it's encouraging to see that people are at least trying to explore the question experimentally.

These approaches are attractive for one main reason, namely, the fact that reductionism has been the single most successful strategy in science. As the English biologist Peter Medawar defines it, "Reductionism is the belief that a whole may be represented as a function (in the mathematical sense) of its constituent parts, the functions having to do with the spatial and temporal ordering of the parts and with the precise way in which they interact." Unfortunately, as I stated at the beginning of this book, it's not always easy to know a priori what the appropriate level of reductionism is for any given scientific problem. For understanding consciousness and qualia there wouldn't be much point in looking at ion channels that conduct nerve impulses, at the brain stem reflex that mediates sneezing or at the spinal cord reflex arc that controls the bladder, even though these are interesting problems in themselves (at least to some people). They would be no more useful in understanding higher brain functions like qualia than looking at silicon chips in a microscope in an attempt to understand the logic of a computer program. And yet this is precisely the strategy most neuroscientists use in trying to understand the higher functions of the brain. They argue either that the problem doesn't exist or that it will be solved some fine day as we plod along looking at the activity of individual neurons.[6]

Philosophers offer another solution to this dilemma when they say that consciousness and qualia are "epiphenomena." According to this view, consciousness is like the whistling sound that a train makes or the shadow of a horse as it runs: It plays no causal role in the real work done by the brain. After all, you can imagine a "zombie" unconsciously doing everything in exactly the same manner that a conscious being does. A sharp tap on the tendon near your knee joint sets in motion a cascade of neural and chemical events that causes a reflex knee jerk (stretch receptors in the knee connect to nerves in the spinal cord, which in turn send messages to the muscles). Consciousness doesn't enter into this picture; a paraplegic has an excellent knee jerk even though he can't feel the tap. Now imagine a much more complex cascade of events starting with long-wavelength light striking your retina and various relays, leading to your saying "red." Since you can imagine this more complex cascade happening without conscious awareness, doesn't it follow that consciousness is irrelevant to the whole scheme? After all, God (or natural selection) could have created an unconscious being that does and says all the things you do, even though "it" is not conscious.

This argument sounds reasonable but in fact it is based on the fallacy that because you can imagine something to be logically possible, therefore it is actually possible. But consider the same argument applied to a problem in physics. We can all imagine something traveling faster than the speed of light. But as Einstein tells us, this "commonsense" view is wrong. Simply being able to imagine that something is logically possible does not guarantee its possibility in the real world, even in principle. Likewise, even though you can imagine an unconscious zombie doing everything you can do, there may be some deep natural cause that prevents the existence of such a being! Notice that this argument does not prove that consciousness must have a causal role; it simply proves that you cannot use statements that begin, "After all, I can imagine" to draw conclusions about any natural phenomenon.

I would like to try a somewhat different approach to understanding qualia, which I will introduce by asking you to play some games with your eyes. First, recall the discussion in Chapter 5 concerning the so-called blind spot—the place where your optic nerve exits the back of your eyeball. Again, if you close your right eye, fix your gaze on the black spot in Figure 5.2 and slowly move the page toward or away from your eye, you will see that the hatched disk disappears. It has fallen into your natural blind spot. Now close your right eye again, hold up the index finger of your right hand and aim your left eye's blind spot at the middle of your extended finger. The middle of the finger *should* disappear, just as the hatched disk does, and yet it doesn't; it looks continuous. In other words, the qualia are such that you do not merely *deduce* intellectually that the finger is continuous—"After all, my blind spot is there"—you literally *see* the "missing piece" of your finger. Psychologists

call this phenomenon "filling in," a useful if somewhat misleading phrase that simply means that you see something in a region of space where nothing exists.

This phenomenon can be demonstrated even more dramatically if you look at Figure 37.1. Again, with your right eye shut look at the small white dot on the right with your left eye and gradually move the book toward you until one of the "doughnuts" falls on your blind spot. Since the inner diameter of the doughnut—the small black disk—is slightly smaller than your blind spot, it should disappear and the white ring should encompass the blind spot. Say the doughnut (the ring) is yellow. What you will see if your vision is normal is a complete yellow homogeneous disk, which will indicate that your brain "filled in" your blind spot with yellow qualia (or white in Figure 37.1). I emphasize this because some people have argued that we all simply ignore the blind spot and don't notice what's going on, meaning that there really is no filling in. But this can't be right. If you show someone several rings, one of which is concentric with the blind spot, that concentric one will look like a homogeneous disk and will actually "pop out" perceptually against a background of rings. How can something you are ignoring pop out at you? This means that the blind spot does have qualia associated with it and, moreover, that the qualia can provide actual "sensory support." In other words, you don't merely deduce that the center of the doughnut is yellow; you literally *see* it as yellow.[7]

Now consider a related example. Suppose I put one finger crosswise in front of another finger (as in a plus sign) and look at the two fingers. Of course, I see the finger in the back as being continuous. I know it's continuous. I sort of see it as continuous. But if you asked me whether I *literally see* the missing piece of finger, I would say no—for all I know, someone could have actually sliced two pieces of finger and put them on either side of the finger in front to fool me. I cannot be certain that I really see that missing part.

Compare these two cases, which are similar in that the brain supplies the missing information both times. What's the difference? What does it matter to you, the conscious person, that the yellow doughnut now has qualia in the middle and that the occluded part of your finger does not? The difference is that *you cannot change your mind* about the yellow in the middle of the doughnut. You can't think, "Maybe it's yellow, but maybe it's pink, or maybe it's blue." No, it's shouting at you, "I am yellow," with an explicit representation of yellowness in its center. In other words, the filled-in yellow is not revocable, not changeable by you.

In the case of the occluded finger, however, you can

FIGURE 37.1   A field of yellow doughnuts (shown in white here). Shut your right eye and look at the small white dot near the middle of the illustration with your left eye. When the page is about six to nine inches from your face, one of the doughnuts will fall exactly around your left eye's blind spot. Since the black hole in the center of the doughnut is slightly smaller than your blind spot, it should disappear and the blind spot then is "filled in" with yellow (white) qualia from the ring so that you see a yellow disk rather than a ring. Notice that the disk "pops out" conspicuously against the background of rings. Paradoxically, you have made a target more conspicuous by virtue of your blind spot. If the illusion doesn't work, try using an enlarged photocopy and shifting the white dot horizontally.

think, "There's a high probability that there is a finger there, but some malicious scientist could have pasted two half fingers on either side of it." This scenario is highly improbable, but not inconceivable.

In other words, I can choose to assume that there might be something else behind the occluding finger, but I cannot do so with the filled-in yellow of the blind spot. Thus the crucial difference between a qualia-laden perception and one that doesn't have qualia is that the qualia-laden perception is irrevocable by higher brain centers and is therefore "tamper-resistant," whereas the one that lacks qualia is flexible; you can choose any one of a number of different "pretend" inputs using your imagination. Once a qualia-laden perception has been created, you're stuck with it. (A good example of this is the dalmatian dog in Figure 37.2. Initially, as you look, it's all fragments. Then suddenly everything clicks and you see the dog. Loosely speaking, you've now got the dog qualia. The next time you see it, there's no way you can avoid seeing the dog. Indeed, we have recently shown that neurons in the brain have permanently altered their connections once you have seen the dog.)[8]

These examples demonstrate an important feature of qualia—it must be irrevocable. But although this feature is necessary, it's not sufficient to explain the presence of qualia. Why? Well, imagine that you are in a coma and I shine a light into your eye. If the coma is not too deep, your pupil will constrict, even though you will have no subjective awareness of any qualia caused by the light. The entire reflex arc is irrevocable, and yet there are no qualia associated with it. You can't change your mind about it. You can't do anything about it, just as you couldn't do anything about the yellow filling in your blind spot in the doughnut example. So why does only the latter have qualia? The key difference is that in the case of the pupil's constriction, there is only one output—one final outcome—available and hence no qualia. In the case of the yellow disk, even though the representation that was created is irrevocable, you have the luxury of a choice; what you can do with the representation is open-ended. For instance, when you experienced yellow qualia, you could say yellow, or you could think of yellow bananas, yellow teeth, the yellow skin of jaundice and so on. And when you finally saw the dalmatian,

FIGURE 37.2 Random jumble of splotches. Gaze at this picture for a few seconds (or minutes) and you will eventually see a dalmatian dog sniffing the ground mottled with shadows of leaves (hint: the dog's face is at the left toward the middle of the picture; you can see its collar and left ear). Once the dog has been seen, it is impossible to get rid of it. Using similar pictures, we showed recently that neurons in the temporal lobes become altered permanently after the initial brief exposure—once you have "seen" the dog (Tovee, Rolls and Ramachandran, 1996). Dalmatian dog photographed by Ron James.

your mind would be poised to conjure up any one of an infinite set of dog-related associations—the word "dog," the dog's bark, dog food or even fire engines. And there is apparently no limit to what you can choose. This is the second important feature of qualia: Sensations that are qualia-laden afford the luxury of choice. So now we have identified *two* functional features of qualia: irrevocability on the input side and flexibility on the output side.

There is a third important feature of qualia. In order to make decisions on the basis of a qualia-laden representation, the representation needs to exist long enough

for you to work with it. Your brain needs to hold the representation in an intermediate buffer or in so-called immediate memory. (For example, you hold the phone number you get from the information operator just long enough to dial it with your fingers.) Again this condition is not enough in itself to generate qualia. A biological system can have other reasons, besides making a choice, for holding information in a buffer. For example, Venus's-flytrap snaps shut only if its trigger hairs inside the trap are stimulated twice in succession, apparently retaining a memory of the first stimulus and comparing it with the second to "infer" that something has moved.

(Darwin suggested that this evolved to help the plant avoid inadvertently shutting the trap if hit by a dust particle rather than a bug.) Typically in these sorts of cases, there is only one output possible: Venus's-flytrap *invariably* closes shut. There's nothing else it can do. The second important feature of qualia—choice—is missing. I think we can safely conclude, contrary to the panpsychists, that the plant does not have qualia linked to bug detection.

In Chapter 4, we saw how qualia and memory are connected in the story of Denise, the young woman living in Italy who suffered carbon monoxide poisoning and developed an unusual kind of "blindsight." Recall that she could correctly rotate an envelope to post it in a horizontal or a vertical slot, even though she could not consciously perceive the slot's orientation. But if someone asked Denise first to look at the slot and then turned off the lights before asking her to post the letter, she could no longer do so. "She" seemed to forget the orientation of the slot almost immediately and was unable to insert the letter. This suggests that the part of Denise's visual system that discerned orientation and controlled her arm movements—what we call the zombie or the how pathway in Chapter 4—not only was devoid of qualia, but also lacked short-term memory. But the part of her visual system—the what pathway—that would normally enable her to recognize the slot and perceive its orientation is not only conscious, it also has memory. (But "she" cannot use the what pathway because it is damaged; all that's available is the unconscious zombie and "it" doesn't have memory.) And I don't think this link between short-term memory and conscious awareness is coincidental.

Why does one part of the visual stream have memory and another not have it? It may be that the qualia-laden what system has memory because it is involved in making choices based on perceptual representations—and choice requires time. The how system without qualia, on the other hand, engages in continuous real-time processing running in a tightly closed loop—like the thermostat in your house. It does not need memory because it is not involved in making real choices. Thus simply posting the letter does not require memory, but choosing which letter to post and deciding where to mail it do require memory.

This idea can be tested in a patient like Denise. If you set up a situation in which she was forced to make a *choice,* the zombie system (still intact in her) should go haywire. For example, if you asked Denise to mail a letter and you showed her two slots (one vertical, one horizontal) simultaneously, she should fail, for how could

the zombie system choose between the two? Indeed, the very idea of an unconscious zombie making choices seems oxymoronic—for doesn't the very existence of free will imply consciousness?

To summarize thus far—for qualia to exist, you need potentially infinite implications (bananas, jaundice, teeth) but a stable, finite, irrevocable representation in your short-term memory as a starting point (yellow). But if the starting point is revocable, then the representation will not have strong, vivid qualia. Good examples of the latter are a cat that you "infer" under the sofa when you only see its tail sticking out, or your ability to imagine that there is a monkey sitting on that chair. These do not have strong qualia, for good reason, because if they did you would confuse them with real objects and wouldn't be able to survive long, given the way your cognitive system is structured. I repeat what Shakespeare said: "You cannot cloy the hungry edge of appetite by bare imagination of a feast." Very fortunate, for otherwise you wouldn't eat; you would just generate the qualia associated with satiety in your head. In a similar vein, any creature that simply imagines having orgasms is unlikely to pass on its genes to the next generation.

Why don't these faint, internally generated images (the cat under the couch, the monkey in the chair) or beliefs, for that matter, have strong qualia? Imagine how confusing the world would be if they did. Actual perceptions need to have vivid, subjective qualia because they are driving decisions and you cannot afford to hesitate. Beliefs and internal images, on the other hand, should not be qualia-laden because they need to be tentative and revocable. So you believe—and you can imagine—that under the table there is a cat because you see a tail sticking out. But there *could* be a pig under the table with a transplanted cat's tail. You must be willing to entertain that hypothesis, however implausible, because every now and then you might be surprised.

What is the functional or computational advantage to making qualia irrevocable? One answer is stability. If you constantly changed your mind about qualia, the number of potential outcomes (or "outputs") would be infinite; nothing would constrain your behavior. At some point you need to say "this is it" and plant a flag on it, and it's the planting of the flag that we call qualia. The perceptual system follows a rationale something like this: Given the available information, it is 90 percent certain that what you are seeing is yellow (or dog or pain or whatever). Therefore, for the sake of argument, I'll assume that it *is* yellow and act accordingly, because if I keep saying, "Maybe it's not yellow," I won't be able to take the next step of choosing an appropriate course of action or thought. In other words, if I treated perceptions as beliefs, I would be blind (as well as being paralyzed with indecision). Qualia are irrevocable *in order to eliminate hesitation and to confer certainty* to decisions.[9] And this, in turn, may depend on which particular neurons are firing, how strongly they're firing and what structures they project to.

•

When I see the cat's tail sticking out from under the table, I "guess" or "know" there is a cat under the table, presumably attached to the tail. But I don't literally see the cat, even though I literally see the tail. And this raises another fascinating question: Are seeing and knowing—the qualitative distinction between perception and conception—completely different, mediated by different types of brain circuitry perhaps, or is there a gray area in between? Let's go back to the region corresponding to the blind spot in my eye, where I can't see anything. As we saw in the Chapter 5 discussion on Charles Bonnet syndrome, there is another kind of blind spot—the enormous region behind my head—where I also can't see anything (although people don't generally use the term "blind spot" for this region). Of course, ordinarily you don't walk around experiencing a huge gap behind your head, and therefore you might be tempted to jump to the conclusion that you are in some sense filling in the gap in the same way that you fill in the blind spot. But you don't. You can't. There is no visual neural representation in the brain corresponding to this area behind your head. You fill it in only in the trivial sense that if you are standing in a bathroom with wallpaper in front of you, you assume that the wallpaper continues behind your head. But even though you assume that there is wallpaper behind your head, you don't literally see it. In other words, this sort of "filling in" is purely metaphorical and does not fulfill our criterion of being irrevocable. In the case of the "real" blind spot, as we saw earlier, you can't change your mind about the area that has been filled in. But regarding the region behind your head, you are free to think, "In all likelihood there is wall-paper there, but who knows, maybe there is an elephant there."

Filling in of the blind spot is therefore fundamentally different from your failure to notice the gap behind your head. But the question remains, Is the distinction between what is going on behind your head and the blind spot qualitative or quantitative? Is the dividing line between "filling in" (of the kind seen in the blind spot) and mere guesswork (for things that might be behind your

head) completely arbitrary? To answer this, consider another thought experiment. Imagine we continue evolving in such a way that our eyes migrate toward the sides of our heads, while preserving the binocular visual field. The fields of view of the two eyes encroach farther and farther behind our heads until they are almost touching. At that point let's assume you have a blind spot behind your head (between your eyes) that is identical in size to the blind spot that is in front of you. The question then arises, Would the completion of objects across the blind spot behind your head be true filling in of qualia, as with the real blind spot, or would it still be conceptual, revocable imagery or guesswork of the kind that you and I experience behind our heads? I think that there will be a definite point when the images become irrevocable, and when robust perceptual representations are created, perhaps even re-created and fed back to the early visual areas. At that point the blind region behind your head becomes functionally equivalent to the normal blind spot in front of you. The brain will then suddenly switch to a completely novel mode of representing the information; it will use neurons in the sensory areas to signal the events behind your head irrevocably (instead of neurons in the thinking areas to make educated but tentative guesses as to what might be lurking there).

Thus even though blind-spot completion and completion behind your head can be logically regarded as two ends of a continuum, evolution has seen fit to separate them. In the case of your eye's blind spot, the chance that something significant is lurking there is small enough that it pays simply to treat the chance as zero. In the case of the blind area behind your head, however, the odds of something important being there (like a burglar holding a gun) are high enough that it would be dangerous to fill in this area irrevocably with wallpaper or whatever pattern is in front of your eyes.

•

So far we have talked about three laws of qualia—three logical criteria for determining whether a system is conscious or not—and we have considered examples from the blind spot and from neurological patients. But you may ask, How general is this principle? Can we apply it to other specific instances when there is a debate or doubt about whether consciousness is involved? Here are some examples:

It's known that bees engage in very elaborate forms of communication including the so-called bee waggle dance. A scout bee, having located a source of pollen, will travel back to the hive and perform an elaborate dance to designate the location of the pollen to the rest of the hive. The question arises, Is the bee conscious when it's doing this?[10] Since the bee's behavior, once set in motion, is irrevocable and since the bee is obviously acting on some short-term memory representation of the pollen's location, at least two of the three criteria for consciousness are met. You might then jump to the conclusion that the bee is conscious when it engages in this elaborate communication ritual. But since the bee lacks the third criterion—flexible output—I would argue that it is a zombie. In other words, even though the information is very elaborate, is irrevocable and held in short-term memory, the bee can only do one thing with that information; only one output is possible—the waggle dance. This argument is important, for it implies that mere complexity or elaborateness of information processing is no guarantee that there is consciousness involved.

One advantage my scheme has over other theories of consciousness is that it allows us unambiguously to answer such questions as, Is a bee conscious when it performs a waggle dance? Is a sleepwalker conscious? Is the spinal cord of a paraplegic conscious—does it have its own sexual qualia—when he (it) has an erection? Is an ant conscious when it detects pheromones? In each of these cases, instead of the vague assertion that one is dealing with various degrees of consciousness—which is the standard answer—one should simply apply the three criteria specified. For example, can a sleepwalker (while he's sleepwalking) take the "Pepsi test"—that is, choose between a Pepsi Cola and a Coca Cola? Does he have short-term memory? If you showed him the Pepsi, put it in a box, switched off the room lights for thirty seconds and then switched them on again, would he reach for the Pepsi (or utterly fail like the zombie in Diane)? Does a partially comatose patient with akinetic mutism (seemingly awake and able to follow you with his eyes but unable to move or talk) have short-term memory? We can now answer these questions and avoid endless semantic quibbles over the exact meaning of the word "consciousness."

•

Now you might ask, "Does any of this yield clues as to where in the brain qualia might be?" It is surprising that many people think that the seat of consciousness is the frontal lobes, because nothing dramatic happens to qualia and consciousness per se if you damage the frontal lobes—even though the patient's personality can be profoundly altered (and he may have difficulty switching attention). I would suggest instead that most of the action is in the temporal lobes because lesions and hyperactivity in these structures are what most often produce striking disturbances in consciousness. For instance, you need the amygdala and other parts of the temporal lobes for seeing the significance of things, and surely this is a vital part of conscious experience. Without this structure you are a zombie (like the fellow in the famous Chinese room thought experiment proposed by the philosopher John Searle[11]) capable only of giving a single correct output in response to a demand, but with no ability to sense the meaning of what you are doing or saying.

Everyone would agree that qualia and consciousness are not associated with the early stages of perceptual processing as at the level of the retina. Nor are they associated with the final stages of planning motor acts when behavior is actually carried out. They are associated, instead, with the intermediate stages of processing[12]—a stage where stable perceptual representations are created (yellow, dog, monkey) and that have meaning (the infinite implications and possibilities for action from which you can choose the best one). This happens mainly in the temporal lobe and associated limbic structures, and, in this sense, the temporal lobes are the interface between perception and action.

The evidence for this comes from neurology; brain lesions that produce the most profound disturbances in consciousness are those that generate temporal lobe seizures, whereas lesions in other parts of the brain only produce minor disturbances in consciousness. When surgeons electrically stimulate the temporal lobes of epileptics, the patients have vivid conscious experiences. Stimulating the amygdala is the surest way to "replay" a full experience, such as an autobiographical memory or a vivid hallucination. Temporal lobe seizures are often associated not only with alterations in consciousness in the sense of personal identity, personal destiny and personality, but also with vivid qualia—hallucinations such as smells and sounds. If these are mere memories, as some claim, why would the person say, "I literally feel like I'm reliving it"? These seizures are characterized by the vividness of the qualia they produce. The smells, pains, tastes and emotional feelings—all generated in the temporal lobes—suggest that this brain region is intimately involved in qualia and conscious awareness.

Another reason for choosing the temporal lobes—especially the left one—is that this is where much of language is represented. If I see an apple, temporal lobe activity allows me to apprehend all its implications almost simultaneously. Recognition of it as a fruit of a certain type occurs in the inferotemporal cortex, the amygdala gauges the apple's significance for my well-being and Wernicke's and other areas alert me to all the nuances of meaning that the mental image—including the word "apple"—evokes; I can eat the apple, I can smell it; I can bake a pie, remove its pith, plant its seeds; use it to "keep the doctor away," tempt Eve and on and on. If one enumerates all of the attributes that we usually associate with the words "consciousness" and "awareness," each of them, you will notice, has a correlate in temporal lobe seizures, including vivid visual and auditory hallucinations, "out of body" experiences and an absolute sense of omnipotence or omniscience.[13] Any one of this long list of disturbances in conscious experience can occur individually when other parts of the brain are damaged (for instance, disturbances of body image and attention in parietal lobe syndrome), but it's only when the temporal lobes are involved that they occur simultaneously or in different combinations; that again suggests that these structures play a central role in human consciousness.

•

Until now we have discussed what philosophers call the "qualia" problem—the essential privacy and non-communicability of mental states—and I've tried to transform it from a philosophical problem into a scientific one. But in addition to qualia (the "raw feel" of sensations), we also have to consider the self—the "I" inside you who actually experiences these qualia. Qualia and self are really two sides of the same coin; obviously there is no such thing as free-floating qualia not experienced by anyone and it's hard to imagine a self devoid of all qualia.

But what exactly is the self? Unfortunately, the word "self" is like the word "happiness" or "love"; we all know what it is and know that it's real, but it's very hard to define it or even to pinpoint its characteristics. As with quicksilver, the more you try to grasp it the more it tends to slip away. When you think of the word "self," what pops into your mind? When I think about "myself," it seems to be something that unites all my diverse sensory impressions and memories (unity), claims to be "in charge" of my life, makes choices (has free will) and seems to endure as a single entity in space and time. It also sees itself as embedded in a social context, balancing its checkbook and maybe even planning its own funeral. Actually we can make a list of all the characteristics of the "self"—just as we can for happiness—and then look for brain structures that are involved in each of these aspects. Doing this will someday enable us to de-

velop a clearer understanding of self and consciousness—although I doubt that there will be a single, grand, climactic "solution" to the problem of the self in the way that DNA is the solution to the riddle of heredity.

What are these characteristics that define the self? William Hirstein, a postdoctoral fellow in my lab, and I came up with the following list:

The embodied self: My Self is anchored within a single body. If I close my eyes, I have a vivid sense of different body parts occupying space (some parts more felt than others)—the so-called body image. If you pinch my toe, it is "I" who experiences the pain, not "it." And yet the body image, as we have seen, is extremely malleable, despite all its appearance of stability. With a few seconds of the right type of sensory stimulation, you can make your nose three feet long or project your hand onto a table (Chapter 3)! And we know that circuits in the parietal lobes, and the regions of the frontal lobes to which they project, are very much involved in constructing this image. Partial damage to these structures can cause gross distortions in body image; the patient may say that her left arm belongs to her mother or (as in the case of the patient I saw with Dr. Riita Hari in Helsinki) claim that the left half of her body is still sitting in the chair when she gets up and walks! If these examples don't convince you that your "ownership" of your body is an illusion, then nothing will.

The passionate self: It is difficult to imagine the self without emotions—or what such a state could even mean. If you don't see the meaning or significance of something—if you cannot apprehend all its implications—in what sense are you really aware of it consciously? Thus your emotions—mediated by the limbic system and amygdala—are an essential aspect of self, not just a "bonus." (It is a moot point whether a pure-bred Vulcan, like Spock's father in the original *Star Trek,* is really conscious or whether he is just a zombie—unless he is also tainted by a few human genes as Spock is.) Recall that the "zombie" in the "how" pathway is unconscious, whereas the "what" pathway is conscious, and I suggest that the difference arises because only the latter is linked to the amygdala and other limbic structures (Chapter 5).

The amygdala and the rest of the limbic system (in the temporal lobes) ensures that the cortex—indeed, the entire brain—serves the organism's basic evolutionary goals. The amygdala monitors the highest level of perceptual representations and "has its fingers on the keyboard of the autonomic nervous system"; it determines whether or not to respond emotionally to something and what kinds of emotions are appropriate (fear in response to a snake or rage to your boss and affection to your child). It also receives information from the insular cortex, which in turn is driven partially by sensory input not only from the skin but also from the viscera—heart, lung, liver, stomach—so that one can also speak of a "visceral, vegetative self" or of a "gut reaction" to something. (It is this "gut reaction," of course, that one monitors with the GSR machine, as we showed in Chapter 9, so that you could argue that the visceral self isn't, strictly speaking, part of the conscious self at all. But it can nevertheless profoundly intrude on your conscious self; just think of the last time you felt nauseous and threw up.)

Pathologies of the emotional self include temporal lobe epilepsy, Capgras' syndrome and Klüver-Bucy syndrome. In the first, there may be a heightened sense of self that may arise partly through a process that Paul Fedio and D. Bear call "hyperconnectivity"—a strengthening of connections between the sensory areas of the temporal cortex and the amygdala. Such hyperconnectivity may result from repeated seizures that cause a permanent enhancement (kindling) of these pathways, leading the patient to ascribe deep significance to everything around him (including himself!). Conversely, people with Capgras' syndrome have reduced emotional response to certain categories of objects (faces) and people with Klüver-Bucy or Cotard's syndrome have more pervasive problems with emotions (Chapter 8). A Cotard's patient feels so emotionally remote from the world and from himself that he will actually make the absurd claim that he is dead or that he can smell his flesh rotting.

Interestingly, what we call "personality"—a vital aspect of your self that endures for life and is notoriously impervious to "correction" by other people or even by common sense—probably also involves the very same limbic structures and their connections with the ventromedial frontal lobes. Damage to the frontal lobes produces no obvious, immediate disturbance in consciousness, but it can profoundly alter your personality. When a crowbar pierced the frontal lobes of a railway worker named Phineas Gage, his close friends and relatives remarked, "Gage wasn't Gage anymore." In this famous example of frontal lobe damage, Gage was transformed from a stable, polite, hardworking young man into a lying, cheating vagabond who could not hold down a job.[14]

Temporal lobe epilepsy patients like Paul in Chapter 9 also show striking personality changes, so much so that some neurologists speak of a "temporal lobe epilepsy personality." Some of them (the patients, not the neurologists) tend to be pedantic, argumentative, egocentric

and garrulous. They also tend to be obsessed with "abstract thoughts." If these traits are a result of hyperfunctioning of certain parts of the temporal lobe, what exactly is the normal function of these areas? If the limbic system is concerned mainly with emotions, why would seizures in these areas cause a tendency to generate abstract thought? Are there areas in our brains whose role is to produce and manipulate abstract thoughts? This is one of the many unsolved problems of temporal lobe epilepsy.

The executive self: Classical physics and modern neuroscience tell us that you (including your mind and brain) inhabit a deterministic billiard ball universe. But you don't ordinarily experience yourself as a puppet on a string; you feel that you are in charge. Yet paradoxically, it is always obvious to you that there are some things you can do and others you cannot given the constraints of your body and of the external world. (You know you can't lift a truck; you know you can't give your boss a black eye, even if you'd like to.) Somewhere in your brain there are *representations* of all these possibilities, and the systems that plan commands (the cingulate and supplementary motor areas in the frontal lobes) need to be aware of this distinction between things they can and cannot command you to do. Indeed, a "self" that sees itself as completely passive, as a helpless spectator, is no self at all, and a self that is hopelessly driven to action by its impulses and urgings is equally effete. A self needs free will—what Deepak Chopra calls "the universal field of infinite possibilities"—even to exist. More technically, conscious awareness has been described as a "conditional readiness to act."

To achieve all this, I need to have in my brain not only a representation of the world and various objects in it but also a representation of myself, including my own body within that representation—and it is this peculiar recursive aspect of the self that makes it so puzzling. In addition, the representation of the external object has to interact with my self-representation (including the motor command systems) in order to allow me to make a choice. (He's your boss; don't sock him. It's a cookie; it's within your reach to grab it.) Derangements in this mechanism can lead to syndromes like anosognosia or somatoparaphrenia (Chapter 7) in which a patient will with a perfectly straight face claim that her left arm belongs to her brother or to the physician.

What neural structure is involved in representing these "embodied" and "executive" aspects of the self? Damage to the anterior cingulate gyrus results in a bizarre condition called "akinetic mutism"—the patient simply lies in bed unwilling to do or incapable of doing anything even though he appears to be fully aware of his surroundings. If there's such a thing as absence of free will, this is it.

Sometimes when there is partial damage to the anterior cingulate, the very opposite happens: The patient's hand is uncoupled from her conscious thoughts and intentions and attempts to grab things or even perform relatively complex actions without her permission. For example, Dr. Peter Halligan and I saw a patient at Rivermead Hospital in Oxford whose left hand would seize the banister as she walked down the steps and she would have to use her other hand forcibly to unclench the fingers one by one, so she could continue walking. Is the alien left hand controlled by an unconscious zombie, or is it controlled by parts of her brain that have qualia and consciousness? We can now answer this by applying our three criteria. Does the system in her brain that moves her arm create an irrevocable representation? Does it have short-term memory? Can it make a choice?

Both the executive self and the embodied self are deployed while you are playing chess and assume you're the queen as you plan "her" next move. When you do this, you can almost feel momentarily that you are inhabiting the queen. Now one could argue that you're just using a figure of speech here, that you're not literally assimilating the chess piece into your body image. But can you really be all that sure that the loyalty of your mind to your *own* body is not equally a "figure of speech"? What would happen to your GSR if I suddenly punched the queen? Would it shoot up as though I were punching your own body? If so, what is the justification for a hard-and-fast distinction between her body and yours? Could it be that your tendency normally to identify with your "own" body rather than with the chess piece is also a matter of convention, albeit an enduring one? Might such a mechanism also underlie the empathy and love you feel for a close friend, a spouse or a child who is literally made from your own body?

The mnemonic self: Your sense of personal identity—as a single person who endures through space and time—depends on a long string of highly personal recollections: your autobiography. Organizing these memories into a coherent story is obviously vital to the construction of self.

We know that the hippocampus is required for acquiring and consolidating new memory traces. If you lost your hippocampi ten years ago, then you will not have any memories of events that occurred after that date. You are still fully conscious, of course, because you have all the memories prior to that loss, but in a very real sense your existence was frozen at that time.

Profound derangement to the mnemonic self can lead to multiple personality disorder or MPD. This disorder is best regarded as a malfunction of the same coherencing principle I alluded to in the discussion of denial in Chapter 7. As we saw, if you have two sets of mutually incompatible beliefs and memories about yourself, the only way to prevent anarchy and endless strife may be to create two personalities within one body—the so-called multiple personality disorder. Given the obvious relevance of this syndrome to understanding the nature of self, it is astonishing how little attention it has received from mainstream neurology.

Even the mysterious trait called hypergraphia—the tendency of temporal lobe epilepsy patients to maintain elaborate diaries—may be an exaggeration of the same general tendency: the need to create and sustain a coherent worldview or autobiography. Perhaps kindling in the amygdala causes every external event and internal belief to acquire deep significance for the patient, so there is an enormous proliferation of spuriously self-relevant beliefs and memories in his brain. Add to this the compelling need we all have from time to time to take stock of our lives, see where we stand; to review the significant episodes of our lives periodically—and you have hypergraphia, an exaggeration of this natural tendency. We all have random thoughts during our day-to-day musings, but if these were sometimes accompanied by miniseizures—producing euphoria—then the musings themselves might evolve into obsessions and entrenched beliefs that the patient would keep returning to whether in his speech or in his writing. Could similar phenomena provide a neural basis for zealotry and fanatacism?

The unified self—imposing coherence on consciousness, filling in and confabulation: Another important attribute of self is its unity—the internal coherence of its different attributes. One way to approach the question of how our account of qualia relates to the question of the self is to ask why something like filling in of the blind spot with qualia occurs. The original motive many philosophers had for arguing that the blind spot is *not* filled in was that there is no person in the brain to fill it in for—that no little homunculus is watching.

Since there's no little man, they argued, the antecedent is also false: Qualia are not filled in, and thinking so is a logical fallacy. Since I argue that qualia are in fact filled in, does this mean that I believe they are filled in for a homunculus? Of course not. The philosopher's argument is really a straw man. The line of reasoning should run, If qualia are filled in, they are filled in for *something* and what is that "something"? There exists in certain branches of psychology the notion of an executive, or a control process, which is generally thought to be located in the prefrontal and frontal parts of the brain. I would like to suggest that the "something" that qualia are filled in for is not a "thing" but simply another brain process, namely, executive processes associated with the limbic system including parts of the anterior cingulate gyrus. This process connects your perceptual qualia with specific emotions and goals, enabling you to make choices—very much the sort of thing that the self was traditionally supposed to do. (For example, after having lots of tea, I have the sensation or urge—the qualia—to urinate but I'm giving a lecture so I choose to delay action until the talk is finished but also choose to excuse myself at the end instead of taking questions.) An executive process is not something that has all the properties of a full human being, of course. It is not a homunculus. Rather, it is a process whereby some brain areas such as those concerned with perception and motivation influence the activities of other brain areas such as ones dealing with the planning of motor output.

Seen this way, filling in is a kind of treating and "preparing" of qualia to enable them to interact properly with limbic executive structures. Qualia may need to be filled in because gaps interfere with the proper working of these executive structures, reducing their efficiency and their ability to select an appropriate response. Like our general who ignores gaps in data given to him by scouts to avoid making a wrong decision, the control structure also finds a way to avoid gaps—by filling them in.[15]

Where in the limbic system are these control processes? It might be a system involving the amygdala and the anterior cingulate gyrus, given the amygdala's central role in emotion and the anterior cingulate's apparent executive role. We know that when these structures are disconnected, disorders of "free will" occur, such as akinetic mutism[16] and alien hand syndrome. It is not difficult to see how such processes could give rise to the mythology of a self as an active presence in the brain—a "ghost in the machine."

The vigilant self: A vital clue to the neural circuitry underlying qualia and consciousness comes from two other neurological disorders—penduncular hallucinosis and "vigilant coma" or akinetic mutism.

The anterior cingulate and other limbic structures also receive projections from the intralaminar thalamic nuclei (cells in the thalamus), which in turn are driven by clusters of cells in the brain stem (including the cholinergic lateral tegmental cells and the pendunculo-pontine cells). Hyperactivity of these cells can lead to visual hallucinations (penduncular hallucinosis), and we

also know that schizophrenics have a doubling of cell number in these very same brain stem nuclei—which may contribute to their hallucinations.

Conversely, damage to the intralaminar nucleus or to the anterior cingulate results in coma vigilance or akinetic mutism. Patients with this curious disorder are immobile and mute and react sluggishly, if at all, to painful stimuli. Yet they are apparently awake and alert, moving their eyes around and tracking objects. When the patient comes out of this state, he may say, "No words or thoughts would come to my mind. I just didn't want to do or think or say anything." (This raises a fascinating question: Can a brain stripped of all motivation record any memories at all? If so, how much detail does the patient remember? Does he recall the neurologist's pinprick? Or the cassette tape that his girlfriend played for him?) Clearly these brain stem and thalamic circuits play an important role in consciousness and qualia. But it remains to be seen whether they merely play a "supportive" role for qualia (as indeed the liver and heart do!) or whether they are an integral part of the circuitry that embodies qualia and consciousness. Are they analogous to the power supply of a VCR or TV set or to the actual magnetic recording head and the electron gun in the cathode-ray tube?

The conceptual self and the social self: In a sense, our concept of self is not fundamentally different from any other abstract concept we have—such as "happiness" or "love." Therefore, a careful examination of the different ways in which we use the word "I" in ordinary social discourse can provide some clues as to what the self is and what its function might be.

For instance, it is clear that the abstract self-concept also needs to have access to the "lower" parts of the system, so that the person can acknowledge or claim responsibility for different self-related facts: states of the body, body movements and so on (just as you claim to "control" your thumb when hitching a ride but not your knee when I tap the tendon with my rubber hammer). Information in autobiographical memory and information about one's body image need to be accessible to the self-concept, so that thought and talk about self are possible. In the normal brain there are specialized pathways that allow such access to occur, but when one or more of these pathways is damaged, the system tries to do it anyway, and confabulation results. For instance, in the denial syndrome discussed in Chapter 7, there is no access channel between information about the left side of the body and the patient's self-concept. But the self-concept is set up to try automatically to include that information. The net result of this is anosognosia or denial syndrome;

the self "assumes" that the arm is okay and "fills in" the movements of that arm.

One of the attributes of the self-representation system is that the person will confabulate to try to cover up deficits in it. The main purposes of doing this, as we saw in Chapter 7, are to prevent constant indecisiveness and to confer stability on behavior. But another important function may be to support the sort of created or narrative self that the philosopher Dan Dennett talks about—that we present ourselves as unified in order to achieve social goals and to be understandable to others. We also present ourselves as acknowledging our past and future identity, enabling us to be seen as part of society. Acknowledging and taking credit or blame for things we did in the past help society (usually kin who share our genes) incorporate us effectively in its plans, thereby enhancing the survival and perpetuation of our genes.[17]

If you doubt the reality of the social self, ask yourself the following question: Imagine that there is some act you've committed about which you are extremely embarrassed (love letters and Polaroid photographs from an illicit affair). Assume further that you now have a fatal illness and will be dead in two months. If you know that people rummaging through your belongings will discover your secrets, will you do your utmost to cover your tracks? If the answer is yes, the question arises, Why bother? After all, you know you won't be around, so what does it matter what people think of you after you're gone? This simple thought experiment suggests that the idea of the social self and its reputation is not just an abstract yarn. On the contrary, it is so deeply ingrained in us that we want to protect it even after death. Many a scientist has spent his entire life yearning obsessively for posthumous fame—sacrificing everything else just to leave a tiny scratchmark on the edifice.

So here is the greatest irony of all: that the self that almost by definition is entirely private is to a significant extent a social construct—a story you make up for others. In our discussion on denial, I suggested that confabulation and self-deception evolved mainly as by-products of the need to impose stability, internal consistency and coherence on behavior. But an added important function might stem from the need to conceal the truth from other people.

The evolutionary biologist Robert Trivers[18] has proposed the ingenious argument that self-deception evolved mainly to allow you to lie with complete conviction, as a car salesman can. After all, in many social situations it might be useful to lie—in a job interview or during courtship ("I'm not married"). But the problem is that your limbic system often gives the game away

and your facial muscles leak traces of guilt. One way to prevent this, Trivers suggests, may be to deceive yourself first. If you actually believe your lies, there's no danger your face will give you away. And this need to lie efficiently provided the selection pressure for the emergence of self-deception.

I don't find Trivers's idea convincing as a *general* theory of self-deception, but there is one particular class of lies for which the argument carries special force: lying about your abilities or boasting. Through boasting about your assets you may enhance the likelihood of getting more dates, thereby disseminating your genes more effectively. The penalty you pay for self-deception, of course, is that you may become delusional. For example, telling your girlfriend that you're a millionaire is one thing; actually believing it is a different thing altogether, for you may start spending money you don't have! On the other hand, the advantages of boasting successfully (reciprocation of courtship gestures) may out-weigh the disadvantage of delusion—at least up to a point. Evolutionary strategies are always a matter of compromise.

So can we do experiments to prove that self-deception evolved in a social context? Unfortunately, these are not easy ideas to test (as with all evolutionary arguments), but again our patients with denial syndrome whose defenses are grossly amplified may come to our rescue. When questioned by the physician, the patient denies that he is paralyzed, but would he deny his paralysis to *himself* as well? Would he do it when nobody was watching? My experiments suggest that he probably would, but I wonder whether the delusion is amplified when others are present. Would his skin register a galvanic response as he confidently asserted that he could arm wrestle? What if we showed him the word "paralysis"? Even though he denies the paralysis, would he be disturbed by the word and register a strong GSR? Would a normal child show a skin change when confabulating (children are notoriously prone to such behavior)? What if a neurologist were to develop anosognosia (the denial syndrome) as the result of a stroke? Would he continue to lecture on this topic to his students—blissfully unaware that he himself was suffering from denial? Indeed, how do I know that I am not such a person? It's only through raising questions such as these that we can begin to approach the greatest scientific and philosophical riddle of all—the nature of the self.

Our revels now are ended. These our actors,
As I foretold you, were all spirits and
Are melted into air, into thin air. . . .

We are such stuff
As dreams are made on,
And our little life
Is rounded with a sleep.   —*William Shakespeare*

During the last three decades, neuroscientists throughout the world have probed the nervous system in fascinating detail and have learned a great deal about the laws of mental life and about how these laws emerge from the brain. The pace of progress has been exhiliarating, but—at the same time—the findings make many people uncomfortable. It seems somehow disconcerting to be told that your life, all your hopes, triumphs and aspirations simply arise from the activity of neurons in your brain. But far from being humiliating, this idea is ennobling, I think. Science— cosmology, evolution and especially the brain sciences—is telling us that we have no privileged position in the universe and that our sense of having a private nonmaterial soul "watching the world" is really an illusion (as has long been emphasized by Eastern mystical traditions like Hinduism and Zen Buddhism). Once you realize that far from being a spectator, you are in fact part of the eternal ebb and flow of events in the cosmos, this realization is very liberating. Ultimately this idea also allows you to cultivate a certain humility—the essence of all authentic religious experience. It is not an idea that's easy to translate into words but comes very close to that of the cosmologist Paul Davies, who said:

> Through science, we human beings are able to grasp at least some of nature's secrets. We have cracked part of the cosmic code. Why this should be, just why *Homo sapiens* should carry the spark of rationality that provides the key to the universe, is a deep enigma. We, who are children of the universe— animated stardust—can nevertheless reflect on the nature of that same universe, even to the extent of glimpsing the rules on which it runs. How we have become linked into this cosmic dimension is a mystery. Yet the linkage cannot be denied.
>
> What does it mean? What is Man that we might be party to such privilege? I cannot believe that our existence in this universe is a mere quirk of fate, an accident of history, an incidental blip in the great cosmic drama. Our involvement is too intimate. The physical species *Homo* may count for nothing, but the existence of mind in some organism on some planet in the universe is surely a fact of fundamental significance. Through conscious beings the universe has generated self-awareness. This can be no trivial

detail, no minor by-product of mindless, purposeless forces. We are truly meant to be here.

Are we? I don't think brain science alone, despite all its triumphs, will ever answer that question. But that we can ask the question at all is, to me, the most puzzling aspect of our existence.

NOTES

1. For clear introductions to the problem of consciousness, see Humphrey, 1992; Searle, 1992; Dennett, 1991; P. Churchland, 1986; P.M. Churchland, 1993; Galin, 1992; Baars 1997; Block, Ramachandran and Hirstein, 1997; Penrose, 1989.
The idea that consciousness—especially introspection—may have evolved mainly to allow you to simulate other minds (which inspired the currently popular notion of a "theory of other minds" module) was first proposed by Nick Humphrey at a conference that I had organized in Cambridge over twenty years ago.

2. Another very different type of translation problem also arises between the code or language of the left hemisphere and that of the right (see note 16, Chapter 7).

3. Some philosophers are utterly baffled by this possibility, but it's no more mysterious than striking your ulnar nerve at the elbow with a hammer to generate a totally novel electrical "tingling" qualia even though you may have never experienced anything quite like it before (or even the very first time a boy or girl experiences an orgasm).

4. Thus an ancient philosophical riddle going back to David Hume and William Molyneux can now be answered scientifically. Researchers at NIH have used magnets to stimulate the visual cortex of blind people to see whether visual pathways have degenerated or become reorganized, and we have also begun some experiments here at UCSD. But to my knowledge, the specific question of whether a person can experience a quale or subjective sensation totally novel to him or her has never been explored empirically.

5. The pioneering experiments in this field were performed by Singer, 1993, and Gray and Singer, 1989.

6. It is sometimes asserted—on grounds of parsimony—that one does not need qualia for a complete description of the way the brain works, but I disagree with this view. Occam's razor—the idea that the *simplest* of competing theories is preferable to more complex explanations of unknown phenomena—is a useful rule of thumb, but it can sometimes be an actual impediment to scientific discovery. Most science begins with a bold conjecture of what might be true. The discovery of relativity, for example, was not

the product of applying Occam's razor to our knowledge of the universe at that time. The discovery resulted from rejecting Occam's razor and asking what if some deeper generalization were true, which was not required by the available data, but which made unexpected predictions (which later turned out to be parsimonious, after all). It's ironic that most scientific discoveries result not from brandishing or sharpening Occam's razor—despite the view to the contrary held by the great majority of scientists and philosophers—but from generating seemingly ad hoc and ontologically promiscuous conjectures that are not called for by the current data.

7. Please note that I am using the phrase "filling in" in a strictly metaphorical sense—simply for lack of a better one. I don't want to leave you with the impression that there is a pixel-by-pixel rendering of the visual image on some internal neural screen. But I disagree with Dennett's specific claim that there is no "neural machinery" corresponding to the blind spot. There is, in fact, a patch of cortex corresponding to each eye's blind spot that receives input from the other eye as well as the region surrounding the blind spot in the same eye. What we mean by "filling in" is simply this: that one quite literally sees visual stimuli (such as patterns and colors) as arising from a region of the visual field where there is actually no visual input. This is a purely descriptive, theory-neutral definition of filling in, and one does not have to invoke—or debunk—homunculi watching screens to accept it. We would argue that the visual system fills in not to benefit a homunculus but to make some aspects of the information explicit for the next level of processing.

8. Tovee, Rolls and Ramachandran, 1996. Kathleen Armel, Chris Foster and I have recently shown that if two completely different "views" of this dog are presented in rapid succession, naive subjects can see only chaotic, incoherent motion of the splotches, but once they see the dog, it is seen to jump or turn in the appropriate manner—emphasizing the role of the "top-down" object knowledge in motion perception (see Chapter 5).

9. Sometimes qualia become deranged, leading to a fascinating condition called synesthesia, in which a person quite literally tastes a shape or sees color in a sound. For example, one patient, a synesthete, claimed that chicken has a distinctly "pointy" flavor and told his physician, Dr. Richard Cytowic, "I wanted the taste of this chicken to be pointed, but it came out all round . . . well, I mean it's nearly spherical; I can't serve this if it doesn't have points." Another patient claimed to see the letter "U" as being yellow to light brown in color, whereas the letter "N" was a shiny varnished ebony hue. Some synesthetes see this union of the senses as a gift to inspire their art, not as brain pathology.

Some cases of synesthesia tend to be a bit dubious. A person claims to see a sound or taste a color, but it turns out that she is merely being metaphorical—much the same way that you might speak of a sharp taste, a bitter memory or a dull sound (bear in mind, though, that the distinction between the metaphorical and the literal is extremely blurred in this curious condition). However, many other cases are quite genuine. A graduate student, Kathleen Armel, and I recently examined a patient named John Hamilton who had relatively normal vision up until the age of five, then suffered progressive deterioration in his sight as a result of retinitis pigmentosa, until finally at the age of forty he was completely blind. After about two or three years, John began to notice that whenever he touched objects or simply read Braille, his mind would conjure up vivid visual images, including flashes of light, pulsating hallucinations or sometimes the actual shape of the object he was touching. These images were highly intrusive and actually interfered with his Braille reading and ability to recognize objects through touch. Of course, if you or I close our eyes and touch a ruler, we don't hallucinate one, even though we may visualize it in our mind's eye. The difference, again, is that your visualization of the ruler is usually helpful to your brain since it is tentative and revocable—you have control over it—whereas John's hallucinations are often irrelevant and always irrevocable and intrusive. He can't do anything about them, and to him they are a spurious and distracting nuisance. It seems that the tactile signals evoked in John's somatosensory areas—his Penfield map—are being sent all the way back to his deprived visual areas, which are hungry for input. This is a radical idea, but it can be tested by using modern imaging techniques.

Interestingly, synesthesia is sometimes seen in temporal lobe epilepsy, suggesting that the merging of sense modalities occurs not only in the angular gyrus (as is often asserted) but also in certain limbic structures.

10. This question arose in a conversation I had with Mark Hauser.

11. Searle, 1992.

12. Jackendorf, 1987.

13. The patient may also say, "This is it; I finally see the truth. I have no doubts anymore." It seems ironic that our convictions about the absolute truth or falsehood of a thought should depend not so much on the propositional language system, which takes great pride in being logical and infallible, but on much more primitive limbic structures, which add a form of emotional qualia to thoughts, giving them a "ring of truth." (This might explain why the more dogmatic assertions of priests as well as scientists are so notoriously resistant to correction through intellectual reasoning!)

14. Damasio, 1994.

15. I am, of course, simply being metaphorical here. At some stage in science, one has to abandon or refine metaphors and get to the actual mechanism—the nitty-gritty of it. But in a science that is still in its infancy, metaphors are often useful pointers. (For example, seventeenth-century scientists often spoke of light as being made of waves or particles, and both metaphors were useful up to a point, until they became assimilated into the more mature physics of quantum theory. Even the gene—the independent particle of beanbag genetics—continues to be a useful word, although its actual meaning has changed radically over the years.)

16. For an insightful discussion of akinetic mutism, see Bogen, 1995, and Plum, 1982.

17. Dennett, 1991.

18. Trivers, 1985.

BIBLIOGRAPHY OF READINGS

Aquinas, St. Thomas. (1989) Excerpts from Book 5: Human nature—embodied spirit. Human abilities—bodily and spiritual. How man knows. In T. McDermott (Ed.), *St. Thomas Aquinas Summa theologiae* (pp. 108–142). Allen, TX: Christian Classic. (Original work published 1265)

Aristotle (1973). Excerpts from de Anima. Books 1 and 3. In J. A. Smith (Trans.), *Introduction to Aristotle* (pp. 155–159, 216–245). Chicago: University of Chicago Press.

Bartlett, Sir F. C. (1932). The method of repeated production. In *Remembering: A study in experimental and social psychology* (pp. 63–94). Cambridge: Cambridge University Press.

Binet, A. & Simon, T. (1905). New methods for the diagnosis of the intellectual level of subnormals. *L'Année Psychologique, 12,* 191–244. Reprinted in E. Kite (Trans.) *The development of intelligence in children* (pp. 37–75). Nashville, TN: Williams Printing Co., 1980.

Chomsky, N. (1959). Verbal behavior, review. *Language* 35:26–58.

Darwin, C. (1873). General principles of expression. In *Expression of the emotions in man and animals* (pp. 27–65). New York: D. Appleton.

Descartes, R. (1972). Selections. In T. S. Hall (Ed.), Treatise of man (pp. 1–5, 19–23, 33–40, 59–90). Cambridge, MA: Harvard University Press. (Original work published 1650)

Ebbinghaus, H. (1964). Our knowledge concerning memory. The method of investigation. In H. A. Ruger and C. E. Bussenius (Trans.) *Memory: A contribution to experimental psychology* (pp. 1–6, 19–33). New York: Dover. (Original work published 1885)

Fechner, G. (1966). Introduction. Outer Psychophysics. In T. B. H. E. Adler, D. H. Howes, & E. G. Boring (Eds.), *Elements of psychophysics.* (pp. 1–18, 38–45). New York: Holt, Rinehart & Winston. (Original work published 1860)

Freud, S. (1910). The origin and development of psychoanalysis (third, fourth and fifth lectures). *American Journal of Psychology* 21:196–218.

Galton, F. (1907). The history of twins. Selection and race. Influence of man upon race. Conclusion. In *Inquiries into Human Faculty and Its Development* (pp. 155–173, 198–207, 216–220). New York: E. P. Dutton.

Gibson, J. J. (1979). The theory of affordances. In *The Ecological Approach to Visual Perception* (pp. 127–143). Hillsdale, NJ: Lawrence Erlbaum.

Hebb, D. O. (1949). The first stage of perception: Growth of the assembly. In *The organization of behavior: A neuropsychological theory* (pp. 60–79). New York: John Wiley & Sons.

Helmholtz, H. von (1995). The facts of perception. In D. Cahan (Ed.), *Science and culture* (pp. 342–366). Chicago: University of Chicago Press. (Original work published 1878)

Hippocrates. (1986). Tradition in medicine. Dreams. Nature of man. In G. E. R. Lloyd (Ed.), J. Chadwick & W. N. Mann (Trans.), *Hippocratic writings* (pp. 70–86, 252–271). New York: Penguin.

Hume, D. (1987). Of the origin of ideas. Of the association of ideas. Of the idea of necessary connection. In C. W. Hendel (Ed.), *An inquiry concerning human understanding* (pp. 26–39, 72–89). New York: Macmillan (Original work published 1748)

James, W. (1984). Emotion. Instinct. In *Psychology: A briefer course* (pp. 324–357). Cambridge, MA: Harvard University Press. (Original work published 1892)

Kant, I. (1978). On the cognitive faculty. In V. L. Dowdell (Ed.), *Anthropology from a pragmatic point of view* (pp. 9–41, 90). Carbondale, IL: Southern Illinois University Press. (Original work published 1798)

Leibniz, G. W. (1996). Book 2, Of ideas. In P. Remnant & J. Bennett (Trans. & Eds.) *New essays on human understanding* (Section 109–145). Cambridge: Cambridge University Press. (Original work published 1765)

Locke, J. (1995). Of ideas in general, and their original. In *An essay concerning human understanding* (pp. 59–70, 92–107). Amherst, NY: Prometheus Books. (Original work published 1689)

McClelland, J. L., Rumelhart, D. E. & Hinton, G. E. (1986). The appeal of parallel distributed processing. In D. E. Rumelhart, J. L. McClelland, & the PDP Research Group, *Parallel distributed processing: Explorations in the microstructure of cognition* (pp. 3–13, 25–40). Cambridge: MIT Press.

Münsterberg, H. (1913). Applied psychology. Means and ends. Vocation and fitness. In *Psychology and industrial efficiency* (pp. 3–10, 17–36). New York: Houghton Mifflin.

Neisser, U. (1967). The cognitive approach. A cognitive approach to memory and thought. In *Cognitive Psychology* (pp. 3–11, 279–305). New York: Meredith.

Pavlov, I. (1957). Lectures on the work of the cerebral hemispheres. In *Experimental psychology and other essays* (pp. 171–187). New York: Philosophical Library. (Original work published 1926)

Piaget, J. (1959). The functions of language in two children of six. In *The language and thought of the child,* Marjorie and Ruth Gabain (Trans.) (3rd ed., pp. 1–49). London: Routledge & Kegan Paul. (Original work published 1926)

Plato (1901). Excerpts from Book VII. Story of the cave. In B. Jowett (Trans.), *The Republic of Plato* (pp. 209–212). New York: Colonial Press. (Original work written ca. 380 B.C.)

Ramachandran, V. S., & Blakeslee, S. (1999). Do Martians see red? In *Phantoms in the brain: Probing the mysteries of the human Mind* (pp. 227–257, 296–298). New York: Quill William Morrow.

Shinn, M. W. (1900). Baby biographies in general. The dawn of intelligence. In *The biography of a baby* (pp. 1–19, 161–181). New York: Houghton Mifflin.

Skinner, B. F. (1957). The mand. In *Verbal behavior* (pp. 35–51). New York: Appleton-Century-Crofts.

St. Augustine of Hippo (1998). Book X. Memory. In H. Chadwick (Trans.), *Saint Augustine Confessions* (pp. 179–201). New York: Oxford University Press. (Original work written 397)

Titchener, E. B. (1927). Ideational type and the association of ideas. In *Experimental psychology: A manual of laboratory practice* (pp. 195–206). New York: Macmillan.

Tolman, E. C. (1948). Cognitive maps in rats and men. *Psychological Review* 55:189–208.

Vygotski, L. S. (1987). Thought and word. In A. Kozulin (Trans. & Ed.), *Thought and language* (pp. 210–214, 217–235, 249–256). Cambridge: MIT Press. (Original work published 1934)

Washburn, M. F. (1907). The difficulties and methods of comparative psychology. The evidence of mind. In *The animal mind* (pp. 1–32). New York: Macmillan.

Watson, J. B. (1913). Psychology as a behaviorist views it. *Psychological Review* 20:158–177.

Wertheimer, M. (1955). Gestalt theory. Laws of organization in perceptual forms. In W. D. Ellis (Ed.), *A source book of Gestalt psychology* (pp. 1–11, 71–88). New York: Humanities Press. (Original work published 1925)

Wundt, W. (1894). Lectures 1 and 30. In J. E. Creighton & E. B. Titchener (Eds.), *Lecture on human and animal psychology* (pp. 1–11, 437–454). New York: Macmillan.

BIBLIOGRAPHY OF BIOGRAPHICAL REFERENCES

Adler, Helmut E. (1996) Gustav Theodor Fechner: A German *Gelehrter.* In G. A. Kimble, C. A. Boneau and M. Wertheimer (Eds.), *Portraits of Pioneers in Psychology, volume 2.* (pp 2–13) Washington, D. C.: American Psychological Association and Mahwah, NJ: Lawrence Erlbaum Associates.

Bartlett, Frederic C. In C. Murchison (Ed.), *A History of Psychology in Autobiography, Volume III.* (pp 39–52) New York: Russell & Russell.

Blumenthal, A. L. (1998) Leipzig, Wilhelm Wundt, and Psychology's Gilded Age. In G. A. Kimble, and M. Wertheimer (Eds.), *Portraits of Pioneers in Psychology, Volume 3.* (pp 31–48). Washington, D. C.: American Psychological Association and Mahwah, NJ: Lawrence Erlbaum Associates.

Bringmann, Wolfgang G., Lück, Helmut E., Miller, Rudolf, Early, Charles E. (1997) *A Pictorial History of Psychology.* Chicago: Quintessence Publishing Co., Inc.

Chadwick, Henry (1991) (Ed. and Trans.), *Saint Augustine Confessions.* (pp ix–xxvi). New York: Oxford University Press.

Reed, Edward S. (1996). James J. Gibson: Pioneer and Iconoclast. In G. A. Kimble, C. A. Boneau and M. Wertheimer (Eds.), *Portraits of Pioneers in Psychology, Volume 2.* (pp. 247–261). Washington, D. C.: American Psychological Association and Mahwah, NJ: Lawrence Erlbaum Associates.

Evans, R. B. (1991) E. B. Titchener on scientific psychology and technology. In G. A. Kimble, M. Wertheimer and C. White (Eds.), *Portraits of Pioneers in Psychology.* (pp. 89–103). Washington, D. C.: American Psychological Association and Hillsdale, NJ: Lawrence Erlbaum Associates.

Fancher, Raymond E. (1996). *Pioneers of Psychology.* New York: Norton.

Fancher, Raymond E. (1998). Alfred Binet, General Psychologist. In G. A. Kimble, and M. Wertheimer (Eds.), *Portraits of Pioneers in Psychology, Volume 3.* (pp. 67–83). Washington, D. C.: American Psychological Association and Mahwah, NJ: Lawrence Erlbaum Associates.

Frederic C. Bartlett in C. Murchison *A History of Psychology in Autobiography, Volume III.* (pp. 39–52). New York: Russell & Russell.

Gleitman, Henry (1991) Edward Chace Tolman: A life of scientific and social purpose. In G. A. Kimble, M. Wertheimer and C. White (Eds.), *Portraits of Pioneers in Psychology.* (pp. 227–241). Washington, D. C.: American Psychological Association and Hillsdale, NJ: Lawrence Erlbaum Associates.

Glickman, Stephen E. (1996) Donald Olding Hebb: Returning the nervous system to psychology, In G. A. Kimble, C. A. Boneau and M. Wertheimer (Eds.), *Portraits of Pioneers in Psychology, Volume 2.* (pp. 227–244). Washington, D. C.: American Psychological Association and Mahwah, NJ: Lawrence Erlbaum Associates.

Helmholtz, Hermann von (1878, 1995). An autobiographical sketch. In D. Cahan (Ed.), *Science and Culture.* (pp 381–392). Chicago: University of Chicago Press.

Kimble, Gregory A. (1991) The spirit of Ivan Petrovich Pavlov. In G. A. Kimble, M. Wertheimer and C. White (Eds.), *Portraits of Pioneers in Psychology.* (pp. 27–40). Washington, D. C.: American Psychological Association and Hillsdale, NJ: Lawrence Erlbaum Associates.

Macnamara, John (1999). *Through the Rearview Mirror: Historical Reflections on Psychology.* Cambridge: MIT Press.

Reed, Edward S. (1997). *From Soul to Mind: The Emergence of Psychology, from Erasmus Darwin to William James.* New Haven: Yale University Press.

Ross, Barbara (1991) William James: Spoiled child of American psychology. In G. A. Kimble, M. Wertheimer and C. White (Eds.), *Portraits of Pioneers in Psychology*. (pp. 13–25). Washington, D. C.: American Psychological Association and Hillsdale, NJ: Lawrence Erlbaum Associates.

Scarborough, Elizabeth and Laurel Furumoto (1987). *Untold Lives: The First Generation of American Women Psychologists*. New York: Columbia University Press.

Sherrill, Jr., Robert (1991) Natural wholes: Wolfgang Kohler and Gestalt theory. In G. A. Kimble, M. Wertheimer and C. White (Eds.), *Portraits of Pioneers in Psychology*. (pp. 257–273). Washington, D. C.: American Psychological Association and Hillsdale, NJ: Lawrence Erlbaum Associates.

Van De Pitte, Frederick P. (1978) Introduction. In V. L. Dowdell (Ed.), *Anthropology from a pragmatic point of view*. (pp. xi–xxii). Carbondale and Edwardsville, IL: Southern Illinois University Press.

Wertheimer, Michael (1991) Max Wertheimer: Modern cognitive psychology and the Gestalt problem. In G. A. Kimble, M. Wertheimer and C. White (Eds.), *Portraits of Pioneers in Psychology*. (pp. 189–207). Washington, D. C.: American Psychological Association and Hillsdale, NJ: Lawrence Erlbaum Associates.

Zigler, Edward & Gilman, Elizabeth (1998) The Legacy of Jean Piaget. In G. A. Kimble, and M. Wertheimer (Eds.) *Portraits of Pioneers in Psychology, Volume 3*. (pp. 145–160). Washington, D. C.: American Psychological Association and Mahwah, NJ: Lawrence Erlbaum Associates.